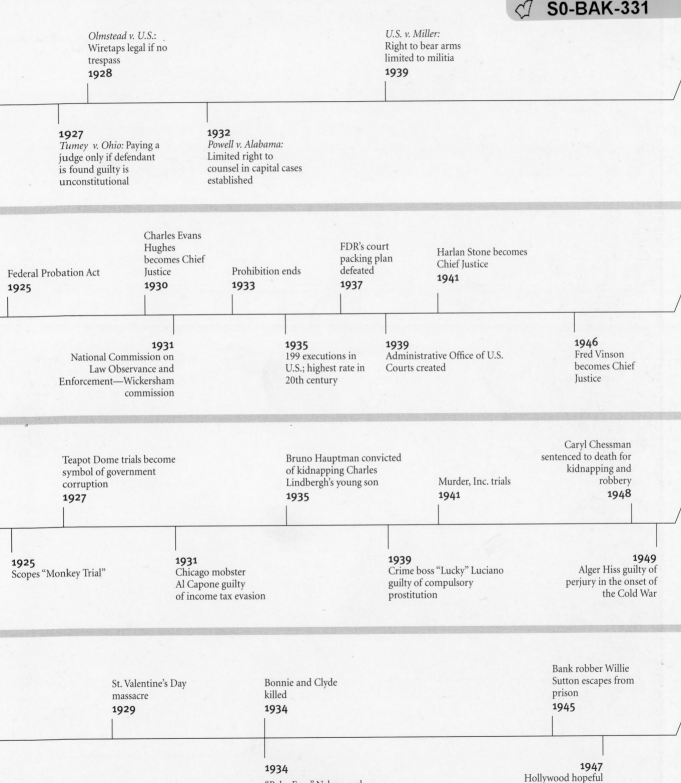

1930   1940   1950

S0-BAK-331

Olmstead v. U.S.: Wiretaps legal if no trespass
1928

U.S. v. Miller: Right to bear arms limited to militia
1939

1927
Tumey v. Ohio: Paying a judge only if defendant is found guilty is unconstitutional

1932
Powell v. Alabama: Limited right to counsel in capital cases established

Charles Evans Hughes becomes Chief Justice
1930

FDR's court packing plan defeated
1937

Harlan Stone becomes Chief Justice
1941

Federal Probation Act
1925

Prohibition ends
1933

1931
National Commission on Law Observance and Enforcement—Wickersham commission

1935
199 executions in U.S.; highest rate in 20th century

1939
Administrative Office of U.S. Courts created

1946
Fred Vinson becomes Chief Justice

Teapot Dome trials become symbol of government corruption
1927

Bruno Hauptman convicted of kidnapping Charles Lindbergh's young son
1935

Murder, Inc. trials
1941

Caryl Chessman sentenced to death for kidnapping and robbery
1948

1925
Scopes "Monkey Trial"

1931
Chicago mobster Al Capone guilty of income tax evasion

1939
Crime boss "Lucky" Luciano guilty of compulsory prostitution

1949
Alger Hiss guilty of perjury in the onset of the Cold War

St. Valentine's Day massacre
1929

Bonnie and Clyde killed
1934

Bank robber Willie Sutton escapes from prison
1945

1934
"Baby Face" Nelson and "Pretty Boy" Floyd killed

1947
Hollywood hopeful Black Dahlia's mutilated body found

America's Courts and the Criminal Justice System

SEVENTH EDITION

DAVID W. NEUBAUER

University of New Orleans

WADSWORTH
™
THOMSON LEARNING

Australia • Canada • Mexico • Singapore • Spain
United Kingdom • United States

To Jeff, Kristen, and Amy

WADSWORTH

THOMSON LEARNING

Executive Editor, Criminal Justice: Sabra Horne
Criminal Justice Editor: Shelley Murphy
Development Editor: Terri Edwards
Assistant Editor: Dawn Mesa
Editorial Assistant: Lee McCracken
Marketing Manager: Jennifer Somerville
Marketing Assistant: Karyl Davis
Project Manager, Editorial Production: Jennie Redwitz
Print/Media Buyer: Tandra Jorgensen
Technology Project Manager: Susan DeVanna

Permissions Editor: Stephanie Keough-Hedges
Production Service: Linda Jupiter, Jupiter Productions
Proofreader: Kay Mikel, WordWorks
Indexer: Paula C. Durbin-Westby
Text/Cover Designer: Liz Harasymczuk
Copy Editor: Sandra Beris
Cover Image: Eyewire
Cover Printer: Phoenix Color Corp.
Compositor/Illustrator: TBH Typecast, Inc.
Printer: R. R. Donnelley/Willard

ExamView® and ExamView Pro® are registered trademarks of FSCreations, Inc. Windows is a registered trademark of the Microsoft Corporation used herein under license. Macintosh and Power Macintosh are registered trademarks of Apple Computer, Inc. Used herein under license.

For permission to use material from this text, contact us by
Web: http://www.thomsonrights.com
Fax: 1-800-730-2215
Phone: 1-800-730-2214

Library of Congress Cataloging-in-Publication Data
Neubauer, David W.
America's courts and the criminal justice system / David W.
    Neubauer.—7th ed.
        p. cm.
    Includes bibliographical references and index.
    ISBN 0-534-56340-6 (alk. paper)
    1. Criminal courts—United States. 2. Criminal justice,
        Administration of—United States. I. Title.

KF9619 .N4 2001
345.73′01—dc21

Instructor's Edition ISBN: 0-534-56341-4

Wadsworth/Thomson Learning
10 Davis Drive
Belmont, CA 94002-3098
USA

For more information about our products, contact us:
Thomson Learning Academic Resource Center
1-800-423-0563
http://www.wadsworth.com

International Headquarters
Thomson Learning
International Division
290 Harbor Drive, 2nd Floor
Stamford, CT 06902-7477
USA

UK/Europe/Middle East/South Africa
Thomson Learning
Berkshire House
168–173 High Holborn
London WC1V 7AA
United Kingdom

Asia
Thomson Learning
60 Albert Street, #15-01
Albert Complex
Singapore 189969

Canada
Nelson Thomson Learning
1120 Birchmount Road
Toronto, Ontario M1K 5G4
Canada

Contents

PART II   LEGAL ACTORS   111

CHAPTER 5
The Dynamics of Courthouse Justice   112

CHAPTER 6
Prosecutors   137

CHAPTER 11
Bail 274

CHAPTER 12
Disclosing and Suppressing Evidence 298

PART V   APPELLATE, LOWER, AND JUVENILE COURTS   451

CHAPTER 17
Appellate Courts   452

Preface

America's Courts and the Criminal Justice System, Seventh Edition, examines the history, traditions, and philosophy underlying our system of justice as it is played out in the criminal court. In a complex, sometimes contradictory, and often fragmented process, defendants are declared innocent or found guilty, and the guilty are sentenced to prison or placed on probation. This book is about the defendants caught up in the process: the three-time losers, the scared young first offenders, and the business executives who are before the court to answer an indictment. But most of all, this book focuses on the prosecutors, judges, defense attorneys, and jurors who are involved in the daily decisions about guilt or innocence, probation or prison.

The impact of these decisions on crime and criminals is the subject of widespread controversy. Concern over how the courts handle criminal cases has been a staple of American political rhetoric since the 1960s. The nature of this public debate, as well as solutions proposed to correct the problems, are integral parts of this book. To be sure, the last decades have witnessed significant deep-seated changes and readjustments in the criminal justice system—given all the public posturing, one would hardly expect less.

This book is written for undergraduate courses that deal with America's criminal courts. Such courses (or parts of courses) are taught in various departments: criminal justice, administration of justice, political science, sociology, psychology, and social welfare. This book highlights not only the pivotal role of the criminal courts within the criminal justice system but also the courts' importance and impact on society as a whole.

America's Courts and the Criminal Justice System, Seventh Edition, focuses on the dynamics of the courthouse. Thus it differs from casebooks, which use appellate court decisions to highlight the history, structure, and philosophy of courts. Although these are important matters, casebooks often project a rather sterile image of courthouse justice and omit what courts do in practice, how they do it, and most importantly, why they do it.

This book's emphasis on the dynamics of courthouse justice grows out of my own field research. Since the 1960s, I have spent considerable time in state and federal courts in all parts of the nation. I have interviewed numerous judges, jurors, prosecutors, defense attorneys, probation officers, jailers, police officers, and defendants. I have observed these officials in action and discussed with them their problems and their views of possible solutions. By the luck of the draw, I have also served on juries in state and federal court. Throughout this book, I have tried to convey to the reader the sense of being in the courthouse.

Writing the Seventh Edition was gratifying and stimulating. It was gratifying to learn that numerous professors, and I hope their students as well, have found the book useful. It was stimulating because it involved closely examining recent changes in both scholarship and public dialogue. The seventh edition offers a current perspective on a continually evolving subject—the criminal court process. In this edition, the chapter structure remains the same as in the previous edition, but new topics are included and new special features have been added.

NEW TOPICS IN THIS EDITION

The courts remain at the center of public attention. I have tried to incorporate as many of these new issues as possible, as well as to highlight recent developments in old areas. Topics new to this edition include these:

- Bounty hunters
- Civil trial of O. J. Simpson

- Community courts
- Declining rates of juvenile crime
- Demise of the Independent Counsel Act
- Drug courts
- Errant judges
- Ineffective assistance of counsel
- Innocents on death row
- Moratorium on the death penalty
- More limits on scientific evidence
- Supreme Court upholds *Miranda*
- Victims' rights amendment
- Violence Against Women Act
- War on Drugs

NEW FEATURES

The Seventh Edition adds a new feature to each chapter entitled The Murder Trial of Shareef Cousin. Cousin was for a time the youngest person on America's death row—he was only sixteen when he was accused of murder. On appeal, however, the murder conviction was overturned and the district attorney chose not to prosecute. Each chapter in the book focuses on an aspect of this case. The goal is to tie the chapter material to this one ongoing and controversial case.

Another new feature in each chapter is entitled A Day in Court. I have combed newspapers across the nation to find articles that give readers a sense of being in court, sitting with the decision-maker. The purpose is to view the process through the eyes of that person, attempting to understand the pressures and frustrations that he or she faces on a daily basis.

The two new features—The Murder Trial of Shareef Cousin and A Day in Court—join two features from the previous editions—Case Close-Up and Controversy—to provide multiple perspectives on the topics discussed in the chapter.

THREE THEMES

In rewriting the Seventh Edition I decided to continue with the three themes introduced in the previous editions. Although they have been with the book since the beginning, the new edition's emphasis on the themes of law on the books, law in action, and law in controversy provides a better focus.

Law on the Books

The starting point of this text is to provide readers with a working knowledge of the major structures and basic legal concepts that underlie the criminal courts. In deciding guilt or innocence and determining the appropriate punishment, the courts apply the criminal law through a complicated process termed criminal procedure. The structure of the courts, the nature of the criminal law they apply, and the procedures followed all have important consequences for how the courts dispense justice. But to understand the legal system, one needs to know more than the formal rules. Also necessary is an understanding of the assumptions underlying these rules, the history of how they evolved, and the goals they seek to achieve. A discussion of the assumptions, history, and goals makes clear that America's criminal justice process is not monolithic but consists of a number of separate and sometimes competing units. It also points out conflicts over the goals the criminal courts are expected to achieve.

Law in Action

Many books leave the false impression that an understanding of the formal law and major structures of the court is all that one needs to know about the criminal courts. This kind of analysis provides only a limited view of how the courts administer justice. The law is not self-executing. It is a dynamic process of applying abstract rules to concrete situations. In making decisions about charges to be filed, the amount of bail to be required, and the sentence the convicted person will receive, judges, prosecutors, and defense attorneys must make choices for which the formal law provides few precise guidelines. Thus, the second theme of this book is law in action, which emphasizes the dynamics of the criminal court process.

An examination of law in action reveals a gap between how the law is supposed to operate and how it is actually applied. For example, the law in theory suggests that the guilt of defendants should be decided by a jury trial. In practice, however, trials are rare. Most defendants plead guilty without a trial. Asking why there is a gap between the law on the books and the law in action is a big step toward understanding the dynamics of courthouse justice.

Courts in Controversy

No treatment of the criminal courts would be complete without a discussion of the problems they are confronting. Are the courts too slow? Are judges too soft in sentencing? Does the criminal court process discriminate against the poor? These are just a few of the questions about the operations of the criminal courts that this book will consider. In turn, many organizations, groups, and individuals have probed the problems facing the criminal courts and proposed reforms. The third theme of this book is to discuss and analyze the controversies surrounding courthouse justice and analyze the reforms that have been suggested for what ails the courts. Not everyone agrees on the types of changes needed. Some argue that certain reforms will produce greater difficulties without solving the original problems. This book examines competing perspectives on the changes and reforms that are being proposed.

PEDAGOGICAL INNOVATIONS

This edition contains an array of pedagogical aids found in the previous edition, including chapter outlines, a running glossary, end-of-chapter critical thinking questions, World Wide Web exercises, and many figures and tables to facilitate student learning.

New to this edition is the inclusion in every chapter of interesting Web addresses and pertinent articles found on InfoTrac College Edition. Rather than waiting until the end of the chapter, these resources challenge the student to become active learners and use the growing power of the World Wide Web as they read. At the end of the chapters there are additional Internet and InfoTrac College Edition resources and exercises that provide search terms, recommended articles, and learning exercises.

SUPPLEMENTS

An extensive package of supplemental aids has been developed to enhance the course and to assist in-

structors and students. The supplemental package includes:

Instructor's Manual

The Instructor's Manual has been revised by William Head. It includes a detailed outline, key terms and concepts, discussion topics and student activities, recommended readings, critical thinking questions, and testing suggestions that will help time-pressed teachers more effectively communicate with their students and also strengthen coverage of course material. Each chapter has multiple choice, true/false, and fill-in-the-blank test items, as well as sample essay questions.

Student Study Guide

The extensive Student Study Guide has been revised by William Head. Because students learn in different ways, a variety of pedagogical aids are included in the guide to help them. Each chapter is outlined, major terms are defined, a summary is included, and sample tests are provided.

Crime & Punishment CD-ROM

The exciting CD-ROM *Crime & Punishment: The Multimedia Simulation of Criminal Sentencing* (packaged with each book) allows students to assume the role of the judge who must impose sentences on convicted felons in six different cases. After reviewing the case files, listening to and watching those involved, and reviewing the criminal statutes, students render the sentences.

Web Site for *America's Courts and the Criminal Justice System*

Designed exclusively for this edition of the text, this Web site—located at http://www.wadsworth.com/product/0534563406s—provides a variety of informative resources and interactive exercises. It takes an in-depth look at chapter-specific cases with a summary of facts, court decision, majority opinion, why the verdict became a law, and related Web links.

Controversies is a topic-specific threaded discussion forum with related Web links. FlashCards provide a glossary of terms. InfoTrac College Edition allows the student and instructor access to a wealth of criminal justice articles. The polling feature gives students an opportunity to cast their vote on a particular issue. Links to reliable periodicals offer another way to search for information on specific topics. Statistics shows the cold facts. Other valuable resources include A Day in Court–Comparative Legal Systems, a link to CourtTV, just for fun links, and Critical Thinking Questions that require students to compare, contrast, analyze, and apply what they have learned.

ExamView®

This computerized testing software helps instructors create and customize exams in minutes. Instructors can easily edit and import their own questions and graphics, change test layout, and reorganize questions. This software also allows instructors to test and grade online. It is available for both Windows and Macintosh.

CNN® Today Video Series

Exclusively from Wadsworth/Thomson Learning, the CNN Today Video Series offers compelling videos that feature current news footage from the Cable News Network's comprehensive archives. *Introduction to Criminal Justice,* Volumes I through IV, provide a collection of three- to five-minute clips on hot topics in criminal justice, such as cybercrime, juveniles behind bars, gender and ethnicity, and more. Available to qualified adopters, these videotapes are great lecture-launchers as well as classroom discussion pieces.

The Wadsworth Criminal Justice Video Library

The Wadsworth Criminal Justice Video Library offers an exciting collection of videos to enrich lectures, including CourtTV videos, many of which are directly correlated to the chapters. Qualified adopters may select from a variety of professionally prepared videos covering various aspects of policing, corrections, and other areas of the criminal justice system. The selections include videos from *Films for the Humanities & Sciences, A&E American Justice Series* videos, *National Institute of Justice:* *Crime File* videos, ABC News videos, and MPI Home Videos.

Careers in Criminal Justice Interactive CD-ROM

This engaging CD-ROM allows students to take an interactive look at the wide range of careers in criminal justice. The self-assessment feature helps steer students to suitable careers based on their personal profiles. They can gather information including job descriptions, salaries, employment requirements, sample tests, and video profiles of criminal justice professionals.

Crime Scenes CD-ROM

The first CD-ROM developed specifically for the introductory criminal justice course, this highly visual, interactive program casts students as the decision-makers as they explore all aspects of the criminal justice system. Exciting videos and supporting documents put students in the middle of a juvenile murder trial, a prostitution case that turns to manslaughter, and several other scenarios. This product received the gold medal in higher education and the silver medal for video interface from *NewMedia Magazine's Invision Awards.*

Mind of a Killer CD-ROM

Based on Eric Hickey's book *Serial Murderers and Their Victims,* this award-winning CD-ROM offers viewers a look at the psyches of the world's most notorious killers. Students can view confessions of and interviews with serial killers, and they can examine famous cases through original video documentaries and news footage. Included are 3-D profiling simulations, which are extensive mapping systems that seek to find out what motivates these killers.

Criminal Justice Internet Investigator III

This fully updated, handy brochure lists the most useful criminal justice links on the Web. It includes the most popular criminal justice sites, featuring those for research, statistics, legal information, general interest, and more.

Seeking Employment in Criminal Justice and Related Fields

Written by J. Scott Harr and Kären Hess, this practical book, now in its Third Edition, helps students develop a search strategy to find employment in criminal justice and related fields. Each chapter includes "insiders' views," written by individuals in the field, who talk about promotions and career planning.

Guide to the Internet for Criminal Justice

Developed by Daniel Kurland and Christina Polsenberg, this easy reference text helps newcomers as well as experienced Web surfers to use the Internet for criminal justice research.

ACKNOWLEDGMENTS

Writing the Seventh Edition was made easier by the assistance and encouragement of people who deserve special recognition. First and foremost I would like to thank the Wadsworth criminal justice team, who provided a fresh perspective on the new edition: Sabra Horne (executive editor), Shelley Murphy (editor), Terri Edwards (developmental editor), Dan Alpert (former criminal justice editor), Jennifer Somerville (marketing manager), Susan DeVanna (technology project manager), and Dawn Mesa (assistant editor). I am also grateful to the gifted production team of Jennie Redwitz, Linda Jupiter, and Sandra Beris, who turned raw manuscript into a polished manuscript and dispensed good cheer along the way. As always, colleagues from a number of schools and institutions offered valuable critiques. They include George Cole (University of Connecticut), Paul Wice (Drew University), Stephan Meinhold (North Carolina-Wilmington), and Chris DeLay (University of Louisiana-Lafayette). At UNO, Lee Brown and Mark Kaplinsky provided valuable research assistance.

Special thanks are due to the reviewers of this edition: Anita Blowers, University of North Carolina, Charlotte; Marc Gertz, Florida State University; Karl Kunkel, Southwest Missouri State University; Donald Walker, Kent State University.

I also wish to gratefully acknowledge the help provided by the reviewers of previous editions: Ruben Auger-Marchand, Indiana University-Purdue University; E. Stan Barnhill, University of Nevada at Reno; Paula M. Broussard, University of Louisiana-Lafayette; Kathleen Cameron-Hahn, Arizona State University; Bill Clements, Norwich University; Beverly Blair Cook, Wisconsin-Milwaukee; Mark Dantzker, Loyola University of Chicago; Max Dery, California State University-Fullerton; Frederick Van Dusen, Palm Beach Community College; Mary Ann Farkas, Marquette University; Roy Flemming, Texas A&M University; David Friedrichs, University of Scranton; Marc Gertz, Florida State University; Gary S. Green, Minot State University; Pamela L. Griset, University of Central Florida; Joseph Hanrahan, Westfield State University; Peter Haynes, Arizona State University; Michael Hazlett, Western Illinois State University; Ed Heck, San Diego State University; Ellen Hochstedler, University of Wisconsin at Milwaukee; Lou Holscher, Arizona State University at Tempe; N. Gary Holten, University of Central Florida; Rodney Kingsnorth, California State University-Sacramento; Jim Love, Lamar University; Patricia Loveless, University of Delaware; David Lukoff, University of Delaware at Newcastle; James Maddex, Georgia State University; Larry Myers, Sam Houston State University; Elizabeth Pelz, University of Houston-Downtown; John Paul Ryan, American Bar Association; Joseph Sanborn, Central Florida; Jose Texidor, Penn State University; Douglas Thomson, University of Illinois-Chicago; David Thysens, Saint Martins College; Russell Wheeler, Federal Judicial Center; Nancy Wolfe, University of South Carolina; Sheryl Williams, Jersey City State College.

As always, my wife and children deserve a special note of thanks for their love and support. I dedicate the book to my children in response to their bemusement at the idea that Daddy was busy writing a book.

David W. Neubauer
Slidell, Louisiana

To the Student

Over the years, the nicest comment I have heard about this book is that students like it. In writing the latest edition I have tried to build on the foundation of the earlier versions by making the book even more student-friendly. This book employs a spiral approach, beginning from a core of information and working outward to cover a wider range of relevant perspectives. I begin with basic building blocks of knowledge and then proceed to use them for a deeper analysis. In each chapter the initial emphasis is on the basics—the later material deals with more complicated issues.

The Seventh Edition contains a number of special features that will help make this introduction to the criminal court process more informative and enjoyable.

RUNNING GLOSSARY AND GLOSSARY

Any text should introduce readers to the basic terminology of a particular field. This is particularly important for a book on the criminal process because the law has a vocabulary all its own. Numerous students have suggested that this book needs a glossary. Indeed, one of my own students commented that the book has lots of "foreign" words—foreign not because they originated in another country but because they are so new.

To aid you, key terms are highlighted throughout the text in boldface type, and a running glossary is provided at the bottom of each page. Another key feature of this edition is the glossary at the back of the book, which is a compilation of the running glossary. Many of the most commonly used legal terms can be found there.

KEY DEVELOPMENTS

To provide a better sense of how the discussion in each chapter relates to material covered in other courses—like Constitutional Law and Criminal Procedure—each chapter contains a figure labeled "Key Developments," which summarizes the major legal developments concerning the topic at hand. I suggest that you use these as cross-references for other courses and also update the material when the Supreme Court hands down new decisions or Congress passes new laws.

IMPORTANT MATERIAL

In each chapter I have also tried to highlight important material in figures. The idea is to provide information on law on the books (definitions and the like) as well as snippets of law in action (basic statistics and so on). In particular, a figure summarizing the steps of the criminal court process is repeated (in an expanded version) in subsequent chapters. The intent is to direct your attention to the interrelated nature of the steps of the process. In addition, these figures provide an overview of the roles that each of the major actors—prosecutor, defense attorney, judge, and victim—play in the process. Because readers are often interested in particular states, a special effort has been made to provide important legal information for all fifty states.

CASE CLOSE-UP

To complement the theme of law on the books, each chapter contains a Case Close-Up. Many of these cases are landmark decisions of the U.S. Supreme Court. Others are less well known but chosen to illustrate the point. Throughout I have tried to get beyond the often dry legal prose to look at the people involved and what happened after their temporary stay in the legal limelight. Thus, each chapter begins with a vignette, which is highlighted in greater depth somewhere in the chapter.

A DAY IN COURT

To complement the theme of law in action, each chapter contains A Day in Court section designed to capture real-life experiences by looking at the people who make the decisions in the courthouse, emphasizing the frustrations they face. Juvenile judges, prosecutors, defense attorneys for those on death row, bounty hunters, and the like are featured.

CONTROVERSY

To complement the theme of courts and controversy, each chapter contains a Controversy box, intended to involve readers in the ongoing debate. Thus I start each Controversy with a question and then ask for your opinion at the end. Most importantly I challenge you to get beyond the immediate, often emotional aspect, and probe more deeply not only into the controversy but also into your own values.

I have tried to capture varying viewpoints in the Controversy sections. I have made no attempt to provide pro and con positions for every issue, but throughout the text as a whole I have tried to balance liberal and conservative views. I do not agree with all of the opinions expressed—and neither should you. However, understanding why people disagree about such matters as plea bargaining and the death penalty is an important part of understanding how courts operate in mediating between conflicting points of view.

THE MURDER TRIAL OF SHAREEF COUSIN

This new feature puts a single face on the material examined in the text. Each chapter features one of the participants involved in this 1995 murder. These vignettes look at the prosecutor, judge, and defense attorney in the case. They also view the process from the perspective of the grieving father and the angry relatives of Shareef Cousin. I avoid trying to provide an answer to the dominant question: Was Shareef Cousin a brutal murderer who was let off on a legal technicality or an innocent defendant wrongly convicted because of prosecutorial misconduct? I let you make your own decision.

CRITICAL THINKING QUESTIONS

Each chapter ends with a set of critical thinking questions. The goal is to have you integrate material from several sections of the chapter. Stated another way, they encourage active learning. It is important that you not be content to let the words just pass in front of your eyes. Instead, you need to think about what you are reading and relate it to your own experiences and your own community. Along the way I hope you come to appreciate how others with different experiences in other types of communities might react differently.

WORLD WIDE WEB RESOURCES AND EXERCISES

In just a few short years the Internet has moved into the mainstream of American life. Most immediately the Web makes learning easier. The Net is chock-full of facts and figures, providing ready access to all matter of knowledge. But at the same time, it requires users to be more aggressive. Many Web pages are nothing more than thinly veiled propaganda pieces, presenting the world from the vantage point of one interest group. Often, factual claims are made without anything to back them up, and closer probing leaves one wondering if they were simply made up. Thus using the Web as a learning tool requires that you analyze the arguments in terms of the perspective of the writer.

To encourage this kind of active, rather than passive, learning, each chapter contains three Web exercises. The first provides a useful URL, the second suggests a Yahoo search, and the third suggests a Web search. In addition, search terms, useful URLs, and uncommon URLs are highlighted. As a bonus feature, some of the more engaging Web sites are noted throughout the text in special boxes. I invite you to browse these interesting sites as you read the chapters. Many provide a real-world look at the chapter's material.

INFOTRAC COLLEGE EDITION RESOURCES AND EXERCISES

InfoTrac College Edition is a comprehensive and powerful reference resource for student research that is available twenty-four hours a day, seven days a week. For the subject of this book—courts and crime—InfoTrac College Edition is the perfect vehicle for finding supplementary information about a topic or locating recent developments. Search terms, recommended articles, and learning exercises are provided at the end of each chapter. In addition, relevant InfoTrac College Edition articles are noted throughout the text in special boxes.

OTHER STUDENT AIDS

Each chapter ends with a conclusion, references, and suggestions for further reading. A detailed index, including authors and subjects, is at the back of the book. Finally, a separate case index of all Supreme Court decisions discussed in the text can also be found at the back of the book.

About the Author

David William Neubauer was born in Chicago. He grew up in Aurora, Illinois, graduating from West Aurora High School in 1962. After receiving an A.B. in political science from Augustana College in Rock Island in 1966, he began graduate work at the University of Illinois, receiving a Ph.D. in 1971.

Neubauer has previously taught at the University of Florida and Washington University in St. Louis. He is now a professor at the University of New Orleans, where he chaired the political science department from 1982 to 1986.

In the mid-1970s, Neubauer served as a consultant to the Federal Judicial Center on two court management projects. From 1978 to 1980, he worked with the American Judicature Society as principal investigator on a project (funded by the National Institute of Justice) concerning court delay reduction. Over the years he has served on review panels for the National Institute of Justice, the Bureau of Justice Statistics, the National Science Foundation, the National Institute of Mental Health, and the National Center for State Courts. He also serves as a consultant to the Metropolitan Crime Commission of New Orleans.

Neubauer is the author of *Judicial Process: Law, Courts, and Politics in the United States, Second Edition* (1997), published by Harcourt Brace Jovanovich, and editor of *Debating Crime: Rhetoric and Reality* (2001), published by Wadsworth.

Courts, Crime, and Controversy

THE MURDER WAS SHOCKING, EVEN IN A CITY RECENTLY PROCLAIMED murder capital of the United States. For their first date, Michael Gerardi gave Connie Babin a single red rose and took her out to dinner at the Port of Call restaurant on the edge of New Orleans' historic French Quarter. As they were returning to his truck parked a block away they were confronted by three black youths. Before Gerardi had a chance to hand over his wallet he was shot in the face. The part-time bartender, who was also a medical student, provided emergency first aid but to no avail. Michael Gerardi was killed during what became known as New Orleans' bloodiest week.

Amid intense local media coverage, the majority African American jury convicted Shareef Cousin of first-degree murder and sentenced him to death. National attention soon focused on the case as well. Shareef Cousin became a poster child for the anti–death penalty movement; he was only sixteen at the time of the murder and thus garnered the dubious distinction of being one of the youngest people on America's death row. ■

The murder in front of the Port of Call restaurant provides but one poignant example that crime has been a pressing national concern for four decades. Newspapers headline major drug busts. Local television news broadcasts graphic footage of the latest murder scene. Not to be outdone, the national media offer tantalizing details on the latest sensational crime or prominent criminal. Meanwhile, official government statistics document high murder rates, and unofficial pollsters report that Americans believe crime rates are too high. These concerns prompt governmental response. Candidates for public office promise that, if elected, they will get tough on criminals. Governmental officials, in turn, announce bold new programs to eradicate street crime, reduce violence, and end the scourge of drugs. Yet, despite all the attention and promises, street crime remains a volatile, persistent, and intractable issue in America (Scheingold 1991).

A good deal of the political rhetoric about crime focuses on the criminal courts. Judges and defense attorneys—much more so than police chiefs and prison wardens—are blamed for high crime rates. Prosecutors are viewed as being too ready to engage in plea bargaining. Judges are accused of imposing unduly lenient sentences. Appellate courts are blamed for allowing obviously guilty defendants to go free on technicalities. Meanwhile, the police complain that Supreme Court decisions handcuff the fight against crime. Victims of crime become frustrated by lengthy trial delays. Witnesses protest wasted trips to the courthouse.

The purpose of this chapter is to build on public perceptions of the criminal courts by focusing on a few basic topics. We begin by discussing where the courts fit in the criminal justice system and how the public perceives the courts. Next, attention shifts to the three activities that set the stage for the rest of the book:

- Finding the courthouse
- Identifying the actors
- Following the steps of the process

As we will see shortly, the judicial process is complicated, so throughout this book we will examine the courts from three perspectives:

- Law on the books
- Law in action
- Courts in controversy

 An easy way to read about crimes making headlines across the United States is to point your browser to **http://www.dailynews.yahoo.com/headlines/cr/**.

For an up-to-date list of Web links, go to **http://www.wadsworth.com/product/0534563406s**.

THE COURTS AND THE CRIMINAL JUSTICE SYSTEM

Fighting crime is a major societal activity. Every year local, state, and federal governments spend $112 billion to apprehend, convict, and punish criminals (Gifford 1999). These tax dollars support an enormous assortment of criminal justice agencies, who in turn employ a large (and growing) number of employees; roughly 2 million people earn their living working in the criminal justice system. These governmental officials are quite busy; every year the police make more than 14.5 million arrests, and every day correctional personnel supervise 6.3 million people. Yet as large as these figures are, they still underestimate societal activity directed against crime. A substantial number of persons are employed in the private sector either directly (defense attorneys and bail agents) or indirectly (locksmiths and security consultants) (Hakim, Rengert, and Shachmurove 1996). There are, for example, more private security guards than public law enforcement officers in the United States (Cunningham, Strauchs, and VanMeter 1991).

The numerous public agencies involved in implementing public policy concerning crime are referred to as the **criminal justice system**. Figure 1-1 depicts the criminal justice system as consisting of three overlapping circles: Police are responsible for apprehending criminals; the courts are responsible for deciding whether those arrested are legally guilty, and if so, determining the sentence; corrections is responsible for carrying out the penalty imposed on the guilty.

The major components of the criminal justice system do not make up a smoothly functioning and internally consistent organization. Rather, the criminal justice system is both interdependent and fragmented.

An Interdependent Criminal Justice System

Viewing the various components of criminal justice as a *system* highlights the fact that these different agencies are interdependent and interrelated (Walker 1992). Police, courts, and corrections are separate governmental institutions with different goals, histories, and operating procedures. Though separate, they are also tied together because they must interact with one another. The courts play a pivotal role within the criminal justice system because many formal actions pertaining to suspects, defendants, and convicts involve the courts. Only the judiciary can hold a suspect in jail prior to trial, find a defendant guilty, and sentence the guilty to prison. Alternatively, of course, the courts may release the suspect awaiting trial, find the suspect not guilty, or decide to grant probation.

The decisions that courts make have important consequences for other components of the criminal justice system. Judges' bail policies, for example,

> **Criminal justice system:** Agencies and institutions directly involved in the implementation of public policy concerning crime, mainly the law enforcement agencies, courts, and corrections.

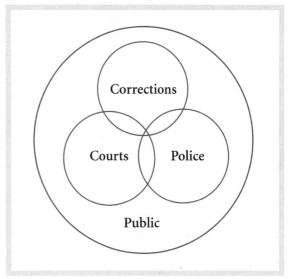

FIGURE 1-1 The Overlapping Circles of the Criminal Justice System

immediately affect what happens to a person arrested by the police; likewise, corrections personnel are affected because the bail policies of the judges control the size of the local jail population. If the decisions made by the courts have important consequences for police and prisons, the reverse is equally true: The operations of law enforcement and corrections have a major impact on the judiciary. The more felons the police arrest, the greater the workload of the prosecutors; and the more overcrowded the prisons, the more difficult it is for judges to sentence the guilty.

> For the latest statistics on the criminal justice system, just point your browser to the Bureau of Justice Statistics Web site at **http://www.ojp.usdoj.gov/bjs/**.
>
> For an up-to-date list of Web links, go to **http://www.wadsworth.com/product/0534563406s**.

A Fragmented Criminal Justice Nonsystem

The system approach to criminal justice dominates contemporary thinking about criminal justice. But not everyone is convinced of the utility of this conceptualization. Some people point to a *nonsystem* of criminal justice. Although the work of the police, courts, and corrections must, by necessity, overlap, this does not mean that their activities are coordinated, or coherent. From the perspective of the nonsystem, what is most salient is the fragmentation of criminal justice. Fragmentation characterizes each component of the criminal justice system. The police component consists of more than 17,000 law enforcement agencies, with varying traditions of cooperation or antagonism. Likewise, the corrections component includes approximately 1,300 state and federal correctional facilities, to say nothing of thousands of local jails. But corrections also encompasses probation, parole, drug treatment, halfway houses, and the like.

The same fragmentation holds true for the courts. In many ways, talking about courts is misleading, because the activities associated with the "court" encompass a wide variety of actors. Many people who work in the courthouse are employed by separate governmental agencies—judges, prosecutors, public defenders, clerks, court reporters, and bailiffs, primarily. Others who work in the courthouse are private citizens, but their actions directly affect what happens in this governmental institution—defense attorneys and bail agents are prime examples. Still others are ordinary citizens who find themselves in the courthouse either because they are compelled to be there—defendants and jurors—or because their activities are essential to case disposition—victims and witnesses.

The fragmentation within the three components of the nonsystem of criminal justice is compounded by the *decentralization* of government. American government is based on the principle of federalism, which distributes governmental power between national (usually referred to as federal) and state governments. In turn, state governments create local units of government, such as counties and cities. Each of these levels of government is associated with its own array of police, courts, and corrections. This decentralization adds tremendously to the complexity of American criminal justice. For example, depending on the nature of the law allegedly violated, several different prosecutors may bring charges against a defendant, including the following: city attorney (local), district attorney (county), attorney general (state), U.S. attorney (U.S. district court), and U.S. attorney general (national).

Needless to say, the fragmentation of the criminal justice nonsystem results in a lack of coordination between the components. Most actors are highly specialized in their particular function and therefore have little concern about the operation of

the system as a whole (Heinz and Manikas 1992). This means that attempts to find solutions to a problem typically involve the interactions of numerous governmental agencies, each with its own set of priorities. Consider a local jail filled to overflowing. When a federal court ordered a county jail to reduce overcrowding, an interagency task force was created to coordinate the response of the county sheriff, city police departments, the state probation department, locally elected judges, and the county governing board. As one would expect, there was considerable tension and conflict among these different organizations (Welsh and Pontell 1991).

 The Criminal Justice Resource Center is a good starting point for links to other criminal justice sites. Go to **http://www.wadsworth.com/**.

For an up-to-date list of Web links, go to **http://www.wadsworth.com/product/0534563406s**.

Tensions and Conflicts

Criminal justice is best viewed as both a system and a nonsystem. Both interdependence and fragmentation characterize the interrelationships between the agencies involved in apprehending, convicting, and punishing wrongdoers. In turn, these structural arrangements produce tensions and conflicts *within* each component. For example, a suburban police department only reluctantly cooperates with its big-city neighbor; the prosecutor loudly condemns the actions of a judge; and the prison warden expresses concern over the activities of halfway houses.

Tensions and conflicts occur also *between* the components of criminal justice. The interrelationships between police, courts, and corrections are often marked by tension and conflict because the work of each component is evaluated by others: The police make arrests, yet the decision to charge is made by the prosecutor; the judge and jury rate the prosecutor's efforts.

Decentralization again plays a role in the inherent tensions and conflicts in the criminal justice nonsystem. For example, it is not unusual to find that the relationship between the city police department and a federal law enforcement agency is marked by friction, nor is it unusual to find that state courts are frustrated by decisions of the federal judiciary.

Tensions and conflicts also result from multiple and conflicting goals concerning criminal justice.

Governmental officials bring to their work different perspectives on the common task of processing persons accused of breaking the law. Tensions and conflicts among police, courts, and corrections, therefore, are not necessarily undesirable; because they arise from competing goals, they provide important checks on other organizations, guaranteeing that multiple perspectives will be heard (Wright 1981).

The Blame Game

Tensions and conflict, though typical and to be expected, can nonetheless be frustrating, particularly to the public, which expects somebody to be responsible for running the war on crime and instead finds constant public bickering. In turn, some public officials seem more intent on blaming another criminal justice official than on working toward a solution. Thus, the blame game is common in criminal justice. Perhaps *The New York Times* (December 9, 1981, 30) said it best when it compared the justice system to Rubik's Cube:

> *It's long been understood that criminal justice is a Rubik's Cube: what the police do will affect what happens in court, which will affect what happens in the jails and prisons. You can't hope to deal with crime better by focusing on any single part—any more than you can solve the cube by concentrating on one square at a time.*
>
> *Yet for years criminal justice officials have responded to public frustration by focusing blame on each other—regarding small matters as well as large. We could hold speedier trials, say court administrators, if only the corrections people would get the prisoners to court on time. We could keep more men on the street, say the police, if only the courts wouldn't tie them up so long when they bring people in. We could send convicts to prison faster, say judges, if only the probation department would prepare pre-sentencing reports on time.*

The editorial concluded that there certainly is plenty of blame to go around but that it is time that various officials begin turning such complaints into questions, and holding each other accountable for the answers.

Because the courts occupy a pivotal role within criminal justice, they are most often the target of this blame game. It is important to emphasize, however, that although some of the blame game is indeed trivial, petty, and personal, a good deal of it

reflects basic organizational structure. Citizens are frustrated because no one seems in charge, but in a basic sense this is by design.

Throughout this book we will discuss efforts to bring greater coherence to the criminal justice system. *Coordination* is now a term heard throughout the system. Particularly in problem areas such as domestic violence and drug abuse, actors in the criminal justice system are instituting innovative programs that join activities, not only of law enforcement, courts, and corrections, but also health care and social services.

 Carl Sessions Stepp, "The Fallout from Too Much Crime Coverage"

COURTS, CRIME, AND THE PUBLIC

Police, courts, and corrections, of course, operate within a wider circle representing the general public. After all, it is the public whose tax dollars support the system. Because the courts occupy a pivotal position within the criminal justice system, the public has high expectations for their performance. Consider, for example, the symbols that surround the courts: the judges' black robes and gavel; Lady Justice's blindfold, the sword and scales of justice; and the Constitution and Bill of Rights. These symbols reinforce the principle that in a democratic society the law places limits on governmental authority.

Public confidence in the judiciary rests on the perception that the process is just, fair, and decent (Walker 2001). In particular, the public looks to the courts as forums of fairness and impartiality, with every citizen accused of a crime allowed to have his or her day in court. At the same time, the public expects the courts to punish wrongdoers. A conviction at trial is a public dramatization that those who violate society's rules will be punished. It also serves as a warning to potential wrongdoers. But at the same time Americans harbor negative symbols of the American judicial process, represented by images of shyster lawyers and legal loopholes that allow the guilty to escape justice.

Public assessments about crime and the courts have remained remarkably constant over the last decades (Myers 1996). Three key sets of attitudes emerge in public opinion polls (Bureau of Justice

Statistics 2000; Gibbs and Hanrahan 1993; McCorkle 1993; Durham 1993).

First, Americans are concerned about crime:

- Eighty-three percent say their best guess is that "the crime rate in this country is going up."

- Thirty-eight percent are afraid to walk alone at night near where they live.

Second, Americans often blame the courts for the crime problem:

- Eighty-two percent believe that courts "do not deal harshly enough with criminals."

- Sixty-eight percent conclude that "the police can't really do much about crime because the courts have put too many restrictions on the police."

- Fifty-five percent believe that "most judges have more sympathy for the criminals than for their victims."

Finally, despite widespread dissatisfaction with the performance of the criminal courts, when asked more questions, Americans are highly supportive of courts and judges. Judges, far more than legislators or public administrators, retain the respect of the public:

- Seventy-five percent believe that judges are generally fair and honest in deciding each case.

- Ninety percent assume that if they were ever accused of a crime they would receive a fair trial.

Public opinions about these matters are not uniform. Perceptions of the courts vary by race. Hispanics are more likely to be dissatisfied with the ability of courts to protect society and also voice concerns about the quality of the courts. African Americans are more likely to be dissatisfied with equality and fairness of the judicial process (Myers 1996).

Broad contours of public opinion aside, individuals often voice their opinions about the criminal court process, and often their views are negative if not hostile. Letters to the editor typically portray the courts as flawed; callers to radio talk shows complain that the system has failed. And in the era of cyberspace, homepages spring up dedicated to "criminal justice reform." In turn, books geared to the general market carry catchy titles such as *The Collapse of Criminal Justice* (Rothwax 1996).

Beyond expressions of individual opinions, a variety of groups attempt to influence criminal justice policy. At the national level, policy debates concerning gun control and victims' rights, to select two areas, are shaped by the actions of several different interest groups (Neubauer 2001). Meanwhile, in local communities, citizen groups pressure mayors and police chiefs to stop crime now. Thus, groups and organizations such as Crimestoppers, neighborhood watch, Crime Commissions, Night Out Against Crime, and Community in Action have become important components of the criminal justice system. In short, although the criminal justice system is almost overwhelmingly governmental, one should not discount the importance of nongovernmental actors, individual as well as collective.

There is a growing recognition at all levels of the criminal justice system of the importance of actively working with (and not against) citizens in the community. Indeed *community* has in recent years become an important word. Community-oriented policing, community courts, community prosecution, and community anticrime programs are examples of innovative efforts involving closer working relationships between justice officials and the broader community. Community antidrug efforts, for example, are premised on the notion that reducing illegal drug use cannot be limited to the efforts of police, courts, and corrections (Weingart, Hartmann, and Osborne 1994). Similarly, solutions to domestic abuse are understood in terms of a collaborative approach among health, justice, and social service professionals (Witwer and Crawford 1995). In important ways the recent emphasis on community efforts represents a major change in thinking; whereas criminal justice officials were once insular, they are now expected to reach out and involve the community.

 Public Agenda Online provides overviews and trends in public opinion. Go to **http://www.publicagenda.org/** and under Issues, select Crime.

For an up-to-date list of Web links, go to **http://www.wadsworth.com/product/0534563406s**.

FINDING THE COURTHOUSE

The criminal justice system, as argued here, is both a system and a nonsystem, tied together by core tasks but also marked by tensions and conflicts. The same

FIGURE 1-2 Overview of Court Structure in the United States

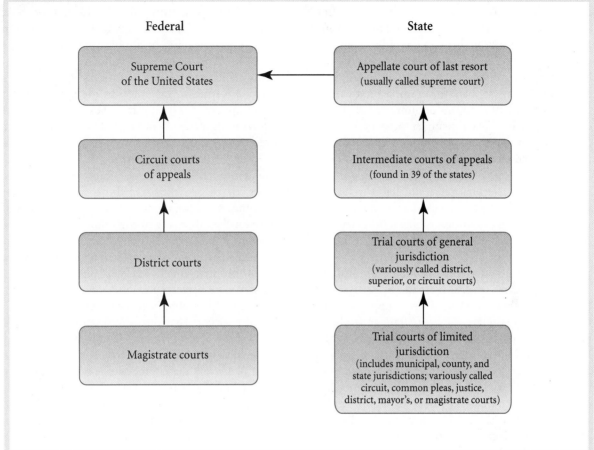

holds true for the courts. Judges, prosecutors, and defense attorneys, for example, share the common task of processing cases but at the same time exhibit different perspectives on the proper outcome of the case. In understanding this complexity, *America's Courts and the Criminal Justice System* examines the nation's judiciary from three complementary perspectives. To oversimplify slightly, Part I is about finding the courthouse, or the basic organization of our court system; Part II concerns identifying the actors in the courthouse; and Part III focuses on following the steps of the process from arrest to appeal.

By rough count there are 17,000 courthouses in the United States. Some are imposing turn-of-the-century buildings noted for their elaborate architecture. Others are faceless modern structures marked by lack of architectural inspiration. A few courts, you might be surprised to learn, are in the front of a funeral parlor or the back of a garage, where justices

of the peace preside in rural areas. Buildings aside, courts are governmental organizations. They are created to hear specific types of cases.

Figure 1-2 offers a preliminary overview of different types of courts in the United States. One distinction is between federal and state courts. The term *dual court system* refers to separate state and federal courts (rarely do cases move from one system to another). The dual court system has tremendous implications for the criminal justice system. In numerous and growing ways laws passed by the U.S. Congress, decisions of the president of the United States, or decisions of the U.S. Supreme Court affect activities of local police departments, local courts, and local corrections. The result is a complicated mosaic.

Another important difference between courts relates to function. Most courts are trial courts. As the name implies, this is where trials are held, jurors sworn, and witnesses questioned. Trial courts are noisy places resembling school corridors between classes. Amidst the noisy crowd you will find lawyers, judges, police officers, defendants, victims, and witnesses walking through the building during working hours. Trial courts, in turn, are divided between major and lower. Lower courts initially process felony cases (set bail, for example) but cannot find the defendant innocent or guilty and therefore cannot sentence. Their primary activity involves processing the millions of minor offenses such as public drunkenness, petty theft, and disorderly conduct. Major trial courts, on the other hand, are responsible for the final phases of felony prosecutions. It is in these courts that defendants charged with crimes such as murder, robbery, burglary, and drug dealing enter a plea of guilty (or occasionally go to trial), and the guilty are sentenced.

Other courts (fewer in number) are appeals courts that review decisions made by trial courts (usually only the major trial courts). Appeals courts review decisions made elsewhere, but no trials are held, no jurors employed, nor witnesses heard. Rather, appellate courts are places where lawyers argue whether the previous decision correctly or incorrectly followed the law. In many ways appellate courts are like a monastery where scholars pore over old books and occasionally engage in polite debates.

In criminal cases defendants who are found guilty by judge or jury have the right to one appeal (findings of not guilty cannot be appealed). Given the growing volume of cases, the federal government and most states have created two levels of appellate courts—intermediate courts, which must hear all cases, and supreme courts, which pick and choose the cases they hear. Although the U.S. Supreme Court stands atop the organizational ladder, it hears only a handful of the cases filed each year (less than 100 per year). Thus its importance is measured not in terms of the number of cases decided but the wide-ranging impact that these few decisions have on all stages of the process.

IDENTIFYING THE ACTORS IN THE COURTHOUSE

Part II focuses on the actors in the courthouse. Enter a trial courtroom and you will observe numerous people either busily engaged in doing something or seemingly doing nothing. Some of the actors in the courthouse are easily identifiable by the clothes they wear. The person sitting high above everyone else wearing the black robes is the judge. The person in handcuffs arrayed in a bright orange jumpsuit is the defendant. And the men and women dressed in uniforms are law enforcement officers. But the roles being performed by the others in attendance are not readily apparent. It is clear that those sitting in front of the railing are more important than those on the other side. Until court proceedings begin, the observer is never sure whether they are victims, defendants, family, witnesses, reporters, potential jurors, or retired citizens whose hobby is court watching. After the proceedings begin, the roles of those on the other side of the railing become more apparent.

Some participants are present on a regular basis, others only occasionally. Many are public employees, but some are private citizens. Using the categories applied to the criminal justice system, Figure 1-3 provides a chart of many of the actors one would expect to see in a courthouse on any given day. Some of the titles vary from place to place. Similarly, the participants vary depending on the type of case. In a murder case, for example, a scientist from the crime lab may be presenting evidence, but in a child sexual abuse case the actors will more likely include a social worker or psychiatrist. Who is present also varies depending on the level of court; minor cases in the lower courts involve far fewer actors than serious felonies in the major trial courts. A brief overview of the main actors will help set the stage.

Prosecutors

The organization of prosecutors in the United States is as fragmented as the courts in which they appear. To limit ourselves only to state courts and state prosecutions, in most states you find one prosecutorial office for the lower courts (typically the city attorney), another for the major trial court (typically called the district attorney or the state's attorney), and yet another at the state level (almost uniformly called the attorney general).

Regardless of the level, prosecutors are the most influential of the courthouse actors. Their offices decide which cases to prosecute, which cases to plea-bargain, and which cases to try. They may also be influential in matters such as setting bail and choosing the sentence.

FIGURE 1-3   Actors in the Courthouse

POLICE
 Federal
 State
 Sheriff
 Local
 Special districts
 Private security
COURTS
 Lawyers
 Prosecutor
 Public defender
 Private defense attorneys
 Judge
 Law clerk
 Court support staff
 Clerk of court
 Court reporter
 Pretrial services
 Bailiff
 Court administrator
 Victim witness assistance program
 Rape crisis center
CORRECTIONS
 Probation officer
 Jail
 Prison
 Drug rehabilitation program
PUBLIC
 Regular participants
 Bail bondsmen
 Newspaper reporter
 Irregular participants
 Defendant
 Victim
 Witness
 Juror
 Victim advocates

Defense Attorneys

The U.S. Constitution guarantees defendants the right to counsel. But for most defendants this abstract "right" collides with economic reality. Up to 80 percent of defendants in large cities cannot afford to hire a lawyer, so the government must provide them with one at government expense. Small counties use the assigned counsel system, whereby the judge appoints a member of the local bar to represent the defendant. Big cities employ the public defender system; indigent defendants are represented by full-time government attorneys who rep-resent all defendants too poor to afford a lawyer. A handful of defendants hire a private lawyer.

Our notions of defense attorneys have been shaped by fictional characters such as Perry Mason, who always was able to show that his client was inno-cent. Realities are strikingly different. Often defense attorneys urge their clients to plead guilty based on the assessment that a jury will find the defendant guilty beyond a reasonable doubt. Even when cases are tried, defense attorneys only occasionally are able to secure a not guilty verdict for their client.

The CourtTV Web site includes a summary of famous cases. Go to **http://www.courttv.com/famous/ index.html**.

For an up-to-date list of Web links, go to **http:// www.wadsworth.com/product/0534563406s**.

Judges

Judges in state courts are by and large elected by the voters. Federal judges, on the other hand, are nomi-nated by the president of the United States and con-firmed by the U.S. Senate.

Judges are the ultimate authority figure in the courthouse because only judges can set bail, only judges can instruct jurors about the meaning of the law, and only judges can impose sentences. Exercis-ing this authority, though, is limited by practical realities, not the least of which is the necessity to move cases. The high volume of court cases means the judges are expected to dispose of cases lest a backlog develop, and the quickest way to dispose of cases is by a plea of guilty. Thus judges must be responsive to prosecutors, defense attorneys, and sometimes even defendants, if they are to achieve their principal goal of disposing of cases.

Defendants and Their Victims

Defendants are, by and large, young, poor, unedu-cated minority males. A large percentage stand accused of property crimes (theft and burglary) or low-level drug offenses. They are hardly the clever and sophisticated criminals portrayed in fiction. This profile has important implications for the judi-cial process. For one, many defendants are too inar-ticulate to help their attorney mount a defense. For another, the fact that the defendants are dispropor-tionately minorities means they are now center stage in the great fault line of U.S. politics—race. Whether the criminal justice system discriminates, either intentionally or unintentionally, against African Americans, Hispanics, or Native Americans is a hot topic and one for which there is no unequivocal answer.

The victims of crime are playing an increasingly important role in the criminal courts. Once banished to a bit part of testifying, they are increasingly demanding major roles in setting bail, agreeing to pleas of guilty, and imposing sentences and release from prison. Groups such as Mothers Against Drunk Driving (MADD) have become a potent political force. Rhetoric aside, it is important to remember that victims often share the same characteristics as their tormentors—they are, by and large, young, poor, undereducated minorities.

FOLLOWING THE STEPS OF THE PROCESS

From arrest to appeal, a case passes through numerous stages. Figure 1-4 presents the steps of criminal procedure in the typical order in which they occur. These steps are meant to provide only a basic overview. The specifics of criminal procedure vary from state to state, and federal requirements differ from state mandates. Moreover, prosecutions of serious crimes (felonies) are more complicated than prosecutions of less serious offenses (misdemeanors). Rest assured that the remainder of the text will complicate this oversimplification. But for now we will focus on a defendant charged with a noncapital state felony.

Crime

There is no way to precisely quantify the amount of crime in the United States, but compared to other industrialized nations it is high. Every year about 12 million serious crimes are reported to the police (many others are never reported and therefore never make the official statistics). Although the media focus on crimes of violence, the overwhelming majority of crimes involve property (burglary and theft primarily). For example, the 15,533 homicides that occur each year account for less than 1 percent (.2%) of serious crime.

Legally, crimes fall into three categories: felonies (in most states punishable by one year or more in prison); misdemeanors (typically punishable by a sentence in the local jail); and ordinance violations (subject to fine or a short jail term). Felonies are filed in major trial courts, whereas misdemeanor and ordinance violations are typically heard in the lower courts.

Arrest

Every year the police make more than 14.5 million arrests for nontraffic offenses. Most are for minor crimes, but 3 million involve serious crimes such as murder, rape, assault, robbery, burglary, and theft. The police are able to make an arrest in only one out of five crimes known to the police. As a result, only a fraction of the nation's major crimes ever reach the courts.

Initial Appearance

An arrested person must be brought before a judge without unnecessary delay. For felony defendants the initial appearance is largely a formality because no plea may be entered. Instead, defendants are told what crime they are alleged to have committed, perfunctorily advised of their rights, and a date for the preliminary hearing is set. For misdemeanor defendants, the initial appearance is typically the defendant's only courtroom encounter; three out of four plead guilty and are sentenced immediately.

Bail

The most important event that occurs during the initial appearance is the setting of bail. Because a defendant is considered innocent until proven guilty, the vast majority of defendants have the right to post bail. But this legal right is tied to the defendant's economic status. Many defendants are too poor to scrounge up the ready cash to pay the bail agent's fee; thus they must remain in jail awaiting trial. The overriding reality, however, is that America's jails are overflowing. As a result, pretrial detention is limited largely to defendants who have committed serious crimes; judges set a very high bail because they don't want these defendants wandering the streets before trial. For defendants charged with less serious crimes, judges and prosecutors may want to keep them in jail while awaiting trial, but

FIGURE 1-4   **Steps of Criminal Procedure**

	Law on the Books	*Law in Action*
Crime	Any violation of the criminal law.	Fourteen million serious crimes reported to the police yearly.
		Property crimes outnumber violent offenses eight to one.
Arrest	The physical taking into custody of a suspected law violator.	About 3 million felony arrests each year.
Initial appearance	The accused is told of the charges, bail is set, and a date for the preliminary hearing is set.	Occurs soon after arrest, which means the judge and lawyers know little about the case.
Bail	Guarantee that a released defendant will appear at trial.	Every day the nation's jails hold over 600,000 pretrial detainees.
Preliminary hearing	Pretrial hearing to determine if probable cause exists to hold the accused.	Cases are rarely dismissed but provides defense attorney a look at the evidence.
Charging	Formal criminal charges against defendant stating what criminal law was violated.	From arrest to the major trial court, half of cases are dropped.
Grand jury	A group of citizens who decide if persons accused of crimes should be charged (indicted).	Grand juries indict the defendants the prosecutor wants indicted.
Arraignment	The defendant is informed of the pending charges and is required to enter a plea.	Felony defendant's first appearance before a major trial court judge.
Evidence	Formal and informal exchange of information before trial.	Prosecutors turn over evidence of guilt in hopes of obtaining a plea of guilty.
	Defense may seek to have evidence suppressed because it was collected in a way that violates the Constitution.	Suppression motions are granted less than 1 percent of the time but are at the heart of major debate.
Plea negotiations	The defendant pleads guilty with the expectation of receiving some benefit.	Ninety to 95 percent of felony defendants admit their guilt.
Trial	A fact-finding process using the adversarial method before a judge or usually a jury of twelve.	Most likely only in serious cases; defendant is likely to be convicted.
Sentencing	Punishment imposed on a defendant found guilty of violating the criminal law.	There are 6.3 million persons in prison, on probation, or on parole.
Appeal	Review of the lower court decision by a higher court.	Only 6 percent of convicted defendants win a significant victory.

the citizens are not willing to invest the tens of millions of dollars needed to build more jails.

Preliminary Hearing

During the preliminary hearing the prosecutor must prove there is probable cause to believe the defendant committed the crime. Probable cause involves two elements: proof that a crime was committed and a linkage between the defendant and that crime. This isn't much of a standard of proof, so most of the time the judge finds that probable cause is present and orders the defendant held for further proceedings. In most courthouses, few cases are dismissed at the preliminary hearing for lack of probable cause.

Charging Decision

Sometime after arrest a prosecutor reviews the case, paying particular attention to the strength of the evidence but also keeping in mind office policies on case priorities. Half the time this review results in dismissal. One out of two defendants is lucky indeed; they are released without the filing of criminal charges. But the other half are in deep trouble; their chances of being found not guilty are now slim indeed.

Grand Jury

Like the preliminary hearing, the grand jury is designed as a check on unwarranted prosecutions. Grand juries are required in all federal felony prosecutions, but only about half of the states use them. If the grand jury thinks there is enough evidence to hold the defendant for trial, they return an indictment (also called a true bill) charging the defendant with a crime. On rare occasions grand juries refuse to indict (such refusal is called a no bill or a no true bill). Legal theory aside, grand juries are dominated by the prosecutor, and they obligingly indict whomever the prosecutor wants indicted.

Arraignment

Although the two terms are often used interchangeably, *arraignment* differs from the *initial appearance*. During arraignment the defendant is given a copy of the formal charges, advised of his or her rights (usually more extensively than at the initial appearance), and for the first time is called upon to enter a plea. Not surprisingly, most defendants plead not guilty, but a handful admit their guilt then and there and enter a plea of guilty. Overall, little of importance happens during arraignment; this legal step is somewhat equivalent to the taking of class attendance.

Evidence

The term *discovery* refers to the exchange of information prior to trial. In some states (but not all) the prosecutor is required to turn over a copy of the police reports to the defense prior to trial. Generally, however, the defense is required to provide the prosecutor with little if any information, an imbalance that attracted considerable public attention during the O. J. Simpson trial. The law aside, many prosecutors voluntarily give defense attorneys they trust extensive information prior to trial, anticipating that the defense attorney will persuade the defendant to enter a plea of guilty.

Motions are simply requests that a judge make a decision. Many motions are made during trial, but a few may be made beforehand. The most significant pretrial motions relate to how the police gathered evidence. Defense attorneys file motions to suppress evidence, that is, to prevent its being used during trial. Motions to suppress physical evidence contend that the police conducted an illegal search and seizure (*Mapp*). Motions to suppress a confession contend that the police violated the suspect's constitutional rights during questioning (*Miranda*).

 The Washtenaw County (Michigan) trial court Web site takes you inside the operating procedures of a trial court, as well as introducing you to the people that work there. Go to **http://www.co.washtenaw.mi.us/ depts/courts/index.htm**.

For an up-to-date list of Web links, go to **http:// www.wadsworth.com/product/0534563406s**.

Plea Negotiations

Most findings of guilt result not from a verdict at trial but from a voluntary plea by the defendant. Ninety percent of all felony convictions are the product of negotiations between the prosecutor and the defense attorney (and sometimes the judge as well). Although the public thinks of plea bargaining as negotiating a sentence less than the maximum, this term represents a variety of different practices and court traditions. At times, bargaining involves negotiations over the seriousness of the offense or over the number of separate charges (called counts).

Trial

Trial by jury is one of the most fundamental rights granted those accused of violating the criminal law. A defendant can be tried either by a judge sitting alone (called a bench trial) or by a jury. A jury trial begins with the selection of twelve jurors (fewer in some cases). Each side makes opening statements, indicating what they think the evidence in the case will show. Because the prosecutor has the burden of proving the defendant guilty beyond a reasonable doubt, he or she is the first to call witnesses. After the prosecution has completed its case, the defense has the opportunity to call its own witnesses. When all the evidence has been introduced, each side makes a closing argument to the jury, and the judge then instructs the jury about the law. The jurors retire to deliberate in secret. Though the details of trial procedure vary from state to state, one factor is constant—the defendant's chances for an acquittal are not good.

Sentencing

Most of the steps of the criminal process are concerned with determining innocence or guilt. As important as this question is, the members of the courtroom work group spend most of their time deciding what sentence to impose on the guilty. Indeed, defendants themselves are often more concerned about how many years they will have to spend in prison than about the question of guilt.

The principal decision the judge must make involves selecting between the option of imposing a prison sentence or placing the defendant on probation. Fines are rarely used in felony cases. The death penalty is hotly debated but in actuality is limited to only some first-degree murder cases. Prison overcrowding is the dominant reality of contemporary sentencing—over 1.4 million inmates are incarcerated in state and federal prisons, and the numbers increase by 8 to 12 percent each year. Only recently has attention begun to focus on the fact that the political rhetoric of "lock them up and throw away the key" has resulted in severe prison overcrowding.

Appeal

Virtually all defendants found guilty during trial contest their fate, filing an appeal with a higher court in hopes that they will receive a new trial. Contrary to public perceptions, defendants are rarely successful on appeal—only one of sixteen appellants achieves a significant victory in the appellate courts. Moreover, appeals are filed in only a small proportion of all guilty verdicts; defendants who plead guilty rarely appeal. Appellate court opinions, however, affect future cases because the courts decide policy matters.

LAW ON THE BOOKS

An important first step in understanding how American courts dispense justice is to learn the basic law underlying the process. The structure of the courts, the legal duties of the main actors, and the steps in the criminal process are all basic to an understanding of how the courts dispense criminal justice. One must also understand the assumptions underlying these rules, the history of how they evolved, and the goals they seek to achieve. These elements constitute law on the books—the legal and structural components of the judiciary. In essence, the starting point in understanding the legal system is knowing the formal rules.

Law on the books is found in constitutions, laws enacted by legislative bodies, regulations issued by administrative agencies, and cases decided by courts. There is little doubt that decisions by the U.S. Supreme Court have far-reaching ramifications. To highlight the importance of court decisions, each chapter's Case Close-Up provides an in-depth look at some of the court decisions that have shaped our nation's criminal justice system (see Case Close-Up: Overview).

LAW IN ACTION

The ongoing public debate over the courts indicates that the criminal courts do not stand in splendid isolation, removed from the rest of society. Rather, their activities are intimately intertwined with other social institutions, community values, public opinion, and the actions (or inactions) of other members of the criminal justice system. This perspective has important consequences for how we study the criminal courts (Neubauer 1997). We need to know not only what the law says (law on the books) but also how the rules are applied (law in action).

In many ways law on the books represents an idealized view of law, one that stresses an abstract set of rules that is so theoretical that it fails to

CASE CLOSE-UP

Overview

 Each chapter of this book features a case that has had a major impact on the criminal justice system. Many of these cases are significant U.S. Supreme Court decisions. Indeed, some of these cases have been absorbed into the English language. *Miranda* and *Mapp*, for example, have almost become household names, and to actors in the system, they are a useful shorthand. Others are less well known but have affected the process in important ways. Throughout I have tried to stress not only the legal principles involved in the decisions but also the nature of the litigants themselves.

incorporate real people. Law on the books provides only an imperfect road map of the day-to-day realities of the courthouse. The concept of law in action, on the other hand, focuses on the factors governing the actual application of the law. It stresses that in the criminal courthouses of the United States, few cases ever go to trial. Most defendants either plead guilty or have their cases dismissed before trial. Instead of the conflict projected by the adversary system, judges, prosecutors, and defense attorneys cooperate on a number of matters. Whereas the main goal of the adversary model is to discover truth and decide guilt, a great deal of the court's attention is directed toward determining the appropriate penalty.

Ours is a law-drenched age. Voters and elected officials alike see the solution to pressing social problems in terms of passing a law. Somehow we are not serious about an issue unless we have a law regulating it, and we are not really serious unless we

have criminal laws. But laws are not self-enforcing. Some people delude themselves by thinking that passing a law solves the problem. This is not necessarily so. Indeed, if the problem persists, frustration sets in. Thus legislatures mandate that drivers purchase automobile insurance, but accident victims become frustrated when they discover the other party has no insurance. Similarly, judges require defendants to pay restitution, but crime victims discover that impoverished defendants (particularly those in prison) have no ability to pay. In the same vein, conservatives call for preventive detention, but jailers find that there are no available jail cells.

In short, there is a wide gap between legal theory (law on the books) and how that law is applied (law in action). Although some persons find this gap shocking, actually it is not; after all, no human institution ever lives up to the high ideals set out for it. If you spend five minutes observing a stop sign on a well-traveled street, you will find that not all

A DAY IN COURT

Overview

 Throughout this book A Day in Court sections focus on law in action, examining the reality of courthouse justice. Sometimes A Day in Court will examine a specific person; other times, an idea or a program. Here is what to expect:

---

cars come to a complete stop, and some do not seem to slow down much at all. Yet at the same time, the stop sign (the law on the books in this example) clearly does affect the behavior of drivers (law in action).

In many ways, Figure 1-4 represents a law-on-the-books model of the criminal court process. The steps seem to suggest a streamlined criminal process, with defendants entering at arrest and steadily and methodically moving through the various stages until conviction, and eventually, sentencing. This is not the reality. The criminal process is filled with numerous detours. At each stage officials decide to advance the defendant's case to the next step, reroute it, or terminate it. The result is that many cases that enter the criminal court process are eliminated during the early stages. Throughout this book A Day in Court sections highlight key dimensions of law in action (see A Day in Court: Overview).

Realizing that law on the books is not the same as the law in action is only the second step in understanding how the courts dispense justice. The crucial task is to understand and explain why the law as practiced differs from the apparent intent of the for-

mal rules. Toward this end a variety of studies have highlighted three important features of the way criminal courts operate: Assembly-line justice, discretion, and the courtroom work group are concepts that describe law in action.

 Lance Hannon, James Defronzo, "The Truly Disadvantaged, Public Assistance, and Crime"

Assembly-line Justice

A basic principle of the American legal system is that each case and each defendant will be considered individually. To some, however, **assembly-line justice** is a more realistic description of how the criminal courts operate. Particularly in the misdemeanor

Assembly-line justice: The operation of any segment of the criminal justice system in which excessive workload results in decisions being made with such speed and impersonality that defendants are treated as objects to be processed rather than as individuals.

and traffic courts of large cities, dispositions are usually made with lightning speed. A person's day in court to answer a charge of speeding may consist of less than a minute before the judge.

Assembly-line justice is partially a reflection of the large numbers of cases that reach the courts. Every year approximately 14 million persons are arrested by the police, 3 million for felonies and the rest for misdemeanors. Because of the large volume, overworked officials are often more interested in moving the steady stream of cases than in individually weighing each case on the scales of justice. Particularly in large cities, there are tremendous pressures to move cases lest the backlog become worse and delays increase. In short, law on the books suggests a justice process with unlimited resources, whereas law in action stresses an administrative process geared to disposing of a large volume of cases.

Discretion

Law on the books projects an image of a legal system that seemingly runs by itself; it is a mechanical process of merely applying rules of law to given cases. Law in action, however, emphasizes a legal system in which the legal actors exercise **discretion** because choices must be made. Prosecutors, for example, exercise discretion in deciding whether to charge a defendant with a violation of the law, and judges clearly exercise discretion when deciding whether to send defendants to prison or place them on probation.

One reason actors in the criminal court community exercise discretion is that the law provides minimal guidance for making decisions. Sentencing provides the clearest example. For each criminal offense, the law specifies a potential range of penalties: probation, prison, or a fine. The legislative law, however, provides only the broadest standards for deciding where in the range of penalties a particular defendant's case should fall. Such discretionary decisions are required at virtually every step of the criminal court process. Judges, prosecutors, and defense attorneys also exercise discretion in an attempt to make the system fair. They seek individualized jus-

tice. In short, law on the books emphasizes a law that is fixed and absolute, whereas law in action emphasizes a law that is flexible, requiring discretion in its application.

The Courtroom Work Group

Although we usually think of the criminal courts in terms of a conflict at trial, a more realistic appraisal is one of limited cooperation among the major participants. Whereas defendants come and go, the judges, prosecutors, and defense attorneys work together daily. They are tied together by more than a shared workplace, the courtroom; each is dependent on the others. Because defense attorneys seldom have resources to investigate a case fully, they are dependent on the prosecutor for access to police reports and the like. Because prosecutors have more cases to try than time to try them, they must rely on guilty pleas from the defense to secure convictions. Because judges want to prevent a backlog of cases from developing, they are dependent on prosecutors and defense attorneys to negotiate pleas. Such cooperation is a two-way street, of course. Actors who work within the system can expect to receive some benefits. Defense attorneys who do not needlessly make additional work for the others are sometimes able to secure a lighter than normal sentence for their clients. On the other hand, actors who challenge the system can expect sanctions. Defendants represented by uncooperative defense counsel sometimes receive longer prison terms than they would otherwise.

This **courtroom work group** is best described as a social organization. No individual actor works in social isolation; each can accomplish tasks only by interacting with the others. The network of cooperation underlying the courtroom community produces a commonly understood set of practices. Courts develop rules of thumb about how certain types of cases will be handled and what penalties will be applied. In short, law on the books stresses conflict at trial, whereas law in action finds a courtroom work group marked by limited cooperation between the key actors.

Discretion: The lawful ability of an agent of government to exercise choice in making a decision.

Courtroom work group: The regular participants in the day-to-day activities of a particular courtroom: judge, prosecutor, and defense attorney interact on the basis of shared norms.

CONTROVERSY

Overview

 To an unprecedented degree the courts in the United States are the subject of seemingly constant criticism and debate. Each chapter of the book examines one or more controversies. Some of these issues involve what cases courts should decide (and which courts should decide them). Others center on the actors in the system, ranging from the diversity of the bench to efforts to better aid victims of crime. Finally, many of the controversies center on the steps of the process, ranging from pretrial release to too many habeas petitions. To look ahead, here are some of the controversies that will be examined in each chapter:

COURTS AND CONTROVERSY

At the heart of the public's concern about crime has been a debate over the actions and inactions of the criminal courts. What the courts do (and don't do) and how they do it (but rarely why) occupies center stage in the nation's continuing focus on crime. Numerous reforms have been suggested, but there is no agreement over what types of change are in order. Even a brief review of the critical comments about the criminal courts discussed so far should indicate the varying and often conflicting views about what is wrong. Throughout this book Controversy sections highlight many issues facing the

courts that are debated today (see Controversy: Overview).

In the public dialogue on the issues facing the criminal courts, conservatives square off against liberals, hard-liners against those said to be soft on crime. This sort of terminology is not very helpful. Such phrases as "soft on crime" attract our attention to questions about the goals of the criminal courts, but they are not useful for systematic inquiry because they are ambiguous and emotional. More constructive in understanding the controversy over the criminal courts are the crime control and due process models developed by Herbert Packer (1968) and discussed by Samuel Walker (2001). In an unemotional way, these two models

FIGURE 1-5	Competing Values in the Criminal Justice System	
	Crime Control Model	*Due Process Model*
Key value	Repress crime.	Protect rights of citizens.
Causes of crime	Breakdown of individual responsibility.	Root causes are poverty and racial discrimination.
Police fact-finding	Most likely to determine guilt or innocence.	Only formal fact-finding can protect the innocent.
Goal of courts	Process guilty defendants quickly.	Careful consideration of each case.
Rights of defendants	Technicalities let crooks go free.	Price we pay for living in a democracy.
Sentencing	Punishment will deter crime.	Rehabilitation will prevent crime.

highlight competing values concerning the proper role of the criminal courts. The conservative crime control model proposes to reduce crime by increasing the penalties on criminals. On the other hand, the liberal due process model advocates social programs aimed primarily at reducing crime by reducing poverty. Figure 1-5 summarizes the two views.

Crime Control Model

The most important value in the **crime control model** is the repression of criminal conduct. Unless crime is controlled, the rights of law-abiding citizens will not be protected, and the security of society will be diminished. Conservatives see crime as the product of a breakdown of individual responsibility and self-control. To reinforce social values of discipline and self-control, and to achieve the goal of repressing crime, the courts must process defendants efficiently. They should rapidly remove defendants against whom there is inadequate evidence and quickly determine guilt according to evidence. The crime control model holds that informal fact-finding—initially by the police and later by the prosecutor—not only is the best way to determine whether the defendant is in fact guilty but is also sufficiently foolproof to prevent the innocent from being falsely convicted. The crime control model, therefore, stresses the necessity of speed and finality in the courts in order to achieve the priority of crime suppression.

According to the crime control model, the courts have hindered effective law enforcement and therefore have produced inadequate protection of society. Advocates of this model are concerned that criminals "beat the system" and "get off easy." In their view the cure is to eliminate legal loopholes by curtailing the exclusionary rule, abolishing the insanity defense, allowing for preventive detention of dangerous offenders, and increasing the certainty of punishment.

 The National Center for Policy Analysis is an advocacy group often associated with the crime control model of criminal justice. For their views on a variety of criminal justice issues go to **http://www.ncpa.org/pi/crime.htm**.

For an up-to-date list of Web links, go to **http://www.wadsworth.com/product/0534563406s**.

Due Process Model

In contrast, the **due process model** emphasizes protecting the rights of the individual. Its advocates are concerned about lawbreaking; they see the need to protect the public from predatory criminals. At the

Crime control model: A perspective on the criminal justice process based on the proposition that the most important function of criminal justice is the repression of crime, focusing on efficiency as a principal measure.

Due process model: A philosophy of criminal justice based on the assumption that an individual is innocent until proven guilty and has a right to protection from arbitrary power of the state.

THE MURDER TRIAL OF SHAREEF COUSIN

Overview

Acting on an anonymous tip, New Orleans police department detectives arrested Shareef Cousin at his home just a few blocks from where Michael Gerardi had been slain. Nine months later the case went to trial. The state's star witness was Connie Babin, the victim's date, who identified Cousin as the attacker. The defense countered with an alibi contending that Cousin was playing basketball about the time of the shooting. After three hours of deliberations the jury in Judge Raymond Bigelow's courtroom unanimously found Cousin guilty of first-degree murder. Following the penalty phase of the trial, Shareef Cousin was sentenced to die by lethal injection.

Amid allegations that the prosecutor had improperly withheld evidence during the trial, the state's case unraveled on appeal, however. The Louisiana Supreme Court reversed on the basis of improper use of hearsay testimony. But there would be no retrial. In January 1999 District Attorney Harry Connick reluctantly dismissed the case. Yet Cousin would not walk away from death row a free man. Earlier he had pled guilty to four armed robberies and is now serving twenty years in Angola, the state's major penitentiary.

Throughout this book we will follow the murder trial of Shareef Cousin. Each chapter will examine one aspect of the prosecution, trial, and appeal of this case. The goal is to illustrate important aspects of the American justice system. Here is what to expect:

To learn more about the murder trial of Shareef Cousin go to **http://www.wadsworth.com/product/ 0534563406s**. This companion Web site provides additional resources, including timelines of key events, list of participants, photos, key documents in the case, newspaper stories of the case, court opinions, motions filed, and much more.

same time, however, they believe that granting too much leeway to law enforcement officials will only result in the loss of freedom and civil liberties for all Americans. This alternative diagnosis stresses different causes of crime. Liberals see crime not as a product of individual moral failure but as the result of social influences (Currie 1985). In particular, unemployment, racial discrimination, and governmental policies that work to the disadvantage of the poor are the root causes of crime; only by changing the social environment will crime be reduced (Currie 1989).

Although adherents of the due process model do not downgrade the need for controlling crime, they believe that single-minded pursuit of such a goal threatens individual rights and poses the threat of a tyrannical government. Thus, the key function of the courts is not the speed and finality projected in the crime control model, but an insistence on careful consideration of each case. The dominant image is one of the courts operating as an *obstacle course*. The due process model stresses the possibility of error in the informal fact-finding process and therefore insists on formal fact-finding, to protect against mistakes made by the police and prosecutors. Proponents of the due process model believe that the courts' priority should be to protect the rights of the individual. Any resulting decrease in the efficiency of the courts is the price we must pay in a democracy based on individual liberties.

The due process model emphasizes the need to reform people through rehabilitation. Community-based sentencing alternatives are considered preferable to the extensive use of prison sentences. Advocates of this approach are concerned that the court system is fundamentally unfair to poor and minority defendants; they therefore support the decisions of the Warren Court expanding protections of criminal defendants.

 The American Civil Liberties Union (ACLU) is often identified with the due process model of criminal justice. For their views on a variety of criminal justice issues go to **http://www.aclu.org**.

For an up-to-date list of Web links, go to **http://www.wadsworth.com/product/0534563406s**.

CONCLUSION

To some, the refusal of District Attorney Harry Connick to try Shareef Cousin a second time represented a miscarriage of justice—a brutal murderer was released on a legal technicality. In the words of Connie Babin, the victim's date for that evening: "You try and do the right thing, and you get kicked in the end" (Coyle 1999). To others, the reversal of the murder conviction meant that justice eventually prevailed—an innocent man had been freed from death row. Throughout the proceedings, the defendant's family alleged racism, prosecutorial misconduct, and underhanded police work. These contrasting reactions illustrate conflicting perspectives on the meaning of justice. They also mirror conflicting views of the purposes of the criminal justice process as summarized in the crime control versus due process models of justice.

The public dialogue and media attention devoted to courts reflect the fact that law is an important part of our culture. Indeed, most Americans possess an elementary knowledge about the criminal courts. They learn in high school civics that a person is presumed innocent until proven guilty. Media coverage of dramatic criminal cases has made them aware of the number of varying steps and procedures involved in a criminal prosecution. Television shows portray some of the difficulties that detectives, prosecutors, and defense attorneys face in fulfilling their responsibilities. Although most people know something about the law, they also know much that is contrary to fact.

Some of these public understandings and misunderstandings about law are the product of education. High school American government and history textbooks, for example, offer a simplified, formal picture of law and the courts, lawyers, and trials. Americans also learn about the legal system by going to the movies, watching television, and reading fiction. At times, persons who rely on these sources are badly misled. Entertainment programs misrepresent the nature and amount of crime in the United States. Because murder makes a much better show than embezzlement or burglary, entertainment rarely shows street crime other than drug offenses.

Television also offers a number of false or doubtful propositions: It tells us, for example, that criminals are white males between the ages of twenty and fifty, that bad guys usually are businesspeople or professional criminals, and that crime is almost always unsuccessful in the end. Television and film also often misrepresent the roles of actors in the legal system. With few exceptions police are in constant action, chasing crooks in cars, running after them on foot, and capturing them only after exchanging gunfire. Perry Mason set the pattern for atypical portrayals of lawyers by always securing his client's acquittal. In addition, entertainment distorts important issues of civil liberties. As soon as we know who did it, and that the guilty crook has been apprehended, the case is solved with no need for the prosecutor to prove the defendant guilty.

These understandings and misunderstandings form the backdrop for this book. The Epilogue will examine in greater depth how and why courts figure so prominently in the public rhetoric over crime.

CRITICAL THINKING QUESTIONS

1. On a large sheet of paper, diagram the criminal justice system in your community. How well do the diagrams in this chapter fit your local community? If you live in a rural area, contemplate how different the system might be in a large city. Conversely, if you live in a big city, what differences would you expect in more rural areas?

2. What private, nongovernmental organizations are important to the criminal justice system of your community?

3. Use newspapers, radio, and criminal justice discussion lists/chat groups to monitor discussions concerning the criminal justice system. Do citizens make distinctions about police, courts, or corrections, or do they lump everything under the general rubric of the criminal justice system?

 WORLD WIDE WEB RESOURCES AND EXERCISES

Web Guides

http://dir.yahoo.com/Society_and_Culture/Crime/
http://dir.yahoo.com/Government/Law/
   Criminal_Justice/
http://dir.yahoo.com/Government/U_S__Government/
   Judicial_Branch/
http://dir.yahoo.com/Society_and_Culture/Crime/
   Outlaws/

Web Search Terms

"Criminal justice"; "administration of justice"

Useful URLs

Sourcebook of Criminal Justice Statistics. This yearly publication runs over 600 pages. As new material becomes available, it is included in the online version: **http://www.albany.edu/sourcebook/.**
CNN.COM offers the latest news about law and crime: **http://www.cnn.com/LAW/.**
The National Consortium for Justice Information and Statistics provides a multifaceted resource for operational criminal justice agencies: **http://www.search.org/.**
The Justice Information Center maintained by the National Criminal Justice Reference Service provides full text of hundreds of government publications: **http://www.ncjrs.org/.**

Uncommon URLs

Famous American Trials offers a fascinating glimpse into trials, old and new, that have shaped U.S. society: **http://www.law.umkc.edu/faculty/projects/ftrials/ftrials.htm.**
Crime Library is a gallery of famous and infamous criminals: **http://www.crimelibrary.com/.**
Cecil Greek's Homepage contains lots of links to criminal justice sites: **http://www.fsu.edu/~crimdo/greek.html.**
Journal of Criminal Justice and Popular Culture features articles on various topics as well as book reviews and movies: **http://www.albany. edu/scj/jcjpc/index.html.**
Famous Cases offers a walk through the history of the FBI: **http://www.fbi.gov/yourfbi/history/famcases/famcases.htm.**

Web Exercises

1. The Internet has been called the world's largest library, and as in any library, the easiest way to retrieve information is to go directly to the place where it is located. Each site on the Web has a unique location called a URL (Uniform Resource Locator).

   One site that contains a wealth of statistical data on the criminal justice system is maintained by the Bureau of Justice Statistics: **http://www.ojp.usdoj.gov/bjs.** Click on Expenditure & Employment and update the employment statistics discussed in this chapter. You can also use this site to add to Figure 1-3 with basic data about numbers of criminal justice agencies and employees.

2. The Internet is not only the world's largest library but also the world's largest library

without a card catalog. Unless you know specifically where to find information (the URL) you can waste a lot of time and become very frustrated in the process. Thankfully, several Web guides organize information around topics. In turn, this information is organized as a menu, which allows you to go from the most general topics (Society and Culture, for example) to specific ones. One of the most popular Web guides is Yahoo. You can access Yahoo either by clicking on Net Search on your browser and then clicking Yahoo or by going directly to Yahoo. The URL for Yahoo is **http://www.yahoo.com**. Once in Yahoo, here are the links to find information about the criminal justice system: **Society and Culture/Crime/ Organizations.**

Look for organizations that span different segments of the criminal justice system and see what they say about coordination.

3.   Select the search engine of your choice and use the search term *administration of justice* to locate three or more groups active in the crime debate. Which Web sites articulate values associated with the crime control model? Which Web sites articulate values associated with the due process model?

 INFOTRAC COLLEGE EDITION RESOURCES AND EXERCISES

Basic Search Terms

Criminal justice, administration of; crime

Recommended Articles

John Diulio, "Federal Crime Policy: Time for a Moratorium"
Kent Roach, "Four Models of the Criminal Process"
Stephen Pomper, "Reasonable Doubts"
Rebecca Porter, "Public Attitudes about Justice System Explored in Survey, Conference"

InfoTrac College Edition Exercises

1.   Using the search term *crime, causes of,* locate one article that reflects the crime control model of criminal justice and another that is based on the due process model of criminal

justice. How did you decide that the articles belong to one category and not the other? Do these two articles make arguments similar or different from those discussed in this book?

2.   Using the search term *criminal justice, administration, of* locate two or more articles that discuss the criminal justice system. To what extent do the articles emphasize the interdependent nature of the criminal justice system? To what extent do they stress the fragmentation of the criminal justice system?

REFERENCES

Bureau of Justice Statistics. 2000. *Sourcebook of Criminal Justice Statistics*—1999. Washington, D.C.: U.S. Department of Justice.

Coyle, Pamela. 1999. "Murder Victim's Date Sticks to Story." *Times-Picayune,* 9 January.

Cunningham, William, John Strauchs, and Clifford VanMeter. 1991. *Private Security: Patterns and Trends.* Washington, D.C.: National Institute of Justice.

Currie, Elliot. 1985. *Confronting Crime: An American Challenge.* New York: Pantheon.

———. 1989. "Confronting Crime: Looking Toward the Twenty-First Century." *Justice Quarterly* 6: 5–15.

Durham, Alexis. 1993. "Public Opinion Regarding Sentences for Crime: Does It Exist?" *Journal of Criminal Justice* 21: 1–11.

Gibbs, John, and Kathleen Hanrahan. 1993. "Safety Demand and Supply: An Alternative to Fear of Crime." *Justice Quarterly* 10: 369–394.

Gifford, Lea. 1999. *Justice Expenditure and Employment, 1995.* Washington, D.C.: U.S. Bureau of Justice Statistics.

Hakim, Simon, George Rengert, and Yochanan Shachmurove. 1996. "Estimation of Net Social Benefits of Electronic Security." *Justice Quarterly* 13: 153–170.

Heinz, John, and Peter Manikas. 1992. "Networks among Elites in a Local Criminal Justice System." *Law and Society Review* 26: 831–861.

McCorkle, Richard. 1993. "Research Note: Punish and Rehabilitate? Public Attitudes toward Six Common Crimes." *Crime and Delinquency* 39: 240–252.

Myers, Laura. 1996. Bringing the Offender to Heel: Views of the Criminal Courts. Pp. 46–61 in *Americans View Crime and Justice: A National Public Opinion Survey,* edited by Timothy Flanagan and Dennis Longmire. Thousand Oaks, CA: Sage Publications.

Neubauer, David. 1997. *Judicial Process: Law, Courts, and Politics in the United States,* 2d ed. Fort Worth: Harcourt Brace.

———. 2001. *Debating Crime: Rhetoric and Reality.* Belmont, CA: Wadsworth.

Packer, Herbert. 1968. *The Limits of the Criminal Sanction.* Palo Alto, CA: Stanford University Press.

Rothwax, Harold. 1996. *The Collapse of Criminal Justice.* New York: Random House.

Scheingold, Stuart. 1991. *The Politics of Street Crime: Criminal Process and Cultural Obsession.* Philadelphia: Temple University Press.

Walker, Samuel. 1992. "Origins of the Contemporary Criminal Justice Paradigm: The American Bar Foundation Survey, 1953–1969." *Justice Quarterly* 9: 47–76.

———. 2001. *Sense and Nonsense about Crime and Drugs,* 5th ed. Belmont, CA: Wadsworth.

Weingart, Saul, Francis Hartmann, and David Osborne. 1994. *Case Studies of Community Anti-Drug Efforts.* Washington, D.C.: National Institute of Justice.

Welsh, Wayne, and Henry Pontell. 1991. "Counties in Court: Interorganizational Adaptations to Jail Litigation in California." *Law and Society Review* 25: 73–102.

Witwer, Martha, and Cheryl Crawford. 1995. *A Coordinated Approach to Reducing Family Violence: Conference Highlights.* Washington, D.C.: National Institute of Justice.

Wright, Kevin. 1981. "The Desirability of Goal Conflict within the Criminal Justice System." *Journal of Criminal Justice* 9: 209–218.

FOR FURTHER READING

Blakey, Edward, and Mary Snyder. *Fortress America: Gated Communities in the United States.* Cambridge, MA: Brookings Institution Press, 1997.

Conley, John. *The 1967 President's Crime Commission Report: Its Impact 25 Years Later.* Cincinnati: Anderson, 1994.

Cook, Kathy, and Hunter Bacot. "Movies in the Classroom: Popular Images of Criminal Justice, Criminology, and the Law." *Journal of Criminal Justice Education* 4 (1993): 199–209.

del Carmen, Rolando. *Criminal Procedure: Law and Practice.* 5th ed. Pacific Grove, CA: Brooks/Cole, 2001.

Flanagan, Timothy, and Dennis Longmire, eds. *Americans View Crime and Justice: A National Public Opinion Survey.* Thousand Oaks, CA: Sage Publications, 1996.

Friedman, Lawrence. *Crime and Punishment in American History.* New York: Basic Books, 1993.

Gaubatz, Kathlyn Taylor. *Crime in the Public Mind.* Ann Arbor: University of Michigan Press, 1995.

Howell, Susan, and Brent Marshall. "Crime and Trust in Local Government: Revisiting a Black Empowerment Area." *Urban Affairs Review* (1997).

Kappeler, Victor, Mark Blumberg, and Gary Potter. *The Mythology of Crime and Justice.* 2d ed. Prospect Heights, IL: Waveland Press, 1996.

Lock, Samuel. *Crime, Public Opinion, and Civil Liberties: The Tolerant Public.* Westport, CT: Praeger Publishers, 1999.

McNeely, Connie. "Perceptions of the Criminal Justice System: Television Imagery and Public Knowledge in the United States." *Journal of Criminal Justice and Popular Culture* 3 (1995): 1–22.

Messner, Steven, and Richard Rosenfeld. *Crime and the American Dream.* Belmont, CA: Wadsworth, 1994.

Sasson, Theodore. *Crime Talk: How Citizens Construct a Social Problem.* New York: Aldine de Gruyter, 1995.

Stalans, Loretta, and Arthur Lurigio. "Public Opinion and the Criminal Justice System." *American Behavioral Scientist* 39 (1996).

Uviller, H. Richard. *Virtual Justice: The Flawed Prosecution of Crime in America.* New Haven: Yale University Press, 1996.

Walker, Samuel. *Popular Justice: A History of American Criminal Justice.* New York: Oxford University Press, 1980.

Wilson, James Q. *Thinking about Crime.* Rev. ed. New York: Basic Books, 1983.

Yanick, Danilo. *Crime, Community, and Local TV News: Covering Crime in Philadelphia and Baltimore.* Newark: Center for Community Development and Family Policy, University of Delaware, 1998.

Zemans, Frances. "The Eye of the Beholder: The Relationship between the Public and the Courts." *Justice System Journal* 15 (1991): 722–740.

The Legal System

Part I examines the legal foundations of the American judicial system, with a particular emphasis on criminal law and the criminal courts.

Chapter 2 provides an overview of law, America's common law heritage, adversarial justice, and the rights of the accused. Particular attention is devoted to how the criminal law defines certain acts as illegal. Topics to be highlighted include the growing use of civil law for what traditionally had been criminal matters and how criminal law is both constant and changing.

Chapter 3 examines the federal court system with its four tiers of courts: magistrate courts, U.S. District Court, U.S. Courts of Appeal, and U.S. Supreme Court. The federal courts also have an important array of administrative mechanisms. Some of the topics of interest include the rising volume of federal caseloads and efforts to federalize state crimes.

Chapter 4 focuses on the organization of state courts, which in most states consists of four levels: minor trial courts, major trial courts, intermediate courts of appeals, and state supreme court. Of special interest are efforts to reform court structures and the consequences of the diversity of judicial bodies. Drug courts are an example of current efforts to modernize the judiciary.

■ ■ ■

Chapter 2

Law and Crime

IN A FLAT, DISEMBODIED MONOTONE, THE COURT CLERK READ THE JURY verdict: "Not guilty." The nation reacted either in stunned silence or jubilant celebration. The verdict, like the thirty-seven-week-long trial of O. J. Simpson, divided the nation, largely along racial lines. But the criminal verdict did not end the matter. Victims of crime are increasingly filing civil lawsuits to right a wrong they believe was done by a criminal court jury. Thus the parents of Nicole Brown Simpson and Ronald Goldman filed a civil action for wrongful death. This time the jury found Simpson liable for the slayings and awarded $33.5 million in damages. Even though the parents were unlikely to collect enough money to cover their legal expenses, they felt that at last justice had been done.

The multiple legal proceedings surrounding the deaths of Nicole Brown Simpson and Ronald Goldman illustrate the complexities of U.S. law. And it is this law that constitutes the basic source of authority for the court. Thus, before we can assess the type of justice produced by the courts, we need to know something about the law that is applied in reaching those results. Bear in mind that the United States has no uniform set of criminal or civil laws. Instead, each jurisdiction enacts its own set of criminal prohibitions, leading to some important variations from state to state. ■

This chapter begins by providing a working definition of law and then examines our common law heritage, including the adversary system and the rights of the accused. Next the discussion shifts from procedure to substance. After looking at differences between civil law and criminal law, we will concentrate on the elements of a crime and legal defenses. The chapter concludes by discussing how American criminal law is both constant and changing and the consequences of this for the criminal courts.

THE BASIS OF LAW

The basis of law can be summarized in two words: human conflict. A controversy over how much money is owed, a quarrel between husband and wife, a collision at an intersection, and the theft of a television set are a few examples of the great number of disputes that arise and threaten to disrupt the normal activities of society. Business, transportation, and everyday activities depend on mechanisms for mediating inevitable human conflicts. Without such mechanisms, individual parties might seek private, violent means of settlement. The legendary feud between the Hatfields and the McCoys illustrates the disruptiveness of blood feuds motivated by revenge—not only in the lives of the individual parties directly involved but also in the larger society.

Law is an everyday word, but as Law Professor Lawrence Friedman (1984, 2) suggests, "It is a word of many meanings, as slippery as glass, as elusive as a soap bubble." Although there are various approaches to defining the term, most scholars define

law as a body of rules enacted by public officials in a legitimate manner and backed by the force of the state (Neubauer 1997). This definition can be broken into four phrases, and each has important implications for how we think about law.

The first element—law is a body of rules—is self-evident. What is not immediately obvious, however, is the fact that these rules and regulations are found in a variety of sources: statutes, constitutions, court decisions, and administrative regulations.

The second element—law is enacted by public officials—is of critical importance. All organizations of any size or complexity have rules and regulations that govern their members. But these private rules are not law under our definition, unless they are recognized by public officials—judges, legislators, and executives in particular.

The third element—law is enacted in a legitimate manner—means that it must be agreed upon ahead of time how the rules will be changed. Thus, legislatures have methods for passing new laws, bureaucrats have procedures for applying those rules, and judges follow a well-known process in interpreting those rules.

The final element—law is backed by the force of the state—says that these rules and regulations would be largely meaningless without sanctions. Thus, what differentiates law from other societal rules is that law has teeth to it. As Daniel Oran's *Law Dictionary for Nonlawyers* (1985) puts it, law is "that which must be obeyed." In most instances, however,

Law: Body of rules, enacted by public officials in a legitimate manner and backed by the force of the state.

it is not necessary to apply legal sanctions, because the threat is enough to keep most people in line most of the time.

It is also important to stress what this working definition of law omits, namely, any mention of justice. In a representative democracy, public perceptions of law embody fundamental notions of justice, fairness, and decency (Walker 2001). It is the potential linking of law and justice (in the form of unjust laws) that also makes law so difficult to define. But law and morality do not necessarily equate. Our working definition of law deliberately excludes any reference to justice because there is no precise legal or scientific meaning to the term. Furthermore, people use *justice* to support particular political and social goals. In the public arena, *justice* is a catchall used in several different ways. As discussed in Chapter 1, backers of the crime control model see justice differently than do supporters of the due process model.

 To further explore legal concepts, go to the Virtual Law Library provided by the Indiana University School of Law– Bloomington: **http://www.law.indiana. edu/v-lib/**.

For an up-to-date list of Web links, go to **http:// www.wadsworth.com/product/0534563406s**.

THE COMMON LAW HERITAGE

The American legal system traces its origins to England and is therefore referred to as Anglo-Saxon or **Anglo-American law**. Common law is utilized in English-speaking nations, including England, Australia, New Zealand, Canada, and the United States. (The only exception is the state of Louisiana, which derives its civil law from the Napoleonic Code and the Continental legal heritage; the state's criminal law, however, derives from the common law.)

The common law first appeared in medieval England after the Norman conquest of England in 1066. The new rulers gradually introduced central governmental administration, including the establishment of courts of law. Initially, the bulk of the

law was local and was administered in local courts or the private courts of the feudal lords. A distinct body of national law began to develop during the reign of Henry II (1154–1189), who was successful in expanding the jurisdiction of the royal courts. The king's courts applied the common customs of the entire realm rather than the parochial traditions of a particular village. Thus, the term **common law** meant general law as opposed to special law; it was the law common to the entire land. During the development of the common law legal system, a distinctive way of interpreting the law gradually emerged. Three key characteristics of this common law heritage stand out: The law was judge-made, based on precedent, and found in multiple sources.

Judge-Made Law

One key characteristic of the common law is that it is predominantly **judge-made law** (rather than legislatively enacted). Until the late nineteenth century there was no important body of statutory law in either England or the United States. Rather, judges performed the task of organizing social relationships through law. In the field of civil law, for example, the common law courts developed the rights and obligations of citizens in such important areas as property, contracts, and torts. Even today American law in these areas is predominantly judge-made.

Similarly, in the field of criminal law, by the 1600s the English common law courts had defined such felonies as murder, suicide, manslaughter, arson, robbery, larceny, rape, and mayhem. Moreover, the legal defenses of insanity, infancy, self-defense, and coercion had also entered the common law. These English criminal law concepts, often with some adaptations, were transplanted to America by the colonists. After the Revolution, those common law crimes considered applicable to local conditions were retained. The process of the courts creating and defining new crimes continued in America during the nineteenth century. During this period

Common law: Law developed in England by judges who made legal decisions in absence of written law. Such decisions served as precedents and became "common" to all of England. Common law is judge-made, it uses precedent, and it is found in multiple sources.

Judge-made law: The common law as developed in form and content by judges or judicial decisions.

Anglo-American law: The American legal system (see common law).

offenses such as conspiracy were developed. Although legislative bodies, not the courts, now define crimes, contemporary statutory definitions often reflect their common law heritage.

 To find historical legal documents like the Constitution and the Magna Carta, just click on **http://www. constitutioncenter.org/** and then go to Historical Documents.

For an up-to-date list of Web links, go to **http:// www.wadsworth.com/product/0534563406s**.

Precedent

A second key characteristic of the common law is the use of **precedent**, often referred to as *stare decisis* ("let the decision stand"). The doctrine of precedent requires a judge to decide a case by applying the rule of law found in previous cases, provided the facts in the current case are similar to the facts in the previous cases. By following previous court decisions, the legal system promotes the twin goals of fairness and consistency. Exhibit 2-1 gives an example of the precedent-based citation system used in American law.

The common law's reliance on precedent reflects a cautious approach to problem solving. Rather than writing a decision attempting to solve the entire range of a given legal problem, common law courts decide only as much of the case as is necessary to resolve the individual dispute. Broad rules and policy directives emerge only through the accumulation of court decisions over time. Unfortunately, many Americans make the mistake of translating the common law heritage, particularly the doctrine of precedent, into a static view of the courts and the law. The entire history of Anglo-American law emphasizes the importance of common law courts shaping old law to new demands. In the words of Justice Oliver Wendell Holmes (1920, 187): "It is revolting to have no better reason for a rule of law than that it was so laid down in the times of Henry IV. It is still more revolting if the grounds

upon which it was laid down have vanished long since, and the rule simply persists from blind imitation of the past."

One way courts achieve flexibility is in adapting old rights to new problems. Another is the ability of courts to distinguish between precedents. Recall that the doctrine of precedent involves previous cases with a similar set of facts. Courts sometimes state that the present set of facts differ from previous decisions and reach a different ruling. Finally, judges will occasionally (but very reluctantly) overturn a previous decision by stating that the previous court opinion was wrong. However, the common law is committed to gradual change in order to maintain stability; it is often said that the law and the courts are conservative institutions.

Multiple Sources of Law

The third key characteristic of the common law is that it is found in multiple sources (a concept sometimes expressed as *uncodified*). In deciding the legal meaning of a given crime (murder, for example), it is not sufficient to look only at the legislative act. One must also know how the courts have interpreted the statute. To aid lawyers and others in determining the legal meaning of crimes, a variety of annotated works contain the law plus commentary (history, explanations, and major court cases discussing the law). Although these annotated works are helpful, they are intended only as guides. They are not official and therefore are not accepted by courts as definitive statements of the law. Depending on the issue, the applicable rules of law may be found in constitutions, statutes, administrative regulations, and court decisions.

Constitutions

Within the hierarchy of law, constitutions occupy the top rung. A **constitution** is the first document that establishes the underlying principles and general laws of a nation or state. The U.S. Constitution is the fundamental law of the land. All other laws—federal, state, or local—are secondary. Similarly, each state has a constitution that is the "supreme law of the state." State courts may use the state constitution

Precedent: A case previously decided that serves as a legal guide for the resolution of subsequent cases.

Stare decisis: Latin phrase meaning "let the decision stand." The doctrine that principles of law established in earlier judicial decisions should be accepted as authoritative in similar subsequent cases.

Constitution: The fundamental rules that determine how those who govern are selected, the procedures by which they operate, and the limits to their powers.

EXHIBIT 2-1 How to Read Legal Citations

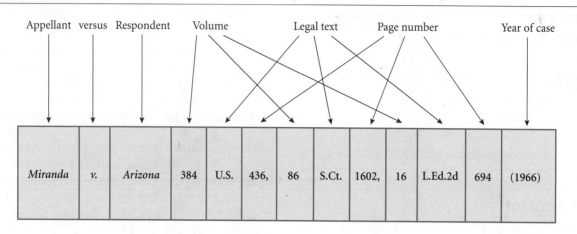

When first confronted with legal citations, students are often bewildered by the array of numbers. But with a few basics in mind, these citations need not be confusing; they are efficient aids in finding court decisions.

The full citation for *Miranda* is as follows: *Miranda v. Arizona,* 384 U.S. 436, 86 S.Ct. 1602, 16 L.Ed.2d 694 (1966). The lead name in the case usually refers to the party who lost in the lower court and is seeking to overturn that decision. That party is called the *appellant.* The second name refers to the other party (or parties) who won at the lower level (in this instance, the state of Arizona). The second party is called the *appellee,* or more simply, the *respondent.* Miranda is the appellant who is seeking to overturn his conviction. The state of Arizona is named as the respondent because criminal prosecutions are brought in the name of the state.

After the names of the parties come three sets of references. All decisions of the U.S. Supreme Court are reported in the *Supreme Court Reports,* which is published by the U.S. Government Printing Office. It is the official reporting system and is abbreviated U.S. In addition, decisions of the Supreme Court are reported in two private reporting systems: the *Supreme Court Reporter,* which is abbreviated S.Ct., and in *Lawyers Supreme Court Reports, Lawyers Edition,* which is abbreviated L.Ed.2d.

The numbers preceding the abbreviation for the volume refer to the volume number. Thus, *Miranda* can be found in volume number 384 of the *Supreme Court Reports.* The numbers after the abbreviation refer to the page number. Thus the *Miranda* decision in volume 384 begins on page 436, and in volume 86 of the *Supreme Court Reporter,* it is on page 1602, and so on. A library usually carries only one of the reporting systems, so the multiple references make it easy to locate the given case, no matter which of the three reporting systems is available.

Decisions of other appellate courts at both the federal and state levels are reported in a similar manner in other volumes.

to invalidate the actions of legislators, governors, or administrators.

Constitutions define the powers that each branch of government may exercise. For instance, Article III of the U.S. Constitution creates the federal judiciary (see Chapter 3).

Constitutions also limit governmental power. Some limitations take the form of prohibitions. Thus, Article I, Section 9, states, "The privilege of the Writ of Habeas Corpus shall not be suspended." Other limitations take the form of specific rights granted to citizens. The clearest example is the first ten amendments to the Constitution, known collectively as the Bill of Rights. For example, the First Amendment begins "Congress shall make no law respecting an establishment of religion, or prohibiting the free exercise thereof." State constitutions also contain bills of rights, many of which are modeled after their national counterpart.

Constitutions also specify how governmental officials will be selected. The U.S. Constitution provides that federal judges shall be nominated by the president, confirmed by the Senate, and serve for "good behavior." Similarly, state constitutions specify that state judges will be selected by election, appointment, or merit (see Chapter 8).

Statutes

The second rung of law consists of **statutes**. Laws enacted by federal and state legislatures are usually referred to as statutory law. The statutory law enacted by local units of government is commonly called a **municipal ordinance**.

Until the latter part of the nineteenth century, American legislatures played a secondary role in the formulation of law. It was not until the twentieth century that state legislatures became the principal source of law (Friedman 1984). A fundamental reason for the growing importance of legislatively enacted statutes was that new types of problems faced a rapidly industrializing society. Questions of how to protect the interests of workers and consumers were much broader in scope than those typically handled by the courts. The common law took decades to develop and refine legal rights and obligations, but the growing needs of an increasingly complex society could not afford the luxury of such a lengthy time frame. Legislators could enact rules of law that were not only much broader in scope than those adopted by judges but were also more precise and detailed. Thus, a great deal of law today is statutory.

Administrative Regulations

The third rung of American law consists of **administrative regulations**. Legislative bodies delegate rule-making authority to a host of governmental bureaucracies variously called agencies, boards, bureaus, commissions, or departments. All levels of government—federal, state, and local—authorize administrative agencies to issue specific rules and regulations consistent with the general principles specified in the statute or municipal ordinance. The Internal Revenue Service, by rule, decides what constitutes a legitimate deduction. State boards, by rule, set standards for nursing homes. Local zoning boards, by rule, decide where restaurants may be built.

> **Statute:** A written law enacted by a legislature.
>
> **Municipal ordinance:** Laws passed by local units of government.
>
> **Administrative regulations:** Rules and regulations adopted by administrative agencies that have the force of law.

Administrative regulations are the newest, fastest-growing, and least-understood source of law. The rules and regulations promulgated by governmental agencies are extensive. The federal bureaucracy alone issues approximately 7,000 rules and policy statements each year. Controlling the actions and inactions of unelected bureaucrats has always been a major concern in the United States. Besides the substantive laws promulgated by administrative agencies, there are also rules and regulations relating to procedure. **Administrative law** concerns the duties and proper running of an administrative agency.

Judicial Decisions

Appellate court decisions also remain an important source of law (Exhibit 2-1). According to the common law tradition, courts do not make law, they merely find it. But this myth, convenient as it was for earlier generations, cannot mask the fact that courts do make law. This tradition, though, suggests a basic difference between legislative and judicial bodies. Legislative bodies are free to pass laws boldly and openly. Moreover, their prescription of the rules is general and all-encompassing. Courts make law more timidly, on a piece-by-piece basis, and operate much more narrowly. In the words of Law Professor Lawrence Friedman (1984), "Legislatures make law wholesale while courts make it retail."

Although American law today is primarily statutory and administrative, vestiges of judge-made law persist. The law governing personal injury (tort) remains principally judge-made law, as do procedural matters such as rules of evidence. The major influence of case law (another term for court decisions), however, is seen in interpreting the law of other sources. The Constitution is a remarkably short document of some 4,300 words, and it is full of generalizations such as "due process of law," "equal protection of the laws," and "unreasonable searches and seizures." The founding fathers left later generations to flesh out the operating details of government. Supreme Court decisions have been primarily responsible for adapting constitutional provisions to changing circumstances. Through an extensive body of case law, the Court has supplied specific meaning to these vague phrases. For this

> **Administrative law:** Law that governs the duties and proper running of an administrative agency.

reason, the Court has often been termed an ongoing constitutional convention (Chapter 17).

Case law is vital in determining the meaning of other sources of law as well. Statutes, for example, address the future in general and flexible language. The interpretations that courts provide can either expand or contract the statute's meaning. No lawyer is comfortable with his or her interpretation of an alleged violation of the criminal law without first checking to see how the courts have interpreted it.

THE ADVERSARY SYSTEM

Law is both substantive and procedural. **Substantive law** creates legal obligations. Tort, contract, property, domestic relations, and inheritance are examples of substantive civil law. Murder, robbery, rape, burglary, and assault are examples of substantive criminal law. **Procedural law**, on the other hand, establishes the methods of enforcing these legal obligations. Trials are the best-known aspect of American procedural law, but trials do not exist alone. Before trial there must be orderly ways to start lawsuits, conduct them, and end them. An important aspect of procedural law centers on the roles lawyers and judges play in the legal process.

The premise of the Anglo-American legal system is that the best way for courts to apply the law is through the **adversary system**, a battle between two differing parties. Under the adversary system the burden is on the prosecutor to prove the defendant guilty beyond a reasonable doubt, and the defense attorney is responsible for arguing for the client's innocence and asserting legal protections. The judge serves as a neutral arbitrator who stands above the fight as a disinterested party, ensuring that each side

> **Substantive law:** Law that deals with the content or substance of the law, for example, the legal grounds for divorce.
>
> **Procedural law:** Law that outlines the legal procedures of process to be followed in starting, conducting, and finishing a lawsuit.
>
> **Adversary system:** A proceeding in which the opposing sides have the opportunity to present their evidence and arguments.

battles within the established rules. Finally, the decision is entrusted to the jury (although in some instances a judge alone may decide). The adversary system reflects two important premises: the need for safeguards and the presumption of innocence.

Safeguards

The first safeguard of the adversary system involves testing evidence. When the two parties approach "the facts from entirely different perspectives and objectives . . . [they] will uncover more of the truth than would investigators, however industrious and objective, seeking to compose a unified picture of what has occurred" (American Bar Association 1970, 3). Through cross-examination, each side has the opportunity to examine witnesses' truthfulness, to probe for possible biases, and to test what witnesses actually know, not what they think they know. The right to cross-examination is protected by the Sixth Amendment: "In all criminal prosecutions, the accused shall enjoy the right . . . to be confronted with witnesses against him."

The adversary system imposes a second type of safeguard by putting power in several different hands. Each actor is granted limited powers, and each has limited powers to counteract the others. If the judge is biased or unfair, the jury has the ability to disregard the judge and reach a fair verdict; if the judge believes the jury has acted improperly, he or she may set aside the jury's verdict and order a new trial. This diffusion of powers in the adversary system incorporates a series of checks and balances aimed at curbing political misuse of the criminal courts.

In diffusing power, the adversary system provides a third safeguard: It charges a specific actor—the defense attorney—with asserting the rights of the accused. Defense attorneys search out potential violations of the rights of the accused. They function as perpetual challengers in the criminal court process and, in theory at least, are ready at every juncture to challenge the government by insisting that the proper procedures be followed.

Presumption of Innocence

One of the most fundamental protections recognized in the American criminal justice process is the **pre-**

sumption of innocence. The state has the burden of proving defendants guilty of alleged crimes; defendants are not required to prove themselves innocent. This difference is fundamental. A moment's reflection makes clear how difficult it would be to prove that something did not happen or that a person did not do an alleged criminal act. Therefore, a defendant is cloaked with the legal shield of innocence during the criminal justice process.

In meeting the obligation to prove the defendant guilty, the prosecution is required to prove the defendant guilty **beyond a reasonable doubt**. This legal yardstick measures the sufficiency of the evidence; it means that the jury must be fully satisfied that the person is guilty. It does not mean the jury must be 100 percent convinced, but it comes close (Oran 1985). The state's burden of proof beyond a reasonable doubt does not require that the state establish absolute certainty by eliminating all doubt whatsoever—only that it eliminate reasonable doubt. This criterion is more stringent than the burden of proof in a civil case, in which the yardstick is the **preponderance of the evidence**, meaning a slight majority of the evidence for one side or the other.

THE RIGHTS OF THE ACCUSED

Procedural law in the United States places a heavy emphasis on protecting the individual rights of each citizen. A key feature of a democracy is the insistence that the prevention and control of crime be accomplished within the framework of law. The criminal process embodies some of society's severest sanctions: detention before trial, confinement in prison

---

Presumption of innocence: The defendant is presumed to be innocent, and the burden is on the state to prove guilt beyond a reasonable doubt.

Beyond a reasonable doubt: Burden of proof required by law to convict a defendant in a criminal case.

Preponderance of the evidence: In civil law, the standard of proof required to prevail at trial. To win, the plaintiff must show that the greater weight, or preponderance of the evidence, supports his or her version of the facts.

---

after conviction, and, in certain limited situations, execution of the offender. Because the powers of the criminal courts are so great, there is concern that those powers not be abused or misapplied. The Judeo-Christian tradition places a high value on the worth and liberty of each individual citizen.

Restrictions on the use and application of governmental power take the form of rights granted to the accused. One of the most fundamental protections is the right to remain silent. Another is the right to a trial by jury. These protections exist not to free the guilty but to protect the innocent (see Figure 2-1). Basing the criminal justice process on the necessity of protecting individual liberties (of the innocent and guilty alike) obviously reduces the effectiveness of that process in fighting crime. To ensure that innocent persons are not found guilty, Anglo-American criminal law pays the price of freeing some of the guilty.

The American tradition of instituting limits on the use of governmental power flows from several basic concerns. The primary justification for providing constitutional safeguards for those caught in the net of the criminal process is to ensure that innocent persons are not harassed or wrongly convicted. The American legal system is premised on a distrust of human fact-finding. Because it fears human errors, the criminal court process provides multiple review points, believing that errors made at one step will be spotted during a later stage. The possibility of wrongly convicting an innocent person arises when honest mistakes are made by honorable people. But it also arises when dishonorable officials use the criminal justice process for less-than-honorable ends. In countries without built-in checks, the criminal justice process provides a quick and easy way for governmental officials to dispose of their enemies. For example, a common ploy in a totalitarian government is to charge persons with the ill-defined crime of being an "enemy of the state." The possibility of political misuse of the criminal justice process by a tyrannical government or tyrannical officials is a major concern in the Anglo-American heritage.

Another reason that democracies respect the rights of those accused or suspected of violating the criminal law is the need to maintain the respect and support of the community. Democratic governments derive their powers from the consent of the governed. Such support is undermined if power is applied arbitrarily. Law enforcement practices that

FIGURE 2-1 Provisions of the U.S. Constitution Dealing with Criminal Procedure

	Constitutional Language
Crime	Article I Section 9.3: No bill of attainder may be passed by the legislature.
	Article I Section 10.1: No state may pass any bill of attainder.
	Article I Section 9.3: The legislature may not pass an ex post facto law.
	Article I Section 10.1: No state may pass an ex post facto law.
Arrest	None
Initial appearance	Amendment VI: Right to know charges.
Bail	Amendment VIII: Right against excessive bail.
Preliminary hearing	Amendment VI: Right to assistance of counsel.
Charging	None
Grand jury	Amendment V: Right to a grand jury for a capital or otherwise infamous crime.
Arraignment	Amendment VI: Right to know charges.
Evidence	Amendment IV: Right against unreasonable search and seizures.
	Amendment V: Right against self-incrimination.
Plea bargaining	None
Trial	Amendment V: Right not to be tried twice for the same crime.
	Amendment VI: Right to a speedy trial; right to an impartial jury; right to a public trial; right to be confronted by witnesses against oneself; right to a jury from state or district where crime shall have been committed; right to obtain witnesses in one's favor; right to conduct cross-examination; right to speak at trial.
Sentencing	Amendment VIII: Right against excessive fines; right against cruel and unusual punishment.
	Amendment XIII: Right against involuntary servitude.
Appeal	Article I Section 9.2: Privilege of the writ of habeas corpus shall not be suspended.

are brutal, random, or overzealous are likely to produce fear and cynicism among the people—lawbreakers and law abiders alike. Such practices undermine the legitimacy that law enforcement officials must have to enforce the law in a democracy. Even in a dictatorship, efforts are often made to portray an image of a fair trial.

A hallmark of American law, then, is that governmental officials must follow a regularized set of procedures in making decisions. The essential goal is to reduce arbitrariness by government officials (Skolnick 1994). In short, we expect our leaders to make decisions according to an agreed-upon set of legal procedures.

Due Process

The principal legal doctrine for limiting the arbitrariness by officials is due process. Due process of law is mentioned twice in the Constitution:

- "No person shall . . . be deprived of life, liberty or property without due process of law." (Fifth Amendment)

- "No state shall deprive any person of life, liberty or property without due process of law." (Fourteenth Amendment)

The concept of **due process of law** has a broad and somewhat elastic meaning, with definitions varying in detail from situation to situation. The core of the

 Mark Goldie, "The Bill of Rights, 1689 and 1998"

Due process of law: A right guaranteed in the Fifth, Sixth, and Fourteenth Amendments of the U.S. Con-idea of due process is that a person should always be given notice of the charges brought against him or her and be provided a real chance to present his or her side in a legal dispute and that no law or government procedure should be arbitrary. The specific requirements of due process vary somewhat, depending on the Supreme Court's latest interpretations of the Bill of Rights.

 You can view the original copy of the Bill of Rights on the Internet thanks to the National Records and Archive Administration at **http://www.nara.gov/ exhall/charters/billrights/billmain.html**.

For an up-to-date list of Web links, go to **http:// www.wadsworth.com/product/0534563406s**.

Bill of Rights

The major obstacle to the ratification of the Constitution was the absence of specific protections for individual rights. Several of the most prominent leaders of the American Revolution opposed the adoption of the Constitution, fearing that the proposed national government posed as great a threat to the rights of the average American as had the king of England. Therefore, shortly after the adoption of the Constitution, ten amendments, collectively known as the **Bill of Rights**, were adopted. Many of these protections—particularly the Fourth, Fifth, Sixth, and Eighth Amendments—deal specifically with criminal procedure.

Originally, the protections of the Bill of Rights restricted only the national government. Through a legal doctrine known as **incorporation**, however, the Supreme Court ruled that the due process clause of the Fourteenth Amendment made some provisions of the Bill of Rights applicable to the states as well. Although not all the protections of the Bill of Rights have been incorporated into the Fourteenth Amendment, all of the major protections now apply

stitution and generally understood to mean the due course of legal proceedings according to the rules and forms established for the protection of private rights.

Bill of Rights: The first ten amendments to the U.S. Constitution, guaranteeing certain rights and liberties to the people.

Incorporation: The theory that the Bill of Rights has been incorporated or absorbed into the due process clause of the Fourteenth Amendment, thereby making it applicable to the states.

to the states as well as the national government (Figure 2-2). The major provisions of the Bill of Rights incorporated through the due process clause of the Fourteenth Amendment are protections against unreasonable searches and seizures (Fourth Amendment); protection against self-incrimination (Fifth); the right to counsel and trial by jury (Sixth); and the prohibition against cruel and unusual punishment (Eighth). Some have aptly called the Bill of Rights a constitutional code of criminal procedure.

State constitutions also contain bills of rights that are increasingly important in determining individual rights and liberties. As the U.S. Supreme Court has become more conservative, state supreme courts have treated state constitutions as an independent basis for establishing rights of privacy and due process.

CIVIL LAW

Most disputes that come to court involve private parties. Conflicts over ownership of property, failure to live up to the terms of a contract, or injuries suffered in an automobile accident are settled on the basis of the body of rules collectively known as **civil law**. These suits are brought because the courts possess powers that private parties do not; courts can order a business to pay another business money owed under a contract, grant a husband and wife a divorce, award monetary damages suffered for an injury received in an automobile accident, and so forth.

A civil suit is brought by a private party to enforce a right or to seek payment for a wrong committed by another private party. But "private parties" are not limited to individual citizens. They may include groups of citizens (advocacy groups and home owners' associations, for example) as well as businesses and the government. Given these "legal fictions," it is best to view civil law as every lawsuit other than a criminal proceeding.

 The premier Web site for legal research is **http:// www.findlaw.com**.

For an up-to-date list of Web links, go to **http:// www.wadsworth.com/product/0534563406s**.

Civil law: Law governing private parties; other than criminal law.

FIGURE 2-2 Cases Incorporating Provisions of the Bill of Rights into the Due Process Clause of the Fourteenth Amendment

First Amendment

Establishment of religion	*Everson v. Board of Education*	1947
Free exercise of religion	*Cantwell v. Connecticut*	1940
Freedom of speech	*Gitlow v. New York*	1925
Freedom of the press	*Near v. Minnesota*	1931
Freedom to peaceably assemble	*DeJong v. Oregon*	1937
Freedom to petition government	*Hague v. CIO*	1939

Second Amendment

Right of the militia to bear arms	[*Presser v. Illinois*, 1886]	NI

Fourth Amendment

Unreasonable search and seizure	*Wolf v. Colorado*	1949
Exclusionary rule	*Mapp v. Ohio*	1961

Fifth Amendment

Grand jury	[*Hurtado v. California*, 1884]	NI
No double jeopardy	*Benton v. Maryland*	1969
No self-incrimination	*Malloy v. Hogan*	1964
Compensation for taking private property	*Chicago, Burlington and Quincy Railroad v. Chicago*	1897

Sixth Amendment

Speedy trial	*Klopfer v. North Carolina*	1967
Public trial	*In re Oliver*	1948
Impartial jury	*Parker v. Gladden*	1966
Jury trial	*Duncan v. Louisiana*	1968
Venue	[Implied in Due Process]	NI
Notice	*Cole v. Arkansas*	1948
Confrontation of witnesses	*Pointer v. Texas*	1965
Compulsory process	*Washington v. Texas*	1967
Assistance of counsel	*Gideon v. Wainwright* (felony)	1963
	Argersinger v. Hamlin (some misdemeanors)	1972

Seventh Amendment

Jury trial in civil cases	[*Walker v. Sauvinet*, 1875]	NI

Eighth Amendment

No excessive bail	[*United States v. Salerno*, 1987]	NI
No excessive fines		NI
No cruel and unusual punishment	*Robinson v. California*	1962

Ninth Amendment

Privacy*	*Griswold v. Connecticut*	1965

---

*The word *privacy* does not appear in the Ninth Amendment (nor anywhere else in the Constitution) but in *Griswold* several justices viewed the Ninth Amendment as guaranteeing that right.

NI—Not incorporated

Adapted from Marvin Zalman and Larry Siegel. 1997. *Criminal Procedure: Constitution and Society,* 2d ed. (Belmont, CA: West/Wadsworth).

A DAY IN COURT

"The French Legal System"

 In French courts, the black robes are worn by lawyers, not judges. They wear red. Lawyers speak only when spoken to, while judges question witnesses. And the jury? Nowhere to be found. Juries don't decide cases in France.

As the French government builds a legal case against seven photographers who pursued Princess Diana in the final hours of her life, prepare to set aside much of what you know about the American legal system. The French legal system is rooted in the Middle Ages, owing more to Napoleon than James Madison.

America boasts an adversarial process that weighs competing rights and turns lawyers into combatants. In France, from start to finish, the process is an inquiry in which the judge is the all-powerful truth-seeker and lawyers are the supporting cast. *"Apres Dieu, c'est lui,"* says Pierre-Philippe Barkats, a lawyer licensed in France and Washington, referring to French judges. "After God, it's the judge." He adds, "This is no O. J. Simpson [trial]."

The first sign of major differences in the two legal systems came as the photographers were taken into custody after Saturday's tragedy. They were held two days without charges being filed. And they had no legal right to see their lawyers during the initial questioning — sure grounds for throwing out a case in the USA.

"The justice system in France would be unconstitutional here," says Tulane University law professor Thomas Carbonneau, who has practiced in France. "They have a very different sense of justice, that it's a job for professionals, not the people. They're less interested in public access to the process." . . .

The probe has no parallel in the U.S. system. The photographers have not been indicted, but a determination has been made that an investigation is warranted. "It's less than indictment, but it's still something significant," says Jonathan Wohl, an American lawyer in Paris. An investigating judge, who has no counterpart in the USA, will conduct the probe in close cooperation with the prosecutor. The judge's investigation could take months. If he decides no charges should be brought, the French prosecutor, unlike American district attorneys, could appeal. But if the judge decides some or all of the photographers should stand trial, the trial will get under way in a formal setting in which the lawyers must be civil and flamboyance is unwelcomed. "Lawyers are rarely celebrities in France," says Axelle Hovine, aide to a judge in Paris. "The judicial process is much more closed."

A panel of judges would preside in the trial phase and question witnesses. Answers could include almost anything, even hearsay evidence that would be barred here. The lawyers can also ask questions, but have no right to cross-examine. The judges are civil servants, not elected or appointed as in the USA. But the fact that they are bureaucrats does not necessarily give them any greater independence, says Carbonneau. "In a celebrity case like this, the judge is going to follow what he believes is the position of the executive branch," says Carbonneau. The French government, he suggests, probably wants the paparazzi punished.

If the photographers are found guilty of anything, it will not be based on the U.S. standard of guilt "beyond a reasonable doubt" but rather the *"conviction intime du juge"*—the judge's [personal] belief of what really happened.

Also highlighting the difference between the two systems is the fact that one of the charges the photographers might face in France does not even exist in the USA: failure to aid someone in danger. It does not require anyone to try to rescue someone, but they must try to get medical or police help. Lawyers for some of the photographers are already insisting that their clients arrived late to the scene and could not have done anything to interfere with rescue efforts.

The charge familiar to Americans is manslaughter. "That's very much the charge you would expect to be brought in the United States," says Laurie Levenson, a Loyola University law professor in Los Angeles. "That is defined as causing a death by reckless and grossly negligent conduct. The big issue in this case is who caused the death."

In a "piggyback" process unfamiliar in the USA, the outcome of the criminal trial—guilt or innocence—will also determine the outcome of the civil suit filed this week by Dodi Fayed's father. There will be no separate civil trial. By contrast, O. J. Simpson was found not guilty of the crime of murdering his former wife and her friend, but a separate jury found him liable for their death.

The French civil system is different in other ways, too. Punitive damage awards, which can run into millions in America, are not allowed in France. And French lawyers work for flat fees, not for a percentage

(continued on following page)

of the damage awards as in the USA. "French lawyers wonder why American lawyers make so much money," says Barkats. One reason is that American jurors are often willing to point the finger of blame in lots of directions. "There are many good causes of action here," says Jack Olender, a Washington, D.C., expert in personal injury law. But one civil charge the photographers could face, invasion of privacy, is far sterner in France than in the USA. Publication of a photo taken in a private place without the subject's permission can be penalized in France. It is unclear whether photographing someone in a car would violate French laws. . . .

In the USA, holding anyone liable in the crash would depend largely on a jury's decision about what caused the accident—photographers in pursuit, or the driver's drunken condition. In France, that determination would be made by judges, not jurors, in a methodical, unsensational atmosphere. "In France, it's much more technical. The judge is the one, like a referee on a tennis court," says French lawyer Barkats.

"He relies very much on common sense. He wants to think. He wants peace. He doesn't want cameras."

Tony Mauro, "The French Legal System," *USA Today* (September 4, 1997).

 To explore how the legal systems of other countries differ from the U.S. system, go to any of these Web sites:

International Web sites from the National Center for State Courts: **http://www.ncsc.dni.us/ COURT/SITES/courts.htm#international**

The International Center: **http://www.ojp. usdog.gov/nij/international/**

The United Nations Crime and Justice Information Network: **http://www.uncjin.org/**

For an up-to-date list of Web links, go to **http:// www.wadsworth.com/product/0534563406s**.

Basis for Filing a Civil Suit

Civil law is considerably more voluminous than criminal law. Figure 2-3 summarizes the major branches of civil law, which form the basis for filing suit in court. **Tort** law involves the legal wrong done to another person. Injuries suffered during automobile accidents are a prime example of tort law. When lawyers speak of an *injury,* however, they do not necessarily mean a physical injury. The term has a broader meaning, including any wrong, hurt, or damage done to a person's rights, body, reputation, or property.

Another type of private law involves **contracts**, or agreements between two or more persons involving a promise (termed a consideration). Insurance policies and bank loans for buying a new car are considered contracts.

Property, which centers on the ownership of things, is another division of private law. Property is

 The premier Web site for legal research is **http:// www.findlaw.com**.

For an up-to-date list of Web links, go to **http:// www.wadsworth.com/product/0534563406s**.

usually divided into *real property* (land and things attached to it) and *personal property* (everything else). Personal property can range from stocks and patents to automobiles and the right to use a famous person's name. But property does not have to be tangible. It may also include ideas. An area of property law that is increasingly important in the computer age is the law of intellectual property (formerly called patent and copyright).

Property received from a person who has died is governed by laws on **inheritance**. The best-known example is a will, a written document telling how a person's property should be distributed after his or her death.

Domestic relations constitutes a major and growing area of law. These family law matters

Tort: A private or civil wrong, not arising as the result of a breach of contract, in which the defendant's actions cause injury to the plaintiff or to property.

Contract: A legally enforceable agreement between two or more parties.

Property: Legal right to use or dispose of particular things or subjects.

Inheritance: Property received from a dead person, either by effect of intestacy or a will.

Domestic relations: Relating to the home; the law of divorce, custody, support, adoption, and so on.

FIGURE 2-3 Major Areas of Civil Law

	Law on the Books	Law in Action
Tort	A legal injury (other than contract) resulting from violating a duty.	Examples: negligence, assault, false arrest, trespass.
Contract	An agreement between two or more parties creating a legally enforceable contract.	Money owed is the major source of cases in small claims courts.
Property	Ownership of a thing: *Real property* Land and things on it. *Personal property* Everything else.	Lawsuits disputing ownership of property are rarer today than 100 years ago.
Domestic relations	Law relating to the home: *Divorce* The ending of a marriage by court order. *Custody* Court determination of care and keeping of children after divorce. *Support* Financial obligation to provide for children after divorce. *Alimony* Court-ordered payments by a divorced husband (or wife) to the ex-wife (or husband) for ongoing personal support. *Adoption* Legally taking a child of another (or, in some states, an adult) as one's own, with all the rights and duties there would have been if the child had been one's own originally.	Domestic relations constitutes the single largest category of cases filed in the major trial courts. • At times civil and criminal issues overlap, most obviously in domestic abuse cases (Chaper 9). • Formally or informally, some big cities have created family courts which handle both civil and criminal matters involving juveniles (Chapter 19). • Many reports of missing children actually involve an ex-spouse who takes a child in violation of court order regarding child custody. • Nonpayment of child support (often called deadbeat dads) is a growing problem.
Inheritance	Receipt of property from a dead person: *Will* A document in which a person tells how his or her property should be handed out after death. *Intestate* Dying without making a will. *Probate* The process of proving that a will is genuine and giving out the property in it.	Courts routinely process probate cases because the will is clear and the amount of money in question is small. On occasion, though, the heirs of the rich and famous have been known to publicly contest the large sums of money left behind.

mainly involve divorce and related issues such as determining child custody, setting levels of child support, allocating economic resources (homes, cars, and savings accounts), and in some states, providing for spousal support (alimony and the like). Some areas of domestic relations overlap with juvenile law (Chapter 19).

Remedies

Individuals, groups, or governments sue because they want something from the other party. What they want is termed a **remedy**. A court's official decision about the rights and claims of each side in a lawsuit is known as a **judgment**. Thus, if the plaintiff wins, the judgment also contains a remedy, which is the relief granted by the court. The remedies granted depend on whether the case involves

Remedy: Vindication of a claim of right. A legal procedure by which a right is enforced or the violation of a right is prevented or compensated.

Judgment: The official decision of a court concerning a legal matter.

FIGURE 2-4   **Major Civil Remedies**

	Law on the Books	*Law in Action*
Declaratory judgment	A court decision declaring the legal rights of the parties.	Principal outcome of divorce cases.
Monetary damages	*Compensatory damages* Payment for actual loses suffered by a plaintiff.	Principal outcome of tort cases.
	Punitive damages Money awarded by a court to a person who has been harmed in a malicious or willful way by another person. The purpose is to warn others.	Rarely awarded. Major source of debate over product liability.
Equity	*Temporary restraining order (T.R.O.)* A judge's order to a person to keep from taking certain action before a full hearing can be held on the question.	Can be granted without the other party present. Expires after a few days.
	Preliminary injunction A judge's order to a person to keep from taking certain action after a hearing but before the issue is fully tried.	During the hearing, both sides present their case. Plaintiff must be able to show irreparable damages will occur if injunction is not issued.
	Permanent injunction A judge's order to a person to keep from taking certain action after the issue has been fully tried.	As with all injunctions, violations are punishable by contempt of court, which can include fines but also jail time.

law or equity. Figure 2-4 summarizes the major civil remedies.

Most civil cases involve a request for monetary damages. The **plaintiff** (the person who starts a lawsuit) demands that the **defendant** (the person against whom a lawsuit is brought) pay money for the plaintiff's legal rights (an injury). For example, in a case involving an automobile accident, the injured party may request a sum of money to pay for hospital expenses, doctors' fees, lost wages, and general "pain and suffering." **Monetary damages** are sums of money that a court orders paid to a person who has suffered a legal injury. There are two principal types of monetary damages in American law. *Compensatory damages* are payments for the actual

harm suffered and may include medical bills, lost income, and pain and suffering. *Punitive damages* are monies awarded to a person who has been harmed in a particularly malicious or willful way. They are not related to the actual cost of the injury or the harm suffered, but are designed to serve as a warning to keep that sort of act from happening again. (Thus both the civil and criminal law involve deterrence.)

Another type of remedy occasionally requested is a **declaratory judgment**, which is a judicial determination of the legal rights of the parties. For example, in prisoner litigation, lawyers seek declaration that prison conditions violate constitutional standards (Chapter 15).

A third type of remedy is called an **injunction** (and comes from another type of law found in

Plaintiff: The person or party who initiates a lawsuit.

Defendant: The person or party against whom a lawsuit or prosecution is brought.

Monetary damage: Compensatory damages—payment for actual losses suffered by a plaintiff. Punitive damages —money awarded by a court to a person who has been harmed in a malicious or willful way.

Declaratory judgment: Judicial pronouncement declaring the legal rights of parties involved in an actual case or controversy.

Injunction: A court order directing someone to do something or to refrain from doing something.

England termed equity or sometimes chancellory law). An injunction is a court order that requires a person to take an action or to refrain from taking an action. For example, a court may issue an injunction prohibiting a company from dumping industrial wastes into a river. To qualify for an injunction, the plaintiff must demonstrate to the court that it will suffer irreparable damages. Consistent with the preventive and remedial heritage of equity, a judge may issue a *preliminary* or *temporary injunction* to stabilize an emergency situation. A *permanent injunction* is granted only after the issues have been fully tried in court. An injunction is a powerful measure that can be enforced by the contempt power of the court. Thus, a person who violates an injunction can be fined or sent to jail.

Using Civil Remedies to Fight Crime

Civil law is having an increasing impact on the criminal justice system (Barrineau 1994). Crime victims are filing civil lawsuits against the criminal defendant, defendants are settling in civil court in lieu of criminal prosecution, and those who perceive that their legal rights have been violated are more willing to sue criminal justice officials.

Victims of crime are increasingly resorting to civil litigation, in addition to victim compensation and restitution, as a means of recovering from the ill effects of crime (Office for Victims of Crime 1992). Moreover, victims' rights advocates are advocating civil remedies as one way for victims to reassert control (Chapter 9). In criminal prosecutions the prosecutor essentially makes all decisions, but in civil litigation it is the plaintiff and plaintiff's lawyer who make the decisions. Although parallel civil and criminal proceedings have been brought for years, they are being used today more frequently than ever before (McCampbell 1995). Three areas—drugs, rape, and drunk driving—illustrate the blending of criminal and civil law.

The overlap between civil and criminal law is highlighted by a number of recent efforts to fight drugs. Legislators at both the state and national levels are passing laws allowing for the seizure of the assets of drug dealers, eviction of residents from public housing if they are convicted of drug possession, and drug testing of employees. Similarly, the California legislature passed a law, prompted by the suicide of actor Carroll O'Connor's son, allowing suspected drug dealers to be sued for any deaths, injuries, or damages they cause. Likewise, nuisance abatement suits have targeted so-called crack houses. These essentially civil laws increase the arsenal of legal weapons law enforcement officials may use against the sale and use of illegal drugs. But some people now wonder whether the use of civil remedies, particularly asset forfeiture, may have gone too far (see Controversy: Should Asset Forfeiture Be Limited?).

Rape victims are pursuing justice in the civil courts at a growing rate, seeking damages from almost anyone they can find who may have shared liability for the rape (Balleza 1991). These lawsuits often proceed on the basis of the legal theory of *premises liability*. In premises liability cases the victim alleges that the owner and/or manager of the property failed to provide adequate security and thereby contributed to the occurrence of the crime. The claims raise issues concerning inadequate security caused by poorly trained security guards, too few security guards, or environmental design flaws. In short, premises liability lawsuits argue that the crime that occurred was foreseeable and the defendant had a legal duty to provide adequate security (Gordon and Brill 1996).

In recent years civil justice has become almost as controversial as criminal justice. Perhaps nowhere is this more apparent than in efforts to curb drunk driving. Seemingly every session, legislatures vote even tougher penalties for driving while intoxicated (Chapter 18). But at the same time, civil lawsuits filed by a person injured in an automobile accident caused by a drunk driver are viewed with skepticism. Tort reformers often implicitly suggest that such lawsuits unnecessarily drive up the already high cost of automobile insurance. It is for this reason that President Clinton labeled Republican-backed tort reform legislation the "drunk driving protection act."

The principal downside of civil remedies is the obvious—few criminal defendants have the economic resources to make litigation financially worthwhile. Indeed, in the most prominent civil lawsuits, the plaintiffs' motives have been primarily vindication, with little likelihood of collecting a dime from Bernhard Goetz, or anything close to the $8.5 million O. J. Simpson was ordered to pay (see Figure 2-5).

Should Asset Forfeiture Be Limited?

 NBC's *Dateline* television series focused on two small Louisiana parishes (the equivalent of counties elsewhere in the United States). Police were accused of targeting innocent motorists on heavily traveled I-10 and seizing their cars for a hefty departmental profit. The law lets police seize property from drivers whom they think may be violating drug laws, even if they don't find any drugs. To recover their property, motorists must first post a $2,500 bond and then wage a long court battle. The local sheriffs and district attorneys told the state legislature that the NBC report was "trash journalism designed to boost ratings." They did, however, acknowledge that their rural jurisdictions totaled $19 million a year—37 percent of all asset forfeitures in the state (Wardlaw 1997). This TV report focused national attention on complaints that some law enforcement officials have abused powers under asset forfeiture.

Asset forfeiture involves governmental seizure of the personal assets obtained from, or used in, a crime. Assets refer to property, businesses, cars, cash, and the like. For example, a car used in the distribution of illegal drugs may be forfeited to the government.

Asset forfeiture was part of British common law as early as 1660. More recently it is identified with the Racketeer Influenced and Corrupt Organizations Act (RICO for short) enacted by Congress in 1970. Congress was concerned about the infiltration of organized crime into the regular business marketplace and sought to discourage such activities by taking away the profits.

One form of asset forfeiture is criminal; a defendant convicted under the RICO law is subject not only to criminal penalties (fines and prison) but also forfeiture of property obtained from the profits of the illegal enterprise. Thus, drug dealers who pour their profits into a restaurant can have the restaurant seized by governmental agents.

But asset forfeiture is not limited to criminal actions. The more potent form of asset forfeiture is civil in nature. The government is proceeding not against a person but against the property in what is termed an *in rem* procedure. (In rem refers to a lawsuit brought against a thing rather than against a person.) In rem lawsuits rest on the legal fiction that the property itself has been charged with a crime and not the owner of the property. As a result it is easier for the government to proceed, because once the property is seized, the burden of proof is on the property owner to show that the property was not used illegally (Cassella 1996).

Through the years Congress has greatly expanded the scope of asset forfeiture (Jensen and Gerber 1996). For example, the Comprehensive Drug Abuse and Control Act of 1970 contains asset forfeiture provisions; the working premise is that illegal drug trafficking is motivated by economic rewards reaped from these illegal activities. Following the federal example, all states except one have enacted asset forfeiture laws.

Asset forfeiture has become big business; $875 million was seized in 1992, declining since then to $650 million a year. Where do these funds go? Under

Civil Liability of Criminal Justice Officials

In the modern era it is not just criminal defendants who find themselves hauled into civil court but police officers and prison guards as well. Increasingly, criminal justice officials find that they must defend themselves against a variety of types of civil lawsuits. Perhaps the best known are cases filed by prison inmates alleging that conditions of confinement constitute cruel and unusual punishment in violation of the Eighth Amendment. These lawsuits have reshaped American prisons in recent years (Chapter 15). More recently the Americans with

Disabilities Act has forced changes in the design of police stations and prisons.

Other civil lawsuits seek monetary damages for misconduct on the part of law enforcement personnel. Most commonly these lawsuits allege the police used excessive force or were negligent in using deadly force. Conversely, some lawsuits center on the inactions of law enforcement or correctional personnel. Local governments have been

In rem: Against a thing; a legal proceeding instituted to obtain decrees or judgments against property.

the "equitable sharing" program of the Department of Justice, any law enforcement agency that participates in the seizure of assets may request part of the monies related to the action, and request they do; 41 percent of local law enforcement agencies participated, with the percentage climbing to 90 percent in jurisdictions with populations of 250,000 or greater.

One concern about asset forfeiture relates to goals. Although initially designed to fight crime by hurting drug dealers and others in the pocketbook, to some the tail now wags the dog; the purpose is to seize cash in order to fund the law enforcement agency. In short, seizing drugs is of little use, because they cannot later be legally sold for a profit; it is better to wait until after the drugs are sold, so that the cash can be seized. To remove such temptations, some argue that forfeiture monies should be placed in the general revenue fund, to be spent on drug education, substance treatment programs, and the like. Under equitable sharing, local police departments can gain windfall profits in the form not only of money but also equipment, cars, and so on (Levy 1996).

Another concern is that current laws make it too easy for law enforcement officials to seize the assets of innocent persons. Defense lawyers and civil libertarians accuse the government of confiscating money or property not only from criminals but also from people with no knowledge they had received proceeds of criminal activities.

The Supreme Court has begun to rein in the government's forfeiture power. In the case of a South Dakota man who had his mobile home and auto body shop seized after being convicted of selling two grams of cocaine, the Court unanimously ruled that the amount seized (almost $43,000) was disproportionate to the crime, basing their reasoning on the Eighth Amendment's little-used ban on excessive fines (*Austin v. U.S.* 1993; Giffuni 1995). The next term, the Court held that the constitutional protections afforded criminal defendants in the Fourth Amendment (unreasonable search and seizure) and the Fifth Amendment (due process and right to notice) also apply in asset forfeiture (*U.S. v. James Daniel Good Real Property* 1993).

But innocent owners can have their assets seized (*Bennis v. Michigan* 1996). Moreover, civil forfeitures do not violate the prohibition against double jeopardy (*U.S. v. Ursery* 1996).

After years of debate Congress passed the Civil Asset Forfeiture Act of 2000, which shifts the burden of proof to the government. The new law also awards lawyers' fees to those who successfully challenge confiscation of property. These changes, though, were strongly opposed by the U.S. Department of Justice. Moreover, proponents labeled the law only a first step.

What do you think? Should more limits be placed on law enforcement officials' ability to seize assets of suspected wrongdoers? Do large financial incentives like these provide too great a temptation?

 To continue the debate you can visit the following Web sites:

Forfeiture Endangers Americans' Rights (FEAR): **http://www.fear.org/**

Liberty Project: **http://www.libertyproject.org/ splash.cfm**

For an up-to-date list of Web links, go to **http:// www.wadsworth.com/ product/0534563406s**.

---

found liable for the death of a person in detention when police officers failed to prevent suicide (Kappeler, Vaughn, and Del Carmen 1991). Similarly, prison officials have been held liable for failure to prevent inmate-against-inmate assaults (Vaughn 1996).

Criminal justice officials also find themselves in civil court as defendants in growing numbers of cases filed by their own employees. Some lawsuits allege discrimination in hiring or promotion. Others argue that the plaintiff was sexually harassed. Chapter 3, on federal courts, will explore how a wide range of federal laws shape the internal operations of law enforcement and corrections.

CRIMINAL LAW

Some disputes are viewed as so disruptive to society that they require special treatment because civil law remedies are not enough. There are several important differences between civil law and **criminal law** (see Figure 2-6 on page 46). One difference centers on who has been harmed. Whereas a breach of the civil law is considered a private matter involving

Criminal law: Laws passed by government that define and prohibit antisocial behavior.

| FIGURE 2-5 | Prominent Examples of Civil Actions Following Criminal Prosecutions |

Person	*Criminal*	*Civil*
Bernhard Goetz	Criminal jury convicted the subway vigilante of illegally having a gun but acquitted of more serious charges after 1984 shooting of a youth Goetz claimed was trying to rob him. The shooting had clear racial overtones (Goetz is white, his victim black).	A 1996 civil jury ordered Goetz to pay $43 million to the man he left paralyzed. It is unlikely that Darrell Cabey, who was paralyzed and suffered brain damage, will be able to collect from the unemployed electrician.
O. J. Simpson	In the televised "trial of the century" the jury acquitted O. J. Simpson of murdering his former wife Nicole Brown Simpson and her friend Ronald Goldman. The verdict divided the nation along racial lines.	A civil jury found Simpson liable for the killings of his ex-wife and her friend. The jury awarded $8.5 million in compensatory damages to Goldman's parents and $25 million in punitive damages. Plaintiff's ability to collect on the judgment is limited because Simpson placed most of his money in retirement accounts that cannot be seized.
Rodney King	Two Los Angeles police officers were acquitted in state court of beating Rodney King, but they were later convicted in federal court (Chapter 3).	The City of Los Angeles settled the civil lawsuit for $3.8 million.
Randall Weaver	After a months-long stand-off, federal agents arrested Randall Weaver at his mountain home in Ruby Ridge, Idaho. During the arrest a fire fight broke out and Weaver's wife was killed. A criminal jury acquitted Weaver of a variety of gun charges.	The U.S. Justice Department paid $3.1 million to settle wrongful death claims against federal agents for the 1992 death of Randall Weaver's wife and son.
Amadou Diallo	Four NYPD officers were acquitted of murder. The Justice Department will not file federal charges.	Lawsuit against the city of New York by the parents pending.

only the individual parties, violations of the criminal law are considered public wrongs. As such, criminal law relates to actions that are considered so dangerous, or potentially so, that they threaten the welfare of society as a whole.

A second difference involves prosecution. Unlike the civil law, in which private parties file suit in court alleging an infringement of private rights, violations of public wrongs are prosecuted by the state.

The type of penalties imposed on law violators is a third difference. In civil law the injured party receives compensation. Violators of the criminal law, however, are punished through the imposition of a prison sentence, a fine, a sentence of probation, or some similar action. In setting penalties, American law often makes a distinction between a misdemeanor and a felony. In general, a **misdemeanor** is a criminal offense less serious than a felony, punishable by a fine or up to a year in jail. But there is no uniform usage or definition of these terms in the United States. Three jurisdictions (Maine, New Jersey, and the District of Columbia) do not use the term **felony** to classify their criminal offenses, and nine others offer no explicit definition. In the thirty-

Misdemeanor: Lesser of the two basic types of crime; usually punishable by no more than one year in prison.

Felony: The more serious of the two basic types of criminal behavior, usually bearing a possible penalty of one year or more in prison.

COURT TV

Cabey v. Goetz

Vigilante Justice: The Civil Trial of Bernhard Goetz

Darrell Cabey, paralyzed in December 1984 when he and several friends were panhandling and asked the defendant for money, sues subway vigilante Bernhard Goetz. As you watch the video, ask yourself the following questions:

1. How does this civil lawsuit differ from a criminal prosecution?
2. Was the difference in the criminal and civil verdicts the result of the difference in venue (the place where the trial was held)? New York City is divided into five boroughs, roughly equivalent to counties. Each borough has its own courts. The criminal trial was held in Manhattan, the prime business district of the city. The civil trial, on the other hand, was held in the Bronx, which is more populated by minorities.
3. Was the dollar amount of the civil verdict too high, too low, or about right? Why?

 Michael Brooks, "Stories and Verdicts: Bernhard Goetz and New York in Crisis"

 Civil complaint against the subway vigilante: **http://192.41.4.29/files/cas91.htm**

For an up-to-date list of Web links, go to **http://www.wadsworth.com/product/0534563406s**.

nine states that use and define the term *felony,* one common method is to define felonies by the place of imprisonment—the convicted are sentenced to death or to imprisonment in the state prison. The alternative approach is to define felonies on the basis of the duration of imprisonment—the convicted are sentenced to death, life imprisonment, or imprisonment for more than one year. A few states define felony in terms of both place and duration (Bureau of Justice Statistics 1987).

The stress on punishment derives from the goal of criminal law to prevent and control crime. It is important to recognize that the criminal law is intended to supplement, not supplant, the civil law. Thus, as discussed earlier, a person may be prosecuted criminally and the victim may also seek to recover civil damages for the same act (see Case Close-Up: Two Verdicts in the O. J. Trials). In automobile accidents involving drinking, for example, the drunk driver may be charged criminally with drunk driving, and the injured party may also file a civil suit seeking monetary damages.

ELEMENTS OF A CRIME

Corpus delicti, a Latin phrase meaning "body of the crime," refers to the essential **elements of a crime**. In defining the elements of a particular offense, criminal laws are based on five general principles. No behavior can be called criminal unless

- a *guilty act* is committed, with a
- *guilty intent,* and
- the *guilty act and the guilty intent are related.*

In addition, a number of crimes are defined on the basis of

- *attendant circumstances* and/or
- *specific results.*

An understanding of the basic concepts embodied in the statutory definitions of crime is essential for correctly interpreting definitions of crime. In turn, these basic concepts produce numerous categories of criminal activities (murder, voluntary manslaughter, and involuntary manslaughter, for example).

Guilty Act

Before there can be a crime, there must be a **guilty act (*actus reus*)**. Thus, criminal liability occurs only after a voluntary act that results in criminal harm. The requirement of a guilty act reflects a

---

Corpus delicti: The body or substance of a crime, composed of two elements—the act and the criminal agency producing it.

Elements of a crime: Five principles of a crime that are critical to the statutory definition of crimes: guilty act, guilty intent, relationship between guilty act and guilty intent, attendant circumstances, and results.

Guilty act (actus reus):   Requirement that, for an act to be considered criminal, the individual must have committed an overt act that resulted in criminal harm (see elements of a crime).

FIGURE 2-6 Differences between Civil and Criminal Law

	Civil	*Criminal*
Moving party	Plaintiff	State
Defending party	Defendant	Defendant
Burden of proof	Preponderance of the evidence	Guilty beyond a reasonable doubt
Jury verdict rules	Less than unanimous (many states)	Unanimous (most states)
Remedy	Monetary damages	Prison or probation
Defendant's testimony	The defendant may be forced to testify	Constitutional right to silence
Right to counsel	No constitutional right to counsel	Constitutional right to counsel
Prosecution	Individual must hire own lawyer	The government through the district attorney
Examples	Tort, contract, property, probate	Assault, theft, burglary

fundamental principle of American law: No one should be punished solely for bad thoughts. Depending on the crime, there are different types of guilty acts. In the offense of possession of an illegal drug, for instance, the guilty act is the possession. Differences in the nature of the guilty act account for many gradations of criminal offenses. To choose one obvious example, stealing property is considered separately from damaging property.

An important subdivision of the guilty act is a class of offenses labeled as **attempts** (for example, attempted burglary or attempted murder). The law does not want a person to avoid legal liability merely because someone or something prevented the commission of a crime. Typically, though, the penalties for attempt are less severe than if the act had succeeded. One result is that in some states, defendants often plead guilty to attempt to reduce the possible severity of the prison sentence.

 To find out what legal resources are available online for your state, just click on **http://dir.yahoo.com/ Government/Law/U_S__States/** and then select your state.

For an up-to-date list of Web links, go to **http:// www.wadsworth.com/product/0534563406s**.

Attempt: An act done with the intent to commit a crime, an overt act toward its commission, the failure to complete the crime, and the apparent possibility of committing it.

Guilty Intent

Every common law crime consists of two elements, the guilty act itself and the accompanying mental state. The rationale is that criminal sanctions are not necessary for those who innocently cause harm. As Justice Holmes once pithily put it, "Even a dog distinguishes between being stumbled over and being kicked." The mental state required for a crime to have been committed is referred to as **guilty intent** or *mens rea* ("guilty mind").

Despite its importance in criminal law, guilty intent is difficult to define because it refers to a subjective condition, a state of mind. Some statutes require only general intent (intent to do something that the law prohibits), but others specify the existence of specific intent (intent to do the exact thing charged). Moreover, legislatively defined crimes have added new concepts of mental state to the traditional ones. Thus crimes differ with respect to the mental state the prosecution must prove existed in order to secure a criminal conviction. Larceny (termed theft in some states), for example, typically requires proof of a very great degree of intent; the prosecutor must prove that the defendant *intentionally* took property to which he *knew* he was not entitled, *intending* to deprive the rightful owner of possession *permanently*. Negligent homicide, on the other hand, is an example of a crime involving a

---

Guilty intent (mens rea): Mental state required for a crime.

lesser degree of intent; the prosecution need only show that the defendant *negligently* caused the death of another. Most crimes require that the defendant knew he or she was doing something wrong. Also, the law assumes that people know the consequences of their acts. Thus, a person cannot avoid legal liability by later saying, "I didn't mean to do it."

Exhibit 2-2 uses the Illinois homicide statute to illustrate how different types of guilty intent lead to varying types of crimes.

Fusion of Guilty Act and Guilty Intent

The criminal law requires that the guilty act and the guilty intent occur together. Here is an example that illustrates this concept of **fusion of the guilty act and guilty intent**: Suppose a husband planned to kill his wife; he purchased some poison but never got around to putting the poison in her drink. The husband returns home late one night, an argument ensues, and he stabs her. In this situation the intent to kill necessary for a murder conviction did not occur along with the death. Therefore, the correct charge would be voluntary manslaughter.

 Formerly called the dictionary for nonlawyers, Oran's dictionary offers nontechnical definitions. See **http://www.wld.com/conbus/orans/**.

For an up-to-date list of Web links, go to **http://www.wadsworth.com/product/0534563406s**.

Attendant Circumstances

Some crimes require the presence, or absence, of **attendant (accompanying) circumstances**. Most states differentiate between classes of theft on the basis of the amount stolen. In Illinois, for example, the law provides that theft of less than $300 is treated as a misdemeanor and more than $300 as a felony. The amount stolen is the attendant circumstance.

Fusion of the guilty act and guilty intent: One of the components of a crime (see elements of a crime). Criminal law requires that the guilty intent and the guilty act occur together.

Attendant (accompanying) circumstances: Conditions surrounding a criminal act, for example, the amount of money stolen in a theft.

Results

In a limited number of criminal offenses the **results** of the illegal act play a critical part in defining the crime. The difference between homicide and battery, for example, depends on whether the victim lived. Similarly, most states distinguish between degrees of battery, depending on how seriously the victim was injured. Note that the concept of results differs from that of intent. In all of the preceding examples, the defendant may have had the same intent. The only difference was how hearty the victim was or perhaps how skillful the defendant was in carrying out his or her intentions.

Based on the five general principles—guilty act, guilty intent, fusion, attendant circumstances, and results—the corpus delicti of each crime (murder, robbery, rape, and burglary, for example) differs (Figure 2-7 on page 51). The elements of a particular crime provide the technical (that is, legal) definitions of a crime. For this reason, criminal statutes must be read closely, because each clause constitutes a critical part of the offense. Before a defendant can be convicted, all the elements of a crime must be proven.

LEGAL DEFENSES

Under the law, individuals may have performed illegal acts but still not be found guilty of a criminal violation because of a legally recognized justification for the actions or because legally they were not responsible for their actions. These **legal defenses** derive from the way crime is defined.

The requirement of a guilty act gives rise to several legal defenses. Above all, criminal acts must be voluntary. Thus, a person who strikes another while suffering an epileptic seizure would not be guilty of battery, because the act (hitting) was not voluntary. Similarly, the law recognizes the defense of duress— unlawful pressure on a person to do what he or she would not otherwise have done. Duress includes force, threat of violence, and physical restraint. In a defense of duress, the defendant is contending, in

Result: A consequence; an outcome.

Legal defense: Legally recognized justification for illegal actions, or acceptance that individuals were not legally responsible for their actions.

CASE CLOSE-UP

Two Verdicts in the O. J. Trials

 The trial of O. J. Simpson has been called the "trial of the century." While some argue that this phrase has become overused, there is little doubt that the trial of O. J. Simpson was the most watched event of its type in history.

The reason for this intense viewer interest is that from the beginning the case seemingly had it all. The shocking news of the murder of Nicole Brown Simpson seemed like an event from a paperback novel: a beautiful blonde and her male companion brutally murdered near her home. The defendant was well known and well liked—a former star football player who after his playing days enjoyed a wide following as a TV sports personality. And to add even more interest, the suspect disappeared in the middle of the night, only to be seen days later by millions of television viewers as the police slowly pursued his white SUV in a surreal chase scene.

Nor was the trial itself an anticlimax. Prominent lawyers basked in the media attention while obscure prosecutors quickly became media celebrities, and a good-natured judge appeared, at times, unable to control the "media circus." For thirty-seven weeks witnesses testified and experts offered their opinions with lawyer pundits quick to label some "flaky" and others just plain wrong. Throughout, the defense kept the focus on the conduct of the Los Angeles police department during the case, alleging, at best, shoddy police work and, at worst, racial bias. But perhaps most importantly of all, the case was widely followed because there was an underlying dramatic tension to the proceedings: Was Simpson innocent or guilty?

Finally, the case went to the jury. After only four hours of deliberation the jury returned a verdict of not guilty. A year after O. J. Simpson was acquitted of criminal charges, the civil trial began. The underlying allegation—O. J. Simpson murdered his ex-wife and Ronald Goldman—remained the same, but the rules in the proceedings were fundamentally different.

The party bringing the lawsuit differs in criminal and civil proceedings. In a criminal prosecution it is the government that files suit. In a civil case it is the injured party. This means that the parties (the families of the deceased in this case) must hire their own lawyers and present their own case. But in this case it also meant that the defendant could not attack the motives and competence of the police (as was done during the criminal trial).

The nature of the accusations also vary. In the criminal trial Simpson was charged with homicide, but in the civil case the allegations involved wrongful death (a type of tort). Instead of having to prove guilty intent, the plaintiff had only to establish that

essence, that he or she should be treated as a victim rather than as a criminal.

The requirement of guilty intent gives rise to several other legal defenses. Some types of persons are considered legally incapable of forming criminal intent and therefore cannot be held criminally responsible for their actions. Children are prime examples. Until children reach a certain age (seven in most states), they are presumed not to be responsible for their actions and therefore cannot be criminally prosecuted. After reaching this minimum age, but before becoming an adult, a child's criminal violations are treated as acts of **juvenile delinquency** (Chapter 19). The premise of juvenile delinquency acts is that people under a certain age have less responsibility for their actions than adults do. The exact age at which a person is no longer considered a juvenile, and can thus be prosecuted as an adult, differs from state to state. As more and more youths are committing violent crimes, states are lowering the age for prosecuting a minor as an adult (see Chapter 19). Similarly, the law assumes that persons with certain types of mental illness are incapable of forming criminal intent. Indeed, the best known, and also most controversial, legal defense is insanity. In Chapter 14 we will examine how insanity and other legal defenses are occasionally used at trial.

Juvenile delinquency: An act committed by a juvenile for which an adult could be prosecuted in a criminal court.

 Crimelynx is the criminal defense lawyer's guide to legal research and investigation on the Internet: **http://www.crimelynx.com/**.

For an up-to-date list of Web links, go to **http://www.wadsworth.com/product/0534563406s**.

O. J. Simpson was negligent, an allegation that is easier to prove because it is a broader concept.

Standards of proof also contrasted during the two proceedings. In a criminal trial the prosecution must prove the defendant guilty beyond a reasonable doubt. But in a civil trial there is a lower standard; the plaintiff must prove the allegations with a "preponderance the evidence," meaning jurors can decide for the plaintiff if they determine there is at least a 50.1 percent probability that Simpson was negligent.

Constitutional protections likewise differ in criminal and civil proceedings. In a criminal case the defendant has a right to remain silent. During the criminal proceedings Simpson largely availed himself of this right. Although he gave a statement at police headquarters a few days after the murder, he did not testify at trial. (His lawyers could have called him to the stand but did not.) But in a civil case the defendant can be forced to testify, and testify Simpson did. Prior to the trial the plaintiff's attorneys took Simpson's deposition. And during trial they called him to the stand as a plaintiff witness. Later the defense also called Simpson to the stand.

Finally, the Simpson cases illustrated important differences in remedies. If Simpson had been found guilty in the criminal case he most certainly would have gone to prison. In the civil case the jury awarded compensatory damages of $8.5 million and $25 million in punitive damages. But this $33.5 million jury award is not self-enforcing. Simpson said he was broke and could not pay. Thus the lawyers for Ronald

Goldman's parents filed separate lawsuits trying to seize assets. Simpson was forced to turn over his Heisman trophy, but it is unlikely that the plaintiffs will ever recover the majority of the damage awards.

Most citizens were more than willing to volunteer themselves as a juror for a day. The verdicts divided Americans citizens largely along racial lines. Whites strongly believed that Simpson literally got away with murder whereas African Americans were more supportive. These sentiments were reversed after the civil trial, with many arguing that justice had finally been done.

 The O. J. Simpson trial produced a variety of reactions. Here are three perspectives on the trials:

Walter L. Gordon III, "Reflections of a Criminal Defense Lawyer on the Simpson Trial"

Steven Fein, Seth J. Morgan, Michael I. Norton, Samuel R. Sommers, "Hype and Suspicion: The Effects of Pretrial Publicity, Race, and Suspicion on Jurors' Verdicts"

Charles Fairfield, "Race, Rage, and Denial: The Media and the O. J. Trials"

 To read more about the O. J. Simpson criminal trial and to view some of the evidence, just click on **http://www.cnn.com/US/OJ/index.html**.

For an up-to-date list of Web links, go to **http://www.wadsworth.com/product/0534563406s**.

CRIMINAL LAW: CONSTANT AND CHANGING

Definitions of crime have changed over time, and this process of change continues today. The criminal law is both constant and changing. Some areas are well settled; typical street crimes such as murder, robbery, theft, and burglary rarely present judges, prosecutors, or defense attorneys with any new issues. But other areas of the law are in flux. Every legislative session produces additions and alterations in the existing criminal code. Some of these changes are narrow and technical. Such legislative changes in the criminal law generate little public interest; this type of lawmaking activity is monopolized by criminal justice professionals — lawyers, police officers, judges, and corrections officers.

But other changes in criminal law are more far-reaching. Stuart Scheingold (1984, 22) underscores the close relationship between politics and the legislative process:

Does not the politicization of crime best explain the odd contours of criminal law controlling gambling, drug use, and sexual behavior? How else are we to understand the passage of these laws and the patterns of inclusion and exclusion? Horse racing is generally legal, but numbers gambling is criminal. Alcohol and Valium may be used legally, while the use of marijuana and cocaine is prohibited. It can hardly be argued that these distinctions reflect some natural moral order. Clearly, some segments are imposing their values on others—perhaps to demonstrate symbolically their superior status or perhaps to protect vested economic interests. Symbolic uses of the criminal law seem to have been paramount in the creation of Prohibition.

EXHIBIT 2-2 How Guilty Intent Produces Different Categories of Homicide

Varying degrees of intent produce different categories of criminal offenses: Although the guilty act is the same, criminal liability varies. Homicide statutes illustrate this important variation. Murder requires proof that the defendant intended to kill or cause great bodily harm. In addition, most state statutes classify deaths resulting from a forcible felony (such as armed robbery) as murder, even though the defendant did not specifically set out to kill the victim. Voluntary manslaughter involves death resulting from a sudden or intense passion. Involuntary manslaughter is involved if death occurred from an act performed recklessly. The following Illinois homicide statute illustrates these differences:

> **9-1. Murder.** *(a) A person who kills an individual without lawful justification commits murder if, in performing the acts which cause death: (1) He either intends to kill or do great bodily harm to that individual or another, or knows that such acts will cause death to that individual or another; or (2) He knows that such acts create a strong probability of death or great bodily harm to that individual or another; or (3) He is attempting or committing a forcible felony other than voluntary manslaughter.*

> **9-2. Voluntary manslaughter.** *(a) A person who kills an individual without lawful justification commits voluntary manslaughter if at the time of the killing he is acting under a sudden and intense passion resulting from serious provocation by: (1) The individual killed, or (2) Another*

whom the offender endeavors to kill, but he negligently or accidentally causes the death of the individual killed. Serious provocation is conduct sufficient to excite an intense passion in a reasonable person. . . .

> **9-3. Involuntary manslaughter and reckless homicide.** *(a) A person who unintentionally kills an individual without lawful justification commits involuntary manslaughter if his acts whether lawful or unlawful which cause the death are such as are likely to cause death or great bodily harm to some individual, and he performs them recklessly, except in cases in which the cause of the death consists of the driving of a motor vehicle, in which case the person commits reckless homicide. (Illinois Revised Statutes: Chapter 38, 1981)*

Note that if death occurred solely because of negligence, no criminal violation is involved. Here the civil law takes over; such wrongful death is considered a private wrong. As we have seen, some defendants are found not guilty of the crime of homicide but found liable for a civil violation of wrongful death.

One major consequence of the definition of different categories of homicide by criminal intent is varying penalties. Under Illinois law, a defendant convicted of murder may be sentenced to death or a minimum of fourteen years in prison. Conviction of voluntary manslaughter carries a maximum sentence of twenty years in prison, involuntary manslaughter ten years, and reckless homicide three years.

Changes in laws dealing with abortion, as well as those regarding obscenity, gambling, flag burning, and drugs, are examples of highly publicized and emotional issues that generate considerable public debate.

Pressures for Changing the Criminal Law

Legislative changes in the criminal codes arise from diverse political factors. One is public concern over rising crime rates. During the 1970s and 1980s, perceptions of crime waves—major increases of armed robberies or rapes, for example—led to public demands that elected officials pass new and tougher laws. More recently, public attention has focused on

drugs, producing a frenzy of antidrug legislation (Chapter 10). Perhaps the clearest contemporary example of public pressure is the passage of laws requiring convicted sex offenders to notify neighbors when they move in. Such laws, called "Megan's laws," are named after Megan Kanka. Jesse Timmendequas, a twice-convicted sex offender, lured the seven-year-old into his house, raping and killing her. In the wake of this tragedy most states have enacted community notification statutes targeting sex offenders. Police, prosecutors, and victims' rights organizations regularly use public concern over rising crime rates to lobby for harsher sentences.

Similarly, the emergence of new forms of unpopular behavior often produces calls for new laws to cover existing loopholes. Computer crimes, child

FIGURE 2-7	Characteristics of the Most Common Serious Crimes

	Law on the Books	*Law in Action*
Homicide	Causing the death of another person without legal justification or excuse.	• Homicide is the least frequent violent crime. • Most often murderers are relatives or acquaintances of the victim.
Rape	Unlawful sexual intercourse with a female, by force or without legal or factual consent.	• Most rapes involve a lone offender and a lone victim, at night.
Robbery	Unlawful taking or attempted taking of property that is in the immediate possession of another, by force or threat of force.	• Half of all robberies involve one offender. • Half of all robberies involve the use of a weapon.
Assault	*Aggravated assault* is the unlawful intentional inflicting of serious bodily injury or unlawful threat or attempt to inflict bodily injury or death by means of a deadly or dangerous weapon with or without actual infliction of injury. *Simple assault* is the unlawful intentional inflicting of less than serious bodily injury without a deadly or dangerous weapon or an attempt or threat to inflict bodily injury without a deadly or dangerous weapon.	• Simple assault occurs more frequently than aggravated assault. • Assault is the most common type of violent crime. • Most assaults involve one victim and one offender.
Burglary	Unlawful entry of any fixed structure, vehicle, or vessel used for regular residence, industry, or business, with or without force, with the intent to commit a felony or larceny.	• Residential property is targeted in two out of three of burglaries.
Larceny (theft)	Unlawful taking or attempted taking of property other than a motor vehicle from the possession of another, by stealth, without force and without deceit, with intent to permanently deprive the owner of the property.	• Pocket picking and purse snatching occur most frequently inside businesses or on street locations. Unlike most other crimes, pocket picking and purse snatching affect the elderly as much as other age groups.
Motor vehicle theft	Unlawful taking or attempted taking of a self-propelled road vehicle owned by another, with the intent of depriving the owner of it permanently or temporarily.	• Motor vehicle theft is relatively well reported to the police. • Vehicles are more likely than other stolen property to be recovered.
Arson	Intentional damaging or destruction or attempted damaging or destruction by means of fire or explosion of the property without the consent of the owner, or of one's own property or that of another by fire or explosives with or without the intent to defraud.	• Single-family residences are the most frequent targets of arson. • Sixteen percent of all structures where arson occurs are not in use.

SOURCE: U.S. Department of Justice, Bureau of Justice Statistics, *Report to the Nation on Crime and Justice,* 2d ed. (Washington, D.C.: Government Printing Office, 1988).

The Question of Civil Liability

 After the criminal charges were dropped against Shareef Cousin, legal attention shifted to the civil law. At first glance the issue seems straightforward. After all, Shareef Cousin's rights were apparently violated—he spent almost two years on Louisiana's death row and almost as long in jail awaiting a new trial that never occurred. But the legal issues are much more complicated and evolving. Legislatures and courts across the nation are debating the question: If an inmate turns out to be wrongfully convicted, does the state owe compensation for the years lost in prison? Or is the restoration of freedom compensation enough? These have become pressing questions in the wake of a wave of persons who have been freed from death row or long prison terms. Only fourteen states and the District of Columbia have enacted laws that create a rational system for paying compensation (Coyle 2000). In the other jurisdictions, these issues are being decided by courts.

In Louisiana the question of compensating the wrongfully incarcerated arose in a lawsuit that was winding its way through the courts at about the same time that Shareef Cousin was being convicted and sentenced to death. Roland Gibson was convicted for the 1967 murder of a New Orleans cab driver and sentenced to life imprisonment. After he spent seventeen years in prison, Gibson's boyhood friend and codefendant, Lloyd West, recanted his claim that Gibson had been the triggerman. A new trial was ordered, but the DA decided not to conduct a retrial. Nonetheless, Gibson still spent eight years in prison after the problem of perjured testimony surfaced.

Following a bench trial, civil court judge Carolyn Gill-Jefferson ruled that the New Orleans police lacked probable cause to arrest Gibson and ordered the city to pay the plaintiff and his family $10.7 million in damages (Finch 1998). But the Louisiana Supreme Court unanimously held that civil trials should not "second-guess" a criminal court finding of probable cause to arrest, even when that evidence later turns out to be false. The court also chastised the trial judge for putting too much weight on the testimony of West, a convicted felon (*Gibson v. New Orleans*, 2000).

Given these legal standards it would be hard for Shareef Cousin to successfully sue the New Orleans police department. And even if he were to win, it would be difficult to collect because the city of New Orleans is cash-starved. In a lawsuit against a private party, the plaintiff is entitled to seize the defendant's assets to pay the judgment. But the federal courts have exempted cities from such possibilities. Thus in the past when plaintiffs have successfully sued the city of New Orleans over matters like police brutality, the city has delayed paying for years. Indeed, some may never collect.

Because state law allows little likelihood that Shareef Cousin could successfully win a civil lawsuit for wrongful conviction, his lawyers turned to federal court, filing a federal civil rights lawsuit (see Chapter 3).

pornography, stalking, and hate crimes provide prime contemporary examples.

Interest groups are another force pressuring legislatures to change the criminal law (Neubauer 2001). Mothers Against Drunk Driving (MADD) mounted a highly successful nationwide effort to increase the penalties for drunk driving (Chapter 18). Likewise, the revolution in rape laws is the product of lobbying by various women's groups. In recent years victims' rights organizations have become a powerful legislative influence (Chapter 9).

Court decisions are another stimulus for legislative alteration of the criminal code. Conflicting appellate court decisions often prompt legislatures' attempts to clarify divergent court standards. Similarly, when a court declares a law unconstitutional, the legislature may pass a new law, trying to remedy the deficiencies of the one struck down.

Thus, after the Supreme Court upheld the Georgia death penalty law but struck down capital punishment laws in other states (*Gregg v. Georgia* 1976), a number of states drafted new laws attempting to reimpose capital punishment within the dictates of the Court's ruling (Chapter 15). In other cases, legislatures may not try to resurrect a law declared invalid by the courts (Wasby 1970). Thus, some laws struck down by the courts remain on the books—unrepealed although unenforced.

Piecemeal Change

Political forces cause changes in the criminal law to occur piecemeal (Berk, Brackman, and Lesser 1977). To be sure, over the last three decades, thirty-four states have codified or substantially revised their criminal codes. But more often, legislatures respond to practical problems in an ad hoc, pragmatic way. As specific deficiencies in the law become evident or new events arise, individual changes designed to cure isolated problems are voted into law. "As a result criminal laws seem to tumble out of our legislatures with great frequency and little reflection. Although there is some movement toward decriminalization of certain behavior, the general tendency is towards proliferation of criminal laws. In America more is often confused with better" (Sigler 1981, 266).

A legislature's choice of what acts to label as criminal has major consequences for how the criminal courts dispense justice.

EFFECTS OF THE CRIMINAL LAW ON THE COURTS

Because the criminal code constitutes the basic source of authority for law enforcement agencies, the way crimes are defined has an important bearing on the entire administration of criminal justice. This principle was articulated early in the nineteenth century by Sir Robert Peel, who was called "the father of the English police" (Skolnick 1994). Peel first reformed the criminal law, under which even minor offenses had carried the death penalty, before introducing a new police system. More recently, the National Advisory Commission on Criminal Justice Standards and Goals (1973, 175) reached a similar conclusion, arguing that substantive criminal law revision "is a necessary concomitant to modernization of the criminal justice system." But such changes are not easily accomplished. Because there is no consensus in American society about what behavior should be criminalized and what penalties should be meted out for infractions, the criminal law is neither clear nor coherent. Thus, proposed alterations in the criminal law prove highly controversial, often pitting due process advocates against crime control adherents.

Chapter 5 will consider in greater detail the relationship between law and discretion. For now we will examine the criminal law and inconsistencies, plea bargaining, and sentencing.

Criminal Law and Inconsistencies

Inconsistencies exist within each criminal code (sometimes referred to as the penal code). Consider

the following. In California, breaking into the glove compartment of a car is punishable by up to fifteen years imprisonment, but stealing the entire car carries a maximum penalty of ten years. In Colorado, stealing a dog is punishable by a maximum sentence of ten years, but killing a dog carries a maximum punishment of six months in jail. These are just two examples cited by Marvin Frankel (a former U.S. district court judge) of what he calls the crazy quilt of state criminal statutes. Not all criminal statutes are this inconsistent, but the examples draw our attention to a major problem: Many states lack a consistent set of criminal definitions and penalties.

Because legislatures change criminal codes piecemeal, the end product is a set of criminal laws with obsolete prohibitions and inconsistent penalties. At times these problems are inadvertent. No one sets out to create such inconsistencies; they just happen. It is not always immediately obvious that changes in one section of the law may be inconsistent with another section of the law. But at other times such contradictions indicate a lack of agreement in American society about what behavior should be criminalized and what penalties are appropriate (Sigler 1981).

In practice, judges and prosecutors attempt to rectify these inconsistencies by informally developing a consistent set of penalties. It should be obvious that the courts must apply the law as they find it. The corollary is that the courts often must rectify inconsistencies in that law. Disparities in possible sentences as provided in state statutes require judges, prosecutors, and defense attorneys to arrive at a workable penalty structure. Society would be outraged if serious crimes elicited the same punishment as minor ones, even if the law technically allowed both categories of offenses to be treated the same way.

 To check out today's news about law just click on **http://www.cnn/law**.

For an up-to-date list of Web links, go to **http://www.wadsworth.com/product/0534563406s**.

Criminal Law and Plea Bargaining

Variations in the definitions of crimes make the criminal courts fertile ground for plea bargaining. In particular, differences in degrees of seriousness provide the means for *charge bargaining* (the defendant pleads guilty to a less serious offense than the one charged). For example, in some states, assault and battery involves five degrees (categories). Although the law must attempt to differentiate between, say, a punch thrown in anger and a deliberate gunshot wound that leaves its victim permanently paralyzed, the existence of many different degrees of seriousness facilitates pleas to less serious offenses. Thus, prosecutors may deliberately overcharge in hopes of inducing the defendant to later plead guilty to a lesser charge (Chapter 13).

Criminal Law and Sentencing

The most obvious way criminal law affects the operations of the criminal courts is in sentencing. As we will discuss in greater detail in Chapters 15 and 16, the legislature establishes sentencing options from which judges must choose. Because of the public's concern about crime, pressures are strong to increase penalties. As a result, legislatures increase the harshness of sentencing, and the courthouse mitigates that harshness. According to Rosett and Cressey (1976, 95), such legislative action and courthouse reactions follow a predictable pattern:

Step I. Laws calling for severe punishments are passed by legislatures on the assumption that fear of great pain will terrorize the citizenry into conformity.

Step II. Criminal justice personnel soften these severe penalties for most offenders (a) in the interests of justice, (b) in the interests of bureaucracy, and (c) in the interests of gaining acquiescence.

Step III. The few defendants who then insist on a trial and are found guilty, or who in other ways refuse to cooperate, are punished more severely than those who acquiesce.

Step IV. Legislatures, noting that most criminals by acquiescing avoid "the punishment prescribed by law," (a) increase the prescribed punishments and (b) try to limit the range of discretionary decision making used to soften the harsh penalties.

Step V. The more severe punishments introduced in the preceding step are again softened for most offenders, as in Step II, with the result that the defendants not acquiescing are punished even more severely than they were at Step III.

This book will return often to the question of whether the legislatures or the courts have adopted the most appropriate stance.

CONCLUSION

The verdicts in the O. J. Simpson trials left citizens divided over where justice lay. Was the criminal jury right (or wrong) in finding Simpson not guilty of murder? Was the civil jury equally right (or wrong) in awarding civil damages? As for Simpson, he kept protesting that the process was unfair because he suffered double jeopardy. Alas for him and a smattering of other criminal defendants, this concept (discussed in Chapter 3) might apply to parallel criminal prosecutions by both the state and national government, but it has nothing to do with parallel criminal and civil actions.

The Simpson trials also illustrate the importance of understanding both law on the books and law in action. The law on the books—first degree murder, in this case—is abstract. The law in action—what victims, defendant, lawyers, judges, and jury do—is concrete. Ultimately the meaning of the law is not what the judge instructs to the jury (law on the books) but the decision reached by the jury (law in action). By voting not guilty, the first jury decided that this conduct was not criminal. By deciding that Simpson was liable, another jury decided that his conduct violated community standards.

What activity should be labeled criminal is the source of constant political discussion. Actions viewed as bad in the past may no longer be considered bad. As society changes, so do public perceptions of public wrongs, and pressures develop to add more activities to the list of officially proscribed ones. Through all of this change, we must not lose sight of the essential fact that law is an integral part of society. Law is not imposed on society; rather it reflects the sociology, economy, history, and politics of society. Law was created to help society, not the other way around.

CRITICAL THINKING QUESTIONS

1. Constitutional rights of the accused is, of course, a controversial topic. The crime control model, in particular, decries letting the obviously guilty go on "technicalities," whereas the due process model emphasizes basic rights. Examining Figure 2-1, what common ground do these two approaches share? Where do they disagree most?

2. All non-English-speaking industrial democracies use the inquisitorial system rather than the adversary system. In this system the judge, not the prosecutor and not the defense attorney, calls witnesses and questions them. Would you prefer being tried under the adversary system or the inquisitorial system? Would you have confidence in the willingness of the judge to equally search out evidence for conviction and evidence for acquittal?

3. If O. J. Simpson had been tried in France, what procedural differences in the case would have occurred? Would the substantive findings also have been different?

4. Each legislative session seems to bring about changes in the laws. For the most recent session of your state legislature, examine the major changes of the law. Which changes seem designed to correct gaps in the law and which ones seem more likely to be exercises in political symbolism (as discussed in Chapter 1 and the Epilogue)?

5. One of the biggest societal changes in recent years has been the rapid expansion of computer technology. How have legislatures responded to crimes involving use of computers? How has the Internet changed the debate over pornography?

WORLD WIDE WEB RESOURCES AND EXERCISES

Web Guides

http://dir.yahoo.com/Government/Law/
http://dir.yahoo.com/Government/Law/Cases/
  OJ_Simpson_Case/

Web Search Terms

"Law," "common law," "criminal law," "asset forfeiture"; "O. J. Simpson"; "subway vigilante"

Useful URLs

Internet Legal Resource Guide is a categorized index of more than 4,000 Web sites in 238 nations: http://www.ilrg.com.

The Legal Information Institute offers a menu of federal and state sources: http://www.law.cornell.edu/topics/criminal.html.

The federal Web locator from the Center for Information Law and Policy is at http://www.infoctr.edu/fwl/.

The state Web locator from the Center for Information Law and Policy is at http://www.law.vill.edu/.

For state resources, go to http://www.findlaw.com and select your state.

Legal research on the Web is at http://www.accd.edu/sac/leassist/la1103/webres.htm.

Uncommon URLs

Anatomy of a Murder offers a trip through our nation's legal system: http://library.thinkquest.org/2760/homep.htm.

Legal History and Philosophy is a site with links to many of the common law classics: http://www.commonlaw.com/.

About.Com/Law shows today's legal headlines: http://law.about.com/newsissues/law/.

Nolo Press is the leading publisher of legal self-help materials: http://www.nolo.com/.

United Kingdom Web sites explain another common law jurisdiction, but there are some important differences: http://www.leeds.ac.uk/law/ccjs/ukweb.htm.

The Subway Vigilante Board Game is a beer-and-pretzel game: http://waggle.gg.caltech.edu/~jeff/games/subwayv.html.

The Five-Hour Law School is a primer that was designed for nonlawyer employees of Thomson Publishing: http://members.aol.com/ronin48th/hope.htm.

Web Exercises

1. One of the major links for doing legal research is FindLaw. Its URL is http://www.findlaw.com/. You can find the U.S. Constitution

by following this path: Laws: Cases and Codes/Constitution. Click on Article III—Judicial Department to read the full article.

Also click on one of the amendments in the Bill of Rights to find annotated information about the meaning of that provision. In particular, examine the Second Amendment and the bearing of arms.

2. Each year more laws are added to the Web. Check to see what is available in your state. Again we will use FindLaw: **http://www.findlaw.com/**. On the menu click State Law Resources.

   The states are arrayed in alphabetical order. Click on your state to get a general sense of what is available. Is the criminal law for your state online? If so, compare the homicide section of your state code to the Illinois statute provided in Exhibit 2-2. (If you are in Illinois, don't get lazy and ignore this assignment! Compare your provisions to those of New York or California.)

3. Update the debate over asset forfeiture by doing a Yahoo search. Access Yahoo at **http://www.yahoo.com**; then click Society and Culture/ Crime/Asset Confiscation.

   You may also want to go directly to Forfeiture Endangers American Rights (F.E.A.R.) at **http://www.fear.org**. This group says it is dedicated to helping forfeiture victims, working to reform draconian forfeiture laws, assisting legal counsel in difficult forfeiture cases, and acting as a watch-dog over governmental forfeiture practices. Where do they fit in the crime control versus due process debate?

 INFOTRAC COLLEGE EDITION RESOURCES AND EXERCISES

Basic Search Terms

Criminal law; asset forfeiture; rape, common law, double jeopardy; United States Constitution, 1st to 10th Amendments

Recommended Articles

Bernard E. Harcourt, "The Collapse of the Harm Principle"

Harper's, "This Is Your Bill of Rights"

Kent Greenawalt, "Justifications, Excuses, and a Model Penal Code for Democratic Societies"

Hossein Esmaeili, Jeremy Gans, "Cultures Colliding in Court"

InfoTrac College Edition Exercises

1. One of the most hotly debated proposed criminal laws involves hate crimes. Using the search term *hate crime, analysis* locate one article on either side of the debate. To what extent does the debate over passage of hate crime laws parallel the divisions discussed by Herbert Packer using the concepts of the due process and crime control models of criminal justice? Here is one article that debates the topic: Elizabeth Birch, Paul Weyrich, "Symposium: Debate for Specific Hate Crime Legislation Protecting Homosexuals."

2. Another hotly debated criminal law is the Internet Decency Act, which Congress has passed twice only to be struck down as unconstitutional by the U.S. Supreme Court. After entering the search term *Telecommunications Act of 1996*, limit the search with the term *pornography*. Locate at least one article on each side of this issue. To what extent do the arguments parallel the debate between adherents of the crime control model versus the proponents of the due process model of criminal justice? To what extent does the debate cross traditional ideological lines? Here are two articles of relevance: William F. Buckley Jr., "Internet: The Lost Fight" and Christopher Harper, "How Free Is the Net?"

REFERENCES

American Bar Association. 1970. *Standards Relating to the Prosecution Function and the Defense Function.* Chicago: American Bar Association.

Balleza, Maureen. 1991. Many Rape Victims Finding Justice Through Civil Courts. *The New York Times,* 20 September, 1.

Barrineau, H. E. 1994. *Civil Liability in Criminal Justice.* 2d ed. Cincinnati: Anderson.

Berk, Richard, Harold Brackman, and Selma Lesser. 1977. *A Measure of Justice: An Empirical Study of Changes in the California Penal Code, 1855–1976.* New York: Academic Press.

Bureau of Justice Statistics. 1987. *State Felony Courts and Felony Laws.* Washington, D.C.: U.S. Department of Justice.

Cassella, Stefan. 1996. "Third-Party Rights in Criminal Forfeiture Cases." *Criminal Law Bulletin* 32: 499–537.

Coyle, Pamela. 2000. "Court to Tackle Issue of Paying Innocent Convicts: N.O. Fighting Damages Awarded to Ex-Inmate." *Times-Picayune,* 16 January.

Finch, Susan. 1998. "Former Inmate Wins Millions: N.O. Owes Money to Innocent Man." *Times-Picayune,* 20 February.

Friedman, Lawrence. 1984. *American Law: An Introduction.* New York: Norton.

Giffuni, Matthew. 1995. "Civil Forfeiture and the Excessive Fines Clause Following *Austin v. United States.*" *Criminal Law Bulletin* 31: 502–533.

Gordon, Corey, and William Brill. 1996. *The Expanding Role of Crime Prevention Through Environmental Design in Premises Liability.* Washington, D.C.: National Institute of Justice.

Holmes, Oliver Wendell. 1920. *Collected Legal Papers.* Boston: Harcourt.

Jensen, Eric, and Jurg Gerber. 1996. "The Civil Forfeiture of Assets and the War on Drugs: Expanding Criminal Sanctions While Reducing Due Process Protections." *Crime and Delinquency* 42: 421–434.

Kappeler, Victor, Michael Vaughn, and Rolando Del Carmen. 1991. "Death in Detention: An Analysis of Police Liability for Negligent Failure to Prevent Suicide." *Journal of Criminal Justice* 19: 381–393.

Levy, Leonard. 1996. *A License to Steal: Forfeiture of Property.* Chapel Hill: The University of North Carolina Press.

McCampbell, Robert. 1995. "Parallel Civil and Criminal Proceedings: Six Legal Pitfalls." *Criminal Law Bulletin* 31: 483–501.

National Advisory Commission on Criminal Justice Standards and Goals. 1973. *Criminal Justice System.* Washington, D.C.: Government Printing Office.

Neubauer, David, ed. 2001. *Debating Crime: Rhetoric and Reality.* Belmont, CA: Wadsworth.

———. 1997. *Judicial Process: Law, Courts, and Politics in the United States.* 2d ed. Fort Worth, TX: Harcourt Brace.

Office for Victims of Crime. 1992. "Civil Legal Remedies for Crime Victims." Washington, D.C.: U.S. Department of Justice.

Oran, Daniel. 1985. *Law Dictionary for Nonlawyers.* 2d ed. St. Paul, MN: West.

Rosett, Arthur, and Donald Cressey. 1976. *Justice by Consent: Plea Bargains in the American Courthouse.* Philadelphia: J. B. Lippincott.

Scheingold, Stuart. 1984. *The Politics of Law and Order.* New York: Longman.

Sigler, Jay. 1981. *Understanding Criminal Law.* Boston: Little, Brown.

Skolnick, Jerome. 1994. *Justice Without Trial: Law Enforcement in a Democratic Society.* 3d ed. New York: Macmillan.

Vaughn, Michael. 1996. "Prison Civil Liability for Inmate-Against-Inmate Assault and Breakdown/ Disorganization Theory." *Journal of Criminal Justice* 24: 139–152.

Walker, Samuel. 2001. *Sense and Nonsense about Crime and Drugs: A Policy Guide.* 5th ed. Belmont, CA: Wadsworth.

Wardlaw, Jack. 1997. "Foster Backs Police Changes." *Times-Picayune,* 2 May.

Wasby, Stephen L. 1970. *The Impact of the United States Supreme Court.* Homewood, IL: Dorsey Press.

FOR FURTHER READING

Bodenhamer, David. *Fair Trial: Rights of the Accused in American History.* New York: Oxford, 1991.

Close, Daryl, and Nicholas Meier. *Morality in Criminal Justice: An Introduction to Ethics.* Belmont, CA: Wadsworth, 1995.

Gardner, Thomas, and Terry Anderson. *Criminal Law.* 7th ed. Belmont, CA: Wadsworth, 2000.

Friedman, Lawrence. *Crime and Punishment in American History.* New York: Basic Books, 1993.

Martin, Susan. "Investigating Hate Crimes: Case Characteristics and Law Enforcement Responses." *Justice Quarterly* 13 (1996): 455–480.

National Crime Prevention Council. *New Ways of Working with Local Laws to Prevent Crime.* Amsterdam, NY: Author, 1996.

Pollock, Joycelyn. *Ethics in Crime and Justice: Dilemmas and Decisions.* 2d ed. Belmont, CA: Wadsworth, 1994.

Samaha, Joel. *Criminal Law.* 6th ed. Belmont, CA: Wadsworth, 1999.

Scheb, John, and John Scheb. *Criminal Law.* 2d ed. Belmont, CA: Wadsworth, 2000.

Smith, Christopher, and John Hurst. "The Forms of Judicial Policymaking: Civil Liability and Criminal Justice Policy." *Justice System Journal* 19 (1997): 341–354.

Walker, Samuel. Popular *Justice: A History of American Criminal Justice.* New York: Oxford University Press, 1980.

Federal Courts

ALFONSO LOPEZ, JR., A TWELFTH GRADER AT EDISON HIGH SCHOOL IN San Antonio, Texas, thought he had found a quick way to make an easy buck. "Gilbert" would pay him forty dollars to take a .38-caliber pistol to school and deliver it to "Jason," who planned to use it in a "gang war." Based on an anonymous tip, school officials confronted Lopez, who admitted carrying the unloaded weapon (but he did have five bullets on his person). Lopez was charged in federal court with violating the Gun-Free School Zones Act of 1990. After a bench trial, Lopez was found guilty and sentenced to six months in prison. The Supreme Court reversed the conviction, however, concluding that the U.S. Congress had no authority to outlaw guns in schools.

The Supreme Court's decision in *U.S. v. Lopez* first attracts our attention because it deals with gun control—one of the truly hot-button issues of American politics. But a closer probing raises other, even more important questions. What should be a federal crime? After all, weapons offenses are usually violations of state law, and indeed Lopez was initially charged in state court; but these charges were dropped after federal officials stepped in. How is it that five conservative judges, appointed by Republican presidents and pledged to getting tough on crime, reversed a conviction that was certainly popular with the American public? After all, Republicans have accused liberal federal judges (seemingly those appointed by Democratic presidents) of being soft on crime.

The issues, both direct and indirect, raised in the case of *U.S. v. Lopez* trace their origins to the early days of the Republic. The founding fathers were deeply divided over which cases federal courts should hear. Indeed, the drafters of the U.S. Constitution were deeply divided over whether there should be any federal courts besides the U.S. Supreme Court. A principal task of this chapter, therefore, is to discuss how the current federal judicial structure—magistrate, district, appellate courts, and the Supreme Court—is a product of over 200 years of political controversy and compromise about the proper role of the federal judiciary. The remainder of the chapter focuses on the specialized courts and the administrative structure. Most importantly, we will discuss the contemporary debate over how many cases are too many for the federal courts to handle, thus illustrating that the controversies continue. But first, to establish some common ground about the often confusing topic of court organization, we begin this chapter by examining some basic principles. ■

BASIC PRINCIPLES OF COURT ORGANIZATION

Much of the American court system is complicated and technical. Even lawyers who regularly use the courts sometimes find the details of court organization confusing. Court nomenclature includes many shorthand phrases that mean something to those who work in the courts daily but can be quite confusing to the outsider who tries to interpret the words in their literal sense. Learning the language of courts is like learning any foreign language— some of it can come only from experience. Before studying the specifics of federal and state courts (Chapter 4), it is helpful to understand the basic principles of court organization. Three concepts— jurisdiction, trial versus appellate courts, and the dual court system—underlie the structure of the American judiciary.

Jurisdiction

Court structure is largely determined by limitations on the types of cases a court may hear and decide. **Jurisdiction** is the power of a court to decide a dispute. A court's jurisdiction can be further classified according to three subcomponents: geographical

Jurisdiction: The power of a court to hear a case in question.

jurisdiction, subject matter jurisdiction, and hierarchical jurisdiction.

Geographical Jurisdiction

Courts are authorized to hear and decide disputes arising within a specified **geographical jurisdiction**. Thus, a California court ordinarily has no jurisdiction to try a person accused of committing a crime in Oregon. Courts' geographical boundaries typically follow the lines of other governmental bodies such as cities, counties, or states.

Two principal complications arise from geographical jurisdiction. First, events that occur on or near the border of different courts may lead to a dispute over which court has jurisdiction. If the laws of the two jurisdictions differ significantly, determination of which law applies can have important consequences for the outcome of the case. Second, a person accused of committing a crime in one state may for whatever reason (flight or happenstance) be in another state when he or she is arrested. **Extradition** involves the surrender by one state (or country) of an individual accused of a crime outside of its own territory and within the territorial jurisdiction of the other state. If an American fugitive has fled to a foreign nation, the U.S. Secretary of State will request the return of the accused under the terms of the extradition treaty the United States has with that country (but a few nations of the world do not have such treaties).

Subject Matter Jurisdiction

Court structure is also determined by **subject matter jurisdiction**. Trial courts of "limited jurisdiction" are restricted to hearing a limited category of cases, typically misdemeanors and civil suits involving small sums of money (termed small claims). U.S. bankruptcy courts, for example, are restricted to hearing bankruptcy cases. State courts typically have traffic courts or juvenile courts, both of which are examples of subject matter jurisdiction. Trial courts of "general jurisdiction" are empowered to

hear all other types of cases within the jurisdictional area. In the state court systems (to be discussed in the next chapter) the county trial court fits here. (See Neubauer 1997 for a discussion of court-developed rules on subject matter jurisdiction of federal courts.)

Hierarchical Jurisdiction

The third subcomponent of jurisdiction is **hierarchical jurisdiction**, which refers to differences in the courts' functions and responsibilities. **Original jurisdiction** means that a court has the authority to try a case and decide it. **Appellate jurisdiction** means that a court has the power to review cases that have already been decided by another court. Trial courts are primarily courts of original jurisdiction, but they occasionally have limited appellate jurisdiction, for example, when a trial court hears appeals from lower trial courts such as mayor's courts or a justice of the peace court. Appellate courts often have a very limited original jurisdiction. The U.S. Supreme Court has original jurisdiction involving disputes between states, and state supreme courts have original jurisdiction in matters involving disbarment of lawyers.

> See the federal judiciary homepage: **http://www.uscourts.gov/**.
>
> For an up-to-date list of Web links, go to **http://www.wadsworth.com/product/0534563406s**.

Trial and Appellate Courts

The second concept embodied in the American court system is the relationship between trial and appellate courts. Virtually all cases, whether civil or criminal, begin in the **trial court**. In a criminal case

---

Geographical jurisdiction: Geographical area over which courts can hear and decide disputes.

Extradition: Legal process whereby officials of one state surrender an alleged criminal offender to officials of the state in which the crime is alleged to have been committed.

Subject matter jurisdiction: Types of cases courts have been authorized to hear and decide.

Hierarchical jurisdiction: Refers to differences in the functions of courts and involves original as opposed to appellate jurisdiction.

Original jurisdiction: Jurisdiction in the first instance; commonly used to refer to trial jurisdiction as compared to appellate jurisdiction. Appellate courts, however, have limited original jurisdiction.

Appellate jurisdiction: The authority of a court to hear, determine, and render judgment in an action on appeal from an inferior court.

Trial court: Judicial body with primarily original jurisdiction in civil or criminal cases. Juries are used and evidence is presented.

the trial court arraigns the defendant, sets bail, conducts a trial (or takes a guilty plea), and, if the defendant is found guilty, imposes sentence. In a civil case the trial court operates in much the same way, ensuring that each party is properly informed of the complaint, supervising pretrial procedures, and conducting a trial or accepting an out-of-court settlement. Because only trial courts hear disputes over facts, witnesses appear only in trial courts. Trial courts are considered finders of fact, and the decision of a judge (or jury) about a factual dispute normally cannot be appealed.

The losing party in the trial court generally has the right to request an appellate court to review the case. The primary function of the **appellate court** is to ensure that the trial court correctly interpreted and applied the law. In performing this function, appellate courts perform another important function: They reexamine old rules, devise new ones, and interpret unclear language of past court decisions or statutes. Appellate and trial courts operate very differently because their roles are not the same. In appellate courts no witnesses are heard, no trials are conducted, and juries are never used. Moreover, instead of a single judge deciding, as in trial courts, a group of judges makes appellate court decisions; there may be as few as three or as many as twenty-eight judges, as in the U.S. Court of Appeals for the Ninth Circuit. In addition, appellate judges often provide written reasons justifying their decisions; trial court judges rarely write opinions.

The principal difference between a trial and an appeal is that a trial centers on determining the facts, whereas an appeal focuses on correctly interpreting the law. This distinction is not absolute, however. Fact-finding in the trial courts is guided by law, and appellate courts are sensitive to the facts of a case.

Dual Court System

America has a **dual court system**: one national court system and also separate court systems in each of the fifty states, plus the District of Columbia as well as the U.S. territories. The result is over fifty-one separate court systems. You will find federal courts in every state and territory of the Union, and a federal court in Alabama operates essentially the same as the counterpart federal court in Wyoming. However, the structural uniformity does not mean that actual practices are identical. On the contrary, there are important variations in how the law is interpreted and applied, an indication that the federal courts are rooted in a heritage that stresses independence, decentralization, and individualism.

Figure 3-1 shows the ordering of cases in the dual court system. The division of responsibilities is not as clear-cut as it looks, however. State and federal courts share some judicial powers. Some acts, for example, selling drugs or robbing banks, are crimes under federal law and under the laws of most states, which means the accused could be tried both in a federal and a state court. Moreover, litigants in state court may appeal to the U.S. Supreme Court, a federal court.

One of the most immediate consequences of the dual court system is the complexity it adds to the criminal justice system. In essence the framers of the U.S. Constitution created two parallel criminal justice systems consisting of their own law enforcement, court structure, and correctional systems. (In virtually all the other federated nations—Germany and Austria for example—the only separate federal courts are found at the highest level.) Of all the levels of complexity created by the dual court system, perhaps the most confusing is the application of the constitutional prohibition against double jeopardy (see Controversy: Should the Double Jeopardy Clause Prohibit Parallel State and Federal Prosecutions? on page 63 and Court TV: *New York v. Nelson* on page 74). It is to the complexities created by federalism that we now turn.

HISTORY OF THE FEDERAL COURTS

At first glance the history of the federal courts appears to be a debate over details of procedure. But a closer look reveals that the political controversies that have shaped the federal judiciary go to the heart of the federal system of government, often involving the allocation of power between the national and the state governments. Thus, any discussion of the

Appellate court: A court that hears appeals from trial courts on points of law.

Dual court system: A court system consisting of a separate judicial structure for each state in addition to a national structure. Each case is tried in a court of the same jurisdiction as that of the law or laws involved.

FIGURE 3-1	Overview of Court Structure in the United States

Federal	State
• Hears cases everywhere in the United States • Decides 46,000 criminal cases a year	• Important variations from state to state • State felony filings outnumber federal by eighty-seven to one.
U.S. Supreme Court • Most powerful court in the world • Virtually complete control over cases it hears • Decisions have completely changed the criminal justice system • Hears only a handful of state criminal cases	**Supreme Court** • Typically has almost total control over cases to be heard • Major policymaker for the state • Final decider of questions of state law • Decides a handful of criminal appeals
U.S. Courts of Appeals • Twelve circuits are organized regionally • Must hear all requests for review • Last stop for the vast majority of defendants convicted in federal court	**Court of Appeals or Appeals Court** • Thirty-nine states have intermediate courts of appeals • Must hear all requests for review • One in sixteen appellants win a significant victory
U.S. District Court • Eighty-nine courts in the continental U.S. • Criminal cases: drugs, fraud, and embezzlement • Civil cases: civil rights, federal statutes, diversity of citizenship	**District, Superior, or Circuit Court** • Organized by county (or groups of counties) • Criminal cases: burglary, theft, drugs, murder, robbery, rape • Civil cases: automobile accidents, divorce, contract, probate
U.S. Magistrate Court • Responsible for preliminary stages of felony cases • Hears a fair volume of minor crimes on federal property • Has responsibility (but not authority) over habeas corpus petitions	**Municipal, City, or Justice of the Peace Court** • In rural areas, judges may be nonlawyers • Handles preliminary stages of felony cases • Criminal cases: petty theft, public drunkenness, disturbing the peace, disorderly conduct • Civil cases: small claims

federal courts in the late twentieth century must begin with two eighteenth-century landmarks—Article III of the U.S. Constitution and the Judiciary Act of 1789. Although there have been important changes since, the decisions made at the beginning of the Republic about the nature of the federal judiciary have had a marked impact on contemporary court structure.

The Federal Judicial Center has created an excellent site on the history of the federal judiciary. Just click on **http://air.fjc.gov/history**.

For an up-to-date list of Web links, go to **http://www.wadsworth.com/product/0534563406s**.

The Constitutional Convention

One major weakness of the Articles of Confederation was the absence of a national supreme court to enforce federal law and resolve conflicts and disputes between courts of the different states. Thus, when the delegates gathered at the Constitutional Convention in Philadelphia in 1787, a resolution was unanimously adopted that "a national judiciary be established." There was considerable disagreement, however, on the specific form that the national judiciary should take. Article III was one of the most hotly debated sections of the Constitution.

The dominant question of whether there should be a federal court system separate from the state sys-

CONTROVERSY

Should the Double Jeopardy Clause Prohibit Parallel State and Federal Prosecutions?

 Lemrick Nelson, Jr., who is black, was acquitted of state charges of murdering Jewish scholar Yankel Rosenbaum during a 1991 race riot in Brooklyn. Yet he was convicted in 1997 in federal court of violating the victim's civil rights. To some, the federal conviction meant that justice was finally done. But to others, the federal prosecution was itself a miscarriage of justice.

Of all the complexities created by the dual court system, perhaps the most confusing to laypersons and lawyers alike is the application of the constitutional prohibition against double jeopardy. The Fifth Amendment provides, "Nor shall any person be subject for the same offense to be twice put in jeopardy of life or limb." How then can a defendant be tried in both state court and federal court for the same crime? The answer is that the double jeopardy clause prevents only trial by the *same* government for the *same* offense (*Bartkus v. Illinois* 1958). This justification has been termed the "dual sovereign" doctrine, because two different sovereign governments (state and federal) are prosecuting the defendant for actions that happen to violate their separate criminal laws. Consider a defendant arrested for robbing a bank. The federal government can try the defendant for robbing a federal bank, and the state government may try the same defendant for robbery. Although the event is the same, it violates both federal and state laws.

The Supreme Court justified its decision on the concerns of federalism; the Court felt that a jurisdiction's interest would be impaired if the jurisdiction (state or federal) was unable to try an individual who had been tried elsewhere facing lesser penalties. Not all agree with this interpretation, however. Critics argue that the dual sovereign exception has no legal or historical basis (Piccarreta and Keenan 1995). The ACLU would bar parallel prosecutions by different governments for the same event, a view shared by sundry defendants who have been acquitted in one court only to be convicted in another. The application

of the double jeopardy clause has in recent years engendered considerable controversy in several highly publicized cases:

- Two Los Angeles police officers were acquitted of state charges in the 1991 beating of Rodney King but were later convicted in federal court of violating his civil rights.
- Four white New York police officers were acquitted in state court of murdering Amadou Diallo in 2000. The U.S. Justice Department later decided against federal prosecution.

These few cases aside, separate state and federal prosecutions are rare. As a practical matter, policies of the U.S. Department of Justice establish a strong presumption against federal reprosecution of a defendant already prosecuted by a state for the same conduct (Litman and Greenberg 1996).

What is perhaps most striking about the controversy over parallel prosecutions by dual sovereigns is that it cuts across the ideological dimensions that structure so much of our nation's debate concerning crime policy. In the Rodney King case, for example, members of the police union readily accepted the ACLU position. Similarly, some groups that are otherwise noted for conservative positions oppose parallel prosecutions. In short, the crime control and due process models are not particularly helpful in understanding this controversy.

What do you think? Are federal prosecutions after failed state prosecutions a good way to remedy miscarriages of justice, or are the rights of defendants unnecessarily placed in jeopardy?

> To continue the debate use the search term *double jeopardy* to locate additional articles on the topic. Here are two: Kelly McMurry, "Fourth Circuit Opens Door to Double Jeopardy" and Donald Dripps, "The Continuing Decline of Finality in Criminal Law."

tems produced two schools of thought. Advocates of states' rights (later called Anti-Federalists) feared that a strong national government would weaken individual liberties. More specifically, they saw the creation of separate federal courts as a threat to the

power of state courts. As a result, the Anti-Federalists believed that federal law should be adjudicated first by the state courts; the U.S. Supreme Court should be limited to hearing appeals only from state courts. On the other hand, the Nationalists (who later called themselves Federalists because they favored ratification of the Constitution) distrusted the provincial prejudices of the states and favored a strong national government that could provide economic and political unity for the struggling new nation. As part of this approach, the Nationalists viewed state courts as incapable of developing a uniform body of federal law that would allow businesses to flourish. For these reasons, they backed the creation of lower federal courts.

The conflict between states' rights advocates and Nationalists was resolved by one of the many compromises that characterized the Constitutional Convention. **Article III** is brief and sketchy, providing only an outline of a federal judiciary: "The judicial Power of the United States, shall be vested in one Supreme Court, and in such inferior Courts as the Congress may from time to time ordain and establish." The brevity of this provision left Congress with the task of filling in much of the substance of the new judicial system.

The Judiciary Act of 1789

Once the Constitution was ratified, action on the federal judiciary came quickly. Indeed, the first bill introduced in the Senate dealt with the unresolved issue of inferior federal courts. The congressional debate included many of the same participants, who repeated all the arguments that were involved in the judiciary debates at the Constitutional Convention. After extensive debate, Congress passed the Judiciary Act of 1789, which laid the foundation for our current national judicial system. The Judiciary Act of 1789 represented a major victory for the Federalists; they were successful in creating separate federal district courts. At the same time, the act was a compromise that allayed some of the Anti-Federalists' fears. The organization of the federal judiciary supported state interests in three ways (Richardson and Vines 1970).

First, the boundaries of the district courts were drawn along state lines; no district encompassed more than one state. Thus, from the outset, the federal judiciary was "state-contained." Even though

> **Article III:** Section of the U.S. Constitution concerning the judicial branch of the national government.

district courts enforced national law, they were organized along local lines, with each district court responsible for its own work under minimal supervision.

Second, by custom the selection process ensured that federal district judges would be residents of their districts. Although nominated by the president, district judges were to be (and are today) local residents, approved by senators from the state, presiding in their home area, and therefore subject to the continuing influence of the local social and political environment (Chapter 8).

Third, the act gave the lower federal courts only limited jurisdiction. The Federalists wanted the full range of federal jurisdiction granted by the Constitution to be given to district and circuit courts. However, to achieve a lower federal court system, they were forced to reduce this demand greatly. But this issue would reappear repeatedly over the next 100 years.

 The Library of Congress provides resources for the U.S. judicial branch: **http://lcweb.loc.gov/global/judiciary.html**.

For an up-to-date list of Web links, go to **http://www.wadsworth.com/product/0534563406s**.

1789–1891

The Judiciary Act of 1789 provided only a temporary compromise on the underlying disagreements between Federalists and Anti-Federalists. The Federalists immediately pushed for expanded powers for the federal judiciary. These efforts culminated in the passage of the Judiciary Act of 1801, which created many new judgeships and greatly extended the jurisdiction of the lower courts. The Federalist victory was short-lived, however. With the election of Thomas Jefferson as president, the Anti-Federalists in Congress quickly repealed the act and returned the federal judiciary to the basic outlines of the previous circuit court system. The 1801 law is best remembered for the resulting lawsuit of *Marbury v. Madison* (1803) in which Chief Justice Marshall created the power of judicial review (the Court can strike down as unconstitutional an act of Congress) (Neubauer 1997).

Between 1789 and 1891 there was general agreement on the inadequacy of the federal judicial system, but the underlying dispute persisted. Congress passed numerous minor bills modifying the system in a piecemeal fashion. Dissatisfaction centered on two principal areas: circuit riding and the appellate court workload.

One of the most pronounced weaknesses of the 1789 judicial structure was circuit riding. The Supreme Court justices, many of them old and ill, faced days of difficult and often impossible travel. In 1838, for example, the nine justices traveled an average of 2,975 miles. Justice McKinley of the circuit that included Alabama, Louisiana, Mississippi, and Arkansas traveled 10,000 miles a year, yet found it impossible to make it to Little Rock. There were numerous complaints from the justices about the intolerable conditions that circuit-riding duties imposed on them.

Beyond the personal discomforts some justices encountered, the federal judiciary confronted a more systemic problem—mounting caseloads. Initially the federal judges of the newly created trial courts had relatively little to do because their jurisdiction was very limited. The Supreme Court likewise had few cases to decide. But the initially sparse workload began to expand as the growth of federal activity, the increase in corporate business, and the expansion of federal jurisdiction by court interpretation created litigation for a court system that was ill equipped to handle it. From the end of the Civil War until 1891, it was not uncommon for a case to wait two or three years after being docketed before it was argued before the Supreme Court. Indeed, by 1890 the high court's docket contained over 1,800 cases. The essential cause was that the high court had to decide every case appealed to it.

 To view pictures of historic federal courthouses go to **http://air.fjc.gov/history/courthouses_frm.html**.

For an up-to-date list of Web links, go to **http://www.wadsworth.com/product/0534563406s**.

Court of Appeals Act of 1891

At first glance the creation of the court of appeals in 1891 appears to be a logical and automatic response to increased federal litigation resulting from a rapidly expanding population and the growth of business following the Civil War. A closer look indicates that it was the culmination of "one of the most enduring struggles in American political history" (Richardson and Vines 1970, 26). There was no debate over the difficulties facing the federal court system. All parties in the controversy agreed that the federal judiciary needed relief; what was in dispute was the nature of the relief.

To solve the burden of mounting litigation in the federal courts, the supporters of states' rights wanted to return cases to the state level by reducing the jurisdiction of federal courts. The supporters of national power, on the other hand, argued for expanding the jurisdiction of federal courts by creating a system of federal appellate courts that would take a great deal of the burden off the high court and also allow the trial courts to function as true trial courts.

The landmark Court of Appeals Act of 1891 represented the climactic victory of the nationalist interests. The law created nine new courts known as circuit courts of appeals. Under this new arrangement, most appeals of trial decisions went to the circuit court of appeals. In short, the creation of the circuit courts of appeals released the high court from hearing many types of petty cases. The high court now had much greater control over its workload and could concentrate on deciding major cases and controversies.

Federal Courts Today

In 1925 Congress passed the Judges Bill, which among other things gave the Supreme Court much greater control over its docket. In 1988 Congress eliminated even more mandatory appeals to the high court. Figure 3-2 summarizes other key developments in the federal judiciary.

The current structure of federal courts is best understood in terms of four layers of courts: magistrate, district, appellate, and Supreme Court. In addition the federal judiciary consists of specialized courts and administrative structures.

U.S. MAGISTRATE JUDGES

U.S. magistrate judges are the federal equivalent of state trial court judges of limited jurisdiction. Although they are officially a subcomponent of the

FIGURE 3-2	Key Developments in the Federal Judiciary		

U.S. Constitution	1787	Article III creates U.S. Supreme Court and authorizes lower federal courts.
Judiciary Act of 1789	1789	Congress establishes lower federal courts.
Marbury v. Madison	1803	The Court has the authority to declare an act of Congress unconstitutional.
Courts of Appeals Act	1891	Modern appellate structure created.
Judges Bill	1925	Supreme Court given control over its docket.
Court Packing Plan	1937	FDR's attempt to pack the Court is defeated.
Administrative Office Act	1939	Current administrative structure created including judicial conference and judicial councils.
Federal Judicial Center	1967	Research and training unit created.
Federal Magistrate Act	1968	Commissioners replaced by U.S. magistrates (later the name is changed to magistrate judges).
Sentencing Commission	1984	Charged with developing sentencing guidelines.
Congressional Act of 1988	1988	Some mandatory appeals to the Supreme Court are eliminated.
Antiterrorism and Effective Death Penalty Act	1996	Severely limit right to state prisoners to file habeas corpus petitions in federal court.

district courts, their duties and workload merit separate discussion. Congress created **U.S. magistrate judges** in 1968 to replace the former position of U.S. commissioners. The purpose was to provide a new first echelon of judicial officers in the federal judicial system to alleviate the increased workload of the U.S. district courts (Puro 1976). The magistrates, as they were originally called, were unhappy over the title, and in 1990 Congress responded to their concerns by including the word *judge;* thus they are now known officially as magistrate judges (Smith 1992).

Magistrate judges are selected by the district court judges. Full-time magistrate judges are appointed for eight-year terms and part-time magistrate judges for four years. They may, however, be removed for "good cause." Except in special circumstances, all must be lawyers. According to the Administrative Office of the U.S. Courts, there are 422 full-time magistrate judges and 77 part-time magistrate judges (the part-time magistrate judges

U.S. magistrate judges: Judicial officers appointed by the U.S. district courts to perform the duties formerly performed by U.S. commissioners and to assist the court by serving as special masters in civil actions, conducting pretrial or discovery proceedings, and conducting preliminary review of applications for post-trial relief made by individuals convicted of criminal offenses.

serve primarily national parks, where the work is seasonal).

Creation of the office raised several constitutional issues, some of which remain under active discussion today (Administrative Office 1993). Magistrate judges perform quasi-judicial tasks and work within the judicial branch of government. They are not, however, Article III judges (that is, they are not nominated by the president nor confirmed by the Senate and therefore do not serve for life). For this reason, several Supreme Court decisions limited the powers of the magistrate judges. In response, Congress passed the 1976 and 1979 Federal Magistrates Acts, which clarified and expanded the scope of the magistrates' power and authority.

Magistrate judges are authorized to perform a wide variety of duties. In felony cases they are responsible for preliminary proceedings, including holding initial appearances, conducting preliminary hearings, appointing counsel for indigents, setting bail, and issuing search warrants. In misdemeanor and petty offense cases, the jurisdiction of magistrate judges is more extensive; they may preside over trials, accept pleas of guilty, and also impose sentences. On the civil side they supervise discovery, review Social Security disability benefit appeals, and even conduct full civil trials with the consent of the litigants. In short, under specified conditions and controls, magistrate judges may perform virtually all tasks carried out by district court judges, except trying and sentencing felony defendants (Smith 1987; Seron 1988). But disputes over their authority continue. In 1991 a bare majority of the Supreme Court decided that magistrate judges may supervise jury selection in a felony trial, thus overruling a contrary decision less than two years old (*Peretz v. U.S.*).

 Click on the Web site of the Federal Magistrate Judges Association at **http://www.fedjudge.org/**.

For an up-to-date list of Web links, go to **http://www.wadsworth.com/product/0534563406s**.

Caseload of U.S. Magistrate Judges

Magistrate judges play an increasingly important role in helping district court judges dispose of their growing caseloads. In a typical year, for example, they handle approximately 650,000 matters for the federal courts, including being involved in some way in 350,000 felony matters. In addition they dispose of over 100,000 misdemeanor and petty offenses.

Given the rising workload of felony cases on the district court docket, magistrate judges are increasingly involved in civil matters—about 163,000 in the most recent year for which statistics are available. Indeed in recent years magistrate judges have presided over 17 percent of civil trials.

Finally, they review but do not decide prisoner petitions, a topic we will address shortly. During 1999, for example, magistrate judges reviewed 25,791 prisoner litigation matters.

U.S. DISTRICT COURTS

Congress has created ninety-four U.S. **district courts** of which eighty-nine are located within the fifty states. There is also a district court in the District of Columbia and four territorial district courts located in Guam, Puerto Rico, the Virgin Islands,

and the Northern Mariana Islands. In the U.S. territories the district courts may also be responsible for local and federal matters.

There is at least one district court in each state; moreover, based on the compromise that produced the Judiciary Act of 1789, no district court crosses state lines. Some states have more than one district court: California, New York, and Texas, for instance, each have four. Because district courts often encompass large geographical areas, some hold court in various locations, or divisions. Some districts have only one division while others have several.

Congress has created 646 district court judgeships for the 94 districts. The president nominates district judges, who must then be confirmed by the Senate (Chapter 8). Once they take the oath of office, they serve during "good behavior," which for practical purposes means for life. The number of judgeships in each district depends on the amount of judicial work as well as the political clout of the state's congressional delegation and ranges from two in sparsely populated Wyoming to twenty-eight in densely inhabited Manhattan (officially called the U.S. District Court for the Southern District of New York).

Judges are assisted by an elaborate supporting cast of clerks, secretaries, law clerks, court reporters, probation officers, pretrial services officers, and U.S. marshals. The larger districts also have a federal public defender. Another important actor at the district court level is the U.S. attorney. There is one U.S. attorney (Chapter 6) in each district, nominated by the president and confirmed by the Senate, but, unlike the judges, he or she serves at the pleasure of the president. The U.S. attorney and his or her staff prosecute violations of federal law and represent the U.S. government in civil cases, which constitute about one third of all civil lawsuits.

The work of the district judges is significantly assisted by 326 **bankruptcy judges**. Although bankruptcy judges are adjuncts of the district courts, they are appointed for fourteen-year terms by the court of appeals in which the district is located. The bankruptcy workload of the district courts is enormous,

District courts: U.S. trial courts established in the respective judicial districts into which the whole United States is divided. These courts are established for the purpose of hearing and deciding cases in limited districts to which their jurisdiction is confined.

Bankruptcy judge: Judge who presides over the legal procedure under federal law by which a person is relieved of all debts after placing all property under the court's authority. An organization may be reorganized or terminated by the court in order to pay off creditors.

with over 1.3 million petitions filed annually. The vast majority of these bankruptcy filings are non-business related, typically involving consumers who cannot pay their bills. The others are filed by businesses big and small. Indeed, companies valued in the billions have declared bankruptcy; obviously such filings create much more work for the judiciary than a bankruptcy petition filed by an individual consumer.

 A list of district courts by state name is available at **http://dir.yahoo.com/Government/ U_S__Government/Judicial_Branch/ Federal_Courts/District_Courts/**.

For an up-to-date list of Web links, go to **http:// www.wadsworth.com/product/0534563406s**.

Caseload of U.S. District Courts

In the federal system, the U.S. district courts are the federal trial courts of original jurisdiction. Table 3-1 provides an overview of case volume in the federal courts. The volume of cases is large and growing. Each year, around 300,000 civil and criminal cases are filed in the U.S. district courts (not including bankruptcy, misdemeanors, and the like). These numbers represent a dramatic increase in workload over the last several decades.

The district courts are the trial courts for all major violations of federal criminal law (magistrate judges hear minor violations). Each year, U.S. attorneys file approximately 60,000 criminal cases, primarily for drug violations, embezzlement, and fraud. For many years federal prosecutions remained fairly constant (roughly 30,000 per year) only to shoot up beginning in 1980. A major part of this upsurge has been due to a dramatic increase in drug prosecutions. Today, drug prosecutions account for 25 percent of all federal criminal cases. Moreover, trials of criminal cases are now more frequent (and also longer) than in years past. Thus although civil, not criminal, cases account for most of the work of the district courts, in some districts criminal filings are limiting the ability of these courts to decide civil cases. (See A Day in Court: Bunton's Rocket Docket.)

Civil lawsuits consume considerably more of the federal courts' time than criminal cases do. Although only a small number of all civil cases are filed in federal courts, these cases typically involve considerably larger sums of money than the cases

filed in state court. Federal court jurisdiction is limited to a few types of cases, primarily involving questions of federal law, diversity of citizenship, and prisoner petitions.

Federal Questions

Article III provides that federal courts may be given jurisdiction over "Cases, in Law and Equity, arising under this Constitution, the Laws of the United States, and Treaties made, or which shall be made under their authority." Cases that fall under this type of jurisdiction are generally referred to as involving a **federal question**. Most federal question cases are filed alleging a violation of a congressional statute. Some of the principal federal laws that are the basis of litigation include Social Security, labor, civil rights, truth in lending, and antitrust. These federal laws are having an increasing impact on state and local criminal justice (see Exhibit 3-1).

Diversity Jurisdiction

Diversity of citizenship cases involve suits between citizens of different states or between a U.S. citizen and a foreign country or citizen. For example, a citizen from California claims to be injured in an automobile accident in Chicago with an Illinois driver and sues in federal court in Illinois since the parties to the suit were of "diverse citizenship." (However, our injured California driver also has the option of suing in state court in Illinois.) In deciding **diversity of citizenship** cases, federal courts apply state (not federal) law (Sloviter 1992). Overall, diversity cases constitute almost one fourth of the civil docket of the district courts, thus making a significant contribution to the workload of the district courts.

In an effort to restrict the types of minor disputes that may be filed in federal court, Congress in 1988 raised the amount-in-controversy threshold from $10,000 to $50,000, and raised it again in 1996 to $75,000. Despite some speculation to the contrary, this change in jurisdictional amount has indeed significantly decreased the number of diversity cases filed in federal courts each year (Flango

---

Federal question: Case that contains a major issue involving the U.S. Constitution or U.S. laws or treaties.

Diversity of citizenship: When parties on the opposite sides of a federal lawsuit come from different states, the jurisdiction of the U.S. district courts can be invoked if the case involves a controversy concerning $75,000 or more in value.

TABLE 3-1 Case Filings in the U.S. Courts

	Total	Criminal	Civil	Prisoner Petitions	Minor Criminal
Supreme Court	7,692				
Courts of Appeals	54,693*	10,251	19,489	17,191	
District Courts	317,000	59,923	203,668	56,603	
Magistrate judges	647,970	350,000	163,218	25,791	109,101

* Includes 7,762 original proceedings and other appeals.

Note: Some of these numbers have been rounded.

SOURCE: L. Ralph Mecham, *Judicial Business of the United States Courts: 1999 Annual Report of the Director* (Washington, D.C.: Administrative Office of the U.S. Courts, 2000).

1991; Kramer 1990). Overall, total diversity filings today remain well below levels of a decade earlier.

Prisoner Petitions

A controversial area of district court jurisdiction involves **prisoner petitions**. Prisoners incarcerated in either federal or state penitentiaries may file a civil suit alleging that their rights under federal law are being violated. (Similar suits may also be filed in state court, where they are called habeas corpus petitions.) Some prisoner petitions contend that the prisoners are being illegally held because they were improperly convicted; for example, they were denied the effective assistance of counsel at trial (discussed further in Chapter 7). Other prisoner petitions relate to the conditions of confinement; for example, the penitentiary is overcrowded or provides inadequate medical assistance (mentioned in Chapter 15). Petitions from state and federal inmates have increased significantly from about 3,500 filings in 1960 to over 56,000 in 1999. Thus, prisoner petitions constitute 25 percent of the total civil caseload as measured by filings. These numbers are being driven by the sharp increase in the prison population. U.S. magistrate judges hear most of these prisoner petitions but are limited to making a recommendation to the U.S. district judge (who typically follows the recommendation). Thus these cases add volume but take little of the district judges' time.

Prisoner petition: Civil lawsuit filed by a prisoner alleging violations of his or her rights during trial or while in prison.

U.S. COURTS OF APPEALS

As mentioned previously, Congress created the courts of appeals in 1891 to relieve the Supreme Court from hearing the growing number of appeals. The courts of appeals are the intermediate appellate courts of the federal system. Originally called circuit courts of appeal, they were renamed and are now officially known as the United States Court of Appeals for the _____ Circuit. Eleven of the circuits are identified by number and another is called the D.C. Circuit (see Figure 3-3).

The courts of appeals are staffed by 179 judges nominated by the president and confirmed by the Senate. As with the district courts, the number of judges in each circuit varies from six (the First Circuit) to twenty-eight (the Ninth Circuit) depending on the volume and complexity of the caseload. Each circuit has a chief judge (chosen by seniority) who has supervisory responsibilities. Several staff positions aid the judges in conducting the work of the courts of appeals. A circuit executive assists the chief judge in administering the circuit. The clerk's office maintains the records. Each judge is also allowed to hire three law clerks. In addition, each circuit has a central legal staff that screens appeals and drafts memorandum opinions.

In deciding cases, the courts of appeals normally utilize rotating three-judge panels. Along with active judges in the circuit, these panels often include visiting judges (primarily district judges from the same circuit) and senior judges. By majority vote, all the judges in the circuit may sit together to

A DAY IN COURT

Bunton's Rocket Docket

In Pecos, Texas, a procession of prisoners captured in the war on drugs is paraded before U.S. District Judge Lucius Bunton. There are no lunch breaks or continuances, and the cases are a blur. Lawyers call it "Bunton's Rocket Docket." The judge has no choice if he wants to keep up with the volume. "You are just running them through here like cattle," he says. . . .

Some in government say the war [on drugs] has made significant progress. But a growing number of judges, defense lawyers and prosecutors say it has had a host of unintended consequences that are jeopardizing the 200-year-old federal court system: Court dockets are choked; probation officers, marshals, and public defenders are overwhelmed; and the balance of power in the courtroom has shifted substantially to the prosecution, impairing the quality of justice that is meted out.

Federal courts . . . now resemble assembly lines, raising serious questions about the integrity of the system.

"It's tenuous," Bunton said, "and in some places, it's broken."

Perhaps most disturbing, although the nation's prisons are bloated, many on the front lines say there has been no serious dent in the drug trade or the violence that attends it.

Congress and the White House declared war on drug traffickers in 1986 by hiring thousands of new law-enforcement officers and passing sweeping laws that carry long, mandatory sentences.

The result has been a record number of arrests and prison terms. . . .

Because they feel overburdened, some judges have placed themselves in the uncharacteristic role of lobbyists with the senators who nominated them.

Bunton has this evidence to make his case: The seven federal judges in the Western District of Texas average 164 cases a year, more than triple the national average. Each judge also averaged 87 trials a year, compared to a national average of 35. Drug cases increased to 886 in 1989 from 272 in 1985.

Bunton's answer is more judges, politics be damned.

"I'm fully cognizant of the fact that the Democratic Congress is not big hog for Republican senators to suggest and the president to appoint a lot of judges," said Bunton, a Democratic appointee. "I don't care if it's a Republican or a Democrat. What I need is a body on the bench to try lawsuits." . . .

Asked what he thinks the war on drugs is accomplishing, Bunton responded: "It's accomplishing full prisons."

---

decide a case or rehear a case already decided by a panel. Such *en banc* hearings are relatively rare, however; in a typical year less than 100 are held throughout the entire nation.

Caseload of U.S. Courts of Appeals

Over the last four decades, the caseload of the courts of appeals has skyrocketed. This dramatic increase in caseload has not been matched by an equivalent increase in judgeships, however. In 1960 there were 68 judgeships compared to 179 today. As a result, the

 To locate the homepage of the court of appeals for your state, click on the following and then the circuit number: **http://dir.yahoo.com/Government/ U_S__Government/Judicial_Branch/ Federal_Courts/Circuit_Courts/**.

For an up-to-date list of Web links, go to **http:// www.wadsworth.com/product/0534563406s**.

number of cases heard per panel has increased from 172 (1960) to 983 (1999).

Approximately 55,000 cases are filed annually. A small number of these cases involve reviews from various administrative agencies such as the Securities and Exchange Commission and National Labor Relations Board. Primarily, the jurisdiction of the courts of appeals consists of criminal appeals, civil

En banc: French term referring to the session of an appellate court in which all the judges of the court participate, as opposed to a session presided over by three judges.

EXHIBIT 3-1 Federal Laws Affecting State and Local Criminal Justice

The impact of federal law on the criminal justice system of the states is most apparent in the decisions of federal courts expanding the rights of those accused of crimes. Under Chief Justice Earl Warren the U.S. Supreme Court sparked a due process revolution (Chapter 17) giving defendants the right to counsel (Chapter 7), broadening notions of a fair trial (Chapter 14), and expanding the right to appeal (Chapter 17). The Court also dealt with sentencing, imposing minimal standards of confinement, and striking down the death penalty (Chapter 15). Perhaps most in the public eye have been decisions restricting police gathering of evidence (Chapter12).

But indirectly, civil lawsuits (or the threat of civil lawsuits) also play an important role. Federal civil law affects the internal operations of criminal justice agencies as well as how these organizations deal with the general public. Here are four types of federal civil cases that have important consequences for state and local criminal justice officials.

- *Civil Rights Violations* Under Section 1983 (originally passed by Congress in 1871) city or state employees may be sued civilly for depriving an individual of his or her constitutional rights (*Monroe v. Pape*, 1967). Moreover, the government, and not just the individual, are liable for damages (*Monell v. Department of Social Services*, 1978). Section 1983 has become second only to prisoner petitions in the number of cases filed in the federal courts (Barrineau 1994). Police officers are sued for

brutality and prison guards are now regularly sued for alleged physical mistreatment.
- *Equal Employment Opportunities* Federal laws relating to equal employment opportunity prohibit discrimination on the basis of race, color, religion, sex, age, national origin, or disability. However, they allow exclusion of members of a "protected class" if there is a bona fide occupational qualification, for example, a valid job-related requirement that is necessary to normal business operation. Thus, criminal justice agencies should avoid height and weight requirements that are not related to job performance.
- *Sex Discrimination* Several federal laws prohibit sex discrimination. Except in rare instances, employers are required to ignore gender when hiring or promoting, provide equal pay to all employees, and treat pregnancy like any other temporary disability (Rubin 1995).
- *Discrimination against the Disabled* The 43 million Americans with disabilities are now protected against discrimination in employment and in their use of public facilities and services (Dooley and Wood 1992). Police departments, in particular, are covered (Smith and Alpert 1993). The Americans with Disabilities Act might have a noticeable impact on the docket of the federal courts, because there is the possibility of a significant number of lawsuits being filed.

---

appeals, and prisoner petitions. Appeals from criminal convictions in the U.S. district courts constitute about 19 percent of the workload of the courts of appeals. Appeals from decisions in civil cases make up the backbone of their caseload with approximately 20,000 heard every year. Finally, the courts of appeals review a large number of prisoner petitions each year. As Chapter 17 will discuss in greater depth, prisoners petitioning the court are rarely successful except in death penalty cases.

A decision by the court of appeals exhausts the litigant's right to one appeal. The losing party may request that the Supreme Court hear the case, but such petitions are rarely granted. As a result the courts of appeals are the "courts of last resort" for virtually all federal litigation. Their decisions end the case; only a tiny percentage will be heard by the nation's highest court.

U.S. SUPREME COURT

The highest court in the nation is composed of nine justices: eight associate justices and one chief justice, who is nominated specifically to that post by the president. Like other judges appointed under Article III of the Constitution, Supreme Court justices are nominated by the president, require confirmation by the Senate, and serve for life.

Cases proceed to the Supreme Court primarily through the **writ of certiorari**, an order to the lower court to send the case records so that the Supreme

Writ of certiorari: Issued from an appellate court for the purpose of obtaining from a lower court the record of its proceedings in a particular case.

FIGURE 3-3   The Federal Judiciary

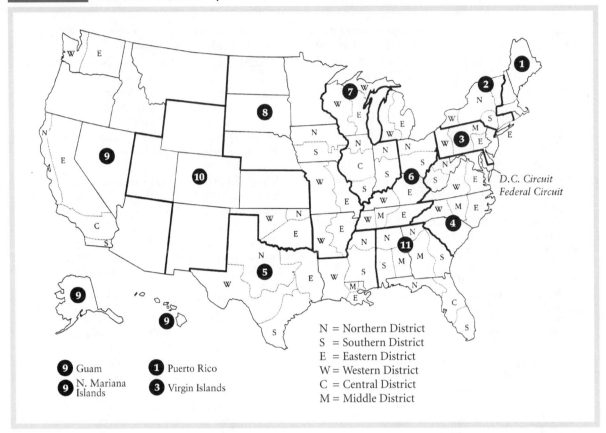

N = Northern District
S = Southern District
E = Eastern District
W = Western District
C = Central District
M = Middle District

9 Guam
9 N. Mariana Islands
1 Puerto Rico
3 Virgin Islands

SOURCE: Russell Wheeler and Cynthia Harrison, *Creating the Federal Judicial System,* 2d ed. (Washington D. C.: Federal Judicial Center, 1994), 26.

Court can determine whether the law has been correctly applied. The Court reviews decisions from the U.S. courts of appeals and state appellate courts of last resort. Although the Supreme Court is the only court in the nation to have authority over all fifty-one separate legal systems, its authority is actually limited.

Caseload of U.S. Supreme Court

With few exceptions, the Court selects which cases it will decide out of the many it is asked to review each year. In deciding to decide, the Court employs the rule of four: Four judges must vote to hear a case before it is placed on the docket. As a result, only a small percentage of the requests for appeals are ever granted. By law and custom a set of requirements must be met before a writ of certiorari (or cert, as it is often called) is granted. In particular, the legal issue must involve a "substantial

federal question." This means state court interpretations of state law can be appealed to the Supreme Court only if there is an alleged violation of either federal law or the U.S. Constitution. For example, a suit contending that a state supreme court has misinterpreted the state's divorce law would not be heard because it involves an interpretation of state law and does not raise a federal question. As a result, the vast majority of state cases are never reviewed by the Supreme Court.

Through its discretionary powers to hear appeals, the high court limits itself to deciding about 80 cases a year. The Court does not operate as the court of last resort, attempting to correct errors in every case in the nation, but rather marshals its time and energy to decide the most important policy questions of the day. The cases granted certiorari reflect conflicting legal doctrines; typically, lower courts have decided similar cases in very different ways. Although the Supreme Court decides a frac-

FIGURE 3-4 **Specialized Federal Courts**

Courts with permanent judges

Court	Level		Jurisdiction
Tax Court	Article I	Trial	Tax disputes
Court of Federal Claims	Article I	Trial	Monetary claims against the federal government
Court of Veterans Appeal	Article I	Trial	Federal veterans' benefits
Court of International Trade	Article III	Trial	Imports of foreign goods
U.S. Court of Appeals of the Armed Forces	Article I	Appellate	Uniform Code of Military Justice
Court of Appeals for the Federal Circuit	Article III	Appellate	Trademarks, patents, foreign trade, claims against the federal government

Courts with judges borrowed from other federal courts

Court	Level	Jurisdiction
Alien Terrorist Removal Court	Trial	Decides whether an alien should be removed from the U.S. on the grounds of being an alien terrorist
Foreign Intelligence Surveillance Court	Trial	Electronic surveillance of foreign intelligence agents
Foreign Intelligence Surveillance Court of Review	Appellate	Electronic surveillance of foreign intelligence agents

SOURCE: Adapted from Lawrence Baum, *American Courts: Process and Policy,* 2d ed. (Boston: Houghton Mifflin, 1990), 37; Lawrence Baum, "Specializing the Federal Courts: Neutral Reforms or Efforts to Shape Judicial Policy?" *Judicature* 74 (1991): 217–224.

tion of all cases filed in the courts, these decisions set policy for the entire nation.

SPECIALIZED COURTS

The magistrate, district, appeals courts, and Supreme Court handle the bulk of federal litigation and therefore are a principal focus of this book. To round out our discussion of the federal judicial system, however, we also need to briefly discuss several additional courts that Congress has periodically created. These courts are called specialized federal courts because they are authorized to hear only a limited range of cases—taxes or patents, for example. They are created for the express purpose of helping administer a specific congressional statute.

Figure 3-4 gives an overview of the specialized federal courts and highlights two important distinctions. First, most specialized courts have permanent, full-time judges appointed specifically to that court. A few specialized courts, however, temporarily borrow judges from federal district or courts of appeals as specific cases arise (Baum 1991).

The second distinction relates to the specialized courts' constitutional status. Judicial bodies established by Congress under Article III are known as **constitutional courts**. The Supreme Court, courts of appeals, and district courts are, of course, constitutional courts. Judicial bodies established by Congress under **Article I** are known as **legislative courts.** Courts presided over by bankruptcy judges and U.S. magistrate judges are examples of legislative courts. The constitutional status of federal courts has important implications for judicial independence. Article III (constitutional court) judges serve for a period that amounts to a lifetime appointment, but Article I (legislative court) judges

Constitutional courts: Federal courts created by Congress by virtue of its power under Article III of the Constitution to create courts inferior to the Supreme Court.

Article I: Section of the U.S. Constitution concerning the legislative branch of the national government.

Legislative courts: Judicial bodies created by Congress under Article I (legislative article) and not Article III (judicial article).

COURT TV

New York v. Nelson

Lemrick Nelson, an African American teen, is charged with the stabbing death of a Hasidic Jewish scholar during a riot in the Crown Heights section of Brooklyn, New York. Violence had erupted in this neighborhood after a Jewish driver's car jumped the sidewalk and killed a seven-year-old black child. Nelson was acquitted after a trial in state court. Later, he was convicted in federal court. While watching the video, keep these questions in mind:

1. How do religious and racial overtones influence perceptions of the crime?
2. How do you view the credibility of the police testimony? How do you react to defense arguments that the police framed Nelson?
3. Federal courts do not permit cameras. How do you think the presence of cameras in the courtroom (Chapter 14) affected the state trial?
4. Why did the federal jury reach a different verdict?
5. Was this an appropriate case for dual prosecutions, or should double jeopardy have prevented a second trial?

---

are appointed for a specific term of office. Moreover, Article III judges are protected against salary reductions while in office. Article I judges enjoy no such constitutional protection. In short, constitutional courts have a greater degree of independence from the other two branches of government than the legislative courts.

The specialized federal courts are overwhelmingly civil in their orientation, handling such matters as patents and tariffs on imported goods. But two specialized courts bear directly on criminal matters: military courts and tribal courts.

Military Justice

Military law provides the legal mechanism for controlling the conduct of military personnel. Congress adopted the Uniform Code of Military Justice in 1950, extending significant new due process rights in courts-martial. The law created the Court of Military Appeals (the name was later changed to the U.S. Court of Appeals for the Armed Forces) com-

posed of three civilian judges appointed for fifteen-year terms by the president. The intent was clearly to extend civilian influence to military law. The Military Justice Act of 1968 contributed to the further civilianization of court-martial. The code covers criminal acts but also can punish acts that are not criminal for civilians (for example, disrespect of an officer). Moreover, on a military base, military justice applies not only to members of the armed services but also to civilian employees, and it covers acts committed on and off a military base (Sherman 1987).

Like other systems of criminal law, the objective of military justice is to provide a forum for determining guilt or innocence. But in addition, court-martials serve the purpose of enforcing order and discipline in the military. In the words of the U.S. Army: "The purpose of military law is to promote efficiency and effectiveness in the military establishment, and thereby to strengthen the national security of the United States." Thus, although military justice is not exempt from the Constitution, it is certainly distinctive. Military justice differs from state and federal justice in the following ways:

- Six-person jury
- A two-thirds majority is sufficient to convict
- Convictions are automatically appealed to a higher military court

Ultimately the case may be appealed to the U.S. Supreme Court, but such cases are rare.

In recent years a few high-profile cases have thrust military justice into the news. Some of the more prominent cases include these:

- Drill Sergeant Delmar Simpson was sentenced to twenty-five years in military prison for raping and abusing more than a dozen trainees at the Aberdeen, Maryland, Army base.
- The Army charged its top enlisted man, Sergeant Major Gene McKinney, with eighteen counts of adultery, maltreatment, and sexual misconduct toward subordinates.
- Murder and hate crimes at Ft. Bragg, North Carolina.
- A U.S. soldier raped a young girl in Okinawa.
- Prosecution of the Marine Corps pilot of an airplane that struck a gondola cable in the Italian Alps, killing the twenty people on board the gondola.

A Federal Civil Rights Lawsuit Is Filed

 Late on the afternoon of January 7, 2000, attorney Clive Stafford-Smith walked the five blocks from his office to the federal courthouse at 500 Camp Street. The date was important. Federal law mandates a one-year statute of limitations in cases like this one. Thus the lawsuit was filed exactly one year after District Attorney Harry Connick decided not to try Shareef Cousin for the Port of Call murder.

Smith had represented Shareef Cousin in the state criminal trial and appeal. But now he was filing a federal civil rights lawsuit. Proceeding to the intake desk of the clerk's office he paid the $150 filing fee and the office time-stamped the lawsuit, entitled "Shareef Cousin, versus Anthony Small." The complaint was given the number 00-0069, indicating that it was the sixty-ninth civil lawsuit filed during the year 2000. The case was then randomly allotted to U.S. district court judge Sarah Vance, who had been appointed to the federal bench in 1994 by President Clinton. As a practicing lawyer she had worked in the civil litigation section of one of the city's largest law firms. As a presiding judge she is noted for running a tight ship, particularly in cases involving felony prosecutions of some of the states top elected officials (Gyan 1997).

The lawsuit names the city of New Orleans and eight individuals as defendants. Some of the defendants were the prosecutors in the state criminal prosecution. The others were New Orleans police officers. The eighty-three-page lawsuit begins: "This civil action arises from the malicious prosecution, wrongful arrest, incarceration and prosecution of plaintiff Shareef Cousin." The lawsuit alleges that the plaintiff's rights were violated under the Civil Rights Act (Chapter 42 of the U.S. Code), particularly Section 1983. The document offers a broad-based indictment of both police and prosecution. Detective Anthony Small, the lead homicide detective in the murder of Michael Gerardi, is accused of being corrupt and fabricating evidence. Assistant District Attorney Roger Jordan is accused of

repeatedly not turning over favorable evidence to the defense. The complaint concludes with a broad-based indictment of racial bias in the police department and Connick's office. The most interesting allegation involves the anonymous "tip" that led to the arrest of Shareef Cousin. Soon after the murder, Crimestoppers offered a $10,000 reward for information about the case. The plaintiff alleges that the tip was bogus—Detective Small had a friend make the call and they later split the reward.

The complaint requests an unspecified amount of damages. In a later letter from one of Cousin's attorneys, however, the lawyer suggested that based on past cases $2.5 million would constitute a justifiable settlement.

The City Attorney for New Orleans defended the police officers. His reply simply denied the allegations, thus providing little guidance as to the defense the city might use in the case. More interesting was the reply from Harry Connick's lawyer, who asserted that the district attorney enjoys absolute immunity from lawsuits (see Chapter 6). The reply also termed the complaint as redundant and immaterial. The judge would later call the document convoluted but refuse to dismiss it.

A month before filing the civil rights lawsuit, attorney Clive-Stafford-Smith and other defense lawyers held a news conference to bestow their first Chef Menteur award (which in French means "big liar"). The recipient was an NOPD homicide detective who allegedly falsified evidence in a trial that resulted in the defendant being acquitted. A longtime homicide detective, who requested that he not be identified by name, scoffed. He said the lawsuits have little to do with the case they claim to address but instead are part of an effort to undermine the credibility of detectives who testify in future cases (Coyle 2000).

The trial is set for spring 2001, but given the heavy docket in the federal court, there is no guarantee that the case will actually be tried then. Make sure to check the Web site for an update.

Tribal Courts

In 1789 Congress designated the Native American tribes as foreign nations to enable the government to sign land and boundary treaties with them. During the nineteenth century U.S. policy was to force Native Americans onto reservations west of the Mississippi River. Today there are about 285 federal and state protected land bases, colloquially called

reservations but technically termed Indian Country (18 U.S.C. sec. 151). The Bureau of Indian Affairs manages federal reservations. On the reservations today, Native Americans enjoy a degree of self-determination and sovereignty, but the degree of self-government varies from tribe to tribe. Moreover, state governments often seek to exert some authority over Indian reservations (Resnik 1995).

The tribe is the basic unit of federal Indian law. Federal legislation protects Native American groups and grants them rights against the federal government. Treaties, for example, give tribes rights to land and hunting, fishing, and water rights. The key elements of American law regarding Native Americans are (1) federal acknowledgment of sovereign governmental powers possessed by Native American groups and (2) a federal trust obligation toward and special federal powers over such groups and their members (Goldberg-Ambrose 1994).

Native American law is a jurisdictional maze of civil and criminal courts affecting Native Americans, as well as non-Native Americans living or operating a business within the jurisdiction of a Native American government (Nielsen and Silverman 1996). Tribal courts total 248, staffed by 271 trial and 39 appellate judges in 27 states. Most were created under the Indian Reorganization Act of 1934, which encouraged self-government through tribal constitutions, organized government, and tribally created courts. Recently Congress mandated a survey of tribal justice systems to examine, among other factors, the capacity of the tribal justice system, volume of the caseload, and facilities, including detention facilities. The Bureau of Justice Statistics (1999) reports in *American Indians and Crime* that Native Americans experience a high rate of violent crimes and are more likely to be victimized by someone of another race; also, 46 percent of all violent victimizations involve a drinking offender.

FEDERAL JUDICIAL ADMINISTRATION

The judicial system created by Congress in the Act of 1789 and subsequent laws can best be characterized in terms of independence, decentralization, and individualism. Courts at all levels enjoyed virtual autonomy. Judges in administrative matters were not only independent of Congress and of the president but of each other as well (Fish 1973). In essence Congress had created a hierarchy of courts that was without direction and without responsibility. "Each judge was left to himself, guided in the administration of his business by his conscience and his temperament" (Frankfurter and Landis 1928, 220).

This situation changed with the passage of the Administrative Office Act of 1939, which largely created the current administrative structure of the federal judiciary. This law illustrates the interplay between judicial administration and politics. During the mid-1930s the conservative majority on the Supreme Court declared many pieces of New Deal legislation unconstitutional. After his reelection in 1936, President Franklin Delano Roosevelt put forth his Court packing plan—the Court would be expanded from nine to fifteen justices, thus allowing FDR to pack the Court with justices more sympathetic to his policies. There was no legal barrier to such actions because the Constitution fails to specify how many justices shall serve on the Court. But the political obstacles proved insurmountable; many of Roosevelt's backers felt that tampering with the Court was a bad idea. The Court packing plan never passed, but it did call attention to the president's complaints that administration of federal court was inefficient. To solve this problem, FDR proposed a national court administrator, to be appointed by the chief justice and with absolute authority to manage the judicial system.

The judiciary opposed the initial legislation as an attack on its heritage of independence, decentralization, and individualism. But at the same time some judges were dissatisfied with the old system of court management because it was located in the Department of Justice, an executive agency. Thus a movement arose among federal judges and national court reformers to clean their own house. The result was a compromise plan; the Administrative Office Act of 1939 was the judiciary's substitute for FDR's court bill. The act expanded the responsibilities of the Judicial Conference, created the Administrative Office of the U.S. Courts, and established the judicial councils. These agencies, along with the office of the chief justice, the Federal Judicial Center, and the more recently created U.S. Sentencing Commission, are the main units involved in administering the federal courts.

 The official site of the Supreme Court of the United States is very good for recent opinions, arguments, and schedules: **http://www.supremecourtus.gov/**.

For an up-to-date list of Web links, go to **http://www.wadsworth.com/product/0534563406s**.

Chief Justice

The chief justice is the presiding officer of the Supreme Court and has supervisory authority over the entire federal judicial system. In fulfilling these duties, the chief justice is allotted an extra law clerk and an administrative assistant to help with the administrative tasks for both the Court and the judicial system as a whole. As head of the federal judiciary, the chief justice is an ex officio member of several important administrative organizations and also appoints persons to key administrative posts. Chief Justice Warren Burger (1969–1986) devoted considerable effort to judicial administration and off the bench was particularly concerned about improving the conditions of American prisons. Current Chief Justice William Rehnquist has often spoken about the need for Congress to increase the number of federal judges, increase the salaries of judges to be competitive with the private practice of law, and reduce the workload of the courts.

Judicial Conference of the United States

The Judicial Conference of the United States is the administrative policy-making organization of the federal judicial system. Its membership consists of the chief justice, the chief judges of each of the courts of appeals, one district judge from each circuit, and the chief judge of the Court of International Trade. The conference meets semiannually for two-day sessions. Because these short meetings are not sufficient to accomplish a great deal, most of the work is done by about twenty-five committees. The committees consist of judges and a few lawyers appointed by the chief judge. In spite of the long hours and unpaid labor, appointments to the committees are coveted. A committee appointment is a status symbol through which judges gain esteem among their peers (Fish 1973). The recommendations of the committees set the agenda for the conference.

The Judicial Conference directs the Administrative Office in administering the judiciary budget and makes recommendations to Congress concerning the creation of new judgeships, increases in judicial salaries, and budgets for court operations. The Judicial Conference also plays a major role in the impeachment of federal judges (a topic discussed in greater depth in Chapter 8). Probably the most important function of the conference is revising the various rules of federal procedure. Proposed changes in the federal rules originate with the Judicial Conference. The Supreme Court can approve, modify, or disapprove these recommendations. Once adopted, the recommendations are transmit-

ted to Congress and automatically become law in ninety days unless Congress acts adversely. In short, the Judicial Conference is a vehicle through which federal judges play a major role in developing policy for the federal judiciary.

Administrative Office of the U.S. Courts

From 1870 to 1939 the U.S. Department of Justice handled the day-to-day administrative tasks of the federal courts. This arrangement generated pervasive conflict because administrative control over the judiciary was in the hands of an executive agency (Fish 1973). Against this backdrop the Administrative Office Act of 1939 created the Administrative Office of the U.S. Courts, a judicial agency. Appointed by the chief justice, the director reports to the Judicial Conference.

Acting as the Judicial Conference's official representative in Congress, the Administrative Office's lobbying and liaison responsibilities include presenting the annual budget requests for the federal judiciary, arguing for the need for additional judgeships, and transmitting proposed changes in court rules. The Administrative Office (AO) is also the housekeeping agency of the judiciary responsible for allotting authorized funds and supervising expenditures. Throughout the year, local federal court staff send the AO a vast array of statistical data on the operations of the federal courts, ranging from the number of filings to the speed of the disposition of cases. The data are published in three separate volumes. The heftiest is the *Annual Report,* which runs hundreds of pages long and is now available on computer tape.

 The Web site of the Administrative Office of the U.S. Courts can be accessed at **http://www.uscourts. gov/**.

For an up-to-date list of Web links, go to **http:// www.wadsworth.com/product/0534563406s**.

Federal Judicial Center

The Federal Judicial Center is the research and training arm of the federal judiciary. Its activities are managed by a director appointed by the board, which consists of the chief justice, the director of the Administrative Office, judges from the U.S. district court, courts of appeals, and bankruptcy court.

One of the principal activities of the Federal Judicial Center is education and training of federal judicial personnel, including probation officers, clerks of court, and pretrial service officers. For example, seminars for newly appointed federal judges are held whenever there is a sufficient number of judges to justify them. The center also conducts research on a wide range of topics, including the work of the magistrate judges, ways of measuring the workload of the courts, and causes of delay.

 Access the Federal Judicial Center at **http://www.fjc.gov/**.

For an up-to-date list of Web links, go to **http://www.wadsworth.com/product/0534563406s**.

Judicial Councils

The judicial council (sometimes referred to as circuit council) is the basic administrative unit of a circuit. Originally the judicial councils were composed of all the active-duty judges of the courts of appeals; in effect the circuit councils consisted of the courts of appeals sitting *en banc* but wearing administrative rather than judicial hats. The judicial councils were restructured and strengthened by congressional legislation in 1981. No longer are all active-duty circuit judges automatically members of the council; rather they decide by majority vote who will sit. In addition, half the membership of the council consists of district judges.

A judicial council is given sweeping authority to "make all necessary and appropriate orders for the effective and expeditious administration of justice within its circuit." Working within this broad mandate, the councils monitor district court caseloads and judicial assignments. Although the law specifies that "all judicial officers and employees of the circuit shall promptly carry into effect all orders of the judicial council," the actual enforcement powers are limited. The major weapons at the councils' disposal are persuasion, peer group pressure, and publicity directed at the judge or judges who are reluctant to comply with circuit policy. At times, for example, circuit councils have ordered that a district judge receive no new cases until his or her docket has been brought up to date. Judicial councils are also authorized to investigate complaints of judicial disability or misconduct (a topic probed in greater detail in Chapter 8).

U.S. Sentencing Commission

The U.S. Sentencing Commission is an independent agency in the judicial branch of government. The commission was created by the Sentencing Reform Act provisions of the Comprehensive Crime Control Act of 1984. Its principal purpose is to establish sentencing policies and practices for the federal courts, including detailed guidelines prescribing the appropriate form and severity of punishment for offenders convicted of federal crimes. Although the development, monitoring, and amendment of the sentencing guidelines is the centerpiece of the agency's work, the commission also provides training, conducts research on sentencing-related issues, and serves as an information resource for Congress, criminal justice practitioners, and the public.

The commission is charged with the ongoing responsibilities of evaluating the effects of the sentencing guidelines on the criminal justice system, recommending to Congress appropriate modifications of substantive criminal law and sentencing procedures, and establishing a research and development program on sentencing issues (Chapter 16).

 Access the United States Sentencing Commission at **http://www.ussc.gov/**.

For an up-to-date list of Web links, go to **http://www.wadsworth.com/product/0534563406s**.

RISING CASELOADS IN THE FEDERAL COURTS

Too many cases has been a significant issue since the early years of the federal judiciary. At first almost all of the nation's judicial business was handled by the state courts—federal jurisdiction was tightly limited by the Judiciary Act of 1789. But with the onset of the Industrial Revolution, the caseload of the federal courts began to grow. This increase in federal judicial business was accelerated by Prohibition, then the New Deal, and even further by federal lawmaking often associated with President Johnson's "Great Society" programs. Growing caseloads in turn prompted changes and additions to the federal judiciary—appellate courts have been added, specialized courts created, and administrative agencies provided for.

FIGURE 3-5   Dramatic Increase in Federal Court Workload

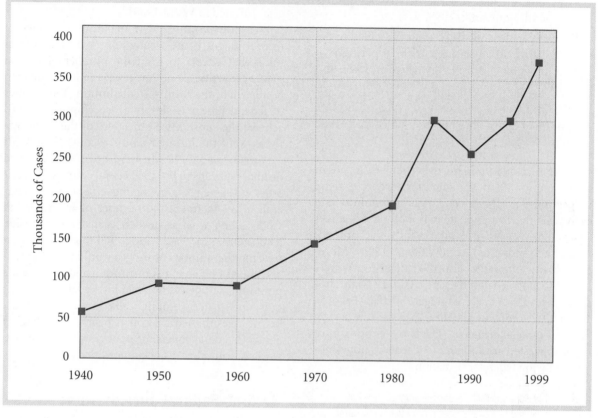

SOURCE: L. Ralph Mecham, *Judicial Business of the United States Courts: 1999 Report of the Director* (Washington, D.C.: Administrative Office of the U.S. Courts, 2000).

Federal caseload growth, therefore, is nothing new. What is new is the pace of that expansion. For most of our nation's history the growth in federal cases was gradual. No longer! Over the last forty years district court filings have more than trebled, and court of appeals cases have increased more than tenfold (Figure 3-5). According to the Administrative Office of the U.S. Courts, federal judges today are faced with unprecedented levels of work. Although there have been small declines in discrete areas of workload, by and large federal judges across the country face a greater number of cases this year than last, and in some instances, are encountering record levels of work.

Dramatic Increase in Workload

"The demands placed on United States judges today are staggering," said L. Ralph Mecham, director of

See the Web site of the Federal Court Clerks' Association at **http://www.id.uscourts.gov/ fcca.htm**.

For an up-to-date list of Web links, go to **http:// www.wadsworth.com/product/0534563406s**.

the Administrative Office of the U.S. Courts. "Jurists at virtually every level of our federal system are facing a greater number of cases, which involve increasingly complex issues, explore novel areas of the law, and consume a larger portion of their time" (Administrative Office 1996). The following are some examples.

• The number of civil rights cases filed in U.S. district courts jumped 86 percent between 1990 and 1995. This increase, when weighted for complexity, equates to fifty-five judgeships solely to handle civil rights cases.

- Filings in U.S. bankruptcy courts doubled over the last decade. Annual bankruptcy filings topped 1.3 million in 1999.

- Approximately one third of all cases filed in the U.S. courts of appeals are prisoner petitions—jumping by nearly 4,700 between 1990 and 1995.

- The number of criminal cases filed in the U.S. courts of appeals has nearly doubled from 1987 until 1995.

The caseload problem is particularly acute in some metropolitan jurisdictions, where federal judges must postpone civil trials for months and even years to accommodate criminal trial schedules (particularly of major drug dealers) in accordance with the Speedy Trial Act (Williams 1993). Moreover, during one recent year the federal courts were forced to stop scheduling new civil jury trials altogether because of a severe budget shortfall (Labaton 1993). Developments like these give rise to the term "federal judicial gridlock." The two solutions most often suggested are adding more federal judgeships and reducing federal jurisdiction.

 "The Supreme Court: A Journey through Time" is presented by CourtTV at **http://www.courttv.com/ multimedia/supremecourt/index.html**.

For an up-to-date list of Web links, go to **http:// www.wadsworth.com/product/0534563406s**.

How Many Federal Judges Are Too Many?

The dramatic increases in federal court cases have not been accompanied by a corresponding increase in the number of federal judgeships, particularly at the appellate level. It is clear that in the short term the number of federal judgeships will be increased, but this process is closely tied to partisan battles in Congress (Chapter 8). More fundamentally, some observers wonder how big the federal judiciary should become.

Judge Jon Newman of the U.S. Court of Appeals for the Second Circuit argues that 1,000 is the effective limit of the federal judiciary. To exceed this number would lead to an inevitable drop in quality of judges, he argues. Judge Joseph Weis of the U.S. Court of Appeals for the Third Circuit agrees, stating, "The Federal courts are like a committee, and

any committee works less efficiently and has a tougher time arriving at a consensus the bigger it gets" (quoted in Wiehl 1990).

To others, imposing a maximum number of federal judges is the wrong approach. Opponents think that efforts to limit the number of federal judges are artificial and imaginary. To Judge Stephen Reinhardt of the Ninth Circuit, limiting the number of federal judges is simply a procedural device to achieve the substantive objectives of the conservatives—shut the little guys out of court (Reinhardt 1993; Newman 1993). In his words, "The right of ordinary citizens to use the Federal courts is in jeopardy. . . . There is a growing movement among Federal judges to freeze the number of judgeships at 1,000, when what is needed is just the opposite, a substantial increase." Judge Reinhardt fears that freezing the number of judges would turn the federal courts into an elitist institution and advance the philosophical agenda of Chief Justice William Rehnquist and Justice Antonin Scalia. Limiting the number of cases the federal courts hear would shut off access to federal courts for poor people, minorities, women, and other disadvantaged persons.

Reduce Federal Jurisdiction?

In the late 1980s, Congress decided for the first time in the nation's history to systematically study the caseload of the federal courts. At the urging of the federal judiciary, Congress created a special study committee with members appointed by the chief justice. In 1990, the *Report of the Federal Courts Study Committee* concluded that "the long-expected crisis of the federal courts, caused by unabated rapid growth in case filings, is at last upon us."

The report makes it abundantly clear that in the committee's view Congress created most of these problems by unwisely expanding federal court jurisdiction, and therefore Congress should act immediately to pass remedial legislation. Alas, having been labeled as the culprit, it is hardly surprising that Congress gave the report a chilly reception (Biskupic 1993). Indeed many of the committee's recommendations had already been considered by Congress and rejected. In short, the nation's top elected lawmakers have been at odds with the nation's top appointed law interpreters for most of this century, and this disagreement is not likely to change.

Arguments based on numbers of cases stress issues of efficiency but typically need to be under-

Should State Crimes Also Become Federal Violations?

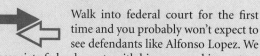 Walk into federal court for the first time and you probably won't expect to see defendants like Alfonso Lopez. We associate federal courts with big cases and important issues. Bank embezzlers and big-time drug dealers are what we expect to see. Street criminals like Lopez are more likely to be found in state courts. But increasingly the dockets of federal courts are being crammed with such criminals. Deciding what should be a federal offense and what should be a state crime is not an easy task—one that says more about the sociology and politics of the nation than its law.

The division of power between the national government and state governments is at times fuzzy. Whereas some ideologues argue for absolute divisions between federal and state power, the reality is that federalism involves shared powers, not necessarily distinct and separate layers of authority.

Under federalism, one of the powers reserved to the states is the power to regulate persons and property in order to promote the public welfare (commonly referred to as police powers). Based on these police powers, state governments and their local subdivisions pass laws to promote the public health, welfare, and safety. Thus, most crimes are defined by the states (see Chapter 2).

Congressional Expansion

Over the years Congress has extended federal criminal jurisdiction beyond the basics centering on federal property and interstate commerce. The underlying motivation has been public concerns (some would say public hysteria) about selected activities. Thus, it is no coincidence that a great deal of the expansion of federal criminal jurisdiction involves public morality in matters like drugs, alcohol, prostitution, and gambling (Meier 1994). The Mann Act (also known as the White Slave Traffic Act) was passed in 1910 after lurid revelations of the growth of prostitution in the United States and fears about importing European women for U.S. brothels. The Harrison Act of 1914 outlawed opium, morphine, heroin, and cocaine because these drugs were associated with deviants (Chinese opium dens and the like). The Volstead Act ushered in Prohibition in 1919, representing the political dominance of rural Protestants over big-city Catholics. The movie *Reefer Madness* is often associated with the federal government's crackdown on marijuana in the 1930s. National attention on the Mafia after World War II

led to the passage of the Racketeer Influenced and Corrupt Organizations Act (RICO) in 1970. More recently, federal attention has focused on guns (see Case Close-Up: *U.S. v. Miller* and the Right to Bear Arms) and yet again on drugs (Brickey 1996).

The same political process continues today, only the specifics have changed. Contemporary demands to expand federal criminal jurisdiction occasionally attract bipartisan support. Recent federal legislation dealing with child pornography falls into this category. But mostly these discussions reflect contrasting partisan and ideological positions. Conservatives generally favor reducing federal court caseloads, but when it comes to some issues, they favor expansion. Some conservative congresspersons, for example, have called for increasing federal criminal jurisdiction to include car-jacking and transferring numerous gun cases from state to federal courts. These efforts, if successful, would potentially result in numerous violent offenders who were armed with a weapon being prosecuted in federal, not state, court.

Democrats oppose such efforts but tend to support expansion of federal criminal law to cover citizens with limited political power. Thus, they favor expanding federal criminal legislation to cover hate crimes, stalking, and violence against women. Moreover, they would allow victims of crimes "motivated by gender" to sue civilly in federal court. And most of all they back gun control as the best strategy for controlling crime. Republicans oppose such efforts.

Judicial Responses

Federal judges, whether appointed by Republican or Democratic presidents, almost uniformly oppose the federalization of state crimes (Schwarzer and Wheeler 1994). Thus, the *Report of the Federal Courts Study Committee* recommended sending drug cases back to state court and eliminating mandatory minimum sentences. Chief Justice Rehnquist (1993) has decried what he calls the near transformation of some federal courts into national narcotics courts. Twenty-five percent of all federal criminal cases are now drug related.

The position of the federal judiciary is that federal jurisdiction should be limited to cases that cannot or should not be brought in state courts. Chief Judge Henry Politz of the Fifth U.S. Court of Appeals expressed the following sentiment: "We ought to be flattered that Congress reacts by saying let's make a

(continued on following page)

federal crime out of it. But don't be fooled by it, we can't handle it." He noted that there are more than 3,000 state trial judges in Texas; by contrast there are 69 federal district judges in the entire Fifth Circuit, which includes not only Texas but also Louisiana and Mississippi (quoted in Voelker 1995).

The Lopez and Morrison Decisions

The *Lopez* case is ultimately significant not because it involves guns but because the Court set limits on what crimes Congress may federalize. Writing for the majority, Chief Justice William Rehnquist stressed that in passing the Gun-Free School Zones Act in 1990 Congress "did not issue any findings showing a relationship between gun possession on school property and commerce."

More recently a bare conservative majority of the Court declared part of the Violence Against Women Act of 1994 unconstitutional (*U.S. vs. Morrison*, 2000). In particular, victims of rape and other violent felonies "motivated by gender" no longer may sue their attackers in federal court (although state remedies are still available).

These decisions have sparked intense debate. To some, concern about overexpansion of federal jurisdiction is a genuine concern in matters like this. But to others the concern over caseload appears to be a façade masquerading conservative antipathy toward gun control and protecting the rights of vulnerable members of society.

Use the search term *crime, federal* to locate additional articles on the topic. Here are two: John Mountjoy, "The Federalization of Criminal Laws" and James Gondles, "The Federalization of Criminal Justice."

In an opinion paralleling the reasoning in *Lopez*, the U.S. Supreme Court declared parts of the Violence Against Women Act unconstitutional. To read the opinion click on the following: **http://supct.law. cornell.edu/supct/html/99-5.ZS.html.**

For an up-to-date list of Web links, go to **http:// www.wadsworth.com/product/0534563406s.**

stood within a more basic framework of political winners and losers. Thus some disagreements reflect divisions along the lines of the due process versus crime control models of justice. But other disagreements reflect institutional differences—the views of federal judges (whether appointed by Republican presidents or Democratic ones) contrast with the views of federal lawmakers. Part of the political battle over federal court jurisdiction involves the scope of federal criminal law. Controversy: Should State Crimes Also Become Federal Violations? explores why this topic cuts across typical ideological perspectives.

CONSEQUENCES OF FEDERAL INVOLVEMENT IN THE CRIMINAL JUSTICE SYSTEM

Crime, Chapter 1 argued, has been a pressing national concern for decades. As a result, national elected officials, whether members of Congress or the president, have often made crime a key cam-

paign issue. In turn, the crime policies of nonelected officials, whether bureaucrats or judges, have been closely scrutinized. Despite all this clamor at the national level, crime remains primarily the responsibility of state and local governments. This imbalance between federal officials' need to be seen as doing something about the crime problem, and their limited jurisdiction to do anything, explains a good deal of the political dynamics of the role of the federal government (and the federal judiciary) in the criminal justice system.

Limited Scope

Although crime receives extraordinary attention from the national government, the role of the federal government in the criminal justice system is limited. The majority of events labeled as crime are violations not of federal law but of state law; as a result the capacity of the federal justice system is limited. Table 3-2 makes the point. The federal system has 6 percent of law enforcement personnel and 9 percent of prison inmates. In terms of numbers of prisoners, this is comparable to Texas (the Lone Star state's 97,000 inmates rank it second

TABLE 3-2 The Limited Scope of Federal Criminal Involvement

Activity	State and Local	Federal	
Law enforcement personnel	828,435	52,105	6%
Supreme Court justices	357	9	2%
Courts of appeals judges	874	179	17%
Major trial court judges	9,763	649	6%
Lower trial court judges	18,317	422	2%
Prison inmates	958,704	95,034	9%
Prisoners under sentence of death	2,723	6	0.2%
Justice system employment	1,635,502	162,202	9%
Correctional officers	352,847	25,515	7%

SOURCES: Brian Reaves, *Federal Law Enforcement Officers, 1993* (Washington, D.C.: Bureau of Justice Statistics, U.S. Department of Justice, 1994); Brian Reaves and Pheny Smith, *Sheriffs' Departments 1993* (U.S. Department of Justice, Washington, D.C. 1996); Kathleen Maguire and Ann Pastore, eds., *Sourcebook of Criminal Justice Statistics—1994* (Washington, D.C.: U.S. Department of Justice, 1995).

behind California). Over the last two decades federal crime has become heavily identified with the war on drugs. Indeed, 44 percent of all federal prosecutions, and 60 percent of all federal inmates, are drug related.

Forum for Symbolic Politics

In spite of the limited scope of its involvement in crime, the federal government remains the focal point of the national debate. Crime is a powerful issue and therefore has attracted a variety of interest groups. Some focus on crime issues directly—for example, the Coalition to Stop Gun Violence, National Association of Chiefs of Police, and National Organization for the Reform of Marijuana Law (NORML). Other interest groups find that crime and crime issues are related to other concerns—the National Rifle Association and the National Association of Attorneys General, for example.

Interest groups have a major impact on public policy. Most directly they lobby on behalf of their members for favorable governmental policies. They can also mount campaigns encouraging their members to write federal officials in favor of (or in opposition to) specific proposals. Some organizations likewise make campaign contributions to selected officials. The National Rifle Association, for instance, contributes to officials who are dubious about gun control, whereas Handgun Control, Inc., supports candidates who favor gun control (Marion 1995).

Many interest group activities are instrumental—that is, they are tied to the passage or defeat of specific legislation. But other activities are more symbolic, seeking to have the values of their organization recognized to the exclusion of other groups, even if the actions have little if any impact. The debate over the death penalty fits here. Congress and the president have debated expanding federal death penalty laws for several decades, but the reality is that any such laws will have limited impact at best.

Federal Dollars

A basic rule of American politics is that citizen demands for services exceed the willingness of voters to raise taxes to pay for those services. Those who one day vocally demand a tax reduction are quick to demand expanded governmental services the next day. Funding the criminal justice system illustrates this equation. Citizens demand that courts "get tough with criminals" but are unwilling to raise taxes for a new jail. Likewise, pleas for more cops on the beat are seldom followed by requests for increased taxes to pay for such increased people power. Faced with these limitations, local and state officials often turn to Washington as a source of

U.S. v. Miller and the Right to Bear Arms

 It is no small irony that in the polemics over gun control the U.S. Constitution is very salient while the U.S. Supreme Court has been very silent. The Second Amendment reads: "A well regulated Militia, being necessary to the security of a free State, the right of the people to keep and bear Arms, shall not be infringed." The high court has addressed the meaning of these archaic words only five times in its history, most recently in 1939.

Jack Miller and Frank Layton drove from Claremore, Oklahoma, to Siloam Springs, Arkansas. Why they were making the trip is unknown; in the quaint words of *The New York Times* ("Supreme Court Bars Sawed-Off Shotgun" 1939), "The record in the case of Miller and Dayton (sic) does not show for what purpose they were taking the sawed-off shotgun across State lines." Both were arrested for transporting a sawed-off shotgun in interstate commerce. The U.S. district court dismissed the indictment on grounds that the National Firearms Act "violates the Second Amendment to the Constitution of the United States" (*U.S. v. Miller et al.* 1939). Alas, for Miller and Layton, the nation's high court reached a very different conclusion.

Writing for a unanimous court, Justice James McReynolds (a jurist noted for his conservative views) explored the history of the Second Amendment, emphasizing that the drafters inserted the phrase "well regulated Militia" very purposefully. "The sentiment of the time strongly disfavored standing armies; the common view was that adequate defense of country and laws could be secured through the Militia—civilians primarily, soldiers on occasion." In short "the right of the people to keep and bear Arms" applied only to militia and not to individual citizens. (States maintained militias until the War of 1812, but their woeful performance against the British army led to their demise, to be replaced by a standing army.)

Since *Miller*, the Supreme Court has declined to directly address the issue. Lower federal courts have upheld firearms regulations either on grounds that the Second Amendment is a collective, not an individual right, or because it has not been incorporated, that is, it limits only the national government, but not state or local entities. Recently, however, the high court (in the tradition of *Lopez*) struck down the part of the Brady Act dealing with background checks, reasoning that the Tenth Amendment prohibits Congress from compelling state law enforcement officers to "administer or enforce a federal regulatory program" (*Printz v. United States*, 1997).

The decision in *U.S. v. Miller* is often mentioned by gun control advocates and just as often ignored by gun rights supporters. The ongoing debate over the meaning of the Second Amendment illustrates the interplay between law on the books and law in action. In terms of law on the books, the Supreme Court has the final say. But in terms of law in action, other branches of government and citizens themselves play a vital role. The Constitution is an important symbol of American society. Labeling a governmental program as constitutional (or unconstitutional) has tremendous consequences. No matter what the Court (and lawyers and judges for that matter) might say, a significant minority of the American public interprets the Second Amendment as creating a personal right to bear arms (and therefore not limited to the militia). Moreover, these views are reinforced by powerful interest groups—most notably the National Rifle Association.

"free" money (with free defined as no local taxes). In turn, federal officials find that appropriating federal money is one way of assuring voters that they take the crime problem seriously.

Congress has authorized spending for a variety of anticrime programs. Some are general in nature, for example, block grants for local projects that reduce crime and improve public safety. Similarly, 60 percent of the research budget of the National Institute of Justice—the principal federal agency involved in the war on crime—is spent on developing new technology for law enforcement and the criminal justice system. Other spending programs are targeted toward specific concerns, for example, domestic violence and victim assistance programs (Chapter 9). Drug and alcohol abuse are also prime targets, as are deadbeat dads. Priorities vary between administrations. Reagan backed preventive detention programs, whereas Clinton supported community-oriented policing and adding 100,000 more cops. Recently, federal funding has become available for building local jails and state prisons. Overall, though, the amount of federal dollars is small compared to what local and state governments spend. Moreover, federal money is often limited to a short period of time (typically three years). After federal funding ends, state or local units of government are expected to take over funding, but often these agencies are strapped for cash, meaning that successful programs are canceled.

The federal government provides state and local criminal justice system support in ways other than just federal dollars. Personnel is one. Federal law enforcement agencies such as the FBI have provided technological support in the form of crime lab analysis, fingerprint identification, and the like.

Today, such help is being extended in the form of joint task forces. Some types of crimes—drug distribution in particular—cross numerous geographical lines and also potentially violate numerous federal and state laws. Because of this, local police departments are cooperating with a wide variety of federal law enforcement agencies in targeting either specific suspects or specific crimes. Wiretapping authority is another form of federal support. The FBI is in a better position both legally and organizationally to tap the telephones of suspected criminals than are local police departments.

CONCLUSION

Street punks like Alfonso Lopez were no doubt on Justice Scalia's mind when he spoke in New Orleans a few years ago, condemning what he called the deterioration of the federal courts. In the 1960s the federal courts had a few judges and small caseloads, but the cases they did hear were "by and large . . . cases of major importance." Today, he argued, the federal courts have more judges and larger caseloads, but many of these cases are "minor" and "routine," concerning "mundane" matters of less import or even "overwhelming triviality" (quoted in Galanter 1988). Thus, to one of the Court's leading conservatives, the federal courts should be returned to their rightful role of deciding major controversies; lesser ones would be banished to state courts.

Other federal judges, whether noted for their liberal, moderate, or conservative views, have also expressed concern about the federalization of state crimes, calling for drug cases to be sent back to state courts where they rightfully belong. But in an era when crime remains a major political issue, rolling back federal jurisdiction to the "good old days" (whenever that might have been) is unlikely to happen. What we learn ultimately is that the jurisdiction of federal courts is determined in no small measure by decisions of elected officials in Congress. In an earlier era federal officials decided that federal law should cover matters such as prostitution, consumption of alcoholic beverages, gambling, and organized crime. Today they focus more on drug dealers, crooks who use guns, and wife beaters.

Federal prosecutions often grab the headlines because the crimes are large or audacious or because the accused are people of prominence. In turn the public by and large identifies the judiciary with federal courts. But we should not be misled. The federal courts are a relatively small part of the nation's judicial system. A major city such as Chicago or Los Angeles prosecutes more felons in a year than the entire federal judiciary. The nature of the crimes brought to federal court differs strikingly from those appearing in state judiciaries, though. State courts handle primarily street crimes that require immediate action—burglary, armed robbery, and murder, for example. By contrast, federal crimes are often paper crimes requiring no immediate action—bank embezzlement and money laundering, for instance. It is to the more common state courts that we turn our attention in the next chapter.

CRITICAL THINKING QUESTIONS

1. To what extent are contemporary debates over the role of the federal government similar to, but also different from, the debates in the late eighteenth century?

2. How would the criminal justice system be different today if the founding fathers had decided not to create a separate system of federal courts and instead allowed federal laws to be enforced in state courts?

3. How would you reduce the federal court caseload? In considering where you would reduce

federal court jurisdiction, also consider where you might increase it. What do your choices reflect about your political values?

4. To what extent does the debate over federalization of state crimes cut across traditional ideological values as represented in the due process model and the crime control model?

5. Federal law enforcement is limited in scope but subject to considerable public attention. Why?

6. Why do opponents of gun control so often ignore *U.S. v. Miller*?

 WORLD WIDE WEB RESOURCES AND EXERCISES

Web Guides

http://dir.yahoo.com/Government/U_S__Government/Judicial_Branch/

Web Search Terms

"Federal courts," "federalization of crime," "double jeopardy"

Useful URLs

The Third Branch, the magazine of the U.S. courts, often contains articles on federal court caseloads: http://www.uscourts.gov/ttb/.

The OYEZ project from Northwestern University offers case summaries, oral arguments, and a virtual tour of the court: http://oyez.nwu.edu/.

See the Commission on Structural Alternatives for the Federal Courts of Appeal at http://app.comm. uscourts.gov/.

The U.S. Marshals Service is America's oldest federal law enforcement agency: http://www.usdoj.gov/marshals/.

The American Bar Association provides a report, "The Federalization of Criminal Law": http://www.abanet.org/crimjust/fedreport.html.

Federal Justice Statistics on the Web are available at http://fjsrc.urgan.org.

Uncommon URLs

Emory Law School's Federal Court Finder provides a U.S. map with easy links: http://www.law.emory.edu/FEDCTS/.

Web Exercises

1. The homepage for the federal courts contains links to all the federal courts and federal judicial agencies. The URL is http://www.uscourts.gov/. Click on the Web sites for the Administrative Office of the U.S. Courts and also the *Third Branch* (the newsletter published by the Federal Judicial Center). Examine recent discussions of federal court caseloads.

2. Yahoo also contains numerous links to federal courts. To access them, first go to Yahoo at http://www.yahoo.com; then click on Government/Judicial Branch/Federal Courts. Don't be dismayed to find many of the same sites as on the U.S. courts homepage. The Web is interrelated, which means there is more than one way to access a specific site. Which route you take is entirely your preference.

   Click on the site for the circuit that governs your state and see what information is available. In particular, do the sites provide information about the number of criminal cases decided each year? Do the data give any indication of the nature of the crimes involved (drugs, bank robbery, for example)? Who do you think the audience is for the Web site—practicing lawyers, potential jurors, the general public?

3. U.S. Supreme Court opinions are available on the Web, which saves the drudgery of walking to the law section of the library and getting your hands dirty on all the dust of older volumes. One of the major links, FindLaw, is at http://www.findlaw.com/. Choose Laws: Cases and Codes/Supreme Court Opinions and search for the court's opinion in *U.S. v. Lopez* using either the citation search (U.S.) or the party (Lopez). (The option of full-text search is not recommended for the novice.)

 INFOTRAC COLLEGE EDITION RESOURCES AND EXERCISES

Basic Search Terms

Federal courts; crime, federal; tribal courts; courts-martial; military courts; constitutional convention; gun control; Rodney King; double jeopardy

Recommended Articles

Donald C. Dilworth, "Blue Ribbon Judicial Panel Will Recommend Fate of Federal Ninth Circuit"

Carrie E. Johnson, "Rocket Dockets: Reducing Delay in Federal Civil Litigation"

Clarissa Campbell Orr, "Court History"

InfoTrac College Edition Exercises

1. Using the search term *crime, federal,* find articles that discuss what types of behavior should be made a federal violation. Based on these articles, discuss what arguments are made suggesting why a crime should be a federal offense. What arguments are made against such proposals? Overall do disagreements reflect philosophical differences of the crime control versus due process model of justice? Here are two suggested articles: Brian Levin, Bruce Fein, "Q. Does America Need a Federal Hate-Crime Law?" and David Savage, "The Chief Lays Down the Law."

REFERENCES

Administrative Office of the U.S. Courts. 1993. *A Constitutional Analysis of Magistrate Judge Authority.* Washington, D.C.: Magistrate Judges Division, Administrative Office of the U.S. Courts.

———. 1996. "Record-Setting Workloads Confront Federal Judges." Press release, June 24. *Http://www.uscourts.gov/ Press_Releases/workld.htm.*

Barrineau, H. E. 1994. *Civil Liability in Criminal Justice.* Cincinnati: Anderson.

Baum, Lawrence. 1991. "Specializing the Federal Courts: Neutral Reforms or Efforts to Shape Judicial Policy?" *Judicature* 74: 217–224.

Biskupic, Joan. 1993. "Congress Cool to Proposals to Ease Load on Courts." *Congressional Quarterly* (April 7): 1073–1075.

Brickey, Kathleen. 1996. "The Commerce Clause and Federalized Crime: A Tale of Two Thieves." *Annals of American Academy of Political and Social Science* 543: 27–38.

Bureau of Justice Statistics. 1999. *American Indians and Crime.* Washington, D.C.: U.S. Department of Justice.

Coyle, Pamela. 2000. "One-Time Murder Suspect Suing City; Inmate Claims Cops Framed Him in Killing." *Times-Picayune,* 11 January.

Dooley, Jeanne, and Erica Wood. 1992. "Opening the Courthouse Door: The Americans with Disabilities Act's Impact on the Courts." *Judicature* 76: 39–41.

Fish, Peter. 1973. *The Politics of Federal Judicial Administration.* Princeton: Princeton University Press.

Flango, Victor. 1991. "Did Increasing the Federal Jurisdictional Amount Have the Predicted Impact on State Courts?" *State Court Journal* (Spring): 21–24.

Frankfurter, Felix, and James Landis. 1928. *The Business of the Supreme Court.* New York: Macmillan.

Galanter, Marc. 1988. "The Life and Times of the Big Six: or, The Federal Courts Since the Good Old Days." Working Paper 9:2, Institute for Legal Studies, University of Wisconsin, Madison.

Goldberg-Ambrose, Carole. 1994. "Of Native Americans and Tribal Members: The Impact of Law on Indian Group Life." *Law and Society Review* 28: 1123–1148.

Gyan, Joe. 1997. "Judge has Tight Grip on Trial." *The Times-Picayune,* 18 May.

Kramer, Larry. 1990. "Diversity Jurisdiction." *Brigham Young University Law Review:* 3–66.

Labaton, Stephen. 1993. "U.S. Judges Refuse to Add Civil Cases, Citing Gap in Funds." *The New York Times,* 9 April.

Litman, Harry, and Mark Greenberg. 1996. "Dual Prosecutions: A Model for Concurrent Federal Jurisdiction." *Annals American Academy of Political and Social Science* 543: 72–86.

Marion, Nancy. 1995. *A Primer in the Politics of Criminal Justice.* New York: Harrow and Heston.

Meier, Kenneth. 1994. *The Politics of Sin: Drugs, Alcohol, and Public Policy.* Armonk, NY: M. E. Sharpe.

Neubauer, David. 1997. *Judicial Process: Law, Courts, and Politics in the United States.* 2d ed. Fort Worth: Harcourt Brace.

Newman, Jon. 1993. "1,000 Judges—The Limit for an Effective Federal Judiciary." *Judicature* 76: 187–188.

Nielsen, Marianne, and Robert Silverman, eds. 1996. *Native Americans, Crime, and Justice.* Boulder, CO: Westview Press.

Piccarreta, Michael, and Jefferson Keenan. 1995. "Dual Sovereigns, Successive Prosecutions, and Politically Correct Verdicts." *Criminal Law Bulletin* 31: 291–304.

Puro, Stephen. 1976. "United States Magistrates: A New Federal Judicial Officer." *Justice System Journal* 2: 141–156.

Rehnquist, William. 1993. "Symposium Spotlights Nation's Drug and Violence Problems." *Third Branch* 25 (July): 1.

Reinhardt, Stephen. 1993. "No. More Cases Should Be Heard." *The New York Times,* 17 May, A11.

Resnik, Judith. 1995. "Multiple Sovereignties: Indian Tribes, States, and the Federal Government." *Judicature* 79: 118–125.

Richardson, Richard, and Kenneth Vines. 1970. *The Politics of Federal Courts.* Boston: Little, Brown.

Rubin, Paula. 1995. "Civil Rights and Criminal Justice: Employment Discrimination Overview." National Institute of Justice, U.S. Department of Justice, Washington, D.C.

Schwarzer, William, and Russell Wheeler. 1994. *On the Federalization of the Administration of Civil and Criminal Justice.* Washington, D.C.: Federal Judicial Center.

Seron, Carol. 1988. "The Professional Project of Parajudges: The Case of U.S. Magistrates." *Law and Society Review* 22: 557–574.

Sherman, Edward. 1987. "Military Law." In *Encyclopedia of the American Judicial System,* edited by Robert Janosik. New York: Charles Scribner's Sons.

Sloviter, Dolores. 1992. "Diversity Jurisdiction Through the Lens of Federalism." *Judicature* 76: 90–93.

Smith, Christopher. 1987. "Who Are the U.S. Magistrates?" *Judicature* 71: 143—150.

———. 1992. "From U.S. Magistrates to U.S. Magistrate Judges: Developments Affecting the Federal District Courts' Lower Tier of Judicial Officers." *Judicature* 75: 210–215.

Smith, Michael, and Geoffrey Alpert. 1993. "Law Enforcement: The Police and the Americans with Disabilities Act—Who Is Being Discriminated Against?" *Criminal Law Bulletin* 29: 516–534.

"Supreme Court Bars Sawed-Off Shotgun." 1939. *The New York Times,* 16 May, 3.

Voelker, Bill. 1995. "Judge: Federal Courts Are Not the Answer." *Times-Picayune,* 1 February, 6.

Wiehl, Lis. 1990. "Drastic Moves Urged to Ease U.S. Courts' Load." *The New York Times,* 23 March.

Williams, Victor. 1993. "Solutions to Federal Judicial Gridlock." *Judicature* 76: 185–186.

FOR FURTHER READING

Banks, Christopher. *Judicial Politics in the D.C. Circuit Court.* Baltimore: The Johns Hopkins University Press, 1999.

Carp, Robert, and Ronald Stidham. *The Federal Courts.* 2d ed. Washington, D.C.: CQ Press, 1990.

Clinton, Robert, Nell Newton, and Monroe Price. *American Indian Law.* 3d ed. Charlottesville, VA: Michie Co., 1991.

Cook, David, Steven Schlesinger, Thomas Bak, and William Rule. "Criminal Caseloads in U.S. District Courts." *American University Law Review* 44 (1995).

Frederick, David. *Rugged Justice: The Ninth Circuit Court of Appeals and the American West, 1891–1941.* Berkeley: University of California Press, 1994.

Fritz, Christian. *Federal Justice in California: The Court of Ogden Hoffman, 1851–1891.* Lincoln: University of Nebraska Press, 1991.

Hall, Kermit, and Eric Rise. *From Local Courts to National Tribunals: The Federal Courts of Florida, 1821–1990.* Brooklyn, NY: Carlson Publishing, 1991.

Hellman, Arthur. *Restructuring Justice: The Innovations of the Ninth Circuit and the Future of Federal Courts.* Ithaca, NY: Cornell University Press, 1990.

Hughes, John. *The Federal Courts, Politics, and the Rule of Law.* New York: HarperCollins, 1995.

"Indian Tribal Courts and Justice: A Symposium." *Judicature* 79 (1995): 110–156.

Levenson, Laurie. "The Future of State and Federal Civil Rights Prosecutions: The Lessons of the Rodney King Trial." *UCLA Law Review* 509 (1994): 509–583.

McLauchlan, William. 1984. *Federal Court Caseloads.* New York: Praeger.

Mecham, L. Ralph. 2000. *Judicial Business of the United States Courts: 1999 Annual Report of the Director.* Washington, D.C.: Administrative Office of the U.S. Courts.

"Native Americans in the Criminal Justice System: Issues of Self-Determination." *Journal of Contemporary Criminal Justice* 14:1 (1998).

Rehnquist, William. *The Historic Impeachments of Justice Samuel Chase and President Andrew Johnson.* New York: William Morrow, 1992.

Sayer, John William. *Ghost Dancing the Law: The Wounded Knee Trials.* Cambridge, MA: Harvard University Press, 1997.

Shattuck, Petra, and Jill Norgren. *Partial Justice: Federal Indian Law in a Liberal-Constitutional System.* New York: Berg Publishers, 1991.

Smith, Christopher. *Judicial Self-Interest: Federal Judges and Court Administration.* Westport, CT: Praeger, 1995.

Smith, Christopher. *United States Magistrates in the Federal Courts: Subordinate Judges* New York: Praeger, 1990.

Spitzer, Robert. *The Politics of Gun Control.* Chatham, NJ: Chatham Publishers, 1994.

Wheeler, Russell, and Gordon Bermant. *Federal Court Governance.* Washington, D.C.: Federal Judicial Center, 1994.

Zelden, Charles. *Justice Lies in the District: The U.S. District Court, Southern District of Texas, 1902–1960.* College Station: Texas A&M University Press, 1993.

Zimring, Franklin, and Gordon Hawkins. "Toward a Principled Basis for Federal Criminal Legislation." *Annals of American Academy of Political and Social Science* 543 (1996): 14–26.

State Courts

AFTER ATTENDING SEVERAL JUDICIAL CONFERENCES AROUND THE NATION, two judges had little trouble identifying the major problems facing the Los Angeles County municipal courts: Soaring drug prosecutions were further crowding jails that were already full. Implementing a solution, however, proved a more troublesome and time-consuming process. In order to establish a drug court the judges needed the active cooperation of other judges, the district attorney, the public defender, treatment providers, and the sheriff. To ensure that these agencies had a voice in the process, a coordinating council was formally established. Finally, after months of meeting and planning, two drug courts were created (Torres and Deschenes 1997).

Discussions of state courts usually contain references to major cases like armed robberies and automobile accidents. But this is only part of their workload. State judges must also adjudicate cases involving wives who want divorces from unfaithful husbands and husbands who physically abuse their wives; juveniles who rob liquor stores and juveniles who simply drink liquor. The contemporary realities reflect an increase in the number of cases placed on the dockets of state courts and rising societal expectations about the administration of justice—while staffing levels remain constant. Thus, although an earlier generation viewed court reform in terms of a neater organizational chart, contemporary discussions are more likely to focus on such topics as finding a better way to handle drug cases.

This chapter examines the structure and functions of state courts. We begin with a discussion of the development of American courts and then divide the somewhat confusing array of state courts into four levels: trial courts of limited jurisdiction, trial courts of general jurisdiction, intermediate appellate courts, and courts of last resort. (Chapter 18 examines the lower courts in depth, and we will discuss juvenile courts in Chapter 19.) We will examine the efforts of court reformers to reorganize state court structure as well as the consequences of court organization for the administration of justice. ∎

HISTORY OF STATE COURTS

Just as American law borrowed heavily from English common law, the organization of American courts reflects their English heritage. But the colonists and later the citizens of the fledgling new nation that called itself the United States of America adapted this English heritage to the realities of the emerging new nation. Issues such as the clash of opposing economic interests, the debate over state versus national power, and outright partisanship have shaped the development of America's fifty diverse state court systems.

Colonial Courts

Early colonial courts were rather simple institutions whose structure replicated English courts in form but not in substance. The numerous, complex, and highly specialized English courts were ill suited to the needs of a small group of colonists trying to survive on the edge of the wilderness, so the colonists greatly simplified the English procedures. As towns and villages became larger, however, new courts were created so that people would not have to travel long distances to have their cases heard. Moreover, a notion of separation of governmental powers began to emerge. In the early days the same governmental body often held executive, legislative, and judicial powers. The county courts, for example, stood at the heart of American colonial government. Besides adjudicating cases, they also performed important administrative functions (Friedman 1985). Gradually, different institutions began to perform these tasks.

Diversity was the hallmark of the colonies, with each colony modifying its court system according to variations in local customs, different religious practices, and patterns of commercial trade. Some of these early variations in legal rulings and court structures have persisted and contribute to the great variety of U.S. court systems today (Glick and Vines 1973).

Early American Courts

After the American Revolution, the functions of state courts changed markedly. Their governing powers were drastically reduced and taken over by the legislative bodies. Moreover, their decisions were often closely watched. The former colonists distrusted lawyers and harbored misgivings about English common law. They were not anxious to see the development of a large, independent judiciary. Thus, state legislatures often scrutinized judicial decisions, and in response to unpopular court decisions, some judges were removed from office or specific courts were abolished.

The distrust of the judiciary increased as courts declared legislative acts favoring free money to be unconstitutional. Such actions were a major source of political conflict between legislatures and courts representing opposing interests. Legislators were more responsive to policies that favored debtors, usually small farmers. Courts, on the other hand, reflected the views of creditors, often merchants. Out of this conflict over legislative and judicial power, the courts gradually emerged as an independent political institution.

 One way to gauge the history of courts is through courthouse architecture. Courthouses were often built in the center of the major town in the county and were also the biggest buildings in the county. Here's a sample of state courthouses that you can see on the Internet:

Texas courthouses: **http://www.telalink.net/ ~scaevola/chtexas.htm**

Florida's historic courthouses: **http://jud10.flcourts. org/Courthouses/courts.htm**

Historic courthouses in California: **http://www. courtinfo.ca.gov/courts/trial/historic/**

For an up-to-date list of Web links, go to **http:// www.wadsworth.com/product/0534563406s**.

Courts in a Modernizing Society

Rapid industrialization following the Civil War produced fundamental changes in the structure of the American judiciary. Increases in population, the growth of cities, and the rise of industrialization greatly expanded the volume of litigation. Moreover, the types of disputes coming to the courts changed as well. Not only did the growth of industry result in disputes over this new wealth, but the concentration of people in the cities (many of whom were immigrants), coupled with the pressures of industrial employment, meant the courts were faced with a new set of problems. The American courts, still reflecting the rural agrarian society of the early nineteenth century, were inadequate in the face of rising demands for services (Jacob 1984).

States and localities responded to the increased volume of litigation in a number of ways. City courts were created to deal with new types of cases in the urban areas. Specialized courts were formed to handle specific classes of cases (e.g., small claims courts, juvenile courts, and family relations courts).

Additional courts were created, often by specifying the court's jurisdiction in terms of a geographic boundary within the city. The development of courts in Chicago illustrates the confusion, complexity, and administrative problems that resulted from this sporadic and unplanned growth. In 1931 Chicago had 556 independent courts; the majority were justice of the peace courts that handled only minor offenses (Glick and Vines 1973).

The jurisdiction of these courts was not exclusive; that is, a case could be brought before a variety of courts depending on the legal and political advantages that each one offered. Moreover, each court was a separate entity; each had a judge and a staff. Such an organizational structure meant there was no way to shift cases from an overloaded court to one with little to do. Each court also produced patronage jobs for the city's political machines.

The sporadic and unplanned expansion of the American court system has resulted in an often confusing structure. Each state system is different. Although some states have adopted a unified court structure, others still have numerous local courts with overlapping jurisdictions. Moreover, there may be major variations in court jurisdiction within a state; the jurisdiction of courts in one county may differ from that in the adjoining county. To reduce confusion, we will examine state courts at four levels: trial courts of limited jurisdiction, trial courts of general jurisdiction, intermediate appellate courts, and courts of last resort. Table 4-1 summarizes the tremendous volume of cases decided each year by state courts.

TRIAL COURTS OF LIMITED JURISDICTION: LOWER COURTS

At the first level of state courts are **trial courts of limited jurisdiction**, sometimes referred to as inferior courts, or more simply, lower courts. There are almost 14,000 trial courts of limited jurisdiction in the United States, staffed by about 18,000 judicial officers. The lower courts constitute 85 percent of all judicial bodies in the United States. The number of

Trial courts of limited jurisdiction: A lower level state court, such as a justice of the peace court, whose jurisdiction is limited to minor civil disputes or misdemeanors.

TABLE 4-1 Case Filings in State Courts

	Civil	Criminal	Domestic	Juvenile	Traffic	Total
Court of last resort						97,000
Intermediate courts of appeals						200,000
Trial courts of general jurisdiction	6,300,000	4,400,000	3,500,000	1,300,000	8,600,000	24,100,000
Trial courts of limited jurisdiction	9,100,000	10,200,000	1,500,000	800,000	45,800,000	67,400,000
Total	15,400,000	14,600,000	5,000,000	2,100,000	54,400,000	91,800,000

Note: These are estimates based on percentages and therefore the numbers may not total.

SOURCE: Brian Ostrom and Neal Kauder, *Examining the Work of State Courts, 1998.* (Williamsburg, VA: National Center for State Courts, 1999).

trial courts of limited jurisdiction varies from none in Idaho, Illinois, Iowa, Massachusetts, Minnesota, South Dakota, and the District of Columbia (where their functions have been absorbed by the major trial courts), to over 2,900 in New York and 2,500 in Texas.

Variously called district, justice, justice of the peace, city, magistrates, or municipal courts, the lower courts decide a restricted range of cases. Most of these courts are created by city or county governments and therefore are not part of the state judiciary. Thus lower courts are typically controlled only by the local governmental bodies that create them and fund them.

The caseload of the lower courts is staggering—over 67 million matters a year, the overwhelming number of which are traffic cases (almost 46 million in any given year) (Table 4-1). The caseload indicates that these are the courts that the average citizen is most likely to come into contact with. For this reason Chapter 18 will examine the lower courts in more depth, highlighting their role in conducting the preliminary stages of felony cases and deciding misdemeanor, traffic, and small claims cases.

 The quickest way to determine if your local courts have Web sites is to go to **http://www.ncsc.dni.us/court/sites/Courts.htm**.

For an up-to-date list of Web links, go to **http://www.wadsworth.com/product/0534563406s**.

TRIAL COURTS OF GENERAL JURISDICTION: MAJOR TRIAL COURTS

At the second level of state courts are the **trial courts of general jurisdiction**, usually referred to as major trial courts. There are an estimated 2,600 major trial courts staffed by over 9,000 judges (Ostrom and Kauder 1999). The phrase *general jurisdiction* means that these courts have the legal authority to decide all matters not specifically delegated to lower courts. The specific division of jurisdiction between the lower courts and the major trial courts is specified by law—statutory or constitutional or both. The most common names for these courts are district, circuit, or superior. The specific names used in all states are listed in Exhibit 4-1.

The geographical jurisdictions of the major trial courts are defined along existing political boundaries, counties primarily. Each court has its own support staff consisting of a clerk of court, a sheriff, and others. In most states the trial courts of general jurisdiction are also grouped into judicial districts or circuits. In rural areas these districts or circuits encompass several adjoining counties. Here the trial

Trial courts of general jurisdiction: The trial courts responsible for major criminal and civil cases.

EXHIBIT 4-1 Major Trial Courts in Different States

Circuit Court
Alabama, Arkansas,[a] Florida, Hawaii, Illinois, Indiana,[b] Kentucky, Maryland, Michigan, Mississippi,[a] Missouri, Oregon, South Carolina, South Dakota, Tennessee,[a] Virginia, West Virginia, Wisconsin

Court of Common Pleas
Ohio, Pennsylvania

District Court
Colorado, Idaho, Iowa, Kansas, Louisiana, Minnesota, Montana, Nebraska, Nevada, New Mexico, North Dakota, Oklahoma, Texas, Utah, Wyoming

Superior Court
Alaska, Arizona, California, Connecticut, Delaware,[a] District of Columbia, Georgia, Maine, Massachusetts, New Hampshire, New Jersey, North Carolina, Rhode Island, Vermont,[c] Washington, New York

Supreme Court
New York[d]

[a] Arkansas, Delaware, Mississippi, and Tennessee have separate chancery courts with equity jurisdiction.
[b] Indiana uses superior and circuit courts.
[c] Vermont also uses district courts.
[d] New York also uses county courts.

SOURCE: David Rottman, Carol Flango, and R. Shedine Lockley. S*tate Court Organization, 1993.* (Washington, D.C.: U.S. Department of Justice, Bureau of Justice Statistics, U.S. Government Printing Office, 1995).

court judges are true generalists who hear a wide variety of cases as they literally ride circuit, holding court in different counties on a fixed schedule. More populated counties have only one circuit or district for the area. Here judges are often specialists assigned to hear only certain types of cases, such as criminal, family, juvenile, civil, and so on. Refer back to Table 4-1 for some basic workload data on the major trial courts.

As discussed in Chapter 3, the lion's share of the nation's judicial business exists at the state, not the federal, level. Twenty-four million cases are filed each year in the nation's state trial courts, more than 100 times the number of similar filings in the federal district courts. Moreover, the types of cases filed in the state courts differ greatly from those going to the

federal courts. Litigants in federal courts are most often big businesses and governmental bodies. In sharp contrast, litigants in state courts are most typically individuals and small businesses.

 One of the leaders in providing useful Web sites is the Superior Court of San Diego County, California: **http://www.sandiego.courts.ca.gov/superior/index.html**.

For an up-to-date list of Web links, go to **http://www.wadsworth.com/product/0534563406s**.

Criminal Cases

Whereas federal courts hear a high percentage of white-collar crimes and major drug distribution cases, state courts decide primarily street crimes. The more serious criminal violations are heard in the trial courts of general jurisdiction. The public associates felonies with crimes of violence such as murder, robbery, and rape, but as we will see in Chapter 10, 90 percent of criminal violations involve nonviolent crimes such as burglary and theft. State courts must also process a rising volume of drug-related offenses, ranging from simple possession of small amounts of illicit drugs to sale of large quantities of cocaine and heroin. Over the last decade and a half criminal cases filed in general jurisdiction courts (primarily felonies) increased 50 percent. Most criminal cases do not go to trial. Thus, the dominant issue in the trial courts of general jurisdiction is not guilt or innocence but what penalty to apply to the guilty.

Civil Cases

The focus on criminal cases in the media might lead one to believe that criminal cases account for the majority of court business. In reality, civil cases dominate the dockets of major trial courts. Press attention also suggests that personal injury lawsuits dominate civil filings. In reality, tort cases make up a relatively small percentage of the docket.

Domestic relations constitutes the single largest category of cases filed in the major trial courts. These family law matters mainly involve divorce and related issues such as determining child custody,

Domestic relations: Relating to the home; the law of divorce, custody, support, adoption, and so on.

THE MURDER TRIAL OF SHAREEF COUSIN

"Doing Time at Tulane and Broad" (Part I)

 The morning sky at the corner of Tulane and Broad is gunmetal gray. . . . Emergency vehicles with lights and sirens a-go-go are so frequent here that no one seems to notice. Also missed in the daily bustle is the grand building on the corner, the building that embodies the very term "Tulane and Broad." The Orleans Parish Criminal Courthouse is so familiar and dirty and, at night, so poorly lit that it fades into background despite the jolting tales of the city inside. . . .

Morning light filters in the north windows in the grand foyer, gray light turning yellow, illuminating dust particles above the expansive marble floor. At this hour, the grand hall emits only the occasional faint echo of hushed conversation or the soft shuffle of an early-rising lawyer's expensive Italian shoes. "It's like a church," one bystander affirms. "It makes you feel guilty before you even get to the courtroom."

Judge Dennis Waldron is one of the first to arrive upon this scene daily, preferring to set his docket in motion at the very unfashionable—for New Orleans—hour of 8:00 A.M. . . . "It's like a train station here," he says, satisfied. "People coming and going; there's something for somebody every day. There is no rehearsal, no reruns. What I like most about a day in this building is the unpredictability of it all."

There are 12 criminal court sections . . . and each day's docket reflects anywhere from 20 to 40 cases in progress. Hundreds of people flock through the courthouse doors for bond hearings, status hearings, arraignments, motions, and pretrial arguments on cases from crack possession to murder, on and numbingly on, all of this dispensed with before actual trials begin later in the day.

Many of the accused in these cases shuffle along wearing international safety orange prison fatigues stamped with "OPP"—Orleans Parish Prison—on the back, their wrists and ankles shackled, deputies flanking them. Down the center of the hall they walk, past the innumerable "bench people" who gather on the seats outside each courtroom. The bench people are witnesses to crimes, victims of crimes and mostly, friends and relatives of the accused. Sometimes these people abide by the No Smoking signs, often they do not. . . .

The improbably named Lark Fall administers to the hurt and the fallen here. Fall, 33, is the answer desk clerk just inside the front door. Her job is to provide courthouse visitors with directions to various courtrooms and agencies, but sometimes she takes on extra duty. Dressed in a sequined "Amazing Grace" T-shirt and poring over sheet music while making notes in the margins, Fall sings.

---

setting levels of child support, allocating economic resources (homes, cars, and savings accounts), and in some states providing for spousal support (alimony and the like). Domestic relations cases account for a full one third of case filings. Moreover, domestic relations cases exhibit the fastest growing part of the civil caseload.

Estate cases (often referred to as probate) are the second most common type of case filed in the states' major trial courts. For those who made a will prior to their death, the courts supervise the distribution of assets according to the terms of the will. For those who failed to make a will before dying, the courts determine which heirs will inherit the estate. Most estate matters present the judge with little if any controversy.

Personal injury cases constitute the third most common type of case filings in state trial courts of general jurisdiction. Tort law covers a wide range of legal injuries. Most involve a physical injury, which can vary from a sprained ankle to wrongful death. Although tort cases may involve a wide range of activities, most stem from accidents involving motor vehicles. Tort cases constitute only about 8 percent of all filings in trial courts of general jurisdiction, but they are the most likely to go to trial. Only the handful that involve large sums of money are likely to be covered in the press. Contrary to popular belief, there has been no "litigation explosion" (Neubauer 1997); tort case filings actually decreased by 1 percent over the last decade (Ostrom and Kauder 1999).

Estate: The interest a person has in property; a person's right or title to property.

Personal injury: Negligence lawsuits, often involving automobile accidents.

It started one day about six years ago. "There was a lady sitting over there on a bench," Fall remembers. "This lady was looking downtrodden. So I started to sing to myself and I saw her pick up a little bit. Since then, whenever I see somebody feeling a little low, I sing—anything from gospel to classical." ...

Numa Bertel loves this story. "Only in New Orleans!" he bellows. "Where else but in a courthouse in New Orleans could you find a young black woman in the hallway singing spirituals to uplift the people coming through the criminal justice system?" Bertel is a veritable lifer here, the chief of the public defender's office and the man to see if you want to know what it's like to love this place.

"The colloquial expression would be: I like to be where the action is," Bertel explains. "The actual expression is: I like life. This is much closer to real life than sitting in a high-rise law office watching corporations function. ... I've been coming into this building every day since '63 and there's hardly a day goes by that there isn't some high drama going here if you know where to look for it—and usually you don't have to look for it. In and out come all the misfortunes and tragedies of the city."

In a first floor corner is Magistrate Court, the first stop in the criminal justice system after arrest and booking. The charges are presented to the accused, a plea is made—99 percent of the time not guilty—and bond is set. Magistrate Court is a microcosm of the criminal justice system, a quick picture. The defendants have generally all been arrested within the past 12 to 24 hours. Dressed in various combinations of OPP fatigues and street clothes, they are, on this day, 20 men in serious need of a good night's sleep, bleary-eyed and unshaven. Statistics tell us at least three-quarters of them are coming down off a buzz from drugs or alcohol.

Bail bondsmen sit in the audience hungrily eyeing these prospective clients like carrion-eaters over road-kill. Magistrate Judge Gerard Hansen whips through the docket. The first guy is fittingly named Lawless. He threw a boat propeller at a guy. Hansen puts bond at $2,000 and moves on. The docket is cluttered with men whose arrest records are stamped CAREER CRIMINAL. Of two suspects busted on an assault charge, one has 12 prior felony arrests and 17 misdemeanors; the other has nine prior felonies, 10 misdemeanors. The next man charged with criminal damage has five prior felony arrests, six misdemeanors ..., and on it goes. ...

In about 24 minutes, Hansen has dispensed with the entire docket. In a few hours, there will be another Magistrate Court session presided over by another judge, 20 more morose citizens will enter the revolving door that is the Orleans Parish criminal justice system.

SOURCE: Christopher Rose, "Doing Time at Tulane and Broad." *The Times Picayune,* September 27, 1998.

A variety of other types of civil cases are also filed in state trial courts of general jurisdiction. Contract cases arise when one party claims that the other party failed to live up to the terms of a contract and asks for monetary damages as compensation. Other cases allege violations of property rights, which typically involve mortgage foreclosures. Thus, most of the other cases are commercial matters, involving businesses in one form or another. Most commercial cases involve debt collection in one form or another.

INTERMEDIATE COURTS OF APPEALS

A century ago state court systems included only a single appellate body—the state court of last resort. Like their federal counterparts, however, state courts have experienced a significant growth in appellate cases that threatens to overwhelm the state supreme court. State officials in thirty-nine states have responded by creating **intermediate courts of appeals,** or ICAs (Exhibit 4-2). The only states that have not followed suit are sparsely populated ones with a low volume of appeals. The ICAs must hear all properly filed appeals. Subsequent appeals are at the discretion of the higher court. Thus a decision by the state's intermediate appellate court is the final one for most cases.

The structure of the intermediate courts of appeals varies in several ways. Twenty-four states organize their ICAs on a statewide basis, and the rest, on a regional basis. In most states these bodies

Intermediate courts of appeals: Judicial bodies falling between the highest, or supreme, tribunal and the trial court; created to relieve the jurisdiction's highest court of hearing a large number of cases.

EXHIBIT 4-2 Intermediate Courts of Appeals (Number of Judges)

Appeals Court
Massachusetts (14)

Appellate Court
Connecticut (9), Illinois (42)

Appellate Division of Superior Court
New Jersey (28)

Appellate Divisions of Supreme Court
New York (48)

Appellate Terms of Supreme Court
New York (15)

Commonwealth Court
Pennsylvania (9)

Court of Appeals
Alaska (3), Arizona (21), Arkansas (6), Colorado (16), Georgia (9), Idaho (3), Indiana(5), Iowa (6), Kansas (10), Kentucky (14), Michigan (24), Minnesota (16), Missouri (32), Nebraska (6), New Mexico(10), North Carolina (12), North Dakota (3),[a] Ohio (65), Oklahoma (12),[b] Oregon (10), South Carolina (6), Tennessee (12),[b] Utah (7), Virginia (10), Washington (23), Wisconsin (15)

Courts of Appeal
California (88), Louisiana (55), Texas (80)

Court of Civil Appeals
Alabama (3)

Court of Criminal Appeals
Alabama (5), Tennessee (9)

Court of Special Appeals
Maryland (13)

District Court of Appeals
Florida (57)

Intermediate Court of Appeals
Hawaii (3)

Superior Court
Pennsylvania (15)

[a] Temporary
[b] Civil only

SOURCE: David Rottman, Carol Flango, and R. Shedine Lockley. *State Court Organization, 1993.* (Washington, D.C.: U.S. Department of Justice, Bureau of Justice Statistics, U.S. Government Printing Office, 1995).

hear both civil and criminal appeals. Alabama and Tennessee, however, have separate courts of appeals for civil and criminal cases. The number of judges in the intermediate courts of appeals ranges from three to the eighty-eight in the California Court of Appeals. Like their federal counterparts, these courts typically employ rotating three-judge panels for deciding cases.

The ICAs handle the bulk of the caseload in the appellate system, and their workload has increased dramatically in the last decade. States have created these courts and given them additional judgeships in hopes of relieving the state supreme courts from crushing caseloads, only to find that the ICAs experience the same problems (Chapter 17). Numerous efforts are under way to increase the efficiency of the appellate process, but not everyone agrees where to draw the line between needed efficiencies and the requirement that justice be done.

Looking ahead, criminal defendants are increasingly likely to appeal their convictions but will find appellate courts markedly unsympathetic to their legal arguments; only one of sixteen receives a major victory (even if temporary). Appellants in civil cases are more likely to persuade a panel of three judges that the trial court erred, but even here trial court decisions are typically affirmed. As we will shortly see, the intermediate appellate courts represent the final stage of the process for most litigants—very few cases make it to the appellate court in the first place, and of those cases only a handful will be heard by the state's highest appellate court.

 For up-to-date statistics on court filings go to the Court Statistics Project in the National Center for State Courts: **http://www.ncsc.dni.us/research/ PROJECTS/Admin2.htm#csp**.

For an up-to-date list of Web links, go to **http:// www.wadsworth.com/product/0534563406s**.

COURTS OF LAST RESORT: STATE SUPREME COURTS

The court of last resort is generally referred to as the **state supreme court**. The specific names vary from

State supreme court: General term for the highest court in a state.

state to state, and to further complicate the picture, Texas and Oklahoma have two courts of last resort—one for civil appeals and another for criminal appeals. The number of supreme court judges varies from a low of three to as many as nine (see Exhibit 4-3). Unlike the intermediate appellate courts, these courts do not use panels in making decisions. Rather, the entire court participates in deciding each case. All state supreme courts have a limited amount of *original jurisdiction* in dealing with matters such as disciplining lawyers and judges. In most states the high court has a purely *discretionary docket;* that is, much like the U.S. Supreme Court, they select only a few cases to hear, but these cases tend to have broad legal and political significance. In states without an intermediate court of appeal, however, the supreme court has no power to choose which cases will be placed on its docket.

The state supreme courts are the ultimate review board for matters involving interpretation of state law. The only other avenue of appeal for a disgruntled litigant is the U.S. Supreme Court, but successful applications are few and must involve important questions of federal law. Although state supreme courts vary greatly in the details of the internal procedures used in deciding cases, most follow procedures that are roughly similar to the U.S. Supreme Court's. State supreme courts, however, tend to have greater caseloads.

Chapter 17 will probe why many state supreme courts have in recent years emerged as significant governmental bodies. In state after state, the supreme courts are deciding issues that have a major impact on the law and government of their jurisdiction (see Case Close-Up: *Wachtler v. Cuomo* and Court Financing).

 The North Carolina court system has won an award for its helpful Web site: **http://www.aoc.state.nc.us/**.

For an up-to-date list of Web links, go to **http://www.wadsworth.com/product/0534563406s**.

COURT UNIFICATION

Since the turn of the last century, the organization of American courts has been a central concern to court reformers who believe that the multiplicity of courts is inefficient (because judges cannot be shifted to meet the caseload needs of other courts)

EXHIBIT 4-3 Courts of Last Resort in Different States (Number of Judges)

Supreme Court
Alabama (9), Alaska (5), Arizona (5), Arkansas (7), California (7), Colorado (7), Connecticut (7), Delaware (5), Florida (7), Georgia (7), Hawaii (5), Idaho (5), Illinois (7), Indiana (5), Iowa (9), Kansas (7), Kentucky (7), Louisiana (8), Michigan (7), Minnesota (9), Mississippi (9), Missouri (7), Montana (7), Nebraska (7), Nevada (5), New Hampshire (5), New Jersey (7), New Mexico (5), North Carolina (7), North Dakota (5), Ohio (7), Oklahoma (9),[a] Oregon (7), Pennsylvania (7), Rhode Island (5), South Carolina (5), South Dakota (5), Tennessee (5), Texas (9),[a] Utah (5), Vermont (5), Virginia (7), Washington (9), Wisconsin (7), Wyoming (5)

Court of Appeals
District of Columbia (9), Maryland (7), New York (7)

Supreme Judicial Court
Maine (7), Massachusetts (7)

Court of Criminal Appeals
Oklahoma (3),[a] Texas (9)[a]

Supreme Court of Appeals
West Virginia (5)

[a] Two courts of last resort in these states.

SOURCE: David Rottman, Carol Flango, and R. Shedine Lockley. *State Court Organization, 1993.* (Washington, D.C.: U.S. Department of Justice, Bureau of Justice Statistics, U.S. Government Printing Office, 1995).

and also inequitable (because the administration of justice is not uniform). Historically, court reform has been associated with implementing a unified court system. Figure 4-1 provides a diagram of a state (Florida) with a unified court system, and Figure 4-2 offers a contrasting diagram of a state (Texas) with limited unification.

The principal objective of a **unified court system** is to shift judicial administration from local

Unified court system: Entails a simplified state trial court structure, rule making centered in the supreme court, system governance authority vested in the chief justice of the supreme court, and state funding of the judicial system with a statewide judicial budget.

| FIGURE 4-1 | Example of a State with a Unified Court Structure |

FLORIDA COURT STRUCTURE

SUPREME COURT
7 justices sit en banc

Case types:
• Mandatory jurisdiction in civil, capital criminal, criminal, administrative agency, juvenile, disciplinary, advisory opinion cases.
• Discretionary jurisdiction in civil, noncapital criminal, administrative agency, juvenile, advisory opinion, original proceeding, interlocutory decision cases.

Court of last resort

DISTRICT COURTS OF APPEAL (5 courts)
61 judges sit in 3-judge panels

Case types:
• Mandatory jurisdiction in civil, capital criminal, administrative agency, juvenile, original proceeding, interlocutory decision cases.
• Discretionary jurisdiction in civil, noncapital criminal, juvenile, original proceeding, interlocutory decision cases.

Intermediate appellate court

CIRCUIT COURTS (20 circuits)
442 judges

Case types:
• Tort, contract, real property rights ($15,001 / no maximum), miscellaneous civil. Exclusive domestic relations, mental health, estate, civil appeals jurisdiction.
• Misdemeanor, DWI/DUI, miscellaneous criminal. Exclusive felony, criminal appeals jurisdiction.
• Juvenile.
• Preliminary hearings.

Jury trials except in appeals.

Courts of general jurisdiction

COUNTY COURTS (67 counties)
254 judges

Case types:
• Tort, contract, real property rights ($2,501 to $15,000), miscellaneous civil. Exclusive small claims jurisdiction ($2,500).
• Misdemeanor, DWI/DUI, miscellaneous criminal.
• Exclusive traffic/other violation jurisdiction, except parking (which is handled administratively).
• Preliminary hearings.

Jury trials except in miscellaneous traffic.

Courts of limited jurisdiction

FIGURE 4-2 **Example of a State with Limited Court Unification**

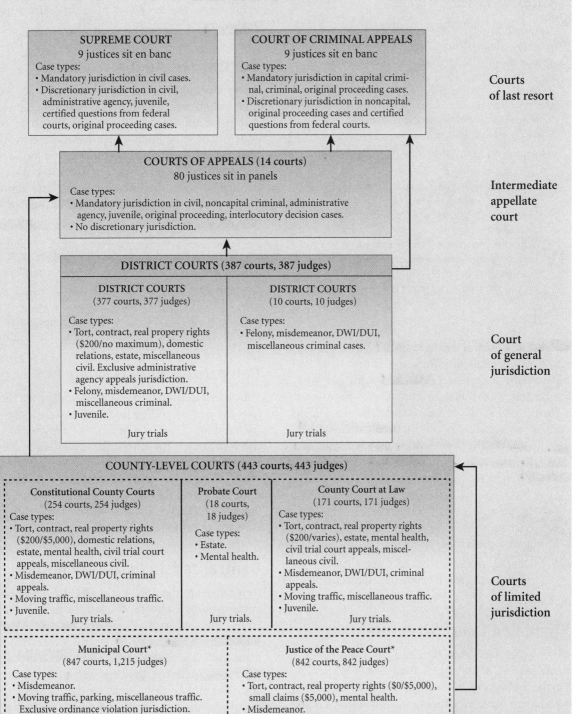

TEXAS COURT STRUCTURE

SUPREME COURT
9 justices sit en banc
Case types:
• Mandatory jurisdiction in civil cases.
• Discretionary jurisdiction in civil, administrative agency, juvenile, certified questions from federal courts, original proceeding cases.

COURT OF CRIMINAL APPEALS
9 justices sit en banc
Case types:
• Mandatory jurisdiction in capital criminal, criminal, original proceeding cases.
• Discretionary jurisdiction in noncapital, original proceeding cases and certified questions from federal courts.

Courts of last resort

COURTS OF APPEALS (14 courts)
80 justices sit in panels
Case types:
• Mandatory jurisdiction in civil, noncapital criminal, administrative agency, juvenile, original proceeding, interlocutory decision cases.
• No discretionary jurisdiction.

Intermediate appellate court

DISTRICT COURTS (387 courts, 387 judges)

DISTRICT COURTS
(377 courts, 377 judges)

Case types:
• Tort, contract, real propery rights ($200/no maximum), domestic relations, estate, miscellaneous civil. Exclusive administrative agency appeals jurisdiction.
• Felony, misdemeanor, DWI/DUI, miscellaneous criminal.
• Juvenile.

Jury trials

DISTRICT COURTS
(10 courts, 10 judges)

Case types:
• Felony, misdemeanor, DWI/DUI, miscellaneous criminal cases.

Jury trials

Court of general jurisdiction

COUNTY-LEVEL COURTS (443 courts, 443 judges)

Constitutional County Courts
(254 courts, 254 judges)
Case types:
• Tort, contract, real property rights ($200/$5,000), domestic relations, estate, mental health, civil trial court appeals, miscellaneous civil.
• Misdemeanor, DWI/DUI, criminal appeals.
• Moving traffic, miscellaneous traffic.
• Juvenile.
Jury trials.

Probate Court
(18 courts, 18 judges)
Case types:
• Estate.
• Mental health.

Jury trials.

County Court at Law
(171 courts, 171 judges)
Case types:
• Tort, contract, real property rights ($200/varies), estate, mental health, civil trial court appeals, miscellaneous civil.
• Misdemeanor, DWI/DUI, criminal appeals.
• Moving traffic, miscellaneous traffic.
• Juvenile.
Jury trials.

Municipal Court*
(847 courts, 1,215 judges)
Case types:
• Misdemeanor.
• Moving traffic, parking, miscellaneous traffic. Exclusive ordinance violation jurisdiction.
• Preliminary hearings.

Jury trials.

Justice of the Peace Court*
(842 courts, 842 judges)
Case types:
• Tort, contract, real property rights ($0/$5,000), small claims ($5,000), mental health.
• Misdemeanor.
• Moving traffic, parking, miscellaneous traffic.
• Preliminary hearings.

Jury trials.

Courts of limited jurisdiction

* Some municipal and justice of the peace courts may appeal to the district court.

COURT TV

California v. Powell

Four Los Angeles police officers are accused of beating Rodney King after a high-speed automobile chase. The trial features the now-famous amateur videotape showing the officers repeatedly swinging their clubs at King. Two of the officers were later convicted in federal court of civil rights violations. While watching the video, keep the following questions in mind:

1. How do racial tensions in the community affect perceptions of the trial?
2. Would the verdict have been different if the case had been tried in Los Angeles?
3. How does the defense use cross-examination to establish the case?
4. Why did the federal government prosecute in federal court after a state court acquittal? Is this a situation where the double jeopardy clause should have barred a second trial?

control to centralized management. The loose network of independent judges and courts would be replaced by a coherent hierarchy with authority concentrated in the state capital. Although court reformers differ about the exact details of a unified court system, their efforts reflect five general principles: a simplified court structure; centralized administration, rule making, and budgeting; and statewide financing (Berkson and Carbon 1978).

The Bureau of Justice Statistics offers a summary of court organization statistics: **http://www.ojp.usdoj. gov/bjs/courts.htm**.

For an up-to-date list of Web links, go to **http:// www.wadsworth.com/product/0534563406s**.

Simplified Court Structure

Court reformers stress the need for a simple, uniform court structure for the entire state. In particular, the multiplicity of minor and specialized courts, which often have overlapping jurisdiction, would be consolidated in one county-level court. This would mean that variations between counties would be eliminated and replaced by a similar court structure

throughout the state. Overall, the court reformers envision a three-tier system: a state supreme court at the top, intermediate courts of appeal where the volume of cases makes it necessary, and a single trial court.

Centralized Administration

Reformers envision the state supreme court, working through court administrators, as providing leadership for the state court system. The state court system would embody a genuine hierarchy of authority, with local court administrators required to follow the policy directives of the central office and in turn be held accountable by the state supreme court. Thus a centralized state office would supervise the work of judicial and nonjudicial personnel.

The Conference of State Court Administrators (COSCA) provides a national forum for improving justice systems: **http://cosca.ncsc.dni.us/**.

For an up-to-date list of Web links, go to **http:// www.wadsworth.com/product/0534563406s**.

Centralized Rule Making

Reformers argue that the state supreme court should have the power to adopt uniform rules that would be followed by all courts in the state. Examples of such rules include procedures for disciplining errant attorneys and time standards for disposing of cases. In addition, judges could be temporarily assigned to other courts to alleviate backlogs and reduce delay. Centralized rule making would shift control from the legislatures to judges and lawyers.

Centralized Judicial Budgeting

Centralized budgeting would give the state judicial administrator (who reports to the state supreme court) the authority to prepare a single budget for the entire state judiciary and send it directly to the legislature. The governor's power to recommend a judicial budget would be eliminated. Likewise, lower courts would be dependent on the supreme court for their monetary needs and unable to lobby local representatives directly. Thus, decisions about allocating funds would be made at the state and not the local level.

Wachtler v. Cuomo and Court Financing

 The governor and the chief judge were longtime friends (and sometimes rivals). Governor Mario Cuomo, a Democrat, had appointed Sol Wachtler, a Republican, chief judge in 1985. And now on the last day of 1990 Cuomo asked Wachtler to administer the oath of office in the paneled chambers of the court of appeals. Neither man could anticipate that within a year they would meet again in another courtroom to do battle over funding the state judiciary. A few weeks into his third term as governor, Mario Cuomo was forced to confront the state's worst financial crisis since the Great Depression. Facing a projected shortfall of $6 billion, Governor Cuomo proposed unprecedented budget cuts throughout the entire New York state government, the courts included. The state judiciary would receive $77 million less than they had requested. Chief Judge Wachtler responded with a lawsuit asserting that the proposed budget cuts violated the doctrine of inherent powers (Glaser 1994).

The doctrine of inherent powers holds that as a coequal branch of government the judiciary has the authority to exercise power reasonably necessary to the performance of judicial functions. American courts have used this doctrine since the early nineteenth century to assert judicial independence. But these efforts were largely limited to matters of judicial housekeeping, such as rules of courtroom decorum, paying jurors, and compensating court-appointed counsel. More recently the doctrine of inherent powers has been evoked to compel the local legislature to create judicial support positions and fund them at adequate levels. Although the doctrine appears to be rather sweeping, its application has typically been limited to specific discrete items, and moreover, appellate courts have imposed important limitations.

Wachtler v. Cuomo was significant because it marked the first substantial use of the doctrine of inherent powers by a state high court against an equal branch of government. It also differed from previous efforts to assert inherent judicial powers because of the large sums of money involved. Unlike previous lawsuits, which involved discrete items amounting to a few thousand dollars or occasionally a million or two, *Wachtler v. Cuomo* centered on the entire budget in the range of $1 billion plus. Funding for the New York judiciary increased significantly in the decade before the lawsuit, rising from $480 million in 1982 to almost $1 billion nine years later. Yet this 86 percent increase could not keep up with demand; caseloads rose swiftly while judicial staffing resources increased only minimally.

Faced with a projected $6 billion deficit, the governor and legislature thought it only fair that the judiciary also absorb some of the budget pain. The initial proposed judicial budget represented an actual decrease of $6.5 million or 0.7 percent from the previous year. The judiciary responded that any cut would unnecessarily weaken the judiciary. Indeed, the chief judge projected 500 layoffs in the court system. After considerable public posturing, the chief judge made good on his threat to file suit in the supreme court (trial court for New York) in Albany County.

The case never came to trial. Amid bantering in the press, the chief judge decided "to cut both his fiscal and public relations losses by ending the year-long conflict" (Glaser 1994, 19). The chief judge called the governor, and an hour later the deal was finalized—judicial budget cuts were largely ended, but the courts would not receive any increases in funding.

Was the lawsuit worth it politically? The legal basis for the judiciary's case was weak. Moreover, public confidence in the judiciary was shaken, and the judiciary's relationship to the other branches of government was strained. According to Howard Glaser, who served as the governor's special assistant (1994, 24): "The ultimate implication of *Wachtler v. Cuomo* is that all parties emerge as losers in an inherent powers conflict of this nature, no matter what the legal outcome of the exercise." Perhaps the headline in *The New York Times* said it best: "Wachtler v. Cuomo = Two Losers."

Although judicial budgets consume a small portion of the entire state budget, they are nonetheless tempting targets when states face difficult fiscal circumstances. This situation is ironic because many fiscal problems of the states stem from public efforts to get tough on crime—judges are expected to send more defendants to prison for longer periods of time. The result is a swelling prison population, which further strains state budgets. At the same time courts are under pressure to produce speedier justice. Again, there is an irony: As court dockets have increased, legislatures have largely been unwilling to add personnel to meet the increasing tide of expectations. In short, the courts are expected to do more with less.

"In Los Angeles County, Two Courts Are Better Than One"

Statewide Financing

Along with centralized judicial budgeting, reformers argue for the adoption of statewide financing of the judiciary. Although courts are mandated by state law, they are often financed in whole or in part by local governments. Given that courts are often not a high priority for local government, they end up with less than adequate local financing. State government, in contrast, has more money and could better support necessary court services. (But as Controversy: The Politics of Court Reorganization highlights, problems of financing courts are not so easily solved. See page 104.)

COURT REFORM: THE EMERGING AGENDA

The assumptions and philosophy of traditional notions of court reform have been called into serious question. A new generation of scholars believes that the old principles of court reorganization hamper creative thinking about the direction court reform should take (Lamber and Luskin 1992; Hudzik 1985; Flango 1994; Scheb and Matheny 1988). One concern is that the concept of a unified court system does not allow for a desirable diversity. The standard blueprint of court organization fails to consider, for example, important differences in the working environment of courts in densely inhabited cities as opposed to those in sparsely populated rural areas.

Modern critics have also charged that traditional concepts of court reform stress abstract ideals of court organization (law on the books) to the neglect of the realities of the courthouse (law in action) (Baar 1980). As a result, court reformers suffer from elite bias. Their perceptions of the problems of the courthouse extend only to cases with policy significance involving major community actors and rarely extend to ordinary cases affecting average citizens. In the biting words of Laura Nader (1992), court reformers talk about "how to rid the . . . courts of 'garbage cases' (e.g., consumer, environmental, feminist issues)." The net result is that problems of battered women and abused children are not considered "real" court

cases, and the difficult questions of child custody are ignored while judges concentrate on the issues raised by big business and big government.

Today court reform concentrates more on how to improve the quality of justice meted out by American courts and less on how to provide a neater organizational chart. The solutions proposed by lawyer elites seem unresponsive to the realities of ordinary cases heard in the nation's trial courts. A judiciary with a clearly delineated organizational structure staffed by judges selected on the basis of merit (Chapter 8) will face the same difficult problems of large caseloads and types of cases—juvenile delinquency, for example—that are difficult to decide. The emerging agenda of court reform includes topics such as improving the efficiency of the appellate courts (Chapter 17) and alternative dispute resolution (Chapter 18). It also includes a focus on case management as a way to reduce delay in the trial courts (Chapter 5).

The emerging agenda on court reform reflects efforts to strengthen the relationship between courts and the communities they serve (Efkeman and Rottman 1997). Perhaps the best known effort is the movement to create community courts (Chapter 18). For now, we will examine the general concept of therapeutic jurisprudence and its most widely known application—drug courts.

 Alcoholism & Drug Abuse Weekly, "New York Drug Reforms Call for Drug Treatment, Not Incarceration"

Therapeutic Jurisprudence

Contemporary court reform involves the creation of specialized courts to deal with specific types of cases. Initially these were called *designer courts* or *boutique courts,* indicating their specialized nature. Common examples include drug court, domestic violence court, family court, juvenile drug court, gun court, drunk driving court, elder court, and reentry court (which deals with prisoners reentering the community).

More recently these specialized courts have been said to rely on therapeutic jurisprudence (Wexler and Winick 1996). Such courts have five essential elements:

1. Immediate intervention
2. Nonadversarial adjudication
3. Hands-on judicial involvement

4. Treatment programs with clear rules and structured goals

5. A team approach that brings together the judge, prosecutors, defense counsel, treatment provider, and correctional staff (Rottman and Casey 1999)

Drug treatment courts are the best-known examples of therapeutic jurisprudence.

 Read about "Drug Courts and Coerced Treatment" on the Web site of Friends of the Addicted for Comprehensive Treatment: **http://www. factadvocates.org/factsheets/**.

For an up-to-date list of Web links, go to **http:// www.wadsworth.com/product/0534563406s**.

Drug Courts

The emergence of **drug courts** illustrates how the judiciary is responding both to increases in caseload and changes in the types of cases being brought to court. In the mid-1980s drug caseloads increased dramatically in courts throughout the country. As a centerpiece of the so-called War on Drugs, elected officials at all levels—federal, state, and local— backed efforts to arrest, prosecute, and imprison persons possessing or selling illegal drugs. As a result, arrests for drug abuse violations represent the largest single category of police activity—over 1,550,000 per year. Moreover, in the major urban areas of the United States the impact of the War on Drugs has been even more dramatic; several large eastern cities experienced 100 percent increases in arrests (Goerdt and Martin 1989).

Some judges and court administrators feared that the first major casualty of the War on Drugs would be the nation's urban trial courts. In the words of one big-city prosecutor: "The situation is desperate. The overload causes backlog; backlog feeds delay; and delay . . . results in the lack of jail and prison space" (Lipscher 1989, 14). Fears of a system breakdown, however, were somewhat overdrawn (Mahoney 1994). One reason is that many prosecutions are straightforward—pleas of guilty are entered

shortly after arraignment. Another reason is that some courts began to experiment with new ways of processing cases by creating drug courts.

Drug courts vary widely in structure, target populations, and treatment programs. The least distinctive way of creating a drug court is to establish one section of court that processes all minor drug cases; the primary goal is to speed up case dispositions of drug cases and at the same time free other judges to expedite their own dockets. Another type of drug court concentrates on drug defendants accused of serious crimes who also have major prior criminal records. These cases are carefully monitored by court administrators to ensure that all other charges are consolidated before a single judge and no unexpected developments interfere with the scheduled trial date (Davis, Smith, and Lurigio 1994).

Still other drug courts emphasize treatment. The assumption is that treatment will reduce the likelihood that convicted drug offenders will be rearrested. Dade County (Miami) Circuit Court is an example of a treatment approach to drug offenders. It has received extensive national publicity because it was the first in the nation. To be eligible, defendants must have no prior felony convictions, must be charged with possession only (not sale), and must admit their drug problem and request treatment. These offenders are diverted into treatment. The sentencing judge, rather than a probation officer, monitors offenders' progress. Participants must periodically report to the drug court judge, who assesses their progress and moves them through the phases of the program.

Within a decade drug courts have moved from experimental innovation to well-established programs. The government lists over 325 drug courts across forty-three states and the District of Columbia. Less formally, drug courts operate in many other jurisdictions as well.

Initial evaluations gave favorable rates of success. For example, in Miami, compared to defendants not in the program, offenders in the Miami drug court treatment program had lower incarceration rates, less frequent rearrests, and longer times to rearrest (Goldkamp and Weiland 1993). Likewise, an evaluation of Broward County, Florida, found that first-time cocaine offenders who were treated were less likely to be rearrested (Terry 1996). But more sophisticated evaluations have reported a different picture. In Washington, D.C., participation in a drug court treatment program has been poor—

Drug courts Specialty courts with jurisdiction over cases involving illegal substances. Drug courts typically stress treatment rather than punishment.

The Politics of Court Reorganization

Judicial reformers have achieved considerable success. Many states have substantially unified their court systems. Significantly, though, only a few states have adopted most or all of the principles suggested by court reformers (Baar 1993). Several states, for example, have adopted a four-tier system (rather than the recommended three tiers) by retaining the lower courts as a separate level rather than combining them with the major trial courts (Flango and Rottman 1992). Along these same lines, the principle of statewide financing has not fared well. In many states the county (or an equivalent unit) still finances the major trial courts to a significant degree (Lim 1987). Moreover, not all reform efforts have been successful. Some states (such as Tennessee) have considered and then rejected constitutional amendments to restructure their courts.

Why have some reform proposals been rejected? Why have the reformers' recommendations been significantly modified? To answer these questions, we need to examine the politics of court reorganization. Battles over court organization are usually presented as dry technical issues involving case volume and efficiency. But such arguments mask the underlying political dynamics.

Support for court reform is concentrated among the elite of the legal profession. The American Bar Association is a long-time advocate of judicial reform. The American Judicature Society was formed in 1913 by elite members of the bar to campaign for improving the courts. Likewise, middle-class reform organizations such as the League of Women Voters endorse the ideals of court reform. More recently, judicial reform has achieved wide official recognition and has become the "government-approved" approach to judicial administration. The National Institute of Justice within the U.S. Justice Department and the quasi-private National Center for State Courts reflect a trend toward greater government involvement and leadership in the reform model of judicial administration (Glick 1988).

But efforts of legal elites to drum up support for court reform are often greeted with disinterest or skepticism. Lawyers reflect divided sentiments over judicial reform. General practice and trial lawyers (who are less likely to be members of the American Bar Association) perceive that court reform would require unnecessary changes in their routines. Judges and other court personnel likewise resist the idea of being forced to learn new procedures if the courts are reorganized. Finally, many of the problems associated with the existing structure of courts are concentrated in the large cities. Rural politicians and rural lawyers, because they see no problems in their own area, are not sympathetic to major overhauls that would not

only forty-one percent of those eligible chose to participate. Moreover, completion of the program took much longer than anticipated; cases were open an average of eleven months as opposed to the six months estimated (Harrell, Cavanagh, and Roman 2000). (See A Day in Court: "DuPage County Says the Jury Is Still Out on Its Fledgling Drug Court.")

CONSEQUENCES OF COURT ORGANIZATION

How the courts are organized and administered has a profound effect on the way cases are processed and on the type of justice that results.

Read "What Is a Drug Court?" on the Web site of the National Association of Drug Court Professionals: **http://www.nadcp.org/**.

Some drug courts have Web sites:

California's Drug Court Project: **http://www. courtinfo.ca.gov/programs/drugcourts/**

King County, Washington: **http://www.metrokc. gov/kcscc/drugcourt/**

St. Mary's Parish, Louisiana: **http://drugcourt.com/ dc/index.html**

Utah's Drug Courts: **http://www.hsdsa.state.ut.us/ Drug_Court.htm**

For an up-to-date list of Web links, go to **http:// www.wadsworth.com/product/0534563406s**.

benefit them but might mean decreased control of local courts (Glick and Vines 1973). It is this public disinterest that explains why members of the Massachusetts legislature "pay little attention to the decisions of the state courts because they see the courts as irrelevant to their political lives. The courts are rarely if ever an issue in their campaigns" (Miller 1993, 41).

The general public has little interest in abstract notions of a cleaner looking organizational chart for the judiciary. Mobilizing public support for court reform, therefore, is not easy. In Oklahoma, voters adopted a more modern court structure only after a series of judicial scandals (Simpson 1991). In Alabama, on the other hand, a nonpolitical group produced consensus that the state needed to modernize.

At times court reform also engenders opposition. Court reform proposals can become a political battleground between political parties (Glick 1988). The party in power often perceives quite correctly that court reform will mean the loss of important patronage positions. Any attempt to unify a state judiciary invariably brings opposition from local governments that wish to retain control of their local courts. Issues of local versus state authority also have important financial dimensions. As a result, most proposals to unify state court systems carry the provision that the state will pay all expenses of the local courts (thus relieving cities of millions of dollars in expense) but allow municipalities to retain revenues derived from court fines and court fees. Finally, nonlawyer judges oppose court reorganization because their jobs would be abolished under plans requiring all judges to be lawyers (Chapter 18). This is why many court reform proposals include "grandfather" clauses allowing nonlawyer judges to remain in office. (A grandfather clause is an exception that allows all those already doing something to continue doing that activity in spite of the new regulation.)

Despite these political obstacles, court reformers have made great strides in altering court structures. The changes adopted in a given state, however, reflect that state's political environment. Alaska and Hawaii have highly unified courts that reflect the way territorial courts developed before statehood. North Carolina's courts are highly consolidated, but elected county clerks remain powerful. Maryland was able to unify its minor courts into a statewide court of limited jurisdiction but was unable to overcome the resistance of the general jurisdiction trial courts, which remain locally funded and administered (Baar and Henderson 1982).

 To continue the debate over court reform here are some good sites for you to visit:

Read about "Various Visions of High Court Reform" on the Web site of the Texas Public Policy Foundation: **http://www.tppf.org/juris/jhigh.htm**.

Read "Court Restructuring: A Position Paper," by New York Chief Justice Judity Kaye, at **http://www.citizensunion.org/court.html**.

For an up-to-date list of Web links, go to **http://www.wadsworth.com/ product/0534563406s**.

Decentralization and Choice of Courts

Although people often talk about the American legal system, no such entity exists. Instead, America has fifty-one legal systems—the U.S. courts and separate courts in each of the fifty states. As Chapter 2 stressed, there are significant differences in the law between each legal system. As a result, lawyers sometimes try to maneuver cases so that they are heard in courts that are perceived to be favorable to their clients (or, alternatively, maneuver to avoid courts that are perceived to be less favorable). For example, some criminal offenses violate both state and federal laws. As a general rule, federal officials prosecute major violations, leaving more minor prosecutions to state officials. Civil litigants may also have choices about where to file suit. For cases with federal jurisdiction, litigants may also choose in which federal court to file. The oil and natural gas industry, for example, prefers to litigate in the Fifth Circuit because this court has historically been supportive of the industry. By contrast, consumer groups prefer to file in the District of Columbia Court of Appeals, because this court has historically supported consumers.

Local Control and Local Corruption

The fifty state court systems are in actuality often structured on a local basis. The officials that staff

A DAY IN COURT

"DuPage County Says the Jury Is Still Out on Its Fledgling Drug Court"

Mark McGee struggled with his cocaine addiction for nearly half his life. The Wheaton man went through numerous treatment programs but, like many addicts, often relapsed. At 42, he was unemployed and staring down another prison sentence for retail theft. McGee decided he'd had enough. "I was tired of the lifestyle," he said. "I tried treatment but the hardest thing for me was that once I got to a certain level, I always managed to sabotage myself. I was afraid of success."

Earlier this month, McGee and two other men became the first graduates of a fledgling drug court in DuPage County that aims to thwart crime by treating drug-addicted criminals. . . . "I've been in prison," McGee said. "Prison is easy. This is hard."

The program has not been without some high-profile failures since its inauguration more than 10 months ago. One man overdosed. Another participant was arrested on reckless homicide charges. He is accused of driving drunk during a crash that killed a family of four in Hanover Park. And officials have stopped taking new applications until at least this spring in order to review the past year and make needed changes.

Still, for the three graduates and roughly 20 others still enrolled, drug court is offering a second chance to avoid prison and lead a sober life. "Anyone who says you're going to save 100 percent is wrong," said William Padish, the first-assistant public defender in DuPage County, who is part of the drug court team. "You can't. But I do think the program promises to do better than what we have been doing. If you can intervene and get these people out of the system, everyone benefits.". . .

DuPage Circuit Judge Ann Jorgensen spearheaded the program and presides over the drug court. But its success hinges on the teamwork of judges, prosecutors, defense attorneys, probation officials, and specialists in substance abuse treatment. The team reviews the arrest and treatment histories of possible participants. To be eligible, a defendant must have been charged with a nonviolent felony, such as drug possession, auto theft or, in McGee's case, repeated retail thefts. The program does not accept those accused of more serious felonies, such as sex crimes, arson, or drug dealing, since they are deemed a greater risk to society.

If accepted, defendants must agree to a strict treatment plan, often including recovery homes, counseling, frequent drug testing and court visits, sobriety meetings, and group sessions. If they reach graduation, the participant's felony arrest is reduced to a misdemeanor conviction with probation. Intense monitoring to respond to program violations is a key component of drug court. Participants appear before Jorgensen each Friday. "They do all the work," Jorgensen said. "Our goal is to give them every tool possible to get through this.". . .

"These courts arose in response to the revolving door of the criminal justice system," said Susan Weinstein, chief counsel for the Alexandria, Virginia–based National Association of Drug Court Professionals. "Prosecutors, defense attorneys, and judges were seeing the same persons over and over and over again. Instead of treating them like criminals, they started treating them as drug-addict criminals.". . .

DuPage's drug court is on hiatus as far as taking new enrollees. . . . "I truly believe in what we are doing," said prosecutor Jennifer Hulvat, a member of the drug court team. "But it's got to have its limitations and safeguards. That's what this pause is for. We have to make sure there's accountability. As a prosecutor, I have to make sure there's protection to the community. That's my utmost responsibility and I can't forget that."

For McGee, recovery has not come easy. He relapsed early after starting the program last January. He admits it's still a day-to-day fight, but one he hopes to win for himself and his two children. He's even started a Friday night club in which other recovering addicts meet at a local treatment center to discuss their progress and give each other support. "It's a struggle," he said. "It's always going to be a struggle. I don't know what tomorrow is going to bring, but I know I'm sober now and I want to stay this way."

SOURCE: Christy Gutowski, "DuPage County Says the Jury Is Still Out on Its Fledgling Drug Court," *Chicago Daily Herald* (November 27, 2000).

these courts—judges and lawyers, prosecutors and defense attorneys—are recruited from the local community they serve and thus reflect the sentiments of that community. As a result, the U.S. system of justice has close ties to local communities and the application of "state" law often has a local flavor. Jurors in rural areas, for example, often have markedly different attitudes toward who is at fault in an accident and the amount of damages that should be awarded.

Local control of justice has the obvious advantage of closely linking courts to the people they serve. But local control has been the incubator for corruption and injustice. Every state invariably has a town or two where gambling and prostitution flourish because the city fathers agree to look the other way. Not surprisingly, they often receive monetary benefits for being so near-sighted. Increasingly, though, such activities attract the attention of state police, state attorney generals, and federal prosecutors.

The locally administered criminal justice system has also been marked by pockets of injustice. At times the police and the courts have been the handmaidens of the local economic elite. In the South the police and the courts hindered efforts to exercise civil rights by arresting or harassing those who sought to register to vote, eat at whites-only lunch counters, or simply speak up to protest segregation.

The dual court system has provided a safety valve for checking the most flagrant abuses of local justice. Often, it is federal—not state or local—officials who prosecute corrupt local officials.

Spectrum: The Journal of State Government, "Drug Crime: The Impact on State Courts"

Be sure to visit Justice Served, a private court management firm, which every year hands out its Top Ten Court Web Site Awards at **http://www.justiceserved.com/**.

For an up-to-date list of Web links, go to **http://www.wadsworth.com/product/0534563406s**.

CONCLUSION

The implementation of drug courts in Los Angles County (and numerous other areas across the nation) illustrates a major shift in thinking about court reform in the United States. Whereas traditional court reform emphasized consolidating various judicial bodies, the emerging agenda encourages the creation of specialized courts. Modern court reform also actively encourages working with members of the community, whereas the older tradition stressed notions of professionalism that disdained popular input. Likewise, court reform in the contemporary context stresses the importance of working with other agencies rather than viewing the judge as a lone authority figure. The next chapter focuses on these other agencies, elaborating on the concept of the courtroom workgroup.

What is perhaps most striking is that the ideas that have dominated discussion of court reform for most of this century are now being quietly buried. Instead of stressing organizational charts and other abstract notions, most efforts to reform the judiciary now focus on more specific matters—reduce court delay and target drug cases for special treatment, for example. Thus, today's court reform is marked by tremendous experimentation at the local level. Judges and other court actors identify a problem and seek solutions, adapting local resources and local understandings in the process. This adaptation to change has always been the hallmark of the American judiciary. Perhaps the only differences today are the rapid pace of change and the public attention paid to these ongoing efforts at judicial reform.

CRITICAL THINKING QUESTIONS

1. Although we typically talk of state courts (as opposed to federal courts), would it be better to talk about local courts? To what extent are there major variations within your state?

2. Compare your state to Figures 4-1 and 4-2. How unified is your state court structure?

3. Have there been discussions in your state of court reorganization? What major interest

groups are urging court reform, and what advantages do they suggest? What interest groups are opposing court reform, and what disadvantages do they cite?

4. Why do crime control advocates often oppose drug courts, and why do due process proponents support drug courts?

5. Make a list of state and local politicians who have been tried in federal court. Were there parallel state investigations or prosecutions? To what extent would corrupt local officials be better off if federal court jurisdiction were limited?

 WORLD WIDE WEB RESOURCES AND EXERCISES

Web Guides

http://dir.yahoo.com/Government/U_S__Government/ Judicial_Branch/State_Courts/

http://dir.yahoo.com/Government/Law/U_S__States/

Web Search Terms

"Courts," "state courts," "drug courts," "court reform," "courthouses"

Useful URLs

The National Center for State Courts provides a variety of reports on caseloads and latest trends. Search under Latest News or Information about the courts: http://www.ncsc.dni.us/.

The book *The State Court Organization 1998* is available online at http://www.ojp.usdoj.gov/bjs/ abstract/sco98.htm.

Read about "Pennsylvania Court Reform Issues" on the Web site of the Pennsylvanians for Modern Courts: http://www.libertynet.org/ pmcpms/Issues.htm.

Read about "Restructuring the Judiciary" on Hawaii's State Judiciary's Web site: http:// www.state.hi.us/jud/ACE.htm.

See "Strategies for Effective Court Reform" on the Web site of Justice for All: http://www.word- wiz72.com/courts.html.

Trial Lawyers for Public Justice is a national public interest law firm that uses trial lawyers to create a more just society: http://www.tlpj.org.

The State Justice Institute was established by federal law to award grants for the improvement of state courts: http://www.statejustice.org/.

The National Drug Court Institute disseminates drug court information and provides training: http://www.drugcourt.org/ndci.htm.

The American University's Drug Court Clearinghouse and Technical Assistance Project can be accessed at http://www.american.edu/justice/.

The National Center for State Courts' Web site is http://www.ncsc.dni.us/.

The National Conference of Appellate Court Clerks' Web site is http://www.ncsc.dni.us/ ncacc/NCACC.html.

To learn more about federal funding, see the Web site of the Drug Courts Program Office: http:// www.ojp.usdog.gov/dcpo/.

Uncommon URLs

Read about "Renovation Kickoff for New High Tech E-Courtrooms" on the Web site of the Maricopa County Superior Court (Phoenix, Arizona): http://www.superiorcourt.maricopa. gov/hightech.html.

The Legal Justice Reform Network is a self-help site for those who believe they have been "judicial victims": http://www.atps.com/uclr/.

See Georgia courthouses: http://www.cviog.uga. edu/Projects/gainfo/courthouses/.

See Indiana county courthouses: http://members. iquest.net/~browns/county/.

See courthouses recorded by the Historic American Buildings Survey (HABS) and the Historic American Engineering Record (HAER): http:// lcweb.loc.gov/rr/print/171_cour.html.

Learn about records kept at courthouses; see the Librarian's Guide to Helping Patrons with Genealogical Research, "Visiting Courthouses," at http://home.tampabay.rr.com/centans/ courthou.html.

Web Exercises

1. FindLaw has information not only on state law but also on state courts. To locate specific information about your state, go to http:// www.findlaw.com/. On the menu, click State Law Resources and then your state. Examine state-level courts. Based on this information,

where would you rank your state on a continuum from consolidated to fragmented?

2. Information on state courts is also available in Yahoo at **http://www.yahoo.com**. Choose Government/Judicial Branch/State Courts, or Government/U.S. States/Your State. Using either path (or preferably, both), find information on trial courts in your state. How easy or difficult is it to locate information? In some states information is easier to locate on the executive and legislative branches than on the judiciary. Is this true in your state? If so, why?

3. Using a search engine such as Alta Vista or Excite, look for information on drug courts. You can access a search engine by clicking Net Search on the browser. In the box marked Search, type the words *drug court.* Look for a drug court near you and examine the site.

4. Using the search engine of your choice use the phrase *court reform* to locate two or more Web sites that deal with this topic. What range of specific topics is included under the general rubric of court reform? To what extent are they consistent or inconsistent with your notions of court reform?

 INFOTRAC COLLEGE EDITION RESOURCES AND EXERCISES

Basic Search Terms

Courts, state courts, drug courts, National Center for State Courts

Recommended Articles

Neeley Tucker, "Seven Vying to Lead D.C. Superior Court"

Jet, "Blacks Have Little Confidence in State, Local Courts"

Spencer Abraham, "The Case for Needed Legal Reform: Frivolous Lawsuits"

UN Chronicle, "Permanent International Criminal Court Established"

InfoTrac College Edition Exercises

1. Using the search term *court administration,* select two articles that discuss state efforts. Does the approach discussed reflect traditional court reform ideas or the emerging agenda of court reform? Here are two possibilities: Major B. Harding, "Preparing Florida Courts for the New Millennium" and Donald C. Dilworth, "BJA Reports Measurement System for Trial Court Performance."

2. Using the search term *drug court,* select two or more articles that discuss this growing phenomenon. What advantages do the writers see for drug courts? What pitfalls do they discuss? Here are two possibilities: Robert Curley, "Drug Court Boom May Bust Treatment Availability" and *Alcoholism & Drug Abuse Weekly,* "Justice-Treatment Relationship Crucial to Drug Court Success."

REFERENCES

Baar, Carl. 1980. "The Scope and Limits of Court Reform." *Justice System Journal* 5: 274–290.

———. 1993. "Trial Court Unification in Practice." *Judicature* 76: 179–184.

Baar, Carl, and Thomas Henderson. 1982. "Organizational Design for State Court Systems." In *The Analysis of Judicial Reform,* edited by Philip Dubois. Lexington, MA: Lexington Books.

Berkson, Larry, and Susan Carbon. 1978. *Court Unification: History, Politics, and Implementation.* Washington, D.C.: National Institute of Law Enforcement and Criminal Justice.

Davis, Robert, Barbara Smith, and Arthur Lurigio. 1994. "Court Strategies to Cope with Rising Drug Caseloads." *Justice System Journal* 17: 1–18.

Efkeman, Hillery, and David Rottman. 1997. "Community-Focused Courts: Progress on a Development Initiative." *State Court Journal* 20: 10–16.

Flango, Victor. 1994. "Court Unification and Quality of State Courts." *Justice System Journal* 16: 33–56.

Flango, Victor, and David Rottman. 1992. "Research Note: Measuring Trial Court Consolidation." *Justice System Journal* 16: 65–74.

Friedman, Lawrence. 1985. *A History of American Law.* 2d ed. New York: Simon & Schuster.

Glaser, Howard. 1994. "*Wachtler v. Cuomo:* The Limits of Inherent Power." *Judicature* 78: 12–24.

Glick, Henry. 1988. *Courts, Politics, and Justice.* 2d ed. New York: McGraw-Hill.

Glick, Henry, and Kenneth Vines. 1973. *State Court Systems.* Englewood Cliffs, NJ: Prentice-Hall.

Goerdt, John, and J. A. Martin. 1989. "The Impact of Drug Cases on Case Processing in Urban Trial Courts." *State Court Journal* 13: 4.

Goldkamp, John, and Doris Weiland. 1993. "Assessing the Impact of Dade County's Felony Drug Court."

National Institute of Justice Research in Brief. Washington, D.C.: U.S. Department of Justice, December.

Harrell, Adele, Shannon Cavanagh, and John Roman. 2000. "Evaluation of the D.C. Superior Court Drug Intervention Programs." Washington, D.C.: National Institute of Justice.

Hudzik, John. 1985. "Rethinking the Consequences of State Financing." *Justice System Journal* 10: 135.

Jacob, Herbert. 1984. *Justice in America.* 4th ed. Boston: Little, Brown.

Lamber, Julia, and Mary Luskin. 1992. "Court Reform: A View from the Bottom." *Judicature* 75: 295–299.

Lim, Marcia. 1987. "A Status Report on State Court Financing." *State Court Journal* 11: 7.

Lipscher, Robert. 1989. "The Judicial Response to the Drug Crisis." *State Court Journal* 13: 13.

Mahoney, Barry. 1994. "Drug Courts: What Have We Learned So Far?" *Justice System Journal* 17: 127–133.

Miller, Mark. 1993. "Lawmaker Attitudes Toward Court Reform in Massachusetts." *Judicature* 77: 34–41.

Nader, Laura. 1992. "Trading Justice for Harmony." *National Institute for Dispute Resolution Forum* (Winter): 12–14.

Neubauer, David. 1997. *Judicial Process: Law, Courts, and Politics in the United States.* 2d ed. Fort Worth: Harcourt Brace.

Ostrom, Brian, and Neal Kauder. 1999. *Examining the Work of State Courts, 1998.* Williamsburg, VA: National Center for State Courts.

Rottman, David, and Pamela Casey. 1999. "Therapeutic Jurisprudence and the Emergence of Problem-Solving Courts." *National Institute of Justice Journal.* (July).

Scheb, John, and Albert Matheny. 1988. "Judicial Reform and Rationalization: The Diffusion of Court Reform Policies among the American States." *Law and Policy* 10: 25–42.

Simpson, Phillip. 1991. "The 1964 State Supreme Court Scandals and the Modernization and Reform of the Oklahoma Judiciary." Paper presented at the annual meeting of the Southwest Political Science Association, San Antonio.

Terry, W. Clinton. 1996. "Felony and Misdemeanor Rearrests of the First Year Cohort of the Drug Court in Broward County, Florida." Paper presented at the annual meeting of the Academy of Criminal Justice Sciences, Las Vegas.

Torres, Sam, and Elizabeth Piper Deschenes. 1997. "Changing the System and Making It Work: The Process of Implementing Drug Courts in Los Angeles County." *Justice System Journal* 19: 267–290.

Wexler, David B., and Bruce J. Winick (eds). *Law in a Therapeutic Key: Developments in Therapeutic Jurisprudence.* Durham, NC: Carolina Academic Press, 1996.

FOR FURTHER READING

Belknap, Michael. *To Improve the Administration of Justice: A History of the American Judicature Society.* Chicago: American Judicature Society, 1993.

Boersema, Craig. "Simplifying the Maze of Nevada's Courts." *Judicature* 78 (1995): 299–303.

Dubois, Philip, ed. *The Politics of Judicial Reform.* Lexington, MA: Lexington Books, 1982.

Edelman, Mark, and Terry Raun. "Does Rural Court Consolidation Save Costs?" *Judicature* 79 (1995): 86–90.

Goldkamp, John. *Justice and Treatment Innovation: The Drug Court Movement; A Working Paper of the First National Drug Court Conference, December 1993.* Washington, D.C.: National Institute of Justice, 1994.

Inciardi, James, Duane McBride, and James Rivers. *Drug Control and the Courts.* Thousand Oaks, CA: Sage Publications, 1996.

Jacob, Herbert. "The Governance of Trial Judges." *Law and Society Review* 31 (1997): 3–27.

Stojkovic, Stan, John Klofas, and David Kalinich. *The Administration and Management of Criminal Justice Organizations: A Book of Readings.* 2d ed. Prospect Heights, IL: Waveland Press, 1994.

Stumpf, Harry, and John Culver. *The Politics of State Courts.* White Plains, NY: Longman, 1992.

Wice, Paul. *Court Reform and Judicial Leadership.* Westport, CT: Praeger, 1995.

Legal Actors

THE LAW IS NOT SELF-EXECUTING. PROSECUTORS, DEFENSE ATTORNEYS, and judges must exercise discretion. The types of people recruited to these positions, the nature of the work they perform, and the pressures they must deal with are the concerns of the five chapters of Part II.

Chapter 5 analyzes the dynamics of courthouse justice, with particular emphasis on how these separate actors work together as a group.

Chapter 6 discusses why the prosecutor is the most important member of the courtroom work group. The discretionary powers of the office structure virtually all of the decisions of the criminal courthouse.

Chapter 7 examines the defense attorney. The nature of the attorney's clientele, the lack of great monetary rewards, and the effects of other members of the courtroom work group help explain why most defense attorneys act nothing like Perry Mason, the famous television figure.

Chapter 8 considers the role of the judge. Of prime concern is how the judge's actions shape and in turn are affected by the courtroom work group.

Chapter 9 discusses the importance of witnesses, victims, and defendants in the decisions made by members of the courtroom work group.

■ ■ ■

The Dynamics of Courthouse Justice

SIXTEEN TIMES WILLIE BARKER'S MURDER CASE WAS SET FOR TRIAL, AND sixteen times it was continued. At first the defense readily agreed, gambling that Barker's codefendant would be found not guilty. Thus, some of the continuances were caused by the six separate trials before the codefendant was finally convicted. Other continuances were granted because of the illness of the police investigator. It was not until five years after arrest that Barker was convicted of murder. To Barker's lawyer, this lengthy delay clearly violated the Sixth Amendment's right to speedy trial. The Kentucky prosecutor replied that the delay did not jeopardize Barker's right to a fair trial.

Barker v. Wingo underscores three key points about criminal case processing in contemporary courts. First, courts deal with lots of cases. From the perspective of victims and defendants, criminal cases are discrete life events, but from the vantage point of judges, prosecutors, and defense attorneys, the docket consists of numerous cases, each demanding the court's time. The pressures to move cases is often referred to as assembly-line justice and is the first concept discussed in this chapter.

Second, the problems in prosecuting and convicting Barker indicate that discretion is often needed in interpreting the law. After all, the meaning of "speedy trial" is not self-evident. As we shall see, the concept of discretion begins to grapple with the day-to-day realities of courthouse dynamics but has several limitations as an explanation for courthouse behavior.

Third, the Barker case shows that case dispositions involve far more than the isolated actions of individual judges. From arrest through trial and sentencing, case dispositions require mutual activity on the part of prosecutors and defense attorneys, to say nothing of police officers and probation officers, bail agents and bailiffs. This chapter discusses the concept of the courtroom work group to analyze the complexities of interaction among courthouse regulars.

This chapter examines the dynamics of courthouse justice by analyzing three major explanations for the great difference between the realities of the courtroom and textbook images of criminal procedure. We will then apply these concepts to one of the most often mentioned problems of American justice—delay. As in the *Barker* case though, we will see that deciding how long is too long is a knotty question. But first let us begin with a tour of a typical U.S. courthouse. ■

THE COURTHOUSE AND THE PEOPLE WHO WORK THERE

Concepts of court jurisdiction and court structure are admittedly intangible notions. Courthouses, on the other hand, are concrete. To be sure, from the outside courthouses appear to be imposing, even forbidding, governmental buildings. But on the inside they are beehives of activity. Most immediately, courthouses are places where you find lawyers arguing before juries, talking to their clients, and conversing with one another. But courthouses also employ numerous nonlawyers who perform vital roles; without clerks and probation officers, bail agents and bailiffs, courthouses could not function. Not to be overlooked, ordinary citizens (whether victims or defendants, witnesses or jurors) also perform important roles in the courthouse.

In trying to understand how lawyers and nonlawyers, regular participants and occasional ones, dispense courthouse justice on a daily basis, it is helpful to start with a walking tour of a courthouse. What goes on inside a courthouse, of course, varies in important ways. In the courthouses of small towns, for example, one finds only a few courthouse regulars who handle many different types of matters. By contrast, in the courthouses of major cities you will find numerous courthouse regulars who specialize in specific duties. Moreover, in some courthouses civil and criminal cases are heard in the same courtroom at the same time; in other jurisdictions civil and criminal cases are separated in time and place. These variations aside, the following provides an overview of a typical day in a medium-sized courthouse in the United States.

 Courtroom 21 is a joint project of the William and Mary College of Law and the National Center for State Courts; this Web site emphasizes technology in the courtroom: **http://www.courtroom21.net/**.

For an up-to-date list of Web links, go to **http://www.wadsworth.com/product/0534563406s**.

The Courthouse

One indication of the low status of the criminal courts is their location. In some cities the criminal courts are carefully tucked away from public view. Security is the most obvious reason for these isolated and inconvenient locations. Since the pretrial detention facilities have often been built next to the courthouse, the entire criminal justice complex is located away from the downtown business center. As a result, victims and witnesses, to say nothing of defendants (out on bail) and family members, face a difficult task in getting to the courthouse. Those using public transportation require several transfers; for those who drive, parking is at a premium because the large parking lots are invariably reserved for the courthouse regulars (Wice 1985).

Having located the courthouse complex, visitors are struck by the architecture of their surroundings. Clustered nearby are older buildings, occupied by bail agents and defense attorneys. Garish neon signs proclaiming "Bail Bonds, 24 Hour Service" compete with unpainted wooden structures to provide a general sense of urban decay. The courthouse building likewise often has a haggard and unkempt look about it. Beneath the veneer of decades of uncleaned grime, though, one sees a once grand building built during an era when citizens took great pride in their public buildings. Although criminal court buildings are constructed in a variety of architectural styles, they nevertheless all seem to present an image of stolidity and unyielding strength.

Entrance is usually gained by climbing an excessive number of steps. For security reasons there is often only one door open, funneling all visitors through a crowded, narrow entranceway. Once inside visitors find themselves in a massive lobby, with an impressively high arched ceiling. In the center of the lobby is the omnipresent information booth, which is invariably unattended. A nearby bulletin board offers the only clue as to what cases are to be found in which courtrooms, but the notices are usually outdated. In a distant corner is a small snack bar and a battery of telephones, a few of which are in service.

The lobby and hallways resound with animated conversations between lawyers, bail agents, bailiffs, defendants, family members, witnesses, and a variety of other interested parties. Indeed, for many bail agents and private criminal lawyers these hallways are their daytime offices. Although courthouses often provide witness reception areas and lawyers' lounges, nearly everyone prefers to be near the action so as not to miss out on a business opportunity or choice bit of gossip.

The Courtroom

After some difficulty, most first-time visitors manage to locate the specific courtroom of interest, entering through a double set of heavy doors, which suggests that this is not an ordinary public building. This initial impression of orderliness under law quickly gives way to a sense of social anarchy. One is immediately confronted with a visual and audio reality far different from that portrayed on television or in the movies. What is happening inside the courtroom is best viewed in terms of sets of actors who congregate in different locations.

In the front is an imposing bench, which dominates the courtroom, literally elevating the black-robed judge on a pedestal. Court begins by the customary call of the crier: "All rise, the court for [blank] county is now in session, the Honorable [blank] [blank] presiding." On cue, the judge strides mindfully from behind a hidden door, law book or case folder tucked under one arm. Just below the bench sits the clerk of court (sometimes called the calendar clerk), who controls the scheduling of cases and keeps the judge apprised of the relevant details of the case. To one side of the bench sits the court stenographer, whose machine mysteriously makes a shorthand record of the proceedings (or at least those parts the judge wishes to be preserved). Also in attendance is a bailiff, who tries to maintain order in the courtroom and also escorts jurors if there is a trial. The judge's staff (who more or less surround the bench) also may include a law clerk and a secretary (who jealously guards access to the judge when he or she is not presiding in the courtroom). Typically, the personal staff has worked with the judge for extended periods of time; indeed the secretary may have occupied that position when the judge was in private practice, and the bailiff was associated with the judge during his or her successful campaign for a seat on the court.

Ten to twenty feet from the front of the bench are two tables reserved for the defense and prosecution, respectively. The district attorney's table is piled high with case folders needed for the day's activities. Somehow, no matter how high the pile of case folders, a file or part of a file invariably is missing, resulting in last-minute scurrying by frantic assistant district attorneys trying to rectify the periodic lapses of the prosecutorial bureaucracy. The mountain of files on the public defender's table nearly matches that of the prosecutor's. The public defender (PD) likewise finds that files are missing or incomplete, resulting in scurrying around looking for missing pieces of paper. When a case involving a private criminal lawyer is called, the PD temporarily gives up the seat at the defense table, but the files remain, an indication that it is really the PD who dominates. Between the bench and the lawyers' table stands a battered wooden podium, which is typically used only for ceremonial occasions, most notably the entering of a plea of guilty by the defendant or arguing before a jury by the lawyers. Otherwise lawyers typically argue while sitting behind the table.

To the side of the bench is the jury box (or in older courthouses two sets of jury boxes, which were alternated depending on the temperature outside). On trial day jurors occupy these seats; when no jury trial is being conducted (which is often), a variety of folks can be found in and around the jury box, waiting, socializing, and occasionally conducting business. Often the easiest to identify are police officers in court to provide testimony. Also in attendance are probation officers, halfway house personnel, and pretrial services representatives. Bail agents also often drop in to make sure that the persons they have posted bail for have indeed arrived as scheduled.

Also sitting in the jury box one is likely to view defendants who have been detained prior to trial. Defendants out on bail sit in the public sector, but those in jail sit in brightly colored uniforms with the name of the county jail readily displayed. Often they are manacled together and are temporarily unchained when their cases are called. Surrounding the defendants, hovering like brooding hens, are the sheriff's deputies. The number of deputies in court provides a pretty good indication of the perceived threat of the defendants; the higher the ratio of guards to prisoners, the more serious the crime and the criminal.

A railing separates the courthouse regulars from the occasional participants. The first row or two are reserved for lawyers waiting for their cases to be called. Sitting in the remaining rows are the defen-

dants (those who have been free on bond or released on their own recognizance), family members, and perhaps a variety of other observers—for example, senior citizens, who enjoy rooting for the prosecutor. Increasingly in contemporary courthouses one will also find victim advocates affiliated with organizations such as victim witness assistance programs, Mothers Against Drunk Driving, child advocates, and rape crisis centers. Like senior citizens, these people make known their desire for harsh punishments. And as the ethnic makeup continues to change, courthouses also increasingly hire translators. Figure 5-1 summarizes the courthouse actors and their main activities.

What is disconcerting to the newcomer to the courtroom is that these actors seem in constant motion. Small groups form and re-form as cases are called and defendants summoned before the bench. In one corner an assistant district attorney (DA) can be seen conversing with an assistant PD, while in the back of the room a private defense attorney is engaged in whispered conversations with the defendant and his mother. Moreover, the cast of characters is ever changing. Many actors are in court for a specific case, and when that case has finished, they leave, often walking to another courtroom where they have other cases to attend. Most exasperating of all, the courtroom alternates between bursts of energy and periods of lethargy. Cases are called, only to be put on hold because one of the needed participants is temporarily busy elsewhere in the courthouse.

Amid these numerous and simultaneous conversations the judge and bailiffs attempt to maintain an acceptable decibel level, but disturbances are commonplace. It must be noted that the chaotic scenes depicted thus far pertain only to those courtrooms where nontrial proceedings are conducted, such as initial appearance, preliminary hearing, motions to suppress evidence, and sentencing. As one moves closer toward trial in a felony case, the courtroom scene becomes more tranquil. The end result is that the trial, which is a statistical rarity, is held in a quiet, sparsely populated courtroom.

 To learn what it takes to become a court reporter, visit **http://www.depo.com/becr.htm**.

For an up-to-date list of Web links, go to **http://www.wadsworth.com/product/0534563406s**.

FIGURE 5-1	Courthouse Actors

	Main Activities
Law Enforcement	
Court security staff	Provide security throughout the courthouse
Sheriff's deputy	Transports prisoners to and from jail
Bailiff	Maintains order in courtrooms
Courts	
Lawyers	
Prosecutor	Government official who conducts criminal proceedings
Public defender	Government attorney who represents indigents
Private defense attorney	Lawyer paid by defendant for representation
Judge	Officer who presides in a court of law
Law clerk	Performs legal research for the judge
Court Support Staff	
Clerk of court	Record keeper, often responsible for jury selection
Court reporter	Makes verbatim transcript of proceedings
Secretary	Handles routine work of judge's office
Translator	Renders another language into English
Court administrator	Supervises and performs administrative tasks for the court
Corrections	
Probation officer	Recommends defendants for probation and monitors their activities
Pretrial services	Handles release of qualified pretrial detainees
Drug rehabilitation program	Recommends defendants for drug rehabilitation and monitors progress
Public	
Regular Participants	
Bail agent	For a fee secures pretrial release for defendants
Newspaper reporter	Provides media coverage of key events
Irregular Participants	
Defendant	Person accused of violating the law
Victim	Person who has suffered a loss due to crime
Witness	Anyone who will testify in court
Jurors	Citizens who will decide guilt or innocence
Rape crisis center	Provides counseling to rape victims
Child advocate	Person who speaks up for child's best interest
Court watchers	Retirees whose hobby is coming to court, or those associated with good-government groups (often intent on proving how little judges work)
Victim-witness assistance program	Public or private agency seeking to improve treatment

Behind the Scenes

Outside the great hall of the courthouse and behind the individual courtrooms are areas where visitors seldom venture. What is immediately obvious is that the steady march of people and the accompanying din of noise are absent. Behind the scenes work the actors who provide essential support for courtroom activities (see A Day in Court: "Those People behind the Scenes").

Courts are paperwork bureaucracies. Even the simplest case requires sheets and sheets of paper: the initial charge, later the indictment, bail release forms, pretrial motions, notice of appearance of counsel, and so on. Most of the behind-the-scenes people process this paperwork. Their actions are almost never visible, but their inactions can make headlines.

Other behind-the-scene actors are managers. A constant complaint is that the courts are mismanaged. Alas, trying to define management in a court setting proves to be elusive. Part of the difficulty is that in many jurisdictions there are three distinct sets of court managers—clerks of court, chief judges, and court administrators—and these three sets of managers are often in competition. Just as important, it is difficult to define what the managers should be doing. There is a fundamental conflict between management—standardized work processes and standard outputs—and the profession of law—individual attention to cases that are fundamentally different. Thus, at the heart of the problem of managing the courthouse is the tension between the rationality of bureaucracy and the antibureaucratic philosophies of judges (Saari 1982).

The **clerk of court,** variously referred to as prothonotary, register of probate, and clerk, is pivotal in the administration of local judiciaries. They are responsible for docketing cases, collecting fees, overseeing jury selection, and maintaining court records. Although these local officials have enormous power, they have been overlooked by academics and reformers alike (Gertz 1977). They have traditionally competed with judges for control over judicial administration (Mays and Taggart 1986). Since they are elected officials in all but six states, they can operate semiautonomously from the judge.

Judges are responsible for court administration, but they have most often been ineffective managers. This is primarily due to the unique environment in which the courts operate. Judges may be held responsible, but they seldom have the necessary authority (Jacob 1997). Moreover, they are not trained in management. The end result is that the lawyers who become judges are not accustomed to analyzing patterns of case dispositions or managing large dockets—the essential skills a manager needs. These problems are reflected in the position of chief judge. Although the chief judge has general administrative responsibilities, the position is really one of "first among equals." Particularly when the chief judge assumes the position by seniority, as many do, there is no guarantee that the person will be interested in management or will be effective at it.

One of the most innovative approaches to court problems has been the creation of a professional group of trained administrators to assist judges in their administrative duties. In short, management—like law—is a profession, and therefore well-trained managers can give the courts what they often have lacked: managerial skill and bureaucratic knowledge. Underlying this theory is the assumption that the managers can perform administrative tasks (case-flow management, budgeting, personnel, and policy development) without interfering in judicial tasks (adjudicating specific cases). But drawing the line between the two has proven to be elusive (Flanders 1991).

The development of the professional position of court administrator has been sporadic (Lawson and Howard 1991). By the 1980s, every state had established a statewide court administrator. The primary duties of these officials are preparing annual reports, summarizing caseload data, preparing budgets, and troubleshooting. Usually, they report to the state supreme court or the chief justice of the state supreme court. Increasingly, trial courts are also employing court administrators. Few, if any, major metropolitan areas are without professional judicial employees (Reinkensmeyer 1991).

Tension between judges and the court administrator may also arise. Some judges are reluctant to delegate responsibility over important aspects of the court's work, such as case scheduling and case-flow management (Mays and Taggart 1986). In practice, the distinction between administration and

---

Clerk of court: An elected or appointed court officer responsible for maintaining the written records of the court and for supervising or performing the clerical tasks necessary to conduct judicial business.

"Those People behind the Scenes"

To David Lawrence, the world of common pleas court depends on a vast, seldom-noticed army that rarely visits a courtroom—a workforce that he divides into "paper people" and "people people."

"Every case has a judge, a defendant, a prosecutor, a defense attorney, two court officers, a stenographer, at least one witness, and two sheriff's deputies if the defendant is in jail," said Lawrence, the court's chief deputy administrator.

"That's what you see in the courtroom. What goes on behind the scenes involves many, many more."

Lawrence oversees his two groups of non-courtroom employees as they guide each criminal case from arrest to final disposition.

The "paper people"—largely clerks and secretaries—track and update the paperwork essential to the resolution of any criminal case.

The "people people" coordinate the work of clerks, stenographers, janitors, and other employees who make sure each case has its day in court.

Together, these two groups account for more than half the 2,000 Common Pleas Court employees. The rest work in other sections—the civil section of the trial division and Family and Orphan courts.

The court employees whose duties relate primarily to criminal cases work for a dozen key agencies that try to move those cases efficiently through the system.

From the time of arrest, Lawrence said, those agencies are busy. One assesses a defendant's ability to afford counsel and eligibility for bail; another coordinates court appearances of the defendant with the schedules of police officers to reduce overtime; another makes sure clerks and defendants are scheduled for court when the case is called.

"There just aren't enough people" in the hidden bureaucracy, he said.

For example, he said, judges outnumber stenographers. That makes it impossible for every judge to be on the bench every day, since some courtrooms wouldn't have anyone to make the official record. . . .

Most significantly, he added, the hidden bureaucracy operates amid other competing bureaucracies.

The interests of each of those bureaucracies—primarily the Police Department, defense bar, district attorney's office, prisons, and sheriff's office—"have a tremendous impact" on case flow, Lawrence said.

"Every action that takes place in the process depends on each of those agencies," he said. "But when the system doesn't work, what do people say? The courts are screwed up."

"Should the courts be the focal point? I guess, because we're the ones charged with dispensing justice and the courts are charged with balancing the diverse interests of all those agencies."

SOURCE: P. Maryniak, "Those People behind the Scenes," *Philadelphia Daily News,* March 13, 1990, 16. Reprinted by permission.

adjudication is not clear-cut. A court administrator's proposal to streamline court procedures may be viewed by the judges as an intrusion on their role in deciding cases. For example, it is not easy to determine whether transferring a judge from one assignment to another is a judicial or nonjudicial responsibility. Substantial confusion still exists over the role of the court administrator (Stott 1982; Hoffman 1991).

Court services bureaus are a major part of sheriff's offices in major cities. See, for example:

> http://www.co.san-diego.ca.us/cnty/
> cntydepts/safety/sheriff/csb/index.html
> (San Diego)
> http://www.cookcountysheriff.org/court/
> (Chicago)
> http://www.open.org/~msheriff/court.htm
> (Indianapolis)

For an up-to-date list of Web links, go to **http://www.wadsworth.com/product/0534563406s**.

DYNAMICS OF COURTHOUSE JUSTICE

The brief tour of the courthouse indicates that justice is very unlike the dramatizations one sees on TV or in the movies. First-time observers find scant relationship between the dynamics of courthouse justice (law in action) and widely held cultural images (law on the books).

- Expecting to see individual trials, they instead witness a parade of defendants and their cases. In particular, newcomers to the courthouse are often struck by the pure volume of cases.

- Expecting the law to provide guidance, they instead find that decisions are not necessarily clear-cut, but that some leeway is available. How else can one explain disagreements over lengths of prison sentences and terms of probation?

- Expecting to observe the conflict (and perhaps even hostility) projected by the adversarial model, courthouse watchers discover cooperation between judges, prosecutors, and defense attorneys. At times conversations become animated, but by and large the verbal exchanges reflect a good amount of badinage.

In exploring these differences, practitioners and scholars have employed three concepts—assembly-line justice, discretion, and courtroom work group (see Figure 5-2).

- Assembly-line justice explains why few cases receive individual treatment.

- Discretion emphasizes that decisions, although guided by law, are not totally determined by rules found in statutes or court decisions.

- The courtroom work group concept stresses the importance of the patterned interactions of judges, prosecutors, and defense attorneys.

As we shall see, each of these explanations is useful in understanding the dynamics of courthouse justice.

ASSEMBLY-LINE JUSTICE

The most commonly advanced reason that criminal courts do not administer justice according to the textbook image is **assembly-line justice**. This orthodox explanation was put forth by the President's Commission on Law Enforcement and Administration of Justice (1967, 31):

> **Assembly-line justice:** The operation of any segment of the criminal justice system in which excessive workload results in decisions being made with such speed and impersonality that defendants are treated as objects to be processed rather than as individuals.

The crux of the problem is that there is a great disparity between the number of cases and the number of judges.

It is not only judges who are in short supply. There are not enough prosecutors, defense counsel, and probation officers even in those courts where some of them are available. The deluge of cases is reflected in every aspect of the courts' work, from overcrowded corridors and courtrooms to the long calendars that do not allow more than cursory consideration of individual cases.

 For photos of Judge Ito's courtroom, see **http://www.ncsc.dni.us/ncsc/ito_ctrm/ito_ctrm.htm**.

For an up-to-date list of Web links, go to **http://www.wadsworth.com/product/0534563406s**.

Strengths of the Explanation

The assembly-line justice explanation highlights some important features of the contemporary courthouse. No one disputes that the volume of cases is large and growing (Chapter 10). Pressures to move cases quickly, lest a backlog develop, are particularly prevalent in large urban areas. In direct and indirect ways, officials view one of their tasks as keeping the docket current, which means that they seldom have much time to spend on any one case.

In devising procedures for handling large caseloads, prosecutors, defense attorneys, and judges often apply several mass-production techniques. One is specialization. This is most readily seen in the operations of big-city public defenders. One assistant will conduct the initial interview with the defendant, another will represent him or her at the initial appearance, and still another will negotiate the plea. Another mass-production technique is group processing. During the initial appearance, felony defendants are often advised of their rights in one large group rather than individually. In big-city misdemeanor courts, group processing may even extend to sentencing, with sentences fixed on the basis of the defendant's membership in a given class rather than detailed consideration of the individual case (Chapter 18).

Weaknesses of the Explanation

Although the assembly-line justice explanation draws our attention to some important aspects of

| FIGURE 5-2 | Three Concepts Explaining the Dynamics of Courthouse Justice | |

Concept	Definition	Examples
Assembly-line justice	The operation of any segment of the criminal justice system with such speed and impersonality that defendants are treated as objects to be processed rather than individuals.	• War on drugs has greatly increased case volume. • Lower courts process felony defendants in groups. • Judges feel pressure to move cases.
Discretion	The authority to make decisions without reference to specific rules or facts.	• Prosecutors decide whether to file criminal charges. • Lower court judges decide on bail amounts. Defense attorneys recommend a plea of guilty or a trial. • Judges choose between prison or probation.
Courtroom work group	The regular participants in the day-to-day activities of a particular courtroom; judge, prosecutor, and defense attorney interact on the basis of shared norms.	• Cooperation more than conflict governs working relationship of courtroom actors. • Case disposition requires joint actions of judge, prosecutor, and defense attorney. • Rules of thumb guide bail release and sentencing.

the criminal courts, it also obscures many important considerations. First of all, this orthodox explanation stresses that excessive caseloads are a modern problem. Repeated references are made to the "rise" of plea bargaining, the "decline" of the trial, and the "twilight" of the adversary system. However, these vivid metaphors distort history. For more than a century, American courts have been faced with caseload pressures. Even more important, plea bargaining predates any of the "modern" problems of the courthouse. Indeed, plea bargaining "began to appear during the early or mid-nineteenth century and became institutionalized as a standard feature of American urban criminal courts in the last of the nineteenth century" (Haller 1979, 273). In short, the historical evidence must be ignored if one tries to explain how justice is administered in the courthouse simply in terms of too many cases resulting from the growth of big cities.

Emphasizing excessive caseloads also fails to consider the types of cases trial courts must decide. Most criminal cases present no disputed questions of law or fact. Although dispute settlement is the function most clearly associated with the courts, in most cases, criminal or civil, the courts are not called on to resolve any actual dispute. Instead, they merely provide a legal and formal authorization to a settlement reached by the lawyers. Thus, most case dispositions reflect **routine administration**: "A matter is routine when a court has no disputed question of law or fact to decide. Routine administration means the processing or approving of undisputed matters" (Friedman and Percival 1976, 267). Most cases end with a plea of guilty (rather than a trial), not because the courthouse has too many cases but because the courts are confronted with a steady stream of routine cases, in which the only major question is the sentence to be imposed. Although judges, prosecutors, and defense attorneys are popularly portrayed as being forced to decide complex legal issues, in reality their courtroom tasks are routine.

Assembly-line Justice Reconsidered

Although heavy caseloads are part of the conventional wisdom surrounding the operations of criminal courts, several studies cast serious doubt on this proposition. A study in Connecticut compared two courts, one with a heavy caseload, another with a light one. It would be logical to expect major differ-

Routine administration: A matter that presents the court with no disputes over law or fact.

"Doing Time at Tulane and Broad" (Part II)

 On this day at the courthouse, the elevators are out of order, the bathrooms are filthy, their fixtures marginally functional. The majesty of this great building stands without human assistance; the mayor's Keep-It-Clean campaign has not made it to Tulane and Broad. The marble floors are unwaxed, the main hallway is un-air-conditioned, and the basement corridor smells like fish. . . .

The defendant in a burglary case in Section B is shackled at the limbs with steel braces. In the courtroom behind him, his wife or girlfriend is crying. He motions with his head for her to come closer but his lawyer raises a hand from across the room to tell her: No. She sits back down, looking across the courtroom at him, searching. He averts his eyes at first, then looks, sees her misery and arches his eyebrows, mugs a little, tries to cheer her up. Two friends on either side of her rub her shoulders. The voices of lawyers arguing motions and the buzzing white noise of the courtroom air-conditioner join together in a fluorescent-tinged droning, the kind of sound into which everything slips away sometimes. . . .

Down in the basement, prospective jurors, culled from state voter and driver's license rosters, are packed into windowless waiting rooms. Josie Windhorst, a state jury commissioner, is in charge here. She paints the best face on the bleak-looking place, talking about the great ideals of democracy, honor, civic duty, and such. The worst thing, really, are the occasional odors that creep in from the coroner's office in the basement annex.

She is like a schoolteacher on a rainy day, trying to keep everyone happy while they fidget and wait. She handles the legion of excuses from those who'd prefer to jettison their duty to the commonwealth. "People have a tendency to reveal to me their entire medical history when all I really want is a doctor's note," she says.

On this day, there will be five trials, about the average number. Windhorst dispatches dozens of prospective jurors to each court for voir dire, the preliminary examination by lawyers of the jurors' fitness to serve. . . .

On this day of five trials, two are for heroin distribution, one is for possession of marijuana and a pistol,

and two are for possession of a crack pipe. "They're kind of legendary around here," says one court official with a roll of his eyes. "Crack pipe cases." They eat the building's resources. The afternoon in both Sections F and J is consumed by cases trying to prove some sorry-looking guy was in possession of a piece of drug paraphernalia. It is the state's duty to do this.

But both cases deadlock at five to one in the jury rooms. A holdout for not guilty in each case prompts mistrial rulings. The juries are thanked and dismissed; the suspects are led back to jail, but not before one of them, in an ill-fitting gray suit, asks for a moment with his father. It turns out not to be a Kodak moment it promised to be; the two start arguing over the defendant's clothes. . . .

It is now late afternoon and trial results trickle in from around the building. In the drugs and weapons case in [Judge] Alarcon's court, the defendant is found guilty. An hour later, the day's third mistrial is declared in one of the heroin cases; this time because of an assistant DA's improper introduction of prejudicial evidence.

At 5:30 P.M., the building is clear except for Judge Julian Parker's courtroom, where the heroin distribution trial of Paul Washington is winding up. Washington was busted with 25 packets of heroin and a loaded .45. If convicted, he'll likely get a life sentence. . . .

A 12-member jury finds Washington guilty, to which the defendant has no visible reaction. As the jurors file out of the courtroom, only one—like Washington, a young black man—looks him in the eye. One of the sisters bolts from the room sobbing while the other quietly buries her head in her hands. As he is led away, Washington looks back over his shoulder to wave good-bye but neither of them sees him.

At 6:45 P.M., two defense attorneys hardly older than the girls' brother comfort them at the top of the steps of the courtroom at Tulane and Broad, and for today at least, court is adjourned.

SOURCE: Christopher Rose, "Doing Time at Tulane and Broad." *The Times Picayune*, September 27, 1998.

ences in how cases were processed and in the substance of justice handed out, but the results indicated that the courts were remarkably similar. Neither court had many trials. In neither did the defense attorneys engage in pitched battle with the prosecution. Both courts set bail in approximately

the same amounts and imposed roughly similar sentences. Each court spent the same amount of time per case, moving through its business "rapidly and mechanically." The only difference was that the busier court was in session longer than the court with fewer cases (Feeley 1979).

A study in Chicago concluded that "variations in caseloads did not affect the guilty plea decision, the sentence in guilty plea cases, or the decision to pursue a case to trial" (Nardulli 1979). In this same vein, practitioners believe that even an adequately funded criminal court system would dispose of relatively few cases by means of a trial (Church 1985). These and other studies clearly suggest that the criminal court process cannot be understood solely on the basis of excessive caseloads, because such an explanation omits too many important considerations (Heumann 1975; Schulhofer 1984).

DISCRETION

Discretion lies at the heart of the criminal justice process. Law Professor Kenneth Culp Davis (1971, 3) authored this often repeated summation:

Engraved in stone on the department of Justice Building in Washington, on the Pennsylvania Avenue side where swarms of bureaucrats and others pass by, are these five words: "Where law ends tyranny begins" (William Pitt).

I think that in our system of government, where the law ends tyranny need not begin. Where law ends, discretion begins, and the exercise of discretion may mean either beneficence or tyranny, either justice or injustice, either reasonableness or arbitrariness.

From the time a crime is committed until after sentence is imposed, **discretion** is exercised every time key decisions are made. The victim may decide not to report the crime to the police. If the crime is reported, the police may decide not to arrest the offender. After arrest, the prosecutor may decide not to prosecute. Once charges have been filed, a lower court judge must set the amount of bail and decide whether there is sufficient probable cause to hold the defendant for the grand jury. In turn, grand juries have discretion over indictments, trial juries over conviction, and the judge over sentencing. Even after sentencing, prison officials may exercise discretion in deciding how much time will actually be served.

As stressed in Chapter 2, the criminal law itself creates discretion. The pretense of the law is that it is

Discretion: The lawful ability of an agent of government to exercise choice in making a decision.

known and precise, but the reality is that the criminal law is evolving and at times ambiguous.

Because no legislature has succeeded in formulating a substantive criminal code which clearly encompasses all conduct intended to be made criminal and which clearly excludes all other conduct, the exercise of discretion in interpreting the legislative mandate is necessary. In part the problem is the result of poor draftsmanship and a failure to revise the criminal law to eliminate obsolete provisions. (LaFave and Scott 1972, 18–19)

Discretion is best defined as "the authority to make decisions without reference to specific rules or facts, using instead one's own judgment" (Cole 1970, 477). Viewed from this perspective, discretion has three major subcomponents: legal judgments, policy priorities, and personal philosophies.

Legal Judgments

Many discretionary decisions in the criminal court process are made on the basis of legal judgments. An example would be a prosecutor who refuses to file a criminal charge because in her legal judgment there is insufficient evidence to prove all the elements of the offense. It is well accepted that decisions made (by lawyers and nonlawyers alike) about the law are a key element in decision making. Some legal judgments stem from a prediction about the likely outcome of a case at a later stage in the proceedings. Consider another situation in which charges are not filed against a defendant. The prosecutor may believe that the defendant did violate the law but that no jury would convict. In a barroom brawl, for example, in which the defendant struck the victim, the prosecutor may believe that a jury would decide that the victim had provoked the assault and therefore acquit.

Policy Priorities

Because criminal laws are so broad and general, they must be selectively enforced. The number of crimes that could be charged is virtually unlimited, but the resources devoted to detecting wrongdoers and processing them through the courts (and later incarcerating them) are limited. Thus, discretionary decisions are often made on the basis of policy priorities. For example, some prosecutors' offices have in-house policies governing prosecutions for minor thefts or embezzlements. Normally, U.S. attorneys will not file embezzlement charges when the suspect is a young employee of a bank who stole small amounts and was fired when discovered, for example. Through policy priorities, court officials try to devote more resources to prosecuting serious crimes, such as murder, rape, and armed robbery, rather than minor offenses.

Personal Philosophies

Some discretionary decisions reflect the decision makers' personal values and attitudes—their personal philosophies. Judges and prosecutors have varying views of what offenses are serious and deserving of a high priority. Differences among judges in the same courthouse are readily apparent. Some differences center on the purpose of the criminal law. Those who believe that the courts can deter crime (through heavy sentences, for example) behave differently from those who discount the role the courts can play in deterrence. Stated another way, the same differences of opinion about crime that characterize society as a whole likewise divide courthouse actors.

THE COURTROOM WORK GROUP

Every day, the same group of courthouse regulars assembles in the same courtroom, sits or stands in the same places, and performs the same tasks as the day before. The types of defendants and the nature of the crimes they are accused of also remain constant. Only the names of the victims and defendants are different. Whereas defendants come and go, the judges, prosecutors, defense attorneys, clerks, and probation officers remain. To even the most casual observer, the courthouse regulars occupy a special status. They freely issue instructions to the temporary visitors to the courthouse (don't smoke, don't talk, don't read the newspaper), although they smoke, talk, and read the newspaper themselves. The ordinary citizens sit on hard benches in the rear of the courtroom and may approach the bench only when specifically requested. The courthouse regulars, on the other hand, enjoy easy access to the front part of the courtroom.

The activities of the courthouse regulars represent a complex network of ongoing social relationships (Blumberg 1970; Neubauer 1974; Flemming, Nardulli, and Eisenstein 1992). These relationships are as important as they are complex. James Eisenstein and Herbert Jacob (1977) have proposed that the best way to analyze the network of ongoing relationships among the courthouse actors is through the concept of the **courtroom work group**. Judges, prosecutors, and defense attorneys are representatives from separate, independent sponsoring institutions. They are drawn together by a common task: Each must do something about a given case. As a result, courthouse regulars work together on a daily basis in ways not envisioned by the formal adversary model (Jacob 1991). In Philadelphia, for example, 83 percent of the district attorneys and public defenders report that they cooperate always or often (Lichtenstein 1984). To understand the extent, as well as the limits of this cooperation, we need to examine both work group formation and the impact of courtroom work groups.

Mutual Interdependence

The criminal courthouse is not a single organization but rather a collection of separate institutions that gather in a common workplace. Whereas most large organizations consist of distinct divisions operating under a central leadership, the criminal courthouse consists of separate institutions without a hierarchical system of control. A judge cannot reward a prosecutor or a public defender who performs well. Rather, each of the courthouse regulars is a representative of a sponsoring institution, which hires and fires them, monitors their activities, and rewards their performance.

None of these actors can perform his or her tasks independently; they must work together. These interactions are critical because none of the courthouse regulars can make decisions independently; each must consider the reactions of others. This is most readily seen in the work of the defense attorney. In representing his or her client, the defense attorney must consider the type of plea agreement the prosecutor may offer, the sentencing tendencies of the judge, the likelihood of a jury verdict of guilty, and the possibility that the probation officer

> **Courtroom work group:**   The regular participants in the day-to-day activities of a particular courtroom: judge, prosecutor, and defense attorney interact on the basis of shared norms.

Massachusetts v. Louise Woodward

Child Killer or Child Lover?

British au pair Louise Woodward is charged with murdering eight-month-old Matthew Eappen. The defense counters that she loved the children and that death occurred because of a previous head trauma. As you watch the video, ask yourself the following questions:

1. A variety of factors have been suggested for why this case attracted so much attention in the United States. They include the nature of the crime, the nature of the victim (a young child), and the status of the defendant (a British citizen). Beyond the specifics of the case, it also represented a variety of issues in American society, including the role of working mothers and the reliability of child care. Which factor or factors explain the widespread public attention to this case?

2. In an unusual move, the judge set aside the jury verdict of second-degree murder and instead found the defendant guilty of involuntary manslaughter. The sentence was for time served— 279 days. In the end, was this compromise decision better or worse than the one produced by the jury and the adversary system?

will recommend probation. Prosecutors and judges are interdependent in similar ways.

Each member of the work group can achieve individual goals and accomplish separate tasks only through work group participation. The actors come to share common interests in disposing of cases. Hence, cooperation—mutual interdependence— within the work group is viewed as leading to mutual benefits. A judge who allows a backlog of cases to develop can expect to feel pressure from other judges (or the chief judge) to dispose of more cases. Assistant prosecutors are judged by their superiors not so much on how many cases they win but on how few they lose. The emphasis is on securing convictions and avoiding acquittals. Defense attorneys face a different set of incentives. Public defender organizations prefer to dispose of cases quickly, because they have a limited number of attorneys to represent a large number of indigents. Private attorneys also need to move cases. Since

most defendants are poor and can afford only a modest fee, private attorneys make a living by representing a large number of clients. Individual fees are insufficient to allow the expenditure of much time on any given case, so a high turnover is needed. In short, all participants receive benefits from disposing of cases without undue effort.

 For a close-up of the victim advocates program of the Adams County sheriff's office, just click on **http://www.co.adams.co.us/sheriff/victim.htm**.

For an up-to-date list of Web links, go to **http://www.wadsworth.com/product/0534563406s**.

Socialization

Court work groups have needs quite apart from the legal mandate of adjudicating cases; they must preserve the ongoing system. A problem common to all organizations is the need to break in new members, a process referred to as socialization. Through socialization newcomers are taught not only the formal requirements of the job (how motions are filed and so on) but also informal rules of behavior. One veteran court aide put it this way:

> *Most of the judges are pretty good—they rely on us. Sometimes you get a new judge who wants to do things his way. We have to break them in, train them. This court is very different. We have to break new judges in. It takes some of them some time to get adjusted to the way we do things. (Wiseman 1970, 99)*

Thus, newcomers learn not only from their peers but also from other members of the social network.

Shared Decision Making

In essence the courtroom is a place where representatives of separate sponsoring institutions, each with its own needs and pressures, end up cooperating on a range of matters. Courtroom work groups affect what decisions are made and how they are made in several ways (Clynch and Neubauer 1981).

Courtroom work groups reflect shared decision making. Judges retain the legal authority to make the major decisions such as setting bail, adjudicating guilt (except when there is a jury trial), and imposing sentences, but they often rely on others. They routinely follow the bail recommendations of the prosecutor, accept guilty plea agreements reached by the defense and prosecution, and follow the recommendations of the probation officer. This does not mean that the judge is without power; the other actors must be sensitive to what the judge might do. Prosecutors (and defense attorneys) know the amount of bail a particular judge has set in past situations, so that is what they recommend in the current case. This shared decision making is highly functional because it diffuses responsibility. Judges, prosecutors, defense attorneys, and others are aware that the decisions they make can turn out to be wrong. Since such dire results cannot be predicted ahead of time, the members of the courtroom work group share a sense that when one of their members looks bad, they all look bad. Decisions therefore are made on a joint basis; if something later goes wrong, work group members have protected themselves: Everyone thought it was a good idea at the time.

The hallmark of work groups is regularity of behavior. This regularity is the product of shared norms about how each member should behave and what decisions are desirable. Courthouse workers can make their common work site a fractious and unpredictable place for carrying out assigned tasks, or, through cooperation, a predictable place to work. The greater the certainty, the less time and resources they need spend on each case. It is the shared norms that provide structure to what otherwise would appear to be an unstructured, almost chaotic, process. One set of shared norms centers on standards of personal and professional conduct. Attorneys are expected to stick by their word and never deliberately mislead. They are also expected to minimize surprises (Eisenstein and Jacob 1977). Another set of shared norms relates to policy standards.

Normal Crimes

As discussed earlier, under Assembly-line Justice, most of the matters before the courts are routine. Although each case is unique, most fall in a limited number of categories. Based on similarities among cases, members of the work group develop concepts about types of crime and criminals. One study has aptly labeled this phenomenon as the concept of the **normal crime** (Sudnow 1965). The legal actors cate-

gorize crimes on the basis of the typical manner in which they are committed, the typical social characteristics of the defendants, the settings of the crimes, and the types of victims. Once a case has been placed into one of these categories, it is usually disposed of on the basis of a set pattern. These policy norms provide a common orientation that accommodates the different demands of the sponsoring institutions. A group sense of justice is the result.

Rewards and Sanctions

Actors who violate these rules of personal and professional conduct can expect sanctions from the other members of the work group. A variety of rewards (carrots) are available as benefits to those who follow the rules. For example, defense attorneys who do not unnecessarily disrupt routines receive greater information from prosecutors (police reports in some jurisdictions) or find they are able to negotiate a sentence that is slightly less severe than normal. In turn, some sanctions (sticks) may be applied to those who do not cooperate. Judges can sanction uncooperative private defense attorneys, for instance, by making them wait for their case to be called. By far the more effective approach is the carrot, because it operates indirectly and is less disruptive. The imposition of sanctions can result in countersanctions being applied, with the result that the network is disrupted even further.

 The Cook County courts provide the public with a Web page of FAQs about courthouses: **http://www. cookcountycourt.org/jury/faq-courthouse.html**.

For an up-to-date list of Web links, go to **http:// www.wadsworth.com/product/0534563406s**.

Variability in Courtroom Work Groups

Virtually all criminal courts studied to date exemplify the patterns just discussed of how courtroom work groups operate, but some important variations need to be considered. Indeed, Flemming, Nardulli, and Eisenstein (1992) argue that this diversity is a major obstacle to understanding America's criminal courts.

- The stability of the work groups varies (Church 1985). Work groups are much more stable in Chicago than in Baltimore, where rotation of key officials' jobs occurs more often

> **Normal crime:** Categorization of crime based on the typical manner in which it is committed, the typical type of defendant who commits it, and the typical penalty to be applied.

and produces numerous disruptions of the ongoing network of relationships (Eisenstein and Jacob 1977).

- Mavericks can be found in most courthouses. Some defense attorneys engage in hostile relations with prosecutors and exhibit many "Perry Mason" attributes of adversarial behavior. They do so at a price, however: They are seldom able to negotiate effectively for good deals.

- There are important variations in how judges control their courtrooms. Some prefer to parcel out decisions to others and are therefore receptive to recommendations from prosecutors, probation officers, and perhaps even defense attorneys. Other judges play a much more dominant role.

- The content of the policy norms varies from community to community. Property crimes are viewed as more threatening in rural areas than in urban ones, so the appropriate penalty for a defendant convicted of burglary in a rural area is more severe than for a defendant convicted in a big city.

To the general public, perhaps the most visible variation between work groups concerns delay. Each courthouse has, over time, evolved a set of expectations about the proper pacing of case dispositions. Some courthouses process cases in a timely fashion, others less so.

THE PROBLEM OF DELAY

Case backlog and trial delay are problems that affect many of the nation's courts. The magnitude of the backlog and the length of the delay vary greatly, depending on the court involved. This was the conclusion of a comprehensive survey (Mahoney et al. 1988) of how long it takes for cases to proceed from arrest to disposition. Clearly, there are degrees of delay. The seventeen courts listed in Table 5-1 fall into three relatively distinct clusters. Seattle and Cincinnati are examples of faster courts—median time of 100 days or less from arrest to disposition. Moderately fast courts—Tucson and Omaha, for example—have disposition times ranging from 100 to 150 days. Finally, in slower courts like Austin and Baltimore the median time is greater than 150 days (Ostrom and Hanson 1999). Stated another way,

delay appears to be a problem in some jurisdictions, but a number of American trial courts handle their cases very expeditiously.

It is best to view delay not as a problem but as a symptom of a problem (Neubauer et al. 1981). In a general sense, the term **delay** suggests abnormal or unacceptable time lapses in the processing of cases. The inherent subjectivity of the term *delay* becomes apparent when we try to define unnecessary delay. The total time that a case is on the court's docket may consist of acceptable time plus unacceptable time. Many empirical measures of delay are actually measures of the total time taken to case disposition. It is better, therefore, to employ a neutral term such as case-processing time (Neubauer 1983).

The difficulties in defining delay help explain why there is no consensus about how long is too long. Past commissions have provided yardsticks ranging from six months to two years (American Bar Association 1968; President's Commission 1967; National Advisory Commission 1973). The most commonly employed benchmark is the recommendation of the American Bar Association that all felony cases reach disposition within one year of filing. Such law-on-the-books efforts to specify time standards are of some use because they provide criteria for assessing current court practices. But from a law-in-action perspective proposed time standards fail to recognize the importance of diversity in case processing.

Consequences of Delay

Concern that "justice delayed is justice denied" is as old as the common law itself. In the thirteenth century, the nobles forced King John to sign the Magna Carta and promise not to "deny or delay right or justice." In the nineteenth century, the novelist Charles Dickens condemned the tortuous process of litigation in the English courts. Cases that take too long to reach disposition are more than a minor inconvenience; the values and guarantees associated with the legal system may be jeopardized. A number of different costs of delay are commonly cited. These perceived costs can be conveniently grouped into four categories: defendant, society, citizen, and resources.

Delay: Postponement or adjournment of proceedings in a case; lag in case-processing time.

TABLE 5-1   Felony Case Disposition Time in Selected Cities (Days from Arrest to Disposition)

City	Percentage Resolved Within		Median Days from Arrest to Disposition
	180 Days	365 Days	
Faster courts			
Seattle, WA	91%	98%	59
Cincinnati, OH	87	97	79
Portland, OR	89	93	85
Santa Clara, CA	78	95	86
Des Moines, IA	87	99	100
Moderate Courts			
Grand Rapids, MI	78	95	104
St. Petersberg, FL	79	94	105
Tucson, AZ	75	91	113
Omaha, NE	84	99	115
Baltimore County, MD	79	98	135
Oakland, CA	59	83	143
Slower Courts			
Baltimore City, MD	57	95	162
Austin, TX	47	79	193
Fort Worth, TX	46	77	195
Sacramento, CA	41	82	224
Birmingham, AL	12	63	304
Hackensack, NJ	12	63	314
All courts combined	**66**	**88**	**126**

SOURCE: Brian Ostrom and Neal Kauder, *Examining the Work of State Courts, 1998* (Williamsburg, VA: National Center for State Courts, 1999).

Defendant's Rights

Historically, court delay was considered a problem because it jeopardized the defendant's right to a speedy trial. The Sixth Amendment provides that "in all criminal prosecutions, the accused shall enjoy the right to a speedy and public trial. . . ." Defendants may languish in jail for a number of months before guilt or innocence is determined. Some suggest that lengthy pretrial incarceration pressures defendants into pleading guilty (Chapter 11). A number of states have enacted speedy-trial laws premised on the need to protect the defendant's rights.

Societal Protection

More recently, delay has been viewed as hampering society's need for a speedy conviction. This view stresses harm done to the prosecution's case. As the case becomes older and witnesses' memories diminish, the defendant's chance for an acquittal rises. Delay also strengthens a defendant's bargaining position. Prosecutors are quicker to accept a plea of guilty and bargain for lesser sentences when dockets are crowded and cases are growing older. Also, when defendants are out on bond and their cases are delayed, there is the potential for additional criminal activity. In short, the state is also viewed as possessing the right to a speedy trial.

Citizens' Confidence and Convenience

Regardless of the costs or benefits to either the defense or the prosecution, a third perspective emphasizes that delay erodes public confidence in the judicial process. Citizens lose confidence in the swiftness or certainty of punishment. Additionally, victims and witnesses may be forced to make repeated, needless trips to the courthouse. Such appearances can cost citizens time and money and ultimately discourage them from prosecution.

Strains on Resources

Delay in disposing of cases strains the resources of the criminal justice system. Pretrial detainees clog jail facilities. Police officers must appear in court on numerous occasions, at public expense. Attorneys are forced to spend time unproductively because of repeated court appearances on the same case. Alas, efforts to reduce delay on the criminal docket may exacerbate delay in the disposing of civil cases.

 See the National Association for Court Management Web site at **http://www.nacmnet.org/**.

For an up-to-date list of Web links, go to **http://www.wadsworth.com/product/0534563406s**.

Assessing the Costs of Delay

Assertions about the costs of delay require careful scrutiny. A general consensus has emerged that delay is a problem facing the courts, but there is no agreement about the particulars. The four perspectives just described stress varying reasons that delay is a problem. Some perceive that lengthy pretrial incarceration forces defendants to enter into detrimental plea bargains. Others, however, portray caseload pressures as forcing prosecutors into offering unduly lenient negotiated bargains. Of course, the four perspectives are not necessarily mutually exclusive. Various observers may share concerns about system resources as well as citizen confidence and convenience. The point is that assessments of the costs of delay are inherently subjective.

The National Center for State Courts has noted that few of the assertions about the social costs of delay have been subjected to empirical examination (Church and McConnell 1978). They find some evidence to indicate that jail overcrowding, failure-to-appear rates, and citizen respect for the judiciary are related to case delay. But they find no support for the assertions that case delay causes deterioration of cases, diminished deterrence, decreased possibilities of rehabilitation, or plea bargaining.

LAW-ON-THE-BOOKS APPROACH TO COURT DELAY

The law-on-the-books approach to court delay (often referred to as conventional wisdom) can be grouped under two headings: (1) resources and workloads and (2) administrative and procedural factors. It is an article of faith among many commentators that the problem of delay results from an imbalance between available resources and mounting caseloads. A common response is to supplement resources—add judges, prosecutors, clerks, and so on. Others urge reducing the number of cases going to court. A traditional view of delay has also identified administrative and procedural factors, stressing the legal and managerial aspects of criminal court processing. Various stages of processing have been mentioned as sources of delay—for example, initial appearance, preliminary hearing, grand jury indictment, and pretrial motions. The recommended solutions involve "streamlining" the courts by eliminating these procedural roadblocks (Church and McConnell 1978).

Unfortunately, the conventional wisdom about court delay rests on an inadequate knowledge base (Gallas 1976) and for this reason has been called into serious question (Church 1982). In *Justice Delayed* (Church et al. 1978), the National Center for State Courts focused on the link between formal aspects of court operations and case-processing time in twenty-one metropolitan courts. These formal aspects constitute the traditional model of court delay and are the factors most often cited by practitioners as the reasons for delay. The study found that the relationships were weak. The size of court was unrelated to delay. Court caseload and the use of trials (as opposed to plea bargaining) also bore little relationship to case-processing time. The type of charging system was the only external variable related to delay; grand jury systems consumed more time.

These findings suggest that the conventional wisdom about court delay needs to be revised. The rationale for reassessment is set forth by Church and McConnell (1978, x): "More study should be devoted to the less formal aspects of courts, especially the network of relationships, motivations, and perceptions among court participants." These findings likewise explain why trying to issue more and

CASE CLOSE-UP

Barker v. Wingo and the Right to a Speedy Trial

 The police arrested two suspects— Willie Barker and Silas Manning—for beating to death an elderly couple in Christian County, Kentucky, with a tire iron. The district attorney had a stronger case against Manning and believed that Barker could not be convicted unless Manning testified against him. Thus, the DA first sought a conviction against Manning. The court-appointed lawyer initially had no objection to continuing the trial; after all, an acquittal could only help Barker.

The Commonwealth of Kentucky, however, encountered more than a few difficulties in its prosecution of Manning. Altogether, six trials were conducted; two ended in hung juries; two others in convictions that were reversed on appeal. Finally, Manning was convicted of murdering one victim, and a sixth trial resulted in a conviction for the other murder.

During these legal maneuverings, Barker was in jail for ten months, which largely explains why it wasn't until the twelfth continuance was requested that the defense filed a motion to dismiss the charges. By the time the Commonwealth was ready to try Barker, another problem arose—the chief investigator on the case was ill; two continuances resulted. Eventually the judge announced that the case would be dismissed if it wasn't tried during the next setting. The trial finally commenced with Manning as the chief prosecution witness; Barker was convicted and given a life sentence.

In assessing these lengthy delays, the opinion of the court notes that "the right to speedy trial is a more vague concept than other procedure rights. It is, for example, impossible to determine with precision when the right has been denied. We can not definitely say how long is too long in a system where justice is supposed to be swift but deliberate" (p. 522). In essence the right to a speedy trial is relative, not absolute. The test would be a balancing test in which the conduct of both the prosecution and the defendant are weighted. Calling the delay "extraordinary," the Court nonetheless ruled that Barker was not seriously prejudiced by the more than five-year delay.

Only in extraordinary circumstances has the Court ordered criminal charges dismissed for lack of timely trial. One such situation involved an eight-year gap between indictment and arrest. The government was negligent in making any effort to track down the defendant, and the defendant was entitled to go free without a trial (*Doggett v. U.S.* 1992).

more rules and regulations eliminating delay is often ineffective.

Speedy-Trial Laws

Besides the provisions of the U.S. Constitution, thirty-five state constitutions have speedy-trial guarantees, but these provisions apply only when the delay has been "extensive." What constitutes unnecessary delay, however, is difficult to pinpoint (see Case Close-Up: *Barker v. Wingo* and the Right to a Speedy Trial). Given the vagueness of these constitutional standards, legislatures have shown considerable interest in putting some teeth into the guarantee of a speedy trial. The best known such effort is the Speedy Trial Act of 1974 (amended in 1979), which specifies time standards for the two primary stages in the federal court process. Thirty days are allowed from arrest to indictment and seventy days from indictment to trial. Certain time periods, such as those associated with hearings on pretrial motions and the mental competency of the defendant, are considered excludable time.

Speedy-trial statutes exist in all fifty states (Misner 1983), but they have a different orientation than their federal counterpart. Most state laws are defendant centered; that is, they are designed to protect defendants from suffering extensive delay, particularly if they are incarcerated prior to trial. By contrast, the federal law is designed to protect the interests of society; that is, a speedy trial is viewed as an important objective irrespective of whether the defendant's interests are in jeopardy. State speedy-trial laws differ among states in many respects, such as what kinds of events count as excludable time, and they vary widely in the amount of time they allow for bringing a case to trial. Among the most restrictive states is California, which specifies fifteen days in felony cases from arrest to indictment and sixty days from indictment to trial. Other states stipulate only that cases be processed with "no unnecessary or unreasonable delay."

 The National Crime Prevention Council has a Web site for court watchers: **http://www.ncpc.org/3bias2dc. htm#top.**

For an up-to-date list of Web links, go to **http:// www.wadsworth.com/product/0534563406s**.

Limits of Speedy-Trial Laws

Efforts to mandate speedy trials are striking in their lack of specifics. These laws are not based on an analysis of why delay occurs. Moreover, they do not provide for any additional resources (more judges or court reporters) to aid the courts in complying. This can produce unforeseen consequences. In a number of federal courts, compliance has come at the price of delaying civil cases. Potential difficulties also arise because not all cases easily fit into the mandated time frames. A major murder case or a complex drug conspiracy trial takes longer to prepare than an ordinary burglary prosecution.

Finally, enforcement is a problem. Ten states provide that the case must be dismissed if the time limits are exceeded. This can result in a guilty defendant's going free because of an administrative problem. It can also allow the prosecutor to procrastinate deliberately because there is too little evidence for conviction and then later blame the judge when the case is dismissed. Other states permit dismissal but allow re-prosecution. The latter approach can undermine the effectiveness of speedy-trial provisions by subjecting defendants to a series of re-prosecutions.

Researchers approach speedy-trial laws with considerable skepticism. Various studies find that such laws have had limited impact in speeding up the flow of cases through the state criminal court process (Nimmer 1978; Church et al. 1978; Mahoney et al. 1988). The primary reason is that most state laws fail to provide the court with adequate and effective enforcement mechanisms. As a result, the time limits specified by speedy-trial laws are seldom a guide to actual practice. One study, however, found that North Carolina's speedy-trial law did indeed speed up the criminal docket, but interestingly, Connecticut's law did not (Marvell and Luskin 1991).

The federal speedy-trial law has proven effective. The average criminal case filed in the federal courts in the early 1970s took seven months to reach a disposition. By the early 1980s, the average case was disposed of in less than three months. Thus, the federal approach of court planning followed by fixed standards works to reduce delay (Garner 1987).

LAW-IN-ACTION APPROACH TO COURT DELAY

The law-on-the-books approach to court delay ignores the dynamics of courthouse justice. All too often, the impression conveyed is that case flow management is somehow removed from other issues in the criminal court process. Case backlogs, trial delay, and case management are intimately intertwined with the dynamics of courthouse justice. The evidence from various studies shows that delay results from the voluntary actions of court participants.

Delay is related not so much to caseload pressure as to the goals of the participants in the decision process. Defense attorneys seek continuances to avoid harsh judges, to maximize their own goals (for example, fee collection and limiting court time), and to satisfy clients. Prosecutors use delay to increase the stakes of plea bargaining or to postpone weak cases they are likely to lose. Judges acquiesce in continuances to pursue their own goals of organizational maintenance and enhancement. Viewed in this context, delay is not simply a question of managing the court docket more efficiently and providing more resources (Flemming, Nardulli, and Eisenstein 1987).

Lawyers and judges are generally content with the existing pace of litigation in their courts. Case-processing time is influenced by shared courthouse norms as to how fast cases ought to move (Church et al. 1978). Practitioners were asked to provide appropriate case-processing times for twelve hypothetical cases, slightly modified from actual cases. Within the four courts studied—the Bronx, Detroit, Miami, and Pittsburgh—there was little systematic disagreement between judges, defense counsel, and prosecutors on the appropriate pace of case dispositions. Between the courts, however, major differences are apparent. Sampling from case files shows that variations in case processing time times closely parallel intercourt differences on attitude measures. Thomas Church (1985, 464) concludes that these findings provide strong support for the existence of

"Court Reform Unclogs Docket"

 Michigan's largest district court used to be a big gallery of congested courtrooms where police and civilian witnesses sometimes nodded off while waiting—often in vain—for hearings to begin. But a new program that began this week appears to end those problems and others that have plagued 36th District Court and tarnished the image of Detroit's criminal justice system.

Initial results from the reform experiment— known as pre-exam waiver hearings—already are startling: It likely will save money, unclog courts, and keep witnesses from showing up for proceedings that never occur. "The potential of this program is tremendous," said Wayne County Prosecutor John O'Hair, a driving force behind the six-month pilot project. "We want to make the criminal justice system as efficient and as pleasant an experience for victims and witnesses as possible."

For six months, O'Hair has worked with a task force of court administrators, police and sheriff's officials, and judges to solve several problems detailed in a three-day *Detroit News* series last December. The reports examined an escalating rate of felony case dismissals within the county. After the series, O'Hair said his office was deluged by letters from residents who had long and usually unpleasant experiences in the court system—especially 36th District Court.

He heard from witnesses who were summoned to court, sometimes repeatedly, "only to be told: 'We don't need you.' When they leave, their attitude is very negative about the entire judicial system," the prosecutor said.

He and the task force decided to employ a preliminary examination waiver program, already used in several smaller district courts of Oakland County. Wayne's pilot program will cost about $150,000, but could save four or five times that amount, officials believe. The concept is simple: Defendants facing drug, gun, or auto theft can waive their preliminary examinations—the court's first look at evidence—one week earlier than normal. . . .

Drug, gun and auto theft cases make up more than half of all criminal cases in 36th District Court. . . .

Early results from the first two days of advance hearings show that 24 defendants—almost 50 percent—accepted waivers and 13 took a plea bargain. Only four defendants failed to appear. . . .

Though the program has garnered mostly support from police, prosecutors, court administrators, and judges, it gets lukewarm response from some defense attorneys. "I'm willing to try this out, but I'm not going to jeopardize my client's rights for speedy docket management," said Sam Chirukian, a veteran defense attorney and chairman of the criminal law section of the State Bar of Michigan.

Other defense attorneys claimed that cases are still being dismissed because large numbers of Detroit police officers don't show up to testify at preliminary exams. "Why would anyone waive the preliminary examination when cops don't show up to court?" asked defense lawyer Stephen Taratuta, head of a group still called the Recorder's Court Bar Association [the court name was changed several years ago]. "We have a motto: Don't waive until you see the whites of the witness's eyes. At 36th District Court, that's pretty rare."

McCree and O'Hair agree that the reform's success relies heavily on whether officers show up in court. Assistant Chief Benny Napoleon of the Detroit Police Department said that since the *News*'s series ran, he has personally investigated any instance of police no-shows. Between January 1 and May 15, records show, 95 officers didn't keep their court dates. Some were ill, forgot, or were on furlough. Most—about 80 percent—were not notified by their superiors or the court, Napoleon said. "We've taken a very serious posture," he added. Officers who miss court dates and fail to provide a good excuse are severely reprimanded, he added.

The new hearing will prompt police and sheriff's deputies to work at a frenetic pace, completing reports within 24 hours of an arraignment and insuring that defendants are brought over from the jail. Prosecutors must have those reports available for the defense attorneys.

The hearing could save the Wayne County Jail thousands of dollars each year by reducing the time defendants spend behind bars. Many drug and gun inmates who plead guilty and don't make bond remain in jail an average of 37 days, court officials said. Under the new program, those defendants would make it through the system in 21 days. With jail costs at $65 per day per inmate, that's an average savings of $1,040 for every inmate who waives the preliminary exam.

The program will save the Detroit Police Department tens of thousands of dollars each year in overtime pay. Officers, who normally would receive 4½ hours of overtime per hearing, will not have to attend waived hearings. "This program will free up officers to respond to calls on the street, where they are needed," said Chief Isaiah McKinnon.

SOURCE: Jim Dyer, "Court Reform Unclogs Docket," *The Detroit News,* June 11, 1998, C1.

a distinctive practitioner attitude regarding proper case-disposition times in each of the four courts.

The dynamics of courthouse justice are equally important in rural courts. Although we commonly associate court delay with large cities plagued by overwhelming crime rates, delay is also a problem in rural courts, where crime is low and case volume not a problem (Miller 1990). Indeed, timely disposition of cases in rural jurisdictions requires courts to move cases at the expense of the friendly atmosphere that governs community life (Fahnestock and Geiger 1993).

Case Scheduling

Waiting is one activity that people in the courthouse inevitably engage in: waiting for a defense attorney or prosecutor who is in another courtroom on another case, waiting for a vital witness to show up, waiting for the court reporter.

From an administrative perspective, the courts are extremely complex institutions. A hearing on a pretrial motion, accepting a guilty plea, or conducting a trial requires that numerous people come together at the same time and place. The disposition of a case often requires the presence of the following individuals: judge, clerk, court reporter, bailiff, defendant, prosecutor, defense attorney, police officer, victim, and witness. Depending on the procedural stage, jurors, a probation officer, a pretrial services representative, and an interpreter may also need to appear.

Many of these people have several different courts to appear in during a single day. Defense attorneys, prosecutors, the probation officer, and the interpreter may have several cases set for the same time. There can be administrative problems, too. Jurors or witnesses may be delayed in traffic. Because of an illegible address, the defendant never receives a notice. Or the jailer may inadvertently forget to include the needed defendant on the day's list. If just one person is late, the others must wait, and if

one person never shows up at all, the hearing must be rescheduled.

Efforts at Coordination

As we have noted previously, the court is actually a collection of separate and independent organizations: judge, police department, prosecutor, sheriff, clerk, and probation officer. Most of these organizations in state court are headed by elected officials, or, like the police, report to elected officials. They have their own bases of power and their own separate legal mandates. Judges thus have limited administrative control (although they are often held responsible when something goes wrong). Not surprisingly judges typically mention as a significant problem "inadequate" control by the courts of the services or functions required to support court operations (Beerhalter and Gainey 1974).

In turn, each of these separate organizations has scheduling problems. Each tries to establish a schedule of court appearances that is best for itself. But such schedules often inconvenience other agencies. For example, the sheriff may decide to bring prisoners to court only once a day. If a defendant is inadvertently left off the day's list, the case must be set for another day.

A major study of the federal courts concluded that most of the best-run district courts held regular meetings of top officials of the various organizations to iron out administrative problems. In the other, less well run courts, each agency head criticized operating procedures of the others as causing delay and inconvenience, but the agency heads never met to work out a coordinated plan (Flanders 1977). A report on the success of four state trial courts in reducing delay pointed to improved communications between the principal agencies as a chief factor. Meeting periodically, the heads of the court agencies were able to share information and work out common problems (Ryan et al. 1981).

CONCLUSION

Discussions of court delay and its consequences all too often are conducted in abstract terms. *Barker v. Wingo,* however, forces one to deal with some of the realities. The Court's opinion is clearly mindful of the fact that to interpret the

right to trial in a manner understood by the drafters of the Constitution would, in all likelihood, result in a brutal murderer being set free. It is one thing to condemn court delay in general and quite another to decide what best to do when prosecution strategy requires trying a codefendant first.

By general consensus, delay constitutes a major problem confronting the American judiciary. In terms of specifics, however, this consensus breaks down. For example, there is no agreement on how to define delay. Not all case-processing time involves delay; time needed for case preparation must be distinguished from unnecessary delay. Similarly, there is no agreement on why delay is a problem. Speedy-trial requirements were originally designed to protect the rights of the accused, but recently the concept is defined in terms of protecting the rights of society.

Barker v. Wingo and our discussion of the problem of delay show that the actual operations of the criminal courts differ greatly from official expectations. Three concepts—excessive caseloads, discretion, and the courtroom work group—attempt to explain this gap between the law in action and the law on the books. Although courts are burdened with too many cases, excessive volume of cases is at best only a partial explanation for the behavior of the criminal courts. More important is the role discretion plays in the court system, shaping the dictates of formal law to the actual cases and defendants that come to the criminal courts. The courtroom work group concept emphasizes the interactions among the key actors in court. The next three chapters will examine in greater depth how prosecutors, defense attorneys, and judges work within the courtroom work group, and why.

CRITICAL THINKING QUESTIONS

1. Take a tour of your local courthouse. How does the description match the one at the beginning of this chapter? Compare notes with other classmates; perhaps they focused on features that you did not.

2. Place yourself in the position of a felony court prosecutor. In what ways does the cooperation of other members of the courtroom work group work to your benefit? How would your answer be different if you approached the question from the vantage point of the judge or the defense attorney?

3. Of the four consequences of delay, which one do you think is the most important, which one the least important?

4. In *Barker v. Wingo* the Court stressed the legitimate reasons for the sixteen trial continuances. But is there a danger that prosecutors might illegitimately seek continuances?

 WORLD WIDE WEB RESOURCES AND EXERCISES

Web Search Terms

"Speedy trial"; "court congestion and delay"; "clerk of court"; "court reporter," "court watchers"; "court services"; "court administrator"

Useful URLs

The National Association for Court Management Web site is **http://www.nacmnet.org/**.

The Bureau of Justice Assistance stresses agency collaboration and crime prevention: **http://www.ojp.usdoj.gov/BJA/**.

FAQs from the American Translator Association can be found at **http://www.atanet.org/frequently.htm**.

The National Court Reporters Association Web site is **http://www.verbatimreporters.com/**.

FindLaw's discussion of the right to a speedy and public trial can be found at **http://caselaw.findlaw.com/data/constitution/amendment06/02.html#1**.

Uncommon URLs

Achieving success as a court reporter requires doing two things at once: **http://www.modbee.com/reports/jobs/20000325_06.html**.

These court watchers in Skokie, Illinois, even have their own Web page: **http://www.skokienet.org/cccwatc1/**.

These court watchers are concerned about gender bias: **http://www.leswhaley.org/watchers.html**.

Cook County court watchers rank the local judges: **http://www.kentlaw.edu/legal_resources/cccw/**.

Go to Courtroom 23 and take a virtual tour of a courtroom in Orange County: **http://www.ninja9.org/courtadmin/mis/courtroom_23.htm**.

To read about how this MADD chapter provides victim advocacy, go to **http://www.columbiasc.com/maddsc/MADD4.htm**.

To read about the Court Security Survey click on this link: **http://aja.ncsc.dni.us/Ctsecurity.html**.

Concerns about courtroom safety are apparent in the following article: **http://sequimgazette.com/News/CountyNews/Courtjudgesfearviole991222.html**.

The Court Reform Committee of the Colorado Bar Association can be accessed at **http://www.cobar.org/comms/crtreform/index.htm**.

Web Exercises

1. Summaries of how the amendments in the Bill of Rights have been interpreted can be found at the following site: **http://www.findlaw.com/laws/constitution**. Click on the Sixth Amendment to find a full legal discussion of the right to a speedy and public trial.

   For future reference, you might want to bookmark this section for two reasons: (1) You won't forget where the information came from, and (2) you won't have to type all those letters next time.

2. Court reform is a topic of constant conversation in legal circles. Do a search on the topic by going to Yahoo: **http://www.yahoo.com**. Then, under Search, type the phrase "court reform." By placing the phrase in quotation marks the search will be limited to hits where the two words are used together. Without the quotation marks the search engine looks for sites with either phrase ("*court*" or "*reform*").

   Select several of these discussions and ask yourself to what extent the right to speedy trial figures in the call for action. Moreover, ask yourself how court reform is viewed by various groups. Is court reform needed to protect the values of the crime control model or the values of the due process model?

3. A growing number of newspapers now have online editions. Some browsers make this service easily available under bookmarks that are built in. Click on Bookmarks and then Newsstand. Or you can go directly to the service at **http://www.naa.org/**. Click the box with the words "SELECT A STATE" inside, and then click on your state. Find the newspaper in your town (or the closest one). Also find a newspaper in a city that is similar to yours in terms of size. Compare the discussion of courts and crime in these two papers. What common elements do you find? How unique is your community?

INFOTRAC COLLEGE EDITION RESOURCES AND EXERCISES

Basic Search Terms

Discretion; court congestion and delay; court administration

InfoTrac College Edition Exercises

1. Using the search terms *court congestion and delay* and/or *speedy trial,* locate two or more articles that discuss court delay. To what extent do the articles stress law-on-the-books solutions or law-in-action reforms? Here are two possible articles: Dwight Aarons, "Getting Out of This Mess" and Major Harding, "Preparing Florida Courts for the New Millennium."

2. Using the search term *criminal justice, administration of,* select two or more articles that discuss problems in the criminal justice system. To what extent do the articles stress assembly-line justice, discretion, or the courtroom work group? To what extent does the choice of problems reflect differences summarized by the due process versus crime control models of justice discussed in Chapter 1? Here are two suggestions: Stephen Pomper, "Reasonable Doubts" and Barbara Dority, "The U.S. Criminal Injustice System."

REFERENCES

American Bar Association Commission on Minimum Standards for Criminal Justice. 1968. *Standards Relating to Speedy Trial.* Chicago: American Bar Association.

Beerhalter, Susan, and James Gainey. 1974. *Minnesota District Court Survey.* Denver: National Center for State Courts.

Blumberg, Abraham. 1970. *Criminal Justice.* New York: Quadrangle Books.

Church, Thomas. 1982. "The 'Old' and the 'New' Conventional Wisdom of Court Delay." *Justice System Journal* 7: 395–412.

———. 1985. "Examining Local Legal Culture." *American Bar Foundation Research Journal:* 449–518.

Church, Thomas, Alan Carlson, Jo-Lynne Lee, and Teresa Tan. 1978. *Justice Delayed: The Pace of Litigation in Urban Trial Courts.* Williamsburg, VA: National Center for State Courts.

Church, Thomas, and Virginia McConnell. 1978. *Pretrial Delay: A Review and Bibliography.* Williamsburg, VA: National Center for State Courts.

Clynch, Edward, and David Neubauer. 1981. "Trial Courts as Organizations: A Critique and Synthesis." *Law and Policy Quarterly* 3: 69–94.

Cole, George. 1970. "The Decision to Prosecute." *Law and Society Review* 4: 331–344.

Davis, Kenneth Culp. 1971. *Discretionary Justice: A Preliminary Inquiry.* Urbana: University of Illinois Press.

Eisenstein, James, and Herbert Jacob. 1977. *Felony Justice: An Organizational Analysis of Criminal Courts.* Boston: Little, Brown.

Fahnestock, Kathryn, and Maurice Geiger. 1993. "'We All Get Along Here': Case Flow in Rural Courts." *Judicature* 76: 258–263.

Feeley, Malcolm. 1979. *The Process Is the Punishment: Handling Cases in a Lower Criminal Court.* New York: Russell Sage Foundation.

Flanders, Steven. 1977. *Case Management and Court Management in United States District Courts.* Washington, D.C.: Federal Judicial Center.

———. 1991. "Court Administration and Diverse Judiciaries: Complementarities and Conflicts." *Justice System Journal* 15: 640–651.

Flemming, Roy, Peter Nardulli, and James Eisenstein. 1987. "The Timing of Justice in Felony Trial Courts." *Law and Policy* 9: 179–206.

Flemming, Roy, Peter Nardulli, and James Eisenstein. 1992. *The Craft of Justice: Politics and Work in Criminal Court Communities.* Philadelphia: University of Pennsylvania Press.

Friedman, Lawrence, and Robert Percival. 1976. "A Tale of Two Courts: Litigation in Alameda and San Benito Counties." *Law and Society Review* 10: 267–302.

Gallas, Geoff. 1976. "The Conventional Wisdom of State Court Administration: A Critical Assessment and an Alternative Approach." *Justice System Journal* 2: 35.

Garner, Joel. 1987. "Delay Reduction in the Federal Courts: Rule 50(b) and the Federal Speedy Trial Act of 1974." *Journal of Quantitative Criminology* 3: 229–250.

Gertz, Marc. 1977. "Influence in Court Systems: The Clerk as Interface." *Justice System Journal* 3: 30–37.

Haller, Mark. 1979. "Plea Bargaining: The Nineteenth-Century Context." *Law and Society Review* 13: 273–280.

Heumann, Milton. 1975. "A Note on Plea Bargaining and Case Pressure." *Law and Society Review* 9: 515–528.

Hoffman, Richard. 1991. "Beyond the Team: Renegotiating the Judge-Administrator Partnership." *Justice System Journal* 15: 652–666.

Jacob, Herbert. 1991. "Decision Making in Trial Courts." Pp. 211–233 in *The American Courts: A Critical Assessment,* edited by John Gates and Charles Johnson. Washington, D.C.: CQ Press.

———. 1997. "Governance by Trial Court Judges." *Law and Science Review* 31: 3–37.

LaFave, Wayne, and Austin Scott. 1972. *Criminal Law.* St. Paul, MN: West.

Lawson, Harry, and Dennis Howard. 1991. "Development of the Profession of Court Management: A History with Commentary." *Justice System Journal* 15: 580–605.

Lichtenstein, Michael. 1984. "Public Defenders: Dimensions of Cooperation." *Justice System Journal* 9: 102–110.

Mahoney, Barry, with Alexander Aikman, Pamela Casey, Victor Flango, Geoff Gallas, Thomas Henderson, Jeanne Ito, David Steelman, and Steven Weller. 1988. *Changing Times in Trial Courts.* Williamsburg, VA: National Center for State Courts.

Marvell, Thomas, and Mary Luskin. 1991. "The Impact of Speedy Trial Laws in Connecticut and North Carolina." *Justice System Journal* 14: 343–357.

Mays, G. Larry, and William Taggart. 1986. "Court Clerks, Court Administrators, and Judges: Conflict in Managing the Courts." *Journal of Criminal Justice* 14: 1–7.

Miller, Fred. 1990. "Delay in Rural Courts: It Exists, But It Can Be Reduced." *State Court Journal* 14: 23–40.

Misner, Robert. 1983. *Speedy Trial: Federal and State Practice.* Charlottesville, VA: The Michie Co.

Nardulli, Peter. 1979. "The Caseload Controversy and the Study of Criminal Courts." *Journal of Criminal Law and Criminology* 70: 89–101.

National Advisory Commission on Criminal Justice Standards and Goals. 1973. *Courts.* Washington, D.C.: U.S. Government Printing Office.

Neubauer, David. 1974. *Criminal Justice in Middle America.* Morristown, NJ: General Learning Press.

———. 1983. "Improving the Analysis and Presentation of Data on Case Processing Time." *Journal of Criminal Law and Criminology* 74: 1589–1607.

Neubauer, David, Marcia Lipetz, Mary Luskin, and John Paul Ryan. 1981. *Managing the Pace of Justice: An Evaluation of LEAA's Court Delay Reduction Programs.* Washington, D.C.: U.S. Government Printing Office.

Nimmer, Raymond. 1978. *The Nature of System Change: Reform Impact in the Criminal Courts.* Chicago: American Bar Foundation.

Ostrom, Brian, and Roger Hanson. 1999. *Efficiency and Timeliness, and Quality: A New Perspective from Nine State Criminal Trial Courts.* Williamsburg, VA: National Center for State Courts.

President's Commission on Law Enforcement and Administration of Justice. 1967. *Task Force Report: The Courts.* Washington, D.C.: U.S. Government Printing Office.

Reinkensmeyer, Marcus. 1991. "Compensation of Court Managers: Current Salaries and Related Factors." *Judicature* 75: 154–162.

Ryan, John Paul, Marcia Lipetz, Mary Luskin, and David Neubauer. 1981. "Analyzing Court Delay-Reduction Programs: Why Do Some Succeed?" *Judicature* 65: 58–75.

Saari, David. 1982. *American Court Management: Theories and Practice.* Westport, CT: Quorum Books.

Schulhofer, Stephen. 1984. "Is Plea Bargaining Inevitable?" *Harvard Law Review* 97: 1037–1107.

Stott, E. Keith. 1982. "The Judicial Executive: Toward Greater Congruence in an Emerging Profession." *Justice System Journal* 7: 152–179.

Sudnow, David. 1965. "Normal Crimes: Sociological Features of the Penal Code in a Public Defender Office." *Social Problems* 12: 254–264.

Wice, Paul. 1985. *Chaos in the Courthouse: The Inner Workings of Urban Criminal Courts.* Westport, CT: Praeger.

Wiseman, Jacqueline. 1970. *Stations of the Lost: The Treatment of Skid Row Alcoholics.* Englewood Cliffs, NJ: Prentice-Hall.

FOR FURTHER READING

Church, Thomas, and Milton Heumann. *Speedy Disposition: Monetary Incentives and Policy Reform in Criminal Courts.* Albany, NY: State University of New York Press, 1992.

Freedman, Warren. *The Constitutional Right to a Speedy and Fair Criminal Trial.* Westport, CT: Greenwood Press, 1989.

Hays, Steven, and Cole Graham, Jr., eds. *Handbook of Court Administration and Management.* New York: Marcel Dekker, 1992.

Lipetz, Marcia. "Routines and Deviations: The Strength of the Courtroom Workgroup in a Misdemeanor Court." *International Journal of the Sociology of Law* 8 (1980): 47–60.

Luskin, Mary. "Social Loafing on the Bench: The Case of Calendars and Caseloads." *Justice System Journal* 12 (1987): 177–195.

Nardulli, Peter. *The Courtroom Elite: An Organizational Perspective on Criminal Justice.* Cambridge, MA: Ballinger, 1978.

Martin, John. *Strategic Planning in the Courts: Implementation Guide.* Denver, CO: Center for Public Policy Studies, 1995.

Ryan, John Paul, Marcia Lipetz, Mary Luskin, and David Neubauer. "Analyzing Court Delay-Reduction Programs: Why Do Some Succeed?" *Judicature* 65 (1981): 58–75.

Stojkovic, Stan, John Klofas, and David Kalinich, eds. *The Administration and Management of Criminal Justice Organizations,* 3d edition. Prospect Heights, IL: Waveland Press, 1999.

Swanson, Charles, and Susette Talarico. *Court Administration: Issues and Responses.* Athens, GA: Carl Vinson Institute of Government, University of Georgia, 1987.

Vaugh, Joseph. *Pursuing Justice: The Management of the Texas Trial Courts.* Huntsville, TX: Criminal Justice Center, Sam Houston State University, 1989.

Walker, Samuel *Taming the System: The Control of Discretion in Criminal Justice, 1950–1990.* New York: Oxford University Press, 1993.

Zaffarano, Mark. "Team Leadership: Using Self-Directed Work Teams in the Courts." *Justice System Journal* 17 (1995): 357–372.

Prosecutors

Even though it might result in some "incompetent, lousy prosecutors getting off," prosecutors should be immune from civil lawsuits, argued an assistant solicitor general in the Bush administration. Granting total immunity to prosecutors will only result in "shredding the Constitution to tiny bits," countered the lawyer for Cathy Burns. At issue was the conduct of Chief Deputy Prosecutor Rick Reed of Muncie, Indiana, who had given poor legal advice to the police. As a result, Cathy Burns had been held on attempted murder charges (later dropped), partly because the prosecutor deliberately misled the trial court judge (Campbell 1990).

The difficulties the nation's highest court faced in trying to draw the line between permissible advocacy and prosecutorial misconduct underscores the influential role prosecutors play in the criminal justice system. More so than judges and defense attorneys, the prosecutor is the most powerful official in the criminal courts. From initial arrest to final disposition, how the prosecutor chooses to exercise discretion determines to a large extent which defendants are prosecuted, the type of bargains that are struck, and the severity of the sentence imposed.

This chapter discusses several factors involved in the work of the prosecutor. We begin by examining the prosecutor's role in the criminal justice system and then consider separately the structure of federal and state prosecutors. Our focus then shifts to actual courtroom behavior, looking at the various roles prosecutors play and the importance of the prosecutor's office, both large and small. But prosecutors do not work in isolation. Thus, the later parts of this chapter look at prosecutors within the context of the courtroom work group and their expanding domain in the criminal justice system. ■

ROLE OF THE PROSECUTOR

The critical importance of the prosecutor stems from the office's central position in the criminal justice system. Whereas police, defense attorneys, judges, and probation officers specialize in specific phases of the criminal justice process, the duties of the prosecutor bridge all of these areas. This means that on a daily basis the prosecutor is the only official who works with all actors of the criminal justice system. As Justice Robert Jackson once remarked, "The prosecutor has more control over life, liberty, and reputation than any other person in America."

Prosecutors stand squarely in the middle of the fragmented nonsystem of criminal justice discussed in Chapter 1. Naturally, the various actors have conflicting views about how prosecutorial discretion should be used—the police push for harsher penalties, defense attorneys for giving their clients a break, and judges to clear the docket. Like big-city mayors, prosecutors occupy uniquely powerful and highly visible positions in a complex and conflict-filled environment. Amid the diffusion of responsibility that characterizes the criminal justice system, power has increasingly been concentrated in the hands of the prosecutor (Misner 1996).

Broad Discretion

A key characteristic of the American prosecutor is broad discretion. Although the prosecutor works in the courthouse, the office of prosecutor is part of the executive branch of government. This independence from the judiciary is vital for the proper functioning of the adversary system, since prosecutors at times challenge judicial decisions. The breadth of prosecutorial power stems from a number of court cases since 1833. Typical is *People v. Wabash, St. Louis and Pacific Railway,* an 1882 decision in which the Illinois Court of Appeals stated that the district attorney "is charged by law with large discretion in prosecuting offenders against the law. He may commence public prosecution . . . and may discontinue them when, in his judgment the ends of justice are satisfied." In decisions like this one, appellate courts have allowed the modern prosecuting attorney to exercise unfettered discretion relating to initiating, conducting, and terminating prosecutions (Jacoby 1980; Albonetti 1987). Figure 6-1 provides an overview of the role of the prosecutor throughout the criminal justice process.

It is only during the trial itself that appellate courts have placed restrictions on the exercise of prosecutorial power. In the context of the adversary system, the prosecutor is expected to advocate the

| FIGURE 6-1 | Role of the Prosecutor in Steps of Criminal Procedure |

	Law on the Books	*Law in Action*
Crime	Must enforce all laws to the fullest.	The impossible legal mandate means that priorities must be established.
Arrest	Little formal role.	In major crimes may advise the police whether there is sufficient evidence of probable cause to arrest.
Initial appearance	Represents the government.	Manages the chaos in the lower court where there are many cases and little is known about the crime or the defendant.
Bail	Typically can make a bail recommendation to the judge.	More influential in setting the bail amount than the defense attorney.
Charging	Exclusive domain of the prosecutor; judges cannot order that a suspect be prosecuted.	Some prosecutors impose stringent charging standards but others defer to the police.
Preliminary hearing	Calls witnesses to establish probable cause to hold the suspect for further proceedings.	Highly successful in having defendant bound over for further proceedings.
Grand jury	Legal advisor to the grand jury and drafts indictments.	Decides which cases will be heard and dominates proceedings.
Arraignment	Formally presents the charges against the defendant to the court.	Half of the cases do not survive to this stage. By taking the case this far, the prosecutor has indicated that the defendant very likely will be found guilty.
Evidence		
Discovery	Important variations in state law regarding how much information must be disclosed prior to trial.	Informally provides trusted defense attorneys with information to induce a plea of guilty.
Suppression motions	Argues that police acted legally in searching the suspect and/or interrogating him.	Very successful in convincing judge to allow evidence to be admitted.
Plea bargaining	Other than a few Supreme Court decisions, the law says little about the DA's role in plea bargaining.	Based on normal penalties, dictates the terms under which defendants plead guilty.
Trial	Presents witnesses proving defendant guilty and urges jury to return a verdict of guilty.	Very successful in gaining convictions.
Sentencing	In many, but not all, jurisdictions, the DA can make a sentencing recommendation to the judge.	Judge is more likely to follow DA's sentencing recommendation than the defense attorney's.
Appeal	Argues before the appellate court why the lower court conviction should stand.	Wins a significant victory in fifteen of sixteen appeals.

guilt of the defendant vigorously. But the prosecutor is also a lawyer and is therefore an **officer of the court**; that is, he or she has a duty to see that justice

Officer of the court: Lawyers are officers of the court and as such must obey court rules, be truthful in court, and generally serve the needs of justice.

is done. Violations of the law must be prosecuted, but in a way that guarantees that the defendant's rights are respected and protected. In 1935 the Supreme Court spelled out the limitations imposed on prosecutors by their obligation as officers of the court: "He may prosecute with earnestness and vigor—indeed, he should do so. But while he may strike hard blows, he is not at liberty to strike foul

CASE CLOSE-UP

Burns v. Reed and Prosecutorial Misconduct

On the evening of September 2, 1982, Cathy Burns called the Muncie, Indiana, police and reported that an unknown assailant had entered her house, knocked her unconscious, and shot her two sons while they slept. The police came to view Burns as their primary suspect, even though she passed a polygraph exam and a voice stress test, submitted exculpatory handwriting samples, and repeatedly denied shooting her sons.

Speculating that Burns had multiple personality disorder, the officers decided to interview her under hypnosis, but they were concerned that hypnosis might be an unacceptable investigative technique. They therefore sought the advice of Rick Reed, chief deputy prosecutor, Delaware County, Indiana, who told the officers they could proceed with the hypnosis. Under hypnosis, Burns referred to the assailant as "Katie" and also referred to herself by that name. Based on this information, Burns was arrested. The next day, during a hearing on the DA's request for a search warrant for Burns's house, one of the officers testified that Cathy Burns had confessed to shooting her children. On this basis a search warrant was issued. Later, Burns sued Reed, proving that neither the officer nor the DA informed the judge that the "confession" was obtained under hypnosis (and therefore not admissible) or that she had consistently denied shooting her sons.

Cathy Burns spent four months in the psychiatric ward of a state hospital. During this time, she was fired from her job as a dispatcher with the Muncie police department, and the state obtained temporary custody of her sons. Medical experts concluded that she did not have multiple personalities, and she was released. The criminal charges against her were later dropped when the judge ruled that the evidence obtained under hypnosis was not admissible.

Cathy Burns filed a civil rights suit (section 1983, discussed in Chapter 2) in the U.S. District Court for the Southern District of Indiana. Before trial the Muncie police department settled for $250,000 (Campbell 1991). But Burns's suit against the DA was dismissed, holding that Reed enjoyed absolute immunity, a position upheld by the U.S. Court of Appeals for the Seventh Circuit (894 F.2d 949, 1990).

Should the DA be immune from a civil lawsuit? Yes, said the Supreme Court, arguing that district attorneys have historically enjoyed absolute immunity. But there are limits, the Court decided: Reed was liable for the legal advice he provided the police. In particular, Justice White's opinion found that there was no historical or common-law support for extending absolute immunity to the investigative or administrative aspects of the prosecutor's job. Indeed, the opinion stated that public officials should be made to hesitate when giving advice that would violate statutory or constitutional rights. Reed's position was supported by the Bush administration and thirty-six state attorney generals. They argued that without immunity, prosecutors might be intim-

---

ones. It is as much his duty to refrain from improper methods calculated to produce a wrongful conviction as it is to use every legitimate means to bring about a just one" (*Berger v. U.S.* 1935).

Moreover, the Supreme Court has held that because prosecutors are officers of the court they have an obligation to provide the defense with information that may show innocence. (Defense attorneys, on the other hand, are under no obligation to provide the prosecution with incriminating evidence.) If prosecutors conceal or misrepresent evidence, such misbehavior can lead to a reversal of the conviction (Chapter 12).

In recent years the Supreme Court has expressed repeated concern about prosecutorial misconduct. Convictions have been reversed because prosecutors were too zealous in their advocacy. But

at the same time the nation's highest tribunal has also decided that prosecutors enjoy absolute immunity from civil lawsuits when acting as courtroom advocates. However, under other conditions, prosecutors may be sued (see Case Close-Up: *Burns v. Reed* and Prosecutorial Misconduct).

Decentralization

Another characteristic of the office of prosecutor is decentralized organization. Although the American prosecutor represents the state in the prosecution of criminal cases, the office is not centralized, as it is in England and most of Europe (Flemming 1990). Instead, prosecution is highly decentralized; there are more than 8,000 federal, state, county, municipal, and township prosecution agencies.

idated by the threat of harassing lawsuits. As a result, DAs might be afraid to prosecute some well-heeled defendants.

The decision in *Burns v. Reed* reaffirmed earlier decisions upholding absolute immunity for prosecutors. In *Imbler v. Pachtman* (1976) the Court said that prosecutors are absolutely immune for their actions in initiating prosecutions and presenting the state's case. This view was based on common law, which made prosecutors immune from suits for malicious prosecution and for defamation of character. This immunity even extended to knowingly using false testimony before the grand jury and at trial. Thus, Reed could not be sued for his actions in supporting the application for a search warrant and presenting evidence at the probable cause hearing. Prosecutorial immunity extended to pretrial court proceedings. The Court, however, drew a line, holding that absolute immunity for section 1983 lawsuits did not apply to state prosecutors giving legal advice to police. In short, advising police during the investigative phase of criminal cases was not intimately associated with the judicial phase of the criminal process. (Three of the justices, however, would hold Reed liable for knowingly misleading the Court during the hearing.)

The Court revisited the issue two years later and laid down a slightly more discernable line of permissible and impermissible conduct. The Court restated that prosecutors have absolute immunity from civil damage suits for actions in connection with the traditional role of courtroom advocacy. But DAs enjoy only "qualified immunity" for other actions. The Court unanimously held that statements made in a news conference were not protected by absolute immunity. But the justices split 5-4 on whether investigative actions by the DA were subject to suit. The bare majority held, "There is a difference between the advocate's role in evaluating evidence, and interviewing witnesses as he prepares for trial . . . and the detective's role in searching for the clues and corroboration that might give him probable cause to recommend that a suspect be arrested" (*Buckley v. Fitzsimmons* 1993).

Civil actions against prosecutors will probably increase over time. Two out of three chief prosecutors in large jurisdictions report they have had one or more civil lawsuits filed against them (DeFrances, Smith, and van der Does 1996). One consequence is that about a third of prosecutors' offices have at least one lawyer who has personal liability insurance for protection in civil lawsuits related to prosecutorial duties.

 The Pittsburgh Post Gazette's award-winning series "Win at All Costs" can be accessed at **http://www.post-gazette.com/win/**.

The Chicago Tribune ran a series "Trial&Error" on how prosecutors violate their oath by hiding evidence in homicide cases: **http://www.chicagotribune.com/news/nationworld/ws/0,1246,21398,00.html**.

For an up-to-date list of Web links, go to **http://www.wadsworth.com/product/0534563406s**.

Commensurate with the nation's often confusing dual court system, separate prosecutors are found in both federal and state courts. The structure, however, is not parallel with court structure, that is, each court does not have attached to it a specific prosecutor. District attorneys, for example, often conduct the trial in the trial court of general jurisdiction and then appeal through both layers of state courts and on rare occasion even to the U.S. Supreme Court (a federal judicial body). Moreover, different prosecutors' offices may handle the same case; sometimes the city attorney conducts the preliminary stages of a felony case in the lower courts and the district attorney prosecutes in the trial court of general jurisdiction.

Figure 6-2 provides a rough overview of typical state and federal prosecutorial structure. Be aware, however, that the apparent hierarchy of prosecutorial structure is an illusion; in the federal courts the U.S. attorneys enjoy considerable autonomy from the U.S. Justice Department, and in the states, local district attorneys are totally separate from state attorney generals. We will begin with prosecution in federal courts and then turn to the more complex realities of state prosecutions.

PROSECUTION IN FEDERAL COURTS

Prosecutions in federal courts are conducted by the U.S. Department of Justice. Billed as the world's largest law firm, the Department of Justice repre-

FIGURE 6-2 Overview of Prosecutors in the Dual Court System

Federal	*State*
Solicitor general • Represents the U.S. government before the U.S. Supreme Court in all appeals of federal criminal cases. • Often appears as amicus in appeals involving state criminal convictions.	**Attorney general** • Chief legal officer of the state. • Civil duties more extensive than criminal. • Has limited authority in criminal prosecutions.
Criminal division • Prosecutes a few nationally significant criminal cases. • Exercises nominal supervision over U.S. attorneys.	**Chief prosecutor** • Has great autonomy in prosecuting felony cases. • Typically argues cases on appeal.
U.S. attorney • Prosecutes the vast majority of criminal cases in federal courts. • Enjoys great autonomy in actions.	**Local prosecutor** • Handles preliminary stages of felony cases. • Prosecutes the large volume of cases in the lower court.

sents the U.S. government in all legal matters not specifically delegated to other agencies. The department is headed by the **U.S. attorney general**, who is a member of the president's cabinet. Top-level officials are presidential appointees who reflect the views of the administration on important policy issues. Day-to-day activities are carried out by a large cadre of career lawyers who enjoy civil service protection and have, over the years, developed invaluable expertise in areas of law. In the words of a twenty-year veteran of the department, "Both civil service attorneys and political appointees influence policy. Wise policy requires cooperation between the two groups" (Landsberg 1993, 276).

The Department of Justice has grown tremendously in recent years. As a direct result of the nation's continuing focus on crime as a major political issue, the Justice Department quadrupled in size from 1981 to 1993 (McGee and Duffy 1997). The Department of Justice is a sprawling series of bureaucracies organized into four major divisions:

• Executive Direction and Management Offices, which include the solicitor general, management oversight, and legislative liaison.

• Litigation Organization, which handles courtroom matters. The major divisions are antitrust, civil, civil rights, criminal, environment, tax, and U.S. attorneys.

• Investigatory and Law Enforcement Offices, which house the FBI, Drug Enforcement Administration (DEA), the U.S. Marshals Service, and the Federal Bureau of Prisons.

• Legal and Policy Office, which includes Immigration and Naturalization Service and Office of Justice Programs, which oversees Bureau of Justice Assistance and other entities.

In terms of prosecution, three entities—solicitor general, criminal division, and U.S. attorneys—are particularly important. We will examine them from the top down, although, as we shall see, there is no hierarchy and considerable autonomy. In addition, in rare situations, federal investigations and prosecutions are conducted by an independent counsel (see Controversy: Does the Federal Government Need an Independent Counsel?).

U.S. attorney general: Head of the Department of Justice; nominated by the president and confirmed by the Senate.

To learn more about the vast bureaucracies included in the U.S. Department of Justice, click on **http://www.usdoj.gov/**.

For an up-to-date list of Web links, go to **http://www.wadsworth.com/product/0534563406s**.

CONTROVERSY

Does the Federal Government Need an Independent Counsel?

The creation of the independent counsel grew out of the Watergate scandal. As evidence mounted that persons high in the Nixon White House were linked to the break-in of the Democratic national headquarters, Attorney General Elliot Richardson resigned rather than fire special prosecutor Archibald Cox, who had demanded secret White House tapes. This act triggered a series of events known as the "Saturday Night Massacre," in which top Justice Department officials resigned. Eventually the tapes were released, impeachment proceedings were instigated, and President Nixon resigned in disgrace, thus avoiding a constitutional crisis.

The Watergate scandal led to public perceptions that high-level administrators were covering up criminal wrongdoing, and Congress responded in 1978 by passing a law creating the independent counsel. The law allows the U.S. attorney general to request an independent counsel to investigate allegations of wrongdoing by high-ranking executive branch officials. The independent counsel is appointed by a special three-judge panel of the D.C. Court of Appeals and is independent of the Justice Department. Congressional legislation created the independent counsel for a five-year period, after which Congress must renew the law.

Every presidential administration, except the Clinton presidency, has opposed the bill and the Department of Justice remains steadfastly opposed, contending that its career officials can conduct independent investigations of suspected criminal wrongdoing free of partisan pressure. The Court, however, has upheld the constitutionality of the law against a challenge that the law is a usurpation of executive authority (*Morrison v. Olson* 1988).

A significant proportion of Congress has viewed the law as symbolically important "to ensure public confidence in unbiased law enforcement." The independent counsel law reflects an institutionalized distrust among Washington elites. Thus Kathy Harringer (1992, 89) concludes that the creation of the independent counsel was merely a symbolic act that allows elected officials to appear to be doing something while avoiding responsibility.

From the beginning the independent counsel law operated under a partisan cloud. In 1992 Republicans in Congress refused to renew the law. They were furious about the independent counsel investigation of the Iran-Contra affair and especially angry about the indictment of former Defense Secretary Caspar Weinberger for allegedly withholding information from Congress. In essence, Republicans saw the independent counsel law as a way for Democrats out of power to harass incumbent Republicans.

This political calculus was, of course, quickly reversed when Democratic Bill Clinton was elected president. In 1994, Congress passed, and the president signed, a new and amended independent counsel law. Support for renewing the law grew as Republicans became interested in investigating Clinton's ties to the Whitewater Development Company (a failed Arkansas land company). Eventually Kenneth Starr was appointed independent counsel. Democrats accused independent counsel Kenneth Starr of abusing his authority by extending his probe into other alleged misdeeds that had no connection to Whitewater. Indeed, Starr's probed lasted over six years and cost approximately $50 million.

Although the mass public is largely uninterested in cries of scandal in Washington, the Starr probe did uncover something that greatly interested the American public: a spicy sex scandal in the White House. Revelations of a sexual encounter between President Clinton and White House intern Monica Lewinsky eventually led Starr to send an impeachment referral to the House of Representatives. The House did vote articles of impeachment, but the Senate refused to convict.

Beyond the inherently partisan debate over the creation of the independent counsel, genuine issues exist. Critics charge that independent counsels have improperly been given unchecked power. Unlike other prosecutors, independent counsels have no restraint of time or money. Even what turn out to be trivial charges can result in lengthy investigations (Roberts and Doss 1997). Moreover, independent counsels have rarely gained convictions against high-ranking federal officials (the seeming target of the original law). For example, independent counsel Donald Smaltz indicated Agriculture Secretary Mike Espy of accepting bribes, but the jury acquitted.

On June 30, 1999 Congress allowed the independent counsel law to expire. Now the Justice Department will investigate allegations of wrongdoing. If the

(continued on following page)

attorney general determines that the department cannot conduct an impartial investigation, then the attorney general (not a three-judge court) will appoint an outside counsel.

What do you think? Some suggest that the nation needs an independent counsel because the federal government cannot be counted on to vigorously investigate wrongdoing by top officials. Others counter that the independent counsel law gave investigators unlimited, unchecked power to go after officials suspected of wrongdoing.

 The Office of the Independent Counsel has a Web site. Go to **http://www.oicstarr.com/** to read the documents in the case against President Bill Clinton.

For an up-to-date list of Web links, go to **http://www.wadsworth.com/product/0534563406s**.

 To continue the debate, see Julie O'Sullivan, "The Independent Counsel Statute: Bad Law, Bad Policy" and Lewis Hapham, "Hide-and-Go-Seek."

Solicitor General

The solicitor general is the third-ranking official in the Justice Department. The solicitor general's principal task is to represent the executive branch in the Supreme Court. But at the same time the justices depend on the **solicitor general** to look beyond the government's narrow interest. Because of the solicitor general's dual responsibility to the judicial and executive branches, the officeholder is sometimes called the Tenth Justice, an informal title that underlines the special relationship with the Supreme Court (Caplan 1988; Meinhold and Shull 1993). The office of the solicitor general is in essence a small, elite, very influential law firm whose client is the U.S. government. The staff consists of twenty-three of the most able attorneys found anywhere.

As the representative of the United States in litigation before the Supreme Court, the solicitor general's office argues all government cases before the Court. For example, the assistant solicitor general argued the major issues in *Burns v. Reed*. But the influence of the office extends further.

Roughly half the work of the solicitor general's office involves coordinating appeals by the federal government. With few exceptions, all governmental agencies must first receive authorization from the solicitor general to appeal an adverse lower-court ruling to the Supreme Court. The office requests Supreme Court review only in cases with a high degree of policy significance and in which the gov-

ernment has a reasonable legal argument. Thus, the solicitor general rejects many cases from governmental agencies because they are not viewed as "cert. worthy" (Puro 1981). In turn the solicitor general has a high rate of success in petitioning the Supreme Court and in winning cases argued on their merits.

Another of the solicitor general's principal functions is to decide when the government will appear as an amicus curiae to urge executive branch policies on the courts in cases in which the federal government is not a direct party (Segal 1988, 1990). By Supreme Court rule, the solicitor general can file an *amicus curiae* ("friend of the court") brief without the permission of the parties to the suit, and the solicitor general is the only amicus regularly given time to argue the case before the Court. Thus, in *Burns v. Reed* the Bush administration made its position known through arguments by an assistant solicitor general, even though the federal government was not a direct party to the case.

 Here is the official Web site of the Office of the Solicitor General, the government's top lawyer before the U.S. Supreme Court: **http://www.usdoj.gov/osg/**.

For an up-to-date list of Web links, go to **http://www.wadsworth.com/product/0534563406s**.

Criminal Division of the Justice Department

The criminal division formulates criminal law enforcement policies over all federal criminal cases, except those specifically assigned to other divisions.

Solicitor general: Third-ranking official in the U.S. Department of Justice who conducts and supervises government litigation in the Supreme Court.

EXHIBIT 6-1 Criminal Division of the U.S. Department of Justice (Selected Units)

Appellate section prepares draft briefs and makes recommendations to the solicitor general as to whether further review of adverse decisions in the district and courts of appeals is necessary. Also argues cases in the courts of appeals.

Asset Forfeiture/Money Laundering section provides centralized management for the asset forfeiture program. The section works with the entire spectrum of law enforcement and regulatory agencies using an interagency, interdisciplinary, and international approach.

Capital Case unit was recently created to oversee the department's handling of capital offenses.

Child Exploitation and Obscenity prosecutes violators of federal criminal statutes relating to child support, sexual exploitation of minors, and obscenity. Includes a subunit devoted to most wanted deadbeat parents.

Computer Crime and Intellectual Property focuses on cybercrime issues.

Executive Office for Organized Crime Drug Enforcement Task Force focuses on the disruption and dismantling of major drug trafficking organizations.

Fraud directs and coordinates the federal effort against fraud and white-collar crime, focusing primarily on complex frauds that involve multidistrict and internal activities, financial institutions, government programs, and so on. The largest component of the criminal division.

Geographic Information System (GIS) works with local police departments on spatial analysis of crime.

Internal Security supervises the prosecution of cases affecting national security, foreign relations, and the export of military and strategic commodities and technology including matters like espionage, sabotage, neutrality, and atomic energy.

International Criminal Investigative Training Assistance Program provides police training to Latin American countries.

Narcotics and Dangerous Drugs section investigates and prosecutes complex, multidefendant narcotics and related money-laundering cases.

Office of Enforcement Operations oversees the use of the sophisticated investigative tools including electronic surveillance.

Office of International Affairs supports government attorneys, both federal and state, regarding questions of foreign and international law.

Office of Policy and Legislation analyzes policy and management issues relating to criminal justice enforcement.

Office of Special Investigation detects and investigates individuals who took part in Nazi-sponsored acts of persecution abroad before and during World War II.

Office of Overseas Professional Development, Assistance, and Training coordinates the training of judges and prosecutors abroad, particularly in Latin America and in Eastern Europe.

Organized Crime and Racketeering coordinates the Justice Department's program to combat organized crime. The principal enforcement efforts are directed toward traditional groups, such as La Cosa Nostra families, and emerging groups from Asia, Europe, and Russia.

Public Integrity oversees the federal effort to combat corruption through the prosecution of elected and appointed public officials at all levels of government.

Terrorism and Violent Crime investigates and prosecutes federal offenses relating to international terrorism incidents that affect U.S. interests. The section also oversees the prosecution of domestic terrorism offenses under federal jurisdiction.

The criminal division, and the ninety-three U.S. attorneys, have the responsibility for overseeing criminal matters under the more than 900 statutes as well as certain civil litigation. Exhibit 6-1 provides an overview of the numerous units within the criminal division, underscoring the complexities of federal prosecution both nationally and internationally. Essentially, the criminal division attorneys prosecute many nationally significant cases, for example, the Unabomber and the Oklahoma City bombing. Through the years the criminal division has also received extensive press coverage for cases involving corrupt government officials, alleged members of organized crime, and major drug-dealing enterprises.

For an update on the organization chart of the criminal division of the Justice Department click on the following: **http://www.usdoj.gov/dojorg.htm**.

For an up-to-date list of Web links, go to **http://www.wadsworth.com/product/0534563406s**.

U.S. Attorneys

The **U.S. attorneys** serve as the nation's principal litigators under the direction of the attorney general. Ninety-three U.S. attorneys are stationed throughout the United States, Puerto Rico, the Virgin Islands, Guam, and the Northern Mariana Islands. U.S. attorneys are appointed by, and serve at the discretion of, the president, with advice and consent of the Senate. One U.S. attorney is assigned to each of the judicial districts, with the exception of Guam and the Northern Mariana Islands, where one serves in both districts. Each U.S. attorney is the chief federal law enforcement officer of the United States within his or her particular jurisdiction. The 93 U.S. attorneys are assisted by 4,700 assistant U.S. attorneys.

U.S. attorneys conduct most of the trial work in which the U.S. attorney is a party. They have three statutory responsibilities:

- the prosecution of criminal cases brought by the federal government,
- the initiation and defense of civil cases in which the United States is a party, and
- the collection of certain debts owed the federal government.

The volume of litigation varies considerably between the districts. U.S. attorneys along the Mexican border, for example, initiate a large number of drug prosecutions. Nonetheless, each district handles a mixture of simple and complex litigation.

U.S. attorneys exercise wide discretion in the use of their resources to further the priorities of the local jurisdictions and needs of their communities. According to the U.S. Department of Justice Web site: "United States Attorneys have been delegated, and will continue to be delegated, full authority and control in the areas of personnel management, financial management, and procurement." Although the criminal division supervises all federal prosecutions, in practice U.S. attorneys enjoy considerable autonomy. This is partly because of tradition—U.S. attorneys were not placed under the direction of the attorney general until 1870, when the Department

of Justice was created. Another factor is remoteness from Washington, D.C.—the ninety-three U.S. attorneys are widely dispersed geographically. The selection process also plays a role. Many U.S. attorneys owe their appointments primarily to persons other than the attorney general or in some cases even the president (Bell 1993). Thus, in the vast majority of cases the decisions are made by U.S. attorneys scattered across the nation rather than the central office based in Washington, D.C.

To locate the Web page of the U.S. attorney in your area, go to the following address: **http://www. usdoj.gov/usao/eousa/usa_websites.html**.

For an up-to-date list of Web links, go to **http://www.wadsworth.com/product/0534563406s**.

PROSECUTION IN STATE COURTS

Decentralization and local autonomy characterize prosecution in state courts. The result is divided responsibility, with state prosecution authority typically found in three separate offices: state, county (or district), and local. At times, the relationship among these separate agencies is marked by competition; various prosecutors jockey to be the first to prosecute a notorious defendant. The existence of separate local prosecutorial agencies also often results in a lack of coordination on common problems. Because most major metropolitan areas encompass numerous counties and cities, gaps in jurisdiction allow sophisticated and organized criminal conspiracies to operate across several boundaries. In response to such problems, some areas have added to the jurisdictional maze by creating special prosecutors' offices to focus on organized crime in designated substantive areas.

We will examine the three major state prosecutors from top down, but bear in mind that each office is separate and not necessarily subject to the dictates of the office above it.

State Attorney General

The position of attorney general, the state's chief legal officer, is typically spelled out in the state's constitution. Among the most important duties are providing legal advice to other state agencies and

U.S. attorneys: Officials responsible for the prosecution of crimes that violate the laws of the United States; appointed by the president and assigned to a U.S. district court.

Florida v. Smith

William Kennedy Smith is accused of rape in the Kennedy family compound in West Palm Beach, Florida. She testifies that "he raped me and I was yelling no." He counters: "How do you defend yourself from someone who says the word *rape* over and over again?" While watching the video, keep the following questions in mind:

1. How does the defense attorney use cross-examination to establish his case?
2. Should the judge have admitted into evidence the testimony of three women who claim they also were forced to have sex with the defendant?
3. What role does the credibility of the witnesses play in the final verdict?
4. How did the defendant's celebrity status help him? Hurt him?

representing the state in court when state actions are challenged. In recent years, attorney generals have focused on their civil responsibilities by emphasizing their role in protecting consumers from various forms of fraud. Thus the typical homepage of the attorney general of a state proclaims how many individual consumer complaints are handled annually (many of which involve motor vehicles and home repair fraud). Many state attorney generals have also been visible in filing consumer lawsuits against major U.S. businesses. The biggest of all involves the suits by over thirty states against the tobacco industry.

State attorney generals have chosen to emphasize their civil responsibilities because they typically have limited authority over criminal matters. Local autonomy is a key characteristic of the office of prosecutor. Generally, state officials do not monitor the activities of local prosecutors. Although the **state attorney general** is the state's chief law enforcement official, his or her authority over local criminal procedures is quite limited. Indeed, in a handful of states, the attorney general has no legal authority to

initiate or intervene in local prosecutions. In other states, this authority is limited to extreme situations. Thus, the state attorney general exercises virtually no control or supervision over chief prosecutors at the county level. This lack of supervisory power, coupled with the decentralization of the office, means that local prosecutors enjoy almost total autonomy. Only the local voters have the power to evaluate the prosecutor's performance, by means of their votes.

 To find the homepage of your state attorney general click on **http://www.naag.org/index2.html**, and then go to "About Your Attorney General." Ask yourself: What is the balance in workload between civil and criminal matters?

For an up-to-date list of Web links, go to **http://www.wadsworth.com/product/0534563406s**.

Chief Prosecutor

The American prosecutor has few direct parallels elsewhere in the world (Flemming 1990). Compared to their counterparts in England and Europe, American prosecutors enjoy unmatched independence and discretionary powers (Albonetti 1987).

Variously called the district attorney, county attorney, or prosecuting attorney (Figure 6-3), the **prosecutor** is the chief law enforcement official of the community. Altogether there are 2,350 chief prosecutors across the nation, employing a staff of 65,000. Structure and workload differ according to the size of the population. The typical office serves a population of 30,000 people, with 157 adult felony arrests in the district with a staff of 8 and a budget of $226,000. But deviations are readily apparent. Big cities (over 500,000) employ a staff of 179 who prosecute 5,964 felonies a year with a budget of $8,500,000. The great majority of the nation's prosecutors' offices, however, are small ones (DeFrances, Smith, and van der Does 1996). Frequently, rural prosecutors are part-time officials who also engage in private law practice. The office has a staff of 4, a caseload of 29 felonies a year, and a budget of $75,000 (Table 6-1 on page 149).

State attorney general: The chief legal officer of a state, representing that state in civil, and under certain circumstances, criminal cases.

Prosecutor: A public official who represents the state in a criminal action.

| FIGURE 6-3 | Chief Prosecutors Who Handle Felony Cases in State Courts |

Title	States
District attorney	Alabama, California, Colorado, Georgia, Kansas, Louisiana, Maine, Massachusetts, Mississippi, Nevada, New Mexico, New York, North Carolina, Oklahoma, Oregon, Pennsylvania, Texas, Wisconsin, Wyoming
County attorney	Arizona, Iowa, Kansas, Minnesota, Montana, Nebraska, New Hampshire, Texas, Utah
State's attorney	Connecticut, Florida, Illinois, Maryland, North Dakota, South Dakota, Vermont
Prosecuting attorney	Arkansas, Hawaii, Idaho, Indiana, Michigan, Missouri, Ohio, Washington, West Virginia
Commonwealth attorney	Kentucky, Virginia
County prosecutor	New Jersey
District attorney general	Tennessee
County and prosecuting attorney	Wyoming
Solicitor	South Carolina
Circuit attorney	Missouri (City of St. Louis)
No local prosecutor	Alaska, Delaware, Rhode Island

Kansas, Missouri, Texas, and Wyoming employ varying names depending on the jurisdiction.

SOURCE: Carol DeFrances, Steven Smith, and Louise van der Does, "Prosecutors in State Courts, 1994." *Bulletin* (Washington, D.C.: Bureau of Justice Statistics, National Institute of Justice, 1996).

Elections are a key characteristic of the office of prosecutor, as 95 percent of chief prosecutors are locally elected officials who serve four-year terms. The exceptions are Alaska, Connecticut, Delaware, the District of Columbia, New Jersey, and Rhode Island, where chief prosecutors are either appointed or are members of the state attorney general's office.

Because of elections, the work of the American prosecutor is deeply set within the larger political process (Worden 1990). For a lawyer interested in a political career, the prosecutor's office offers a launching pad. Indeed, prosecutors "virtually own the politically potent symbols of 'law and order' politics" (Flemming, Nardulli, and Eisenstein 1992). Numerous governmental officials—governors, judges, and legislators—began their careers as crusading prosecutors (Schlesinger 1966). Most prosecutors, however, do not plan to enter politics. Studies in Wisconsin and Kentucky, for example, indicated that more than half of the prosecutors

had no further political ambitions. They viewed the office as useful for gaining visibility before establishing a private law practice (Jacob 1966; Engstrom 1971). In Wisconsin district attorneys are remaining in office longer but rarely use the position as a springboard for other partisan offices. Instead, former district attorneys practice private law or assume other positions in the public sector—judge primarily (Jones 1994).

The tremendous power of the prosecutor means that political parties are very interested in controlling the office. The chief prosecutor has numerous opportunities for patronage. In some communities, partisan considerations play a large role in the hiring of assistant district attorneys (Eisenstein, Flemming, and Nardulli 1988). Political parties may also want one of their own serving as district attorney in order to guarantee that their affairs will not be closely scrutinized and to act as a vehicle for harassing the opposition.

TABLE 6-1 Profile of Chief Prosecutors' Offices

	All Offices	Population over 500,000	Population under 500,000 (full-time)	Part-time Office
Number of offices	2,343	127	1,533	683
Population served	29,480	724,418	43,812	16,196
Adult felony arrests	157	5,964	264	29
Staff size	8	179	10	4
Budget	$226,000	$8,500,000	$255,000	$75,000
Criminal cases closed	985	23,389	1,201	586
Percent convicted	87%	75%	87%	88%
DNA evidence used	42%	95%	47%	23%
Unavailability of prosecution witness	44%	82%	50%	22%
Speedy trial restrictions	13%	36%	16%	0%

SOURCE: Carol DeFrances, Steven Smith, and Louise van der Does. "Prosecutors in State Courts, 1994." *Bulletin* (Washington, D.C.: Bureau of Justice Statistics, National Institute of Justice, 1996).

 Here are three prosecutors' offices with informative Web sites:

Marion County (Indiana): **http://www.ci. indianapolis.in.us/pros/index.htm**

San Angelo (Texas): **http://www.tgcl.co. tom-green.tx.us/datty/**

Mercer County (New Jersey): **http://www. mercerpros-nj.com/**

For an up-to-date list of Web links, go to **http:// www.wadsworth.com/product/0534563406s**.

Local Prosecutor

Variously called city attorneys, solicitors, or the like, little is known about the activities of local prosecutors, although recent estimates place their numbers at about 5,700. In some jurisdictions **local prosecutors** are responsible for the preliminary stages of felony cases as they are processed in the lower courts. In these jurisdictions, it is the local prosecutor (not the chief prosecutor) who represents the government at the initial appearance, argues bond amounts, and conducts the preliminary hearing. These decisions may have important consequences for later stages of the felony prosecution, but the chief prosecutor's office has no direct control over these matters.

Local prosecutors, however, are primarily responsible for processing the large volume of minor criminal offenses disposed of in the lower courts. Public drunkenness, petty theft, disorderly conduct, and minor assaults are the staple of these judicial bodies (Chapter 18).

THE PROSECUTOR AT WORK

The word *lawyer* usually evokes the image of someone arguing before a jury. Until the mid-twentieth century, this was a good description. The most famous lawyers of their day—Clarence Darrow, who argued the Scopes "monkey trial" in 1925, for example—were skilled trial orators. But times have changed. The majority of American lawyers never try a case (Heinz and Laumann 1982). However, the prosecutor's office is one place where trials are still

Local prosecutors: General term for lawyers who represent local governments (cities and counties, for example) in the lower courts; often called city attorneys or solicitors.

an important part of what lawyers do. The activities of American lawyers, particularly prosecutors, can be conveniently divided into five categories: fighting, negotiating, drafting, counseling, and administering (Neubauer 1997).

Fighting

A trial lawyer must be a fighter who likes to question witnesses, object to other lawyers' questions, and appeal to juries. A criminal case does not arrive in the prosecutor's office neatly packaged and awaiting the summoning of a jury. One of the most vital skills of an attorney is taking a disorganized case and preparing it for trial. Such case preparation and the eventual trial involve numerous tactical decisions. Will this person make a good witness? How can we show the jury the strongest points of the case while minimizing the weaknesses? What type of defense is the opposition likely to mount, and how can it be countered? How can we introduce a vital piece of evidence on the borderline of admissibility? A working knowledge of the rules of evidence is the starting point. But perhaps equally important is insight into the psychological and sociological dynamics of juries, judges, defendants, and witnesses. What looks like an unbeatable case to a law professor may appear to be a difficult one to a seasoned trial prosecutor.

Negotiating

Only a handful of cases are ever tried; the rest are "pled out" or dismissed. One of the most important tasks of the prosecutor is to **negotiate** with the opposition. Reputation as a trial attorney is an important factor in negotiations. If you consider the skills necessary for artful and effective negotiation, you can see why poor trial attorneys tend to make poor negotiators as well. Like trial work, negotiating requires numerous tactical decisions. Based on the type of case and the nature of the defense attorney, would it be best to divulge the prosecutor's whole case, in the hope of inducing a guilty plea? Or would it be better to play it close to the vest and tell the opposition nothing? During negotiations, attorneys must constantly reevaluate the weaknesses of their own case and the strengths of the opposition's. For example, a victim's reluctance to testify may necessitate a lesser sentence.

Drafting

Courts, as stressed in Chapter 5, are paper bureaucracies. No case can advance from one step to the next without the proper paperwork. The clerk of the court is primarily responsible for keeping these papers in order, but the prosecutor is charged with drafting—preparing—these vital documents. Search warrants, for example, are often prepared by the prosecutor's office. When charges are filed, the prosecutor must specify the section of the criminal code that the defendant has allegedly violated. The prosecutor must also prepare motions involving defense allegations that evidence was improperly seized or that a confession was coerced. Most of the prosecutor's legal research involves preparing such motions and **briefs** (the technical term for the form in which written arguments are presented to the court).

At the close of the trial, the prosecutor is involved in the preparation of the final charge to the jury, and if a conviction is appealed, the prosecutor must prepare and argue before the appellate court. If documents are not properly prepared, the case may be irretrievably lost, or much extra effort may have to be expended later to remedy the initial mistake.

Counseling

A critical aspect of a lawyer's responsibility is advising and counseling clients. Just as patients judge doctors by their bedside manner, lawyers are often measured by their friendly, courteous, and understanding relationship with their clients. In the prosecutor's case, the counseling dimension is complicated by the fact that the prosecutor's client is the state. Nonetheless, prosecutors spend part of their time talking to victims, witnesses, and police officers. Before trial, attorneys prepare witnesses by going over the questions to be asked, advising them how to testify, and telling them of matters to be avoided. A poorly coached witness can easily cause an acquittal or a hung jury.

Negotiate: Discuss, arrange, or bargain about a settlement or compromise between the parties of a lawsuit.

Brief: A written statement submitted by the attorney arguing a case in court. It states the facts of the case, presents legal arguments in support of the moving party, and cites applicable law.

Prosecutors also counsel victims of crimes about why a plea bargain was negotiated or why the charges were dropped. A victim may want to prosecute to the fullest, but the prosecutor may believe that no crime was committed. Prosecutors must also advise police about why a case is weak, what additional evidence is needed, and so on.

Administering

Like the other members of the courtroom team, prosecutors handle a large volume of cases (Jacoby 1980). A major concern of prosecutors is administration—keeping the cases moving. In doing so, they carry out a number of important administrative responsibilities. In some jurisdictions, prosecutors are responsible for setting dates for trial; as the case approaches trial, they must make sure subpoenas are issued for all the witnesses they plan to call. Faced with numerous cases, district attorneys and their top aides must decide how to allocate resources. For example, should some attorneys be shifted from an existing section to make room for a new division specializing in child abuse cases?

In the largest offices, simply keeping the bureaucracy running—hiring new assistants, promoting assistants, preparing and fighting for the budget—consumes major amounts of time. In a survey of prosecutors, workload problems were ranked most significant, followed by prison crowding and jail crowding. These three problems reflect an unfortunate combination of too many criminals and too few staff members to handle them (McEwen 1995).

THE PROSECUTOR'S OFFICE AT WORK

In the courtroom one's attention normally gravitates toward the individual lawyers as they call witnesses, ask questions, and cross-examine the opponent's witnesses. These individual activities, however, must be understood within the larger context in which they occur. Although there are a large number of small prosecutors' offices, the bulk of prosecution occurs in offices with dozens to hundreds of assistants. Exhibit 6-2 provides an overview of the complexities of the nation's largest district attorney's office, Los Angeles County. Clearly, prosecution involves more than the acts of individual and isolated lawyers.

Assistant District Attorneys

The day-to-day work of the prosecutor's office is executed by over 30,000 assistant district attorneys. The recruiting, training, socializing, and supervising of these assistants have a major bearing on the exercise of prosecutorial power and discretion.

Most assistant district attorneys (sometimes called deputy district attorneys) are hired immediately after graduation from law school or after a short time in private practice. Usually, they have attended local law schools rather than the nation's most prestigious law schools (whose graduates prefer higher-status, better-paying jobs in civil practice). In the past, many prosecutors hired assistants on the basis of party affiliation and the recommendations of ward leaders and elected officials. Increasingly, however, greater stress is being placed on merit selection, a trend exemplified by the Los Angeles prosecutor's office—the nation's largest, with more than 1,000 lawyers—where hiring is done on a civil service basis.

The turnover rate among assistant district attorneys is high. Most serve an average of two to four years before entering private practice. Low salaries are one reason for the high turnover. Although starting salaries are generally competitive with those in private law offices, the salary levels after a few years are markedly lower. The nature of the office is another reason for the high turnover. Prosecutors' offices present numerous openings for assistants, but only a few chiefs are needed. After a couple of years on the job, assistant DAs have learned about all they will learn—there are only a few ways to prosecute a burglary case and only a few possible defenses to counter. Assistants looking for new challenges either turn for promotion to an elite, specialized unit within the office (armed robbery or murder, for example), where trials are more numerous and more demanding, or they enter private practice. Finally, turnover is a product of assistants growing tired of the job. With its never-ending stream of society's losers, the criminal courthouse can become a depressing place to work (see A Day in Court: "The Good Fight Takes Its Toll" on page 154). Moreover, regular trial work creates numerous physical and psychological pressures. In the words of a former New Orleans prosecutor, "The average trial assistant leaves work every day with a huge stack of

EXHIBIT 6-2   The Nation's Largest DA's Office

This exhibit is a slightly condensed version of the home-page of the Los Angeles County district attorney's office (http://da.co.la.ca.us/oview.htm).

The Los Angeles County district attorney's office handles a staggering workload. Approximately 70,000 felonies, 280,000 misdemeanors, and 650,000 family support cases—that's 1,000,000 cases—are being handled by the 988 prosecutors in the office annually. The following are brief descriptions of the bureaus, special units, and programs which constitute the Los Angeles County District Attorney's Office.

A.C.T. (Abolish Chronic Truancy) Places prosecutors in the schools to work with administrators, teachers, parents, and students to intervene at the very beginning of the truancy cycle.

Auto Insurance Fraud A special group of expert prosecutors works with investigators to combat this multi-million dollar problem.

Bad Check Enforcement Program This very successful program (paid for by bad check writers) obtains payment on bad checks and also teaches people how to handle their personal finances.

C.A.P.O.S. (Crimes Against Peace Officers Section) Provides attorneys to prosecute crimes against peace officers.

Child Abduction This special unit is in touch with agencies across the country and the world to obtain the return of children illegally taken by noncustodial parents.

Child Abuse Prosecutors are specially trained to handle these very sensitive cases.

Consumer Protection Attorneys prosecute crimes in the marketplace, seeking to assure that citizens will get a dollar's value for a dollar spent. A special section deals with the growing problem of elder abuse.

Crime Prevention Programs advise citizens on how to avoid becoming crime victims and keep them abreast of current laws. Early intervention programs for youth address truancy, gangs, and drugs.

Election Code Violations are a priority because the sanctity of the ballot box is essential in a democracy.

Environmental Toxic waste violators and others who endanger the environment face felony prosecution.

Family Support Establishes paternity for children born out of wedlock and enforces the rights of all children to their legally entitled support, including medical coverage.

Family Violence Prosecutors handle this hidden crime, help victims to obtain restraining orders, and provide referrals to appropriate social agencies for further help.

Gang Leaders and their followers are prosecuted by the Hardcore Gang Unit, which works with local law enforcement to investigate serious gang-related crimes.

Grand Jury Presentations by the District Attorney involve complex criminal cases and sensitive cases, such as child abuse, for which the Grand Jury may be the appropriate forum.

papers under his arm. The grind can really wear you down. There's just too much work" (Perlstein 1990).

Although many assistants view their job as a brief waystation toward a more lucrative and more varied private practice, some see the position as a permanent career position. In Wisconsin the average tenure is about six years, and perhaps just as importantly, some assistants advance to become the elected DA in their county, run for the position in a neighboring county, or make other lateral moves (Jones 1994).

Learning the Job

Law schools provide an overview of major areas of the law—criminal law, criminal procedure, torts, and contracts, to name just a few. But they give their students very little exposure to how law is actually practiced. Thus, the typical assistant DA, having just passed the bar examination, comes to the job having little familiarity with the day-to-day realities of the profession. Here is how one lawyer described his first days on the job:

For the first week or two, I went to court with guys who had been here. Just sat there and watched. What struck me was the amount of things he [the prosecutor] has to do in the courtroom. The prosecutor runs the courtroom. Although the judge is theoretically in charge, we're standing there plea bargaining and calling the cases at the same time and chewing gum and telling the people to quiet down and setting bonds, and that's what amazed me. I never thought I would learn all the terms. What bothered me also was the paperwork. Not the Supreme Court decisions, not the mens rea or

Hate Crimes The office is dedicated to eradicating hate crimes in Los Angeles County.

Insurance Fraud Expert prosecutors and investigators are zeroing in on the rings which operate massive workers' compensation and automobile fraud mills.

Juvenile Cases are handled by a separate division within the DA's office. The program seeks to help those who can be helped and to punish those who deserve punishment.

Legislation As the chief prosecutor of the most populous county in California, the DA develops the kind of state and federal legislation needed to control crime.

Local Law Enforcement Assisted by the DA through legal advice, training programs, and when requested, help in investigations.

Major Frauds These sophisticated swindles must be handled by experienced prosecutors committed to convicting and imprisoning these con artists.

Narcotics A special prosecution unit works with the police to arrest major dealers, seize narcotics and dealer assets, and get dealers off the streets.

Nursing Home Abuse The DA is tightening up enforcement to stop nursing home abuse, punish the guilty, and protect victims and potential victims.

Official Misconduct A special prosecution unit targets crimes by public officials.

Organized Crime DA investigators and prosecutors work with federal, state, and local agencies to halt organized crime intrusions.

O.S.H.A. (Occupational Safety and Health Administration) The DA insists on strong enforcement of felony laws to protect workers.

Police Misconduct Including uncalled-for violence and shootings, this is a continual concern and is prosecuted by a special prosecution unit.

Real Estate Frauds Unit dedicated to prosecuting those who prey on low-income and unsophisticated victims.

S.A.G.E. (Strategy Against Gang Environment) The DA's office goes into various cities and obtains injunctions against gang activity.

Sexual Crimes A unit of highly trained and skilled prosecutors who seek to assist the victims as well as convict the guilty.

The Speakers Bureau This office program provides experts to meet with the public to discuss criminal justice issues and the services of the DA's office.

T.R.A.P. (Task Force for Regional Auto Theft Prevention) A multiagency task force, including the DA's office, to attack the problem of large-scale auto theft rings.

Victims Victim Advocates in the District Attorney Victim-Witness Assistance Program. Advocates counsel crime victims as well as assist them in obtaining state compensation.

Witnesses Aided by the Victim-Witness Assistance Program and by the Bureau of Investigation to facilitate their appearance and assure their personal security.

any of this other stuff, but the amount of junk that's in those files that you have to know. We never heard about this crap in law school. (Heumann 1978, 94)

For decades, the position of assistant district attorney has provided new attorneys with the opportunity to serve an apprenticeship in legal practice. But the training was almost exclusively on the job; it was not unusual for recent law school graduates with no experience to be sent into court on their first day on the job. One assistant summed up the office tradition as follows: "They have a very unique way of breaking people in. They say, 'Here's a file. There's the jury. Go try it.'"(Flemming, Nardulli, and Eisenstein 1992). More recently, large prosecutors' offices have begun to train new employees more systematically. After a week of general orienta-

tion to the different divisions of the office, new assistants are allowed to watch various proceedings and observe veteran trial attorneys at work. Such formalized indoctrination is still relatively rare, however.

New assistants quickly learn to ask questions of more experienced prosecutors, court clerks, and veteran police officers, who are willing to share their knowledge about courtroom procedures. Through this socialization process, assistants learn important unwritten rules about legal practice. In the courthouse environment, there have developed shared conceptions of what types of violations should be punished and the appropriate penalties to be applied to such violations. Assistants learn that their performance (and chances for promotion) are measured by how promptly and efficiently they dispose of cases. They become sensitive to

"The Good Fight Takes Its Toll"

 I chose to become an assistant district attorney for that most noble and banal of reasons: I wanted to help people. Growing up in New York City, I had always been appalled by the crime and thought I could do something about it. At law school graduation I was a fireball, full of energy and the conviction that I could make a difference. But I wasn't prepared for the kind of uphill battle I would face.

My colleagues and I jumped right into combat together, and for a while it was exhilarating. Our first year was a blur of thousands of misdemeanors and countless hours in court. Cases such as shoplifting, marijuana possession, and disorderly conduct landed on our desks in heaps and were disposed of in short order. We took our mission seriously and gave our all (at first) to insisting on a few more days of community service or a few more dollars in restitution.

We were proud to be the good guys, and we had some great times together. Several nights a week we would make a beeline to the local bar to blow off steam, shoot some pool, and trade horror stories. There were crazies of all kinds, like the defendant who mooned the judge or the guy who was convinced he was being stalked by Roberta Flack. We laughed through our exhausted haze and formed friendships that would last a lifetime.

As we gained experience our cases got more serious, but the problems remained the same. A victim called police demanding that someone be arrested. A few days later, when the legal machine had been set in motion and that someone was in jail, the victim would refuse to cooperate. Others were too terrified to testify, and who could blame them? They knew all too well how the system worked and that there was no guarantee the defendants would stay in jail.

Star Witnesses

Then there were those who were a little too enthusiastic about testifying. An alarming number of people, I discovered, thought nothing of lying under oath for revenge in hopes of getting money in future civil lawsuits—or simply because they liked being the center of attention.

I was suckered by a flaky yet sympathetic girl who wept in my office and showed me horrifying photos of bruises inflicted by her boyfriend. She was a nobody, and the boyfriend was wealthy and powerful. He was convicted based mainly on those photos and the testimony of the girl's friend. It was only months later, after the defense attorney hired an expert to examine the photos, that we realized they were fakes and our victim was a liar.

Witnesses were not our only frustration. Defense attorneys called us racists and zealots, and they reserved even worse epithets for the police. The judges indulged these attacks, which was even more infuriating. They sneered at us and scorned our determinedly polite requests for higher bail, longer sentences.

In most courtrooms, there was no limit to what the defense could insinuate or even claim outright without a shred of evidence to back it up. Assistants who objected were silenced and overruled. Ridiculous requests for obscure, irrelevant paperwork were granted, delaying trials for days. Endless, frivolous motions were entertained, necessitating reams of wasted paper.

We were expected to live up to an unrealistic standard, and as frustrating as that was, it was somehow a source of pride. Nobody in the outside world could ever comprehend what our lives were like. We stood up to unbelievable pressure, and we fought the good fight; in spite of the stress, we loved what we did.

Burnout Begins

I left all that behind when I experienced the predictable burnout. The bad times had begun to outweigh the good, and worse than that I had stopped caring. I dreaded what fresh horrors each day would bring instead of looking forward to the challenges. I was disillusioned and discouraged and really just wanted to wash my hands of the whole thing: the crumbling building, the endless parade of ruined lives and misery, the wasted time, the constant arguing.

So I turned in my badge and became a civilian. There wasn't that much about the office that I expected to miss. But I was wrong. I miss it every day—from the lousy coffee to the camaraderie of the court officers to the 2 A.M. giddiness of the complaint room.

The work I have done since then feels like a pale shadow of the life I used to lead. And while the stress is gone, so too is the thrill. Nothing else will ever match the terror, the joy, the pride, and the sorrow I felt as an assistant district attorney in Manhattan.

SOURCE: Page Bondor, "The Good Fight Takes Its Toll," *ABA Journal*, 86 (2000): 104.

hints—for example, if a judge complains that a backlog is developing because prosecutors are bringing too many minor cases, the new assistant usually gets the message that he or she is pressing too hard. Promotions are also related to the candidates' reputations as trial attorneys. Assistants are invariably judged by the number of convictions they obtain. In the courthouse environment, however, not losing a case has a higher value than winning. Thus, assistants learn that if the guilt of the defendant is doubtful or the offender is not dangerous, it is better to negotiate a plea than to disrupt the courtroom routine by attempting to gain a jury conviction.

Promotions and Office Structure

As assistants gain experience and settle into the courthouse routine, they are promoted to more demanding and also more interesting tasks. Promotions are related to office structure (Flemming, Nardulli, and Eisenstein 1992). Small prosecutors' offices usually employ vertical prosecution, in which one prosecutor is assigned responsibility for a case from intake to appeal (Nugent and McEwen 1988). In these offices, assistants are promoted by being assigned more serious cases. However, such an assignment system is administratively burdensome in large courthouses; assistants would spend much of their time moving from one courtroom to another and waiting for their one or two cases to be called. Therefore, most big-city prosecutors employ horizontal prosecution, in which prosecutors are assigned to specific functions, such as initial appearance, charging, preliminary hearing, grand jury, trial, and appeal. On a regular basis, one or two attorneys are systematically assigned to one courtroom with a given judge. Through time, prosecutors come to know the judge's views on sentencing and the like. Under horizontal prosecution, assistants are promoted by being assigned to courtrooms with more serious felonies.

Over the past decades, specialization has become increasingly common in chief prosecutors' offices, particularly those found in densely populated jurisdictions. Often it is the most experienced trial attorneys who staff these positions. Specialized units dealing with murder, sexual assault, armed robbery, and major drug crimes are the most prestigious, mainly because trial work is both plentiful and challenging.

 For up-to-date statistics on prosecution from the Bureau of Justice Statistics, go to **http://www.ojp.usdoj.gov/bjs/pros.htm**.

For an up-to-date list of Web links, go to **http://www.wadsworth.com/product/0534563406s**.

Supervision

Assistant district attorneys are supervised by a bureau chief, who is supposed to ensure that they follow policies of the office. However, for several reasons, assistant DAs enjoy fairly great freedom.

Office policies are often general and somewhat vague. In small offices, they are seldom even put in writing. Official and unofficial policies are simply part of what the assistant learns informally; for this reason, it is hard for the bureau chief to enforce them. In large offices, decentralized work assignments means supervisors can exert limited control over specific cases or individual assistants. Assistant district attorneys spend most of their time not in the central office but in the courtroom. Indeed, in crowded courthouses, trial assistants often have offices adjoining the judge's chambers and only rarely appear in the prosecutor's office at all. It is therefore difficult for supervisors to observe and monitor the assistant district attorney's activities. Each assistant has dozens of cases that require individual decisions on the basis of specific facts, unique witness problems, and so on. A supervisor has no way to monitor such situations except on the basis of what the assistant orally reports or writes in the file. Here, as elsewhere, information is power. Assistants can control their supervisors by selectively telling them what they think they should know (Neubauer 1974).

Perhaps most important, assistant district attorneys are professionals, licensed by society to exercise special powers, most of which involve their ability to exercise judgment. Assistants view their brief tenure in office as an apprenticeship for learning the practice of law. Attempts by supervisors to control the work of the assistants tend to erode the morale of the office; assistants do not appreciate feeling that their professional status has been reduced to that of a clerk.

Attempts at Greater Supervision

The traditional form of prosecutorial management is centered on autonomy; each individual assistant district attorney is granted a great deal of freedom to make his or her own decisions. The Erie, Pennsylvania, DA's office is typical: It "promulgated few formal written policies, gave most of its assistants fairly wide latitude to dispose of cases in ways consistent with the general aim of the office, and relied on informal supervision" (Eisenstein, Flemming, and Nardulli 1988, 215).

Concerned that autonomy allows too much unchecked discretion, many prosecutors have attempted to exert greater supervision by adopting a rigid system of office policies. Some forbid any charge reductions whatsoever for some types of defendants (habitual offenders) and for serious charges such as armed robbery, burglary, weapons, and hard drugs (Eisenstein, Flemming, and Nardulli 1988). To ensure compliance with these detailed office policies, formal, detailed, bureaucratic enforcement mechanisms are imposed. Typical is DuPage County, Illinois, where the DA's office "was highly centralized, rigidly enforcing the 'bottom-line' pleas established by the indictment committee. The DA's office relied on a formally structured hierarchy to administer its policies" (215). Chief prosecutors believe that these management systems monitor prosecutorial discretion, minimize differences between individual assistants, and concentrate scarce crime-fighting resources (Jacoby 1980).

The content of office policy, case-assignment procedures, and the degree of supervision shape assistant district attorneys' work lives. When offices review all case files to ensure that policies have been followed, some assistants feel uncomfortable, as if they were not completely trusted and had to be watched. Moreover, reductions in individual discretion increase the general level of tension in the office. One trial assistant related how a colleague was summarily fired on the same day he violated office policy on plea bargaining. All the assistants resented and feared the administrator who fired him (Eisenstein, Flemming, and Nardulli 1988, 215).

PROSECUTORS AND COURTROOM WORK GROUPS

Prosecutors spend most of their time working directly with other members of the courtroom work group. Even when interviewing witnesses or conducting legal research, the prosecutor is anticipating the reactions of judges and defense attorneys. Thus, the activities of prosecutors can be understood only within the setting of the courtroom work group (Worden 1990).

The prosecutor is the most important member of the work group. Prosecutors set the agenda for judges and defense attorneys by exercising discretion over the types of cases filed, the nature of acceptable plea agreements, and the sentences to be handed out. Prosecutors also control the flow of information about cases through providing access to police arrest reports, laboratory tests, and defendants' past criminal histories. By stressing certain information or withholding other facts, prosecutors can influence the decisions of judges and defense attorneys.

As the dominant force in the courtroom work group, prosecutors clearly set the tone for plea bargaining. This is how one veteran explained his perspective:

> I get so damned pissed off and tired of these guys who come in and cry, "My guy's got a job" or "My guy's about to join the army," when he's got a rap sheet as long as your arm. His guy's a loser, and he's wailing on my desk about what a fine man he is. What really wins me is the guy who comes in and says, "O.K., what are we going to do with my criminal today? I know he has no redeeming social value. He's been a bad son of a bitch all his life, so just let me know your position. But frankly, you know, my feeling is that this is just not the case to nail him on. We all know if he does something serious, he's going." And before long the guy who approaches it this way has you wrapped around his little finger. (Carter 1974, 87)

Prosecutors' actions, in turn, are influenced by other members of the courtroom work group. Through the socialization process, assistant district attorneys internalize the accepted ways of doing things in the courthouse, learning to plead cases out on the basis of normal crimes (discussed in Chapter 5). Prosecutors who stray too far from the shared norms of the courtroom work group can expect sanctions. The judge may informally indicate that the state is pushing too hard for a harsh sentence or may publicly chastise a district attorney in open court, thus threatening the attorney's status among peers. The defense attorney may not agree to a prosecutor's request for a continuance or may employ delaying tactics to impair the state's efforts to schedule cases, thus further disrupting the prosecutor's efforts to move cases. (The prosecutor, of course, is not without countersanctions. These will be discussed in the next two chapters.)

Operating within the constraints of the courtroom work group, effective assistant DAs are those who make tactical decisions that maximize their objectives. Experienced prosecutors, for example, know which defense attorneys can be trusted, granting these people greater access to information about the case and listening to them more when the case involves unusual circumstances. Prosecutors also quickly learn the tendencies of the judge. No experienced prosecutor can afford to ignore how the judge wishes the courtroom to be run.

Although the prosecutor is generally the most important member of the courtroom work group, work groups show considerable variability. There are differences between one community and the next, and in big-city courthouses, there are often differences from courtroom to courtroom. Conflicting goals and varying political styles are two factors that account for contrasting work groups.

 Elizabeth Galzer, "How Federal Prosecutors Can Reduce Crime"

Conflicting Goals and Contrasting Work Groups

On the surface, the goals of prosecutors seem the model of simplicity: Their job is to convict the guilty. But a closer examination shows that the goals are not as clear-cut as they first appear. Prosecutors define their main job in different ways. Some serve as trial counsel to the police department, advocating the department's views in court. Others act as "house counsel" to the police, giving legal advice to the department on enforcement practices that will withstand challenges in court. Still others consider themselves representatives of the court, enforcing rules designed to control police practices. Finally, some prosecutors stress their role as elected officials, trying to reflect the opinion of the community in making their decisions (LaFave 1965).

The uncertainties about which of these tasks should come first produce marked diversity among prosecutors. Therefore, William McDonald (1979) cautions that we must consider the domains of the prosecutor not as fixed by law and tradition but rather as blurred, evolving, and open to negotiation. A study of prosecutors' offices in San Diego and Oakland highlighted this diversity. Even though both were operating within the same legal environment of the state of California, Pamela Utz (1979) discovered contrasting operating styles. The prosecutor's office in San Diego reflects an adversarial model. Assistant district attorneys presume that cases are serious, they routinely overcharge, and they set plea bargaining terms so high that many cases are forced to trial. Because there is a pronounced distrust of defense attorneys, plea bargaining involves a gamelike atmosphere. In general, the San Diego office is dedicated to the "full enforcement" of the law.

The operating style in Oakland, on the other hand, reflects a magisterial model. Office policies determine which types of cases represent serious violations of the law and set strict standards in terms of charging. The office philosophy is that if the case is not "prison material," there should be no trial. Plea bargaining proceeds on the basis that defense attorneys are fellow professionals. Overall, there appears to be more of a search for the truth in Oakland than in San Diego.

The contrasts in operating style between San Diego and Oakland parallel differences in other states. In a survey of prosecutors in Kentucky (Engstrom 1971), almost half stated that they viewed their job in terms of being a law enforcement official (the adversarial model found in San Diego). The remainder came closer to the magisterial model of Oakland. The differing orientations of American prosecutors appear to be related to varying goals: Prosecutors with a law enforcement orientation are more likely to stress punishing the guilty, and those with an alternative approach are more likely to define their major goal as securing convictions (Eisenstein 1978).

Political Styles and Contrasting Work Groups

The prosecutor's role within the courtroom work group also needs to be understood within the broader political context in which the office functions. This was the conclusion of Roy Flemming's (1990) study of nine prosecutors' offices in three states (Illinois, Michigan, and Pennsylvania). Because they exercise broad discretion (in the context of decentralization and local autonomy), elected prosecutors choose political styles. This choice is both personal and strategic. It depends first on the prosecutor's satisfaction or dissatisfaction with the office's status within the courthouse community. It also depends on the prosecutor's perception of the value of conflict as a means of changing the office's status.

Prosecutors satisfied with the status of the office adopt an "office conservator" style. Office conservators accept the status quo. Continuity is often a key consideration; former assistants are elected with the blessings of the previous officeholder and the support of the local political establishment. Once in office, conservators do not deliberately step on toes—if they push for change, it generally comes as a response to the requests of others. Montgomery County, Pennsylvania, provides an example. The newly elected DA retained the preexisting staff intact. He did fashion some guidelines regarding guilty pleas, but they were flexible, symbolic gestures—signals that a changing of the guard had taken place, not a revolution. Most important, however, the DA tolerated the judges' traditional dominance of the courthouse community.

Prosecutors who are less content with the status of their offices face a more complicated set of choices. They must decide whether conflict is an effective tool for them to use. Courthouse insurgents are very dissatisfied with the status quo and are prepared to do battle to change it. They do not shy away from open conflict, nor do they hesitate to challenge the courthouse community in the pursuit of their goals. DuPage County, Illinois, is an example. The state's attorney was an outsider to the county who won the office by narrowly defeating the Republican party's favored candidate in a bitterly fought, mud-slinging primary. Perceiving that the office failed to stand up to defense attorneys, the new state's attorney turned the office inside out. Immediately after election, he eliminated the part-time staff, hired aggressive assistants, and instituted policies severely restricting plea bargaining. Moreover, the insurgent DA minced no words in publicly criticizing judges and defense attorneys.

Policy reformers are also dissatisfied with the status quo, but unlike courthouse insurgents, they are cautious, often conciliatory, and sometimes more subtle in their approach. Upon taking office, they gradually move to tighten their offices' guilty plea policies, encourage more assertive attitudes among their assistants, and try to develop innovative approaches to prosecutorial work. They do not shrink from trying to alter their relationships with judges. Erie, Pennsylvania, provides a case in point. Embittered by the decline of the office when he left as an assistant to enter private practice, the new Erie prosecutor bucked the political establishment and decisively trounced the incumbent in the Democratic party primary to win the office. However, his plans to restore the respect of the office clashed with the docket policies of the court. Rather than fighting openly, the Erie DA mounted an indirect campaign to wrest control of the docket from the judges.

Flemming's study highlights two aspects of prosecutorial behavior that are not immediately obvious. First, differences in political styles crossed party lines; these are not Republican or Democratic styles. Second, differences in political styles were not necessarily constant through time. In several communities, a district attorney was initially elected as an insurgent or a policy reformer but through the years came to adopt a conservator style.

 Christopher Darden, "Trials of a Former Black Prosecutor"

THE EXPANDING DOMAIN OF THE PROSECUTOR

Throughout the twentieth century the domain of the prosecutor has been expanding, and pressures to place greater authority in the hands of the prosecutor are likely to continue (Figure 6-4 on page 160). Within the fragmented, sometimes nonsystem, of criminal justice the prosecutor is in the best position to provide coordination. Moreover, with crime as a dominant issue in elections, the prosecutor is uniquely able to capitalize on his or her role as the community's chief law enforcement official and promise the voters to expand crime-fighting efforts. We will examine two types of programs that exemplify the contemporary expansion of the domain of the prosecutor: improving police-prosecutor relationships and community prosecution.

Improving Police-Prosecutor Relationships

Police and prosecutors are commonly viewed as members of the same crime-fighting team, but a closer look reveals a more complex reality. Police and prosecutors have varying perspectives on the law. To the police, the case is closed when the suspect is arrested, but prosecutors stress that they often need additional information to win in court (Stanko 1981).

THE MURDER TRIAL OF SHAREEF COUSIN

DA Harry Connick Defends His Aggressive Tactics

District Attorney Harry Connick, Sr. has been a fixture in New Orleans political life for almost three decades. (His son, Harry Connick, Jr. is a popular musician and actor.) Connick and his wife ran a record store to pay his way through school. After graduating from Tulane Law School, he worked for the New Orleans Legal Aid Bureau and as an Assistant United States Attorney for the Eastern District of Louisiana. In 1973 he challenged embattled District Attorney Jim Garrison and won.

New Orleans District Attorney Jim Garrison had arrested businessman Clay Shaw in 1965 on the charge of conspiracy to assassinate President John F. Kennedy. At first, Garrison spoke of a "homosexual thrill killing" but later expanded the investigation to include conspiracy theories. Two years later the jury deliberated less than an hour in acquitting Shaw. Nationally, the city became associated with conspiracy theories and government plots to kill the president. Locally, community leaders thought that Garrison had embarrassed the city and sought a candidate who would restore civic pride. Connick proved to be their man.

After almost thirty years in office Connick remains at the epicenter of controversy, mostly of his own making. Internally, some assistants have chafed under his tight management control. One hardworking assistant who thought she was unfairly fired appealed all the way to the U.S. Supreme Court (only to lose). Externally, Connick has been quick to publicly condemn those who don't share his law-and-order philosophy. Numerous judges (some of whom previously worked in his office) have been singled out for harsh criticism relating to bail setting, interpretations of the law, or sentencing predilections (see Chapter 7).

By the mid-1990s the Orleans Parish district attorney was again attracting national attention, this time over the issue of prosecutorial misconduct and innocents on death row (see Chapter 17). In *Kyles v. Whitely* the U.S. Supreme Court used strong language to condemn the office for not disclosing exculpatory evidence in a death penalty case (see Chapter 12). After five trials, Connick eventually dismissed the charges in that case. The same issue became pivotal in the murder trial of Shareef Cousin. On the night of the murder Connie Babin told police that things were so confusing that she doubted she could identify the killer. Yet this key witness statement was not given to the defense. Connick and his assistants have contended that they are under no legal obligation to disclose such information, but the vast majority of lawyers and judges strongly disagree.

The Shareef case is not the only case to cause Connick public embarrassment in recent years. A dying former prosecutor told his best friend that he had concealed evidence that could have cleared John Thompson, who had been convicted of murder and sentenced to death (Bell, 1999). For the first time in his twenty-five years as district attorney, Connick asked a judge to put off the execution of a man his office had put on death row.

Harry Connick Sr. easily won reelection in 1978, 1984, and 1990. But the 1996 campaign resembled a bare-knuckled political brawl, with the candidates attacking the fitness of their opponent to hold public office. The underlying issue was race. Connick, who is white, ran for reelection in a city with a 64 percent black voting population. His major challenger was former judge Morris Reed, an African American, who charged that Connick's office was racially biased and it was time to elect a black DA. Connick won, though, by putting together a biracial coalition, benefiting greatly from the backing of Mayor Marc Morial, the city's top black elected official. In all likelihood, 1996 was Connick's last election—he will be seventy-six in 2002 when he must run again.

 To learn more about the trial of Clay Shaw, go to **http://reitzes.www4.50megs.com/chron.html**.

A good Web site on New Orleans and the Garrison investigation can be accessed at **http://mcadams.posc.mu.edu/garrison.htm**.

The homepage of the New Orleans District Attorney is located at **http://www.noda.new-orleans.la.us/**.

For an up-to-date list of Web links, go to **http://www.wadsworth.com/product/0534563406s**.

 For more about the Shareef Cousin trial, type in the search words *dead teen walking* and read the section "The Prosecution."

Inadequate police reports present a classic illustration of noncoordination within the criminal justice system. Prosecutors depend on the police for their raw materials. The thoroughness of police investigations and the quality of their arrests directly affect the likelihood of the prosecutor obtaining a conviction. A survey of 225 (mostly big-city) prosecutors indicated that 66 percent cited inadequate

FIGURE 6-4	**Key Developments Concerning the Prosecutor**	
Berger v. United States	1935	The prosecutor's primary interest is in doing justice, not simply winning cases.
Imbler v. Pachtman	1976	Prosecutors enjoy absolute immunity from civil liability when initiating and pursuing a criminal prosecution.
Morrison v. Olson	1988	Independent counsel law is constitutional.
Burns v. Reed	1991	Prosecutors enjoy only qualified immunity from lawsuits concerning advice given to the police.
Buckley v. Fitzsimmons	1993	Prosecutors enjoy only qualified immunity from civil lawsuits for actions during criminal investigations and statements made during news conferences.
Kalina v. Fletcher	1997	A prosecutor may be sued for making false statements of fact in an affidavit in support of an arrest warrant.

police preparation of crime reports as a major problem in their offices (Nugent and McEwen 1988). Among commonly mentioned problems, names and addresses of victims and witnesses are lacking; full details of how the crime was committed are missing; and vital laboratory reports are not forwarded on time. Faced with incomplete or inaccurate police reports, the prosecutor may be forced to drop charges (see Chapter 10).

The National Institute of Justice (1988) has sponsored research on ways to strengthen the working relationships between police and prosecutors. Some of the questions of greatest interest include:

- What is a "good" arrest from the viewpoint of the police? Of the prosecutor?
- Why do a small percentage of officers make half the arrests resulting in conviction?
- Once the arrest is made, what is the best way to ensure that the prosecutor gets the information needed?
- How can cooperation on case preparation be fostered?

Police and prosecutors in several jurisdictions have adopted strategies to improve coordination and communication among themselves (Buchanan 1989). In Indianapolis, for example, the prosecutor has funded a computer message system that enables attorneys in the office to transmit notes, case dispositions, and subpoenas directly to police officers at their work location. In Alameda County, California, and Montgomery County, Maryland, "street jump" narcotics officers and prosecutors consult frequently, both in person and over the telephone, to build cases that meet the requirements of the search-and-seizure law. In Seattle, sex crime investigators and prosecutors interview child victims together so that they can understand the case better and make decisions that will lead to success in court.

A few agencies have gone further: They have institutionalized teamwork and made communication between investigators and prosecutors a top priority. In Multnomah County, Oregon, the Organized Crime/Narcotics Task Force has brought together twelve investigators from several area agencies and two prosecutors from the district attorney's office. There is daily informal contact about the progress of pending cases. Moreover, prosecutors act as consultants to the police during the investigative phase. Thus, investigators can get answers to difficult legal questions in a few minutes, just by walking down the hall.

Programs like these indicate that despite a long history of difficulties some agencies apparently are bridging the gap. But a word of caution is in order. No research to date has systematically evaluated these programs to indicate their overall effectiveness. Until such research is conducted, there is no way of knowing which programs may or may not prove effective in other communities.

Community Prosecution

The historic image of the district attorney stresses case processing—the DA files charges and doggedly pursues a conviction. But this traditional image is becoming blurred as locally elected prosecutors respond to a wide variety of social problems such as domestic violence (Chapter 9), drug abuse (Chapter 10), disorder on city streets (Chapter 18), and growing numbers of juvenile offenders (Chapter 19). In responding to these types of social problems, which often reflect disintegrating neighborhoods, prosecutors today are more likely to stress problem-oriented approaches. At times the specifics are hard to pin down because the approaches are truly shaped to local needs rather than national program guides (Coles and Earle 1996). But these new approaches have three elements in common (Jacoby 1995):

- the recognition that crime prevention is a legitimate prosecutorial goal;

- the most effective results are obtained within small, manageable geographic areas; and

- change is more likely to occur through cooperative efforts or partnerships, rather than prosecutorial dictates.

The Neighborhood District Attorney approach in Multnomah County (Portland, Oregon) provides a case in point. Business leaders in Lloyd District (an inner-city neighborhood) called for more police protection as well as the assignment of a special prosecutor to the district (for which they provided one year's funding). Citizen demands were invariably expressed in traditional law enforcement terms—more police, more arrests, and more convictions, particularly of repeat offenders. The Lloyd District special prosecutor, however, quickly saw that people's concerns were more immediate than he had imagined. "They wanted something done about prostitution, public drinking, drug use, vandalism, assaults, littering garbage, and 'car prowls' (thefts from cars)" (Boland 1996, 36). Although none of these problems (except thefts from cars) fits traditional notions of serious crime, they nonetheless raise serious concern among citizens. (This approach clearly emphasizes the activities of the local courts—discussed in Chapter 18.)

As the program developed, several distinctive features became apparent. For one, the assistant DA used the laws in new ways, including using civil remedies to fight crime (Chapter 2). Perhaps most importantly the program was problem-oriented—rather than focusing on individual arrestees, the Neighborhood District Attorney addressed prob-

lems from a larger perspective, with long-term goals in mind. Ultimately what emerged was an approach, not a program. Rather than being guided by clear-cut procedures, Portland has adopted a highly flexible organization that can meet the different needs of different neighborhoods (Boland 1996). Overall, community prosecution stresses a proactive approach—rather than reacting to crime through prosecution these programs stress crime prevention (Coles and Kelling 1999).

 To learn more about community prosecution across the nation, go to the following:

Indianapolis: **http://www.ci.indianapolis.in.us/ pros/street_level_advocacy.htm**

Washington, D.C.: **http://www.usdoj.gov/usao/ dc/cp/cp.html**

Maryland: **http://www.lib.jjay.cuny.edu/len/97/ 10oct/html/feature.html**

For an up-to-date list of Web links, go to **http:// www.wadsworth.com/product/0534563406s**.

CONCLUSION

The impact of *Burns v. Reed* is still unfolding. Carol Burns was last reported working as a supervisor in a discount department store in Muncie, richer by her civil settlement with the police (minus lawyers' fees). Her suit against Reed, however, was still pending—the nation's highest court held only that she had a right to sue, not that she would win that suit. As for Rick Reed, the aftermath has been more promising—he is now the district attorney for Delaware County, Indiana, the voters evidently not convinced that his behavior was out of line.

From a broader perspective, *Burns v. Reed* and other lawsuits claiming prosecutorial misconduct are likely to have minimal impact. For years courts have granted prosecutors wide-ranging discretionary powers. The exercise of this discretion shapes the dynamics of the courthouse. In effect, all others involved in the criminal courts—judges, defense attorneys, probation officers, juries, witnesses, and so on—must react to the decisions made by the prosecutor. But the law imposes few formal restrictions on the use of these discretionary powers. Prosecutors' offices are decentralized, autonomous, and headed by locally elected officials. Moreover, the assistants, who make most of the key decisions, are generally fresh out of law school and have little background in how the law is actually administered.

This does not mean that prosecutorial discretion is uncontrolled; rather, it is influenced by other members of the courtroom work group. Through the socialization process and the occasional application of sanctions, new prosecutors are educated in the norms of the courtroom work group.

CRITICAL THINKING QUESTIONS

1. Robert Misner (1996) argues that given the fragmented nature of the criminal justice system (Chapter 1) over the last thirty years responsibility has increasingly been centralized in the hands of the district attorney. What factors support this assessment?

2. Should state attorney generals be given authority to supervise locally elected district attorneys? How would such increased authority alter the criminal justice system?

3. How much authority should assistant district attorneys be given? As licensed attorneys, should they be given a large amount of discretion to dispose of cases on the basis of their best judgment, or should they have more limited authority so that the office employs a uniform policy?

4. In terms of the three political styles—office conservator, courthouse insurgent, and policy reformer—which best describes your local prosecutor?

5. Community prosecution stresses the need for the prosecutor to reach out to the community, but what does community mean? Is this reform based on a naive assumption that all members of the same geographic entity share similar views? How might different "communities" within the same city (or perhaps county) stress different law enforcement priorities?

 WORLD WIDE WEB RESOURCES AND EXERCISES

Web Guides
http://dir.yahoo.com/Society_and_Culture/Crime/ Law_Enforcement/District_Attorneys/

Web Search Terms
"Attorney general"; "solicitor general"; "U.S. attorney"; "United States Department of Justice"

Useful URLs
Visit the National Association of Attorneys General: **http://www.naag.org/**.

Visit the Web site of the National District Attorneys Association, "The Voice of America's Prosecutors," at **http://www.ndaa.org/**.

The American Prosecutors Research Institute, the research, training, and technical affiliate of the National College of District Attorneys, provides continuing legal education and training for prosecutors: **http://www.law.sc.edu/ncda/index.htm**.

Uncommon URLs

Read about "The Epidemic of Prosecutorial Misconduct" on the Web site of the Association of Americans for Constitutional Laws and Justice: **http://www.pixi.com/~itmc/ProsecutorialMisconduct.html**.

Visit the Mean Justice homepage: **http://home.earthlink.net/~ehumes/**.

Truth in Justice works to free wholly innocent men and women convicted of crimes they did not commit, and to prevent wrongful convictions: **http://www.truthinjustice.org/**.

Web Exercises

1. The U.S. Department of Justice maintains a major Web site. Access it using the following URL: **http://www.usdoj.gov**. Under Justice Department Press Releases, sample the press releases of the attorney general and those of the U.S. attorneys. To what extent do they reflect a focus on similar types of crimes? To what extent do they reflect an emphasis on very different types of activities? Overall, what does this Web site suggest about the difference between federal prosecutors and state prosecutors?

2. A growing number of district attorneys' offices have created Web pages. To access these sites conduct a search by going to Yahoo: **http://www.yahoo.com**. Then choose **Society and Culture/Crime/Law Enforcement/District Attorneys**.

   Select two homepages and compare them to the Los Angeles County District Attorney's office homepage (see Exhibit 6-2 on page 152). Overall, do you think these homepages provide useful information, or does the information amount to little more than public relations?

3. A growing number of communities are instituting some form of community prosecution. Access these experiences using the search engine of your choice. Type in the phrase "*community prosecution*" and select three dif-

ferent programs. Compare the information with the discussion in the text. Do these programs appear to differ in major ways from the way prosecutors have historically run their offices, or are these programs just old wine in new bottles?

INFOTRAC COLLEGE EDITION RESOURCES AND EXERCISES

Basic Search Terms

United States Department of Justice; prosecution; malicious prosecution; public prosecutors, state attorneys general; special prosecutor, community prosecution; prosecutorial misconduct; city attorney; attorneys; government attorneys.

Recommended Articles

Anthony Annucci, "Effective Strategies for Managing Litigation and Working with Attorneys General Offices"

Eric Waltenburg and Bill Swinford, "Tactics of State Attorneys General"

Ted Gest and Lincoln Caplan, "Bill Clinton's Man to See"

Kevin Flynn, "Departing U.S. Attorney Quietly Makes an Imprint"

InfoTrac College Edition Exercises

1. Use the search phrase *community prosecution* and answer the following questions: What advantages are portrayed for community prosecution? What negatives are mentioned? In general, do the articles support or refute the discussion in the text of the expanding domain of the prosecutor. Here are two articles: Catherine M. Coles and George L. Kelling, "Prevention through Community Prosecution" and Susan Weinstein, "Community Prosecution: Community Policing's Legal Partner."

2. Using the search term *prosecutorial misconduct* and/or *malicious prosecution,* locate two or more articles on the topic. How significant do they see the problem—is it major or minor? What remedies do they recommend? Here are two articles: Rick Bierschbach, "Fixing a Broken Frame" and "One Bite at the Apple."

REFERENCES

Albonetti, Celesta. 1987. "Prosecutorial Discretion: The Effects of Uncertainty." *Law and Society Review* 21: 291–313.

Bell, Griffin. 1993. "Appointing United States Attorneys." *Journal of Law and Politics* 9: 247–256.

Bell, Rhonda. 2001. "Evidence Flap Has DA on Defensive: Connick Insists Case an Aberration." *Times-Picayune,* May 31, 1991, A1.

Boland, Barbara. 1996. "What Is Community Prosecution?" *National Institute of Justice Journal* 231 (August): 35–40.

Buchanan, John. 1989. "Police-Prosecutor Teams: Innovations in Several Jurisdictions." *NIJ Reports* 214 (May/June): 2–8.

Campbell, Linda. 1990. "Court Urged to Protect Prosecutors." *Chicago Tribune,* 29 November.

———. 1991. "High Court Reduces Prosecutor Immunity." *Chicago Tribune,* 31 May.

Caplan, Lincoln. 1988. *The Tenth Justice: The Solicitor General and the Rule of Law.* New York: Vintage.

Carter, Lief. 1974. *The Limits of Order.* Lexington, MA: D. C. Heath.

Coles, Catherine, and Ronald Earle. 1996. "The Evolution of Problem-Oriented Prosecution." Paper presented at the annual meeting of the American Criminological Association, Chicago, Illinois, November.

Coles, Catherine, and George Kelling. 1999. "Prevention Through Community Prosecution." *The Public Interest* 36: 69.

DeFrances, Carol, Steven Smith, and Louise van der Does. 1996. "Prosecutors in State Courts, 1994." *Bulletin.* Washington, D.C.: Bureau of Justice Statistics, National Institute of Justice.

Eisenstein, James. 1978. *Counsel for the United States: U.S. Attorneys in the Political and Legal System.* Baltimore: Johns Hopkins University Press.

Eisenstein, James, Roy Flemming, and Peter Nardulli. 1988. *The Contours of Justice: Communities and Their Courts.* Boston: Little, Brown.

Engstrom, Richard. 1971. "Political Ambitions and the Prosecutorial Office." *Journal of Politics* 33: 190.

Flemming, Roy. 1990. "The Political Styles and Organizational Strategies of American Prosecutors: Examples from Nine Courthouse Communities." *Law and Policy* 12: 25.

Flemming, Roy, Peter Nardulli, and James Eisenstein. 1992. *The Craft of Justice: Politics and Work in Criminal Court Communities.* Philadelphia: University of Pennsylvania Press.

Harriger, Kathy. 1992. *Independent Justice: The Federal Special Prosecutor in American Politics.* Lawrence: University Press of Kansas.

Heinz, John, and Edward Laumann. 1982. *Chicago Lawyers: The Social Structure of the Bar.* New York: Russell Sage Foundation.

Heumann, Milton. 1978. *Plea Bargaining.* Chicago: University of Chicago Press.

Jacob, Herbert. 1966. "Judicial Insulation—Elections, Direct Participation, and Public Attention to the Courts in Wisconsin." *Wisconsin Law Review:* 812.

Jacoby, Joan. 1980. *The American Prosecutor: A Search for Identity.* Lexington, MA: D. C. Heath.

———. 1995. "Pushing the Envelope—Leadership in Prosecution." *Justice System Journal* 17: 291–308.

Jones, David. 1994. "Prosecutorial Tenure in Wisconsin." Paper presented at the Midwest Criminal Justice Association Meeting, Chicago, September.

LaFave, Wayne. 1965. *Arrest: The Decision to Take a Suspect into Custody.* Boston: Little, Brown.

Landsberg, Brian. 1993. "The Role of Civil Service Attorneys and Political Appointees in Making Policy in the Civil Rights Division of the U.S. Department of Justice." *Journal of Law and Politics* 9: 275–289.

McDonald, William. 1979. "The Prosecutor's Domain." In *The Prosecutor,* edited by William McDonald. Newbury Park, CA: Sage.

McEwen, Tom. 1995. *National Assessment Program: 1994 Survey Results.* Washington, D.C.: National Institute of Justice.

McGee, Jim and Brian Duffy. 1997. *Main Justice: The Men and Women Who Enforce the Nation's Criminal Laws and Guard Its Liberties.* New York: Simon & Schuster.

Meinhold, Stephen and Steven Shull. 1993. "Policy Congruence Between the President and the Solicitor General." Paper presented at the Midwest Political Science Association, 16 April.

Misner, Robert. 1996. "Recasting Prosecutorial Discretion." *Journal of Criminal Law and Criminology* 86: 717–758.

National Institute of Justice. 1988. "Police-Prosecutor Coordination." Washington, D.C.: U.S. Department of Justice.

Neubauer, David. 1974. *Criminal Justice in Middle America.* Morristown, NJ: General Learning Press.

———. 1997. *Judicial Process: Law, Courts, and Politics in the United States.* 2d ed. Fort Worth: Harcourt Brace.

Nugent, Hugh, and Thomas McEwen. 1988. *Prosecutor's National Assessment of Needs.* Washington, D.C.: National Institute of Justice, U.S. Department of Justice.

Perlstein, Michael. 1990. "DA's Office Suffers as Prosecutors Flee to Better Pay, Hours." *The Times-Picayune,* 22 July, B1.

Puro, Steven. 1981. "The United States as Amicus Curiae." In *Courts, Law and Judicial Processes,* edited by S. Sidney Ulmer. New York: Free Press.

Roberts, Robert, and Marion Doss. 1997. "Prosecutor in the Cross Hairs: The Federal Independent Counsel Law Comes Under Fire." Paper presented at the annual meeting of the Academy of Criminal Justice Sciences, Louisville, Kentucky, March.

Schlesinger, Joseph. 1966. *Ambition and Politics: Political Careers in the United States.* Chicago: Rand McNally.

Segal, Jeffrey. 1988. "Amicus Curiae Briefs by the Solicitor General During the Warren and Burger Courts: A Research Note." *Western Political Quarterly* 41: 135–144.

———. 1990. "Supreme Court Support for the Solicitor General: The Effect of Presidential Appointments." *Western Political Quarterly* 42: 137–152.

Stanko, Elizabeth. 1981. "The Arrest Versus the Case." *Urban Life* 9: 295–414.

Utz, Pamela. 1979. "Two Models of Prosecutorial Professionalism." In *The Prosecutor,* edited by William McDonald. Newbury Park, CA: Sage.

Worden, Alissa Pollitz. 1990. "Policymaking by Prosecutors: The Uses of Discretion in Regulating Plea Bargaining." *Judicature* 73: 335–340.

FOR FURTHER READING

Baker, Mark. *D.A.: Prosecutors in Their Own Words.* New York: Simon & Schuster, 1999.

Baker, Nancy. *Conflicting Loyalties: Law and Politics in the Attorney General's Office, 1789–1990.* Lawrence: University Press of Kansas, 1992.

Clayton, Cornell. *The Politics of Justice: The Attorney General and the Making of Legal Policy.* Armonk, NY: M. E. Sharpe, 1992.

———, ed. *Government Lawyers: The Federal Legal Bureaucracy and Presidential Politics.* Lawrence: University Press of Kansas, 1995.

Dewey, Thomas. *Twenty Against the Underworld.* Garden City, NY: Doubleday, 1974.

Gomme, Ian, and Mary Hall. "Prosecutors at Work: Role Overload and Strain." *Journal of Criminal Justice* 23 (1995): 191–200.

Heilbroner, David. *Rough Justice: Days and Nights of a Young D.A.* New York: Pantheon, 1990.

Jones, David. "Judicial Federalism and Prosecutorial Vindictiveness: State Responses to Bordenkircher and Goodwin." *Journal of Crime and Justice* 20 (1997): 73–96.

Salokar, Rebecca. *The Solicitor General: The Politics of Law.* Philadelphia: Temple University Press, 1992.

Sanders, Andrew, ed. *Prosecution in Common Law Jurisdictions.* Brookfield, VT: Dartmouth Publishing, 1996.

Defense Attorneys

CLARENCE EARL GIDEON HAD BEEN IN AND OUT OF PRISON SINCE THE age of fourteen. His brushes with law had been minor—public drunkenness and petty theft primarily—but now he faced a much more serious charge—burglarizing a poolroom in Bay Harbor. As he stood before the judge, he appeared to be a shipwreck of a man; his wrinkled face and trembling hands suggested a person much older than fifty-one. Yet "a flame still burned inside Clarence Earl Gideon . . . he had a fierce feeling that the State of Florida had treated him wrongly" (Lewis 1972, 6). He demanded the court appoint a lawyer to defend him. The trial judge flatly refused; unrepresented by counsel, Gideon was found guilty. But on appeal he was luckier. The Supreme Court plucked this obscure case from the bowels of the criminal justice system to issue a landmark decision; all indigent defendants were entitled to court-appointed counsel in felony trials. *Gideon v. Wainwright* (1963) was a victory not only for Clarence Earl Gideon, but, more importantly, sent shock waves through the criminal justice system.

The Court's decision in *Gideon* underscores the importance of the lawyers in the criminal justice system. In America the phrase *defense attorney* makes most people think of Perry Mason. As rerun on late-night television, the fictionalized character of Perry Mason embodies our image of the defense attorney fighting to free his falsely accused client—and always succeeding. The public often contrasts this favorable image with a less complimentary one of real attorneys. Concerned about rising crime rates, many Americans view the defense attorney as a conniver who uses legal technicalities to free the guilty. In the eyes of other members of the legal profession, the defense attorney is a virtual outcast who knows little about the law and who may engage in unethical behavior. To a client, the one whose future is literally in the lawyer's hands, the defense attorney is often perceived as just another member of the courthouse gang who does not fight hard enough.

This chapter assesses these conflicting images in terms of the daily realities of the small proportion of the legal profession who represent defendants accused of violating the criminal law. The picture is a complicated one. Some defense attorneys suffer from the shortcomings mentioned by their critics; others do not. But all face day-to-day problems and challenges that are not usually encountered by the bulk of American lawyers who represent higher status clients. The key topics of this chapter are the factors influencing the type of legal assistance available to those who appear in criminal courts: the legal right to counsel, the tasks defense attorneys perform, their relationship with courtroom work groups, the nature of the criminal bar, the relationship between lawyer and client, and, finally, the various systems for providing legal assistance to the poor. ■

THE RIGHT TO COUNSEL

Like many other provisions of the Constitution, the Sixth Amendment has a different meaning today than it did when it was first ratified. In a landmark decision, the U.S. Supreme Court held that based on the Sixth Amendment's provision of **right to counsel**, indigent defendants charged with a felony are entitled to the services of a lawyer paid for by the government (see Case Close-Up: *Gideon v. Wainwright* and the Right to Counsel). Later, the Sixth Amendment right to counsel was extended to juvenile court proceedings as well (*In re Gault* 1967). But

as so often happens, answering one question raised several new ones. In the wake of the *Gideon* decision, the Court wrestled with issues regarding the right to counsel concerning (1) nonfelony criminal prosecutions, (2) stages of the criminal process, (3) ineffective assistance of counsel, and (4) self-representation. Figure 7-1 lists key developments in the right to counsel (see page 170).

Nonfelony Criminal Prosecutions

The *Gideon* ruling was limited to state felony prosecutions. Did the newly discovered constitutional right to court-appointed counsel also extend to those accused of minor violations (misdemeanor or ordinance violations)? In *Argersinger v. Hamlin* (1972) the Court ruled that "absent a knowing and intelligent waiver, no person may be imprisoned for any offense, whether classified as petty, misdemeanor, or felony, unless he was represented by counsel." But

Right to counsel: Right of the accused to the services of a lawyer paid for by the government, established by the Sixth Amendment and extended by the Warren Court (*Gideon v. Wainwright*) to indigent defendants in felony cases.

CASE CLOSE-UP

Gideon v. Wainwright and the Right to Counsel

 From his prison cell Clarence Earl Gideon drafted a petition that, despite the garbled prose of a man with no real education, nonetheless raised a major legal principle:

> *When at the time of the petitioners trial he ask the lower court for the aid of counsel, the court refused this aid. Petitioner told the court that this [Supreme] Court made decision to the effect that all citizens tried for a felony crime should have aid of counsel. The lower court ignored this plea. (Lewis 1972)*

Every year thousands of pauper petitions like this are sent to the Supreme Court; few are ever heard. But this petition struck a responsive cord. The Court signaled the importance of the issue when it appointed Abe Fortas, one of the best known lawyers in Washington, D.C., to represent Gideon. (Fortas would later be appointed to the Court.)

In what became officially known as *Gideon v. Wainwright*, the Court forcefully noted that "in our adversary system of criminal justice, any person, haled into court, who is too poor to hire a lawyer, cannot be assured a fair trial unless counsel is provided for him. This seems to us to be an obvious truth. . . ." The Court's decision in *Gideon* underscores the importance of the lawyers in the criminal justice system.

The Sixth Amendment states that "in all criminal prosecutions, the accused shall enjoy the right . . . to have the assistance of counsel for his defence." As written by the framers over 200 years ago, this constitutionally protected right to counsel meant only that the judge could not prevent a defendant from bringing a lawyer to court. (In England defendants had been convicted despite requests to have their lawyers present.) Thus, the Sixth Amendment affected only those who could afford to hire their own lawyers.

Beginning in the 1930s the Supreme Court took a more expansive view of the right to counsel. Criminal defendants in federal cases were entitled to a court-appointed lawyer if they were too poor to hire their own. But a different rule prevailed in the state courts. Only defendants accused of a capital offense were entitled to court-appointed counsel; indigent defendants charged with ordinary felonies or misdemeanors were not (*Betts v. Brady*). Thus, a significant number of defendants in state courts had to face the legal maze of criminal proceedings by themselves. The inequity of this situation was spelled out by the Supreme Court in 1956 in *Griffin v. Illinois:* "There can be no equal justice where the kind of trial a man gets depends on the money he has."

Gideon v. Wainwright (1963) significantly expanded the legal meaning of the right to counsel. As

---

several years later, the justices declined to extend the *Argersinger* decision, holding that a defendant is guaranteed the right to legal counsel, paid by the state if necessary, only in cases that actually lead to imprisonment, not in all cases in which imprisonment is a potential penalty (*Scott v. Illinois* 1979). The net effect of the *Scott* case was to limit the right to counsel in nonfelony prosecutions, particularly if the guilty faced only paying a fine (see Chapter 18).

Stages of the Criminal Process

The *Gideon* ruling spawned another important question: When in the criminal process does the right to counsel begin (and end)? Note that the Sixth Amendment provides for the right to counsel in "all criminal prosecutions," so it is not limited to the trial itself. The Supreme Court adopted a "criti-

 To learn more about the Sixth Amendment and the right to counsel go to **http://caselaw.findlaw.com/ data/constitution/amendment06/10.html**.

For an up-to-date list of Web links, go to **http:// www.wadsworth.com/product/0534563406s**.

cal stages" test, under which a defendant is entitled to legal representation at every stage of prosecution "where substantial rights of the accused may be affected," requiring the "guiding hand of counsel" (*Mempa v. Rhay* 1967). As Figure 7-2 (page 171) summarizes, indigent defendants have a right to court-appointed counsel from the time they first appear before a judge until sentence is pronounced and the first appeal concluded. (The only exception is the grand jury, whose peculiar practices will be examined in Chapter 10.) As a general rule, defenoccasionally happens, the Court reversed its earlier precedent in *Betts*.

> *Governments, both state and federal, quite properly spend vast sums of money to establish machinery to try defendants accused of crime. Lawyers to prosecute are everywhere deemed essential to protect the public's interest in an orderly society. Similarly, there are few defendants charged with crime, few indeed, who fail to hire the best lawyers they can get to prepare and present their defenses.*
>
> *That the government hires lawyers to prosecute and defendants who have the money hire lawyers to defend are the strongest indications of the widespread belief that lawyers in criminal courts are necessities, not luxuries. The right of one charged with crime to counsel may not be deemed fundamental and essential for fair trials in some countries, but it is in ours.*

Now, all indigent defendants charged with a felony were entitled to the services of a lawyer paid by the government, irrespective of whether they were on trial in state or federal court.

A later decision partially extended the Sixth Amendment to cover misdemeanor cases in lower courts (*Argersinger v. Hamlin* 1972). Moreover, the right to counsel is not limited just to trial but extends throughout the criminal prosecution. Indigent defendants are entitled to court-appointed counsel during critical stages of the proceedings, including interrogation in the police station, police lineups, and the pre-

liminary hearing. After conviction, the right to counsel extends to the first appeal (but not habeas corpus proceedings).

Gideon proved to be a major transforming event in the American criminal justice system. It was the first major decision of the Warren Court's revolution in criminal justice. But unlike other decisions, it proved not to be controversial. The court's rationale focusing on basic fairness and the importance of lawyers gave it widespread legitimacy. Moreover, *Gideon* focused on the need for a lawyer at the trial itself. Later decisions—*Miranda* in particular—restricted police gathering of evidence and proved to be highly contentious.

 You can view Clarence Gideon's handwritten petition by clicking on **http://www.constitutioncenter.org/resources/supreme_court/4b2.asp** or **http://www.aclumontana.org/rights/gideon.html**.

The full opinion in *Gideon v. Wainwright* is available at **http://supct.law.cornell.edu/supct/**. In the Quick Search box, type *Gideon*.

To listen to the oral argument in *Gideon,* go to **http://oyez.at.nwu.edu/cases/cases.cgi.** Under Search by Title, insert *Gideon.*

For an up-to-date list of Web links, go to **http://www.wadsworth.com/product/0534563406s**.

dants have a Sixth Amendment right to the assistance of counsel once any adversary proceedings have begun (*Brewer v. Williams* 1977).

The right to counsel in the pretrial stage is much more limited, however. Applying the critical stages test, subsequent decisions held that defendants have the right to court-appointed counsel during custodial interrogations (*Miranda v. Arizona*) and police lineups (*U.S. v. Wade 1967, Kirby v. Illinois* 1972). However, merely being detained by the police is not sufficient grounds to guarantee a right to counsel (*United States v. Gouveia* 1984). (The controversy surrounding the extension of the right to counsel in the police station will be examined in Chapter 12.)

The right to counsel also extends to certain post-trial proceedings, but as in pretrial proceedings, the right to counsel is more limited. Working

on the assumption that a person's right to an appeal can be effective only if counsel is available, the Court held that indigents have the right to court-appointed counsel for the appeal (*Douglas v. California* 1963), as well as free trial transcripts (*Griffin v. Illinois* 1956). The Burger Court, however, rejected attempts to extend the Douglas ruling beyond the first appeal. Thus, in discretionary appeals and appeals to the Supreme Court, indigent defendants have no right to court-appointed counsel (*Ross v. Moffitt* 1974). One consequence of the Ross decision is that defendants sentenced to death must rely on voluntary counsel in pursuing postconviction remedies. Besides appeal, the right to counsel in post-trial proceedings also includes probation and parole revocation hearings (*Gagnon v. Scarpelli* 1973).

Some states have gone considerably further than others in mandating counsel for situations in

| FIGURE 7-1 | Key Developments in the Right to Counsel |

Sixth Amendment	1791	"In all criminal prosecutions the accused shall enjoy the right ... to have the assistance of counsel for his defense."
Powell v. Alabama	1932	Indigent defendants in a capital case in state court have a right to court-appointed counsel.
Johnson v. Zerbst	1938	Indigent defendants in federal court are entitled to court-appointed counsel.
Betts v. Brady	1942	Indigent defendants in a noncapital case in state court have no right to appointed counsel.
Gideon v. Wainwright	1963	Indigents in state court have the right to appointed counsel (Betts overruled).
Douglas v. California	1963	Indigents have right to court-appointed counsel during the first appeal.
In re Gault	1967	Juveniles are covered by the Sixth Amendment's right to counsel.
Argersinger v. Hamlin	1972	Limited right of nonfelony defendants to have court-appointed counsel.
Faretta v. California	1975	Defendants have the right to self-representation.
Strickland v. Washington	1984	Defense attorney is ineffective only if proceedings were unfair and the outcome would have been different.
Martinez v. Court of Appeal of California	2000	Defendants have no Sixth Amendment right to represent themselves on appeal.
Roe v. Flores-Ortega	2000	A lawyer's failure to file an appeal does not necessarily constitute ineffective assistance of counsel.

which the Supreme Court has not yet acted or has not required counsel under the Sixth Amendment. Examples of this expanded right to counsel in other criminal and quasi-criminal proceedings include ordinance violations, termination of parental rights, civil commitments of mental patients, postconviction petitions, and prison disciplinary hearings (Bureau of Justice Statistics 1988; Spangenberg et al. 1986a).

Ineffective Assistance of Counsel

But is it enough to have a lawyer? Must the lawyer also be competent and effective? The Supreme Court recognized the effective assistance of counsel as essential to the Sixth Amendment guarantee (*McMann v. Richardson* 1970). The Court's most significant holding came in 1984 in *Strickland v. Washington,* in which an "objective standard of reasonableness" was set forth as the proper criterion to be applied in making a determination of the ineffectiveness of counsel. Speaking for the Court, Jus-

tice Sandra Day O'Connor emphasized that the "benchmark for judging any claim of ineffectiveness must be whether counsel's conduct so undermined the proper functioning of the adversarial process that the trial cannot be relied on as having produced a just result." In short, appellate courts must reverse only if the proceedings were fundamentally unfair and the outcome would have been different if counsel had not been ineffective. This standard places a heavy burden on the claimant; there are few appellate court reversals on these grounds. Indeed, the Court recently held that a lawyer's failure to file an appeal does not necessarily constitute ineffective assistance of counsel (*Roe v. Flores-Ortega* 2000).

Self-Representation

Can defendants represent themselves if they wish? An important qualification was added to *Gideon* when the Supreme Court ruled that defendants have a constitutional right to self-representation. This

| FIGURE 7-2 | Right to Counsel During Steps of Felony Crime Procedure |

	Extent of Right	*Supreme Court Case*
Crime	No lawyer required	
Arrest	No lawyer required	
Initial appearance	Lawyer required if critical stage	*Coleman v. Alabama* (1970)
Bail	Lawyer required if critical stage	*Coleman v. Alabama* (1970)
Charging	No lawyer required	
Preliminary hearing	Lawyer required	*Coleman v. Alabama* (1970)
Grand jury	No lawyer allowed	
Arraignment	Lawyer required	*Hamilton v. Alabama* (1961)
Evidence		
Interrogation (preindictment)	Lawyer on request	*Miranda v. Arizona* (1966)
Interrogation (postindictment)	Lawyer required	*Massiah v. U.S.* (1964)
Lineup (preindictment)	No lawyer required	*Kirby v. Illinois* (1972)
Lineup (postindictment)	Lawyer required	*U.S. v. Wade* (1967)
Plea bargaining	Lawyer required	*Brady v. U.S.* (1970) *Tollett v. Henderson* (1973)
Trial	Lawyer required	*Gideon v. Wainwright* (1963)
Sentencing	Lawyer required	*Mempa v. Rhay* (1967)
Probation revocation	Lawyer in court's discretion	*Gagnon v. Scarpelli* (1973)
Parole revocation	Lawyer in board's discretion	*Morrissey v. Brewer* (1972)
Appeal		
First appeal	Lawyer required	*Douglas v. California* (1963)
Discretionary appeal	No lawyer required	*Ross v. Moffitt* (1974)

means that criminal defendants have the right to proceed *pro se* (Latin for "in his or her own behalf"). The Court, however, did establish limits. Defendants who wish to represent themselves must show the trial judge that they have an ability to conduct the trial. The defendant need not have the skills and experience of a lawyer, but the judge may not deny self-representation simply because the defendant does not have an expert knowledge of criminal law and procedure (*Faretta v. California* 1975). This decision has been qualified by the Court's recognition that the trial judge may appoint standby counsel when defendants choose to represent themselves (*McKaskle v. Wiggins* 1984). Standby counsel is available during the trial to consult with the defendant, but it is the defendant, not the standby lawyer, who makes the decisions.

The Sixth Amendment right to self-representation, however, is limited to trial; state appellate courts can deny a defendant the right to represent himself or herself on appeal (*Martinez v. Court of Appeal of California* 2000).

Self-representation occurs occasionally, most typically when the defendant strongly distrusts the criminal justice system or becomes frustrated with the perceived incompetence of court-appointed counsel. Perhaps the oddest case of self-representation is that of Colin Ferguson. Ferguson fired into a crowded Long Island Railroad commuter train, killing six passengers and wounding nineteen others. Ferguson claimed that he acted out of a sense of "black rage"; his lawyer argued he was insane. Ferguson then dismissed his court-appointed lawyer, who objected that the trial would become a complete circus because "a crazy man cannot represent himself." The prediction proved accurate. During his opening statement Ferguson said there were "93 counts in the indictment, only because it matches the year 1993" (McQuiston 1995). Broadcast nation-wide on Court TV, the trial, and inevitable guilty verdict, was perceived as not a trial but a spectacle and underlined the limits of self-representation.

 Nancy Gibbs and David Jackson describe how Theodore Kaczynski made a circus of his terrorist bombing trial in their article, "In Fits and Starts."

DEFENSE ATTORNEYS AT WORK

Lawyers are expected to be advocates for their clients' cases, arguing for legal innocence. As one defense counsel phrased it, "If the attorney does not appear to be taking the side of the defendant, then no one will" (Neubauer 1974, 73). But the zealous advocacy of a client's case is not the same thing as winning at all costs. As a member of the legal profession, a lawyer's advocacy of a client's case is limited by professional obligations. Like prosecutors, defense attorneys are officers of the court, who must fulfill their responsibilities within the framework established by legal ethics. They cannot deliberately mislead the court by providing false information. Nor can they knowingly allow the use of perjured testimony.

At virtually all stages of the criminal justice process, defendants may have the guiding hand of counsel (Figure 7-3). We can best understand the multiple (and sometimes conflicting) responsibilities of defense attorneys by examining their work in fighting, negotiating, drafting, counseling, and administering.

Fighting

The defense attorney's objectives are diametrically opposed to those of the prosecutor. Whereas the state seeks to prove the defendant guilty, defense attorneys seek to disprove the criminal charges. Under the adversary system, their task is to zealously advocate their clients' cases, to ensure that the defendants receive justice. The defense attorney's role as fighter is most visible during trial. Through cross-examination, defense attorneys search for weaknesses in the state's case. By calling their own witnesses, they seek to convince the jury that there is a reasonable doubt about the defendant's guilt.

Throughout the trial, the defense attorney manages the case and must make important tactical and strategic decisions. (Chapter 14 will discuss some of the factors guiding such decisions.)

Negotiating

The defense attorney's role as advocate is not confined solely to trial. Because of the lawyer's dual role as advocate and counselor, there are different ways of assessing the work performed. How do we define winning? For Perry Mason, winning meant an acquittal. Real-life defendants usually define winning in the same way. A study of more than 2,000 Florida prisoners demonstrated that defendants believed it was their lawyers' job to "get them off, no matter how guilty they were" (Kerper 1972). Such expectations are unrealistic, however. As the American Bar Association's Standards on the Administration of Justice spell out, lawyers who define success as gaining an acquittal are doomed to disappointment. An experienced Los Angeles public defender explains:

> What is our job as a criminal lawyer in most instances? Number one is . . . no kidding, we know the man's done it, or we feel he's done it, he may deny it, but the question is: Can they prove it? The next thing is: Can we mitigate it? Of course you can always find something good to say about the guy—to mitigate it. Those are the two things that are important, and that's what you do. (Mather 1974, 278)

Thus, many defense attorneys define winning in terms of securing probation, staying away from a felony conviction by accepting a plea to a misdemeanor, or avoiding a long prison sentence. Such alternative goals to gaining an outright acquittal focus on sentencing, whereas the prescribed role of advocate centers on contesting guilt. One attorney put it this way: "Given the situation, what is the best that can be done for my client?" (Neubauer 1974, 74). Often, the best that can be done for the client is to negotiate the best possible deal (Chapter 13).

 To learn how defense attorneys defend drug cases click on **http://dpa.state.ky.us/~rwheeler/drugs/leo.htm**.

For an up-to-date list of Web links, go to **http://www.wadsworth.com/product/0534563406s**.

FIGURE 7-3	**Role of Defense Attorney in Typical Felony Case**
Crime	Counsels the client about the crime charged.
Arrest	Rarely present.
Initial appearance	Typically just met the client, so advises client to say nothing during the court proceedings.
Bail	Argues for client's release on bail.
Charging	May use informal ties with prosecutor to argue for charging client with less serious offense.
Preliminary hearing	Good opportunity to find out what really happened in the case.
Grand jury	Tells client to take the Fifth Amendment; grand jury transcript may be useful for discovery.
Arraignment	Chance to talk to the client and may suggest entering a plea of guilty.
Evidence	Requests (formally or informally) discovery information from the prosecutor; files motions to suppress confession and/or search and seizure.
Plea bargaining	Negotiates with the district attorney (sometimes judge as well) for most beneficial deal possible.
Trial	Typically stresses that the prosecutor has not proved the defendant "guilty beyond a reasonable doubt."
Sentencing	Argues for sentence at the low end of the normal penalty scale.
Appeal	Files notice of appeal and writes appellate brief. Common grounds for arguing for a new trial are (1) judge improperly admitted evidence, (2) prosecutor's closing argument was inflammatory, (3) judge erred in instructions to the jury. Unlikely to be involved after right of appeal has been exhausted.

Drafting

Under the adversary system, defense attorneys are also responsible for protecting the defendant's constitutional rights. One of the defense attorney's roles is to keep the adversary system honest. Defense attorneys question whether the police and prosecutor have acted properly. Most of these activities occur when the attorneys file motions they have drafted to suppress confessions or evidence because the police acted improperly (Chapter 12). Defense attorneys may also file motions for change of venue (place for holding the trial; see Chapter 14) because of prejudicial pretrial publicity.

Counseling

One of the most important tasks of defense attorneys is **counseling**. As advocates, defense attorneys are expected to champion their clients' cases. But as

Counseling: Legal advice provided by lawyers to their clients.

counselors, they must advise their clients about the possible legal consequences involved. Lawyers must fully and dispassionately evaluate the strengths and weaknesses of the prosecutor's case, assess the probable success of various legal defenses, and—most important—weigh the likelihood of conviction or acquittal. In appraising risks and outlining options, lawyers interpret the law to their clients, who are often unversed in what the law considers important, what the law demands, and what the law views as irrelevant. (A later section of this chapter will examine why the counseling role is a difficult one for the defense attorney.)

Administering

Like prosecutors, defense attorneys represent numerous clients at the same time. Moreover, the cases are all at different stages of the criminal court process. Defense attorneys must keep numerous balls in the air, trying to meet various scheduled court appearances: initial appearances, bail hearings, arraignments, pretrial motions, plea bargaining

The New York State Defenders Association offers defense news and hot topics: **http://www.nysda.org/**.

For an up-to-date list of Web links, go to **http://www.wadsworth.com/product/0534563406s**.

sessions, trial settings, and sentencing hearings. On a typical day, defense attorneys must appear in several different courts; they thus spend part of their day waiting for everyone else to assemble. Besides scheduling court appearances, defense attorneys are also responsible for other administrative duties: making sure that necessary witnesses are subpoenaed to be in court, filing motions on time, and so on.

The fact that a lawyer represents numerous defendants means that there is often insufficient time to investigate each case thoroughly. Like judges and prosecutors, defense attorneys must be able to process many cases. Consider the assessment by a public defender of a former colleague: "She wasn't a good PD [public defender] in the sense that she couldn't handle cases on a volume basis. She wanted to act like a private lawyer and the office couldn't afford to give her that much time. She was eased out of the office" (Platt and Pollock 1974, 254).

DEFENSE ATTORNEYS AND COURTROOM WORK GROUPS

How defense attorneys perform their multiple tasks as fighters, negotiators, counselors, drafters, and administrators is directly related to their relationship with other members of the courtroom work group. Usually, assistant public defenders are permanently assigned to a single courtroom and work every day with the same judge, the same prosecutor(s), the same court reporter, and the same clerk of court. Similarly, private defense attorneys— although they practice before several judges—are a permanent fixture in the criminal courts, for a handful of lawyers dominate the representation of fee-paying criminal defendants in any city.

This daily interaction of the criminal bar with the court community shapes the type and quality of legal representation received by those accused of violating the law. Whereas the adversary system stresses the combative role of the defense attorney, the day-to-day activities of the courtroom work group stress cooperation (see A Day in Court: "Legal Workload Frustrating to Both Sides"). The legal system, civil and criminal, is based on controversy. Norms of cooperation work to channel such controversy into constructive avenues. All too often, advocacy is falsely equated with antagonism. Although defense attorneys exchange pleasantries with judges and prosecutors, their personal contacts with these officials outside the courtroom are limited (Mather 1974).

Another qualification to bear in mind is that cooperative attorneys do not bargain every case; they also take cases to trial. If the defense attorney thinks the prosecutor is driving too hard a bargain or that the state cannot prove its case to the jury, a trial will be recommended. Furthermore, there is no evidence that cooperative attorneys do not argue the case to the best of their abilities during a trial.

 The National Association of Defense Lawyers (NACDL) discusses issues in criminal defense: **http://www.criminaljustice.org/**.

For an up-to-date list of Web links, go to **http://www.wadsworth.com/product/0534563406s**.

Rewards and Sanctions

Defense attorneys who maintain a cooperative stance toward judges, prosecutors, and clerks can expect to reap some rewards. Defense attorneys have limited (in some instances, nonexistent) investigative resources. Prosecutors can provide cooperative defense attorneys with information about the cases by letting them examine the police reports, revealing the names of witnesses, and so on.

The court community can also apply sanctions to defense attorneys who violate the norms. Some sanctions work indirectly, by reducing a lawyer's income-generating ability. The clerk may refuse to provide beneficial case scheduling, or the judge may drag out a trial by continuously interrupting it for other business. Other sanctions are more direct. A judge can criticize a lawyer in front of his or her client (thus scaring away potential clients in the courtroom) or refuse to appoint certain attorneys to represent indigents—a significant source of income for some lawyers (Nardulli 1978). A final category of sanctions involves the prosecutor's adopting a tougher stance during bargaining by not reducing

A DAY IN COURT

"Legal Workload Frustrating to Both Sides"

 Meet David Thalheimer, assistant district attorney, and Kathleen Knese, assistant public defender, who bring you sharply different perspectives on the state of justice in Philadelphia's criminal courts. Take yesterday, when Thalheimer and Knese squared off in Common Pleas Courtroom 315 with 12 felony cases. One case ended with a guilty plea—the other 11 were postponed for a myriad of reasons. Defendants failed to show, the defense wasn't ready, a defendant lacked a lawyer, the DA's office lost a case file, a police witness was out having back surgery.

"Probably the worst day I've ever had," said Thalheimer, 30, a prosecutor since June. "This is frustrating!" he exclaimed at a break, referring to five defendants who failed to appear—two of them repeat no-shows and accused drug dealers. "Today was a crummy day. I achieved very little."

"What's frustrating," countered Knese, 29—after weathering a 102-degree fever to be in court—"is that there is this push to just dispose of cases. That doesn't leave a lot of time for individual one-on-one justice for my clients. We don't want to be seen as just a plea mill."

Thalheimer and Knese, though, share the common bond of overworked, underpaid assistant DAs and public defenders, who juggle a dozen cases or more every day in a beleaguered criminal court system overflowing with cases.... Both Thalheimer and Knese know they're making far less money than they would make in private practice. In fact, Thalheimer was making that kind of money; he gave up a $60,000-a-year job at a corporate law firm—Dechert, Price and Rhoads—to join the DA's office at half the salary.

"At Dechert Price," he said, "I spent my time researching arcane legal issues for corporations. Here, I meet the people, every day." After the corporate decorum of Dechert Price, Thalheimer says one thing that raises his frustration with his job is the shabby milieu of City Hall. "It smells of sewers and reeks of human waste," he said. "These are the halls of justice."

Knese . . . said making money has never been her goal in life, being a public defender was. . . . Knese's biggest frustration, unlike Thalheimer's, isn't the courts' sluggishness, it's what she sees as their frenzied pace. Like Thalheimer, Knese handles felony waivers—in which defendants waive their right to a jury trial and have their cases heard by a judge. Her workload—40 cases a week—is brutalizing.

"The felony waiver program is extremely tiring and stressful," she said. "You're holding the lives of 40 people in your hands. It's difficult to explain to my clients: 'I'd like to spend more time with you, but I have eight other clients today.'" Add onto that an increasing public clamor for stiff jail terms for drug dealers—and decreasing public tolerance for a defendant's rights—and you have a sense of Knese's existence. . . .

Public Defender Ben Lerner, who's headed the Defender's Association for 15 years, contends with the same budget problems as [other criminal justice agencies]—plus a distinct lack of public support—for the job of protecting defendants' constitutional rights. Lerner noted that when the local defenders association was cited as the best in the nation last year by the National Bar Association, no public official offered congratulations. Like his DA counterpart, Lerner painted a portrait of a system under siege, "drowning" in a sea of drug cases. He said the low pay and long hours are exacting a heavy toll on his staff. "More people [public defenders] are leaving in their most productive years," he said. "And when you have more inexperienced people, it has an impact on the whole system."

SOURCE: J. Grace, "Legal Workload Frustrating to Both Sides," *Philadelphia Daily News,* March 13, 1990, 21. Reprinted by permission.

 Here are three Web sites that provide an overview of the functions and structures of public defenders' offices:

Maryland Office of Public Defender: **http://www.opd.state.md.us/**

Oklahoma Indigent Defense System: **http://www.state.ok.us/~oids/**

South Carolina Commission on Indigent Defense: **http://www.scoid.state.sc.us/**

For an up-to-date list of Web links, go to **http://www.wadsworth.com/product/0534563406s**.

charges or by recommending a prison sentence that is longer than normal.

Sanctions against defense attorneys are seldom invoked, but when they are, they can have far-reaching effects. Every court community can point to an attorney who has suffered sanctions, with the result that the attorney either no longer practices criminal law in the area or has mended his or her ways.

Variations in Cooperation

Defense attorneys are the least powerful members of the courtroom work group. Because of the numerous sanctions that can be applied to defense attorneys, they are forced into a reactive posture.

Prosecutors assess a defense attorney in terms of "reasonableness"—that is, ability to "discern a generous offer of settlement and to be willing to encourage his client to accept such an offer" (Skolnick 1967, 58). Based on this criterion, Skolnick put attorneys into three categories. One category consisted of defense attorneys who handled few criminal cases. One might suppose that prosecutors would prefer dealing with such inexperienced attorneys, but they did not. Because these attorneys did not know the ropes, they were too unpredictable and often caused administrative problems. In another category were attorneys who had active criminal practices and maintained a hostile relationship with the prosecutor's office. Known as "gamblers," these attorneys exemplified the aggressive, fighting advocate, but because they either won big or lost big, they also served to show the other attorneys the disadvantage of this posture. The final category of attorneys consisted of public defenders and private attorneys who represented large numbers of defendants. These attorneys worked within the system.

 The Association of Federal Defense Attorneys (AFDA) hosts a Web site for criminal defense attorneys, law school students, and the interested general public: **http://www.afda.org**.

For an up-to-date list of Web links, go to **http://www.wadsworth.com/product/0534563406s**.

An Assessment

Are criminal defense attorneys, especially public defenders and regular private attorneys, the co-opted agents of a court bureaucracy or simply calculating realists? This question has preoccupied research on defense attorneys for almost thirty years (Flemming 1986b).

Some studies argue that defense attorneys' ties to the court community mean that defendants' best interests are not represented. David Sudnow (1965) argued that public defenders became co-opted when public defenders and prosecutors shared common conceptions of what Sudnow called "normal crimes." Public defenders were more interested that a given case fit into sociological cubbyholes than in determining whether the event met the proper penal code provisions. As a result, the public defenders seldom geared their work to securing acquittals for their clients. Thus, from the beginning, the presumption of guilt permeated the public defenders' assessment of cases.

Although Sudnow believed private attorneys were not similarly co-opted, Abraham Blumberg (1967) concluded that all defense attorney regulars were double agents. His study of a large New York court likened the practice of law to a confidence game in which both the defendant and the defense attorney must have larceny at heart; a con game can be successful only if the "mark" is trying to get something for nothing. Judges and prosecutors depended on the defense attorneys to pressure defendants to plead guilty. Blumberg placed great stress on the fact that it is the defense attorney who first suggests a guilty plea to the defendant—a suggestion that a number of defendants initially respond to in a negative way because they expect their attorney to be their champion. In short, both Sudnow and Blumberg portray defense attorneys as ideological and economic captives of the court rather than aggressive advocates.

However, other studies have concluded that defendants' best interests are not eroded when their attorneys adopt a cooperative posture within the courtroom community. Indeed, Jerome Skolnick (1967) suggested that the clients do better as a result of a cooperative posture. Working within the system benefits the client, because the prosecutor will be more amenable to disclosing information helpful to the defense, the bargains struck will be more favorable, and the defendant will not be penalized for the hostility of the defense attorney. Furthermore, attorneys identified as agitators may harm their clients' causes because prosecutors and judges will hand out longer sentences. Neubauer's (1974) study of Prairie City, Illinois, also found that attorneys who remain on good terms with other members of the courtroom work group function better as counselors, because they are better able to predict the reactions of the court community to individual cases. In short, the studies by Skolnick (1967), Neubauer (1974), and Mather (1974) conclude that attorneys who work within the system are best able to develop a realistic approach to their work, based on experience and knowledge of how their clients will fare.

These assessments of defense attorneys' performance within the courtroom work group have been drawn primarily from studies of individual courts. Peter Nardulli (1986) offers a much-needed comparative evaluation of nine counties. By and large, the performance of regular and outsider defense attorneys differs very little. In particular, there is little empirical evidence to suggest that insiders systematically manipulate the system to their clients' benefit. To those who control the dispositional process, certainty, uniformity, and routine are extremely important. Thus, once established, norms about normal pleas affect cases involving both insiders and outsiders.

 Joseph McSorley, "'Criminal Lawyers' or 'Lawyer Criminals'"

THE CRIMINAL BAR

Law offices of solo practitioners are a permanent feature of urban architecture. They can be found huddled around the stone edifice of the criminal courts and near the neon lights proclaiming "Harry's 24-Hour Bail Bonds." In Detroit they are called "the Clinton Street Bar" and in Washington, D.C., "the Fifth Streeters"—titles that are not meant to be complimentary. These lawyers spend little time in their offices; they are most often at the courthouse, socializing with other members of the courtroom work group. Their proximity to the criminal courts and the sparseness of the law books in their offices are good indicators that the law practiced from these offices bears little resemblance to images of defense attorneys presented in television's

Perry Mason or *L.A. Law.* A number of factors account for the low economic and professional status of the criminal bar.

 Michael Depp, "Defensive Starters"

Diversity and Stratification of the Legal Profession

The practice of law is not a single, unified profession. Rather, there are important distinctions within the legal profession, based partially on the law school attended and the place of work. An interdisciplinary team, law professor John Heinz and sociologist Edward Laumann, conducted a comprehensive study of the diverse tasks that characterize the social role of lawyers. Based on extensive interviews with practicing attorneys *Chicago Lawyers: The Social Structure of the Bar* (1982) reported dramatic differences among several sorts of lawyers.

One difference in the social structure of the bar involves specialization. Most lawyers never handle criminal cases, largely because other areas of the law are much more lucrative. Moreover, the practice of criminal law is also becoming a highly specialized area. The increase in appellate court decisions involving criminal law and criminal procedure requires a large investment of a lawyer's time and energy to keep abreast of changes in the law.

Chicago Lawyers found that the most important differentiation within the legal profession involved which clients were served. Some lawyers represent large organizations (corporations, labor unions, or government). Others represent mainly individuals. By and large, lawyers operate in one of these two hemispheres of the profession; seldom, if ever, do they cross the equator separating these very different types of legal work. The corporate client sector involves large corporate, regulatory, general corporate, and political lawyers. The personal client sector is divided into personal business and personal plight lawyers (divorce, tort, and so on).

The bulk of the attorneys who appear in criminal court are drawn from the personal client sector. They are often referred to as solo practitioners because they practice alone or share an office with another attorney. For this group of courtroom regulars, criminal cases constitute a dominant part of their economic livelihood. Thus, studies of private attorneys in different cities report that the bulk of nonindigent defendants are represented by a handful of attorneys (Nardulli 1986; Neubauer 1974).

Not all private defense attorneys, however, fall into the category of sometimes unethical, poorly trained wholesalers. This pattern appears to predominate in America's older central cities. Newer cities tend to have a different type of defense attorney—younger, more skilled, and more committed to providing quality representation. Moreover, the old-time solo practitioner is a vanishing breed. A study of private defense bars in nine U.S. cities reported that as the older attorneys of this type die or retire they are not being replaced (Wice 1978). Part of the reason is economic pressure. Public defenders are now available to provide legal services. Younger attorneys are also more professionally and ethically committed to providing high-quality legal services to criminal indigents. They prefer working for public defenders' offices, rather than eking out a living as a solo practitioner.

 If you're thinking of going to law school, be sure to check out the *Pre-Law Handbook* from the University of Richmond at **http://www.richmond.edu/~polisci/prelaw/**.

For an up-to-date list of Web links, go to **http://www.wadsworth.com/product/0534563406s**.

Environment of Practice

It is no accident that in many large cities there is a distinct criminal bar. Low status, difficulty in securing clients, and low fees are three factors that affect the availability of lawyers to represent those accused of violating the law.

Low Status

Most lawyers view criminal cases as unsavory. Representing criminal defendants also produces few chances for victory; most defendants either plead guilty or are found guilty by a judge or jury. Moreover, many lawyers who represent middle-class clients do not want accused drug peddlers brushing shoulders in the waiting room with their regular clients. Also, despite the legal presumption of innocence, once defendants are arrested, the public assumes they are guilty. As a result, the general public perceives attorneys as freeing known robbers and

rapists to return to the streets. "Realistically, a lawyer who defends notoriously unpopular clients becomes identified in the public's mind, and not infrequently in the mind of his own profession, with his client" (Kaplan 1973).

Securing Clients

To earn a living, lawyers first need clients. Attorneys working in the personal client sector of the legal profession seldom have a regular clientele. Accordingly, a part of their time is spent securing clients. The criminal lawyer's most important commodity in securing clients is his or her reputation, which often develops on the basis of the lawyer's handling of a specific case. A lawyer's reputation is important in several ways. First, defendants want a specific attorney to represent them, not a firm of lawyers. Second, attorneys who do not practice criminal law often refer clients to a specific lawyer who does. Finally, a repeat offender may seek out the previous attorney, if he or she felt the lawyer provided good representation in the past.

In securing clients, some defense attorneys rely on police officers, bail agents, and court clerks to give their names to defendants who need counsel. In addition, solo practitioners are known as "joiners"; they make their names known by belonging to as many groups as possible. The need to secure clients is also a reason solo practitioners are often active in local politics. Not only do their names become familiar, but their hopes for a future appointment, perhaps as a judge, are also thus improved (Wice 1978).

Fees

Obtaining clients is only half the problem facing private attorneys who represent criminal clients. The second half is getting paid. "Criminal lawyers are more concerned than other lawyers with collection of the fee—after all, their clients are mostly criminals" (Lushing 1992, 514). The lawyer's fee in a criminal case is generally a flat fee paid in advance. The three most important considerations in setting the fee are the seriousness of the offense, the amount of time it will take the lawyer to deal with the case, and the client's ability to pay. Well-known criminal lawyers, for example, often charge their prosperous clients considerable fees. There has been a myth that criminal lawyers receive fabulous salaries. Although a few have become quite wealthy, most earn a modest middle-class living (Wice

1978). Of course, many defendants are so impoverished that they cannot afford to hire a private attorney at all.

 If you wonder what they teach in law school, check out this Web site of law school course outlines: **http://www.ilrg.com/students/outlines/**.

For an up-to-date list of Web links, go to **http://www.wadsworth.com/product/0534563406s**.

PROVIDING INDIGENTS WITH ATTORNEYS

Indigents are defendants who are too poor to pay a lawyer and therefore are entitled to a lawyer for free. Indigent defendants, rather than those who can afford to hire their own lawyer, dominate the criminal court process. Three quarters of state prison inmates had a court-appointed lawyer to represent them for the offense for which they were serving time. In urban courthouses, the indigency rate is a little higher: 80 percent of felony defendants are too poor to hire their own lawyer (Smith and DeFrances 1996). Obviously, the Supreme Court's decision in *Gideon*, requiring the state to provide attorneys for indigents, applies to a substantial number of criminal defendants.

Although the Supreme Court has essentially mandated the development of indigent defense systems, it has left the financing and type of delivery system up to states and counties, which have considerable discretion in adopting programs (Worden and Worden 1989). As with other aspects of America's dual court system, the characteristics of defense systems for the indigent vary considerably (Lee 1992). In most jurisdictions, local governments are solely responsible for providing criminal defense for the poor. Twenty-four states organize indigent defense services on a county level, and three others employ a district- or circuit-organized system. In seventeen states, the state government is responsible. To confuse matters further, six states' defense systems for the indigent are organized on both state and county levels.

Indigent: A person too poor to hire a lawyer.

How best to provide legal representation for the poor has been a long-standing vital issue for the courts and the legal profession. In the United States, there are three primary methods: assigned counsel (attorneys appointed by the judge on a case-by-case basis), contract systems (attorneys hired to provide services for a specified dollar amount), and public defender (a salaried public official representing all indigent defendants). Figure 7-4 on page 181 shows the type of system used in the majority of counties in each state. Each system has its supporters and critics. The ongoing debate over the advantages and disadvantages of these three systems highlights some important issues about the quality of legal representation provided the poor.

 For updated indigent defense statistics, go to **http://www.ojp.usdoj.gov/bjs/id.htm**.

For an up-to-date list of Web links, go to **http://www.wadsworth.com/product/0534563406s**.

Assigned Counsel

The assigned counsel system reflects the way professions such as law and medicine traditionally respond to charity cases: Individual practitioners provide services on a case-by-case basis. **Assigned counsel systems** involve the appointment by the court of private attorneys from a list of available attorneys. The list may consist of all practicing attorneys in the jurisdiction, or, more commonly, those attorneys who volunteer. Three out of four counties use ad hoc assigned counsel systems, in which individual private attorneys are appointed by individual judges and provide representation on a case-by-case basis. The other counties use coordinated assigned counsel systems and have an administrator who oversees the appointment of counsel and develops a set of standards and guidelines for program administration (Houlden and Balkin 1985). (Coordinated systems are sometimes indistinguishable from public defender programs.)

The assigned counsel system, used in half of all U.S. counties, nonetheless serves less than one third

Assigned counsel system: Arrangement that provides attorneys for persons who are accused of crimes and are unable to hire their own lawyers. The judge assigns a member of the bar to provide counsel to a particular defendant.

THE MURDER TRIAL OF SHAREEF COUSIN

Limitations Facing the Defense

 "I could win most of my cases if it weren't for the clients. . . . They will waltz into the witness box and blurt out things which are far better left unblurted" (Mortimer, 1984, 11). This sentiment from the fictional British defense attorney Rumpole is shared by many real-life American attorneys, who might embellish by saying, "Clients blurt out things to the police that are better left unblurted."

Late on the afternoon of March 27, 1995, the police arrested the defendant at his house and took him to the homicide division (located in central police headquarters). With his mother present, the police interrogated Cousin. Although he confessed to participating in four armed robberies, he did not directly admit to murdering Michael Gerardi in front of the Port of Call restaurant. However, when he was handed a copy of a police report about the murder, he immediately noted that the murder occurred on March 3, not February 3, as the report erroneously recorded. If he would have taken the stand in his own defense, then the jury would almost certainly have been able to learn this damning tidbit.

Shareef Cousin was also very unlikely to take the stand in his own defense because of his past conduct. During police questioning he admitted to participating in four armed robberies and he later pled guilty to those crimes (see Chapter 13). As discussed in Chapter 14, defendants enjoy the protection against self-incrimination; that is, they cannot be forced to testify against themselves. But if a defendant takes the stand, then the prosecution can impeach the defendant's credibility by introducing evidence of past felony convictions. Thus, if Cousin took the witness stand in his own defense, the jury would learn of these crimes, several of which appeared to parallel the murder in front of the Port of Call restaurant.

Another limitation the defense had to work around was the defendant himself. It appears from the court record that Cousin was unpredictable. Outside of the presence of the jury, the defense hinted at medical and psychiatric issues but never presented them to the jury. This much is known, however. In the fall of 1994 Cousin spent several months in a hospital and the admitting physician was a child psychiatrist. Moreover, during the sentencing phase of trial, Cousin made an angry statement of innocence, one that most certainly worked to the advantage of the prosecution.

Finally, the defense was forced to defend Cousin without any help from his family. Jumping ahead to material covered in Chapter 16, by the time of the penalty phase of the first-degree murder trial, family members firmly believed that the justice system was racist and would therefore not participate, not even to the extent of the mother pleading for the jurors to spare her son's life.

Given these limitations, the defense proceeded on two fronts. One was to stress that Shareef Cousin had an alibi. The other was to limit the evidence the state could present at trial. Toward this end the defense filed a series of motions, one of which was successful. The prosecution wanted to introduce the testimony of the victims of the four previous armed robberies. The trial judge ruled that the evidence of such signature crimes could be introduced at trial. But the appellate court overturned the trial judge, ruling, "The four prior armed robberies are not sufficiently distinctive or similar to the offense charged to justify their admission in evidence." But the other efforts by the defense to limit the evidence that the prosecution could introduce—motions to suppress physical evidence and motions to suppress identification—were not successful.

 To read more about the Shareef Cousin trial, type in the search words *dead teen walking* and read the section, "The Defense."

---

of the nation's population. It predominates in small counties with less than 50,000 residents, where there is not a sufficient volume of cases to support the costs of a public defender system.

Critics contend that the assigned counsel system results in the least qualified lawyers being appointed to defend indigents. In most counties, the only attorneys who volunteer are either young ones who desire courtroom experience or those who seek numerous appointments to make a living. Even

where appointments are rotated among all members of the practicing bar (as in New Jersey or Houston, Texas), there is no guarantee that the lawyer selected is qualified to handle the increasing complexity of the criminal law; the appointee may be a skilled real estate attorney or a good probate attorney, but these skills are not readily transferable to the dynamics of a criminal trial.

The availability of lawyers willing to serve as assigned counsel is directly related to financial com-

FIGURE 7-4   State Defense Systems, by Type, in Majority of Counties

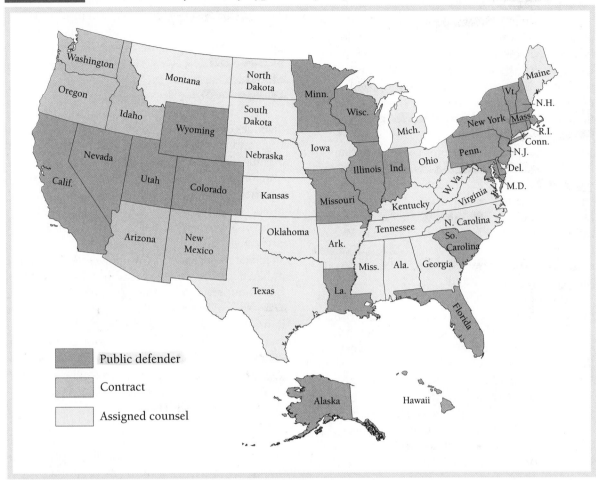

Public defender

Contract

Assigned counsel

SOURCE: Bureau of Justice Statistics, *Criminal Defense for the Poor, 1986* (Washington D.C.: U.S. Department of Justice, 1988).

pensation. In the past, a number of jurisdictions expected attorneys to represent indigents as part of their professional responsibility, without being paid (*pro bono*). Today, however, the majority of assigned counsel are paid. Most commonly, lawyers are compensated for such defense work on the basis of separate hourly rates for out-of-court and in-court work. However, hourly fees for in-court felony work usually range far below the fees charged in private practice. Critics contend that inadequate compensation pressures attorneys to dispose of such cases quickly, in order to devote time to fee-paying clients (Moore 1965, 283).

The widely held assumption that rates of compensation are directly related to the quality of criminal defense representation has been challenged by a recent study. The extent of effort of lawyers in

Michigan who handled appellate representation did not vary significantly in relation to the rate of compensation. Overall, professional role expectations of lawyers may be of greater influence on their work than financial considerations (Priehs 1999).

Contract Systems

Contract systems are a relatively new way to provide defense services. A **contract system** involves bidding by private attorneys to represent all criminal

Contract system: System of providing counsel for indigents under which the government contracts with a law firm to represent all indigents for the year in return for a set fee.

defendants found indigent during the term of the contract, in return for a fixed payment. Such systems are used in 11 percent of U.S. counties (Bureau of Justice Statistics 1988), and there is reason to believe it will become a more rather than less popular option in the future (Worden 1991). Contract systems are most often found in counties with populations of less than 50,000, where the key feature is that they place an absolute budget limit on defense services for the indigent.

The primary advantage of contract systems is that they limit the costs government must pay for indigent defense. Critics counter with two types of concerns. The first is that contract programs will inevitably lead to a lower standard of representation through the bidding system, which emphasizes cost over quality. The second is that the private bar will no longer play an important role in indigent defense (Spangenberg Group 2000).

The contract system was held unconstitutional in Arizona when the Arizona Supreme Court held that the Mohave County contract system, which assigned defense representation of the indigent to the lowest bidder, violated the Fifth and Sixth Amendments because the system (1) did not take into account the time the attorney is expected to spend on a case, (2) did not provide for support staff costs, (3) failed to take into account the competence of the attorney, and (4) did not consider the complexity of the case (*Smith v. State* 1984). Likewise, courts in several other states have found legal defects in contract systems that result in inadequate funding levels (Spangenberg Group 2000).

A study in Michigan found that competitive bidding is indeed less expensive than the alternatives, but at the same time raises questions about the implications of this financial advantage for program quality. The findings also suggest that contracting, paradoxically, is adopted in small jurisdictions whose bars cannot support competitive bidding; as a result, these jurisdictions pay a high price for this type of program (Worden 1993).

 The Office of Justice Programs has a Web page on indigent defense: **http://www.ojp.usdoj.gov/ indigentdefense**.

For an up-to-date list of Web links, go to **http:// www.wadsworth.com/product/0534563406s**.

Public Defender

The **public defender** is a twentieth-century response to the problem of providing legal representation for the indigent. Public defender programs are public or private nonprofit organizations with full- or part-time salaried staff who represent indigents in criminal cases in the jurisdiction.

Started in Los Angeles County in 1914, public defender offices spread slowly. By 1965 the National Legal Aid and Defender Association—the national organization that promotes better legal representation for indigents in civil as well as criminal cases—reported programs in only 117 counties. Since 1965 public defender programs have spread rapidly because of Supreme Court decisions (*Gideon* and later *Argersinger*), as well as increased concern for more adequate representation of indigents. Today the public defender system is used in 37 percent of all U.S. counties, representing approximately 70 percent of all indigents nationwide. It predominates in most big cities and has also been adopted in numerous medium-sized jurisdictions. Seventeen states have established statewide, state-funded programs. The remaining public defender programs are funded by local units of government and operate autonomously, without any central administration (Bureau of Justice Statistics 1988; Spangenberg et al. 1986a).

Proponents of the public defender system cite several arguments in favor of its adoption. One is that a lawyer paid to represent indigents on a continuous basis will devote more attention to cases than a court-appointed attorney who receives only minimal compensation. Moreover, many members of the practicing bar like the idea that they no longer have to take time away from fee-paying cases to meet their professional obligations.

A second advantage often claimed for the public defender system is that it provides more experienced, competent counsel. Because public defenders concentrate on criminal cases, they can keep abreast of changes in the law, and the day-to-day courtroom work keeps their trial skills sharp. The public defender is also likely to be more knowledgeable about informal norms and is therefore in a better

Public defender: An attorney employed by the government to represent indigent defendants.

position to counsel defendants and negotiate the best possible deal.

Finally, a public defender system assures continuity and consistency in the defense of the poor (Silverstein 1965). Public defenders are usually able to provide early representation, entering the case at the initial appearance. Moreover, issues that transcend individual cases—criteria for pretrial release, police practices, and so forth—are more likely to be considered by a permanent, ongoing organization than under appointment systems.

 Visit Public Defenders in the Neighborhood and read about how "A Harlem Law Office Stresses Teamwork, Early Investigation": **http://www.ncjrs.org/txtfiles/163061.txt**.

For an up-to-date list of Web links, go to **http://www.wadsworth.com/product/0534563406s**.

Assessing the Merits of Public Defenders

Critics contend that public defenders—as paid employees of the state—will not provide a vigorous defense because they are tied too closely to the courtroom work group. Several studies have investigated this concern by comparing the adequacy of representation provided by assigned counsel to that of public defenders' offices. The dominant conclusion is that there is not much difference (Flemming 1989; Wice 1985). The National Center for State Courts drew the following conclusions from the nine jurisdictions it studied: (1) Attorneys for indigent defendants resolved their cases more expeditiously than privately retained counsel. (2) Defense attorneys for the indigent gained as many favorable outcomes (acquittals, charge reductions, and short prison sentences) for their clients as privately retained attorneys did for their clients. (3) Indigent defense attorneys and prosecuting attorneys were equally experienced (Hanson, Hewitt, and Ostrom 1992). Likewise, the outcomes of criminal appeals do not vary between public defenders and privately retained counsel (Williams 1995).

Problems often identified with public defenders are in reality not all that unique. Rather, they reflect difficulties associated with lawyers—whether paid or court appointed—who maintain close ties with other members of the courtroom work group. James

Eisenstein, Roy Flemming, and Peter Nardulli (1988) found several characteristics of court communities that impede vigorous defense of poor clients. First, the structure of defense for the indigent creates financial disincentives. Public defenders are usually paid less than prosecutors; young attorneys are attracted to the position only because it offers trial experience. Second, public defenders' offices are usually not well insulated from pressures that discourage vigorous advocacy. They receive funds from county agencies, which seek to keep expenditures low and also discourage the reappointment of attorneys who are gung-ho advocates.

Many scholars have insisted that indigent defenders (assigned counsel, contract lawyers, and public defenders) survive only because the lawyers do not really fight against, but rather cooperate with, the state as it prosecutes and convicts defendants. Indeed, some scholars portray lawyers appointed by the court as "cop-out artists," more geared to negotiating a plea than fighting the other members of the criminal justice system.

The Public Defender: The Practice of Law in the Shadows of Repute offers a radically different view of public defense attorneys. Lisa McIntyre (1987) demonstrates that public defense lawyers are indeed free to defend their clients zealously. She found that in the courts of Cook County, Illinois, public defenders are adversarial and even combative opponents of the state's prosecutorial apparatus. McIntyre argues, in fact, that the office of the public defender survives because its effective advocacy for its clients bolsters the legitimacy of the court system.

Why then does the public defender's image not reflect this? The freedom to defend against the state cannot include the freedom to embarrass it. Hence, the complexity of the public defender's institutional role requires that the office not advertise its successes. McIntyre shows that the public defender's office deliberately retains its image of incompetency in order to guarantee its continued existence: Public defenders may practice good law, but they must do it in the darker shadows of repute.

The long-standing debate over the adequacy of court-appointed counsel is beginning to give way to a new reality—large governmental expenses. Images and myths play a central role in the debate over funding levels for court-appointed lawyers (see Controversy: Are We Spending Too Little or Too Much on Indigent Defense?).

CONTROVERSY

Are We Spending Too Little or Too Much on Indigent Defense?

 Important ideological differences are apparent in discussions over court-appointed counsel. Although all camps agree that basic notions of equity and fairness require that indigents have counsel during trial, the scope of this right is disputed. Crime control advocates are concerned that government spends too much money on providing the poor with lawyers, whereas due process proponents are worried that government is spending too little.

Crime Control Perspective: We Spend Too Much

Between 1976 and 1986 the cost of providing defense services for the indigent increased fivefold (Spangenberg et al. 1986b; Bureau of Justice Statistics 1988). More recently the estimated number of cases is 8 million each year with spending at about $2 billion (Blum 1995). Hardest hit by the expansion of legal rights and consequent increase in costs have been local governments and, secondarily, state governments. Indeed the burden is highest in communities with the greatest needs and fewest resources—those with high crime rates and large populations of the poor.

As expenditures for defense services for the indigent have risen dramatically, there has been a noticeable trend toward containing the costs. One technique is the adoption of stringent indigency standards. Although this has been common practice in some courts, big-city judges rarely inquire into the financial capabilities of defendants to determine whether they satisfy the court's definition of indigency. Most seem to feel that if a defendant is willing to settle for a public defender, then he or she is not likely to possess the funds necessary to hire a private attorney (Wice 1985). However, a report funded by the National Institute of Justice stresses that courts should not assume all criminal defendants who request court-appointed attorneys are indigent. To reduce the costs to taxpayers, courts should screen applications "to ensure that only the truly indigent are provided representation at public expense" (Spangenberg et al. 1986b, 69).

Another way of containing governmental expenses is cost recovery. In screening applications for defense services for the indigent, many courts now distinguish between defendants so poor that they are exempt from paying any costs of their defense and a new category of "partially indigent" defendants who may be able to pay a portion of the costs (Lee 1992). Although cost recovery is not a new idea, these efforts seldom generated significant revenue until recently. The most promising new approach is to try to collect contributions from the partially indigent prior to the disposition of the case. "From a practical standpoint,

See FAQs from the Marion County, Indiana, public defender at **http://www.indygov.org/pubdef/ FAQ.htm**.

For an up-to-date list of Web links, go to **http:// www.wadsworth.com/product/0534563406s**.

LAWYERS AND CLIENTS

The adversary system is premised on a good working relationship between lawyer and client. In order to be an effective advocate and counselor, the lawyer must know all the facts of a case. For this reason, the American legal system surrounds the attorney-client relationship with special protections. Statements made by a client to his or her attorney are considered **privileged communication**, which the law protects from forced disclosure without the client's consent. The attorney-client privilege extends not only to statements made by the client but also to any work product developed in representing the client.

Based on trust and a full exchange of information, the attorney assumes the difficult task of advocating a client's case. In civil litigation the relationship between lawyer and client is often (but not always) characterized by such trust and full disclosure (Cox 1993). In criminal cases, however, the relationship is more likely to be marked by distrust

Privileged communications: A recognized right to keep certain communications confidential or private.

defendants appear to be more willing to voluntarily contribute to their costs of representation before disposition than being requested to pay after entering a plea or having been found guilty" (Spangenberg et al. 1986b, 70).

Due Process Perspective: We Spend Too Little

Due process advocates, on the other hand, are concerned that government is spending too little on indigent defense (Margulies 1989). Typical is a *Chicago Tribune* editorial headlined "Paying for Justice" (2000) arguing that it "is not too much to say that many poor people are in prison who would be free if they had the legal representation that many affluent people do—and vice versa."

From the perspective of the due process model, oppressive caseloads are the single greatest obstacle to effective representation (Gershman 1993). Underfunding indigent defense produces high caseloads. The National Advisory Commission on Criminal Justice Standards and Goals recommends that a maximum effective felony caseload per attorney per year be 150 cases. Yet in many jurisdictions it is typically much higher: Each Connecticut public defender, for example, faces annual caseloads of up to 1,000 clients (Cauchon 1999). High caseloads undermine the ability of lawyers to even meet their clients in a timely fashion. Consider Minneapolis. In past years, the public defender saw the client the same day he or she was appointed; now getting to see a client is a major event, according to one assistant public defender (Blum 1995).

Evidence to support the due process argument is all too easy to come by (Smothers 1994). For three years in a row the federal courts ran out of money that Congress provided for paying court-appointed counsel. More recently Congress eliminated the Post-Conviction Defender Organization, which provided for the appointment and compensation of qualified lawyers in federal habeas corpus death penalty cases. The lack of attorneys available to defend death row inmates is a major point of contention over the death penalty (Chapters 15 and 17). Indeed the American Bar Association urged abolition of the death penalty, primarily because of the lack of lawyers for death row inmates.

At the state level, the American Bar Association's Special Committee on Funding for the justice system found that in many parts of the nation the justice system is on the verge of collapse because of a crisis in funding (McWilliams 1993). In an era when slogans about getting tough on criminals dominate elections, elected officials view funding indigent defense as increasingly unpopular politically. In Virginia, for example, the legislature is reluctant to increase funding for court-appointed lawyers; indeed the maximum a lawyer may receive in defending a client facing death row is $845 (Cauchon 1999). And a federal judge ordered the state of Illinois to reduce the backlog of cases of the agency that appeals convictions of indigent prison inmates (Parsons 1996).

What do you think? Should government be spending less money or more money on court-appointed counsel for the indigent?

---

and hostility. Indeed, more than half of defendants are described by their attorneys as passive participants in the overall defense, and 10 percent are described by their attorneys as recalcitrant, that is, rarely or never accepting the attorney's advice (Bonnie et al. 1996).

Lawyers View Their Clients

Attorneys with public clients labor in the shadow of the public defender stereotype. Whether they actually work as public defenders makes no difference; their clients give them little respect and distrust them. As one attorney phrased it, "The standard joke around this county is, 'Do you want a public defender or a real attorney?'" (Flemming 1986a, 257).

Getting along with clients is one of the most difficult tasks of public defenders. Client disrespect irritates attorneys, sours their associations with clients, and makes the job less pleasant. As one public defender complained, "It is frustrating to have to constantly sell yourself" to clients (Flemming 1986a, 258). Many eventually leave the job because of the difficulty of dealing with their clients (Platt and Pollock 1974).

Refusal to cooperate, deception, and dishonesty are serious problems public attorneys face in dealing with their clients (Flemming 1986a). At times, defendants tell their attorneys implausible stories, invent alibis, or withhold key information. The defendant's lack of candor greatly complicates the job of the attorney in representing him or her. Evasions and deceptions can affect tactical and strategic decisions.

COURT TV

The Greatest Trials of All Time

The Scottsboro Boys

Nine young black boys were arrested for raping a white woman while aboard a freight train. They were taken to the county seat at Scottsboro, Alabama, and thus the case became known as that of "The Scottsboro Boys." A month later the nine were convicted, and several were sentenced to die. As you watch the video, keep the following questions in mind:

1. In 1931 segregation was the rule of law in the South. In cases like this, how did white officials use the law to preserve their way of life? How did civil rights groups like the NAACP use such cases to advance their goal of desegregation? Why was the Communist Party so interested in this case?

2. At the time of this trial, the nation was in the depths of the Great Depression. How did these economic conditions affect perceptions of the crime and attitudes toward "colored" (as African Americans were referred to then) defendants?

3. Lynchings were common during this period. How did the threat of mob violence influence the conduct of the trial and later the appellate court decisions?

4. What major changes did the U.S. Supreme Court make in the right to counsel? Do you think the Court was influenced more by the facts of this case or changing views of the law?

Lynn Mather (1974) describes a case in which a public defender went to trial at the request of a client who claimed she had no prior record. To the attorney's surprise, the defendant's pre-sentence report revealed that she had a five-year history of similar crimes. She was sentenced to prison. The public defender said that his client "fooled everyone."

The lack of trust in the lawyer-client relationship may stem from the necessity for the lawyer to prepare the client for a less than total victory. To return to the counselor role, the defense attorney may at some point have to inform the defendant that imprisonment is a likely result, given the crime, the prior record, facts of the case, and so forth. Since defendants involved in the criminal process often don't look beyond the present, postponing bad news from day to day, such statements are not to their lik-

ing. Preparing the client for the possibility of conviction clashes with traditional notions that the attorney should always win.

Ultimately, it is the defendant's choice whether to accept the attorney's advice to plead guilty or to go to trial. Lawyers differ in their ability to influence their clients. Private attorneys find their advice accepted more readily than court-appointed lawyers do. This difference partially accounts for the type of commitment the defendant has made. The indigent defendant has no choice in receiving the services of a public defender or assigned counsel, whereas defendants with private attorneys have a choice and have shown their commitment by paying a fee.

 In "Equal Before Law" public defender Tamara Rice Lave wrestles with the question: How can you represent *those* people?

Defendants View Their Lawyers

Public clients have doubts about the status of their lawyers, are skeptical about their skills as advocates, and are worried about whose side the lawyers are on. Thus, many defendants view their lawyers, whether public or private, with suspicion, if not bitterness. This is particularly the case with court-appointed attorneys, whom many defendants consider the same as any other government-paid attorney. Some defendants think that public defenders will not work hard on their cases because they are paid whether they win or not. To others, the defense attorney has ambitions to become a judge or prosecutor and therefore does not want to antagonize the court system by fighting too hard. Overall, then, many defendants view the public defender as no different from the prosecutor. In prison, "PD" stands not for "public defender" but for "prison deliverer." In what has become a classic statement, a Connecticut prisoner responded to Jonathan Casper's (1972) question as to whether he had a lawyer when he went to court, with the barbed comment, "No, I had a public defender."

A partial explanation for a breakdown of trust between the client and public defender involves the absence of one-to-one contact. Most public defenders' offices are organized on a zone basis. Attorneys are assigned to various courtrooms and/or responsibilities—initial appearance, preliminary hearing, trial sections, and so on. Each defendant sees several public defenders, all of whom are supposed to be working for him or her. This segmented approach to representation for indigents decreases the likelihood that a bond of trust will develop between attorney and client. It also increases the probability that some defendants will be overlooked and no attorney will work on their cases or talk to them. One can certainly understand the frustration of this thirty-three-year-old accused murderer with no previous record:

> "I figured that with he being my defense attorney, that as soon as that grand jury was over—because he's not allowed in the hearing—that he would call me and then want to find out what went on. After that grand jury I never saw him for two months." "You stayed in jail?" "Yeah." (Casper 1972, 8)

Quite clearly, not all defendants' criticisms of their attorneys are valid. But valid or not, defendants' lack of trust and confidence in their lawyers is a major force in shaping the dynamics of courthouse justice. Defendants try to con their attorneys, and the lawyers respond by exhibiting disbelief when defendants state unrealistic expectations or invent implausible alibis. For an attorney, failure to gain "client control" can lead to a bad reputation in the courthouse and jeopardize his or her own position within the courtroom work group (Eisenstein, Flemming, and Nardulli 1988).

 For practical tips on what to do until you see your public defender, look at **http://www.indygov.org/pubdef/case.htm**.

For an up-to-date list of Web links, go to **http://www.wadsworth.com/product/0534563406s**.

CONCLUSION

From the bleak perspective of his prison cell Clarence Gideon had no way of knowing that his petition to the Supreme Court would have the impact it did. Overnight Gideon went from defending himself to having Abe Fortas—one of the nation's most prestigious lawyers—represent him. Following the Supreme Court reversal of his conviction, Clarence Earl Gideon was given a new trial. His court-appointed lawyer discovered evidence suggesting that the man who had accused Gideon of burglarizing the poolroom had himself committed the crime. Moreover, as a result of the *Gideon* decision, thousands of other prison inmates in Florida and elsewhere were freed.

Nor could Gideon have realized that his name would become associated with a landmark Supreme Court decision. He achieved no small degree of legal immortality. His case has been chronicled by *New York Times* reporter Anthony Lewis (1972) in *Gideon's Trumpet*. *Gideon v. Wainwright* transformed the law, signaling a due process revolution in the rights of criminal defendants. Gideon himself was not transformed, however. He avoided any more major brushes with the law, but he died penniless on January 18, 1972, in Ft. Lauderdale, Florida.

The travails of Clarence Earl Gideon illustrate the importance of legal access to the legal system. Perhaps nowhere else is there a greater contrast between the images and the realities of the criminal court process than in the activities of the defense attorney. Unlike Perry Mason, who always defended innocent clients successfully, most defense attorneys deal with a steady stream of defendants who are in fact guilty, and their representation focuses on plea bargaining.

CRITICAL THINKING QUESTIONS

1. The public generally views defense attorneys as too zealous in their advocacy of obviously guilty clients, while many scholars portray an image of defense attorneys, particularly public defenders, as too willing to plead their clients guilty. What do you think? What evidence would you cite for either position?

2. In what ways have contemporary decisions by the U.S. Supreme Court modified the original meaning of the Sixth Amendment? Is the original intent of the Sixth Amendment relevant in today's world?

3. What factors hinder a defense attorney in his or her attempt to protect the rights of the defendant? Think of both system factors and individual ones.

4. What are the major contrasts in the work-a-day world of private defense attorneys and court-appointed lawyers?

5. Should all attorneys be required to provide *pro bono* defense for indigents? Would such activities improve the image of the bar? Would such activities be in the best interests of the defendants?

6. If you had been arrested, which would you rather have: a private lawyer or a public defender?

 WORLD WIDE WEB RESOURCES AND EXERCISES

Web Guides

http://dir.yahoo.com/Entertainment/Humor/Jokes/Lawyer_Jokes/

http://dir.yahoo.com/News_and_Media/Television/Shows/Lawyer_Shows/

Web Search Terms

"Adversary system"; "defense attorneys"; "public defender"; "right to counsel"; "Gideon v. Wainwright"; "indigent defense"

Useful URLs

Justice Lives, which bills itself as fighting for small businesses, the middle class, and the poor, offers this view of the right to counsel: **http://justicelives.com/**.

Visit the American Civil Liberties Union (ACLU) Web site: **http://www.aclu.org**.

Access the American Bar Association Division for Legal Services at **http://www.abanet.org/legalservices**.

The National Legal Aid and Defender Association is a nationwide network of persons, programs, and organizations committed to equal access to justice for the poor: **http://www.nlada.org/**.

The Colorado Public Defender's Office may be accessed at **http://www.state.co.us/gov_dir/pdef_dir/pd.htm**.

The Florida Public Defender's Office is at **http://www.nettally.com/fpda/**.

The Georgia Indigent Defense Council can be found at **http://www.gidc.com/**.

Comprehensive information and resources for attorneys and law librarians may be accessed at **http://www.law.com/**.

The Law Reform Network advocates reforming the adversary system: **http://www.lawreform.net/adversary.htm**.

Visit the Spangenberg Group at **http://www.spangenberggroup.com/**.

Contracting for Indigent Defense Services: A Special Report is available online at **http://www.ncjrs.org/pdffiles1bja/181160.pdf**.

Uncommon URLs

To view a photo of the nine young black men dragged off the train in Scottsboro, Alabama, click on **http://www.aclumontana.org/rights/powell.html**. The case became known as *Powell v. Alabama.*

Read "The Right to Counsel in Student Due Process Hearings: How Much Process is Due?" at **http://www.campusoutreachservices.com/counsel.htm**.

For "Ten Tips on Hiring a California DUI Lawyer over the Telephone" see **http://topgundui.com/hiring.htm**.

Web Exercises

1. The American Bar Association has always had an active interest in providing legal services for the poor. Here is their URL: **http://www.abanet.org/legalserv/**. What services does the ABA provide, and what changes would they like to see?

2. A limited amount of information on indigent defense is available from the Bureau of Justice Statistics at **http://www.ojp.usdoj.gov/bjs/**. Choose Courts and Sentencing Statistics/Indigent Defense and update the material in this chapter on the major methods of providing indigents with defense attorneys.

3. The reality of being a defense attorney is strikingly different from fictional images portrayed by Perry Mason and others. One way to explore what defense attorneys really do is by examining their role in defending those

accused of violating drug laws. Go to the Web site **http://dpa.state.ky.us:80/~rwheeler/drugs/leo.htm**. How does this discussion differ from fictional notions of defense attorneys defending clients who are factually innocent?

 INFOTRAC COLLEGE EDITION RESOURCES AND EXERCISES

Basic Search Terms

Defense attorney; defense, criminal; right to counsel; attorneys; solo practitioners; attorneys, bar association; attorneys, attorney and client; public defender; Gideon v. Wainwright

Recommended Articles

Angela D. McCravy, "Self-Representation and Ineffective Assistance of Counsel"

Donald A. Dripps, "Ineffective Assistance of Counsel"

Joseph Hall, "Guided to Injustice . . . Indigent Defendants and Public Defense"

InfoTrac College Edition Exercises

1. Using the search term *right to counsel*, locate articles on the subject and answer the following question: In discussing the concept of right to counsel do the articles proceed from a crime control or a due process perspective? Here are two possibilities: Martin Gardner, "The Sixth Amendment Right to Counsel" and Burke Kappler, "Small Favors."

2. Using the search terms *defense, criminal*, or *public defender* select two or more articles on the topic. Do they discuss the role of lawyers more in terms of law on the books or in terms of law in action? Here are two possibilities: Spencer M. Aronfeld, "Go Solo without Starving" and Cornelius Nestler, "Faulty System or Ineffective Defense Counsel?"

REFERENCES

Blum, Andrew. 1995. "Defense of Indigents: Crisis Spurs Lawsuits." *National Law Journal,* 15 May.

Blumberg, Abraham. 1967. "The Practice of Law as a Confidence Game." *Law and Society Review* 1: 15–39.

Bonnie, Richard, Norman Poythress, Steven Hoge, John Monahan, and Marlene Eisenberg. 1996. "Decision-Making in Criminal Defense: An Empirical Study of Insanity Pleas and the Impact of Doubted Client Competence." *Journal of Criminal Law and Criminology* 87: 48–77.

Bureau of Justice Statistics. 1988. *Criminal Defense for the Poor, 1986.* Washington, D.C.: U.S. Department of Justice.

Casper, Jonathan. 1972. *American Criminal Justice: The Defendant's Perspective.* Englewood Cliffs, NJ: Prentice-Hall.

Cauchon, Dennis. 1999. "Indigents' Lawyers: Low Pay Hurts Justice?" *USA Today,* 3 February.

Cox, Gail. 1993. "Hellish Clients, Big Trouble." *National Law Journal* 15 (February 15): 1.

Eisenstein, James, Roy Flemming, and Peter Nardulli. 1988. *The Contours of Justice: Communities and Their Courts.* Boston: Little, Brown.

Flemming, Roy. 1986a. "Client Games: Defense Attorney Perspectives on Their Relations with Criminal Clients." *American Bar Foundation Research Journal:* 253–277.

———. 1986b. "Elements of the Defense Attorney's Craft: An Adaptive Expectations Model of the Preliminary Hearing Decision." *Law and Policy* 8: 33–57.

———. 1989. "If You Pay the Piper, Do You Call the Tune? Public Defenders in America's Criminal Courts." *Law and Social Inquiry* 14: 393–405.

Gershman, Bennett. 1993. "Defending the Poor." *Trial* 29: 47–51.

Hanson, Roger, William Hewitt, and Brian Ostrom. 1992. "Are the Critics of Indigent Defense Counsel Correct?" *State Court Journal* (Summer): 20–29.

Heinz, John, and Edward Laumann. 1982. *Chicago Lawyers: The Social Structure of the Bar.* New York: Russell Sage Foundation.

Houlden, Pauline, and Steven Balkin. 1985. "Costs and Quality of Indigent Defense: Ad Hoc vs. Coordinated Assignments of the Private Bar Within a Mixed System." *Justice System Journal* 10: 159–172.

Kaplan, John. 1973. *Criminal Justice: Introductory Cases and Materials.* Mineola, NY: Foundation Press.

Kerper, Hazel B. 1972. *Introduction to the Criminal Justice System.* St. Paul, MN: West.

Lee, Monica. 1992. "Indigent Defense: Determination of Indigency in the Nation's State Courts." *State Court Journal* (Spring): 16–23.

Lewis, Anthony. 1972. *Clarence Earl Gideon and the Supreme Court.* New York: Random House.

Lushing, Peter. 1992. "The Fall and Rise of the Criminal Contingent Fee." *Journal of Criminal Law and Criminology* 82: 498–568.

Margulies, J. 1989. "Resource Deprivation and the Right to Counsel." *Journal of Criminal Law and Criminology* 80: 673–725.

Mather, Lynn. 1974. "The Outsider in the Courtroom: An Alternative Role for the Defense." In *The*

Potential for Reform of Criminal Justice, edited by Herbert Jacob. Newbury Park, CA: Sage.

McIntyre, Lisa. 1987. *The Public Defender: The Practice of Law in the Shadows of Repute.* Chicago: University of Chicago Press.

McQuiston, J. T. 1995. "In the Bizarre L.I.R.R. Trial, Equally Bizarre Confrontations." *The New York Times,* 5 February.

McWilliams, J. Michael. 1993. "The Erosion of Indigent Rights." *ABA Journal* 79 (March): 8.

Moore, Michael. 1965. "The Right to Counsel for Indigents in Oregon." *Oregon Law Review* 44: 255–300.

Mortimer, John. 1984. *Rumpole for the Defense.* New York: Penguin Books.

Nardulli, Peter. 1978. *The Courtroom Elite: An Organizational Perspective on Criminal Justice.* Cambridge, MA: Ballinger.

———. 1986. "'Insider' Justice: Defense Attorneys and the Handling of Felony Cases." *Journal of Criminal Law and Criminology* 77: 379–417.

Neubauer, David. 1974. *Criminal Justice in Middle America.* Morristown, NJ: General Learning Press.

Parsons, Christi. 1996. "State Offers Judge a Plan to Cut Defender's Backlog." *Chicago Tribune,* 20 April.

"Paying for Justice." 2000. *Chicago Tribune,* 16 January.

Platt, Anthony, and Randi Pollock. 1974. "Channeling Lawyers: The Careers of Public Defenders." In *The Potential for Reform of Criminal Justice,* edited by Herbert Jacob. Newbury Park, CA: Sage.

Priehs, Richard. 1999. "Appointed Counsel for Indigent Criminal Appellants: Does Compensation Influence Effort?" *The Justice System Journal* 21: 57–79.

Silverstein, Lee. 1965. *Defense of the Poor.* Chicago: American Bar Foundation.

Skolnick, Jerome. 1967. "Social Control in the Adversary System." *Journal of Conflict Resolution* 11: 52–70.

Smith, Steven, and Carol DeFrances. 1996. "Indigent Defense." Washington, D.C.: Bureau of Justice Statistics.

Smothers, Ronald. 1994. "Court-Appointed Defense Offers the Poor a Lawyer, but the Cost May Be High." *The New York Times,* 14 February, A9.

Spangenberg Group. 2000. *Contracting for Indigent Defense Services: A Special Report.* Washington, D.C.: Bureau of Justice Statistics.

Spangenberg, Robert, Beverly Lee, Michael Battaglia, Patricia Smith, and A. David Davis. 1986a. *National Criminal Defense Systems Study: Final Report.* Washington, D.C.: Bureau of Justice Statistics, U.S. Department of Justice.

Spangenberg, Robert, Richard Wilson, Patricia Smith, and Beverly Lee. 1986b. *Containing the Cost of Indigent Defense Programs: Eligibility Screening and Cost Recovery Procedures.* Washington, D.C.: National Institute of Justice, U.S. Department of Justice.

Sudnow, David. 1965. "Normal Crimes: Sociological Features of the Penal Code in a Public Defender Office." *Social Problems* 12: 209–215.

Wice, Paul. 1978. *Criminal Lawyers: An Endangered Species.* Beverly Hills, CA: Sage.

———. 1985. *Chaos in the Courthouse: The Inner Workings of the Urban Criminal Courts.* New York: Praeger.

Williams, Jimmy. 1995. "Type of Counsel and the Outcome of Criminal Appeals: A Research Note." *American Journal of Criminal Justice* 19: 275–285.

Worden, Alissa Pollitz. 1991. "Privatizing Due Process: Issues in the Comparison of Assigned Counsel, Public Defender, and Contracted Indigent Defense Systems." *Justice System Journal* 14: 390–418.

———. 1993. "Counsel for the Poor: An Evaluation of Contracting for Indigent Criminal Defense." *Justice Quarterly* 10: 613–637.

Worden, Alissa Pollitz, and Robert Worden. 1989. "Local Politics and the Provision of Indigent Defense Counsel." *Law and Policy* 11: 401–424.

FOR FURTHER READING

Bright, Stephen. "Counsel for the Poor: The Death Sentence Not for the Worst Crime, But for the Worst Lawyer." *Yale Law Journal* 103 (1994): 1835–1884.

Gershman, Bennett. "Themes of Injustice: Wrongful Convictions, Racial Prejudice, and Lawyer Incompetence." *Criminal Law Bulletin* 29 (1994): 502–515.

Goodpaster, Gary. 1986. "The Adversary System, Advocacy, and Effective Assistance of Counsel in Criminal Cases." *New York University Review of Law and Social Change* 14: 90.

Hanson, Roger, William Hewitt, Brian Ostrom, and Christopher Lomvardias. *Indigent Defenders: Get the Job Done and Done Well.* Williamsburg, VA: National Center for State Courts, 1992.

Schrager, Sam. *The Trial Lawyer's Art.* Philadelphia: Temple University Press, 1999.

Seron, Carroll. *The Business of Practicing Law: The Work Lives of Solo and Small-Firm Attorneys.* Philadelphia: Temple University Press, 1996.

Stone, Christopher. "Community Defense and the Challenge of Community Justice." *National Institute of Justice Journal* (August, 1966): 41–45.

Uphoff, Rodney. "The Criminal Defense Lawyer: Zealous Advocate, Double Agent, or Beleaguered Dealer?" *Criminal Law Bulletin* 28 (1992): 419–456.

Wasserman, David. *A Sword for the Convicted: Representing Indigent Defendants on Appeal.* Westport, CT: Greenwood Press, 1990.

Judges

To U.S. DISTRICT JUDGE HAROLD BAER, JR., THE EIGHTY POUNDS OF cocaine could not be introduced as evidence because the police lacked probable cause to search the trunk of Carol Bayless's car. New York City's mayor and police chief quickly denounced the judge's decision. Within a few days Republicans nationwide joined in the attack; soon-to-be presidential nominee Bob Dole called for the judge's impeachment. In turn, the White House, its eyes on the election calendar, threatened to ask Judge Baer (a Clinton appointee) to resign. After an unusual rehearing, Judge Baer reversed himself and allowed the drugs to be admitted during trial.

The heated political attacks on Judge Baer raise deep-seated questions about judicial independence in the United States. Had the judge made a bad ruling? If so, are the resulting political denunciations an example of holding governmental officials, judges included, accountable for their actions? Or had the judge decided the controversial case properly? If so, the resulting judge-bashing is an indication that judges can be intimidated. Whatever one's opinion, Judge Baer's decisions and the resulting controversy dramatize the importance of judges in the criminal justice system.

The purpose of this chapter is to untangle the conflicting notions about what judges do and how they do it. The chapter begins by examining the powers and responsibilities of the judge and how various pressures (the large number of cases, for example) have eroded the ideal image of a judge's power. Next, the judge will be considered as a member of the courtroom community. A judge's actions are shaped and influenced by actions of prosecutors and defense attorneys, among others. At the same time, the type of justice handed out varies from one judge to another. A persistent concern is whether judges are as qualified as they should be. Therefore, three suggestions for improving the quality of the judiciary will be examined: merit selection, increased training, and mechanisms for removing unfit judges. ■

THE POSITION OF JUDGE

For most Americans, the judge is the symbol of justice. Of all the actors in the criminal justice process, the public holds the judge most responsible for ensuring that the system operates fairly and impartially. And most certainly the trappings of office—the flowing black robes, the gavel, and the command "all rise" when the judge enters the courtroom—reinforce this mystique. As important as these symbols are, they sometimes raise obstacles to understanding what judges actually do and how they influence the criminal justice process. The vast array of legal powers often cause us to overestimate the actual influence of the judge by ignoring the importance of the other actors in the courtroom work group. At the same time, the mystique of the office often results in an underestimation of the role of the judge. Judges are not merely impartial black-robed umpires who hand down decisions according to clear and unwavering rules. "This view of the judge as an invisible interpreter of the law, as a part of the courtroom with no more individual personality than a witness chair or a jury box, is a fiction that judges themselves have done much to perpetuate" (Jackson 1974, vii).

Benefits of the Job

In discharging their duties, judges enjoy some distinct benefits of the office. Traditionally, they have been given a high level of prestige and respect (Wice 1991). Lawyers address the judge as "your honor," and everyone rises when the judge enters or leaves the courtroom. Judges also enjoy other trappings of the office. Federal judges enjoy life terms, as do judges in a handful of states. More commonly, terms of office for state judges range from six to ten years, considerably longer than those of other public officeholders—a reflection of the independence of the American judiciary.

For many lawyers, a judgeship is the capstone to a successful career. Judicial salaries are not the highest incomes in the legal profession, but they are higher than the average of other criminal justice personnel. Annual salaries of general jurisdiction trial judges range from $77,340 to $136,700. The average is about $100,000. For some lawyers, a judicial salary represents an increase over that received in private practice, and it is certainly more secure. For others, however, a judgeship represents a significant decrease in earning power. For example, it is not at all unusual to find lawyers in federal court who are paid more than the judges.

Many judgeships carry with them considerable patronage powers. Court positions—bailiffs, clerks, commissioners, reporters, probation officers, and secretaries—must be filled. Because these positions are usually not covered by civil service, judges can award jobs to friends, relatives, campaign workers, and party leaders. In some cities, judicial staff positions are significant sources of party patronage.

Frustrations of the Job

Because of the pressures of today's criminal justice system, the ideals surrounding the judge are not always borne out by the reality. One of the most frustrating aspects of being a judge is the heavy caseload and corresponding administrative problems (Rosen 1987). Thus, instead of having time to reflect on challenging legal questions or to consider the proper sentence for a convicted felon, trial judges must move cases, acting more like administrators in a bureaucracy than judicial sages. As a New York judge put it:

> It is clear that the "grand tradition" judge, the aloof brooding charismatic figure in the Old Testament tradition, is hardly a real figure. The reality is the working judge who must be politician, administrator, bureaucrat, and lawyer in order to cope with a crushing calendar of cases. A Metropolitan Court Judge might well ask, "Did John Marshall or Oliver Wendell Holmes ever have to clear a calendar like mine?" (Blumberg 1967, 120)

Moreover, the judge's actions are limited by the system—lawyers are late, court documents get lost, jails are crowded. Added to these general constraints is the overall low prestige of criminal court judges, who occupy the lowest rung within the judicial system. Like the other actors in the criminal justice system, the judge becomes tainted by close association with defendants who are perceived as society's outcasts.

Thus, the frustrations of the criminal trial court judge are many. Some judges prefer the relative peace of civil court, where dockets are less crowded, courtrooms quieter, legal issues more intriguing, and witnesses more honest than in the criminal court atmosphere of too many cases, too much noise, too many routine (and often dull) cases, and too many fabricated stories. Other judges, however, like the camaraderie of the criminal court.

JUDGES AT WORK

The formal powers of judges extend throughout the criminal court process. From arrest to final disposition, the accused face judges whenever decisions affecting their futures are made (Figure 8-1). Judges set bail and revoke it; they determine whether there is sufficient probable cause to hold defendants; they rule on pretrial motions to exclude evidence; they accept pleas of guilty; if there is a trial, they preside; and after conviction, they set punishment. Throughout the process judges are expected to discharge these powers and responsibilities judiciously and without the appearance of impropriety.

Although we tend to think of judges primarily in terms of presiding at trials, their work is much more varied. In the course of their work day, they conduct hearings, accept guilty pleas, impose sentences, or work in their offices (called **chambers**). In carrying out the responsibilities of the office, judges mainly react to the work of prosecutors and defense attorneys. We will examine the variety of tasks judges engage in, using the same categories employed in Chapters 6 and 7: fighting, negotiating, drafting, counseling, and administering.

Fighting

Serving as an umpire during trial is a primary task of judges. Seven out of ten judges with a criminal assignment report that on a typical day they preside over a trial (Ryan et al. 1980). While presiding at a trial, judges are expected to be neutral and not intervene to the undue advantage of either side. Because no legal code can furnish clear, unambiguous rules for every case, judges must use discretion in determining how the law applies to the particular facts of the case. They are the final arbiters of the law for the legal questions that may arise during trials: what questions may be asked potential jurors, what evidence is admissible, what instructions of law should be given the jury. Incorrect rulings on such matters may result in an appellate court ruling that judicial error has been committed and a new trial is required.

Chambers: The private office of a judge.

FIGURE 8-1	Role of Judges in the Steps of Criminal Procedure (Typical Felony Case)		
	Lower Court	*Major Trial Court*	*Appellate Court*
Crime			Appellate court opinions are the final word on interpreting criminal laws passed by the legislature.
Arrest	Occasionally signs arrest warrants.		Wrestles with legality of police arrest in context of question of illegal search and seizure.
Initial appearance	Informs defendant of pending charges, appoints counsel for indigents.		
Bail	Sets initial bail amount.	May alter bail amount.	Rarely decides that bail is excessive.
Charging		No authority to intervene.	
Preliminary hearing	Presides over preliminary hearing.		
Grand jury		Chief judge has nominal supervision over the grand jury.	
Arraignment		Informs defendant of pending charges and enters defendant's plea.	
Evidence	Signs search warrants. In rural areas may advise police on wording of search warrant.	Rules on suppression motions involving illegal search and seizure, custodial interrogation, and lineups.	Rulings establish boundaries for search and seizure, custodial interrogation, and lineups.
Plea bargaining	Judges rely on pleas to dispose of large dockets.	Some judges actively participate whereas others are passive.	Rarely rules that plea of guilty was not voluntary.
Trial	Rarely held.	Presides at trial. Rules on admissibility of evidence. Instructs jury as to law applicable to the case.	Decides if evidence was properly admitted. Decides if trial judge properly instructed jury as to the law.
Sentencing	Typically imposes "normal penalties."	Increasingly difficult and controversial task.	In some jurisdictions must interpret sentencing guidelines.
Appeal	Rare except in some drunk driving convictions.	Notice of appeal filed in trial court.	Rarely reverses trial judge.

Negotiating

Most criminal convictions result not from a finding of guilt but from the defendant's plea of guilty. Negotiating activities are a common part of the judge's work day. Judges vary greatly in the extent to which they participate in plea bargaining negotia-tions. Some are active participants; along with prosecutors and defense attorneys, they discuss the evidence in the case, the type of charge to which the defendant will plead, and the sentence to be imposed. Others refuse to participate. In these cases, the defense and prosecution take into consideration the judge's past practices.

Drafting

Only on rare occasions do trial judges draft legal opinions setting forth reasons for their decisions. However, they do rule on numerous legal motions drafted by the prosecution or defense. They are required by law to sign search warrants. They must rule on defense motions to exclude evidence because of improper police conduct. Most of these matters are fairly routine and receive only brief examination by the judge. Contrary to popular perceptions, trial judges in criminal cases seldom decide complex legal issues. However, drafting documents and keeping up with the law are tasks judges commonly engage in.

Counseling

Prosecutors and defense attorneys must deal with clients, but trial judges have no direct counseling role. Indeed, canons of judicial ethics generally prohibit judges from dealing directly with victims, witnesses, defendants, or police officers. Occasionally, however, lower court judges offer advice to police officers on how to draft a warrant properly. Similarly, some judges try to ensure that jurors and witnesses are treated fairly and courteously. Overall, counseling activities are not part of the trial judge's common work day.

Administering

Judges must also be administrators. Judges try to keep their dockets (the calendar of cases scheduled to be heard) current. One major management task is the scheduling of cases. Dates for hearing pretrial motions and for trial must be established. The judge's degree of generosity in granting attorneys' requests for continuances (additional time) greatly affects how speedily or slowly cases are disposed of. Another major management problem is keeping track of the cases and all the papers involved in a specific case. Lost cases or lost papers can have serious consequences. Assisting judges in these administrative tasks are bailiffs, clerks, and/or law clerks. In large courts, the administrative tasks are so time-consuming that one judge, designated chief judge, devotes almost full time to administering the court. In a growing number of courts, particularly in large ones, court administrators may also be present.

CRIME & PUNISHMENT

State of Illinois v. Jane Maloy

Joseph Greene is walking home from his night job when he is approached from behind, thrown against a car, and poked in the back with a sharp object. His wallet is removed. Cries for help summon a nearby police officer who sees the defendant Jane Maloy throw down a knife. She runs but is later subdued and arrested. After watching the CD, you should be able to discuss the following questions:

1. Do you think the defendant's statement helps or harms her cause? As a judge, are you more or less inclined to show leniency after her statement?
2. Do you think the statement of the victim helps or harms the state's case? As a judge, are you more or less inclined to impose a sentence toward the harsher end of the continuum?
3. In reviewing the presentence investigation, which factors point to a sentence on the harsh side? Which factors point to a sentence on the lenient side?
4. In what ways does the Maloy prosecution represent an atypical armed robbery case and an atypical armed robbery defendant?
5. Did the prosecutor deliberately overcharge in this case? If the defendant has been charged with armed robbery, then what justification is there for the state also to charge assault and battery?

JUDGES WITHIN THE COURTROOM WORK GROUP

The public believes judges are the principal decision makers in courts. Often they are not. Instead, they defer to the judgments of other members of the courtroom work group—prosecutors, witnesses, defense attorneys, psychiatrists, clerks, jail wardens, and probation officers—who may have a greater knowledge about particular cases. Thus, judges often accept bail recommendations offered by prosecutors, plea agreements struck by defense and prosecution, and sentences recommended by the probation officer. In short, although judges still retain the formal legal powers of their office, they often informally share these powers with other members of the courtroom work group.

THE MURDER TRIAL OF SHAREEF COUSIN

Judge Raymond Bigelow, Ex-Prosecutor

Raymond Bigelow first ran for a judgeship in 1992, but lost. The following year another vacancy opened up. In a crowded field of five Bigelow won a plurality in the first election and won outright with 54 percent of the vote in the runoff, defeating Harry Tervalon, a former policeman, prosecutor, and public defender. During his campaign Bigelow stressed the rights of victims. "It seems to me that the victims are kind of lost, kind of shuffled aside," he said, promising to devise "creative ways to provide victims with comfort" (Cooper, 1993).

Prior to becoming a judge, Bigelow was first assistant district attorney in Orleans Parish, a powerful position that runs the day-to-day operations of the office. Thus he enjoyed the political backing of his boss, DA Harry Connick (see Chapter 6). Indeed, Bigelow is one of several judges who had previously worked for Connick. But on the bench Bigelow's former boss and political mentor became his sharpest critic. In more than a dozen trials of defendants charged with possessing crack cocaine Judge Bigelow found them innocent, ruling that simply possessing a crack pipe with residue invisible to the naked eye does not prove a defendant intended to possess cocaine. To Connick, the law is clear—they are smoking crack and should be punished. The appellate court, though, upheld Judge Bigelow's rulings. (The DA could have charged the defendants with the less serious offense of possession of drug paraphernalia, but chose not to.)

The long-running legal battle over the status of crack pipes was the second time Connick and Bigelow faced off. In another case, the judge ordered prosecutors to give defense attorneys a list with potential jurors' arrests and convictions, saying both sides should have access to the same information. Connick refused and appealed, but the state supreme court let Bigelow's order stand.

In terms of case processing time (see Chapter 5) Orleans Parish Criminal District Court is one of the fastest in the nation. Some judges, though, are faster than others and Judge Bigelow is certainly one of these. In his section of court the median time from arraignment to disposition is approximately thirty-one days. But even in speedy sections of court, complicated cases like murder take longer to reach disposition than more simple cases like possession of illegal drugs. Nonetheless, in the murder trial of Shareef Cousin Judge Bigelow moved with dispatch; the case was tried seven months after indictment and less than eleven months after the crime.

Predictably, both sides strenuously disagreed with some of Judge Bigelow's decisions during the trial. The defense objected to the improper use of rebuttal witnesses (an issue they would win on appeal). On the other hand, the prosecution objected to his decision to allow the defense several extra days to prepare for the penalty phase of the trial. Most importantly, the judge refused to grant a motion for a new trial. Cousin's supporters were quick to claim that the black defendant was being "railroaded." They speculated that Bigelow did not want to appear to be soft on crime by granting a new trial for an accused killer because he was up for reelection in a few months. In the words of Reverend Raymond Brown, a local minister and supporter of the Cousin family, "The judge is afraid of the backlash" (Charles, 1996).

Bigelow was reelected to a full six-year term, easily defeating veteran defense attorney Donald Ray Pryor. Bigelow, then forty-nine, garnered all the major endorsements in the race. He promised to keep his court's docket as low as possible and to refuse unjustified requests for continuances. According to Pryor, Bigelow's attitude often works to the disadvantage of low-income defendants.

Sanctions can be applied against judges who deviate from the consensus of the courtroom work group. Defense attorneys and prosecutors can foul up judges' scheduling of cases by requesting continuances or failing to have witnesses present when required. Particularly in big-city courts, judges who fall too far behind on disposing of the docket feel pressures from other judges, especially the chief judge. Judges who fail to move their docket may be transferred to less desirable duties (for instance, traffic court or juvenile court).

By no means are judges totally controlled by the courtroom work group. As the most prestigious members of the group, they can bring numerous pressures to bear on prosecutors, defense attorneys, and others. A verbal rebuke to a defense attorney in open court or an informal comment to the head prosecutor that the assistant is not performing

A DAY IN COURT

"'Frustrated' Judge Gets the Gridlocked System Moving"

 It's the criminal justice version of a run-down rowhouse—a small, utilitarian courtroom with little charm and no amenities.

Four of the 14 overhead fluorescent lights are out; the strip of blue carpeting under the defense and commonwealth tables looks as if it's never been vacuumed; aged parchment shades cover the windows.

It's not pretty. And neither is the situation that Common Pleas Judge Norman Ackerman has to deal with on this Monday morning in Courtroom 615.

As Assistant District Attorney Tariq Karim El-Shabazz put it, "This is a real Murphy's Law day."

Defense attorneys who are scheduled to appear are at trials in other counties, states and City Hall courtrooms; defendants and complaining witnesses show up only to leave frustrated over more delays; there are snafus and postponements and long, long waits.

"This case is 546 days old, you'd better have a good reason," Ackerman admonishes Shabazz and public defender Pat Mandracchia, who seek a continuance in a drug case for reasons they refuse to disclose—probably because the defendant is cooperating with the state's investigation.

Throughout the morning, as he reviews the status of cases before him, Ackerman expresses frustration with the delays. The cases before him have been pending for an average of 462 days—more than a year and three months.

Ackerman is a waiver judge who presides over non-jury trials and proceedings. There are 15 cases before him. Six will be continued. One was listed in error. Eight will proceed, but only because of his diligence. He stays on the bench all day—from 9:30 A.M. until 5:15 P.M. with one 10-minute recess and a 50-minute lunch break, through interminable waits for private counsel and other delays—virtually forcing cases through the system.

Case in point: Attorney J. Michael Farrell, scheduled to be in court on a drug case, sent a message that he was in court in New Jersey on a last-minute matter. Ackerman was angry.

"If you practice law in Philadelphia, I expect Philadelphia cases to take precedence. This case is 497 days old, which is bothersome to the court."

And instead of continuing the case again, Ackerman waited it out.

"We'll be here all afternoon. Tell him to call when he gets back," Ackerman instructed the court crier to tell Farrell's office.

When Farrell finally called, he was told to report immediately. He roared down I-95 from Trenton—calling from his car with reports of heavy traffic—and finally burst into the courtroom in a breathless rush, well after 4 P.M., to have his case heard.

"We need 30 more like him," court crier Pat West says of Ackerman, a gray-haired man with a calm temperament who is uniformly described as dedicated and hard-working.

In an interview later, Ackerman acknowledges his frustration with the system.

"Sure I'm frustrated. What do you do? I was practicing law for close to 30 years before I came on the bench and you reach a situation when you're elevated to the bench and you want to make a significant contribution to the court system...."

He said he and the other judges who are new to the bench—he was appointed in June 1988—are trying to make defense attorneys realize that repeated continuances will not be tolerated.

That attitude and some innovative programs are making things better, he said. Waiver judges are now disposing of more cases on a daily basis than are coming into the system, and "that's a great sign." ...

At 5:30 P.M., as dusk begins to fall and Judge Ackerman takes off his robe, he ends a day that was as productive as possible; a day in which he was tough and human and determined to get some work done.

They should all be like him.

SOURCE: J. Porter, "'Frustrated' Judge Gets the Gridlocked System Moving," *Philadelphia Daily News,* March 13, 1990, 5. Reprinted by permission.

satisfactorily are examples of judicial actions that can go a long way toward shaping how the courtroom work group disposes of cases (see A Day in Court: "'Frustrated' Judge Gets the Gridlocked System Moving").

The amount of influence judges actually exert on the other members of the courtroom work group varies. Some judges are active leaders of the courtroom work group; they run "tight ships," pressuring attorneys to be in court on time, for example. These judges participate fully in courthouse dynamics. On the other hand, some judges have a laissez-faire attitude, allowing the attorneys as many continuances as they request. Such judges have in essence abdicated responsibility to prosecutors, defense attorneys, and others.

In large courts "judge shopping" is a common practice. By the strategic use of motions for continuances and motions for a change of judge, defense attorneys maneuver to have their clients' cases heard by the judge they perceive as most favorable. Such judge shopping is the most direct evidence of variations between judges. Although organizational pressures work to provide a certain degree of consistency among judges, any examination of a multi-judge court immediately shows that judges differ in terms of sentences handed out, the ways they run their courtroom, and the number of cases pending. A knowledge of these judicial differences is often as necessary for the practicing attorney as mastery of law and rules of procedure.

QUALITY AND QUALIFICATION OF JUDGES

In large measure, the quality of justice depends on the quality of the judges who dispense it. As the noted American jurist Benjamin Cardozo once put it, "In the long run, there is no guarantee of justice except the personality of the judge" (Cardozo 1921, 149). Unfortunately, there is no agreed-upon set of criteria about what personality good judges should have—to say nothing about their legal talent and insight into human affairs.

The difficulties of establishing the qualities of a good judge, to say nothing of determining what constitutes a poor judge, are summarized by the President's Commission on Law Enforcement and Administration of Justice (1967, 66): "Although it is possible to identify such factors as professional incompetence, laziness, or intemperance which should disqualify a lawyer from becoming a judge, it is much more difficult to choose confidently the potentially superior judge from among a number of aspirants who appear generally qualified."

Although many factors have a bearing on the quality of judicial personnel—salary, length of term, prestige, independence, and personal satisfaction with the job—the factor considered most important

by legal reformers is judicial selection. The training of judges and removal of poor judges are additional methods prominently mentioned for upgrading the quality of judges.

VARYING ROADS TO A JUDGESHIP

A variety of methods are used to select judges: partisan elections, nonpartisan elections, merit selection (usually referred to as the *Missouri Bar Plan*), or appointment. In some states, different procedures are used for different levels of the judiciary. Figure 8-2 reveals definite regional patterns in the methods of judicial selection. Partisan elections are concentrated in the South, nonpartisan elections in the West and upper Midwest, legislative elections and executive appointments in the East, and merit selection west of the Mississippi River.

However, formal selection methods (law on the books) are far less important in determining which lawyers reach the bench than informal methods (law in action). How selection is conducted establishes the actual routes to who becomes a judge (Graham 1990a). When a judicial vacancy occurs, interim selection methods are needed. Appointment by governors and merit selection predominate in filling temporary vacancies. Nationwide, half of all trial judges initially received their position through some form of interim selection (Ryan et al. 1980). Thus, a combination of formal selection procedures and initial selection methods account for how trial judges first arrive on the bench.

Executive Appointments

In the early years of the Republic, judges were selected by executive appointment or elected by the legislature. Today, these methods of judicial selection are used in only a handful of jurisdictions. Three states use election by the legislature, and a few others still employ appointment by the governor. All Article III federal judges are selected by executive appointment. A number of studies have examined the political dynamics involved in the selection of federal judges (Goldman 1997; Slotnick 1988; Goldman and Slotnick 1999).

The U.S. Constitution specifies that the president has the power to nominate judges with the ad-

FIGURE 8-2 Initial Selection of State Judges (Trial Courts of General Jurisdiction)

Partisan Election	Nonpartisan Election	Merit	Appointment
Alabama	California	Alaska	Maine (G)
Arkansas	Florida	Arizona	New Hampshire (G)
Illinois	Georgia	Colorado	New Jersey (G)
Indiana	Idaho	Connecticut	Rhode Island (G)
Louisiana	Kentucky	Delaware	South Carolina (L)
Mississippi	Michigan	District of Columbia	Virginia (L)
Missouri*	Minnesota	Hawaii	
New York	Montana	Iowa	
North Carolina	Nevada	Kansas	
Pennsylvania	North Dakota	Maryland	
Tennessee	Ohio	Massachusetts	
Texas	Oklahoma	Nebraska	
West Virginia	Oregon	New Mexico	
	South Dakota	Utah	
	Washington	Vermont	
	Wisconsin	Wyoming	

L = Legislative appointment; G = Gubernatorial appointment

*Partisan election in nonmetropolitan circuits

SOURCE: American Judicature Society, *Judicial Selection in the United States: A Compendium of Provisions,* 2d ed. (Chicago: American Judicature Society, 1993).

vice and consent of the Senate (Simon 1993). Based on this constitutional authorization, both the president and the Senate have a voice in the selection process. When a judgeship becomes vacant, the deputy attorney general of the U.S. Department of Justice (the executive official authorized by the president to handle judicial nominees) searches for qualified lawyers by consulting party leaders of the state in which the vacancy occurred, campaign supporters, U.S. senators, and prominent members of the bar. This initial and private screening has been known to take a year or longer when there are conflicts within the president's party over who should be selected.

After the president has submitted his nomination for the vacant judicial post, the process shifts to the Senate. Most nominations are routine. After a hearing by the Senate Judiciary Committee, the full Senate usually confirms, most often without a negative vote being cast. If the nomination is contro-

versial, the committee hearings and Senate vote become the focus of great political activity. For example, after months of public debate, the Senate narrowly defeated President Ronald Reagan's nomination of Robert Bork as associate justice of the Supreme Court.

Senators also influence federal judicial selections through the informal power of senatorial courtesy. Senators expect to be consulted before the president nominates a person for a judicial vacancy from their state if the president belongs to the same party. A senator who is not consulted may declare the nominee personally unacceptable, and senators from other states—finding strength in numbers—will follow their colleague's preferences and not approve the presidential nomination. Through this process, senators can recommend persons they think are qualified (former campaign managers come to mind) or exercise a direct veto over persons they find unacceptable (political enemies, for example).

Although the **American Bar Association (ABA)**, the national lawyers' association, enjoys no formal role in the screening of nominees for the federal bench, it plays an increasingly influential role through its Standing Committee on Federal Judiciary (Slotnick 1983). The committee investigates potential nominees by consulting with members of the legal profession and law professors. It then ranks the candidates as "exceptionally well qualified," "well qualified," "qualified," or "unqualified." Although the president has the sole power to nominate, most presidents do not wish to name someone who will later be declared unqualified. Therefore, the deputy attorney general usually seeks the ABA's recommendations prior to nomination, and some potential nominees are eliminated in this way. This process produces federal judges with two defining attributes: They belong to the president's party, and they have often been active in politics.

State appointive systems resemble the presidential system for selecting federal judges, except that with **gubernatorial appointments** there is no equivalent of senatorial courtesy at the state level. As with federal appointees, governors tend to nominate those who have been active in their campaigns. At times, governors have been known to make appointments to strengthen their position within a geographical area or with a specific group of voters. In recent years some governors have allowed bar associations to examine the qualifications of potential nominees. State bar associations are gaining influence, much like the ABA influence on federal judicial appointees. However, governors have greater independence to ignore bar association advice.

 Dick Durbin, John Ashcroft, "Q: Is the GOP Causing a Vacancy Crisis in the Federal Judiciary?"

Election of Judges

More than half the states select judges through popular **judicial elections**. The concept of an elected

judiciary emerged during the Jacksonian era as part of a larger movement aimed at democratizing the political process. It was spearheaded by reformers who believed that an elitist judiciary did not square with the ideology of a government controlled by the people (Dubois 1980). According to this philosophy, there should be no special qualifications for public office; the voters (not the elites) should decide who is most qualified.

In some states judges are selected using partisan elections (the nominee's political party is listed on the ballot). Historically this approach enabled party bosses to use judicial posts as patronage to reward the party faithful. In other states judges are selected using nonpartisan elections (no party affiliations are listed on the ballot). Nevertheless, even where nonpartisan elections are employed, partisan influences are often present (law in action); judicial candidates are endorsed or nominated by parties, receive party support during campaigns, and are readily identified with party labels.

Campaigns for American judgeships are generally low-key, low-visibility affairs marked by the absence of controversy and low voter turnout (Hojnacki and Baum 1992; Champagne and Thielemann 1991). However, in recent years some contests (particularly for state supreme court seats) have been contentious and costly election battles. Millions of dollars in campaign contributions flowed into appellate court races in states like Ohio, Idaho, Illinois, Michigan, and Florida, among other states (Glaberson 2000). Some of the money came from groups like the U.S. Chamber of Commerce and insurance companies that sought to elect business-friendly judges who would back tort reform (Stone 2000). On the other side of the equation lawyers who most often represent plaintiffs in personal injury law suits contribute substantial sums of money to opposing candidates.

The general lack of information and the low levels of voter interest give incumbent judges important advantages in running for reelection. The prestigious title of *judge* is often listed on the ballot in front of the judge's name. For this reason, few local lawyers wish to challenge a sitting judge. Once a judge is selected, either through an election or an appointment to fill a midterm vacancy, the chances of being voted out of office are small. Few sitting judges are even opposed for reelection; of those challenged, few are ever voted out of office (Dubois 1984; Neubauer 1997). Yet the possibility exists. The best known such case was that of Chief Justice Rose

---

American Bar Association (ABA): The largest voluntary organization of lawyers in the United States.

Gubernatorial appointment: Method of judicial selection in which the governor appoints a person to a judicial vacancy without an election.

Judicial election: Method of judicial selection in which the voters choose judicial candidates in a partisan or nonpartisan election.

Bird of the California Supreme Court. She was strongly opposed by conservatives, particularly for her opposition to the death penalty, and was defeated in a retention election in November 1986 (Wold and Culver 1987). More recently, other incumbent state supreme court justices in Washington, Louisiana, and Tennessee have been voted out of office in hard-fought campaigns.

 The League of Women Voters offers a Voters' Guide to Judicial Elections: **http://www.ca.lwv.org/lwvc.files/ judic/**.

For an up-to-date list of Web links, go to **http:// www.wadsworth.com/product/0534563406s**.

Merit Selection

"Remove the courts from politics" has been the long-standing cry of judicial reformers, who point to three adverse effects of the popular election of judges. First, popular election fails to encourage the ablest lawyers to seek judicial posts. It works to discourage qualified persons from considering running, because they wish to avoid the ordeal of an election. Second, popular election suggests the appearance of impropriety, because it provides an incentive for judges to decide cases in a popular manner: "An elective system does little to dissuade minority groups from believing that an elected judge must pander to the popular viewpoint in order to remain in judicial office" (National Advisory Commission 1973, 146). Third, the elective system is a contest in which the electorate is least likely to be informed about the merits of the candidates. Implicit in these and other arguments of judicial reformers is the identification of poor judges with political hacks subservient to the party that initially slated them for a judgeship.

To cure these ills, legal reformers advocate merit selection, also known as the **Missouri Bar Plan**, because that state was the first to adopt it in 1940. Merit selection has won increasing acceptance. The American Bar Association officially endorsed the concept in 1990. At present, thirty-four states and the District of Columbia use the merit system, at least at some level of their state court system (see again Figure 8-2 on page 199). In addition, a number of other states have actively considered adopting merit selection. The growing importance of merit selection is demonstrated by the fact that all states that have altered judicial selection techniques in recent years have adopted some form of the Missouri Bar Plan. Even in states that have not formally adopted merit selection, governors often use "voluntary merit plans" to fill temporary vacancies (Dubois 1980).

Merit selection is actually a hybrid system that incorporates elements from other judicial selection methods: gubernatorial appointment, popular election, citizen involvement, and—most important—a formalized role for the legal profession. In its present form, merit selection involves the establishment of a judicial nominating commission composed of lawyers and laypersons, who suggest a list of qualified nominees (usually three) to the governor (Henschen, Moog, and Davis 1990). The state's chief executive makes the final selection but is limited to choosing from those nominated by the commission. After a short period of service on the bench (usually one year), the new judge stands uncontested before the voters. The sole question is, "Should Judge X be retained in office?" If the incumbent judge wins a majority of affirmative votes, he or she earns a full term of office. Each subsequent term is secured through another uncontested "retention ballot" (Hall and Aspin 1992). Most judges are returned to the bench by a healthy margin, often receiving 70 percent of the vote. Only a handful of judges have been removed from office. Over a thirty-year period, for example, fifty trial and appellate courts court judges were defeated in 3,912 retention elections in ten states. Twenty-eight of these defeats occurred in Illinois, which requires a judge to receive a minimum of 60 percent of the popular vote to remain on the bench (Aspin et al. 2000).

Although backers of the Missouri Bar Plan contend that it will significantly improve the judges selected and remove the courts from politics, studies of the merit selection system in operation have reached different conclusions. The politics of judicial selection has been altered but not removed; in fact, removing politics does not seem possible. What the reformers presumably mean is the removal of "partisan" politics. In operation, the Missouri Bar Plan has reduced the influence of political parties, while at the same time greatly increased the power of the legal profession (Watson and Downing 1969).

Missouri Bar Plan: The name given to a method of judicial selection combining merit selection and popular control in retention elections.

CONSEQUENCES OF JUDICIAL SELECTION

The debate over the best method for selecting state judges has raged for decades. Partisan and nonpartisan elections, employed in a majority of states, are supported by those who believe elections are the most appropriate method for guaranteeing the popular accountability of state judicial policy makers. Critics, on the other hand, assert that elections are fundamentally inconsistent with the principle of judicial independence, which is vital for neutral and impartial judicial decision making. Less philosophically, these competing perspectives find expression in tension between the legal profession and political parties over influencing judicial selections. The different methods of judicial selection heighten or diminish the influence of the bar or the influence of political parties.

This debate indicates that methods of judicial selection are perceived to have important consequences. Three topics stand out. One centers on which system is "best." The second relates to similarities in judges' backgrounds. The third involves efforts to produce a more diverse judiciary.

 Gerald F. Richman, "The Case for Merit Selection and Retention of Trial Judges"

Which System Is Best?

In evaluating which selection system is best, a key criterion is whether one system produces better judges than another. Judicial folklore has long held that particular systems may produce superior judges. Several studies have systematically analyzed this folklore. Because it is impossible to evaluate a normative concept such as "best," it is necessary to rephrase the question empirically. That is, do judges selected by one method differ from those selected by others? Researchers use measurable judicial credentials, such as education and prior legal experience, as indicators of judicial quality. These studies point to two different types of conclusions.

From the standpoint of individuals who wish to become judges, methods of judicial selection make a difference, but not much. When legislators appoint judges, it is quite clear that former legislators are more likely to be selected than in other systems.

Similarly, elective systems elevate to the bench a higher proportion of persons who have held local political office. By contrast, when the governor appoints, the system benefits those who have held state office (such as legislators). These differences may be evaluated by asking what systems appear to favor candidates with local political office—which typically means the district attorney. Under the Missouri Bar Plan and elective systems, former DAs are more often selected as judges. When the executive or legislature makes the selection, fewer DAs become judges. The differences between systems are pronounced. In California, for example, which governor makes the appointment has an impact on who becomes a judge (Dubois 1985).

From a broader perspective, methods of judicial selection have only a marginal influence on the types of lawyers who become judges. Whether elected by the voters, appointed by the governor, or selected through merit plans, state judges are more alike than different. In terms of personal background characteristics such as prior political experience, ties to the local community, political party affiliation, and quality of legal education, the systems of judicial selection do not appear to produce very different types of judges (Emmert and Glick 1987, 1988; Flango and Ducat 1979). In short, methods of judicial selection are not related to judges' personal characteristics in the way the debate in the literature would have us believe (Canon 1972; Nagel 1973). Thus, there is no systematic evidence that one selection system produces better judges than another selection system.

The conventional wisdom among political scientists that selection method has no meaningful impact has recently been challenged. A study of six states matched them according to selection systems and region—Rhode Island and Virginia use legislative appointment; Pennsylvania and West Virginia employ partisan elections; and Connecticut and New Jersey utilize gubernatorial appointment. Policy decisions of the state supreme courts indicated that judges selected in partisan elections reacted to public opinion, whereas those appointed by the governor were free of this constraint (Pinello 1995).

Similarities in Judges' Backgrounds

Although the United States uses a variety of methods for selecting judges, it is important to note that judges share some important similarities, which may be of even greater importance than the differences. In general, judges are males from the upper middle class, and their backgrounds reflect the attributes of that class: They are more often white and Protestant, and they are better educated than the average American.

Another similarity among judges is that most were born in the community in which they serve. Trial court judges are usually appointed from particular districts; the persons appointed were often born in that area and attended local or state colleges before going on to a law school within the state. (The only major exception is in New England, where the schools have a strong regional orientation.)

Finally, judges are seldom newcomers to political life. Almost three out of four state supreme court judges have held a nonjudicial political office. Trial court judges also have held prior office—most often district attorney or state legislator. Eighty percent of federal judges had prior governmental experience. Before becoming judges, they had some familiarity with the range of public issues that governments as well as courts must address. Because of these factors, few political mavericks survive the series of screens that precede becoming a judge. The process tends to eliminate those who hold views and exhibit behavior widely different from the mainstream of local community sentiment.

 The National Association of Women Judges maintains a Web site at **http://www.nawj.org**.

For an up-to-date list of Web links, go to **http://www.wadsworth.com/product/0534563406s**.

Diversity and the Judiciary

The dominant profile of judges as white males has begun to change, but to some, change has not come fast enough (see Controversy: Is Gender Bias a Significant Problem in the Courts?). Since the presidency of Jimmy Carter an increasing number of federal court vacancies have been filled with female jurists. During his single term in office, President Jimmy Carter appointed significant numbers of women (forty) and blacks (fifty-five) to the federal bench. Ronald Reagan, during his two terms, named twenty-four women to the federal district courts, and George Bush nominated twenty-nine during his single term. Bill Clinton outstripped the other three presidents during his first six years in office. Overall,

there was a 55 percent increase in nontraditional judges in active service from the day Clinton was first elected (Goldman and Slotnick 1999). Altogether he achieved a record proportion of women and minorities: about 60 percent of all appointees to the federal bench (Goldman 1995; Goldman and Saronson 1994).

The picture of state judges is significantly more complicated. Until this century, the number of women judges in America was so small that they could be counted on one hand. The twentieth century began witnessing changes, though not very quickly. By 1950, women had achieved at least token representation on the bench. It was not until 1979, however, that every state could report that its bench included at least one woman judge (Carbon 1984). Information about the gender of local officeholders is sketchy, but recent estimates place the number of women on the bench as anywhere from 10 percent to 15 percent (Maule and Parry 1997). Overall the number of women holding judicial positions on major trial courts increased 54 percent from 1987 to 1994 and 80 percent on the state supreme courts (Martin 1999). This growth parallels increases in the number of women lawyers (Martin 1990). Significant growth in the number of women lawyers began in the 1970s, and by 1992, approximately 19 percent of the legal profession was made up of women. It was estimated that by the year 2000 women would constitute 25 percent of the legal profession (Martin 1999). Thus, there is every expectation that the proportion of women on the bench will continue to grow.

With the increasing number of women serving on the state and federal benches, there is an understandable interest in probing the "difference" women may bring to the bench (Martin 1993). Speculation by affirmative action activists has suggested that female judges would be more liberal than male jurists. Some studies report gender differences (but often the differences are at best small). For example:

- An analysis of appellate judges' votes in obscenity, job discrimination, and search and seizure cases found that women judges were more liberal than men only in cases involving employment discrimination (Songer, Davis, and Haire 1994).

- Research on appellate courts finds that women judges tend to be the strongest supporters of

Is Gender Bias a Significant Problem in the Courts?

The last several decades have witnessed a monumental change in the gender composition of the American workforce. Not only are a higher percentage of women working outside the home, but women are also increasingly working in what had once been considered male-only professions. Law most certainly is a case in point. Today, women constitute anywhere from one third to one half of all law students, and as discussed in this chapter, now make up over 10 percent of the nation's judges. In turn many female lawyers have been at the forefront of arguing cases, big and small, that affect the role of women in society (Ogden 1996).

One of the areas of most concern to the women's rights movement is gender bias. Thirty-six states have created task forces to investigate gender bias in the legal system. Some state task forces defined gender bias in terms of decisions made based on stereotypes about men and women; others stressed insensitivity toward certain aspects of men's and women's lives; and still others emphasized intentional bias and ill will. Regardless of the precision of the definition, a team of researchers from Boise State University found these reports to be remarkably consistent. The state task forces consistently found gender bias in four areas of the legal system: domestic violence, sexual assault, divorce, and behavior toward female workers (Hemmens, Strom, and Schlegel 1997).

Domestic violence is one area in which the state task force studies found gender bias to be most common. Some members of the courtroom work group believe that domestic violence is a private matter and should not be dealt with in the court system. Indeed one male district judge was quoted as saying slapping around the wife was justified.

Sexual assault is another area in which women experience gender bias. Sexual assault is underreported because women believe they will not be believed and will themselves be blamed. Moreover, women perceive that reporting sexual assault will result in a revictimization, with past sexual history of the female (more so than the male) thrown open to scrutiny.

Divorce cases are another area in which the possibility of gender bias looms. The state task force reports unanimously found that women suffer from gender bias in terms of awarding alimony, division of property, and child support. The courts, on the other hand, appear to be biased against fathers in child custody awards.

Finally, the thirty-six state task force reports found gender bias against female lawyers and court employees. Of principal concern is offensive and intolerable actions toward women participants in the legal system. The most common form of gender bias mentioned was the practice of judges and attorneys addressing female lawyers in a demeaning manner. Female lawyers, more so than their male counterparts, were addressed by their first names. Moreover, terms like "sweetie," "little lady lawyer," "pretty eyes," and "dear" were used. Another common form of gender bias suffered by female attorneys (and judges as well) is sexist remarks or jokes. Gender bias also affects hiring and promotion. Female lawyers perceive that it is harder to get hired, and once hired they are paid less and have fewer opportunities for promotion.

women's rights claims, regardless of their ideology (Palmer 2001).

- In Pennsylvania women judges are somewhat harsher in sentencing criminal defendants. Notably they are particularly hard toward repeat minority offenders (Steffensmeier and Hebert 1999).

But other studies find no gender differences among judges. For example,

- A study of Justice Sandra Day O'Connor, the first woman to serve on the U.S. Supreme Court, concludes, "Overall, the findings presented here do very little to support the assertion that O'Connor's decision making is distinct by virtue of her gender" (Davis 1993, 139).

- In a major state trial court, the gender of the judge made little difference on how assets were distributed after divorce (Crowe 1994).

- Analysis of over 2,100 written opinions from 1992 to 1995 indicated that male and female federal district court judges were not significantly different when it came to their decisions (Stidham and Carp 1997).

It is important to underscore that these findings are based on reports of specific events ("have you ever had remarks made about your looks?") as well as perceptions of gender bias or problems. Women consistently reported problem areas at higher levels than men. Answers to questions like those asked in surveys, of course, can be understood in different ways. Perhaps women are oversensitive to these issues (or alternatively, males are oblivious). Another stumbling block is the difficulty in estimating the true extent of the gender bias problem. Perceptions of bias could be the product of an isolated few who have contact with many female lawyers and judges, or they could be the result of persistent practices by numerous male lawyers and judges.

Given the problems of using perceptions alone to document a social problem such as gender bias, it is important to look for independent validation. For this reason *America's Courts and the Criminal Justice System* examines domestic violence (Chapter 9). For now let us examine the admittedly complex topic of divorce. Not all studies of actual court awards (as opposed to perceptions of court awards) agree. Lenore Weitzman's pioneering study *The Divorce Revolution* (1985) concludes that no-fault divorce laws have had a negative impact on the economic status of divorcing women. Herbert Jacob (1988), on the other hand, finds that no-fault divorce improved the economic position of divorcing women in one key area and in other areas had no impact. As I conclude elsewhere, "The underlying problem for women and their children who go through a divorce is not the laws that govern divorce, but the economics of divorcing couples, something that judges and legislatures are largely unable to alter" (Neubauer 1997, 343).

These issues aside, perceptions of gender bias are a serious matter because they affect litigants' perceptions of the fairness of justice. If litigants and/or their lawyers perceive that they are treated differently, they have less confidence in the process of justice, irrespective of the outcome of the case. It is also important to underscore that the gender bias issues investigated must be taken seriously because they directly affect the lives of many women and their children as well. Moreover, the issues are some of the most explosive facing the justice system and have become in a relatively few years important public issues.

Gender bias is not a problem created by the court system but a reflection of prevailing attitudes in society. Although "current laws and affirmative action plans have furthered women's equality, they cannot by themselves change the attitudes of individuals. It is the individual attitudes that require change if gender bias is to be eradicated" (Hemmens, Strom, and Schlegel 1997, 31).

What do you think? Is gender bias a serious problem in the nation's courthouses? Have you seen or experienced biased behavior by lawyers, judges, or other court personnel? If you are troubled by using individual reports to make the case for gender bias, what alternative methods would you use to study the problem?

 To learn more about gender bias, visit the Clearinghouse on Racial/Ethnic and Gender Bias at the National Center for State Courts at **http://www. ncsc.dni.us/is/clrhouse.htm**, and the National Judicial Education Program Task Force on Gender Bias in the Courts at **http://www.nowldef.org/ html/njep/history.htm**.

For an up-to-date list of Web links, go to **http:// www.wadsworth.com/product/0534563406s**.

Perhaps the best summary is that drawing conclusions about the difference women make on the bench is still problematical (Davis, Haire, and Songer 1993).

The American Judicature Society reported in 1973 that slightly more than 1 percent of state judges were black. By the mid-1980s the percentage had increased to 3.8 percent. Thus, Barbara Luck Graham (1990b) found 714 black state court judges covering forty-one states in 1986. The underrepresentation of blacks on the bench is partially a reflection of the paucity of black attorneys (25,000 out of a total pool of over 750,000). But underrepresentation is also a product of how judges are selected. Black judges are more likely to be found in states using appointment either by the governor or the legislature; they are less likely to be selected in states using elections (Graham 1990a). In 1991 the Supreme Court held that the Voting Rights Act of 1965, as amended in 1982, applies to judicial elections (*Chisom v. Roemer* and *Houston Lawyers' Association v. Attorney General of Texas*). The rulings pave the way for major changes in the forty-one states, particularly in the South, that use elections for at least some of their judges (Smith and Garmel 1992) (see Case Close-Up: *Chisom v. Roemer* and Diversity and the Bench).

Chisom v. Roemer and Diversity and the Bench

Janice Clark had always wanted to be a judge. As a practicing lawyer she seemed to possess the education and experience necessary to don the black robes, but she still faced an insurmountable barrier. The problem was not gender—after all, women were being elected to the bench on a regular basis all over the United States. Rather, the insurmountable barrier was race. White voters rarely voted for black candidates; indeed as a black candidate for a judgeship, she received only 3.2 percent of the white vote. So as lawyers often do, she filed suit in the U.S. District Court for the Middle District of Louisiana. Her lawsuit alleged that electing judges from multimember districts diluted black voting strength in violation of the Voting Rights Act.

Janice Clark's lawsuit raises some deep-seated questions about who our judges are and how best to select them. Should the backgrounds matter? Is it enough to have a bench composed of fair and impartial individuals? Or does the appearance of justice also require that our judges broadly reflect the society they serve and protect? Just as importantly, the Clark lawsuit called into question how judges are selected. Are some methods of judicial selection systematically related to choosing judges with certain types of backgrounds?

Janice Clark's lawsuit was a class action brought by black voters and black lawyers qualified to be elected judges in Louisiana. Local civil rights groups as well as several national organizations, including the Lawyer's

Committee for Civil Rights under Law, joined the suit. The nominal defendant was the governor of the state. Also appearing for the defendants were attorneys representing the Louisiana District Judges Association and the Orleans Trial Judges Association (*Clark et al. v. Edwin Edwards et al.* 1988).

U.S. District Judge John Parker's opinion stressed that, of the 156 district court judgeships in Louisiana, only two were held by black judges. The reason was that judgeships were elected from the entire judicial district, which had the effect of "diluting black voting strength," a violation of the Voting Rights Act. This case was one of several filed in the federal courts, and the underlying legal issue was eventually settled at the appellate level in *Chisom v. Roemer* (1991) and *Houston Lawyers' Association v. Attorney General of Texas* (1991). The basic legal issue hinged on an interpretation of the Voting Rights Act of 1965 as amended in 1982. The Fifth Circuit ruled that judges do not fall under the law. But *Chisom* held otherwise, finding that judges were indeed covered by the Voting Rights Act.

Crossing this important threshold means that in drawing election districts (either for legislatures or judges) the lines may not dilute minority voting. This conclusion is based on repeated findings of the existence of racially polarized voting; that in an election contest pitting a black candidate against a white one, white voters rarely cast their ballot for the black candidate (Engstrom 1989).

JUDICIAL EDUCATION

The various methods of judicial selection recruit amateurs to the bench who have no practical experience or systematic exposure to the judicial world. Many new judges find that being a judge varies greatly from what they had expected.

Newly appointed federal judges, for example, experience three general kinds of problems (Carp and Wheeler 1972). First is mastering new areas of substantive and procedural law. In sharp contrast to private lawyers, who specialize in a few areas of the law, judges must be generalists. They must rule on a diverse range of legal matters, some of which they were exposed to in law school but some of which are entirely new. A second set of problems facing new

judges is administrative in nature. Supervising the court staff, efficiently and wisely using their time, and managing the hundreds of cases on the court's docket are types of problems many judges have never previously faced. Finally, new judges experience psychological discomfort in adjusting to their new job. Some judges have difficulty abandoning the adversary role that marked their previous legal careers. As one judge indicated, "The major problem along these lines is that a judge has got to look at both sides of the case, whereas an attorney need only look at one."

But judges do have help in learning how to deal with the problems facing them. Fellow judges are the foremost training agents. Through informal exchanges, as well as formal meetings, judges discuss common problems and possible techniques. Law-

The essential problem is that judges are elected from judicial districts (typically one or more counties), with multiple judgeships elected at large. These long-time practices make the remedy difficult. Several states, Arkansas, Louisiana, and Mississippi among them, have created black majority subdistricts—some judges continue to be elected from the entire jurisdiction while others are selected only from one area of the district (Smothers 1996). The result is that blacks are elected in these districts. Critics of these developments worry that judges will engage in "home cooking." One study, however, found no evidence that judges elected from subdistricts in Louisiana (all of whom are black) sentence defendants from their electoral district any differently from defendants outside of their voting area (Kirksey 1997).

The future of this line of decisions is cloudy. In a series of sharply divided decisions, the nation's highest court has struck down majority-minority congressional districts, ruling that the district lines were primarily motivated by race and not justified by legitimate state interests (*Bush v. Vera* 1996; *Shaw v. Hunt* 1996; *Miller v. Johnson* 1995; *Abrams et al. v. Johnson et al.* 1997). Nonetheless, challenges to judicial election and selection procedures under the Voting Rights Act have been mounted in fifteen states (Scruggs, Mazzola, and Zaug 1995).

The impact of *Chisom* is still unfolding. In Louisiana, vacant judgeships were selected in single-member districts (instead of several judges in at-large elections), resulting in several minorities gaining the bench. In Arkansas, ten judicial seats were created in predominantly black subdistricts carved from five of the state's twenty-four judicial districts. In Georgia the governor settled a lawsuit with black plaintiffs that will pave the way for an immediate and dramatic increase in the number of black judges. Though it is likely that the major impact of *Chisom* will be in southern states (because they have significant minority populations), northern states also will feel its effects. In New York, for example, a gubernatorial task force concluded that the state's method of selecting trial court judges probably violated the Voting Rights Act because of its "uniformly poor" record of placing black, Hispanic, and female lawyers on the bench.

Janice Clark's legal argument eventually became the law of the land. The series of Supreme Court cases firmly established the principle that judges cannot be elected in ways that place minority candidates at an unfair disadvantage. But the eventual impact is far from certain. Each of the states with a significant minority population differs somewhat in tradition and method of judicial selection, factors that shape the emerging systems of judicial selection. But for Janice Clark the outcome was both immediate and positive. She ran again for the major trial court bench in Baton Rouge and won, taking the oath of office on January 1, 1993. She has already generated headlines. When a high-ranking state police official publicly complained about one of her decisions, she took to the bench and scolded the official, explaining that the problem was not her interpretation of the law but how badly the legislature had written the state's gaming law in the first place. Her unusual candor aside, it will be many years before we know if minority judges have a long-term impact on the type of justice meted out in courthouses across America.

---

yers who appear in court are another source for what the law says in an area new to the judge. Local court staff often provide new judges with advice on administrative or procedural matters. In the end, however, judges must rely on themselves. Through reading in the law library and seeking out knowledgeable persons, judges engage in self-education.

Judicial training schools and seminars have developed to ease the adjustment problems of new judges. Such programs are by no means limited to new judges. Even veterans of the bench may benefit from a systematic exposure to administrative techniques for keeping the docket current or from seminars on rapidly changing areas of the law, such as sentencing guidelines (Claxton 1992).

Judicial education in America caught on during the 1960s. Until then, the idea that judges should go back to school was not widely accepted—mainly because it might appear to downgrade the judiciary, which was supposed to know the law. Under the prodding of the American Bar Association and Supreme Court Justice Tom Clark, judicial education programs were developed. In 1956 the Institute for Judicial Administration initiated seminars for state appeals court judges. The National Judicial College conducts one- to four-week summer courses for trial judges. The Federal Judicial Center conducts seminars for newly appointed federal judges, as well as continuing education seminars for veteran judges. Other such national programs have sprung up. At the state level, however, institutionalization of training programs for new judges and yearly educational conferences for all judges have been slower to develop (Stein 1986).

The National Judicial College hosts a Web site at **http://www.judges.org/**.

The National Clearinghouse for Judicial Education Information features its programs at **http://jeritt.msu.edu**.

For an up-to-date list of Web links, go to **http://www.wadsworth.com/product/0534563406s**.

JUDGING THE JUDGES

Judicial selection techniques attempt to recruit Solomon-like figures to the bench. Judicial education programs help beginning judges learn their new roles and keep veteran judges abreast of changes in the law. The troublesome problem still remains, however: What should be done about unfit judges? Despite the lack of clarity in what attributes a good judge should possess, one central conclusion stands out: A few judges do not fulfill minimal standards. A few are senile, prejudiced, vindictive, tyrannical, lazy, and sometimes corrupt. Proper judicial conduct is indispensable to the confidence of the people in their judiciary, confidence that itself is indispensable to the rule of law. In recent years such confidence has been eroded by questions of judicial misconduct in a variety of states, including California, Illinois, Florida, New York, Oklahoma, Rhode Island, Pennsylvania, and New Hampshire.

Judicial Independence

A critical issue in judging the judges is how to devise a system for removing unfit judges while at the same time guaranteeing **judicial independence**. At times critics attempt to remove a judge from office, not because of his or her misconduct, but solely because of displeasure with the substance of the judge's decisions. Clearly, protections against unpopular court rulings constitute the hallmark of an independent judiciary. Yet judicial independence is not an end in itself. As University of Chicago Law Professor Philip Kurland has put it, "The provisions for securing the independence of the judiciary were not created for

> **Judicial independence:** Normative value that stresses a judge should be free from outside pressure in making a decision.

COURT TV

Michigan v. Kevorkian

Dr. Death or Angel of Mercy?

Dr. Jack Kevorkian has helped 130 people commit suicide. Four times the state of Michigan prosecuted him for violating the state prohibition on assisted suicide, and four times the jury acquitted or could not reach a decision. But now Dr. Kevorkian has thrown down the gauntlet, having videotaped a death in which he directly administered the lethal drugs. As you watch the video, ask yourself the following questions:

1. What problems does the judge face in conducting a trial in a highly publicized and emotionally charged case like this one? What special problems does the judge confront in presiding over a trial in which the defendant represents himself? How do the judge's decisions affect the trial?

2. Why did the jury convict in this case but not previous ones? Is this the type of case in which juries might engage in jury nullification (Chapter 14)? Was the compromise verdict unexpected?

3. What contrasting views of law do the participants express? In what ways is Dr. Kevorkian's crusade to change suicide laws similar to or different from past social justice crusades, including antiwar protests and the civil rights movement?

the benefit of the judges, but for the benefit of the judged" (quoted in Byrd 1976, 267). Controversy: Is Judicial Independence Being Undermined? explores this topic in a contemporary setting.

Judicial Misconduct

Systems for removing or disciplining unfit judges must not only strike a balance between judicial accountability and judicial independence, they must also grapple with the wide range of misbehavior encompassed by the phrase *judicial misconduct* (Begue and Goldstein 1987). Most directly, judicial misconduct involves corruption. In recent years judges in big cities such as Chicago, New York, and Philadelphia have been accused of (and sometimes convicted of) such criminal offenses as taking bribes and fixing traffic tickets. But not all judicial misconduct is so

Is Judicial Independence Being Undermined?

It was not just the decision by U.S. District Judge Harold Baer, Jr., to suppress the eighty pounds of cocaine and heroin that caused the controversy, but the reasoning behind it. The police searched Carol Bayless's car after watching four men who had delivered packages to the auto flee when they recognized a police officer (Neumeister 1996). This did not constitute probable cause for a search (Chapter 12) Judge Baer ruled, because in that neighborhood such actions were understandable, not suspicious. The Washington Heights area of New York City is noted not only for its high crime rates but also for its reputation for police brutality and police corruption. Indeed, a number of officers in Harlem's Thirtieth Precinct were convicted for stealing drugs and then selling them.

According to legal experts, Judge Baer's ruling (*U.S. v Bayless*), although controversial, was well within the law and not likely to be overturned. But these opinions did not deter the unprecedented political firestorm that broke out during the 1996 election season. New York Mayor Rudolph Giuliani and Police Commissioner William Bratton assailed the judge's decision for tossing out $4 million in drugs. The local decision soon became a national controversy as well. Senator Bob Dole, soon to be the Republican nominee for president, called for Judge Baer's impeachment. Republican House Speaker Newt Gingrich charged that Baer's ruling was "the perfect reason why we are losing our civilization." The White House immediately sought to diffuse the issue by calling the judge's ruling "wrong-headed"—and the press secretary threatened to ask him to quit. Within a few weeks the specific issue was defused when Judge Baer reinstated the evidence, deciding after hearing additional testimony that the police were indeed justified in searching the vehicle.

In "Judicial Decision Making and the Impact of Election Year Rhetoric" Jennifer Segal (2000) notes that the critiques were indeed unsubstantiated. The data indicate that not only is Baer no friend to defendants, neither are his Democratic colleagues in the Southern District of New York.

The Judge Baer incident, however, left a lingering residue and served to reopen the debate over judicial independence. Nor was this the only such incident during recent election years, which found judges, both state and federal, the subject of attack.

- A coalition of New York City's anticrime and victims' rights organizations called for the impeachment of Judge Lorin Duckman; the Brooklyn judge released Benito Oliver on bail for a domestic violence arrest, and Oliver later killed his ex-girlfriend (Purdy and Van Natta 1996).

- Justice Penny White of the Tennessee Supreme Court was voted off the bench in a retention election because she voted in a death penalty case to allow the defendant to put on evidence in mitigation (Bright 1997).

- Justice David Lanphier lost a retention election when a cluster of special interest groups campaigned for his removal over displeasure with selected decisions rendered by the Nebraska Supreme Court (Reid 1999).

- H. Lee Sarokin, U.S. Court of Appeals for the Third Circuit (based in Philadelphia), resigned. Appointed to the district court by President Carter in 1979, he was elevated by President Clinton in 1994. Dole had singled him out for attack, particularly for his 1991 ruling in favor of a homeless man who was ejected from a New Jersey public library for poor hygiene. "The constant politicization of my tenure has made 'my' lifetime dream impossible" (Mauro 1996).

In the wake of the Judge Baer incident, Chief Justice William Rehnquist, in a rare public speech, voiced concern about judicial independence. Without directly mentioning the Baer controversy, the chief justice, noted for his conservative positions, stated, "There is a wrong way and right way to go about putting a popular imprint on the judiciary" (Carelli 1996). Similarly, four judges of the Second Circuit Court of Appeals (which includes New York) condemned the attacks and labeled the White House threat "an extraordinary intimidation."

Appointments to the federal bench have become a centerpiece in the tension between Republicans and Democrats. Early in the campaign Senator Dole fired a salvo at his rival, President Bill Clinton, over federal judges. Hoping to make President Clinton's nominations to the federal bench a key campaign issue, Dole described federal judges as "root causes" of an explosion of crime in America (Tackett 1996). In pointed language he labeled four of the president's judicial appointments as members of a "judicial hall of shame." Democrats were quick to point out that Dole had voted to confirm 182 of the 185 judges nominated by Clinton, including 2 he harshly criticized.

(continued on following page)

Political divisions over judicial decision making carried over into President Clinton's entire second term. With a Democrat in the White House but the Republicans in control of the Senate, prospects for smooth sailing in filling judicial vacancies were not favorable. Senator Orrin Hatch (R-Utah), chairman of the Senate Judiciary Committee, slowed down consideration of Clinton nominees with only a few being confirmed.

Throughout the years criticism of decisions of federal judges has usually been followed by cries to remove tenure. This also proved to be the case in 1997. Some Republicans openly called for the impeachment of federal judges who had rendered decisions that conservatives disapproved of. Moreover, in Louisiana, a Republican candidate for the U.S. Senate promised to abolish lifetime tenure for "liberal" judges (no mention was made of "conservative" judges, however, evidently implying they could remain on the bench as long as they liked). But very little has come of repeated efforts to change the system of tenure for federal judges.

Amidst this political clatter, Law Professor Stephen Burbank (1987), a member of the National Commission on Judicial Discipline and Removal, reminds us that judicial independence is a means to an end rather than an end itself. Attacks on the federal judiciary are hardly new. President Jefferson tried to remove Justice Samuel Chase as part of a campaign to "reform" the federal judiciary. In the 1960s a nationwide campaign was launched by the ultra-conservative John Birch

Society to impeach Chief Justice Earl Warren. During the 1968 presidential election, candidate Richard Nixon attacked the Supreme Court, promising to remake the high court in his own image (Chapter 17). But almost invariably challenges to judicial independence fail (Friedman 1998).

Criticism is one thing, undermining judicial independence is another. "Courts are not independent when state judges are voted off the bench because of unpopular decisions by their courts, and when federal judges reverse decisions or resign from the bench after a barrage of criticism" (Bright 1997, 167).

What do you think? Where do you draw the line between fair criticism of judges and intimidation? Do you think federal judges would decide cases differently if they served for set terms rather than for life?

To continue the debate point your browser to:
The ABA Standing Committee on Judicial Independence: **http://www.abanet.org/judind/home.html**
Citizens for Independent Courts: **http://www.constitutionproject.org/cfic.html**
Brennan Center for Justice: **http://www.brennancenter.org/**

For an up-to-date list of Web links, go to **http://www.wadsworth.com/product/0534563406s**.

venal; sometimes it involves improper or bizarre behavior on the bench (Wice 1991). Exhibit 8-1 summarizes some recent cases that illustrate the range of behavior.

The most difficult situations involve judges of advanced years whose mental capacity has become impaired. After years of dedicated service, with no hint of scandal, and exemplary conduct on the bench, a judge might become senile. State supreme court justices in California and Vermont, for example, have been deemed too old and too senile to continue to dispense justice. Accordingly, a growing number of states impose mandatory retirement ages for judges. The Supreme Court has ruled that state laws requiring judges to retire at seventy years of age do not violate the federal Age Discrimination in Employment Act (*Gregory v. Ashcroft* 1991). In another widely followed case, the nation's highest

court upheld the prison sentence of David Lanier, a state judge from Dyersburg, Tennessee. Judge Lanier had been convicted in federal court of sexually attacking five women in his courthouse. He had not been prosecuted in state court, nor had the state's conduct commission taken action, many said because the judge was politically well connected and his brother was the county prosecutor. The decision strengthened federal civil rights laws (Chapter 3), but the opinion stopped short of recognizing a federal right not to be raped by a state official (*U.S. v. Lanier* 1997). Figure 8-3 (page 212) summarizes the Supreme Court cases affecting judges.

Formal methods for removing unfit judges—recall elections and impeachment proceedings—are generally so cumbersome that they have seldom been used. Moreover, these techniques are better directed at corrupt judges than those whose behav-

EXHIBIT 8-1	Examples of Errant State Judges

- Pennsylvania Supreme Court Justice Rolf Larsen was removed from office in 1994 by the Pennsylvania Senate after being convicted of arranging to have a doctor prescribe drugs in the name of court employees. A House impeachment report also accused Larsen of favoritism by giving friends and supporters special treatment in deciding whether to accept an appeal (Jesdanun 1994).
- Illinois Supreme Court Chief Justice James Heiple stepped down as chief justice after being censured by the Illinois Courts Commission for disobeying police during traffic stops and using his position to avoid traffic tickets. Heiple faced impeachment proceedings in the legislature (Armstrong and Pearson 1997). Heiple was the author of the fiercely disputed 1994 Baby Richard decision, which gave custody to the biological father, thus taking the boy away from his adoptive parents (Neubauer 1997).
- New York Supreme Court (the state's major trial court) Judge Duckman was alleged by the Commission on Judicial Conduct of being biased toward prosecutors and making disparaging remarks toward women and blacks in his court (Dao 1996).
- An Ohio judge was suspended after he dismissed a child-rape case because a prosecution witness was twenty minutes late (Panel Suspends 1994).

- Florida Circuit Judge Michael Blackstone resigned rather than contest allegations that he abused lawyers, made arbitrary decisions, and lied under oath about these matters ("This Week in Review" 2000).
- The Maryland Judicial Commission issued a warning to a Montgomery County circuit judge who told an eleven-year-old female sexual assault victim that "it takes two to tango" ("Maryland Judge Warned" 2000).
- Colfax County (New Mexico) Magistrate Archie Valdez agreed to a temporary suspension without pay pending resolution of indictments charging sexual misconduct, bribery, and battery (Lezon 2000).
- The Commission on Judicial Performance recommended a public admonishment for an Orange County (California) judge for making inappropriate comments to parties involved in three criminal cases (Pfeifer 2000).
- Judge Calvin Hotard of Second Parish Court Jefferson Parish (Louisiana) retired from the bench in the wake of judiciary commission allegations of helping five criminal defendants in exchange for sexual favors (Louwagie 2000).

ior is improper or whose advanced age has caught up with them. A more workable method for dealing with judicial misconduct is the judicial conduct commission.

State Judicial Conduct Commissions

In 1960 California became the first state to adopt a modern and practical system for disciplining its judges. In response to the mounting public clamor for accountability on the part of government officials, every state has followed California's pioneering lead (Brooks 1985). Under the California model, a **judicial conduct commission** is created as an arm of the state's highest court. The members of the commission consist of judges, lawyers, and promi-

nent laypersons. They investigate allegations of judicial misconduct and, when appropriate, hear testimony. If the commission finds in favor of the judge, the investigation is closed and the matter is permanently concluded (Miller 1991). Confidentiality is essential, lest a judge's reputation be tarnished by a crank complaint. Many complaints are issued by disgruntled litigants, whose charges amount to simple displeasure that the judge did not rule in their favor. If the complaint has merit, the commission may recommend a sanction of private admonishment, public censure, retirement, or removal. The state supreme court retains the final power to discipline errant judges (Gardiner 1986).

Although commissions are armed with the potent weapon of a public recommendation, they prefer to act more informally. If the information gathered suggests judicial misconduct, the commission holds a confidential conference and discusses the matter with the judge, who has an opportunity to rebut the charges. The commission may try to correct the matter; a judge with a substance abuse problem, for example, is encouraged to enroll in a

Judicial conduct commission: An official body whose function is to investigate allegations of misconduct by judges.

FIGURE 8-3	Key Developments Concerning Judges	
Gregory v. Ashcroft	1991	State laws requiring judges to retire at seventy do not violate the federal Age Discrimination in Employment Act.
Chisom v. Roemer; Houston Lawyers' Association v. Attorney General of Texas	1991	Judges are covered by the Voting Rights Act.
U.S. v. Lanier	1997	The trial court improperly ruled that state judges are not covered by federal civil rights laws, but there is no federal right not to be raped.

treatment program. If the problems are serious, continuous, or not immediately solvable, the commission usually seeks to force the voluntary retirement of the judge. The informal pressures and the threat of bringing public proceedings are often powerful enough to force the judge in question off the bench. The complaints and investigations remain confidential unless the commission finds it necessary to seek a reprimand or removal before the state supreme court.

 FAQs from the State of Illinois Judicial Inquiry Board can be found at **http://www.state.il.us/jib/faq.htm**.

For an up-to-date list of Web links, go to **http://www.wadsworth.com/product/0534563406s**.

Federal Conduct and Disability Act

In 1980 Congress passed the first major change since 1939 in the self-governance mechanism of the federal judiciary. The Judicial Councils Reform and Judicial Conduct and Disability Act lays out a precise and exacting mechanism for acting on complaints against federal judges (Neisser 1981; Burbank 1987). Complaints are initially heard by the judicial councils (the administrative arm of each U.S. court of appeals). Most result in either a finding of no misconduct or the imposition of nonpublic sanctions. However, if there is substantial evidence of serious misconduct, the judicial council sends a written report to the Judicial Conference, which may recommend that the U.S. House of Representatives begin impeachment procedures.

Article II of the Constitution provides for the removal of the president, vice president, or civil officers of the United States—including federal judges —for crimes of "treason, bribery, or other high crimes and misdemeanors." The House must first vote articles of impeachment specifying the specific charges. **Impeachment** does not mean conviction, but rather allegations of wrongdoing—roughly equivalent to a grand jury indictment. The trial on the articles of impeachment is conducted before the Senate. Conviction requires a two-thirds vote of the senators present and carries with it **removal** from office and disqualification from holding any future office. Historically, in functioning as both judge and jury in impeachment trials, all Senators observed the testimony and cross-examination of witnesses. But in the modern era, the press of legislative business makes this time-consuming process unworkable. Therefore, in 1986 the Senate made the historic decision to establish a twelve-person Impeachment Committee to receive evidence and take testimony prior to the trial on the Senate floor (Heflin 1987).

An unprecedented series of allegations of misconduct against federal judges since 1981 highlights the interlocking relationships between criminal prosecutions, impeachment, and the new statutory scheme (Exhibit 8-2). The impeachment proceedings against U.S. District Judge Alcee Hastings raised the most difficult questions: Unlike Claiborne and Nixon, he was never convicted of a criminal offense. Hastings, the first black federal judge ever appointed in Florida, was indicted for soliciting a $150,000 bribe from two convicted racketeers. A jury acquitted the judge but found the codefendant guilty. Nonetheless, the judicial council of the

Impeachment: Official accusation against a public official brought by a legislative body seeking his or her removal.

Removal: To dismiss a person from holding office.

EXHIBIT 8-2 Federal Judges Who Have Faced Disciplinary Action (Typical Felony Case)

Judge	Allegations	Criminal	Outcome
U.S. District Judge Harry Claiborne (District of Nevada)	Accepting a bribe in a criminal case over which he was presiding.	Jury acquitted on the charge of bribery but convicted on income tax evasion.	While serving a two-year sentence in federal prison, the Senate found Claiborne guilty on three of four impeachment articles by the required two-thirds vote and removed him from the bench (1986).
Chief Judge Walter Nixon (Southern District of Mississippi)	The judge falsely denied before a federal grand jury that he had intervened in a state narcotics case involving the son of a friend.	Convicted of perjury.	While serving his sentence at Eglin Air Force Base in Florida, the Senate removed Nixon from the federal bench (1989).
U.S. District Judge Alcee Hastings (Southern District of Florida)	Accused of soliciting a $150,000 bribe from two convicted racketeers.	Acquitted, but the jury found the codefendant guilty.	The judicial council of the Eleventh Circuit and the Judicial Conference concluded that Hastings was not only guilty but had also fabricated his defense. The House of Representatives, by an overwhelming margin, voted seventeen articles of impeachment and the Senate ousted Hastings from office in 1989.
U.S. District Judge Robert Aguilar (Northern District of California)	Told an acquaintance about a government wiretap in a racketeering investigation and obstructing a grand jury investigation by lying to FBI agents about the matter.	Convicted in 1990 on two counts of obstructing justice. The Ninth Circuit reversed but the Supreme Court reinstated the wiretap conviction (*U.S. v. Aguilar* 1995).	The judge remained on the bench during his appeal but was limited to trying civil cases. After another conviction and yet another appellate reversal, Aguilar resigned from the bench apparently in exchange for criminal charges being dropped.
U.S. District Judge Robert Collins (Eastern District of Louisiana)	Accused of taking a $100,000 bribe from a drug smuggler. The FBI raided his office and found marked bills.	First federal judge in history to be convicted of bribery.	While serving a seven-year prison sentence and facing impeachment proceedings, Collins resigned from the bench before formal Senate action was taken.
U.S. District Judge Brian Duff (Northern District of Illinois)	Temper as black as judicial robe and shoot-from-the-lip courtroom manner. Highest rate of reversal in the Chicago courthouse.	None.	Amidst reports of a Justice Department complaint filed with the Judicial Counsel for the Seventh Circuit, the judge stepped down with possibility of a reduced caseload after three years. Judge Duff cited medical problems (Robinson 1996).

Eleventh Circuit and the Judicial Conference concluded that Hastings was not only guilty but had also fabricated his defense. Hastings argued that racial motivations lay behind the impeachment proceedings. In 1988 the House of Representatives, by an overwhelming margin, voted seventeen articles of impeachment, and the Senate ousted Hastings from office in 1989. In a strange twist, Hastings was then elected to Congress.

The situations of these six federal judges are truly exceptional. Prior to the 1980s, only four federal judges had been removed, the most recent in 1936. But these statistics obscure the fact that many misconduct and disability problems of federal judges are resolved informally by the judiciary itself. In turn, these informal methods have been greatly strengthened by the enactment of the federal judicial discipline statute (Fitzpatrick 1988).

CONCLUSION

The controversy surrounding Judge Baer's decision to suppress the eighty pounds of drugs found in the trunk of Carol Bayless's car serves as a case in point of a theme developed in Chapter 1—judges much more so than police officers or prison officials are held responsible for the nation's high crime rate. The different policy perspectives of crime control and due process adherents regarding the proper scope of police conduct become personalized in decisions like this. To some the public criticism was justified and served to change a bad ruling. To others the political maelstrom was just another example of judge-bashing, which undermines judicial independence. The issues are obviously complex. *The New York Times,* sometimes accused of a liberal bias, editorialized that the decision was an instance of judicial malpractice that undermines respect for the legal system. But after the judge reversed himself, the same paper opposed partisan efforts to undermine the judiciary.

These high-profile controversies, however, are far removed from the realities of law in action in the trial courts. The workaday world of the trial judge bears little resemblance to the high expectations we have about the role of the judge. The trial judge is expected to dispose of a large caseload but is often frustrated by the lack of preparation of the attorneys, missing defendants, misplaced files, little time to reflect, and, probably most important, insufficient control over many vital aspects of the case. For these and other reasons, judges depend on other members of the courtroom work group. Some depend heavily on the prosecutors and defense attorneys and probation officers, feeling content to let them make the difficult decisions. Others are much more active participants and are truly leaders of the courtroom work group.

To a large extent the public's impression of justice is shaped by the trial judge's demeanor and the dignity the judge imparts to the proceedings. Given the very high ideals society holds for judges, however, not all measure up. To a certain extent, this is because we expect too much of judges, as if we think merely placing a black robe on a lawyer will eradicate all the shortcomings the person already had. Ultimately, the judges range in quality from some who are highly competent and extremely dedicated, to many who are average, to a few who fall below minimal standards.

CRITICAL THINKING QUESTIONS

1. Which method of judicial selection (election, appointment, or merit selection) do you think is best? What does your choice reveal about your personal attitudes? Stated another way, do you think the legal profession should have more say in judicial selection (merit) or less influence (elections)?

2. For your state, examine judicial selection in terms of both law on the books (formal method of judicial selection) and law in action (actual practices).

3. At what point are efforts to remove "unfit judges" really efforts to remove judges because of decisions they have made?

4. American society has high expectations for judges, yet the actions of judges are constrained by other members of the courtroom

work group. To what extent is criticism of judges, whether local or national, really criticism of the actions and inactions of prosecutors and defense attorneys?

5. Does underrepresentation of women on the bench hurt justice? Would citizens' views of the fairness of courts improve if more nontraditional persons became judges?

 WORLD WIDE WEB RESOURCES AND EXERCISES

Web Guides

http://dir.yahoo.com/Government/Law/U_S__States/
http://dir.yahoo.com/Government/U_S__ Government/Judicial_Branch/

Web Search Terms

"Judges"; "judicial misconduct"

Useful URLs

The American Judicature Society Web site is at http://www.ajs.org.

The National Association of Judicial Educators Web site is at http://www.dcr.net/~aragorn/.

The Brennan Center for Justice offers "Q and A about Judicial Independence": http://www.brennancenter.org/resources/resources_jiqanda.html.

The Institute for Court Management (ICM) can be found at http://www.ncsc.dni.us/ICM/index.html.

The Fund for More Modern Courts is a nonpartisan, nonprofit, statewide court reform organization for New York: http://www.moderncourts.org/.

Visit the National Association of State Judicial Educators at http://nasje.unm.edu/.

Uncommon URLs

Bad Judges and What to Do About Them comes from a disgruntled Arizona lawyer: http://www.primenet.com/~nolawyer/.

Visit The Committee to Expose Dishonest and Incompetent Attorneys and Judges at http://www.amoralethics.com/.

The American Judges Association is at http://aja.ncsc.dni.us/.

The Alliance for Justice's Judicial Selection Project stresses securing access to justice: http://www. afj.org/jsp/home.html.

The Center for Judicial Accountability is a national, nonpartisan organization, documenting how judges break the law and get away with it: http://www.judgewatch.org/.

The Justice Web Collaboratory is a joint project of the Chicago-Kent College of Law and the National Center for State Courts: http://judgelink.org/.

Judicial Watch is an ethical and legal "watchdog" over our government, legal, and judicial systems, with a conservative orientation: http://www.judicialwatch.org/.

Web Exercises

1. How easy is it to find the location of your state's judicial conduct commission? Start by going to http://www.findlaw.com/, and then choose State Law Resources/State Name. The first place to look is under the state supreme court.

    If you are successful in locating any information, ask yourself how helpful this information is. If you were a citizen with a complaint about a judge, how easy or difficult would it be to seek remedial action?

2. Judicial selection is often a hot subject. Search for information by going to Yahoo at http://www.yahoo.com, and then choose Society and Culture/Crime. Search for "*judicial selection.*" What types of groups appear to be involved? What arguments do they use to buttress their position that a change is needed?

3. Humor is a long-time staple of the courthouse. The following site contains some all-time favorites of what can go wrong: http://pubweb.acns.nwu.edu/~bil874/comedy/occup/lalawless.htm. Ask yourself why these situations are so humorous. Is it the lawyer or the judge who isn't thinking? Or are these situations humorous because lay citizens have such limited knowledge of law and court procedures?

INFOTRAC COLLEGE EDITION RESOURCES AND EXERCISES

Basic Searches

Judges, judicial searches; judicial candidates; disqualification of judges; women judges; African American judges

Recommended Articles

Jose Angel Gutierrez, "Experiences of Chicana County Judges in Texas Politics"

Richard H. Middleton, Jr., "Remembering Two Giants of Judicial Independence"

Erwin Chemerinsky, "When Do Lawmakers Threaten Judicial Independence?"

"One Man's Activist: What Republicans Really Mean When They Condemn Judicial Activism"

Glen Krutz, Richard Fleisher, and Jon Bond, "From Abe Fortas to Zoe Baird: Why Some Presidential Nominations Fail in the Senate"

Stephen Williams, "Judges in the Dock"

Ebony, "Judges with Clout"

InfoTrac College Edition Exercises

1. Using the search term *judicial selection* and/or *judges elections,* locate two or more articles on the topic. What advantages and disadvantages are discussed for electing judges? How often do criticisms of current methods of judicial selection stress decisions that the writer thinks are wrong?

2. Using the search term *judicial activism,* select two or more articles that discuss the U.S. Supreme Court. To what extent are discussions of judicial activism understood using the concepts of due process and crime control models of criminal justice?

REFERENCES

Armstrong, Ken, and Rick Pearson. 1997. "Heiple Quits as Top Justice, Stays on Court." *Chicago Tribune,* 3 May.

Aspin, Larry, William Hall, Jean Bax, and Celeste Montoya. 2000. "Thirty Years of Judicial Retention Elections: An Update." *The Social Science Journal* 37:1.

Begue, Yvette, and Candace Goldstein. 1987. "How Judges Get into Trouble." *The Judges Journal* 26: 8.

Blumberg, Abraham. 1967. *Criminal Justice.* Chicago: Quadrangle Books.

Bright, Stephen. 1997. "Political Attacks on the Judiciary." *Judicature* 80: 165–173.

Brooks, Daniel. 1985. "Penalizing Judges Who Appeal Disciplinary Sanctions: The Unconstitutionality of 'Upping the Ante.'" *Judicature* 69: 95–102.

Burbank, Stephen. 1987. "Politics and Progress in Implementing the Federal Judicial Discipline Act." *Judicature* 71: 13–28.

Byrd, Harry. 1976. "Has Life Tenure Outlived Its Time?" *Judicature* 59: 266–277.

Canon, Bradley. 1972. "The Impact of Formal Selection Processes on the Characteristics of Judges–Reconsidered." *Law & Society Review* 6: 579–594.

Carbon, Susan. 1984. "Women in the Judiciary." *Judicature* 65: 285.

Cardozo, Benjamin. 1921. *The Nature of the Judicial Process.* New Haven, CT: Yale University Press.

Carelli, Richard. 1996. "Independent Judiciary Vital, Rehnquist Says." *Times-Picayune,* 27 April.

Carp, Robert, and Russell Wheeler. 1972. "Sink or Swim: The Socialization of a Federal District Judge." *Journal of Public Law* 21: 359–394.

Champagne, Anthony, and Greg Thielemann. 1991. "Awareness of Trial Court Judges." *Judicature* 74: 271–277.

Charles, Alfred. 1996. "Teen Denied Murder Retrial." *Times-Picayune,* 2 July.

Claxton, Charles. 1992. "Characteristics of Effective Judicial Education Programs." *Judicature* 76: 11–14.

Cooper, Christopher. 1993. "Bench Hopefuls: Educate Offenders." *Times-Picayune,* 14 October.

Crowe, Nancy. 1994. "Gender and Asset Settlements in Divorce Proceedings." *Law and Courts Newsletter* (Winter): 7–16.

Dao, James. 1996. "Panel Is to File Charges Against Brooklyn Judge." *The New York Times,* 23 April.

Davis, Sue. 1993. "The Voice of Sandra Day O'Connor." *Judicature* 77: 134–139.

Davis, Sue, Susan Haire, and Donald Songer. 1993. "Voting Behavior and Gender on the U.S. Court of Appeals." *Judicature* 77: 129–133.

Dubois, Philip. 1980. *From Ballot to Bench: Judicial Elections and the Quest for Accountability.* Austin: University of Texas Press.

———. 1984. "Voting Cues in Nonpartisan Trial Court Elections: A Multivariate Assessment." *Law & Society Review* 18: 395–436.

———. 1985. "State Trial Court Appointments: Does the Governor Make a Difference?" *Judicature* 70: 20–28.

Emmert, Craig, and Henry Glick. 1987. "Selection Systems and Judicial Characteristics: The Recruitment of State Supreme Court Judges." *Judicature* 70: 228–235.

———. 1988. "The Selection of State Supreme Court Justices." *American Politics Quarterly* 16: 445–465.

Engstrom, Richard. 1989. "When Blacks Run for Judge: Racial Divisions in the Candidate Preferences of Louisiana Voters." *Judicature* 73: 87–89.

Fitzpatrick, Collins. 1988. "Misconduct and Disability of Federal Judges: The Unreported Informal Responses." *Judicature* 71: 282–283.

Flango, Victor Eugene, and Craig Ducat. 1979. "What Differences Does Method of Judicial Selection Make? Selection Procedures in State Courts of Last Resort." *Justice System Journal* 5: 25–44.

Friedman, Barry. 1998. "Attacks on Judges: Why They Fail." *Judicature* 81: 150–156.

Gardiner, John. 1986. "Preventing Judicial Misconduct: Defining the Role of Conduct Organizations." *Judicature* 70: 113–121.

Glaberson, William. 2000. "Fierce Campaigns Signal a New Era for State Courts." *Times-Picayune,* 5 June.

Goldman, Sheldon. 1995. "Judicial Selection under Clinton: A Midterm Examination." *Judicature* 78: 276–291.

———. 1997. *Picking Federal Judges: Lower Court Selection from Roosevelt through Reagan.* New Haven, CT: Yale University Press.

Goldman, Sheldon, and Matthew Saronson. 1994. "Clinton's Nontraditional Judges: Creating a More Representative Bench." *Judicature* 78: 68–73.

Goldman, Sheldon, and Elliot Slotnick. 1999. "Clinton's Second Term Judiciary: Picking Judges Under Fire." *Judicature* 82: 264–285.

Graham, Barbara Luck. 1990a. "Do Judicial Selection Systems Matter? A Study of Black Representation on State Courts." *American Politics Quarterly* 18: 316–336.

———. 1990b. "Judicial Recruitment and Racial Diversity on State Courts: An Overview." *Judicature* 74: 28–34.

Hall, William, and Larry Aspin. 1992. "Distance from the Bench and Retention Voting Behavior: A Comparison of Trial Court and Appellate Court Retention Elections." *Justice System Journal* 15: 801–813.

Heflin, Howell. 1987. "The Impeachment Process: Modernizing an Archaic System." *Judicature* 71: 123–125.

Hemmens, Craig, Kristin Strom, and Elicia Schlegel. 1997. "Gender Bias in the Courts: A Review of the Literature." Paper presented at the Academy of Criminal Justice Sciences, Louisville, Kentucky.

Henschen, Beth, Robert Moog, and Steven Davis. 1990. "Judicial Nominating Commissioners: A National Profile." *Judicature* 73: 328–334.

Hojnacki, Marie, and Lawrence Baum. 1992. "Choosing Judicial Candidates: How Voters Explain Their Decisions." *Judicature* 75: 300–309.

Jackson, Donald. 1974. *Judges.* New York: Atheneum.

Jacob, Herbert. 1988. *Silent Revolution: The Transformation of Divorce Law in the United States.* Chicago: University of Chicago Press.

Jesdanun, Nick. 1994. "Pennsylvania Judge Impeached." *Times-Picayune,* 25 May.

Kirksey, Jason. 1997. *Sentencing Behavior of Judges Elected from Subdistrict.* Unpublished Ph.D. dissertation, Department of Political Science, University of New Orleans.

Lezon, Dale. 2000. "Magistrate Agrees to Voluntarily Step Down." *Albuquerque Journal,* 12 September.

Louwagie, Pam. 2000. "Judge Ends His Tarnished Career." *Times-Picayune,* 15 September.

Martin, Elaine. 1990. "Men and Women on the Bench: Vive la Différence?" *Judicature* 73: 204–208.

———. 1993. "Women on the Bench: A Different Voice?" *Judicature* 77: 126–128.

———. 1999. "Women Judges: The Next Generation." In *Women in Politics: Outsiders or Insiders? A Collection of Readings,* edited by Lois Duke Whitaker. Upper Saddle River, NJ: Prentice Hall.

Maule, Linda, and Janine Parry. 1997. "Women in Municipal Government." Paper presented at the Southwestern Social Science Association, New Orleans, 27 March.

Mauro, Tony. 1996. "Appeals Judge Steps Down After Dole Attacks." *USA Today,* 5 June.

"Maryland Judge Warned for Scolding Sex Victim." 2000. *Associated Press,* 22 June.

Miller, Benjamin. 1991. "Assessing the Functions of Judicial Conduct Organizations." *Judicature* 75: 16–19.

Nagel, Stuart. 1973. *Comparing Elected and Appointed Judicial Systems.* Beverly Hills, CA: Sage.

National Advisory Commission on Criminal Justice Standards and Goals. 1973. *Courts.* Washington, D.C.: U.S. Government Printing Office.

Neisser, Eric. 1981. "The New Federal Judicial Discipline Act: Some Questions Congress Didn't Answer." *Judicature* 65: 143–160.

Neubauer, David. 1997. *Judicial Process: Law, Courts, and Politics in the United States.* 2d ed. Fort Worth: Harcourt, Brace.

Neumeister, Larry. 1996. "Criticized Judge Reinstates Evidence." *The New York Times,* 2 April.

Ogden, Carla. 1996. "The Impact of Women Justices on the Political and Legal Environment: A Longitudinal Analysis of the Minnesota Supreme Court." Paper presented at the Midwest Political Science Association, Chicago.

Palmer, Barbara. 2001. "Women in the American Judiciary: Their Influence and Impact." *Women and Politics* (forthcoming).

"Panel Suspends Impatient Judge." 1994. *The Times-Picayune,* 10 February, B-3.

Pfeifer, Stuart. 2000. "State Panel Urges Punic Admonishment for Judge." *Los Angeles Times,* 27 June.

Pinello, Daniel. 1995. *The Impact of Judicial-Selection Method of State-Supreme-Court Policy: Innovation, Reaction and Atrophy.* Westport, CT: Greenwood Press.

President's Commission on Law Enforcement and Administration of Justice. 1967. *Task Force Report: The Courts.* Washington, D.C.: U.S. Government Printing Office.

Purdy, Matthew, and Don Van Natta. 1996. "Before the Murder, A Judicial Skirmish." *The New York Times,* 14 March.

Reid, Traciel. 1999. "The Politicization of Retention Elections: Lessons from the Defeat of Justices Lanphier and White." *Judicature* 83: 68–77.

Robinson, Mike. 1996. "Abrasive, Erratic Judge Sidelined." *Times-Picayune,* 12 October.

Rosen, Ellen. 1987. "The Nation's Judges: No Unanimous Opinion." *Court Review* 24: 5.

Ryan, John Paul, Allan Ashman, Bruce Sales, and Sandra Shane-Dubow. 1980. *American Trial Judges.* New York: Free Press.

Scruggs, Anna, Jean-Claude Mazzola, and Mary Zaug. 1995. "Recent Voting Rights Act Challenges to Judicial Elections." *Judicature* 79: 34–41.

Segal, Jennifer. 2000. "Judicial Decision Making and the Impact of Election Year Rhetoric." *Judicature* 84: 26–33.

Simon, Paul. 1993. "The Exercise of Advice and Consent." *Judicature* 76: 189–191.

Slotnick, Elliot. 1983. "The ABA Standing Committee on Federal Judiciary: A Contemporary Assessment." *Judicature* 66: 385–393.

———. 1988. "Federal Judicial Recruitment and Selection Research: A Review Essay." *Judicature* 71: 317–324.

Smith, Nancy, and Julie Garmel. 1992. "Judicial Election and Selection Procedures Challenged under the Voting Rights Act." *Judicature* 76: 154–155.

Smothers, Ronald. 1996. "Arkansas Plan to Promote Election of Black Judges Brings a Familiar Challenge." *The New York Times,* 8 April.

Songer, Donald, Sue Davis, and Susan Haire. 1994. "A Reappraisal of Diversification in the Federal Courts: Gender Effects in the Courts of Appeals." *Journal of Politics* 56: 276–291.

Stein, Mary Lou. 1986. "Judicial Education: How Does Your State Measure Up?" *The Judges Journal* 25: 28.

Steffensmeier, Darrell, and Chris Hebert. 1999. "Women and Men Policymakers: Does the Judge's Gender Affect the Sentencing of Criminal Defendants?" *Social Forces* 77: 1163.

Stone, Peter. 2000. "Jousting Over Judges." *The National Journal,* 24 June.

Stidham, Ronald, and Robert Carp. 1997. "Judges' Gender and Federal District Court Decisions." Paper presented at the Southwestern Political Science Association, New Orleans.

Tackett, Michael. 1996. "Dole Fires a Salvo at Clinton, Judges." *Chicago Tribune,* 20 April.

"This Week in Review." 2000. *St. Petersburg Times,* 3 September.

Watson, Richard, and Ronald Downing. 1969. *The Politics of the Bench and Bar: Judicial Selection under the Missouri Nonpartisan Court Plan.* New York: John Wiley.

Weitzman, Lenore. 1985. *The Divorce Revolution: The Unexpected Social and Economic Consequences for Women and Children in America.* New York: Free Press.

Wice, Paul. 1991. *Judges and Lawyers: The Human Side of Justice.* New York: HarperCollins.

Wold, John, and John Culver. 1987. "The Defeat of the California Justices: The Campaign, the Electorate, and the Issue of Judicial Accountability." *Judicature* 70: 348–355.

FOR FURTHER READING

Allison, Garland. "Delay in Senate Confirmation of Federal Judicial Nominees." *Judicature* 80 (1996): 8–15.

Barrow, Deborah, Gary Zuk, and Gerard Gryski. *The Federal Judiciary and Institutional Change.* Ann Arbor: University of Michigan Press, 1996.

Bright, Stephen. "The Past and Present of Judicial Independence." *Judicature* 80 (1996): 117–122.

Bushnell, Eleanore. *Crimes, Follies, and Misfortunes: The Federal Impeachment Trials.* Champaign: University of Illinois Press, 1992.

Champagne, Anthony, and Judith Haydel, eds. *Judicial Reform in the States.* Lanham, MD: University Press of America, 1993.

Drachman, Virginia. *Sisters in Law: Women Lawyers in Modern American History.* Cambridge, MA: Harvard University Press, 1998.

Epstein, Cynthia. *Women in Law.* 2d ed. Urbana: University of Illinois Press, 1993.

Gerhardt, Michael. *The Federal Impeachment Process: A Constitutional and Historical Analysis.* Princeton, NJ: Princeton University Press, 1996.

Gryski, Gerard, Gary Zuk, and Deborah Barrow. "A Bench That Looks Like America? Representation of African-Americans and Latinos on the Federal Courts." *Journal of Politics* 56 (1994): 1076–1086.

Hall, William, and Larry Aspin. 1987. "What Twenty Years of Judicial Retention Elections Have Told Us." *Judicature* 70: 340–347.

Lovrich, Nicholas, and Charles Sheldon. "Is Voting for State Judges a Flight of Fancy or a Reflection of Policy and Value Preferences?" *Justice System Journal* 16 (1994): 57–71.

Lyles, Kevin. *The Gatekeepers: Federal District Courts in the Political Process.* Westport, CT: Praeger, 1997.

Palmer, Vernon P. *Mixed Jurisdictions Worldwide: The 3rd Legal Family.* Cambridge, MA: Cambridge University Press, 2001.

Satter, Robert. *Doing Justice: A Trial Judge at Work.* New York: Simon and Schuster, 1990.

Sheldon, Charles, and Linda Maule. *Choosing Justice: The Recruitment of State and Federal Judges.* Pullman: Washington State University Press, 1997.

Spohn, Cassia. "The Sentencing Decisions of Black and White Judges: Expected and Unexpected Similarities." *Law and Society Review* 24 (1990): 1197–1216.

Stidham, Ronald, Robert Carp, and Donald Songer. "The Voting Behavior of President Clinton's Judicial Appointees." *Judicature* 80 (1996) 16–28.

Van Tassel, Emily Field, and Paul Finkelman (eds.). *Impeachable Offenses: A Documentary History from 1878 to the Present.* Washington: Congressional Quarterly, Inc., 1999.

Volcansek, Mary. *Judicial Impeachment: None Called for Justice.* Urbana: University of Illinois Press, 1993.

Washington, Linn. *Black Judges on Justice: Perspectives from the Bench.* New York: The New Press, 1994.

Defendants and Victims

THE FIRST OFFICER ON THE SCENE DESCRIBED PERVIS TYRONE PAYNE as looking like "he was sweating blood." The officer's partner followed the trail of blood into the kitchen where he found Charissee Christopher and her two-year-old daughter Lacie butchered to death. After returning a verdict of guilty of two counts of first-degree murder, the trial proceeded to the penalty phase of a capital murder prosecution. The defense called four witnesses who testified that Payne was a very caring person but had such a low score on an IQ test that he was mentally handicapped. The prosecutor countered by calling the victim's grandmother to the stand, who testified that three-year-old Nicholas (the lone survivor) kept asking why his mother didn't come home, and he cried for his sister. During closing argument the prosecutor made maximum use of this emotional testimony, imploring the jury to make sure that Nicholas would know later in life that justice had been done in his mother's brutal slaying. The Memphis, Tennessee, jury imposed the death penalty.

The difficulty with the grandmother's testimony is that, just a couple of years before, the Supreme Court had ruled that such emotional statements are inadmissible because they tend to mislead jurors. But in the interim, the membership of the Court had changed, with the addition of two conservatives appointed by Republican presidents. By agreeing to hear the case, the Court was signaling that it might be willing to reverse itself and allow victim impact statements during sentencing.

Payne v. Tennessee directs our attention to both defendants and their victims. All too often, when we think about the criminal courts, our minds immediately focus on the members of the courtroom work group: prosecutors, defense attorneys, and judges. We are less likely to think about the other participants: victims, witnesses, or even defendants. Yet these other actors are also important.

Victims greatly influence workload. Courts are passive institutions. They do not seek out cases to decide; rather, they are dependent on others to bring matters to their attention. How many cases are filed, as well as what kinds of cases are brought to court, is determined by the decisions of others—police, victims, and those who violate the law in the first place. Thus, the courtroom work group has very little control over its workload. Second, victims, witnesses, and defendants are the consumers of the court process. Democratic governments are expected to be responsive to the wishes and demands of their citizens; victims and witnesses often complain about how the courts handle their cases. Victims and defendants are both subjects and objects of the criminal justice process. Their importance for how the courtroom work group administers justice on a day-to-day basis is the subject of this chapter. ■

DEFENDANTS

In some ways those accused of violating the criminal law are a diverse lot. Although many defendants are economically impoverished, their numbers also include high-ranking government officials, businesspeople, and prominent local citizens. An indicator of the diversity of defendants centers on how often they are involved with the criminal justice system. At one end of the spectrum are those who are arrested once and are never involved again. At the other end are a small group of career criminals who are responsible for a disproportionate share of offenses (Chaiken and Chaiken 1991; Moore, et al. 1984). To complicate matters further, there are indications of a generational effect. People locked behind bars or on probation are twice as likely to have been victims of childhood abuse as the general population (Harlow 1999). Violent offenders are much more likely to have experienced abuse and violence in their families (Bureau of Justice Statistics 1988).

Moreover, conviction of a parent is correlated with the likelihood of a child being convicted (Rowe and Farrington 1997). Whether it is possible to predict who will become a career criminal, however, is subject to extensive debate.

Characteristics of Defendants

Aside from certain aspects of diversity, the majority of violators conform to a definite profile. Compared to the average citizen, felony defendants are significantly younger, overwhelmingly male, disproportionately members of racial minorities, more likely to come from broken homes, less educated, more likely to be unemployed, and less likely to be married. By the time the court sorting process has ended, those sentenced to prison consist of an even higher proportion of poor, young, illiterate, minority males (Table 9-1).

Three characteristics of defendants—gender, poverty, and race—figure prominently in discussions

TABLE 9-1 Profile of State Prison Inmates

Male	95%
White	35%
35 or younger	68%
Married	18%
Never married	55%
Raised primarily in single-parent home	43%
Prior incarceration of immediate family member	36%
High school dropout	65%
Prior adult incarceration	55%
Prior conviction	81%
Unemployed before arrest	33 %
Offense committed under the influence of drugs	31%
Offense committed under the influence of alcohol	32%
Violent offense conviction	47%
Property offense conviction	25%

Source: U.S. Department of Justice, Bureau of Justice Statistics, *Survey of State Prison Inmates, 1991* (Washington, D.C.: USGPO, 1993); James Lynch, Steven Smith, Helen Graziadei, and Tanutda Pittayathikhun, *Profile of Inmates in the United States and in England and Wales, 1991* (Washington, D.C.: Bureau of Justice Statistics, U.S. Department of Justice, 1994).

of crime and crime policy and therefore deserve expanded treatment.

For the most up-to-date statistics on defendants, go to **http://www.ojp.usdoj.gov/bjs/** and click on criminal offenders.

For an up-to-date list of Web links, go to **http://www.wadsworth.com/product/0534563406s**.

Overwhelmingly Male

Defendants are overwhelmingly male. A look at Table 9-1 shows that 95 percent of prisoners are male. The male domination of crime is the subject of a book with the provocative title *Just Boys Doing Business: Men, Masculinities and Crime* (Newburn

and Stanko 1994). To be sure, rates of female involvement in the justice system have been increasing in recent years, but in terms of absolute number still fall well below those of males. Not only are women less likely to be arrested, but when prosecuted they are charged with less serious offenses. Women in prison for crimes such as robbery, burglary, and drug dealing were more likely to have had a male accomplice who played a primary role (Alarid et al. 1996).

Mostly Underclass

Typical felony defendants possess few of the skills needed to compete successfully in an increasingly technological society. They are drawn from what sociologists call the urban underclass (Jencks and Peterson 1991). The association of crime with poverty explains why the overwhelming number of crimes are committed for economic motives—burglary, theft, and drug sale primarily. Although crimes of violence dominate the headlines, most defendants are not dangerous; they are charged with property or drug offenses.

Racial Minorities Overrepresented

Race remains a divisive issue in American politics, and nowhere is this more evident than in the area of crime. African Americans, Hispanics, and Native Americans are imprisoned at a significantly higher rate than whites. At the same time, it is important to stress that historically whites constituted the majority of those in prison, a fact conveniently ignored on some radio and TV discussions.

Why minorities are overrepresented in the criminal justice system is a topic of considerable importance (and therefore addressed in several later chapters). To some it is an indication that minorities are more likely to be poor and therefore more likely to commit crimes for economic advancement. Others counter that discrimination is the reason; minorities are more likely to be targeted by criminal justice officials and also more likely to receive a harsh sentence. Whatever the cause, the impact is enormous. One in three young black males is in trouble with the law, either in prison, on probation, or parole (Cass 1995).

Nicole Walker, "Why Women Are Committing More Crimes"

Defendants in Court

The **defendant** is supposed to stand at the center of the criminal court drama. Yet the typical felony defendant is largely powerless to control his fate—more an object to be acted upon than the key to what happens. Because most defendants are poor and uneducated, they are ill equipped to deal with the technical abstractions of the criminal court process. Many are incapable of understanding even the simplest instructions about the right to bail or the presumption of innocence. Many are too inarticulate to aid their attorneys in preparing a defense. Many hold unfavorable attitudes toward the law and the criminal justice system and thus regard the judge and all other court personnel, including their defense attorneys, with hostility and distrust. As a result, the huge majority of defendants

> *submit to the painful consequences of conviction but do not know for certain whether they committed any of the crimes of which they are accused. Such defendants are so unschooled in law that they form no firm opinion about their technical innocence or guilt. Neither do they actually agree or disagree that it is just to punish them. (Rosett and Cressey 1976, 146)*

The nature of the clientele makes criminal courts a depressing place to work. Judges, prosecutors, and defense attorneys seldom come away from their day's activities with a sense of accomplishment, for many of the criminal cases involve such social problems as drug addiction, marital problems, lack of education, and mental illness, over which the court personnel have no control. Many cases stem from disputes between people who know one another. An in-depth study of felony case dispositions in New York City summed it up this way:

> *The incidents that give rise to arrest are frequently not the kind that the court system is able to deal with satisfactorily. At the root of much of the crime brought to court is anger—simple or complicated anger between two or more people who know each other. Expressions of anger result in the commission of technical felonies, yet defense attorneys, judges, and prosecutors recognize that*

> *in many cases conviction and prison sentences are inappropriate responses. High rates of dismissal or charge reduction appear to be a reflection of the system's effort to carry out the intent of the law—as judges and other participants perceive it—though not necessarily the letter of the law. (Vera Institute of Justice 1981, xv)*

Court personnel have little empathy with or understanding of the types of defendants whose fates they must decide. Members of the courtroom work group are essentially middle class. Little in their backgrounds or training has equipped them to deal with violations of the law committed by the poor.

 Joy Parker-Jiminez, "An Offender's Experience with the Criminal Justice System"

COURTS THROUGH THE EYES OF VICTIMS AND WITNESSES

Traditionally, victims and witnesses have been the forgotten participants in the criminal justice system. Fictional and nonfictional treatments of the court process direct attention to the criminal as victim rather than to the victim as victim (Elias 1986). Thus, although the literature on offenders is enormous, less is known about victims. In the view of many, the courts, along with the rest of the criminal justice community, have ignored the interests of victims and witnesses.

Frustrations in Coping with the Process

Crime victims once played a prominent role in the criminal process. Before the American Revolution, victims were the central figures in the criminal justice drama. Criminals' fates were closely tied to their victims' wishes. When crime became viewed as an offense against the state, the victim was assigned a subordinate role (Elias 1986). As prosecutorial dominance increased, the power of the victim declined (Chapter 6). Victims lost control over their cases, and their role was reduced to initiating investigations by complaining to the police and testifying for the prosecution as just another piece of evidence in

Defendant: The person or party against whom a lawsuit or prosecution is brought.

the state's presentation of damning facts against the accused (Karmen 2001).

Several studies have documented the hardships victims and witnesses face while participating in the criminal court process (McDonald 1976; Cannavale and Falcon 1976; Connick and Davis 1983). Although some are minor inconveniences, such as getting to the courthouse and finding a parking place, other hardships are more significant:

- Trial delays, which result in frequent travel and wasted time.
- Long waits in uncomfortable surroundings.
- Inadequate notification of court dates.
- General lack of knowledge about the criminal justice system and courtroom procedure.
- Wages lost for time spent going to court.
- Property that may be kept as evidence for a long time or never returned.
- Fear of the defendant or retaliation from the defendant's associates.
- A sense that criminal justice personnel are indifferent to their plight.

A Day in Court: Trial by Ordeal for Waiting Witnesses focuses on some of the frustrations of witnesses in Philadelphia.

Travails of Testifying

Victims and witnesses also face major problems while testifying in court. Because few people are accustomed to testifying, lawyers must coach their witnesses ahead of time to answer only the question asked, to speak forcefully (but not belligerently), and not to become rattled by cross-examination. Even after such preparation, many witnesses are uncomfortable during cross-examination, as the defense attorney tests their memory, challenges their veracity, or even suggests that they were somehow responsible for their own victimization. After enduring cross-examination, some victims report feeling as though they, and not the offender, have been portrayed as the criminal to the jury.

Most of what we know about the ordeal of testifying in court comes from studies of rape victims (Resick 1984). The dominant conclusion is that the victim, rather than the defendant, is put on trial. Testifying in court provokes anxiety for several months, exacerbating psychological distress (Steketee and Austin 1989). Holmstrom and Burgess (1983), both of whom counsel rape victims in Boston City Hospital, followed the cases of fourteen women who testified in court during a rape trial. They concluded that the trauma is often significant, because the victim must publicly repeat in detail how the rape occurred. The type of defense employed by the defense attorney also has an impact on the victim's adjustment to the crime. A defense claim that the woman consented to sex is injurious, because it puts the victim on trial and calls into question her discouragement of the perpetrator of the crime (Steketee and Austin 1989). Moreover, the defense often seeks to blame the victim by suggesting that she consented, did not resist, was provocatively dressed, and so on. It can take little to discredit the victim. Following the Holmstrom and Burgess study, most states have passed legislation limiting inquiry into a rape victim's past sexual conduct.

 To view the court process from the perspective of a victims' advocate, go to Kathy Copley's Web site at **http://cuppp.campbellsvil.edu/~victadv/**.

For an up-to-date list of Web links, go to **http://www.wadsworth.com/product/0534563406s**.

Surprising Support for the System

Somewhat surprisingly, despite the problems and frustrations experienced, victims and witnesses still express overall support for the court process (Hagan 1983). In Milwaukee, those surveyed indicated that they were satisfied or very satisfied with the handling of their case by the police (81 percent), district attorney (75 percent), and judge (66 percent). Less than 15 percent said that they were dissatisfied (Knudten et al. 1976). Favorable judgments were independent of whether a victim was satisfied with the eventual outcome of the case.

VICTIMS AND WITNESSES THROUGH THE EYES OF THE COURT

The criminal courts confront a double bind with regard to victims. On the one hand, victims are valued for the cases they bring to the system; their mis-

A DAY IN COURT

Trial by Ordeal for Waiting Witnesses

 Summoned by a silent alarm tripped by burglars at his church—again—the good reverend was on a holy mission as he sped to the scene from his home. He caught the two men, who turned out to be brothers, in the kitchen of the Old Zion Lutheran Church, Broad Street near Mount Vernon in North Philadelphia. There the two suspects met the wrath of the Rev. Carl Heinrich Schmutzler, who held them for police. . . .

The arrests were in October 1989. And as one of the accused in this case repeatedly fails to show up in court, Schmutzler doggedly clings to his sense of civic responsibility. "[Witnesses] are called, and we are supposed to be here. I've lost as much as 4½ hours in one day," Schmutzler said yesterday outside a Common Pleas courtroom. "It's an enormous waste of time. I understand people who don't want to cooperate with police because frankly, it's a hassle. . . . The system is inefficient."

Witnesses in other cases throughout City Hall criminal courtrooms echoed Schmutzler's frustration with a legal system that seems hell-bent on testing their endurance. Yesterday was Beverly Wilson's third time in court as a witness to the theft of her $9,600 1986 Buick Century. Last June she showed up, but the defendant didn't. She wasn't excused until 2 P.M., she said. "I sat there a long time like I am now," said Wil-

son, who occasionally dozed off while waiting to be called. The accused car thief, Kenneth Diprinzio, was nonchalant when asked about his non-appearance at the June hearing. "I didn't feel like it," he said. "I knew what would happen." Diprinzio, 36, pleaded guilty yesterday to stealing Wilson's car and driving under the influence of alcohol. For her perseverance, Wilson heard the court order Diprinzio to pay her restitution. She wasn't impressed. "Depending on him is like depending on a child," she said.

Meanwhile, Schmutzler . . . found that he too would have to wait for justice. One of the burglary defendants, Sherman Pointer, 24, who signed his own bail note in November, then failed to show up for his arraignment last year, left the court flat again yesterday. Common Pleas Judge Mary D. Collins issued a second warrant for Pointer, who is free on $25,000 bail. Schmutzler, who said he arrived at City Hall as told at 8 A.M., only found out that he wouldn't be needed to testify when he approached an assistant district attorney around 10:30 A.M. "As a witness you get no information whatsoever. You are told where to come and when, and you just sit there and wait. You're lucky if something happens," the minister said.

SOURCE: J. Sills, "For Waiting Witnesses, It's Trial by Ordeal," *Philadelphia Daily News*, March 13, 1990, p. 15. Reprinted by permission.

---

fortunes become the raw material of the court process (Figure 9-1). On the other hand, individual victims represent a potential source of irrationality in the process. The personal and often emotional involvement of victims in the crime experience can generate particularized demands for case outcomes that have little to do with the public interest. Thus, at times members of the courtroom work group perceive that the victim's demands for public justice actually mask a desire for private vengeance (Hagan 1983).

Lack of Cooperation

Many victims and witnesses are reluctant to become involved in the criminal justice process. Over half of all major crimes are never reported to the police; even when they are, not all victims wish to prosecute. They may fear reprisal by the suspect, or they

may prefer not to go through the ordeal of the court process. Some specific witness-related problems include giving the police incorrect addresses, refusing to sign a complaint, failing to show up in court, and offering testimony that is confused, garbled, or contradicted by other facts. Witness-related problems result in a significant number of cases in which the prosecutor refuses to file charges or the case is later dismissed. In Indianapolis, for example, 40 percent of cases dropped from the process before trial were attributed to witness problems. Cities with comparable figures are Golden, Colorado (20 percent), New Orleans (40 percent), and Los Angeles (70 percent) (Boland et al. 1982).

Not all uncooperative behavior can be blamed on victims and witnesses, however; the court process can be equally at fault. In Washington, D.C., a study focusing on what it called "noncooperative" witnesses reported that 41 percent were never told

FIGURE 9-1	Major Activities of Victims in Steps of the Court Process	
	Law on the Books	*Law in Action*
Crime	No general requirement to report crimes to the police.	Thirty-eight percent of personal and household crimes are reported to the police.
Arrest	A citizen's arrest is the taking of a person into physical custody, by a person other than a law enforcement officer, for the purpose of delivering the person to the custody of a law enforcement officer.	• The vast majority of arrests are made by law enforcement officers. • Citizen arrests may result in injury to the victim and may also result in civil lawsuits.
Initial appearance	Open to the public.	Very unlikely for victim to be present because unlikely to know timing of the event.
Bail	VRA provides victims have a right to be heard if present and to submit a statement "to determine a release from custody."	Victims are very rarely present.
Charging	Victim has no role and the VRA states that "nothing in this article shall provide grounds for the victim to challenge the charging decision."	Reluctance or refusal of victims to cooperate is a key reason for case dismissal.
Preliminary hearing	Besides the right to notice and be present, the VRA is silent on the role of victims during this stage.	Victims rarely testify because hearsay evidence is admissible.
Grand jury	Grand jury can subpoena victim to testify.	In grand jury states, victim likely to be subpoenaed to testify.
Arraignment	VRA provides that victims of crimes have the right to notice of proceedings like this.	Victims are rarely present.
Evidence	In some jurisdictions defense is entitled to see a copy of victim's statement to the police.	Even if not required, some DAs disclose victim's statement in hopes of inducing a guilty plea.
Plea bargaining	VRA: victim may be heard and submit a statement during an acceptance of a negotiated plea.	Some jurisdictions allow victims to be heard as to the plea bargain but few actually appear.
Trial	If they are to testify, victims generally cannot view the trial (wording in the VRA concerning public proceedings might change this law).	Victim's testimony is a key part of the trial.
Sentencing	VRA: victims may be heard and submit a statement during sentencing.	Victims are unlikely to appear.
Appeal	Like other court proceedings, appellate argument is open to the public.	Victims are very unlikely to be present.

VRA = Proposed Victims' Rights Amendment to the U.S. Constitution.

that they should contact the prosecutor, 62 percent were never notified of court appearances, and 43 percent stated that the police, prosecutor, and judge all failed to explain the witnesses' rights and duties. Apart from this failure to communicate, the report also concluded that prosecutors misinterpreted the witnesses' intentions and therefore regarded them as uncooperative, when such a conclusion was premature at best and incorrect at worst. Other reports have found that the longer the case is delayed, the

A Victim's Guide to the D.C. Criminal Justice System can be found at **http://www.ojp.usdoj.gov/BJA/ html/victsguide.htm**.

For an up-to-date list of Web links, go to **http:// www.wadsworth.com/product/0534563406s**.

more likely it is that witnesses will not appear when summoned (Cannavale and Falcon 1976).

Characteristics of Victims

How a case is handled is determined by the identity of the victim as well as that of the offender (Hagan 1983). Prosecutors allocate their limited resources to the cases they believe constitute the most "trouble." Not surprisingly, such judgments correlate with the desire for high conviction rates. Prosecutors assume that judges and juries will find the claims of certain kinds of victims credible and acceptable, but not the claims of others (Stanko 1981-1982). The troubles of older, white, male, employed victims are considered more worthy of public processing (Myers and Hagan 1979), whereas victims of violent crime tend to be young, nonwhite males, divorced or never married, low income, and unemployed (Bureau of Justice Statistics 1988; Elias 1986). For example, legal outcomes in murder cases were related to the race, gender, and conduct of victims at the time of the incident (Baumer, Messner, and Felson 2000).

Prior Relationships between Defendants and Victims

Perhaps the most important victim characteristic that influences case processing centers on the prior relationship between defendants and victims. The following case is illustrative.

> An auxiliary police officer watched a woman approach a man as he emerged from a liquor store. It was dark. The officer thought he saw a knife flash in her hand, and the man seemed to hand her some money. She fled, and the officer went to the aid of the victim, taking him to the hospital for treatment.
>
> The officer saw the woman on the street a few days later and arrested her for first degree robbery on the victim's sworn complaint. It was presumably a "high quality" arrest—identification of the

perpetrator by an eyewitness, not from mugshots or a lineup, but in a crowd. Yet, shortly thereafter, this apparently airtight case was dismissed on the prosecutor's motion.

> What the victim had not explained to the police was that the defendant, an alcoholic, had been his girlfriend for the past five years; that they had been drinking together the night of the incident; that she had taken some money from him and got angry when he took it back; that she had flown into a fury when he then gave her only a dollar outside the liquor store; and that she had slashed at him with a pen knife in anger and run off. He had been sufficiently annoyed to have her charged with robbery, but, as the judge who dismissed the case said, "He wasn't really injured. Before it got into court they had kissed and made up." In fact, the victim actually approached the defense attorney before the hearing and asked him to prevail upon the judge and the Assistant District Attorney (ADA) to dismiss the charges against his girlfriend. (Vera Institute of Justice 1981, xxii)

This case is one of many cited by the Vera Institute that show the importance of the prior relationship between defendants and victims.

Prior relationships between defendants and victims are more common than generally assumed. In half of all felony arrests in New York, the victim had a prior relationship with the defendant. Prior relationships were frequent in cases of homicide and assault, in which they were expected, but they were also frequent in cases of robbery, in which they were not. Other studies reach a similar conclusion. Nationwide, roughly half of all violent crimes (rape, assault, and robbery) are committed by relatives, friends, or acquaintances of the victim (Bureau of Justice Statistics 1987). Homicides, in particular, are usually committed not by strangers but by someone the victim knows by sight (Hewitt 1988). Criminal court officials often regard crimes involving people who know one another as not very serious, viewing them as private disputes rather than offenses against the entire community.

Domestic Violence

The prior relationship between victims and defendants is most apparent in crimes against women. Men are more likely to experience violent victimization compared to women. But the nature of these events differs greatly. Women are about six times more likely than men to experience violence committed by an intimate (Bachman and Saltzman 1995). The most recent statistics indicate about 1,000,000 incidents of intimate violence occur each year. In 85 percent of these incidents women are the victims (Bureau of Justice Statistics 2000).

The prior relationship between victim and offender causes particular problems for law enforcement officials in the area of domestic violence (Buzawa and Buzawa 1996). Many women call the police in order to stop the violence but later have a change of heart and refuse to sign a complaint. Historically, police officers made an arrest only as a last resort—taking the suspect into custody seemed to be the only way to ensure no more violence that night. Over the last thirty years, however, advocacy groups for battered women and victims' advocacy groups have worked vigorously for policy changes designed to make the criminal justice system treat domestic violence as a serious offense. Jeffrey Fagan (1996) has given this movement a name in his aptly titled book, *The Criminalization of Domestic Violence*.

The question of what constitutes the most effective criminal justice response, however, has stirred considerable controversy. The police have been urged to make more arrests and prosecutors file charges no matter the wishes of the victim. Whether these mandatory arrest policies are effective has been questioned, however (Hirschel et al. 1992). Researchers report that arrest reduces domestic violence in some cities but increases it in others (Schmidt and Sherman 1993). Although there is considerable debate over whether mandatory arrest policies actually work, there is little doubt that courts are now handling a higher number of these cases; 91 percent of prosecutors nationwide cite domestic violence crimes as a workload problem (McEwen 1995).

Legal sanctions against domestic violence are not limited to the criminal law. Victims of domestic violence may request a **civil protection order**. Recent legislative changes in most jurisdictions now make these court orders easier to obtain. They are no longer limited to women who have filed for divorce and may be issued on an emergency basis without the other party being present. However, civil protec-

---

 To get a better sense of how courts handle domestic violence cases, go to any of the following court Web sites:

> Delaware County (Ohio): **http://www.municipalcourt.org/dv.asp**
>
> Family Law Court in San Diego County (California): **http://www.sandiego.courts.ca.gov/superior/courts/domestic.html**
>
> Palm Beach County (Florida): **http://www.pbcountyclerk.com/**
>
> The Municipal Court of Seattle (Washington): **http://www.cityofseattle.net/courts/prob/dvprob.htm**

For an up-to-date list of Web links, go to **http://www.wadsworth.com/product/0534563406s**.

---

tion orders are not self-enforcing. There is even a danger that a civil protection order may induce a false sense of security among some women who are at risk of continued battery from a former intimate.

AIDING VICTIMS AND WITNESSES

For decades, reformers have urged that victims and witnesses be accorded better treatment.

- In 1931 the National Commission on Law Observance and Enforcement concluded that effective administration of public justice required willing witnesses, but testifying in court imposed unreasonable burdens on citizens.

- A 1938 American Bar Association report found that witness fees were deplorably low, courthouse accommodations uncomfortable, and witnesses were frequently summoned to court numerous times only to have the case continued.

But it was not until the 1960s that attention was seriously devoted to the problems faced by victims and witnesses in the court and ways to improve the situation (Karmen 2001).

- In 1967 the President's Commission on Law Enforcement and Administration of Justice highlighted a "growing concern that the average citizen identifies himself less and less with the criminal process and its officials."

Civil protection order: Court order requiring a person to stay away from another person.

THE MURDER TRIAL OF SHAREEF COUSIN

The Anguish of the Victims

For the last several decades, the politics of victims, and not the rights of defendants, have dominated criminal justice policy making. The anguish of the victims in the Port of Call murder case, and their alternating emotions, provide a poignant close-up.

"My life is like a black void, a hole. I can't sleep at night and I watch television until the wee hours of the morning," testified Sal Gerardi, the victim's father. His body heaving with sobs, he described roaring across Interstate 10 toward New Orleans after hearing that his son had been shot (Varney, 1996b). One can only speculate that this victim statement during the penalty phase of the Shareef Cousin murder trial had a powerful impact on the jurors. It was all the more powerful because none of Cousin's relatives would take the witness stand to offer a counter emotion to taking Cousin's life.

When the guilty verdict was announced, Sal Gerardi dropped to one knee and crossed himself. Afterwards he commented, "There still really isn't any satisfaction," and then added, "I feel sorry for their family because they've lost a son now, too" (Varney, 1996a).

The emotions of the victims were radically different two years later when DA Harry Connick announced that he would not retry Cousin. Connie Babin, now married, said the dismissal stung: "I am frustrated, I am devastated, I am angry. I am sad. I am frightened. I am all of those things." She recounted the travails of having testified. Over the past four years, vandals had struck her home, callers had harassed her on the phone, and someone had hanged her in effigy in her front yard. On the witness stand defense attorneys attacked her credibility; outside the courtroom she was branded a racist.

But overall Babin blamed herself. "I was in such a state that night. I was on a mental shutdown, and I wasn't able to express myself." She went on to say, "I am sorry. I messed up, the DA messed up, but I didn't mess up that badly." She remained adamant that Cousin was the murderer (Coyle, 1999).

 To read more about the Shareef Cousin trial, type in the search words *dead teen walking* and read the section, "From Father to Son."

In recent years, concern for victims and witnesses of crime has risen to a crescendo. Crime victims have been the subject of considerable research and have also received special attention from the White House.

- In 1982, the President's Task Force on Victims of Crime stressed the need for achieving a balance between the needs and rights of the victim and those of the defendant.

Public and governmental concern over the plight of victims has prompted numerous pieces of legislation (Figure 9-2). The first federal law was passed in 1982; the Victim and Witness Protection Act required greater protection of victims and witnesses in federal cases from intimidation by defendants or their associates. The act also mandated guidelines for fair treatment of victims and witnesses in federal criminal cases. The Victims of Crime Act of 1984 authorized federal funds for state victim programs. Spurred by these concerns, every state has passed comprehensive legislation protecting the interests of victims. In short, a wide variety

of programs have been adopted in recent years to improve the treatment crime victims receive from the criminal justice system (Young 1990). The three most common types of initiatives are (1) victim/witness assistance programs, (2) victim compensation programs, and (3) victim's bill of rights.

 The focal point of the federal government's response to victims of crime is the Office for Victims of Crime in the U.S. Department of Justice. Its Web site stresses resources for helping crime victims: **http://www.ojp.usdoj.gov/ovc/**.

For an up-to-date list of Web links, go to **http://www.wadsworth.com/product/0534563406s**.

Victim/Witness Assistance Programs

Victim/witness assistance programs encourage cooperation in the conviction of criminals by reducing the inconvenience citizens face when appearing in court (Finn 1986). Typical activities

| FIGURE 9-2 | Key Developments in Law Relating to Victims |

National Crime Victims' Week	1980	Annual event focusing on the plight of crime victims.
Victim and Witness Protection Act	1982	Enhance and protect the necessary role of crime victims and witnesses in the criminal justice process.
Victims' Rights Amendments	1982	California is first state to adopt.
Victim of Crimes Act	1984	Established Crime Victim Fund from fines, penalties, and bond forfeitures of convicted federal criminals.
Booth v. Maryland	1987	In capital cases, victim impact statements are unconstitutional because they introduce the risk of imposing the death penalty in an arbitrary and capricious manner.
South Carolina v. Gathers	1989	Characteristics of the victim are irrelevant during death penalty deliberations.
Payne v. Tennessee	1991	The Eighth Amendment creates no bar to the introduction of victim impact statements during sentencing.
Simon & Schuster v. New York State Crime Victims Board	1991	Declared unconstitutional New York's "Son of Sam" law, which sought to prevent criminals from profiting from their crimes.
Violence Against Women Act	1994	Comprehensive law creating a variety of programs to strengthen law enforcement, prosecution, and victim services in cases involving crimes against women.
The Antiterrorism and Effective Death Penalty Act	1996	A federal court must impose mandatory restitution, without consideration of the defendant's ability to pay.
Victims' Rights Amendment	1996	VRA proposed in the U.S. Congress.
	2000	VRA withdrawn in face of virtual defeat.

include providing comfortable and secure waiting areas, assisting with the prompt return of stolen property that has been recovered, and providing crisis intervention. These programs also provide victims and witnesses with a clearer understanding of the court process by distributing brochures, explaining court procedures, and notifying witnesses of upcoming court dates (Webster 1988). Of particular concern is victim and witness intimidation. Intimidation can be either case specific—threats or violence intended to dissuade a witness from testifying in a specific case—or community-wide—acts by gangs or drug-selling groups intended to foster a general atmosphere of fear and noncooperation within a neighborhood or community (Healey 1995).

Today, virtually all jurisdictions of any size have established programs aimed at helping crime victims cope with the hardships of victimization and deal with the often troublesome demands of the criminal justice system. Most are based in criminal justice agencies (prosecutors', police, and sheriffs'

offices), but others are independently operated multiservice agencies (Finn and Lee 1988). Often the title is *Victim Services*.

Evaluations of victim/witness assistance programs have yielded mixed results. In Prince George's County, Maryland (Norton 1983) and Peoria, Illinois (National Institute of Justice 1982), a victim's willingness to cooperate in the future was positively associated with considerate treatment by criminal justice personnel. Thus, victims and witnesses receiving help were more likely to appear when summoned than those who had not been aided. But no such impact was found in Brooklyn (Davis 1983) or Houston (Skogan and Wycoff 1987). Those helped by the program appeared at the same rate as those who were not aided, and there was no change in the rate of case dismissals. Although the Brooklyn project's services were highly rated by users, they did not affect users' opinions of the court system. Most disturbing of all, in Houston there was some evidence that the program had negative consequences.

Andrew Karmen (2001) suggests that one explanation for these research findings is that expectations of significant improvements in case outcomes were based on faulty assumptions. The presumption is that the adjudication process is characterized by an adversarial model. The reality is that the courtroom work group has a mutual interest in processing large numbers of cases expeditiously. Thus, whereas victims see their situations as unique events that deserve careful and individual consideration, judges, prosecutors, and defense attorneys see them as routine occurrences, to be disposed of based on "going rates."

 Victim/Witness Assistance Unit of the prosecutor's office in Golden (Colorado): **http://www.co.jefferson. co.us/dpt/da/vw.htm**

Victim Services Unit of the District 27 District Attorney (Oklahoma): **http://www.state.ok.us/~okda27/ victmser.htm**

Victim-Witness Assistance Program of the Commonwealth's Attorney for the City of Virginia Beach (Virginia): **http://www.city.virginia-beach. va.us/courts/oca/vw.htm**

Victim-Witness Assistance Program of the Cook County (Illinois) State's Attorney: **http://www. statesattorney.org/victim/victimwi.htm**

For an up-to-date list of Web links, go to **http:// www.wadsworth.com/product/0534563406s**.

Victim Compensation Programs

The criminal justice system in the United States is offender-oriented, focusing on the apprehension, prosecution, and punishment of wrongdoers. While emphasizing the rehabilitation of offenders, the system has done little to help victims recover from the financial and emotional problems that they suffer.

Civil lawsuits are of little relevance, because most criminal defendants have no money to pay monetary damages for personal injuries or damage to property. An increasingly common technique is restitution, in which the court orders the defendant to pay the victim for the losses suffered (see Chapter 15). But a major shortcoming of restitution is the fact that in many crimes no offender is convicted. Even if convicted, many defendants have little or no ability to provide adequate compensation to a victim. And once restitution is ordered, the victim's

---

COURT TV

Vermont v. Grace

Christine Grace is charged with the murder of her abusive boyfriend and uses the battered woman's defense. While watching the video, keep the following questions in mind:

1. How do the witnesses in this case differ from those seen in the movies and in TV dramas?
2. What line of questioning does the defense use to impeach the credibility of the prosecution's key witnesses?
3. Why did the defense call their client to the stand? Does her testimony help or hurt her case?
4. How does this case relate to the issue of domestic violence?

---

likelihood of collecting is not good (Davis, Smith, and Hillenbrand 1992).

When restitution by the offender is inadequate or impractical, compensation by a third party (an insurance company, for example) is the only alternative. But many victims, because they are poor, do not have insurance covering medical expenses or property losses. The government is another sort of third party. Victim compensation programs rest on the premise that the government should counterbalance losses suffered by victims of criminal acts. The first compensation program in the United States began in California in 1965. Similar programs quickly emerged in a few other states.

In 1984 Congress passed the Victims of Crime Act, which established a Crime Victims Fund administered by the Office for Victims of Crimes within the U.S. Department of Justice. The fund is financed primarily from fines collected under the Criminal Fine Enforcement Act of 1984 (Parent, Auerbach, and Carlson 1992).

The federal backing has now spurred all states to enact legislation providing compensation for at least certain classes of crime victims. The staffs are small, however, and relatively few claims are filed—under 100,000 during a typical year. Most programs provide for recovery of medical expenses and some lost earnings; none reimburses the victim for lost or damaged property. The maximum amount that can be paid in damages ranges from $10,000 to $25,000.

Victim compensation programs appear to provide clear benefits to victims of crime, but the actual

CRIME & PUNISHMENT

The State of Illinois v. Bobby Hart

Bobby Hart and Chris Murphy have been living together for several years and are now the parents of a young son. Their relationship, however, has been marred by past instances of domestic violence. Fairly recently, Chris Murphy instructed Bobby Hart to leave the house, but instead of leaving he held out a knife. The court granted Murphy a restraining order, but Hart violated the court order by breaking into the house. After watching the CD, you should be able to discuss the following questions:

1. How serious is this case? In answering this question, consider the severity of the past injuries to Chris Murphy. Also weigh how badly she was physically injured during the events surrounding this prosecution.
2. Both the victim and the defendant express concern about their young son. What sentence would be in the best interest of the child?
3. In deciding a sentence, what factors in the presentence investigation do you think are most important?
4. In deciding a sentence, how much weight do you give the statements made by the defendant and the victim?
5. What does this case illustrate about restraining orders?
6. What deterrent effect do you think the sentence will have in this case?

results of such programs require careful scrutiny. Preliminary evaluations of compensation programs have yielded findings disappointing for administrators (Karmen 2001). Compensation programs are intended to improve the attitudes of victims toward the criminal justice system, but this improvement does not occur (Doerner 1980). Indeed, cumbersome administrative procedures lead to added frustrations and increased alienation. The central problem, however, is that few victims of violent crimes apply for benefits, and even fewer claimants receive any money. The fact that only half (Elias 1986) to two thirds (McCormack 1991) of the claimants are awarded some compensation is related primarily to strict eligibility requirements. Most states require that the victim report the crime to police within a specified period after it occurs and agree to assist in the prosecution of the offender. "This requirement

eliminates many domestic violence, child abuse, and sexual assault victims who either are afraid to report or decide not to prosecute for other pragmatic reasons" (McCormack 1991, 338). Most states also have a "family exclusion" clause, which makes victims living in the same household as the offender ineligible. Crime victims must also be "innocent" victims (those to whom no contributory fault can be ascribed). Finally, maximum awards for seriously injured victims are set at unrealistically low levels. Thus, these programs are designed more to spread the limited funds around, rather than to concentrate on a few badly injured victims.

 For information on the victim compensation program in your state, go to **http://mova.missouri.org/viccomp.htm**.

For an up-to-date list of Web links, go to **http://www.wadsworth.com/product/0534563406s**.

Victim's Bill of Rights

Nowhere is the awakened concern about victims of crime more readily apparent than in proposals for a victim's bill of rights (see Exhibit 9-1). Apart from sharing the title, however, these proposals vary markedly, reflecting different philosophies. In 1982 the President's Task Force on Victims of Crime submitted sixty-eight separate recommendations aimed at achieving a balance between the needs and rights of the victim and those of the defendant. Also in 1982 California voters approved Proposition 8 by a two-to-one margin. Known as the "Victim's Bill of Rights," it added twelve controversial provisions to the state constitution and the criminal code. These versions of the victim's bill of rights reflect the rallying cry of the law-and-order movement, which accuses the courts of protecting the rights of defendants rather than those of victims. Premised on the notion that defendants escape too easily from the court process, these proposals stress substantive changes in the law, such as abolishing the exclusionary rule, limiting bail, restricting plea bargaining, and imposing stiffer sentences.

Other proposed victim's bills of rights are less ideological, emphasizing improvements in court procedures to better the lot of victims and witnesses. For example, the National Conference of the Judiciary on the Rights of Victims of Crime adopted a Statement of Recommended Judicial Practices, sug-

EXHIBIT 9-1 Text of Proposed Victims' Rights Amendment

105th CONGRESS
1st Session
S.J. RES. 6
IN THE SENATE OF THE UNITED STATES
JANUARY 21, 1997

Mr. KYL (for himself, Mrs. FEINSTEIN) introduced the following joint resolution; which was read twice and referred to the Committee on the Judiciary

JOINT RESOLUTION

Proposing an amendment to the Constitution of the United States to protect the rights of crime victims.

Resolved by the Senate and the House of Representatives of the United States of America in Congress assembled (two thirds of each House concurring therein), That the following article is proposed as an amendment to the Constitution of the United States, which shall be valid for all intents and purposes as part of the Constitution when ratified by the legislatures of three-fourths of the several States within seven years from the date of its submission by the Congress:

SECTION 1. Each victim of a crime of violence, and other crimes that Congress may define by law, shall have the rights to notice of, and not to be excluded from all public proceedings relating to the crime; To be heard, if present, and to submit a statement at a public pre-trial or trial proceedings to determine a release from custody, an acceptance of a negotiated plea, or a sentence; To the rights described in the proceedings portions of this section at a public parole proceedings, or at a non-public parole proceedings to the extent they are afforded to the convicted offender; To notice of a release pursuant to a public or parole proceedings or an escape; To a final disposition of the proceedings relating to the crime free from unreasonable delay; To an order of restitution from the convicted offender; To have the safety of the victim considered in determining any release from custody; And To notice of the rights established by this article; however, the rights to notice under this section are not violated if the proper authorities make a reasonable effort, but are unable to provide the notice, or if the failure of the victim to make a reasonable effort, to make those authorities aware of the victim's whereabouts prevents that notice.

SECTION 2. The victim shall have standing to assert the rights established by this article. However, nothing in this article shall provide grounds for the victims to challenge a charging decision or conviction; to obtain a stay of trial; or to compel a new trial. Nothing in this article shall give rise to a claim for damages against the United States, a State, a political subdivision, or a public official, nor provide grounds for the accused or convicted offender to obtain any form of relief.

SECTION 3. The Congress and the States shall have the power to enforce this article within their respective Federal and State jurisdictions by appropriate legislation, including the power to enact exceptions when required for compelling reasons for public safety or for judicial efficiency in mass victim cases.

SECTION 4. The rights established by this article shall apply to all proceedings that begin on or after the 180th day after the ratification of this article.

SECTION 5. The rights established by this article shall apply in all Federal and State proceedings, including military proceedings to the extent that Congress may provide by law, juvenile justice proceedings, and collateral proceedings such as habeas corpus, and including proceedings in any district or territory of the United States not within a State.

gesting (1) fair treatment of victims and witnesses through better information about court procedures, (2) victim participation and input through all stages of judicial proceedings, and (3) better protection of victims and witnesses from harassment, threats, intimidation, and harm.

Most recently, discussions of the victim's bill of rights have shifted from the state to the national level (see Controversy: Should the Victims' Rights Amendment Be Adopted?).

Julie Brienza, "Crime Victim Laws Sometimes Ignored"

AIDING OR MANIPULATING VICTIMS?

After a long period of neglect, aiding victims has become good politics. These efforts are backed by a national movement for the rights of crime victims.

The Victims' Rights Movement

Organizing crime victims is a difficult task. Aside from having been harmed by criminals, victims as a group have very little in common (Karmen 2001).

CONTROVERSY

Should the Victims' Rights Amendment Be Adopted?

 Efforts to protect the rights of victims began with the passage in virtually all jurisdictions of victims' rights legislation. These activities soon expanded to include a demand that these protections be given even greater force of law by placing them in state constitutions, and the public has responded with overwhelming support. Thirty-two states have passed victims' rights amendments to their state constitutions, and others are considering adding similar amendments. In 1996, for example, all eight proposed state constitutional amendments handily passed with an average of 85 percent approval.

Having achieved considerable success at the state level, victims' rights groups are now pressing for an amendment to the U.S. Constitution. The National Victims' Constitutional Amendment Network is a coalition of dozens of victims' organizations focusing on protecting the rights of crime victims. The current proposal reads very differently from many earlier proposals—of special note is that it makes no mention of tougher sentences for those convicted or of abolishing the exclusionary rule (see Exhibit 9-1). Just as importantly, it prohibits civil lawsuits from being filed to ensure its enforcement.

The victims' rights amendment (VRA) was first proposed during the Annual National Crime Victims' Rights Week in 1966. Not coincidentally this was an election year, and the proposal soon became part of national election campaigns. It was not, however, a divisive issue because the proposed amendment had bipartisan support in Congress. In 1996 and 2000, each party's presidential candidate endorsed it.

However, proposals to amend the U.S. Constitution are frequently offered but rarely adopted. Amending the Constitution is a difficult and complicated task, requiring a two-thirds vote in both houses of Congress and ratification by three quarters (thirty-eight) of the states. In its 200 plus–year history the document has been amended twenty-seven times (the first ten amendments, or Bill of Rights, were adopted soon after the signing of the Constitution). Since 1997 both the Senate and House judiciary committees have held hearings on the resolution, but in 2000 Senate backers withdrew the legislation rather than see it defeated.

Senator Dianne Feinstein (D-California) is a co-sponsor of the proposed amendment, arguing the Constitution protects the rights of criminal defendants but "crime victims, families, survivors have no rights at all, according to the Constitution of the United States" (Cannon 1996). If the victims' rights amendment is adopted, victims of violent crimes would have the following rights:

- Allowed to be present at major stages of a criminal case
- Permitted to make views known during a plea of guilty and sentencing
- Spared delays in defendants' trials
- Notified of any release or escape of the offender
- Guaranteed full restitution by the offender

The most fundamental concern expressed about the proposed victims' rights amendment is that its guiding assumption—victims are being excluded from the judicial process—is patently false. Unlike many nations of the world, in the United States all steps of the criminal process (except grand jury proceedings) are mandated to be open to the public. Victims are excluded from trial only when they will be witnesses, and this is happening more often because of another facet of the victims' rights movement—victim impact statements. More substantively, critics make the following points:

Despite these obstacles, victim advocacy groups have become a powerful political voice.

The emergence of the victims' rights movement reflects several parallel trends. One is the law-and-order rhetoric of the 1960s, which emphasized the harm criminals do to victims. Another is the women's rights movement, which came to take a special interest in crimes involving women. A key feature of the feminist movement is its emphasis on grassroots activism. Thus, a logical extension of the women's movement was to form local programs to aid women who had been victims of rape or spousal abuse (Weed 1995).

The victims' rights movement involves people striking back to turn tragedy into action and rage into reform (Office for Victims of Crime 1998). The best known of these organizations is Mothers Against Drunk Driving (MADD). Founded by

- *Prosecutors may not want to give rights to some victims.* Victims (like defendants) are a diverse lot, and some prosecutors may decide it is in the best interests of justice to ignore some of their wishes. For example, some victims are also defendants in other cases. And to complicate matters further, what if gang members wished to be notified when rival gang members were about to be released from prison?
- *The costs will be enormous.* The notification requirements appear to be sensible and straightforward until one calculates the high volume of cases processed each year. Serious felony cases typically require numerous court hearings, which would require separate notification for each hearing. Given that some victims change addresses often, timely notification could prove costly. In all likelihood the amendment would increase paperwork considerably, but local governments are unlikely to spend tax dollars to hire additional personnel.
- *States are already doing a lot.* Critics wonder why a federal constitutional amendment is needed when states have already taken significant steps to help crime victims. Notifying victims, for instance, has become standard practice, with 97 percent of district offices routinely notifying victims of felonies of the outcomes in their cases (DeFrances, Smith, and van der Does 1996). As discussed in Chapter 3, some are concerned over the federalization of state crimes. Is this another area in which the federal government is unnecessarily usurping the grounds usually reserved for the states?
- *Endless litigation will ensue.* Opponents of the victims' rights amendment also foresee the possibility of endless litigation, which will only undermine the effective administration of justice. One issue sure to arise is definitional. Who is a victim? What of the family? What of friends? What if victims disagree? Consider also the difficulty appellate courts will face in resolving potential conflicts

between rights of the accused and rights of crime victims. There is a distinct possibility that some criminal convictions will be overturned because trial judges tipped the scale in favor of the victim, resulting in an unfair trial.
- *More frustration will result.* Finally, opponents are concerned that the victims' rights amendment will increase, not decrease, frustrations victims experience. What if victims oppose a plea bargain only to find that the judge approves the standard plea for such a charge? How will victims react when they urge a stiff sentence and the judge imposes a lower sanction based on the going rate?

What do you think? Would adopting the victims' rights amendment to the U.S. Constitution genuinely improve the plight of victims of crime, or is it another example of manipulating the plight of victims for political ends? Is this an area where states should have great freedom to act but the national government only a limited role? In the end, would a victims' rights amendment be effective or just window dressing?

Marlene A. Young, Roger Pilon, "Should We Amend the Constitution to Protect Victims' Rights?"

To continue the debate, click on the following sites, which offer contrasting views on the wisdom of passing the Victims' Rights Amendment:

National Victims' Constitutional Amendment Network: **http://www.nvcan.org/**.

American Civil Liberties Union: **http://www.aclu.org/congress/congresssearch.html**. (use the search term *"victims"*)

For an up-to-date list of Web links, go to **http://www.wadsworth.com/product/0534563406s**.

Candy Lightner, whose daughter was killed by a drunk driver, MADD has become the nation's largest victim advocacy group (Chapter 18). A check of the Internet reveals numerous other groups. Many of these groups are local, emphasizing various types of victims ranging from those harmed by drunk drivers to battered women. These grassroots operations function loosely under the national umbrella organization, the National Organization of Victim

Assistance, which provides a larger focus for their specialized concerns.

Today the victims' rights movement involves a loose coalition of local, state, and national organizations with wide-ranging interests. Their activities constitute a full-blown social movement that seeks to place the interests of crime victims into the mainstream of American political discourse. Although diverse in origins, the victims' rights movement

CASE CLOSE-UP

Payne v. Tennessee and Victim Impact Statements

Pervis Tyrone Payne spent the morning injecting cocaine and drinking beer. The early afternoon found him driving around town with a friend, each taking turns reading a pornographic magazine. Around three in the afternoon Payne returned to his apartment complex, only to find his girlfriend wasn't home yet. Instead, uninvited, he entered the apartment of his neighbor, twenty-eight-year-old Charissee Christopher and her two children, Lacie (two years old) and Nicholas (three years old). Payne soon began making sexual advances, but when she resisted he became violent. After hearing a "blood-curdling scream," a neighbor called the police, who arrived just as Payne, covered in blood, was leaving the apartment. Inside, they encountered a horrifying scene. Blood covered the walls and floor throughout the unit. Charissee and her daughter were lying dead on the kitchen floor, stabbed numerous times with a butcher knife. Miraculously, Nicholas survived despite deep knife wounds.

For over a full page, Chief Justice William Rehnquist emphasizes facts like these, clearly directing the reader to the brutal nature of the crime before proceeding to examine the legal issue: Should victim impact statements be admissible during the sentencing phase of capital murder trials?

Payne was convicted of two counts of first-degree murder and one count of first-degree assault. During the sentencing phase of the trial the defense called Payne's parents, his girlfriend, and a clinical psychologist, each of whom testified as to various mitigating aspects of his background and character. He was considered a "loving and caring person." Moreover, his low IQ marked him as mentally handicapped.

The state countered with the testimony of Charissee's mother. She testified that the surviving child "cries for his mom. He doesn't seem to understand why she doesn't come home. And he cries for his sister."

During closing arguments the prosecutor made maximum use of this emotional testimony. She acknowledged there was nothing the jury could do to ease the pain of the families involved in this case. Nor could they do anything about the victims—Charissee and her dead daughter:

> But there is something you can do for Nicholas. Somewhere down the road Nicholas is . . . going to want to know what type of justice was done. He is going to want to know what happened. With your verdict you will provide the answer.

The jury unanimously sentenced Payne to death, and the Tennessee Supreme Court affirmed, calling the emotional testimony of the grandmother "technically irrelevant."

Moving beyond the grisly facts of the case, the legal issue was one of precedent. In two recent decisions (*Booth v. Maryland*, 1987, and *South Carolina v. Gathers*, 1989) the Court, by a five to four vote, held that victim impact statements are unconstitutional because they create an unacceptable risk that a jury may impose the death penalty in an arbitrary and capricious manner. Rehnquist sweeps aside these objections. Admitting that stare decisis is the pre-

---

shares a common ideology seeking to demonstrate the triumph of good over evil. Thus, the movement resonates with a moral view of crime held by many average citizens (Weed 1995).

 Julie Brienza, "Crime Victim Laws Sometimes Ignored"

Differing Goals

The victims' rights movement reflects the mutual interests of a strange set of political bedfellows, which explains why, beneath the rhetoric about

aiding victims of crimes, there are important disagreements over goals and priorities (Viano 1987) (see Case Close-Up: *Payne v. Tennessee* and Victim Impact Statements). A study of a victims' rights organization in Alabama found that the membership was disproportionately white and female, with blacks excluded from potential membership. These results suggest that the victims' rights movement is becoming polarized, with some most concerned with secondary victimization and others more focused on punishment of defendants (Smith and Huff 1992). Similarly, a study in the state of Washington found that groups supporting the Community Protection Act reflected a punitive orientation toward defendants more so than an effort to aid vicferred course because it promotes evenhanded and predictable legal principles, nonetheless the Court in the past has reversed previous decisions when they "are unworkable or are badly reasoned." The Court held that the Eighth Amendment does not prohibit the sentencing jury in a capital case from considering victim impact statements relating to the victim's personal characteristics and the emotional impact of the murder on the victim's family.

Justice Thurgood Marshall thundered back in a biting dissent: "Power, not reason, is the new currency of this Court's decision making." Marshall was working on two fronts. First, he was highlighting the fact that the conservatives on the Court had usually emphasized the importance of precedent, but now were willing to look the other way when precedent was inconvenient. Further, Marshall was calling attention to the change in membership on the Court. In particular, Justice Lewis Powell, a moderate appointed by a Republican president, had been replaced by a more conservative justice. As we shall see in Chapter 17, Reagan's appointment shifted the Court to the right, and once in control, the conservative majority discovered that it no longer preferred precedent as a policy. Thus, the decision in Payne reflects more a change of court personnel than changes in the law.

Victim impact statements are supported by the National District Attorneys Association. They are opposed by the National Association of Criminal Defense Lawyers. Following *Payne*, forty-one states and the federal government grant the right in most cases for the victim to address the court during sentencing.

But are victim impact statements sound criminal justice policy? The National Victim Center and other victims' groups support giving victims a voice in the process, rather than reducing them to being a mere statistic. By venting their anger and frustrations they are better able, proponents contend, to get on with their lives. But critics fear that the venting of frustrations can demean the judicial process. As a certain death sentence was about to be pronounced against Richard Allen Davis for sexually molesting and then killing Polly Klaas (discussed in Chapter 16), Davis told the court that Polly's father had sexually molested her, a charge that crime-victim advocates labeled outrageous and sickening.

Incidents like this one lead critics to wonder whether victim impact statements help victims; perhaps the possibility of speaking in court at a much later date unnecessarily prolongs the grieving process of victims. Victims are not encouraged to reach a sense of closure until they testify (or in some cases until the defendant is actually executed). Moreover, there is concern that judges and juries may view some victims as more valuable to society than others. What if the deceased led a less than exemplary life? If the victim's character can be used as an aggravating factor during death penalty deliberations, might it also be used in mitigation (Finn-DeLuca 1994)?

Amidst the debate over law on the books, it is important to focus on law in action (Donahoe 1999). Apart from a few high-profile cases of rape and/or murder, the majority of victims do not exercise that option. There is strong likelihood that more upper-status victims will choose to participate, perhaps further skewing the justice process along social-economic lines. But this might not prove to be the case. A carefully controlled study in Bronx County, New York, found that victim impact statements neither increased officials' consideration of harm to victims nor resulted in generally harsher sentencing decisions (Davis and Smith 1994).

tims of sexual assault (Scheingold, Olson, and Pershing 1994). These differing goals explain why victims' rights laws and constitutional amendments are so contradictory.

Do Victims Benefit?

Everyone agrees that victims and witnesses should be treated better during the court process. But political rhetoric should not be allowed to obscure some important issues. Although enthusiasm for helping victims is clearly growing, the willingness to pay for the necessary services is not always present. Overall, legislators and other government officials find vot-

ing for victim-oriented legislation politically advantageous, but when it comes to voting money for another "welfare program," they are much more hesitant.

Moreover, it is unclear how much aid victims and witnesses receive from these programs. Once enacted, programs do not always work as intended. Elias (1993) concluded that victim compensation laws were exercises in symbolic politics. Few claimants ever received compensation; the laws provided "political placebos," with few tangible benefits for victims.

Victim/witness assistance programs appear to be important first steps in providing better services to citizens who find themselves thrust into the criminal court process, but not all agree that the benefits of these programs actually aid the victim. Sociologist William McDonald (1976) charges that "some projects that are billed as 'assisting victims' are more accurately described as assisting the criminal justice system and extending government control over victims. Whether the victims so controlled would regard the project as 'assisting' them is problematic" (35). Some victims do not wish to become involved.

The important question is at whose expense should victims be compensated? Some versions emphasize protecting the rights of victims by deny-

ing privileges and benefits to suspects, defendants, and prisoners. This type of victim's bill of rights is the most recent example of the conflict between the due process model and the crime control model (highlighted in Chapter 1). Other versions emphasize improving the welfare of victims at the expense of the privileges and options enjoyed by members of the courtroom work group (Karmen 2001).

 Chester Hicks, "The Rights of Crime Victims: Does Legal Protection Make a Difference?"

CONCLUSION

The future of both Pervis Tyrone Payne and his victim are difficult to predict. Payne sits on Tennessee's death row. Having lost on appeal to the Supreme Court, his lawyers hope to set aside the death penalty during further rounds of habeas corpus review. Meanwhile he sits in his cell, wondering whether he will die or not. Predicting the future of Nicholas is even more difficult. At his young age, his mind might be able to block out the memories of seeing his mother and younger sister murdered in his presence. But there is still a good chance of flashbacks and antisocial behavior, which psychologists label post-traumatic stress disorder. It is possible that as he grows up Nicholas will himself shift from victim to defendant. As we learned in this chapter, many defendants arrested for violent crimes were themselves the victims of violent acts as children.

The perhaps troubling future of Nicholas highlights some of the contradictions still apparent in how society reacts to victims. Today there is less tendency to blame victims (particularly rape victims) for causing their own misfortune. But such tendencies are more muted. Instead numerous groups are ready to step forward and call for helping victims. Some of these same voices who are quick to champion the cause of victims are just as quick to denounce what has become popularly called the abuse excuse.

Victims and witnesses provide the raw material for the court process. The complaints they bring, the credibility of their stories, and their willingness to participate directly affect the courtroom work group's activities. But members of the

courtroom work group do not respond uncritically to the demands for their services. They find some stories more believable than others and some claims more worthy than others. The clientele shapes the criminal court process in a less obvious way. Most defendants are young, male, illiterate, impoverished members of minority groups. Many victims share similar traits. They are also poor, unversed in the ways of the courts, and, disproportionately, members of minority groups. The net result is that the criminal courts are poor people's institutions. They share many characteristics of other institutions (such as welfare offices and charity hospitals) that deal almost exclusively with the poor. Unlike the middle class, the poor are accustomed to accepting the conditions they find themselves in. They do not protest long waits before government officials can see them, nor do they demand that the building they wait in offer amenities. In cities with separate civil and criminal courts, the former are usually newer and cleaner, reflecting their middle-class clientele. Such contrasts emphasize that in the criminal courts victims and witnesses often exert little influence over the disposition of the cases in which they are involved.

CRITICAL THINKING QUESTIONS

1. In what ways are victims and defendants similar? In what ways are they different? Is there any difference in the characteristics of victims and defendants when the victim is a male as opposed to when the victim is a female?

2. Many of the discussions of crime suggest that smart defendants are able to beat the rap by pleading insanity (Chapter 14), slanting their testimony at defense counsel urging (Chapter 7), and exploiting legal loopholes such as the exclusionary rule (Chapter 12). Given the profile of the typical criminal defendant, how realistic are these assumptions of a smart crook?

3. To some, the victims' rights movement is more an exercise in symbolic politics than a substantive program. Thus some critics argue that many of these programs are really more interested in severe punishment of the defendant than in helping victims adjust socially, economically, or psychologically to the new role as victim. Which dimensions of helping victims reflect the crime control model? Which dimensions reflect the due process model?

4. Would your views on victim impact statements be different if the U.S. Supreme Court had chosen a less emotional case to consider in deciding their constitutionality? Overall, do you think victim impact statements correctly allow victims a voice in the process or just add unnecessary emotionalism?

 WORLD WIDE WEB RESOURCES AND EXERCISES

Web Guides

http://dir.yahoo.com/Society_and_Culture/Crime/
http://dir.yahoo.com/Society_and_Culture/Crime/
   Victims__Rights/
http://dir.yahoo.com/Society_and_Culture/Crime/
   Types_of_Crime/Domestic_Violence/
http://dir.yahoo.com/Entertainment/Humor/
   Job_Humor/Law_Enforcement/

Web Search Terms

"Victims"; "victims' advocates"; "victims' rights amendment"; "domestic violence"

Useful URLs

The ABA Commission on Domestic Violence references a variety of studies and statistics: **http://www.abanet.org/domviol/home.html.**

The Violence Against Women Office is located in the U.S. Department of Justice: **http://www.ojp.usdoj.gov/vawo/.**

The Criminal Justice Legal Foundation is a nonprofit public interest law organization dedicated to restoring a balance between the rights of crime victims and the criminally accused: **http://cjlf.org/.**

The National Coalition against Domestic Violence is dedicated to the empowerment of battered women and their children: **http://www.ncadv.org/.**

The National Organization for Victim Assistance is the largest umbrella organization offering assistance to victims: **http://www.try-nova.org/.**

The National Association of Crime Victims Compensation Board provides information on victim compensation programs in the states: **http://www.mailbag.com/users/derene/home.html.**

Uncommon URLs

The Pennsylvania Coalition Against Domestic Violence is located at **http://www.pcadv.org/.**

The Virginia Poverty Law Center, Inc. provides legal help for victims of domestic violence or sexual assault at **http://www.vplc.org/.**

The Jacksonville (North Carolina) Web page on domestic violence can be seen at **http://jpd.onslowonline.net/Violence/intro.htm.**

Dumb Crooks offers true stories of mentally challenged criminals: **http://www.dumbcrooks.com/main.htm.**

The Missouri Victim Assistance Network is a good example of a state-level organization. The Web site provides lots of links useful to state citizens: **http://mova.missouri.org/.**

Safe Horizon offers a tour of a domestic violence shelters: **http://www.dvsheltertour.org/.**

Crime Victims' Rights offers a conservative perspective: **http://www.victimsrights.org/.**

Victim Service Council of the St. Louis Prosecuting Attorney's Office can be viewed at **http://mova.missouri.org/members/vsc.htm.**

Web Exercises

1. The number of victims' rights organizations is growing, and you can locate many of them by

using the following Yahoo search: Society and Culture/Crime/Victims'Rights/Organizations.

Access several organizations and ask yourself the following questions. Does the name of the organization provide a good description of the organization? What types of crime are mentioned? To what extent does gender play a major or minor role in the stated purpose of the organization? In terms of crime control model versus due process model, do the organizations appear to be geared to punishing defendants or providing social and psychological support for crime victims?

2 What's your favorite dumb crook joke? Check out the dumb crook Web site: Dumb crooks **http://www.dumbcrimes.com**, homepage for the TV show *America's Dumbest Criminals.* Why are these tales so popular? What do they suggest about charges that smart crooks know how to beat the system using technicalities?

3. The National Victims' Constitutional Amendment Network supports amending the U.S. Constitution to recognize "the fundamental rights of crime victims to be treated with dignity, fairness, and respect by the criminal justice system." Access their homepage (**http://www.nvc.org**) and determine who supports their efforts (both individuals and organizations). What arguments do they make in urging that "Statutes are NOT Enough"?

Unlike many other advocacy groups, they choose to include arguments from opponents. Does this enhance their credibility as an organization? How powerful are the negative arguments they include?

Use the Web site to determine the current status of the victims' rights amendment. The homepage provides links to individual states. Click on your state to find out what type of victims' rights law and constitutional provisions amendments affect your jurisdiction. In particular, what notification rights exist in your state? Some states are creating Web sites to notify victims and others of pending parole releases, and so on. Access one of these pages and ask yourself how easily an average citizen would be able to locate the desired information.

INFOTRAC COLLEGE EDITION RESOURCES AND EXERCISES

Basic Search Terms

Criminals; African American criminals; women criminals; recidivists; victims of crimes; victims' rights amendment; rape victims; rape victim services; victim impact statements

Recommended Articles

Barry Yeoman, "Bad Girls"
Diane S. Young and Carrie Smith, "When Moms Are Incarcerated"
J. P. Tremblay, "Empowering the Victim: California Shifts the Focus of Justice"
James Ferguson, "Civil Justice for Crime Victims"
Amy K. Phillips, "Thou Shalt Not Kill Any Nice People"
Stuart W. Fors and Dean G. Rojek, "The Effect of Victim Impact Panels on DUI/DWI Rearrest Rates"
Sue Carter, "Media Insensitivity to Victims of Violence"
Cathy Spatz Widom, "Childhood Sexual Abuse and Its Criminal Consequences"
"From a Crime Victim in Texas" (the story of a crime victim who became active in the criminal justice system)

InfoTrac College Edition Exercises

1. Using the search term *victims' rights amendment,* find one article that supports the passage of this law and another that opposes it. To what extent are the arguments similar to or different from those discussed in the text? To what extent do differences of opinion fall along the lines of the due process versus the crime control model of justice?

2. Using the search term *women criminals,* find two or more articles that discuss why women commit fewer crimes than men but that rates of female involvement in the criminal justice system have been increasing in recent years.

REFERENCES

Alarid, Leanne, James Marquart, Velmer Burton, Francis Cullen, and Steven Cuvelier. 1996. "Women's Roles in Serious Offenses: A Study of Adult Felons." *Justice Quarterly* 13: 431–454.

Bachman, Ronet, and Linda Saltzman. 1995. "Violence Against Women: Estimates from the Redesigned Survey." U.S. Department of Justice, Bureau of Justice Statistics.

Baumer, Eric, Steven Messner, and Richard Felson. 2000. "The Role of Victim Characteristics in the Disposition of Murder Cases." *Justice Quarterly* 17: 281–308.

Boland, Barbara, Elizabeth Brady, Herbert Tyson, and John Bassler. 1982. *The Prosecution of Felony Arrests.* Washington, D.C.: Institute for Law and Social Research.

Bureau of Justice Statistics. 1987. *Violent Crime by Strangers and Non-Strangers.* Washington, D.C.: U.S. Department of Justice.

———. 1988. *Report to the Nation on Crime and Justice: The Data.* 2d ed. Washington, D.C.: U.S. Department of Justice.

———. 2000. "Intimate Partner Violence." U.S. Department of Justice, Bureau of Justice Statistics.

Buzawa, Eve, and Carl Buzawa. 1996. *Domestic Violence: The Criminal Justice Response,* 2d ed. Thousand Oaks, CA: Sage.

Cannavale, F., and W. Falcon. 1976. *Witness Cooperation.* Lexington, MA: D.C. Heath.

Cannon, Angie. 1996. "Bill Spells Out Rights of Victims." *Times-Picayune,* 23 April.

Cass, Connie. 1995. "1 in 3 Young Black Men Run Afoul of Law." *Times-Picayune,* 5 October.

Chaiken, Marcia, and Jan Chaiken. 1991. *Priority Prosecution of High-Rate Dangerous Offenders.* Washington, D.C.: National Institute of Justice.

Connick, Elizabeth, and Robert Davis. 1983. "Examining the Problems of Witness Intimidation." *Judicature* 66: 438–447.

Coyle, Pamela. 1999. "Murder Victim's Date Sticks to Story." *Times-Picayune,* 9 January.

Davis, Robert. 1983. "Victim/Witness Noncooperation: A Second Look at a Persistent Phenomenon." *Journal of Criminal Justice* 11: 287–299.

Davis, Robert, and Barbara Smith. 1994. "The Effects of Victim Impact Statements on Sentencing Decisions: A Test in an Urban Setting." *Justice Quarterly* 11: 453–469.

Davis, Robert, Barbara Smith, and Susan Hillenbrand. 1992. "Restitution: The Victim's Viewpoint." *Justice System Journal* 15: 746–758.

DeFrances, Carol, Steven Smith, and Louise van der Does. 1996. "Prosecutors in State Courts, 1994." *Bulletin.* Washington, D.C.: Bureau of Justice Statistics.

Doerner, William. 1980. "Impact of Crime Compensation on Victim's Attitudes Toward the Criminal Justice System." *Victimology* 5: 61–77.

Donahoe, Joel. 1999. "The Changing Role of Victim Impact Evidence in Capital Cases." *Western Criminology Review* 2:1.

Elias, Robert. 1986. *The Politics of Victimization: Victims, Victimology and Human Rights.* New York: Oxford University Press.

———. 1993. *Victims Still: The Political Manipulation of Crime Victims.* Thousand Oaks, CA: Sage.

Fagan, Jeffrey. 1996. *The Criminalization of Domestic Violence: Promises and Limits.* Washington, D.C.: National Institute of Justice.

Finn, Peter. 1986. "Collaboration Between the Judiciary and Victim-Witness Assistance Programs." *Judicature* 69: 192–198.

Finn, Peter, and Beverley Lee. 1988. *Establishing and Expanding Victim-Witness Assistance Programs.* Washington, D.C.: National Institute of Justice.

Finn-DeLuca, Valerie. 1994. "Victim Participation at Sentencing." *Criminal Law Bulletin* 30: 403–428.

Hagan, John. 1983. *Victims Before the Law: The Organizational Domination of Criminal Law.* Toronto: Butterworth's.

Harlow, Caroline. 1999. "Prior Abuse Reported by Inmates and Probationers." Washington, D.C.: Office of Justice Programs, U.S. Department of Justice, NCJ 172879.

Healey, Kerry. 1995. "Victim and Witness Intimidation: New Developments and Emerging Responses." Washington, D.C.: National Institute of Justice.

Hewitt, John. 1988. "The Victim-Offender Relationship in Convicted Homicide Cases: 1960–1984." *Journal of Criminal Justice* 16: 25–33.

Hirschel, J. David, Ira Hutchison, Charles Dean, and Anne-Marie Mills. 1992. "Review Essay on the Law Enforcement Response to Spouse Abuse: Past, Present and Future." *Justice Quarterly* 9: 247–284.

Holmstrom, Lynda, and Ana Burgess. 1983. *The Victim of Rape: Institutional Reactions.* New Brunswick, NJ: Transaction Publishers.

Jencks, Christopher, and Paul Peterson, eds. 1991. *The Urban Underclass.* Washington, D.C.: Brookings Institution.

Karmen, Andrew. 2001. *Crime Victims: An Introduction to Victimology.* 4th ed. Belmont, CA: Wadsworth.

Knudten, Richard, Anthony Meader, Mary Knudten, and William Doerner. 1976. "The Victim in the Administration of Criminal Justice: Problems and Perceptions." Pp. 115–146 in *Criminal Justice and the Victim,* edited by William McDonald. Newbury Park, CA: Sage.

McCormack, Robert. 1991. "Compensating Victims of Violent Crime." *Justice Quarterly* 8: 329–346.

McDonald, William, ed. 1976. *Criminal Justice and the Victim.* Newbury Park, CA: Sage.

McEwen, Tom. 1995. *National Assessment Program: 1994 Survey Results.* Washington, D.C.: National Institute of Justice.

Moore, Mark, Susan Estrich, Daniel McGillis, and William Spelman. 1984. *Dangerous Offenders: The Elusive Target of Justice.* Cambridge, MA: Harvard University Press.

Myers, Martha, and John Hagan. 1979. "Private and Public Trouble: Prosecutors and the Allocation of Court Resources." *Social Problems* 26: 439–451.

National Institute of Justice. 1982. *Exemplary Projects: Focus for 1982—Projects to Combat Violent Crime.* Washington, D.C.: U.S. Department of Justice.

Newburn, Tim, and Elizabeth Stanko, eds. 1994. *Just Boys Doing Business: Men, Masculinities and Crime.* London: Routledge.

Norton, Lee. 1983. "Witness Involvement in the Criminal Justice System and Intention to Cooperate in Future Prosecutions." *Journal of Criminal Justice* 11: 143–152.

Office for Victims of Crime. 1998. "From Pain to Power: Crime Victims Take Action." Washington, D.C.: U.S. Department of Justice.

Parent, Dale, Barbara Auerbach, and Kenneth Carlson. 1992. *Compensating Crime Victims: A Summary of Policies and Practices.* Washington, D.C.: National Institute of Justice, U.S. Department of Justice.

Resick, Patricia. 1984. "The Trauma of Rape and the Criminal Justice System." *Justice System Journal* 9: 52–61.

Rosett, Arthur, and Donald Cressey. 1976. *Justice by Consent.* Philadelphia: J.B. Lippincott.

Rowe, David, and David Farrington. 1997. "The Familial Transmission of Criminal Convictions." *Criminology* 35: 177–201.

Scheingold, Stuart, Toska Olson, and Jana Pershing. 1994. "Sexual Violence, Victim Advocacy, and Republican Criminology: Washington State's Community Protection Act." *Law and Society Review* 28: 729–763.

Schmidt, Janell, and Lawrence Sherman. 1993. "Does Arrest Deter Domestic Violence?" *American Behavioral Scientist* 36: 601–615.

Skogan, Wesley, and Mary Ann Wycoff. 1987. "Some Unexpected Effects of a Police Service for Victims." *Crime and Delinquency* 33: 490–501.

Smith, Brent, and C. Ronald Huff. 1992. "From Victim to Political Activist: An Empirical Examination of a Statewide Victims' Rights Movement." *Journal of Criminal Justice* 20: 201–215.

Stanko, Elizabeth. 1981–1982. "The Impact of Victim Assessment on Prosecutors' Screening Decisions: The Case of the New York County District Attorney's Office." *Law and Society Review* 16: 225–239.

Steketee, Gail, and Anne Austin. 1989. "Rape Victims and the Justice System: Utilization and Impact." *Social Service Review* 63: 285–303.

Varney, James. 1996a. "Teen-Ager Gets Death for Killing Slidell Man; Family Silent in Court." *Times-Picayune,* 27 January.

———. 1996b. "Teen Guilty of Murder Outside Quarter Lounge." *Times-Picayune,* 31 January.

Vera Institute of Justice. 1981. *Felony Arrests: Their Prosecution and Disposition in New York City's Courts.* Rev. ed. New York: Longman.

Viano, Emilio. 1987. "Victim's Rights and the Constitution: Reflections on a Bicentennial." *Crime and Delinquency* 33: 438–451.

Webster, Barbara. 1988. *Victim Assistance Programs Report Increased Workloads.* Washington, D.C.: National Institute of Justice.

Weed, Frank. 1995. *Certainty of Justice: Reform in the Crime Victim Movement.* New York: Aldine de Gruyter.

Young, Marlene. 1990. "Victim Assistance in the United States: The End of the Beginning." *International Review of Victimology* 1: 181–199.

FOR FURTHER READING

Gender

Belknap, Joanne. *The Invisible Woman: Gender, Crime and Justice.* Belmont, CA: Wadsworth, 2001.

Frohman, Lisa. "Constituting Power in Sexual Assault Cases: Prosecutorial Strategies for Victim Management." *Social Problems* 45 (1998): 393–427.

Greenfeld, Lawrence, and Tracy Snell. "Women Offenders." Washington, D.C. Bureau of Justice Statistics, NCJ 175688, 1999.

Klein, Ethel, Jacquelyn Campbell, Esta Soler, and Marissa Ghez. *Ending Domestic Violence: Changing Public Perceptions/Halting the Epidemic.* Newbury Park, CA: Sage, 1997.

Matoesian, Gregory. *Reproducing Rape: Domination Through Talk in the Courtroom.* Chicago: University of Chicago Press, 1993.

Simon, Rita, and Jean Landis. *The Crimes Women Commit, The Punishments They Receive.* New York: Lexington Books, 1991.

Ward, Colleen. *Attitudes Toward Rape—Feminist and Social Perspectives.* Thousand Oaks, CA: Sage, 1996.

Wonders, Nancy. "Women's Work? The Contradictory Implications of Courses on Women and the Criminal Justice System." *Journal of Criminal Justice Education* 4 (1993): 79–100.

Imprisonment

Morris, Norval. 1974. *The Future of Imprisonment.* Chicago: University of Chicago Press.

Poverty

Backstrand, John, Don Gibbons, and Joseph Jones. "Who Is in Jail? An Examination of the Rabble Hypothesis." *Crime and Delinquency* 38 (1992): 219–229.

Dunaway, R. Gregory, Francis Cullen, Velmer Burton, and T. David Evans. "The Myth of Social Class and Crime Revisited: An Examination of Class and Adult Criminality." *Criminology* 38 (2000): 589–613.

Short, James. *Poverty, Ethnicity, and Violent Crime.* Boulder, CO: Westview Press, 1997.

Race

Cao, Liqun, Anthony Adams, and Vickie Jensen. "A Test of the Black Subculture of Violence Thesis: A Research Note." *Criminology* 34 (1997): 367–379.

Flowers, Ronald. *Minorities and Criminality.* Westport, CT: Greenwood, 1990.

Free, Marvin. *African Americans and the Criminal Justice System.* New York: Garland, 1997.

LaFree, Gary, and Katheryn Russell. "The Argument for Studying Race and Crime." *Journal of Criminal Justice Education* 4 (1993): 273–289.

Lynch, Michael, and E. Britt Patterson, eds. *Justice with Prejudice: Race and Criminal Justice in America.* Albany, NY: Harrow and Heston, 1996.

Mann, Coramae Richey. *Unequal Justice: A Question of Color.* Bloomington: Indiana University Press, 1993.

Walker, Samuel, Cassia Spohn, and Miriam DeLone. *The Color of Justice.* 2d ed. Belmont, CA: Wadsworth, 2000.

Victims

Boles, Anita, and John Patterson. *Improving Community Response to Crime Victims.* Thousand Oaks, CA: Sage, 1997.

Chermak, Steven. *Victims in the News: Crime and the American News Media.* Boulder, CO: Westview Press, 1995.

Davis, Robert, Arthur Lurigio, and Wesley Skogan. *Victims of Crime.* 2d ed. Newbury Park, CA: Sage, 1997.

Fletcher, George. *With Justice for Some: Victims' Rights in Criminal Trials.* New York: Addison-Wesley, 1995.

Horney, Julie, and Cassia Spohn. "The Influence of Blame and Believability Factors on the Processing of Simple versus Aggravated Rape Cases." *Criminology* 34 (1996): 135–162.

McCoy, Candace. *Politics and Plea Bargaining: Victim's Rights in California.* Philadelphia: University of Pennsylvania Press, 1993.

Sarnoff, Susan. *Paying for Crime: The Policies and Possibilities of Crime Victim Reimbursement.* Westport, CT: Praeger, 1996.

Sebba, Leslie. *Third Parties: Victims and the Criminal Justice System.* Columbus: Ohio State University Press, 1996.

Processing
the Accused

THE FIVE CHAPTERS OF PART III FOLLOW THE STEPS OF CRIMINAL PROSE-
cution from arrest to the determination of guilt or innocence. The central
concerns are why many cases are eliminated from the process early and why
most cases end not with a trial but rather with a plea of guilty.

Chapter 10 looks at case attrition. Well before trial, many cases are eliminated
by actions of prosecutors, grand juries, and/or judges.

Chapter 11 focuses on the American bail system, examining why some defendants await trial in jail whereas others receive pretrial release.

Chapter 12 considers the preparation of cases for trial. The primary topics are
discovery and controversial Supreme Court decisions concerning the suppression of evidence.

Chapter 13 discusses plea bargaining—a much publicized but little understood part of the criminal court process. Central topics include why cases are
pled out and whether plea bargaining is fair.

Chapter 14 examines the trial itself: jury selection, presentation of evidence,
and the eventual jury verdict. Even though only a handful of cases go to trial,
jury verdicts nonetheless have a major impact on how the courts exercise
discretion.

. . .

Arrest to Arraignment

LIKE THOUSANDS OF OTHERS ARRESTED ON FRIDAY, DONALD LEE McLaughlin had to wait in jail three to five days before a judge was available to conduct a probable cause hearing. The U.S. Constitution requires a more prompt hearing, argued the public defender for County of Riverside, California. Not practical, countered the lawyer for the county, stressing the realities of the contemporary criminal justice system in large urban areas—thousands of arrests, overcrowded jails, and lack of availability of judges, to say nothing of defense attorneys and prosecutors. It is in this context that the high court had to decide whether a "prompt hearing" meant twenty-four hours or thirty-six hours or forty-eight hours.

County of Riverside v. McLaughlin highlights the importance of the early stages of a felony prosecution. At first glance, though, the numerous preliminary stages of a prosecution seem to be only of procedural interest, with cases moving automatically from arrest to charging through preliminary hearing and grand jury before arriving at the major trial court. But a closer look indicates that at numerous stages during these early proceedings, prosecutors, judges, police officers, and victims have the option of advancing a case to the next step, seeking an alternative disposition, or dropping the case altogether. These screening decisions result in significant case attrition, with half of all felony arrests being dropped at some point after arrest and before arraignment.

This chapter examines the early stages of a criminal case, focusing on when and why case attrition occurs. The discussion begins with crime and the arrests that sometimes follow. Our attention then shifts to events in the courthouse, including initial appearance, charging, preliminary hearing, grand jury, and (for some cases) arraignment in the trial court of general jurisdiction. ■

CRIME

Beginning in the early 1960s, the United States experienced a dramatic increase in crime. For almost two decades, crimes known to the police increased much faster than the growth in population. In the early 1980s, however, the crime rate reached a plateau, and in the 1990s it decreased considerably. The peaks and valleys of the official crime figures, however, are largely irrelevant to the general public. Rather, the public continues to perceive (no matter what the official figures say) that crime is on the increase. These fears are in turn reinforced by extensive media coverage, particularly of violent crime.

The most publicized measure of crime is the Federal Bureau of Investigation's (FBI) yearly publication *Uniform Crime Reports,* which divides criminal offenses into two categories. **Type I offenses** consist of eight crimes and are referred to as **index crimes**. These crimes produce headlines about ris-

ing crime rates. Note that some serious street crimes (such as sale of drugs) are not included. Moreover, white-collar crimes committed primarily by the upper class—fraud and stock manipulations, for instance—are also excluded, even though their economic costs are greater than the costs of crimes committed by the poor. Contrary to public perceptions, most felony arrests are for nonviolent offenses involving burglary and larceny; property crimes outnumber violent offenses by a ratio of eight to one (Federal Bureau of Investigation 2000).

Type II offenses are the less serious, but more numerous, crimes that range from theft to simple assault. Interestingly, drug crimes are counted as Type II offenses.

A major weakness of the *Uniform Crime Reports* is that they are based only on crimes known to the police. But only a fraction of the number of crimes actually committed are reported to the police. Of the personal and household offenses measured in the National Crime Victimization Survey's yearly sample of households, 38 percent had been reported to the police—a rate of reporting that has remained basically unchanged since 1980 (Bureau of Justice Statistics 2000a). What this means is that the official FBI crime statistics actually underestimate the total amount of crime in the United States.

No matter which set of statistics you examine and what you choose to emphasize, the United

Type I offenses: Serious crimes of homicide, rape, arson, aggravated assault, robbery, burglary, auto theft, and larceny, according to the FBI's *Uniform Crime Reports;* also called index crimes.

Index crimes: The specific crimes used by the FBI when reporting the incidence of crime in the United States in the *Uniform Crime Reports.*

States has a much higher level of crime than any other Western industrial democracy. No wonder crime continues to be a concern of the general public and an issue in any number of contests for elective office at all levels of government.

 Edward L. Glaeser, Bruce Sacerdote, "Why Is There More Crime in Cities?"

 For more information about the purposes and advantages of the Uniform Crime Reports and the National Crime Victimization Survey, see "The Nation's Two Crime Measures," available at **http://www.ojp.usdoj.gov/bjs/abstract/ntmc.htm**.

For an up-to-date list of Web links, go to **http://www.wadsworth.com/product/0534563406s**.

ARREST

Of the crimes brought to the attention of the police, 21 percent result in an arrest. The police clearance rate by arrest varies greatly by the type of crime involved. The clearance rate for violent crimes is 50 percent, compared to 18 percent for property crimes (Federal Bureau of Investigation 2000).

Every year the police make an estimated 14 million **arrests** for nontraffic offenses—mostly minor ones such as simple assault, public drunkenness, disorderly conduct, petty theft, and possession of small amounts of illegal drugs. However, 2.3 million of these arrests are for the serious crimes of homicide, rape, arson, aggravated assault, robbery, burglary, auto theft, and larceny. Figure 10-1 displays recent arrest data by major categories of relevance to the major trial courts.

These arrests are the overwhelming source of criminal cases filed in the courts; only a handful of prosecutions begin with an indictment, for example. Figure 10-2 summarizes the steps of criminal procedure.

Quality of Arrests

The police have a lot to do with what happens in court after arrest. For years, studies have called for

Arrest: The physical taking into custody of a suspected law violator or juvenile.

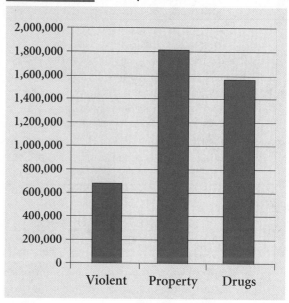

FIGURE 10-1 Felony Arrests

SOURCE: Federal Bureau of Investigation. 2000. *Uniform Crime Reports for the United States—1999* (Washington, D.C.: U.S. Government Printing Office, 2000).

improvement in the investigative and evidence-gathering functions of the police. Prosecutors in particular often complain that the police tend to be sloppy in their investigations, sometimes missing important evidence and improperly seizing, marking, or storing the items they do gather. A review of over 14,000 arrests in the District of Columbia reached the following conclusions (Forst, Lucianovic, and Cox 1977):

- When the arresting officer recovers tangible evidence, the prosecutor is considerably more likely to convict the defendant.

- When the police locate cooperative witnesses for the prosecutor, the probability of conviction is significantly enhanced.

- When the police are able to make the arrest soon after the offense, tangible evidence is more often recovered, and conviction is more likely.

Individual police officers have varying degrees of success in providing the prosecutor with sufficient evidence for a conviction. A seven-city study found that 12 percent of the officers produced half of all convictions, whereas 22 percent produced no arrests resulting in conviction. This difference in performance did not spring from the personal characteristics of the officers or their experience. Rather,

FIGURE 10-2   **Steps of Criminal Procedure**

	Law on the Books	*Law in Action*
Crime	Any violation of the criminal law.	
	• *Felony* The more serious of the two types of criminal behavior, usually bearing a possible penalty of one year or more in prison.	• Property crimes outnumber violent offenses by eight to one among Type 1 offenses.
	• *Misdemeanor* Lesser of the two basic types of crime, usually bearing a possible penalty of no more than one year in jail.	• The most common misdemeanors include public drunkenness, disorderly conduct, assault, and theft.
Arrest	The physical taking into custody of a suspected law violator.	• 2.3 millions felony arrests yearly. • 11.7 million misdemeanor arrests yearly.
Initial appearance	The accused is told of the charges, advised of rights, bail is set, and a date for the preliminary hearing is set.	• Occurs in lower courts. • Many misdemeanor defendants plead guilty.
Charging	Formal criminal charges against defendant stating which criminal law(s) was violated.	• From arrest to arraignment half of felony arrests are terminated, downgraded, or diverted in some manner.
	• *Information* Formal accusation of a crime made by the prosecutor.	• Defendant's chances of getting off are better during these private sessions in the prosecutor's office than during public trials in the courthouse.
	• *Complaint* Formal accusation of a crime supported by oath or affirmation of the victim.	
	• *Arrest warrant* An official document signed by a judge accusing an individual of a crime and authorizing law enforcement personnel to take the person into custody.	• Complaints very rarely used in felony prosecutions.
	Prosecutor is supposed to prosecute all known criminal conduct.	Presecutor exercises discretion in deciding which charges should be filed.
	Prosecutor controls charging decision.	Some prosecutors allow police input into the charging decision.
Preliminary hearing	A pretrial hearing to determine if there is probable cause to hold the accused for further proceedings.	In many jurisdictions the preliminary hearing is brief with a strong probability that the case will proceed.
Grand jury	Required for felony prosecutions in nineteen states and the federal courts.	• Typically not a major decision maker.
	Grand juries have extensive powers, not possessed by law enforcement, to investigate crimes.	• Prosecutor dominates grand jury proceedings, deciding which cases will be presented and which charges filed.
	• *Indictment* Formal accusation of a crime, made against a person by a grand jury, upon the request of the prosecutor.	• The investigatory powers of the grand jury are most likely to be used in cases involving major drug rings, governmental corruption, and significant white-collar crime.
	• *Subpoena* Court order requiring the person to either appear before the grand jury and/or produce documents.	
Arraignment	Stage of the criminal process in which the defendant is formally informed of the charges pending and must enter a plea.	• A significant milestone because it indicates that the evidence against the defendant is strong and a conviction is likely.

CRIME & PUNISHMENT

The Commonwealth of Massachusetts v. Darnell Jameson

Darnell Jameson is arrested after making a $100 drug sale to an undercover agent. A search warrant later turns up a large quantity of cocaine and a handgun. Jameson cooperates with the police in contacting his major drug supplier, but the sting goes awry. Jameson pleads guilty to three charges: distribution and manufacture of a Class B substance; possession of a controlled substance; and possession of a dangerous weapon without a permit. After watching the CD, you should be able to discuss the following questions:

1. What factors indicate that Darnell Jameson is a good candidate for drug treatment? What factors indicate that he is not a good candidate for drug treatment? In what ways does answering these questions largely determine the sentence to be imposed?

2. What is your reaction to Darnell Jameson's statement? Do you think he is sincere when he says he wants to put this behind him, or do you think he is merely saying what he hopes will produce leniency?

3. In choosing the sentence, what weight do you give to Jameson's cooperation with the police?

4. Both prosecution and defense agree that Darnell Jameson has a substance abuse problem (although there are slight differences in how this problem is articulated). They differ as to the response, however. How do the sentencing arguments reflect the crime control model and due process model?

5. How do the sentencing arguments reflect different understandings of the war on drugs?

6. Would the Jameson case be better handled in a drug court?

the most important factor was the successful officers' "persistence in finding and interviewing witnesses and in supporting witnesses through the trial, as well as being particularly conscious of the gathering and maintenance of evidence" (Forst et al. 1981).

Police departments also differ in the quality of arrests referred to the district attorney. When prosecutors deal with numerous police departments, some departments often have a better record of forwarding evidence necessary for a successful conviction. In Salt Lake City, for example, prosecutors accept 85 percent

of the felony arrests made by the sheriff's office, compared with 67 percent of those made by the police department. The same pattern appears in Los Angeles: 86 percent acceptance for sheriff's arrests, compared with 60 percent for police arrests (Brosi 1979). Such statistics support prosecutors' perceptions that some police agencies conduct more thorough investigations than others (Neubauer 1974b).

 The ACLU provides an online *bustcard,* which discusses what to do if you are stopped by the police: **http://www.aclu.org/issues/criminal/bustcardtext. html**.

For an up-to-date list of Web links, go to **http:// www.wadsworth.com/product/0534563406s**.

Swelling Criminal Dockets

Even though serious crime has decreased significantly during the last decade, court dockets keep growing. As stressed in Chapter 5, the workload of the criminal courts is large and growing.

- In the federal courts, the number of suspects prosecuted by U.S. attorneys more than doubled between 1980 and 1998 with 78,172 persons prosecuted annually (Bureau of Justice Statistics 2000b).

- In state courts, felony filings increased 65 percent from 1984 to 1998 (Ostrom and Kauder 1999).

Most state trial court systems were unable to keep pace with the increasing volume of criminal cases. The number of cases disposed of each year is less than the number filed. According to the National Center for State Courts (1993, 13), this growth in caseloads has serious implications: "Cases are being handled less expeditiously than previously and courts are accumulating problems that must be confronted in subsequent years."

From the early 1980s until now, a good deal of the growth in felony caseloads has been drug related. Every year the police arrest 1,550,000 persons for drug-related offenses, a 125 percent increase since 1980. On the other hand, the number of suspects investigated for non-drug-related violations increased by only 76 percent during the same period (Bureau of Justice Statistics 2000b). The results are readily obvious when one examines court dockets.

- The number of federal suspects prosecuted for drug violations increased 160 percent between 1980 and 1993. Today, 43 percent of all federal prosecutions involve drugs.

- In the state courts, drug trafficking convictions account for one fifth of all felony convictions, which is more than double the number in the 1980s (Bureau of Justice Statistics 1995).

The massive increase in law enforcement efforts directed against drug use is clearly overloading the criminal courts. In federal courts, new drug laws that impose much harsher automatic sentences are making defendants more reluctant to plead guilty and much more willing to go through long trials. State prosecutors in large urban areas likewise see the enormous effort against drugs as sapping resources, overloading the system, and making it difficult to respond adequately to other types of crime. The major response by courts has been the creation of drug courts (Chapter 4).

Of all the social problems that wind their way into the courts in one form or another, none has a bigger impact than drugs. Irrespective of whether the drugs are legal (alcohol) or illegal (cocaine), a substantial number of prosecutions are directly or indirectly related to drug use/abuse. As important as drug policy is to the judiciary, however, it is difficult to provide an objective assessment, much less suggest viable alternatives (see Controversy: Is It Time to Rethink the War on Drugs?).

 Spectrum, "Drug Crime: The Impact on State Courts"

INITIAL APPEARANCE

The **initial appearance** occurs within a few hours or a few days of arrest. It is at this stage that most misdemeanor defendants enter a plea of guilty and are sentenced immediately (Chapter 18). For those arrested on a felony, however, a plea is not possible because the initial appearance occurs in a trial court

Initial appearance: Shortly after arrest the suspect is brought before a judicial official who informs the person of the reason for the arrest, and if the case is a felony, bond is set.

of limited jurisdiction, which has no authority to accept a plea. Thus, the initial appearance is typically a brief affair, as little is known about the crime or the alleged criminal. At times suspects insist on telling their side of the story, but the judge typically cautions that anything said can be used against the defendant. Lawyers provide the same advice. One author has likened the sea of humanity in initial appearance court to "Hell's Waiting Room" (see A Day in Court on page 254).

In all large jurisdictions, and many medium-sized ones as well, the public defender's office assigns an assistant to the initial appearance court to provide instant legal advice for the indigents who need it. Private attorneys may also appear, but they typically tell the court that they are representing the defendant only for this particular hearing (an indication that an agreement on payment of fees has yet to be arranged).

CHARGING

The criminal court process begins with the filing of a formal written accusation alleging that a specified person or persons committed a specific offense or offenses. The **charging document** includes a brief description of the date and location of the offense. All the essential elements (*corpus delicti*) of the crime must be specified. These accusations satisfy the Sixth Amendment provision that a defendant be given information upon which to prepare a defense. Applicable state and federal law governs technical wording, procedures for making minor amendments, and so on.

There are four types of charging documents: complaint, information, arrest warrant, and indictment (which will be discussed later). Which one is used depends on the severity of the offense, applicable state law, and local customs. A **complaint** must be supported by oath or affirmation of either the victim or the arresting officer. It is most commonly

Charging document: An information, indictment, or complaint that states the formal criminal charge against a named defendant(s).

Complaint: In civil law, the first paper filed in a lawsuit. In criminal law, a charge signed by the victim that a person named has committed a specified offense.

CONTROVERSY

Is It Time to Rethink the War on Drugs?

U.S. drug policy dates from the Harrison Narcotics Act of 1914, when the federal government for the first time outlawed certain drugs. But modern strategy dates to 1968 when President Nixon was elected after a campaign denouncing a breakdown in "law and order." The administration soon announced a war on drugs, largely targeting heroin being imported from the Mideast. In various ways all subsequent presidents have waged a war on drugs. President Carter focused on marijuana. President Reagan announced another war on drugs, and the first lady was identified with a "Just Say No" program. President Bush was the first to establish a drug czar. President Clinton elevated the position to cabinet status.

The war on drug rhetoric emphasizes the social problems associated with drug abuse. There is no doubt that drug addiction produces untold human suffering in the United States. And there is little doubt that drugs are also associated with crime. The National Institute of Justice's Arrestee Drug Abuse Monitoring (ADAM, for short) reports that approximately two thirds of those arrested show evidence of recent use of illegal drugs (crack, methamphetamines, marijuana, for example) and/or legal drugs (alcohol primarily). As a result, a substantial proportion of offenders need drug treatment (Falkin, Prendergast, and Anglin 1994). (See Controversy: Should Defendants Be Forced to Take a Drug Test? in Chapter 11).

The association of drug abuse with crime has become an axiom among the general public, but research suggests a more ambiguous pattern. For one, a large number of people who use illegal drugs hold jobs, and the only laws they violate are those making drug possession illegal. Moreover, the notion that reducing drug supplies will reduce certain types of other crimes fails to take into account that drug use and abuse is a way of life for some. Thus, most researchers suggest that drug use acts as an accelerator of some antisocial behavior such as crime, and merely eliminating drug use (which is unlikely) would not result in a substantial reduction in crime.

Historians suggest that medical or scientific knowledge about the harm of drugs has never played a significant role in formulating U.S. drug policy. Rather U.S. policy has been driven by the desire to control groups considered threats to the existing social order. Thus the Harrison Act targeted opium (used by Chinese in California), marijuana (smoked by Mexican Americans in the Southwest), and cocaine (allegedly being used by blacks in the South).

Viewing drug policy not in terms of the physical dangers of drugs but rather the perceived social dangers from those using drugs explains why it is so difficult to differentiate between legal drugs and illegal drugs, and also confounds any distinction between drug use and drug abuse. Moreover, this perspective suggests that as social perceptions change so does drug policy. Prohibition outlawed alcohol but has long since been repealed. More recently cocaine initially caused little social concern when it was being used by stars and starlets in Hollywood but sparked great alarm when it spread to young males in the ghettos.

The direct association of drugs with crime, plus their indirect link to marginal groups, suggests why the war on drugs enjoys widespread public support. Beneath the broad consensus supporting the war on drugs, however, there is a growing disquiet. Off the record, some criminal justice officials guardedly express reservations about the war on drugs. In print, some scholars increasingly voice the urgent need to rethink the war on drugs. The following three books reflect the concerns of those who apparently swim upstream in criticizing the war on drugs.

In *Drug War Politics: The Price of Denial,* Eva Bertram and her colleagues (1996) argue that punitive approaches that seek to control the supply of drugs by massive interdiction efforts and punishment have been a failure. Despite expenditures of billions on drug control annually in the United States, the supply of drugs reaching the country is high, and the availability of drugs to users has not been affected. Failure, however, only convinces the advocates of the war on drugs that greater efforts need to be taken. In short, in the war on drugs, nothing succeeds like failure.

It is not just the failure to reduce drug supply (or demand) that concerns critics, but also the social impact of these efforts. In *Reckoning: Drugs, the Cities, and the American Future,* sociologist Elliott Currie condemns current drug policy for destroying inner-city communities:

The failure of American drug policy is depressingly apparent. Twenty years of the "war" on drugs have jammed our jails and prisons, immobilized the criminal justice system in many cities, swollen the ranks of the criminalized and unemployable minority poor, and diverted desperately needed resources from other social needs. Yet the drug crisis is still very much with us. (1993, 3)

(Chapter 15 will further examine whether drug prosecutions fall disproportionately on minorities.)

Making an objective assessment of the war on drugs is unlikely, however. In *The Politics of Sin: Drugs, Alcohol, and Public Policy,* Kenneth Meier (1994) argues that as a political issue the drug problem has advantages "because it is so readily transformed into new and yet more alarming images" (Sharp 1994, 14). In short, drug policy has joined Social Security as a third-rail issue of American politics—touch it and you die. By linking drugs with sin, the issue has become a moral crusade in which facts are irrelevant and moral rhetoric everything.

Critics of the war on drugs do not necessarily advocate drug legalization, a proposal that is so abstract that it fails to offer practical alternatives. Rather, Bertram and her colleagues suggest that we should replace the punitive law enforcement approach with a public health approach. In short, laws outlawing drugs, particularly major drug imports, would continue to play a role, but more emphasis would be placed on prevention and treatment. In this regard, there is a major concern that existing substance abuse programs, although more than adequate to handle those whose health insurance will pay for coverage, is totally inadequate for those who have no resources to pay for such treatment.

The public support and the private disquiet over the war on drugs reflects the differences between the crime control and due process models of criminal justice. Three points—focusing on causes, equality, and punishment—are at issue.

- The crime control model begins with the judgment that drug abuse is caused by a breakdown of individual responsibility; hence Nancy Reagan's often repeated phrase "Just Say No." The due process model views substance abuse as a disease; just saying no to diabetes is clearly counterproductive and so is just saying no to addiction.

- According to the crime control model, the solution is punishment. Arrest and conviction will serve as a lesson to the violator and will also deter others. The due process model replies that filling the prisons is costly and ineffective. It is therefore more effective and also less costly to emphasize rehabilitation programs.

- The due process model is very concerned that current drug policies fall unequally on racial minorities. The crime control model counters with seeming banal indifference: "You do the crime you serve the time."

What do you think? Does the nation need to change its drug policies to place more emphasis on public health matters (treatment and prevention) and less on law enforcement (arrest, conviction, and imprisonment)? Asked another way, is drug policy an effective way of dealing with drug use/abuse or an excuse to ignore the problems of the poor and minorities?

Gary E. Johnson, "The Case for Drug Legalization"

Charles B. Rangel, "Why Drug Legalization Should Be Opposed"

To continue the debate point your browser to the following sites, which offer dramatically different views on U.S. drug policy:

The Office of Drug Control Policy is the White House agency that spearheads the war on drugs: **http://www.whitehousedrugpolicy.gov/**.

The Drug Reform Coordination Network offers its drug library at **http://www.druglibrary.org/**.

For an up-to-date list of Web links, go to **http://www.wadsworth.com/product/0534563406s**.

---

used in prosecuting misdemeanor offenses or city ordinance violations. An **information** is virtually identical in form to the complaint, except that it is signed by the prosecutor. It is required in felony prosecutions in most states that do not use the grand jury. In grand jury states, an information is used for initiating felony charges pending grand jury action. An **arrest warrant** is issued by a judicial officer—usually a lower court judge. On rare occasions, the warrant is issued prior to arrest, but for most street crimes, the police arrest the suspect and then apply for an arrest warrant. Some states require that the prosecutor approve the request in writing before an arrest warrant can be issued.

Information: A formal accusation charging someone with the commission of a crime, signed by a prosecuting attorney, which has the effect of bringing the person to trial.

Arrest warrant: A document issued by a judicial officer authorizing the arrest of a specific person.

A DAY IN COURT

"Hell's Waiting Room"

 It's past midnight and the bench is full. At one end of the well-worn pine slab on which new prisoners sit, a gaunt woman with a deeply lined face slumps against the wall muttering and coughing, her face covered by a gauze hospital mask. Three hookers, regular visitors to the San Francisco County Jail, are taking off their spike heels—potential weapons—and trading them in for jail-issue pale blue polyester socks tossed to them by a sheriff's deputy.

"I didn't do nothing. Nothing!" says a young man in handcuffs waiting to be booked. "All I did was not check in with my parole officer and you throw me around," he says in the general direction of a group of San Francisco cops standing at the desk.

When Randy Duane Nichols is called, a roughly handsome man with sandy red hair rises from the bench and steps forward to one of the three booking windows to be processed by a deputy. A jailhouse tattoo—a swirl of roses and his initials—adorns his neck. Nichols smirks, swaggers, and stares defiantly as his mug shot is taken. Unlike the others on the bench, Nichols has a long history of criminal activity that includes drug charges, assaults, and long stretches in state prison, a deputy notes. Captured this evening during one of the periodic police sweeps for parolees wanted back by the State Department of Corrections, Nichols is headed back to prison in a few days.

"You're on the bus, Gus," says the deputy as Nichols is led across the hall to the process tank, the cramped, fetid holding area for male prisoners awaiting assignment to a cell.

Inmates like Nichols, the hookers, the gasping drug addict, and those who loudly protest their innocence are an every hour fact of life inside the jail. From the mentally ill to homeless drunks to violent felons to parole violators returning to prison—the county jail is the processing center for anyone charged with a crime in San Francisco.

Over a three-week period spent inside County Jail One, the intake facility for San Francisco prisoners on the sixth floor of the Hall of Justice on Bryant Street, the *Examiner* was able to witness the inner workings of the lock-up. It was an education in the lives of the city's underclass, a world of petty thievery, poverty, madness, and despair.

Mostly hidden from public view, the jail is like a massive sieve for alleged wrongdoers caught by the police. The bench, where all prisoners begin their jail sojourn, could be the waiting room in hell. Gathered there are what sociologist, prison critic, and former convict John Irwin calls the rabble of society, those persons too detached, disreputable or lost to make it on the outside. Sometimes, they're just plain unlucky. . . .

The Traffic

The seemingly endless traffic of prisoners in and out of custody makes for a tense atmosphere. Dank hallways echo with the metallic clank of jail doors opening and closing, a noisy elevator creaks back and forth bringing police officers and their prisoners into the jail. The air inside is hot and close, ventilation is poor, and the rank smell of body odor and sweat is a constant.

Many of those here "are not normal," says Sheriff Hennessey. "There are a lot of drunks, sick people, and addicts. A lot of them are mad as hell at being there. It can be a stressful environment, a harsh, ugly world." For many of those dragged into the jail, it is a place to sleep, to receive a little medical care, perhaps to see a psychiatrist. For others, it is the first stop on the way to a long prison term. Sheriff Hennessey estimates that a quarter of the inmates are in need of psychiatric care and that three-quarters have a serious drug problem.

Says Alisa Riker, the director of a jail program to release misdemeanor inmates on their own recognizance: "The jail is an incredibly expensive homeless shelter, an incredibly expensive detox center, an incredibly expensive drug treatment center and it's an incredibly inept way to handle social problems. But these problems are not being dealt with in other ways."

SOURCE: A. Lin Neumann, "Hell's Waiting Room," *San Francisco Examiner* (September 28, 1998).

Law on the Books: Prosecutorial Control

Through the charging decision, the prosecutor controls the doors to the courthouse. He or she can decide whether charges should be filed and what the proper charge should be. Although the law demands prosecution for "all known criminal conduct," the courts have traditionally granted prosecutors wide discretion in deciding whether to file charges (Baker 1933). For example, there are no legislative or judicial standards governing which cases merit prosecution and which should be declined. Moreover, if a prosecutor refuses to file charges, no review of this decision is possible; courts have consistently refused to order a prosecutor to proceed with a case.

Law in Action: Police Influence

Although the prosecutor has the legal authority to dominate the charging process, some choose to share this authority with the police. An American Bar Foundation study concluded that some prosecutors defer to the police (Miller 1969). In these communities the police file criminal charges with minimal supervision by the prosecutor. In essence, these prosecutors have transferred their decision-making power to the police (Mellon, Jacoby, and Brewer 1981). In other jurisdictions, the prosecutor retains the formal authority to file charges, but the police influence the prosecutor's decision. Studies of Oakland (Skolnick 1993) and Seattle (Cole 1970) indicate that the police and prosecutor jointly discuss cases before charges are filed. The police have considerable influence during such interchanges, pressuring prosecutors to overcharge defendants or to file charges even though the evidence is weak.

In communities where prosecutors choose to control the filing of criminal charges, a substantial percentage of persons arrested are released without the filing of criminal charges. This author analyzed all nontraffic arrests for a month in a medium-sized Illinois community and found that a third of police arrests resulted in no criminal charges being filed (Neubauer 1974a). Another study likewise concluded that in court systems with strong prosecutorial screening, up to half of all felony arrests do not result in criminal charges (Boland, Mahanna, and Sones 1992).

Law in Controversy: Should Prosecutors Set High Standards for Charging?

One of the major recommendations of the National Advisory Commission on Criminal Justice Standards and Goals (1973) was that prosecutors should exercise the dominant role in the charging decision. The primary justification is efficiency. Removing cases that are weak or do not warrant prosecution

eliminates the need for judges and other court personnel to devote time to them. Moreover, civilian witnesses and police officers are not required to appear, which translates into additional savings on police overtime and allows civilians and police alike to use their time in more productive ways.

However, the law-on-the-books argument in favor of prosecutorial control of the charging decision on the basis of "efficiency" neglects a key element of law in action:

Those who have studied the pretrial screening process have failed to see it as part of either the prosecutorial system or the criminal justice system. The result is, in part, a failure to see pretrial screening as part of a continuum rather than as an isolated act and as a means to an end, the disposition of a case, rather than as a goal in itself. Screening cannot be separated from the larger system of which it is part if it is to be evaluated. (Jacoby 1977, 12)

In this connection, the importance of the relationship between the police and the prosecutor must not be overlooked. Police departments resist prosecutorial control of the charging decision. Every arrest rejected by the prosecutor is viewed as an implicit criticism of the arresting officer. When District Attorney Harry Connick established a tough screening policy in New Orleans, the case rejection rate went up to 46 percent. The police responded publicly, refusing to believe that they were "wrong" in half the arrests they made. Such practices can have consequences at the polls. In another jurisdiction where a DA rejected a lot of arrest warrant requests, it upset the police. Thus when he started to run for reelection, he found he had no support from the Fraternal Order of the Police and dropped out of the race. The message was clear: "If you get on the wrong side of the cops, they'll screw you" (Flemming, Nardulli, and Eisenstein 1992, 46).

Moreover, in some jurisdictions the police rely on the initial charging policies of the prosecutor to protect them from civil lawsuits for false arrest. Accommodating prosecutors file charges they would otherwise reject, just to convince the defendant that the arrest was lawful, or require the defendant to sign a release waiving any claim of false arrest. Tough prosecutorial screening policies disrupt such arrangements. In addition, the police may rely on overcharging as a means of developing snitches: They promise to drop charges if the arrestee agrees to cooperate. Prosecutorial dominance of the charging decision obviously alters such practices (McDonald 1976). As a result, some prosecutors choose to maintain good working relationships with their police departments and to demonstrate that they are part of the law enforcement team by granting police a major voice in the charging decision.

PRELIMINARY HEARING

An arrested person is entitled to a timely hearing before a neutral judge to determine whether probable cause exists to detain the defendant prior to trial (*Gerstein v. Pugh* 1975). But how timely is timely? An individual may be jailed for up to forty-eight hours without a hearing before a magistrate to determine whether his or her arrest was proper. Justice O'Connor's opinion cited burdened criminal justice systems and said local courts need flexibility to combine the probable cause hearing with a bail hearing or arraignment (see Case Close-Up: *County of Riverside v. McLaughlin* and a Prompt Hearing before a Magistrate).

Law on the Books: Weighing Probable Cause

The **preliminary hearing** (or *preliminary examination,* as it is called in some states) represents the first time that a case is reviewed by someone other than a law enforcement official. Usually held before a lower court judge, the preliminary hearing is designed "to prevent hasty, malicious, improvident, and oppressive prosecutions, to protect the person charged from open and public accusations of crime, to avoid both for the defendant and the public the expense of a public trial, to save the defendant from the humiliation and anxiety involved in public prosecution, and to discover whether or not there are substantial grounds upon which a prosecution may be based" (*Thies v. State* 1922). In states with no grand jury, the preliminary hearing is the sole procedure for determining whether sufficient evidence exists to justify holding the defendant. In grand jury states,

the preliminary hearing **binds over** the accused for possible indictment. A magistrate's ruling that there is insufficient evidence does not necessarily end the case; the prosecutor can take the case directly to the grand jury (Gilboy 1984).

During a preliminary hearing, the state does not have to prove the defendant guilty beyond a reasonable doubt, as would be required during a trial. Rather, all that is necessary is that the prosecutor establish **probable cause** that a crime has been committed and that the defendant committed it. Usually, hearsay evidence (secondhand evidence) is admissible. Generally, the defense does not have the right to cross-examine witnesses, although some states and some judges permit attorneys to ask witnesses questions. The situation in Chicago illustrates the diversity of practices. During most preliminary hearings, evidentiary rules are not strictly enforced. But in murder cases, the judge permits hearsay testimony only for minor matters. For critical matters, such as the identification of the assailant, the judge insists on the testimony of witnesses to the occurrence (Gilboy 1984).

Law in Action: Variations in Using the Preliminary Hearing

Defense attorneys weigh several factors in deciding whether to demand a preliminary hearing or waive it (Flemming 1986). Practices of the local prosecutor are one important consideration. If the district attorney's files are open and plea-bargaining policies are well known, it is viewed as time-consuming and redundant to hold a preliminary hearing. Second, strategic and tactical considerations are involved. Waiving the preliminary hearing may reflect an assessment that the information to be gained from holding a preliminary hearing does not outweigh the potential damage to the defendant's case (for example, the publicity that may surround a rape case). A third factor is client control. Defense attorneys sometimes insist on a preliminary hearing to

---

Preliminary hearing: A pretrial hearing to determine whether there is probable cause to hold the accused for the grand jury.

Bind over: If at the preliminary hearing the judge believes that sufficient probable cause exists to hold a criminal defendant, the accused is said to be bound over for trial.

Probable cause: Standard used to determine whether a crime has been committed and whether there is sufficient evidence to believe a specific individual committed it.

CASE CLOSE-UP

County of Riverside v. McLaughlin
and a Prompt Hearing before a Magistrate

 Beyond the bare facts that he was arrested in Riverside County, California, little is known about Donald Lee McLaughlin. Who he was, why he was arrested, and whatever happened to his case quickly became irrelevant. For whatever reason, the public defender's office decided that the facts of his case made him an ideal candidate to be used as a plaintiff in a suit filed in federal court. The office was prepared to challenge countywide practices; a plaintiff was needed and at the last minute McLaughlin's name was inserted. Thus, McLaughlin's name went first in a class action lawsuit filed on behalf of McLaughlin and all other individuals in the same situation. The class action status was important for two reasons. First, it meant that the lawsuit could be heard in court even after his particular case had been resolved. Otherwise the lawsuit would be dismissed as moot (no longer needing a decision because the case had already been decided). Second, the class action status meant that any potential decision by a court would affect not just the individual plaintiff but all others who were arrested in the same situation. Class action suits, like this one, are the typical way of bringing lawsuits seeking systematic changes in policy. In short, the particulars of Donald Lee McLaughlin's case were much less important than what happened to defendants like him in the future.

McLaughlin v. County of Riverside raised the difficult question of how prompt is prompt. California law mandated a probable cause hearing of all those arrested without a warrant within forty-eight hours of arrest, weekends and holidays excluded. Thus, an individual arrested late in the week may in some cases be held for as long as five days before appearing before a neutral judicial official; over the Thanksgiving holiday a seven-day delay is possible. The U.S. district court agreed with part of McLaughlin's plight and ordered a probable cause hearing within thirty-six hours of arrest. Having lost in the trial court, the county appealed (hence the names changed place, with the county now listed as the moving party). The Ninth Circuit affirmed the district court's decision, and the county appealed to the U.S. Supreme Court, which granted cert.

Although *County of Riverside v. McLaughlin* appears to be a minor quibble over a few hours, the underlying issues are much more fundamental, centering on where to strike the balance between an individual's right to liberty and society's need for effective law enforcement. The Supreme Court has allowed police officers to make arrests, based upon their own assessment of probable cause, without first obtaining a warrant. To counterbalance this privilege, the Court established that an individual arrested without a warrant is entitled to a prompt judicial determination of probable cause afterward. In *Gerstein v. Pugh* they wrestled with this issue and held that the defendant was entitled to a timely determination. The Court ruled that the thirty-day wait in Florida was too long, but failed to be much more specific. As a result, Gerstein "created a nationwide divergence in postarrest and pretrial procedures and subjected some individuals to what numerous courts and commentators believed to be unjustifiably prolonged restraints of liberty following their arrests" (Perkins and Jamieson 1995, 535).

Justice Sandra Day O'Connor, the most centrist justice on the Court (Chapter 17), wrote the opinion of the Court, and her opinion reflects the ability to strike a compromise. The earlier decision in *Gerstein,* she wrote, provided flexibility to law enforcement but not a blank check. She recognized that the standard of "prompt" has proven to be vague and therefore has not provided sufficient guidance. In the future, prompt shall be defined in most circumstances as forty-eight hours—a time period she labeled as "practical compromise between the rights of individuals and the realities of law enforcement." Because of paperwork, the transporting of prisoners from jails to courthouses, and the availability of magistrates, hearings cannot be arranged instantly. Moreover, records will have to be reviewed, charging documents drafted, appearance of counsel arranged, and bail set. To O'Connor a twenty-four-hour rule would compel local governments across the nation to speed up their criminal justice mechanisms substantially, presumably by allotting local tax dollars to hire additional police officers and magistrates. What is perhaps most striking is how forthright the opinion is in recognizing that law on the books must take into account law in action.

What is most interesting about the four dissenters is their ideological mix. The three moderates agreed with the lower courts that the thirty-six hour standard was best. But Justice Antonin Scalia, one of the Court's most conservative members, would fix the time at twenty-four hours, a standard he says existed in the common law from the early 1800s.

COURT TV

Campbell v. Florida

Driving While Black

Nathan Campbell, a twenty-seven-year veteran police officer, was arrested by a white member of the Orlando, Florida, sheriff's office. The officer claims Campbell committed two traffic violations. Campbell counters that he was stopped because of his race. Campbell is charged with a variety of crimes, including resisting arrest. As you watch the video, ask yourself the following questions:

1. Given that the traffic stop was made at night and the driver was going at high speed, how credible is Campbell's claim that he was pulled over because he was black? Conversely, would the white officer have responded differently if the police officer he stopped had been white?

2. Going beyond the specifics of the Campbell case, reflect on how the traffic practices of the Orlando sheriff's office relate to Controversy: Is It Time to Rethink the War on Drugs?, which is presented in this chapter. To what extent does the war on drugs have a black face?

3. In the stops featured in this video, did the police engage in illegal search and seizures (Chapter 12)? Did the police have probable cause to search Campbell's vehicle after arrest?

4. To what extent does the jury's compromise verdict reflect trials as balancing wheels (Chapter 14)? Would the jury verdict have been different if the police video did not exist?

impress on their client the gravity of the situation. Finally, the preliminary hearing gives the defense attorney an overview of the evidence against the client and provides the opportunity for discovery (see Chapter 12).

The tactical decision of holding or waiving the preliminary hearing highlights the complexity of the preliminary hearing from the law-in-action perspective. Although the legal purpose of the preliminary hearing is simple, the actual conduct of these hearings is quite complex. In some courts, they may last an hour or more; in others, they consume only a few minutes. In some jurisdictions, preliminary hearings are an important stage in the proceedings, but in others, they are a perfunctory step, in which probable cause is found to exist in virtually every case. This variability makes it difficult to generalize about the importance of the preliminary hearing, but studies do reveal four major patterns.

Preliminary Hearings Seldom Held

In some jurisdictions, preliminary hearings are almost never held. The federal courts are the prime example. The majority of federal criminal cases begin not with an arrest but with a grand jury indictment, which means there is no need for a preliminary hearing. But even when there is a street arrest, it is common practice in federal courts to seek a grand jury indictment before the ten-day period required for conducting the preliminary hearing. Thus, probable cause hearings are held in a very small percentage of cases in the federal courts.

Short and Routine Preliminary Hearings

It is most common for preliminary hearings to be short and routine. A typical case involves a police detective testifying (from a police report he did not write) to the effect that Mrs. Jones reported a crime committed. Then a minimal amount of information is presented as to why the police arrested Mr. Smith. The total time consumed is generally no more than a minute or two. Such short and routine preliminary hearings seldom result in a finding that probable cause does not exist. This author's own study of Prairie City, Illinois, for example, documented that only 2 percent of the defendants had their cases terminated at the preliminary hearing (Neubauer 1974b). Defense attorneys often view such judicial proceedings as useless and are therefore inclined to waive them.

Preliminary Hearing as a Minitrial

For decades, Los Angeles has used the preliminary hearing in a unique way. A minitrial takes place, in which the prosecution calls all of its principal witnesses, and the defense is allowed to call witnesses and cross-examine the state's witnesses. Despite the time-consuming process of conducting a minitrial, it is rare that the court finds no probable cause; about 10 percent of cases are dismissed or reduced to a misdemeanor at this stage (Greenwood et al. 1976). This low rate reflects extensive prosecutorial screening before the preliminary hearing. Although it screens few cases out of the system, the preliminary hearing in Los Angeles has a major impact on the court process, because a transcript of the proceedings is made. Many cases are disposed of not by a guilty plea or a trial but by the opposing parties submitting the transcript to a judge (submission on the transcript). After reading the transcript, the judge usually finds the defendant guilty after a brief bench trial (Mather 1974).

Preliminary Hearing as a Screening Device

In most jurisdictions, the preliminary hearing is largely ceremonial, resulting in few cases being screened out of the criminal process; but in a few courts, it is quite significant. In Brooklyn, for example, the preliminary hearing is a major stage of the proceedings. Because the prosecutor has not previously reviewed the case, it is left to the judge to separate the strong cases from the weak ones; 65 percent of felony cases are disposed of by dismissal or reduction to a less serious misdemeanor during the preliminary hearing (McIntyre and Lippman 1970).

 The Delaware Public Defender offers a useful Web site providing an overview of procedures in felony cases: **http://www.state.de.us/pubdefen/jdeffelo.htm**.

For an up-to-date list of Web links, go to **http://www.wadsworth.com/product/0534563406s**.

Law in Controversy: Political Realities

McIntyre (1968) explored what he called the "judicial dominance of the charging process" in Chicago. After a routine felony arrest, the Chicago police alone decided whether to file a complaint. Thus, the state's attorney did not review a case prior to filing. It was therefore the judge's responsibility to screen cases. Of the approximately 16,000 preliminary hearing cases yearly in Chicago, 20 percent were bound over to the grand jury. Of the remainder, a large number were dismissed or reduced to misdemeanor charges. (In the 1980s, however, a new state's attorney installed a Felony Review Unit to give his office greater control over the workload.) McIntyre argues that the judicial dominance of the charge process was based on important political realities. The judges "were less susceptible to criticisms for showing leniency" than were the police or prosecutor. Thus, the preliminary hearing allowed the police to build an impressive record of "crime clearance rates," unhampered by a lack of prosecution. At the same time, these procedures allowed the prosecutor to point to a high conviction rate (after the preliminary hearing) without the necessity of

making decisions that could be viewed as unduly lenient.

GRAND JURY

Whereas grand juries make accusations, trial juries decide guilt or innocence. Institutions similar to grand juries existed in ancient Greece, Rome, Scandinavia, and Normandy. The grand jury emerged in English law in 1176, during a political struggle among King Henry II, the church, and noblemen. At first, criminal accusations originated with members of the grand jury themselves, but gradually this body came to consider accusations from outsiders as well. Initially the grand jurors heard witnesses; later they also came to consider accusations brought by prosecutors.

After the American Revolution, the **grand jury** was incorporated into the Fifth Amendment to the Constitution, which provides that "no person shall be held to answer for a capital, or otherwise infamous crime, unless on a presentment or indictment of a grand jury." The archaic phrase "otherwise infamous crime" has been interpreted to mean felonies. This provision, however, applies only to federal prosecutions. In *Hurtado v. California* (1884), the Supreme Court held that states have the option of using either an indictment or an information. In nineteen states the grand jury is the exclusive means of initiating prosecution for all felonies. In a few, it is required only for capital offenses. In the remainder the grand jury is an optional investigative body (Figure 10-3).

Grand juries are impaneled (formally created) for a set period of time—usually three months. During that time, the jurors periodically consider the cases brought to them by the prosecutor and conduct other investigations. If a grand jury is conducting a major and complex investigation, its time may be extended by the court. The size of grand juries varies greatly, from as few as six jurors (Indiana), to sixteen or seventeen, to as many as twenty-three. Grand jurors are normally randomly selected in a manner similar to the selection of trial jurors. In

Grand jury: A group of citizens who decide whether persons accused of crimes should be indicted (true bill) or not (no true bill).

FIGURE 10-3	Grand Jury Requirements

Grand Jury Indictment Required	Grand Jury Indictment Optional	Grand Jury Lacks Authority to Indict
All crimes	Arizona	Pennsylvania
New Jersey	Arkansas	
South Carolina	California	
Tennessee	Colorado	
Virginia	Idaho	
All felonies	Illinois	
Alabama	Indiana	
Alaska	Iowa	
Delaware	Kansas	
District of Columbia	Maryland	
Georgia	Michigan	
Hawaii	Missouri	
Kentucky	Montana	
Maine	Nebraska	
Mississippi	Nevada	
New Hampshire	New Mexico	
New York	North Dakota	
North Carolina	Oklahoma	
Ohio	Oregon	
Texas	South Dakota	
West Virginia	Utah	
Capital crimes only	Vermont	
Connecticut	Washington	
Florida	Wisconsin	
Louisiana	Wyoming	
Massachusetts		
Minnesota		
Rhode Island		

SOURCE: Deborah Emerson, *Grand Jury Reform: A Review of Key Issues* (Washington, D.C.: Department of Justice, National Institute of Justice, 1983).

a handful of states, however, judges, county boards, jury commissioners, or sheriffs are allowed to exercise discretion in choosing who will serve on the grand jury.

Law on the Books: Shield and Sword

The two primary functions of grand juries have been aptly summarized in the phrase "shield and sword" (Zalman and Siegel 1997). *Shield* refers to the protections the grand jury offers, serving as a buffer between the state and its citizens, preventing the government from using the criminal process against its enemies. *Sword* refers to the investigatory powers of this body (Alpert and Petersen 1985).

If the grand jury believes there are grounds for holding the suspect for trial, they return an **indictment**, also termed a **true bill**, meaning that they find the charges to be true. Conversely, if they find the charges insufficient to justify trial, they return a no bill or **no true bill**.

Many legal protections found elsewhere in the criminal court process are not applicable at the grand jury stage. One unique aspect of the grand

Indictment: A formal accusation of a criminal offense made against a person by a grand jury.

True bill: A bill of indictment by a grand jury.

No true bill: The decision of a grand jury not to indict a person for a crime.

jury is secrecy. Because the grand jury may find insufficient evidence to indict, it works in secret in order to shield those merely under investigation from adverse publicity. By contrast, the rest of the criminal court process is required to be public. Another unique aspect is that indictments are returned by a plurality vote; in most states, half to two thirds of the votes are sufficient to hand up an indictment. Trial juries can convict only if the jurors are unanimous (or, in four states, nearly unanimous). Finally, witnesses before the grand jury have no right to representation by an attorney, whereas defendants are entitled to have a lawyer present at all vital stages of a criminal prosecution. Nor do suspects have the right to go before the grand jury to protest their innocence or even to present their version of the facts.

In furtherance of its investigative powers, grand juries have the authority to grant **immunity** from prosecution. The Fifth Amendment protects a person against self-incrimination. In 1893 Congress passed a statute that permitted the granting of **transactional immunity**. In exchange for a witness's testimony, the prosecutor agrees not to prosecute the witness for any crimes admitted—a practice often referred to as "turning state's evidence." The Organized Crime Control Act of 1970 added a new and more limited form of immunity. Under **use immunity**, the government may not use a witness's grand jury testimony to prosecute that person. However, if the state acquires evidence of a crime independent of that testimony, the witness may be prosecuted. The Supreme Court has held that use immunity does not violate the Fifth Amendment's prohibition against self-incrimination (*Kastigar v. United States* 1972). Use immunity gives witnesses less protection than does transactional immunity. A witness may not refuse the government's offer of immunity, and failure to testify may result in a jail term for contempt of court.

The investigative powers of the grand jury to gather evidence are also seen in its **subpoena power**. Under the court's authority, the grand jury may issue a subpoena requiring an individual to appear before the grand jury to testify and/or bring papers and other evidence for its consideration. Failure to comply with a subpoena (or offer of immunity) is punishable by **contempt**. A person found in contempt of the grand jury faces a fine or being jailed until he or she complies with the grand jury request. Thus, contempt of the grand jury is potentially open ended—as long as the grand jury is in existence and as long as the person refuses to comply, the person can sit in jail. Critics contend that some prosecutors call political dissidents to testify to find out information unrelated to criminal activity.

The contempt power can also be used for punishment. A prosecutor may call a witness, knowing that he or she will refuse to testify, and then have the witness jailed. In this way, a person can be imprisoned without a trial. This has happened mainly to newspaper reporters. In *Branzburg v. Hayes* (1972), the Supreme Court ruled that journalists must testify before a grand jury. Some journalists have gone to jail rather than reveal their confidential sources, because they believe that to do so would erode the freedom of the press protected by the First Amendment.

Law in Action: Prosecutorial Domination

The work of the grand jury is shaped by its unique relationship with the prosecutor. In most states, grand juries are considered part of the judicial branch of government. In theory at least, the prosecutor functions only as a legal adviser to the grand jury, but in practice, the prosecutor dominates. Grand jurors hear only the witnesses summoned by the prosecutor, and, as laypersons, they are heavily influenced by the legal advice of the prosecutor. Indeed, the high court has recently ruled that the government is under no obligation to disclose to the

Immunity: A grant of exemption from prosecution in return for evidence or testimony.

Transactional immunity: Absolute protection against prosecution for any event or transaction about which a witness is compelled to give testimony or furnish evidence.

Use immunity: A witness may not be prosecuted based on grand jury testimony he or she provides but may be prosecuted based on evidence against the witness acquired independently from that testimony.

Subpoena (power): An order from a court directing a person to appear before the court and to give testimony about a cause of action pending before it.

Contempt (of court): The failure or refusal to obey a court order; may be punished by fine or imprisonment.

grand jury evidence that tended to clear the defendant. (This is one of a number of significant developments in the way criminal procedure has been shaped by the courts—see Figure 10-4.) Justice Scalia's opinion stressed that the grand jury is an institution separate from the courts and beyond the court's supervisory power (*U.S. v. Williams* 1992).

The net result is that grand juries often function as a rubber stamp for the prosecutor. A study of the Harris County (Houston, Texas) grand jury found that the average time spent per case was only five minutes; in 80 percent of the cases, there was no discussion by members of the grand jury; rarely did members voice a dissent; and finally, the grand jury approved virtually all of the prosecutor's recommendations (Carp 1975). Similarly, federal grand juries returned more than 17,000 indictments in one recent year, but only sixty-eight no true bills. In Chicago, grand juries indicted 100 percent of the murder cases presented (Gilboy 1984). In short, grand juries generally indict whomever the prosecutor wants indicted.

Nor are no true bills necessarily an indication that grand juries fulfill a significant screening function. A prosecutor who believes a case is weak subtly conveys this feeling. One assistant prosecutor this author interviewed says that grand jurors "get the feeling when we're not pressing a case real hard" (Neubauer 1974b, 134). In turn, the secrecy of the grand jury proceedings may lead prosecutors to use it as a "safety valve." That is, if a case involves a prominent citizen, has received extensive publicity, or both, the prosecutor may hesitate to dismiss the case even though a conviction appears unlikely.

 You can read about one federal grand juror's experience by going to **http://www.udayton.edu/~grandjur/recent/juror.htm**.

For an up-to-date list of Web links, go to **http://www.wadsworth.com/product/0534563406s**.

Law in Controversy: Reform the Grand Jury?

The grand jury system has been the object of various criticisms. In theory, the grand jury serves as a watchdog on the prosecutor, but some portray the grand jury as "the prosecutor's darling," a "puppet," or a "rubber stamp." To William Campbell (1973), U.S. District Court judge for the Northern District

of Illinois, "The grand jury is the total captive of the prosecutor who, if he is candid, will concede that he can indict anybody at any time, for almost anything, before any grand jury" (174). These concerns have prompted a call for the abolition of the grand jury. Early in the twentieth century, judicial reformers succeeded in abolishing grand juries in some states. More recently, such abolition efforts have not been successful, however, because they require a constitutional amendment.

Today, critics call for reforming the grand jury (Brenner 1998). Often these calls are based on concerns that grand jury proceedings have been misused to serve partisan political ends, harassing and punishing those who criticize the government. The cases most often cited include prominent opponents of the Vietnam War (Deutsch 1984). The leading advocate for Federal Grand Jury Reform is the National Association of Criminal Defense Lawyers (2000). This organization advocates a Citizens Grand Jury Bill of Rights, which among other things would grant witnesses the right to the presence of counsel during testimony; require prosecutors to disclose evidence that might exonerate the target; and allow targets of investigations to testify (Lefcourt 1998).

ARRAIGNMENT

Arraignment occurs in the trial court of general jurisdiction. During the arraignment the defendant is formally accused of a crime (either by an information or indictment), and the defendant is called upon to enter a plea. Thus, initial appearance and **arraignment** are similar in that the defendant must be informed with some specificity about the alleged criminal actions. The major difference is that felony defendants are not allowed to enter a plea (either innocent or guilty) in a lower court because that court lacks jurisdiction to take a plea and to sentence.

Procedurally, the arraignment provides the court the opportunity to ensure that the case is on track for disposition. Thus the judge summons the defendant, verifying not only the name but the

---

Arraignment: The stage of the criminal process in which the defendant is formally told the charges and allowed to enter a plea.

FIGURE 10-4	Key Developments Concerning Criminal Procedure

Crime

Lanzetta v. New Jersey	1939	A law is unconstitutional if it forbids an act in terms so vague that "men of common intelligence must necessarily guess at its meaning."
U.S. v. Lopez	1995	U.S. Congress does not have the authority under the commerce clause to prohibit guns in schools.

Arrest

Chimel v. California	1969	During a search incident to arrest, the police may search only the person and the area within the immediate vicinity.
Payton v. New York	1980	Unless the suspect gives consent, or an emergency exists, an arrest warrant is necessary if an arrest requires entry into a suspect's private residence.

Initial appearance

Sixth Amendment	1791	"In all criminal prosecutions, the accused shall enjoy the right . . . to be informed of the nature and cause of the accusation."
Coleman v. Alabama	1970	Defendant has a right to counsel if the initial appearance is a "critical stage" in the proceedings.

Charging

Sixth Amendment	1791	"In all criminal prosecutions, the accused shall enjoy the right . . . to be informed of the nature and cause of the accusation."
People v. Wabash, St. Louis and Pacific Railway	1882	Prosecutor has discretion in beginning prosecutions and may terminate them when, in his (or her) judgment, the ends of justice are satisfied.
Burns v. Reed	1991	Prosecutor enjoys absolute immunity to civil lawsuit for all actions involving the adversary process.

Preliminary hearing

Gerstein v. Pugh	1975	Arrested persons are entitled to a "prompt" hearing and thirty days is too long.
County of Riverside v. McLaughlin	1991	A jurisdiction that provides judicial determinations of probable cause within forty-eight hours of arrest will, as a general matter, comply with the promptness requirement.
Press Enterprises v. Superior Court	1986	The preliminary hearing must be open to the public.

Grand jury

Fifth Amendment	1791	"No person shall be held to answer for a capital, or otherwise infamous crime, unless on a presentment or indictment of a grand jury."
Hurtado v. California	1884	States are not required to use a grand jury in charging felonies.
U.S. Congress	1893	Prosecutors may grant a witness transactional immunity for testimony before the grand jury.
Organized Crime Control Act	1970	Prosecutors may grant a witness use immunity for testimony before the grand jury.
Kastigar v. U.S.	1972	Use immunity does not violate the Fifth Amendment protection against self-incrimination.
Branzburg v. Hayes	1972	Journalists have no constitutional right to maintain their confidentiality of their news sources when subpoenaed before grand juries and are compelled to give testimony.
U.S. v. Williams	1992	Prosecutors are under no obligation to present exculpatory evidence to the grand jury.
Campbell v. Louisiana	1998	A white criminal defendant may challenge his conviction on grounds that blacks were discriminated against in the selection of grand jurors.

Arraignment

Sixth Amendment	1791	"In all criminal prosecutions, the accused shall enjoy the right . . . to be informed of the nature and cause of the accusation."
Hamilton v. Alabama	1961	Defendant has the right to court-appointed counsel if indigent.

address where he or she resides and also that the defendant is represented by counsel. The lawyer provides a formal notification to the court that he or she represents the defendant in this matter. The arraignment also provides the opportunity for miscellaneous matters, particularly confirming the pretrial release status (Chapter 11) of the defendant. But most importantly, the arraignment means that the defendant must enter a plea. For those who refuse, the judge will enter a plea of not guilty. Typically defendants plead not guilty and a trial date (or other key event) is established. A handful of defendants enter a plea of not guilty by reason of insanity (Chapter 14). A significant proportion, though, enter a plea of guilty. In New Orleans, for example, one out of four defendants pleads guilty at arraignment, which results in a significant reduction in case processing time (Neubauer 1996).

The arraignment is rarely a major decision-making stage in the process. Rather, its real importance is measured more indirectly. The arraignment is important because it signifies to all members of the courtroom work group that the defendant is in all probability guilty and that the likelihood of being found not guilty is now slim. Thus, from the perspective of law-in-action, the arraignment says something very important about case attrition.

 The Maricopa County Sheriff's Office (Phoenix, Arizona) provides a live jail cam; you can view bookings: **http://www.mcso.org/**.

For an up-to-date list of Web links, go to **http://www.wadsworth.com/product/0534563406s**.

LAW-IN-ACTION PERSPECTIVE: CASE ATTRITION

The law-on-the-books perspective suggests a mechanical process—cases move almost automatically from one pretrial stage to the next. In sharp contrast the law-in-action perspective emphasizes a dynamic process—cases are likely to be eliminated during these early stages.

A detailed picture of case attrition emerges in a study of thirty urban prosecutors. For every 100 arrests, 24 are rejected, diverted, or referred to other jurisdictions during prosecutorial screening (Figure 10-5). Of those that survive the initial hurdle, 21 are

later dismissed by the prosecutor through a ***nolle prosequi*** (no prosecution). When this happens, the case is said to be "nolled," "nollied," or "nol. prossed." Overall, only 55 of the 100 arrests are carried forward to the trial stage.

The high attrition rate of felony cases early in the process contrasts sharply with the small percentage of acquittals during the trial phase. Once cases reach the felony court, relatively few are dismissed. Most end in either a plea or a trial (Boland, Mahanna, and Sones 1992). These statistics underscore the fact that decisions made during early steps of felony prosecutions are much more important in terminating cases than the later activities of judges and juries.

However, there are important variations between courts in the stage at which case attrition occurs. These variations reflect differences in state law, the structure of courts, and local traditions. Consider prosecutorial screening. In states with two levels of trial courts and dual prosecutors, felony court prosecutors have no control over the charging decisions made by local prosecutors in the lower courts. Similarly, some states allow police officers to use arrest warrants for filing charges without prosecutorial review (Jacoby 1977). Thus, a critical stage for case screening and case attrition in one court may be of little importance in another jurisdiction. In Los Angeles and Detroit, for example, prosecutors make the important screening decisions, meaning that the preliminary hearing is relatively unimportant. By contrast, in Brooklyn and Houston, prosecutors tend to defer to the police during the charging phase, resulting in significant case attrition at the preliminary hearing (McIntyre and Lippman 1970).

WHY ATTRITION OCCURS

Case attrition is the product of a complex set of factors, including the relationships between the major actors in the criminal justice system, the patterns of informal authority within the courtroom work group, the backlog of cases on the court's docket,

Nolle prosequi: The ending of a criminal case because the prosecutor decides or agrees to stop prosecuting. When this happens the case is "nollied," "nolled," or "nol. prossed."

FIGURE 10-5   Case Attrition of Felony Arrests in Twenty-Eight Urban Prosecutors' Offices

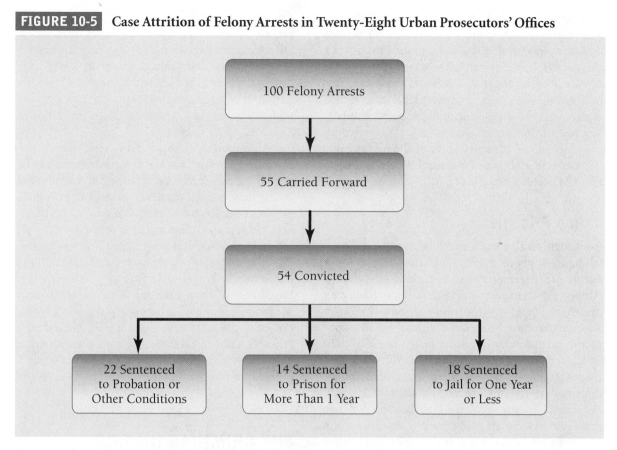

SOURCE: Barbara Boland, Paul Mahanna, and Ronald Sones, *The Prosecution of Felony Arrests, 1988* (Washington, D. C.: U.S. Department of Justice, Bureau of Justice Statistics, 1992).

and community standards defining serious criminal activity. We can best examine why attrition occurs by using the three facets of discretion discussed in Chapter 5: legal judgments, policy priorities, and personal standards of justice. Like other attempts to understand discretion, these categories are not mutually exclusive—some screening decisions are based on more than one criterion.

Legal Judgments

Legal judgments are the most important reason that cases drop by the wayside after arrest and before arraignment. Prosecutors, judges, and grand jurors begin with a basic question: Is there sufficient evidence to prove the elements of the offense? (Cole 1970; Feeney, Dill, and Weir 1983). One assistant district attorney phrased it this way: "When I examine the police report I have to feel that I could go to trial with the case tomorrow. All the elements of

prosecution must be present before I file charges" (Neubauer 1974b, 118).

More broadly, when prosecutors in fifteen urban jurisdictions were asked whether they would accept or decline prosecution for thirty standard cases, the legal-evidentiary strength of the case emerged as the most important factor (Jacoby et al. 1982). Witness problems (discussed in Chapter 9) constitute a specific type of legal-evidentiary problem. Three out of four prosecutors cite victim reluctance as a source of problems of felony case prosecution in their office, a percentage that reaches an astronomical 92 percent in urban areas with over half a million people (DeFrances, Smith, and van der Does 1996).

Focusing on the strength of the state's case introduces an important change in evaluative standards. From an initial concern with *probable cause*, the emphasis shifts to whether it is a *prosecutable case*. At the preliminary hearing, the judge determines whether there is probable cause—that a crime has been committed and there are grounds to believe that the suspect committed it. From the prosecutor's perspective, however, probable cause is too gross a yardstick; even though it is present, a case may still be legally weak. Thus, a prosecutable case is not merely one that satisfies the probable cause standard required of police in making an arrest and used by the judge in the administration of the preliminary hearing. Rather, it is a case that meets the standards of proof necessary to convict.

Policy Priorities

Case attrition also results from general prosecutorial policies about priority of cases. Prosecutors devote greater resources to more serious offenses (Gilboy 1984; Jacoby et al. 1982). At times, these case priorities are reflected in office structure; district attorneys around the nation have established priority prosecution programs that focus on major narcotics dealers, organized crime, sex offenders, and the like. Just as important, prosecutors employ informal criteria that govern allocation of scarce resources. For example, some U.S. attorneys will not prosecute bank tellers who embezzle small amounts of money, get caught, and lose their jobs. The stigma of being caught and losing the job is viewed as punishment enough. Similarly, numerous local and state prosecutors have virtually decriminalized possession of small amounts of marijuana by refusing to file charges. Based on informal office policies, district attorneys are reluctant to prosecute intrafamily assaults, neighborhood squabbles, and noncommercial gambling.

 Lisa Frohmann, "Constituting Power in Sexual Assault Cases: Prosecutorial Strategies for Victim Management"

Personal Standards of Justice

Personal standards of justice—attitudes of members of the courtroom work group about what actions should not be punished—constitute the third category of criteria that explain case attrition. When McIntyre (1968) studied screening in Chicago, he found that many cases are dropped or reduced for reasons other than failure to establish guilt. Even if the evidence is strong, defendants might not be prosecuted if their conduct and background indicate that they are not a genuine threat to society. In Detroit, among other places, a different phrase is used—"Prosecution would serve no useful purpose"—but the thought is the same. Across the nation these reasons for rejection are included under the category "interests of justice" (Boland, Mahanna, and Sones 1992).

An important dimension of personal standards of justice involves a subjective assessment on the part of the prosecutor that the case is not as serious as the legal charge suggests. In most courthouses, officials refer to some cases as "cheap" or "garbage" cases. Rosett and Cressey (1976) provide the following example. An old man stumbled drunkenly into a liquor store waving a cap pistol and demanding a bottle of whiskey. Even though all the elements of the offense of armed robbery were clearly present, the judge, complaining witness, and prosecutor did not take the case seriously. It was viewed as a "cheap" robbery. Decisions not to file charges in cheap cases reflected the effort of court officials to produce substantive justice.

THE CRIMINAL JUSTICE WEDDING CAKE

The tyranny of criminal justice statistics is that they treat all cases in the same way. A homicide counts the same as a $75 theft, which under state law is petty larceny but is reported as a major felony in the *Uniform Crime Reports* (adopted in the 1930s). Merely counting the number of criminal events gets in the way of understanding how and why court officials treat murder cases differently from petty thefts. To understand case attrition, Samuel Walker (2001) suggests that it is useful to view criminal justice as a wedding cake (Figure 10-6).

The wedding cake model is based on the observation that criminal justice officials handle different kinds of cases very differently. Within each layer, there is a high degree of consistency; the greatest disparities are found between cases in different layers. An examination of these layers illuminates the paradox of American criminal justice: "The problem is not that our system is too lenient, or too severe; sadly, it is both" (Zimring, O'Malley, and Eigen 1976).

FIGURE 10-6   The Criminal Justice Wedding Cake

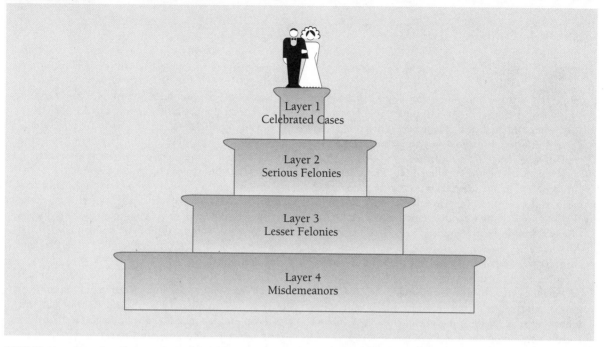

SOURCE: From Samuel Walker, *Sense and Nonsense about Crime and Drugs: A Policy Guide*, 5th ed. (Belmont, CA: Wadsworth, 2001).

Celebrated Cases

The top layer of the criminal justice wedding cake consists of a few celebrated cases. O. J. Simpson is clearly the most celebrated of the modern celebrated cases. The names of the defendants and the types of crimes they are accused of, of course, vary. But here is a sampling of the cases that have dominated the national news over the last several years:

- The shooting of West African immigrant Amadou Diallo by four New York police officers.

- The murder in Jasper, Texas, of James Byrd, Jr. by defendants who were allegedly members of the so-called Aryan Nation.

- Theodore Kaczynski (better known as the Unabomber), accused of mailing bombs—which killed or maimed—to various people he considered representative of the technological society he hated.

- The trial and conviction of Terry Nichols and Timothy McVeigh for the bombing of the federal building in Oklahoma City.

These types of cases are particularly newsworthy either because of the number of persons killed, the bizarre nature of the crime, or the prominence of the defendant. Likewise, local communities may have a few celebrated cases, either because a local notable has been charged with a serious crime or because the crime itself was particularly heinous.

From the moment these cases begin, criminal justice officials treat them as exceptional, making sure that every last detail of the judicial process is followed. The cases are also extraordinary because they frequently involve the rarest of criminal court events—the full jury trial. To the fascination of the viewing and reading public, controversial matters are aired in public. As in morality plays of old and soap operas of today, public attention is focused on the battle between good and evil, although who is playing which role is not always obvious.

These celebrity cases are most likely to be broadcast on TV, with the cable station Court TV providing a daily dose. Because of the publicity surrounding them, celebrated cases have a tremendous impact on public perceptions of criminal justice. On one level, these cases reinforce the textbook notion that defendants will receive their day in court, complete with a Perry Mason–type defense counsel and an attentive jury. But on another level, celebrated

New Orleans' Bloodiest Week in Memory

The story of the murder of Michael Gerardi was as poignant as it was brutal. He had met Connie Babin just several nights before at a Mardi Gras party. He repeatedly called her, and on their first date he gave her a red rose.

His murder at the Port of Call restaurant was but one of what *The Times-Picayune,* New Orleans' only major daily newspaper, headlined the "Bloodiest Week in Memory." In just seven days twenty-one people had died, and nine others were wounded ("A Week of Violence" 1995). Some were domestic homicides. Others appeared to be drug-related—a very elastic term that the police use to encapsulate everything from attempts to rob drug dealers, to fights over territory, to retaliation for selling bogus drugs. Other violence occurred during the course of armed robberies.

The murder of Michael Gerardi was not the most shocking of all that took place that week. That dubious distinction went to the murder of police officer Ronald Williams, Jr., age twenty-five, Cuong Vu, seventeen, and his sister Ha Vu, twenty-four, at the Vu family restaurant in eastern New Orleans. They were murdered execution-style by Antoinette Frank, a New Orleans police officer who was Ronald Williams' partner. She is currently on Louisiana's death row.

The murder wave in the first week of March 1995 solidified in the citizens' minds that their city was indeed a dangerous place. Just the year before, it had been identified as the murder capital of the nation. And 1995 proved to be even worse, with a total of 421 murders. Moreover, 60 percent of the black residents reported that they heard gunfire a few times a year or even a few times a month (Howell 2000).

In high-profile murders the police are under considerable pressure to solve the crime by making an arrest. This public pressure always produces the uncomfortable fear that the police might act in haste and arrest the wrong person. This point was made in the federal civil rights lawsuit filed by Cousin's attorneys (see Chapter 3). The complaint mentions the newspaper article with the title "Bloodiest Week" and charges that the mayor and the police chief were under political pressure to solve the crime. The complaint goes on to inject race into the discussion, arguing that Police Chief Pennington, who is African American, "voiced his desire to do more for people in the French Quarter, due to the racially biased notion that murders in that part of town are somehow more important than deaths of poorer people in other sections of the city" (*Cousin v. Small,* 2000).

Since 1995 the number of murders in New Orleans has declined dramatically, dipping to a low of 162 in 1999 (Philbin 2001). Moreover, fewer black residents now report hearing gunshots on a regular basis. In the public's mind the reduction in crime in the Crescent City is related to major changes in the activities of the police department. Amid widespread scandal in the department and general views of ineffectiveness, the newly elected mayor hired Pennington as the city's police chief. But Pennington often complained that the city had too few police officers, and that those they had were underpaid.

This situation changed dramatically after another French Quarter murder, just a few blocks from the Port of Call, in December 1996. Shortly after arriving for work on Sunday morning a waitress at the Louisiana Pizza Kitchen found three co-workers dead in the deep freezer, gunshot victims; a fourth person was in serious condition. (The murderers were arrested shortly thereafter and later convicted.) The following Thursday a large contingent of French Quarter residents and merchants marched on City Hall, demanding that the City Council do something to shore up the police department. Within weeks new taxes were imposed and the police budget was increased. In the aftermath, as noted, crime in the city did go down—although not all agree that police department actions are the cause. Still, the overall impact is clear—the police are making more arrests, which results in more cases being filed in Criminal District Court (see Chapter 4) and more jail cells needed for those arrested (see Chapter 11). As was stressed in this chapter, an overwhelming number of those felony arrests are for drugs—almost two-thirds of all case filings in the city.

For more information about crime and the police in New Orleans go to **http://www.nopdonline.com**.

For an up-to-date list of Web links, go to **http://www.wadsworth.com/product/0534563406s**.

To read more about the Port of Call murder, search on *dead teen walking* and read the section, "A Fatal Date."

cases highlight the public's worst fears—the rich often get off scot-free because they can afford an expensive attorney. All too many seem to beat the rap. People assume that the court process ordinarily functions this way, but in fact it does not. Celebrated cases are atypical; they do not reflect how the courts operate on a day-to-day basis.

Serious Felonies

The second layer of the wedding cake consists of serious felonies. The courtroom work group distinguishes between this level and the next on the basis of three main criteria: the seriousness of the crime, the criminal record of the suspect, and the relationship between the victim and the offender. The guiding question is, "How much is the case worth?"

Serious cases end up on the second layer; the "not-so-serious" ones on the third. Murders, armed robberies, and most rapes are treated by all members of the courtroom work group as serious felonies, with the result that there is less likelihood the suspect will be released on bail (Chapter 11). In addition, at this level, there is more pretrial maneuvering (Chapter 12), with less chance that the sides can reach a plea agreement (Chapter 13), and a strong likelihood of trial (Chapter 14) and eventually an appeal (Chapter 17).

Lesser Felonies

There is, of course, no automatic formula for sorting cases into serious and not-so-serious felonies; the key is a commonsense judgment about the facts of the case. What first appears to be a serious offense might be downgraded because the victim and the offender knew one another. For example, what starts out as an armed robbery might later be viewed as essentially a private disagreement over money owed, with the criminal act a means of seeking redress outside accepted channels. On the other hand, a suspect's long criminal record might transform an otherwise ordinary felony into a serious one, at least in the eyes of the prosecuting attorney.

Analysis of the true seriousness of a case is part of the everyday language of the courthouse actors. Serious cases are routinely referred to as "heavy" cases or "real" crimes, and the less serious ones as "garbage," "bullshit," or simply not real crimes. The practical consequences are that second-layer felonies are given considerable attention, whereas third-layer crimes receive less attention and are treated in a routine and lenient manner.

The Lower Depths

The bottom layer of the criminal justice wedding cake is a world unto itself, consisting of a staggering volume of misdemeanor cases, far exceeding the number of felony cases. About half are "public order" offenses—disorderly conduct, public drunkenness, disturbing the peace, and so on. Only about a third involve crimes against property or persons, many of which are petty thefts or physical disagreements between "friends" or acquaintances. Rarely do these defendants have any social standing. In the eyes of the courtroom work group, few of these cases are worth much, and relatively little time is devoted to their processing. They are usually handled by a different court from the one that handles felony cases and processed in a strikingly different way. Dispositions are arrived at in a routine manner. Defendants are arraigned en masse. Guilt is rarely contested. Even more rarely are the punishments harsh. For these reasons, the lower courts will be treated separately in Chapter 18. Although these crimes are minor, Wesley Skogan (1990) suggests that there is a link between disorder and serious crime, a link that contributes to the spiraling decline of some inner-city neighborhoods.

CONCLUSION

One could hardly label Donald Lee McLaughlin a bit player in the case that bears his name. He was more of a prop, no more than a convenient arrest, at least from the perspective of the public defender's office in Riverside, California. A live body was needed to challenge systematic practices, and he was chosen and then promptly vanished from public awareness.

The debate among the nine justices over twenty-four hours versus thirty-six versus forty-eight seems at best arcane. But this debate illustrates the overriding reality of the modern age—at times, the rights of individuals must be considered not just on their own merits but also in the context in which they are raised. Individually providing each defendant a probable cause hearing within twenty-four hours would cause no disruption to the system. But providing potentially hundreds of suspects a day such a right runs smack into logistical problems—transporting prisoners from distant jails, hiring more magistrates, making sure that police reports are quickly available, and the like.

What is ultimately important about *County of Riverside v. McLaughlin* is that it focuses attention on what is otherwise an invisible time period in the history of a felony prosecution. The specific steps of criminal procedure are important because they help to ensure fairness in the process. But equally important is the substance of the decisions made. In statistical profile, the process resembles a funnel—wide at the top, narrow at the end. Fewer than half of all crimes are ever reported to the police. Only one in five of the crimes known to the police results in an arrest. Thus, most crimes never reach the courts. Of the small subset of criminal events referred to court officials, half are dropped following prosecutorial screening, preliminary hearings, or grand jury deliberations. Prosecutors and judges decline to prosecute or later dismiss charges that have been filed because the case lacks sufficient evidence, falls too low on the priority list, or is viewed as a "cheap" case. The wedding cake model highlights this sorting process. Considerable resources are devoted to serious felonies. Lesser felonies receive less attention; they are more likely to be filtered out of the system.

The decisions made at these early points set the tone of cases moving through the criminal court process. Quantitatively, the volume of cases is directly related to screening decisions. In many areas, it is common for roughly half of the defendants to have their charges dismissed during these early stages. Qualitatively, screening decisions greatly influence later stages in the proceedings. Most directly, plea bargaining reflects how cases were initially screened. For instance, it is a long-standing practice in many courts for prosecutors to overcharge a defendant by filing accusations more serious than the evidence indicates, in order to give themselves leverage for later offering the defendant the opportunity to plead to a less serious charge. Thus, the important decisions about innocence or guilt are made early in the process by judges and prosecutors, not, as the adversary system projects, late in the process by lay jurors.

CRITICAL THINKING QUESTIONS

1. If you were to start from scratch, how would you design the FBI's *Uniform Crime Reports*? In particular, would you collect information in parallel with state criminal law? As the categories stand now, there is little relationship between felonies and Type I offenses. In your redesign, would the data collected be similar or different from that now gathered in the National Crime Victimization Survey?

2. How long before an arrested person has the right to be brought before a neutral judicial official? Do you think it was proper for the Court to take into account law-in-action factors such as case volume in deciding *County of Riverside*?

3. In your community, at what stage does case attrition occur? Do you detect any public displeasure with how the process currently operates?

4. If you were the prosecutor, what arguments would you make to the police chief(s) regarding a policy of careful screening of cases soon after arrest? Conversely, what arguments do you think law enforcement officials make?

5. To what extent do the issues of weeding out weak cases cut across ideological dimensions? In particular, the crime control model may offer contradictory advice. On the one hand it suggests prosecution of all wrongdoers to the fullest extent of the law, but on the other hand values efficiency, emphasizing the early elimination of weak cases so that scarce resources can be concentrated on the strong prosecutions.

6. Do you know of any local crimes that fit the celebrated cases category of the criminal justice wedding cake? Why did these cases re-

ceive such attention? Are they similar or different from cases that receive extensive coverage in the media?

WORLD WIDE WEB RESOURCES AND EXERCISES

Web Guides

http://dir.yahoo.com/Society_and_Culture/Crime/
http://dir.yahoo.com/Government/Law/Jury_Duty/ Grand_Jury/
http://dir.yahoo.com/Health/Pharmacy/Drugs_and_ Medications/Drug_Policy/U_S__War_on_Drugs/

Web Search Terms

"War on drugs"; "grand jury"; "preliminary hearing"

Useful URLs

Federal Bureau of Investigation *Uniform Crime Reports* are available at **http://www.fbi.gov/ ucr.htm.**
For the latest National Crime Victimization Survey go to **http://www.ojp.usdoj.gov/bjs/cvict.htm.**
The Bureau of Justice Statistics provides comprehensive statistics at **www.ojp.usdoj.gov/bjs.**
Arrestee Drug Abuse Monitoring (ADAM) provides data on recent drug use among those arrested: **http://www.adam-nij.net/.**
The Lycaeum Drug War Library houses a collection of papers, letters, and articles on ending the war on drugs: **http://www.lycaeum.org/ drugwar/.**

Uncommon URLs

The Federal Grand Jury Web site was created by two law professors to let people know what grand juries are and what they do: **http://www. udayton.edu/~grandjur/.**
The Pacific Crest Biodiversity Project provides an activist's guide to getting arrested and going to trial: **http://www.pcbp.org/arrest.htm.**
Citizens' self-arrest form from the University of Oklahoma police department is available at **http://www.ou.edu/oupd/selfarr2.htm.**
The California Grand Jury Association can be accessed at **http://www.cgja.org/.**

To learn more about efforts at grand jury reform, go to **http://www.criminaljustice.org** and locate the Federal Grand Jury Reform report.

Web Exercises

1. Examine the latest crime victimization data summarized in the *Sourcebook of Criminal Justice Statistics* at **http://www.albany.edu/ sourcebook.** How do victimization rates vary according to gender, race, and size of community?

2. Do a Web search to find out where various groups stand concerning the war on drugs. If you are using Yahoo, here are the commands: **http://www.yahoo.com, Society and Culture/Crime/War on Drugs.**

   Do these groups appear to be supportive of or hostile to the war on drugs? What arguments do they make for continuing (ending) the war on drugs? Do these groups appear to be representative of public views? If not, why not?

3. Examine the governmental policy on drugs as represented by the Office of National Drug Policy, which is located at the following Web site: **www.whitehousedrugpolicy.gov.** Does current drug control policy appear to reflect the crime control model or the due process model? How does current governmental drug policy treat the problem of court overload?

INFOTRAC COLLEGE EDITION RESOURCES AND EXERCISES

Basic Search Terms

Arrest, criminal statistics; narcotics, control of; drug abuse; legalization of narcotics; grand jury; preliminary examinations

Recommended Articles

Bruce A. Jacobs and Jody Miller, "Crack Dealing, Gender, and Arrest Avoidance"
Thomas D. Colbridge, "Protective Sweeps"
John C. Hall, "Police Use of Nondeadly Force to Arrest"
Lisa A. Regini, "Searching Pagers Incident to Arrest"
Columbia Journalism Review, "Statistics/Crime Rates"
Nicole Walker, "Why Women Are Committing More Crimes"
Amanda Ripley, "A New Killing Season?"

Daniel C. Richman, "Grand Jury Secrecy: Plugging the Leaks in an Empty Bucket"

Erich Goode, "Strange Bedfellows: Ideology, Politics, and Drug Legalization"

InfoTrac College Edition Exercises

1. Using the search term *legalization of narcotics,* find one article on each side of the debate. To what extent do differences of opinion about crime reflect the crime control versus the due process model of criminal justice?

REFERENCES

"A Week of Violence: 21 Dead, 9 Wounded in New Orleans' Bloodiest Week in Memory." 1995. *Times-Picayune,* 5 March.

Alpert, Geoffrey, and Thomas Petersen. 1985. "The Grand Jury Report: A Magic Lantern or an Agent of Social Control?" *Justice Quarterly* 2: 23–50.

Baker, Newman. 1933. "The Prosecutor-Initiation of Prosecution." *Journal of Criminal Law, Criminology and Police Science* 23: 770–796.

Bertram, Eva, et al. 1996. *Drug War Politics: The Price of Denial.* Berkeley: University of California Press.

Boland, Barbara, Paul Mahanna, and Ronald Sones. 1992. *The Prosecution of Felony Arrests, 1988.* Washington, D.C.: U.S. Department of Justice, Bureau of Justice Statistics.

Brenner, Susan. 1998. "Is the Grand Jury Worth Keeping?" *Judicature* 81: 190–199.

Brosi, Kathleen. 1979. *A Cross-City Comparison of Felony Case Processing.* Washington, D.C.: Institute for Law and Social Research.

Bureau of Justice Statistics. 1995. *Drugs and Crime Facts, 1994.* Washington, D.C.: U.S. Department of Justice.

———. 2000a. *Criminal Victimization, 1998.* Washington, D.C.: U.S. Department of Justice.

———. 2000b. *Federal Criminal Case Processing, 1998.* Washington, D.C.: U.S. Department of Justice.

Campbell, William. 1973. "Eliminate the Grand Jury." *Journal of Criminal Law and Criminology* 64: 174–182.

Carp, Robert. 1975. "The Behavior of Grand Juries: Acquiescence or Justice?" *Social Science Quarterly* 853–870.

Cole, George. 1970. "The Decision to Prosecute." *Law and Society Review* 4: 313–343.

Currie, Elliott, *Reckoning: Drugs, the Cities, and the American Future.* 1993. New York: Hill and Wang.

DeFrances, Carol, Steven Smith, and Louise van der Does. 1996. "Prosecutors in State Courts, 1994." *Bulletin.* Washington, D.C.: Bureau of Justice Statistics.

Deutsch, Michael. 1984. "The Improper Use of the Federal Grand Jury: An Instrument for the Internment of Political Activists." *Journal of Criminal Law and Criminology* 75: 1159–1189.

Falkin, Gregory, Michael Prendergast, and M. Douglas Anglin. 1994. "Drug Treatment in the Criminal Justice System." *Federal Probation* 58: 31–36.

Federal Bureau of Investigation. 2000. *Uniform Crime Reports for the United States—1999.* Washington, D.C.: U.S. Government Printing Office.

Feeney, Floyd, Forrest Dill, and Adrianne Weir. 1983. *Arrests Without Conviction: How Often They Occur and Why.* Washington, D.C.: U.S. Department of Justice, National Institute of Justice.

Flemming, Roy. 1986. "Elements of the Defense Attorney's Craft: An Adaptive Expectations Model of the Preliminary Hearing Decision." *Law and Policy* 8: 33–57.

Flemming, Roy, Peter Nardulli, and James Eisenstein. 1992. *The Craft of Justice: Politics and Work in Criminal Court Communities.* Philadelphia: University of Pennsylvania Press.

Forst, Brian, Frank Leahy, Jean Shirhall, Herbert Tyson, and John Bartolomeo. 1981. *Arrest Convictability as a Measure of Police Performance.* Washington, D.C.: U.S. Department of Justice, National Institute of Justice.

Forst, Brian, J. Lucianovic, and S. Cox. 1977. *What Happens After Arrest? A Court Perspective of Police Operations in the District of Columbia.* Washington, D.C.: Law Enforcement Assistance Administration.

Gilboy, Janet. 1984. "Prosecutors' Discretionary Use of the Grand Jury to Initiate or to Reinitiate Prosecution." *American Bar Foundation Research Journal* 1984: 1–81.

Greenwood, Peter, Sorrel Wildhorn, Eugene Poggio, Michael Strumwasser, and Peter Deleon. 1976. *Prosecution of Adult Felony Defendants in Los Angeles County: A Policy Perspective.* Lexington, MA: D. C. Heath.

Howell, Susan. 2000. *1998 Quality of Life Survey; Orleans and Jefferson Parishes.* Unpublished manuscript, Department of Political Science, University of New Orleans.

Jacoby, Joan. 1977. *The Prosecutor's Charging Decision: A Policy Perspective.* Washington, D.C.: U.S. Government Printing Office.

Jacoby, Joan, Leonard Mellon, Edward Ratledge, and Stanley Turner. 1982. *Prosecutorial Decisionmaking: A National Study.* Washington, D.C.: U.S. Department of Justice, National Institute of Justice.

Lefcourt, Gerald. 1998. "Curbing the Abuse of the Grand Jury." *Judicature* 81: 196–197.

Mather, Lynn. 1974. "Some Determinants of the Method of Case Disposition: Decision-Making by

Public Defenders in Los Angeles." *Law and Society Review* 8: 187–216.

McDonald, William, ed. 1976. *Criminal Justice and the Victim*. Newbury Park, CA: Sage.

McIntyre, Donald. 1968. "A Study of Judicial Dominance of the Charging Decision." *Journal of Criminal Law, Criminology and Police Science* 59: 463–490.

McIntyre, Donald, and David Lippman. 1970. "Prosecutors and Disposition of Felony Cases." *American Bar Association Journal* 56: 1154–1159. `

Meier, Kenneth. 1994. *The Politics of Sin: Drugs, Alcohol, and Public Policy*. New York: M. E. Sharpe.

Mellon, Leonard, Joan Jacoby, and Marion Brewer. 1981. "The Prosecutor Constrained by His Environment: A New Look at Discretionary Justice in the United States." *Journal of Criminal Law and Criminology* 72: 52–81.

Miller, Frank. 1969. *Prosecution: The Decision to Charge a Suspect with a Crime*. Boston: Little, Brown.

National Advisory Commission on Criminal Justice Standards and Goals. 1973. *Report on Courts*. Washington, D.C.: U.S. Government Printing Office.

National Association of Criminal Defense Lawyers. 2000. "Citizens Grand Jury Bill of Rights." (www.criminaljustice.org).

National Center for State Courts. 1993. *State Court Caseload Statistics: Annual Report, 1991*. Williamsburg, VA: Author.

Neubauer, David. 1974a. "After the Arrest: The Charging Decision in Prairie City." *Law and Society Review* 8: 495–517.

———. 1974b. *Criminal Justice in Middle America*. Morristown, NJ: General Learning Press.

———. 1996. "A Tale of Two Cities: A Comparison of Orleans and Jefferson Parish, Louisiana." Paper presented at the annual meeting of the Academy of Criminal Justice Sciences, Louisville, Kentucky, March 17.

Ostrom, Brian, and Neal Kauder. 1999. *Examining the Work of State Courts, 1998*. Williamsburg, VA: National Center for State Courts.

Perkins, David, and Jay Jamieson. 1995. "Judicial Probable Cause Determinations After *County of Riverside v. McLaughlin*." *Criminal Law Bulletin* 31: 534–546.

Philbin, Walt. 2001. "Murder Rate Up Sharply in 2000." *Times-Picayune*, 1 January.

Rosett, Arthur, and Donald Cressey. 1976. *Justice by Consent: Plea Bargaining in the American Courthouse*. Philadelphia: J. B. Lippincott.

Sharp, Elaine. 1994. *The Dilemma of Drug Policy*. New York: HarperCollins.

Skogan, Wesley. 1990. *Disorder and Decline: Crime and the Spiral of Decay in American Neighborhoods*. Berkeley: University of California Press.

Skolnick, Jerome. 1993. *Justice Without Trial*. 3d ed. New York: Macmillan.

Walker, Samuel. 2001. *Sense and Nonsense about Crime and Drugs: A Policy Guide*. 5th ed. Belmont, CA: Wadsworth.

Zalman, Marvin, and Larry Siegel. 1997. *Criminal Procedure: Constitution and Society*. 2d ed. Belmont, CA: Wadsworth.

Zimring, Franklin, Sheila O'Malley, and Joel Eigen. 1976. "Punishing Homicide in Philadelphia: Perspectives on the Death Penalty." *University of Chicago Law Review* 43: 227–252.

FOR FURTHER READING

Abadinsky, Howard. *Drugs: An Introduction*. 4th ed. Belmont, CA: Wadsworth, 2001.

Blank, Blanche Davis. *The Not So Grand Jury: The Story of the Federal Grand Jury System*. Lanham, MD: University Press of America, 1993.

Duffee, David, and Bonnie Carlson. "Competing Value Premises for the Provision for Drug Treatment for Probationers." *Crime and Delinquency* 42 (1996): 574–592.

Frankel, Marvin, and Gary Naftalis. *The Grand Jury: An Institution on Trial*. New York: Hill and Wang, 1977.

Inciardi, James, Duane McBride, and James Rivers. *Drug Control and the Courts*. Thousand Oaks, CA: Sage, 1996.

Jenkins, Phillip. "'The Ice Age' The Social Construction of a Drug Panic." *Justice Quarterly* 11 (1994): 7–32.

Meier, Robert, and Gilbert Geis. *Victimless Crimes? Prostitution, Drugs, Homosexuality, Abortion*. Los Angeles: Roxbury, 1997.

Menard, Scott. "The 'Normality' of Repeat Victimization from Adolescence through Early Adulthood." *Justice Quarterly* 17 (2000): 543–574

Messner, Steven, and Richard Rosenfeld. *Crime and the American Dream*. Belmont, CA: Wadsworth, 1994.

National Center for State Courts. 1999. *State Court Caseload Statistics: Annual Report, 1997*. Williamsburg, VA: Author.

Sheley, Joseph. *Criminology: A Contemporary Handbook*. Belmont, CA: Wadsworth, 1991.

Weiss, Robert, Richard Berk, and Catherine Lee. "Assessing the Capriciousness of Death Penalty Charging." *Law and Society Review* 30 (1996): 607–632.

Zimring, Franklin, and Gordon Hawkins. *The Search for Rational Drug Control*. Cambridge: Cambridge University Press, 1992.

Bail

ANTHONY SALERNO, ORGANIZED CRIME BOSS, WAS INDICTED ON TWENTY-nine counts of labor racketeering, extortion, gambling, and conspiracy to murder. Based on past practices, there is little doubt that Salerno would have been held in jail in an indirect manner until his trial—bond would have been set so high that he would not have been able to post the necessary cash and collateral. But Rudolph Giuliani, U.S. attorney, sought to detain Salerno directly. A recently passed federal law allowed a judge to refuse to set bail if the defendant might harm others while out on bail. The judge found that Salerno met the criteria and ordered him held in jail until trial.

The decision in *Salerno* represents one of the few times that the Supreme Court has wrestled with the Eighth Amendment's clause that "excessive bail shall not be required." To crime control model advocates, the historical right to bail needs to be modified in the face of pretrial releases of defendants who commit new crimes while out on bail. To due process model supporters, the original understanding that defendants merely charged with a crime shouldn't have to pay a penalty is as applicable today as when the Bill of Rights was adopted. But does this debate about law on the books really matter? From the perspective of law in action, jails are so full today that laws allowing judges to detain certain defendants prior to trial are merely toothless tigers.

The *Salerno* case underscores the importance of pretrial detention decisions. Bail represents a defendant's first major encounter with the courts. For various fees, depending on the crime, the accused can purchase freedom and return to home and family. But defendants who cannot post bond must await trial in jail, suffering many of the same penalties normally reserved only for those who have been found guilty. This chapter examines how America's system of pretrial release works, the factors that shape its operation, and the consequences of decisions about bail. Some of the key areas discussed include concerns that bail discriminates against the poor, fears that bail exposes the public to risks of being victimized, and the question of whether defendants released on bail later appear for trial. ■

LAW ON THE BOOKS: THE MONETARY BAIL SYSTEM

Bail is a guarantee. In return for being released from jail, the accused promises to return to court as needed. This promise is guaranteed by posting money or property with the court. If the defendant appears in court when requested, the security is returned. If he or she fails to appear, the security can be forfeited. The practice of allowing defendants to be released from jail pending trial originated in thirteenth-century England, largely as a convenience to local sheriffs. The colonists brought the concept of bail with them across the Atlantic. It eventually became embedded in the Eighth Amendment, which provides that "excessive bail shall not be required." Although the Supreme Court has never decided whether the excessive bail clause establishes a right to **bail**, federal law and most state constitutions create such a right (Nagel 1990). There are limitations,

Bail: The security (money or bail bond) given as a guarantee that a released prisoner will appear at trial.

however. Because no security is considered large enough to deter accused persons from fleeing to save their lives, defendants accused of capital offenses have no right to bail. Similarly, courts have historically refused to allow bail if there is a risk of flight or if the defendant, upon release, might obstruct justice (Berg 1985).

Bail Procedures

Shortly after arrest, a defendant is brought before a lower court judge, who sets the conditions of release. Bail procedures vary according to the seriousness of the crime. Those arrested for minor misdemeanors can be released fairly quickly by posting bail at the police station. In most communities, the lower court judges have adopted a fixed bail schedule (also known as an emergency bail schedule), which specifies an exact amount for each offense.

Bail procedures for felony or serious misdemeanor cases are considerably more complex. The arrestee must appear before a lower court judge for the setting of bail, so those accused of serious crimes remain in police custody for a number of hours before they have the opportunity to make bail.

Pretrial FAQs are provided by the California Association of Pretrial Services at **http://www. napsa.org/docs/faq.htm**.

For an up-to-date list of Web links, go to **http://www.wadsworth.com/product/0534563406s**.

Forms of Bail

Once bail has been set, a defendant can gain pretrial release in four basic ways. First, the accused may post the full amount with the court in the form of a **cash bond**. All of this money will be returned when all court appearances are satisfied. Because it requires a large amount of cash, this form of bail is seldom used. If, for example, bail is set in the amount of $10,000, most persons, particularly felony defendants, cannot raise that much money easily and quickly.

The second method for securing pretrial release is a **property bond**. Most states allow a defendant (or friends or relatives) to use a piece of property as collateral. If the defendant fails to appear in court, the property is forfeited. Property bonds are also rare, because courts generally require that the equity in the property must be double the amount of the bond. Thus, a $10,000 bond requires equity of at least $20,000.

A third alternative for making bail is **release on recognizance** (ROR for short). Judges release a defendant from jail without monetary bail if they believe the person is not likely to flee. Such personal bonds are used most often for defendants accused of minor crimes and for those with substantial ties to the community.

Because many of those arrested lack ready cash, do not own property, or lack the needed social clout, the first three options for making bail are only abstractions. Many of those released prior to trial use the fourth method: They hire a **bail agent** (often

called bail bondsman) to post bail, who posts the amount required and charges a fee for services rendered, usually 10 percent of the amount of the bond. Thus, a bail agent would normally collect $1,000 for writing a $10,000 bond. None of that money is refundable.

In America's system of monetary bail, those who are rich enough can buy their freedom and await trial on the streets. But the poor await trial in jail. On any given day, there are over 600,000 persons in jail (not prison), half of whom have not been convicted of any crime. Such average daily population figures greatly underestimate the high volume of transactions that occur. Unlike prisons, where the annual turnover of the population is relatively small, large numbers of individuals pass through the revolving door of the jail, "moving into, out of, and back into, the facility during any given year" (Backstrand, Gibbons, and Jones 1992). In a typical year, there are more than 13 million entries and exits about equally divided between admissions and releases (Bureau of Justice Statistics 1993). The median length of stay is three days; a very large number of defendants are released on bail after spending several days in jail while friends or relatives try to obtain the necessary funds to meet the bondsman's fee.

Conflicting Theories of Bail

Administration of bail has been greatly influenced by a long-standing disagreement over the purposes of bail. The basic question is whether society should grant a pretrial release to a defendant who is probably guilty. The Continental legal system answers no, and pretrial release is very limited in Europe. By contrast, American law is deeply suspicious of the possibility of a misuse of official power and refuses to allow officials to detain anyone merely accused of a crime, except under very limited circumstances. Conflicts arise from the clash of these two perspectives.

Adherents of the due process model stress that the only purpose of bail is to ensure that the defendant appears in court for trial. The basis of this view is the premise of the adversarial system that a person is innocent until proven guilty and therefore should not suffer any hardships, such as a stay in jail while awaiting trial. According to this view, a judge should calculate bail solely on the basis of what amount will guarantee the availability of the accused for court hearings.

Cash bond: Requirement that money be posted to secure pretrial release.

Property bond: Use of property as collateral for pretrial release.

Release on recognizance (ROR):   The release of an accused person from jail on his or her own obligation rather than on a monetary bond.

Bail agent (bondsman):   A person whose business it is to effect release on bail for persons held in custody by pledging to pay a sum of money if a defendant fails to appear in court as required.

FIGURE 11-1 Key Developments Regarding Bail

Eighth Amendment	1791	Excessive bail shall not be required.
Stack v. Boyle	1951	Bail set at a figure higher than an amount reasonably calculated to ensure the defendant's presence at trial is excessive.
Bail Reform Act	1966	Creates a presumption favoring pretrial release of federal arrestees.
Schilb v. Kuebel	1971	Illinois' bail deposit system is constitutional.
Bail Reform Act	1984	In setting bail the judge may consider danger to the community.
U.S. v. Salerno	1987	Federal preventative detention law does not violate the Eighth Amendment.
U.S. v. Montalvo-Murillo	1990	Defendant has no "right" to freedom when a detention hearing was not held at the time of his first appearance; this failure was a minor statutory violation.
Kansas v. Henricks	1997	Upholds Kansas' Sexually Violent Predator Act, which permits the state to keep sexual offenders in a mental institution after they complete a criminal sentence.

The assumption that bail should be set solely to assure the defendant's appearance in court does not do away with the central issues raised by practices in the Continental legal system—what to do with potentially dangerous defendants or those who might commit additional crimes while awaiting trial. Supporters of the crime control model therefore stress that bail should be used to protect society. This perspective is reflected in law in action: Informally, judges deliberately set bail so high that defendants perceived to be dangerous will be unable to post bail and therefore await trial in jail. More recently, preventive detention has been formally authorized in some jurisdictions. Figure 11-1 summarizes key developments in the law regarding bail.

The competing perspectives of ensuring appearance at trial and protecting society affect the daily realities of bail setting in ways that will be discussed throughout this chapter.

LAW IN ACTION: THE CONTEXT OF BAIL SETTING

Deciding whom to release and whom to detain pending trial poses critical problems for American courts. At the heart of the matter are efforts to balance the conflicting theories of bail. The realities of the bail system in the United States reflect an attempt to strike a balance between the legally recognized purpose of setting bail to assure reappearance for trial and the working perception that some defendants should not be allowed out of jail until their trial. As Roy Flemming argues, one can imagine two improbable extremes. On the one hand, the courts could release all defendants prior to trial. On the other, they could hold every suspect. But neither of these extremes is possible. Freeing all those accused of murder, robbery, and rape is not politically feasible, no matter what the chances are of the accused later appearing in court. Similarly, jailing them all is not possible, because prisons are simply not large enough. Nevertheless, court officials must make decisions every day that balance these competing demands (Flemming 1982).

Legal protections such as the right to bail are meaningful only in the context of the policies that execute those protections. Only rarely do judges directly decide that a defendant should remain in jail pending trial. Rather, this important decision is made indirectly, when the amount of bail is fixed. The higher the bail, the less likely the accused will be able to secure pretrial release. As the amount of bail increases, fewer defendants are able to secure pretrial release (Zeisel 1979).

Trial court judges have a great deal of discretion in fixing bail. Statutory law provides few specifics about how much money should be required, and appellate courts have likewise spent little time deciding what criteria should be used. Although the Eighth Amendment prohibits excessive bail, appellate courts will reduce a trial judge's bail amount only in the rare event that flagrant abuse can be proved. In practice, then, trial court judges have virtually unlimited legal discretion in determining the amount of bail.

The range of choices available to court officials is referred to as the context of bail setting. Uncertainty, risk, and jail overcrowding are the primary political and institutional factors that shape pretrial release policy in any given court.

 The Web site of Action Bail Bonds promises to tell you everything about the bail bond process: **http://www.actionbail.com/**.

For an up-to-date list of Web links, go to **http://www.wadsworth.com/product/0534563406s**.

Uncertainty

Uncertainty is a major problem facing court officials in making bail decisions. A few short hours after arrest, the defendant appears in court for bail setting. Because of this short time span, only a limited amount of information is available. The details of the alleged crime—the who, what, when, where, and especially the why—are troublingly vague. Thus, the judge must set bail on the basis of little information about the strength of the evidence against the accused (Nagel 1983).

Compounding the information void is the lack of adequate facts about the defendant's past criminal history. In many courts, police "rap sheets" (lists of prior arrests) are available but typically contain information only on prior arrests, not on how the case was eventually disposed of—dismissal, plea, or imprisonment, for example. Of course, defendants may volunteer information about their backgrounds and prior experience with the court, but court officials understandably treat this information as unreliable. Faced with limited information, some of which may prove to be inaccurate, court officials must nonetheless make a number of decisions. Is this specific defendant likely to appear in court? Is he or she dangerous to the community? In the context of the crime and the defendant, what is "reasonable" bail? Because of the scarcity of knowledge, defendants may be classified incorrectly as good or bad candidates for release.

Risk

The uncertainty court officials face during bail setting is aggravated by the risks involved. Potentially, any defendant released on bail may commit another crime. This is how one judge expressed this risk factor:

> If you let [the defendant] out on personal recognizance, with the understanding that he would reappear again for trial, and then the victim was badly injured, or killed, you have the problem of the newspapers coming [out] in a very critical vein. You have to have some security for the particular judge. (Suffet 1966, 323)

Police groups, newspapers, district attorneys, and the general public may criticize a judge severely for granting pretrial release to defendants. In New York City, for example, a judge was nicknamed "Turn 'Em Loose Bruce" by the Patrolman's Benevolent Association. The judge was later reassigned to civil court after a series of public controversies about his setting low bail for defendants accused of violent crimes.

It is important to recognize that in bail setting judges and other court officials may make two types of mistakes. Type 1 errors involve releasing a defendant who later commits another crime or fails to appear in court. Type 2 errors involve detaining a suspect who should have been released. These two types of errors are inversely related; that is, the more type 2 errors, the fewer type 1. However, type 2 errors are largely hidden; they appear only if a major tragedy occurs, such as a suicide in jail. Type 1 errors, on the other hand, form the stuff of which newspaper headlines are made. In short, judges face public criticism mainly for type 1 errors. In assessing risk factors, court officials tend to err on the conservative side, preferring to make type 2 rather than type 1 errors.

Jail Overcrowding

The context of bail setting involves not only uncertainty and risk but also available resources. The principal limiting factor is the size of the local jail. Simply stated, jails are filled to capacity. In the decade from 1983 to 1993 the jail population more than doubled. Today there are approximately 600,000 inmates in local jails (Figure 11-2). Although construction has added thousands of new beds over the years, capacity remains at 93 percent, meaning that there is little ability to put more arrestees in jail without releasing others (Bureau of Justice Statistics 2000). The problem is most acute in

FIGURE 11-2 Growth in U.S. Jail Population

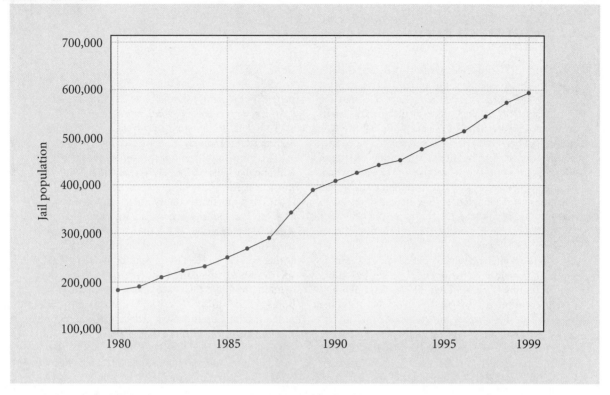

SOURCE: *Sourcebook of Criminal Justice Statistics.* www/albany.edu/sourcebook. Table 6.25.

eight states where the total jail population exceeds jail capacity. Likewise, the nation's largest cities face acute overcrowding problems; in jails with 1,000 or more inmates, the occupancy rate stands at 111 percent (Perkins, Stephan, and Beck 1995). Thus, like prisons (discussed in Chapter 15), jails face serious overcrowding problems. Indeed prison overcrowding is a principal cause of jail overcrowding. With prisons filled to overflowing, recently sentenced defendants must often spend time in local jails awaiting a vacant cell in the state prison.

Jails filled to overcapacity force court officials to make uncomfortable decisions (see A Day in Court: Get Outta Jail Free). Although they may believe that the defendant should be held in jail awaiting trial, they may realize that arrestees who have committed more serious offenses have already filled the jail. Thus, as jails become overcrowded or threaten to exceed their capacity, bail-setting practices become more lenient (Roth and Wice 1980; Flemming 1982). Figure 11-3 on page 281 summarizes bail and pretrial release practices as seen by law on the books and law in action.

THE PROCESS OF BAIL SETTING

Court officials respond to the context of bail setting (uncertainty, risk, and limited jail capacity) through general guidelines concerning the proper amount of bail (shared norms in terms of the courtroom work group concept developed in Chapter 5). Judges do not ponder each case as an isolated event; rather, bail guidelines provide cues for evaluating specific cases. In essence, bail setting "involves a search by officials to establish whether or not they should follow custom" (Flemming 1982, 29). In some communities, these normal bail amounts are specified in written guidelines (Jones and Goldkamp 1991). In most communities, they operate informally but have a major impact nonetheless. Two factors are particularly important in shaping bail guidelines:

A DAY IN COURT

Get Outta Jail Free

Criminals in Jefferson County don't need a get out of jail free card. Most times they never see the inside of the county jail. With only 33 spaces available and serious crime recently on the rise, the need to open the new county jail becomes ever more pressing. The county sheriff's department has filing cabinet drawers full of warrants for people to serve time in the county jail. Meanwhile, every weekend the sheriff and the judges must make some tough decisions on who to release to make room for new arrests.

Such was the case with Bruce Hanlin, 18, of Steubenville. He was convicted on Thursday of murder and four other charges after the Nov. 25 shooting death of Donald J. Hamann III, 23, of Mingo Junction. Had there been enough space, Hanlin might have been in the county jail the day of that shooting serving time for charges including carrying a concealed weapon. In a seven-month period, he was charged with 17 misdemeanors during four arrests. His total municipal court sentence was 210 days but he was out because the county jail was full. . . .

Municipal Court Judge Richard Powell said he's forced to play a dangerous shell game. "My biggest fear is releasing someone because of no room and that person going out and committing a really violent act," Powell said. "When you have the choice of domestic violence, driving under the influence, drug dealer, or burglar, who are you going to pick to release?". . .

Abdalla keeps a list of prisoners like a baseball coach keeps a list of players.

"On the weekend, I look at the board (list of prisoner names) and write down the names before I go home so I can make a decision on who is released to make room for someone more serious. That's no way to run a jail. The judges have to make the same decisions. You have to worry about some idiot after you release them going out and hurting someone. The people of this county should be irate," Abdalla said. . . .

If you do the crime, you don't do the time.

That has become the motto of people charged with misdemeanors in Jefferson County.

There are only 33 jail spaces available at the county jail. The new jail will have 120 cells, with about 40 of those cells for misdemeanor crimes. The lack of jail space has handcuffed county judges on sentences. . . .

Ohio law requires a person convicted of DUI to spend 72 hours in jail. The county courts are forced to use a three-day driver intervention program as a substitute for jail time. The people convicted of DUI spend a weekend talking with counselors about their drinking problem. "The law doesn't say to do the 72 hours when you feel like it," Toronto county court Judge Joseph Corabi said. According to the county sheriff's department, more than 400 people are waiting to serve time in jail for DUI. . . .

Not having room at the county jail has an effect on other court programs, especially community service, Corabi said. "If you sentence someone to community service, they figure what can they do to me if I don't show up. When the jail opens, I'll be getting a lot more phone calls to let their sons, daughters, or friends out of jail," he said.

Municipal Court Judge Richard Powell said not having any cells for female prisoners is common knowledge among the community. Females charged with petty theft come into court knowing they aren't going to jail. Powell is forced time after time to suspend the sentence or spend about $50 to $70 a day to house the woman in another county jail.

SOURCE: Mark Law, "With Jail Space Tight, Prisoners Get a Free Pass," *The Herald Star* (May 5, 1997), 1.

---

the seriousness of the crime and the prior criminal record of the defendant. As will become apparent, situational justice also comes into play.

Seriousness of the Crime

By far the most important consideration in establishing bail tariffs is the seriousness of the crime. The more serious the crime, the higher the amount of bail. For example, a study of bail practices in seventy-two cities found that 86 percent of the judges believed that the seriousness of the charge was the most important pretrial release criterion in their city. The assumption underlying this belief is that the more serious the crime, the greater the defendant's inclination to forfeit bail, and, therefore, the greater the financial costs should be for such flight (Wice 1974). This proposition is confirmed by a Bureau of Justice Statistics report on the nation's seventy-five most populous counties. When bail was

FIGURE 11-3 Bail and Pretrial Release

	Law on the Books	Law in Action
Right to bail	Based on the Eighth Amendment and the presumption of innocence until proven guilty, U.S. law creates a general right to bail.	• The average daily jail population is approximately 600,000; over 13,000,000 admissions to local jails each year. • Jails house about a third of all persons incarcerated in the United States.
Capital cases	Defendants awaiting trial on a murder charge that carries the death penalty have no right to bail.	
Methods of release	• *Cash* Defendant may post the full amount of the bond with clerk of court. • *Property* A piece of property with equity of twice the amount of bail posted with the clerk. • *Release on recognizance (ROR)* Released without posting collateral. • *Bail bondsmen (agents)* Post bond with the court for a fee (typically 10 percent of the bond).	• Most often used in minor offenses processed in the lower courts. • Used on rare occasions. • Used in lesser felonies. • Lower court defendants typically plead guilty at first appearance. • Prefer clients accused of less serious, nonviolent crimes.
Preventive detention	Two out of three jurisdictions allow the court to refuse to set bail if the defendant might flee and/or may be a risk to others.	• Jail overcrowding is the norm so in many jurisdictions preventive detention is never formally used. • Historically, judges set high bail amounts to accomplish the same goal.
Jails	Typically funded by local governments, jails hold suspects awaiting trial, house inmates awaiting transfer to state prisons, and confine those serving short sentences.	• The U.S. has 3,365 jails. • Forty-seven jails are privately owned or operated. • Annual cost per inmate is $15,000-plus.

set at $50,000 or more, only one out of eight defendants were eventually released. By contrast, when bail was set under $5,000, six out of ten defendants obtained release prior to case disposition (Bureau of Justice Statistics 1993). As a result, defendants charged with murder were the least likely to be granted pretrial release (16 percent), whereas those accused of drug or property crimes were released 66 percent of the time (Hart and Reaves 1999). Stated another way, the severity of the charge is inversely related to bail release.

Prior Criminal Record

A second criterion used in setting the amount of bond is the defendant's prior criminal record. Defendants with prior criminal records typically

have bond set higher than normal for the offense charged. Eighty-five percent of the judges in one survey reported using the defendant's prior criminal record and found it important (Wice 1974). For this reason, in New York City defendants with prior criminal records were more likely to await trial in jail (Nagel 1983; Sviridoff 1986). Nationwide, the lowest probability of release is found for defendants with multiple prior convictions or with a felony conviction record (Bureau of Justice Statistics 1993).

 The latest pretrial release and detention statistics are available at http://www.ojp.usdoj.gov/bjs/stssent.htm.

For an up-to-date list of Web links, go to http://www.wadsworth.com/product/0534563406s.

Situational Justice

The use of bail tariffs enables the courts to set bail rather rapidly for most defendants. After a consideration of the charge and the prior record, the judge announces the bail amount or grants a recognizance bond. However, not all bail settings are automatic. Judges often seek situational justice, in which they weigh the individual facets of the case and the defendant. Because they have so little information, judges may construct honesty tests such as the following.

> *"Have you ever been arrested anywhere in the world since the day you were born to this day?" The defendant replied that he was arrested two or three years ago. "What for?"*
>
> *"I forget," the defendant answers.*
>
> *"Weren't you arrested this year? In April? Weren't you in the Wayne County jail for a day or so? On the 26th?" The judge asks the questions without giving the defendant a chance to reply.*
>
> *After pausing a moment, the judge informed the defendant he had a "pretty bad memory" and added, "Have to have a bondsman for people with bad memories.". . .*
>
> *The defendant then spoke up and told the judge that he hadn't thought it was very important to remember the charge in the earlier case. The judge smiles. "You didn't think it was very important? Well, bond isn't either." (Flemming 1982, 57)*

The use of honesty tests is but one illustration of the fact that the demeanor of the defendant influences bail setting. Cooperative defendants are more likely to gain pretrial release (Snyder 1989; Frazier, Bock, and Henretta 1980).

BAIL SETTING AND THE COURTROOM WORK GROUP

Bail setting usually involves a unilateral decision-making process—the judge reviews the case and sets a bond amount (Flemming 1982). However, there are direct and indirect ways for members of the courtroom work group to influence this decision.

Influence of the Prosecutor

Next to the judge, the prosecutor is the most important actor in setting bail. The prosecutor is often present when bail is set. Over time, judges come to know and respect the prosecutor's assessments. An excellent study of bail setting in the New York criminal court explores the interaction among judge, prosecutor, and defense attorney, observing over 1,400 bail settings. Eighty-seven percent of the time the judge, prosecutor, and defense attorney agreed on how much bond should be required, accepting the prevailing bail guidelines. When the participants disagreed, the prosecutor was more influential than the defense attorney. When prosecutors considered the judge's initial bail suggestion too low, they were successful 80 percent of the time in getting the amount increased. When the situation was reversed, the defense attorney was less successful. The author of the study concluded that the prosecutor's ability to influence bail setting derived from the fact that the judge and prosecutor held similar views about the proper amount of bail (Suffet 1966).

 The American Jail Association (AJA) is a national nonprofit organization dedicated to supporting those who work in and operate our nation's jails: **http://www.corrections.com/aja/**.

For an up-to-date list of Web links, go to **http://www.wadsworth.com/product/0534563406s**.

Geographic Differences

Pretrial release policies and practices vary widely in America's criminal courts. The most recent National Jail Census illustrates this point. The highest numbers of jail inmates per 100,000 state residents were found in Georgia (328), Louisiana (377), Texas (307), and Tennessee (282). The lowest rates occurred in Iowa (57), North Dakota (57), and Maine (57) (Perkins, Stephan, and Beck 1995).

At first glance, these differences in the use of pretrial detention might seem related to the amount and severity of crime in the community, but this proves not to be the case. Even when studies include controls for the seriousness of the crime, states still differ widely in ROR use, cash bail amounts, and overall pretrial release rates. The only conclusion is that defendants' chances of pretrial release are heavily dependent on the community where they are arrested (Thomas 1970).

There are major differences in bail-setting policies between Detroit and Baltimore. Detroit granted ROR for almost half the cases, compared with only 12 percent in Baltimore. Likewise, the typical cash bail in the Motor City was less than half the amount required in Baltimore (Flemming 1982). These variations reflect important differences in the political dynamics surrounding pretrial release policies and procedures. In the Flemming study, both Detroit and Baltimore faced a jail crisis marked by overcrowding, riots, and unsanitary conditions. In Detroit the federal court imposed a maximum capacity on the jail population. This court order forced the judges of Detroit Recorder's Court to alter their bail policies and practices. In Baltimore, on the other hand, the federal court ordered some improvements in the local jail but did not impose a cap on the jail population. The Baltimore courts were not under the same pressure as their counterparts in Detroit to make changes.

The disparities between the two cities ran deeper than the specifics of the federal court order. In Detroit, pro-defendant groups were politically active, and the judges could not ignore their demands. By contrast, the dominant political culture in Baltimore was conservative. Pro-defendant groups in particular and black political activity in general were not very influential. Thus, within the context of bail setting (uncertainty, risk, and limited jail resources), the political environment of Detroit supported bail reform, whereas the dynamics of Baltimore supported more punitive policies.

BAIL BONDSMEN

Clustered around urban courthouses are the bright neon lights of the bail bondsmen. Boldly proclaiming "Bail Bonds, 24-Hour Service," they are a constant reminder that freedom is available, for a price. Bail bondsmen are as important to America's monetary bail system as they are controversial. To judicial reformers, they are parasites who prey on human misery. Abolition of bail bondsmen is a key objective of many reformers, and five states (Kentucky, Oregon, Wisconsin, Nebraska, and Illinois) have eliminated bail bonding for profit (Bureau of Justice Statistics 1988). In other states, bondsmen are far less active than they were before the advent of the bail reform movement, writing fewer bonds (Sviridoff 1986). Despite frequent criticisms and efforts to abolish them, they continue to play an important role in the pretrial processing of defendants in many jurisdictions.

Published material about bail bondsmen has been strongly biased because the literature has been mostly reform-oriented. Grand jury investigations, legislative studies, journalistic exposés, and the reports of two national commissions have portrayed bondsmen as fixers of cases and corrupters of courthouses. They are viewed as essential links in the chain of official corruption. To Forrest Dill, however, these studies leave the simplistic impression that the bondsman is an isolated sore. Based on studying bail bondsmen in two California cities, he comments that their links to official corruption, "contain an element of truth, of course, but it is hardly surprising that bail bondsmen in corrupt jurisdictions participate in corrupting practices" (1975, 643). To understand the role of bondsmen in the criminal justice system, one must examine two aspects of their existence: the business setting and the court setting.

 Bad Boyz Bail Bonds—**http://www. badboyzbailbonds.com** has the trademark of "In Jail, We Bail."™

For an up-to-date list of Web links, go to **http:// www.wadsworth.com/product/0534563406s**.

The Business Setting

Bail bondsmen are businesspeople, but their business is unique. By allowing commercial intermediaries to post bond, the state has created a business operation within the criminal courts. In essence, the bondsman is a private government subcontractor; key decisions on pretrial release have been transferred from public officials to private parties, who represent neither the interests of the courts nor those of the defendant.

Bail bondsmen make money by providing a specialized form of insurance. For a nonrefundable fee, they post a bond with the court. If the defendant does not appear for trial, the bondsman is responsible for the full amount of the bond. For assuming this risk, he or she is permitted to charge a fee, usually 10 percent of the face amount of the bond. Rarely, however, do bail bondsmen post a cash surety directly with the court. Instead, they purchase a surety bond from a major insurance company, which charges 30 percent of the bondsman's fee. Thus, if the total amount of the bail is $1,000, the bondsman receives $100 from the client and keeps $70 of it. Because the profit margin in each case is seldom large, bondsmen need to find plenty of clients willing to purchase their services, while simultaneously accepting only those who present a minimal risk of fleeing.

Competition among local bondsmen to gain "good" clients is stiff. Bondsmen employ several techniques to ensure a steady supply of clients. Defendants with prior court experience know how to contact bondsmen who have provided reliable service in the past. Third parties are also a frequent (and sometimes controversial) source of referrals. Defense attorneys sometimes refer a client to a bondsman (often expecting future favors in return). Likewise, police officers, court clerks, or bailiffs may steer defendants toward bondsmen. Such referrals are sometimes an attempt to be helpful, but more often there is an expectation that the person making the referral will be compensated in some way.

Once contact has been made, the bondsman must decide whether to take the arrestee as a client. They consider the following types of defendants bad risks: first offenders (because they are likely to panic); recidivists whose new crime is more serious than previous ones; and violent defendants (they may harm the bondsman). In assessing which defendants are financially reliable, bondsmen use the very criteria ignored by the court: employment history, family situation, and roots in the community. Contrary to popular belief, bondsmen do not accept just anyone as a client. They prefer to write bonds when the bail is low, because their risks are then also low. Thus, many bondsmen make a living by posting bond for numerous defendants accused of minor crimes and an occasional large bond when repayment is assured.

After a bondsman has decided to accept a defendant as a client, a key factor determining whether there will be a bond forfeiture is the degree of supervision the bondsman exercises over the client. Although some bondsmen work long and hard to maintain contact with their clients, most are quite lax (Wice 1974). Once a defendant skips, however, the bondsmen attempt to find the person; they have extraordinary legal powers over bailed defendants who jump bond.

As a condition of posting bail, the bondsman requires the client to sign a contract waiving any protections against extradition and allowing the bondsman to retrieve the defendant from wherever he or she may have fled. These powers exceed any possessed by law enforcement officials. For example,

a bondsman can retrieve a fugitive much more easily than the police can. (See A Day in Court: "So I'm a Bounty Hunter; You Got a Problem with That, Pal?")

Bail Bondsmen and the Courtroom Work Group

Experienced bail bondsmen are on a first-name basis with such court personnel as sheriffs, bailiffs, clerks, and prosecutors, who represent a vital part of their business. Each of these officials can help or hinder the bondsman. As one bondsman noted, "The court clerk is probably one of the most important people I have to deal with. He moves cases, he can get information to the judge, and he has control over various calendar matters. When he's not willing to help you out, he can make life very difficult. He knows he's important, and he acts like it" (Dill 1975, 658). Bondsmen often contribute financially to judges' reelection campaigns. The relationships between bail bondsmen and the courts are reciprocal.

One way in which bondsmen help the courts is by managing the population of arrested persons. Without bail bondsmen, the courts would be faced with an intolerably large jail population or would be forced to make major alterations in their procedures. For decades, bail bondsmen have been the easiest way out of this dilemma. At the same time, bondsmen may also help the court prevent some defendants from being released. When court officials desire that a particular defendant not be released, the bondsmen usually cooperate by refusing to post surety (Dill 1975).

The major financial risk facing bondsmen is that clients will jump bond and fail to appear in court, in which case the entire amount of the bond will have to be made good. Yet in many cities, forfeited bonds regularly go uncollected. Part of this practice is legitimate. To encourage bondsmen to seek out and find those who have fled, courts allow a grace period before bonds are forfeited. But the key reason that many bonds go uncollected is the discretionary power of judges to relieve bondsmen from outstanding bonds. In many cities, bondsmen will not have to pay a bond forfeiture if they can convince the judge that they made every effort to find the missing client (Wice 1974). These considerations cannot fully explain all of the uncollected bonds. Judges are deliberately not trying to collect. Given the help the bondsmen offer the courts, the

A DAY IN COURT

"So I'm a Bounty Hunter; You Got a Problem with That, Pal?"

I wonder whether this is the best time to admit this, but shy is not my style so here goes: I'm proud to call myself a bounty hunter.

No, I'm not talking about the kind of bounty hunter who has been getting so much ink lately—the ones who kick down doors at the wrong houses, or shoot first and ask questions later, or beat up bail jumpers before handing them over to the police.

I'm talking about the bounty hunters like myself and others whose work I respect and admire—professionals who have captured dangerous fugitives after everyone else has given up, who take the time and trouble to make sure they have the right suspect, who treat bounty hunting as a job that needs to be done well and not as an opportunity to play Steve McQueen or Clint Eastwood.

And make no mistake: Like any profession, the field of bounty hunting draws its share of bad actors. I have seen bounty hunters slap people around for no reason other than to satisfy their own sadistic impulses. That's why I have no trouble with those who argue that we need more regulation—perhaps a licensing system and formal training courses. As far as I'm concerned, that can only make the good bounty hunters better and get rid of the bad ones.

Bounty hunting is an accepted part of the criminal justice system. Some of my colleagues hate the term "bounty hunter" and prefer the term "bail enforcement agent." They can call themselves whatever they want. Bounty hunter is fine with me. . . .

The courts depend on us. Without bounty hunters, most bail jumpers would probably never come to trial. The police just wouldn't have the time, or the resources, to catch them all. And we can do things the police can't—something I learned early in my career. Take the case of Ricki and Dee, two women in their twenties awaiting trial on drug charges. I had traced them to a house in the nearby town of Paso Robles. I planned to arrest them, but first I told my pals in the Paso Robles police department. Some of them were standing on the front lawn when I knocked on the door. A woman talked to me through the screen door, but wouldn't open it or let me in. I sensed from her nervous behavior that one or both women were hiding inside. I went around to the side of the house, where I spotted an open window. In a flash, I leaped over the sill and landed in the kitchen.

There was Ricki. I led her out the front door to the waiting cops. I went back into the house to do a more thorough search, and I found Dee hiding in a bathroom. My leap through the window caused quite a stir. I heard a deputy sheriff say, "Gee, I wish I could do that." He wasn't talking about my leaping ability. He was talking about entering the house without a search warrant. So why can I enter a house if the cops can't? Because the courts long ago decided that a defendant, in accepting a bond, is agreeing to allow the bondsman to come after him if he fails to come to court.

Sound too harsh? Remember, we are dealing with accused and convicted criminals whose friends and families have put up the money for their bonds. If they don't show up for trial, their loved ones get hurt. I don't have a lot of sympathy for them.

That's also why I don't apologize for some of my tactics. When I'm trying to trace a skip, I will do anything to get information, including telling outright lies. I will even pretend I am a friend or a relative. My thinking is: They lied to me when they said they would show up for court, so I see nothing wrong with lying to bring them back. Bounty hunting is a head game, and the name of the game is scam. . . .

So when you wonder about bounty hunters and what they do, remember Mr. Rapist. Sure, we need to be careful about who does bounty hunting and how they do it. But while you're sleeping tonight, remember that bounty hunters are hiding in back alleys, crouching on rooftops and lying in muddy fields to track down fugitives who never make it to "America's Most Wanted." Let's not lose sight of who the bad guys really are.

SOURCE: Mackenzie Green, "So I'm a Bounty Hunter; You Got a Problem with That, Pal?" *The Star Tribune* (September 21, 1997), 21A.

 Mackenzie Green is the owner of a San Francisco bail bond firm. Her Web site, Bounty Hunters Online, can be reached at **http://www.onworld.com/BHO/index.html**.

For an up-to-date list of Web links, go to **http://www.wadsworth.com/product/0534563406s**.

 John Elvin, "The Strong Arm of the Law"

major way the courts can reciprocate is by not trying to collect bond forfeitures.

EFFECTS OF THE BAIL SYSTEM

Even though defendants detained before trial are presumed innocent until proven guilty, they suffer many of the same disadvantages as those incarcerated after conviction. Economically, they often lose their jobs. Psychologically, they are subjected to stress, anxiety, and isolation. Physically, they are held in a violence-prone atmosphere. The President's Commission on Law Enforcement and Administration of Justice (1967) chose the following examples to dramatize the human toll that pretrial detention can exact.

- A man was jailed on a serious charge brought last Christmas Eve. He could not afford bail and spent 101 days in jail until a hearing. Then the complainant admitted the charge was false.

- A man spent two months in jail before being acquitted. In that period he lost his job, and his car, and his family was split up. He did not find another job for four months.

In a variety of ways, detained defendants are at a disadvantage during pretrial preparation, plea bargaining, trial, and sentencing.

Jail Conditions

In an influential 1965 book *Ransom: A Critique of the American Bail System,* Ronald Goldfarb described the conditions of jails in the United States as "the ultimate ghetto." Overcrowding was typical and idleness the norm. Food was of low quality and nutritionally poor. Medical care all too often was totally lacking. The environment was brutal; the threat of attack, including homosexual rape, was always present. Three decades after Goldfarb wrote *Ransom,* jails are in "an increasing sense of crisis" (Mays and Thompson 1991). They are the dumping grounds for the arrested criminal, the chronic drunk, the drunk drivers, the mentally ill, the homeless, and juveniles who could be anything from runaway to amoral killer. "The general public and the media ignore jails unless there are escapes, fires, suicides, riots, or titillating tales of corruption or wrongdoing by the staff or elected sheriff" (Kerle 1991).

The impetus for improving jail conditions has come from a steady stream of lawsuits filed by prisoners in federal court, contending that the conditions in the county jails violate the Eighth Amendment prohibition against "cruel and unusual punishment." As a result, federal court supervision of local jails is extensive. Of the 505 jurisdictions with at least 100 jail inmates, 57 percent are under court order to improve one or more conditions of confinement, usually overcrowded living conditions, inadequate recreational facilities, and deficient medical services (Bureau of Justice Statistics 1993). Improving local jails, however, faces numerous obstacles, including trying to coordinate the activities of numerous governmental agencies (Chapter 1) and the reluctance to spend taxpayers' money to "coddle" criminals. Moreover, attempts to choose a site for a new jail typically result in a "not in my back yard" (NIMBY) impasse (Welsh 1995). Thus litigation, although it has produced change, has done so slowly.

Case Disposition

Pretrial detention has a great impact on the legal processing of defendants.

> *Viewed from the perspective of maintaining the plea-bargaining system, pretrial detention and demoralizing conditions in jails are highly functional. They discourage the defendant from bargaining too hard; they place a high price upon filing motions or demanding a trial. . . . This is not to argue that those in authority consciously plan rotten jails; clearly most are concerned about jail conditions. But it is to suggest that such conditions are functional, do serve the needs of the production ethic that dominates our criminal justice system. (Casper 1972, 67)*

The discriminatory impact of bail has been the subject of considerable research. Do defendants in jail have higher rates of conviction and imprisonment? Data on felony defendants in the nation's seventy-five largest cities indicate that detained defendants were convicted 78 percent of the time compared to 66 percent for defendants who had been released (Hart and Reaves 1999). Earlier data from the Manhattan Bail Project, the first systematic investigation of the effects of bail on the criminal court process, clearly showed that detained defendants also had a greater likelihood of being sentenced to prison and for longer terms than those who post bond (Ares, Rankin, and Sturz 1963).

There is widespread agreement in the literature about the central proposition: Jailed defendants are more likely to be convicted and (once convicted) more likely to be sentenced to prison than those who have obtained pretrial release. What is in dispute is the interpretation of these findings. Do these disparities result because the lack of pretrial release imposes additional burdens on the defendants? Or are these disparities a statistical artifact of a preselection process? Given that bail tariffs increase with the severity of the crime and the length of the prior record, one might reasonably expect that these defendants would end up disadvantaged, but for good reason.

John Goldkamp (1980) has attempted to answer this difficult question through a sophisticated analysis of more than 8,000 criminal cases in Philadelphia. Goldkamp found that jailed defendants did not differ from their bailed counterparts in terms of findings of guilt. At all the significant stages—dismissal, diversion, and trial—jailed defendants were as likely as bailed ones to receive a favorable disposition of their cases. When it came to sentencing, however, jailed defendants were more likely to be sentenced to prison, although the length of the sentence was not related to bail status. Similarly, a three-city study (Eisenstein and Jacob 1977) revealed that there was no uniform impact of bail status on either findings of guilt or sentencing (although in some cities in some situations there was an impact). Does bail status negatively affect the defendant's case? Perhaps the best response is provided by Goldkamp: "It depends."

Failure to Appear

Defendants who have gained pretrial release do not always appear in court when required. Skipping bail has several consequences. First, bail is forfeited. Second, a warrant is issued for the suspect's arrest. This warrant, termed a **bench warrant** or a *capias*, authorizes the police to take the person into cus-

> **Bench warrant (capias):**   An order issued by the court itself, or from the bench, for the arrest of a person; it is not based, as is an arrest warrant, on a probable cause showing that a person has committed a crime, but only on the person's failure to appear in court as directed.

tody. The person must be delivered to the judge issuing the warrant and cannot be released on bail. Finally, failure to appear often subjects the defendant to a separate criminal charge of bond jumping.

How often bailed defendants fail to appear in court is subject to considerable debate (Wice 1974). One Bureau of Justice Statistics study of the nation's seventy-five largest jurisdictions reported that 24 percent of the released defendants missed one or more court dates. But this estimate appears to overstate the problem because it defined nonappearance as missing a single court date. Probably more accurate is the estimate of 8 percent of released defendants who failed to appear and were still fugitives at the end of the year-long study (Bureau of Justice Statistics 1993).

Defendants who fail to appear do not always intend to do so. Failure-to-appear rates are closely related to practices within the court. A number of defendants do not show up because they were not given clear notice of the next appearance date. Another way in which courts themselves contribute to nonappearances is by lengthy delay in disposing of cases. As the time from arrest to trial increases, the rate of nonappearances rises even faster (Bureau of Justice Statistics 1993).

> For 101 excuses why defendants fail to appear in court, see: **http://athenabb.com/101excuses.htm**.
>
> For an up-to-date list of Web links, go to **http://www.wadsworth.com/product/0534563406s**.

BAIL REFORM BASED ON THE DUE PROCESS MODEL

America's system of monetary bail has been the subject of extensive debate for decades. The fairness and effectiveness of pretrial release and detention have been questioned from two conflicting perspectives. The bail reform movement of the 1960s and 1970s was largely concerned with correcting inequities. Requiring suspects to buy their freedom was viewed as unfairly discriminating against the poor. Bail reform based on the values of the due process model are reflected in the Bail Reform Act of 1966, which created a presumption favoring pretrial release. Unless the judge is convinced that pretrial release "will not reasonably assure the appearance of the person as required," the defendant is to be released. To make bail fairer, reformers advocated adopting a 10 percent bail deposit and institutionalizing pretrial service programs. These programs offered new ways to accomplish the purpose of bail: to guarantee appearance for trial.

Ten Percent Bail Deposit

Bail agents charge a nonrefundable 10 percent fee for posting bond. Since they seem to perform few services for their fee and have often been linked with corruption, bail reformers have attempted to legislate an economic end run around these third-party operators. In a handful of jurisdictions, defendants may gain pretrial release by posting 10 percent of the face amount of the bond with the court. At this point, there is no difference between what the bail agent charges and what the court requires. But when the defendant makes all scheduled court appearances, the court will refund 90 percent of the amount posted. (The remaining 10 percent covers the administrative costs of the program.) Defendants who fail to appear are still liable for the full face amount of the bond. The 10 percent bail deposit program directly threatens the bail bond industry. In Illinois, the first state to adopt this program, bail agents have virtually disappeared. In other states, however, agents have been successful in defeating such proposals in the legislature.

 Thomas J. Wolf, "What United States Pretrial Services Officers Do"

Pretrial Service Programs

Bail reformers have been critical of traditional methods of bail setting because the court does not directly focus on whether the defendant is likely to appear in court. What were first called bail reform projects but are now termed pretrial service programs seek to remedy this deficiency by determining which defendants are good risks. First developed and tested by the Vera Institute of Justice in New York City, the program works as follows. A program worker interviews the defendant shortly after arrest about family ties, employment history, length of time in the community, prior criminal record, and (in a growing number of areas) results of post-arrest drug tests. Persons deemed good risks are recom-

mended for release on recognizance. Not all defendants are eligible for the program, however; those arrested for serious charges such as murder, armed robbery, or sale of drugs are usually excluded. After release, the pretrial service agency makes follow-up contacts to ensure that the defendant knows when the court appearance is scheduled and will show up.

The guiding assumption of the Vera Project is that defendants with ties to the community are not likely to flee. By providing information about these ties (which normally is not available when bail is set), the program provides a more workable way for making sure that the wrong persons are not detained prior to trial. Research has confirmed the operating assumption. Where pretrial service programs have been tried, the rate of nonappearance for those released on recognizance has been lower than for those released through bail agents (Wice 1974). Supporters also argue that such programs save money. Because more people are being released, costs for holding defendants in jail are significantly reduced. More recently, pretrial service programs have been adopted as a means for relieving jail overcrowding (Bureau of Justice Statistics 1988). Hundreds of such programs now operate throughout the nation.

Pretrial service agencies must operate in a very restricted political atmosphere. In an era dominated by anticrime rhetoric, programs aimed at helping people accused of crimes face an uphill battle. Moreover, there are often conflicts among judges, court administrators, prosecutors, defense attorneys, and the police about who will control and administer the programs (Wice 1974). In an effort to head off possible negative public relations, pretrial service programs have maintained a conservative stance by selecting only the most reliable persons for pretrial release. As a result, pretrial service agencies end up concentrating government resources on those least in need. The initial concern was with truly poor defendants, many from the inner cities and ethnic minorities. But in practice, bail reform has been least able to help this group. A study of the pretrial release program in Charlotte, North Carolina, found that most of the defendants released by the program would have been released on recognizance anyway or would have been able to hire a bail agent. Thus, the pretrial release program made only a slight dent in the percentage of defendants released prior to trial (Clarke, Freeman, and Koch 1976). These and other studies reveal a major

Awaiting Trial in Foti's Fortress

 Because he was charged with a capital offense, Shareef Cousin was not eligible for bail. Therefore, he awaited trial (and later retrial) in what is officially known as the Orleans Parish Prison. Informally, the facility is referred to as Foti's Fortress, a tribute to one of the most powerful officials in the area, Criminal Sheriff Charles Foti, Jr. In a city in which prisons are a growth industry, Sheriff Foti is one of the most ambitious entrepreneurs in town.

When Foti was first elected in 1973, the inmate population was less than eight hundred. Today the total number of local, state, and federal inmates is over 7,000, making it one of the largest jail populations in the country. What is collectively referred to as the Orleans Parish Prison (OPP) is in actuality thirteen separate buildings that sprawl over a twelve-block area, interspersed between the New Orleans police department headquarters, the district attorney's office, criminal district court, municipal court, and traffic court.

Some of the growth in jail capacity was spurred by federal lawsuits over conditions of confinement (Chapter 15). Old Parish Prison, for example, constructed in 1929, was in danger of being closed by the federal courts in the 1970s because of poor safety and sanitary conditions. The growth in the local jail population is also due to the increased arrest activity of the New Orleans police department. As the police have become more proactive (Chapter 10) they have made more arrests, requiring more cells. Another factor is prison overcrowding at the state level (Chapter 15). With the state prisons filled to overflowing, many prisoners are held in local jails, like Orleans Parish Prison, until they can be transferred to state prisons.

In turn, the sheriff has effectively mobilized public opinion to support building more prisons. During peak arrest periods (Mardi Gras, for instance) the sheriff constructed a tent city on vacant land near the other prisons (Cooper 1993). These temporary facilities drew the ire of neighborhood residents and the ACLU, creating political pressures for a more permanent solution. The sheriff has likewise cleverly publicized the problem of overcrowding. In the news media it became known as the "Foti Walk." Local television stations routinely broadcast videotapes of a line of jeering criminals being released from OPP because of overcrowding.

How this prison expansion has been financed remains a persistent and mysterious issue in New Orleans politics. The sheriff takes the position that as an independently elected official he does not have to share financial information with the public, so no one knows how much money the office has or where it comes from. The city is obligated under federal court order to pay $19.65 a day per prisoner but is often late in making payments. Thus, Sheriff Foti finds it more profitable to hold prisoners for the state, which pays $22 per day, or for the federal government.

A complex of this size and magnitude has its problems. One is escapes. In 1993, for example, fifteen prisoners escaped, but the sheriff did not notify the public for several weeks (Woods 1993). Another is inmate deaths. In 1999, for instance, diabetic inmate JoAnn Johnson died while in custody, prompting a protest rally in front of the jail and the filing of a federal lawsuit by the ACLU, which alleged inadequate medical care.

Despite these periodic public relations problems, Sheriff Foti is one of the most popular local officials. He has been reelected every four years with little or no opposition. This is partly due to the variety of non-law enforcement programs he sponsors, including a Halloween haunted house for teens and an annual Thanksgiving dinner for the elderly. He also takes pride in a number of programs for prisoners, including the Prison Art Program, which has literally "painted the town" by creating colorful, large-scale murals on public buildings, and the About Face Program, which provides an innovative approach aimed at helping inmates learn how to redirect their lives. But critics claim that in reality Foti places a low priority on programs to assist prisoners in learning a skill or learning to read (Cooper 1993).

 For a firsthand view of the Orleans Parish Criminal Sheriff's Office, visit the Web site: **http://www.opcso.org/**.

For an up-to-date list of Web links, go to **http://www.wadsworth.com/product/0534563406s**.

gap between the theory of pretrial service programs and their actual implementation (Flemming, Kohfeld, and Uhlman 1980). Overall, pretrial service agencies seem to release those who would have posted cash bail anyway (Bynum 1982). In most jurisdictions, the overall pretrial release rate is more dependent on jail capacity than on the reform efforts (Mahoney 1976).

The District of Columbia Pretrial Services Agency is one of the nation's most active and can be visited at **http://www.gwu.edu/~pretrial/**.

For an up-to-date list of Web links, go to **http://www.wadsworth.com/product/0534563406s**.

BAIL REFORM BASED ON THE CRIME CONTROL MODEL

During the 1980s, concern shifted to the link between bail and crime. Allowing dangerous defendants to post bail was viewed as unnecessarily jeopardizing the public. Critics urged the adoption of preventive detention. Detaining some suspects without bail is designed to adapt constitutional provisions to the current realities of high crime rates. To a great extent, the demand for preventive detention reflects a backlash against the bail reform movement of the 1960s (Walker 1989). Bail reform based on the values of the crime control model are reflected in the 1984 Bail Reform Act, which made wholesale revisions in the earlier law. Its emphasis on protecting the safety of the community represents a major shift in philosophy. In setting bail, a federal judge may now consider danger to the community and may deny bail altogether when the accused is found to be a "grave danger to others." Whereas release of the defendant was the primary intent of the earlier law, detention plays a prominent role in the new one. Bail reform based on the crime control model focuses on two topics: pretrial crimes and preventive detention.

 Here are some Web sites that provide an inside view of jails:

Niagara County (New York): **http://www.ncsd.com**
Sangamon County (Springfield, Illinois): **http://www.fgi.net/sheriff/jail.html**
Chesapeake (Virginia): **http://www.chesapeake.va.us/services/depart/sheriff/sheriff/correct.htm**

For an up-to-date list of Web links, go to **http://www.wadsworth.com/product/0534563406s**.

Pretrial Crimes

Most of the attention in the contemporary discussion of bail focuses on defendants who commit additional crimes while on pretrial release. Individual occurrences are easy to find, and adherents of the crime control model are quick to highlight them in their arguments for preventive detention. But how common are such events?

Numerous studies of pretrial crime have been conducted. The dominant conclusion is that arrests of pretrial releasees for serious crimes are relatively infrequent, and convictions for such crimes are even less frequent (Jackson 1987; Walker 1989). At first glance, this does not appear to be the case. Two studies report that about 15 percent of those released were rearrested while on pretrial conditional release (Toborg 1983; Reaves and Perez 1994). But a simple measure of rearrest distorts the true picture. Many of those rearrested were initially arrested for a misdemeanor and later arrested for another minor offense. A better measure is the percentage of all persons arrested for a felony, released on bail, and later arrested for another felony. Depending on the study, the pretrial crime rate ranges from 5 to 7 percent (Gottfredson 1974; Toborg 1983). The relative infrequency of serious pretrial crime makes its prediction especially difficult (Jackson 1987), not to say suspect. Nonetheless, as a tool in predicting risk, many jurisdictions are now adopting mandatory pretrial drug testing. (See Controversy: Should Defendants Be Forced to Take a Drug Test?)

Preventive Detention

Should defendants be held in jail awaiting trial with no right to bail? Adherents of the crime control model assume that current bail practices do not successfully restrain dangerous defendants. They point to defendants who commit crimes while out of jail on pretrial release. The suggested alternative is **preventive detention**, which allows judges to hold suspects without bail if they are accused of committing a dangerous or violent crime and locking them up is deemed necessary for community safety.

About three fifths of the states have enacted laws that allow courts to consider public safety, danger to the community, jeopardy to others, or similar general reasons in setting conditions of release or in

Preventive detention: Holding a defendant in custody pending trial in the belief that he or she is likely to commit further criminal acts or flee the jurisdiction.

CONTROVERSY

Should Defendants Be Forced to Take a Drug Test?

 The dual concerns of failure to appear and committing additional crimes while out on bail have become focused on pretrial drug-testing programs.

There is little doubt that drug use among those arrested is high—in a typical year the percentage of male arrestees testing positive for recent illegal drug use is approximately 75 percent. This estimate is based on data gathered by the Arrestee Drug Abuse Monitoring (ADAM) program, which was formerly known as Drug Use Forecasting (DUF). The ADAM program tests arrestees in thirty-five cities for recent use of illicit drugs ("Arrestee Drug Abuse Monitoring" 2001).

Pretrial drug-testing programs are based on the following assumptions: First, knowledge of a defendant's drug use at the time of arrest—obtained through a drug test—provides an important predictor of pretrial misconduct. Second, monitoring drug use during the pretrial periods, coupled with sanctions, will reduce the risk of pretrial misconduct (Henry and Clark 1999).

The District of Columbia Pretrial Services Agency was the first to implement pretrial drug testing as part of the bail process. Demonstration programs to replicate the D.C. program were established with federal funding in six other cities. In addition, other jurisdictions have created somewhat similar programs (Pretrial Services Resource Center 1999).

In the federal courts Operation Drug TEST (Testing Effective Sanctions and Treatments) was implemented in 1997. It requires that all defendants arrested will be tested and the results reported to the courts, prosecutors, and defense attorneys. Refusal by a defendant to submit to a drug test is not the basis for detention.

Pretrial drug testing rests on the assumption that the most frequent serious offenders are also the heaviest drug users. Research, however, questions the utility of such programs in reducing pretrial rearrests and increasing court appearances. A study of three drug-testing programs found no differences in terms of rearrest or failure to appear rates (Visher 1992; Goldkamp and Jones 1992). "The lack of predictive power is not surprising from a statistical perspective because drug use is very common among arrestees and pretrial misconduct a relatively rare event" (Belenko, Mara-Drita, and McElroy 1992, 577).

To be worthwhile, pretrial drug-testing programs must be able to improve predictive accuracy beyond that offered by other readily existing data such as prior arrest records and ties to the community. To assess the effectiveness of drug testing, researchers examined six sites. The findings showed that, except for heroin use, pretrial drug testing did not appear to help predict rearrests and that, except for cocaine use, testing did not help identify those who would fail to appear for trial. The best predictor of rearrest turned out to be the number of prior arrests, not drug use. Surprisingly, first-time arrestees who tested positive for any illicit substance were better risks for release than repeat offenders who did not test positive for recent drug use (Rhodes, Hyatt, and Scheiman 1996).

Beyond the cost of conducting drug tests is the expense of treating addicts. Throughout the United States, programs to treat those addicted to alcohol and/or illicit drugs are plentiful for those covered by medical insurance but sparse for those without coverage (which tends to be those involved in the criminal justice system). Overall, treatment options for drug-dependent arrestees are limited.

What do you think? Are pretrial drug-testing programs effective in reducing failure to appear rates and pretrial crimes? Or are pretrial drug-testing programs ineffective because they are based on faulty assumptions?

 For the latest statistics on drug use, point your browser to **http://www.adam-nij.net**.

For an up-to-date list of Web links, go to **http://www.wadsworth.com/product/0534563406s**.

denying release altogether. These laws take various forms, including exclusion of certain crimes from automatic bail eligibility, limitations on the right to bail for those previously convicted, and revocation of pretrial release when there is evidence that the accused committed a new crime (Bureau of Justice Statistics 1988; Goldkamp 1985).

The best-known example of preventive detention is the Bail Reform Act of 1984, which authorizes preventive detention for federal defendants accused of serious crimes. After a detention hearing, the defendant may be held in jail without bail for up to ninety days pending trial if the judge finds "clear and convincing evidence" that (1) there is a serious

U.S. v. Salerno and Preventive Detention

 The eighty-eight-page federal grand jury indictment charged that Anthony Salerno, the alleged "boss of the Genovese Crime Family of La Cosa Nostra," and fourteen other members described as associates violated twenty-nine federal laws ranging from Racketeer Influenced and Corrupt Organizations Act (RICO) violations, mail fraud, wire fraud, and extortion to gambling and conspiracy to commit murder. The front-page article in *The New York Times* was quick to note that the indictments followed an earlier *New York Times* series detailing how the mob had infiltrated concrete companies to control construction of high-rise buildings in Manhattan, including Trump Plaza (Lubasch 1986).

In past cases like this, bond had typically been set in the millions with the amount calculated to virtually assure that the defendant would be unable to raise the necessary funds and therefore wait trial in jail. But in this case Rudolph Giuliani, U.S. attorney for the Southern District of New York (primarily Manhattan), chose to seek preventive detention. The Bail Reform Act of 1984 allows a federal court to detain an arrestee pending trial if the government demonstrates by clear and convincing evidence that no release condition "will reasonably assure . . . the safety of any other person and the community." During the detention hearing, the U.S. attorney introduced evidence gathered through court-ordered wiretaps and also two potential trial witnesses, who asserted that Salerno personally participated in two murder conspiracies. The district court granted the government's detention motion.

Salerno appealed and the Second Circuit struck down the law as unconstitutional. Other circuits, though, had reached a different conclusion. An indication that the Court was anxious to hear a case like this one could be seen in the speed of the appellate process; on January 21, 1987, just ten months after arrest, the Court heard oral argument.

That the majority of the Court adheres to the crime control model on this issue is made abundantly clear in the opening paragraph (after the statement of the facts). Chief Justice William Rehnquist's opinion begins by stressing the reasonableness of the statute: Responding to "the alarming problem of crimes com-

mitted by person on release . . ." Congress passed the Bail Reform Act of 1984 as the solution to a "bail crisis in the federal courts." As for the Eighth Amendment, the opinion stresses "Nothing in the text of the Bail Clause limits permissible government considerations solely to questions of flight." Thus Congress was justified in allowing the courts to deny bail, not only if there is a danger of flight but also if the person poses a danger to others.

The three dissenting justices clearly express values of the due process model. In Thurgood Marshall's biting words, the Bail Reform Act of 1984 represents the first time Congress "declares that a person innocent of any crime may be jailed indefinitely, pending the trial of allegations which are legally presumed to be untrue." Such practices are "consistent with the usages of tyranny and excesses of bitter experience teaches us to call the police state." Likewise in dissent John Paul Stevens argues that depriving persons of vital rights on the basis of predictions of future dangerousness is unconstitutional.

Beneath the debate over how best to reduce crime runs an important issue of how to interpret the Constitution (Chapter 17). One theory, usually associated with conservatives, is strict constructionism—the document should be interpreted on the basis of the original intent of the framers. Another theory, usually identified with liberals, is adaptationist—the meaning of the document should be adjusted to changing conditions of society. The *Salerno* opinion dramatically illustrates that when it comes to rights of criminal defendants these positions are reversed. Conservatives stress the need to adapt the Constitution to the pressing current problem of crime, whereas liberals emphasize that the framers were indeed correct in suspecting that the government is capable of tyranny.

 The following articles provide contrasting opinions about preventive detention:

Michael Corrado, "Punishment, Quarantine, and Preventive Detention"

Michael Davis, "Preventive Detention, Corrado, and Me"

risk that the person will flee; (2) the person may obstruct justice or threaten, injure, or intimidate a prospective witness or juror; or (3) the offense is one of violence or one punishable by life imprison-

ment or death. The law also creates a presumption against pretrial release for major drug dealers (Berg 1985). The Supreme Court has upheld the Bail Reform Act, ruling that Congress enacted preventive detention not as a punishment for dangerous individuals but as a potential solution to the pressing social problem of crimes committed by persons on bail (see Case Close-Up: *U.S. v. Salerno* and Preventive Detention).

Are preventive detention laws merely exercises in symbolic politics, or do they have substantive impact? Experience with state preventive detention statutes suggests that they are rarely implemented (Toborg and Bellassai 1986). This was certainly the case in Washington, D.C. (whose law served as the basis for the 1984 federal law). Prosecutors rarely requested detention hearings, and fewer than two out of every thousand felony defendants were formally detained (Thomas 1976). To avoid the law's elaborate procedural requirements, prosecutors relied on the traditional practice of using high monetary bail amounts as a covert form of preventive detention (Cohen 1985). It is also worth noting that, considering severe jail overcrowding at the state and local level, preventive detention laws are doomed to a symbolic status unless there are massively expensive efforts to greatly increase jail capacity.

Experience at the federal level, however, suggests a more complicated pattern. The Bail Reform Act of 1984 is being implemented on a substantial scale. Detention hearings are being held and defendants detained without bail being set. In the most recent year for which data are available, over 26,000 detention hearings were held, with 75 percent of the defendants (19,254) ordered detained (Bureau of Justice Statistics 1999). But what of those defendants the government wished to detain but the court refused? Interestingly, only 0.3 percent committed a violent crime; clearly most defendants whom the government feared would commit an act of violence did not do so (Bak 1994). However, other evidence suggests that the effects of the law are actually quite muted. A detailed analysis of the U.S. District Court for the Eastern District of California found that the overall detention rate, and the average detention length, remained unchanged. The greatest impact was felt by drug offenders, for whom rates of detention significantly increased (Kingsnorth et al. 1987). Similarly, a Bureau of Justice Statistics study (1988) indicates that pretrial detention is being used as an alternative to the setting of high monetary bonds to hold defendants prior to trial. In short, the new law has changed procedures but seems to have had relatively little impact on overall detention policy.

Civil libertarians view preventive detention laws as a threat to constitutional values. Predictions of the dangerousness of arrestees prove to be very unreliable. According to Ewing (1991), for every accurate prediction of dangerousness, there are two inaccurate predictions. Various studies indicate that the criteria used in setting bail are poor predictors of the likelihood that the defendant will later appear in court as scheduled or will commit further crimes while out on bail (Goldkamp 1983). Therefore, civil libertarians advocate reducing trial court delay (Chapter 5) as a better approach to reducing crimes committed while defendants are out on bail. Critics also contend that preventive detention measures will have little effect on the crime rate (Walker 1989).

CONCLUSION

U.S. v. Salerno marked a turning point in the lives of both participants. *Fortune* magazine once described Anthony "Fat Tony" Salerno as the richest and most powerful mobster in America. But at the age of seventy-four he was sentenced to 100 years in prison. The future for U.S. attorney Rudolph Giuliani was strikingly different. He resigned his office several years later to run successfully for mayor of New York, with crime as his lead issue. In 1997 he was overwhelmingly reelected. In 2000 he withdrew from a promising race for U.S. Senate after being diagnosed with prostate cancer.

Beyond the people associated with *U.S. v. Salerno*, the case itself has a couple of unusual features. In deciding to decide about preventive detention, the Court clearly selected the best fact situation for its purposes. If the Court intended, as it probably did, to uphold preventive detention laws, then what better case than a reputed mobster accused of several murders? This interpretation of the Court's choice is reinforced by another unusual feature: By the time the Court made its decision, Salerno had already been convicted. Thus, by all legal standards the justices should have declared the issue of preventive detention for

Salerno to be moot because he was now being held in jail as a convicted felon, not merely as a person accused of a crime. Overall, the Court appeared to be in a rush to put its stamp of approval on a law reflecting the crime control model.

Bail serves several purposes in the American court system, some legally sanctioned, others definitely extralegal. Bail is used to guarantee a defendant's appearance at trial, to protect society by holding those perceived to be dangerous, to punish those accused (but not yet convicted) of violating the law, and to lubricate the system by softening defendants up to enter a plea of guilty. These varying purposes are partially the result of the tension between conflicting principles. Although the law recognizes that the only legal purpose of bail is to guarantee a suspect's future appearance at trial, court officials perceive a need to protect society. Out of these conflicting principles arise compromises.

 Anthony Salerno died in prison in 1992. To view his grave site, go to **http://www.findagrave.com** and search under the name *Anthony Salerno.*

For an up-to-date list of Web links, go to **http://www.wadsworth.com/product/0534563406s**.

CRITICAL THINKING QUESTIONS

1. How does bail and bail setting illustrate the differences between law on the books and law in action?

2. In what ways do crime control model advocates approach bail differently than do backers of due process model values?

3. How does the courtroom work group constrain the judge in bail setting?

4. Examine the local papers. Have there been reports of defendants committing crimes while out on bail? Have there been reports of poor conditions in the local jail? How might these reports affect bail setting?

5. Talk with judges, prosecutors, and defense attorneys about the relationship between pretrial release and the following two factors: jail capacity and length of time between arrest and disposition. (You may wish to review Chapter 5.)

6. Are preventive detention laws effective, or are they exercises in symbolic politics?

 WORLD WIDE WEB RESOURCES AND EXERCISES

Web Guides

http://dir.yahoo.com/Society_and_Culture/Crime/Law_Enforcement/Bail_Enforcement_Agents/
http://dir.yahoo.com/Business_and_Economy/Shopping_and_Services/Financial_Services/Personal_Finance/Bail_Bonds/
http://dir.yahoo.com/Society_and_Culture/Crime/Law_Enforcement/Wanted/

Web Search Terms

"Bail"; "pretrial release"; "jail"; "bounty hunters"; "pretrial services agency"; "preventive detention"; "excessive bail"

Useful URLs

The American Jail Association is a national nonprofit organization dedicated to supporting those who work in and operate our nation's jails: **http://www.corrections.com/aja/**.

The Bureau of Justice Statistics provides up-to-date jail statistics at **http://www.ojp.usdoj.gov/bjs/jails.htm**.

Crimestoppers USA focuses on arresting fugitives: **http://www.crimestopusa.com/**.

The National Association of Pretrial Services Agencies represents professionals in the field: **http://napsa.org/index.htm**.

The Jail Operations Section of the National Sheriffs' Association offers correspondence courses and provides technical assistance: **http://www.sheriffs.org/**.

The Pretrial Services Resource Center is a clearinghouse for information on pretrial issues and a technical assistance provider: **http://www.pretrial.org/**.

For more than thirty-five years the Vera Institute of Justice has been the pioneering organization in pretrial practices: **http://www.verg.org**.

Uncommon URLs

The following bail agents provide interesting and sometimes colorful Web sites:
Athena Bail Bonds: **http://athenabb.com/**
Bail Bond Recovery Resource Center: **http://www.pimall.com/nais/bailr.html**
Excalibur Bail Recovery Agency: **http://www.bhunted.com/home.htm**

Fort Worth Bounty Hunting Association: **http://web2.airmail.net/jdt/**

Jail Net: **http://www.jail.net/**

National Surety Services of Florida, Inc.: **http://www.bailbonding.com/**

Pretrial Services of the Arizona Superior Court in Pima County offers insights into a court-sponsored agency: **http://www.sc.co.pima.az.us/pretrial/**.

Pretrial Services Agency of the U.S. District Court for New Mexico is an example of a federal court agency: **http://www.nmcourt.fed.us/ptdocs/**.

PX Direct sells inmate uniforms, jail cell equipment, and so on: **http://www.pxdirect.com/**.

Pennsylvania Crimestoppers can be found at **http://www.pacrimestoppers.org/**.

Private Investigators Mall bills itself as "The Web's First Shopping Mall of Private Investigators": **http://www.pimall.com/**.

"Wanted" posters from the United States Postal Inspection Service can be found at **http://www.usps.gov/websites/depart/inspect/wantmenu.htm**.

Web Exercises

1. The online version of the *Sourcebook of Criminal Justice Statistics* contains the most recent data available. In particular, information on pretrial release of federal defendants can easily be found at the following URL: **http://www.albany.edu/ sourcebook/**.

   Under Section 5 look for information on pretrial release to answer the following two questions: What percentage of released federal defendants had no violation? What percentage of federal defendants were held under preventive detention?

2. A growing number of bail agents have Web sites. The following Yahoo search will locate some (although a search engine using the key words "*bail agents*" or "*bail bondsmen*" will yield more): **http://www.yahoo.com/, Business and Economy/Companies/Financial Services/ Personal Finance/Bail Bonds**. From the list provided, choose three that are geographically close to you and compare their Web sites. Which one would you call if a friend or relative needed to post bond? Do the Web sites provide any information on types of clients that they prefer? Overall, how do these ads compare to ads for lawyers, doctors, insurance agents, or other personal services?

3. "Wanted: Dead or Alive" posters became the basis for nineteenth-century legendary heroes. The twenty-first-century equivalent can be found on the Internet. The bail industry's showcase to display "bond skips" can be found at **http://www.bailjumpers.net/**. Compare the number of fugitives who have skipped bail to those who have never been arrested. How do these lists differ from those maintained by law enforcement (the FBI, for example)? Overall, does there appear to be a profit motive mentioned for seeking out fugitives?

 INFOTRAC COLLEGE EDITION RESOURCES AND EXERCISES

Basic Search Terms

Bail; pretrial release; mandatory drug testing, evaluation; bounty hunters; bail bondsmen

Recommended Articles

Loren Buddress, "Federal Probation and Pretrial Services—A Cost-Effective and Successful Community Connections System"

Christian Parenti, "I Hunt Men"

"Aggressive Drug-Fighting Efforts Reduce Use among Pennsylvania Inmates"

Barry Lester, "Drug-Addicted Mothers Need Treatment, Not Punishment"

Rolando del Carmen and Maldine Beth Barnhill, "Legal Issues in Juvenile Drug Testing"

"New Jersey Court Allows Drug Test Search, Finding Reasonable Suspicion"

Jeffrey Fagan and Martin Guggenheim, "Preventative Detention and the Judicial Prediction of Dangerousness for Juveniles: A Natural Experiment"

InfoTrac College Edition Exercises

1. The debate over preventive detention offers a classic difference between advocates of the crime control and the due process model. Using the search term *preventive detention,* find articles that debate this topic and analyze their arguments.

2. Using the search term *pretrial services,* find two or more articles that discuss this topic. What advantages are portrayed for these programs? Why do bail agents often oppose these governmental programs?

REFERENCES

Ares, Charles, Ann Rankin, and Herbert Sturz. 1963. "The Manhattan Bail Project: An Interim Report on the Use of Pretrial Parole." *New York University Law Review* 38: 67–92.

"Arrestee Drug Abuse Monitoring Program." 2001. Washington, D.C.: National Institute of Justice. http://www.adam-nij.net/.

Backstrand, John, Don Gibbons, and Joseph Jones. 1992. "Who Is in Jail? An Examination of the Rabble Hypothesis." *Crime and Delinquency* 38: 219–229.

Bak, Thomas. 1994. "Defendants Who Avoid Detention: A Good Risk?" Washington, D.C.: Administrative Office of the United States Courts.

Belenko, Steven, Iona Mara-Drita, and Jerome McElroy. 1992. "Drug Tests and the Prediction of Pretrial Misconduct: Findings and Policy Issues." *Crime and Delinquency* 38: 557–582.

Berg, Kenneth. 1985. "The Bail Reform Act of 1984." *Emory Law Journal* 34: 687–740.

Bureau of Justice Statistics. 1988. *Pretrial Release and Detention: The Bail Reform Act of 1984.* Washington, D.C.: U.S. Department of Justice.

———. 1993. *Jail Inmates 1992.* Washington, D.C.: U.S. Department of Justice.

———. 1999. *Federal Pretrial Release and Detention, 1996.* Washington, D.C.: U.S. Department of Justice.

———. 2000. *Jail Statistics.* (http://www.ojp.usdoj.gov/bjs/jails.htm)

Bynum, Tim. 1982. "Release on Recognizance: Substantive or Superficial Reform?" *Criminology* 20: 67–82.

Casper, Jonathan. 1972. *American Criminal Justice: The Defendant's Perspective.* Englewood Cliffs, NJ: Prentice-Hall.

Clarke, Stevens, Jean Freeman, and Gary Koch. 1976. *The Effectiveness of Bail Systems: An Analysis of Failure to Appear in Court and Rearrest While on Bail.* Chapel Hill: Institute of Government, University of North Carolina.

Cohen, Fred. 1985. "Special Feature: An Introduction to the New Federal Crime Control Act." *Criminal Law Bulletin* 21: 330–337.

Cooper, Christopher. 1993. "Wish Comes True: Prison Space for 7,140." *Times-Picayune,* 20 October.

Dill, Forrest. 1975. "Discretion, Exchange and Social Control: Bail Bondsmen in Criminal Courts." *Law and Society Review* 9: 639–674.

Eisenstein, James, and Herbert Jacob. 1977. *Felony Justice: An Organizational Analysis of Criminal Courts.* Boston: Little, Brown.

Ewing, Charles. 1991. "Preventive Detention and Execution: The Constitutionality of Punishing Future Crimes. "*Law and Human Behavior* 15: 139–165.

Flemming, Roy. 1982. *Punishment Before Trial: An Organizational Perspective on Felony Bail Process.* New York: Longman.

Flemming, Roy, C. Kohfeld, and Thomas Uhlman. 1980. "The Limits of Bail Reform: A Quasi Experimental Analysis." *Law and Society Review* 14: 947–976.

Frazier, Charles, E. Wilbur Bock, and John Henretta. 1980. "Pretrial Release and Bail Decisions: The Effects of Legal, Community and Personal Variables." *Criminology* 18: 162–181.

Goldfarb, Ronald. 1965. *Ransom: A Critique of the American Bail System.* New York: Harper and Row.

Goldkamp, John. 1980. "The Effects of Detention on Judicial Decisions: A Closer Look." *Justice System Journal* 5: 234–257.

———. 1983. "Questioning the Practice of Pretrial Detention: Some Empirical Evidence from Philadelphia." *The Journal of Criminal Law and Criminology* 74: 1556–1588.

———. 1985. "Danger and Detention: A Second Generation of Bail Reform." *Journal of Criminal Law and Criminology* 76: 1–74.

Goldkamp, John, and Peter Jones. 1992. "Pre-Trial Drug-Testing Experiments in Milwaukee and Prince George's County: The Context of Implementation." *Journal of Research in Crime and Delinquency* 29: 430–465.

Gottfredson, Michael. 1974. "Empirical Analysis of Pretrial Release Decisions." *Journal of Criminal Justice* 2: 287.

Hart, Timothy, and Brian Reaves. 1999. *Felony Defendants in Large Urban Counties, 1996.* Washington, D.C.: Bureau of Justice Statistics.

Henry, D. Alan, and John Clark. 1999. "Pretrial Drug Testing: An Overview of Issues and Practices." *Bulletin,* Bureau of Justice Assistance (NCJ 176341).

Jackson, Patrick. 1987. "The Impact of Pretrial Preventive Detention." *Justice System Journal* 12: 305–334.

Jones, Peter, and John Goldkamp. 1991. "The Bail Guidelines Experiment in Dade County, Miami: A Case Study in the Development and Implementation of Policy Innovation." *Justice System Journal* 14: 445–476.

Kerle, Kenneth. 1991. "Introduction." In *American Jails: Public Policy Issues,* edited by Joel Thompson and G. Larry Mays. Chicago: Nelson-Hall.

Kingsnorth, Rodney, Carole Barnes, Cynthia Davis, Tina Hodgins, and Camille Nicholes. 1987. "Preventive Detention: The Impact of the 1984 Bail Reform Act in the Eastern Federal District of California." *Criminal Justice Policy Review* 2: 150–173.

Lubasch, Arnold. 1986. "Reputed Mob Leader Among 15 Indicted on Racketeering Counts." *The New York Times,* 21 March.

Mahoney, Barry. 1976. "Evaluating Pretrial Release Programs." Paper presented at the annual meeting of the American Political Science Association, Chicago.

Mays, G. Larry, and Joel Thompson. 1991. "The Political and Organizational Context of American Jails."

In *American Jails: Public Policy Issues*, edited by Joel Thompson and G. Larry Mays. Chicago: Nelson-Hall.

Nagel, Ilene. 1983. "The Legal/Extra-Legal Controversy: Judicial Decisions in Pretrial Release." *Law and Society Review* 17: 481–515.

Nagel, Robert. 1990. "The Myth of the General Right to Bail." *Public Interest* 98: 84–97.

Perkins, Craig, James Stephan, and Allen Beck. 1995. *Jails and Jail Inmates 1993–94*. Washington, D.C.: U.S. Department of Justice, Bureau of Justice Statistics.

President's Commission on Law Enforcement and Administration of Justice. 1967. *Task Force Report: The Courts*. Washington, D.C.: U.S. Government Printing Office.

Pretrial Services Resource Center. 1999. *Integrating Drug Testing into a Pretrial Service System: 1999 Update*. Washington, D.C.: Bureau of Justice Assistance, U.S. Department of Justice.

Reaves, Brian, and Jacob Perez. 1994. *Pretrial Release of Felony Defendants, 1992*. Washington, D.C.: U.S. Department of Justice, Bureau of Justice Statistics.

Rhodes, William, Raymond Hyatt, and Paul Scheiman. 1996. "Research in Brief: Predicting Pretrial Misconduct with Drug Tests of Arrestees." Washington, D.C.: National Institute of Justice.

Roth, Jeffrey, and Paul Wice. 1980. *Pretrial Release and Misconduct in the District of Columbia*. Washington D.C.: Institute for Law and Social Research.

Snyder, Elizabeth. 1989. "Toward an Integrative Theory on Courtroom Decision Making: Observations on Bail Setting and Sentencing." Paper presented at the 1989 Midwest Political Science Association Convention, Chicago, April.

Suffet, Frederick. 1966. "Bail Setting: A Study of Courtroom Interaction." *Crime and Delinquency* 12: 318–331.

Sviridoff, Michele. 1986. "Bail Bonds and Cash Alternatives: The Influence of 'Discounts' on Bail-Making in New York City." *Justice System Journal* 11: 131–147.

Thomas, Wayne. 1970. *The Current State of Bail Reform: Bail Projects*. Davis, CA: Center on the Administration of Justice.

———. 1976. *Bail Reform in America*. Berkeley: University of California Press.

Toborg, Mary. 1983. "Bail Bondsmen and Criminal Courts." *Justice System Journal* 8: 141–156.

Toborg, Mary, and John Bellassai. 1986. *Public Danger as a Factor in Pre-Trial Release*. Washington, D.C.: Toborg Associations, Inc., in cooperation with the National Association of Pre-Trial Service Agencies.

Visher, Christy. 1992. *Pretrial Drug Testing*. Washington, D.C.: National Institute of Justice, U.S. Department of Justice.

Walker, Samuel. 1989. *Sense and Nonsense About Crime: A Policy Guide*. 2d ed. Pacific Grove, CA: Brooks/Cole.

Welsh, Wayne. 1995. *Counties in Court: Jail Overcrowding and Court-Ordered Reform*. Philadelphia: Temple University Press.

Wice, Paul. 1974. *Freedom for Sale*. Lexington, MA: Lexington Books.

Woods, Keith. 1993. "The Wall Builder." *Times-Picayune*, 13 September.

Zeisel, Hans. 1979. "Bail Revisited." *American Bar Foundation Research Journal* 1979: 769–789.

FOR FURTHER READING

Corrado, Michael. "Punishment and the Wild Beast of Prey: The Problem of Preventive Detention." *Journal of Criminal Law and Criminology* 86 (1996): 778–814.

Devine, F. E. *Commercial Bail Bonding: A Comparison of Common Law Alternatives*. Westport, CT: Greenwood, 1991.

Hirschel, J. David, and Charles Dean. "The Relative Cost-Effectiveness of Citation and Arrest. *Journal of Criminal Justice* 23 (1995): 1–12.

Katz, Charles, and Cassia Spohn. "The Effect of Race and Gender on Bail Outcomes: A Test of an Interactive Model." *Americana Journal of Criminal Justice* 19 (1995): 161–184.

Kerle, Kenneth. *American Jails: Looking to the Future*. Woburn, MA: Butterworth-Heinemann, 1998.

Mieckowski, Tom, and Kim Lersch. "Drug Testing in Criminal Justice: Evolving Uses, Emerging Technologies." *National Institute of Justice Journal* (December 1997): 9–15.

Robinson, Jerome, and James Jones. "Drug Testing in a Drug Court Environment: Common Issues to Address." Washington, D.C.: U.S. Department of Justice, Drug Courts Program Office (NCJ 181103), 2000.

Thompson, Joel, and G. Larry Mays, eds. *American Jails: Public Policy Issues*. Chicago: Nelson-Hall, 1991.

Vance, Neil, and Ronald Stupak. "Organizational Culture and the Placement of Pretrial Agencies in the Criminal Justice System." *Justice System Journal* 19 (1997): 51–76.

Wolf, Thomas. "The Mirmont Evaluation: Drug Treatment as a Condition of Pretrial Release." *Federal Probation* 58 (1994): 34–45.

Disclosing and Suppressing Evidence

Just before midnight, eighteen-year-old Lois Ann Jameson (not her real name) left the downtown theater where she worked and walked the two blocks to her normal bus stop. A half hour later she alighted in her neighborhood for her usual short walk home. The only unusual event was a strange car, which suddenly veered in front of her. A young Hispanic man got out, grabbed her with one hand, and placed the other over her mouth while dragging her into the parked car. He drove twenty minutes into the desert, where he tore off her clothes and raped her. In a strange twist of circumstances, the assailant drove Lois Ann Jameson back to her neighborhood. Once she was home, she immediately called the police. To Detective Carroll Cooley, Jameson's story was not only somewhat contradictory but also offered few leads. Jameson couldn't provide a very good description of her attacker. The only lead was her detailed description of the car—an old model, light green, clean on the outside, and dirty brown upholstery on the inside. Moreover, in the back seat of the car was a loop of rope designed to help rear-seat passengers in pulling themselves up. This description eventually led Detective Cooley to a house on the west side of town where he found a car exactly as described (Baker 1983). The subsequent interrogation and conviction of Ernesto Miranda was to change the landscape of American criminal justice.

The *Miranda* warnings are the most controversial part of the Supreme Court's revolution in criminal justice. Responding to criticisms that police procedures were unfair and that the police were not adhering to the procedural requirements of the law, the Supreme Court imposed additional restrictions on police investigative techniques, such as searches, interrogations, and lineups. The Court's decisions produced extensive national controversy. But in turn, subsequent Courts, dominated by appointees of Republican presidents, have significantly curtailed (but not eliminated) these earlier decisions.

This chapter examines some of the diverse activities that may occur between arraignment and final disposition (either a guilty plea or a trial). The first topic will be the gathering of evidence, which is termed discovery. Next will be a discussion of how and why some evidence is excluded from trial. ■

DISCOVERY

The informal and formal exchange of information between prosecution and defense is referred to as **discovery**. Laboratory reports, fingerprint results, ballistics tests, statements of witnesses, defendants' confessions, and police reports are examples of information that prosecutors often gather and defense attorneys want to know before trial. Such knowledge can help each party strengthen its own case as well as plan responses to the opposition's litigation strategy.

Discovery seeks to ensure that the adversary system does not give one side an unfair advantage over the other. The guiding assumption of the adversary system is that truth will emerge after a struggle at trial. But as Justice William Brennan (1963) asked, should this struggle at trial be a sporting event or a quest for the truth? Historically, civil trials were largely sporting events, in which the outcome depended heavily on the technical skills of

the lawyers. In an effort to eliminate the worst aspects of such contests, the Federal Rules of Civil Procedure were adopted in 1938, and most states have since followed the federal example. By these rules, prior to trial, every party in a civil action is entitled to the disclosure of all relevant information in the possession of any person, unless that information is privileged (Wright 1994). These discovery rules are intended to make a trial "less a game of blind man's bluff and more a fair contest with the basic issues and facts disclosed to the fullest practicable manner" (*U.S. v. Procter and Gamble Co.,* 1958). There has been a long-standing debate, however, over the extent of pretrial discovery in criminal cases.

Law on the Books:
Rules Requiring Disclosure

Although there is a very broad power of discovery in civil proceedings, there is no general constitutional right to discovery in a criminal case (*Weatherford v. Bursey,* 1977). Courts have expressed concern that requiring too much prosecutorial disclosure might result in the defendant's taking undue advantage (*State v. Tune,* 1953). For example, the defendant,

Discovery: Pretrial procedure in which parties to a lawsuit ask for and receive information such as testimony, records, or other evidence from each other.

FIGURE 12-1		Key Developments in Criminal Discovery Law
Jencks v. U.S.	1957	Prior inconsistent statements of a witness must be made available to defense counsel.
Brady v. Maryland	1963	Due process of law is violated when prosecutors conceal evidence that might be favorable to the defense.
Williams v. Florida	1970	Requiring defense to disclose an alibi defense prior to trial does not violate the defendant's privilege against self-incrimination.
U.S. v. Agurs	1976	Under *Brady*, the prosecutor must disclose evidence only if such evidence would have been persuasive and produced reasonable doubt about guilt.
Weatherford v. Bursey	1977	No general constitutional right to discovery in criminal cases.
Kyles v. Whitley	1995	Materiality of evidence not disclosed determined by looking at the effect of all of the evidence, not simply one item.
Wood v. Bartholomew	1995	Failure of prosecutor to turn over inadmissible polygraph evidence was not a *Brady* violation.
Strickler v. Greene	1999	Even though petitioner was not given exculpatory evidence, there was no *Brady* violation because there was no prejudice.

knowing of the state's case, might procure perjured testimony or might harass and intimidate witnesses who are likely to testify (Saltzburg 1983).

The type of information that is discoverable varies considerably from state to state. Some jurisdictions allow only limited discovery: The trial court has the discretion to order the prosecutor to disclose the defendant's confession and/or other physical documents, but that is all. Other jurisdictions take a middle ground: Discovery of confessions and physical evidence is a matter of right, but discovery of other items (witnesses' statements, for example) is more difficult. Finally, a few states have adopted liberal discovery rules: There is a presumption strongly in favor of prosecutorial disclosure, with only certain narrow exceptions. Figure 12-1 summarizes significant developments in criminal discovery law.

Because of growing discontent with the discovery system, American courts have cautiously expanded mandatory disclosure by the prosecutor. In *Jencks v. U.S.* (1957), the Court ruled that prior inconsistent statements of a witness must be made available to the defense. This decision was later strengthened in *Brady v. Maryland* (1963), in which the Supreme Court held that due process of law is violated when prosecutors conceal evidence that might be favorable to the defense. Read together, these decisions stand for the proposition that, as officers of the court, prosecutors can no more suppress evidence than they can knowingly use perjured

testimony. Note that *Brady* rests on constitutional grounds and not statutory law as do state laws.

Brady applies only to exculpatory evidence (evidence tending to show the defendant's innocence). Needless to say, this standard requires a judgment call on the part of prosecutors, and in recent years the Court has ruled that prosecutors have been too narrow in their interpretation. In *Kyles v. Whitley* (1995) the prosecutor failed to disclose statements of two of four witnesses and other evidence relating to Kyles's car. In a five-to-four decision, Justice David Souter wrote that the test was a cumulative one looking at all the evidence not disclosed, and not just isolated pieces. Moreover, to gain a new trial, the defense need only show a reasonable probability of a different result (not a preponderance of the evidence). (On retrial, three juries declined to convict Kyles and charges were dropped.)

Law in Action: Informal Prosecutorial Disclosure

Discovery rules are vitally important to defense attorneys. In states that grant defense considerable discovery rights, the lawyer can go straight to the prosecutor's files and obtain the essentials of the state's case against the defendant. By learning the facts of the prosecutor's case, the defense attorney need not face the difficult task of trying to force his client to voluntarily disclose this information.

Across the nation, "nearly all lawyers interviewed felt that clients' veracity is questionable and in need of thorough verification. This forces the attorney to devote extra hours, frequently wasted, verifying a client's version of the facts, which also puts a strain on their relationship—especially when the attorney is forced to confront the defendant with his prevarications" (Wice 1978, 45).

In jurisdictions that grant limited discovery rights to the defense, defense attorneys must be more resourceful in determining what actually happened. A variety of proceedings not directly designed for discovery purposes can be used for that purpose. At the preliminary hearing, intended to test the sufficiency of the evidence for holding the defendant, the defense hears at least part of the story of some critical witnesses. Similarly, during a hearing on a pretrial motion to suppress evidence, the testimony of key government witnesses may yield important new facts relevant to a trial defense. But eventually, defense attorneys may be forced to confront their clients about inconsistencies (or worse) in their statements, a confrontation that can strain lawyer-client relationships (Chapter 7).

Some prosecutors have an office policy prohibiting assistant prosecutors from disclosing any information not required by law (see A Day in Court: "Lawyers Claim DAs Exclude Evidence"). But it is more usual that assistant DAs voluntarily disclose certain aspects of the state's case to defense attorneys. Such informal discovery operates within the norms of cooperation of courtroom work groups. Defense attorneys who maintain good relationships with prosecutors and are viewed as trustworthy receive selected information about the case. Conversely, defense attorneys who maintain hostile relationships with the prosecutor and/or represent clients who are viewed as troublemakers (the two frequently go together) find the prosecutors holding the cards as tightly to the vest as the law allows.

Informal prosecutorial disclosure does not stem from sympathy for the defendant, but rather from a long-held courthouse theory that an advance glimpse at the prosecutor's case encourages a plea of guilty. From the perspective of the prosecutor, defendants often tell their lawyers only part of what happened. Therefore, the defense attorney who learns what evidence the prosecutor possesses can use it to show the defendant that contesting the matter may be hopeless. The following events concerning a liquor store burglary provide a good illus-

tration. The client told his attorney that the police had stopped him several blocks from the alleged break-in and that he had nothing to do with it. The prosecutor relayed a different version. According to the police reports, the squad car was on routine patrol checking stores. When the squad car pulled into the parking lot, its headlights illuminated someone inside the store. The officers went to the back of the store and observed a suspect leaving the store and entering a car. They chased the car, stopped it several blocks away, discovered that the car was "loaded with goodies," and arrested the defendant. After such disclosures, the prosecutors contend that the lawyer will go back to his client and say, "You lied to me, you bastard. Tell me the truth or I'll pull out of the case" (Neubauer 1974, 200). Of course, prosecutors are not likely to reveal the weaknesses in their case—only the strengths.

Informal prosecutorial discovery greatly encourages pleas of guilty. Paul Wice (1978) reports that in courthouses where prosecutors emphasize closed discovery, there is often a failure to plea bargain, and a large number of cases go to trial, frequently without a jury. Overall, in courthouses where prosecutors have adopted open discovery policies, pleas of guilty are entered sooner, resulting in a significantly smaller backlog than is found in most cities with closed discovery.

Law and Controversy: Requiring Reciprocal Disclosure

Defense attorneys understandably press for broader discovery laws. A major issue in broadening discovery involves the extent to which the defense should also be required to disclose relevant materials in its possession. The guiding light, as articulated by prosecutors and law-and-order advocates, is that the trial should be a level playing field for all parties; both sides should be prevented from attempting to conduct a trial by ambush.

Reciprocal disclosure by the defense takes several forms. Some jurisdictions require that the defense file a notice of **alibi defense** (the crime was committed while the defendant was somewhere

> **Alibi defense:**   A defense alleging that the defendant was elsewhere at the time of the crime he or she is charged with.

"Lawyers Claim DAs Exclude Evidence"

 In overturning Curtis Kyles's conviction and death penalty sentence in the 1984 murder of Gentilly housewife Delores Dye, the U.S. Supreme Court took aim squarely at Orleans Parish prosecutors, tagging them with misconduct for illegally withholding evidence that tended to undermine their case against Kyles. In a scathing 1995 opinion, the normally mild-mannered Justice David Souter said prosecutors have an "inescapable" duty to disclose such information to defense attorneys, unless the adversary system of justice is to descend to a gladiatorial level unmitigated by any prosecutorial obligation for the sake of truth.

Strong words, indeed. Among defense attorneys and courtroom junkies across the land, "Kyles" has become a household word, much as "Brady" did after the 1963 *Brady v. Maryland* decision in which the high court first asserted that a fair trial requires prosecutors to turn over evidence favorable to the defense. But if the Kyles case has resonated nationally, the public scolding has had little practical effect closer to home, defense attorneys say. Orleans Parish prosecutors still routinely withhold evidence, especially in high-profile cases, they say. "This is a pattern and a practice, and if anything, it has gotten worse," said Denise LeBoeuf, who handles capital cases throughout Louisiana. "It is worse than anywhere else in the state."

[District Attorney Harry] Connick and his staff disagree. They say they turn over exculpatory evidence, evidence favorable to a defendant, and are well aware of their obligation to do so. "We are not frivolous about it and even if we know the son-of-a-bitch did it, if it is exculpatory, he is entitled to it and we turn it over," Connick said. Camille Buras, Connick's top assistant, praised the office's record and estimated only 10 convictions since 1974 have been reversed on grounds that prosecutors withheld favorable evidence. The issue of how much information prosecutors must disclose is constantly evolving, and differences of opinion exist among judges at Criminal District Court and their counterparts on appeals courts, Buras said. . . .

But local defense attorneys—who say if they gave their opponents a "Brady" test, they'd fail it—are not the only critics. . . . Increasingly, Orleans Parish Criminal Court judges are voicing their dismay. Whether prosecutors met their duty to turn over favorable information has surfaced as an issue in several recent cases:

- "The DA's office doesn't understand it," fumed Judge Calvin Johnson from the bench during the trial of two former police officers charged with aggravated rape of a girl. Only after Johnson tacitly threatened to grant a new trial did prosecutors turn over material in dispute, including a statement in which the girl said one of the two officers asked her to have sex. The jury convicted the men of sexual battery, a significantly lesser charge. . . .
- In a murder trial last month, Judge Frank Marullo slammed prosecutors for withholding a witness's statement. Marullo went one step farther, and, in a highly unusual move, told jurors before opening statements that prosecutors had "neglected" to give the defense attorney information that a witness had described a mustached perpetrator who was 10 years younger and at least three inches shorter than the bald, clean-shaven defendant. He was convicted of second-degree murder.
- Two murder cases in the past six months ended in mistrials after defense attorneys complained that information that surfaced during testimony and that defense attorneys felt would have helped their cases was not made available when they asked for it before trial. Judge Denis Waldron and Julian Parker, both former prosecutors, stopped the trials.

SOURCE: Pamela Coyle, "Lawyers Claim DAs Exclude Evidence," *Times-Picayune*, September 21, 1997.

else), complete with a list of witnesses to be called to support the alibi (*Williams v. Florida,* 1970). Such pretrial notice enables the prosecutor to investigate the backgrounds of these witnesses and thus be prepared to undermine the defendant's contention that he or she was somewhere else when the crime was committed. In the same vein, some states mandate that defense must disclose to the prosecution prior to trial that an insanity plea will be entered or that expert witnesses will be called. A few states mandate that the defense must turn over to the prosecutor in advance of trial the names, addresses, and statements of any witnesses (other than the defendant) it intends to call at trial.

The Constitution limits reciprocal discovery, however. Unlike civil proceedings, criminal defendants enjoy the privilege against self-incrimination (Chapter 2). Thus efforts in some states to require the defense to turn over to the prosecutor prior to trial statements from expert witnesses that it does not intend to call at trial are probably unconstitutional. And as the trial of O. J. Simpson demonstrated, prosecutorial enforcement of reciprocal discovery is not straightforward. The defense team stated that they would disclose only when an expert witness wrote the final report (even though the defense had been orally informed of the findings).

 Therese M. Myers, "Reciprocal Discovery Violations: Visiting the Sins of the Defense Lawyer on the Innocent Client"

THE EXCLUSIONARY RULE AND THE SUPREME COURT

The most controversial of the Supreme Court's criminal justice decisions have concerned how the police gather evidence. For example, the rape conviction of Ernesto Miranda in 1966 was overturned because the police had not advised him of his constitutional right to remain silent before he confessed. In 1961, Dollree Mapp's pornography conviction had been reversed because the police had illegally searched her house. In both cases, otherwise valid and trustworthy evidence was excluded from trial. These cases are applications of the exclusionary rule.

The **exclusionary rule** prohibits the prosecutor from using illegally obtained evidence during a trial. It is the Supreme Court's sole technique for enforcing several vital protections of the Bill of Rights. Its adoption has been justified on three grounds. The first is a normative argument: A court of law should not participate in or condone illegal conduct. The second reflects an empirical assessment: Excluding evidence will deter law enforcement officials from

> **Exclusionary rule:**   A rule created by judicial decisions holding that evidence obtained through violations of the constitutional rights of the criminal defendant must be excluded from the trial.

illegal behavior. The final justification is based on experience: Alternative remedies, such as civil suits for damages against police officers for misconduct, are unworkable.

The exclusionary rule is commonly associated with the search and seizure of physical evidence, but in fact there are three distinct exclusionary rules. One applies to the identification of suspects. In *U.S. v. Wade* (1967), the high court held that police lineups constitute a critical stage of the prosecutorial process, so defendants have the right to be assisted by counsel. In later decisions, identifications of suspects were excluded from trial because the lineups had been improperly conducted. The other exclusionary rules relate to confessions and searches.

CONFESSIONS

For almost seventy years, the Supreme Court has struggled to place limits on how police interrogate suspects (see Figure 12-2). The traditional rule was that only confessions that were "free and voluntary" would be admitted at trial. Confessions obtained by physical coercion (beatings or torture, for example) were not allowed into evidence because they were not trustworthy; someone in fear of a beating is likely to say what his or her antagonists want to hear. In the 1930s, the Court rejected confessions based on physical coercion, and subsequently such practices largely ceased. The Court was then confronted with the slightly different issue of confessions obtained as a result of lengthy interrogations, psychological ploys, and the like. The Court reasoned that confessions based on psychological coercion should be rejected just as if they were based on physical coercion, because such statements were not likely to be free and voluntary. But it is not easy to define what constitutes psychological coercion. In more than twenty cases, the Court sought to spell

 Richard A. Leo, Richard J. Ofshe, "The Consequences of False Confessions: Deprivations of Liberty and Miscarriages of Justice in the Age of Psychological Interrogation"

Paul G. Cassell, "Protecting the Innocent from False Confessions and Lost Confessions—and from *Miranda* (A response to Leo and Ofshe)"

FIGURE 12-2	Key Developments in Interrogation Law	
Fifth Amendment	1791	"No person . . . shall be compelled in any criminal case to be a witness against himself. . . ."
English Common law	19th century	Involuntary confessions are not admissible in court.
Brown v. Mississippi	1936	Use of physical coercion to obtain confessions violates the due process clause of the Fourteenth Amendment.
Ashcraft v. Tennessee	1944	Psychologically coerced confessions are not voluntary and therefore not admissible in court.
Miranda v. Arizona	1966	Suspect's due process rights were violated because he had not first been advised of his right to remain silent and to have an attorney present during a custodial interrogation.
Harris v. New York	1971	Voluntary statements made by the defendants who had not been properly warned of their constitutional rights could be used during trial to impeach their credibility when they took the witness stand in their own defense and contradicted the earlier statements.
New York v. Quarles	1984	Overriding considerations of public safety justified the police officer's failure to provide *Miranda* warnings before asking questions about the location of a weapon apparently abandoned just before arrest.
Duckworth v. Eagan	1989	Altered warnings have been upheld. Advising a suspect that counsel could be appointed only "if and when you go to court" does not render *Miranda* warnings inadequate.
Illinois v. Perkins	1990	A law enforcement officer can pose as a prison inmate and elicit a confession from an actual inmate, even though the officer gives no *Miranda* warnings about the inmate's constitutional rights.
Minnick v. Mississippi	1990	Once a suspect has invoked his or her right to counsel, police may not resume interrogation without the suspect having his or her attorney present.
Pennsylvania v. Muniz	1990	Police officers may ask suspected drunken drivers routine questions and videotape their answers without warning them of their rights.
Arizona v. Fulminate	1991	A coerced confession does not automatically overturn a conviction.
Davis v. U.S.	1994	Police do not need to stop questioning a suspect who makes an ambiguous statement about wanting an attorney.
Dickerson v. U.S.	2000	*Miranda* has become embedded in police practices and the Court will not overrule it.

out what factors the trial court should use in deciding what constitutes psychological coercion, but the standards announced were far from precise.

The Warren Court Changes the Rules

In an attempt at greater precision, the Court under the leadership of Chief Justice Earl Warren adopted specific procedures for police interrogations. In the path-breaking decision of *Miranda v. Arizona* (1966) the Court imposed what are widely known as

Miranda warnings. The police are required to tell a suspect:

- You have the right to remain silent.
- Anything you say can and will be used against you in a court of law.
- You have the right to talk to a lawyer and have him or her present with you while you are being questioned.
- If you cannot afford to hire a lawyer, one will be appointed to represent you before any questioning, if you wish.

In addition, the Court shifted the burden of proof from the defense, which previously had to prove that a confession was not "free and voluntary," to the police and prosecutor, who now must prove that they have advised the defendant of his or her constitutional rights (see Case Close-Up: *Miranda v. Arizona* and Limiting Police Interrogations).

The Burger and Rehnquist Courts Limit *Miranda*

The Court under the leadership of Chief Justice Warren Burger limited *Miranda*'s application by carving out exceptions. Here are the two most prominent examples:

- Voluntary statements made by the defendants who had not been properly warned of their constitutional rights could be used during trial to impeach their credibility when they took the witness stand in their own defense and contradicted the earlier statements (*Harris v. New York*, 1971).

- Overriding considerations of public safety justified the police officer's failure to provide *Miranda* warnings before asking questions about the location of a weapon apparently abandoned just before arrest (*New York v. Quarles*, 1984).

The Rehnquist Court has likewise moved to narrow the application of *Miranda* protections, as the following cases illustrate.

- Police officers may ask suspected drunken drivers routine questions and videotape their answers without warning them of their rights (*Pennsylvania v. Muniz*, 1990).

- Altered warnings have been upheld. Advising a suspect that counsel could be appointed only "if and when you go to court" does not render *Miranda* warnings inadequate (*Duckworth v. Eagan*, 1989).

- Police do not need to stop questioning a suspect who makes an ambiguous statement about wanting an attorney (*Davis v. U.S.*, 1994).

However, the Rehnquist Court is not always unsympathetic to the plight of criminal defendants. One six-to-two decision seemed to take *Miranda* protections a step further. The Court overturned a capital murder conviction, holding that once a suspect has invoked his or her right to counsel, police may not resume interrogation without the suspect

having his or her attorney present (*Minnick v. Mississippi*, 1990). The Rehnquist Court also recently declined to overrule *Miranda*. Writing for seven justices, Chief Justice Rehnquist opined, "Whether or not this court would agree with *Miranda*'s reasoning and its rule in the first instance, *stare decisis* weighs heavily against overruling it now." Moreover, "*Miranda* has become embedded in routine police practice to the point where the warnings have become part of our national culture" (*Dickerson v. U.S.*, 2000).

 To read the opinion of the court in *Dickerson v. U.S.* go to **http://findlaw.com/**. Under Laws click on U.S. Supreme Court and then go to 2000 decisions. For contrasting views on *Dickerson*, point your browser to:
http://www.aclu.org/features/f041900a.html
http://www.law.utah.edu/Cassell/Overhaul Miranda?

For an up-to-date list of Web links, go to **http://www.wadsworth.com/product/0534563406s**.

SEARCH AND SEIZURE

The Fourth Amendment provides that "the right of the people to be secure in their persons, houses, papers, and effects against unreasonable search and seizure, shall not be violated." But what constitutes an **unreasonable search and seizure**?

Historically, the gathering of physical evidence was governed by the common law rule that "if the constable blunders, the crook should not go free." This meant that if the police conducted an **illegal search and seizure** (search without probable cause), the evidence obtained could still be used. Evidence was admitted in court if it was reliable, trustworthy, and relevant. How the police obtained the evidence was considered a separate issue. Thus, there were no effective controls on search and seizure; law enforcement officials who searched illegally faced no sanctions.

Unreasonable search and seizure: The Fourth Amendment provides for protection against unreasonable search and seizure, or the illegal gathering of evidence, but was not very effective until the adoption of the exclusionary rule, barring the use of evidence obtained through an unreasonable search and seizure (*Mapp v. Ohio*, 1961).

Illegal search and seizure: An act in violation of the Fourth Amendment of the U.S. Constitution.

CASE CLOSE-UP

Miranda v. Arizona and Limiting Police Interrogations

By the age of twenty-three Ernesto Miranda had compiled a long police record. His mother had died when he was three, and he later drifted apart from his father. He dropped out of Queen of Peace grammar school in Mesa, Arizona, after the eighth grade, and shortly thereafter was arrested for car theft. By the age of eighteen his police blotter showed six arrests and four prison sentences. A stint in the military to turn his life around quickly degenerated into his problems in civilian life—after going AWOL, he was given an undesirable discharge. But at twenty-three he appeared to have turned the corner. His boss at the produce company described him as "one of the best workers I ever had." Indeed, on Wednesday he worked from 8:00 P.M. to 8:00 A.M. and had barely slept an hour when the police knocked on the front door.

Stating that they didn't want to talk in front of his common-law wife, the police took him to a Phoenix, Arizona, police station. A lineup of three other Hispanics from the city jail was quickly assembled. Lois Ann Jameson viewed the four men but could only state that Miranda's build and features were similar to her assailant. In the interrogation room, Miranda asked how he did, and Detective Cooley replied, "You flunked." At first Miranda maintained his innocence, but after two hours of questioning he signed a written confession admitting guilt. His subsequent trial was short and perfunctory. The only prosecution exhibit was the signed confession. The defense attorney offered no evidence and called no witnesses. Nor did the defense call the defendant, out of fear that the jury would learn of his extensive criminal background. Needless to say, the jury quickly returned guilty verdicts for kidnapping and rape.

The interrogation of Ernesto Miranda was in most ways unremarkable. It most certainly lacked the blatant brutality and duress at the center of earlier Supreme Court decisions on the limits of police interrogation. What was missing, however, was any advice to Ernesto about his rights under the Constitution. Indeed, the police testified that they never told Miranda that he didn't have to talk to the police, nor did they advise him of his right to consult with an attorney. (According to Miranda, the police promised to drop other charges if he confessed to the rape.) These facts highlighted the giant chasm between the principles of the Constitution and the realities of police stations in America.

Early in the twentieth century, the Supreme Court modified the common law tradition by adopting the exclusionary rule, holding that the Fourth Amendment barred the use of evidence secured through an illegal search and seizure (*Weeks v. U.S.,* 1914). But this ruling was applied very narrowly. Only federal law enforcement officials were covered; state law enforcement officials were exempt. After World War II, the Court extended the privacy component of *Weeks* to the states. But the divided Court refused to impose the exclusionary rule (*Wolf v. Colorado,* 1949). Although a few states—for instance, California—did adopt it, many took no effective action to curb illegal searches. Twelve years later, the *Wolf* decision was overturned by a bare five-to-four vote. In a bellwether decision, the exclusionary rule was extended to the states in *Mapp v. Ohio* (1961). Evidence obtained during an illegal search would no longer be admitted in either federal or state courts. Figure 12-3 on page 308 describes the key developments in search-and-seizure law.

The conservative majorities of both the Burger and Rehnquist Courts have limited the application of the exclusionary rule by creating numerous exceptions.

- Police should ordinarily knock and announce their identity before entering a home with a search warrant, but an unannounced entry may be reasonable if police fear physical violence or destruction of evidence (*Wilson v. Arkansas,* 1995).

- Once the police have stopped a car for a traffic infraction, they may go on to request the driver's permission to search the car for drugs without first informing him that the routine stop is over and that he is, in fact, free to go on his way (*Ohio v. Robinette,* 1996).

- A person running at the sight of a police officer could justify the police conducting a stop-and-frisk search (*Illinois v. Wardlow,* 2000).

By 1966 the Supreme Court had been grappling with the issue of confessions for three decades. In the 1930s the Supreme Court rejected confessions based on physical coercion (beatings with rubber hoses and the like). By the 1940s and 1950s attention shifted to confessions produced as a result of psychological coercion (long periods of interrogation or improper promises, for example). Despite these numerous cases, the standards for interrogating suspects were still far from clear.

Chief Justice Earl Warren's opinion in *Miranda* expressed concern over the "police-dominated" atmosphere of interrogation rooms and held that warnings were required to counteract the inherently coercive nature of station house questioning. But in reality *Miranda* created no new rights—under American law, suspects have never been required to talk to the police, and the right to counsel extends to the police station as well as the courthouse. In essence the Court held that the Fifth Amendment privilege against self-incrimination was as applicable to interrogation by the police before trial as questioning by the prosecutor during trial.

Miranda v. Arizona is the Warren Court's best known and, arguably, most controversial decision extending constitutional rights to those accused of violating the criminal law. The four dissenting justices criticized the ruling on both constitutional and practical grounds. To Justice Byron White, the *Miranda* rule was "a deliberate calculus to prevent interrogation, to reduce the incidence of confessions, and to increase the number of trials." Police, prosecutors, and public officials likewise criticized the ruling, and it became a key plank in Richard Nixon's law-and-order campaign in 1968 (Chapter 17). With four Nixon-appointed justices, the Burger Court began narrowing *Miranda,* but the holding itself has not been overturned. Indeed, *Miranda* has now become settled law, deeply imbedded in the constitutional fabric of our nation.

 Warren's handwritten notes on the *Miranda* decision and Brennan's responses are available through the manuscript division of the Library of Congress: **http://lcweb.loc.gov/exhibits/treasures/trr038.html**.

For an up-to-date list of Web links, go to **http://www.wadsworth.com/product/0534563406s**.

 Owen Einspahr, "The Interview Challenge"

Michael R. Napier, Susan H. Adams, "Magic Words to Obtain Confessions"

On rare occasions. though, the Rehnquist Court does place limits on the ability of the police to search.

• Bus and train passengers have an expectation of privacy when they put their luggage into an overhead rack (*Bond v. U.S.,* 2000).

• Police cannot stop and search a person for a gun solely because they received an anonymous tip (*Florida v. J. L.,* 2000).

Nonetheless, four decades later, the exclusionary rule requirements remain highly controversial. (See Controversy: Should the Exclusionary Rule Be Abolished? on page 310.) Critics and supporters of the exclusionary rule agree on one central point: The grounds for a lawful search are complex and highly technical. Search and seizure is one of the most difficult areas of Supreme Court decision making, and few think that the system works particularly well (Bradley 1993). Searches fall into two broad categories: searches based on a warrant and warrantless searches.

 The following sites provide information about the Fourth Amendment:

> **http://www.nolo.com/encyclopedia/articles/crim/search_seizure.html**
> **http://law.about.com/newsissues/law/cs/searchseizure/**

For an up-to-date list of Web links, go to **http://www.wadsworth.com/product/0534563406s**.

Search Warrants

A **search warrant** is a written document, signed by a judge or magistrate, authorizing a law enforcement officer to conduct a search. The Fourth Amendment

Search warrant: A written order, issued by judicial authority, directing a law enforcement officer to search for personal property and, if found, to bring it before the court.

FIGURE 12-3   Key Developments in Search-and-Seizure Law

Fourth Amendment	1791	"The right of the people to be secure in their persons, houses, paper, and effects against unreasonable searches and seizures, shall not be violated, and no Warrants shall issue, but upon probable cause, supported by Oath or affirmation, and particularly describing the place to be searched, and the persons or things to be seized."
Weeks v. U.S.	1914	The exclusionary rule established for federal prosecutions.
Wolf v. Colorado	1949	The exclusionary rule is applicable to the federal courts and the states that choose to adopt it.
Mapp v. Ohio	1961	The exclusionary rule applies to the states as well as the federal government (overturning Weeks and Wolf).
Terry v. Ohio	1968	Police officers may conduct a frisk of the outer clothing on the basis of reasonable suspicion that a crime is being contemplated.
Chimel v. California	1969	In a search incident to an arrest, the police may search only the defendant's person and the area within the immediate vicinity.
U.S. v. Leon	1984	Creates a limited "good faith exception."
Illinois v. Krull	1987	Good faith exception applied to a warrantless search, even when the state statute was later found to violate the Fourth Amendment.
Maryland v. Garrison	1987	Evidence is admissible even though the specifics in the search warrant were inaccurate.
Illinois v. Rodriguez	1990	Police officers were acting in good faith when the victim allowed entry into her apartment even though she no longer resided with the defendant.
Arizona v. Evans	1995	Traffic stop that led to the seizure of drugs was legal, even though the arrest warrant, which was the basis of the search, was improper because it was based on a computer error.
Knowles v. Iowa	1998	Issuing a speeding ticket does not give police authority to search the car.
Illinois v. Wardlow	2000	A person running at the sight of a police officer could, in some cases, justify the police conducting a stop-and-frisk search.
Bond v. U.S.	2000	Bus and train passengers have an expectation of privacy when they put their luggage into an overhead rack.
Florida v. J.L.	2000	Police cannot stop and search someone solely because they received an anonymous tip.

specifies that "no Warrants shall issue, but upon probable cause, supported by Oath or affirmation, and particularly describing the place to be searched and the Persons or things to be seized." A study by the National Center for State Courts provides considerable insight into how search warrants are obtained (Van Duizend, Sutton, and Carter 1984).

Once a police officer decides that a search warrant is necessary, the officer usually goes back to the station house to prepare the application, affidavit, and warrant. Three alternative procedures are used. In a few jurisdictions, search warrant applications are prepared by a deputy prosecutor on the basis of information provided by the officer. In other localities, the prosecutor systematically reviews all search warrant applications before they are presented to the magistrate. Finally, in rural areas, a significant number of warrants are obtained by telephone.

Next, the applicant goes to the courthouse or (if court is not in session) to the home of a judge. The review seldom takes long, typically consisting of a hushed conversation at the bench or a presentation in chambers after the judge has called a brief recess. Outright rejection is rare. "Most of the police officer interviewees could not remember having a search warrant application turned down" (Van Duizend, Sutton, and Carter 1984).

The final step is the execution of the warrant. The officer serves the warrant, conducts the search, and seizes evidence. Officers mainly search private residences and impound vehicles for drugs or stolen goods. Statutory law generally requires that the officer file a "return" in court, indicating what items were seized, if any.

The authors concluded, "It is a sizable overstatement . . . to say that the warrant review process routinely operates as it was intended. For example, it was clear in many cases that the review process was largely perfunctory, and apparent that some judges regarded themselves more as allies of law enforcement than as independent reviewers of evidence" (Van Duizend, Sutton, and Carter 1984).

The Police Executive Research Forum analyzed the impact of the reasonable, good faith exception to the exclusionary rule created by the *Leon* ruling in the same seven cities studied by the National Center for State Courts. All search warrant applications made during comparable three-month periods before and after the *Leon* decision were reviewed. The study found that *Leon* had limited impact on police policies and practices. The number and content of warrants did not change. Although *Leon* gave the police added incentives to secure warrants, there was no discernible increase in the number of search warrants requested. Overall, the impact on judicial suppression of evidence was virtually nonexistent. Out of 2,115 applications, only 1 was rejected by a judge (Uchida et al. 1988).

 Thomas D. Colbridge, "Search Incident to Arrest: Another Look"

Warrantless Searches

Obtaining a search warrant is still a relatively rare phenomenon, although more frequent than in the days before *Mapp*. For a host of reasons, police officers and even some judges view the process of securing a search warrant as burdensome and time-consuming. It is therefore not surprising that many law enforcement officers regard the search warrant as the option of last resort. In their eyes, there are many easier ways to get the evidence or otherwise make a case against the accused.

The majority of searches are conducted without warrant. One common form of **warrantless search** is a **consent search**. The person must freely and vol-

> **Warrantless search:** Search without a search warrant.
> **Consent search:** A person, place, or moveables may be lawfully searched by an officer of the law if the owner gives free and voluntary consent.

untarily consent to be searched, but law enforcement officers indicate that consent is the easiest thing in the world to obtain. As one Mountain City detective explained, you just make an offer that cannot be refused:

> *[You] tell the guy, "Let me come in and take a look at your house." And he says, "No, I don't want to." And then you tell him, "Then I'm going to leave Sam here, and he's going to live with you until we come back [with a search warrant]. Now we can do it either way." And very rarely do the people say, "Go get your search warrant then." (Van Duizend, Sutton, and Carter 1984)*

The police may also lawfully search without a warrant if the search is incident to a lawful arrest or if the evidence is in **plain view**.

The precise meaning of "probable cause" remains elusive, however. The grounds for a warrantless search vary, depending on what is being searched. The Supreme Court is more likely to find a search to be reasonable if a person is searched, as opposed to a search of an area where the person has a property interest (home or business, for example) (Segal 1984). Figure 12-4 on page 312 presents an overview of the issues surrounding disclosure and suppression of evidence discussed so far.

THE EXCLUSIONARY RULE AND THE COURTROOM WORK GROUP

The police must often make immediate decisions about searching or interrogating a suspect. In street arrests, officers do not have time to consult an attorney about the complex and constantly evolving law governing these areas. These on-the-spot decisions may later be challenged in court as violations of suspects' constitutional rights. Even though the exclusionary rule is directed at the police, its actual enforcement occurs in the courts, particularly the trial courts.

 Lisa A. Regini, "The Motor Vehicle Exception: When and Where to Search"

> **Plain view:** If police happen to come across something while acting within their lawful duty, that item may be used as evidence in a criminal trial even if the police did not have a search warrant.

CONTROVERSY

Should the Exclusionary Rule Be Abolished?

 The exclusionary rule was controversial when it was adopted in 1961 and remains so four decades later. In a 1981 speech, President Reagan's strong words expressed the views of the crime control model, which call for the abolition of the exclusionary rule:

> The exclusionary rule rests on the absurd proposition that a law enforcement error, no matter how technical, can be used to justify throwing an entire case out of court, no matter how guilty the defendant or how heinous the crime. The plain consequence of treating the wrongs equally is a grievous miscarriage of justice: the criminal goes free; the officer receives no effective reprimand; and the only ones who really suffer are the people of the community.

But to law professor Yale Kamisar (1978), illegal conduct by the police cannot so easily be ignored. Here is how he states the due process model case for the exclusionary rule:

> A court which admits [illegally seized evidence] . . . manifests a willingness to tolerate the unconstitutional conduct which produced it. How can the police and the citizenry be expected to "believe that the government truly meant to forbid the conduct in the first place." A court which admits the evidence in a case involving a "run of the mill" Fourth Amendment violation demonstrates an insufficient commitment to the guarantee against unreasonable search and seizure. . . . It signifies the government officials need not always be subjected to the same rules of conduct that are commands to the citizens.

While the *Mapp* decision remains controversial, the nature of the debate has changed. Initially, critics called for abolition of the exclusionary rule (Oaks 1970; Wilkey 1978); now, they just suggest modifications. This shift in thinking is reflected in the Reagan administration's Attorney General's Task Force on Violent Crime (1981). Although composed largely of long-standing critics of the exclusionary rule, the final report called only for its modification, not its abolition.

Among the alternatives proposed, former Chief Justice Warren Burger has urged an "egregious violation standard" (*Brewer v. Williams*, 1977). Others have proposed an exception for reasonable mistakes by the police (Fyfe 1982). To critics, modifications along these lines would reduce the number of arrests lost because of illegal searches, and the sanction would be more proportional to the seriousness of the Fourth

Pretrial Motions

A defense attorney who believes that his or her client was identified in a defective police lineup, gave a confession because of improper police activity, or was subjected to an illegal search can file a motion to suppress the evidence. Most states require that **suppression motions** be made prior to trial.

During the hearing on these pretrial motions, the defense attorney usually bears the burden of proving that the search was illegal or that the confession was coerced. The only exception involves an allegation that the *Miranda* warnings were not given, in which case the state has the burden of proof. The judge's ruling in the pretrial hearing is binding on the later trial.

Suppression motion: Request that a court of law prohibit specific statements, documents, or objects from being introduced into evidence in a trial.

Pretrial hearings on a motion to suppress evidence are best characterized as "swearing matches." As one defense attorney phrased it, "The real question in Supreme Court cases is what's going on at the police station" (Neubauer 1974, 167). Seldom is there unbiased, independent evidence of what happened. The only witnesses are the participants—police and defendant—and, not surprisingly, they give different versions. Thus, *Miranda* "just moves the battleground from the voluntariness of the confession back to the voluntariness of the waiver. . . . The police have done pretty well with these swearing contests over the years" (quoted in Cipes 1966, 55).

Suppression motions focus on the facts of the case. This dispute over the facts structures and apportions the roles that the police, defense attorneys, judges, and prosecutors play. Because they must search out the issues, defense attorneys are forced into a catalytic role. By virtue of their power as fact finders at hearings, judges become the su-

Amendment violation. The Supreme Court, however, has recognized an "honest mistake" or a "good faith" exception to the exclusionary rule only in extremely narrow and limited circumstances (*U.S. v. Leon,* 1984; *Illinois v. Krull,* 1987). The high court is increasingly leaning in this direction. Thus when Arizona police seized marijuana in the car of Isaac Evans, they were able to use it in court even though the arrest warrant was erroneously listed on a police computer. Rehnquist's opinion stressed that rights to privacy are not violated when there is a "good faith" exception for human error. But in a concurring opinion, three justices stressed that the police cannot rely on a computerized system that "routinely leads to false arrests" (*Arizona v. Evans,* 1995).

When the Republican party gained control of both houses of Congress in 1995, conservatives increased their efforts to modify the exclusionary rule. As part of the "Contract with America," conservative House Republicans pledged to approve a bill that would let federal courts admit evidence obtained without a warrant if police appeared to have tried to obey the constitutional ban on unreasonable searches. Similarly, some Senate Republicans proposed legislation that would wipe out *Miranda* rules and also kill the exclusionary rule (Congressional Quarterly 1996). These efforts to overturn Supreme Court decisions proved unsuccessful.

The Rehnquist Court includes six justices who have publicly criticized *Mapp.* Yet this working majority has apparently been unable to agree among themselves as to how to replace *Mapp* while prohibiting truly bad-faith searches by the police. As a result, predicting the future of *Mapp* is problematical at best.

What do you think? Should the exclusionary rule be abolished outright, given "good faith exceptions," or kept in its present form? If one admits that there are problems in its current application, what realistic alternatives might restrain law enforcement from potentially conducting blatant and flagrant searches in violation of the Fourth Amendment?

Timothy Lynch, "In Defense of the Exclusionary Rule"

John A. Wasowicz, "Exclusionary Rule: A Twentieth-Century Invention"

To continue the debate over the exclusionary rule, go to these sites:

American Civil Liberties Union: **http://www.aclu.org**

National Center for Policy Analysis: **http://www.ncpa.org**

The Cato Institute: **http://www.cato.org**

National Association of Criminal Defense Lawyers: **http://www.criminaljustice.org**

For an up-to-date list of Web links, go to **http://www.wadsworth.com/product/0534563406s**.

preme umpires that legal theory indicates they should be. Prosecutors, in contrast, play a relatively passive role. Although pretrial motions place prosecutors in a defensive posture, they are not at a major disadvantage, because the police are usually able to provide information indicating compliance.

Defense Attorney As Prime Mover

Because defense attorneys have the responsibility of protecting the constitutional rights of their clients, they are the prime movers in suppression matters. Unless the defense objects, it is assumed that law enforcement officials have behaved properly.

Filing a pretrial motion to suppress evidence may produce benefits for the defense. If the motion is granted, the defense wins, because the prosecutor will usually dismiss the case for lack of evidence. Even if the motion is denied, the defense may be able to discover information that may later prove valuable at trial. Moreover, filing a pretrial motion keeps options open; plea bargaining remains a possible course of action.

Despite these apparent advantages, defense attorneys face major barriers in raising objections. Possible violations of *Mapp* or *Miranda* do not come into the lawyer's office prepackaged, just awaiting a court hearing. Successful motions to suppress require a thorough knowledge of appellate court decisions that are ever changing.

Defense attorneys must frame the issue and determine whether enough facts exist to support the contention. According to many defense attorneys, the police follow proper procedures most of the time. Thus, the task of the lawyer is to separate the out-of-the-ordinary situation from the more numerous ones in which the police have not violated Supreme Court rulings. This winnowing is not easy. One lawyer commented,

FIGURE 12-4   Overview: Disclosing and Suppressing Evidence

	Law on the Books	Law in Action
Discovery	Pretrial procedure in which parties to a lawsuit ask for and receive information such as witnesses' statements, expert witnesses' reports, and lab reports.	In a number of jurisdictions informal prosecutorial disclosure means that defense attorneys who maintain a cooperative stance toward the district attorney will be able to view most or all of the state's case prior to trial.
Brady material	Prosecutor must turn over exculpatory evidence to the defense prior to trial.	Some defense attorneys assert that some prosecutors do not always live up to their constitutional obligation.
Rules of evidence	In jurisdictions with more open discovery, defense is entitled to see witnesses' statements and lab reports before trial.	Prosecutors who maintain an open discovery policy experience quicker pleas of guilty and less case backlog.
Reciprocal discovery	Requirement that defense disclose to the prosecutor various material prior to trial.	In era of "get tough with criminals," an increasingly popular response by legislatures.
Lineups	The suspect has a right to have an attorney present. In addition the lineup must represent the description given by the witness.	The police routinely take a picture of the persons in the lineup, which is typically sufficient to prove to the court that the lineup was indeed representative.
Interrogations	Method of acquiring evidence in the form of information or confessions from suspects by police.	Suspects who provide incriminating statements are more likely to be charged with a crime, more likely to be convicted, and more likely to be punished severely.
Physical coercion	Statements made to the police obtained by the use of physical force or the threatened use of physical force are not admissible because they are untrustworthy.	• Historically, there is every reason to believe that physically coerced confessions were common. • In contemporary practice, believable reports of physical coercion are extremely rare.
Psychological coercion	Fifth Amendment protection against self-incrimination means that any statement elicited by the police cannot be used in court if the statement is not "free and voluntary."	• During the 1940s and 1950s the Supreme Court found that a number of confessions were inadmissible because of psychological coercion. • Difficulty of applying this standard on a case-by-case basis led the Court to announce *Miranda* warnings.
Miranda warnings	Prior to interrogation the police must warn a suspect that (1) you have the right to remain silent; (2) anything you say can and will be used against you in a court of law; (3) you have the right to talk to a lawyer and have him or her present with you while you are being questioned; and (4) if you cannot afford to hire a lawyer, one will be appointed to represent you before any questioning, if you wish.	• Three out of four suspects waive their *Miranda* rights (Leo 1996a). • Police use advising of *Miranda* rights to gain the confidence of the suspect.

(continued from previous page)

Search and seizure	Legal term found in the Fourth Amendment referring to the searching for and carrying away of evidence by police during a criminal investigation.	• In street crimes, police officers must make quick decisions about searching a person or car for contraband. • Most often occurs in drug and weapons offenses.
Search warrant	A written order, issued by judicial authority, directing a law enforcement officer to search for property, and if found, to bring it before the court.	• Judges or magistrates rarely scrutinize them closely. • Police are often successful in obtaining suspect's consent for a voluntary search.
Consent search	Law enforcement officials are under no requirement to tell the suspect that they do not have the right to search.	• Suspects are surprisingly willing to consent to search of person or car.
Incident to a valid arrest	After a valid arrest, the police officer may search to protect himself or herself and to prevent the destruction of contraband.	• Some officers have been known to search and then fabricate probable cause for arrest.
Plain view	Law enforcement officers may search and seize any contraband or illegal substances or items if they are in the immediate vision of the officers.	• Some law enforcement officers allegedly search in hidden areas but later testify the material was in plain view.

Illegal searches are hard to get at. . . . The defendant doesn't know if the police had probable cause. Sometimes the police get an anonymous phone call that a burglary is in progress. . . . Or the police get a tip that guns are in a car. Well, the prosecutor doesn't tell you that. You have to root around to find out if probable cause existed. You have to ask, "How did the police get to it in the first place?" A search without probable cause is hard to find out about. (Neubauer 1974, 173)

In trying to discover the facts of the situation, attorneys often get no help from their clients. As the lawyer just quoted went on to say, "For the defendant the case starts when he's arrested. Search and seizure and probable cause, however, start before that."

In deciding whether to make a motion to suppress evidence, defense attorneys are influenced by the informal norms of the courtroom work group. Pretrial motions require extra work, not only for the defense attorney but for the judge and prosecutor as well. Defense attorneys who file too many frivolous motions or use them to harass the judge and/or prosecutor can be given a variety of sanctions. One prosecutor told this author about a defense attorney who had filed numerous motions in a case, just to make the DA work harder. After winning a motion unexpectedly, he gloated over the victory, to which the DA replied simply that he might have won the battle, but not the war. In a subsequent case, the defense attorney's client received a sentence that was harsher than normal. As a result, the defense attorney is now much more selective in filing pretrial motions.

The Defensive Posture of the Prosecutor

Suppression motions represent only liabilities for prosecutors. At a minimum, they must do extra work. At worst, they may lose the case entirely. Even if they win the suppression motion, they may have to expend extra effort defending that decision on appeal, where they may lose.

Despite these drawbacks, prosecutors maintain the upper hand. For once, they need only defend, because the defense attorney bears the burden of proof. Because the police control the information involved, prosecutors are generally in a favorable position to argue against excluding evidence. For example, the police are usually able to obtain the

THE MURDER TRIAL OF SHAREEF COUSIN

The DA Fails to Disclose a Witness Statement

The first police unit arrived at the Port of Call restaurant at 10:28 P.M., only two minutes after the dispatcher logged the first call for assistance. As other units also arrived, some officers secured the chaotic murder scene while others searched for witnesses. They quickly determined that Connie Babin—Michael Gerardi's date—was a witness and took her statement. She answered some questions but had trouble articulating the answers to many questions. The officers noted that she was hysterical and could not speak in complete sentences. She told the police that she did not get a good look at the gunman and probably would not be able to identify him.

Three days later, during an interview in her house, she stated that she was not wearing her glasses or contact lenses on the night of the murder and could only see patterns and shapes. Thus, she could describe the murderer only as a black male in his late teens, five feet seven or eight inches tall, with curly hair and an "old man's face," wearing colorful socks. These statements would come to dominate later proceedings but not the trial itself—because the prosecutor chose not to disclose these statements to the defense prior to trial.

When Shareef Cousin became a suspect three weeks later, Detective Anthony Small compiled a photographic lineup and Connie Babin made a positive identification of Cousin as the murderer. At trial, she repeated the positive identification.

The defense learned of the existence of her statements through an anonymous tip (identified only as "an honest police officer" in Cousin's federal lawsuit). Once the existence of these witness statements became known the defense moved for a new trial, but the judge denied the motion. Later, the issue took center stage in the appeal to the Louisiana Supreme Court.

Why didn't DA Harry Connick's office disclose these statements (Chapter 8)? The brief for the State of Louisiana offers a tortured explanation at best. According to lawyers for Connick, somewhat similar statements had been disclosed prior to trial. Therefore "even if the transcribed statement did contain information that could be considered exculpatory, the evidence was merely cumulative and there is no reasonable probabil-

ity that, had the evidence been disclosed to the defense, the result of the proceeding would have been different."

On appeal, the Louisiana Supreme Court dismissed the prosecutor's argument, calling the statement "obviously exculpatory," citing Brady and Kyles (*State v. Shareef Cousin* 1998). The issue resurfaced again during preparation for the second trial. The trial judge issued what is for Louisiana a broad discovery order, requiring the prosecutor to turn over all evidence (except lawyer work product). This unusual remedy had been upheld in a previous case in which Connick's office had failed to disclose (*State v. Duc Nguyen* 1998) and the high court sanctioned its use in this case as well (*State v. Cousin* 1998—KK-3171).

Would the disclosure of the statements made by Connie Babin have mattered? In all likelihood, if the defense had known of these statements, the dynamics of the trial would have been fundamentally different. According to the news account (borne out by reading the actual transcript), on cross-examination Cousin's defense team "tried to pick delicately at Babin's story" (Varney 1996). Moreover, the defense argued during later motions that they were afraid to explore the issue of eyesight, fearing that the prosecutor was laying a trap.

To most observers the revelation of Babin's initial statement that she would never be able to identify the murderer doomed subsequent prosecutions. Essentially, the state's case was reduced to a single witness (see Chapter 14) and with that witness identification called into question, a conviction would be highly unlikely.

Jurors and laypersons give eyewitness testimony a great deal of credibility, but psychologists are more skeptical. Read Torun Lindholm and Sven-Ake Christianson, "Intergroup Biases and Eyewitness testimony."

To find out more about the decision not to retry Shareef Cousin for murder, search on the term *follow-up (Shareef Cousin)*.

---

defendant's signature on the *Miranda* warning form, which indicates compliance with Supreme Court requirements (see Exhibit 12-1). Similarly, in a search-and-seizure case, the officers are familiar

enough with the law to know how to testify in order to avoid suppression of evidence. Of course, the DA can dismiss a case that presents potential problems, thus avoiding a public hearing on the matter.

EXHIBIT 12-1 Sample Custodial Interrogation Form

KENNER POLICE DEPARTMENT   A   47408

REV. 11/76   ADVICE OF RIGHTS   KENNER, LA.

DAY_____ DATE _____ TIME _____ COMPLAINT NO. _____

LOCATION_____

NAME _____

BIRTH DATE _____ RACE _____ SEX _____ AGE_____

ADDRESS_____CITY_____ STATE _____

HIGHEST GRADE COMPLETED SCHOOL _____

ABILITY TO READ: ☐ YES   ☐ NO
ABILITY TO WRITE: ☐ YES   ☐ NO

☐ I am investigating -- or --
☐ You are under arrest for alleged -- Violation of _____

_____ Relative to_____

According to provisions in the Constitution of the United States and of the State of Louisiana it is my duty to inform you that:

1. You have the right to remain silent.
2. Anything you say may be used against you in court.
3. You have a right to consult with and obtain the advice of an attorney before answering any questions.
4. If you cannot afford an attorney, the court will appoint an attorney to represent and advise you.
5. You have a right to have your attorney present at the time of any questioning or giving of any statement.
6. If you decide to answer questions now without an attorney present, you will still have the right to stop answering at any time until you talk to an attorney.

DO YOU UNDERSTAND WHAT I HAVE JUST READ TO YOU?   ☐ YES ☐ NO

     NOTE: IF THE PERSON DOES NOT FULLY UNDERSTAND AND INTELLIGENTLY AND VOLUNTARILY WAIVE THE RIGHT OF COUNSEL, HE CANNOT BE QUESTIONED. IF THE PERSON AT ANY TIME DURING THE QUESTIONING ASKS NOT TO BE QUESTIONED FURTHER OR INDICATES IN ANY MANNER THAT HE DOES NOT WISH TO BE QUESTIONED, THEN THE QUESTIONING MUST CEASE.

ARE YOU WILLING TO ANSWER QUESTIONS AT THIS TIME WITHOUT A LAWYER?   ☐ YES ☐ NO
HAVE ANY THREATS OR PROMISES BEEN MADE TO YOU OR HAS PRESSURE OF ANY KIND BEEN APPLIED TO INDUCE YOU TO ANSWER QUESTIONS OR TO GIVE UP ANY OF YOUR RIGHTS?   ☐ YES ☐ NO
WITH FULL KNOWLEDGE OF MY RIGHTS I WISH TO WAIVE ALL PRIVILEGES AGAINST SELF INCRIMINATION AND MAKE A STATEMENT ABOUT MY KNOWLEDGE OF THIS CRIME.   ☐ YES ☐ NO

_____
               Signature of Person Receiving Rights

I have read and explained the RIGHTS OF AN ARRESTEE OR SUSPECT to the person named above, and he . . .
☐ SIGNED, WAIVING HIS RIGHTS
☐ SIGNED AS UNDERSTANDING, NOT WAIVING RIGHTS
☐ REFUSED TO SIGN
☐ WAS UNDECIDED, CONSEQUENTLY WAS ADVISED NOT TO SIGN
☐ PREFERS TO SPEAK WITH ATTORNEY BEFORE MAKING DECISION
☐ OTHER - (EXPLAIN IN REMARKS)

CONCLUDED: DAY_____ DATE _____TIME _____

RIGHTS READ BY_____

WITNESS_____

WITNESS _____

REMARKS_____

_____

KPD-122

Federal guidelines for searching and seizing computers may be seen at **http://www.web-police. org/wp_guidelines.html**.

For an up-to-date list of Web links, go to **http:// www.wadsworth.com/product/0534563406s**.

Trial Judges As Decision Makers

The decision to suppress evidence rests with the trial judge. After hearing the witnesses and viewing the physical evidence (if any), the judge makes a ruling based on appellate court decisions. Thus, trial court judges are key policy makers in applying and implementing Supreme Court decisions concerning confessions and search and seizure.

As noted earlier, a pretrial motion is essentially a clash over the facts. The trial court judge possesses virtually unfettered discretion in making findings of fact. Judges' backgrounds predispose them to be skeptical of defense motions to suppress. As noted in Chapter 6, many judges were once prosecutors, whose courtroom arguments supported the police. These inclinations are reinforced by the selection process. Judges are by and large appointed by governors or presidents, who are often critical of appellate court restrictions on gathering of evidence by the police, or elected by the public in campaigns that stress crime reduction. For these reasons, trial judges do not regularly grant defense motions to suppress evidence.

On appeal, upper courts examine whether the law was correctly applied by the trial judge, but they rarely scrutinize the facts to which the law was applied. Such deference is based on the trial judge's proximity to the event. Only trial judges have the opportunity to observe directly how witnesses testify—their responsiveness to questions or their attempts at concealment. Such nuances are not reflected in the trial court transcript. Moreover, when "an appeals court reverses in one of these cases they are saying that another judge abused his discretion. They are understandably reluctant to do so" (Neubauer 1974, 175).

Police Testimony

At the center of court hearings on police practices and defendants' rights are events that happened out in the field or in the police station. Although police

COURT TV

Florida v. Wuornos

Predatory Prostitute or Victim of Her Own Life?

Eileen Wuornos is a highway hooker who is tried for killing one of her clients and later pleads guilty to six other, similar homicides. To the prosecution she is a cold-blooded murderer, but the defense counters that she killed in self-defense. As you watch the video, ask yourself the following questions.

1. Chapter 9 discussed victims and the politics of victims' rights. To what extent is Eileen Wuornos a victim? To what extent does she abuse the victim excuse?
2. Was police trickery proper in obtaining a confession from Wuornos? Would the verdict have been different if the police testified from notes made during the interrogation rather than making a video of the confession?
3. To what extent does this case represent a reversal of typical gender stereotypes? How does the case and sentencing relate to the discussion of discrimination and gender (Chapter 16)?

are increasingly using video technology to document crime scenes and to record a suspect's behavior during sobriety tests, they are less likely to use it for custodial interrogations (Leo 1996b). What is known in court therefore is largely the product of police testimony.

Richard Leo (1996a) observed 122 interrogations in a major urban police department and reported the following. Detectives begin by cultivating the suspect, getting him to make eye contact and engage in conversation. The *Miranda* warnings are useful for this purpose because they induce suspects to respond to questions. Thus three out of four suspects waive their *Miranda* warnings. Next the detective states that his (occasionally her) job is to discover the truth and typically shares with the suspect some of the evidence in the case. A two-pronged approach is being used. One is the use of negative incentives, tactics that suggest the suspect should confess because of no other plausible course of action. The other is the use of positive incentives, tactics that suggest the suspect will in some way feel better or benefit if he or she confesses. The results were as follows:

- No incriminating statement (36 percent)
- Incriminating statement (23 percent)
- Partial admission (18 percent)
- Full confession (24 percent)

A suspect's decision to provide detectives with incriminating information was fateful. Those who incriminated themselves were more likely to be charged with a crime, less likely to have their case dismissed, more likely to enter a plea of guilty, more likely to be convicted, and more likely to receive more punishment than their counterparts who did not provide incriminating statements.

LAW AND CONTROVERSY: COSTS OF THE EXCLUSIONARY RULE

A key issue in the ongoing debate over the exclusionary rule centers on its costs. In a widely cited dissent, Chief Justice Burger summed up the critics' position as follows: "Some clear demonstration of the benefits and effectiveness of the exclusionary rule is required to justify it in view of the high price it exacts from society—the release of countless guilty criminals" (*Bivens v. Six Unknown Federal Narcotics Agents*, 1971).

Assessing the number of convictions lost because of the exclusionary rule is difficult, for reasons discussed in Chapter 10. Case attrition occurs at numerous stages of the proceedings and for various reasons. Several studies shed considerable light on the topic.

Exclusionary rules can lead to the freeing of apparently guilty defendants during prosecutorial screening. Prosecutors may refuse to file charges because of a search-and-seizure problem, a tainted confession, or a defective police lineup. However, this occurs very infrequently. The comptroller general (1979) examined case rejections by U.S. attorneys and found that search and seizure was cited as the primary reason 0.4 percent of the time. Similarly, a study of seven communities reports that an average of 2 percent of the rejections were for *Mapp* or *Miranda* reasons (Boland et al. 1982). The most controversial study analyzed 86,033 felony cases rejected for prosecution in California. The National Institute of Justice (NIJ) report found that 4.8 percent were rejected for search-and-seizure reasons. The NIJ conclusion that these figures indicated a "major impact of the exclusionary rule" has been challenged as misleading and exaggerated (Davies 1983). Indeed, compared to lack of evidence and witness problems, *Mapp* and *Miranda* are minor sources of case attrition.

After charges are filed, case attrition can also occur when judges grant pretrial motions to suppress, but a nine-county study concluded that relatively few pretrial motions to suppress evidence are filed (Nardulli 1983). In less than 8 percent of the cases did the defense file one or more motions to exclude evidence. Once filed, pretrial motions are rarely successful. Challenges to identifications or confessions were granted 5 percent of the time. Challenges to gathering physical evidence were somewhat more likely to be granted by the judge, but the rate was still only 17 percent. Interestingly, not all defendants who were successful in having evidence suppressed escaped conviction; some were convicted anyway. Similarly, a study in seven jurisdictions found that 1.5 percent of the defendants were allowed to go free as a result of a successful motion to suppress physical evidence (Uchida and Bynum 1991).

Piecing together the various stages of the criminal court process leads to the conclusion that the exclusionary rule has a marginal effect on the criminal court system (Nardulli 1983). Examining case attrition data from California, Davies (1983) calculated that 0.8 percent of arrests (8 out of 1,000) were rejected because of *Mapp* and *Miranda*. As for cases filed, Nardulli calculated for his nine communities that 0.57 percent of convictions (6 out of 1,000) were lost because of exclusionary rules. Moreover, of the lost convictions, only 20 percent were for serious crimes. Weapons cases and drug cases are those most likely to involve questions about police conduct.

A special panel of the American Bar Association (1988) has likewise concluded that constitutional protections of the rights of criminal defendants do not significantly handicap police and prosecutors in their efforts to arrest, prosecute, and obtain convictions for the most serious crimes. Although many people blame the failures of the criminal justice system on judges' concern for defendants' rights, the blame is misplaced. The main problem is that the criminal justice system is stretched too thin, the ABA concluded.

CONCLUSION

In many ways Ernesto Miranda fit the pattern of those arrested by the police—a young minority male with little education and few job prospects. But the eventual outcome of his case was hardly typical. His case was heard by the nation's highest court, and he not only won the right to a new trial but also established new law in the process. Unlike most defendants whose cases are quickly forgotten, his name became a code word of crime and rights of criminal defendants.

If *Miranda* the legal principle was to endure, Miranda the man was less fortunate. Initially, his chances of gaining an acquittal during retrial looked promising indeed. After all, the state's only evidence—the signed confession—had been ruled to be inadmissible evidence. It turned out, however, that while in jail Ernesto Miranda had admitted details of the crime to his common-law wife, who by now had grown afraid of him. She testified for the state, and after an hour and a half of deliberations, the jury found Miranda guilty of rape and kidnapping a second time. After serving his prison term, Ernesto Miranda was living in a Phoenix flophouse when he became involved in a barroom quarrel over small change in a poker game. A large knife normally used to harvest lettuce ended his life. It is no small irony that the Phoenix police read Miranda's killer his *Miranda* rights when they arrested him.

This chapter has examined several important aspects of what occurs while cases are being prepared for trial. One is discovery, the formal or informal exchange of information between prosecution and defense. What information is subject to discovery varies greatly. As a rule, defense attorneys who are cooperative members of the courtroom work group receive more information than others. Another important aspect of preparing for trial centers on suppression of evidence. Confessions and physical evidence that have been illegally obtained cannot be used at trial. If the defense believes that there have been illegal actions by the police, it files a pretrial motion to suppress the evidence. Prosecutors are usually in a favorable position to show that the evidence was obtained legally.

CRITICAL THINKING QUESTIONS

1. In civil cases each party is entitled to all the information in the possession of the other side (unless that information is privileged). Why are discovery rules in criminal cases different?

2. To what extent do prosecutorial policies that restrict the sharing of information with defense attorneys other than what is legally required represent a contradiction in the crime control model? On the one hand, the crime control model suggests that criminal defendants (and their lawyers) shouldn't receive any breaks. But on the other hand, the crime control model stresses efficiency so that scarce resources can be concentrated on apprehending and convicting the guilty.

3. When the Court announced its decision in *Miranda v. Arizona* in 1966, the decision sparked massive controversy and was a major issue in the 1968 presidential campaign. Yet over time it has become much more accepted than the Court's decision in *Mapp v. Ohio* regarding search and seizure. What factors might explain this apparent shift in assessments?

4. A number of conservatives call for eliminating or restricting the exclusionary rule in street crimes. Yet some conservatives also call for a more draconian rule in white-collar crimes, suggesting that the financial records of a person or a business should be given special protections under the Fourth Amendment. Are these arguments consistent or simply a case of whose ox is being gored? How would these arguments play out if a substantial citizen in the community (whose financial records are being requested) is under investigation for major drug dealings?

5. To what extent is the continuing controversy over search-and-seizure law really a debate over the war on drugs? Recall the controversy in Chapter 8 centering on judicial independence, in which a federal judge in New York suppressed a goodly amount of illegal drugs.

WORLD WIDE WEB RESOURCES AND EXERCISES

Web Guides

http://dir.yahoo.com/Government/U_S_ _
Government/Judicial_Branch/Supreme_Court/
Court_Decisions/Specific_Cases/
Miranda_v_ _Arizona/

Web Search Terms

"Discovery+criminal"; "Miranda"; "exclusionary rule"; "search and seizure"

Useful URLs

CNN's Legal Survival Guide discusses "What Is the Miranda Warning?" at **http://www.courttv.com/legalhelp/lawguide/criminal/91.html**.

Uncommon URLs

Search and Seizure Bulletin is available at **http://www.policecenter.com/**. And while visiting the site, you might want to take the following quiz: **http://www.policecenter.com/bulletins/quiz.shtml**.

Time to overhaul Miranda? University of Utah law professor Paul Cassell is the leading conservative critic of *Miranda* and *Mapp*: **http://www.law.utah.edu/Cassell/**.

Search and Seizure Law for New York Law Enforcement Officers can be found at **http://www.gouldlaw.com/ss-toc.htm**.

Judge Scott J. Silverman (Dade County Court) offers "Criminal Discovery in Florida": **http://www.fl.judges.com/articles/96discov.htm**.

Learn about Ernesto Miranda, *Miranda v. Arizona*, and the Miranda rights at **http://www.io.com/~mcapra/miranda/rights.html**.

Read "Invoking the Miranda Right to Counsel: The Defendant's Burden" by Kimberly A. Crawford: **http://www.emergency.com/miranda.htm**.

Web Exercises

1. Access the following two cases on the Internet: *Miranda v. Arizona* at **http://www.law.cornell.edu/supct/cases/** and *Terry v. Ohio* at **http://www.findlaw.com/casecode/Supreme.html**.

   Read the two decisions not so much for the specific legal issues but for the tone of the opinions. How do these opinions differ in their treatment of police investigation? Do the opinions give direct or indirect evidence of what has happened in the two years that separate the decisions—riots and protests against the Vietnam War?

2. Using Alta Vista or another search engine, search for the phrase "*exclusionary rule.*" Based on the articles found, what is the current status of efforts to abolish or modify the exclusionary rule?

3. Using excite.com or another search engine, search using the phrase "*exclusionary rule*" and find two or more Web sites that discuss the topic. Web sites rarely indicate directly what political philosophy they reflect. It is important, therefore, for the student to analyze the message. Which one comes closest to the crime control model? Which more clearly reflects a due process model? Are they similar or different in the legal information provided?

INFOTRAC COLLEGE EDITION RESOURCES AND EXERCISES

Basic Search Terms

Miranda rule; police questioning; exclusionary rule (evidence); probable cause; searches and seizures; discovery (laws); Mapp v. Ohio; Miranda v. Arizona; self-incrimination

Recommended Articles

Anne Bowen Poulin, "Prosecutorial Discretion and Selective Prosecution: Enforcing Protection after *United States v. Armstrong*"

Richard A. Leo, "Inside the Interrogation Room"

Cathy Young, "*Miranda* Morass"

Bruce Fein and Stephen J. Schulhoffer, "Q: Should the High Court Let Police Avoid Giving the Miranda Warning?"

Thomas Y. Davies, "Recovering the Original Fourth Amendment"

Leonard W. Levy, "Origins of the Fourth Amendment"

InfoTrac College Edition Exercises

1. Using the search term *Miranda rule* or *police questioning,* find one article on each side of the issue. In what ways does this debate reflect differences between the crime control and the due process models of criminal justice? To what extent is the debate largely symbolic—what proof is offered that defendants are really going free?

2. Using the search terms *searches and seizures* or *exclusionary rule,* find one article on each side of the issue. In what ways does this debate reflect differences between the crime control and the due process models of criminal justice? To what extent is the debate largely symbolic—what proof is offered that defendants are really going free?

REFERENCES

American Bar Association. 1988. *Criminal Justice in Crisis.* Chicago: Author.

Attorney General's Task Force on Violent Crime. 1981. *Final Report.* Washington, D.C.: U.S. Department of Justice.

Baker, Liva. 1983. *Miranda: Crime, Law and Politics.* New York: Atheneum.

Boland, Barbara, Elizabeth Brady, Herbert Tyson, and John Bassler. 1982. *The Prosecution of Felony Arrests.* Washington, D.C.: Institute for Law and Social Research.

Bradley, Craig. 1993. *The Failure of the Criminal Procedure Revolution.* Philadelphia: University of Pennsylvania Press.

Brennan, William. 1963. "The Criminal Prosecution: Sporting Event or Quest for Truth?" *Washington University Law Quarterly* 279–294.

Cipes, Robert. 1966. "Crime, Confessions and the Court." *Atlantic Monthly* 55.

Comptroller General of the United States. 1979. *Impact of the Exclusionary Rule on Federal Criminal Prosecutions.* Washington, D.C.: General Accounting Office.

Congressional Quarterly. 1996. "House Republicans Advance Six Anti-Crime Bills." *1995 Congressional Quarterly Almanac.* Washington, D.C.: Author.

Davies, Thomas. 1983. "A Hard Look at What We Know (and Still Need to Learn) About the 'Costs' of the Exclusionary Rule: The NIJ Study and Other Studies of 'Lost Arrests.'" *American Bar Foundation Research Journal* 611–690.

Fyfe, James. 1982. "In Search of the 'Bad Faith' Search." *Criminal Law Bulletin* 18: 260–265.

Kamisar, Yale. 1978. "Is the Exclusionary Rule an 'Illogical' or 'Unnatural' Interpretation of the Fourth Amendment?" *Judicature* 78: 83–84.

Leo, Richard. 1996a. "Inside the Interrogation Room." *Journal of Criminal Law and Criminology* 86: 266–303.

———. 1996b. "The Impact of *Miranda* Revisited." *Journal of Criminal Law and Criminology* 86: 621–692.

Nardulli, Peter. 1983. "The Societal Cost of the Exclusionary Rule: An Empirical Assessment." *American Bar Foundation Research Journal* 585–609.

Neubauer, David. 1974. *Criminal Justice in Middle America.* Morristown, NJ: General Learning Press.

Oaks, Dallin. 1970. "Studying the Exclusionary Rule in Search and Seizure." *University of Chicago Law Review* 37: 665–753.

Reagan, Ronald. 1981. Speech in New Orleans, quoted in *The New York Times,* 29 September.

Saltzburg, Stephen. 1983. "Discovery." In *Encyclopedia of Crime and Justice,* edited by Sanford Kadish. New York: Free Press.

Segal, Jeffrey. 1984. "Predicting Supreme Court Cases Probabilistically: The Search and Seizure Cases, 1962–1981." *American Political Science Review* 78: 891–900.

Uchida, Craig, Timothy Bynum, Dennis Rogan, and Donna Murasky. 1988. "Acting in Good Faith: The Effects of *United States v. Leon* on the Police and Courts." *Arizona Law Review* 30: 467–495.

Uchida, Craig, and Timothy Bynum. 1991. "Search Warrants, Motions to Suppress and 'Lost Cases': The Effects of the Exclusionary Rule in Seven Jurisdictions." *Journal of Criminal Law and Criminology* 81: 1034–1066.

Van Duizend, Richard, L. Paul Sutton, and Charlotte Carter. 1984. *The Search Warrant Process.* Williamsburg, VA: National Center for State Courts.

Varney, James. 1996. "Date Sure Teen was Quarter Killer." *Times-Picayune,* 25 January.

Wice, Paul. 1978. *Criminal Lawyers: An Endangered Species.* Newbury Park, CA: Sage.

Wilkey, Malcolm. 1978. "The Exclusionary Rule: Why Suppress Valid Evidence?" *Judicature* 62: 214–232.

Wright, Charles. 1994. *Hornbook on Federal Courts.* 5th ed. St. Paul, MN: West.

FOR FURTHER READING

Altman, David. "Fifth Amendment—Coercion and Clarity: The Supreme Court Approves Altered Miranda Warnings." *Journal of Criminal Law and Criminology* 80 (1990): 1086–1111.

Brandt, Charles. *The Right to Remain Silent.* New York: St. Martin's Press, 1991.

Brooks, Peter. *Troubling Confessions: Speaking Guilt in Law and Literature*. Chicago: University of Chicago Press, 2000.

Davey, Joseph. "The Death of the Fourth Amendment under the Rehnquist Court: Where Is the Original Intent When We Need It?" *Journal of Crime and Justice* 17 (1994): 127–143.

Decker, John. *Revolution to the Right: Criminal Procedure Jurisprudence during the Burger-Rehnquist Court Era*. Hamden, CT: Garland, 1994.

Geller, William. *Videotaping Interrogations and Confessions*. Washington, D.C.: National Institute of Justice, U.S. Department of Justice, 1993.

Kassin, Saul, and Karlyn McNall. "Police Interrogations and Confessionals: Communicating Promises and Threats by Pragmatic Implication." *Law and Human Behavior* 15 (1991): 233–254.

Leo, Richard. "*Miranda*'s Revenge: Police Interrogation as a Confidence Game." *Law and Society Review* 30 (1996): 259–288.

Leo, Richard, and George Thomas. *The* Miranda *Debate: Law, Justice, and Policing*. Boston: Northeastern University Press, 2000.

Rutledge, Devallis. *Criminal Interrogation: Law and Tactics*. Placerville, CA: Copperhouse Publishing, 1994.

Schlesinger, Steven. *Exclusionary Injustice: The Problem of Illegally Obtained Evidence*. New York: Marcel Dekker, 1977.

Zalman, Marvin, and Larry Siegel. *Criminal Procedure: Constitution and Society*. Belmont, CA: Wadsworth, 1997.

Chapter 13

Negotiated Justice
and the Plea of Guilty

CHARGED WITH TWO COUNTS OF GAMBLING, BOTH FELONIES, RUDOLPH Santobello pled guilty to a single count of possession of gambling records, a misdemeanor. Just as importantly, the prosecutor agreed to make no recommendation as to the sentence. But Santobello's sentencing hearing was delayed for several months, and in the interim the initial judge had retired and another prosecutor had replaced the one who had negotiated the plea of guilty. Apparently ignorant of his colleague's commitment, the new DA demanded the maximum sentence, and the new judge agreed, imposing a one-year jail term. The justices of the U.S. Supreme Court were concerned about the failure of the prosecutor's office to honor the commitment it had made to induce the guilty plea. Others were no doubt concerned whether Santobello, who had a long and serious criminal record, should have been allowed to plead guilty with such a light sentence in the first place.

Santobello v. New York highlights the importance of guilty pleas. Although the average American equates criminal justice with trials, only a handful of defendants are ever tried. Instead, most convictions result not from a guilty verdict following a contested trial but rather from a voluntary plea by the accused. Views about this common practice differ. To some it erodes the cornerstones of the adversary system: the presumption of innocence and the right to trial. To others it enables the guilty to escape with a light penalty. To still others it is a modern-day necessity if the courts are to dispose of their large caseloads. All agree, however, that it is the most important stage of the criminal court process. ■

THE MANY FACES OF PLEA BARGAINING

Guilty pleas are the bread and butter of the American criminal courts. They outnumber trials by more than five to one at the federal level and by about ten to one at the state and local levels (Bureau of Justice Statistics 1984). The data in Figure 13-1 demonstrate the pervasiveness of guilty pleas. Most guilty pleas are the result of plea bargaining. The prosecutor, defense attorney, defendant, and sometimes the judge reach an accommodation on the disposition of the case. **Plea bargaining** can best be defined as the process through which a defendant pleads guilty to a criminal charge with the expectation of receiving some consideration from the state.

Plea bargaining is hardly new. There is considerable evidence that it became a common practice in state courts sometime after the Civil War (Alschuler 1979; Friedman 1979; Sanborn 1986). In federal courts the massive number of liquor cases stemming from Prohibition led to the institutionalization of plea bargaining in the first third of this century (Padgett 1990). What is new is the amount of attention plea negotiations now receive. During the early decades of this century, it was only sporadically discussed. The crime surveys of the 1920s reported the dominance of plea bargaining (Illinois Association 1929; Moley 1928), but most courts persistently denied its existence. It was not until the 1960s that plea bargaining emerged as a controversial national issue.

One indication of this controversy is the language used to describe negotiated settlements in criminal cases. Currently, the two most popular names are *plea bargaining* and *plea negotiation*. These terms, often used interchangeably, evoke negative images suggesting that the courts are "bargaining with criminals" (Sanborn 1986). Even more pejorative phrases, such as "copping a plea" or "striking a deal," are sometimes used. Moreover, court officials disagree about what is meant by plea bargaining. Some prosecutors refuse to admit that they engage in bargaining; they simply call it something else (Miller, McDonald, and Cramer 1978).

Plea bargaining is a general term that encompasses a wide range of practices. Table 13-1 on page 325 shows the extensive differences among jurisdictions in the ratio of pleas to trials. In some courthouses, trials are rare indeed. In others, they are more common. Any discussion of negotiated justice must start with the recognition that there are important variations both in the types of plea agreements negotiated and the process by which such agreements are reached.

> **Plea bargaining:** The process by which a defendant pleads guilty to a criminal charge with the expectation of receiving some benefit from the state.

| FIGURE 13-1 | Trial Rates for Typical Felonies |

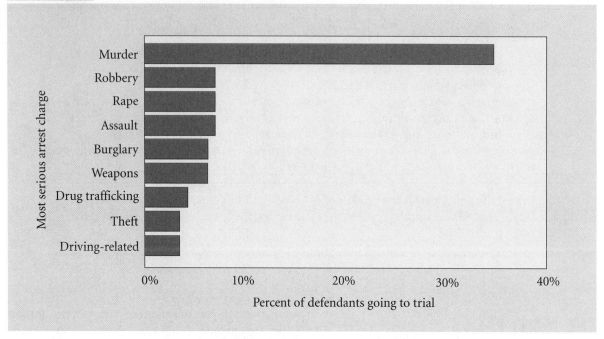

SOURCE: Timothy Hart and Brian Reaves, *Felony Defendants in Large Urban Counties, 1996*. Washington, D.C.: Bureau of Justice Statistics, 1999.

 For an article on the history of plea bargaining in one Massachusetts county, go to **http://www.yale.edu/yalelj/109/109-5ab.html**.

For an up-to-date list of Web links, go to **http://www.wadsworth.com/product/0534563406s**.

 George Fisher, "Plea Bargaining's Triumph"

LAW ON THE BOOKS: TYPES OF PLEA AGREEMENTS

The types of plea agreements found in a given jurisdiction reflect the legal definitions of crimes and the penalty structure provided for them (Chapter 2). The close relationship between plea bargaining practices and the state's criminal code is illustrated by Donald Newman's (1966) study of plea bargaining in Wisconsin, Michigan, and Kansas. The following common type of burglary case illustrates the point: A defendant was arrested in the act of stealing appliances from a warehouse sometime before dawn. The defendant had gained entry by forcing a rear door with a crowbar.

- In Wisconsin the defendant would probably be charged with burglary and plead on the nose to that offense.

- In Michigan the suspect would likely be charged with breaking and entering in the nighttime and later plead to the reduced charge of breaking and entering in the daytime.

- In Kansas the initial charge would be first-degree burglary, with a later plea to the lesser offense of third-degree burglary.

Such differences in customary ways of dealing with cases are largely the result of differences in sentencing structure in the states. In Wisconsin, sentencing laws are flexible, leaving great discretion to the judge, so guilty pleas involve little explicit bargaining. In Michigan and Kansas, statutes have fixed sentencing to allow for little judicial discretion in sentencing. As a result, these states are marked by widespread use of explicit bargaining, especially charge reduction bargaining (Newman 1966). Often, members of the courtroom work group enter into plea agreements because they perceive the

TABLE 13-1 Number of Pleas per Trial, Caseloads, and Crime Rates
(Based on All Felony Arrests) for Selected Jurisdictions

Jurisdiction	Pleas per Trial	Pleas and Trials	Index Crime Rate	Population
Geneva, Illinois	37	680	6,400	278,000
Manhattan, New York	24	17,033	13,800	1,428,000
Cobb County, Georgia	22	1,456	8,800	298,000
Littleton, Colorado	19	699	8,400	330,000
Golden, Colorado	18	1,129	5,200	374,000
Rhode Island	15	3,250	9,100	947,000
Colorado Springs, Colorado	12	809	8,200	317,000
St. Louis, Missouri	10	2,533	14,300	453,000
Salt Lake City, Utah	9	1,338	11,700	619,000
Lansing, Michigan	8	1,057	6,300	272,000
Tallahassee, Florida	7	684	12,000	202,000
Washington, D.C.	5	4,024	10,000	638,000
New Orleans, Louisiana*	4	3,103	9,600	557,000
Portland, Oregon*	4	2,986	11,200	563,000
Jurisdiction median	11	1,400	9,400	414,000

•Approximately half the trials in New Orleans and Portland are bench trials (heard by a judge only, without a jury). When bench trials are excluded, both jurisdictions still have a plea-to-trial ratio below the 14-jurisdiction median.

SOURCE: Bureau of Justice Statistics, "The Prevalence of Guilty Pleas," in *Bureau of Justice Statistics Special Report* (Washington, D.C.: U.S. Department of Justice, 1984).

penalties to be inappropriately harsh (Thomson and Ragona 1987).

Sentencing provisions in many states are severe because those who draft the laws have in mind the worst offenders: professional, hardened, and violent criminals. But courtroom work groups rarely encounter such stereotypical bad guys. Most defendants are less threatening and less dangerous than the formal law envisions. When legislative definitions of serious offenses are at odds with the courts' definitions of serious and threatening violations, plea bargaining provides the flexibility to make adjustments and produce substantive justice.

The Newman study, although dated, highlights important differences in the types of plea agreements that result from negotiations. Typically, plea agreements take one of three forms: charge bargaining, count bargaining, and/or sentence bargaining. These plea agreements are often explicit: The defendant pleads guilty with a specific understanding. Others are implicit: The defendant pleads guilty in

general anticipation of receiving a lenient sentence (Padgett 1985). Figure 13-2 summarizes the different types of plea bargaining.

Charge Bargaining

One type of plea agreement is termed **charge bargaining**. In return for the defendant's plea of guilty the prosecutor allows the defendant to plead guilty to a less serious charge than the original one filed. For example, the defendant would plead guilty to robbery rather than the original charge of armed robbery. Or the defendant enters a plea of guilty to misdemeanor theft rather than the initial accusation of felony theft. The principal effect of a plea to a less serious charge is to reduce the potential sentence.

Charge bargaining: The defendant pleads guilty to a less serious charge than the one originally filed, which reduces the potential sentence.

FIGURE 13-2   Forms of Plea Bargaining

	Law on the Books	Law in Action
Plea bargaining	The process by which a defendant pleads guilty to a criminal charge with the expectation of receiving some benefit from the state.	• The majority of findings of guilt occur because of plea bargaining. • The proportion of pleas (as opposed to trials) varies among jurisdictions.
Charge bargaining	• The defendant pleads guilty to a less serious charge than the one originally filed. • Pleading to a less serious charge reduces the potential sentence the defendant faces.	• Courthouse norms control allowable reductions. • Some prosecutors deliberately overcharge so it appears that the defendant is receiving a break.
Count bargaining	• The defendant pleads guilty to some, but not all, of the counts contained in the charging document. • Pleading guilty to fewer counts reduces the potential sentence the defendant faces.	• Some prosecutors deliberately file additional charges so they can dismiss some later on, making it appear the defendant got a good deal. • In multiple-count charges, sentences are typically served concurrently (not consecutively) so the "sentence reduction" the defendant receives is largely illusionary.
Sentence bargaining	• The defendant pleads guilty knowing the sentence that will be imposed. • The sentence in the sentence bargain is less than the maximum.	• Sentences are based on normal penalties. • Because the normal penalty for an offense is less than the maximum, defendants appear to get off lightly.

Some offenses carry a stiff maximum sentence. A plea to a lesser charge therefore greatly reduces the possible prison term the defendant will have to serve.

Bargains for reduced charges are most commonly found in jurisdictions where the state's criminal code is rigid and/or where prosecutors routinely overcharge to begin with. Thus, some charge reductions reflect the probability that the prosecutor would not be able to prove the original charge in a trial.

Count Bargaining

Another common type of plea agreement is called **count bargaining**. In return for the defendant's plea of guilty to one or more counts in the indictment or information, the prosecutor dismisses the remain-

ing charges. For instance, a defendant accused of three separate burglaries pleads guilty to one burglary count, and the two remaining criminal charges are dismissed. Count bargaining is often used when the defendant has engaged in essentially a single criminal act but the law specifies several separate and often technical criminal violations. For example, in a forgery case, the defendant may be charged not only with forgery but also with uttering (circulating) a forged document and with obtaining property by false pretenses.

Like a charge reduction agreement, a count bargain reduces the defendant's potential sentence but in a very different way. A person charged with multiple counts theoretically can receive a maximum sentence of something like 135 years, a figure arrived at by multiplying the number of charges by the maximum jail term for each charge and assuming that the judge will sentence the defendant to serve the sentences consecutively (one after another). Such figures are often unrealistic, because sentences are typically imposed concurrently (to run at the same time). In practice, the defendant will often re-

Count bargaining: The defendant pleads guilty to some, but not all, of the counts contained in the charging document, which reduces the potential sentence.

ceive the same penalty no matter how few (or how many) charges are involved.

Sentence Bargaining

The third common form of plea agreement is called **sentence bargaining**. A plea of guilty is entered in exchange for a promise of leniency in sentencing. There may be a promise that the defendant will be placed on probation or that the prison term will be no more than a given figure, say, five years. In a sentence bargain, the defendant typically pleads to the original charge (often termed a **plea on the nose**). In some jurisdictions, however, sentence bargaining operates in conjunction with count bargaining and/or charge reduction bargaining.

In sentence bargaining, the defendant invariably receives less than the maximum penalty. To some, this is an indication that defendants get off too easily, but in fact only defendants with long criminal records who have committed particularly heinous crimes would receive the maximum anyway. In practice, courts impose sentence on the basis of normal penalties for specific crimes involving common types of defendants. In sentence bargaining, the sentence agreed to is the one typically imposed in similar cases.

 The most recent criminal case processing statistics are available from the Bureau of Justice Statistics at **http://www.ojp.usdoj.gov/bjs/cases.htm**.

For an up-to-date list of Web links, go to **http://www.wadsworth.com/product/0534563406s**.

LAW IN ACTION: BARGAINING AND CASELOADS

The common explanation for plea bargaining is that the courts have too many cases. Plea bargaining is usually portrayed as a regrettable but necessary expedient for disposing of cases. In Chapter 5, it was argued that although this explanation contains some truth it obscures too many important facets of what the courts do and why they do it. Certainly the press of cases and lack of adequate resources shape the criminal court process, plea bargaining included (Worden 1990). Certainly, because prosecutors need to move cases, they agree to more lenient pleas than they might prefer.

But the caseload hypothesis cannot explain why plea bargaining is as prevalent in courts with relatively few cases as it is in courts with heavy caseloads (Eisenstein and Jacob 1977). Variations in plea bargaining rates among the fourteen jurisdictions bear this out. Among the jurisdictions with a high ratio of pleas to trials are four suburban counties (Geneva, Illinois; Cobb County, Georgia; Golden and Littleton, Colorado) that have generally low crime rates and average or below-average caseloads. With the exception of Manhattan, there does not appear to be a strong association between the size of the caseload and the plea-bargaining rate. The vast differences among jurisdictions in the ratio of pleas to trials primarily reflect differences in the prosecution and the police, not in crime rates or court resources (Boland and Forst 1985).

A similar conclusion emerges from a study of Miami, Pittsburgh, Detroit, and the Bronx. Members of the courtroom work group were presented with twelve hypothetical cases and asked, "Assuming that prosecution, defense, and the court have adequate resources to deal with their caseloads in a fair and expeditious manner, how do you believe this case should be resolved?" (Church 1985, 474). The responses indicated that relatively few of the cases would be disposed of by a trial. Furthermore, there was little support for the notion that practitioners considered negotiated guilty pleas a necessary but illegitimate response to inadequate court system resources (see A Day in Court: "Where 'Swift' Justice Means Just That").

A study of El Paso, however, did find some support for the excessive caseload hypothesis. An examination of the plea-bargaining ban by the prosecutor over a fifteen-year period found a considerable increase in the proportion of cases going to jury trial and a substantial but gradual decrease in the disposition rate. But the authors go on to suggest that the plea-bargaining ban was not the result of a carefully planned policy innovation but rather evolved from a conflict between the district attorney and the judges (Holmes, Daudistel, and Taggart 1992).

Sentence bargaining: The defendant pleads guilty knowing the sentence that will be imposed; the sentence in the sentence bargain is less than the maximum.

Plea on the nose: The defendant pleads guilty to the charges contained in the indictment or bill of information.

A DAY IN COURT

"Where 'Swift' Justice Means Just That"

All day long handcuffs snapped in Judge Anthony J. DeFino's courtroom. The defendants stood before the bench in fours and threes pleading guilty in Room 738 in City Hall. "They dispose of a lot of cases here, I'll tell you," said an officer stationed in the Common Pleas courtroom with the "rocket docket"—a court where the aim is to speed up justice partly with fast-track guilty pleas.

Yesterday, DeFino fast-forwarded 46 criminal cases involving about 16 defendants and sentenced several. He also accepted 26 guilty pleas.

"Guilty," said defendants charged with possessing cocaine with intent to distribute.

"Guilty," said a man whose shoplifting haul included $93.99 worth of razor blades.

"Guilty," said a man accused of robbery—and for that matter, of "robbing people since he was 12 years old."

Snap, snap. And the prisoners were cuffed and back in custody.

"Every day this courtroom works, [it] generally saves another courtroom a week," said Assistant District Attorney Evan Silverstein. Saving time is the big idea behind this "Expedited Case Management" program, set up in January to eliminate trials with inevitable outcomes, and make sure other cases are really ready when they go to trial. Lawyers assigned to the court from the district attorney's office and Public Defender Association say they work together for faster resolution. In the first month, 547 cases were closed.

If DeFino was quick, lawyers said Judge Legrome Davis, regularly assigned to the courtroom, is quicker. In addition to negotiated guilty pleas, the rocket docket includes case consolidations of several charges against the same defendant. That way, one judge knows the whole record when setting sentence. But yesterday wasn't as busy as usual, said DeFino, who started at 9:21 A.M. and reluctantly ended at 3:25 P.M. when he ran out of defendants.

"Maybe we could scour the courts and see if we could get some other defendants to plead," said Assistant DA Charles Junod, after a sheriff's officer replaced the last pair of handcuffs.

Snap.

SOURCE: R. Smith, "Where 'Swift' Justice Means Just That," *Philadelphia Daily News*, March 13, 1990, 20. Reprinted by permission.

LAW IN ACTION: BARGAINING AND DISCRETION

The principal weakness of the excessive caseload hypothesis is that it assumes a purely mechanical process, ignoring the underlying dynamics. It seems to suggest that if there were only more judges, more prosecutors, more defense attorneys, and more courtrooms, there would be many more trials, and the penalties imposed on the guilty would also increase. Such a view ignores discretion inherent in the criminal justice process. Plea bargaining is a response to some fundamental issues, the first of which centers on the question of guilt.

Presumption of Factual Guilt

The process of negotiated justice does not operate in isolation from the other stages of the criminal court process. What has gone before—for example, the setting of bail, the return of a grand jury indictment, and the prosecutor's evaluation of the strengths of a case—significantly affects how courts dispose of cases on a plea. The opposite is equally true. Throughout the history of a case, decisions on bail, indictment, and screening have been premised on the knowledge that the majority of defendants end up pleading guilty.

Recall from Chapter 10 that the bulk of legally innocent defendants are removed from the criminal court process during the screening process through the preliminary hearing, grand jury, or the prosecutor's charging decision. By the time a case reaches the trial stage, the courtroom work group presumes that the defendant is probably guilty. Survival through the prior processing means that prosecutors, defense attorneys, and judges alike perceive that trial defendants are in serious trouble (Eisenstein and Jacob 1977).

The following case illustrates what some court officials term a *dead bang* or a *slam dunk* case with very strong evidence against the defendant, who has no credible explanation indicating innocence (Mather 1974).

> *A neighbor saw a young black man entering the rear door of the house. The police were called and arrested the defendant, Ronald Phillips (not his actual name but the case is a real one nonetheless) within a block of the house in possession of a color TV set. According to Phillips, the TV came from his "aunt's" house.*

One Illinois state's attorney summarized the strong evidence of guilt in such cases: "The pervasiveness of the facts should indicate to any competent attorney that the element of prosecution is present and a successful prosecution is forthcoming" (Neubauer 1974, 200). Likewise, one study estimated that about 50 percent of the cases in Philadelphia were "hopeless" or devoid of triable issues of law (Schulhofer 1984).

No two cases are ever the same, of course. Many discussions of plea bargains leave the false impression that the attorneys haggle only over the sentence. In fact, courtroom work groups spend a lot of time discussing and analyzing how the crime was committed, the nature of the victim, the types of witnesses, and the character of the defendant (Maynard 1988). In many cases, there is little likelihood that the defendant will be acquitted outright; there is only the possibility that he or she might be convicted of a less serious offense. The question of what charge the facts will support is an important part of plea bargaining.

Costs and Risks of Trial

The possibility of trial greatly influences negotiations. Trials are a costly and time-consuming means of establishing guilt. For example, to try a simple burglary case would take from one to four days (depending on the jurisdiction) and require the presence of the judge, bailiff, clerk, defense attorney, prosecutor, and court reporter. During this period, none of them could devote much time to the numerous other cases requiring disposition. Also, each would be forced to spend time preparing for this trial. A trial would also require the presence of numerous noncourt personnel: police officers, witnesses, victims, and jurors. For each of these persons, a trial represents an unwanted intrusion into their daily lives.

COURT TV

New Mexico v. Gilbert

Ambush or Intruder?

Terri Gilbert was charged with first-degree murder and tampering with evidence after shooting her estranged husband. The prosecution claimed she created an ambush; the defendant contended that she was acting in self-defense. As you watch the video, ask yourself the following questions:

1. If you were the prosecutor, would you have offered to allow Terri Gilbert to plead guilty to a lesser offense? If you were the defense attorney, would you have advised your client to plead guilty to a lesser charge (and if so, which one)?
2. How do the rules of evidence (discussed in Chapter 14) affect what evidence the jury is allowed to hear and see? Would the jury verdict have been different if the jury had been allowed to hear additional facts?
3. Defense attorneys rarely call their clients to testify at trial (Chapter 7). Why did the defense decide to call Terri Gilbert to the stand? What risks did they run in making this decision?

Based on these considerations, all members of the courtroom work group have a common interest in disposing of cases and avoiding unnecessary trials. Their reasons may differ. Judges and prosecutors want high disposition rates in order to prevent case backlogs and to present a public impression that the process is running smoothly. Public defenders prefer quick dispositions because they lack enough people to handle the caseload. Private defense attorneys are dependent on high case turnover to earn a living, because most of their clients can afford only a modest fee. In short, all members of the courtroom work group have more cases to try than time or resources to try them (Eisenstein and Jacob 1977).

To a large extent, then, a trial is a mutual penalty that all parties seek to avoid through plea bargaining. To be sure, not all trials are avoided. But through plea bargaining, scarce trial resources can be applied to the cases that need to be tried.

What to Do with the Guilty

The adversary proceedings of trial are designed to resolve conflict over guilt or innocence. In practice, however, it is not the issue of legal guilt that is most often in dispute but rather what sentence to impose on the guilty. Sentencing decisions involve more than the verdict of guilt or innocence presented at trial; they incorporate difficult issues of judgment about the type of crime and the nature of the defendant. Moreover, because of the standards of evidence, the information relevant to sentencing is not easily introduced at trial (Mather 1979). Unlike a trial, plea bargaining does focus on what to do with an offender, particularly, how much leniency is appropriate.

Criminal statutes are broad; the courtroom work group is called upon to apply these broad prohibitions to specific and variable cases. The participants are concerned with adjusting the penalties to the specifics of the crime and the defendant. In the interest of fairness, they seek to individualize justice. Consider a case with two codefendants of unequal culpability—an armed robbery involving an experienced robber who employed a youthful accomplice as a driver. Technically, both are equally guilty, but in the interest of fairness and substantive justice, the prosecutor may legitimately decide to make a concession to the young accomplice but none to the prime mover. How members of the courtroom work group individualize justice is greatly shaped by the criminal code under which they work.

BARGAINING AND THE COURTROOM WORK GROUP

Plea bargaining is a contest involving the prosecutor, defendant, defense counsel, and, at times, the judge. Each party has its own objectives. Each attempts to structure the situation to its own advantage by employing tactics to improve its bargaining position. Each defines success in terms of its own objectives. Among the conflicting objectives, accommodations are possible, because each side can achieve its objectives only by making concessions on other matters. Plea bargaining is typical of "most bargaining situations which ultimately involve some range of possible outcomes within which each party would rather make a concession than fail to reach agreement at all" (Schelling 1960, 70). Bargaining is also possible because each of the legal actors understands the realities of law in action: the presumption of guilt, the costs and uncertainties of trial, and the

concern with arriving at an appropriate sentence. All these factors influence bargaining positions.

Prosecutors

To the prosecutor, a plea bargain represents the certainty of conviction without the risks of trial. Recall that prosecutors emphasize convictions. Because they value the deterrent objectives of law enforcement, they prefer that a guilty person be convicted of some charge rather than escape with no conviction at all. Not incidentally, guilty pleas can also give the prosecutor a favorable image in the public mind, because a plea also counts as a conviction.

The certainty and finality of a defendant's pleading guilty contrast sharply with the potential risks involved in a trial (Worden 1990). During trial, a number of unexpected events can occur, most of which work to the detriment of the prosecutor. The victim may refuse to cooperate. Witnesses' testimony may differ significantly from earlier statements made in investigative reports. A witness may make an unfavorable impression on the jury. There is always the possibility that a mistrial will be declared—the judge ends the trial without a verdict because of a major defect in the proceedings. Even after a jury verdict of guilty, the appellate courts may reverse, and the whole process must be repeated.

Plea bargains are useful to prosecutors in other ways. For example, prosecutors use plea bargains to reward cooperative defendants. A typical example is a crime involving a major figure and a secondary one. In exchange for providing evidence against the major figure, the secondary one may be allowed to enter a plea to a less serious charge. Such a deal greatly increases the likelihood that the major figure will be convicted.

In seeking a conviction through a guilty plea, the prosecutor is in a unique position to control the negotiating process. To begin with, the prosecutor proceeds from a position of strength: In most cases, the state has sufficient evidence for conviction. If, however, the case is weak, the prosecutor can avoid the embarrassment of losing a case at trial by either dismissing it altogether or offering such a good deal that the defendant cannot refuse.

To improve their bargaining position, some prosecutors deliberately overcharge. "Sure, it's a lever," says one San Francisco prosecutor, referring to his office's practice of charging every nonautomobile homicide as murder. With unusual candor he adds, "And we charge theft, burglary, and the possession of burglar's tools, because we know that if we charged only burglary there would be a trial" (Alschuler 1968, 90). This is not a universal practice, however (Levin 1977).

Prosecutors, of course, control several of the forms of plea bargaining. They are in a position to offer a charge reduction or a count bargain. They can threaten to throw the book at a defendant who does not plead, or they may refuse to bargain at all. If the crime is a serious one and the defendant is viewed as very dangerous, the prosecutor may force the defendant either to plead on the nose, with no sentencing concessions, or to run the risk of trial and a harsher sentence for not having cooperated.

Defendants

If pleas give prosecutors what they want (convictions), why do defendants plead guilty? To understand plea bargaining, it is important to recognize that it is often in the defendant's best interest to give up the right to be presumed innocent at a trial. The primary benefit of a plea is the possibility of a lenient sentence.

Around the courthouse, it is a common perception that defendants who refuse to plead guilty receive harsher sentences. For example, a judge may impose a stiffer sentence because the defendant compounded the crime by lying on the witness stand or getting some friends to perjure themselves. Or a prosecutor may agree not to invoke state "career criminal" provisions, which impose higher penalties for those with a prior felony conviction.

Pleading guilty may also benefit defendants in ways not directly related to sentencing. For defendants who are unable to post bail, a guilty plea can mean an immediate release (either on probation or for time served). By pleading, the accused can also avoid conviction for a crime with an undesirable label (for instance, rape or drunk driving). The defendant can plead to an offense with a less pejorative title, also avoiding the embarrassing publicity of a trial.

Ultimately, defendants must decide whether to go along with the plea bargain or take their chances at trial (see A Day in Court: "The Name of the Game Is Plea Bargaining"). Few defendants are in a position to make a reasoned choice between the advantages of a plea and those of a trial; most are poor, inarticulate, and have little formal education. For these defendants, the experience in the courts is like their life on the streets: They learn to go along.

Often softened up by the experience in jail awaiting trial, many defendants find that entering a plea is the best way to go along and avoid the possibility of even harsher penalties.

Defense Attorneys

If the prosecutor enters negotiations from a position of strength, the opposite is true of defense attorneys, who have few bargaining chips. However, they may attempt to gain some tactical advantages through various maneuvers. If the defendant is out on bail, they can seek to drag out the case in hopes that witnesses and victims will lose interest or otherwise become unavailable. For another, they may file pretrial motions to suppress the confession or evidence that was seized. But if the chances of winning at trial are not high—and they rarely are—defense attorneys must also consider the strong possibility that after a trial conviction the defendant may be penalized with a higher prison sentence.

The decision-making process for defense attorneys involves three phases. First, the defense attorney must assess the offer for a guilty plea, weighing the potential costs of delay against the likely outcome of a trial. Second, the defense attorney negotiates the terms of a plea bargain; if the initial offer is better than average, negotiations are less intense than if it is below average. Third, the defense attorney counsels the defendant, who may or may not accept the offer (Emmelman 1996).

The lawyer's main resource in negotiating a plea agreement is his or her knowledge of the courtroom work group—the types of pleas the prosecutor usually enters, the length of sentence the judge normally imposes in similar cases, and so on. Defense attorneys act as classic negotiators, trying to get the best deal possible for their clients while

 For contrasting views on plea bargaining from members of the courtroom workgroup go to:

The Criminal Defense Lawyer As Effective Negotiator: A Systemic Approach: **http://dpa.state.ky.us/ advocate/sept98/systematic.html**.

Andrew L. Sonner, State's Attorney for Montgomery County, Rockville, Maryland, provides a concept paper on plea bargaining at **http://www.abanet. org/ceeli/conceptpapers/CrimProcedure/ crimpro1.html**.

For an up-to-date list of Web links, go to **http:// www.wadsworth.com/product/0534563406s**.

"The Name of the Game Is Plea Bargaining"

 The public defender stuck a patent-leather loafer on the lowest rung of the holding cell and wedged an elbow in between the gray steel bars. "Cedric," he said quietly, "Cedric, listen to me, please."

Cedric looked back at him without an emotion crossing the flat, black expanse of his face. "Cedric, how are we going to explain the coats in the back of the car?" the defender asked. "Somebody's going to want to know how they got there."

The pale sunlight came into the cell in neat squares through the wire mesh windows. On the floor behind Cedric, bundled heaps of men tried to escape into unconsciousness. Every now and then one would mumble in his half-sleep or lash out with a savage elbow to protect his floorspace.

"Uh, look," Cedric said, the barest of smiles on his lips. "We just say somebody threw them there, you know, was running by and threw them in."

Kent Brody, the defender, took his foot off the cross-bar and looked directly at Cedric. They were both young, each almost with a baby face, but more than just jail bars separated them. "Cedric, there comes a time to face facts," Brody said. "The facts of the case are against you. We both know it. They offered a better deal than I thought. They offered flat time on the armed robbery and that would cover the arson and the probation violation. I assumed they'd give a spread, but they are offering you flat time, Cedric."

Cedric was not impressed. He gripped the bars, but casually, his slim body leaning gently against the steel, he said nothing.

"OK," said Brody. "Four years is a long time, but armed robbery carries a minimum of four to life, Cedric. You don't want it. OK. But if you get convicted, it won't be the minimum."

There was a pause and Cedric spoke softly. "Fight it," he said.

"Sure," Brody said. "Fine. OK now, so what's our defense? How'd the stuff get in the car, Cedric?"

Cedric Malthia may not know much about the law, but he knows what he likes. And he doesn't like the idea of going to prison for four years in exchange for saying he held up a clothing store at gun point. No, for a four-year sentence he was not going to say it.

Now if Brody had gotten him the deal he asked for, it might have been different. If that gun had been made to magically disappear and he had been offered two on a simple robbery, now that he might go along with. He might save the state the trouble of proving him guilty for that. He might take the plea bargain if they would agree to two. . . .

But Cedric was not cooperating. Not yet, anyway. For while the system may be in a hurry, Cedric had nothing but time.

SOURCE: Excerpted from *Chicago Sun-Times* article by Roger Simon. Copyright *Chicago Sun-Times*, 1975. Reprinted with permission.

explaining to the clients the realistic alternatives. As noted in Chapter 7, these two roles can conflict. A defense attorney may negotiate what he or she considers the best deal under the circumstances, only to have the client refuse to go along.

Judges

Several factors limit a judge's ability to control, supervise, or participate in plea bargaining. Given the division of powers in the adversary system, judges are reluctant to intrude on prosecutorial discretion. Many of the key bargaining mechanisms—specifically, the charges filed and the charges the defendant is allowed to plead to—are controlled by the prosecutor. Thus, when a prosecutor, defense attorney, and defendant have agreed either to a count bargain or a charge reduction bargain, the judge has no legal authority to refuse to accept the plea.

Even more fundamentally, the judge knows relatively little about each case. Only the prosecutor, defendant, and defense attorney know the evidence for and against the defendant. Without a knowledge of why the parties agreed to plea-bargain, it is obviously difficult for a judge to reject a plea agreement. In short, the judge is dependent on the prosecutor and, to a lesser extent, the defense attorney.

Within these constraints, judges have some ability to shape the plea-bargaining process. The extent to which they are involved in the process varies greatly. A survey of state trial court judges (Ryan and Alfini 1979) revealed four basic patterns.

- Some judges are actively involved in plea nego- tiations, offering recommendations about case disposition. Seven percent of the judges sur- veyed fell into this category.

- Other judges are indirectly involved, review- ing the recommendations made by defense and prosecutor. Twenty percent of the judges re- ported such participation.

- A small percentage of judges (4 percent) attend plea discussions but do not participate.

- The majority of judges do not attend plea- negotiating sessions. Thus, their role is limited to ratifying agreements reached by others. Fully 69 percent of the judges fit into this category.

Even judges who only ratify plea negotiations can have an important impact on the process. Regu- lar members of the courtroom work group know the sentence the judge is likely to impose. Therefore, they negotiate case dispositions that incorporate these sentencing expectations. On rare occasions, judges may reject a plea agreement. Such rejections serve to set a baseline for future negotiations.

The extent to which a judge is actively involved in plea-bargaining negotiations is influenced by a number of factors. One is the judge's perception of his or her own negotiating skills. Judges who view themselves as effective negotiators are more likely to be active participants. Judges in large cities are also more likely to be active participants (Ryan and Alfini 1979). More stable courtroom work groups likewise tend to encourage the involvement of judges (Worden 1995). On the other hand, state rules and state court decisions may discourage judges' involvement. Some states have adopted clear statements prohibiting judges from participating in plea negotiations. In these states, judicial participa- tion is rare (Ryan and Alfini 1979). It appears that a judge's participation is shaped by the judge's indi- vidual talents as well as the type of court over which he or she presides.

DYNAMICS OF BARGAINING

Negotiating is a group activity, typically conducted in busy, noisy, public courtrooms. In such a court- room, the initial impression is of constant talking and endless movement. While the judge is hearing a pretrial motion in one case, a prosecutor and de- fense attorney are engaged in an animated conversa- tion about a charge reduction in another. Mean- while, in more hushed tones, a public defender is briefing his client about why a continuance will be requested, and nearby, a mother is talking to her son who is being held in jail. These numerous conversa- tions occur while other participants continually move in and out. Police officers leave after testifying in a motion to suppress, bail agents arrive to check on their clients, clerks bring in new files, and lawyers search for the prosecutor assigned to their case. Occasionally, the noise becomes so loud that the judge or bailiff demands silence—a request that us- ually produces only a temporary reduction in the decibel level.

On the surface, courtrooms appear disorgan- ized. In fact, there is an underlying order to the diverse activities that occur (Maynard 1984). Inter- action norms control the face-to-face encounters of the participants. Decision-making norms govern the substance of the negotiations.

Interaction Norms

Courtrooms are the site of numerous simultaneous conversations. Despite the seeming chaos, a certain kind of order governs who talks to whom, when, and where. Physically, the courtroom is divided into three distinct regions. The first is the audience sec- tion, where defendants, friends, family, and wit- nesses are allowed. A railing divides this public section from the lawyers' region. Here, activity tends to occur around one or more tables reserved for the lawyers. The jury box is considered part of the lawyer's turf because prosecuting and defense attor- neys may use it to conduct their negotiations and conferences. The third area is the judge's region, with a raised bench and a witness stand (which is unused during pretrial matters). In front of the bench and to the side are desks for clerks, court recorders, and often a probation officer (Maynard 1984).

In this physical setting, a decided social order governs who talks to whom and when. Participants accord the highest ranking to judicial encounters. The judge's activities dominate all other courtroom interactions. When the judge calls a case, the other participants involved in that matter are immedi- ately expected to drop all other business and pro- ceed to the front of the court. Next in order of social importance are negotiatory encounters that take place between the lawyers. The two parties do not sit down and discuss all of their cases one by one; rather, negotiations occur in fits and starts. For example, a discussion about a plea in exchange for time served may be interrupted when the judge calls another case and resumed later when both lawyers are free. The lowest social ranking is given to lawyer-client encounters. These conversations occur largely at the convenience of the lawyer. Clients are expected to be ready when the lawyers inquire about the facts of the case or want to relay information about ongoing plea negotiations. A conversation initiated by a client is not viewed as obligatory; that is, the lawyer can end it at any time, something that would not happen in a lawyer-lawyer interchange. Prosecutors will not interrupt a lawyer's conversation with a client although the judge will (Maynard 1984).

Decision-Making Norms

Through working together on a daily basis, the members of the courtroom work group come to understand the problems and demands of the others. They develop shared conceptions of how certain types of cases and defendants should be treated. Everyone except the outsider or the novice knows these customs of the courthouse.

As we have seen, plea bargaining is a complex process that exhibits variations among jurisdictions. Nonetheless, studies in different courts reveal important similarities in shared norms. The most important is the seriousness of the offense. The more serious the crime charged, the harder the prosecutor bargains (Mather 1979; Nardulli, Flemming, and Eisenstein 1984). The next most important factor is the defendant's criminal record. Those with prior convictions receive fewer concessions during bargaining (Alschuler 1979; Nardulli 1978; Springer 1983; Smith 1986). Another key consideration is the strength of the prosecutor's case. The stronger the evidence against the defendant, the fewer concessions offered (Adams 1983; Smith 1986).

These shared norms structure plea negotiations. In each courtroom work group, there is a well-understood set of allowable reductions. Based on the way the crime was committed and the background of the defendant, nighttime burglary will be reduced to daytime burglary, drunkenness to disturbing the peace, and so on. Writing about a mis-

demeanor court, Malcolm Feeley (1979) offers an economic analogy of shared norms:

> *It is the salesman's stock-in-trade to represent a "going rate" as if it were a special sale price offered only once. The gap between theoretical exposure and the standard rate allows defense attorneys and prosecutors to function much the same way, making the defendant think he is getting a special "deal" when in fact he is getting the standard rate. Together prosecutors and defense attorneys operate like discount stores, pointing to a never-used high list price and then marketing the product as a supposedly "special" sale price, thereby appearing to provide substantial savings to those who act quickly.* (191)

Contrary to many popular fears, defendants are not allowed to plead to just any charge. If a defendant has been charged with armed robbery, the defense attorney knows that the credibility of her bargaining position will be destroyed if she suggests a plea to disturbing the peace. Such a plea would be out of line with how things are normally done.

Courtroom work groups have similar shared norms about sentencing. On the basis of these shared norms, all parties know what is open for bargaining and what is not. The shared norms provide a baseline for disposing of specific cases. Upward or downward adjustments are made, depending on the circumstances of the individual case.

Why Cases Go to Trial

Although most cases are disposed of by a guilty plea, an important 2 percent to 10 percent of defendants are tried. Cases go to trial when the parties cannot settle a case through negotiation. In large measure, the factors that shape plea bargaining—the strength of the prosecutor's case and the severity of the penalty—are the same ones that enter into the decision to go to trial. Defense attorneys recommend a trial when the risks of trial are low and the possible gains are high.

This broad calculation leads to two very different types of trial cases. In one, the possible gains for the defendant are high because there is a chance of an acquittal. There may be reasonable doubt that the defendant committed any crime, or two sets of witnesses may tell conflicting versions of what happened (Neubauer 1974). A second category of cases going to trial involves situations in which the prison

TABLE 13-2   Percentage of Indicted Cases That Went to Trial

	Homicide	Sexual Assault	Robbery	Burglary	Larceny	Drugs
Indianapolis, Indiana	38%	18%	21%	14%	12%	9%
Los Angeles, California	29	20	12	7	5	7
Louisville, Kentucky	57	27	18	13	10	11
Manhattan, New York	25	12	11	9	8	8
New Orleans, Louisiana	22	18	16	5	7	7
Rhode Island	44	22	10	1	3	2
St. Louis, Missouri	36	23	15	4	6	6
Salt Lake City, Utah	64	18	19	7	6	4
San Diego, California	37	2	12	6	5	3

SOURCE: Bureau of Justice Statistics, *Report to the Nation on Crime and Justice,* 2d ed. (Washington, D.C.: U.S. Department of Justice, 1988), p. 84.

sentence will be high. Even though a judge or jury is not likely to return a verdict of not guilty, the defendant may still decide that the slim possibility of an acquittal is worth the risk of the trial penalty.

However, not all trial cases are the result of such rational calculations. Some defendants insist on a trial, no matter what. Judges, prosecutors, and defense attorneys label as irrational defendants who refuse to recognize the realities of the criminal justice system and insist on a trial even when the state has a strong case (Neubauer 1974).

The net effect of these considerations is that some types of cases are more likely to go to trial than others. Table 13-2 presents data highlighting variation in trial rates in typical felonies. Although trial rates vary from city to city, the same pattern holds in most jurisdictions. Property offenses (burglary and larceny) are much less likely to go to trial than homicide, sexual assault, or robbery. Mather (1974) suggests that property crimes are least likely to go to trial because the state is apt to have a strong case (usually buttressed by the presence of indisputable physical evidence), and the prison sentence will not be long. Serious crimes such as murder, rape, and robbery are much more likely to be tried. In some crimes of violence, there may be reasonable doubt, because the victim may have provoked the attack. Moreover, a convicted defendant is likely to serve a long prison term and is therefore more disposed to take a chance on an outright acquittal.

Jury Trial Penalty

Although most defendants plead guilty, a significant minority of cases do go to trial. As previously indicated, it is a common assumption in courthouses around the nation that defendants who do not enter a plea of guilty can expect to receive harsher sentences. Typically called the jury trial penalty, the notion reflects the philosophy, "He takes some of my time, I take some of his." Here, time refers to the hours spent hearing evidence presented to a jury (Uhlman and Walker 1980). This is how one judge expressed his philosophy:

> If someone has a trial and it's apparent that there is some question of a good defense . . . then the sentence is probably no harsher than it would have been if he'd entered a plea. It's a delight to have a good trial, handled by a good attorney. He knows what he is doing and comes up with sharp things during the trial. . . . But I think there are times when you see a completely frivolous trial which . . . is a waste of everyone's time. Take the guy who is caught with his hand in the till, and there's no question but that he's guilty. And the case is still tried, and his hands are still in the till, and he hasn't been able to get them out, and you wonder why he's wasted everyone's time. (Heumann 1978, 142)

Several studies provide empirical documentation for these courthouse perceptions (Brereton and

Casper 1981–1982). In a major eastern city "the cost of a jury trial for convicted defendants in Metro City is high: sentences are substantially more severe than for other defendants" (Uhlman and Walker 1980, 337). However, such findings have not gone unchallenged. Research on some other courts was unable to document the existence of a jury trial penalty (Rhodes 1978). In their three-city study, Eisenstein and Jacob (1977) concluded that "the effect of dispositional mode was insignificant in accounting for the variance in sentence length" (270). Read together, these various studies suggest that it is difficult to draw conclusions about nationwide practices, because of the tremendous discrepancies among jurisdictions. Moreover, it appears that the jury trial penalty may be applied more selectively than earlier research indicated.

Despite the uncertainty over the extent of the jury trial penalty, the U.S. Supreme Court has clearly sanctioned the practice. A Kentucky defendant accused of forging an $88 check was offered a five-year prison sentence if he entered a plea of guilty. But the prosecutor indicated that if the defendant rejected the offer the state would seek to impose life imprisonment because of the defendant's previous two felony convictions. Such stepped-up sentences for habitual criminals were allowed at that time by Kentucky law. The defendant rejected the plea, went to trial, was convicted, and was eventually sentenced to life imprisonment. In *Bordenkircher v. Hayes* (1978), the high court held, "The course of conduct engaged in by the prosecutor in this case, which no more than openly presented the defendant with the unpleasant alternative of forgoing trial or facing charges on which he was plainly subject to prosecution" did not violate constitutional protections. In dissent, however, Justice Powell noted that the offer of five years in prison "hardly could be characterized as a generous offer." He was clearly troubled that "persons convicted of rape and murder often are not punished so severely" as this check forger. See Figure 13-3 for other key legal developments involving plea bargaining.

COPPING A PLEA

"Your honor, my client wishes at this time to withdraw his previous plea of not guilty and wishes at this time to enter a plea of guilty." In phrases similar to this one, defense attorneys indicate that the case is about to end; the defendant is ready to plead. A plea of guilty is more than an admission of conduct; it is a conviction that also involves a defendant's waiver of the most vital rights of the court process: presumption of innocence, jury trial, and confrontation of witnesses (*Boykin v. Alabama*, 1969).

As recently as the 1960s, the process of entering a plea of guilty was usually brief and informal. Because the courts and the legal process as a whole were reluctant to recognize the existence of plea bargaining, little statutory or case law guided the process. Under the leadership of Chief Justice Warren Burger, however, the U.S. Supreme Court sought to set standards for the plea bargaining process (see Case Close-Up: *Santobello v. New York* and Honoring a Plea Agreement on page 339).

Questioning the Defendant

In limited circumstances a defendant will enter a plea of *nolo contendere*—Latin for "I will not contest it." Although a plea of nolo contendere has the same results in criminal proceedings as a plea of guilty, it cannot be used in a subsequent civil proceeding as a defendant's admission of guilt. Thus, this plea is usually entered when civil proceedings and liabilities may result. Most defendants plead guilty to one or more charges listed in the charging document. Before a defendant's plea of guilty can be accepted, the judge must question the defendant. This was not always the case; judges once merely accepted the attorney's statement that the defendant wanted to plead guilty. But in *Boykin v. Alabama* the Supreme Court ruled: "It was error, for the trial judge to accept petitioner's guilty plea without an affirmative showing that it was intelligent and voluntary."

The judge inquires whether the defendant understands the nature of the charge and the possible penalty upon conviction, whether any threats were made, if the defendant is satisfied with the services of defense counsel, and whether the defendant realizes that a plea waives the right to a jury trial. A typical *Boykin* form is shown in Exhibit 13-1. Such

---

Nolo contendere: Latin phrase meaning "I will not contest it." A plea of "no contest" in a criminal case means that the defendant does not directly admit guilt but submits to sentencing or other punishment.

***Boykin* form:** Document intended to show that the defendant entered a guilty plea voluntarily and intelligently, understanding the charges and consequences of conviction (*Boykin v. Alabama*, 1969).

FIGURE 13-3	**Key Developments Involving Plea Bargaining**	
Boykin v. Alabama	1969	When a defendant enters a plea of guilty, the judge must determine if the plea is knowingly entered and completely voluntary.
Brady v. U.S.	1970	Even though the defendant pled guilty to avoid the possibility of a death penalty, the plea was voluntary and intelligently made and therefore not coerced.
Alford v. North Carolina	1971	Given the defendant's desire to avoid the death penalty and the existence of substantial evidence of guilt, the plea of guilty was valid even though the defendant denied guilt.
Santobello v. New York	1971	When a plea rests in any significant degree on a promise or agreement of the prosecutor, so that it can be said to be a part of the inducement or consideration, such promise must be fulfilled.
Bordenkircher v. Hayes	1978	It is not a violation of due process for a prosecutor to threaten defendants with other criminal prosecutions so long as the prosecutor has probable cause to believe that the accused has committed the offense.
Ricketts v. Adamson	1987	Prosecutor allowed defendant to plead guilty to second-degree murder, contingent upon his testimony against the codefendant. When defendant refused to so testify, the DA prosecuted him for first-degree murder. The defendant was not protected by double jeopardy because he breached the plea agreement.
Alabama v. Smith	1989	Defendant was successful in having his original guilty plea vacated. After trial conviction the judge imposed a substantially more severe sentence than under the plea agreement. Court held that the enhanced sentence was not vindictiveness because the trial judge had more information available as a result of the trial.
U.S. v. Mezzanatto	1995	Federal prosecutors may use statements made by a defendant during plea bargaining to cross-examine the defendant at trial.

questioning serves to ensure that the guilty plea reflects the defendant's own choice, is made with a general understanding of the charges and consequences of conviction, and has not been improperly influenced by the prosecution, law enforcement officials, or the defendant's own attorney. Such questioning also provides an official court record, which prevents defendants from later contending they were forced to plead guilty.

Accepting a Plea

Judges have discretion in deciding whether to accept the defendant's plea of guilty. In one capital murder case, the defendant protested his innocence but entered a plea of guilty anyway, saying, "I pleaded guilty on second-degree murder because they said there is too much evidence, but I ain't shot no man. . . . I just pleaded guilty because they said if I didn't they would gas me for it. . . . I'm not guilty but

I pleaded guilty." The Supreme Court held that given the defendant's desire to avoid the death penalty and the existence of substantial evidence of guilt, the plea of guilty was valid (*Alford v. North Carolina*, 1971).

Some judges accept *Alford* pleas—in which the defendant pleads guilty while claiming innocence. They are viewed as a way of speeding up the clogged judicial process. Superficially, the defendant "saves face," but for all practical purposes the *Alford* plea has the same effect as a conventional guilty plea and results in the same punishment. Other judges refuse to accept a plea of guilty unless the defendant fully admits guilt. According to Superior Court Judge Martin McKeever of Connecticut, *Alford* pleas fly "in the face of what crime and punishment should be all about." Thus he does not accept pleas "in cases where culpability is so obvious that the public has a right to know about it" (quoted in Steinberger 1985).

EXHIBIT 13-1 A Typical *Boykin* Form

PARISH OF ORLEANS

STATE OF LOUISIANA

SECTION "J"

JUDGE LEON A. CANNIZZARO, JR.

STATE OF LOUISIANA   CASE NO. _____

VERSUS   VIO:R.S. _____

_____

WAIVER OF CONSTITUTIONAL RIGHTS / PLEA OF GUILTY

I, _____ , before my Plea of GUILTY to the crime of _____ ,
have been informed and understand the charge of which I am pleading guilty. _____
(Defendant's Initials)

I understand that I have a right to trial by Judge or Jury and if convicted a right to appeal and by entering a plea
of guilty in this case I am waiving my rights to trial and appeal. _____
(Defendant's Initials)

The acts constituting the offense to which I am pleading guilty have been explained to me as well as the fact that
for this crime I could possibly receive a sentence of _____ . _____
(Defendant's Initials)

I understand that by pleading guilty that I am waiving my right to confront and cross-examine the witnesses who
accuse me of the crime charged, and to compulsory process of the court to require witnesses to appear and testify
for me. _____
(Defendant's Initials)

I am entering a plea of guilty to this crime because I am, in fact, Guilty of this crime. _____
(Defendant's Initials)

I have not been forced, threatened, or intimidated into making this plea. _____
(Defendant's Initials)

I am fully satisfied with the handling of my case by my attorney and the way in which my attorney has
represented me. _____
(Defendant's Initials)

I further understand that I am waiving my right against self-incrimination, that at my trial I would not have to
testify, and if I did not testify, neither the Judge nor the Jury could hold that against me. I also give up the right
not to say anything against myself, or against my interest, such as I am doing by pleading guilty. _____
(Defendant's Initials)

I understand that if I elected to have a trial I have a right to have competent counsel to represent me at trial, but
by entering the plea of guilty, I am waiving these rights. _____
(Defendant's Initials)

If a plea bargain agreement has been made I understand that no other promises which may have been made to
me other than as set out hereinabove in this plea bargain are enforceable or binding. _____
(Defendant's Initials)

_____   _____
DATE   DEFENDANT

_____   _____
JUDGE   ATTORNEY FOR THE DEFENDANT

The Judge has addressed me personally as to all of these matters and has given me the opportunity to make any
statement I desire.

_____
DEFENDANT

CASE CLOSE-UP

Santobello v. New York and Honoring a Plea Agreement

 Rudolph Santobello was indicted on two counts: Promoting Gambling in the First Degree, and Possession of Gambling Records in the First Degree, both felonies under New York law. After negotiations with the prosecutor's office in the Bronx, Santobello entered a plea to the lesser included offense of Possession of Gambling Records in the Second Degree, and the prosecutor also agreed to make no recommendation as to the sentence. Months lapsed, though, before sentencing. A new defense attorney was hired, and he moved to suppress the evidence on grounds of an illegal search and seizure. The trial judge retired. Another assistant DA assumed control over the case (it is unclear whether his predecessor was promoted or resigned to take a job in private practice). Thus months later, when Santobello appeared for sentencing, the new prosecutor recommended the maximum one-year sentence. The judge quickly imposed this sentence, leaving no doubt of his thoughts about the defendant. Reading the probation report he said: "I have here a history of a long, long serious criminal record. . . . He is unamenable to supervision in the community. He is a professional criminal." The judge concluded by regretting that a one-year sentence was all he was allowed to impose.

Chief Justice Warren Burger was beginning his second term on the court. Despite being a product of the law-and-order movement, his decision begins by noting the sloppiness apparent in the DA's office. "This record represents another example of an unfortunate lapse in orderly prosecutorial procedures, in part, no doubt, because of the enormous increase in the workload of the often understaffed prosecutor's office." But, most notably, he continues the theme of workload by coming out strongly in favor of guilty pleas:

The disposition of criminal charges by agreement between the prosecutor and the accused, sometimes loosely called "plea bargaining," is an essential component of the administration of justice. Disposition of charges after plea discussions is not only an essential part of the process but a highly desirable part.

The Burger Court decision in *Santobello* in essence brought plea bargaining out of the closet. This is the Court's first look at a state noncapital punishment plea. As for the specific issue, "When a plea rests in any significant degree on a promise or agreement of the prosecutor, so that it can be said to be part of the inducement or consideration, such promise must be fulfilled."

The net effect was to suggest that state pleas proceed under Rule 11 of the Federal Rules of Criminal Procedure, which requires the parties to disclose in open court the nature of the plea agreement.

In hindsight what is perhaps most notable is that a justice appointed by the President as representative of his law-and-order philosophy readily embraces plea bargaining. Within just two years Nixon's crime commission denounced the practice and called for its abolition within five years, a call that was doomed to failure from the beginning.

Placing the Plea Agreement on the Record

For years, plea negotiations were officially considered taboo. As a result, the taking of a plea was often a sham. The defendant was expected to lie and deny that a deal had been made. This is how one defendant described his experience:

Did your lawyer tell you how to answer them beforehand?

No, but you know how to answer them. He [the judge] asked me, you know, like had you ever been—you haven't been offered any kind of deal or nothing. He didn't put in that word, but it was meant the same thing. You have to say "No." If

anybody's in the courtroom, you gotta make a little show for them. (Casper 1972, 84)

To prevent the possibility of covering up plea bargaining, some courts now require that a plea agreement be placed on the record. Either a law enforcement officer or the prosecutor states that if a trial were held the evidence would show the defendant to be guilty and then proceeds to summarize the evidence sufficient to prove each of the elements of the offense. The defendant then has the opportunity to offer any corrections or additions. This public disclosure allows defendants and attorneys to correct any misunderstandings. Indeed the Federal Rules of Criminal Procedure make this practice mandatory in federal courts.

To ensure fairness in negotiations between defense and prosecution, the law now gives defendants a limited right to withdraw a guilty plea. In *Santobello v. New York* (1971) Chief Justice Warren Burger wrote, "When a plea rests in any significant degree on a promise or agreement of the prosecutor, so that it can be said to be a part of the inducement or consideration, such promise must be fulfilled." Subsequent decisions likewise held that defendants must live up to their end of the plea agreement (*Ricketts v. Adamson*, 1987).

LAW IN CONTROVERSY: ABOLISHING PLEA BARGAINING

Chief Justice Burger's opinion in *Santobello* supports plea bargaining because it contributes to the efficiency of the criminal justice processes. But some people find justifying plea bargaining merely on the basis of expediency to be unconvincing. What of justice? some legitimately ask. (See Controversy: Who Benefits from Plea Bargaining? on page 342.)

Doubts about plea bargaining have resulted in attempts in some jurisdictions to abolish or reform the practice. Such efforts conform to one of the most controversial recommendations of the National Advisory Commission on Criminal Justice Standards and Goals (1973):

> As soon as possible . . . negotiations between prosecutors and defendants—either personally or through their attorneys—concerning concessions to be made in return for guilty pleas should be prohibited. In the event that the prosecution makes a recommendation as to sentence, it should not be affected by the willingness of the defendant to plead guilty to some or all of the offenses with which he is charged. A plea of guilty should not be considered by the court in determining the sentence to be imposed. (46)

This recommendation was prompted by the commission's view that plea bargaining produces undue leniency.

The main weakness of the commission's recommendation to abolish plea bargaining is that it fails to recognize the importance of law in action. Rosett and Cressey (1976) make this point forcefully:

> These proposals ignore the underlying conflicts to which negotiation is a response. They assume

that justice can be administered without confronting these differences. They seek an idealized criminal law that is clear and precise, and that does not have to accommodate messy disagreements and accidents. Such proposed cures are futile. (95)

Faced with mounting public criticism and professional concern, prosecutors and judges in a number of American communities have altered traditional plea-bargaining practices. Claims that plea bargaining has been abolished or that major reforms have been instituted require critical analysis. As a result of a growing number of studies of such efforts, some important areas of interest can be highlighted.

 Michael Gorr, "The Morality of Plea Bargaining"

Are the Changes Implemented?

In analyzing the impact of changes in plea-bargaining practices, a basic question is whether the changes are indeed implemented. Written policy changes do not always alter the behavior of court actors. For example, efforts in Denver to adopt mandatory pretrial conferences met with resistance from defense attorneys and others. As a result, the programs did not have their intended impact and were later dropped (Nimmer and Krauthaus 1977). A similar pattern was observed in a northern California county. After the grand jury publicly criticized plea bargaining for undue leniency, the prosecutor responded by trying to eliminate plea bargaining. The defense attorneys then began to take more cases to trial. After the state lost twelve out of sixteen jury verdicts, the prosecutor quietly returned to the old policies (Carter 1974). Of course, not all efforts at reform are short-lived. Separate efforts in Detroit to use pretrial conferences (Nimmer and Krauthaus 1977) and to abolish plea bargaining in cases involving the Michigan Felony Firearm Statute (Heumann and Loftin 1979) were successfully implemented.

Is Discretion Eliminated or Just Moved Elsewhere?

Even when programs are successfully implemented, they may not have the impact intended. Discretion

THE MURDER TRIAL OF SHAREEF COUSIN

Pleading Guilty to Four Armed Robberies

"The defendant appeared before the bar of the court attended by Willard Hill. Through counsel, the defendant withdrew the former plea of not guilty and tendered to the court a plea of guilty as charged to R.S. 3 (Cts) 14; 64."

The legal and bureaucratic prose of this docket entry of September 28, 1995, gives little indication of the importance of the event. Shareef Cousin and his lawyer Willard Hill entered a plea of guilty to three armed robberies charged in case number 375-893 and another armed robbery in case number 377-134. (Although Cousin would not be sentenced until after the murder trial, the record indicates that a twenty-year sentence had been agreed upon.) The pleas were entered while both sides were busily preparing for the upcoming murder trial and had major impacts on subsequent developments.

First, the pleas of guilty virtually guaranteed that Shareef Cousin would not testify at trial. If he had taken the stand in his own defense the prosecution would have impeached his credibility by introducing certified copies of his four previous armed robbery convictions. Indeed, this would have provided the prosecution a back-door method of introducing what the law terms "signature crimes"—crimes committed by a criminal in a recurring and unique way.

Second, the four prior convictions were used during the penalty phase of the first-degree murder trial. Each of the four victims testified about the terror they experienced when robbed at gunpoint. One victim, for example, identified Shareef Cousin as the one who used a shotgun in a carjacking in which his five-year-old daughter was present.

Third, the prosecution used the prior convictions to rule out mitigating circumstances during the penalty phase. One mitigating factor recognized by Louisiana law is that the defendant had no significant prior history of criminal activity. The defense now could not argue that issue to the jury.

Finally, two of the armed robberies were committed along with codefendant James Rowell. During trial, Rowell became a turncoat prosecution witness; he was supposed to testify that Cousin had bragged of committing a murder but did not (see Chapter 14). The prosecution's attempt to impeach the credibility of its own witness would be the principal reason for appellate court reversal (Chapter 17).

Two days after the jury recommended that Shareef Cousin die by lethal injection for the murder of Michael Gerardi, the defendant and his lawyers appeared before Judge Bigelow for sentencing on the four armed robbery pleas. After imposing the twenty-year sentence the judge allowed Cousin to fire his trial lawyers. The new counsel was Clive Stafford-Smith, who would later argue the appeal (Chapter 17) and file the federal civil rights lawsuit discussed in Chapter 3. Stafford-Smith immediately moved to set aside the four guilty pleas, arguing that Cousin had entered the pleas on "erroneous advice of counsel." Moreover, the motion argues that Cousin was factually innocent of two of the four crimes charged (Cousin admitted only to being in the car when the codefendants committed the armed robberies). The judge denied the motion and the state's Fourth Circuit Court of Appeals agreed.

Anti–death penalty activists contend that Cousin was coerced into pleading to armed robbery, but the court record offers a different conclusion. On March 27, 1995, NOPD officer Christy Williams asked Shareef Cousin (with his mother present) what he knew about the carjacking on March 4 and he replied: "It was me, Dwayne, James, and Brent." After Dwayne committed the carjacking, "I jumped in the car." Moreover, during the penalty phase of the trial, defense attorney Willard Hill admitted that Shareef had committed some despicable acts. As for the judge, he commented, "Some of us might agree he was going to receive a relatively light sentence for the armed robberies—twenty years. I think as part of the plea, Mr. Hill may have mistakenly thought he wouldn't be convicted in the murder trial."

(Chapter 5) in the criminal justice system has been likened to a hydraulic process. Efforts to control discretion at one stage typically result in its displacement to another part of the process. Thus, the result of "abolishing" or "reforming" plea bargaining is often that the activity simply moves elsewhere. Such

a hydraulic process occurred in California after the voters approved Proposition 8 in 1982. One of the key provisions of this victim's bill of rights (see Chapter 9) prohibits plea bargaining for twenty-five of the most serious crimes. The ban applied only to the major trial court, however. Proposition 8 did not

CONTROVERSY

Who Benefits from Plea Bargaining?

Some people within the court system are concerned that plea bargaining reduces the courthouse to a place where guilt or innocence and prison or probation are negotiated in the same way as one might haggle over the price of copper jugs at a Turkish bazaar (Rubin 1976). They see it as justice on the cheap—inherently destructive of the concept that the rule of law exists to protect society. Others outside the legal system are concerned that plea bargaining works to make the jobs of the judge, prosecutor, and defense attorney much easier but sacrifices the legitimate interests of the police, victim, witnesses, and the public in general.

But primarily opposition to plea bargaining reflects different ideological preferences. What is particularly interesting is that civil libertarians as well as spokespersons for law and order see plea bargaining as a danger, but often for different reasons.

Does Plea Bargaining Sacrifice Defendants' Rights?

Supporters of the values of the due process model are concerned that plea bargaining undercuts the protections afforded individuals. This view is aptly expressed by the leading academic critic of plea bargaining, Law Professor Albert Alschuler (1975): "The plea bargaining system is an inherently irrational method of administering justice. . . . Today's guilty-plea system leads even able, conscientious, and highly motivated attorneys to make decisions that are not really in their clients' interests" (1180).

A prime concern of due process adherents is that a criminal court process geared to produce guilty pleas negates the fundamental protection of the adversary system—a public trial in which the defendant is presumed innocent—since plea bargaining discourages trials by imposing a penalty on those who lose at trial. They therefore advocate abolishing bargaining and increasing the number of trials. However, such a position ignores the reality of criminal courts: In most cases, there is no substantial disagreement over the facts. Moreover, civil libertarian critics look to the jury as the proper forum for sifting guilt from innocence. Yet experienced trial attorneys often have grave doubts about such an approach. In the words of a Los Angeles public defender: "If you've

got an exceptional case—one which is weak and there's a good chance that the defendant may be innocent—then you don't want to take it before a jury because you never know what they'll do" (Mather 1974, 202).

Another concern is that in a criminal court process geared to guilty pleas, an innocent defendant might be forced to enter a plea of guilty. Consider the statement of a minor Louisiana politician who contended that he was forced into pleading guilty to charges of vote fraud despite his innocence: "I was faced with six felonies and 41 years. . . . I didn't have the time or money to clear my name" (Degruy and Simon 1977, 1). It is difficult to evaluate such a statement, for any protestations of innocence after entering a plea of guilty are obviously self-serving. Given that courts are human institutions, it is likely that innocent defendants have sometimes been pressured to plead, but there is no evidence that this is a systemic problem. Cases of doubtful validity are screened throughout the court process, and the majority of defense attorneys will not let their clients enter a plea unless they are convinced there is enough evidence for a guilty verdict. However, due process advocates suspect that even defendants who are guilty receive few advantages by entering a plea.

Do the Guilty Benefit?

If advocates of due process are worried that plea bargaining jeopardizes the rights of the individual, the backers of the crime control model express the opposite concern. They believe that plea bargaining allows defendants to avoid conviction for crimes they actually committed, results in lenient sentences, and in general gives criminal wrongdoers the impression that the courts and the law are easily manipulated.

In particular, the police would much prefer a conviction on the crime charged than a plea to a lesser one. In the words of one detective in downstate Illinois, "When we arrest them, they should be found guilty on that charge, not some lesser charge. I don't believe in reduced charges; they should be made to answer" (Neubauer 1974, 61).

It is not a difficult task to single out individual cases in which these law enforcement criticisms of plea bargaining have merit. But the argument ob-

(continued on following page)

scures too much. In particular, it confuses cause with effect. A bargained agreement on reduced charges, for example, may be the product of initial overcharging and/or of evidence problems that surface later. Moreover, such criticisms suggest that in plea bargaining anything goes—the prosecutor and judge will make any deal to dispose of a case. In reality, each court employs a more or less consistent approach to what charge or count reductions are customary, plus a set of sentencing rules of thumb. A comparison of 1,533 plea cases with 279 trial cases in six jurisdictions supports this interpretation (Smith 1986). Defendants who gain the most from plea bargaining are the less serious, marginal offenders, in cases lacking in evidence. By contrast, defendants in serious cases who have prior criminal histories do not benefit. In short, plea bargaining appears to reflect a rational rather than a coercive process.

Many of the law enforcement criticisms of plea bargaining may be reduced to an overall displeasure with the leniency of the courts. Whether sentences are too harsh or too lenient should be a separate issue from the vehicle for reaching these sentencing dispositions.

What do you think? Does plea bargaining sacrifice the rights of the defendant or do the guilty benefit?

 "Should We Really 'Ban' Plea Bargaining? The Core Concerns of Plea Bargaining Critics" at **http://www. law.emory.edu/ELJ/volumes/spg98/guido.html**.

Steven Silverblatt discusses "The Problem with Plea Bargaining" at **http://home.dti.net/open/ coercion.html**.

For an up-to-date list of Web links, go to **http:// www.wadsworth.com/product/0534563406s**.

abolish plea bargaining but rather relocated it to the lower court, where the proportion of bargained cases increased (McCoy 1984). Indeed, the overall level of plea bargaining increased. Far from helping the victims of crime, the acceleration of plea bargaining prevented both victims and defendants from understanding the reasons for convictions and sentences (McCoy 1993).

Alaska provides another clear example. In that state, the attorney general forbade assistant prosecutors from engaging in plea bargaining or from making sentencing recommendations to the judge. Judges complained that their responsibilities increased dramatically, meaning they have very little opportunity to give sentencing thorough consideration (Rubenstein and White 1979, 277). The hydraulic process seems to explain why a recent reevaluation of Alaska's plea-bargaining ban found clear evidence of both evolution and decay in the policy. For example, charge bargaining had reemerged in most of the state (Carns and Kruse 1992).

 For an update on the Alaskan plea bargaining ban, go to the Alaska Judicial Council Web site at **http:// www.ajc.state.ak.us/Reports/pleafram.htm**.

For an up-to-date list of Web links, go to **http:// www.wadsworth.com/product/0534563406s**.

Do Offsetting Changes Occur?

Efforts to abolish or change plea-bargaining practices may produce offsetting changes. This was the conclusion of an excellent in-depth study of a Michigan county (Church 1976). After a law-and-order antidrug campaign, the newly elected prosecuting attorney instituted a strict policy forbidding charge-reduction plea bargaining in drug sale cases. One result was an increased demand for trials, although it was not as great as some judges feared. But at the same time, outright dismissals because of insufficient evidence increased. Moreover, a much greater percentage of defendants were sentenced as juveniles rather than adults, so that they would not have a felony record. Most important, plea bargaining involving defense attorneys and judges continued in drug cases, and the assistant prosecutor's ability to control the disposition of the case weakened.

Efforts to increase sentence severity by abolishing or constraining plea bargaining are not always successful. When the Coast Guard effectively eliminated plea bargains in special courts-martial, there was no increase in sentence severity (Call, England, and Talarico 1983). In short, attempts to abolish plea bargaining often produce a number of offsetting changes because overall policies fail to consider the reasons for negotiations.

CONCLUSION

Most of the Supreme Court decisions highlighted in this book deal with serious crimes—murder and the death penalty quite often. Perhaps the Court decided to decide *Santobello* because the underlying charge was a minor one. After all, establishing new rules for plea bargaining would prove less controversial if the crime was not a conviction for violence. Nonetheless, it is still curious that Burger's opinion states so many negatives about Santobello, leaving little doubt that this small-time alleged member of one of New York's crime families was hardly a model citizen. As for Santobello, the man, little else is known. In covering the case *The New York Times* discusses only the legal issues, and not the local man whose name is now enshrined in a major Supreme Court pronouncement.

Plea bargaining vividly illustrates the difference between law on the books and law in action. The rules of criminal procedure, decisions of appellate courts, and theories of the adversary system suggest that the trial is the principal activity of the criminal courts. Instead, plea bargaining is the predominant activity. Bargaining is best understood not as a response to the press of cases but as an adaptation to the realities of the types of cases requiring court disposition. In most cases, there is little question about the defendant's legal guilt. A trial is a costly and sometimes risky method of establishing that guilt, and it cannot wrestle with the most pressing issue: what sentence to impose on the guilty. Finally, through plea bargaining, courthouse officials are able to individualize justice. In short, it is neither necessary nor desirable that every defendant have a trial.

It is important to bear in mind, however, that plea bargaining is not one single easily definable practice. All the complexities and differences of America's legal system are reflected in the wide variety of practices collectively referred to as plea bargaining. It has been defined here as the process by which a defendant pleads guilty to a criminal charge with the expectation of receiving some consideration from the state. Some bargains are explicit; others are implicit. Some defendants plead guilty on the nose, others after a charge reduction, still others after count bargaining, and finally, some after sentence negotiations. Equally varied are the processes through which such bargains are reached. Different persons with divergent concerns have observed roughly similar plea-bargaining practices and procedures and reached very different conclusions about the justice dispensed and the improvements needed.

CRITICAL THINKING QUESTIONS

1. Of the three states analyzed by Newman—Wisconsin, Michigan, and Kansas—which most closely resembles your state? How is your state similar or different in terms of sentencing discretion? How might this affect the types of plea agreements reached in your state?

2. Should a defendant be allowed to plead guilty without fully admitting guilt? Would you limit *Alford* pleas to situations in which the defendant wishes to avoid the death penalty? Would you allow white-collar defendants to enter *Alford* pleas? Some federal judges will not because they perceive that high-ranking corporate officials want to end the criminal cases without accepting full responsibility for their actions.

3. What types of plea agreements were involved in *Santobello*—charge, count, or sentence? Was the nature of the agreement implicit or explicit? How would you characterize the working relationships between defense and prosecution in *Santobello*?

4. Do defendants benefit from plea bargaining in terms of lower sentences, or is plea bargaining largely a shell game in which defendants are manipulated to think they are receiving a good deal?

 WORLD WIDE WEB RESOURCES AND EXERCISES

Web Search Terms

"Plea bargaining"

Useful URLs

To further explore the Alaskan ban on plea bargaining, go to **http://www.ajc.state.ak.us/Reports/pleafram.htm**.

This site offers a defense attorney's views on plea bargaining: **http://www.thebestdefense.com/criminal process/thecase/bargaining.html**.

Uncommon URLs

Read "Plea Bargaining: Active Learning in a Course on the Courts" by Valerie Hans at **http://www.udel.edu/cte/aboutteach/fall99/hans.html**.

Web Exercises

1. Rule 11 of the Federal Rules of Criminal Procedure deals with plea bargaining. The Federal Rules can be found at **http://www.courtrules.org/frc.htm**. Select Procedure Rule 11. Why do you think the rule is so detailed?

   Many states also have placed their rules of procedure on the Web. Search for the applicable rule in your state. Is it as detailed as the federal rule?

2. Using Yahoo, do a search for *"plea bargain."* (The use of quotation marks is important!) Find news stories of cases in which plea bargains have been accepted (or rejected). What societal reactions appear to be most important? Are the people quoted more likely or less likely to believe that the plea bargain achieved a just result?

3. Use Alta Vista or another search engine to search for articles on plea bargaining. Read several articles. Do the materials appear to be favorable to plea bargaining or opposed to its use? Do the articles appear to reflect the due process model or the crime control model? What types of factual situations are used to advance the author's position?

4. Use a search engine to search on the phrase *"plea bargaining."* (Again, the use of quotation marks is important; you will find that this search yields different results from one limited to *"plea bargain."*) Examine several sites that discuss plea bargaining and examine the reasons they advance for why plea bargaining should be retained or why it should be abolished.

 INFOTRAC COLLEGE EDITION RESOURCES AND EXERCISES

Basic Searches

Plea bargaining

Recommended Articles

Michael Gershowitz, "Waiver of the Plea-Statement Rules"

InfoTrac College Edition Exercises

According to Peter Nardulli (1978), defenders of plea bargaining tend to see guilty pleas occurring when the state has a very strong case, whereas opponents tend to see it occurring most frequently when the evidence is weak. Analyze this proposition using the search term *plea bargaining* and find two or more article that discuss plea bargaining.

REFERENCES

Adams, Kenneth. 1983. "The Effect of Evidentiary Factors on Charge Reduction." *Journal of Criminal Justice* 11: 525–538.

Alschuler, Albert. 1968. "The Prosecutor's Role in Plea Bargaining." *University of Chicago Law Review* 36: 50–112.

———. 1975. "The Defense Attorney's Role in Plea Bargaining." *Yale Law Journal* 84: 1179–1314.

———. 1979. "Plea Bargaining and Its History." *Law and Society Review* 13: 211–246.

Boland, Barbara, and Brian Forst. 1985. "Prosecutors Don't Always Aim to Pleas." *Federal Probation* 49: 10–15.

Brereton, David, and Jonathan Casper. 1981–1982. "Does It Pay to Plead Guilty? Differential Sentencing and the Functioning of Criminal Courts." *Law and Society Review* 16: 45–70.

Bureau of Justice Statistics. 1984. "The Prevalence of Guilty Pleas." *Bureau of Justice Statistics Special Report*. Washington, D.C.: U.S. Department of Justice.

Call, Jack, David England, and Susette Talarico. 1983. "Abolition of Plea Bargaining in the Coast Guard." *Journal of Criminal Justice* 11: 351–358.

Carns, Teresa White, and John Kruse. 1992. "Alaska's Ban on Plea Bargaining Reevaluated." *Judicature* 75: 310–317.

Carter, Lief. 1974. *The Limits of Order*. Lexington, MA: D.C. Heath.

Casper, Jonathan. 1972. *American Criminal Justice: The Defendant's Perspective*. Englewood Cliffs, NJ: Prentice–Hall.

Church, Thomas. 1976. "Plea Bargains, Concessions and the Courts: Analysis of a Quasi-Experiment." *Law and Society Review* 10: 377–389.

———. 1985. "Examining Local Legal Culture." *American Bar Foundation Research Journal* 1985: 449–518.

Degruy, Pierre, and John Simon. 1977. "Poll Official 'Forced' into Guilty Plea." *New Orleans Times-Picayune,* 14 April.

Eisenstein, James, and Herbert Jacob. 1977. *Felony Justice.* Boston: Little, Brown.

Emmelman, Debra. 1996. "Trial by Plea Bargain: Case Settlement as a Product of Recursive Decisionmaking." *Law and Society Review* 30: 335–360.

Feeley, Malcolm.1979. *The Process Is the Punishment: Handling Cases in a Lower Criminal Court.* New York: Russell Sage Foundation.

Friedman, Lawrence. 1979. "Plea Bargaining in Historical Perspective." *Law and Society Review* 13: 247–259.

Heumann, Milton. 1978. *Plea Bargaining: The Experience of Prosecutors, Judges, and Defense Attorneys.* Chicago: University of Chicago Press.

Heumann, Milton, and Colin Loftin. 1979. "Mandatory Sentencing and the Abolition of Plea Bargaining: The Michigan Felony Firearm Statute." *Law and Society Review* 13: 393–430.

Holmes, Malcolm, Howard Daudistel, and William Taggart. 1992. "Plea Bargaining and State District Court Caseloads: An Interrupted Time Series Analysis." *Law and Society Review* 26: 139–160.

Illinois Association for Criminal Justice. 1929. *The Illinois Crime Survey.* Chicago: Blakely.

Levin, Martin. 1977. *Urban Politics and the Criminal Courts.* Chicago: University of Chicago Press.

Mather, Lynn. 1974. "Some Determinants of the Method of Case Disposition: Decision-Making by Public Defenders in Los Angeles." *Law and Society Review* 8: 187–216.

———. 1979. *Plea Bargaining or Trial?* Lexington, MA: D.C. Heath.

Maynard, Douglas. 1984. *Inside Plea Bargaining: The Language of Negotiation.* New York: Plenum Press.

———. 1988. "Narratives and Narrative Structure in Plea Bargaining." *Law and Society Review* 22: 449–481.

McCoy, Candace. 1984. "Determinate Sentencing, Plea Bargaining Bans, and Hydraulic Discretion in California." *Justice System Journal* 9: 256–275.

———. 1993. *Politics and Plea Bargaining: Victim's Rights in California.* Philadelphia: University of Pennsylvania Press.

Miller, Herbert, William McDonald, and James Cramer. 1978. *Plea Bargaining in the United States.* Washington, D.C.: National Institute of Law Enforcement and Criminal Justice.

Moley, Raymond. 1928. "The Vanishing Jury." *Southern California Law Review* 2: 97.

Nardulli, Peter. 1978. *The Courtroom Elite: An Organizational Perspective on Criminal Justice.* Cambridge, MA: Ballinger.

Nardulli, Peter, Roy Flemming, and James Eisenstein. 1984. "Unraveling the Complexities of Decision Making in Face-to-Face Groups: A Contextual Analysis of Plea-Bargained Sentences." *American Political Science Review* 78: 912–928.

National Advisory Commission on Criminal Justice Standards and Goals. 1973. *Courts Report.* Washington, D.C.: U.S. Government Printing Office.

Neubauer, David. 1974. *Criminal Justice in Middle America.* Morristown, NJ: General Learning Press.

Newman, Donald. 1966. *Conviction: The Determination of Guilt or Innocence Without Trial.* Boston: Little, Brown.

Nimmer, Raymond, and Patricia Krauthaus. 1977. "Plea Bargaining Reform in Two Cities." *Justice System Journal* 3: 6–21.

Padgett, John. 1985. "The Emergent Organization of Plea Bargaining." *American Journal of Sociology* 90: 753–800.

———. 1990. "Plea Bargaining and Prohibition in the Federal Courts, 1908–1934." *Law and Society Review* 24: 413–450.

Rhodes, William. 1978. *Plea Bargaining: Who Gains? Who Loses?* Washington, D.C.: Institute for Law and Social Research.

Rosett, Arthur, and Donald Cressey. 1976. *Justice by Consent.* Philadelphia: J. B. Lippincott.

Rubenstein, Michael, and Teresa White. 1979. "Plea Bargaining: Can Alaska Live Without It?" *Judicature* 62: 266–279.

Rubin, Alvin. 1976. "How We Can Improve Judicial Treatment of Individual Cases Without Sacrificing Individual Rights: The Problems of the Criminal Law." *Federal Rules of Decisions* 70: 176.

Ryan, John Paul, and James Alfini. 1979. "Trial Judges' Participation in Plea Bargaining: An Empirical Perspective." *Law and Society Review* 13: 479–507.

Sanborn, Joseph. 1986. "A Historical Sketch of Plea Bargaining." *Justice Quarterly* 3: 111–138.

Schelling, Thomas. 1960. *The Strategy of Conflict.* Cambridge, MA: Harvard University Press.

Schulhofer, Stephen. 1984. "Is Plea Bargaining Inevitable?" *Harvard Law Review* 97: 1037–1107.

Smith, Douglas. 1986. "The Plea Bargaining Controversy." *Journal of Criminal Law and Criminology* 77: 949–957.

Springer, J. Fred. 1983. "Burglary and Robbery Plea Bargaining in California: An Organizational Perspective." *Justice System Journal* 8: 157–185.

Steinberger, Barbara. 1985. "Alford Doctrine Popular in State's Courts." *New Haven Register,* 9 June.

Thomson, Douglas, and Anthony Ragona. 1987. "Popular Moderation versus Governmental Authoritarianism: An Interactionist View of Public Sentiments Toward Criminal Sanctions." *Crime and Delinquency* 33: 337–357.

Uhlman, Thomas, and Darlene Walker. 1980. "'He Takes Some of My Time: I Take Some of His': An Analysis of Judicial Sentencing Patterns in Jury Cases." *Law and Society Review* 14: 323–342.

Worden, Alissa Pollitz. 1990. "Policymaking by Prosecutors: The Uses of Discretion in Regulating Plea Bargaining." *Judicature* 73: 335–340.

———. 1995. "The Judge's Role in Plea Bargaining: An Analysis of Judges' Agreements with Prosecutor's Sentencing Recommendations." *Justice Quarterly* 12: 257–278.

FOR FURTHER READING

Fitzgerald, Oonagh. *The Guilty Plea and Summary Justice: A Guide for Practitioners.* Toronto: Carswell, 1990.

Gertz, Marc. "The Dynamics of Plea Bargaining in Three Countries." *Criminal Justice Review* 1 (1990): 48–63.

Lynch, David. "The Impropriety of Plea Agreements: A Tale of Two Counties." *Law and Social Inquiry* 19 (1994): 115–136.

McCoy, Candace. *Politics and Plea Bargaining: Victim's Rights in California.* Philadelphia: University of Pennsylvania Press, 1993.

Nardulli, Peter, James Eisenstein, and Roy Flemming. *The Tenor of Justice: Criminal Courts and the Guilty Plea Process.* Champaign: University of Illinois Press, 1988.

Nasheri, Hedieh. 1998. *Betrayal of Due Process: A Comparative Assessment of Plea Bargaining in the United States and Canada.* Lanham, MD: University Press of America.

Pritchard, David. "Homicide and Bargained Justice: The Agenda-Setting Effect of Crime News on Prosecutors." *Public Opinion Quarterly* 50 (1986): 143–159.

Steinberg, Allen. "From Private Prosecution to Plea Bargaining: Criminal Prosecution, the District Attorney, and American Legal History." *Crime and Delinquency* 30 (1984): 568–592.

Trials and Juries

"Why Isn't Sam Sheppard in Jail?" screamed the headline of a front-page editorial in a prominent Cleveland newspaper. For weeks vivid headlines like these made it clear that the press thought the police were not pressing hard enough in arresting Dr. Samuel Sheppard—a socially prominent physician—for the brutal murder of his wife. Live radio coverage of the coroner's inquest contributed to the intense media scrutiny; for six hours Dr. Sheppard was questioned (without counsel) about his activities that night. During trial, jurors were allowed to read the daily press coverage of the trial. After conviction, Sheppard served twelve years in prison before the Supreme Court reversed the conviction, likening the trial to a "Roman holiday" (*Sheppard v. Maxwell,* 1966). In holding that prejudicial pretrial publicity denied Sheppard the right to a fair and impartial trial, the Court set off a long and often heated battle over where freedom of the press ends and the right to a fair trial begins.

Trials attract more attention than any other step of the judicial process. The national media provide detailed accounts of the trials of celebrities like Sam Sheppard and O. J. Simpson. The local media offer extensive coverage of the trials of local notables, brazen murderers, and the like. Books, movies, and television use courtroom encounters to entertain. The importance of trials, however, extends far beyond the considerable public attention lavished on them. They are central to the entire scheme of Anglo-American law. Trials provide the ultimate forum for vindicating the innocence of the accused or the liability of the defendant. For this reason, the right to be tried by a jury of one's peers is guaranteed in several places in the Constitution. ■

Given the marked public interest in trials, as well as their centrality to American law, we would expect trials to be the prime ingredient in the criminal court process. They are not. Trials are relatively rare events. As Chapter 12 established, roughly 95 percent of all felony convictions result from guilty pleas. In a very fundamental sense, then, a trial represents a deviant case. But at the same time, the few cases that are tried have a major impact on the operations of the entire criminal justice system. Trials are the balance wheel of the process, determining how members of the courtroom work group bargain cases.

HISTORY OF TRIAL BY JURY

The primary purpose of the jury is to prevent oppression by the government and provide the accused a "safeguard against the corrupt or overzealous prosecutor and against the compliant, biased, or eccentric judge" (*Williams v. Florida,* 1970). Ideally, juries are made up of fair-minded citizens who represent a cross section of the local community. Once selected, their role is to judge the facts of the case. During trial, the judge rules on questions of law, but the jury decides the weight of the evidence and the credibility to give to the testimony of witnesses.

Trial juries are also called **petit juries**, to differentiate them from grand juries. The jury system represents a commitment to the role of laypeople in the administration of justice. The views and actions of judges and lawyers are constrained by a group of average citizens who are amateurs in the ways of the law (Kalven and Zeisel 1966).

English Roots

The trial by jury has roots deep in Western history. Used in Athens five or six centuries before the birth of Christ, juries were later employed by the Romans. They reappeared in France during the ninth century and were transferred to England from there. However, these early bodies served purposes vastly different from those of the modern institution. For

Petit jury: A trial jury as distinguished from a grand jury.

example, in England prior to 1066, settling disputes by a trial took one of two forms. *Trial by compurgation* was based on a community approach. If the defendant could recruit thirty men to certify that he was an honorable person, then he was considered truthful. *Trial by ordeal* involved subjecting the accused to torture by fire or water. Those who survived were considered truthful because God had directed it. The American Puritans tested the truthfulness of witnesses by dunking them in a pond; those who sank were lying.

The concept of the jury functioning as an impartial fact-finding body was first formalized in the Magna Carta of 1215, when English noblemen forced the king to recognize limits on the power of the Crown.

> *No Freeman shall be taken or imprisoned, or be disseized of his Freehold, or Liberties, or free Customs, or be outlawed, or exiled or otherwise destroyed, nor will we pass upon him nor condemn him but by lawful judgment of his peers or by Law of the Land. We will sell to no man, we will not deny or defer to any man, either justice or right.*

This protection applied only to nobility (freemen). Its extension to the average citizen occurred several centuries later. Like much of English law, this early trial system was clearly oriented to protecting property rights.

In the centuries after the Magna Carta, the legal status of the jury continued to evolve. Early English juries did not determine guilt or innocence. They were composed of witnesses to a crime and served to compel testimony of witnesses to a crime (who were required to testify), thus functioning much like the modern-day grand jury. Only later did they become impartial bodies, selected from citizens who knew nothing of the alleged event.

 Jeffrey Robert White, "The Civil Jury: 200 Years Under Siege"

Colonial Developments

By the time the U.S. Constitution was written, jury trials in criminal cases had been in existence in England for several centuries. This legal principle was transferred to the American colonies and later written into the Constitution. The pivotal role that the right to trial by jury plays in American law is underscored by the number of times it is mentioned in the Constitution.

Article III, Section 2, provides that "the trial of all crimes, except cases of impeachment shall be by jury and such trial shall be held in the state where the said crimes shall have been committed." This section not only guarantees the right to a trial by jury to persons accused by the national government of a crime but also specifies that such trials shall be held near the place of the offense. This prevents the government from harassing defendants by trying them far from home.

The Sixth Amendment guarantees that "in all criminal prosecutions, the accused shall enjoy the right to a speedy and public trial, by an impartial jury." The requirement of a public trial prohibits secret trials, a device commonly used by dictators to silence their opponents.

The Seventh Amendment provides: "In suits at common law . . . the right to trial by jury shall be preserved." This provision is a historical testament to the fact that the framers of the Constitution greatly distrusted the judges of the day.

LAW ON THE BOOKS: THE CONSTITUTION AND TRIAL BY JURY

Throughout most of our nation's history, the three broad constitutional provisions dealing with trial by jury had little applicability in state courts. The U.S. Constitution applied only to trials in federal courts; trials in state courts were governed by provisions found in state constitutions, provisions that varied in important ways. These practices changed dramatically, however, during the Warren Court revolution in criminal justice (Chapter 17). In a pathbreaking case the Supreme Court ruled that the jury provisions of the Sixth Amendment applied to state as well as federal courts (*Duncan v. Louisiana*, 1968). (Technically, the Sixth Amendment was incorporated into the due process clause of the Fourteenth Amendment, which restricts state power.) Subsequent decisions grappled with the problem of defining the precise meaning of the right to trial by jury. (Figure 14-1 summarizes key decisions.) The most important issues concerned the scope of the right to a jury trial, the size of the jury, and unanimous versus non-unanimous verdicts.

FIGURE 14-1		Key Developments Concerning the Right to Trial by Jury
Magna Carta	1215	English noblemen have the right to a trial by a jury of peers.
U.S. Constitution Article III, Sec. 2	1789	The trial of all crimes shall be by jury and shall be held in the state where the crime was allegedly committed.
Sixth Amendment	1791	"In all criminal prosecutions, the accused shall enjoy the right to a speedy and public trial, by an impartial jury."
Seventh Amendment	1791	Right to a trial by a jury in civil suits under common law.
Griffin v. California	1965	The privilege against self-incrimination prohibits the prosecutor from commenting on the defendant's failure to testify during trial.
Sheppard v. Maxwell	1966	The defendant was denied a fair trial because of prejudicial pretrial publicity.
Duncan v. Louisiana	1968	The due process clause of the Fourteenth Amendment incorporates the Sixth Amendment's right to a jury trial.
Baldwin v. New York	1970	Defendants accused of petty offenses do not have the right to be tried by a jury of their peers.
Williams v. Florida	1970	State juries are not required by the U.S. Constitution to consist of twelve members.
Johnson v. Louisiana	1972	Federal criminal juries must be unanimous.
Apodaca v. Oregon	1972	There is no federal requirement that state juries must be unanimous.
Taylor v. Louisiana	1975	Women cannot be excluded from juries.
Ballew v. Georgia	1978	Six is the minimum number for a jury.
Burch v. Louisiana	1979	Six-member criminal juries must be unanimous.
Chandler v. Florida	1981	The right to a fair trial is not violated by electronic media and still photographic coverage of public judicial proceedings.
Batson v. Kentucky	1986	If a prosecutor uses peremptory challenges to exclude potential jurors solely on account of their race, the prosecutor must explain his or her actions.
Georgia v. McCollum	1992	The defense is prohibited from excluding jurors based on race.
Daubert v. Merrell Dow	1993	The trial judge must ensure that any and all scientific evidence is not only relevant but reliable.
J.E.B. Petitioner v. Alabama	1994	Lawyers may not exclude potential jurors from a trial because of their gender.
U.S. v. Scheffer	1998	Doubts about the accuracy of lie detector tests justifies banning their use in court.
Kumho Tire v. Carmichael	1999	*Daubert* standards for scientific testimony apply to nonscientific testimony as well.
Apprendi v. New Jersey	2000	Any fact that increases the penalty for a crime beyond the prescribed statutory maximum must be submitted to a jury.
Portuondo v. Agard	2000	Prosecutors can tell jurors that the defendant's presence during trial helps them tailor their testimony to fit the evidence.

Famous Trials, by Law Professor Doug Linder, offers a fascinating view of many of the trials that have shaped our nation's history: **http://www.law.umkc.edu/ faculty/projects/ftrials/ftrials.htm**.

For an up-to-date list of Web links, go to **http:// www.wadsworth.com/product/0534563406s**.

Scope of the Right to a Trial by Jury

Although juries are considered "fundamental to the American scheme of justice" (*Duncan v. Louisiana*, 1968), not all persons accused of violating the criminal law are entitled to a trial by jury. Youths prosecuted as juvenile offenders have no right to have their cases heard by a jury (Sanborn 1993). Similarly, adult offenders charged with **petty offenses** enjoy no right to be tried by a jury of their peers. The Sixth Amendment covers only adults charged with serious offenses. In this context, "no offense can be deemed 'petty' for the purposes of the right to trial by jury where imprisonment for more than six months is authorized" (*Baldwin v. New York*, 1970). As a result, drunk drivers in five states—Louisiana, Mississippi, Nevada, New Jersey, and New Mexico—have no right to a jury trial if they face a jail term of six months or less (*Blanton v. City of North Las Vegas*, 1989). Some state constitutions, however, guarantee a jury trial to anyone facing any criminal charge whatsoever, including traffic offenses.

Jury Size

During the fourteenth century, the size of English juries became fixed at twelve. Although some colonies experimented with smaller juries in less important trials, the number twelve was universally accepted by the time of the American Revolution. However, in *Williams v. Florida* (1970), the Supreme Court declared that the number twelve was a "historical accident, wholly without significance except to mystics," and therefore not required by the Constitution. The Court concluded that the six-person jury used in Florida in noncapital cases was large enough to promote group deliberations and to provide a fair possibility of obtaining a representative cross section of the community. Attempts to use juries with even fewer than six members were struck down by *Ballew v. Georgia* (1978). The defendant's misdemeanor conviction by a five-member jury was reversed because "the purpose and functioning of the jury in a criminal trial is seriously impaired, and to a constitutional degree, by a reduction in size to below six members."

Use of six-member juries has been suggested as a way to relieve congestion of court calendars and reduce court costs for jurors (National Advisory Commission 1973). Thirty-three states have specifically authorized juries of fewer than twelve (see Figure 14-2), but most allow smaller juries only in misdemeanor cases. In federal courts, defendants are entitled to a twelve-person jury unless the parties

Petty offense: A minor criminal offense that does not entitle the defendant to a trial by jury.

FIGURE 14-2 State Provisions on Size of Criminal Juries

Twelve-member juries required

Alabama, Hawaii, Illinois, Maine, Maryland, New Jersey, North Carolina, North Dakota, Rhode Island, Vermont, West Virginia, Wisconsin

Juries of fewer than twelve specifically authorized

Alaska, Arizona, Colorado, Connecticut, Florida, Georgia, Idaho, Indiana, Iowa, Kansas, Kentucky, Louisiana, Massachusetts, Michigan, Minnesota, Mississippi, Missouri, Montana, Nebraska, New Hampshire, New Mexico, New York, Ohio, Oklahoma, Oregon, South Carolina, South Dakota, Tennessee, Texas, Utah, Virginia, Washington, Wyoming

Juries of fewer than twelve permitted by agreement

Arkansas, California, Delaware, Nevada, Pennsylvania

SOURCE: Based on data from National Center for State Courts, *Facets of the Jury System: A Survey* (Denver: 1976), pp. 41–44.

---

agree in writing to a small jury, but six-member juries in federal civil cases are quite common.

There has been a good deal of debate over whether small juries provide the defendant with a fair trial. Critics contend that six-member juries are more likely to ignore conflicting points of view and be too hasty in reaching a verdict (Saks 1996). Social science evidence suggests there are few differences between six- and twelve-person juries. For example, small and large juries spend about equal time deciding similar cases (Pabst 1973). Research also indicates that small juries do not exclude important points of view in reaching a verdict (Roper 1979). In terms of the types of verdicts reached, however, the evidence is mixed. A few studies suggest that case outcomes are about the same regardless of jury size. But other studies indicate that twelve-member juries are more likely to vote for the plaintiff in civil cases and to be more generous in their financial awards (Zeisel and Diamond 1974; Beiser 1975). Similarly, a study of 110 juries and 1,000 jurors concluded that large juries are slightly more likely to be unable to reach a verdict than smaller ones.

Providing a dissenter with an ally increases the ability of the dissenter to resist pressures to conform (Roper 1980).

Unanimity

The requirement that a jury reach a unanimous decision became a firm rule in England during the fourteenth century. An agreement by all of the jurors seemed to legitimize the verdict, giving the community a sense that the conclusion must be correct. However, the Supreme Court altered this assumption in a pair of 1972 decisions. It held that verdicts in federal criminal trials must be unanimous, but it affirmed state courts' findings of guilty by votes of nine to three and ten to two (*Johnson v. Louisiana*, 1972; *Apodaca v. Oregon*, 1972). Most state constitutions specifically require unanimous verdicts in criminal trials; only five states (Louisiana, Montana, Oregon, Oklahoma, and Texas) permit non-unanimous criminal verdicts. In any case, six-member juries must be unanimous (*Burch v. Louisiana*, 1979).

To allow non-unanimous verdicts would protect against one or two jurors' refusing to go along with the conclusion of their colleagues, no matter what the evidence. It would reduce the expensive and time-consuming process of conducting a second trial, and it would probably reduce deliberation time. Opponents of non-unanimous verdicts argue that the Burger Court misread the history of the jury, with the result that a basic constitutional right is being sacrificed. They point out that proof beyond a reasonable doubt has not been shown if only some of the jurors vote to convict. These concerns receive some empirical support (Zeisel 1982). A carefully controlled experiment compared unanimous to non-unanimous juries and found that non-unanimous juries tend to be hung less often, deliberate less thoroughly, and result in less satisfied jurors (Hastie, Penrod, and Pennington 1984).

LAW ON THE BOOKS: SELECTING A FAIR AND UNBIASED JURY

Before the first word of testimony, trials pass through the critical stage of jury selection. Many lawyers believe that trials are won or lost on the basis of which jurors are selected. Juries are chosen in a process that combines random selection with deliberate choice. If juries are to function as a fair and impartial body that carefully weighs the facts of the case, it is important that fair and impartial jurors be initially selected. The question of whether the three stages of jury selection—compiling a master list, drawing the *venire*, and conducting the *voir dire*—actually produce fair and impartial juries has been the subject of much concern.

Master Jury List

The first step in jury selection is the compilation of a master jury list. Juries are supposed to be made up of fair-minded laypeople, representatives of the community in which the defendant allegedly committed the crime. Therefore, the first step in jury selection is the development of procedures that will produce a representative cross section of the community. These sentiments are reflected in the Federal Jury Selection and Service Act of 1968, which was designed to ensure that "no citizen shall be excluded from service as a grand or petit juror in the district courts of the United States on account of race, color, religion, sex, national origin, or economic status." This act was prompted by evidence that selection of federal juries was systematically biased. Similar concerns have been expressed about jury selection at the state level (Fukurai, Butler, and Krooth 1991).

Voter registration lists are the most frequently used source for assembling names for the **master jury list** (sometimes called jury wheel or master wheel). These lists have major advantages: They are readily available, frequently updated, and collected in districts within judicial boundaries. However, basing the master jury list on voter registration tends to exclude the poor, the young, racial minorities, and the less educated (Kairys, Kadane, and Lehorsky 1977).

> **Master jury list:** A list of potential jurors in a court's district from which a representative cross section of the community in which a crime allegedly was committed can be selected for a trial. It is usually compiled from multiple sources, such as voter registration lists, driver's license lists, utility customer lists, and telephone directories. Also called jury wheel or master wheel.

Because of these limitations, many states as well as the federal government either require or allow the use of other sources—city or telephone directories, utility customer lists, or driver's license lists—in drawing up the master list. The use of multiple sources achieves a better cross section of the community on jury panels (Munstermann and Munstermann 1986; Newman 1996).

Jury panels can be challenged if they fail to include racial or other minorities. Appellate courts have ruled that the master jury list must reflect a representative and impartial cross section of the community. Blacks, Mexican Americans, and women cannot be systematically excluded from petit juries solely on the basis of race or sex. This does not mean that every jury must include blacks, Mexican Americans (*Castenada v. Partido*, 1977), or women (*Taylor v. Louisiana*, 1975). But such parties may not be denied the opportunity to be chosen for jury service equally with others in the community. However, the requirement of a representative cross section of the community applies only to jury pools. The Court held that this standard does not apply to the juries chosen from the pool (*Holland v. Illinois*, 1990).

 For FAQs on the jury selection process from the Cook County (Illinois) court, see **http://www. cookcountycourt.org/jury/faq-selection.html**.

For an up-to-date list of Web links, go to **http:// www.wadsworth.com/product/0534563406s**.

Venire

The second step in jury selection is the drawing of the **venire** (or jury pool). Periodically, the clerk of court, or jury commissioner, determines how many jurors are needed for a given time. A sufficient number of names is then randomly selected from the master jury list, and the sheriff issues a summons for these citizens to appear at the courthouse for jury duty. The number of citizens who merely ignore their summons is increasing nationwide, however; estimates place the nonresponse rate at 20 percent (Boatright 1999; Losh, Wasserman, and Wasserman 2000).

Venire: A group of citizens from which members of the jury are chosen.

Not all those summoned will actually serve on the venire. Virtually all states have laws that require jurors to be citizens of the United States, residents of the locality, of a certain minimum age, and able to understand English. Most states disqualify convicted felons and insane persons. Persons who fail to meet these requirements are eliminated from the venire. Others will be excused because of **statutory exemptions**. The identities of those exempted from jury duty by statute vary greatly but commonly include government officials, medical personnel, ministers, educators, and lawyers. Those not exempt by law may still be excused if they can convince the judge that jury duty would entail an undue hardship.

Although serving on a jury is a right and privilege of citizenship, many people consider it a nuisance. Indeed, in some jurisdictions, 60 percent of all persons whose names are pulled from the master jury list return their questionnaires asking to be excused. The responses of court officials to these requests play a major role in determining the makeup of juries. In some areas, all requests are automatically granted, on the assumption that any person who does not want to serve will not be a good juror. Especially likely to be excused on this basis are women, blue-collar workers, the young, and the old (van Dyke 1977). But in other areas, only a few requests involving extreme hardship are granted. Citizens who are not excused from jury duty eventually receive a summons, ordering them to appear at the courthouse on a given date. The clerk's office randomly selects a number of potential jurors from the venire and directs them to a specific courtroom. It is from this jury pool that a trial jury will be selected.

Voir Dire

The final step in jury selection is the **voir dire** (French legal term for "to speak the truth"), which involves the preliminary examination of a prospective juror in order to determine his or her qualifications to serve as a juror. The prospective jurors are

Statutory exemptions: Rules adopted by legislatures exempting certain types of persons or occupations from jury duty.

Voir dire: French legal phrase meaning "to speak the truth." The process by which prospective jurors are questioned to determine whether there is cause to excuse them from the jury.

questioned by the attorneys and/or judge about their backgrounds, familiarity with the case, friendship or acquaintance with persons involved in the case (defendant, witness, or lawyer), attitudes about certain facts that may arise during trial, and any other matters that may reflect on their willingness and ability to judge the case fairly and impartially.

If it develops during the questioning that a juror cannot fairly judge the case, the juror may be **challenged for cause** by either the defense or the prosecution. The presiding judge rules on the motion and, if it is sustained, the juror is excused. In practice, few challenges for cause are made, and even fewer are sustained. **Peremptory challenge** is the second—and much more important—technique used by the prosecution and the defense in influencing who will sit on the jury. Each side has a limited number of peremptory challenges that can be used to exclude a juror. Based on hunch, insight, whim, prejudice, or pseudoscience, a lawyer may peremptorily exclude a juror without giving a reason.

Attorneys have traditionally enjoyed unrestricted freedom to exercise peremptory challenges. For decades, the Supreme Court tacitly protected the practice of some prosecutors who used peremptory challenges to keep blacks off the jury in any case involving a black defendant. But in *Batson v. Kentucky* (1986), the Court reversed its earlier policy. If a prosecutor uses peremptory challenges to exclude potential jurors solely on account of their race, the prosecutor must explain his or her actions and may be ordered to change tactics. Moreover, a criminal defendant may object to race-based exclusions of jurors through peremptory challenges whether or not the defendant and the excluded jurors share the same race (*Powers v. Ohio*, 1991). And in a move backed by prosecutors, the Court held that the defense is also prohibited from excluding jurors based on race (*Georgia v. McCollum*, 1992).

The battleground over the proper use of peremptory challenges next shifted to gender. The Court extended *Batson* to cover gender jury bias, holding in a civil action that lawyers may not exclude potential jurors from a trial because of their sex

(*J.E.B. Petitioner v. Alabama ex rel T.B.,* 1994 or T.B., 1994). The *Batson* line of decisions is having a major impact on how lawyers exercise their discretion in using peremptory challenges, and some commentators are even suggesting the need to eliminate peremptory challenges all together (Steinberg 1991).

 Harper's, "Fear of a Black Jury"

Jury Duty

Every year, thousands of Americans are called to serve as jurors. Unfortunately, many jurors experience great frustration in the process. They are made to wait hours in barren courthouse rooms; the compensation is minimal, and not all employers pay for the time lost from work; and some potential jurors are apprehensive about criminals and courthouses. A Day in Court: "The Verdict: Juries Work" recounts the experiences of one such juror.

In spite of these hardships, most citizens express an overall satisfaction with jury duty. Of 3,000 jurors surveyed, almost 90 percent stated that they were favorably impressed with jury duty. Overall, they "view their experience as a precious opportunity of citizenship rather than an onerous obligation" (Pabst 1973, 10). Just as important, there is every indication that jurors take their job seriously.

Considerable attention is being devoted to reducing the inconvenience of jury duty. Courts in all states use a juror call-in system. In these jurisdictions, jurors can dial a number to learn whether their attendance is needed on a particular day during their term of service. In addition, an increasing number of courts are reducing the number of days a person remains in the jury pool. Traditionally, jurors were asked to serve for a full thirty days. Although only a few jurors were needed for a particular day, the entire pool had to be present in the courthouse each and every working day. Increasingly, however, jurors are asked to serve for only a few days. An approach known as the one-day/one-trial jury system requires each juror to serve either for one day or for the duration of one trial. The person is then exempt from jury duty for a year or more (Kasunic 1983). The one-day/one-trial jury system is much more efficient than older practices because it spares many citizens the inconvenience of waiting in courthouses with no trials to hear.

Challenge for cause: Method for excusing a potential juror because of specific reasons such as bias or prejudgment; can be granted only by the judge.

Peremptory challenge: Method for excusing a potential juror without specifying the reason.

A DAY IN COURT

"The Verdict: Juries Work"

The timing couldn't have been much worse. I had been home from South Africa just a couple of hours that Wednesday night when my husband handed me the message from the jury commissioner at Criminal District Court: I had missed my first day of jury duty.

Weasel out of it, a naughty voice from within said. A three-week stint out of the country, more than 20 hours in airplanes and an out-of-whack body clock that kept ticking seven hours ahead were surely a pretty good argument.

But I didn't put up much of a fight and agreed to show up with the other 200 or so men and women summoned to the courthouse basement at Tulane Avenue and Broad Street every Monday and Wednesday for the rest of May.

Justice Wheels Grind Slow

Aside from jockeying for one of the few reserved parking spaces, waiting was the worst part—hours-long waits either reading outdated magazines and chatting with strangers in a crowded, stuffy basement lounge, or sitting solemnly in a freezing courtroom.

Potential jurors waited in the lounge each morning until we were summoned to courtrooms to be questioned by defense attorneys and prosecutors, who both explained that they were seeking 12 "fair and impartial" people to decide the guilt or innocence of an accused person.

To the prosecutor that meant weeding out those soft hearted jurors who might waffle when it comes to issuing a guilty verdict, or be reluctant to hand down a harsh sentence. For example, the slightest pause or hint of uncertainty when a prosecutor asked, "Can you consider the death penalty," often landed unsuspecting men and women back in the basement lounge.

To the defense attorneys, finding a fair and impartial juror meant just the opposite. An overly enthusi-

astic or confident response on the death penalty question often hastened a return downstairs.

After the questioning (called voir dire), each side is allowed by law to dismiss 12 potential jurors—known as peremptory challenges—without having to provide a reason satisfactory to the judge. It's a tricky and often discriminatory process used sometimes to purposely exclude certain kinds of jurors from certain kinds of cases—for example, African Americans in cases involving race, women in cases involving rape, and men in child support cases. For amusement, those of us waiting our turn often tried to figure out which jurors would pass those unspoken tests.

Weighing Case Seriously

Of course, news reporters rarely pass those tests. Defense attorneys often figure we may know a bit too much about the case, and prosecutors figure we're all bleeding-heart liberals. So, one or the other issues a challenge. But I passed the test once, before a no-nonsense judge who called the first 12 potential jurors then swore the same group in just minutes later.

Considering the number of murder cases being heard every day at the court house, this case was minor: A man accused of making a false bomb threat. It didn't take long to reach a verdict, but I was pleasantly surprised by how seriously we all took our civic responsibility. We deliberated thoroughly, argued a few points back and forth and decided he was guilty. All the while, we never lost sight of the fact that, no matter how insignificant the case may have seemed, a man's future hung in the balance.

The jury process is imperfect. But my firsthand experience gave me more confidence that, despite its flaws, it often achieves what it seeks: justice.

SOURCE: Lisa Frazier, "The Verdict: Juries Work," *Times-Picayune*, May 30, 1994.

LAW IN ACTION: CHOOSING A JURY BIASED IN YOUR FAVOR

The National Advisory Commission (1973) has succinctly summarized the official—that is to say, the law-on-the-books—purpose of jury selection as follows: "A defendant is entitled to an unbiased jury; he

is not entitled to a jury biased in his favor" (p. 99). Members of the courtroom work group are reluctant to formally question this pious wisdom, but informally their actions are strikingly different. Particularly through selective use of peremptory challenges lawyers for both prosecution and defense seek jurors predisposed to their side. This is the major reason why in some areas the voir dire has become a time-consuming process (Sipes 1988). Some cases have consumed six weeks or more in the jury selection process, but it is usually accomplished in less than two hours.

Through educating jurors, trial lawyers seek decision makers who are comfortable with their approach. Through hiring jury consultants, trial lawyers aggressively seek to identify jurors who will be biased in their favor.

Educating Jurors

Attorneys use voir dire for purposes other than eliminating bias. The questioning of jurors develops rapport between the attorneys and the jurors. Voir dire also gives lawyers the opportunity to influence jurors' attitudes and perhaps their later vote. As the nationally recognized lawyers F. Lee Bailey and Henry Rothblat (1971, 83) have said: "As you interrogate the jurors you meet them personally for the first time. You are given a chance to start selling the defense. Your questions should educate each prospective juror to the legal principles of your defense." Defense attorneys in particular view the voir dire as necessary for ensuring that potential jurors will presume that the defendant is innocent until proven guilty. Many lawyers view this questioning as the final safeguard against unstated biases or prejudices by jurors, ensuring a fair and dispassionate jury.

 To find out more about jury consultant Dr. Jo-Ellan Dimitrius and her newly formed consulting firm, go to **http://www.vindim.com/**.

For an up-to-date list of Web links, go to **http://www.wadsworth.com/product/0534563406s**.

Jury Consultants

In recent years, attorneys have employed social scientists to aid them in a more systematic use of the voir dire. By determining the social characteristics and attitudes of the local population that would be beneficial to the accused, lawyers could reject some jurors while retaining others. The O. J. Simpson defense team, for example, hired Dr. Jo-Ellan Dimitrius, the head of Trial Logistics (Gollner 1995). Consultants who offer scientific jury selection are quick to point to cases in which the winning side used their techniques. But no one has yet produced convincing evidence that advice on jury selection made the difference. Indeed, the effects of scientific jury selection are modest at best. The most valuable aid social science consultants can offer is to help attorneys develop trial presentations that are clear and convincing (Diamond 1990). Often, jury consultants advise their client not on selection but rather deselection of jurors—avoiding potential jurors who would be adverse to their side.

OPENING STATEMENTS

Once the jury has been selected and sworn, the trial begins. (See Figure 14-3.) Regardless whether a trial proceeds with six or twelve jurors, it is a common practice in many courts to select several **alternate jurors**, who will serve if one of the regular jurors must withdraw during the trial.

The prosecution and defense are allowed (but not required) to make brief **opening statements**. The purpose of opening statements is to advise the jury of what the attorney intends to prove and how such proof will be offered. Opening statements are not evidence; the attorneys offer the jurors "road maps" to guide them through the case. The lawyers are limited to statements of what they actually believe will be presented as the trial progresses (*United States v. Dinitz*, 1976).

THE PROSECUTION PRESENTS ITS CASE

After the opening statements, the prosecution presents its main evidence. How the prosecutor proceeds is affected by two important aspects of the law: the presumption of innocence and rules of evidence.

Alternate juror: Juror(s) chosen in excess of minimum number needed, in case one or more jurors is unable to serve for the entire trial.

Opening statement: Address made by attorneys for both parties at the beginning of a trial in which they outline for the jury what they intend to prove in their case.

FIGURE 14-3	Steps of the Process: Trials

	Law on the Books	*Law in Action*
Trial	The adversarial process of deciding a case through the presentation of evidence and arguments about the evidence.	Only a handful of felonies and even fewer misdemeanors are decided by trial.
Bench trial	Trial before a judge without a jury.	Defense prefers when the issues are either highly technical or very emotional.
Jury trial	A group of average citizens selected by law and sworn in to look at certain facts and determine the truth.	Introduces public standards of justice into the decision-making process.
Jury selection	Process of selecting a fair and impartial jury.	Each side seeks to select jurors who are biased in its favor.
Master jury list	Potential jurors are selected by chance from a list of potential jurors. List should reflect a representative cross section of the community.	Selecting only from registered voters or the like means that the poor, the young, and minorities are less likely to be called.
Venire	A group of citizens from which jury members are chosen (jury pool).	Judges vary in their willingness to excuse potential jurors because of hardship.
Voir dire	The process by which prospective jurors are questioned to determine whether there is cause to excuse them from the jury.	Lawyers use questioning to predispose jurors in their favor.
Peremptory challenge	Each side may exclude a set number of jurors without stating a reason	Both sides use peremptory challenges to select a jury favorable to their side.
Challenge for cause	A judge may dismiss a potential juror if the person cannot be fair and objective.	Rarely granted.
Opening statements	Lawyers discuss what the evidence will show.	Lawyers use to lead the jury to a favorable verdict.
Prosecutor's case-in-main	The main evidence offered to prove the defendant guilty beyond a reasonable doubt.	Defense suggests that the prosecution has not met its burden of proof.
Witness	A person who makes a statement under oath about the events in question.	Through cross-examination, defense undermines the credibility of the witness.
Expert witness	A person possessing special knowledge or experience who is allowed to testify not only about facts but also about conclusions he or she has drawn.	Some expert witnesses testify only for one side or the other because their conclusions are predictable.
Defense's case-in-main	Evidence that defense may present. Because the defendant is innocent until proven guilty, the defense is not required to present evidence.	Defense may rest without calling witnesses because jurors expect to hear reasons why they shouldn't convict.

(continued from previous page)

Witness	The defendant may waive his or her privilege against self-incrimination and testify.	Defense attorneys are reluctant to call the defendant to the stand particularly if there is a prior conviction.
Rebuttal	Evidence that refutes or contradicts evidence given by the opposing party.	Prosecutor will call witnesses to undermine a defendant's alibi.
Closing arguments	After all the evidence has been presented, each side sums up the evidence and attempts to convince the jury why their side should win.	Many trial attorneys believe that a good closing argument will win the case.
Prosecution	Because the prosecution bears the burden of proof, the prosecutor goes first and last.	The district attorney's first closing argument provides an orderly summary of the evidence.
Defense	Closing argument of the defense highlights the evidence leading to a not guilty verdict.	Typically stresses that the prosecutor has failed to prove the defendant guilty beyond a reasonable doubt.
Prosecution	Rebuts defense allegations.	Impassioned statement, calling upon jurors to do their duty and convict the guilty.
Jury instructions	Explanations by the judge informing the jury of the law applicable to the case.	Legal language difficult for average citizens to follow.
Jury deliberations	• Jurors are repeatedly instructed not to talk about the case . • Jurors deliberate in private. • Jurors select a foreperson and discuss the case. • Jurors may request further instructions from the judge. • Jurors take an oath to follow the law as instructed by the judge.	• Jurors routinely talk with other jurors about the case. • Higher status individuals participate more. • The first vote is usually decisive. • Such requests produce great anxiety among lawyers. • Some juries introduce popular law into the decision-making process.
Verdict	Decision that the defendant is either guilty or not guilty (acquittal).	• Juries convict three out of four times. • Jury verdicts often reflect a compromise.
Hung jury	Jury is unable to reach a verdict.	Defense attorneys consider a hung jury an important victory.
Post-verdict motions	Motions filed by the defense after conviction and before sentencing.	Judge must accept a verdict of not guilty.
Motion in arrest of judgment	Defense argues that the jury could not have reasonably convicted the defendant based on the evidence presented.	Trial judges are very reluctant to second-guess jury verdicts and almost never grant this motion.
Motion for a new trial	Defense argues that the trial judge made mistakes and therefore a new trial should be held.	On very rare occasions trial judges admit that an error occurred and set aside a jury verdict of guilty.

Burden of Proof

One of the most fundamental protections recognized in the American criminal justice process is the presumption of innocence. The state has the burden of proving the defendant guilty of the alleged crime; the defendant is not required to prove himself or herself innocent. This difference is a fundamental one. A moment's reflection will give an idea of how hard it would be to prove that something did not happen or that a person did not commit an alleged criminal act, for it is very difficult to rule out all possibilities. Therefore, a defendant is cloaked with the legal shield of innocence throughout the criminal justice system.

In meeting the obligation to prove the defendant guilty, the prosecution is required to prove the defendant guilty beyond a reasonable doubt. **Reasonable doubt** is a legal yardstick measuring the sufficiency of the evidence. This burden of proof does not require that the state establish absolute certainty by eliminating all doubt—just reasonable doubt. In attempting to show the defendant guilty beyond a reasonable doubt the prosecutor calls witnesses and introduces physical evidence based on the rules of evidence.

Types of Evidence

The state tries to convince the jury to return a guilty verdict by presenting **evidence**. Evidence can be classified into real evidence, testimony, direct evidence, and circumstantial evidence. **Real evidence** includes objects of any kind—guns, maps, records, and documents, for example. The bulk of the evidence during a criminal trial consists of **testimony**—statements by competent witnesses. **Direct evidence** is eyewitness

---

Reasonable doubt: The state of mind of jurors when they do not feel a moral certainty about the truth of the charges and when the evidence does not exclude every other reasonable hypothesis except that the defendant is guilty as charged.

Evidence: Any kind of proof offered to establish the existence or nonexistence of a fact in dispute, for example, testimony, writings, other material objects, demonstrations.

Real evidence: Objects, such as fingerprints, seen by the jury.

Testimony: The giving of evidence by a witness under oath.

Direct evidence: Evidence derived from one or more of the five senses.

---

evidence. Testimony that a person was seen walking in the rain is direct evidence that a person walked in the rain. Indirect evidence is called **circumstantial evidence**. Circumstantial evidence can be used to prove the truth or falsity of a fact at issue. Testimony that the person was seen indoors with wet shoes is circumstantial evidence that the person had walked in the rain.

The presentation of evidence during trial is governed by principles called rules of evidence. A trial is an adversary proceeding in which the rules of evidence resemble the rules of a game, with the judge acting as an impartial umpire. These rules of evidence have developed primarily out of appellate court decisions. Although they may seem to be a fixed set of legal rules, they are not. Like all other legal principles, they are general propositions that courts must apply to specific instances. During such applications, judges use a balancing test, carefully weighing whether the trial would be fairer with or without the piece of evidence in question (Rothstein 1970). Nowhere is the adaptability of rules of evidence more apparent than in the area of scientific evidence.

The purpose of the adversary process is to get at the truth, and the primary purpose of rules of evidence is to help achieve this end. For instance, a judge who feels that the jury would give certain evidence undue weight or would be greatly prejudiced will not allow that evidence to be presented. However, some rules of evidence have purposes other than truthfulness. Because the law seeks to protect the secrecy of communications (legally called **privileged communications**) between doctor and patient, lawyer and client, and husband and wife, such communications are not normally admissible in open court. Similarly, under the exclusionary rule (Chapter 12), illegally seized evidence is inadmissible (even if trustworthy), because the law seeks to discourage such activities. Most of the major rules of evidence, however, are directed at achieving the truth. These principles may be briefly summarized under the headings of trustworthiness and relevance.

Circumstantial evidence: An indirect method of proving the material facts of a case; testimony that is not based on the witness's personal observation of the material events.

Privileged communications: A recognized right to keep certain communications confidential or private.

The Legal Information Institute provides an excellent overview of evidence at **http://www.law.cornell.edu/topics/evidence.html**.

The Federal Rules of Evidence can be found at **http://www.law.cornell.edu/rules/fre/overview.html**.

For an up-to-date list of Web links, go to **http://www.wadsworth.com/product/0534563406s**.

Rules of Evidence: Trustworthiness

The basic criterion for admissibility of evidence is **trustworthiness**. The object of the evidentiary system is to ensure that only the most reliable and credible facts, statements, and testimony are presented to the fact-finder. The **best-evidence rule** illustrates the point. Ordinarily only the original of a document or object is admissible, because a copy or facsimile may have been altered. Similarly, a judge may rule that a person of unsound mind or a very young child is not a competent witness, because he or she might not understand what was seen or heard. The mere fact that evidence is legally ruled to be competent does not, of course, mean that the jury must believe it. A wife's alibi for her husband may be competent evidence, but the jury may choose not to believe her.

Hearsay is secondhand evidence. It is testimony that is not based on personal knowledge but is a repetition of what another person has said: "My brother Bob told me he saw Jones enter the store that evening." The general rule is that hearsay evidence is not admissible because it is impossible to test its truthfulness; there is no way to cross-examine as to the truth of the matter. There are exceptions, however. In some situations, dying declarations constitute an exception to the hearsay rule. There are many such exceptions; the rules for whether or not hearsay may be used are among the more complex in the law.

Rules of Evidence: Relevance

To be admissible, evidence must not only be trustworthy but also relevant; there must be a valid reason for introducing the statement, object, or testimony. Evidence not related to an issue at trial is termed **immaterial** or **irrelevant**. If, for example, a defendant is accused of murder, the issue is whether he killed the deceased. Evidence regarding motive, intention to commit the offense, and ability to commit the offense would all be relevant. But information about the defendant's character—prior convictions or a reputation for dishonesty, for instance—would not normally be admissible, because it is not material to the issue of whether the defendant committed this crime. However, if the defendant were to testify, such evidence would be admissible during rebuttal for the sole purpose of **impeaching** (casting doubt on) his or her credibility.

 For actual case histories of how forensics solves crimes go to **http://www.forensic-lab.com/casehist/index.html**.

For an up-to-date list of Web links, go to **http://www.wadsworth.com/product/0534563406s**.

Scientific Evidence

Scientific evidence like blood, bloodstains, hairs, fibers, firearms, tool marks, and fingerprints are now routinely admitted into evidence if they meet the traditional yardsticks of the rules of evidence—trustworthiness and relevance. But when the technologies for gathering and measuring these forms of evidence first emerged, their use as evidence was far from routine. Moreover, not all evidence based on "science" is necessarily admissible. Polygraph examinations and testimony gained from hypnosis are generally not admissible as evidence.

Trustworthiness: Basic criterion for the admissibility of evidence, which seeks to ensure that only the most reliable and credible facts, statements, and testimony are presented to the fact-finder.

Best-evidence rule: Rule requiring that someone coming into court must bring the best available original evidence to prove the questions involved in the case.

Hearsay: An out-of-court assertion or statement, made by someone other than the testifying witness, which is offered to prove the truth of testimony. Hearsay evidence is excluded from trials unless it falls within one of the recognized exceptions.

Immaterial: Evidence that neither proves nor disproves the issue of a trial.

Irrelevant: Testimony that has no bearing on the issue of a trial.

Impeach: To question the truthfulness of a witness's testimony.

The Greatest Trials of All Time

The Trial of Sam Sheppard

When Dr. Sam Sheppard was tried for murdering his pregnant wife, it was the trial of the century of its day. From the beginning, the police didn't believe the suspect's story about an intruder, and the evidence during the first trial appeared to be overwhelming. Yet Dr. Sheppard maintained his innocence and eventually won a key Supreme Court victory. As you watch the video, ask yourself the following questions:

1. To what extent was the jury influenced by publicity about matters outside the courtroom? Why did the U.S. Supreme Court decide to make this a pathbreaking decision about prejudicial pretrial publicity (Chapter 14)?
2. Public reaction to the criminal justice decisions of the Warren Court are often negative, yet this case seems more sympathetic. Why are reactions to this decision different? Is it because it dealt with the conduct of the trial rather than limits on police investigation? Or is it because Sheppard had a high-profile attorney? Would reaction have been different if he had been convicted during the second trial?
3. What similarities do you find between the murder case of Marilyn Sheppard and other high-profile murder cases, like those of Nicole Simpson and Jon Benet Ramsey? What are the differences?

Separating science from pseudoscience is never an easy task. For seventy years the "general acceptance" test was the dominant standard for determining the admissibility of novel scientific evidence at trial.

> Just when a scientific principle or discovery crosses the line between the experimental and demonstrable stages is difficult to define. Somewhere in this twilight zone the evidential forces of the principle must be recognized, and while courts will go a long way in admitting expert testimony deduced from a well-recognized scientific principle or discovery, the thing from which the deduction is made must be sufficiently established to have gained general acceptance in the particular field in which it belongs. (Frye v. U.S. *D.C. Cir., 1923*)

In the modern era some courts rejected the "general acceptance" prong of the *Frye* test, holding that this nose-counting approach was no longer adequate in the face of rapid developments in science (Labaton 1990). Following this trend, the Supreme Court rejected the *Frye* standard, arguing that it had been replaced by the Federal Rules of Evidence. The Court assigned federal judges an active role in screening scientific evidence. "The trial judge must ensure that any and all scientific testimony or evidence is not only relevant but reliable" (*Daubert v. Merrell Dow Pharmaceuticals Co.* 1993). *Daubert* has particular applicability in civil cases, where critics argue that "junk science" (unreliable findings by persons with questionable credentials) is producing too many civil lawsuits.

The use of DNA (deoxyribonucleic acid) as evidence has sparked considerable debate. Initially judges and lawyers debated whether such evidence was admissible, but those legal battles have now been resolved. One dimension of the contemporary debates focuses on the reliability of crime labs. In a basic sense, crime labs have become a victim of their own success—eight out of ten report that their caseloads have grown faster than their budgets (Beaupre 1996). And as will be discussed in Chapter 17, there are demands that old cases be reopened so that DNA tests (not available at the time of the original trial) be performed.

Objections to the Admission of Evidence

During trial, attorneys must always be alert, ready to make timely objections to the admission of evidence. After a question is asked but before the witness answers, the attorney may **object** if the evidence is irrelevant, immaterial, or hearsay. The court then rules on the objection, admitting or barring the evidence. The judge may rule immediately or may request the lawyers to argue the legal point out of the hearing of the jury (this is termed a side-bar conference). If the objection is to a line of testimony, it may be necessary for the jury to retire to the jury room while the judge hears the testimony and makes a ruling. If the testimony is admissible, it is then repeated before the jury.

Occasionally, inadmissible evidence will inadvertently be heard by the jury. For example, in

Objection: The act of taking exception to a statement or procedure during a trial.

answering a valid question, a witness may overelaborate. When this occurs and the attorney objects, the judge will instruct the jury to disregard the evidence. But even with such a cautionary warning, jurors may still be influenced by that piece of evidence. If the erroneous evidence is deemed so prejudicial that a warning to disregard is not sufficient, the judge may declare a **mistrial**.

THE DEFENSE PRESENTS ITS CASE

We might expect a trial to be a battle along the lines of "You did it"; "No, I didn't." However, such a view greatly oversimplifies the tactical decisions involved. In deciding on the defense strategy at trial, the attorney must carefully consider the strengths and weaknesses of the state's case, the character of the defendant, and how credible the defense witnesses may be. In weighing how jurors are likely to react, defense attorneys invariably start from a position of weakness. They are seldom able to pick cases they wish to try. If the prosecutors consider the case to be weak, they may dismiss it rather than risk an acquittal or offer such a good deal that the defendant cannot turn it down. Defense attorneys are sometimes forced to trial even when they believe the client's story is implausible or dishonest.

The defense must also consider whether the trial should be before a jury or only the judge (a **bench trial**). Most states allow defendants to waive their right to a jury trial and be tried by a judge; the other states require the agreement of the prosecution also. Studies indicate that a judge is more likely to find guilt than a jury. In some instances, however, the defense attorney may wish to avoid a jury trial, either because of the inflammatory nature of the alleged offense or because the legal defense will be of a technical nature that a jury is not likely to understand. Most trials are jury trials.

In deciding on a strategy the defense must weigh reasonable doubt, calling the defendant as a witness, alibi defenses, affirmative defenses, and challenging scientific evidence.

> **Mistrial:**   Invalid trial.
> **Bench trial:**   A trial conducted without a jury in which the judge tries the facts.

Reasonable Doubt

Because the defendant is presumed innocent, the defense does not have to call any witnesses or introduce any evidence. Through cross-examination, the attorney can try to undermine the state's case and create in the jury's mind a reasonable doubt as to whether the defendant committed the crime. The key to such a strategy is the skillful use of the right to confront witnesses, one of the criminal court procedures enumerated in the Sixth Amendment: "In all criminal prosecutions, the accused shall enjoy the right . . . to be confronted with witnesses against him." One meaning of this provision is that the defendant must be present during trial—that is, the state cannot try defendants who are absent. (Defendants who disrupt the trial may be removed, however.) The right to be confronted with witnesses guarantees the right to **cross-examination**. A fundamental tenet of the adversary system is the need to test evidence for truthfulness, and the primary means of testing the truthfulness of witnesses is cross-examination.

If a defendant has no valid defense but will not plead guilty, the defense attorney's only choice is to force the state to prove its case and hope to create a reasonable doubt in the minds of the jury. But many experienced defense attorneys consider this to be the weakest kind of defense. They believe that to gain an acquittal the defense must give the jury something to "hang their hat on." Thus, they must consider whether to let the defendant testify.

The Defendant As Witness

The most important part of defense strategy is the decision whether the defendant will testify. The Fifth Amendment protection against **self-incrimination** means that the defendant cannot be compelled to be a witness against himself. If the defendant chooses not to testify, no comment or inference can be drawn from this fact. The prosecutor cannot argue before the jury, "If he is innocent, why doesn't he take the stand and say so?" (*Griffin v. California,*

> **Cross-examination:**   At trial, the questions of one attorney put to a witness called by the opposing attorney.
> **Self-incrimination:**   Forcing a suspect to provide evidence against him- or herself; prohibited by the Fifth Amendment.

1965). Nonetheless, jurors are curious about the defendant's version of what happened. They expect the defendant to protest innocence; in the secrecy of the jury room, they can ponder aloud why the defendant refused to testify.

Defendants may, of course, waive the privilege against self-incrimination and take the stand in their own defense. In deciding whether the defendant should testify, the defense attorney must consider whether the story is believable. If it is not, the jury will probably dismiss it, thus doing more harm to the defendant's case than if he or she had not testified at all.

Like any other witness, a defendant who takes the stand is subject to cross-examination. Because cross-examination is broader than direct examination, the defendant cannot tell a mere part of the story and conceal the rest. Once the defendant chooses to testify, the state can bring out all the facts surrounding the event testified to. Just as important, once the defendant has taken the stand, the state can impeach the defendant's credibility by introducing into evidence any prior felony convictions. The defense attorney must make the difficult decision whether to arouse the jury's suspicion by not letting the accused testify or letting the defendant testify and be subjected to possibly damaging cross-examination.

Alibi Defense

In an **alibi defense**, defendants argue that they were somewhere else at the time the crime was committed. Witnesses may be called to testify that during the time in question the defendant was drinking beer at Mary's or shopping downtown with some friends. Some states require that defendants provide a notice of an alibi defense prior to trial, along with a list of witnesses to be called to support this assertion. A notice of alibi defense gives the prosecution the opportunity to investigate the witnesses' story before trial. Prosecutors who suspect that witnesses have carefully rehearsed the alibi testimony can use clever cross-examination to ask questions out of sequence, hoping to catch each witness in a series of contradictions. Prosecutors can also call rebuttal

> **Alibi defense:** A defense alleging that the defendant was elsewhere at the time of the crime he or she is charged with.

witnesses to suggest that the witnesses were long-time friends of the defendant, who are likely to lie.

Affirmative Defenses

An **affirmative defense** goes beyond denying the facts of the prosecutor's case; it sets out new facts and arguments that might win for the defendant. In essence, affirmative defenses are legal excuses that should result in a finding of not guilty. They also require the defense to assume the burden of proving its case. The state still has the ultimate duty of proving the defendant guilty beyond a reasonable doubt. But under an affirmative defense, the defense has "the burden of going forward with the evidence." From the defendant's perspective, an affirmative defense is tricky, for it often means that the defendant admits the prosecutor's case. Moreover, juries often view such a defense strategy as an attempt by the defendant to wiggle out of a guilty verdict.

There are several types of affirmative defenses. One is **self-defense,** which is the right of a person to use force upon another person in order to protect him- or herself. Another affirmative defense is **duress,** which means a person is compelled to do something he or she does not want to do. Yet another is **entrapment,** which is the act of a law enforcement agent inducing a person to commit a crime that the person was not otherwise disposed to commit. By far the best known and also most controversial affirmative defense is the insanity defense. (See Controversy: Should the Insanity Defense Be Abolished?)

Challenging Scientific Evidence

In recent years a prominent version of the reasonable doubt defense has been a direct attack on the

> **Affirmative defense:** Without denying the charge, defendant raises extenuating or mitigating circumstances, such as insanity, self-defense, or entrapment.
>
> **Self-defense:** The right to use physical force against another person who is committing a felony, threatening the use of physical force, or using physical force.
>
> **Duress:** Unlawful pressure on a person to do what he or she would not otherwise have done.
>
> **Entrapment:** The act of a government official or agent inducing a person to commit a crime that the person would not have committed without the inducement.

THE MURDER TRIAL OF SHAREEF COUSIN

Two Trial-Day Surprises

 In fictional courtrooms, trials proceed in an orderly manner with predictable outcomes. In real-world courtrooms, however, trials are sometimes disjointed, with unexpected developments. During the murder trial of Shareef Cousin both sides experienced trial-day surprises. For the prosecution, a key witness became a turncoat. For the defense, a few frames of a videotape blurred the much-heralded alibi defense.

During its case-in-main the prosecution called a variety of law enforcement officers who testified about the crime scene, provided diagrams of the crime scene, and so on. The coroner was also called to the stand to testify as to the cause of death. But establishing that a crime had been committed was the easy part. Tying the crime to Shareef Cousin proved much more difficult. Several witnesses testified that they were only "reasonably certain" that Cousin was the killer. Thus, for the prosecution, the trial hinged on one and only one witness—the victim's date. Connie Babin forcefully identified Shareef Cousin as the murderer. As discussed in Chapter 12, the defense could not vigorously cross-examine her because they did not know of her previous statements about being unable to identify any suspect.

To bolster the credibility of Connie Babin's eyewitness identification, the prosecution called James Rowell, a sixteen-year-old friend of the defendant, who had earlier admitted to committing several armed robberies with Cousin (Chapter 13). During opening arguments the DA had promised jurors that Rowel would testify that Shareef Cousin had bragged that he had shot a man outside a French Quarter restaurant during a botched robbery. But when Rowell took the stand he would only say that that was the story the DA wanted him to testify to. Faced with a turncoat witness, prosecutor Roger Jordan asked Judge Bigelow to declare him a hostile witness and now tried to rehabilitate their own

witness. Thus the prosecution called Rowell's attorney, who testified that his client had boasted of killing someone. Indeed, Cousin was reputed to have said that after killing someone he would find killing easier the next time. But was this hearsay testimony solely to impeach the credibility of the witness, or did the prosecution offer this testimony as proof of the crime? The appeal (Chapter 17) would center on this question.

For the defense, the trial hinged on the jury believing that Shareef Cousin had an alibi for the time of the crime. According to Eric White, a basketball coach with the New Orleans Recreation Department, Shareef Cousin had been his star player the night of March 2, 1995, coming off the bench to score ten points in a come-from-behind victory. Because the game ran late, he didn't drop Cousin off at his house until about 10:45 (some twenty minutes after the murder occurred). On cross-examination, however, the prosecution introduced a videotape of the game and under hard questioning the coach was forced to admit that the quarters were actually six minutes long, not the eight he had testified to. Moreover, a clock in the gym seemed to suggest the game ended much earlier than his testimony indicated. The prosecution also pressed hard on a previous statement in which White had said the game ended about 9:20 or 9:25. In short, the prosecution used cross-examination to shred the alibi defense. Although the defense had stressed briefly Cousin's alibi throughout the five-day trial, Hill only mentioned it during his thirty-minute closing argument.

The defense rested without calling Cousin to the stand, probably because of his previous convictions for four armed robberies.

At 11:30 on Friday night the jury returned a unanimous verdict of guilty of first-degree murder. Their next task would be to decide whether Shareef Cousin would spend the rest of his life in prison or die by lethal injection (Chapter 16).

scientific evidence introduced by the prosecution. In particular, the way evidence was gathered, preserved, and analyzed by experts has been the centerpiece of several major trials. Most prominently, the O. J. Simpson defense team stressed the mishandling of evidence, suggesting that any subsequent analysis, no matter how precise, was unbelievable. This case thrust crime labs under the microscope, and the

results were not always flattering. One result was a comprehensive investigation of the FBI crime lab, which highlighted numerous problems (U.S. Department of Justice 1997). The report resulted in disciplinary action against several lab employees, a total revamping of the lab, and notification of fifty prosecutors that FBI lab problems could affect their cases (Sniffen 1997).

CONTROVERSY

Should the Insanity Defense Be Abolished?

 The insanity defense, one of the most hotly debated topics in criminal law, is rooted in a fundamental concept of Anglo-American law: that a person should not be punished for what he or she cannot help doing. Thus, under the concept of mens rea, an insane person is not criminally responsible for his or her acts, because he or she is incapable of having criminal intent (Chapter 2).

But what degree of insanity, mental illness, or mental disease makes a person blameless for otherwise criminal acts? This question has been debated for centuries. At the heart of contemporary discussions are marked philosophical divergences within American society concerning an individual's responsibility for his or her own acts. The lack of agreement is reflected in major differences among states concerning the extent to which a person's mental faculties must be impaired before he or she is considered insane. The standards for insanity found in U.S. jurisdictions are shown in the table on page 367.

Varying Standards

The oldest test of insanity is the **McNaughton rule**, which grew out of the murder of a private secretary to Sir Robert Peel, the British prime minister. In 1843 the English House of Lords ruled that to establish a defense on the basis of insanity it is necessary to prove clearly that at the time of committing an act, the accused party was "laboring under such a defect of reason from disease of the mind as not to know the nature and quality of the act he was doing, or if he did know it that he did not know he was doing what was wrong." Lawyers call this the *cognitive test* because the language hinges on knowing the difference between right and wrong. The McNaughton rule (sometimes spelled M'Naghten) is by far the most restrictive standard. Psychiatrists believe that the "right and wrong" test is difficult to apply and fails to take into account what we

have learned about human behavior since the test was developed over 150 years ago. Nonetheless, sixteen jurisdictions currently utilize a modified version of the McNaughton test (Keilitz and Fulton 1984).

A few states supplement the McNaughton rule with a slightly broader test of **irresistible impulse**. According to this standard, a defendant is insane if he or she was compelled by an irresistible impulse (owing to a mental disease or defect that prevented the person from controlling his or her actions) even though he or she knew the act was wrong (Sigler 1981). In recent years a number of states have followed the lead of the American Law Institute (ALI) and adopted a **substantial capacity** guideline. This test states that "A person is not responsible for criminal conduct if at the time of such conduct and as a result of mental disease or defect he lacks substantial capacity either to appreciate the criminality of his conduct or to conform his conduct to the requirements of the law." The ALI standard has been characterized as a modernized combination of the McNaughton and the irresistible impulse tests; it is used in the federal courts and twenty-four states (Keilitz and Fulton 1984).

Finally, three states (Idaho, Montana, and Utah) have abolished the use of the insanity defense altogether. However, psychiatric evidence is allowed on the issue of whether there is an intent to commit a crime (Bureau of Justice Statistics 1988).

Usually, a defendant who uses an insanity defense enters a dual plea of not guilty and not guilty by reason of insanity. The burden of proof is on the prosecution to prove that the defendant committed the crime in question, but the defense bears the burden of proof as to the defendant's insanity.

The Debate

The insanity defense has sparked considerable controversy. The public perceives the insanity defense as a dodge used by tricky lawyers trying to gain sympa-

---

McNaughton rule: Oldest and most restrictive standard of insanity as legal defense, essentially requiring that the accused not be able to distinguish between right and wrong; currently applied in a modified version in sixteen jurisdictions.

Irresistible impulse: A test of insanity under which a person is driven to commit an act by an urge that cannot be resisted or overcome because mental disease or derangement has destroyed the freedom of

will, the power of self-control, and the ability to choose.

Substantial capacity: A person is not responsible for criminal conduct if at the time of such conduct and as a result of mental disease or defect he or she lacks substantial capacity either to appreciate the criminality of the conduct or to conform his or her conduct to the regiments of the law.

thy for their guilty clients, who avoid punishment by pretending they are insane. When the jury acquitted would-be presidential assassin John Hinckley, Jr., as "not guilty by reason of insanity," there was a heated outcry against the verdict, even though Hinckley was then confined to a mental institution. Public and professional displeasure produced a rush to reform the insanity defense. For example, twelve states have greatly altered the traditional insanity defense and made available the verdict "guilty but mentally ill" (Bureau of Justice Statistics 1988; Klofas and Yandrasits 1989). This verdict is an alternative to, but does not preclude, a verdict of "not guilty by reason of insanity" (Gardner 1985). Defendants found guilty but mentally ill are treated in a mental institution until recovery and then transferred to a prison to serve the remainder of the sentence.

This debate resurfaced during the trial of Theodore Kaczynski. The alleged Unabomber refused to allow his lawyer to plead not guilty by reason of insanity and he was subsequently convicted.

The often heated debate over the insanity defense is largely symbolic, however. Because the public remains skeptical about the insanity defense, defense attorneys seldom use it as a trial strategy, and jurors even more rarely find defendants not guilty by reason of insanity. One study found that of the 2 million criminal prosecution cases in one year, only 1,625 defendants were found not guilty by reason of insanity (Steadman et al. 1982). Moreover, numerous states make incarceration in a mental institution mandatory if the defendant is found not guilty by reason of insanity. Indeed, such defendants are usually held in a mental institution for a longer period of time than they might have been held in prison had they been found guilty of the crime they were charged with. For these reasons lawyers consider insanity a defense of last resort.

What do you think? Should the insanity defense be abolished, restricted, or kept the way it is? In particular, do you think that defendants fake insanity, or are defendants really insane and therefore not responsible for their actions? If you were a juror, what types of evidence would convince you to return a verdict of not guilty by reason of insanity?

 Timothy W. Maier, "One Flew into the Cuckoo's Nest"

Richard E. Vatz, Lee S. Weinberg, "The Insanity Defense: Unconscionable Impact on Victims of Violence"

 To continue debating this topic, point your browser to:

http://www.psych.org/public_info/insanity.cfm
http://www.diminishedcapacity.com/

For an up-to-date list of Web links, go to **http://www.wadsworth.com/product/0534563406s**.

Standards for Insanity Used by the States and the U.S. Courts

Insanity Standard	Jurisdiction
McNaughton rule	Arizona, Florida, Iowa, Kansas, Louisiana, Minnesota, Mississippi, Nebraska, Nevada, New Jersey, North Carolina, Oklahoma, Pennsylvania, South Carolina, South Dakota, and Washington
Irresistible impulse	Colorado, Georgia, New Mexico, and Virginia
Substantial capacity	All federal circuits, Alabama, Alaska, Arkansas, California, Connecticut, Delaware, District of Columbia, Hawaii, Illinois, Indiana, Kentucky, Maine, Maryland, Massachusetts, Michigan, Missouri, Ohio, Oregon, Tennessee, Texas, Vermont, West Virginia, Wisconsin, and Wyoming
Other	New Hampshire, New York, North Dakota, and Rhode Island
No standard	Idaho, Montana, Utah

SOURCES: Adapted from Ingo Keilitz and Junius P. Fulton, *The Insanity Defense and Its Alternatives: A Guide for Policymakers* (Williamsburg, VA: National Center for State Courts, 1984), p. 15; Bureau of Justice Statistics, *Report to the Nation on Crime and Justice*, 2d ed. (Washington, D.C.: U.S. Department of Justice, 1988).

REBUTTAL

After the defense rests its case, the prosecution may call rebuttal witnesses, whose purpose is either to discredit the testimony of a previous witness or discredit the witness. The prosecutor may call a **rebuttal** witness to show that the previous witness could not have observed what she said she did because she was somewhere else at the time. Or the prosecutor may call witnesses or otherwise present evidence to show that the previous witnesses have dishonorable reputations. The rules of evidence regarding rebuttal witnesses are complex. In general, evidence may be presented in rebuttal that could not have been used during the prosecution's main case. For example, the prosecution may legitimately inform the jury of the previous convictions of defendants who take the stand, in an attempt to impeach their credibility.

CLOSING ARGUMENTS

After the prosecution and defense have rested (that is, completed the introduction of evidence), each side has the opportunity to make a closing argument to the jury. **Closing arguments** allow each side to sum up the facts in its favor and indicate why it believes a verdict of guilty or not guilty is in order. The prosecutor goes first, carefully summing up the facts of the case and tying together into a coherent pattern what appeared during the trial to be isolated or unimportant matters. The prosecutor calls upon the jurors to do their duty and punish the defendant, who has committed the crime. The defense attorney goes next, highlighting the evidence favorable to the defendant, criticizing the witnesses for the state, and showing why they should not be believed. The defense also calls upon the jurors to do their sworn duty and return a not guilty verdict. Because the prosecutor bears the burden of proof, he or she has the opportunity to make one last statement to the jury, refuting the defense arguments.

In closing arguments to the jury, lawyers muster all the art, craft, skill, and guile of their profession.

Closing arguments are often the most dramatic parts of the trial. However, there is a fine line between persuasiveness and unnecessary emotionalism. Jury verdicts have been reversed on appeal because the prosecutor interjected prejudicial statements into the closing argument.

JURY INSTRUCTIONS

Although the jury is the sole judge of the facts of the case, the judge alone determines the law. Therefore, the court instructs the jury as to the meaning of the law applicable to the facts of the case. These **jury instructions** begin with discussions of general legal principles (innocent until proven guilty, guilty beyond a reasonable doubt, and so forth). They follow with specific instructions on the elements of the crime in the case and what specific actions the government must prove before there can be a conviction. If the defendant has raised a defense such as insanity or duress, the judge instructs the jury as to the meaning of the defense according to the law in that jurisdiction. (In a few states, judges are also allowed to comment on the evidence. That is, they can express their own views on the credibility of the witnesses, and so on.)

Finally, the judge instructs the jury on possible verdicts in the case and provides a written form for each verdict of guilty and not guilty. Depending on the state or federal law involved, the jury may also have the option of choosing alternative forms of guilty verdicts, called lesser included offenses. In a murder case, for example, the jury may find the defendant guilty of murder in the first degree, murder in the second degree, or manslaughter—or they may acquit on all charges.

The judge and the trial attorneys prepare the jury instructions during a special **charging conference** that precedes jury deliberations. Each side drafts suggested instructions, and the judge chooses the ones most appropriate. If the judge rejects a given instruction, the lawyer enters an objection on the record, thus preserving the issue for later appeal.

Rebuttal: The introduction of contradictory evidence.

Closing argument: Statement made by an attorney at the end of the presentation of evidence in which the attorney summarizes the case for the jury.

Jury instructions: Directions given by a judge to the members of the jury informing them of the law applicable to the case.

Charging conference: Meeting attended by judge, prosecutor, and defense attorney during which the judge's instructions to the jury are discussed.

Particularly in technical cases such as embezzlement or fraud, the judge's charge to the jury can greatly affect the final verdict. If the judge adopts a very narrow definition of the crime in question, the instructions to the jury virtually mandate an acquittal. The instructions are written out, signed by the judge, and then read to the jury. Some judges allow the jurors to take a copy of the instructions into the jury room as a guide.

Jury instructions represent a formal, detailed lecture on the law. Because faulty jury instructions are a principal basis for appellate court reversal, judges are careful in their wordings and deliberate in their manner. Unfortunately, the result is a pitifully low rate of juror comprehension; lay jurors are ill-equipped to understand the extensive legal jargon presented by the judge in rapid-fire manner. There have been some efforts to increase jurors' understanding of these vital matters (Ellwork, Sales, and Alfini 1982; Severance and Loftus 1982). One experiment found that clarifying the meaning of the judge's charge to the jury did increase understanding, but jurors still did not have an accurate knowledge of the law. The jury instructions stressed that a defendant is presumed innocent until proven guilty by the evidence beyond any reasonable doubt; yet after hearing and reading the modern instruction on this matter, only 50 percent of the jurors understood that the defendant did not have to present any evidence of innocence and 10 percent were still uncertain what the presumption of innocence was (Strawn and Buchanan 1976). The major difficulty in improving jury comprehension is the complexity of the law itself; it is difficult to translate into plain English the subtleties of meaning of certain legal terms and the intentional vagueness of the law ("reasonable person" and "preponderance of the evidence" come quickly to mind) (Steele and Thornburg 1991). One solution to teaching jurors complex legal concepts is the use of simple graphics in conjunction with written jury instructions (Dattu 1998). Social science research on jurors' lack of comprehension of instructions has produced some legal changes. Surprisingly, however, the courts seem more responsive than legislatures to these findings (Tanford 1991).

JURY DELIBERATIONS

How juries decide has long fascinated lawyers and lay people alike. There is a great deal of curiosity about what goes on behind the locked jury room door. During the trial, jurors are passive observers who are not allowed to ask questions and are usually prohibited from taking notes. But after the judge reads the jury instructions, the lawyers, judges, and defendants must wait passively, often in tense anticipation, for the jury to reach a verdict. The only hints of what is occurring during **jury deliberations** occur on the rare occasions when the jurors request further instructions from the judge about the applicable law or ask to have portions of the testimony read in open court.

What Motivates a Jury?

Because jury deliberations are secret, research on what factors motivate a decision must be conducted indirectly. Much of what we know about how juries decide is based either on observing mock juries or asking jurors to recall what occurred in the jury room. A team of researchers at the University of Chicago Law School conducted the major studies on jury deliberation. They found that rates of participation varied with social status: Men talked more than women, better educated jurors participated more frequently, and persons with high-status occupations were more likely to be chosen as foremen (Strodtbeck, James, and Hawkins 1957; Simon 1967). Discussions among jurors mostly concern court procedures, opinions about the trial, and personal reminiscences; there is far less discussion of the testimony or the judge's instructions to the jury (James 1958).

Juries usually reach a verdict after short deliberations. Interviews in more than 200 criminal cases in Chicago and Brooklyn revealed that juries usually take a vote as soon as they retire to chambers. In 30 percent of these cases, only one vote was necessary to reach a unanimous verdict. In 90 percent of the rest, the majority on the first ballot eventually won out (Broeder 1959). Most important, a lone juror rarely produced a hung jury. The psychological pressures associated with small-group discussions are so great that a single juror can buck predominant sentiment only if he or she can find at least one ally. Thus, jury deliberations "do not so much decide the case as bring about a consensus" (Kalven and Zeisel 1966, 488). If the jury does become deadlocked and cannot reach a verdict, the trial ends

Jury deliberations: The action of a jury in determining the guilt or innocence, or the sentence, of a defendant.

with a **hung jury**. The prosecutor then has the option of trying the defendant again.

Reports of apparent increases in the number of hung juries across the nation have caused concern among policy makers in recent years. But the data do not bear out these concerns. In federal trials the rate of hung juries has been low and stable for years, averaging about 3 percent per year. In state courts in large urban counties there is some variation but the rate is about 6 percent (Hannaford, Hans, and Munsterman 1999).

 Joseph Ward, "The Danger of Deadlock: Coercion in the Courtroom"

Are Juries Biased?

But what of jury bias? Do different groups of jurors decide differently? In terms of gender, race, age, and education, jurors who vote to convict aren't very different as a group from jurors who vote to acquit (Mills and Bohannon 1980). Moreover, a study of thirty-eight sexual assault trials found that evidence was the primary factor. Jurors were influenced by extralegal factors, but these effects were largely limited to weak cases in which the state presented little hard evidence (Reskin and Visher 1986). Although there is some evidence that extralegal factors play a role, American juries appear to perform remarkably well on the whole, deciding primarily on the basis of legal factors (Ford 1986).

THE VERDICT

Once the jury informs the judge that a decision has been reached, the lawyers and the defendant gather in the courtroom. After the foreman announces the **verdict**, either party may request that the jury be polled individually, with each juror voicing his or her vote in open court.

How often do juries convict? Given that the vast majority of cases have already been dismissed or disposed of by a plea of guilty, one might expect that the defendant's chances of winning at trial are roughly fifty-fifty, but the real odds are significantly higher.

Hung jury: A jury that is unable to reach a verdict.
Verdict: The decision of a trial court.

In the aftermath of the jury verdict finding O. J. Simpson not guilty, numerous calls were heard to reform the jury system, arguing that juries are too prone to acquit. But the data point in the opposite direction. In federal courts juries convict 82 percent of the time in nondrug cases and 87 percent of the time in drug prosecutions. Data from various states point in the same direction; juries convict two-thirds of the time in criminal cases (Roper and Flango 1983; Vidmar et al. 1997).

Do juries view cases differently than judges? Harry Kalven and Hans Zeisel (1966) attempted to answer this question by comparing verdicts reached by juries to the decisions judges would have made in more than 3,500 criminal trials. Overall, they found that judges and juries agreed more than three out of four times, which suggests that the evidence in the case is the primary factor shaping the jury's verdict. Judges and juries disagreed 22 percent of the time, with the juries voting acquittal when the judges would have convicted.

Two studies have challenged the conclusion that judges convict at a higher rate than juries. Robert Roper and Victor Flango (1983) examined data for all fifty states and found that juries convicted felons at a much higher rate than did judges, but judges convicted nonfelons at a much higher rate than juries did. James Levine (1983) probed data from the federal courts and reached the same conclusion: Juries convicted defendants accused of felonies more often than judges did. Thus, disagreements between judge and jury appear to vary according to the seriousness of the offense.

POST-VERDICT MOTIONS

A trial verdict of **acquittal** (not guilty) ends the case. The defendant can leave the courthouse a free person. Bond is immediately canceled, and the person cannot be charged with the same offense again. A verdict of guilty, however, means that further proceedings will occur; the defendant must be sentenced (Chapters 15 and 16) and in all likelihood will appeal (Chapter 17).

If the jury returns a verdict of guilty, the defendant still has certain opportunities to be retried or

Acquittal: The decision of the judge or jury that the defendant is not guilty.

to have the conviction dismissed. A guilty defendant may file **post-verdict motions**, which are heard prior to sentencing. These motions give the defense attorney the opportunity to reargue alleged mistakes made at trial. The trial judge may have a change of mind and become convinced that some ruling made against the defendant was erroneous.

Post-verdict motions generally fall into two categories. One is a *motion in arrest of judgment*, which argues that errors in the actual trial require that the case be dismissed and the defendant discharged. In essence, counsel asks the court to reverse the jury's decision. A common ground for such a motion is the assertion that the evidence was insufficient for the jury to return a verdict of guilty. A second type of post-verdict motion is a *motion for a new trial*. It asserts that serious errors were made at trial (either by the trial judge or by the prosecutor), so the guilty verdict should be set aside and a new trial granted. The most common grounds for such a motion are newly discovered evidence and errors committed during trial or pretrial hearings. Post-verdict motions are largely a formality; few are ever granted.

LAW IN ACTION: TRIALS AS BALANCING WHEELS

Trials exert a major influence on the operation of the entire criminal court process. Although only a handful of cases go to trial, the possibility of trial operates as a balancing wheel on all other cases. Assessments of the chances of losing at trial are an important basis for the exercise of prosecutorial discretion during screening. The likelihood of conviction determines the negotiating position of lawyers during plea bargaining. Thus, jury trials must be measured not only in terms of their impact on specific cases but also on how the decisions reached affect similar cases in the future.

Popular Standards of Justice

Juries introduce the community's conscience and commonsense judgments into judicial decisions. The University of Chicago jury project (Broeder 1959)

> **Post-verdict motions:** Various motions made by the defense after a jury conviction in hopes of gaining a new trial.

TABLE 14-1 Federal Jury Conviction Rates for Selected Regulatory Crimes

	Jury Conviction Rate	Number of Jury Trials
National defense	83%	143
Selective service	82%	809
Immigration	80%	1,084
Food and drug	80%	376
Obscenity	72%	258
Antitrust	39%	257
Civil rights	36%	536
Migratory birds	36%	358

SOURCE: James Levine, "Using Jury Verdict Forecasts in Criminal Defense Strategy," *Judicature* 66 (1983): 448. Reprinted by permission.

found that popular standards of justice are by far the major reason for disagreement between judge and jury. The result is jury legislation—a jury's deliberate modification of the law to make it conform to community views of what the law ought to be (Kalven and Zeisel 1966). The data in Table 14-1 show how popular standards of justice affect the criminal courts. Federal jury conviction rates vary substantially according to the crime charged. Whereas four out of five of those accused of violating food and drug laws were convicted, only one in three defendants charged with migratory bird and civil rights offenses were found guilty. Rural juries appear to be dubious about laws that restrict hunting privileges, and for many years Southern juries (as well as some Northern ones) have questioned federal laws against racial discrimination. Thus, federal defendants accused of these crimes have a good chance of finding friendly juries ready to come to their rescue (Levine 1983). Similarly, state juries are less likely to convict if they perceive that the potential sentence is too severe (as when a defendant charged with drunken driving, who caused no damage or injury, stands to lose his or her driver's license for a long time). Jury verdicts thus establish boundaries on what actions the local community believes should and should not be punished. One of the most prominent examples involves Dr. Jack Kevorkian, who was tried on several occasions for violating Michigan's assisted-suicide law, but jurors steadfastly refuse to convict. However, when he later directly helped a person commit suicide the jury did convict.

In recent years the importance of juries introducing popular standards into the justice system has been associated with the concept of **jury nullification**—the right of juries to nullify or refuse to apply law in criminal cases despite facts that leave no reasonable doubt that the law was violated (Brown 1997). Some advocates of jury nullification base their ideas on the need to reduce governmental intrusion into citizens' lives. Others are motivated by concern over racial injustice. As a protest against racial discrimination in the criminal justice system, law professor Paul Butler (1995), for instance, urges African American jurors to acquit African American defendants who may be "technically guilty" of nonviolent regulatory offenses like drug possession, and to consider jury nullification for nonviolent crimes like theft. To some, the verdict in the O. J. case was a classic example, with African American jurors voting to acquit on the basis of a historical legacy of discrimination, reinforced by detective Mark Fuhrman's reputation for using racially offensive terms.

Judges are quick to denounce jury nullification because they feel that the rule of law is undermined. But others counter that juries have been refusing to follow the law for centuries, and they have every right to send a message by not following a law they find, for whatever reason, to be flawed. Contemporary discussions focus on whether juries should be told they have the right to disregard the judge's jury instructions and substitute their own views (Galiber et al. 1993).

Paul Jackson, "Jurors Flex Their Muscles"
Clay S. Conrad, "Jury Nullification"

Uncertainty

Jury trials also affect the criminal court system by introducing uncertainty into the process. During a trial, the legal professionals are at the mercy of the witnesses, whose behavior is somewhat unpre-

dictable. What a witness says and how he or she says it often means the difference between conviction and acquittal (Eisenstein and Jacob 1977). The presence of juries adds yet another layer of unpredictability to the process. Stories about irrational juries form part of the folklore of any courthouse. Here are two examples. During jury deliberations in a drug case, two jurors announced that "only God can judge" and hung the jury by refusing to vote. After an acquittal in a burglary case, a juror put her arm around the defendant and said, "Bob, we were sure happy to find you not guilty, but don't do it again" (Neubauer 1974, 228). Legal professionals resent such intrusions into their otherwise ordered world; they seek to reduce such uncertainties by developing the norms of cooperation discussed throughout this book. Viewed in this light, plea bargaining serves to shield the system from a great deal of the uncertainty that results when lay citizens are involved in deciding important legal matters.

PREJUDICIAL PRETRIAL PUBLICITY

The conviction of Dr. Sam Sheppard for bludgeoning his wife to death in her bedroom, and later reversal by the Supreme Court (see Case Close-Up: *Sheppard v. Maxwell* and Prejudicial Pretrial Publicity), raised the issue of **prejudicial pretrial publicity**. The Court, in holding that Sheppard had been denied a fair and impartial trial, set off a long and heated battle over fair trial versus freedom of the press.

When a New Orleans trial judge issued a gag order forbidding the press from publishing testimony revealed in open court during a pretrial hearing, the Supreme Court held that this ruling infringed on freedom of the press (*Times-Picayune v. Schulingkamp* 1975). Gag orders pose another problem: A journalist who prints information in violation of a court order can be sentenced to jail for contempt of court, even if an appellate body later rules that the trial judge's order was illegal.

Jury nullification: Idea that juries have the right to refuse to apply the law in criminal cases despite facts that leave no reasonable doubt that the law was violated.

Prejudicial pretrial publicity: Prejudicial information, often inadmissible at trial, which is circulated by the news media before a trial and which reduces the defendant's chances of a trial before an impartial jury.

CASE CLOSE-UP

Sheppard v. Maxwell and Prejudicial Pretrial Publicity

 On July 4, 1954, Marilyn Sheppard—the pregnant wife of Dr. Samuel Sheppard—was bludgeoned to death in the upstairs bedroom of the couple's home in a fashionable Cleveland suburb. The case produced some of the most sensational press coverage the country had witnessed. While it was not the crime of the century, it was certainly the crime of the decade. Sheppard told the police that he was asleep on a sofa when he was awakened by his wife's screams. Rushing upstairs, he grappled with the intruder, only to be struck unconscious by a blow to the head. Sheppard was taken to his family's medical clinic, where he was treated by his brother, also a doctor. From the outset officials focused suspicion on Sheppard. They interrogated him while he was still at the clinic and continued to question him for several weeks.

The official investigation was prodded by extensive media coverage, which was critical of how the police handled the case. Day after day vivid headlines called for the arrest of Dr. Sheppard and implied that the police were going easy because he and his family were socially prominent. To add fuel to the fire the paper published a front-page editorial headlined "Why Don't Police Quiz Top Suspect," claiming somebody "was getting away with murder." At the coroner's inquest Dr. Sheppard's attorney was present but not allowed to participate. Live radio broadcast the six-hour questioning of Sheppard about his activities the night of the murder and about his lovers before that night. Six weeks after the murder Sheppard was indicted.

The case came to trial two weeks before the general election in which the judge was seeking reelection and the prosecutor was running for municipal court judge. The names and addresses of potential jurors were published in the paper, resulting in letters and phone calls concerning the trial. The courtroom was so packed that reporters were allowed to sit behind the defense table, meaning that Sheppard could not converse privately with his lawyer. Indeed, the din was so great that the judge installed a loudspeaker in a vain effort to allow the spectators to hear the witnesses. A radio station carried a daily broadcast from the courtroom. Every day newspapers printed trial testimony verbatim; no effort was made to prevent the jury from reading these accounts, even when evidence was ruled inadmissible. Not surprisingly, after a nine-week trial in which jurors were free to return home every night, Sheppard was convicted of second-degree murder.

Sheppard spent twelve years in prison. A string of appeals and habeas corpus petitions were denied. Eventually the family hired a young Boston lawyer, F. Lee Bailey, who would go on to become one of the most famous and controversial lawyers in the United States. Indeed, Bailey figured prominently in a trial that later received extensive media coverage—the murder trial of former football star and TV commentator O. J. Simpson. Bailey convinced the high court to hear the Sheppard case and won a stunning victory.

Justice Tom Clark held that prejudicial pretrial publicity denied Sheppard the right to a fair and impartial trial (*Sheppard v. Maxwell*, 1966). But finding that pretrial publicity can be prejudicial is a far easier task than deciding how to control it. The essential problem underlying the issue of prejudicial pretrial publicity is that two key protections of the Bill of Rights are on a collision course. The Sixth Amendment guarantees defendants the right to a trial before an impartial jury; decisions about guilt or innocence must be based on what jurors hear during the trial, not what they have heard or read outside the courtroom. At the same time, the First Amendment protects freedom of the press; what reporters print, say on radio, or broadcast on television is not subject to prior censorship. Without the First Amendment, there would be no problem; courts could simply forbid the press from reporting anything but the bare essentials of a crime. Although this is the practice in England, such prior restraints are not allowed in the United States. To Justice Clark the answer to this dilemma lay in controlling the flow of information. In his words, "The carnival atmosphere at trial could easily have been avoided since the courtroom and courthouse premises are subject to the control of the court."

But decades later trial courts still struggle to strike the balance between freedom of the press and the rights of criminal defendants. Perhaps the biggest difference is that the television (which was in its infancy when Sheppard was first tried) is now a dominating presence.

 To learn more about the Sam Sheppard trial, go to **http://dir.yahoo.com/Government/Law/Cases/ Sam_Sheppard_Case/**.

For an up-to-date list of Web links, go to **http:// www.wadsworth.com/product/0534563406s**.

Pretrial publicity does affect juries. A team of researchers from Columbia University provided one set of "jurors" with prejudicial news coverage of a case and a control group with "nonprejudicial" information. After listening to an identical trial involving a case in which the guilt of the defendant was greatly in doubt, the study found that 78 percent of the "prejudiced jurors" voted to convict, compared with only 55 percent of "nonprejudiced jurors" (Padawer-Singer and Barton 1975). Likewise, a study of two highly publicized cases concluded that even modest pretrial publicity can prejudice potential jurors against a defendant and that self-reports of impartiality should not be taken at face value (Moran and Cutler 1991).

Very few criminal trials, however, involve prejudicial pretrial publicity; news reports seldom extend beyond police blotter coverage. Indeed, the conditions necessary for media coverage to prejudice jurors to the extent that they are unable to decide a case based on courtroom evidence are likely to occur in only 1 of every 10,000 cases (Frasca 1988). But when there is extensive pretrial publicity, the jury selection process is greatly strained. Voir dire is geared to ferreting out ordinary instances of unfairness or prejudice, not to correcting the possibility of a systematic pattern of bias. For example, if an attorney excuses all jurors who have heard something about the case at hand, he or she runs the risk of selecting a jury solely from the least attentive, least literate members of the general public. On the other hand, if an attorney accepts jurors who assert that they will judge the case solely on the basis of testimony in open court, he or she is still not certain that the juror— no matter how well-intentioned—can hear the case with a truly open mind.

In trying to reconcile conflicting principles involved in the First and Sixth amendments, trial courts employ (singly or in combination) three techniques—limited gag orders, change of venue, or sequestering of the jury. Each of these methods suffers from admitted drawbacks (Kramer, Kerr, and Carroll 1990).

 To see which trials are being broadcast today, go to **http://www.courttv.com/**.

For an up-to-date list of Web links, go to **http://www.wadsworth.com/product/0534563406s**.

Limited Gag Order

The First Amendment forbids the court from censoring what the press writes about a criminal case, but it says nothing about restricting the flow of information to the media. Thus, in notorious cases in which it seems likely that selecting a jury may be difficult, judges now routinely issue a limited **gag order** forbidding those involved in the case—police, prosecutor, defense attorney, and defendant—from talking to the press. Violations are punishable as **contempt of court** (disobeying a judge's order). Since these people know the most about the case (and often have the most to gain from pretrial publicity), the net effect is to dry up news leaks. However, consistent with the First Amendment, the press is free to publish any information it discovers. The greatest difficulty is that one of the people involved in the case may secretly provide information, in violation of the judge's order. The judge can then subpoena the reporter and order disclosure of the source. Reporters believe that identifying their sources will dry up the flow of information, so they refuse to testify. They are cited for contempt and go to jail. Thus, the court may infringe on freedom of the press when its intent is simply to guarantee another Bill of Rights protection—the right to a fair trial.

Change of Venue

The term **venue** refers to the place where a case is tried. If the court is convinced that a case has received such extensive publicity that picking an impartial jury is impossible, the trial may be shifted to another part of the state. If a case has received statewide coverage, however, such a change is of limited use. In the Oklahoma City bombing case, the judge moved the federal trial to another part of the circuit (Denver) stating "There is so great a prejudice against these two defendants in the state of Oklahoma that they cannot obtain a fair and impartial

Gag order: A judge's order that lawyers and witnesses not discuss the trial with outsiders.

Contempt of court: The failure or refusal to obey a court order; may be punished by a fine or imprisonment.

Venue: The geographic location of a trial, which is determined by constitutional or statutory provisions.

Should Cameras Be Allowed in the Courtroom?

The rise of the electronic media has added a new dimension to the defendant's right to a fair trial. Trials, of course, are open to the public, and journalists are free to observe and report on courtroom proceedings. However, since the sensational Lindbergh trial of the 1930s, radio and television coverage of the judicial process has been limited. German immigrant Bruno Hauptman was accused of kidnapping and murdering the son of the famous aviator Charles Lindbergh. Because it was perceived that the daily press coverage of the trial was excessive, rules of court came to forbid cameras or recording devices in the courthouse. That is why television stations have historically hired artists to provide sketches of courthouse scenes for the nightly news.

Restrictions on cameras in the courtroom are changing, however. The Supreme Court unanimously held that electronic media and still photographic coverage of public judicial proceedings does not violate a defendant's right to a fair trial; states are therefore free to set their own guidelines (*Chandler et al. v. Florida*, 1981). Since then, the barriers against cameras in the courtroom have fallen in state after state. The U.S. Judicial Conference adopted a resolution allowing each court of appeals to decide whether cameras should be allowed (but only a few circuits have acted favorably). Just as importantly, only two states still prohibit all forms of electronic coverage of criminal court proceedings: Thirty-five states allow electronic coverage of criminal trials (Alexander

(continued on following page)

trial" (Queary 1996). This move greatly displeased the victims who wished to attend the trial.

Defense attorneys face a difficult tactical decision in deciding whether to request a **change of venue**. They must weigh the effects of prejudicial publicity against the disadvantages of having a trial in a more rural and conservative area, where citizens are hostile to big-city defendants (particularly if they are black). Prosecutors generally oppose such moves because they believe that the chances of conviction are greater in the local community. To justify this position, prosecutors cite the expense of moving witnesses, documents, and staff to a distant city for a long trial.

Sequestering the Jury

A prime defect in the trial of Dr. Sheppard was the failure to shield the jury from press coverage of the

ongoing trial. Indeed, jurors read detailed newspaper stories of the trial, which included inadmissible evidence. One remedy that is common in trials involving extensive media coverage is to **sequester the jury**. The jurors live in a hotel, take their meals together, and participate in weekend recreation together. Sheriff deputies censor newspapers and mail going to the jury and shut off television news. The possibility of being in virtual quarantine for six weeks or eight weeks, or in some cases even longer, makes many citizens reluctant to serve. When sequestering is probable, the jury selected runs the risk of including only those citizens who are willing to be separated for long periods of time from friends, family, and relatives, who can afford to be off work, who are unemployed, or who look forward to a Spartan existence. At a minimum sequestration is a trying experience for the jurors and may result in an unfair verdict (Levine 1996).

Change of venue: The removal of a case from one jurisdiction to another. It is usually granted if the court believes that, due to prejudice, a defendant cannot receive a fair trial in the area where the crime occurred.

Sequester: To isolate members of a jury from the community until they have reached a final verdict.

(continued from previous page)

1996). State rules and guidelines include many specific restrictions designed to prevent disruptions of the proceedings—limiting the number of cameras in the courtroom and prohibiting camera operators from moving around the courtroom while the trial is in session. The scope of permissible coverage varies greatly though. In some states, the consent of the parties is required, meaning either side can veto coverage of the proceedings. In others, the news media need only receive permission from the trial judge to broadcast the proceedings.

Some people complain that televising trials distorts the process by encouraging the participants to play to the camera (Thaler 1994). They also argue that by covering only sensational trials and presenting only the most dramatic moments of hours of testimony, television stations fail to portray the trial process accurately. Others argue that cameras in the courtroom have a valuable educating role, providing the public with a firsthand view of how court proceedings operate. Law professor Donna Demac argues that televising court proceedings ultimately leads to greater trust in government: "Many people suspect that the legal system dispenses a different standard of justice for the wealthy," but the more the people see the system firsthand, the greater the chance that the system will be fair (quoted in Scardino 1989). Indeed, two separate studies found that viewers of a television trial of moderate interest became more knowledgeable about the judicial process (Alexander 1991; Raymond, 1992). As to the possibility of the camera disrupting judicial proceedings, a detailed study of Florida, where the guidelines are the most liberal of any state allowing camera coverage, concluded: "Broadcast journalists who follow state guidelines present coverage which, upon close examination by presiding judges, participating attorneys and jurors, is perceived as undistorted" (Alexander 1991).

The widely televised trial of O. J. Simpson is clearly causing rethinking about cameras in the courtroom. Perceptions that lawyers were playing to the cameras apparently had an impact in several highly publicized cases that followed: The trial judge refused to allow broadcasts of the trial. In the trial of Susan Smith, a South Carolina woman accused of drowning her two infant sons, the judge allowed live broadcast of all pretrial hearings but ruled that "There is an absolute likelihood that broader coverage in the courtroom would interfere with the due process of this trial and pose a risk to this case" (Holland 1995). Similarly, the judge barred cameras from the California trial of the man accused of kidnapping and killing Polly Klaas (Chapter 16). Bucking this trend, however, the judge allowed coverage of the trial of four police officers accused of murdering Amadou Diallo.

What do you think? Should cameras be allowed in the courtroom or should the nation return to its former ban on electronic media in the courthouse? Does the educative role of watching real trials outweigh the possibilities that lawyers will play to the cameras? Watch a trial broadcast on CourtTV and systematically examine whether witnesses, lawyers, or judges seem distracted by the cameras. Just as importantly, ask yourself about the educational value of such broadcasts.

 To continue debating whether cameras should be allowed in courtrooms, point your browser to:

> http://www.nysda.org/Hot_Topics/Cameras_in_the_Court/cameras_in_the_court.html

> http://www.mediastudies.org/courts/mauro.html

> http://www.ibiblio.org/nppa/sherer/npp3.html

The following jurisdictions make their rules for cameras in the courtroom available on the Web:

Arizona: **http://www.supreme.state.az.us/media/cameras.htm**

California: **http://www.courtinfo.ca.gov/reference/cameras-sectionf.htm**

Missouri: **http://www.courtrules.org/camera.htm**

Second U.S. Circuit Court of Appeals: **http://www.nylj.com/rules/scpf.html**

For an up-to-date list of Web links, go to **http://www.wadsworth.com/product/0534563406s**.

 Jennifer L. Reichert, "New York Judge Rules Ban on Cameras in Court Unconstitutional"

CONCLUSION

After twelve years in prison Sheppard was retried. The prosecution put on essentially the same case but they now faced one of the top defense attorneys in the nation. F. Lee Bailey tore into the prosecutor's witnesses and in closing argument likened the prosecution's case as "ten pounds of hogwash in a five-pound bag." After deliberating for less than twelve hours the jury returned a verdict of not guilty. But for Sam Sheppard liberty proved short-lived. He died in 1970, probably sent to an early grave by journalistic excess.

The Sheppard murder trial has been called the "first trial of the century," second only in celebrity status to the trial of O. J. Simpson. The legacy of the Sheppard case lived on not only in the important Supreme Court decision that it spawned but also in fiction—the TV series and later movie *The Fugitive*. More recently the family has again sought to clear Dr. Sheppard's name. They blame the murder on a former gardener and argue that DNA evidence conclusively proves that an innocent man was convicted amidst a media spectacle. However, in 2000 a Cleveland jury refused to find Sam Sheppard innocent, thus dealing a fatal legal blow to his son's efforts to clear his father's name.

In many ways highly publicized jury trials for defendants—whether well known like Sam Sheppard and O. J. Simpson or hardly known at all—are the high point of the judicial process. Indeed, along with Lady Justice, jury trials stand as the primary symbol of justice. In turn, many Supreme Court decisions emphasize the importance of adversarial procedures at trial. Yet in examining the realities of trial, we are presented with two contradictory perspectives: Full-fledged trials are relatively rare, yet trials are an important dimension of the court process. Every year 2 million jurors serve in some 200,000 civil and criminal cases. Although only a relative smattering of cases are ever tried, the possibility of trial shapes the entire process. Thus, long after trials have declined to minimal importance in other Western nations, the institution of the trial jury remains a vital part of the American judicial process. Nowhere is this more apparent than in criminal justice. Given the availability of counsel, any defendant, no matter how poor and no matter how inflamed the public

is about the crime allegedly committed, can require the state to prove its case.

CRITICAL THINKING QUESTIONS

1. What impact does the jury system have on the rest of the criminal justice system? How would criminal justice function differently if defendants had no right to a trial by a jury of their peers, which is the situation in virtually all of the non–Common Law nations of the world?

2. If you are in a federal courthouse and observe a six-member jury, what type of case is being tried? Why?

3. Compare two recent trials in your community. What were the similarities and differences in terms of jury selection, the prosecutor's case-in-main, the defense strategy, and the verdict? If possible, compare a murder trial to one involving a major felony. In what ways are murder trials different from, say, a trial for armed robbery or rape?

4. In the wake of the O. J. Simpson verdict of not guilty, many commentators spoke about the collapse of the jury system. Were these sentiments driven by the one verdict or were there other reasons? Conversely, the conviction in the Oklahoma City bombing trial restored faith in the system. Were these sentiments tied to this one verdict or had other changes occurred?

5. Why are some jury verdicts popular and others not? To what extent do differences of opinion over the fairness of a jury verdict reinforce notions that equate justice with winning (Chapter 2)?

 WORLD WIDE WEB RESOURCES AND EXERCISES

Web Guides

http://dir.yahoo.com/Government/Law/Jury_Duty/
http://dir.yahoo.com/Government/Law/Cases/
http://dir.yahoo.com/Society_and_Culture/Crime/
Evidence/

Web Search Terms

"Jury"; "jury consultants"; "DNA"; "evidence"; "cameras in the courtroom"; "insanity defense"; "jury nullification"; "DNA testing"

Useful URLs

The American Academy of Forensic Sciences is a professional society dedicated to the application of science to the law: http://www.aafs.org/.

Crime scene investigation can be found at http://police2.ucr.edu/csi.html.

Read jury news from the research division of the National Center for State Courts at http://www.ncsc.dni.us/research/jurors/Jurynews.htm.

The Jury Research Institute provides trial consulting services: http://www.jri-inc.com/.

National Court Reports Association is a trade association with a Web page at http://www.verbatimreporters.com/.

Uncommon URLs

The Fully Informed Jury Association seeks to restore the political function of government: http://www.fija.org/.

The Insanity Defense and the Unabomber offers important insights at http://www.law.cornell.edu/background/insane/INSANE.html.

Visit the Juror's Web Site: http://members.tripod.com/~jctMac/jurynull.html

The Jury Rights Project educates jurors about their right to acquit people who have been accused of victimless crimes and thereby veto bad laws: http://www.levellers.org/jrp/.

A growing number of states place their rules of evidence online, including Pennsylvania (http://www.pennlegal.com/) and Texas (http://tarlton.law.utexas.edu/texas/rcve_toc.htm).

Web Exercises

1. Watch a criminal trial on CourtTV. How do prosecutors use the rules of evidence to prove the defendant guilty? What type of strategy does the defense use? A listing of current trials can be found at http://www.courttv.com.

2. Using the search engine of your choice, use the terms "*DNA testing*" or "*scientific evidence*" to locate articles on the latest developments in scientific evidence. What issues are presented? To what extent does the discus-

sion of these issues parallel differences of opinion embodied in the due process versus crime control models of justice?

3. Using the search engine of your choice, search for the term "*jury nullification*" to locate information on the topic. Do supporters of jury nullification form a full-fledged movement or are they isolated groups of one or two people? To what extent do opinions about jury nullification reflect ideological differences of the due process model versus the crime control model? To what extent do the views instead reflect a form of populist protest against the justice system?

INFOTRAC COLLEGE EDITION RESOURCES AND EXERCISES

Basic Searches

Jury; cameras in the courtroom; insanity defense; right to trial by jury; jury nullification; DNA testing

Recommended Articles

Richard E. Vatz, Lee S. Weinberg, "The Unabomber's Twisted Saga"

Julie Brienza, "Camera-Access Bill Approved by U.S. House"

Dan Johnson, "Witness: A Weak Link in the Judicial System"

Jet, "Lawyer's Comments about Race Leads to Mistrial in Murder Case"

Erick J. Haynie, "Populism, Free Speech, and the Rule of Law: The 'Fully Informed' Jury Movement and Its Implications"

InfoTrac College Edition Exercises

1. Using the search term *jury members,* select two or more articles that discuss jury bias and/or jury diversity. What problems do these articles discuss and what reforms are recommended?

2. Using the search term *jury,* select two or more articles that discuss jury reform. What problems do these articles identify and why? What solutions do they recommend? Do the articles represent similar or different social and/or political agendas?

3. Using the search term *DNA testing, evidence,* or *DNA testing, laws,* select two or more arti-

cles that discuss the advantages and/or drawbacks of expanding the use of DNA evidence in criminal trials. To what extent do these articles reflect concerns associated with the due process or the crime control models of justice?

REFERENCES

Alexander, S. L. 1991. "Cameras in the Courtroom: A Case Study." *Judicature* 74: 307–313.

———. 1996. "The Impact of *California v. Simpson* on Cameras in the Courtroom." *Judicature* 79: 169–175.

Bailey, F. Lee, and Henry Rothblat. 1971. *Successful Techniques for Criminal Trials*. New York: Lawyers Cooperative.

Beaupre, Becky. 1996. "Politics, Pressure Strain Crime Labs." *USA Today*, 21 August.

Beiser, Edward. 1975. "Six-Member Juries in the Federal Courts." *Judicature* 58: 424.

Boatright, Robert. 1999. "Why Citizens Don't Respond to Jury Summonses, and What Courts Can Do about It." *Judicature* 82: 156–165.

Broeder, D. W. 1959. "The University of Chicago Jury Project." *Nebraska Law Review* 38: 744–760.

Brown, Darryl. 1997. "Jury Nullification Within the Rule of Law." *Minnesota Law Review* 81: 1149–1200.

Bureau of Justice Statistics. 1988. *Report to the Nation on Crime and Justice*, 2d ed. Washington, D.C.: U.S. Department of Justice.

Butler, Paul. 1995. "Racially Based Jury Nullification: Black Power in the Criminal Justice System." *Yale Law Journal* 105: 677–725.

Dattu, Firoz. 1998. "Illustrated Jury Instructions." *Judicature* 82: 79–83.

Diamond, Shari. 1990. "Scientific Jury Selection: What Social Scientists Know and Do Not Know." *Judicature* 73: 178–183.

Eisenstein, James, and Herbert Jacob. 1977. *Felony Justice: An Organizational Analysis of Criminal Courts*. Boston: Little, Brown.

Ellwork, Amiram, Bruce Sales, and James Alfini. 1982. *Making Jury Instructions Understandable*. Charlottesville, VA: The Michie Co.

Ford, Marilyn. 1986. "The Role of Extralegal Factors in Jury Verdicts." *Justice System Journal* 11: 16–39.

Frasca, Ralph. 1988. "Estimating the Occurrence of Trials Prejudiced by Press Coverage." *Judicature* 72: 162–169.

Fukurai, Hiroshi, Edgar Butler, and Richard Krooth. 1991. "Cross-Sectional Jury Representation or Systematic Jury Representation? Simple Random and Cluster Sampling Strategies in Jury Selection." *Journal of Criminal Justice* 19: 31–48.

Galiber, Joseph, Barry Latzer, Mark Dwyer, Jack Litman, H. Richard Uviller, and G. Roger McDonald. 1993. "Law, Justice, and Jury Nullification: A Debate." *Criminal Law Bulletin* 29: 40–69.

Gardner, Thomas. 1985. *Criminal Law: Principles and Cases*. 3d ed. St Paul, MN: West.

Gollner, Phillip. 1995. "Consulting by Peering into Minds of Jurors." *The New York Times*, 7 January, A25.

Hannaford, Paula, Valerie Hans, and G. Thomas Munsterman. 1999. "How Much Justice Hangs in the Balance? A New Look at Hung Jury Rates." *Judicature* 83: 59–67.

Hastie, Reid, Steven Penrod, and Nancy Pennington. 1984. *Inside the Jury*. Cambridge, MA: Harvard University Press.

Holland, Jesse. 1995. "Susan Smith Judge Bars TV Cameras From Murder Trial." *Times-Picayune*, 25 June.

James, Rita. 1958. "Status and Competence of Jurors." *American Journal of Sociology* 69: 563–570.

Kairys, David, Joseph Kadane, and John Lehorsky. 1977. "Jury Representativeness: A Mandate for Multiple Source Lists." *California Law Review* 65: 776–827.

Kalven, Harry, and Hans Zeisel. 1966. *The American Jury*. Boston: Little, Brown.

Kasunic, David. 1983. "One Day/One Trial: A Major Improvement in the Jury System." *Judicature* 67: 78–86.

Keilitz, Ingo, and Junius Fulton. 1984. *The Insanity Defense and Its Alternatives: A Guide for Policymakers*. Williamsburg, VA: National Center for State Courts.

Klofas, John, and Janette Yandrasits. 1989. "'Guilty but Mentally Ill' and the Jury Trial: A Case Study." *Criminal Law Bulletin* 24: 424.

Kramer, Geoffrey, Norbert Kerr, and John Carroll. 1990. "Pretrial Publicity, Judicial Remedies, and Jury Bias." *Law and Human Behavior* 14: 409–438.

Labaton, Stephen. 1990. "DNA Fingerprinting Is Facing Showdown at an Ohio Hearing." *The New York Times*, 22 June.

Levine, James. 1983. "Using Jury Verdict Forecasts in Criminal Defense Strategy." *Judicature* 66: 448–461.

———. 1996. "The Impact of Sequestration on Juries." *Judicature* 79: 266–272.

Losh, Susan, Adina Wasserman, and Michael Wasserman. 2000. "Reluctant Jurors: What Summons Responses Reveal about Jury Duty Attitudes." *Judicature* 83: 304–311.

Mills, Carol, and Wayne Bohannon. 1980. "Jury Characteristics: To What Extent Are They Related to Jury Verdicts?" *Judicature* 64: 22–31.

Moran, Gary, and Brian Cutler. 1991. "The Prejudicial Impact of Pretrial Publicity." *Journal of Applied Social Psychology* 21: 345–367.

Munstermann, G. Thomas, and Janice Munstermann. 1986. "The Search for Jury Representativeness." *Justice System Journal* 11: 59–78.

National Advisory Commission on Criminal Justice Standards and Goals. 1973. *Courts.* Washington, D.C.: U.S. Government Printing Office.

Neubauer, David. 1974. *Criminal Justice in Middle America.* Morristown, NJ: General Learning Press.

Newman, Ted. 1996. "Fair Cross-section and Good Intentions: Representation in Federal Juries." *Justice System Journal* 18: 211–232.

Pabst, William. 1973. "What Do Six-Member Juries Really Save?" *Judicature* 57: 6–11.

Padawer-Singer, Alice, and Alice Barton. 1975. "The Impact of Pretrial Publicity on Jurors' Verdicts." In *The Jury System in America: A Critical Overview,* edited by Rita James Simon. Beverly Hills, CA: Sage.

Queary, Paul. 1996. "Bombing Trial Moved to Denver Because of Bias." *Times-Picayune,* 27 February.

Raymond, Paul. 1992. "The Impact of a Televised Trial on Individuals' Information and Attitudes." *Judicature* 75: 204–209.

Reskin, Barbara, and Christine Visher. 1986. "The Impacts of Evidence and Extralegal Factors in Jurors' Decisions." *Law and Society Review* 20: 423–439.

Roper, Robert. 1979. "Jury Size: Impact on Verdict's Correctness." *American Politics Quarterly* 7: 438–452.

———. 1980. "Jury Size and Verdict Consistency: 'Line Has to Be Drawn Somewhere'?" *Law and Society Review* 14: 972–995.

Roper, Robert, and Victor Flango. 1983. "Trials Before Judges and Juries." *Justice System Journal* 8: 186–198.

Rothstein, Paul. 1970. *Evidence in a Nutshell.* Minneapolis: West.

Saks, Michael. 1996. "The Smaller the Jury, the Greater the Unpredictability." *Judicature* 79: 263—265.

Sanborn, Joseph. 1993. "The Right to a Public Jury Trial: A Need for Today's Juvenile Court." *Judicature* 76: 230–238.

Scardino, Albert. 1989. "Steinberg Live: Courtroom TV Is a Fixture, Even as New York Is Deciding." *The New York Times,* 22 January, E7.

Severance, Lawrence, and Elizabeth Loftus. 1982. "Improving the Ability of Jurors to Comprehend and Apply Criminal Jury Instructions." *Law and Society Review* 17: 153–198.

Sigler, Jay. 1981. *Understanding Criminal Law.* Boston: Little, Brown.

Simon, Rita James. 1967. *The Jury and the Defense of Insanity.* Boston: Little, Brown.

Sipes, Dale. 1988. *On Trial: The Length of Civil and Criminal Trials.* Williamsburg, VA: National Center for State Courts.

Sniffen, Michael. 1997. "FBI Lab Problems Are Widespread." *Times-Picayune,* 14 February.

Steadman, Henry, John Monahan, Sharon Davis, and Pamela Robbins. 1982. "Mentally Disordered Offenders: National Survey of Patients and Facilities." *Law and Human Behavior* 6: 31–38.

Steele, Walter, and Elizabeth Thornburg. 1991. "Jury Instructions: A Persistent Failure to Communicate." *Judicature* 74: 249–254.

Steinberg, Marvin. 1991. "The Case for Eliminating Peremptory Challenges." *Criminal Law Bulletin* 27: 216–229.

Strawn, David, and Raymond Buchanan. 1976. "Jury Confusion: A Threat to Justice." *Judicature* 59: 478–483.

Strodtbeck, F., R. James, and C. Hawkins. 1957. "Social Status in Jury Deliberations." *American Sociological Review* 22: 713–719.

Tanford, J. Alexander. 1991. "Law Reform by Courts, Legislatures and Commissions Following Empirical Research on Jury Instructions." *Law and Society Review* 25: 155–176.

Thaler, Paul. 1994. *The Watchful Eye: American Justice in the Age of the Television Trial.* Westport, CT: Praeger.

U.S. Department of Justice/Office of Inspector General. 1997. *The FBI Laboratory: An Investigation into Laboratory Practices and Alleged Misconduct in Explosives-Related and Other Cases.* (April). http://www.usdoj.gov/oig/fbilab1/fbi1toc.htm.

van Dyke, Jon. 1977. *Jury Selection Procedures: Our Uncertain Commitment to Representative Panels.* Cambridge, MA: Ballinger.

Vidmar, Neil, Sara Beale, Mary Rose, and Laura Donnelly. 1997. "Should We Rush to Reform the Criminal Jury?" *Judicature* 80: 286–290.

Zeisel, Hans. 1982. "The Verdict of Five Out of Six Civil Jurors: Constitutional Problems." *American Bar Foundation Research Journal*: 141–156.

Zeisel, Hans, and Shari Diamond. 1974. "Convincing Empirical Evidence on the Six Member Jury." *University of Chicago Law Review* 41: 281–295.

FOR FURTHER READING

Abramson, Jeffrey. *We, the Jury: The Jury System and the Ideal of Democracy.* New York: Basic Books, 1994.

Brill, Steven, ed. *Trial by Jury: The Tactics, Deals and Decisions That Determined the Outcome of 17 of the Decade's Biggest Legal Cases.* Englewood Cliffs, NJ: Simon and Schuster, 1990.

Broady, David. "Balancing Jury Secrecy and the Rule of Law: The Second Circuit's Guide to Removing Nullifying Jurors." *Justice System Journal* 20 (1998): 113–120.

Boatright, Robert. "The 21st-Century American Jury: Reflections from the Cantigny Conference." *Judicature* 83 (2000): 288–297.

Chiasoon, Lloyd. *The Press on Trial: Crimes and Trials as Media Events.* Westport, CT: Praeger, 1997.

Fahringer, Herald. "The Peremptory Challenge: An Endangered Species?" *Criminal Law Bulletin* 31 (1995) 400–463.

Gardner, Thomas and Terry Anderson. *Criminal Evidence: Principles and Cases.* Belmont, CA: Wadsworth, 2001.

Goldfarb, Ronald. *TV or Not TV: Television, Justice, and the Courts.* New York: New York University Press, 1998.

Giles, Robert and Robert Snyder, eds. *Covering the Courts: Free Press, Fair Trials and Journalistic Performance.* New Brunswick: Transaction Publishers, 1999.

Horowitz, Irwin, and Thomas Willging. "Changing Views of Jury Power: The Nullification Debate, 1787–1988." *Law and Human Behavior* 15 (1991): 165.

Loftus, Elizabeth, and Katherine Ketcham. *Witness for the Defense.* New York: St. Martin's Press, 1991.

National Institute of Justice. *Eyewitness Evidence: A Guide for Law Enforcement.* Washington, D.C.: U.S. Department of Justice, 1999.

Munsterman, G. Thomas, Paula Hannaford and G. Marc Whitehead, eds. *Jury Trial Innovations.* Williamsburg, VA: National Center for State Courts, 1997.

Insanity and Other Affirmative Defenses

Bonnie, Richard, Norman Poythress, Steven Hoge, John Monahan, and Marlene Eisenberg. "Decision-Making in Criminal Defense: An Empirical Study of Insanity Pleas and the Impact of Doubted Client Competence." *Journal of Criminal Law and Criminology* 87 (1996) 48–76.

Caplan, Lincoln. *The Insanity Defense and the Trial of John W. Hinckley, Jr.* Boston: D. R. Godine, 1984.

Jenkins, Pamela, and Barbara Davidson. "Battered Women in the Criminal Justice System: An Analysis of Gender Stereotypes." *Behavioral Sciences and the Law* 8 (1990): 161–170.

Miller, Kent, and Michael Radelet. *Executing the Mentally Ill: The Criminal Justice System and the Case of Alvin Ford.* Newbury Park, CA: Sage, 1993.

Morris, Norval. *The Brothel Boy and Other Parables of the Law.* New York: Oxford University Press, 1992.

Simon, Rita James. *The Jury and the Defense of Insanity.* 2d ed. Boston: Little, Brown, 1998.

Scientific Evidence and DNA

Foster, Kenneth and Peter Huber. *Judging Science: Scientific Knowledge and the Federal Courts.* Cambridge, MA: MIT Press, 1999.

Freeman, Michael and Helen Reece, eds. *Science in Court.* Brookfield, VT: Ashgate Publishing, 1998.

Huber, Peter. *Galileo's Revenge: Junk Science in the Courtroom.* New York: Basic Books, 1991.

Huff, C. Ronald, Ayre Rattner, and Edward Sagarin. *Convicted but Innocent: Wrongful Conviction and Public Policy.* Newbury Park, CA: Sage, 1996

Kaye, D. H. *Science in Evidence.* Cincinnati: Anderson Publishing, 1997.

Ragle, Larry. *Crime Scene.* New York: Avon Books, 1995.

Sentencing the Guilty

SENTENCES ARE THE CURRENCY OF THE REALM. REFORMERS, LAW PROFESSORS, and appellate courts spend most of their time debating and analyzing how courts determine guilt or innocence. But judges, prosecutors, defense attorneys, and defendants focus much of their attention on sentencing. Will the defendant be granted probation? If not, how many years in prison will be imposed? These are the main topics that fuel the dynamics of courthouse justice.

Sentencing is involved in both the beginning and the end of the criminal justice system. For society, sentencing is the starting point: The reasons for punishing law violators establish the very purpose of the criminal justice system. For the defendant, sentencing is the last step in the process—whether he or she will be sentenced to prison or placed on probation will be decided. The courts stand in the middle; they must wrestle with a host of conflicting considerations, some of which have no easy answers. Dissatisfaction with how the courts perform these tasks is widespread and long-standing.

Chapter 15 considers the legal basis of judicial discretion in sentencing. Of particular interest are the why, the who, and the what of sentencing. Asking *why* we sentence provokes fundamental disagreement. Asking *who* sentences highlights the important role that legislative and executive agencies play in sentencing. Asking *what* sentences may be imposed draws our attention to the limited options available for punishing wrongdoers—typically prison or probation.

Chapter 16 examines how courtroom work groups choose between prison and probation. The choices judges actually make are criticized from both sides; to some sentences are too harsh, whereas others argue that sentences are too lenient. Still others are concerned that sentencing is unfair.

■ ■ ■

Sentencing Options

It was two o'clock in the morning and William Furman, a seventh-grade dropout, was intent on burglary. Awakened by a strange noise, William Micke, father of five, went downstairs to investigate. In his haste to flee, Furman tripped over a washing machine cord on the back porch, discharging his gun and hitting Micke through a closed solid plywood door. Although the killing was accidental, Georgia law authorized the death penalty. Judge and jury agreed with this policy, and William Furman was sentenced to death.

Like so many other capital cases, the Furman conviction was appealed to the U.S. Supreme Court. Indeed, 118 cases were on the Court's docket that day. Like the rest of the nation, the highest court had been wrestling with the moral issue of who deserves to die in the electric chair, and like the rest of the nation, it was badly divided over the matter. Thus, of the 118 cases reviewed by the Court on June 28, 1971, thirty-three death row inmates were spared because of various procedural defects during trial. In almost all of the other cases, the Court extended previous stays of execution, thus deciding to decide the case another day. In an unexpected move, however, Furman's appeal was granted certiorari. Along with another murder case from California and rape convictions from Georgia and Texas, the Supreme Court agreed for the first time to hear arguments as to whether the imposition of the death penalty constitutes "cruel and unusual punishment," as prohibited by the Eighth Amendment. The Court's first, tentative, groping answer came a year later. By the slimmest of margins the Court declared all existing death penalty laws unconstitutional, and in the process irrevocably altered the debate over what punishments are appropriate for those who violate the criminal law. ■

The debate over the death penalty is the most obvious example of the unprecedented attention the nation has devoted over the last decades to crime. In large measure, the public holds judges, from the Supreme Court on down, responsible for high rates of crime and points to decisions such as *Furman* as examples. Understanding the dissatisfaction with sentencing and the sentencing reforms that have resulted requires an understanding of the legal basis of sentencing. This chapter focuses on the why, the who, and the what of sentencing. Punishments are shaped by philosophical and moral considerations. Asking *why* we sentence focuses attention on the competing justifications for sentencing. Probing *who* should make these choices reveals the complex sentencing structure in the United States. Although the public associates the judge with sentencing, closer scrutiny indicates that other branches of government share sentencing responsibility as well. Finally, examining the *what* of sentencing shows that a variety of sentences may be imposed on the guilty, including prison, probation, intermediate sanctions, fines, and restitution. And most controversial of all, a penalty of death may be imposed upon a select number of defendants found guilty at trial.

WHY DO WE SENTENCE?

"An eye for an eye, a tooth for a tooth."
"Lock 'em up and throw away the key."
"Let this sentence be a warning to others."
"Sentencing should rehabilitate the offender."

These statements—variously drawn from the Bible, newspaper headlines, casual conversations, and statements by court officials—demonstrate that there is no consensus on how the courts should punish the guilty. Retribution, incapacitation, deterrence, and rehabilitation are the four principal justifications offered. These sentencing philosophies differ in important ways. Some focus on past behavior, whereas others are future-oriented. Some stress that the punishment should fit the crime, whereas others emphasize that punishment should fit the criminal. These issues influence contemporary thinking about sentencing.

Retribution

"An eye for an eye, a tooth for a tooth." This Old Testament phrase expresses the oldest of sentencing philosophies (see Exhibit 15-1). What is most distinctive about **retribution** is its focus on past behavior; the severity of the punishment is directly tied to the seriousness of the crime. This concept is based on strongly held moral principles—individuals are held responsible for their own actions. Because they have disregarded the rights of others or otherwise upset the social order, criminals are wicked people and therefore deserve to be punished. Punishing wrongdoers also reflects a basic human emotion, the desire for revenge: Because the victim has suffered, the criminal should suffer as well.

Retribution: A concept that implies the payment of a debt to society and thus the expiration of one's offense.

EXHIBIT 15-1   Old Testament View of Sentencing

> When one man strikes another and kills him, he shall be put to death. Whoever strikes a beast and kills it shall make restitution, life for life. When one man injures and disfigures his fellow-countryman, it shall be done to him as he has done; fracture for fracture, eye for eye, tooth for tooth; the injury and disfigurement that he has inflicted upon another shall in turn be inflicted upon him.
>
> —Leviticus 24:17–22

The concept of retribution clearly stands for punitive sentencing, but a closer probing reveals important subtleties involving limits on sentencing. Because society as a whole is punishing the criminal, individuals are not justified in taking the law into their own hands. Moreover, in applying sanctions, the severity of the punishment is limited to the severity of the injury of the victim. This is how Leviticus 24:20 differs from other ancient notions about punishment. Note also that retribution provides for reconciliation—through punishment, the offenders are said to have paid their debt to society.

From biblical times through the eighteenth century, retribution provided the dominant justification for punishment. Beginning with the Enlightenment, however, retribution lost much of its influence. Criminal penalties based on revenge began to be viewed as barbaric, and more utilitarian reasons for sentencing were preferred. More recently, since the 1970s, retribution has once again attracted the interest of scholars and criminal justice reformers, who use a more humane phrasing: deserved punishment. According to one of the leading exponents, Andrew von Hirsch (1976), "Someone who infringes the rights of others . . . does wrong and deserves blame for his conduct. It is because he deserves blame that the sanctioning authority is entitled to choose a response that expresses moral disapproval; namely punishment." This punishment should be administered in accordance with the principle of **just deserts**: The severity of the sanction should be pro-

portionate to the gravity of the defendant's criminal conduct.

As a sentencing philosophy, retribution suffers from several limitations. Its focus on crimes of violence offers little apparent guidance for sentencing the far more numerous defendants who have committed property violations. Its moralistic emphasis on individual responsibility does not fit well with modern explanations of human behavior based on social, physical, and psychological factors. Its emphasis on vengeance does not easily square with constitutional limits on governmental power (individual rights) that are fundamental to a representational democracy. Most important, though, it emphasizes the past behavior of the defendant and exhibits no concern for future criminal activity. Some studies demonstrate that extended periods of custody may actually increase the likelihood that an inmate will commit future criminal acts. Thus, sentencing on the basis of retribution may prove to be contrary to the goal of crime reduction.

Incapacitation

"Lock them up and throw away the key." Average citizens, outraged by a recent, shocking crime, often express sentiments like this. The assumption of **incapacitation** is that crime can be prevented if criminals are physically restrained. The theory of isolating current or potential criminals differs from the theory of retribution in two important ways. First, it is future-oriented: The goal is to prevent future crimes, not punish past ones. Second, it focuses on the personal characteristics of the offender—the type of person committing the crime is more important than the crime committed. Unlike rehabilitation, however, incapacitation has no intention of reforming the offender.

Since ancient times, societies have banished persons who have disobeyed the rules. England transported criminals to penal colonies, such as Georgia and Australia. Russia exiled dissidents to cold, distant Siberia, where they could not threaten the government. More commonly, nations have used prisons to isolate guilty offenders, preventing them from committing additional crimes in the

Just deserts: Punishment for criminal wrongdoing should be proportionate to the severity of the offense.

Incapacitation: Sentencing philosophy that stresses crime prevention through isolating wrongdoers from society.

community. Some people likewise justify the death penalty on the basis that it prevents future crimes.

Incapacitation is probably the most straightforward justification offered for punishing wrongdoers. As a sentencing philosophy, however, it suffers from important limitations. It cannot provide any standards about how long a sentence should be. Unlike retribution, it does not imply any limits on sentencing. Indeed, the goal of crime prevention may be used to justify severe sanctions for both trivial and serious offenses. Moreover, isolation without efforts directed toward rehabilitation may produce more severe criminal behavior once the offender is released. Prisons "protect the community but that protection is only temporary. They relieve the community responsibility by removing the offender, but they make successful reintegration of the offender into the community unlikely" (National Advisory Commission 1973). Finally, applying the incapacitation theory to the fullest would require the building of many more prisons, at great expense.

The incapacitation theory of sentencing has never been well articulated. Its assumptions about crime and criminals are simplistic. But in recent years a more focused variant, **selective incapacitation**, has received considerable attention. Research has shown that a relatively small number of criminals are responsible for a large number of crimes (Haapanen 1989). For example, some burglars commit many such offenses before they are caught. These findings have led to an interest in targeting dangerous offenders (Chaiken and Chaiken 1990). Some studies estimate that sending serious offenders to prison for longer periods of time will result in a significant reduction in crime (Shinnar and Shinnar 1975). Not all researchers agree, however, that selective incapacitation will greatly reduce crime (Van Dine, Conrad, and Dinitz 1979). Critics argue that even though some offenders may be imprisoned others on the verge of criminality are ready to take their places. Moreover, it is unclear how multiple repeat offenders can be singled out from the garden-variety crooks. At issue is whether we have the knowledge or technology to make accurate predictions of future criminal activity by convicted defendants (Visher 1987). Indeed recent research suggests that selective incapacity notions perform extremely poorly in terms of both reliability and validity (Auerhahn 1999).

 David Dolinko, "Justice in the Age of Sentencing Guidelines"

Deterrence

"Let this sentence be a warning to others." Phrases like this reflect one of the more modern and also most widely held justifications for punishment. According to **deterrence theory**, the purpose of punishment is the prevention of future crimes. Unlike retribution and incapacitation, this theory offers ideas about the causes of crime and how to alter them. Deterrence is not content to punish the given wrongdoer, rather it seeks to prevent other potential offenders from committing crimes. Deterrence, however, does not propose to change offenders—just deter them. Much like rehabilitation, deterrence argues that the punishment should fit the criminal. Note that this is a different concern from that of retribution theory, in which the punishment should fit the crime.

A nineteenth-century British lawyer, reformer, and criminologist, Jeremy Bentham, first articulated the deterrence theory. To Bentham, punishment based on retribution was pointless and counterproductive. Instead, sanctions should be used to further society's goal of preventing crime. Punishment can therefore be justified only if it can be shown that more "good" results when punishment is inflicted than when it is withheld. Bentham believed that human behavior is governed by individual calculation: People seek to maximize pleasure and minimize pain. Under this utilitarian theory, the basic objective of punishment is to discourage crime by making it painful. Because people seek to minimize pain, they will refrain from activities such as crimes, which result in painful sanctions.

Contemporary discussions of deterrence theories incorporate two subconcepts, which are often

Selective incapacitation: Sentencing philosophy that stresses targeting dangerous offenders for lengthy prison sentences.

Deterrence theory: The view that sure and swift punishment will discourage others from similar illegal acts.

confused. **General deterrence** is the idea that the general populace will be discouraged from committing crimes by observing the public example of the punishment of wrongdoers. It has a strong education component, and public perceptions of punishment are very important. **Special deterrence** (which is sometimes called specific or individual deterrence) is concerned with producing changes in the behavior of the individual defendant. It seeks individualized punishment in the amount and kind necessary so that the criminal will not commit future crimes. A difficulty with deterrence theory is that the goals of general and special deterrence can be incompatible. The severity of the punishment needed to impress the general population with the price of committing a particular crime may be higher than that needed to deter the individual defendant from future crimes.

Notions of deterrence form the core of contemporary discussions about sentencing. In a general sense, many people refrain from committing illegal acts because they fear the consequences of being convicted. After a party, for example, an intoxicated guest may take a taxi home rather than run the risk of being arrested and disgraced by a drunken driving conviction. In this situation, one can easily argue that the threat of punishment does deter. In terms of other applications, however, the picture becomes much cloudier.

The exact nature of the role that deterrence plays and the extent to which sentencing policies affect crime and criminals is unclear. An extensive literature examines deterrence but reaches no firm conclusions. Some studies find a deterrent effect, and others do not (Nagin 1998). Although discussions of deterrence are usually coupled with calls for increasing the severity of sentences, some research suggests that certainty of punishment is more of a deterrent than the severity of punishment (Wilson 1983). Moreover, deterrence rests on the assumption of rational, calculating behavior. Many crimes (particularly crimes of violence) are committed on the spur of the moment. Other offenses are committed while the defendant is under the influence of drugs or alcohol. For these reasons, many observers question whether court sentences—particularly severe ones—do indeed deter.

Rehabilitation

The most appealing modern justification for imposing punishment is to restore a convicted offender to a constructive place in society through vocational, educational, or therapeutic treatment. The idea of **rehabilitation** assumes that criminal behavior is the result of social, psychological, or physical imperfections and that the treatment of such disorders should be the primary goal of corrections. Success means assessing the needs of the individual and providing a program to meet those needs. Ultimately, then, offenders are not being punished but treated, not only for their own good but also for the benefit of society. Under rehabilitation, sentences should fit the offender rather than the offense. Thus, rehabilitation shares a common orientation with deterrence-crime reduction. But they differ in a fundamental way: Rehabilitation assumes that human behavior can be altered.

The concept of rehabilitation has dominated thinking about sentencing throughout the twentieth century. It has provided the intellectual linchpin for such important developments as probation, parole, and indeterminate sentencing. Most court personnel and correctional officials have strongly favored rehabilitation. It has also enjoyed widespread public support; almost three out of four persons favor the idea that the main emphasis in prisons should be to help the offender become a productive citizen.

During recent decades the rehabilitative ideal has been challenged on both empirical and normative grounds. Growing evidence shows that rehabilitative programs do not substantially reduce the later criminality of their clients (Blumstein et al. 1983). California, for example, where the rehabilitative model had been most completely incorporated, was also marked by high rates of recidivism (repeat criminal behavior). To some, the key weakness of rehabilitation is that people cannot be coerced to change. This is reflected in the fact that some prisoners participate in prison rehabilitation programs, such as counseling, job training, and religious services, out of a desire to gain an early release—not because they wish to change their behavior. Doubts have also been expressed as to whether the causes of

---

General deterrence: Concept stressing that punishment will deter the general populace.

Special deterrence: Concept stressing that punishment will deter the person being sentenced.

Rehabilitation: The notion that punishment is intended to restore offenders to a constructive role in society; based on the assumption that criminal behavior is a treatable disorder caused by social or psychological ailments.

FIGURE 15-1	Contrasting Sentencing Philosophies

Retribution	Punishment inflicted on a person who has infringed on the rights of others and so deserves to be penalized to a degree commensurate with the crime.	• Focuses on the crime committed (not the defendant). • Limits punishment to the harm done to the offender.
Incapacitation	Deprives a convicted person of the capacity to commit crimes against society by detention in prison.	• Focuses on defendant's past history. • Can lead to very unequal sentences because minor offenses can be punished more severely than major ones.
Deterrence	Punishment of criminals to prevent future crimes.	• Based on Bentham's utilitarian theory. • General deterrence (directed toward the general populace) differs from special deterrence (the specific defendant).
Rehabilitation	The process of restoring a convicted offender to a constructive place in society through some form of vocational, educational, or therapeutic treatment.	• Focuses on the defendant rather than the crime committed. • Dominant sentencing philosophy for most of the twentieth century. • Under what conditions defendants can be rehabilitated is subject to extensive debate.

crime can be diagnosed and whether enough is yet known about major behavior modification.

Apart from the empirical question of whether rehabilitation programs have been successful, concern has also been voiced that sentencing structures based on the rehabilitative ideal grant too much discretion to judges and parole boards. As a result of this discretion, the humanitarian goal of rehabilitation can serve to mask punishment. In most prisons, rehabilitation programs are minimal or nonexistent. Yet judges often sentence in the hope of rehabilitating the offender; this may produce lengthier prison sentences. Thus, to critics, sentencing an offender according to the rehabilitative ideal may be more punitive than sentencing for the sake of punishment alone.

Competing Sentencing Philosophies

Justifications for punishing wrongdoers are based on religious and moral views of right and wrong as well as empirical perceptions of human behavior (see Figure 15-1). Of the four philosophies—retribution, incapacitation, deterrence, and rehabilitation—none alone is adequate; the various goals must be balanced. Therefore, elements of each of these four philosophies have been incorporated into society's efforts to control crime. Sentencing decisions also reflect ambivalent expectations about the causes of crime, the nature of criminals, the role of the courts in reducing crime, and the likely results of following these philosophies. The limitations of historical sentencing philosophies has led a small band of adherents to pioneer a new way of thinking about criminals and their victims. (See Controversy: Should Restorative Justice Replace Revenge-based Sentencing?)

Since the late 1970s the reasons for sentencing have been the subject of intense debate. After three quarters of a century, the intellectual dominance of the rehabilitative ideal began to crumble and then collapse. Scholars and others began to explore alternative justifications for imposing punishment on wrongdoers. This has resulted in widespread sentencing reforms, many of which focus on who should have the authority to impose a sentence and what limits should be placed on that authority.

WHO SHOULD DECIDE THE SENTENCE?

From the inside looking out, sentencing is a judicial function. With a few exceptions, only the judge has the legal authority to send the guilty to prison or grant probation. From the outside looking in,

Should Restorative Justice Replace Revenge-based Sentencing?

After imposing a prison sentence on a rapist, Justice John Kelly observed that the victim was no less distraught than she had been throughout the court proceedings. So before he called the next case, he asked the victim to approach the bench. Speaking briefly and quietly, he concluded with these words, "You understand that what I have done here demonstrates conclusively *that what happened was not your fault.*" Hearing these words she began to weep and ran from the courtroom. Several days later the Australian judge called the family and learned that his words had been words of vindication for the woman; they marked the beginning of her psychological healing. Her tears had been tears of healing. In *Restoring Justice,* Daniel Van Ness and Karen Strong (1997) use this example to emphasize their central theme—sentencing should promote healing. The restorative justice movement seeks to replace retribution with restoration. In essence, the failures of the contemporary criminal justice system are traced to the historical emphasis on vengeance.

Restorative justice is based on three distinct elements (Galaway and Hudson 1996):

- Crime is primarily a conflict between individuals, which results in injuries (physical and/or psychological) to victims, the community, and the offender as well. Therefore, crime is only secondarily a violation of governmental laws.
- The principal aim of the criminal justice system should be to repair these injuries. Therefore, pro-

moting peace and reconciling parties is much more important than punishing the guilty.
- The criminal justice system should facilitate involvement of victims, offenders, and the community. Therefore, lay citizens should play a central role in the criminal justice system, and professionals (police, prosecutors, judges, and probation officers, for example) should play less of a role.

Proponents stress that restorative justice is a way of thinking and is not tied to any specific program.

Clearly, proponents of restorative justice reject the crime control model's emphasis on punishment. In their view vengeance is counterproductive. But at the same time, they view the due process model as not going far enough. The rehabilitative model targets offenders but provides no healing for victims and fails to address the trauma they have experienced.

Skeptics voice concern that restorative justice means considerably different things to different people. Indeed, by stressing abstract concepts rather than pointing to specific programs, proponents make it somewhat difficult to discuss restorative justice because many of the examples singled out as successful implementation are drawn from other countries. This notion of all things to all people is reinforced by evolving terminology. What started out as victim-offender reconciliation programs (VORPs) became mediation and then changed to dialogue, until today they are called conferences. The movement is also maddeningly vague about important specifics center-

however, sentencing responsibility involves all three branches of government—legislative, executive, and judicial. The result is a varied and complex sentencing structure that has changed greatly over the last thirty years (Tonry 1999).

Through most of the twentieth century, sentencing was exercised within broad limits set by the legislature, which prescribed maximum sentences. The judicial branch of government had primary authority over who went to prison, and an executive agency—parole boards—controlled the length of the prison term. Since the mid-1970s, dramatic changes have been made in the laws under which offenders are sent to prison and in the mechanisms that control how long they stay there. Legislatures have increased their control over the sentencing process, and the judiciary and the parole boards have

taken steps to formalize and regularize their exercise of discretion in applying sanctions. The result has been a significant narrowing of sentencing discretion in most states (see Figure 15-2 on page 392).

Legislative Sentencing Responsibility

Legislatures are initially responsible for creating sentencing options. Recall from Chapter 2 that there can be no crime and no punishment without law. Legislative sentencing responsibility is expressed in the criminal codes enacted by legislative bodies.

Legislatures specify terms of imprisonment in two different ways. Consistent with the goal of rehabilitation, which dominated correctional thinking

ing on which victims would be most amenable to conferencing, which offenders are willing to frankly confront the harm they have done to others, and what is meant by that always-elusive contemporary buzz-word—community.

If skeptics seem somewhat receptive to this new idea, critics express open hostility about subjecting a victim to another, possibly equally as damaging, encounter with the defendant. Typical was the person on an Internet discussion list who wanted to know why victims should be forced to bargain with a person who has caused them harm? Perhaps victims do not want to go through the process because of legitimate concerns (unnecessarily revisiting the original trauma) or out of shortsightedness (holding on to the role of victim is comfortable). Overall, it is clear that the restorative justice understanding of victims is far different from those views that stress punishment and not forgiveness (discussed in Chapter 9).

Restorative justice appears to straddle core cultural values, reinforcing key norms such as healing while challenging social understandings such as punishment. The differences of opinion among supporters reflects this duality. To some, restorative justice programs should work within the criminal justice system, diverting the guilty from imprisonment. But to others, restorative justice should work outside the criminal justice system, offering a full-fledged alternative aimed at replacing this system. To complicate matters further, some advocates are, in essence, antigovernment, envisioning a criminal justice system with fewer professionals, particularly police and prosecutors. These opposing views within the movement

make predictions about the future of restorative justice difficult. Based on experience with alternative dispute resolution (examined in Chapter 18), programs that work within the system are more likely to be adopted than those that refuse to make accommodations with existing criminal justice agencies.

What do you think? Should our current criminal justice system, which is often equated with a revenge-based system, be replaced by restorative justice? What types of victims might be most amenable to conferencing? What types of defendants are most likely to express remorse? What elements of the community would be most supportive of restorative justice?

 To continue the debate over restorative justice, go to

Restorative Justice: Healing the Effects of Crime: **http://www.restorativejustice.com/**
Victim-Offender Mediation Center: **http://www.voma.org/**

For an up-to-date list of Web links, go to **http://www.wadsworth.com/product/0534563406s**.

 Emilio C. Viano, "Restorative Justice for Victims Offenders: A Return to American Traditions"

James Turpin, "Restorative Justice Challenges Corrections"

through most of this century, state legislatures adopted indeterminate (often called indefinite) sentences, based on the idea that correctional personnel must have discretion to release an offender when treatment has been successful. States with **indeterminate sentences** stipulate a minimum and maximum amount of time to be served in prison—one to five years, three to ten years, twenty years to life, and so on. At the time of sentencing, the offender knows the range of the sentence and knows that parole is a possibility after the minimum sentence, minus good time, has been served. How long the

person actually remains in prison is determined by the parole authority, based on its assessment of the offender's progress toward rehabilitation.

Because of growing disillusionment with the rehabilitative model and the rise of the concept of deserved punishment, determinate sentences have become more popular. **Determinate sentences** (sometimes called fixed sentences) consist of a specified number of years rather than a range of years. For example, the judge must sentence the defendant to imprisonment for five years, or ten years, or whatever the legislature specifies for a particular offense.

Indeterminate sentence: A sentence that has both a minimum and maximum term of imprisonment, the actual length to be determined by a parole board.

Determinate sentencing: A term of imprisonment, imposed by a judge, that has a specific number of years.

FIGURE 15-2 Changing Sentencing Structures in the United States		
	Most of Twentieth Century	*Since the Mid-1970s*
Legislative responsibility	• Legislators provided wide parameters for possible sentences. • Little guidance provided about who should be placed on probation. • Little guidance offered on how long a prison sentence should be.	Perceiving that judges are unduly lenient, legislatures have adopted sentencing guidelines, mandatory minimums, and three-strike laws (Chapter 16).
Judicial responsibility	• Judges had wide discretion in deciding upon a specific sentence. • Actual sentences imposed could vary significantly from judge to judge.	• Judges' sentencing discretion has been greatly curtailed. • Judges complain that they are unable to shape sentences to real crimes committed by real criminals.
Executive responsibility	Correction officials enjoyed wide discretion in awarding good time and deciding when to place a convict on parole.	• Good time and parole have been abolished or greatly restricted in most jurisdictions. • Prison overcrowding has resulted in even wider discretion for correction officials.

In a perceptive analysis of sentencing policy, Rosett and Cressey (1976) suggest that legislatures are involved in a severity-softening-severity process. Severe criminal laws are passed, on the assumption that the fear of pain will terrorize the citizenry into conformity. However, court officials soften these penalties, because most of the offenders do not fit the criteria the legislatures initially had in mind. Finding that the severe sentences are not being handed out, the legislatures pass even more severe laws, and the process is repeated.

In recent decades there has been considerable rethinking of the purposes of punishment and the sentences created to carry out those purposes. Numerous legislative bodies have enacted major changes in sentencing laws, aiming to reduce the amount of discretion exercised by actors in the other branches of government. A number of states have restricted the carte blanche authority historically granted judges and have also limited (and in some cases abolished) the discretion of parole boards to release prisoners (Griset 1991). Chapter 16 will explore in more detail issues related to mandatory minimums, sentencing guidelines, and the like.

Judicial Sentencing Responsibility

Only judges have the authority to choose among the sentencing options provided by the legislature. Other members of the work group may recom-

mend, but only the judge can decide. Of course, there are some minor exceptions to this general proposition. A few jurisdictions allow an appeal of the sentence. In capital punishment cases, only the jury can decide whether to impose the death penalty. In addition, a few states provide for jury-determined sentences for certain types of crimes. These minor exceptions aside, American judges traditionally have enjoyed virtually unlimited judicial sentencing responsibility.

Wide judicial discretion in sentencing reflected the rehabilitative model, which stressed that punishment should fit the criminal. No two crimes or criminals are exactly alike; sentences should therefore be individualized, with judges taking these differences into account. But there is no agreement on what factors should increase the penalty or reduce it.

By the mid-1970s wide judicial discretion came under attack from both ends of the political spectrum. Advocates of the due process model of criminal justice expressed concern that judicial sentencing discretion is too vast, resulting in inequities like racial discrimination (Frankel 1972). Conversely, proponents of the crime control model expressed concern that too much judicial discretion led to unduly lenient sentences. These twin political movements, although contradictory, led legislatures to greatly reduce judicial sentencing discretion. Thus, an increasing number of jurisdictions are narrowing judicial discretion over sentencing in some manner (Bureau of Justice Statistics 1998).

Visit these Web sites:

Georgia Board of Pardons and Paroles: **http:// www.pap.state.ga.us/**

Missouri Board of Probation and Parole: **http:// www.corrections.state.mo.us/division/prob/ prob.htm**

U.S. Parole Commission: **http://www.usdoj.gov/ uspc/**

Pennsylvania Board of Probation and Parole: **http:// www.pbpp.state.pa.us/**

South Carolina Department of Probation, Parole, and Pardon Services: **http://www.state.sc.us/ppp/**

For an up-to-date list of Web links, go to **http:// www.wadsworth.com/product/0534563406s**.

Executive Sentencing Responsibility

Most sentences imposed by judges are actually carried out by officials of the executive branch. Collecting fines is the responsibility of the judiciary, but sentences of probation or prison are generally part of executive sentencing responsibility. The decisions made by governors, parole boards, and departments of corrections play a major role in sentencing.

Few prisoners serve their maximum terms of imprisonment. Each year over 700,000 inmates are released from prison to serve the remainder of their sentences in the community. Indeed, only one out of five of these prisoners is released because his or her sentence has expired; the vast majority are released after serving only a part of the prison term imposed by the judge (Bureau of Justice Statistics 1998). These prisoners are often released conditionally; that is, they are subject to supervision. The criteria for early release are established and administered by correctional officials. The most common forms of early release are parole, good time, and (to a lesser extent) executive clemency.

Parole is the conditional release of an inmate from incarceration, under supervision, after a portion of the prison sentence has been served. A parole officer supervises the conditions of release, and any rule violations or new crimes can result in a return

to prison for the balance of the unexpired term. **Parole boards**, which are usually appointed by the governor, vary greatly in their discretionary authority. Nearly 713,000 persons are on parole (Bureau of Justice Statistics 2001).

There is another way in which decisions made by the executive branch affect how long an inmate must stay in prison. In most states prisoners are awarded **good time**—days off their minimum or maximum terms for good behavior or participation in various vocational, educational, and treatment programs. The amount of good time that can be earned varies from five days a month to forty-five days a month in some states. Correctional officials find these sentence-reduction provisions necessary for the maintenance of institutional order and as a mechanism to reduce overcrowding. They usually have discretion in awarding good time.

State governors, as well as the President of the United States, have the power to pardon any prisoner in their jurisdiction, reduce the sentence, or make the prisoner eligible for parole (Moore 1989; Ruckman 1997). **Pardons** are not a common method of prisoner release, however; only a small group of inmates receive executive clemency each year.

How long an offender will be imprisoned depends not only on the length of the sentence imposed by the judge but also on the criteria parole boards use in granting a conditional release and on the way correctional officials compute good time. In a fragmented criminal justice system, such executive powers are clearly necessary. Based on experience with the offender and other information, parole and correctional officials may be in a better position than the sentencing judge to know when the inmate is ready for release. These powers also allow the executive to mute sentencing disparities.

The use of these powers is being questioned today. Prisoners and ex-prisoners are strong critics of

---

Parole board: An administrative body whose members are chosen by the governor to review the cases of prisoners eligible for release on parole. The board has the authority to release such persons and to return them to prison for violating the conditions of parole.

Good time: A reduction of the time served in prison as a reward for not violating prison rules.

Pardon: An act of executive clemency that has the effect of releasing an inmate from prison and/or removing certain legal disabilities from persons convicted of crimes.

Parole: Early release from prison on the condition of good behavior.

The Karla Faye Tucker Story

The Law versus the Lord

Karla Faye Tucker faces execution in Texas for a brutal double murder fourteen years ago. While in prison she had a religious conversion and now is remorseful. Religious groups argue her life should be spared while one of the victims advocates her death. Should her life be spared? As you watch the video, ask yourself the following questions:

1. How do the four major sentencing philosophies—retribution, incapacitation, deterrence, and rehabilitation—apply in this case?

2. Is there a double standard in the United States about executing women versus men? How does the discussion in the text of discrimination and gender (Chapter 16) apply to arguments about executing Karla Faye Tucker?

3. The double murder received extensive publicity and the appeal for mercy widespread media coverage. How does this media attention help or hurt Karla Faye Tucker? Would the jury have been as likely to impose the death penalty if the case had not received such extensive coverage? Would the push for mercy have been more or less successful without the extensive media scrutiny?

4. Texas is the lethal injection capital of the United States. Would a jury in another state have been as likely to impose the death penalty in a case like this? Would a commutation of the death sentence have been more likely in another state?

good behavior or program participation. In the majority of jurisdictions, parole boards have discretionary authority to release prisoners after they have served a fraction of the sentence—often one third. Nearly all states have legislative statutes defining general criteria for parole release. However, in some states, the District of Columbia, and the federal system, the discretion of the parole board to release prisoners is limited by explicit parole guidelines enacted by the legislature or voluntarily adopted by parole boards.

Despite efforts to reduce the use of parole and curb the power of parole boards, burgeoning prison populations increasingly force correctional officials to use parole as a backdoor solution to prison overcrowding (Kelly and Ekland-Olson 1991). Thus, nationwide there has been a dramatic increase in the number of persons under parole supervision.

 The details of sentencing structure vary in important ways from jurisdiction to jurisdiction. To determine the sentencing structure in your state, examine the Bureau of Justice Statistics Report, *1996 National Survey of State Sentencing Structures,* available online at **http://www.ncjrs.org/courdocs.htm#169270**.

For an up-to-date list of Web links, go to **http://www.wadsworth.com/product/0534563406s**.

extensive parole authority, because the prisoners cannot predict when they will be released. A convict may be denied parole after only a brief hearing. Moreover, because release is tied to rehabilitation, prisoners can deceive parole and prison officials. Some may attend church on Sunday or enroll in rehabilitation programs during the week not out of any desire to change but to gain an early release.

This questioning of parole boards' authority has led to significant changes in some jurisdictions in recent years. The fourteen states that have adopted determinate sentencing generally do not allow discretionary release by parole boards. Inmates are released from prison when they have served their original sentence, minus time off for

WHAT SENTENCE SHOULD BE IMPOSED?

What types of sentences should be imposed upon the guilty? Today, answers center on prison and probation, with a hot debate over the death penalty. But throughout history sentences were very different. Flogging, the stocks, exile, chopping off a hand, and branding are just a few examples of punishments historically inflicted on the guilty. Today such sanctions are viewed as violating the Constitution's prohibition against cruel and unusual punishment. In their place, we use imprisonment, probation, intermediate sanctions, fines, and restitution. Many states also make formal provisions for capital punishment, but the death penalty is rarely used. In essence, these forms of punishment are tools created under the sentencing structure to advance society's theories of punishment. They are the

FIGURE 15-3	Sentencing Options

	Law on the Books	*Law in Action*
Prison	A correctional facility for housing adults convicted of felony offenses, usually under the control of state government.	• Almost 1.4 million adults are in prison. • Six percent of inmates are female. • Forty-five percent of prison inmates are black.
Parole	Adults conditionally released to community supervision after serving part of a prison term. The parolee is subject to being returned to prison for rule violations or other offenses.	• Over 700,000 are on parole from state or federal prison. • Twelve percent of parolees are women. • Fifty-three percent of parolees are white.
Probation	Punishment for a crime that allows the offender to remain in the community without incarceration but subject to certain conditions.	• Over 3,775,000 adults are under federal, state, or local jurisdiction on probation. • Half of all offenders on probation are on probation for a felony.
Intermediate sanctions	A variety of punishments that are more restrictive than traditional probation but less stringent than incarceration.	• Much less costly than imprisonment. • Community service requires offender to perform public service such as street cleaning or hospital volunteer work.
Fines	A sum of money to be paid to the government by a convicted person as punishment for an offense.	• Often used in misdemeanors. • Recent research shows that it can be effectively used in select felonies.
Restitution	Requirement that the offender pay to the victim a sum of money to make good the loss.	• Most defendants are so poor that they cannot reasonably be expected to make restitution.
Capital punishment	The use of the death penalty (execution) as the punishment for the commission of a particular crime.	• Over 3,450 prisoners are on death row. • Sixty-eight executions during 1998. • Fifty-five percent of death row inmates are white.

options from which the sentencing judge must choose (see Figure 15-3).

One can approach the question of which penalty should be imposed upon the guilty from either a micro or macro perspective. The micro perspective focuses on a specific defendant convicted of a crime. It is from this perspective that victims often view sentencing, and from this vantage point they are often critical of the judge's (or sometimes the legislature's) choice, arguing that the sentence is too lenient. It is vitally important, however, to assess such criticisms from a macro perspective. From this vantage point, prisons are already overcrowded, the caseloads of probation officers overwhelming. It is for this reason that judges occasionally address crime victims and explain the painfully obvious—to send this defendant to prison will require correc-

tional officials to release someone who is possibly an even greater threat to the community.

A thoughtful crime policy requires balancing the micro and macro perspectives. Alas, such balancing is not only difficult in the abstract but must be attempted in a highly emotional setting. The next chapter will examine how the courtroom work group decides on the specific penalty for a convict. For now we will examine the various options available, beginning with that most distinctly American invention, the prison.

 For the most up-to-date statistics on corrections, go to **http://www.ojp.usdoj.gov/bjs/correct.htm**.

For an up-to-date list of Web links, go to **http://www.wadsworth.com/product/0534563406s**.

IMPRISONMENT

Although it was used from time to time throughout history, **imprisonment** (incarceration) has become the dominant form of punishment only during the last two centuries. The United States imprisons a larger share of its population than any other nation. More than 2 million inmates are currently housed in prisons and jails. One reason for this high rate of imprisonment is the length of sentences; prison sentences in the United States are quite long compared to those imposed in Europe, where it is rare for a defendant to be sentenced to more than five years.

 For a sense of what it is like to be a prisoner, go to The Black People's Prison Survival Guide: **http://www. cs.oberlin.edu/students/pjaques/etext/ prison-guide.html**.

See also Prison Life Inside the California Department of Corrections: **http://www.inmate.com/inmates/ davidcdc.htm**.

For an up-to-date list of Web links, go to **http:// www.wadsworth.com/product/0534563406s**.

Prison Overcrowding

The political rhetoric of getting tough on criminals (Chapter 1) clearly has had an impact—prisons are filled to overflowing (Rhodes 1990). Prison overcrowding has become the dominant reality of criminal justice policy. Figure 15-4 shows how the size of the prison population has skyrocketed in recent years, more than tripling from the 1970s to the 1990s. And the trend continues; every year record-high levels of prisoners are reported, with increases averaging from 8 percent to 12 percent. It is worth noting that skyrocketing prison populations occurred during a period when crime rates (Chapter 10) were largely constant and now are falling (Arvanites 1992).

Conditions of Confinement Lawsuits

Numbers of prisoners provide only part of the picture. Rapid increases in the size of the prison population occurred during the same time that federal courts began to demand improvements in prison conditions. Prison conditions have often been described as substandard. Although a few prisons resemble college campuses, many are old and run-down. Overcrowding results in inadequate security for inmates, with assaults and homosexual rapes a constant part of prison life.

Traditionally, courts followed a hands-off policy regarding prisons, choosing not to interfere in their internal administration. But this policy began to change in 1964 when the Supreme Court held that prison wardens could be sued civilly in federal courts (*Cooper v. Pate*, 1964). By the 1970s the federal courts began to scrutinize the operations of correctional institutions to ensure compliance with the Eighth Amendment's protection against cruel and unusual punishment (DiIulio 1990). Prisoners have sued, in what are often termed **conditions of confinement lawsuits**, contending that state officials have deprived them of their constitutional rights, such as adequate medical treatment, protection against excessive force by correctional officers, violence by other inmates, due process in disciplinary hearings, and access to law libraries (Hanson and Daley 1995). Figure 15-5 summarizes key developments in the law concerning imprisonment.

The entire prison systems of at least nine states have been declared unconstitutional. Individual prisons have been found constitutionally defective in many others. Similar litigation concerning prison conditions and overcrowding is pending in other states as well. The net effect was that for many years most states operated all or part of their correctional systems under a federal court order, which usually specifies a maximum prison population, requires physical conditions to be upgraded, increases the number of prison guards, upgrades the quality of the food, and mandates minimal medical facilities. In the last two decades, federal judges in virtually all states have ordered state governments to alter dramatically the way in which they operate their prisons and jails (Chilton 1991; Crouch and Marquart 1990; Taggart 1989). These federal court orders have had a significant effect on transforming prison conditions, particularly in the South (Feeley and Rubin 1998).

Imprisonment: Placing a person in a prison, jail, or similar correctional facility as punishment for committing a crime.

Conditions of confinement lawsuit: Lawsuit brought by a prisoner contesting prison conditions.

FIGURE 15-4 Growing Prison Population

SOURCE: Bureau of Justice Statistics, U.S. Department of Justice, *Prisoners in 1999* (Washington, D.C.: U.S. Government Printing Office, 2000).

FIGURE 15-5 Key Developments Concerning Imprisonment

Eighth Amendment	1791	Excessive bail shall not be required, nor excessive fines imposed, nor cruel and unusual punishments inflicted.
Cooper v. Pate	1964	Prisoners can sue prison officials in federal court.
Ruiz v. Estelle	1980	U.S. District Court declares that conditions of confinement in the Texas prison system are unconstitutional.
Estelle v. Gamble	1976	Deliberate indifference to serious medical needs of prisoners constitutes the unnecessary and wanton infliction of pain, and thus violates the Eighth Amendment.
Rhodes v. Chapman	1981	Double-celling and crowding do not necessarily constitute cruel and unusual punishment.
Whitley v. Albers	1986	A prisoner shot in the leg during a riot does not suffer cruel and unusual punishment if the action was taken in good faith to maintain discipline rather than for the mere purpose of causing harm.
Wilson v. Seiter	1991	Prisoners contesting conditions of confinement in federal court must show that prison officials acted with "deliberate indifference" to prisoner needs and living conditions.
Prison Litigation Reform Act	1996	Relief granted to state prisoners must be narrowly drawn and the court must terminate.
Miller v. French	2000	Upheld the Prison Litigation Reform Act, saying Congress could lawfully impose a ninety-day time limit to rule on prison condition lawsuits.

It is now harder to challenge prison conditions in federal court, however. The Rehnquist Court created a new standard under the Eighth Amendment, holding that the prisoner must show a "deliberate indifference" on the part of prison officials (*Wilson v. Seiter,* 1991). And in 1996 Congress passed the Prison Litigation Reform Act, which terminated federal court supervision of state prisons. Nonetheless, state correctional officials are aware that slipping back to old practices will result in future litigation.

 To learn more about prisoners' rights, go to these sites:

> http://www.aclu.org/issues/prisons/
> hmprisons.html
> http://www.wehelpyou.cc/

For an up-to-date list of Web links, go to http://www.wadsworth.com/product/0534563406s.

 For contrasting views on the Prison Litigation Reform Act of 1996, read Sarah Vandenbraak, "PLRA: A Step in the Right Direction" and John Boston, "PLRA Is Not the Answer."

High Costs

Getting tough on criminals is popular, yet public opinion polls show that spending money for more prisons is not a high priority for the general public. Prisons are costly to build and even more costly to maintain. Estimates of the costs of constructing a single cell for a prisoner range from $75,000 to $100,000 (Clear and Cole 2000). The costs of incarcerating a prisoner (clothes, food, and guards, primarily) depend on the level of confinement and also vary from state to state, ranging from $20,000 to $30,000 per prisoner per year. Exhibit 15-2 shows that building a 500-cell prison runs $337,500,000 over thirty years.

Faced with swelling prison populations and federal court orders over conditions of confinement, state legislatures have been faced with spending enormous sums of money to build new prisons and upgrade existing ones. Prison construction during the 1990s was a growth industry, with 213 state and federal prisons built during the first five years at an estimated $30 billion ("In '90s, Prison," 1997). Despite large expenditures, no state has been able to build prisons fast enough to keep ahead of surging prison admissions. On December 31, 1999, state prisons were operating at between 1 percent and 17 percent above capacity, while federal prisons were operating at 32 percent above capacity (Bureau of Justice Statistics 2001).

Some states have declared an emergency situation, thus triggering the early release of certain types of prisoners. Rhode Island, for example, granted ninety days of good time to all prisoners. States that fail to take such action face sanctions from federal judges. Contempt of court, hefty fines, and judicially mandated release of prisoners are some of the remedies federal judges have imposed on state and local officials who have failed to take action to solve prison overcrowding (Clear and Cole 2000).

The long-standing political debate over sentencing has now given way to the overriding reality of a severe shortage of prison cells. State after state is discovering that the political rhetoric of the late twentieth century to get tough on criminals by sending more people to prison for longer periods must give way to the fiscal realities of the twenty-first century—adjusting sentencing policies to fit prison capacity. Almost out of desperation, states are now turning to alternative penalty programs that resemble ideas that were tried and largely discarded a decade ago.

EXHIBIT 15-2 Financial Projections Over Thirty Years for Building a New 500-Cell Prison

	Cells	1-year total	30-year total
Construction costs	500 × $75,000	$37.5 million	$ 37.5 million
Incarceration costs	500 × $20,000	$10.0 million	$300.0 million
Totals		$47.5 million	$337.5 million

THE MURDER TRIAL OF SHAREEF COUSIN

Doing Time on the Farm

On July 2, 1996, Judge Bigelow denied defense motions for a new trial and officially ordered that Shareef Cousin die by lethal injection. Soon after, Cousin was transported to Louisiana's death row, which was featured in the movie *Dead Man Walking*. During 1996, Cousin was one of nine prisoners added to the death row population. One would be executed and another removed following a successful appeal. Altogether, at the end of the year sixty-three men sat on death row awaiting their fate; two-thirds were, like Cousin, black.

After the district attorney decided not to try Cousin a second time for murder, he was returned to the Louisiana State Penitentiary (LSP) at Angola, which is the largest maximum security prison in the United States. It houses some 5,100 men, three-quarters of whom are black and 85 percent of whom will die within its walls.

Angola has been a prison since the end of the Civil War. The penitentiary sits on the site of a plantation that derived its name from the area in Africa that provided the slave labor. The prison is divided into six self-contained units, many of which are called camps. Camp F constitutes death row. Each has its own warden, kitchen, and so on. According to the Louisiana State Penitentiary Museum Web site, "LSP consists of 18,000 acres of the finest farmland in the south. It is ideally situated for the prison as it is located in a rural area, surrounded on three sides by the Mississippi River, and bordered on the fourth side by the rugged Tunica Hills." The location is "ideal" in the sense that it is virtually escape-proof because it is so isolated. But this isolation also symbolizes one of the oldest of American traditions—NIMBY (or Not in My Backyard). The rural area has embraced the prison because it provides employment for 1,517 correctional officers plus a host of medical and support staff. Many of these are third- or fourth-generation employees, some of them living right on the prison grounds.

At Angola, the principal activity is farming. The majority of medium and maximum security inmates work eight hours per day, five days per week, growing corn, soybeans, cotton, and food for the prison. The rural nature of the prison was featured in the 1998 documentary film *The Farm: Angola USA*. It is also famous for its annual prison rodeo held every October. The rural focus of Angola is in stark contrast to its principal inhabitants—inmates from big cities. LSP provides some rehabilitation programs—education and self-help groups, primarily—but these programs are limited.

At one time Angola was one of the most violent in the United States, notorious for beatings, rapes, and murder. In 1973, for example, there were forty prison murders. In 1971 the first lawsuit protesting conditions of confinement was filed. In 1975 the federal courts took over the entire prison system, finding conditions at Angola "shock the conscience of any right-thinking person" and flagrantly violate basic constitutional requirements" (*Williams v. Edwards*). In the words of U.S. District Judge Frank Polozola, who has been overseeing the state prison system since 1973, when he first visited Angola "he couldn't tell the difference between guards and inmates" partly because guards did not wear uniforms and some "trusties" carried guns (Wardlaw 1998). The state has been forced to spend massive amounts of money to improve conditions. Improvement in conditions have been major. For example, inmate murder is now a rarity. Finally in 1999 the federal court order was dissolved. Although Louisiana is now in full control of its adult prison system, there is still the possibility that, if the state backslides, a new round of federal litigation would begin.

After the murder charges were dismissed, Shareef Cousin returned to Angola, this time in the general population. He later was transferred to the Washington Correctional Institute, another Louisiana prison. In the fall of 2000 a phone call to his lawyer in the federal civil rights lawsuit (see Chapter 3) was apparently misrouted. Guards overheard his conversation, which indicated he had committed theft, and he was placed in administrative segregation. He then filed a prisoner petition in federal court contending that his right to counsel was violated. According to his handwritten petition, he is prisoner #363553 in Sleet 4, 4s cell #8. Check the Web site for future developments.

 For some views of life inside Angola, go to:

The Louisiana State Penitentiary Museum: **http://www.angolamuseum.org/**

"Fixin' to Die": The Louisiana Prison Hospice: **http://www.npha.org/fixin.html**

Prison art by Kevin Seward, inmate at Louisiana State Prison: **http://prisonart.virtualave.net/**

For an up-to-date list of Web links, go to **http://www.wadsworth.com/product/0534563406s.**

Watch the SuperMax prison in Wisconsin being built: **http://supermax.jobsight.net/public/sitepic.stm**.

For an up-to-date list of Web links, go to **http://www.wadsworth.com/product/0534563406s**.

PROBATION

Probation is the primary alternative to imprisonment. It is also the most commonly used sanction in the United States; about four times as many offenders are placed on probation every year as are sent to prison. Altogether, almost 3.8 million adults are on probation, a number that represents a doubling during the last decade. The increasing use of probation is a direct reflection of the serious problem of prison overcrowding. Ironically, it has resulted in a significant amount of "probation crowding" (overload of the probation system equivalent to prison overcrowding) (Byrne, Lurigio, and Baird 1989). Figure 15-6 shows that probation crowding is rising more dramatically than prison overcrowding. As a result, probation officers often must handle excessive caseloads.

Unlike incarceration, **probation** is designed as a means of maintaining control over offenders while permitting them to live in the community (under supervision). The practice of probation initially evolved from the efforts of judges to lessen the excessively harsh penalties of the common law by suspending sentences. It was not until the early twentieth century that the probation movement gained real momentum as a social reform, and by 1920 it had become widely accepted (McCarthy and McCarthy 2001). Today the major justification is that prisons are inappropriate places for some defendants, and limited supervision is a better way to rehabilitate criminals. Youthful or first-time offenders may only become embittered if mixed in prison with hardened criminals; they may end up learning more sophisticated criminal techniques. But most important, probation is significantly less expensive than imprisonment.

State and federal laws grant judges wide discretion in deciding whether to place a defendant on probation. Generally, statutes allow probation when it appears that

1. the defendant is not likely to commit another offense;
2. the public interest does not require that the defendant receive the penalty provided for the offense; and
3. the rehabilitation of the defendant does not require that he or she receive the penalty provided for the offense.

Legislative provisions regarding who may be placed on probation vary considerably from state to state. Some states have statutes prohibiting certain types of offenders—typically rapists and other violent offenders—from receiving probation.

Often the sentencing judge imposes a prison sentence but then suspends its execution and places the offender on probation instead. A sentence of probation is often used in conjunction with some other form of nonprison sanction, such as a fine, restitution, or required attendance at a drug or alcohol rehabilitation center.

Offenders placed on probation must agree to abide by certain rules and regulations prescribed by the sentencing judge. Termed conditions of probation, these rules typically include keeping a job, supporting the family, avoiding places where alcoholic beverages are sold, reporting periodically to the probation officer (Chapter 16), and not violating any law. Because probation is a judicial act, the judge can revoke probation and send the defendant to prison if the conditions of probation are violated.

One topic of particular interest is the effectiveness of probation. Some studies report high rates of recidivism (the repetition of criminal behavior) among probationers. One federal study, for example, found an alarmingly high rate of recidivism—43 percent among probationers (Langan and Cunniff 1992). Such high failure rates seem to suggest limited or cautious use of probation for felons. But these conclusions concerning rampant recidivism have been challenged by other studies that report much lower rates of recidivism—the imprisonment rate in New Jersey, for example, is 9 percent, which closely resembles Kentucky and Missouri. These findings suggest that for some felony offenders probation is not an unreasonable option, especially for drug offenders, who tend to have low rates of recidivism (Whitehead 1991).

Probation: Punishment for a crime that allows the offender to remain in the community without incarceration but subject to certain conditions.

Mario A. Paparozzi, "Reinventing Probation from the Top Down"

FIGURE 15-6 Growth in Probation Population

SOURCE: Bureau of Justice Statistics, *Correctional Populations in United States, 1997* (Washington, D.C.: U.S. Department of Justice, 1999).

INTERMEDIATE SANCTIONS

There is growing concern that the United States relies much too heavily on imprisonment and probation. Prison is viewed as too harsh (as well as unavailable) for many defendants, while probation is really unsupervised. Alternative sentences that lie somewhere between prison and probation are often referred to as **intermediate sanctions.** Intermediate sanctions begin with probation with limited supervision, move along a continuum of intrusiveness and control, and end with penal incarceration. Punishments of this type include community-based penalties such as substantial fines, community service, restitution, intensive probation, electronic monitoring, house arrests, shock incarceration, boot camp, and treatment (Morris and Tonry 1990; Parent et al. 1997).

Intensive supervised probation (ISP) is one commonly used intermediate sanction. Routine probation typically involves minimal supervision and is designed for low-risk defendants. But prison overcrowding means that probation increasingly deals with persons convicted of felonies, who are a higher risk. ISP may involve once-a-day meetings between probation officers and offenders, closer monitoring of the offender's activities, and rehabilitation- and work-related efforts. Although ISP has been called the most promising criminal justice innovation in decades, evaluations find mixed results. "The ambiguous results of these programs indicate that assumptions about the ability of ISPs to produce practical results—relieve prison crowding, lower costs, and control crime—may not have been well-founded. . . . It appears not that the ISPs themselves have failed, but that the objectives set for them may be overly ambitious, raising expectations they have been unable to meet" (Petersilia and Turner 1993). The issue of costs provides a good example. Although ISP is designed to reduce costs, intensive supervision can mean increased probation failure rates, which translates into more offenders being placed in costly prison cells (Clear and Cole 2000).

 Cheryl Crawford, Vincent Talucci, "Partnerships for Public Safety"

FINES

The imposition of a **fine** is one of the oldest and also one of the most widely used forms of punishment.

Intermediate sanctions: Variety of sanctions that lie somewhere between prison and probation.

Fine: A sum of money to be paid to the state by a convicted person as punishment for an offense.

CRIME & PUNISHMENT

The State of Illinois v. Stephanie Caneelly

Stephanie Caneelly was observed by an undercover police officer putting on clothes in Bloomingdale's department store and walking out without paying. She has been charged with grand theft because the value of the merchandise was more than $250. After watching the CD, you should be able to answer the following questions:

1. Sentencing reflects four dominant philosophies: retribution, incapacitation, deterrence, and rehabilitation. Which philosophy is most applicable in this case? Which is least applicable?
2. The defendant doesn't make a statement on her own behalf. Does this influence the sentence imposed?
3. No victim is present. As a sentencing judge, does this influence your decision?
4. How realistic is the prosecutor's recommendation of four years in prison? After all, the case does not involve violence, and the defendant has only one prior conviction for a minor offense.
5. How realistic is the defense offer of restitution? Stephanie Caneelly is earning a little above the minimum wage and has four children and a husband to support.
6. In imposing sentence, should the gender of the defendant matter? Is this the type of case in which a woman might be sentenced more leniently than a man committing the same offense?

Fines are used extensively for traffic offenses and minor ordinance violations, generating well over $1 billion annually for local governments. Judges in the lower courts impose a fine alone or in combination with other sanctions in about 86 percent of their cases. But the imposition of fines is not confined to the lower courts. In the major trial courts, a fine, either alone or together with other sanctions, is imposed in almost 45 percent of the cases. First offenders with a known ability to pay are most likely to be sentenced in this way (Cole et al. 1988).

The limited use of fines as punishment in felony cases contrasts sharply with practices in some Western European countries. Some countries have adopted sentencing policies that explicitly make fines the sentence of choice for many offenses, including some crimes of violence that would result in jail sentences in many American courts. In Germany, for example, a major legislative goal is to minimize the imposition of jail terms of less than six months. Instead, German courts make extensive use of "day fines," which enable judges to set fines at amounts reflecting the gravity of the offense but also taking into account the financial means of the offender (Hillsman and Mahoney 1988). In the United States the day fine concept has been relabeled "structured fines" and is being recommended as a less costly sentencing option than imprisonment (Bureau of Justice Statistics 1996).

American judges frequently cite the poverty of offenders as an obstacle to the broader use of fines as sanctions (Gillespie 1988–1989). Nonetheless, some courts regularly impose fines on persons whose financial resources are extremely limited and are successful in collecting those fines. Recent research suggests that fines can be collected. Performance can be improved substantially if administrators systematically apply collection and enforcement techniques that already exist and have been proven effective (Hillsman and Mahoney 1988; Cole 1992). Moreover, skepticism about the use of fines is beginning to erode; in Maricopa County (Phoenix), Arizona, for example, the day fine program was successful in diverting offenders from routine supervision probation and in encouraging greater financial payments while maintaining public safety (Turner and Greene 1999).

RESTITUTION

Restitution is the requirement that the offender provide reparation to the victim for the harm caused by the criminal offense. Requiring defendants to compensate victims (giving something back) for their losses was customary in ancient civilizations, particularly for the people in the time of the Old Testament. But as the government replaced the victim as the principal party in the criminal prosecution, restitution fell into decline; offenders paid fines to the government rather than restitution to the victim (Tobolowsky 1993). Beginning in the mid-1960s, the idea of **restitution** became the focus of renewed

Restitution: To restore or to make good on something; for example, to return or pay for a stolen item.

interest and is now being touted as one of the criminal justice system's more creative responses to crime (McCarthy and McCarthy 2001). Nearly all states have enacted laws providing for the collection and distribution of restitution funds. Restitution efforts generally take one of two forms—direct or symbolic (Galaway 1988).

In **direct restitution**, the offender is required, as a condition of probation, to make monetary payments to the victim. As a criminal sanction, it is largely restricted to property crimes, since it has little relevance if violence figured in the commission of the offense. Although direct restitution has many supporters, some are concerned that if it is used as the sole sanction, it could allow some offenders to purchase a relatively mild punishment. As a practical matter, however, the typical property offender lacks the financial resources to compensate the victim. As we saw in Chapter 9, the 1996 Congressional Act requires the federal court to impose mandatory restitution, without consideration of the defendant's ability to pay. Thus, there is a danger that court-imposed restitution can only increase victim dissatisfaction when the offender doesn't pay. Nonetheless, close program monitoring of offenders, coupled with greater program attention to victims, can increase offenders' compliance with restitution orders (Davis and Bannister 1995).

In **symbolic restitution**, the offender makes reparation for the harm done in the form of good works benefiting the entire community rather than the particular individual harmed. Such work is often called community service. The offender is required to perform a specified number of hours of public service work, such as collecting trash in parks or working in a social service agency. This sanction is most often used when there is no direct victim of the offense—for example, in convictions for drunk driving.

 Visit the Restitution Help Line: **http://www.link.ca/ ~chelsom/resthelp.html**.

For an up-to-date list of Web links, go to **http:// www.wadsworth.com/product/0534563406s**.

Direct restitution: The defendant pays money directly to the victim of the crime.

Symbolic restitution: The defendant performs community service.

THE DEATH PENALTY

Of all the forms of punishment, the **death penalty** is by far the most controversial, but it is also the least used; only a handful of offenders potentially face the ultimate sanction society can impose on the guilty.

Capital punishment was once almost the only penalty applied to convicted felons. By the time of the American Revolution, the English courts had defined over 200 felonies, all of which were **capital offenses.** However, many death penalties were not carried out; instead, offenders were pardoned or banished to penal colonies. Over time, courts and legislatures began to recognize other forms of punishment, such as imprisonment and probation. By 1970, all but nine U.S. jurisdictions provided for the death penalty, but its imposition was limited to murder, treason, and (largely in the South) rape.

Throughout the twentieth century, the number of executions fell steadily (Figure 15-7). Between 1930 and 1967, nearly 3,800 persons were put to death. During the peak years of 1935 and 1936, nearly 200 executions occurred each year. But executions declined substantially every year thereafter; they averaged only twenty-one per year between 1960 and 1967. From 1967 to 1972, an unofficial moratorium on executions existed. Since 1976, the highest number of executions in any one year was seventy-four.

Abolition of the death penalty has been a hot political issue. Opponents contend that it is morally wrong for the state to take a life, it has no deterrent value and is inherently discriminatory. These arguments have led all Western democracies except the United States to abolish the death penalty. Supporters counter that retribution justifies the taking of a life and that the death penalty does deter; they are generally unconcerned or unconvinced about allegations of discriminatory impact. (See Controversy: Should a Moratorium on the Death Penalty Be

Death penalty: Capital punishment, or executions by the state for purposes of social defense. *Gregg v. Georgia,* 1976, upheld constitutionality of rewritten state capital punishment laws struck down by *Furman v. Georgia,* 1972.

Capital punishment: Use of the death penalty as the punishment for the commission of a particular crime.

Capital offense: Any crime punishable by death.

FIGURE 15-7 Persons Executed in the United States, 1930–1999

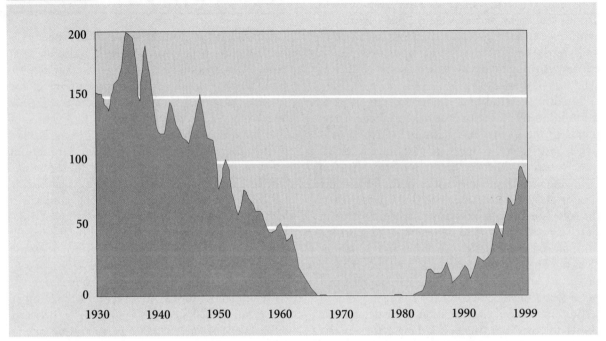

SOURCE: Tracy Snell, *Capital Punishment 1998* (Washington, D.C.: Bureau of Justice Statistics, U.S. Department of Justice, 2000).

Imposed?) For the last several decades, the debate over the death penalty has largely focused on Supreme Court decisions.

Look at Texas Death Row Statistics: **http://www.tdcj.state.tx.us/statistics/stats-home.htm**.

Read the Death Row Book: **http://www.editionnine. deathrowbook.com/deathrow.htm**.

For an up-to-date list of Web links, go to **http://www.wadsworth.com/product/0534563406s**.

Eighth Amendment Standards

Is capital punishment consistent with the Eighth Amendment's prohibition against **cruel and unusual punishment**? The Supreme Court first addressed this question in its 1972 landmark decision in *Furman v. Georgia*, which invalidated all thirty-seven state death penalty statutes (see Case Close-Up: *Fur-*

man v. Georgia and Cruel and Unusual Punishment on page 406). The Court was deeply divided, however, with every justice writing a separate opinion.

Furman v. Georgia raised more questions than it answered and state legislatures attempted to write new capital punishment laws consistent with the Eighth Amendment. By 1976, thirty-seven states had enacted new legislation designed to avoid the arbitrary application of capital punishment. These laws took two forms. Some states passed mandatory death penalty laws, which removed all discretion from the process by requiring that anyone convicted of a capital offense be sentenced to death. Other states enacted guided discretion statutes, which required judges and juries to weigh various aggravating and mitigating circumstances in deciding whether or not a particular defendant should receive the death penalty (Blankenship et al. 1997).

These new laws were tested in a series of five companion cases, collectively known as the death

Cruel and unusual punishment: Punishment, by the government, that is prohibited by the Eighth Amendment.

Furman v. Georgia: Supreme Court ruling that statutes leaving arbitrary and discriminatory discretion to juries in imposing death sentences are in violation of the Eighth Amendment.

CONTROVERSY

Should a Moratorium on the Death Penalty Be Imposed?

Anthony Porter was two days away from dying by lethal injection when the Illinois Supreme Court intervened holding that his IQ of 51 dictated that his mental competency be examined. Northwestern University Professor David Protess and his journalism students delved into Porter's case and found that he had not committed the pair of 1982 murders (McCormick 1999). Another suspect later confessed.

In the wake of the Porter case, Illinois Governor George Ryan, a Republican, declared a temporary halt to executions in his state. In his words: "I now favor a moratorium, because I have grave concerns about our state's shameful record of convicting innocent people and putting them on death row." Illinois had already freed thirteen death row prisoners because DNA evidence, witnesses who recanted, or independent investigations showed their innocence. Moreover, according to the *Chicago Tribune*, thirty-three death row inmates were defended by attorneys who were later disbarred or suspended and forty-six convictions were obtained through questionable testimony of jailhouse informants (Stern 2000).

Over the last several years different groups, most notably the American Bar Association, have called for moratoriums on the death penalty. Illinois, however, has been the only state to actually implement a moratorium. Indeed, governors in other states showed little inclination to follow the lead of the Land of Lincoln.

The focus on innocents on death row represents the latest round in a long-running debate over the death penalty. Not surprisingly there are profound ideological differences on the three central issues in the death penalty debate: morality, deterrence, and fairness (Chapter 17). To advocates of the due process model of criminal justice, the death penalty is immoral because the state should not take a life. To proponents of the crime control model the death penalty is moral because the defendant has already taken a life. To advocates of the due process model, the death penalty is not a deterrent because many of those who commit murder are incapable of rational

calculations. To proponents of the crime control model the death penalty is a deterrent because some who might murder refrain from doing so because they know they might themselves die.

To advocates of the due process model the death penalty is unfairly administered. They stress that racial minorities are more likely than whites to be executed (Chapter 16). They also believe that too many people on death row are innocent or their trials involved procedural irregularities (Chapter 17). To this the proponents of the crime control model respond that the fairness of the death penalty is unimportant or unproven. They believe that blacks are no more likely to be executed than whites. They also argue that the review process works because appeals have freed the few innocents who were wrongfully convicted.

What do you think? Of the three main issues in the death penalty debate—morality, deterrence, and fairness—which provides the best argument for abolishing the death penalty? Which one offers the best grounds for keeping the death penalty? Do you think that the issue of innocents on death row justifies a moratorium on the death penalty?

To continue the debate, point your browser to these sites:

Pro Death Penalty: **http:// www.prodeathpenalty.com**

Campaign to End the Death Penalty: **http:// www.ncadp.org/**

For an up-to-date list of Web links, go to **http:// www.wadsworth.com/product/0534563406s**.

Will Manning, Jacqueline Rhoden-Trader, "Rethinking the Death Penalty"

William Tucker, "The Chair Deters"

Carl M. Cannon, "The Problem with the Chair"

penalty cases (***Gregg v. Georgia***, 1976). Again, the Court was badly divided, but a seven-justice majority agreed that the death penalty did not constitute cruel and unusual punishment under all circumstances. Next, the Court considered under what circumstances the death penalty was unconstitutional.

Gregg v. Georgia: Supreme Court ruling that (1) the death penalty is not, in itself, cruel and unusual punishment, and (2) a two-part proceeding—one for the determination of innocence or guilt and the other for determination of the sentence—is constitutional and meets the objections noted in *Furman v. Georgia*.

CASE CLOSE-UP

Furman v. Georgia and Cruel and Unusual Punishment

William Furman, a seventh-grade dropout, was twenty-six at the time he broke into William Micke's home and accidentally killed him. Prior to trial, Furman was committed to the Georgia Central State Hospital for a psychiatric examination. The unanimous conclusion of the hospital staff was that William Furman had a mild to moderate mental deficiency, with psychotic episodes associated with convulsive disorder, and was legally insane. After several months of psychiatric treatment, the hospital determined that Furman was still mentally ill but that he now knew the difference between right and wrong (Georgia's insanity test) and was also able to cooperate with his counsel. Furman was convicted of murder and sentenced to death. The U.S. Supreme Court consolidated Furman's appeal with three others. These four cases had little in common except that all the victims were white, all the defendants were black, and all four had been sentenced to death following conviction (Meltsner 1973).

The Legal Defense Fund of the NAACP represented many of these death row inmates, Furman included. Initially the Legal Defense Fund (LDF for short) had concentrated on achieving integration, winning the monumental school desegregation case of *Brown v. Board of Education.* But by the early 1960s the LDF expanded its activities to include representing Southern blacks on death row. To the NAACP the imposition of the death penalty was racially moti-

vated. By 1971 they had won some important procedural battles, but these issues were quickly drying up. Somewhat unexpectedly, the Court decided in *Furman* to consider directly whether the death penalty was consistent with the Eighth Amendment.

Briefs supporting abolition of the death penalty were filed by a broad array of groups, including a group of governors, prison officials, religious leaders, and the American Civil Liberties Union. Surprisingly, support for the death penalty was thin. Besides answering briefs filed by the attorney generals of the three affected states—Georgia, Texas, and California—few groups filed in support of the death penalty.

An unexpected development led to the postponement of oral argument. In September 1971, Justices Hugo Black and John Harlan resigned from the Supreme Court for health reasons. The resignations meant that for the first time in thirty years an American president would have two Supreme Court vacancies to fill at the same time. President Nixon eventually chose Justices Lewis Powell and William Rehnquist (Chapter 17).

Thus, it wasn't until January 1972, that the death penalty cases were actually argued. The Court clearly signaled the importance of the issue by allotting a full four hours for oral argument. The lawyers argued over what the somewhat archaic eighteenth-century phrase "cruel and unusual punishment" meant in the twentieth century. To Stanford Law Professor Tony

---

Mandatory death penalty laws were struck down because they failed to focus on the circumstances of the case. Thus, the death penalty provisions in twenty-one states were invalidated; the death sentences imposed on hundreds of offenders in those states were modified to life imprisonment. Guided discretion death penalty laws, on the other hand, were upheld: "The concerns expressed in *Furman* that the penalty of death not be imposed in an arbitrary or capricious manner can be met by a carefully drafted statute that ensures that the sentencing authority is given adequate information and guidance."

For a death penalty law to be constitutional, the high court ruled, it must provide for a bifurcated process. During the first, or guilt, phase of the trial, the jury considers only the issue of guilt or innocence. If the jury unanimously convicts for a crime

carrying the death penalty, then the jury reconvenes. During the second, or penalty, phase of the trial, the jury considers aggravating and mitigating circumstances and then decides whether to impose the death penalty. If the death penalty is not imposed, the defendant is usually sentenced to life imprisonment. (See Figure 15-8 on page 408.)

Contemporary Death Penalty Laws

Many state legislatures, citing public opinion polls showing that a majority of citizens favor the death penalty for murder, quickly revised their laws to conform with those upheld in the death penalty cases. Today, thirty-eight states and the federal government (covering roughly 90 percent of the nation's population) have death penalty laws on the books. All death penalty laws encompass murder. The death penalty

Amsterdam (representing the LDF), the standard should be whether a punishment, if evenhandedly applied, would be unacceptable to contemporary standards of decency. University of Texas Law School Professor Charles Alan Wright (representing the state of Texas) set out to refute Professor Amsterdam, arguing that executing only one out of a hundred rapists did not violate the Eighth Amendment. After hearing four hours of arguments from a variety of lawyers, the Court took the case under advisement, providing no hint when or how it would decide.

Shortly after ten o'clock on the morning of June 29, 1972, the last day of the term, the nine justices took their seats behind the bench, and the crowd fell silent awaiting decisions in several important cases. The first was *Furman*. Lawyers for the LDF were elated; all state death penalty laws were struck down. But as they began to read the opinion itself, their initial elation gave way to anxiety. Like the American public, the justices of the Supreme Court proved to be deeply divided over who should die and who should live. Each justice penned a separate opinion. Among the five justices in the majority, two argued that capital punishment constituted cruel and unusual punishment under all circumstances. But the other three justices in the majority wrote more narrowly, expressing concern that the death penalty was selectively applied. Justice Potter Stewart likened the randomness of the death penalty to being struck by lightning. The three justices believed the death penalty violated the Eighth Amendment because existing death penalty laws allowed too much discretion and therefore opened the door to discriminatory practices.

The four dissenting justices (all Nixon appointees) likewise expressed divergent views about why they believed capital punishment was consistent with the Eighth Amendment. Chief Justice Burger clearly favored the use of the death penalty and argued that legislatures should be able to retain capital punishment if they chose to do so. Justice Harry Blackmun, on the other hand, expressed his "distaste, antipathy, and indeed, abhorrence, for the death penalty" but concluded that abolition should be left to elected legislatures. (Just before his retirement, Blackmun reversed this position.)

Within minutes the story began to appear on the major wire-service tickers. A few governors and correctional officials supported the decision. But mostly the reactions were negative. Indeed, by the time the evening papers went to press, a few members of Congress had already proposed a constitutional amendment to overturn *Furman*. Soon after the initial shock subsided, lawyers in state capitols across the nation began to write new laws.

The divergent approaches adopted by the five justices in the majority meant that *Furman v. Georgia* set no precedent. Although the Court ruled that existing laws did not pass constitutional muster, the wording left open the possibility that future laws, more narrowly drafted, might comply with the Eighth Amendment to the Constitution. Thus, as often happens, a significant Supreme Court decision spawned further litigation. The second time around, the Court would provide a different answer to the question of who deserves to die.

for crimes other than murder has been struck down. According to the Supreme Court, rape is not a grave enough offense to justify the imposition of the death penalty (*Coker v. Georgia*, 1977). Thirteen states and the District of Columbia do not have capital punishment statutes (Figure 15-9).

State death penalty laws have some differences (Acker 1993). For one, they vary in the specific types of homicide cases that are death-eligible. They also differ in terms of a minimum age at which the death penalty may be imposed. Twelve jurisdictions set the minimum age at sixteen, four set it at seventeen, and fourteen set it at eighteen. New York, which most recently passed a death penalty law, specifies nineteen, and eight states do not specify a minimum age. Defendants who were fifteen or younger at the time they committed murder may not be executed (*Thompson v. Oklahoma*, 1988). But

the Supreme Court refused to set aside the death penalty for defendants who were seventeen at the time of the crime (*Stanford v. Kentucky*, 1989).

Important variations also exist in how often states use their death penalty laws. Three states have no one on death row, and some states rarely impose the death penalty. A few jurisdictions, particularly in the South and West, regularly use capital punishment (Figure 15-10).

Appeals and Evolving Standards

Like all defendants found guilty, those sentenced to death are entitled to appellate court review. In death penalty cases, however, special provisions govern appeal. Except for Arkansas, all jurisdictions with death penalty statutes provide for automatic review after a sentence of death is imposed. This review is

FIGURE 15-8	Key Developments Concerning Capital Punishment	
Eighth Amendment	1791	Excessive bail shall not be required, nor excessive fines imposed, nor cruel and unusual punishments inflicted.
Witherspoon v. Illinois	1968	Prospective jurors cannot be excluded because they oppose the death penalty.
Furman v. Georgia	1972	All existing death penalty laws invalidated; five-judge majority expresses different reasons for this action.
Gregg v. Georgia	1976	• Death penalty laws do not constitute cruel and unusual punishment under all circumstances. • Mandatory death penalty laws struck down.
Coker v. Georgia	1977	Rape is not a grave enough offense to justify the imposition of the death penalty.
Pulley v. Harris	1984	The Eighth Amendment does not require states to assess whether a sentence of death is compared to other cases to determine whether the sentence is proportional.
Lockhart v. McCree	1986	Potential jurors may be excluded if they oppose the death penalty. Thus, a death-qualified jury was upheld (overturning *Witherspoon v. Illinois*).
Thompson v. Oklahoma	1988	Defendants who were fifteen or younger at the time they committed murder may not be executed.
Stanford v. Kentucky	1989	It is not unconstitutional to apply the death penalty to persons who are convicted of murder when they were seventeen.
Penry v. Lynaugh	1989	It is constitutional to execute mentally retarded persons.
Simmons v. South Carolina	1994	Defense may tell jurors that the only alternative to a death sentence is life without parole.
Harris v. Alabama	1995	States may give judges the power to sentence a capital defendant to death even if the jury votes not to impose the death penalty.
Ramdass v. Angelone	2000	Upheld sentence of death even though jurors were not told that defendant would not be eligible for parole if sentenced to life in prison.
Williams v. Taylor	2000	Upheld a section of the Anti-Terrorism and Effective Death Penalty Act intended to shorten time between sentencing and execution.

undertaken regardless of the defendant's wishes and is conducted by the state's highest appellate court, bypassing any intermediate courts of appeals. Next, a writ of certiorari may be filed with the U.S. Supreme Court. Even though the chances of four justices voting to hear the case are not high, they are much higher than for ordinary criminal appeals. Having exhausted these appellate remedies, defendants sentenced to death often file numerous writs of habeas corpus in the state and federal courts, although this practice changed greatly in 1996 (Chapter 17).

The review process in death penalty cases is quite lengthy. The sixty-eight prisoners executed during 1998 had been under sentence of death an average of ten years and ten months—three months less than that for inmates executed in 1997 (Snell 2000). Critics objected to the old habeas corpus system because it allowed condemned prisoners constant opportunities for review and resulted in lengthy delays.

The lengthy appellate process is partly due to evolving standards concerning the application of the death penalty. The Supreme Court has become America's life-and-death tribunal. No other Supreme Court in history has been as preoccupied with the questions of when life begins and when a state may snuff one out. The following three issues illustrate some of the questions the Court has faced in the aftermath of the *Gregg* decision.

One long-standing issue has been the exclusion of persons opposed to the death penalty from juries

| FIGURE 15-9 | Jurisdictions without a Death Penalty |

Alaska	Minnesota
District of Columbia	North Dakota
Hawaii	Rhode Island
Iowa	Vermont
Maine	West Virginia
Massachusetts	Wisconsin
Michigan	

SOURCE: Tracy Snell, *Capital Punishment 1998* (Washington, D.C.: Bureau of Justice Statistics, U.S. Department of Justice, 2000).

| FIGURE 15-10 | Prisoners under Sentence of Death, by Region |

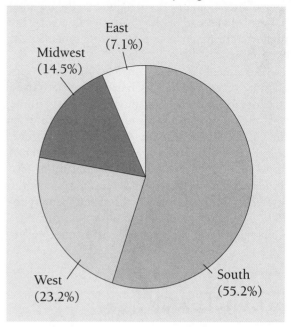

SOURCE: Tracy Snell, *Capital Punishment 1998* (Washington, D.C.: Bureau of Justice Statistics, U.S. Department of Justice, 2000).

in capital cases. In 1968 the Warren Court rejected the classic "hanging jury." *Witherspoon v. Illinois* (1968) held that states cannot exclude from juries in capital cases any persons who voice general objections to the death penalty or express religious scruples against its imposition. However, the more conservative Rehnquist Court has limited *Witherspoon* (*Wainwright v. Witt*, 1985), ruling that the Constitution does not prohibit the removal for cause of prospective jurors whose opposition to the death penalty is so strong that it would prevent or substantially impair the performance of their duties as jurors at the sentencing phase of the trial (*Lockhart v. McCree*, 1986). The erosion of *Witherspoon* clearly works to the advantage of the prosecution, which can use voir dire to select a "death-qualified" jury.

There is also considerable disagreement over whether *Gregg* required proportionality review. Proportionality is the concept that state supreme courts should compare each death sentence with sentences imposed in cases throughout the state, to determine whether the cases are being handled in an even-handed way. The Supreme Court upheld the death sentence in a California murder case, holding that a proportionality review by an appellate court was not a constitutional requirement (*Pulley v. Harris*, 1984). Many state laws, however, mandate such a review.

A third issue relates to Eighth Amendment concerns about the execution of the mentally retarded. The Court provided conflicting answers in an opinion written by Justice Sandra Day O'Connor (who has been the swing vote in many death penalty cases). The defendant had an IQ between 50 and 63 and the mental age of a six-and-a-half-year-old. The Court sent the case back to the lower court because of the failure of the trial judge to provide the jury with instructions that the defendant's mental retardation could be considered a mitigating circumstance. But at the same time, the Court concluded that there is insufficient evidence of a national consensus against executing mentally retarded people convicted of capital murder to find that it is categorically prohibited by the Eighth Amendment (*Penry v. Lynaugh*, 1989).

Three decades after upholding the death penalty, the Supreme Court still struggles with procedural permutations. During the 1980s the Court was often badly divided; many significant holdings were decided by a bare five-to-four majority. By the 1990s, however, the Court had clearly shifted toward favoring the death penalty.

Death Row Inmates

As a result of post-*Gregg* statutes, almost 3,500 prisoners are under a sentence of death. Death row inmates are predominantly male (a scant 1 percent are female), are disproportionately non-white (45 percent), have never completed high school

(62 percent), and have a prior felony conviction (65 percent). The median age is twenty-eight at the time of arrest. Figure 15-10 highlights the regional pattern of the use of the death penalty, with the highest percentage of those awaiting execution in the South.

On January 16, 1977, convicted murderer Gary Gilmore's execution by a Utah firing squad attracted considerable national and international attention, not only because he was the first person executed in the United States since the unofficial moratorium began in 1967, but also because Gilmore had opposed all attempts to delay the execution. Five hundred persons have been executed since the Supreme Court reinstated the death penalty in 1976. The most common methods of execution are lethal injection (twenty states), electrocution (four-teen), lethal gas (six), hanging (three), and firing squad (two).

A sentence of death does not necessarily mean that the offender will be executed. From 1976, when the death penalty was upheld, through the end of 1998, a total of 5,709 prisoners were under a sentence of death. Of those, 500 were executed. An additional 2,137 had their death sentences vacated on appeal or commuted by the governor, or else they died in prison. The others remain on death row pending the outcome of their appeals (Snell 2000).

 To take a virtual tour of a death row cell, go to **http://www.dc.state.fl.us/oth/vtour/index.html**.

For an up-to-date list of Web links, go to **http://www.wadsworth.com/product/0534563406s**.

CONCLUSION

The issues raised in *Furman v. Georgia* thirty years ago are still with us. Although public support for the death penalty has increased, we as a nation execute very few defendants. Often unrecognized is the fact that murder (the only crime for which the death penalty is allowed) constitutes only a tiny percentage of crime. The public's demands that something be done about "rising" crime rates has directly and indirectly affected the why, who, and what of sentencing.

During the last three decades, there has been an unprecedented public debate over *why* we sentence. The previously dominant goal of rehabilitation has come under sharp attack, and many voices urge that punishment should instead be based on the principle of just deserts. After nearly forty years of stability, the indeterminate sentencing system has been rejected in state after state.

Intense interest in crime has also produced major alterations in *who* has the authority to sentence. The mix of sentencing responsibilities has changed in major ways. Legislators have inserted themselves more directly in the sentencing process, reducing the sentencing discretion of judges in many jurisdictions. Legislatures have also restricted parole board authority over early release in some jurisdictions and abolished parole altogether in a few areas.

The *what* of punishment has likewise come under intense scrutiny. Prison overcrowding has become the dominant issue. Probation overcrowding is an equally pressing, if less visible, problem. Perhaps more pressing than the debate over capital punishment is the lack of a national debate over prison overcrowding. Our nation's emphasis on getting tough on criminals is apparently a policy without costs, until we total the bill for building and maintaining prisons. Although citizens and public officials want to send even more offenders to prison, they are unwilling to expend large sums of tax dollars to build the needed facilities. Thus, sentencing is likely to remain an important public policy issue for the foreseeable future.

CRITICAL THINKING QUESTIONS

1. In what ways is restorative justice similar to the four dominant sentencing philosophies of retribution, incapacitation, deterrence, and rehabilitation? In what ways is restorative justice different from these four sentencing philosophies?

2. Should the punishment fit the crime or should the punishment fit the criminal? In what ways do the four sentencing phi-

losophies provide different answers to this question?

3. What is the mix of legislative, judicial, and executive sentencing responsibilities in your state? What changes, if any, have occurred over the last decade in the balance of sentencing responsibilities?

4. Under contemporary standards, would the *Furman* case be considered a death-eligible case?

5. Public criticisms of lenient sentencing tend to occur in a select number of either violent crimes or highly unusual circumstances. In what ways do such discussions deflect attention from the question of what the appropriate sentence should be for the bulk of defendants convicted of nonviolent crimes (burglary and theft, for example) and also drug-related crimes?

 WORLD WIDE WEB RESOURCES AND EXERCISES

Web Guides

http://dir.yahoo.com/Society_and_Culture/Crime/Correction_and_Rehabilitation/
http://dir.yahoo.com/Society_and_Culture/Crime/Correction_and_Rehabilitation/Sentencing/
http://dir.yahoo.com/Society_and_Culture/Crime/Correction_and_Rehabilitation/Death_Penalty/
http://dir.yahoo.com/Government/Law/Criminal_Justice/Restorative_Justice/

Web Search Terms

"Prison"; "probation"; "restorative justice"; "death penalty"

Useful URLs

The American Correction Association, a multidisciplinary organization of professionals representing all facets of corrections and criminal justice, including federal, state, and military: http://www.corrections.com/aca/.
Visit these related sites:
Bureau of Justice Statistics Corrections Statistics: http://www.ojp.usdoj.gov/bjs/correct.htm
Federal Bureau of Prisons: http://www.bop.gov/

National Institute of Corrections: http://www.nicic.org/
The Corrections Connection: http://www.corrections.com/
Focus on the Death Penalty is a comprehensive resource that includes history, U.S. Supreme Court cases, and statistics: http://www.uaa.alaska.edu/just/death/.

Uncommon URLs

The Civil Rights Lawyers Defense Team handles parole matters: http://www.parole.cc/.
Restitution Incorporated promotes healing between victim and offender: http://www.restitutioninc.org/.
The Center for Restorative Justice and Mediation provides current information: http://ssw.che.umn.edu/rjp/default.html.
Visit the Restorative Justice Project: http://www.fresno.edu/dept/pacs/rjp.html.
The Other Side of the Wall offers news about prison issues: http://www.prisonwall.org/.
Visit the Anamosa State Penitentiary (formerly the Iowa Men's Reformatory) at http://www.geocities.com/Heartland/2201/oldphoto.htm.
Look at the famous Alcatraz Island: http://www.alcatrazhistory.com/.
Ken Light Texas Death Row offers photos and articles about life on death row: http://sightphoto.com/sightphoto/Light/light_texas.html.

Web Exercises

1. If your state department of corrections has a Web page, access it and ask yourself the following questions: Does it discuss costs (and increases in costs) of incarcerating prisoners? Does it indicate whether any or all prisons have been under federal court order? Overall, what image does the information project?

2. Using the data provided by your state department of corrections, chart the growth in the prison population in your state over the last decade. Is the rate of increase similar to, or different from, the rate of increase nationwide (Figure 15-4)?

3. Two of the groups most active in advocating restorative justice are Restorative Justice: Healing the Effects of Crime (http://www.restorativejustice.com/) and the Mennonite

Central Committee **(http://www.mcc.org/ programs/crime/restorative-justice.html)**. Examine their homepages and answer the following questions: In what ways do their arguments appear to be working within dominant American thought patterns about victims? In what ways are they challenging dominant thought patterns about punishment?

 INFOTRAC COLLEGE EDITION RESOURCES AND EXERCISES

Basic Searches

Punishment; prisons; pardon; imprisonment; capital punishment; cruel and unusual punishment; probation; fines (penalties); restorative justice; Prison Litigation Reform Act of 1966; executions

Recommended Articles

William C. Collins, Darlene C. Grant, "The Prison Litigation Reform Act"

Alcoholism & Drug Abuse Weekly, "California Alternative-Sentencing Program Seeks Greater Participation"

InfoTrac College Edition Exercises

1. Using the search term *prisons* or *imprisonment,* find two or more articles that discuss the problem of prison overcrowding. Why do the authors think that prison overcrowding is a problem, and what solutions do they suggest?

2. Using the search term *restorative justice,* find two or more articles that discuss the topic and answer the following questions: Do the authors support restorative justice? If so, what benefits do they cite? If not, what downside do they see? What types of crimes would restorative justice be most suited for? What types of defendants? What types of victims?

REFERENCES

Acker, James. 1993. "Doing the Devil's Work: Toward Model Death Penalty Legislation." *Criminal Law Bulletin* 29: 219–247.

Arvanites, Thomas. 1992. "Increasing Imprisonment: A Function of Crime or Socioeconomic Factors?" *American Journal of Criminal Justice* 17: 19–38.

Auerhahn, Kathleen. 1999. "Selective Incapacitation and the Problem of Prediction." *Criminology* 37: 703–734.

Blankenship, Michael, James Luginbuhl, Francis Cullen, and William Redick. 1997. "Juror Comprehension of Sentencing Instructions: A Test of Tennessee's Death Penalty Process." *Justice Quarterly* 14: 325–357.

Blumstein, Alfred, Jacqueline Cohen, Susan Martin, and Michael Tonry, eds. 1983. *Research on Sentencing: The Search for Reform.* Washington, D.C.: National Academy Press.

Bureau of Justice Statistics. 1996. *How to Use Structured Fines (Day Fines) as an Intermediate Sanction.* Washington, D.C.: U.S. Government Printing Office.

———. 1998. *1996 National Survey of State Sentencing Structures.* Washington, D.C.: U.S. Department of Justice.

———. 2001 "Prison Statistics." http://www.ojp.usdoj. gov/bjs/prisons.htm.

Byrne, James, Arthur Lurigio, and Christopher Baird. 1989. "The Effectiveness of the New Intensive Supervision Programs." *Research in Corrections* 2: 1–15.

Chaiken, Marcia, and Jan Chaiken. 1990. *Redefining the Career Criminal: Priority Prosecution of High-Rate Dangerous Offenders.* Washington, D.C.: U.S. Department of Justice.

Chilton, Bradley. 1991. *Prisons Under the Gavel: The Federal Takeover of Georgia Prisons.* Columbus: Ohio State University Press.

Clear, Todd, and George Cole. 2000. *American Corrections.* 5th ed. Belmont, CA: Wadsworth.

Cole, George. 1992. "Using Civil and Administrative Remedies to Collect Fines and Fees." *State Court Journal* 16: 4–10.

Cole, George, Barry Mahoney, Marlene Thornton, and Roger Hanson. 1988. "The Use of Fines by Trial Court Judges." *Judicature* 71: 325–333.

Crouch, Ben, and James Marquart. 1990. "Resolving the Paradox of Reform: Litigation, Prisoner Violence, and Perceptions of Risk." *Justice Quarterly* 7: 103–123.

Davis, Robert, and Tanya Bannister. 1995. "Improving Collection of Court-Ordered Restitution." *Judicature* 79: 30–33.

DiIulio, John, ed. 1990. *Courts, Corrections, and the Constitution: The Impact of Judicial Intervention on Prisons and Jails.* New York: Oxford University Press.

Feeley, Malcolm, and Edward Rubin. 1998. *Judicial Policy Making and the Modern State: How the Courts Reformed America's Prisons.* New York: Cambridge University Press.

Frankel, Marvin. 1972. *Criminal Sentences: Law Without Order.* New York: Hill and Wang.

Galaway, Burt. 1988. "Restitution As Innovation or Unfilled Promise?" *Federal Probation* 52: 3–14.

Galaway, Burt, and Joe Hudson, eds. 1996. *Restorative Justice: International Perspectives.* Monsey, NY: Criminal Justice Press.

Gillespie, Robert. 1988–1989. "Criminal Fines: Do They Pay?" *Justice System Journal* 13: 365–378.

Griset, Pamala. 1991. *Determinate Sentencing: The Promise and the Reality of Retributive Justice.* Albany: State University of New York Press.

Haapanen, Rudy. 1989. *Selective Incapacitation and the Serious Offender: A Longitudinal Study of Criminal Career Patterns.* New York: Springer-Verlag.

Hanson, Roger, and Henry Daley. 1995. *Challenging the Conditions of Prisons and Jails.* Washington, D.C.: Bureau of Justice Statistics, U.S. Department of Justice.

Hillsman, Sally, and Barry Mahoney. 1988. "Collecting and Enforcing Criminal Fines: A Review of Court Processes, Practices, and Problems." *Justice System Journal* 13: 17–36.

"In '90s, Prison Building by States and U.S. Government Surged." *New York Times,* 1997. 8 August, A15.

Kelly, William, and Sheldon Ekland-Olson. 1991. "The Response of the Criminal Justice System to Prison Overcrowding: Recidivism Patterns among Four Successive Parolee Cohorts." *Law and Society Review* 25: 601–620.

Langan, Patrick, and Mark Cunniff. 1992. *Recidivism of Felons on Probation, 1986–89.* Washington, D.C.: National Institute of Justice, U.S. Department of Justice.

McCarthy, Belinda, and Bernard McCarthy. 2001. *Community-Based Corrections.* 4th ed. Belmont: Wadsworth Publishing.

McCormick, John. 1999. "Coming Two Days Shy of Martyrdom." *Newsweek,* 15 February.

Meltsner, Michael. 1973. *Cruel and Unusual Punishment: The Supreme Court and Capital Punishment.* New York: Random House.

Moore, Kathleen Dean. 1989. *Pardons: Justice, Mercy and the Public Interest.* New York: Oxford University Press.

Morris, Norval, and Michael Tonry. 1990. *Between Prison and Probation: Intermediate Punishments in a Rational Sentencing Structure.* New York: Oxford University Press.

Nagin, Daniel. 1998 "Criminal Deterrence Research at the Outset of the Twenty-First Century." In *Crime and Justice: A Review of Research* (Vol. 23), edited by Michael Tonry. Chicago: University of Chicago Press, 1998.

National Advisory Commission on Criminal Justice Standards and Goals. 1973. *Corrections.* Washington, D.C.: U.S. Government Printing Office.

Parent, Dale, Terrence Dunworth, Douglas McDonald, and William Rhodes. 1997. "Intermediate Sanctions." Washington, D.C.: National Institute of Justice.

Petersilia, Joan, and Susan Turner. 1993. *Evaluating Intensive Supervision Probation/Parole: Results of a Nationwide Experiment.* Washington, D.C.: National Institute of Justice.

Rhodes, Susan. 1990. "Democratic Justice: The Responsiveness of Prison Population Size to Public Policy Preferences." *American Politics Quarterly* 18: 337–375.

Rosett, Arthur, and Donald Cressey. 1976. *Justice by Consent: Plea Bargains in the American Courthouse.* Philadelphia: J. B. Lippincott.

Ruckman, P. S. 1997. "Executive Clemency in the United States: Origins, Development, and Analysis (1900–1993)." *Presidential Studies Quarterly* 27: 251–271.

Shinnar, Shlomo, and Reuel Shinnar. 1975. "The Effects of the Criminal Justice System on the Control of Crime: A Quantitative Approach." *Law and Society Review* 9: 581–611.

Snell, Tracy. 2000. *Capital Punishment 1998.* Washington, D.C.: Bureau of Justice Statistics, U.S. Department of Justice.

Stern, Andrew. 2000. "Illinois Governor Halts Executions Pending Review." Reuters, 23 January.

Taggart, William. 1989. "Redefining the Power of the Federal Judiciary: The Impact of Court-Ordered Prison Reform on State Expenditures for Corrections." *Law and Society Review* 23: 241–272.

Tobolowsky, Peggy. 1993. "Restitution in the Federal Criminal Justice System." *Judicature* 77: 90–95.

Tonry, Michael. 1999. "Reconsidering Indeterminate and Structured Sentencing." Office of Justice Programs, Washington, D.C.: U.S. Department of Justice.

Turner, Susan and Judith Greene. 1999. "The FARE Probation Experiment: Implementation and Outcomes of Day Fines for Felony Offenders in Maricopa County." *The Justice System Journal* 21: 1–21.

Van Dine, Stephen, John Conrad, and Simon Dinitz. 1979. *Restraining the Wicked.* Lexington, MA: Lexington Books.

Van Ness, Daniel, and Karen Heetderks Strong. 1997. *Restoring Justice.* Cincinnati: Anderson.

Visher, Christy. 1987. "Incapacitation and Crime Control: Does a 'Lock 'Em Up' Strategy Reduce Crime?" *Justice Quarterly* 4: 513–544.

von Hirsch, Andrew. 1976. *Doing Justice.* New York: Hill and Wang.

Wardlaw, Jack. 1998. "Accord Returns Angola to Louisiana Control." *Times-Picayune,* 25 September.

Whitehead, John. 1991. "The Effectiveness of Felony Probation: Results from an Eastern State." *Justice Quarterly* 8: 525–543.

Wilson, James Q. 1983. *Thinking About Crime: A Policy Guide.* 2d ed. New York: Basic Books.

FOR FURTHER READING

Byrne, James, Arthur Lurigio, and Joan Petersillia, eds. *Smart Sentencing: The Emergence of Intermediate Sanctions.* Newbury Park, CA: Sage, 1992.

Christianson, Scott. *With Liberty for Some: 500 Years of Imprisonment in America.* Boston: Northeastern University Press, 1998.

Crouch, Ben, and James Marquart. *Appeal to Justice: Litigated Reform of Texas Prisons.* Austin: University of Texas Press, 1989.

DiIulio, John. *No Escape: The Future of American Corrections.* New York: Basic Books, 1991.

Hudson, Joe, and Burt Galaway. 1996. *Introduction to Restorative Justice: International Perspectives,* edited by Burt Galaway and Joe Hudson. Monsey, NY: Criminal Justice Press.

Lin, Ann Chih. *Reform in the Making: The Implementation of Social Policy in Prison.* Princeton: Princeton University Press, 2000.

Mauer, Marc. *The Race to Incarcerate.* New York: The New Press, 1999.

Simon, Jonathan. *Poor Disciple: Parole and the Social Control of the Underclass, 1890–1990.* Chicago: University of Chicago Press, 1994.

Welch, Michael. *Punishment in America: Social Control and the Ironies of Imprisonment.* Thousand Oaks, CA: Sage Publications, 1999.

Zimring, Franklin, and Gordon Hawkins. *The Scale of Imprisonment.* Chicago: University of Chicago Press, 1991.

Death Penalty

Abbott, Geoffrey. *Lords of the Scaffold: A History of the Executioner.* New York: St. Martin's Press, 1991.

Baldus, David, George Woodworth, and Charles Pulaski. *Equal Justice and the Death Penalty: A Legal and Empirical Analysis.* Boston: Northeastern University Press, 1990.

Bedau, Hugo Adam, ed. *The Death Penalty in America: Current Controversies.* New York: Oxford University Press, 1996.

Berns, Walter. *For Capital Punishment: Crime and the Morality of the Death Penalty.* New York: Basic Books, 1991.

Borg, Marian. "The Southern Subculture of Punitiveness? Regional Variation in Support for Capital Punishment." *Journal of Research in Crime and Delinquency* 34 (1997): 24–45.

Haines, Herbert. *Against Capital Punishment: The Anti-Death Penalty Movement in America, 1972–1994.* New York: Oxford University Press, 1996.

Latzer, Barry. 1998. *Death Penalty Cases.* Boston: Butterworth-Heineman, 1988.

Paternoster, Raymond. *Capital Punishment in America.* New York: Lexington, 1992.

Radelet, Michael, Hugo Adam Bedau, and Constance Putnam. *In Spite of Innocence: Erroneous Convictions in Capital Cases.* Boston: Northeastern University Press, 1993.

Streib, Victor. *A Capital Punishment Anthology.* Cincinnati: Anderson, 1996.

Wright, Harold, Robert Bohm, and Katherine Jamieson. "A Comparison of Uninformed and Informed Death Penalty Opinions: A Replication and Expansion." *American Journal of Criminal Justice* 20 (1995): 57–87.

Sentencing Decisions

TWELVE-YEAR-OLD POLLY KLAAS WAS KIDNAPPED FROM A SLUMBER party in her home while her mother and little sister slept in the next room. Her two friends were found a short time later, bound and gagged, and were able to provide a general description of the bearded intruder. For nine weeks, hundreds of law enforcement officers and thousands of volunteers attempted to find the girl, but to no avail. Just before Christmas, the bad news came. Polly had been killed shortly after her abduction.

The police arrest of parolee Richard Allen Davis did little to calm an angry public. The kidnapping and murder of Polly Klaas was blamed on a badly flawed criminal justice system that failed to keep a dangerous person like Davis behind bars. The murder of Polly Klaas, and the extensive national media coverage that surrounded it, sparked another round of get-tough-with-crooks legislation. Whereas earlier laws resulted in mandatory minimums, abolition of parole, and sentencing guidelines, the focus now shifted to "three strikes and you're out" laws. ■

While public attention focuses on the sentences handed out in the handful of sensational cases such as the Polly Klaas murder (refer to the wedding cake analogy used in Chapter 10), judges must wrestle with the sentence to impose upon the almost 900,000 felons convicted each year. The problems members of the courtroom work group face in reaching these sentencing decisions are captured by the powerful symbol of Lady Justice. Held high in her right hand are the scales of justice, symbolizing fairness in the administration of justice. Draped across her eyes is a blindfold, suggesting that all who come before her will receive impartial justice. Grasped low in her left hand is a sword, standing for the power and might of law. Replicas of Lady Justice adorn the exteriors of many American courthouses, but whether the sentencing process inside the courtrooms lives up to those high ideals is open to question.

The scales of justice are the starting point in examining sentencing. This chapter begins by focusing on who is and who is not sentenced to prison, granted probation, or executed. First, we need to know what factors judges and other members of the courtroom work group weigh in deciding between prison or probation. Normal penalties are the most important consideration in sentencing. Based on the seriousness of the offense and the defendant's prior record, courthouses have developed going rates, which are used as parameters in fine-tuning a sentence for a given offender.

The blindfold is the next major topic. Sentences imposed on the guilty are expected to be fair and just. Many observers argue that they are not; disparities and discrimination in sentencing are major topics of concern. Numerous studies probe the extent to which economic status, age, gender, and race improperly pierce the judicial blindfold when sentences are imposed.

The sword of justice will also be discussed. Whereas some worry that the scales of justice are tipped, others are concerned that the sword of justice is sheathed. Frustration over rising crime rates has given rise to charges that judges are too lenient. Demands that sentences be more certain as well as more severe have become a staple of American politics. Legislators have responded by increasing the severity of some punishments and altering sentencing structures in hopes of producing greater predictability in sentencing. Sentencing guidelines are now the centerpiece in discussions of increasing the predictability of sentencing as well as increasing the severity of the penalty.

COURTROOM WORK GROUPS AND SENTENCING DECISIONS

Sentencing is a joint decision-making process. Although only judges possess the legal authority to impose sentence, other members of the courtroom work group are also influential (Figure 16-1). The extent of this influence varies from jurisdiction to jurisdiction and from judge to judge. Where sentence bargaining predominates, for example, the judge almost invariably imposes the sentence that the prosecutor and defense attorney have already

| FIGURE 16-1 | The Courtroom Work Group and Sentencing |

	Law on the Books	*Law in Action*
Probation officer	Conducts pre-sentence investigation (PSI).	• Judges most often follow the recommendation in PSI. • Studies disagree whether the sentencing decision is guided by PSI or provides a paper rationale for an already agreed-upon sentence.
Prosecutor	In most jurisdictions the DA makes a sentencing recommendation to the judge.	• Judges are more likely to impose the sentence recommended by the DA than by the defense attorney. • Plea bargaining decisions greatly influence the potential sentence.
Defense attorney	During the sentencing hearing, defense attorney argues for the court to show leniency to the defendant.	• Pleas for leniency are viewed as efforts to impress the client and the client's family and therefore are often ignored. • Defense attorneys with good working relationships with the other members of the courtroom work group are influential in achieving lenient sentences in selected instances.
Judge	By law, the only person who can impose sentence. Mandatory sentence and sentencing guidelines restrict the judges' discretion in a growing number of jurisdictions.	• Judges most often sentence within the normal penalty structure. • Judges often criticize legislatures for restricting judicial sentencing discretion.

agreed upon. Where count and charge bargaining is used, the actors reach agreements based on past sentencing patterns of the judge. The most significant actors in sentencing are probation officers, prosecutors, defense attorneys, and (of course) judges.

Probation Officers

Probation officers perform two major functions in the sentencing process. One is the supervision of offenders after a sentence of probation has been imposed (Clear and Cole 2000). The other is investigation prior to sentencing.

The primary purpose of a **pre-sentence investigation** (PSI) is to help the judge select an appropriate sentence by providing information about the crime and the criminal. Most often, the PSI is

ordered by the court following the defendant's conviction. A date is set for sentencing the offender, and meanwhile the probation officer conducts the investigation (see A Day in Court: Probation Officers Classify Defendants). The report is based on police reports, prosecutor's records, an interview with the offender, and perhaps a talk with the defendant's family as well. A typical pre-sentence report contains a description of the offense, the defendant's version of the crime, the person's prior criminal record and social history, and a psychological evaluation (if needed). The pre-sentence report gives the judge, who must select the proper sentence, an appropriate database. This is particularly important when the defendant has entered a plea of guilty, because then the judge knows little about the particulars of the crime or the background of the offender.

Beyond providing background information, many pre-sentence reports also include a recommendation of an appropriate sentence. However, some judges will not allow a recommendation, claiming that this is the prerogative solely of the

> **Pre-sentence investigation:** Investigation by a probation department into circumstances surrounding a crime in order to help judges make appropriate sentencing decisions.

A DAY IN COURT

Probation Officers Classify Defendants

 PO [probation officers] did not so much process individuals as they processed types of individuals who had been labeled in particular ways. . . . [They] used a three-fold typology of criminal defendants which was based on the defendant's risk of recidivism.

1. Low-risk defendants were usually in trouble with the criminal justice system for the first time, were between the ages of 18 and 25, and were either attending university or had a steady job. These defendants, therefore, had much to lose by possessing a criminal record and they took their current involvement with the courts seriously. As one PO put it, "These people have made one screwy mistake and it's shaken them up so much we'll probably never see them again." For example, one defendant had been convicted of attempted theft after he had altered a sales receipt to obtain items he hadn't paid for. This defendant was unusually cooperative during the interview and expressed concern about the fact that business associates and local bankers would find out about the criminal record he now possessed. His PO told me, "I don't think we'll see him come through here again. This was his first offense and I think it really made an impression on him."

2. High-risk defendants usually had at least two prior arrests and convictions, little formal education, and were seen as unwilling or unable to hold a steady job. Often, they were perceived as not taking their involvement with the courts seriously. For these reasons, POs saw these defendants as likely to be in and out of trouble for much of their adult lives. For example, a defendant had been convicted of burglary and had several other theft-related convictions. In addition, he had never held a job for more than three months at a time. The PO who handled the case told me: "This [defendant] is just too lazy to work. . . . He commits these burglaries because of that. I'll bet ya we see this guy again. He's definitely [high-risk] material."

3. The final category of defendants consisted of individuals whose risk of recidivism was neither definitely high or low, but was seen as problematic. Some of these defendants had been in trouble with the law before, generally involving minor offenses such as shoplifting. Others possessed characteristics of alcoholism or a "bad attitude," which POs considered likely to be related to future criminal behavior. While there was no specific set of characteristics which defined this category of defendants, POs pointed out that what they did share was the potential for "heading for trouble." For example, a defendant had been convicted of theft and had two prior theft-related convictions. However, he also was working two jobs to pay off a student loan and return to the university. The PO described the defendant's risk of recidivism in the following way: "It is hard to tell with him. He's got these [prior offenses], but he's got these things [two jobs, a car] going for him. If he was in a situation where he could steal, I don't know."

What was important for POs was that, whatever the problem, these defendants were "workable." As one PO put it: "I spend the most time with these [defendants]. I try to make them aware of alternatives . . . or refer them for heavy-duty counseling, or do some things myself so hopefully they won't get in trouble again."

SOURCE: Jack Spencer, "Accounts, Attitudes, and Solutions: Probation Officer Defendant Negotiations of Subjective Orientations." *Social Problems* (1983) 30: 570–581. Reprinted by permission.

court. Even if there is no explicit recommendation, most PSIs leave little room for doubt about what the probation officer thinks the sentence should be. If probation is recommended, the report usually includes a suggested level of supervision (ranging from intensive through regular to minimal), a listing of special conditions of probation, a plan for treatment, and an assessment of community resources available to facilitate rehabilitation.

Probation officers clearly play a significant role in the sentencing process. Judges are very likely to impose the sentence recommended in the PSI. The seminal study by Carter and Wilkins (1967) found a 95 percent rate of agreement between the judge and the probation report when probation was recommended and an 88 percent rate of agreement when the report opposed probation. Thus, although sentencing judges are not required to follow such recommendations, they usually do (Campbell, McCoy, and Osigweh 1990; Hagan 1977).

There is considerable disagreement, however, over the actual influence of probation officers in the sentencing process. On the one hand, some studies suggest that judges seriously consider the recommendations and use them to guide their decisions. Walsh (1985), for example, concludes that judges lean heavily on the professional advice of probation officers. On the other hand, some researchers argue that probation officers have little real influence on the sentencing process. Kingsnorth and Rizzo (1979) report that probation recommendations have been supplanted by plea bargaining. In jurisdictions where sentence bargaining predominates, prosecutors and defense attorneys usually talk to the probation officer before the PSI is submitted to the court. The conversation indicates what information should be stressed to justify the sentence already agreed upon. The probation report then provides a rationale after the fact. According to Hagan, Hewitt, and Alwin (1979), the probation officer's role in sentencing is largely ceremonial. By and large, recommendations by probation officers "do not influence judicial sentencing significantly but serve to maintain the myth that criminal courts dispense individual justice" (Rosencrance 1988, 236).

 For an insider's view of what a federal probation officer does, go to **http://www.uic.edu/~jmaghan/intern/postperm.html**.

For an up-to-date list of Web links, go to **http://www.wadsworth.com/product/0534563406s**.

Prosecutors

Prosecutors can influence the sentencing decision in several important ways. By agreeing to a count or charge bargain, prosecutors limit the maximum penalty the judge may impose. During the sentencing hearing, prosecutors can bring to the court's attention factors that are likely to increase the penalty—for example, that the victim was particularly vulnerable or that the defendant inflicted great harm on the victim. Alternatively, prosecutors can bring out factors that would lessen the penalty—for example, the defendant's cooperation with the police.

Finally, prosecutors may make a specific sentencing recommendation. If, for example, there has been a sentence bargain, the prosecutor will indicate

the penalty agreed on, with the usual result that the judge will adopt that recommendation as the sentence. When such prosecutorial recommendations are based on office policy, they can have the positive effect of muting sentencing disparities among the different judges. In some courts, however, prosecutors are not allowed to make sentencing recommendations, because sentencing is viewed solely as a judicial responsibility.

Defense Attorneys

The defense attorney's role in sentencing begins early in the history of a case. The decision whether to go to trial or to enter a guilty plea is partially based on the attorney's assessment of the sentence likely to be imposed. Based on the knowledge of what sentences have been handed out to past defendants accused of similar crimes and with similar backgrounds, the attorney must advise the client as to the probable sentence.

At the same time, the defense attorney seeks to obtain the lightest sentence possible. One way to accomplish this goal is to maneuver the case before a judge with a lenient sentencing record. Another way is to discuss the case with the prosecutor in hopes that he or she will agree to (or at least not oppose) a recommendation of probation in the presentence investigation. Defense attorneys also try to emphasize certain circumstances that make the defendant look better in the eyes of the judge, prosecutor, and probation officer. They may try to downplay the severity of the offense by stressing the defendant's minor role in the crime or the fact that the victim was not without blame; or they may have friends or employers testify about the defendant's general good character and regular employment.

Overall, though, defense attorneys are less influential than prosecutors. Judges and prosecutors typically view defense attorneys' arguments for leniency as efforts to impress their clients with the fact that they tried as hard as they could.

 The National Association of Sentencing Advocates is a professional membership organization of sentencing advocates and defense-based mitigation specialists: **http://www.sentencingproject.org/nasa/index.html**.

For an up-to-date list of Web links, go to **http://www.wadsworth.com/product/0534563406s**.

Judges

Courtroom work groups impose informal limits on how judges exercise their formal legal authority to impose sentences. Judges are well aware that the disposition of cases is related to plea bargaining, which in turn depends on being able to anticipate the sentencing tendencies of judges. Judges share in a framework of understandings, expectations, and agreements that are relied upon to dispose of most criminal cases. If a judge strays too far from expectations by imposing a sentence either substantially more lenient or more severe than the one agreed on by defendant, defense lawyer, and prosecutor, it becomes more difficult for the prosecutor and defense counsel to negotiate future agreements (Rosett and Cressey 1976).

In working within the limits established by the consensus of the courtroom work group, judges are also constrained because the other members of the work group have more thorough knowledge of the details of the defendant and the nature of the crime. In particular, a judge's sentencing decision is restricted by the bargains struck between prosecution and defense. Indeed, judges who enjoy stable relationships with the prosecutors who practice before them are more likely to defer to those prosecutors' sentencing recommendations (Worden 1995).

Judges, though, are not without influence. They are the most experienced members of the courtroom team, so their views carry more weight than those of the relatively inexperienced prosecutors or defense attorneys. The particular judge's attitudes on sentencing are reflected in the courtroom work group's common understanding of what sentences are appropriate.

For a look inside a probation office, go to:
Santa Clara County (California): **http:// claraweb.co.santa-clara.ca.us/probation/ Adult.htm**
Suffolk County (New York): **http://www.co.suffolk. ny.us/probation/**
Pima County (Arizona): **http://www.sc.co.pima. az.us/apo/**
Marion County (Indiana): **http://www.ci. indianapolis.in.us/probation/**
For an up-to-date list of Web links, go to **http:// www.wadsworth.com/product/0534563406s**.

NORMAL PENALTIES AND SENTENCING DECISIONS

Sentencing involves a two-stage decision-making process. After conviction, the first decision is whether to grant probation or to incarcerate the defendant. If incarceration is chosen, the second decision is determining how long the sentence should be. Table 16-1 indicates that for the more than 800,000 adults found guilty of a felony in state courts every year, 69 percent are incarcerated (either in prison or jail), with the remaining 31 percent sentenced to probation. Thus, for every 100 felons sentenced, 31 are granted probation and 69 are incarcerated (38 in prison and 31 in jail) (Levin, Langan, and Brown 2000).

Making these sentencing decisions is not an easy task; most judges say that sentencing is the most difficult part of their job. The frustrations of sentencing stem in part from the need to weigh the possibility of rehabilitation, the need to protect the public, popular demands for retribution, and any potential deterrent value in the sentence (see Chapter 15). Of course, courtroom work groups do not consider these competing perspectives in the abstract. They must sentence real defendants found guilty of actual crimes. Each defendant and crime is somewhat different. Sentences are expected to be individualized—to fit the penalty to the crime and the defendant.

In seeking individualized sentences, courtroom work groups employ **normal penalties** (Sudnow 1965). Based on the usual manner in which crimes are committed and the typical backgrounds of the defendants who commit them, courtroom work groups develop norms of what penalties are appropriate for given categories. The normal sentences are not used mechanically; rather, they guide sentencing. It is within the context of these normal penalties that individualization occurs. Upward and downward adjustments are made.

Different courtroom work groups employ varying concepts of normal penalties. From one courtroom to the next, there are important differ-

---

Normal penalties: Norms for proper sentencing based on the crime committed and the defendant's prior record.

TABLE 16-1 Types of Sentences Imposed by Conviction Offense

	Prison (%)	Jail (%)	Probation (%)
All offenses	38	31	31
Violent offenses	57	22	21
Murder	92	3	5
Sexual assault	63	16	21
Robbery	73	14	13
Aggravated assault	42	30	28
Other violent	38	34	27
Property offenses	34	28	38
Burglary	45	26	29
Larceny	31	32	37
Fraud	26	24	50
Drug offenses	35	37	28
Possession	29	41	30
Trafficking	39	33	27
Weapons offenses	40	27	33
Other offenses	31	32	37

SOURCE: David Levin, Patrick Langan, and Jodi Brown. *State Court Sentencing of Convicted Felons, 1996* (Washington, D.C.: Bureau of Justice Statistics, U.S. Department of Justice, 2000).

Seriousness of the Offense

The most important factor in setting normal penalties is the seriousness of the offense. The more serious the offense, the less likely the defendant will be granted probation (Table 16-1). Also, the more serious the offense, the longer the prison sentence. These conclusions are hardly surprising. Society expects that convicted murderers will be punished more severely than defendants found guilty of theft. What is important is how courtroom work groups go about the task of deciding what offenses are serious.

When weighing the seriousness of the offense, courtroom work groups examine the harm or loss suffered by the crime victim in what they perceive to be the "real offense" (what really happened, not the official charge). This information is provided either in the pre-sentence report or by the police arrest report. By focusing on the real offense, judges can counteract charge bargaining. For example, pre-sentence reports for simple robbery cases sometimes include the type of weapon used. Thus, the defendant who has been found guilty only for unarmed robbery may often be sentenced on the basis that he really committed an armed robbery. The opposite also happens. By examining the prior relationship between the defendant and the victim, the courtroom work group may perceive that the underlying crime is a squabble among friends and therefore less serious than the official charge indicates (Vera Institute of Justice 1977).

Sentencing on the basis of seriousness is one of the principal ways courts attempt to arrive at consistent sentences. Most courts employ a rank ordering that incorporates the full range of offenses—from the most serious crimes of armed robbery and rape, through middle-level crimes of domestic homicide, to the lowest level of forgery, theft, and burglary. One reason that sentences appear to critics to be lenient is that most cases are distributed on the lowest level of this ranking.

 Michael D. Norman, Robert C. Wadman, "Utah Pre-sentence Investigation Reports: User Group Perceptions of Quality and Effectiveness"

Prior Record

After the seriousness of the offense, the next most important factor in sentencing is the defendant's

ences in the threshold for granting probation. Likewise, once it has been decided that a defendant should be imprisoned, there are important differences in the factors used to determine the length of that sentence. Stated another way, courtroom work groups tend to look at the same set of general factors when passing sentence, but there is no uniformity in the relative weights that are assigned these factors. Nonetheless, normal penalties governing appropriate sentences for defendants take into account the seriousness of the crime, the prior criminal record, and any aggravating or mitigating circumstances.

prior record. As the prior record increases, so does the sentence. In choosing between probation and imprisonment, the courtroom work group carefully considers the defendant's previous criminal involvement. Often, a single previous conviction is sufficient ground for denying probation (Neubauer 1974). If the decision has been made to sentence the offender to prison, the prior record also plays a role in setting the length of incarceration. A study of seven cities found that a previous incarceration increased the length of the sentence (Welch and Spohn 1986).

How courts assess prior records varies. Some consider only previous convictions, whereas others look at arrests as well. In addition, courtroom work groups often consider the length of time between the current offense and the previous one. If there has been a significant gap, the defendant will often receive a sentence more lenient than normal. On the other hand, if the previous conviction is a recent one, this is often taken as an indication that the defendant is a "bad actor," and the severity of the punishment will increase. Finally, the prior record is assessed within the context of the severity of the crime itself. A study of federal defendants found that prior record had its greatest impact on less serious offenses. "When the crime is perceived as being less serious, individual factors such as prior record seem to be given relatively more weight than when the crime is more serious—there uniformly 'let the punishment fit the crime' seems to be more important" (Tiffany, Avichai, and Peters 1975, 379).

Aggravating or Mitigating Circumstances

In passing sentence, judges and other members of the courtroom work group consider not only the formal charge but also the way the crime was committed. Prosecutors and defense counsel engage in a careful calculation of moral turpitude, examining the nature of the crime and the role of the victim (McDonald, Rossman, and Cramer 1979). Some of the aggravating circumstances that lead to a higher penalty are the use of a weapon and personal injury to the victim. For example, an offender who pistol-whipped an elderly woman during a mugging would receive a higher penalty than one who only threatened the victim with a weapon.

Mitigating factors include youth of the defendant, lack of mental capacity, and role (principal or secondary actor) in the crime. One of the most important mitigating factors is the perceived social stability of the defendant. Marital status, relationship with the family, length of employment, and prior alcohol or drug abuse are considered to be indicators of social stability or instability. Social stability is a particularly important predictor of judges' sentencing, especially when probation is under consideration.

Law in Controversy: Uncertainty and Public Opinion

Sentencing is more art than science. Judges, prosecutors, probation officers, and defense attorneys are well aware that they will make mistakes in considering the seriousness of the offense, the prior record of the defendant, aggravating or mitigating circumstances, and the stability of the defendant. Uncertainty is ingrained in the process. They may send someone to prison who should not be there or impose a prison sentence longer than necessary. Or they may err in the opposite direction: A defendant recently granted probation may commit a serious and well-publicized crime. Note that only the second type of error will reach public attention; mistakes of the first kind may appear, but only well after the fact.

The uncertainties inherent in sentencing are particularly important at a time when public opinion is critical of the courts and sentencing. The majority of Americans feel that sentences are too lenient. In response, courts are sentencing a higher proportion of defendants to prison. Prisons are overcrowded, adding further complexity to the difficult task of arriving at a fair and appropriate sentence.

DISCRIMINATION AND SENTENCING

The ideal of equal justice under the law means that all persons convicted of the same offense should receive identical sentences. But not all deviations from equality are unwarranted. The law also strives for individualized dispositions, sometimes reflecting varying degrees of seriousness of the offense, sometimes reflecting varying characteristics of the offender.

What one person may perceive as unfairness, another may see as justifiable variation. Discussions about unwarranted variation in sentencing employ two widely used terms—discrimination and disparity. Although widely used, these terms are rarely defined consistently. Moreover, the concepts overlap somewhat. Nonetheless, for our purposes they should be treated as involving distinct phenomena.

Disparity, discussed in more detail later in the chapter, refers to inconsistencies in sentencing; the decision-making process is the principal topic of interest. **Discrimination,** on the other hand, refers to illegitimate influences in the sentencing process; defendants' attributes are the primary focus. Legal factors like seriousness of the offense and the prior criminal record of the defendant are considered legitimate factors. Sentencing discrimination exists when some illegitimate attribute is associated with sentence outcomes after all other relevant variables are adequately controlled. These objectionable influences are referred to as extralegal variables (Walker, Spohn, and DeLone 2000).

Imbalance versus Discrimination

No one doubts that the criminal justice system reflects an imbalance in terms of the types of people caught in its web. Whether we examine arrests, prosecutions, convictions, and/or sentences, the statistical profile highlights the same imbalance—poor, young minority males are disproportionately represented.

Evidence of imbalance in outcomes, however, is not proof of discrimination. Imbalance could be the result of legally relevant factors discussed earlier in this chapter (such as seriousness of the offense and prior record). In making claims about discrimination, researchers want to make sure they are comparing cases that are truly similar. By way of illustration, consider two defendants of different races who have received different sentences. One of the defendants is a first offender who pled guilty to burglary and received one year probation. The other has two prior felony convictions and was convicted by a jury of simple robbery and sentenced to three years in prison. Irrespective of which offender was

> **Discrimination:** Illegitimate influences in the sentencing process based on the characteristics of the defendants.

CRIME & PUNISHMENT

The State of Illinois v. Nikita McNutt

Nikita McNutt entered into the bedroom of the thirteen-year-old daughter of the woman he lived with. He later pled guilty to aggravated criminal sexual assault. After watching the CD you should be able to discuss the following questions:

1. What sentence should be imposed on Nikita McNutt? Sentencing reflects four dominant sentencing philosophies—retribution, incapacitation, deterrence, and rehabilitation. Which philosophy is most applicable in this case? Which sentencing philosophy is least applicable in this case?
2. What facts support the prosecutor's statement that this is a serious case? What facts support the defense view that this is not a serious case?
3. The victim does not testify but her mother does. Would the testimony of the thirteen-year-old girl have made a difference?
4. Using the sentencing guidelines, what sentence would this defendant receive in Minnesota?
5. Is this a case where the victim's impact statement helps, hinders, or makes no difference in aiding the judge to determine the appropriate sentence?

---

white or black, we would not conclude solely on this evidence that the sentences were discriminatory. Rather, we would want to compare a number of cases involving similar crimes and defendants with similar backgrounds.

In trying to ensure that like cases are being compared, researchers use statistical controls. A variety of statistical procedures allow researchers to compare first offenders to other first offenders, and burglars to other burglars. Only after legally relevant variables have been held constant can claims about the existence (or absence) of discrimination be made.

Earlier studies often failed to employ appropriate statistical features. They considered only the single variables of race and sentencing, for example, and found racial discrimination in the sentencing. When these studies were reanalyzed, Hagan (1974) found that claims of racial discrimination were not supported by the data.

Conflicting Findings

Numerous studies have probed the extent to which a defendant's attributes, such as economic status, gender, and race, pierce the judicial blindfold when sentences are imposed. The results are provocative, not only because they raise important issues of equality before the law but also because they frequently appear to contradict one another. For example, Eisenstein and Jacob (1977) conclude from a study of sentencing in Baltimore, Chicago, and Detroit that "blacks are not treated worse than whites"; but Lizotte (1978) uses some of the same data from Chicago to calculate that "the 'cost' of being a black laborer is an additional 8.06 months of prison sentence."

Some studies find patterns of discrimination, and others do not. Clearly, sentencing discrimination involves complex issues, and researchers disagree over how best to study it. The discussion that follows examines the research concerning discrimination under the headings of economic status, gender, race in sentencing, and race in capital punishment.

DISCRIMINATION AND ECONOMIC STATUS

The courts are a sorting process. At several stages during the process, it is obvious that access to economic resources makes a difference, with the poor receiving less preferential treatment. For example, the poor are less likely to be released on bail prior to trial and also are less likely to be able to hire a private attorney. These differences during processing carry over to sentencing: Defendants who are not released on bail or represented by a court-appointed attorney are granted probation less often and are given longer prison sentences.

Outcome differences based on economic status are, therefore, readily apparent in sentencing. The provocative title of a recent book by Jeffrey Reiman (2001), *The Rich Get Richer and the Poor Get Prison,* reflects this fact. Prisons are indeed the modern equivalent of the poorhouse. Do these patterns indicate that courts discriminate against the poor in sentencing, or are they the product of other, legally permissible, factors? A number of studies yield conflicting and complex answers.

Some studies conclude that unemployment affects sentencing decisions (Chiricos and Bales 1991; Walsh 1987). Other studies find that unemployment has no significant influence on sentencing (Clarke and Koch 1976; Myers and Talarico 1986a).

A recent study comparing two cities highlights the complexity of the relationship between economic status and sentencing. In Kansas City unemployment had a direct effect on the decision to grant probation but none on the length of imprisonment. In Chicago, on the other hand, unemployment had no effect on the decision to grant probation but directly affected sentence length. Perhaps most importantly, unemployment interacted with race and ethnicity. If the offender was white, unemployment status had no effect. For black or Hispanic young males, though, unemployment was related to harsher sentencing. Nobiling, Spohn, and DeLone (1998) conclude that certain types of unemployed offenders are perceived as "social dynamite." The term social dynamite is used to characterize the segment of the deviant population seen as particularly threatening and dangerous. Viewed from this perspective, economic status appears to be a dimension of social stability considered by the courtroom work group during sentencing.

DISCRIMINATION AND GENDER

Crime, Chapter 9 emphasized, is predominantly (but not exclusively) a male enterprise. Sixteen percent of adults convicted each year are women (Levin, Langan, and Brown 2000), and 6 percent of the prison population are women. The marked imbalance between male and female defendants complicates efforts to examine gender-based differences in sentencing outcomes. Researchers, nonetheless, focus on two key questions: Why are women increasingly being sentenced to prison? and Why are women sentenced more leniently than men? The results of research on gender and sentencing reveal a complex sentencing process.

Why Are Women Increasingly Being Sentenced to Prison?

During the past decade the number of women incarcerated in state and federal prisons has increased dramatically. The almost 91,000 women under the jurisdiction of state and federal authorities stands in sharp contrast to the 23,000-plus held in 1985 (Bureau of Justice Statistics 2001). This increase of almost 400 percent in the number of women prisoners outpaces the increase in male inmates.

Much of this growth in the number (and rate) of women imprisoned is attributed to the war on drugs. The number of women incarcerated for drug offenses increased 432 percent from 1986 to 1991 (Bureau of Justice Statistics 1997). Citing evidence like this, Meda Chesney-Lind (1997) concludes that the war on drugs has translated into a war on women. In other words, women have been the silent targets of punitive responses against drug use, coupled with get-tough sentencing policies such as sentencing guidelines, mandatory minimums, and three-strikes laws. As a result, the criminal justice system now seems more willing to incarcerate women.

Are Women Sentenced More Leniently Than Men?

A variety of studies document the more lenient sentencing of women compared to men. That is, compared to male defendants, women are more likely to be granted probation and also more likely to receive shorter prison sentences. In *The Invisible Woman,* Joanne Belknap (2001) aptly summarizes the three competing hypotheses concerning the treatment of women by the criminal justice system: (1) chivalry or paternalistic treatment, (2) the evil woman, and (3) equal treatment.

The chivalry/paternalism hypothesis stresses that men are unwilling to punish women because they don't believe that a woman could really be a criminal (Moulds 1978). Paternalism emphasizes the notion that women are childlike, and therefore "women are incapable of achieving, nor are they in fact held to, the same standards of personal responsibility as are men" (Rapaport 1991, 368). In essence, gender stereotypes lead predominantly male criminal justice officials to treat women in a protective manner.

The evil woman hypothesis focuses on traditional sex role expectations. This hypothesis emphasizes that women lose the advantages normally provided by chivalry and paternalism when they are convicted of "manly" crimes such as robbery or assault. This evil woman view argues that women might actually be treated more harshly than men when they deviate from stereotypical sex role expectations (Weisheit and Mahan 1988).

The third hypothesis is that men and women are actually treated equally during sentencing. Pennsylvania sentencing data indicate that "when men and women appear in (contemporary) criminal court in similar circumstances and are charged with similar offenses, they receive similar treatment" (Steffensmeier, Kramer, and Streifel 1993). Studies in Kentucky (Crew 1991), Detroit (Spohn and Spears 1997), and Milwaukee (Steury and Frank 1990) likewise report no significant gender-based decisions. Boritch (1992, 293) writes that "some of the less severe treatment of women is attributable to the fact that women usually are less serious offenders than men," and therefore studies using appropriate statistical controls for legally relevant variables find less evidence of differential leniency in the severity of sanctions.

In *Gender, Crime, and Punishment* Kathleen Daly (1994) fleshes out this argument. She selected forty male-female pairs of apparently similar crimes and then analyzed transcripts of the court proceedings. She concludes that women were involved in less serious crimes, and this factor (not gender) explains "lenient" treatment.

Contemporary researchers now explicitly reject the chivalry/paternalism and evil woman explanations. Nonetheless, concern remains that different criteria influence the legal processing of male and female offenders. Erez (1992) reports that gender role expectations and stereotypes guide parole decision making, and Rapaport (1991, 367) argues that "there is a form of gender bias inimical to the interests of women in our capital punishment law."

 Angela Y. Davis, "Women in Prison"

DISCRIMINATION AND RACE

Critics of the criminal justice system view the high rates of arrest and imprisonment for blacks and other minorities as evidence of racial discrimination. Although the law contains no racial bias, these critics claim that, because criminal justice officials exercise discretion, discrimination can and often does occur. (See Controversy: Should Federal Penalties for Crack Be Lowered to Remove Racial Disparities?)

There are more studies of racial discrimination at the sentencing stage than at any other decision

CONTROVERSY

Should Federal Penalties for Crack Be Lowered to Remove Racial Disparities?

 Crack is a cheap, smokable form of cocaine that provides a quick high, and carries a long federal prison term. Powder cocaine, on the other hand, carries a significantly lesser sentence. Under federal law, 5 grams of crack triggers the same mandatory five-year prison term for first offenders as does 500 grams of powder cocaine. (Most state codes make no such distinction.)

The difficulty is that the sentences are based on the weight of the drug and not the weight of the active ingredient in the drug. Through the years, sentencing disparities like this have been common but have rarely entered public discussion. In this case the debate centers on who uses these drugs. Crack cocaine is more likely to be used by blacks and powder by whites. The undeniable result is a racial imbalance—88 percent of all people prosecuted in federal courts for trafficking in crack cocaine are black.

Some in law enforcement believe that such sentencing disparities are justified because crack is a more serious problem than powder cocaine. Crack is more often sold by gangs and used by poor people, who in their desperation to repeat the quick high that crack affords, commit robbery or worse to get the money to buy more. Indeed, law enforcement officials often insist that crack is behind a large percentage of the crime they see (Hodges 1997).

When faced with crime issues, Congress increasingly asks the U.S. Sentencing Commission to study the matter, and study they did. The Sentencing Commission concluded that crack is somewhat more addictive and more closely associated with other crime than is powder cocaine. But the analysis of federal sentencing decisions also documents racial imbalance. The Commission therefore recommended narrowing the sentencing disparity significantly, arguing that a two to one disparity would be more fitting. But thus far Congress has failed to act. In fact, in 1995, Congress voted to uphold the disparity, and riots broke out in various federal prisons.

The U.S. Supreme Court has likewise shown no enthusiasm for tackling this divisive issue. The justices rejected, without comment, the argument that federal sentencing laws are racially discriminatory in treating crack cocaine dealers more severely than traffickers of powder cocaine ("Court: Sentences for Crack" 1997).

The Clinton administration also handled the issue ever so cautiously. Initially the administration opposed any changes in the penalty for crack cocaine (clearly fearing to make it a Republican election issue). But in 1997 the administration softened its stance, proposing to reduce the current 100 to 1 ratio to 10 to 1 by *increasing* the penalties for possession of powder cocaine. This proposal drew negative comments from the congressional black caucus, which argues there should be no racial disparity.

What do you think? Are the differences in cocaine sentencing fair? Should the apparent racial discrepancy in sentencing drug offenders be a matter of concern? Is crack cocaine more addictive than powder cocaine and therefore more likely to be linked with crime? If you favor reducing the disparity in sentencing between crack and powder cocaine, would you do so by reducing the penalty for crack cocaine or raising the sanction for powder cocaine? Overall, do you think Congress is justified in imposing a mandatory minimum for drug crimes, or do mandatory minimums end up producing an irrational sentencing structure with minor offenders being punished more severely than major ones?

 To continue the debate, go to the following sites and search for crack cocaine:

The Sentencing Project: **http://www.sentencingproject.org/** (go to Publications)

Policy.com: **http://www.policy.com/**

Office of National Drug Court Policy: **http://www.whitehousedrugpolicy.gov/**

National Institute of Drug Abuse: **http://www.nida.nih.gov/**

Families Against Mandatory Minimums: **http://www.famm.org/**

For an up-to-date list of Web links, go to **http://www.wadsworth.com/product/0534563406s**.

 Alcoholism & Drug Abuse Weekly, "Drop in Violent Crime Linked to Crack Decline"

Alcoholism & Drug Abuse Weekly, "Senate Supports Tougher Penalties for Powder Cocaine Offenses"

point in the criminal justice system. Studies conducted from the 1930s through the 1960s often reported that extralegal factors such as race were responsible for differences in sanctions. These original findings, however, have not stood up to further analysis, because they failed to use appropriate statistical techniques. When Hagan (1974) reexamined the data from early studies, he found that the relationship between the race of the offender and the sentence handed out was not statistically significant.

Contemporary research using appropriate statistical techniques has produced conflicting findings. Some researchers conclude that blacks are sentenced more harshly than whites, others that there are no differences, and still others that blacks are sentenced more leniently (Walker, Spohn, and DeLone 2000). The first group is research reporting that blacks are sentenced more harshly than whites (Spohn and Holleran 2000; Zatz 1984; Steffensmeier, Ulmer, and Kramer 1998). A prominent example of this type of conclusion is based on a study of six American cities. In three Southern cities, blacks were sentenced to prison more often than whites. No such differences were found in Northern jurisdictions, however (Welch, Spohn, and Gruhl 1985). Overall, though, these studies report modest levels of racial discrimination; racial discrimination affects some forms of sentencing (probation decisions rather than sentencing length) and is confined to less serious cases (Spohn and Cederblom 1991).

A second group of studies fail to find a link between race and sentencing (Klein, Petersilia, and Turner 1990; Myers and Talarico 1986a; Kramer and Steffensmeier 1993). Research in diverse geographical locations reports the absence of consistent evidence of systematic racial discrimination in sentencing. Perhaps typical is a study of sentencing in federal courts, which found that from 1986 to 1988 "white, black, and Hispanic offenders received similar sentences, on average, in Federal district courts." After sentencing guidelines were imposed in 1989, Hispanic and black offenders were slightly more likely than white offenders to be sentenced to prison, but these apparent racial differences were directly attributable to characteristics of offenses and offenders (McDonald and Carlson 1993).

Finally, a few studies conclude that blacks are sentenced more leniently than whites (Bernstein, Kelly, and Doyle 1977). For example, research in Atlanta found that black defendants received the same sentences as whites after taking into account seriousness of the offense, prior record, and so on. In analyzing sentences handed down by individual judges, however, a more complex pattern emerged. Some judges were clearly anti-black, others pro-black, and some nondiscriminatory (Gibson 1978).

Given these inconsistent findings, it is difficult to draw firm conclusions. A prominent summary of the literature argues that the contemporary sentencing process, while not racially neutral, is not characterized by "a widespread systematic pattern of discrimination" (Blumstein et al. 1983, 93). Thus, while a few studies suggest overt racial discrimination, most find more subtle and indirect racial effects (Zatz 1987; Spohn and Spears 1996).

 Carolyn Wolpert, "Considering Race and Crime: Distilling Nonpartisan Policy from Opposing Theories"

DISCRIMINATION AND CAPITAL PUNISHMENT

Capital punishment has figured prominently in studies of racial discrimination in sentencing. Marked racial differences in the application of the death penalty in the South provide the most obvious historical evidence of racial discrimination in sentencing. From 1930 to 1966, 2,306 prisoners were executed in the South, and 72 percent of them were black. This proportion is dramatically higher than the ratio of blacks in the overall population or the ratio of blacks convicted of capital offenses. The racial gap was even more pronounced in rape cases. Only the South executed rapists, and 90 percent of those executed for rape were black. Those most likely to be executed were blacks who had raped white women (Wolfgang and Riedel 1973).

Offender-Victim Dyad

The executions in the South clearly show major racial differences. As indicated earlier, however, racial imbalances in outcomes do not necessarily prove discrimination. Interestingly, many studies found that the most obvious factor—race of the defendant—was not as important as the race of the offender in combination with the race of the victim. The offender-victim dyad, ordered according to the perceived seriousness of the offense, is

1. black offender, white victim;
2. white offender, white victim;
3. black offender, black victim; and
4. white offender, black victim.

Research on the offender-victim dyad established that blacks killing or raping whites were found to be most likely to be executed; conversely, whites killing or raping blacks were least likely to receive the death penalty. These findings have been interpreted as indicating that severe punishments were motivated by a desire to protect the white social order. Some also argue that black lives were not valued as much as white lives. A variety of studies indicate that the use of the death penalty in the South was racially discriminatory (Hindelang 1972). A different conclusion emerges for the North. Studies of the death penalty in Northern states find no evidence of racial discrimination (Kleck 1981).

The following advocacy groups identify race and the death penalty as a significant problem:

Amnesty International: "Race Drives Use of Death Penalty": **http://amnestyusa.org/news/1999/ usa05181999.html**

American Civil Liberties Union (ACLU): "Double Justice: Race and the Death Penalty": **http:// www.aclu.org/issues/death/death5.html**

National Association for the Advancement of Colored People (NAACP): **http://www.naacp. org/**

For an up-to-date list of Web links, go to **http:// www.wadsworth.com/product/0534563406s**.

Evidence of Discrimination since *Gregg*

Major racial differences in execution rates, together with studies finding racial discrimination in the application of the death penalty, figured prominently in the opinions of several justices when the Supreme Court struck down state death penalty laws in 1972 (*Furman v. Georgia*). The Court later upheld guided discretion statutes designed to reduce or eliminate the arbitrariness with which the death penalty is imposed. Since *Gregg v. Georgia* in 1976, several studies report evidence of racial discrimina-

tion in the application of post-*Gregg* death penalty laws (Keil and Vito 1990).

The prosecution of homicide cases involves several discretionary decisions that can affect the use of capital punishment (Weiss, Berk, and Lee 1996). From the time the police classify a homicide until the case is presented in court, significant changes in the characterization of the homicide can occur. Several studies find that racial discrimination exists in the pretrial stages of decision making for potential capital murder prosecutions (Sorensen and Wallace, 1999). For example, a study of more than 1,000 homicide defendants in Florida compared original police classifications with the charges later filed by the prosecutor. Blacks accused of killing whites were the most likely to have the charges upgraded to a death-eligible charge and least likely to be downgraded (Radelet and Pierce 1985). Similarly, in South Carolina, the race of the victim was found to be a significant factor structuring the district attorney's decision to request capital punishment. For black offenders who killed white victims, the prosecutor was forty times more likely to request the death penalty than in the case of black defendants accused of killing other blacks (Paternoster 1984).

Jet Magazine, "Jet Study Shows Justice Department Lawyers Seek Death Penalty Most for Minorities"

Evidence of No Discrimination since *Gregg*

Findings that the application of the death penalty remain racially biased despite the apparent protections required by *Gregg* have been challenged by a study of all death-eligible cases appealed to the Louisiana Supreme Court from 1979 through 1984 (Klemm 1986). The initial analysis revealed the impact of extralegal variables. The chance of receiving a death sentence steadily decreased as one moved down the scale of offender-victim dyads. These findings clearly paralleled earlier ones in other states. More sophisticated analysis, however, highlighted the importance of legal variables.

Unlike previous researchers, Klemm also examined how the crime was committed. The prior relationship of the offender to the victim emerged as an important factor. Primary homicides are crimes of passion involving persons who knew one another. Nonprimary homicides occur during the commission of another felony (most typically, armed robbery), and the victim is a total stranger. Those convicted of nonprimary homicides were more likely to receive a sentence of death, regardless of the race of the offender or the race of the victim. Thus, the chances of receiving a death sentence were greater if the victim was a stranger.

Overall, the race of the victim had only an indirect effect in Louisiana. Likewise a study of the use of the death penalty in Texas prior to *Furman* finds some remarkable parallels to the findings from Louisiana. In particular, nonprimary homicides were more likely to result in the imposition of the death penalty (Ralph, Sorensen, and Marquart 1992).

McCleskey v. Kemp Bars Social Science Evidence

The Supreme Court squarely addressed the issue of racial discrimination in capital punishment in a controversial 1987 decision (*McCleskey v. Kemp*). At issue was a study in Georgia that the application of capital punishment was related to the offender-victim dyad. Defendants convicted of killing a white victim were four times more likely to receive a sentence of death than those found guilty of slaying a black victim. These racial differences remained even after controls for such relevant factors as prior record and type of homicide were introduced. The authors conclude that Georgia had a dual system of capital punishment, based on the race of the victim (Baldus, Pulaski, and Woodworth 1983).

By a five-to-four vote, the majority rejected claims that statistical studies indicated that the state's death penalty law was "wanton and freakish" in application. To Justice Lewis Powell, "Disparities are an inevitable part of our criminal justice system." The opinion argued that the statistics do not prove that race enters into any capital sentencing decisions or that race was a factor in McCleskey's case.

Overall, as the Court has become more supportive of the death penalty, it has become less inclined to consider social science evidence that might show patterns of racial discrimination (Acker 1993). Nonetheless, critics continue to point to patterns of discrimination in the application of the death penalty. In 1997 the American Bar Association called for a moratorium on the death penalty partially based on concerns about the lack of fair use. These same concerns motivated Justice Harry Blackmun to shift his position on the death penalty just before his retirement (Exhibit 16-1).

EXHIBIT 16-1 Justice Blackmun's Dissent

From this day forward, I no longer shall tinker with the machinery of death. For more than 20 years I have endeavored—indeed, I have struggled, along with a majority of this Court—to develop procedural and substantive rules that would lend more than the mere appearance of fairness to the death penalty endeavor. . . .

Rather than continue to coddle the Court's delusion that the desired level of fairness has been achieved and the need for regulation eviscerated, I feel morally and intellectually obligated simply to concede that the death penalty experiment has failed. It is virtually self-evident to me now that no combination of procedural rules or substantive regulations ever can save the death penalty from its inherent constitutional deficiencies. The basic question—does the system accurately and consistently determine which defendants "deserve" to die?—cannot be answered in the affirmative. . . .

The problem is that the inevitability of factual, legal and moral error gives us a system that we know must wrongly kill some defendants, a system that fails to deliver the fair, consistent and reliable sentences of death required by the Constitution.

—Justice Harry Blackmun dissenting in *Callins v. James*, 1994

 For discussions about race and the death penalty from a variety of perspectives, go to the following:

ABA Focus on Law Studies: **http://www.abanet. org/publiced/focus/spr97rac.html**

Policy.com: **http://www.policy.com**

National Center for Policy Analysis: **http://www. ncpa.org/**

For an up-to-date list of Web links, go to **http:// www.wadsworth.com/product/0534563406s**.

DISPARITIES AND SENTENCING

Unlike discrimination, which focuses on attributes of defendants, disparity centers on the process that sentences defendants. Thus, **disparity** refers to

Disparity: Unequal sentences resulting from the sentencing process itself.

inconsistencies in sentencing resulting from the decision-making process. The most commonly cited types of sentencing disparity involve geography (variations across jurisdictions) and judicial backgrounds and attitudes (variations between judges within the same jurisdiction).

The Geography of Justice

What counts against defendants is not only what they do but also where they do it. Significant variations in the sentencing patterns of judges in different judicial districts within the same political jurisdiction is referred to as the geography of justice. The frequency of fines, probation, or imprisonment varies from county to county. Similar differences occur among the states in convicts imprisoned per 100,000 people (Figure 16-2).

Geographical differences in justice are the product of a number of factors, including the amount of crime, the effectiveness of the police in apprehending offenders, and the types of screening employed by the court. Also, some courts deal with more serious offenses, as well as with a greater number of defendants having prior records. But even after controlling for such factors, it is apparent that important geographic differences remain (Rengert 1989; Gertz and Price 1985; Myers and Talarico 1987).

Overall, it appears that the South imposes harsher sentences than other regions. Executions, for example, are concentrated in this region. Similarly, urban courts make greater use of probation and shorter prison terms than their rural counterparts (Austin 1981). Such geographic patterns demonstrate that court officials, drawn as they are from the local communities, vary in their views of what offenses are the most serious as well as what penalty is appropriate (Myers and Talarico 1986b; Myers and Reid 1995).

Judges' Backgrounds and Attitudes

What counts against defendants is not only what they do and where they do it but also which judge will impose sentence. Sentencing disparities based on the judge have fascinated social scientists for decades. A study of women's court in Chicago is typical of this interest. Cameron (1964) found that the proportion of shoplifting defendants placed on probation ranged from a low of 10 percent for one judge

to a high of 62 percent for another. Although such sentencing disparities may be due to variations in the seriousness of the cases heard, differences in judges' backgrounds and attitudes are a more likely cause.

Judges come to the bench from a variety of backgrounds. We might reasonably expect these differences to be reflected in varying patterns of judicial behavior, and studies of judicial decision making support this proposition. U.S. district court judges appointed by Democratic presidents are more likely to decide for the defendant than those appointed by Republican presidents (Carp and Rowland 1983). However, a study of Georgia judges also found that such background variables as age, gender, religion, and experience as a district attorney were poor predictors of sentencing severity (Myers and Talarico 1987).

Variations in judges' backgrounds are associated with different perceptions of what crimes are serious as well as the relative weights to be assigned to conflicting sentencing goals. Several studies have directly examined judicial attitudes and sentences imposed (Green 1961; Gibson 1980). Hogarth (1971) reports that in Ontario, Canada, magistrates who stressed deterrence were more likely to favor prison sentences over other forms of sentencing. Conversely, magistrates who were more treatment-oriented used suspended sentences, fewer fines, and relatively few and relatively short jail sentences.

Although the public views judges as either harsh or lenient sentencers, detailed studies indicate that the pattern is far more complex. It is an accepted fact that judges have different sentencing tendencies. Some have reputations for handing out stiff sentences. "Maximum Max" or "Mean Geraldine" are examples of the colorful labels used by members of the courtroom work group to characterize such judges. Others are known for lenient sentences. "Cut 'em loose Bruce" is one name given such a judge by courthouse regulars. The sentences of most judges fall somewhere in between these extremes. Because they are less distinctive, these courtroom actors seldom get colorful nicknames. Thus a study of federal judges reports that the twenty-nine judges whose general sentences were in the middle range in most cases nonetheless varied in individual instances; each had a sentence ranked among the ten most severe in at least one case and a sentence ranked among the ten least severe in another case (Partridge and Eldridge 1974).

FIGURE 16-2 Number of Prisoners in State Institutions per 100,000 Civilian Population

SOURCE: Bureau of Justice Statistics, U.S. Department of Justice, *Prisoners in 1999* (Washington, D.C.: U.S. Government Printing Office, 2000).

INCREASING THE PREDICTABILITY OF SENTENCING

Disparities and discrimination in sentencing have concerned scholars, practitioners, and offenders themselves for most of this century. Nonetheless, evidence of unequal sentencing uncovered by researchers did not spur efforts to take corrective action (Forst 1982). During the late 1960s and early 1970s, an unusual (and temporary) political coalition developed between liberals and conservatives. Both sides found considerable fault in existing sentencing practices. But their reasons reflected fundamental differences.

Law in Controversy: Reducing Judicial Discretion

Adherents of the due process model were concerned that excess of discretion resulted in a lack of fairness in sentencing. They perceived that criminal justice officials, ranging from police officers to parole boards, were making decisions in a discriminatory manner, especially on the basis of race. They were also concerned that judges' sentencing discretion resulted in sentencing disparities. Thus, the political left saw determinate sentences as a means of reducing individual discretion and thereby (presumably) reducing disparity and discrimination.

Adherents of the crime control model were far more concerned that excess of discretion resulted in the lack of effective crime control. They perceived that criminal justice officials were making decisions that produced undue leniency and lack of certainty in sentencing. Concern about disparity or discrimination was not part of the agenda. In particular, they viewed trial judges as all too ready to impose sentences well below the statutory maximum. They perceived that parole boards were too willing to release prisoners early; they were shocked that prisoners were back on the streets on parole well before the maximum sentence had expired. To conservatives, the essential problem was that sentencing was not reducing crime. In an effort to make sentencing more effective, a "justice" model of sentencing came into increasing prominence. Wrongdoers should be punished on the principle of just deserts, which implies a certainty and uniformity of punishment (Chapter 15).

Despite their different concerns, liberals and conservatives defined the problem in similar terms: The criminal laws permitted too much latitude in sentencing, providing judges with little or no guidance on how to determine the proper sentence for each individual case. This coalition therefore sought greater predictability in sentencing. The development of explicit sentencing standards has dominated criminal justice reforms during the past decades. Initially, legislative bodies directly established standards through determinate sentencing laws (Griset 1991).

Law on the Books: Determinate Sentencing Returns

In response to criticisms of the rehabilitation model, with its emphasis on indeterminate sentences and discretionary parole release, a number of states have adopted determinate or fixed sentencing laws (see Chapter 15). These new sentencing laws are based on the assumption that judges should give offenders a specific amount of time to serve rather than a minimum and a maximum. The change to determinate sentencing is usually accompanied by a move to abolish release on parole as well. Under determinate sentencing, the prisoner is automatically released to community supervision at the end of the term.

Maine was the first to enact determinate sentencing laws in 1976; since then, several other states have also adopted this approach. (See Figure 16-3 on page 434 for a summary of key developments concerning sentencing.) The statutory systems in these states vary widely. At one end of the continuum is

Maine's law, which retains the broad discretion of judges to determine the time to be served in prison. Because of the abolition of parole, however, prisoners can predict at sentencing when they will be released. At the other end of the continuum is California's Uniform Determinate Sentencing Law, which abolished parole release for most prisoners and enacted detailed statutory sentencing standards. The determinate sentencing laws of other states fall in between those of Maine and California; they provide more guidance to judges than the former but less than the latter.

Law in Action: Diverse Impacts

Whether determinate sentencing laws are seen as successful depends somewhat on one's political vantage point. Some adherents hoped that these laws would increase the certainty of punishment (and, in some cases, the severity as well); others feared that prison populations would swell. A number of studies have investigated the impact of determinate sentencing laws in terms of probation, length of prison sentence, and prison populations. The findings indicate that the impacts are diverse.

An offender's chance of receiving probation declined in California (McCoy 1984), but there was no change in Colorado (Covey and Mande 1985). Analysis of sentence length yields a slightly different pattern. In Indiana (Clear, Hewitt, and Regoli 1979) there was a projected 50 percent increase in the actual length of sentence for first offenders, yet in North Carolina (Clarke 1984) increase in sentence length was less severe. Finally, researchers have examined overall prison population. In California (Casper, Brereton, and Neal 1982), as in other states (Carroll and Cornell 1985), there have been significant increases in the prison population following the passage of determinate sentencing legislation.

The lack of clear findings is not surprising. The American legal system consists of numerous independent units, and the laws in question vary in important ways. In reviewing the sentencing developments since the mid-1970s, Michael Tonry (1993) noted that they have been unprecedented in their diversity. Moreover, the specifics of determinate sentencing laws may not be important. Evaluations of long-term trends show that the growth in prison population was much more a continuation of the previous trends than a change attributable to alterations in sentencing laws (Marvell and Moody 1996; Blumstein et al. 1983).

THE MURDER TRIAL OF SHAREEF COUSIN

The Jury Chooses Death

"Today we focus on the character of the man that you found guilty as charged of first degree murder. That's the character of Shareef Cousin." With these words, Assistant DA Roger Jordan began the penalty phase of the murder trial. In urging the jury to recommend the death penalty, Jordan emphasized two aggravating circumstances: (1) the killer was perpetrating, or attempting to perpetrate, an armed robbery, and (2) the especially heinous, atrocious, and cruel manner of the crime.

Toward those ends the prosecution called six witnesses. The first was Sal Gerardi, who tearfully offered a victim impact statement (see Chapter 9) about how empty his life had become since his son's murder. Next, the state called the four victims of the armed robberies (see Chapter 13) who testified about the terror they experienced. Donald Rhodes, for example, was walking a few blocks from the Port of Call restaurant when Shareef Cousin pointed a gun in his face. After giving him his wallet and watch, Shareef walked a few steps and then turned around, pointing his gun at Rhodes in the firing position. Finally, the prosecution called detective Christy Williams, who introduced into evidence Cousin's confession to the four armed robberies. (Since Cousin did not take the witness stand in his own defense, the jury had not known of the previous armed robbery convictions.)

The defense countered with only three witnesses who offered substantive testimony. The first was Richard Collins from Worcester, Massachusetts, where Shareef Cousin had lived for a while with his older brother. Collins testified that the boy "was like a son to me" and was doing well in school until he left for New Orleans in the spring of 1994. Two New Orleans teachers were also called to testify that Cousin did well in their math classes (although under cross-examination one admitted that at times he had been a discipline problem).

Perhaps what was most significant about the defense during the penalty phase was who wasn't called. Outside of the jury, attorney Willard Hill informed the court of an ongoing problem during the trial: "But it has become more acute as a result of the verdict rendered on Friday. I am referring to the reluctance of his family members, for whatever reason, to testify in this case.... We have spent many hours with the family trying to convince them to testify in this case. It has been our advice—our strong recommendation to the family that they do so. They have refused."

Events outside the courtroom (and therefore not observed by the jury) flesh out what Hill alluded to. Family members orchestrated a demonstration on the courthouse steps, claiming authorities vigorously pressed their case against Cousin because "white people consider themselves superior to black people" (Varney 1996).

In short, the jury never heard the other family members plea for mercy, imploring the jury to spare Shareef Cousin's life. During closing arguments Hill tried to highlight the good aspects of Cousin's short life. He seemed to do well when a positive male role model was present, Hill asserted, but seemed to fall off the wagon when he returned from living with his brother near Boston.

During closing arguments the prosecution pressed home the brazen nature of the armed robberies. Referring to Cousin's character witnesses the DA drove home his point: "They didn't see the face that was pointing a gun. . . ." In midsentence, Shareef Cousin exploded, jumping from his seat and shouting "I wasn't out there. I'm innocent." His attorney ordered him to sit down and the judge threatened to remove him from court. But the damage had been done. Seizing the opportunity, Roger Jordan pointed at Cousin and argued "that is the face that Michael Gerardi saw. That's the face that he saw and the anger in his eyes, with a gun in his hand."

Several hours later the jury returned and Judge Bigelow read into the record their verdict:

Having found the below listed statutory aggravating circumstance or circumstances, and after consideration of the mitigating circumstances offered, the jury unanimously determines that the defendant should be sentenced to death. The aggravating circumstance: That the victim in this murder was killed when the offender was engaged in the perpetration or attempted perpetration of an armed robbery.

On July 2, 1996 Judge Bigelow formally imposed sentence, writing on the standard court form that the sentence for Shareef Cousin was "death by lethal injection."

Helen Prejean, "Letter from Death Row"

For more about age and the death penalty, type in the search words *dead teen walking* and read the section, "The Kids on Row."

FIGURE 16-3	Key Developments in Sentencing	
Determinate sentencing	Early twentieth century	In most jurisdictions the judge imposes a specific number of years of imprisonment.
Indeterminate sentencing	Through 1970s	Based on the rehabilitation model, many jurisdictions allow judge to impose a sentencing range. Corrections officials and parole boards decide the actual length of time served.
Maine	1976	First state in modern era to return to determinate sentencing.
Mandatory minimums	1960s	Most jurisdictions require that a defendant serve a minimum prison sentence for selected offenses.
California, Illinois, and Indiana	1977	Determinate sentencing laws enacted.
Minnesota	1980	First state to create a sentencing commission and adopt sentencing guidelines.
Sentencing Reform Act	1984	Federal sentencing guidelines adopted and parole abolished in federal courts effective 1987.
McCleskey v. Kemp	1987	Court rejects use of statistical information to prove racial discrimination in the use of the death penalty.
Mistretta v. U.S.	1989	Federal sentencing guidelines and Sentencing Commission do not violate constitutional separation of powers.
Megan's Law	1994	Following the rape and murder of seven-year-old Megan Kanka, New Jersey passes law requiring convicted sex offenders to register with local police departments.
Polly's Law	1994	California passes three-strikes law named after murder victim Polly Klaas.
"Three Strikes and You're Out"	1993–1995	Twenty-four states and the federal government pass three-strikes laws.
Truth in Sentencing Laws	1990s	First enacted in 1984, Truth in Sentencing Laws require offenders to serve a substantial portion of their prison sentence. Most often applied for violent offenses.
San Diego County v. Romero	1996	California Supreme Court holds judges have discretion in counting prior convictions.
Edwards v. U.S.	1997	Court refuses to hear challenge that federal sentencing laws dealing with crack are racially discriminatory.
Aimee's Law	1999	Proposed federal law named after murder victim Aimee Willard, a college athlete killed by a parolee. Law would encourage states to incarcerate individuals convicted of murder, rape, or child molestation.

SENTENCING GUIDELINES

The problems with the determinate sentencing reforms of the late 1970s were predictable—legislative bodies had neither the time nor the skills to enact detailed sentencing rules. Thus, during the 1980s efforts to provide certainty and consistency in sentencing took on a different form. Legislatures created commissions that devised detailed sentencing rules, and the legislatures then enacted these guidelines into law.

At the national level, Congress created the U.S. Sentencing Commission in 1984 to develop guidelines for sentencing federal offenders. Over strong objections the federal sentencing guidelines went

CASE CLOSE-UP

Mistretta v. U.S. and Sentencing Guidelines

 The opinion of the Court is remarkably silent about the background of John Mistretta. All that is known is that he sold cocaine (probably a small amount) to an undercover federal narcotics agent. Like countless other federal drug charges, Mistretta's indictment would probably have resulted in a plea of guilty and a minor sentence. But Mistretta had the misfortune of being charged a month after the federal sentencing guidelines became effective. Thus, through happenstance, Mistretta's name became forever linked to the bold sentencing experiment of the 1980s—sentencing guidelines.

Defense attorneys across the nation vehemently opposed the new scheme, arguing the guidelines would send a lot more people to prison for a lot longer periods of time. A number of federal judges likewise opposed the guidelines, believing that the congressional legislation represented a slap in the face, an indication that judges' discretion could no longer be trusted.

The judges of the Western District of Missouri (where Mistretta was indicted) were divided over the matter. In a highly unusual maneuver, the trial judges considered the matter as a group and issued what amounted to a collective decision (normally found only at the appellate level). The majority of trial judges in the district rejected legal challenges to the new sentencing scheme. (One judge dissented, however.) As a result, Mistretta pled guilty and was sentenced to eighteen months in prison.

The trial court decision was appealed to the Court of Appeals for the Eighth Circuit, but before the appeal could be heard, another virtually unprecedented legal maneuver occurred: The U.S. Supreme Court, citing the "imperative public importance" of the issue, granted certiorari.

In an eight-to-one decision written by Justice Harry Blackmun (a Nixon appointee who was nonetheless known for a moderate-to-liberal bent on the Court), the Court upheld the law. At the center of the controversy was the composition of the seven-member commission, which by law must include three federal judges. Blackmun wrote that the independent commission "unquestionably is a peculiar institution within the framework of our government." Nonetheless, merely because it is an anomaly or innovation does not mean that the federal sentencing law violated constitutional requirements of separation of powers among the branches of government or delegated excessive authority to the sentencing commission.

The lone dissenter was Justice Antonin Scalia (the Court's most conservative member). He rejected arguments that this case was about comingling of the branches of government. Rather, in his opinion, this case was about "the creation of a new branch altogether, a sort of junior-varsity Congress." In short, Article I, which deals with Congress, was at stake and not Article III, which hinges on judicial independence.

Many federal judges firmly opposed the federal sentencing guidelines, with somewhere between 100 to 150 declaring the law unconstitutional. Numerous others found the law defective on statutory grounds or found ways to avoid its application. Thus *Mistretta* is important because the high court chose not to confront Congress. Although on many issues the Rehnquist Court is deferential to Congress, when it comes to deciding the proper role of the federal judiciary under Article III, the Court has challenged Congress at times. But in *Mistretta* the Court decided that this was not an issue worthy of a confrontation.

into effect on November 1, 1987. By an eight-to-one vote, the Supreme Court upheld the guidelines (see Case Close-Up: *Mistretta v. U.S.* and Sentencing Guidelines).

At the state level, sentencing guidelines operate in seventeen states, and five more have appointed commissions to implement or study this approach (Frase 1995). There are, however, important differences in how guidelines are written.

Law on the Books: Voluntary versus Presumptive Guidelines

Sentencing guidelines provide a recommended sentencing range based on the seriousness of the offense and the criminal history of the offender. In arriving at a sentence, judges first calculate the severity of the crime. Next, with the help of probation officers, the judge computes the criminal history score (the lower the number the better for the defendant). The recommended sentence is then located in the appropriate grid. The sentencing grid used in Minnesota illustrates how sentencing guidelines operate (Exhibit 16-2).

The impact of the recommended sentence depends on whether the jurisdiction has adopted voluntary or presumptive sentencing guidelines. Voluntary sentencing guidelines are most commonly employed. Recommended sentencing ranges are derived by analyzing the types of sanctions judges in the jurisdiction have imposed in various types of cases in the past. Thus, descriptive guidelines codify past sentencing practices as standards for future cases. Once adopted, these guidelines may be used by judges voluntarily, but they are advisory only. Voluntary sentencing guidelines do not have the force of law, and noncompliance by a judge creates no right to appeal the sentence.

Presumptive sentencing guidelines, on the other hand, are prescriptive because they express what sentence should be imposed, regardless of existing practices (Kramer, Lubitz, and Kempinen 1989). Once adopted, these guidelines must be followed by the sentencing judges. If a sentence is imposed outside of the guidelines, the judge must provide reasons for the deviation. Both defendants and prosecutors have the right to have the sufficiency of that explanation reviewed by an appellate court. Thus presumptive, or prescriptive, guidelines have substantial legal authority.

Law in Action: Varied Impacts

The impact of sentencing guidelines varies according to the type of guidelines used. In jurisdictions employing voluntary sentencing guidelines, not all judges actually use the guidelines when imposing sentence and even fewer judges provide reasons for sentences outside the guidelines. As a result, in Florida the guidelines did not reduce sentencing disparity. In Maryland the findings were somewhat more ambiguous with reports of modest decreases in disparity in at least some of the four test sites (Carrow 1984).

Presumptive sentencing guidelines, as you might expect, achieve a much higher rate of judicial compliance. As a result, they have helped reduce sentencing disparity. Overall, racial, ethnic, and gender differences in sentencing generally decline (Parent et al. 1996; Kramer and Ulmer 1996). Dis-

parity reductions, though, tend to erode somewhat over time.

Minnesota's sentencing guidelines provide a case in point. They appear to have achieved their goals of more predictable, more uniform, and more socioeconomically neutral sentencing. During the first year of operation, the law achieved significant increases in both uniformity and neutrality. But not all judicial discretion was eliminated; the law allowed judges some leeway. Over time, judges came to follow the guidelines less faithfully, but uniformity of sentencing remained well above pre-guideline levels (Miethe and Moore 1989). Overall, the Minnesota sentencing guideline law has been more successful than other sentencing reforms. The chief reason for this success, at least in the areas governed by the guidelines, is that the state's sentencing guidelines were backed by the weight of law (Moore and Miethe 1986).

Sentencing guideline laws are associated with increases in sentencing severity. This has been the experience in Minnesota (Tonry 1987), Pennsylvania (Kramer and Lubitz 1985), and Florida (Holten and Handberg 1990). The same holds true at the federal level. In 1987 federal prisons held about 42,000 inmates. By 1999 the federal prison population had increased to 135,246 prisoners. There is, however, a debate in the literature whether increasing prison populations are attributable to sentencing guidelines or simply reflect long-term trends (D'Alessio and Stolzenberg 1995; Moody and Marvell 1996).

 The following Web sites provide information on sentencing in their jurisdictions:

United States Sentencing Commission: **http://www.ussc.gov/**

Minnesota Sentencing Commission: **http://www.msgc.state.mn.us/**

North Carolina Sentencing Commission: **http://www.aoc.state.nc.us/www/copyright/commissions/sentcom/index.htm**

State of Washington Sentencing Guidelines Commission: **http://www.sgc.wa.gov/**

The Pennsylvania Commission on Sentencing: **http://pcs.la.psu.edu/**

New Jersey Sentencing Guidelines: **http://www.judiciary.state.nj.us/sentguid.htm**

For an up-to-date list of Web links, go to **http://www.wadsworth.com/product/0534563406s**.

EXHIBIT 16-2 Minnesota Sentencing Grid

Severity level of conviction offense		Criminal history score						
		0	**1**	**2**	**3**	**4**	**5**	**6 or more**
Murder, 2nd degree (intentional murder, drive-by-shootings)	X	306 *299–313*	326 *319–333*	346 *339–353*	366 *359–373*	386 *379–393*	406 *399–413*	426 *419–433*
Murder, 3rd degree Murder, 2nd degree (unintentional murder)	IX	150 *144–156*	165 *159–171*	180 *174–186*	195 *189–201*	210 *204–216*	225 *219–231*	240 *234–246*
Criminal sexual conduct, 1st degree Assault, 1st degree	VIII	86 *81–91*	98 *93–103*	110 *105–115*	122 *117–127*	134 *129–139*	146 *141–151*	158 *153–163*
Aggravated robbery, 1st degree	VII	48 *44–52*	58 *54–62*	68 *64–72*	78 *74–82*	88 *84–92*	98 *94–102*	108 *104–112*
Criminal sexual conduct, 2nd degree (a) & (b)	VI	21	27	33	39 *37–41*	45 *43–47*	51 *49–53*	57 *55–59*
Residential burglary Simple robbery	V	18	23	28	33 *31–35*	38 *36–40*	43 *41–45*	48 *46–50*
Nonresidential burglary	IV	12*	15	18	21	24 *23–25*	27 *26–28*	30 *29–31*
Theft crimes (over $2,500)	III	12*	13	15	17	19 *18–20*	21 *20–22*	23 *22–24*
Theft crimes ($2,500 or less) Check forgery ($200–$2,500)	II	12*	12*	13	15	17	19	21 *20–22*
Sale of simulated controlled substance	I	12*	12*	12*	13	15	17	19 *18–20*

Note: The left-hand column ranks the seriousness of the offense according to ten categories. The upper rows provide a seven-category criminal history score, calculated by summing the points allocated to such factors as the number of previous convictions, the total times incarcerated, whether the offender was on probation or parole, employment status or educational achievement, and the offender's history of drug and/or alcohol abuse. After calculating the offense severity ranking and the criminal history score, the judge determines the recommended sentence by finding the cell of the sentencing grid in the applicable row and column. The cells above the bold line call for sentences other than imprisonment; these numbers specify months of supervision. The cells below the bold line contain the guideline sentence expressed in months of imprisonment. The single number is the recommended sentence. The range extends plus or minus 5 to 8 percent from the guideline sentence. By law first-degree murder is excluded from the guidelines and continues to have a mandatory life sentence.

*One year and one day.

SOURCE: Minnesota Sentencing Guidelines Commission, 1981, p. 23.

Law in Controversy: Has Too Much Discretion Been Removed?

Federal sentencing guidelines remain highly controversial (Stith and Cabranes, 1998). Indeed many federal judges, probation officers, defense attorneys, and even some prosecutors resent and resist the guidelines. According to Michael Tonry (1993), the federal sentencing guidelines "are a failure and should be radically revised or repealed." In support of this conclusion he offers the following arguments. First, the guidelines are unduly harsh, as reflected in the dramatic increase in the federal prison population. Second, the guidelines have failed to reduce disparities in federal sentencing. Finally, the guidelines contribute to unfairness in sentencing because they are rigid and complex. Judges are specifically not allowed to consider the defendant's employment status or family life in passing sentence. (A Day in Court: "Drug Sentence Draws Wrath of Judges" provides an example of the type of sentencing decisions judges feel are unjust.)

State guidelines are not as controversial, mainly because they are more diverse and often allow greater discretion to judges. But this greater flexibility has also lessened their impact. Moreover, not all efforts to develop sentencing guidelines have been successful. Some efforts foundered because legislatures were unwilling to devote sufficient resources to the task. But mainly the political culture of the state was not conducive to generating the necessary consensus needed to develop and implement guidelines (Tonry 1991).

Consider New York (Griset 1995). The members of the New York commission reflected the same political divisions as were found in the state's criminal justice policy-making circles. Unlike Minnesota, where the commission members were all committed to sentencing reform and shared a vision for sentencing guidelines, the New York commissioners were torn by internal factionalism and saw themselves as representing the partisan interests of their

background (Gizzi 1992). Thus, New York, and other states such as Vermont, have been unsuccessful in developing and implementing sentencing guidelines.

INCREASING THE SEVERITY OF THE PENALTY

The majority of Americans believe that prison sentences are too lenient (Krisberg 1988), and elected officials often express these views (Thomson and Ragona 1987). Thus, when confronted with a crime problem, legislators respond by sounding a clarion call to get tough with criminals. Such actions reflect the notion that increasing the severity of the penalty will deter criminals and reduce crime. These ideas are more often justified by moral claims than supported by valid scientific evidence. Researchers are skeptical that this type of deterrent effect actually exists.

Law on the Books: Mandatory Minimum Sentences

Mandatory minimum sentencing laws are one method legislatures use to increase the severity of sentencing. These types of laws are typically enacted in response to allegations that lenient judges are allowing many serious offenders (particularly violent ones) to go free. (The "proof" of this proposition is often limited to one or two highly publicized cases.) Virtually all states have passed mandatory minimum sentencing laws.

Typically, **mandatory minimum sentencing** laws require that offenders convicted of certain offenses must be sentenced to a prison term of not less than a specified period of years, and nonprison sentences (such as probation) are expressly precluded. In short, a term of imprisonment is mandated regardless of the circumstances of the offense or the background of the individual.

In recent years the most popular mandatory minimum laws have supposedly targeted violent offenders with previous felony convictions. (See Controversy: Should "Three Strikes and You're Out"

Jeffrey T. Ulmer, John H. Kramer, "The Use and Transformation of Formal Decision-Making Criteria: Sentencing Guidelines"

Joseph S. Hall, "Guided to Injustice? The Effect of the Sentencing Guidelines on Indigent Defendants and Public Defense"

Mandatory minimum sentencing: Minimum required penalty specified for a certain crime.

A DAY IN COURT

"Drug Sentencing Draws Wrath of Judges"

Washington—Except for a speeding ticket, 19-year-old filing clerk Margaret Mitchell had never been in trouble with the law before. But because she wanted money to buy Christmas presents, she welcomed an offer from her brother's friend to earn $250 by carrying crack from Los Angeles to Las Vegas. She was caught at the bus station with 504.9 grams of crack in a gym bag.

The law left no choice for U.S. District Judge Harry Hupp of Los Angeles. Last October he ordered her to prison for 10 years without parole. That's more than the average federal sentence in 1990 for homicide (six years, eight months), robbery (eight years), and sex offenses (five years, one month). "Make no mistake, she deserved punishment, but 10 years is out of whack," Hupp, an appointee of former President

Reagan, said Friday. "Here's a young person at the beginning of her life and suddenly the world has closed in on her. This is not the type of case to lock 'em up and throw the key away."

Such stiff prison terms have provoked protests from a growing number of federal judges—including many tough law-and-order Reagan nominees—who say they are routinely forced to hand out unjustifiably harsh punishment to minor, first-time drug offenders. One Reagan appointee quit in protest. "The bottom line is we're putting people in prison who don't belong there—and the prisons are bulging at the seams," U.S. District Judge Robert McNichols of Spokane, Wash., said.

SOURCE: Aaron Epstein, "Drug Sentencing Draws Wrath of Judges," *The Times-Picayune*, May 1993.

Laws Be Passed?) Through the years legislative bodies have also enacted mandatory minimums for crimes that are particularly unpopular at the moment. Listed here are some of the most prominent examples:

- Short minimum prison sentences for those who use (or in some instances merely possess) firearms. For example, the Michigan Felony Firearm Statute requires an additional two-year prison sentence for those who possess firearms while committing felonies.

- Mandatory jail sentences for certain types of repeat drunk drivers. For example, Mothers Against Drunk Driving (MADD) has effectively lobbied statehouses for mandatory prison sentences for those convicted of drunk driving (Chapter 18).

- Possession of certain drugs with intent to sell often receives mandatory minimums. Federal law, for example, mandates a five-year minimum prison sentence for possession of cocaine.

Most recently mandatory minimum legislation has taken on a new direction. Now called Truth in Sentencing laws, these laws would required offenders to a serve a substantial portion of their prison term (often 85 percent) before release. Most typi-

cally these laws are targeted for crimes of murder, child molestation, and sexual assaults (Ditton and Wilson 1999).

Visit the Web site of Families Against Mandatory Minimums (FAMM), a national organization of citizens working to repeal statutory mandatory minimum sentences: **http://www.famm.org/**.

For an up-to-date list of Web links, go to **http:// www.wadsworth.com/product/0534563406s**.

Law in Action: Nullification by Discretion

Mandatory minimum sentencing laws have proven popular because they promise certainty of punishment. "If Every Criminal Knew He Would Be Punished If Caught" is the title of an article by James Q. Wilson (1973). He argued that the way to improve the deterrent effect of the law is to concentrate on increasing the certainty—but not necessarily the severity—of punishment. But researchers caution that administering the law is seldom that automatic.

Sharp increases in formal penalties tend to be sidestepped by those who apply the law. "No one

Should "Three Strikes and You're Out" Laws Be Passed?

 The kidnapping and murder of Polly Klaas focused the nation's attention on violent, predatory criminals. The man convicted of the crime, Richard Allen Davis, was an ex-con who had recently been released from prison on parole. The news coverage of the kidnapping and eventually the arrest fed the nation's fears that no one was safe, not even those who lived in a tranquil small town like Petaluma, California. At fault were not only societal outcasts like Richard Allen Davis, but also a criminal justice system that was a failure (Surette 1996).

Faced with an unsettled public, elected officials sought to reassure them by taking dramatic action. Thus, the murder of Polly Klaas became the reference event for passing "three strikes and you're out" legislation.

The basic arguments advanced by proponents of the three-strikes concept parallel the crime control model, which has dominated American thinking since the 1960s. First, incapacitating chronic offenders who have demonstrated by their acts that they are both dangerous and unwilling to reform will protect the public. Moreover, repeat offenders will be deterred because they will be off the streets.

Critics countered that substantial increases in the use of imprisonment over the past decade have had little if any effect on violent crime rates. Life terms for three-time losers will require the allotment of expensive prison cells to offenders who are well past their peak ages of criminal conduct. Moreover, the criminal courts will be overburdened—demands for jury trials will rise, speedy dispositions will decrease, and costs for indigent defense will increase. These adherents of the due process model argue that spending the same amount of money in other areas would produce a much greater reduction in crime than three-strikes laws (Greenwood et al. 1996).

Court arguments aside, public support for three-strikes laws was overwhelming—over 80 percent in some polls. Thus in quick order, between 1993 and 1995, elected officials in twenty-four states and the federal government enacted new laws using the "three strikes" moniker. What was left largely unspoken during the debate was the fact that for many years most states have had provisions in their laws for enhanced sentencing of repeat offenders.

The three-strikes laws that were passed had substantial differences (Clark, Austin and Henry, 1998). Although all the statutes increased sentences substantially, they differed in the number and types of offenders affected. The federal crime law, for example, affected only the small number of defendants in federal courts who had accumulated three convictions for crimes involving serious injuries to their victims. The California law, on the other hand, was far broader. It mandated twenty-five years to life in prison for an offender convicted of any felony following two prior convictions for serious crimes (Greenwood et al. 1996).

Were these laws effective? Outside of California, three-strikes provisions rarely applied. These laws have had minimal impacts because they were drafted to apply to only the most violent repeat offenders, the very defendants already covered by habitual offender laws and also the very offenders who fare the worst under existing normal penalties (Clark, Austin, and Henry 1997).

California's law potentially has greater impact because it was more loosely drafted. Because any

should assume that any judicial outcome can be made truly 'mandatory'—discretion removed from one place in the criminal justice system tends to reappear elsewhere in it" (Wilson 1983, 187). At a variety of points in the application of legal sanctions—police arrest, prosecutorial discretion, jury conviction, and sentencing—discretion may be exercised to offset the severity of the penalty (McCoy 1984).

A reduction in the number of arrests is one type of discretionary reaction that may occur when the severity of the penalty is increased. This clearly occurred when Connecticut's governor tried to crack down on speeders by imposing a mandatory loss of the driver's license; arrests for speeding decreased after the severe penalties were announced, apparently because the police and other legal officials perceived that the penalty was too severe for the offense (Campbell and Ross 1968).

An increase in prosecutorial discretion may also compensate for an increase in the harshness of sentencing. Prosecutors often respond to new leg-felony can be a third strike, life sentences can be imposed for relatively minor nonviolent crimes. Thus, the California law applies to criminals with a record of one or more violent or serious felonies. After one such crime ("strike"), the sentence for any new felony is doubled. After two strikes, a new felony requires a term of twenty-five years to life. In less than two years 3,371 defendants were sentenced under the third strike and almost 28,000 under the second strike (Criminal Justice Consortium 1997).

Stepping back from predictions about the immediate future, three-strikes laws are the most recent example of spasmodic attempts by the public, and the politicians they elect, to respond in an extreme manner to what is perceived as skyrocketing crime rates and an unduly lenient criminal justice system. These outbursts are followed by adaptation by members of the courtroom work group. This happened following the Rockefeller drug law of 1972 and the 1980s victim's bill of rights in California. Prosecutors, for example, can manipulate case records to downgrade the seriousness of the offense in order to bring sentencing exposure into line with what prosecutors and judges think are appropriate levels. Political scientists Malcolm Feeley and Sam Kamin (1996) argue therefore that "researchers should guard against being caught up in the rhetoric of the symbolic crusade lest they contribute to it."

Adaptive behavior is readily apparent in the California Supreme Court's decision holding that judges don't have to impose life sentences on repeat criminals if they think the punishment is too harsh (*San Diego County v. Romero* 1996). Later the court held that juvenile convictions likewise need not be counted (*San Diego County v. Garcia* 1999). In essence, the California high court held that the law went too far and judges should use discretion.

Although courtroom work groups typically find ways to adapt to broad demands for more punitive

sanctions, this does not imply that get-tough measures like three strikes have no impact. For one, the law significantly disrupted the efficiency of the work group, making the prediction of case outcomes more difficult (Harris and Jesilow 2000). For another, these efforts have through the years systematically ratcheted up the penalty structures, leading to the anomaly highlighted in Chapter 15—prison populations continue to swell despite the fact that crime is falling. Finally, the law is applied unevenly, with some defendants receiving harsh sentences for minor crimes. In one extreme case the defendant was sentenced to twenty-five years in prison for stealing $35.98.

What do you think? Are three-strikes laws an appropriate and effective response to violent crimes by predators? Or do you think that these laws are overreactions? Given that adaptation by the courtroom work group seems inevitable, why do legislatures periodically pass such laws?

 To continue debating the topic, point your browser to

California Criminal Law Observer: The "Three Strikes and You're Out" Law: **http://www. silicon-valley.com/3strikes.html**

Families to Amend California's 3-Strikes (FACTS): **http://www.facts1.com/**

For an up-to-date list of Web links, go to **http:// www.wadsworth.com/product/0534563406s**.

 Robert N. Scola, Jr., H. Scott Fingerhut, "Tough Times in the Sunshine State"

John R. Schafer, "The Deterrent Effect of Three-Strikes Laws"

John J. Dilulio, Jr., "Against Mandatory Minimums"

---

islative actions by reducing the number of charges for that category. In 1973 the New York legislature enacted a tough new antidrug law that provided stiff mandatory sentences (up to life) and sought to prevent plea bargaining. Indictments for drug violations in New York State remained constant through the first year of the law's implementation, but the number fell by 14 percent the next year (Association of the Bar of the City of New York Drug Abuse Council 1976). Thus, prosecutors may choose to file charges for an offense that does not

carry the most severe penalties when they anticipate that judges and juries will be reluctant to convict.

A decrease in the number of convictions may also occur when legislators increase the severity of punishment. The most commonly cited example is capital punishment in late-eighteenth- and early-nineteenth-century England, when most felonies were punishable by death. Judges often strained to avoid convicting defendants by inventing legal technicalities (Hall 1952). Similarly, in New York State,

Maximum Security
Crime Behind Bars

Maximum security takes viewers behind the walls of Walpole Penitentiary in Massachusetts. Follow the corrections officers who investigate crime among 700 of the state's most dangerous offenders. As you watch the video, ask yourself the following questions:

1. How does life inside Walpole reinforce citizens' images of what a prison is like? How does life inside the prison challenge citizens' images of what a prison is like?
2. What implications of the nation's policy of imposing long sentences affect the running of a prison like Walpole?
3. How does the violent environment inside the prison affect the inmates? How does the environment affect the corrections officers?

after the tough drug law was passed, the number of convictions dropped.

After conviction, judges are reluctant to apply the severe penalty (Ross and Foley 1987). When Chicago traffic court judges sought to crack down on drunk drivers by voluntarily agreeing to impose a seven-day jail term, the penalty was rarely applied (Robertson, Rich, and Ross 1973).

There is clearly a relationship between punishment policy and the system that administers it. Through the discretionary actions of police, prosecutors, judges, and juries, harsh penalties are nullified. The more severe the penalty, the less likely it will be imposed when its severity exceeds what is viewed as appropriate. The final result is that more produces less. Stepping up the severity of the punishment does not increase the threat of punishment; it reduces it.

Law in Controversy:
Negative Side Effects

One reason legislators find raising penalties so attractive is that they appear to be fighting crime but do not have to increase appropriations. It is a policy apparently without costs; the public will be appeased without the painful necessity of voting in higher taxes. But a number of studies suggest that increasing the severity of the punishment produces negative side effects (referred to by economists as hidden costs and others as unanticipated consequences). That is, harsher laws have impacts, but often not the ones intended.

One negative side effect of increasing the severity of punishments centers on the greater time, effort, and money courts must expend. Faced with severe sanctions, defendants demand more trials, which consumes more court time. This clearly happened in New York State. Before the 1973 drug law, 6.5 percent of the drug cases went to trial; after it, 13.5 percent (Association of the Bar 1976). As a result, a backlog of cases developed, delays increased, and the certainty and speed of conviction declined. Moreover, the courts were forced to spend $55 million to comply with the law.

Another unintended consequence is that increasing the severity of penalties increases the pressure to plea bargain. To ensure convictions, avoid expensive and time-consuming trials, and give expression to their views of benevolence, prosecutors and judges try to get a guilty plea in return for a lesser sentence (Wilson 1983). To cite but one example, Illinois prosecutors allowed first-time drunk driving offenders to plead to reckless driving, which did not carry a mandatory one-year suspension of the driver's license (Neubauer 1974).

Critics are also concerned that mandatory minimum sentencing legislation results in a rigid, mechanical, and inflexible overreaction to problems of judicial discretion. By requiring every single defendant convicted under the same statute to serve the identical sentence, it threatens to create a system so automatic that it may operate in practice like a poorly programmed robot. In the words of U.S. District Court Judge Vincent Broderick, "The most frustrating aspect of mandatory minimum prison sentences is that they require routinely imposing long prison terms based on a single circumstance, when other circumstances in the case cry out for a significantly different result. The same sentence is mandated for offenders with very different criminal backgrounds and whose roles differ widely one from another" (Vincent and Hofer 1994). There are more than 100 federal mandatory minimum penalties located in 60 criminal statutes. The large number of mandatory minimums makes it difficult to develop a fair and equitable sentencing structure.

CONCLUSION

Richard Allen Davis was convicted of first-degree murder and sentenced to death. But as mentioned in Chapter 9, he used the sentencing hearing to make yet another dramatic statement, accusing the father of sexual misconduct with his daughter.

Whether the "three strikes and you're out" laws passed in the aftermath of the Polly Klaas kidnapping and murder will have a lasting impact is open to question. The essential difficulty is that the criminals who figure prominently in the media bear little resemblance to the ones who appear before U.S. judges every day. While the replica of Lady Justice on the outside of the courthouse contemplates justice in the abstract, judges inside the courthouse must pass judgment on real-life defendants, not the stereotypical villains who dominate the rhetoric of elected officials. In deciding whether to send an offender to prison or grant him or her probation, the scales of justice require the judge (and other members of the courtroom work group) to weigh the normal penalty for the offense, the seriousness of the crime, and the defendant's prior record and social stability. The resulting decisions have become the focus of heated public debate.

To some, American courthouses do not mete out fair and impartial justice. These critics find that the blindfold is improperly pierced by sentences that are discriminatory and/or disparate. To others, American courthouses hand out sentences that are too lenient. These critics argue that wielding the sword of justice will protect the public from crime. These dual concerns have prompted numerous changes since the mid-1970s. Determinate sentencing laws, mandatory minimum sentencing provisions, and sentencing guidelines are the most prominent changes undertaken.

Sentencing is likely to remain on the nation's political agenda. All too often, members of the public, as well as elected officials, have ignored an important reality: Prison populations are swelling. America sends more people to prison than any other Western nation, and the rate of incarceration is growing steadily. The result is severe prison overcrowding, compounded by federal court orders requiring major improvements in prison conditions. Limitations on the capacity and quality of prisons create a political dilemma. Although citizens and public officials want to send even more offenders to prison for longer periods of time, they are unwilling to spend large sums of tax dollars to build the needed facilities. Sentencing is thus likely to remain an important public policy issue for the foreseeable future. Alas, in the end, Lady Justice appears to cost more than the public is able or willing to spend.

CRITICAL THINKING QUESTIONS

1. Within the courtroom work group, which actor is the most influential in sentencing decisions? Why? How might influence vary from one courtroom to the next?

2. In what ways do the crime control model and the due process model differ over the issues of disparity and discrimination in sentencing?

3. In what ways do sentencing guidelines reflect normal penalties? In what ways do they differ?

4. To what extent can slight variations in the defendant's background produce markedly different sentences? In Exhibit 16-2 calculate the recommended sentence for a defendant convicted of second-degree assault. How much does the sentence change if the criminal history score is a 2 or a 3? Do you think this is too much variation to be determined by a mathematical calculation?

5. How have public demands to "get tough with crooks" changed the sentencing process in the last two decades? Why do courtroom work groups resist such efforts and often subvert them?

 WORLD WIDE WEB RESOURCES AND EXERCISES

Web Guides

http://dir.yahoo.com/Society_and_Culture/Crime/
    Correction_and_Rehabilitation/

http://dir.yahoo.com/Society_and_Culture/Crime/
    Correction_and_Rehabilitation/Sentencing/

http://dir.yahoo.com/Society_and_Culture/Crime/
Correction_and_Rehabilitation/Sentencing/
Mandatory_Minimum_Sentences/

http://dir.yahoo.com/Society_and_Culture/Crime/
Correction_and_Rehabilitation/Death_Penalty/

Web Search Terms

"Sentencing"; "sentencing commission"; "sentencing guidelines"; "mandatory minimums"

Useful URLs

The Sentencing Project is a source for criminal justice policy analysis, data, and program information for policy makers and the public: **http://www.sentencingproject.org/**.

Bureau of Justice Statistics sentencing statistics are available at **http://www.ojp.usdoj.gov/bjs/sent.htm**.

Bureau of Justice Statistics death penalty statistics are available at **http://www.ojp.usdoj.gov/bjs/cp.htm**.

Uncommon URLs

Coalition for Federal Sentencing Reform is united by a concern that the federal sentencing guidelines are not fulfilling their promise: **http://www.sentencing.org/**.

Citizens for Effective Justice is working toward changes that would reduce crime and prison overcrowding through an alternative sentencing program that combines punishment and rehabilitation: **http://www.reducecrime.org/**.

The National Association of Sentencing Advocates is a professional membership organization of sentencing advocates and defense-based mitigation specialists: **http://www.sentencingproject.org/nasa/index.html**.

Aimee's Law is dedicated to preserving the memory of Aimee Willard: **http://www.geocities.com/~aimeeslaw/**.

Davrie Communications asserts that, although the current federal sentencing regime leaves little room to maneuver, steps can be taken to position defendants for the most advantageous programs allowed by the Bureau of Prisons: **http://www.davrie.com/PreSentencing.htm**.

The Criminal Justice Division of the Alteo Group provides advocacy services under the federal sentencing guidelines: **http://www.alteo.com/cj/**.

Web Exercises

1. The Bureau of Justice Statistics publishes a variety of statistics on sentencing, which can be found at the following URL: **http://www.ojp.usdoj.gov/bjs/welcome.html**. Access the site, and under Courts and Sentencing, find the most recent report "Felony Sentences in State Courts." Use these data to update the information in Table 16-1.

   At the same site under the heading Corrections, examine the summary statistics provided. Compare this information to the discussion of normal penalties. What evidence do you find to support the discussion that seriousness of the crime and prior record of the defendant are key factors in sentencing?

2. Several Web sites are devoted to capital punishment and represent a broad array of views buttressed by facts. Using the search engine of your choice, locate these pages. If you are using Yahoo, the commands are as follows: **http://www.yahoo.com/Society_Culture/Crime/Death_Penalty**.

   Select one group from "Opposing Views" and another from "Supporting Views." Compare these Web sites, asking yourself the following questions: What arguments do the two sides make, and what evidence do they use to support their positions? It is also important to analyze issues that are not addressed. What do opponents of the death penalty have to say about deterring crime? What do supporters have to say about the death penalty being fairly (or unfairly) applied?

3. To monitor the latest discussions on sentencing guidelines, do a subject search with the search engine of your choice. With Alta Vista the commands are as follows: **http://altavista.com/**. Under Search, click the Web, and then click English.

   For your subject search, type "*sentencing guidelines*" and press Enter. Pick out three Web pages and see how their discussions relate to topics discussed in the chapter, particularly whether the guidelines produce injustice by removing too much discretion from the judge. Overall, do the Web sites support or oppose sentencing guidelines?

 INFOTRAC COLLEGE EDITION RESOURCES AND EXERCISES

Basic Searches

Sentences; mandatory sentences; pre-sentence investigation reports; sentencing guidelines; discrimination in criminal justice administration; prison sentences

Recommended Articles

Ian F. Haney Lopez, "Institutional Racism: Judicial Conduct and a New Theory of Racial Discrimination"

Celia C. Lo, Richard C. Stephens, "Drugs and Prisoners: Treatment Needs on Entering Prison"

Josie Glausiusz, "The Crack Kid Myth"

InfoTrac College Edition Exercises

1. Using the search term *discrimination in criminal justice administration,* find two or more articles that discuss racial discrimination in sentencing. To what extent do they make the distinction between imbalance and discrimination?

2. Using the search term *sentences,* locate two or more articles that research the sentencing process. What information do they provide about the operation of normal penalties?

REFERENCES

Acker, James. 1993. "A Different Agenda: The Supreme Court, Empirical Research Evidence, and Capital Punishment Decisions, 1986–1989." *Law and Society Review* 27: 65–86.

Association of the Bar of the City of New York Drug Abuse Council. 1976. *The Effects of the 1973 Drug Laws on the New York State Courts.* New York: Author.

Austin, Thomas. 1981. "The Influence of Court Location on Types of Criminal Sentences: The Rural-Urban Factor." *Journal of Criminal Justice* 9: 305–316.

Baldus, David, Charles Pulaski, and George Woodworth. 1983. "Comparative Review of Death Sentences: An Empirical Study of the Georgia Experience." *Journal of Criminal Law and Criminology* 74: 661–53.

Belknap, Joanne. 2001. *The Invisible Woman: Gender, Crime, and Justice.* 2d ed. Belmont, CA: Wadsworth.

Bernstein, Ilene Nagel, William Kelly, and Patricia Doyle. 1977. "Societal Reaction to Deviants: The Case of Criminal Defendants." *American Sociological Review* 42: 743–95.

Blumstein, Alfred, Jacqueline Cohen, Susan Martin, and Michael Tonry, eds. 1983. *Research on Sentencing: The Search for Reform.* Vol. 1. Washington, D.C.: National Academy Press.

Boritch, Helen. 1992. "Gender and Criminal Court Outcomes: An Historical Analysis." *Criminology* 30: 293–317.

Bureau of Justice Statistics. 1997. *Correctional Populations in the United States, 1995.* Washington, D.C.: U.S. Department of Justice.

———. 2001. *Prison Statistics.* http://www.ojp.usdoj.gov/bjs/prisons.htm, 19 February.

Cameron, Mary. 1964. *The Booster and the Snitch.* Glencoe, IL: Free Press.

Campbell, Curtis, Candace McCoy, and Chimezie Osigweh. 1990. "The Influence of Probation Recommendations on Sentencing Decisions and Their Predictive Accuracy." *Federal Probation* 54: 13–21.

Campbell, Donald, and H. Laurence Ross. 1968. "The Connecticut Crackdown on Speeding: Times-Series Data in Quasi-Experimental Analysis." *Law and Society Review* 3: 33–54.

Carp, Robert, and C. K. Rowland. 1983. *Policymaking and Politics in the Federal District Courts.* Knoxville: University of Tennessee Press.

Carroll, Leo, and Claire Cornell. 1985. "Racial Composition, Sentencing Reforms, and Rates of Incarceration, 1970–1980." *Justice Quarterly* 2: 473–490.

Carrow, Deborah. 1984. "Judicial Sentencing Guidelines: Hazards of the Middle Ground." *Judicature* 68: 161–171.

Carter, Robert, and Leslie Wilkins. 1967. "Some Factors in Sentencing Policy." *Journal of Criminal Law, Criminology and Police Science* 58: 503–514.

Casper, Jonathan, David Brereton, and David Neal. 1982. *The Implementation of the California Determinate Sentencing Law.* Washington, D.C.: U.S. Department of Justice.

Chesney-Lind, Meda. 1997. *The Female Offender: Girls, Women and Crime.* Thousand Oaks, CA: Sage.

Chiricos, Theodore, and William Bales. 1991. "Unemployment and Punishment: An Empirical Assessment." *Criminology* 29: 701–724.

Clark, John, James Austin, and D. Alan Henry. 1997. *"Three Strikes and You're Out": A Review of State Legislation.* Washington, D.C.: National Institute of Justice.

———. 1998. "'Three Strikes and You're Out': Are Repeat Offender Laws Having Their Anticipated Effects?" *Judicature* 81: 144–154.

Clarke, Stevens. 1984. "North Carolina's Determinate Sentencing Legislation." *Judicature* 68: 140–152.

Clarke, Stevens, and Gary Koch. 1976. "The Influence of Income and Other Factors on Whether Criminal Defendants Go to Prison." *Law and Society Review* 11: 57–92.

Clear, Todd, and George Cole. 2000. *American Corrections.* 5th ed. Belmont, CA: Wadsworth.

Clear, Todd, John Hewitt, and Robert Regoli. 1979. "Discretion and the Determinate Sentence: Its Distribution, Control and Effect on Time Served." *Crime and Delinquency* 24: 428–445.

"Court: Sentences for Crack Are Fair." 1997. *Times-Picayune,* 15 April.

Covey, Herbert, and Mary Mande. 1985. "Determinate Sentencing in Colorado." *Justice Quarterly* 2: 259–270.

Crew, B. Keith. 1991. "Sex Differences in Criminal Sentencing: Chivalry or Patriarchy?" *Justice Quarterly* 8: 59–84.

Criminal Justice Consortium. 1997. "Count of Prisoners Sentenced for Third and Second Strike Cases." http://www.cjc

D'Alessio, Stewart, and Lisa Stolzenberg. 1995. "The Impact of Sentencing Guidelines on Jail Incarceration in Minnesota." *Criminology* 33: 283–302.

Daly, Kathleen. 1994. *Gender, Crime, and Punishment.* New Haven, CT: Yale University Press.

Ditton, Paula and Doris Wilson. 1999. *Truth in Sentencing in State Prisons.* Washington, D.C.: Bureau of Justice Statistics.

Eisenstein, James, and Herbert Jacob. 1977. *Felony Justice: An Organizational Analysis of Criminal Courts.* Boston: Little, Brown.

Erez, Edna. 1992. "Dangerous Men, Evil Women: Gender and Parole Decision-Making." *Justice Quarterly* 9: 105–126.

Feeley, Malcolm, and Sam Kamin. 1996. "The Effect of 'Three Strikes and You're Out' on the Courts: Looking Back to See the Future." In *Three Strikes and You're Out: Vengeance as Public Policy,* edited by David Shichor and Dale Sechrest. Thousand Oaks, CA: Sage.

Forst, Martin. 1982. "Sentencing Disparity: An Overview of Research and Issues." In *Sentencing Reform: Experiments in Reducing Disparity,* edited by Martin Forst. Beverly Hills: Sage.

Frase, Richard. 1995. "State Sentencing Guidelines: Still Going Strong." *Judicature* 78: 173–179.

Gertz, Marc, and Albert Price. 1985. "Variables Influencing Sentencing Severity: Intercourt Differences in Connecticut." *Journal of Criminal Justice* 13: 131–139.

Gibson, James. 1978. "Race as a Determinant of Criminal Sentences: A Methodological Critique and a Case Study." *Law and Society Review* 12: 455–478.

———. 1980. "Environmental Restraints on the Behavior of Judges: A Representational Model of Judicial Decision Making." *Law and Society Review* 14: 343–370.

Gizzi, Michael. 1992. "Thinking about Sentencing Reform: What Makes Sentencing Commissions Work?" Paper presented at the annual meeting of the American Political Science Association, September 3–6.

Green, Edward. 1961. *Judicial Attitudes in Sentencing.* New York: St. Martin's Press.

Greenwood, Peter, C. Peter Rydell, Allan Abrahamse, Jonathan Caulkins, James Chiesa, Karyn Model, and Stephen Klein. 1996. "Estimated Benefits and Costs of California's New Mandatory Sentencing Law." In *Three Strikes and You're Out: Vengeance as Public Policy,* edited by David Shichor and Dale Sechrest. Thousand Oaks, CA: Sage.

Griset, Pamala. 1991. *Determinate Sentencing: The Promise and the Reality of Retributive Justice.* Ithaca, NY: State University of New York Press.

———. 1995. "Determinate Sentencing and Agenda Building: A Case Study of the Failure of a Reform." *Journal of Criminal Justice* 23: 349–362.

Hagan, John. 1974. "Extra-Legal Attributes and Criminal Sentencing: An Assessment of a Sociological Viewpoint." *Law and Society Review* 8: 357–381.

———. 1977. "Criminal Justice in Rural and Urban Communities: A Study of the Bureaucratization of Justice." *Social Forces* 55: 597–612.

Hagan, John, John Hewitt, and Duane Alwin. 1979. "Ceremonial Justice: Crime and Punishment in a Loosely Coupled System." *Social Forces* 58: 506–527.

Hall, Jerome. 1952. *Theft, Law and Society.* Indianapolis: Bobbs-Merrill.

Harris, John, and Paul Jesilow. 2000. "Its Not the Old Ball Game: Three Strikes and the Courtroom Workgroup." *Justice Quarterly* 17: 185–204.

Hindelang, Michael. 1972. "Equality Under the Law." Pp. 312–323 in *Race, Crime and Justice,* edited by Charles Reasons and Jack Kuykendall. Pacific Palisades, CA: Goodyear.

Hodges, Sam. 1997. "Should Federal Punishments for Crack, Powder Be Closer?" *Mobile Register,* 22 June, A-20.

Hogarth, John. 1971. *Sentencing as a Human Process.* Toronto: University of Toronto Press.

Holten, N., and R. Handberg. 1990. "Florida's Sentencing Guidelines: Surviving—But Just Barely." *Judicature* 73: 259–267.

Keil, Thomas, and Gennaro Vito. 1990. "Race and the Death Penalty in Kentucky Murder Trials: An Analysis of Post-*Gregg* Outcomes." *Justice Quarterly* 7: 189–207.

Kingsnorth, Rodney, and Louis Rizzo. 1979. "Decision-Making in the Criminal Courts: Continuities and Discontinuities." *Criminology* 17: 3–14.

Kleck, Gary. 1981. "Racial Discrimination in Criminal Sentencing: A Critical Evaluation of the Evidence with Additional Data on the Death Penalty." *American Sociological Review* 46: 783–805.

Klein, Stephen, Joan Petersilia, and Susan Turner. 1990. "Race and Imprisonment Decisions in California." *Science* 247: 812–816.

Klemm, Margaret. 1986. *The Determinants of Capital Sentencing in Louisiana, 1979–1984*. Unpublished Ph.D. dissertation, University of New Orleans.

Kramer, John, and Robin Lubitz. 1985. "Pennsylvania Sentencing Reform: The Impact of Commission-Established Guidelines." *Crime and Delinquency* 31: 481–500.

Kramer, John, Robin Lubitz, and Cynthia Kempinen. 1989. "Sentencing Guidelines: A Quantitative Comparison of Sentencing Politics in Minnesota, Pennsylvania, and Washington." *Justice Quarterly 6:* 565–587.

Kramer, John and Darrell Steffensmeier. 1993. "Race and Imprisonment Decisions." *The Sociological Quarterly* 34: 357–376.

Kramer, John and Jeffrey Ulmer. 1996. "Sentencing Disparity and Departures from Guidelines." *Justice Quarterly* 13: 81–106.

Krisberg, Barry. 1988. "Public Attitudes About Criminal Sanctions." *The Criminologist* 13: 1–21.

Levin, David, Patrick Langan, and Jodi Brown. 2000. *State Court Sentencing of Convicted Felons, 1996*. Washington, D.C.: Bureau of Justice Statistics, U.S. Department of Justice.

Lizotte, Alan. 1978. "Extra-Legal Factors in Chicago's Criminal Courts: Testing the Conflict Model of Criminal Justice." *Social Problems* 25: 564–580.

Marvell, Thomas, and Carlisle Moody. 1996. "Determinate Sentencing and Abolishing Parole: The Long-Term Impacts on Prisons and Crime." *Criminology* 34: 107–128.

McCoy, Candace. 1984. "Determinate Sentencing, Plea Bargaining Bans, and Hydraulic Discretion in California." *Justice System Journal* 9: 256–275.

McDonald, Douglas, and Kenneth Carlson. 1993. *Sentencing in the Federal Courts: Does Race Matter? The Transition to Sentencing Guidelines, 1986–1990*. Washington, D.C.: Bureau of Justice Statistics.

McDonald, William, Henry Rossman, and James Cramer. 1979. "The Prosecutorial Function and Its Relation to Determinate Sentencing Structures." In *The Prosecutor,* edited by William McDonald. Beverly Hills, CA: Sage.

Miethe, Terance, and Charles Moore. 1989. "Sentencing Guidelines: Their Effect in Minnesota." Washington, D.C.: U.S. Department of Justice, Bureau of Justice Statistics.

Moody, Carlisle, and Thomas Marvell. 1996. "The Uncertain Timing of Innovations in Time Series: Minnesota Sentencing Guidelines and Jail Sentences—A Comment." *Criminology* 34: 257–267.

Moore, Charles, and Terance Miethe. 1986. "Regulated and Unregulated Sentencing Decisions: An Analysis of First-Year Practices under Minnesota's Felony Sentencing Guidelines." *Law and Society Review* 20: 253–278.

Moulds, Elizabeth. 1978. "Chivalry and Paternalism: Disparities of Treatment in the Criminal Justice System." *Western Political Science Quarterly* 31: 416–440.

Myers, Laura, and Sue Titus Reid. 1995. "The Importance of County Context in the Measurement of Sentencing Disparity: The Search for Routinization." *Journal of Criminal Justice.* 23: 233–241.

Myers, Martha, and Susette Talarico. 1986a. "The Social Contexts of Racial Discrimination in Sentencing." *Social Problems* 33: 237–251.

———. 1986b. "Urban Justice, Rural Injustice? Urbanization and Its Effect on Sentencing." *Criminology* 24: 367–391.

———. 1987. *The Social Contexts of Criminal Sentencing.* New York: Springer-Verlag.

Neubauer, David. 1974. *Criminal Justice in Middle America.* Morristown, NJ: General Learning Press.

Nobiling, Tracy, Cassia Spohn, and Miriam DeLone. 1998. "A Tale of Two Counties: Unemployment and Sentence Severity." *Justice Quarterly* 15: 459–485.

Parent, Dale, Terence Dunworth, Douglas McDonald, and William Rhodes. 1996. *The Impact of Sentencing Guidelines.* Washington, D.C.: National Institute of Justice.

Partridge, Anthony, and William Eldridge. 1974. *The Second Circuit Sentencing Study: A Report to the Judges of the Second Circuit.* Washington, D.C.: Federal Judicial Center.

Paternoster, Raymond. 1984. "Prosecutorial Discretion in Requesting the Death Penalty: A Case of Victim-Based Racial Discrimination." *Law and Society Review* 18: 437–478.

Radelet, Michael, and Glenn Pierce. 1985. "Race and Prosecutorial Discretion in Homicide Cases." *Law and Society Review* 19: 587–621.

Ralph, Paige, Jonathan Sorensen, and James Marquart. 1992. "A Comparison of Death-Sentenced and Incarcerated Murderers in Pre-*Furman* Texas." *Justice Quarterly* 9: 185–209.

Rapaport, Elizabeth. 1991. "The Death Penalty and Gender Discrimination." *Law and Society Review* 25: 367–384.

Reiman, Jeffrey. 2001. *The Rich Get Richer and the Poor Get Prison: Ideology, Class, and Criminal Justice.* Boston: Allyn & Bacon.

Rengert, George. 1989. "Spatial Justice and Criminal Victimization." *Justice Quarterly* 6: 543–564.

Robertson, Leon, Robert Rich, and H. Laurence Ross. 1973. "Jail Sentences for Driving While Intoxicated in Chicago: A Judicial Action That Failed." *Law and Society Review* 8: 55–68.

Rosencrance, John. 1988. "Maintaining the Myth of Individualized Justice: Probation Presentence Reports." *Justice Quarterly* 5: 235–256.

Rosett, Arthur, and Donald R. Cressey. 1976. *Justice by Consent*. Philadelphia: J. B. Lippincott.

Ross, H. Laurence, and James Foley. 1987. "Judicial Disobedience of the Mandate to Imprison Drunk Drivers." *Law and Society Review* 21: 315–323.

Sorensen, Jon and Donald Wallace. 1999. "Prosecutorial Discretion in Seeking Death: An Analysis of Racial Disparity in the Pretrial Stages of Case Processing in a Midwestern County." *Justice Quarterly* 16: 559–578.

Spohn, Cassia, and Jerry Cederblom. 1991. "Race and Disparities in Sentencing: A Test of the Liberation Hypothesis." *Justice Quarterly* 8: 305–328.

Spohn, Cassia, and David Holleran. 2000. "The Imprisonment Penalty Paid by Young, Unemployed Black and Hispanic Male Offenders." *Criminology* 38: 281–307.

Spohn, Cassia, and Jeffrey Spears. 1996. "The Effect of Offender and Victim Characteristics on Sexual Assault Case Processing Decisions." *Justice Quarterly* 13: 649–679.

———. 1997. "Gender and Sentencing of Drug Offenders." Paper presented at the annual meeting of the American Society of Criminology, San Diego, California.

Steffensmeier, Darrell, John Kramer, and Cathy Streifel. 1993. "Gender and Imprisonment Decisions." *Criminology* 31: 411–438.

Steffensmeier, Darrell, Jeffrey Ulmer, and John Kramer. 1998. "The Interaction of Race, Gender, and Age in Criminal Sentencing: The Punishment Cost of Being Young, Black, and Male." *Criminology* 36: 763–798.

Steury, Ellen Hochstedler, and Nancy Frank. 1990. "Gender Bias and Pretrial Release: More Pieces of the Puzzle." *Journal of Criminal Justice* 18: 417–432.

Stith, Kate, and Jose Cabranes. 1998. *Fear of Judging: Sentencing Guidelines in the Federal Courts*. Chicago: University of Chicago Press.

Sudnow, David. 1965. "Normal Crimes: Sociological Features of the Penal Codes in a Public Defender Office." *Social Problems* 12: 254–264.

Surette, Ray. 1996. "News from Nowhere, Policy to Follow: Media and the Social Construction of 'Three Strikes and You're Out.'" In *Three Strikes and You're Out: Vengeance as Public Policy*, edited by David Shichor and Dale Sechrest. Thousand Oaks, CA: Sage.

Thomson, Douglas, and Anthony Ragona. 1987. "Popular Moderation Versus Governmental Authoritarianism: An Interactionist View of Public Sentiments Toward Criminal Sanctions." *Crime and Delinquency* 33: 337–357.

Tiffany, Lawrence, Yakov Avichai, and Geoffrey Peters. 1975. "A Statistical Analysis of Sentencing in Federal Courts: Defendants Convicted After Trial, 1967–1968." *Journal of Legal Studies* 10: 369–390.

Tonry, Michael. 1987. *Sentencing Reform Impacts*. Washington, D.C.: U.S. Government Printing Office.

———. 1991. "The Politics and Processes of Sentencing Commissions." *Crime and Delinquency* 37: 307–329.

———. 1993. "The Failure of the U.S. Sentencing Commission's Guidelines." *Crime and Delinquency* 39: 131–149.

Varney, James. 1996. "Killer's Family Accuses Justice System of Racism." *Times-Picayune*, 30 January, B1.

Vincent, Barbara, and Paul Hofer. 1994. *The Consequences of Mandatory Minimum Prison Terms: A Summary of Recent Findings*. Washington, D.C.: Federal Judicial Center.

Vera Institute of Justice. 1977. *Felony Arrests: Their Prosecution and Disposition in New York City's Courts*. New York: Author.

Walker, Samuel, Cassia Spohn, and Miriam DeLone. 2000. *The Color of Justice: Race, Ethnicity, and Crime in America*. 2d ed. Belmont, CA: Wadsworth.

Walsh, Anthony. 1985. "The Role of the Probation Officer in the Sentencing Process." *Criminal Justice and Behavior* 12: 289–303.

———. 1987. "The Sexual Stratification Hypothesis and Sexual Assault in Light of the Changing Conceptions of Race." *Criminology* 25: 153–173.

Weisheit, Ralph, and Sue Mahan. 1988. *Women, Crime and Criminal Justice*. Cincinnati: Anderson.

Weiss, Robert, Richard Berk, and Cathrine Lee. 1996. "Assessing the Capriciousness of Death Penalty Charging." *Law and Society Review* 30: 607–638.

Welch, Susan, and Cassia Spohn. 1986. "Evaluating the Impact of Prior Record on Judges' Sentencing Decisions: A Seven-City Comparison." *Justice Quarterly* 3: 389–408.

Welch, Susan, Cassia Spohn, and John Gruhl. 1985. "Convicting and Sentencing Differences Among Black, Hispanic and White Males in Six Localities." *Justice Quarterly* 2: 67–80.

Wilson, James Q. 1973. "If Every Criminal Knew He Would Be Punished If Caught." *New York Times Magazine*, 28 January.

———. 1983. *Thinking About Crime: A Policy Guide*. 2d ed. New York: Basic Books.

Wolfgang, Marvin, and Marc Riedel. 1973. "Race, Judicial Discretion, and the Death Penalty." *Annals of the American Academy of Political and Social Science* 407: 119–133.

Worden, Alissa. 1995. "The Judge's Role in Plea Bargaining: An Analysis of Judges' Agreement with

Prosecutor's Sentencing Recommendations." *Justice Quarterly* 12: 257–278.

Zatz, Marjorie. 1984. "Race, Ethnicity, and Determinate Sentencing: A New Dimension to an Old Controversy." *Criminology* 22: 147–171.

———. 1987. "The Changing Forms of Racial/Ethnic Biases in Sentencing." *Journal of Research in Crime and Delinquency* 24: 69–92.

FOR FURTHER READING

Alozie, Nicholas, and C. Wayne Johnson. "Probing the Limits of the Female Advantage in Criminal Processing: Pretrial Diversion of Drug Offenders in an Urban County." *Justice System Journal* 21 (2000): 239–259.

Caulkins, Jonathan, C. Peter Rydell, William Schwabe, and James Chiesa. *Mandatory Minimum Drug Sentences: Throwing Away the Key or the Taxpayers Money?* Santa Monica, CA: Rand Corporation, 1997.

Christianson, Scott. *With Liberty for Some: 500 Years of Imprisonment in America.* Boston: Northeastern University Press, 1998.

Diaz-Cotto, Juanita. *Gender, Ethnicity, and the State: Latina and Latino Prison Politics.* Albany: State University of New York Press, 1996.

Free, Marvin. *African Americans and the Criminal Justice System.* New York: Garland, 1997.

Kempf-Leonard, Kimberly, and Lisa Sample. "Disparity Based on Sex: Is Gender-Specific Treatment Warranted?" *Justice Quarterly* 17 (2000): 89–128.

Irwin, John, and James Austin. *It's About Time: America's Imprisonment Binge.* 2d ed. Belmont, CA: Wadsworth, 1997.

Lynch, Michael, and E. Britt Patterson. *Race and Criminal Justice.* Fairfax, VA: Harrow and Heston, 1996.

Marquart, James, Sheldon Edland-Olson, and Jonathan Sorensen. *The Rope, the Chair, and the Needle: Capital Punishment in Texas, 1923–1990.* Austin: University of Texas, 1994.

Morris, Norval, and David Rotman, eds. *The Oxford History of the Prison.* New York: Oxford University Press, 1996.

Myers, Martha. *Race, Labor and Punishment in the New South.* Columbus: Ohio State University Press, 1998.

National Council on Crime and Delinquency. *National Assessment of Structured Sentencing.* Washington, D.C.: Bureau of Justice Assistance, 1996.

Parent, Dale, Terence Dunworth, Douglas McDonald, and William Rhodes. 1997. *Mandatory Sentencing.* Washington, D.C.: National Institute of Justice.

Pollock-Byrne, Jocelyn. *Women, Prison, and Crime.* Pacific Grove, CA: Brooks/Cole, 1990.

Rossi, Peter, and Richard Berk. *Just Punishments: Federal Guidelines and Public Views Compared.* Hawthorne, NY: Aldine de Gruyter, 1997.

Russell, Gregory. *The Death Penalty and Racial Bias: Overturning Supreme Court Assumptions.* New York: Greenwood, 1994.

Ulmer, Jeffrey. *Social Worlds of Sentencing: Court Communities Under Sentencing Guidelines.* Albany: State University of New York Press, 1997.

Wicharaya, Tamasak. *Simple Theory, Hard Reality: The Impact of Sentencing Reforms on Courts, Prisons, and Crime.* Albany: State University of New York Press, 1995.

Appellate, Lower, and Juvenile Courts

PART V EXAMINES SEVERAL SPECIALIZED COURTS THAT ARE IMPORTANT FOR the criminal justice system. Some of these judicial bodies are separate and distinct from other courts—appellate courts, for example. Others are considered special courts whether they are separate and distinct or not. They are special courts because they handle a specific type of case. Juvenile courts differ from those that process adults accused of violating the criminal law because juvenile law is distinctive.

Chapter 17 focuses on appellate courts, which are designed to provide a second look at how the case was handled in the lower courts. Although few guilty defendants successfully challenge their convictions, the public is convinced that courts are releasing countless guilty defendants on technicalities.

Chapter 18 discusses the nation's lower courts, which process literally millions of less serious offenses each year. Increasingly, however, these minor matters loom large in terms of criminal justice policy making. Clearly domestic violence and drunk driving are two topics that criminal justice officials cannot dismiss as unimportant.

Chapter 19 considers juvenile courts, which deal with millions of children each year. The cases that attract the most attention are those in which children are accused of adult crimes involving violence. But these are relatively few compared to the millions of juveniles who appear in these courts each year because of less serious adult violations as well as "crimes" that only juveniles can commit. To complicate matters further, some of these juveniles have not committed any criminal act; rather, they are before the court because their parents have abused or neglected them.

■ ■ ■

Appellate Courts

ROGER COLEMAN, AN APPALACHIAN COAL MINER, WAS CONVICTED OF rape and murder in the small town of Grundy, Virginia, and sentenced to death. After his first appeal was unsuccessful, Coleman sought further review by filing a writ of habeas corpus. Alas, his lawyer filed the notice of appeal with the Virginia Supreme Court one day late, and the case was dismissed.

Should this error by his lawyer prevent Coleman from having federal courts also review his case? Proponents of the crime control model argue that Coleman is a textbook example of endless appeals, and therefore he shouldn't be allowed yet one more review. Supporters of the due process model, on the other hand, counter that basic fairness is far more important than failure to comply with a narrow technical requirement.

Coleman v. Thompson highlights the importance of appellate court decisions. To be sure, appellate courts decide far fewer cases than the trial courts. Nonetheless, the relative handful of cases decided by the appellate courts are critically important for the entire judicial process. Whereas the decisions of trial court judges are binding only on that judge, the decisions of appellate court judges are binding on all judges within the jurisdiction. It is through written opinions that appellate judges engage in significant policy making. Thus, ultimately the decisions of a group of judges not only determine the results of the case (the fate of individual defendants like Roger Coleman) but also, and more importantly, shape the law by providing the reasons for the decisions reached. *Coleman v. Thompson* also symbolizes how the relative handful of death penalty decisions receive a disproportionate share of appellate court time and attention.

Appellate courts subject the trial court's action to a second look, examining not a raw dispute in the course of being presented, but rather a controversy as already packaged and decided. This second look provides a degree of detachment, perspective, and opportunity for reflection by a group of judges. By providing the loser at trial with the possibility of rescrutiny, appellate review lends legitimacy to the adjudicative process. ■

NATURE OF THE APPELLATE PROCESS

One of the few aspects of the American judicial process about which there is a consensus is that every loser in a trial court should have the right to appeal to a higher court. Appellate courts were created partly because of the belief that several heads are better than one. In essence, the decisions of a single judge are subjected to review by a panel of judges who are removed from the heat engendered by the trial and are consequently in a position to take a more objective view of the questions raised. They operate as multimember or collegial bodies, with decisions made by a group of judges. There may be as few as three judges or as many as twenty-eight (as in the U.S. Ninth Court of Appeals). In the courts of last resort all judges typically participate in all cases. On intermediate appellate courts, on the other hand, decisions are typically made using rotating three-judge panels. But in important cases all judges may participate (this is termed an **en banc** hearing). In unraveling the complexities of the review process, it is helpful to begin by asking why appellate courts exist and why dissatisfied litigants are permitted to appeal.

> **En banc:** French term referring to the session of an appellate court in which all the judges of the court participate, as opposed to a session presided over by three judges.

The Purposes of Appeal

The most obvious function of appellate courts is **error correction**. During trial a significant portion of the decision making is spur of the moment. As one trial judge phrased it, "We're where the action is. We often have to 'shoot from the hip' and hope you're doing the right thing. You can't ruminate forever every time you have to make a ruling. We'd be spending months on each case if we ever did that" (quoted in Carp and Stidham 1990, 256). As reviewing bodies, appellate courts oversee the work of the lower courts, ensuring that the law was correctly interpreted and applied. Thus, the error correction function of appellate review protects against arbitrary, capricious, or mistaken decisions by a trial court judge.

The other primary function of appellate courts is **policy formulation**. The law-making function focuses on situations in which appellate courts fill in the gaps in existing law, clarify old doctrines, extend existing precedent to new situations, and on occasion even overrule previous decisions. Thus, through policy formulation, appellate courts shape the law in response to changing conditions in society. Stated another way, error correction is concerned primarily with the effect of the judicial process upon individual litigants, whereas policy formulation involves the impact of the appellate court decision on other cases.

 Tracy Raffles Gunn, "Preserving Error in Jury Trials: Rules to Remember"

Scope of Appellate Review

A basic principle of American law is that the losing party has the **right to one appeal**. But at the same time it is important to stress that the defendant has now lost his or her legal shield of innocence. The individual is no longer considered innocent until proven guilty but rather now stands, in the eyes of the law, guilty. This has important implications for bail. Guilty defendants no longer have a right to bail; courts may set a bail amount (typically in higher amounts than prior to trial), but many defendants wait out their appeal in prison.

Although American law recognizes the right to one appeal, the scope of appellate review is subject to several important limits, exceptions, and refinements. Appeals, for example, may be filed only by parties who have lost in the lower court. But prosecutors may not appeal not guilty findings. The Fifth Amendment guarantees, "Nor shall any person be subject for the same offense to be twice put in jeopardy of life or limb." This provision protects citizens from **double jeopardy** (a second prosecution of the same person for the same crime by the same sovereign after the first trial). Double jeopardy serves the purpose of preventing repeated harassment of an accused person. Thus, once a not guilty verdict is returned in a criminal case, jeopardy is said to attach, and the prosecutor cannot appeal.

Appeals are also discretionary; that is, the losing party is not required to seek appellate court review. The lone exception involves capital punishment cases. When a jury imposes a sentence of death, the case must be appealed regardless of the defendant's wishes. Typically, this automatic review is heard directly by the state supreme court, thus bypassing any intermediate courts of appeals. The mandatory appeal requirements in capital punishment cases aside, in all other cases, civil and criminal, appeal is discretionary.

There are also limits on when cases may be appealed. As a general rule, the losing party may only appeal from a final judgment of the lower court. In this context, a judgment is considered final when it ends the action in the court in which it was brought and nothing more is to be decided. In very limited situations, however, litigants may appeal certain types of **interlocutory** (nonfinal) orders. Prosecutors may file an interlocutory appeal on certain pretrial rulings that substantially hinder the

Error correction: Appellate courts seek to correct legal errors made in lower courts.

Policy formulation: Function of appellate courts to make new law and adjust existing law to changing circumstances.

Right to one appeal: U.S. law generally grants the loser in trial court the right to a single appeal, which the upper court must hear.

Double jeopardy: Fifth Amendment prohibition against a second prosecution after a first trial for the same offense.

Interlocutory: Provisional; temporary; while a lawsuit is still going on.

state's ability to proceed to trial. For example, if the trial court suppressed a defendant's confession or excluded physical evidence because of an illegal search and seizure, the prosecution may file an interlocutory appeal arguing that the judge's ruling was in error.

Appeals are also restricted to questions of law; findings of fact are not appealable. Because they have not been directly exposed to the evidence, appellate courts are reluctant to second-guess findings of fact made by lower tribunals. Thus, appellate courts hear no new testimony and consider no new evidence. Rather they focus on how decisions were made in the trial court, basing their review on the appellate court record. Questions of law that are commonly raised on appeal include defects in jury selection, improper admission of evidence during the trial, and mistaken interpretations of the law. The appellant may also claim constitutional violations, including illegal search and seizure or improper questioning of the defendant by the police (see Chapter 12). Finally, some defendants who have pled guilty may seek to set aside the guilty plea because of ineffective assistance of counsel or because the plea was not voluntary.

Appeals are also confined to issues properly raised in the trial court. Recall from Chapter 14 that during trial attorneys must make timely objections to the judge's rulings on points of law. When an attorney makes such an objection, and the trial judge overrules it, there is a disagreement over a point of law and the issue has been preserved for appeal.

Appeals in criminal cases have also historically been limited in the United States (but interestingly not England) to findings of guilt. That is, a defendant cannot appeal the sentence imposed as being too harsh (nor can the prosecutor appeal a sentence as too lenient). This restriction is changing, however, in a few states. In recent years a handful of states have allowed defendants to appeal the sentence imposed by the trial judge (Di Pietro 1991; Williams 1992).

Finally, the right to appeal is limited to a single appeal, within which all appealable issues have to be raised. Appeals from U.S. district courts and most appeals from state courts of general jurisdiction are heard by intermediate courts of appeals. In the less populous states, which do not have intermediate appellate bodies, the initial appeal is filed with the court of last resort (see Chapter 4). These courts

have **mandatory appellate jurisdiction,** which means they must hear all properly filed appeals. But after the first reviewing body has reached a decision, the right to one appeal has been exhausted. The party that loses the appeal, however, may request that a higher court review the case again, but such appeals are discretionary; the higher court does not have to hear the appeal. The U.S. Supreme Court and most state supreme courts have largely **discretionary appellate jurisdiction,** which means that they can pick and choose which cases they will hear. The bulk of appeals are decided by intermediate courts of appeals and are never heard by state or national supreme courts. Figure 17-1 shows the appellate court structure of the states.

 Raymond T. Elligett, Jr., "Top 10 Appellate Mistakes"

APPELLATE COURT PROCEDURES

Appellate court procedures reflect numerous variations among the nation's fifty-one legal systems. Nonetheless, each judicial system utilizes essentially the same six steps (Meador 1974). Figure 17-2 summarizes the appeals process.

In recent years, however, traditional appellate court procedures have been modified because of exponential increases in appellate court filings. Appellate court caseloads have been increasing more rapidly than those of the trial courts. By way of illustration, appeals filed in the U.S. courts of appeals have increased by a whopping 705 percent from 1961 to 1983. Today, federal appellate courts hear over 50,000 cases per year. Appeals heard by state courts have likewise grown rapidly, doubling about every decade since World War II (Marvell 1989). Today, state appellate courts hear about 300,000

Mandatory appellate jurisdiction: Jurisdiction that a court must accept. Cases falling under a court's mandatory jurisdiction must be decided officially on their merits, though a court may avoid giving them full consideration.

Discretionary appellate jurisdiction: Jurisdiction that a court may accept or reject in particular cases. The Supreme Court has discretionary jurisdiction over most cases that come to it.

| FIGURE 17-1 | Organizing States by Appellate Court Structure |

Court of Last Resort Only	Court of Last Resort and One Intermediate Appellate Court		One Court of Last Resort and Two Intermediate Appellate Courts	Two Courts of Last Resort and One Intermediate Appellate Court
Delaware	Alaska	Massachusetts	Alabama	Oklahoma*
Maine	Arizona	Michigan	New York	Texas
Montana	Arkansas	Minnesota	Pennsylvania	
New Hampshire	California	Mississippi	Tennessee	
Nevada	Colorado	Missouri		
Rhode Island	Connecticut	Nebraska		
South Dakota	Florida	New Jersey		
Vermont	Georgia	New Mexico		
West Virginia	Hawaii*	North Carolina		
Wyoming	Idaho*	North Dakota*		
	Illinois	Ohio		
	Indiana	Oregon		
	Iowa*	South Carolina*		
	Kansas	Utah		
	Kentucky	Virginia		
	Louisiana	Washington		
	Maryland	Wisconsin		

*Court of Last Resort assigns cases to intermediate appellate court.

SOURCE: David Rottman, Carol Flango, Melissa Cantrell, Randall Hansen, and Neil La Fountain, *State Court Organization 1998* (Williamsburg, VA: National Center for State Courts, 2000).

appeals every year (Ostrom and Kauder 1999). To accommodate the steadily rising volume of appeals, reviewing bodies now often use expedited processing for some cases (Hanson 1996).

Notice of Appeal

An appeal does not follow automatically from an adverse trial court judgment. Rather, the **appellant** (the losing party in the lower court) must take affirmative action to set an appeal in motion. The first step consists of filing a **notice of appeal**. Rules of appellate procedure fix a precise time—usually thirty or sixty days—within which this short written statement must be filed.

Appellate Court Record

After the notice of appeal has been filed, the next step is preparing and transmitting the record. The **appellate court record** consists of the materials that advance to the appellate court. Many of these items—papers and exhibits—are already in the case file. A major item not in the clerk's office is the transcript of the testimony given at the trial. To include this in the record, the court reporter prepares a typewritten copy and files it with the court.

Appellant: The party, usually the losing one, that seeks to overturn the decision of a lower court by appealing to a higher court.

Notice of appeal: Written document filed with the clerk of court stating that the defendant in the criminal case plans to appeal.

Appellate court record: Papers, documents, exhibits, as well as the transcript of the trial, which are submitted to the appellate court for review.

FIGURE 17-2   **Steps of Criminal Procedure: Appeal and Post-Conviction Remedies**

	Law on the Books	*Law in Action*
Appeal	Legal challenge to a decision by a lower court.	Virtually certain if the defendant is convicted at trial.
Mandatory	Appellate court must hear the case.	Many appeals are "routine," which means they have little likelihood of succeeding.
Discretionary	Appellate court may accept or reject.	Appellate courts hear a very small percentage of discretionary appeal cases.
Notice of appeal	Written statement notifying the court that the defendant plans to appeal.	Standards for indigent defenders mandate that an appeal must be filed.
Appellate court record	The transcript of the trial along with relevant court documents.	Some appellate courts prefer a focused record of contested matters whereas others want the entire record.
Briefing the case	Written statement submitted by the attorney arguing a case in court.	Defense lawyers make numerous arguments in hopes that one will be successful.
Oral argument	Lawyers for both sides argue their cases before appellate court justices, who have the opportunity to question lawyers.	Judges often complain that they learn little during oral argument. To expedite decision making, some courts limit oral argument to select cases.
Written opinion	Reasons given by appellate courts for the results they have reached.	Only appellate court opinions are considered precedent. Many appellate courts no longer issue written opinions in straightforward matters.
Disposition		
Affirmed	Appellate court decision that agrees with the lower court decision.	Seven out of eight criminal appeals are affirmed.
Remanded	Case is sent back to the lower court for a hearing on a specific issue.	Often an indication that the appellate court is troubled by the judge's action but doesn't wish to reverse.
Reversed and remanded	The lower court decision is set aside and further proceedings may be held.	Defendants are very often reconvicted following retrial.

Briefing the Case

The third step in the appeal process consists of writing briefs. A **brief** is a written argument that sets forth the party's view of the facts of the case, the issues raised on appeal, and the precedents supporting their position. First, the appellant's brief is filed, which lists alleged errors on questions of law that were made at trial. Next, the winning party in the lower court (termed the **appellee,** or **respondent**) files a brief setting forth arguments as to why the original decision of the lower court is legally correct and should stand. The appellant then has the option of filing a reply brief.

Oral Argument

The lawyers for both parties are allotted a limited time to argue their side of the case before the appellate court panel. The appellant's oral argument, for

Brief: A written statement submitted by the attorney arguing a case in court. It states the facts of the case, presents legal arguments in support of the moving party, and cites applicable law.

Appellee (respondent):   A party, usually the winning party, against whom a case is appealed.

example, briefly discusses the facts on which the cause of action is based, traces the history of the case through the lower courts, and presents legal arguments as to why the decision of the trial court was erroneous. **Oral argument** provides the opportunity for face-to-face contact between judges and lawyers. In this phase, judges typically ask lawyers questions about particular issues in the case.

Eliminating oral argument is one type of expedited procedure. Many judges view oral arguments as not particularly helpful in deciding routine cases (Wasby 1982). Thus, some courts have eliminated oral argument altogether in straightforward cases. By ruling solely on the basis of the appellate court record, judges conserve some of their time.

 The Oyez Project at Northwestern University provides links to oral arguments in many of the Supreme Court's most important decisions: **http://oyez. nwu.edu/**.

For an up-to-date list of Web links, go to **http:// www.wadsworth.com/product/0534563406s**.

Written Opinion

After the case has been argued, the court recesses to engage in group deliberations. Decisions are made in private conference, with one judge in the majority assigned the task of writing the opinion, which summarizes the facts of the case and discusses the legal issues raised on appeal. If the case is an easy one, the **opinion** of the court may be short, perhaps no more than a page or two. But if the legal issues are important or complex, the court's opinion may run dozens of pages. Some legal issues have such fine distinctions or involve such a number of conflicting legal issues that the judges do not always agree among themselves as to the correct answer. Judges who disagree with the majority often write **dissenting opinions,** explaining why they believe their fellow judges reached the wrong conclusions.

Opinion preparation consumes more of appellate judges' time than any other activity, and for this reason the opinion-writing process is a prime candidate for increasing the efficiency of appellate courts. Appellate courts as diverse as Louisiana (Neubauer 1985) and New Hampshire (Douglas 1985) are therefore deciding some cases by summary affirmation, in which the court affirms the decision of the lower court without providing a written opinion and often without granting oral argument as well.

Many courts are reluctant to take the drastic step of not writing opinions, even in selected cases. Therefore, a more common practice is curtailing opinion publication; the litigants are given written reasons for the decision reached, but the opinion is not published and therefore may not be cited as precedent. Unpublished opinions are used in error correction cases when the court is applying existing law (Songer 1990). They save considerable judicial time because unpublished opinions need not be as polished as published opinions.

 Jennifer S. Carroll, "Appellate Specialization and the Art of Appellate Advocacy"

Disposition

The court's opinion ends with a disposition of the case. The appellate court may **affirm** (uphold) the judgment of the lower court. Or the court may modify the lower court ruling by changing it in part, but not totally reversing it. Alternatively, the previous decision may be **reversed** (set aside) with no further court action required. A disposition of **reversed and remanded** means that the decision of the lower court is overturned and the case is sent back to the lower court for further proceedings, which may include holding a hearing or conducting a new trial. Often the defendant is tried a second time, but not always. Finally, the case may be

Oral argument: The part of the appellate court decision-making process in which lawyers for both parties plead their case in person before the court.

Opinion: The reasons given for the decision reached by an appellate court.

Dissenting opinion: An opinion written by a judge of an appellate court in which the judge states the reasons for disagreeing with the majority decision.

Affirm: In an appellate court, to reach a decision that agrees with the result reached in the case by the lower court.

Reverse: In an appellate court, to reach a decision that disagrees with the result reached in the case by the lower court.

Reversed and remanded: Decision of an appellate court that the guilty verdict of the lower court be set aside and the case be retried.

remanded to the lower court with instructions for further proceedings (Neubauer 1992).

Appellate courts modify, reverse, remand, or reverse and remand, only if they find **error,** that is, a mistake made by a judge during the trial. If the error is substantial, it is called **reversible error** by the higher court. If the error is minor, it is called **harmless error** (Traynor 1970). The appellate court may find error but affirm the lower court anyway.

CRIMINAL APPEALS

The bulk of trial court filings are never appealed because the case is settled without a trial—civil cases are negotiated and criminal cases are plea-bargained. As a result, only a small percentage of state trial court cases are reviewed by higher courts. The majority of appeals involve civil cases, but the number of criminal appeals has increased dramatically since the 1960s.

Law on the Books: Expanded Opportunity to Appeal Criminal Convictions

For decades, most defendants found guilty by judge or jury did not appeal because they could not afford the expense. This pattern changed significantly in the early 1960s. A series of important Warren Court decisions, based on the equal protection clause of the Fourteenth Amendment, held that economically impoverished defendants cannot be barred from effective appellate review. Indigent defendants, therefore, are entitled to a free trial court transcript (*Griffin v. Illinois,* 1956) and a court-appointed lawyer (*Douglas v. California,* 1963). Indigents, however, are not normally provided free legal service to pursue discretionary appeals (*Ross v. Moffitt,* 1974).

> **Remand:** In an appellate court, to send a case back to the court from which it came for further action.
>
> **Error:** A mistake made by a judge in the procedures used at trial, or in making legal rulings during the trial, that allows one side in a lawsuit to ask a higher court to review the case.
>
> **Reversible error:** An error made at trial serious enough to warrant a new trial.
>
> **Harmless error:** An error made at trial that is insufficient grounds for reversing a judgment.

As a result of these rulings, it is now rare for a convicted defendant not to appeal from a trial verdict of guilty. Indeed, indigent defendants have everything to gain and nothing to lose by filing an appeal. For example, if the appeal is successful, but the defendant is reconvicted following a new trial, the sentencing judge cannot increase the sentence out of vindictiveness (*North Carolina v. Pearce,* 1969; *Texas v. McCullough,* 1986). See Figure 17-3 for a summary of key developments concerning appeals. The Warren Court decisions expanding the opportunity for indigent defendants to appeal produced an exponential increase in the number of criminal appeals filed. Whereas criminal appeals composed only 10 percent to 15 percent of total appeals prior to 1963, two decades later they constituted about 45 percent of total appellate volume (Bureau of Justice Statistics 1985).

Law in Action: Defendants Rarely Win on Appeal

Criminal appeals are drawn from a fairly narrow stratum of the most serious criminal convictions in the trial courts (Davies 1982). For example, over half the criminal appeals filed in five appellate courts stem from convictions for crimes of violence (homicides and armed robberies, primarily). And as you might expect from our discussions of plea bargaining, these appeals cases typically involve substantial sentences (60 percent appealed from sentences of six or more years in prison) (Chapper and Hanson 1990). In short, criminal appeals are atypical of crimes prosecuted in the trial courts.

Criminal appeals are also by and large routine because they seldom raise meritorious issues (Wold and Caldeira 1980). Current standards of effective assistance of counsel force lawyers to appeal, no matter how slight the odds of appellate court reversal. As a result, a significant number of criminal appeals lack substantial merit. According to one intermediate appellate court judge, "If 90 percent of this stuff were in the United States Post Office, it would be classified as junk mail" (Wold 1978).

Criminal appeals rarely succeed; appellate courts often find that no reversible error was committed during the trial court proceedings. Thus, the vast majority of criminal appeals affirm the conviction. Roughly speaking, defendants win on appeal only one out of eight times. A closer look, though, indicates that an appellate court reversal produces

FIGURE 17-3	Key Developments Concerning Appeal

U.S. Constitution, Article I	1789	The Privilege of the Writ of Habeas Corpus shall not be suspended unless when in Cases of Rebellion or Invasion the public Safety may require it.
Fifth Amendment	1791	Prohibited double jeopardy.
Griffin v. Illinois	1956	Indigents are entitled to a free trial court transcript.
Douglas v. California	1963	Indigents are entitled to a court-appointed attorney during first appeal.
Fay v. Noia	1963	Warren Court decision greatly expanded the right of state prisoners to file habeas corpus petitions in federal court.
North Carolina v. Pearce	1969	If the appeal is successful, the sentencing judge cannot increase the sentence if the defendant is later reconvicted.
Ross v. Moffitt	1974	Indigent defendants are not entitled to a court-appointed lawyer for discretionary appeals.
Stone v. Powell	1976	Burger Court decision held that federal courts cannot consider Fourth Amendment search-and-seizure questions in habeas corpus proceedings.
Coleman v. Thompson	1992	Death row inmate whose lawyers filed papers late has no further right to federal court review.
Antiterrorism and Effective Death Penalty Act	1996	State inmates are typically limited to only one review of their prisoner petition in federal courts.
Felker v. Turpin	1996	Upheld the Antiterrorism and Effective Death Penalty Act.
Roe v. Flores-Ortega	2000	A lawyer's failure to file an appeal does not necessarily violate the right to counsel.
Williams v. Taylor	2000	Under the Antiterrorism and Effective Death Penalty Act a federal judge can reject an inmate's claim only if the state court used an unreasonable interpretation of federal law.
Edwards v. Carpenter	2000	Limited state prisoner access to federal courts based on claims that their lawyers gave them inadequate help.

only minor victories for some criminal defendants. For example, some "reversals" produce a modification but do not otherwise disturb the conviction (Neubauer 1992). Moreover, if the appellate court reverses and remands the case to the lower court for a new trial, half of the defendants are convicted a second time (Roper and Melone 1981). While the public perceives that many criminals are freed on technicalities, in reality appellate court reversals are relatively rare. Overall, only about one out of every sixteen criminal appeals produces a tangible victory for the defendant (Neubauer 1991).

What is even more interesting is the types of cases in which reversals occur. A study of appeals in Louisiana discovered that defendants convicted of nonviolent offenses and who received a relatively lenient sentence were the most likely to win on appeal. Conversely, defendants convicted of violent offenses and sentenced to lengthy prison terms were the least likely to win on appeal. Reading the court's opinions suggests that this pattern of winners and losers is far from random. Rather, the appellate court justices strain to find ways to affirm convictions in crimes such as murder and armed robbery when the defendant has a long criminal record.

 All of the U.S. Courts of Appeals have Web sites. As a start, go to these:

http://www.tourolaw.edu/2ndcircuit/
http://www.ca5.uscourts.gov/
http://www.ca7.uscourts.gov/
http://www.ca9.uscourts.gov/

For an up-to-date list of Web links, go to **http://www.wadsworth.com/product/0534563406s**.

POST-CONVICTION REVIEW

After the appellate process has been exhausted, state as well as federal prisoners may challenge their convictions in federal courts on certain limited grounds. These post-conviction remedies are termed collateral attacks, because they are attempts to avoid the effects of a court decision by bringing a different court proceeding. Although they are filed by prisoners who have been convicted of a criminal offense, they are civil matters. Thus, they are filed against the prison warden. The Case Close-Up in this chapter illustrates this. When Roger Coleman appealed, the case title was *Coleman v. Commonwealth of Virginia.* But after the right to appeal had been exhausted, he later filed a habeas petition in federal court, and the case was captioned *Coleman v. Thompson.* The warden, Thompson, is considered a nominal respondent because no actions on his part are at issue. Thompson is merely a stand-in; the defendant contends he is being illegally detained because of the actions of the trial judge.

How Post-Conviction Remedies Differ from Appeals

Post-conviction remedies differ from appeals in several ways that have important implications for the criminal justice system. First, they may be filed only by those actually in prison. Second, they may raise only constitutional defects, not technical ones. Third, they may be somewhat broader than appeals. While appeals are limited to objections made by the defense during the trial, post-conviction petitions can bring up issues not raised during trial, assert constitutional protections that have developed since the original trial, and contest conditions of confinement. Finally, post-conviction remedies in state courts are unlimited in number; a prisoner can file numerous petitions at all levels of the court system.

Coleman v. Thompson illustrates these factors. Coleman was eligible to file because he was in prison. His petition listed six different constitutional violations of his rights. Moreover, many of these points had not been argued on appeal. Finally, the petition had been filed not only in two state courts, but was now filed in the U.S. District Court for the Western District of Virginia, reviewed by the

Fourth Circuit Court of Appeals, and now being considered by yet another federal court—the U.S. Supreme Court.

The most common type of post-conviction relief is **habeas corpus** (Latin for "you have the body"). Protected by the U.S. Constitution, it is a judicial order to someone holding a person to bring that person immediately before the court. Article I provides that "the Privilege of the Writ of Habeas Corpus shall not be suspended unless when in Cases of Rebellion or Invasion the public Safety may require it." This provision traces its roots to seventeenth-century England, when the king's officers often detained citizens without ever filing charges. The writ of habeas corpus has been described as the "great writ," because it prevents the government from jailing citizens without ever filing charges. Many totalitarian regimes have no such protections; even some Western democracies allow the police or prosecutors to detain a person suspected of a crime for up to a year without formally accusing the person of any wrongdoing.

Originally, habeas corpus was regarded as an extraordinary means to determine the legality of detention prior to trial. But the great writ of liberty has undergone considerable transformation in recent decades.

 Federal Rule of Appellate Procedure Number 22: Governing Habeas Corpus Proceedings by Indigents is available online: **http://www.ck10.uscourts.gov/circuit/titleVI.html**.

For an up-to-date list of Web links, go to **http://www.wadsworth.com/product/0534563406s**.

Expansion under the Warren Court

In three 1963 decisions, the Warren Court greatly expanded the application of habeas corpus, making it much easier for state prisoners to seek judicial relief in the federal courts (*Fay v. Noia,* 1963; *Towsend v. Sain,* 1963; and *Sanders v. U.S.,* 1963).

Habeas corpus: Latin phrase meaning "you have the body"; a writ inquiring of an official who has custody of a person whether that person is being lawfully imprisoned or detained.

CASE CLOSE-UP

Coleman v. Thompson and Federal Court Scrutiny of State Court Convictions

 Roger Coleman was convicted of rape and murder in the small coal-mining town of Grundy, Virginia. The Virginia Supreme Court affirmed both the conviction and the imposition of the death penalty. Coleman then filed a habeas corpus action, which raised numerous federal constitutional claims that had not been raised on direct appeal. After a two-day hearing, the County Circuit Court again ruled against Coleman. The volunteer attorneys who argued the appeals, however, were unfamiliar with Virginia rules of appellate procedure, some of the most complicated in the nation. Thus, they filed the notice of appeal with the Virginia Supreme Court one day late, and the case was dismissed for this procedural reason.

Some observers thought there were solid grounds for further review, including evidence that a local juror told friends he wanted to hear the case to nail the defendant. But when the habeas corpus petition was filed in U.S. district court, it was rejected without a hearing. The federal judge ruled that Coleman had procedurally defaulted his claims in state court and therefore also waived his right to review in federal courts.

The opinion of the Supreme Court was delivered by Justice Sandra Day O'Connor. It begins, "This is a case about federalism. It concerns the respect that federal courts owe the States...." Her opinion stresses that federal courts will not review a question of federal law decided by a state court if the decision of that court rests on an independent and adequate aspect of state law. The Court was also unconcerned about attorney error. O'Connor wrote that after the first appeal, Coleman had no right to counsel, and therefore "any attorney error that led to the default of Coleman's claims in state court cannot constitute cause to excuse the default in federal habeas."

In a forceful dissent Justice Harry Blackmun wrote, "One searches the majority's opinion in vain . . . for any mention of petitioner Coleman's right to a criminal proceeding free from constitutional defect or his interest in finding a forum for his constitutional challenge to his conviction and sentence of death." The dissent terms the majority opinion's emphasis on federalism as cavalier, arguing, "The form of Federalism embraced by today's majority bears little resemblance to that adopted by the Framers of the Constitution."

The decision in *Coleman* sparked a debate over whether it is fair to penalize the prisoner for his lawyer's mistake. Calling the conclusion "bizarre," the editorial writers of *The New York Times* argued that the Court's opinion reflects "a cramped distortion of federalism's scheme of justice under the Constitution. In the name of states' rights, the Court has produced a terrible injustice" ("Federalism Despoiled" 1991). Others, however, applauded the Court's decision, hailing it as another effort to reduce federal review of state death penalty decisions.

Virginia executed Coleman in 1992. But the controversy over his guilt resurfaced eight years later. Three newspapers have filed suit seeking new DNA testing in the case (Masters 2000). Thus even in death Roger Coleman became enmeshed in yet another controversy surrounding the death penalty: Should death row inmates have the right to new DNA testing that might show their innocence?

These decisions opened the floodgate for federal review. The annual number of habeas corpus petitions jumped from 2,000 in 1960 to over 68,000 in 1996. Whether the actual workload of the federal courts increased as rapidly as the number of petitions is an open question. Most decisions are made on the basis of written records; more time-consuming evidentiary hearings are relatively rare. How often prisoners actually win depends on the time period being considered. In 1970, more than 12,000 petitions were granted—an indication that state courts were

slowly adopting the new procedural requirements of the Warren Court revolution in criminal justice. By the 1980s, however, prisoners were rarely successful; fewer than 2 percent gained release.

Contraction under the Burger and Rehnquist Courts

Warren Court decisions expanding habeas corpus relief have steadily been cut back in recent years by a more conservative Supreme Court. The Burger

New Jersey v. Landano

Wrong Man Walking

In 1977, Vincent Landano was convicted of murdering an off-duty police officer. After serving twelve years in prison Landano was released because the prosecutor had withheld evidence at trial, including a statement from the only eyewitness identifying another man as the killer. As you watch the video, ask yourself the following questions:

1. Do you agree with the opinion of one observer that *New Jersey v. Landano* represents a textbook case of where the criminal justice system doesn't work? How is your assessment of whether the system works or doesn't work influenced by the final verdict in the case?
2. Landano is able to gain a new trial based on the work of a lawyer who was working pro bono. Does this case support the proposition that those in prison should have greater access to court-appointed lawyers, or are the facts of this case so unique that one cannot fairly draw any conclusions?
3. Is there prosecutorial misconduct in this case? Was the police investigation fundamentally biased? If so, should either or both of these factors justify damages in a civil lawsuit?

Court restricted the grounds for prisoner petitions, ruling that if state courts provide a fair hearing, federal courts cannot consider Fourth Amendment search-and-seizure questions in habeas corpus proceedings (*Stone v. Powell*, 1976).

The Rehnquist Court repeatedly tightened restrictions on prisoner petitions (*Butler v. McKeller*, 1990; *Saffle v. Parks*, 1990; *McClesky v. Zant*, 1991; *Keeney v. Tamayo-Reyes*, 1992).

Congress Greatly Restricts Federal Habeas

For over two decades Congress considered proposed changes in habeas corpus proceedings (Smith 1995). This inconclusive debate was shattered by the Oklahoma City bombing in 1995. Victims were anxious to channel their grief into tangible reform, and one avenue was habeas corpus reform (Gest 1996). Thus,

as the 1996 elections loomed, Congress passed the Antiterrorism and Effective Death Penalty Act. In terms of habeas corpus the act does the following:

- Creates one-year deadlines for filing habeas petitions.
- Limits successive petitions.
- Restricts the review of state prisoner petitions if the claim was adjudicated on the merits in state courts.
- A "certificate of appealability" is required before a habeas petition may be appealed to a federal court of appeals.
- Decisions of a federal appellate panel are not appealable by writ of certiorari to the Supreme Court.

Moving with unusual speed, the Court agreed to hear a challenge to the new law within two months of passage. During a rare June hearing the justices expressed skepticism about Congress curtailing the power of the Supreme Court. In the end a unanimous court held that the law was constitutional because appeal to the Supreme Court was still technically possible under a 200-year-old and rarely successful route of direct appeal to the Court (*Felker v. Turpin*, 1996). The decision was predicted to speed up the pace of executions. This ruling and others principally affect death penalty cases. (See A Day in Court: "A Self-Appointed Lawyer for the Nation's Condemned.")

STATE SUPREME COURTS

As courts of last resort, state supreme courts have the final authority on the issues most basic to citizens' daily lives. There is no typical state supreme court. Indeed some aren't even called supreme court but rather court of appeals, supreme judicial court, court of criminal appeals, or supreme court of appeals. More importantly, the role that state supreme courts play is affected by the control these judicial bodies exercise over their dockets. Perhaps just as importantly is the exact wording of the state constitution. But these legal factors only partially explain the policy-making role of state supreme courts. Perhaps nowhere is this more obvious than in death penalty appeals.

A DAY IN COURT

"A Self-Appointed Lawyer for the Nation's Condemned"

 On Elisabeth Semel's bulletin board is a *New Yorker* cartoon that shows a man with a thick briefcase walking into an empty prison cell: "Hi, I'm your court-appointed lawyer," he announces. "Whoa! Don't tell me you've been executed already." While it may have been a mordant joke for *New Yorker* readers, for Ms. Semel it defines, in a fundamental way, the parameters of her life. Death row. Incompetent, court-appointed lawyers. Speeded-up executions.

"You're in crisis mode all the time," said Ms. Semel, who was at her desk in her office on Capitol Hill, talking between phone calls, existing, it seemed, on mineral water, lattes, and passion for her work as the director of the American Bar Association's Death Penalty Representation Project. Right now she needs to find volunteer lawyers for dozens of death row inmates in Texas, Virginia, Alabama, and Georgia who are without representation and are facing strict deadlines for filing state and federal appeals. At the same time, two men on federal death row in Indiana are several weeks from execution.

Ms. Semel has been a criminal defense lawyer for 25 years. Three years ago, she left the highly successful San Diego law firm she had helped found and, taking a pay cut of more than 50 percent, moved across the country to revive the bar association's death penalty project. California has executed only eight people since capital punishment was reinstated in 1976, and it provides better counsel and more resources than most other states for those charged with capital murder. Ms. Semel wanted to work on behalf of death row inmates in states like Texas, which has executed 232 people since 1976, and Virginia, which has executed 76, that provide the fewest legal resources.

"I wanted closer proximity to death," she said, paraphrasing the title of a book about a group of crusading lawyers in Atlanta who represent death row inmates. The obstacles were enormous. The federal government had eliminated all financing to help states with capital appeals, and Congress had passed a bill to speed up review of these cases in federal court.

And she would be trying to recruit big law firms to take cases pro bono at a time when they were increasingly focused on profits.

She has on a wall a photograph of Calvin E. Swann, the first Virginia inmate to have his scheduled execution halted by Gov. James S. Gilmore III, who commuted the sentence to life in prison. One of Mr. Swann's relatives has inscribed it to his lawyers: "The Family!!!! With deepest gratitude." Ms. Semel helped find the New York law firm that took the case.

These days she worries about Juan Garza and David Hammer, the first federal prisoners scheduled to be executed since 1963. Both have clemency petitions before President Clinton. The combination of recent Justice Department findings of geographic and racial disparities in the federal system and the public's growing doubts about the fairness of the administration of the death penalty, Ms. Semel said, "call on the president to refuse to permit these executions to go forward." Mr. Garza, whose case she has been actively involved in, was convicted of three drug-related murders. But Ms. Semel never refers to him, or any of her former clients, as a murderer. "That's not how you define a human being," she said. "A human being is always more than the worst thing he's ever done. Do you deny the crime an individual has been convicted of, or the fact that he's guilty? No. But that's not who he is." . . .

She was probably destined to be a lawyer, she said. "The law is the greatest opportunity if you have a passion for advocacy," she said. "The death penalty is my civil rights issue," she added. "It's the ultimate expression of the legal system's unequal treatment of people who are poor, and people of color."

She gets to her office most days by 7:30. She has one lawyer on staff and one assistant. By 11 p.m., she is still working, returning e-mail messages. This is not the sort of schedule that leaves much room for a personal life. Running is how she relaxes. . . .

SOURCE: Sara Rimer, "A Self-Appointed Lawyer for the Nation's Condemned," *New York Times,* October 30, 2000.

Law on the Books:
State Supreme Courts
and Discretionary Dockets

In states that have not created intermediate courts of appeals, the responsibility for appellate review falls directly on the state supreme court. In such circumstances, the state's highest court finds itself relegated to dealing with a succession of relatively minor disputes, devoting its energies to error correction rather than to more time-consuming efforts to shape the law of the state.

By contrast, in the forty states and the District of Columbia that have created intermediate courts

CONTROVERSY

Should Federal Courthouse Doors Be Closed to State Prisoners?

 The right of convicted offenders to seek virtually unlimited review through habeas corpus proceedings has sparked a heated debate (Robbins 1990). Some people would keep the doors of the federal courts wide open to state prisoners; others would slam the doors firmly shut in most cases.

Some proposals to restrict habeas corpus relief are based on problems of judicial administration: Post-conviction petitions contribute to the heavy caseload of the federal courts, are sometimes frivolous, and undermine the value of a final determination of guilt. But most restrictive efforts are anticrime proposals. Typical is the letter President Reagan wrote Congress urging passage of remedial legislation: "As a result of judicial expansion of the habeas corpus remedy, state prisoners are now free to relitigate their convictions and sentences endlessly in the lower federal courts" (quoted in Remington 1988). Conservatives stress that a criminal trial is a procedure that determines the defendant's guilt or innocence, not a game in which the accused may elude justice for any imperfection (Fein 1994).

Writs of habeas corpus play a particularly important role in capital punishment cases. After exhausting appellate remedies, defendants engage in lengthy challenges to the sentence of death by filing multiple writs of habeas corpus in various state and federal courts. Chief Justice William Rehnquist has criticized his colleagues for providing capital offenders with "numerous procedural protections unheard of for other crimes" and "for allowing endlessly drawn out legal proceedings."

Others counter that the death penalty is qualitatively different from other types of sanctions, so multiple scrutiny of such cases is more than justified. The argument for keeping the federal courthouse doors open is forcefully stated by Justice John Paul Stevens, who notes that federal habeas proceedings reveal deficiencies in 60 percent to 70 percent of the capital cases (*Murray v. Giarratano*, 1989). Advocates of this policy also argue not only should there be no rush to judgment but death row inmates should have access to legal assistance, yet often don't. The majority of

post-conviction cases are *pro se*—the prisoner is appearing on his or her own behalf. Recall from Chapter 7 that the Court has held that there is no right to counsel after the first appeal has been exhausted. Many death row defendants must rely on overworked volunteer attorneys (Applebome 1992).

The Antiterrorism and Effective Death Penalty Act has altered the debate in major ways. Some observers predict that the rate of executions will increase significantly. Others think that state courts will be more rigorous in scrutinizing death penalty cases, knowing that the federal courts will now play a much more limited role.

What do you think? Should the federal courthouse doors be reopened to state prisoners, particularly those on death row, to ensure that justice is not short-circuited? Or should the federal courthouse doors remain as they are now, with only one federal review (unless the case presents an extraordinary issue)? Asked another way, where should the line be drawn between the interests of justice (ensuring that only the truly guilty are executed) and the need for finality (many of the habeas petitions raise issues that are very unlikely to succeed)?

 To continue the debate, go to the following sites:

Southern Center for Human Rights: **http://www.schr.org/reports/report.html**

National Center for Policy Analysis: **http://www.ncpa.org/crime** and search for "habeas corpus"

For an up-to-date list of Web links, go to **http://www.wadsworth.com/product/0534563406s**.

 Burke W. Kappler, "Small Favors: Chapter 154 of the Antiterrorism and Effective Death Penalty Act, the States, and the Right to Counsel"

Dwight Aarons, "Getting Out of This Mess: Steps Toward Addressing and Avoiding Inordinate Delay in Capital Cases"

of appeals, it is the lower appellate courts that are primarily concerned with error correction. This leaves the state's highest court free to devote more attention to cases that raise important policy questions (Tarr and Porter 1988). Discretionary review

at the highest level transforms the nature of the judicial process. The high court is no longer merely reacting to disputes brought to it by disgruntled litigants; rather it is selecting those disputes in which it chooses to participate. In sum, the architecture of the system tells the judges of the top court to be creative (Carrington, Meador, and Rosenberg 1976). In states with intermediate courts of appeals, the court of last resort is characterized by high discretion and low caseloads. A substantial portion of their work consists of reviewing petitions and then deciding the petitions granted.

 A growing number of state supreme courts have Web sites, including

Arizona: **http://www.supreme.state.az.us/ azsupreme/**

New Jersey: **http://www.judiciary.state.nj.us/ supreme/index.htm**

Ohio: **http://dir.yahoo.com/Government/Law/ U_S__States/**

Virginia: **http://www.sconet.state.oh.us**

For an up-to-date list of Web links, go to **http:// www.wadsworth.com/product/0534563406s**.

Law in Action: State Supreme Courts as Policy Makers

Americans have long paid attention to the U.S. Supreme Court, but they have tended to overlook state supreme courts. In recent years, scholars have sought to remedy this oversight, focusing on the significant role state courts of last resort play in governmental policy making.

Applications of U.S. Supreme Court decisions is one way that state supreme courts participate in policy making. Although in theory federal law is supreme over conflicting state law, in practice state supreme courts do not invariably follow authoritative pronouncements of the nation's highest court (Tarr 1982). Noncompliance has been most pronounced in race relation cases, with southern state supreme courts often aiding and abetting their state's massive resistance to desegregation (Tarr and Porter 1988). Noncompliance has also occurred in a variety of states, extending over many types of cases. In areas such as police interrogations and search and seizure, state supreme courts have, on occasion, refused to accept the constitutional principles enunciated by the Supreme Court (Johnson and Canon 1984). Short of noncompliance, state supreme courts may erode Constitutional standards adopted by the nation's highest court. This clearly occurred in the area of police interrogations, with

most state supreme courts carving out exceptions to *Miranda* (Gruhl 1981).

Interpretations of state constitutional provisions is another way that state supreme courts act as important governmental policy makers. The phrase **new judicial federalism** refers to the movement in the state supreme courts to reinvigorate state constitutions as sources of individual rights over and above the rights granted by the federal Constitution. New judicial federalism occurred partially as a response to the Burger Court's unwillingness to continue, or even in some cases maintain, the Warren Court's understanding of civil liberties (Galie 1987). Just as important, though, new judicial federalism reflects the growing understanding that the federal Constitution establishes minimum guarantees of individual rights rather than maximum protections (Emmert and Traut 1992). In some instances, for example, state supreme courts have interpreted state bill of rights provisions regarding criminal procedures more expansively than the equivalent sections of the U.S. Bill of Rights. Researchers have identified hundreds of state supreme court decisions that interpret state charters as more rights-generous than their federal counterpart (Fino 1987).

The image of the new judicial federalism is that of a wholly liberal legal movement, but recent research suggests a more complex pattern. An examination of all fifty state supreme courts' criminal procedure decisions based on state constitutional law decided from the late 1960s to the end of 1989 found a "hidden conservatism." Two thirds of the criminal rulings endorsed—"not repudiated"—the conservative holdings of the U.S. Supreme Court (Latzer 1991). Indeed, in some states, conservatives have succeeded in changing the thrust of new judicial federalism.

Law in Controversy: State Supreme Courts and Death Penalty Cases

State supreme courts reveal pronounced differences in their handling of death penalty cases. In California (Emmert and Traut 1996) and New Jersey, for

New judicial federalism: Movement in state supreme courts to reinvigorate states' constitutions as sources of individual rights over and above the rights granted by the U.S. Constitution.

example, the state supreme courts are openly hostile to the imposition of the death penalty. New Jersey's highest court has thrown out all but one of the twenty-nine death sentences it has reviewed (Sullivan 1991). At the other extreme is Georgia, whose supreme court is very likely to uphold the imposition of a sentence of death. Other states fit somewhere in between. The Louisiana Supreme Court, for example, has through the years thrown out roughly half of the sentences of death it has reviewed, but has upheld the rest. (See Controversy: Innocent on Death Row?)

Differences in how state courts of last resort respond to death penalty appeals is not random. Supreme court justices in states with competitive judicial elections are more likely to uphold death sentences (Brace and Hall 1997). In particular, liberal justices facing reelection with possible close margins of victory are more likely to conceal their opposition to the death penalty; they cast votes reflecting their constituents' opinions. Nowhere is the role of state supreme courts more important than in the ongoing Controversy: Innocent on Death Row?

 The Christian Century, "States Review Death Penalty"

THE U.S. SUPREME COURT AND CRIMINAL JUSTICE POLICY

"I'll appeal all the way to the Supreme Court" is a familiar phrase. Alas, it is not very realistic. The jurisdiction of the U.S. Supreme Court is almost exclusively discretionary; that is, it can pick and choose the cases it wishes to decide. Most of the time it decides not to decide. Of the roughly 92 million lawsuits filed in the United States every year, only about 7,000 will ever be appealed to the nation's highest court; and from this small number, the justices will select a mere handful, about 90 in recent years, for briefing, argument, and written decision. Moreover, of this small number, criminal cases constitute an even smaller percentage; in a typical year only 26 criminal decisions are reviewed by the Supreme Court with full opinion.

The importance of the Supreme Court, then, is measured not in terms of quantity but quality. Pres-

idents Ronald Reagan and George Bush made five appointments to the nation's highest court; their choices were intended to move the court in a more conservative direction. Have the Republican presidents been successful? Figure 17-4 charts Supreme Court support for the rights of criminal defendants, showing a major decline over the last two decades. To fully understand today's practices, it is helpful to place the Rehnquist Court in historical perspective. Competing claims that a Court is "too conservative" or "too liberal" can be understood only on the basis of the Court's performance in other periods (Wasby 1993).

Informally, scholars refer to Court eras according to the chief justice. Thus the Warren Court refers to the period from 1953 to 1969 in which Earl Warren (a former Republican governor of California appointed by President Eisenhower) was chief justice. Because the associate justices change, however, these references provide only informal guides to the dominant thinking of the court. For example, the liberal heritage of the Warren Court does not firmly emerge until President Kennedy's appointment of Justice Arthur Goldberg in 1961 (Segal and Spaeth 1989). Nonetheless, an examination of the Warren Court, Burger Court, and now the Rehnquist Court offers a useful summary of major differences in the direction of criminal justice policy.

 CourtTV offers an innovative Web site, The Supreme Court: A Journey Through Time, at **http://www. courttv.com/multimedia/supremecourt/index.html**.

For an up-to-date list of Web links, go to **http:// www.wadsworth.com/product/0534563406s**.

The Warren Court (1953–1969)

Although it is now over thirty years since Chief Justice Earl Warren stepped down, the **Warren Court** (1953–1969) commands our attention because in the areas of civil liberties and civil rights it remains the benchmark against which subsequent periods of the Supreme Court will be measured. The Warren Court revolutionized constitutional law and American society as well, giving to minorities victories they had not been able to obtain from reluctant

Warren Court: The Supreme Court under the leadership of Chief Justice Earl Warren (1953–1969).

CONTROVERSY

Innocent on Death Row?

For six weeks Ron Williamson sat in his cell next to the Oklahoma electric chair screaming, "I am an innocent man!" Just five days before his scheduled execution his public defender persuaded a U.S. district judge that his state trial had serious constitutional flaws. Before the former professional baseball player was retried, however, the Innocence Project at the Benjamin Cardozo Law School arranged for new DNA testing. The results conclusively showed that Williamson was indeed innocent of the rape and murder of Debra Sue Carter.

In *Actual Innocence,* Barry Scheck, Peter Neufield, and Jim Dwyer (2000) use the Williamson case and others to argue that many convicts are wrongly on death row. By their count over the last decade sixty-nine people were sent to prison and death row for crimes they did not commit. Similarly, an influential article, "A Broken System: Error Rates in Capital Cases," examines 5,760 capital verdicts imposed between 1973 and 1995 (Liebman, Fagan, and West 2000a). The authors report that 68 percent of all verdicts fully reviewed were found to be so seriously flawed that they had to be scrapped and retried. And where retrials were known, only 18 percent resulted in the reimposition of the death penalty (Liebman, Fagan, and West 2000b). Studies like these lead proponents of the due process model to argue that "for every seven people executed in this country since 1976, when the Supreme Court reinstated capital punishment, an eighth person—completely innocent—has been condemned to die and later exonerated" (American Civil Liberties Union 2000).

But not all are convinced that the capital appeals process is broken. Barry Latzer and James Cauthen (2000) argue that the statistical conclusions cited above are flawed. They distinguish between two types of errors: conviction errors and sentencing errors. Their analysis shows that conviction errors constitute only a small percentage of appellate court reversals in capital cases. It is sentencing errors, then, that dominate reversals and this is to be expected because capital cases receive much closer scrutiny than noncapital appeals. Overall, advocates of the crime control model argue that the process is working—the few wrong trial court verdicts are indeed identified and corrected on appeal.

In recent years the debate over innocents on death row has focused on DNA testing (Chapter 14). To be sure, some who have been freed from death row or life imprisonment were later found to be innocent because of witnesses who lied at trial. But some like Williamson have been freed after reexamination of trial evidence using advanced DNA testing techniques that were not available during the original trial. Barry Sheck, for one, argues that all convicts on death row should legally be entitled to have the original evidence retested. Conservatives quickly counter that calls for retesting are yet another delaying tactic for defendants who were convicted on the basis of overwhelming physical and testimonial evidence.

What do you think? Do the number of innocent persons released from death row or life imprisonment indicate that the capital appeals process is broken or that it is actually working as it should? Do you think that all convicts on death row should have the right to have physical evidence retested using more advanced DNA techniques or should such requests be granted only upon a strong showing that the suspect might indeed be innocent?

For contrasting views about innocents on death row, go to

"Innocence" Critique: **http://www.prodeathpenalty.com/Innocence.htm**

The Innocence Project: **http://www.cardozo.yu.edu/innocence_project/**

For an up-to-date list of Web links, go to **http://www.wadsworth.com/product/0534563406s**.

Peter Vilbig, "Innocent on Death Row"

"Wrong Guy, Good Cause" (protesting the death penalty)

John Leo, "An Innocent Martyr?" (media bias against capital punishment)

Elizabeth King, "DNA Threatening Court Credibility?"

legislatures and recalcitrant executives. Thus, the Warren Court revolution reflects a distinct departure from earlier Courts, which were often characterized as conservative.

The Warren Court first captured national attention with its highly controversial 1954 decision invalidating racial segregation in the public schools (*Brown v. Board of Education,* 1954). In addition, the

FIGURE 17-4 Declining Support by the Supreme Court for Rights of Criminals

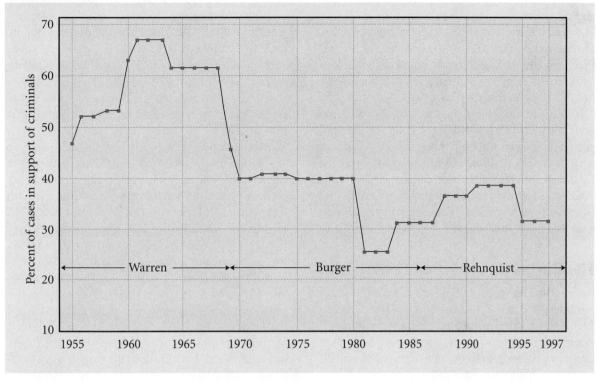

Note: The data were smoothed using a running median using 53R'H (Frederick Hartwig with Brian Dearing, *Exploratory Data Analysis,* Beverly Hills, CA: Sage, 1979).

SOURCE: Adapted from Lee Epstein, Thomas Walker, and William Dixon, "The Supreme Court and Criminal Justice Disputes: A Neo-Institutional Perspective," *American Journal of Political Science* 33 (1989) 834. Updated by Harold Spaeth, *United States Supreme Court Judicial Data Base, 1953–1997 Terms.* Ann Arbor, MI: Inter-University Consortium for Political and Social Research, 2001.

Court first confronted the difficult problem of defining obscenity and considerably narrowed the grounds for prosecution of obscene material (*Roth v. U.S.,* 1957). What produced the greatest controversy, however, was the adoption of a series of broad rules protecting criminal defendants.

During the 1960s, the Supreme Court for the first time attempted to exercise strong policy control over the administration of criminal justice. The nation's highest court began to apply to state courts some of the more specific requirements of the Bill of Rights. Earlier opinions enunciating vague standards of "due process" were replaced by decisions specifying precise rules. The Bill of Rights was seemingly transformed from a collection of general constitutional principles into a code of criminal procedure. These sweeping changes in constitutional interpretation have been called the "due process revolution."

Listing the significant Warren Court criminal justice decisions virtually constitutes a review of the major chapters of this book. The right to counsel was expanded (*Gideon v. Wainwright,* 1963, discussed in Chapter 7); limits were placed on prosecutorial power (Chapter 6); courts were compelled to bring defendants before a judge without unnecessary delay (Chapter 10); restrictions were placed on police searches (*Mapp v. Ohio,* 1961, Chapter 12); limits on police interrogations were mandated (*Miranda v. Arizona,* 1966, Chapter 12); jury selection was significantly changed to ensure equality and fairness (Chapter 14); the death penalty was declared unconstitutional (Chapters 15 and 16); the ability of the guilty to appeal their convictions was made easier (this chapter); and the right of convicts to file habeas corpus petitions was also greatly expanded (also this chapter).

If nothing else, the Warren Court put the issues of criminal justice on its docket and eventually on the nation's agenda as well. There was a persistent increase in the number of civil liberties cases heard every term, as well as the number of civil liberties cases decided in a liberal direction.

The Warren Court revolution in areas as diverse as segregation and pornography, school prayer, and reapportionment greatly changed American society. But many of these changes were far from popular. The Supreme Court's attempt to nationalize, rationalize, and constitutionalize the criminal justice system came at a time of increasing crime in the streets, riots in big cities, political violence protesting the Vietnam war, and, most tragically of all, assassinations of American leaders. To the public, there appeared to be a connection between the new trends of what was seen as judicial permissiveness and the breakdown of law and order. Supreme Court justices were accused of "coddling criminals" and "handcuffing the police." This controversy became the focus of national debate.

The Burger Court (1969–1986)

During the 1968 presidential campaign, Republican candidate Richard Nixon made the Warren Court's decisions on criminal procedure a major issue. He promised to appoint "strict constructionists" to the Court, and after his election he made good on this promise. With his four appointments, Nixon achieved remarkable success in remodeling the Court. After Warren Burger, Harry Blackmun, Lewis Powell, and William Rehnquist took the bench, support for civil liberties quickly began to diminish, dropping from 80 percent in 1968 to only 34 percent in 1985 (Segal and Spaeth 1989).

The Nixon Court was named after the new Chief Justice, Warren Burger. While on balance the **Burger Court** (1969–1986) was more conservative than its predecessor, there was no constitutional counterrevolution, only modest adjustment. The withdrawal from Warren Court decisions were most apparent in criminal justice. *Miranda* was weakened but not overturned. Similarly, despite clamor by conservatives, *Mapp* was not overruled, although the Court began creating "good faith" exceptions to the exclusionary rule (see Chapter 12). To be sure, the death penalty was reinstated, but overall the Burger Court did not cut back on Warren Court criminal procedure rulings as much as had been expected.

Just as important, the Burger Court began to tackle new sets of issues not previously treated. In sex discrimination, women were not given as complete protection as had been given to racial minorities, but the tone was moderate to liberal, not conservative (Wasby 1993). Plea bargaining was openly discussed, and rather than abolishing it (as some conservatives urged), the Burger Court sought to regularize its practice (Chapter 13). And in one of the most controversial decisions ever issued, the Burger Court struck down a variety of requirements that interfered with a woman's right to obtain an abortion (*Roe v. Wade*, 1973).

Amid this diversity, it is hard to capture the essence of the Burger Court. Indeed, it is probably best characterized by the headline, "Pragmatism, Compromise Marks Courts: Tricky Track Record Harder to Categorize than Pundits Predicted" (Wasby 1993, 17). The Burger Court in the eighties was dominated by a four-judge center bloc—Blackmun, Powell, Stevens, and White—who needed only one additional vote to carry the day. Powell was the most centrist of the centrist justices on most other matters, and for this reason he was often called upon to craft the majority opinion when the Court was split five to four. Overall, the Burger Court was composed of seven justices appointed by Republican presidents. (President Carter did not have an opportunity to name a justice to the Court.) Yet President Reagan sought to remake this Republican body in his even more conservative image.

 The recently redesigned U.S. Supreme Court Web site provides easy access to current cases and past ones as well: **http://www.supremecourtus.gov/**.

For an up-to-date list of Web links, go to **http://www.wadsworth.com/product/0534563406s**.

The Rehnquist Court (1986–)

Presidents Ronald Reagan and George Bush continued the Republican policy of appointing conservatives to the court. The **Rehnquist Court** (1986–) officially began when William Rehnquist was elevated from associate justice to chief justice. Unofficially, it is likely to be dated with the 1988 appointment of Anthony Kennedy, who provided a

---

Burger Court: The Supreme Court under the leadership of Chief Justice Warren Burger (1969–1986).

Rehnquist Court: The Supreme Court under the leadership of Chief Justice William Rehnquist (1986–).

TABLE 17-1   Supreme Court Justices in Order of Seniority

Name	Year of Birth	Home State	Year of Appointment	President	Senate Vote
William Rehnquist*	1924	Arizona	1971	Nixon	65–33
John Paul Stevens	1920	Illinois	1975	Ford	78–0
Sandra Day O'Connor	1930	Arizona	1981	Reagan	99–0
Antonin Scalia	1936	New York	1986	Reagan	98–0
Anthony Kennedy	1936	California	1988	Reagan	97–0
David Souter	1940	New Hampshire	1990	Bush	90–9
Clarence Thomas	1948	Georgia	1991	Bush	52–48
Ruth Bader Ginsburg	1933	New York	1993	Clinton	96–3
Stephen Breyer	1938	Massachusetts	1994	Clinton	87–9

•William Rehnquist was promoted from associate justice to chief justice in 1986.

conservative vote far more dependably than did his predecessor Lewis Powell. Thus, it was during the 1988 term that the Rehnquist Court seemed to come of conservative age by cutting back abortion rights, condoning mandatory drug testing, and permitting capital punishment for juveniles and retarded persons convicted of murder. And as we have emphasized in this chapter, it virtually eliminated the right of convicts to seek habeas corpus relief.

But other Rehnquist Court decisions cannot necessarily be easily categorized as conservative; for example, the high court upheld flag burning and unanimously ruled that mistaken jury instructions can never be considered harmless error. And most interestingly, the Court announced a new constitutional right grounded in the Eighth Amendment's prohibitions against excessive fines; these limits place brakes on the government's aggressive use of its authority under the drug forfeiture laws (Chapter 3). The Court's conservative justices have been criticized for their activist inclination to disregard precedent (Smith and Hensley 1993). For example, the 1991 decision permitting victim impact testimony in capital sentencing hearings (*Payne v. Tennessee,* discussed in Chapter 9) directly overturned precedents that were merely two and four years old (*Booth v. Maryland,* 1987; *South Carolina v. Gathers,* 1989).

There is little doubt that the Rehnquist Court is more conservative on many issues than its predecessors. Perhaps Law Professor Yale Kamisar said it best

in his comment that the Rehnquist Court "gives weight to the needs, convenience, and practical problems of law enforcement" (quoted in Wicker 1991). Overall, the Court is increasingly pragmatic but still very conservative.

Decisions reflect shifting alliances of the justices. Firmly on the right are Antonin Scalia, Clarence Thomas, and William Rehnquist, with Anthony Kennedy often joining. Arrayed more to the left are John Paul Stevens, Ruth Bader Ginsburg, Stephen Breyer, and David Souter. It is Sandra Day O'Connor who often holds the balance of power.

The six conservative justices who were appointed by Republican presidents, however, do not always agree among themselves. O'Connor's deference to legislatures, for example, is at times at odds with Scalia's bold libertarian brand of conservatism. As a result, the conservative Rehnquist Court has not always been consistently conservative (Rosenberg 1993). In short, the voting alliances of the justices cannot always be neatly divided into liberal and conservative camps.

With the retirement of Byron White, President Clinton became the first Democratic president in twenty-six years to make an appointment to the high court. He chose Ruth Bader Ginsburg. With his second appointment, he elevated Stephen Breyer to the high court (Table 17-1). Both have been moderates who on some cases forge an alliance with the centrist justices.

THE MURDER TRIAL OF SHAREEF COUSIN

A Reversal on Narrow Grounds

 Because the jury had imposed the death penalty, the conviction of Shareef Cousin was appealed directly to the Louisiana Supreme Court. The fact that it took longer for the appellate court to review the case (twenty-two months) than it took to get the case to trial (ten months) is a reflection of how seriously these matters are treated. Some of this time lapse occurred because both sides requested additional time to prepare their briefs. In addition, the state's highest court also found that the original trial court record was defective and ordered the clerk of court for Criminal District Court to resubmit the entire record. The final record is nothing if not voluminous. Besides the briefs and the filings, there are twenty-two volumes of trial court transcripts. Stacked one atop the other, the complete record (without the cardboard box) stands twenty-six inches tall.

The brief on appeal for the appellant runs eighty-one pages and argues that forty-nine errors occurred during the trial proceedings. By contrast, the brief of the State of Louisiana, the appellee, provides forty-five pages of refutation. The court heard oral argument in December 1997 with a total of eighty minutes allotted to both sides.

To ensure that the workload is distributed equally, the Louisiana Supreme Court assigns opinion writing on a rotating basis. Thus by rotation the opinion was assigned to Justice Harry Lemmon. After working as a chemist for four years and serving in the army for two years, Lemmon graduated cum laude from Loyola University School of Law. He practiced law for several years before being elected to the state's intermediate court of appeals in 1970. Ten years later he was elected to the Louisiana Supreme Court.

Justice Lemmon's seventeen-page opinion focuses primarily on the evidence introduced by the prosecution to impeach the credibility of James Rowell, their turncoat witness (see Chapter 14). His prior statements were hearsay but nonetheless admissible for the purposes of establishing a prior inconsistent statement—he had indeed earlier stated that he had a conversation with Shareef Cousin two days after the murder. But the prosecutor went too far when he introduced that evidence to show the substantive guilt of the defendant,

the opinion noted. Moreover, the prosecutor compounded the error by "flagrant misuse" of hearsay evidence during closing arguments.

As for the prosecutor's failure to disclose the key statements from Connie Babin, the opinion largely ducks the issue. At one point the court says that the evidence was clearly exculpatory (and therefore should have been given to the defense), but in a footnote says it does not reach the issue because the defense now knew about the statement.

But if the court thought it could duck the contentious issue of prosecutorial misconduct, it was mistaken. For the next year and a half the lawyers battled over the scope of discovery. Eventually, the state's high court granted broad discovery rights to the defense (see Chapter 12).

While examining the voluminous appellate court record I made a surprise finding—a 10×12×4 inch box is included. Inside are hundreds of letters addressed to the Justice of the Supreme Court, Louisiana Supreme Court. I sampled a few that had been opened. Although handwritten, the letters were similar, urging the court to reverse Cousin's conviction because he was too young to die and also his alibi showed that he was innocent. Clearly, the murder trial of Shareef Cousin had become a national and in some case an international cause célèbre, with anti–death penalty groups urging concerned citizens to write the court. There was no indication, however, that the letters had been read by any of the justices; indeed, most had never been read at all—they were still sealed, taking up space in the clerk of court's office.

 To view how anti–death penalty groups tried to rally support for Shareef Cousin, go to **http://www. ncadp.org/motivate.html.**

For an up-to-date list of Web links, go to **http:// www.wadsworth.com/product/0534563406s**.

 To read national coverage of the reversal, search for "New Trial Granted to Shareef Cousin."

The Post-Rehnquist Court

During the 2000 presidential campaign the future composition of the Court was a minor issue. Amid rumors that at least three justices (Rehnquist among them) wished to retire, the two major candidates offered contrasting views about how they would fill potential vacancies: Democratic nominee Al Gore suggested he would nominate middle-of-the-road justices, while Republican George W. Bush expressed strong preferences for justices on the very right.

Following the election, the current membership of the Court became the dominating topic. With ballot problems in Florida, the five conservatives on the Court ruled that the vote counting should end, thus ensuring that George W. Bush would become the nation's forty-third president (*Bush v. Gore*, 2000). The sharp division on the nation's highest judicial body has muddied the waters of future appointments to the Court. If George W. Bush attempts to appease the right wing of the Republican Party by nominating justices in the mold of Scalia and Thomas, then he risks defeat in the U.S. Senate. If, on the other hand, he chooses to nominate more moderate justices he risks alienating a key political base and risks defeat in the 2004 presidential election. Either way, the direction he attempts to lead the Supreme Court might become the defining issue in his presidency.

The Supreme Court in Broad Perspective

Newspaper coverage of the Supreme Court tends to reflect the play by play of an athletic event, with each decision in the term described as a "victory" or "defeat" for conservatives or liberals. Unfortunately what gets lost in this commentary is the broader perspective. Overall, the decisions of the Supreme Court swing back and forth much like a pendulum on a clock. Far from being random, however, these swings reflect major political movements in the nation. Most directly this occurs because of the swing of electoral politics; presidential appointments control the composition of the bench and may temper the speed, if not shift the direction, of the Court. Somewhat indirectly public opinion also affects the justices' lives and may serve to curb them when they threaten to go too far or too fast in their rulings. "But changes in the direction of the Court are ultimately moderated by its functioning as a collegial body, in which all nine justices share power and compete for influence" (O'Brien 1988, 13). The Court thus generally shifts direction gradually, incorporating and accommodating the views of new appointees. Ultimately these long-term trends, more so than individual decisions, have the most influence.

CONCLUSION

Roger Coleman died in the Virginia electric chair, but the controversy over the Supreme Court decision continues. To some observers, it represented a much-needed step of reducing a long, drawn-out review process. To others, it reflected a hollow formalism devoid of considerations of justice. Ultimately, though, it was a law passed by Congress, more so than any decisions by the Supreme Court, that has recently altered post-conviction reviews in federal courts.

The right to one appeal is being increasingly used. Appellate court caseloads have grown dramatically in recent years. The explosive growth in appellate court caseloads not only reflects the greater willingness of litigants to ask reviewing bodies to correct errors but also represents the greater role appellate courts play in policy making. U.S. Supreme Court decisions have important impacts on the criminal justice system. But the nine justices are often as divided over the correct answer to a legal problem as is society. Thus, predicting specific case outcomes is difficult; indeed, the conservative Rehnquist Court has not always ruled in a predictably conservative manner.

CRITICAL THINKING QUESTIONS

1. Do you think the Supreme Court was correct in ruling that Roger Coleman should not have his murder conviction reviewed in federal court because his lawyer filed the notice

of appeal one day late? Would your answer be the same or different if this was not a death penalty case? Would your answer be the same or different if the basis of the review would be procedural as opposed to the substance of the evidence?

2. In the public's mind, at least, appellate courts drag on endlessly and result in a lack of finality in the process. Do you think this is a significant problem, or is it merely one of appearance?

3. How does the appeal and review process in a capital murder case differ from the appeal and review process in a serious felony?

4. Why are most findings of guilt at the trial level not appealed? In what ways are appellate cases unrepresentative of trial court cases?

5. In what ways do expedited processing techniques represent what Howard (1981) has called a shift from handcrafted to mass production techniques? Some lawyers object because traditional procedures are being altered. In what ways might justice suffer? In what ways do expedited processing techniques actually provide better justice because judicial time is more focused on difficult cases?

6. Based on material in this chapter and earlier ones, what have been the significant differences in decisions between the Warren Court, the Burger Court, and the Rehnquist Court? In particular, consider Court decisions related to right to counsel (Chapter 7), bail (Chapter 11), right to trial (Chapter 14), the death penalty (Chapter 15), and habeas corpus.

 WORLD WIDE WEB RESOURCES AND EXERCISES

Web Guides

http://dir.yahoo.com/Government/Law/U_S__States/ (Select "State," and then go to judicial branch.)
http://dir.yahoo.com/Government/U_S__ Government/Judicial_Branch/Federal_Courts/ Appeals_Courts/

Web Search Terms

"Habeas corpus"; "Anti-Terrorism and Effective Death Penalty Act"

Useful URLs

Visit CNN'S Supreme Court Center: http://www.cnn.com/LAW/scotus/.

See the Supreme Court Resource Center from Findlaw.com: http://supreme.lp.findlaw.com/supreme_court/.

See the Supreme Court from *USA Today*: http://usatoday.com/news/court/courtfront.htm.

The Legal Information Institute at Cornell University includes lots of information about the Supreme Court as well as the full text of many opinions in a searchable format: http://supct.law.cornell.edu/supct.

Uncommon URLs

The Virtual Supreme Court is a teaching tool to explore the role of the judiciary in deciding how to interpret the words of the Constitution: http://www.law.upenn.edu/fac/bwoodhou/vsc/.

The Georgia Association of Criminal Defense Lawyers disseminates information about the Anti-Terrorism and Effective Death Penalty Act: http://www.gacdl.org/habeas.htm.

The Supreme Court Historical Society offers insights into the Court's history and also provides an online gift service: http://www.supremecourthistory.org.

The Colorado State Public Defender provides an appellate brief online at http://www.state.co.us/gov_dir/pdef_dir/library/e_garcia/garcia%20toc.htm.

The State Appellate Defender Organization (Michigan) provides lots of information about appeals on its Web site: http://www.sado.org. Of special interest is "How to Seek Judicial Review of Your Felony Conviction and Sentence" at http://www.sado.org/fbull.htm.

The Center on Wrongful Convictions of Northwestern University has freed several falsely accused convicts from death row: http://www.law.nwu.edu/depts/clinic/wrongful/.

The DNA Testing Program of the Oklahoma Indigent Defense System can be accessed at http://www.state.ok.us/~oids/.

The National Committee to Prevent Wrongful Executions is a bipartisan committee of death penalty supporters and opponents who are concerned about the risk of wrongful executions: http://www.constitutionproject.org/.

Web Exercises

1. Read press accounts of recent U.S. Supreme Court decisions to see if the Court continues to give limited support to the rights of criminal defendants. One of the most widely read national newspapers has a useful archive of coverage of cases during the current year and preceding ones as well: **http://www.usatoday. com/Index/Supreme Court.**

2. Jerry Goldman at Northwestern University has created an award-winning Web site, Oyez Oyez Oyez, which provides access to oral argument and the Court's opinion announcement. Many of the cases highlighted in the Case Focus in each chapter are now available (you will need RealAudio, however). Locate it through **http://oyez.nwu.edu/.**

    Once on the site you can access specific opinions either by title, case citation, subject, or decision date. Tune into *Felker v. Turpin* to hear the lawyers argue the case and the justices ask questions.

3. Biographies of Supreme Court justices, past and present, are readily available on the Web through **http://www.yahoo.com/Government/ U_S__Government/Judicial_Branch-Supreme_ Court/Justices/.**

    Pick a justice from the conservative camp and one from the moderate wing. Compare their careers. Besides the appointing president, are there any differences in backgrounds related to law school attended, type of law practiced, governmental service, and the like?

4. One of the most hotly contested death penalty case centers on Mumia Abu-Jamal, who was convicted of murdering a Philadelphia police officer. The battle to free him revolves around habeas corpus filings. Choose the search term *Mumia Abu-Jamal* and find one Web site on each side of the issue. Two possibilities are Mumia Abu-Jamal's Freedom Journal (**http://www.mumia.org/**) and Justice for Police Officer Daniel Faulkner (**http:// www.danielfaulkner.com/**).

    In examining these sites ask yourself what is more important: the procedures in the case or the substance of the matter? Moreover, how does this case relate to Controversy: Should Federal Courthouse Doors Be Closed to State Prisoners?

INFOTRAC COLLEGE EDITION RESOURCES AND EXERCISES

Basic Searches

Appellate courts; appellate procedure; courts of appeal; briefs; certiorari; waiver of appeal; court of last resort; Supreme Court, United States; Supreme court; Antiterrorism and Effective Death Penalty Act of 1996; habeas corpus; Warren, Earl; Burger, Warren; Rehnquist, William

Recommended Articles

Speedy Rice, "Preserving Your Evidence and Record for Appeal"

Jennifer L. Reichert, "Ninth Circuit Should Remain Intact, Commission Says"

"Legal Malpractice in the Criminal Context: Is Postconviction Relief Required?"

Andrew Peyton Thomas, "Penalty Box: A Much-Needed Reform Seemed Poised to Hasten Executions"

Andrew Phillips, "The Long Needle of Justice"

"'Serious Error' Found in Death Penalty System"

InfoTrac College Edition Exercises

1. Using the search term *United States, Supreme Court,* locate two or more articles that discuss the current decisions of the Court relating to criminal justice. To what extent do the authors think that the decisions are too liberal or too conservative?

2. Using the search terms *capital punishment; capital punishment, cases,* or *capital punishment, law regulations,* locate two or more articles that discuss the length of time from a sentence of death to execution. To what extent do the authors think that delay is good or bad? Why?

3. Using the search term *habeas corpus,* find articles that relate to contemporary practices and answer the following questions: To what extent are discussions of habeas corpus practices dominated by death penalty cases? In discussing habeas corpus, to what extent do the authors come closer to the crime control model or the due process model of criminal justice?

REFERENCES

American Civil Liberties Union. 2000. "Act Now to Stop the Execution of the Innocent." http://www.aclu.org/death-penalty/.

Applebome, Peter. 1992. "Indigent Defendants, Overworked Lawyers." *The New York Times,* 18 September.

Brace, Paul and Melinda Gann Hall. 1997. "The Interplay of Preferences, Case Facts, Context, and Rules in the Politics of Judicial Choice." *Journal of Politics* 59: 1206–1241.

Bureau of Justice Statistics. 1985. "Bulletin: The Growth of Appeals, 1973–83 Trends." Washington, D.C.: U.S. Department of Justice.

Carp, Robert, and Ronald Stidham. 1990. *Judicial Process in America.* Washington, D.C.: Congressional Quarterly Press.

Carrington, Paul, Daniel Meador, and Maurice Rosenberg. 1976. *Justice on Appeal.* St. Paul, MN: West.

Chapper, Joy, and Roger Hanson. 1990. "Understanding Reversible Error in Criminal Appeals." *State Court Journal* 14: 16–24.

Davies, Thomas. 1982. "Affirmed: A Study of Criminal Appeals and Decision-Making Norms in a California Court of Appeal." *American Bar Foundation Research Journal* 1982: 543–648.

Di Pietro, Susanne. 1991. "The Development of Appellate Sentence Review in Alaska." *Judicature* 75: 143–153.

Douglas, Charles. 1985. "Innovative Appellate Court Processing: New Hampshire's Experience with Summary Affirmance." *Judicature* 69: 147–156.

Emmert, Craig, and Carol Ann Traut. 1992. "State Supreme Courts, State Constitutions, and Judicial Policymaking." *Justice System Journal* 16: 37–48.

———. 1996. "An Integrated Model of Judicial Decisonmaking: The California Justices and Capital Punishment." Paper presented at the annual meeting of the Midwest Political Science Association, Chicago, April 19.

"Federalism Despoiled." 1991. *The New York Times,* 27 June.

Fein, Bruce. 1994. "Don't Play Criminals' Game." *USA Today,* 15 April, 11.

Fino, Susan. 1987. *The Role of State Supreme Courts in the New Judicial Federalism.* Westport, CT: Greenwood.

Galie, Peter. 1987. "State Supreme Courts, Judicial Federalism and the Other Constitutions." *Judicature* 71: 100–110.

Gest, Ted. 1996. "The Law That Grief Built." *U.S. News and World Report,* 29 April, 58.

Gruhl, John. 1981. "State Supreme Courts and the U.S. Supreme Court's Post-Miranda Rulings." *Journal of Criminal Law and Criminology* 72: 886–913.

Hanson, Roger. 1996. *Time on Appeal.* Williamsburg, VA: National Center for State Courts.

Howard, J. Woodford. 1981. *Courts of Appeal in the Federal Judicial System: A Study of the Second, Fifth, and District of Columbia Circuits.* Princeton, NJ: Princeton University Press.

Johnson, Charles, and Bradley Canon. 1984. *Judicial Policies: Implementation and Impact.* Washington, D.C.: Congressional Quarterly Press.

Latzer, Barry. 1991. "The Hidden Conservatism of the State Court 'Revolution.'" *Judicature* 74: 190–197.

Latzer, Barry, and James Cauthen. 2000. "Capital Appeals Revisited." *Judicature* 84: 64–71.

Liebman, James, Jeffrey Fagan, and Valerie West. 2000a. "A Broken System: Error Rates in Capital Cases, 1973–1999." *Texas Law Review* 73: 1862.

———. 2000b. "Death Matters: A Reply to Professors Latzer and Cauthen." *Judicature* 84: 72–77.

Marvell, Thomas. 1989. "State Appellate Court Responses to Caseload Growth." *Judicature* 72: 282–289.

Masters, Brooke. 2000. "Another Look at '92 Execution Backed." *Washington Post,* 11 November.

Meador, Daniel. 1974. *Appellate Courts: Staff and Process in the Crisis of Volume.* St. Paul, MN: West.

Neubauer, David. 1985. "Published Opinions Versus Summary Affirmations: Criminal Appeals in Louisiana." *Justice System Journal* 10: 173–189.

———. 1991. "Winners and Losers Before the Louisiana Supreme Court: The Case of Criminal Appeals." *Justice Quarterly* 8: 85–106.

———. 1992. "A Polychotomous Measure of Appellate Court Outcomes: The Case of Criminal Appeals." *Justice System Journal* 16: 75–87.

O'Brien, David. 1988. "The Supreme Court: From Warren to Burger to Rehnquist." *PS* 20: 13.

Ostrom, Brian, and Neal Kauder. 1999. *Examining the Work of State Courts, 1998.* Williamsburg, VA: National Center for State Courts.

Remington, Frank. 1988. "Post-Conviction Review: What State Trial Courts Can Do to Reduce Problems." *Judicature* 72: 53–57.

Robbins, Ira. 1990. "Death Penalty Habeas Corpus: Defining the Issues." *Judicature* 73: 215–219.

Roper, Robert, and Albert Melone. 1981. "Does Procedural Due Process Make a Difference? A Study of Second Trials." *Judicature* 65: 136–141.

Rosenberg, Yale. 1993. "Two Judicious Surprises: The Supreme Court Reinforces Both Federal Habeas Corpus and Miranda." *Criminal Law Bulletin* 29: 418–427.

Scheck, Barry, Peter Neufeld, and Jim Dwyer. 2000. *Actual Innocence: Five Days to Execution and Other Dispatches from the Wrongfully Convicted.* New York: Doubleday.

Segal, Jeffrey, and Harold Spaeth. 1989. "Decisional Trends on the Warren and Burger Courts: Results from the Supreme Court Data Base Project." *Judicature* 73: 103–107.

Smith, Christopher. 1995. "Federal Habeas Corpus Reform: The State's Perspective." *Justice System Journal* 18: 1–11.

Smith, Christopher, and Thomas Hensley. 1993. "Assessing the Conservatism of the Rehnquist Court." *Judicature* 77: 83–89.

Songer, Donald. 1990. "Criteria for Publication of Opinions in the U.S. Courts of Appeals: Formal Rules versus Empirical Reality." *Judicature* 73: 307–313.

Sullivan, Joseph. 1991. "New Jersey's Highest Court Defends Its Course." *The New York Times,* 4 August, E16.

Tarr, G. Alan. 1982. "State Supreme Courts and the U.S. Supreme Court: The Problem of Compliance." In *State Supreme Courts: Policymakers in the Federal System,* edited by Mary Cornelia Porter and G. Alan Tarr. Westport, CT: Greenwood.

Tarr, G. Alan, and Mary Cornelia Porter. 1988. *State Supreme Courts in State and Nation.* New Haven, CT: Yale University Press.

Traynor, Roger. 1970. *The Riddle of Harmless Error.* Columbus: Ohio State University Press.

Wasby, Stephen. 1982. "The Functions and Importance of Appellate Oral Argument: Some Views of Lawyers and Federal Judges." *Judicature* 65: 340–353.

———. 1993. *The Supreme Court in the Federal Judicial System.* 4th ed. Chicago: Nelson-Hall.

Wicker, Tom. 1991. "Dee Brown and You." *The New York Times,* 15 May, A15.

Williams, Jimmy. 1992. "Sentencing Guidelines and the Changing Composition of Criminal Appeals: A Preliminary Analysis." *Judicature* 76: 94–97.

Wold, John. 1978. "Going Through the Motions: The Monotony of Appellate Court Decisionmaking." *Judicature* 62: 58–65.

Wold, John, and Greg Caldeira. 1980. "Perceptions of 'Routine' Decision-Making in Five California Courts of Appeal." *Polity* 13: 334–347.

FOR FURTHER READING

Amar, Akhil Reed. *The Constitution and Criminal Procedure: First Principles.* New Haven, CT: Yale University Press, 1997.

Biskupic, Joan, and Elder Witt. *The Supreme Court at Work.* Washington, D.C.: CQ Publishing, 1996.

Bureau of Justice Statistics. *Prisoner Petitions in the Federal Courts, 1980–1996.* Washington, D.C.: Author, 1997.

Decker, John. *Revolution to the Right: Criminal Procedure during the Burger-Rehnquist Court Era.* Hamden, CT: Garland, 1994.

Hall, Melinda Gann. "Electoral Politics and Strategic Voting in State Supreme Courts." *Journal of Politics* 54 (1992): 427–446.

Hanson, Robert, and Henry Daley. *Federal Habeas Corpus Review.* Williamsburg, VA: National Center for State Courts, 1995.

Hickey, Thomas. "A Double Jeopardy Analysis of the Medgar Evers Murder Case." *Journal of Criminal Justice* 23 (1995): 41–51.

Hoffman, Joseph, and Lauren Robel. "Federal Court Supervision of State Criminal Justice Administration." *Annals of the American Academy* 543 (1996): 154–166.

Kincaid, John. "The New Federalism Context of the New Judicial Federalism." *Rutgers Law Journal* 26 (1995): 913–979.

Latzer, Barry. *State Constitutions and Criminal Justice.* Westport, CT: Greenwood, 1991.

Lopeman, Charles. *The Activist Advocate: Policy Making in State Supreme Courts.* Westport, CT: Praeger, 1999.

Marvell, Thomas. "The Effectiveness of Flexible Assignment of Appeals Between Supreme and Intermediate Courts." *Judicature* 78 (1995): 292–298.

McCoy, Candace, and Illya Lichtenberg. "Providing Effective Habeas Counsel for Indigents in Capital Cases." *The Justice System Journal* 21 (1999): 81–87.

O'Brien, David. *Storm Center: The Supreme Court in American Politics.* 5th ed. New York: W. W. Norton, 1999.

Perry, Barbara. *The Priestly Tribe: The Supreme Court's Image in the American Mind.* Westport, CT: Praeger, 1999.

Schwartz, Bernard. *The Warren Court: A Retrospective.* New York: Oxford University Press, 1996.

Tarr, G. Alan, ed. *Constitutional Politics in the States: Contemporary Controversies and Historical Patterns.* Westport, CT: Greenwood, 1996.

Williams, Jimmy. "Type of Counsel and the Outcome of Criminal Appeals: A Research Note." *American Journal of Criminal Justice* 19 (1995): 275–285.

The Lower Courts

THE LYNCH CITY POLICE COURT MEETS EVERY THURSDAY NIGHT, Judge C. B. Russell presiding. Like many others born and raised in the small towns of Kentucky's coal mining region, Russell dropped out of high school and worked in the coal mines. Later he was elected judge. During one session Judge Russell found Lonnie North guilty of drunk driving and sentenced him to thirty days in jail. But Kentucky law allows only a fine for Lonnie North's charge. It seems that the nonlawyer judge had exceeded his legal authority.

On appeal North's lawyers argued that defendants cannot receive due process of law when the judge is not a lawyer. Chief Justice Warren Burger's majority opinion disagreed, arguing that rural courts, with nonlawyer judges, were convenient to the citizens, providing simple and speedy justice. But critics wonder if convenient and speedy may not equate all too often to rough justice. ∎

North v. Russell is a rare case—the nation's highest court almost never hears appeals from the trial courts of limited jurisdiction, preferring instead to concentrate on the more intellectually challenging legal issues raised by murderers and drug dealers who have been found guilty in the major trial courts. Nonetheless, countless Lonnie Norths appear in the nation's lowest courts every day. These are the courts that process the millions of Americans accused each year of disturbing the peace, shoplifting, being drunk, and driving too fast. Individually, these cases may appear to be minor—almost petty—but collectively, the work of the lower courts is quite important.

This chapter discusses the rapid, rough justice dispensed by the lower courts. We begin with an examination of the scope of the lower courts and then consider their problems. As we shall see, many of the criticisms stem from the great flexibility exercised by judges and prosecutors as they try to produce substantive justice, rather than simply adhering to procedures. Moreover, lower courts exhibit immense variation—big-city courts function very differently from their counterparts in rural areas. The next two sections, therefore, consider the different issues presented in rural justice of the peace courts as opposed to the big-city municipal courts. Finally, we examine alternative dispute resolution (ADR), which is designed to reduce the caseloads of the courts by providing nonadversarial alternatives to traditional courtroom procedures.

SCOPE OF THE LOWER COURTS

At the first level of state courts are **trial courts of limited jurisdiction,** sometimes referred to as **inferior courts,** or more simply, **lower courts.** Although these minor courts stand at the bottom of the judicial hierarchy, the base is much larger than the typical pyramid diagram suggests. Indeed, when we count up the number of courts, judges, and cases

> **Trial courts of limited jurisdiction:** A lower level state court, such as a justice of the peace court, whose jurisdiction is limited to minor civil disputes or misdemeanors.
>
> **Inferior court (lower court):** Term for a trial court of limited jurisdiction; also may refer to any court lower in the judicial hierarchy.

TABLE 18-1 Volume of Cases Filed in Lower Courts and Major Trial Courts in a Year (millions)

	Lower Courts	Major Trial Courts
Criminal	10.2	4.4
Juvenile	.8	1.3
Traffic/ordinance violations	45.8	8.6
Domestic relations	1.5	3.5
Civil	9.1	6.3
Total	67.4	24.1

SOURCE: Brian Ostrom and Neal Kauder, *Examining the Work of State Courts, 1998.* (Williamsburg, VA: National Center for State Courts, 1999).

filed in courts all across the nation, the numbers are dominated by the nation's lowest judiciary. The 13,748 lower courts constitute 84 percent of all judicial bodies, and the 17,974 lower court judges make up 66 percent of all state judges. Table 18-1 highlights the large volume of cases heard by the lower courts: The 67 million-plus case filings represent about 75 percent of yearly state court filings. These filing figures require closer examination because they are often bandied about in the debate over the litigation explosion.

The precise jurisdiction of lower courts varies from place to place. In some states major trial courts in rural areas hear traffic cases and the like because there are few lower courts. Moreover, in six states and the District of Columbia, the lower courts have been consolidated with the major trial courts; as a result, statistical comparisons between these jurisdictions and the other forty-four states are difficult at best. Nonetheless, the workload of the lower courts can usefully be examined in terms of felony criminal cases, nonfelony criminal cases, and civil cases.

Felony Criminal Cases

Lower court jurisdiction typically includes the preliminary stages of felony cases (Chapter 4). Thus, after an arrest a judge in a trial court of limited jurisdiction will hold the initial appearance, appoint counsel for indigents, and conduct the preliminary hearing. Later the case is transferred to a trial court of general jurisdiction for trial (or plea) and sentencing. Note also, from Figure 18-1, that lower court judges typically sign search warrants—a decision that may prove crucial for decisions in the major trial court.

 Perhaps nowhere is the old saying "Fact is stranger than fiction" more true than on reality television. A number of these shows use the lower courts as their setting. Two of the most popular are *People's Court* (**http://peoplescourt.warnerbros.com/**) and *Judge Judy* (**http://www.judgejudy.com/home/main.asp**).

For an up-to-date list of Web links, go to **http://www.wadsworth.com/product/0534563406s**.

Nonfelony Criminal Cases

Typically, criminal cases are divided into felony and misdemeanor, a distinction that fits nicely with the work of the trial courts of general jurisdiction. But for the lower courts, a broader concept of nonfelony cases is best. Nonfelony includes not only misdemeanors but also ordinance violations and traffic cases.

A **misdemeanor** is a crime punishable by fine and/or imprisonment, usually in a city or county jail, for a period of less than one year. Misdemeanors are enacted by state legislative bodies and cover the entire state. **Ordinance,** on the other hand, are laws passed by a local governing body such as a city council. They are similar in effect to a legislative statute, but they apply only to the locality, and any fine that is assessed for violations goes to the local government, not to the state. It is typical for ordinances to prohibit the same type of conduct (disorderly conduct, public drunkenness, for example) as state misdemeanors. Ordinance violations are technically noncriminal, which means that they are easier to prosecute. At times police prefer to arrest a suspect for an ordinance violation because it presents fewer legal obstacles to gaining a conviction.

Traffic offenses commonly refer to a group of offenses involving self-propelled motor vehicles, which range from infractions (punishable by fine but not incarceration) to minor misdemeanors. Traffic offenses include parking violations, violations of equipment standards, speeding, and the like. The volume is quite large, although the exact numbers are not known for reasons that relate directly to the position of the lower courts in the judicial hierarchy. Because the lower courts are not typically part of the state judiciary, they are not required to report case filings with the court administrator. Speeding is the most common traffic offense, along with driving without a license and driving while a license is suspended or revoked. Traffic tickets can be big money-makers for local governments.

Traffic cases are one area where court caseloads have actually declined in recent years, while the rest of state court caseloads continue to grow. From 1990 to 1995 traffic cases declined by 20 percent because, increasingly, less serious traffic cases are being decriminalized or transferred to an executive branch hearing for what is essentially an administrative (rather than a judicial) proceeding (Ostrom and Kauder 1996). Overall, traffic constitutes 68 percent of lower court caseloads. The most watched aspects of traffic cases are prosecutions for drunk driving.

 The National Traffic Law Center of the American Prosecutors Research Institute provides information on topics ranging from blood alcohol level to vehicular homicide: **http://www.ndaa.org/apri/NTLC/Index.htm**.

For an up-to-date list of Web links, go to **http://www.wadsworth.com/product/0534563406s**.

Civil Cases

On the civil side, the lower courts decide disputes under a set dollar amount, often referred to as small claims. The term small claims refers not to a substance but a process. **Small claims courts** handle

Misdemeanor: Lesser of the two basic types of crime; usually punishable by no more than one year in prison.

Ordinance: A law enacted by a local governmental body for the regulation of some activity within the community.

Traffic offenses: A group of offenses, including infractions and minor misdemeanors, relating to the operation of self-propelled motor vehicles.

Small claims court: A lower level court whose jurisdiction is limited to a specific dollar amount, for example, damages may not exceed $1,500.

| **FIGURE 18-1** | **Steps of Criminal Procedure in Lower Courts for Nonfelony Cases** |

	Law on the Books	*Law in Action*
Crime	*Misdemeanor* Crime punishable by fine or local jail for less than one year. *Ordinance violation* Law passed by local government similar to a misdemeanor. *Traffic offense* Relating to motor vehicle.	With the exception of drunk driving and domestic violence, the criminal law has changed little in the last decades.
Arrest	*Arrest* Taking of a person into custody for the purpose of charging him or her with a crime. *Citation* Written order issued by a law enforcement officer notifying a defendant to appear in court. *Complaint* Sworn statement by victim alleging that a specific person has committed a specified crime.	• Assaults (minor): 1,294,000. • Drunkenness and other liquor law: 1,255,000. • Disorderly conduct: 745,000. • Driving under the influence: 1,314,000. • Petty theft: 1,000,000 plus. • Weapons: 172,400. • Vandalism: 278,200.
Initial appearance	Suspects are told the charges pending; lower court judges can take a plea in nonfelony cases.	• Often held within twenty-four hours of arrest. • Two out of three defendants plead guilty during the first appearance.
Bail	Money posted for bail or for a citation may be forfeited as an alternative to appearance in court.	Many suspects plead guilty immediately, so bail release doesn't come into play.
Preliminary hearing	Preliminary hearings are not applicable in nonfelony cases.	
Charging	Charges are filed by police (based on an arrest or citation) or directly by the victim (complaint).	• Prosecutor and judge typically proceed on the basis of the police arrest. • The judge may view the crime as less serious than the police.
Grand jury	Grand juries are not applicable to nonfelony cases.	
Arraignment	Arraignments in trial courts of general jurisdiction are not applicable in nonfelony cases.	
Evidence	Lower court judges have authority to sign search warrants.	Search warrants are very rare in nonfelony cases.
Plea negotiations	Misdemeanor defendants sentenced to jail have a right to counsel (*Argersinger v. Hamlin*).	Few defendants have an attorney, so defendants must negotiate on their own.
Trial	Defendants have a constitutional right to a trial by jury only if the offense is punishable by imprisonment for more than six months (*Baldwin v. New York*).	• Trials are rare indeed. • Defendants charged with drunk driving may demand trial, particularly if they have a previous drunk driving conviction.
Sentencing	Defendants may not be jailed because they are unable to pay a fine (*Tate v. Short*).	• Fines predominate. • Jail sentences (short) sometimes imposed.
Appeal	Appeals from lower courts are heard by trial court of general jurisdiction or intermediate court of appeals.	• Very few defendants appeal. • Appeals may occur following drunk driving convictions.

A DAY IN COURT

"(Traffic) Crime and Punishment"

Guy says, well, even if he did weave totally out of his lane three times as he talked on the car phone, as alleged, what was the big deal? Nobody else was on the road. Except the cop.

"Guilty," says Judge Ian M. O'Flaherty.

Woman says, yes, she was in the right-turn-only lane while stopped at a light, because she was going to turn to get gas, but her fuel warning light blinked off, so when the stoplight changed to green, she decided to turn left, after checking for cars, of course.

"Guilty."

Guy tries to prove that the '97 sticker on his license plate belongs there and was not, say, lifted from some other car. Here's a registration, he says.

"Sir," O'Flaherty says, "I'm reading it. It says it expires 10/31/96. I can't do a lot of things, but I can read."

Same guy produces another registration card. It's for a '98 sticker. Zero for 2. "Any other paper you'd like to show me?" O'Flaherty says.

"No, sir," the guy says. "That's all I have."

Can't blame a guy for trying.

"Guilty."

How can you not laugh? "My job is not to laugh," O'Flaherty says back in his chambers. And he doesn't, at least not while sitting on the bench, listening with a blank face, exuding courtesy, giving the Traffic Court defendants every chance to explain, buying a fair number of their stories, but not most.

O'Flaherty, 50, could be one of the guys on a Smith Brothers cough-drop box, except the hair and beard are gray. He's been a General District Court judge in Fairfax County for nearly seven years, a job that requires him to spend every other month hearing the traffic cases that fill at least four courtrooms at the judicial center in Fairfax City every workday.

His domain this day is Courtroom 1B, a modern, windowless arena that takes on the aura of church during Traffic Court, because the alleged sinners are arrayed in rows of long pews, awaiting redemption or punishment. The accusers, the cops, sit in the first two rows, clutching paperwork from the days and nights in dispute. O'Flaherty enters from a side door, not to the usual cry of "All rise!" but to "Remain seated!" He thinks a judge is just a judge, not the king.

It would seem to be one of life's more satisfying, well-positioned jobs. Unlike the rest of us, who can't do a thing about the macho cases and airheads who infest our roadways, O'Flaherty controls the fate of hundreds of alleged miscreants, the ones who've opted not to prepay a ticket but to try to find

---

cases ranging from a low of $1,000 in some states to a high of $10,000 in others (the median is $2,000). The trend is clearly in an upward direction. The largest number of cases falling under these dollar amounts are debt collection, primarily involving nonpayment for goods purchased or services rendered. Another major category includes landlord-tenant disputes—mostly claims by landlords against tenants concerning past-due rent, evictions, and property damage. A smaller number of small claims cases involve alleged property damage, largely stemming from automobile accidents.

In most states streamlined procedures have been adopted to provide quick, inexpensive processing by dispensing with strict rules of evidence and the right to trial by jury (Goerdt 1992). Accordingly, small claims cases are less formal and less protracted than other civil cases.

PROBLEMS OF THE LOWER COURTS

It is the quantity of caseload that makes the trial courts of general jurisdiction so qualitatively important. Individually the cases may be minor, but collectively they are of critical importance because these are the matters that bring typical citizens to court. Jury duty aside, an appearance in lower court is for many citizens their only direct encounter with the judiciary, and these encounters in turn shape citizens' perceptions of the quality of justice meted out by all courts, whether state or federal, trial or appellate.

For decades, reformers have criticized the lower courts, highlighting a variety of problems. Only a shadow of the adversary model of criminal justice mercy, the ones charged with DUI, the ones charged with driving without a valid license. There being no jury in Traffic Court, O'Flaherty is the trier of fact and deliverer of sentence. You can nail those puppies, right, judge? "I can't feel like I'm a vigilante," O'Flaherty says. "My job is to sit there as detached as possible."

Considering. Considering O'Flaherty drives. He knows. He sees. This is a man who takes Route 1, not Interstate 95, when he and his wife drive to Richmond to see her sister. Too much weirdness on 95. He won't drive the Capital Beltway if he can help it, nor drive after 10 P.M., when the drunks are plentiful. Out there, he says, "it's getting worse and worse all the time."

Most of the worse and worse is being committed by basically good people who have screwed up with their cars. "There are too few roads and too many cars around here, and under the right circumstances, they boil over," O'Flaherty says. They get behind, then speed up to catch up. But what does it get them? An extra minute? "What are you going to do with this minute?" he says. "Save the world? Cure AIDS?"

Because most violators aren't career maniacs, O'Flaherty doesn't speechify or condemn to Hell. Many defendants are harder on themselves than he is. Most have never been to court, and their nervousness is tangible. If the defendant is contrite, made a simple mistake, or was just absent-minded, the punishment isn't much, because merely being there

is enough to make most think twice down the road, literally.

At one point, a defendant apologizes for causing an accident. "I've seen only a few people in my life deliberately run into someone," O'Flaherty replies. "The rest is just a mistake." He makes two exceptions. If you've driven really fast—more than 90 mph—he'll make you miserable. As an assistant commonwealth's attorney, he went to accident scenes in which sheets covered bodies. What worries him is that the mass of traffic is moving ever faster, so the really aggressive have to move faster still, to be able to do what they do best: bob and weave. O'Flaherty will make you spend a night in jail for every mile per hour above 90 you go.

Lying is the other exception. If he thinks you're making it up as you go, you're toast. Better to promptly plead guilty than try to shovel. He doesn't have any cases of wildly aggressive behavior this day, in part because none of the accusers is a state trooper, the guys who do most of the patrolling on the interstates, where the most madness happens. He doesn't even have a lot of cases, at least for Traffic Court. He finishes by 11:30, having dealt with 68 defendants in two hours, a fast day.

"I love this job," he says. Of course, he does have to drive to and from it.

SOURCE: Steve Twomey, "(Traffic) Crime and Punishment," *Washington Post*, June 9, 1997.

can be found in these courts. Few defendants are represented by an attorney. Trials are rare. Informality, rather than the rules of courtroom procedure, predominates. Jail sentences are imposed, sometimes with lightning speed. In short, practices that would be condemned if they occurred in higher courts are commonplace in the lower courts. Is this justice? The President's Commission on Law Enforcement and Administration of Justice (1967, 128) found the conditions of the lower courts disquieting.

The commission has been shocked by what it has seen in some lower courts. It has seen cramped and noisy courtrooms, undignified and perfunctory procedures, and badly trained personnel. It has seen dedicated people who are frustrated by huge case loads, by the lack of opportunity to examine cases carefully, and by the impossibility of devising constructive solutions to the problems of offenders. It has seen assembly-line justice.

An observer's most lasting impression of such courts is the nonjudicial atmosphere of the proceedings. The process instills little respect for the criminal justice system in defendants, witnesses, observers, or court officials. To identify the most pressing problems of the trial courts of limited jurisdiction, the American Judicature Society surveyed six states: Colorado, Illinois, Louisiana, New Hampshire, New Jersey, and Texas. They found the problems confronting the lower courts to be as varied as the courts themselves, but four are particularly important: inadequate financing, inadequate facilities, lax procedures, and unbalanced caseloads (Ashman 1975).

Inadequate Financing

Generally, lower courts are funded locally. Sparsely populated counties and small municipalities often lack funds to staff and equip their courts adequately. Even when funds are available, there is no guarantee that local governments will spend money on the lower courts. In many cities, these courts are expected to produce revenue for local governments. Indeed, some court officials now realize that monitoring financial reports on a regular basis, coupled with a systematic collection program, can net considerable additional revenue (Burrell 1997). Even though they may generate a fairly large amount of income by assessing fines and imposing court costs, the local courts have no control over how these funds are spent. For example, 150 Texas municipal courts had revenues five times greater than their operating expenses. Yet over half of these courts lacked adequate courtrooms, office space, and the like (Ashman 1975). The remainder of the funds went to pay for city services. In short, local funding has meant inadequate financing for the nation's lowest tribunals.

Inadequate Facilities

Lower court courtrooms are often crowded and noisy, with a hundred or more people forced to spend hours waiting for their minute before the judge. Some are makeshift, hastily created in the side of a store or the back of a garage. Such courtroom conditions lack dignity and leave a bad impression, suggesting that the judiciary is more interested in collecting the fine for speeding than in bothering to do justice. Such inadequate facilities are detrimental to the attitudes of the defendant, prosecutor, judge, and all others involved in the justice process.

Lax Court Procedures

Besides singling out inadequate facilities, critics of lower courts often cite lax court procedures in the day-to-day administration of these courts. Many trial courts of limited jurisdiction do not have written rules for the conduct of cases. Conventional bookkeeping methods are often ignored. How much fine money was collected and how it was spent is often impossible to determine. You can find some information in the city budget but not the court records; this frustrates any attempts to assess the effectiveness of these courts.

Unbalanced Caseloads

Many lower courts are characterized by moderate to heavy caseloads, but others appear to have little to do. Because of unbalanced caseloads, some courts have huge backlogs for which they are unequipped. But because these courts are locally controlled, there is no way to equalize the workload.

Unbalanced caseloads are the clearest indication that any generalizations about the problems of the lower courts must be coupled with the observation that the nation's lowest tribunals are tremendously varied. From state to state, between one county and its neighboring county, and even within a city, wide discrepancies exist in the quality of justice rendered. There is no easy way to determine what is wrong (or even what is right) about these courts. Because of the wide disparity, it is best to examine the rural justice of the peace courts separately from the urban municipal courts. Although they share many problems, they are also sufficiently different to warrant separate treatment.

RURAL JUSTICE

More than 60 million Americans get their justice off the main road. Although the United States is increasingly a nation where most people live in big cities and surrounding suburbs, roughly 25 percent of the population still live and work in small towns and rural areas. For them, the law is meted out in rural courthouses that are more numerous than usually imagined—79 percent of the 3,082 courts of general jurisdiction in the United States are in rural areas. These rural courthouses are often presided over by part-time judges and administered by overworked and underpaid court clerks. It is clear that there are marked differences between urban and rural criminal justice. Compared to their big-city counterparts, rural courts exhibit three special features: lower caseload, lack of resources, and greater familiarity (Bartol 1996).

Lower Caseloads

Caseloads in rural courts are lighter than those in suburban or urban courts. Moreover, in rural areas serious crimes are exceptional—less than 1 percent of all arrests in rural counties are for homicide, robbery, and rape (Thompson 1996). But this does not mean that rural citizens do not experience crime. To be sure, urban crime is roughly three times higher than rural crime, but over the last decades rural crimes have increased at the same rate as big-city crimes. And some types of crime—drunk driving and fraud, for example—are more prevalent in rural areas. In addition, the isolation of rural areas makes them attractive for certain types of crime seldom found in big cities—cattle rustling, marijuana raising, and poaching, for example. Law enforcement officials also recognize that rural areas may be attractive because their settings are fairly insulated from government and citizen monitoring. Rural settings may harbor hate groups, militia, and others who bill themselves as antigovernment. In recent years the United States has experienced a series of unrelated standoffs between law enforcement and private citizens in Ruby Ridge (1992), Waco (1993), and the Republic of Texas (1997), several of which ended with violent confrontations.

 Patrick C. Jobes, "Residential Stability and Crime in Small Rural Agricultural and Recreational Towns"

Lack of Resources

Although rural courts have lower caseloads, this does not mean that they don't face problems processing the workload. Rural courts receive less federal money and have a lower local tax base than larger counties (McDonald, Wood, and Pflug 1996). As a consequence, court facilities are often outmoded and salaries are low. Moreover, the small size of the courthouse staff in rural courts means that the staff must be generalists rather than specialists.

Lack of resources is a particular problem in criminal cases in which defendants are indigent (Chapter 7). Since few attorneys practice law in the county, the defense pool is limited. These built-in limitations have been compounded in recent years by cutbacks in federal funding—rural areas have been hardest hit by drastic reductions in publicly funded legal services to the poor, with the result being ever greater injustice for nonurban residents.

Familiarity

Justice in rural areas involves fewer agencies and also fewer personnel than urban or suburban systems. Whereas big-city courts are characterized by the interface of numerous bureaucracies, in rural areas contacts are invariably one-on-one (Weisheit, Wells, and Falcone 1995). The active bar consists of a dozen or fewer members, including the prosecutor, the judge, and the lawyer who represents the local government. Often, there are five or fewer sheriff's deputies and a single probation officer, each of whom is known to the judge. The clerk's office typically consists of two or three long-term employees. In short, "fewer than 30 people routinely work together, a group about the size of a small family reunion" (Fahnestock 1991, 14).

Not only is the number of actors in rural courts small, but their interactions are frequent and long-term. By and large, justice is administered by those who grew up in the community, and they are bound together by long-standing social and family networks. As a result, rural courts place greater emphasis on informal mechanisms of social control, whereas urban courts are more legalistic and formal (Weisheit, Wells, and Falcone 1995).

 To learn more about the unique problems of rural justice, point your browser to the Small Town and Rural Crime Page maintained by Dr. Ralph Weisheit of Illinois State University: **http://www.ilstu.edu/depts/cjs/rural.htm**.

For an up-to-date list of Web links, go to **http://www.wadsworth.com/product/0534563406s**.

Assessing Rural Justice

The most commonly mentioned aspect of rural justice is comity. Generally it speaks of a friendly social atmosphere and a group harmony. But in this context, it also can mean "You scratch my back, and I'll scratch yours." It's not always a conscious thing. The judge and the prosecutor are friends. Sometimes they're related. "There's a lack of an independent judiciary and a weak adversary process in many parts of rural America," says social activist Kathryn Fahnestock (Sitomer 1985). "Community knowledge is substituted for the Constitution," she says. A study in a North Carolina county reported that the court tended to rubber-stamp police and prosecutorial decisions, citizens were arrested capriciously, unduly high bail was set, and defendants were often pressured into pleading guilty.

To Albert Barney, longtime chief justice of Vermont's supreme court, and to other critics, local mores and loyalty tend to work against an effective justice system in small towns. In Barney's words,

"It's all in the name of protecting the community" (Sitomer 1985). Consequently, the process is sometimes more convenient than constitutional, more community-oriented than concerned with individual rights. In many places, lack of funds, lack of expertise, inadequate knowledge about proper procedures, and even unfamiliarity with constitutional mandates have often resulted in an uneven, unequal, unresponsive judicial process. Defendants who are not part of the community (either socially or geographically) may be at a disadvantage. According to the Rural Justice Center, "What they want to do is preserve the peace and traditional community values" at the expense of minorities, the poor, and those considered "outsiders" (Sitomer 1985).

Citizens of small towns and rural areas beg to differ with their often urban-based critics. They are fearful of trying to impose urban solutions on rural problems. In the context of rural America, discussions of court reform typically center on the justice of the peace.

JUSTICE OF THE PEACE COURTS

In rural areas, the lower courts are collectively called **justice of the peace** courts. The officeholder is usually referred to simply as a **JP.** This system of local justice traces its origins to fourteenth-century England, when towns were small and isolated. The JP system developed as a way to dispense simple and speedy justice for minor civil and criminal cases. The emphasis was decidedly on the ability of local landowners, who served as part-time JPs, to decide disputes on the basis of their knowledge of the local community.

The small-town flavor of the JP system persists today. By and large, present-day JPs are part-time nonlawyers who conduct court at their regular place of business—the back of the undertaker's parlor, the front counter of the general store, or next to the grease rack in the garage. The nation has more than 15,000 JPs, most of whom are locally elected officials serving short terms. Some serve *ex officio*—many

small-town mayors also serve as judges in city court. Although a few earn a comfortable income from the job, the salaries are low for the most part. Moreover, support personnel are often limited. In the smaller courts, the JP's spouse may serve as clerk, but many courts have no clerks at all.

Critics argue that the JP system has outlived its purpose. It may have met the needs of the small, isolated towns of a century ago, but it is out of step with the modern era. Some lower courts administer fair and evenhanded justice, but all too many do not. Critics doubt whether the current diversified and fragmented JP system can ever deliver fair, impartial, and evenhanded justice. Efforts at improving the quality of justice dispensed by the rural lower courts focus on abolition of the JP courts and upgrading the quality of the personnel. Elimination of the **fee system** has also been recommended.

 A few justices of the peace maintain Web sites, including these:

Denton (Texas): **http://www.co.denton.tx.us/dept/ JP6/jp6.htm**

Spring (Texas): **http://nashforjp.com/**

Swanzey (New Hampshire): **http://top.monad.net/ ~shamrockrlestate/**

For an up-to-date list of Web links, go to **http:// www.wadsworth.com/product/0534563406s**.

Abolition of the JP System

The ultimate goal of judicial reformers is to abolish the JP system altogether. A major defect is that JP courts are not part of the state judiciary; they are controlled only by the local governmental bodies that create them and fund them. Only recently have judicial conduct commissions (Chapter 8) been granted the authority to discipline or remove local judges who abuse their office.

Nor are the activities of the lower courts subject to appellate scrutiny. Rarely are trial courts of limited jurisdiction courts of record; no stenographic record is kept of the witnesses' testimony or the judges' rulings. When a defendant appeals, the appeal is heard by a trial court of general jurisdiction. This court must conduct an entirely new trial, taking the testimony of the same witnesses and

---

Justice of the peace (JP):   A low-level judge, sometimes without legal training, typically found in rural areas of some states, empowered to try petty civil and criminal cases and to conduct the preliminary stages of felony cases.

Fee system: A system that pays the judicial officer directly from fees assessed against the guilty.

hearing the same attorneys' arguments as the lower court did. This is called a *trial de novo.* The trial de novo system needlessly increases the caseload of the state trial courts. But by far the major weakness of the system is that it insulates the lower court from scrutiny. No opportunity exists for higher courts to correct errors in court procedure, the denial of defendants' constitutional rights, or erroneous interpretations of criminal law. The absence of appellate court review also hides patterns and practices that, although not illegal, are nonetheless problems—for example, disparaging remarks by the judge (Bing and Rosenfeld 1974).

Some reformers would unify state courts into a three-tier system, consisting of a single trial court, an intermediate appellate court, and a supreme court (Chapter 4). This reform would abolish the justice of the peace, require all judges to be lawyers, and eliminate the trial de novo system.

Reformers have had only limited success in their efforts to abolish the JP system. One major obstacle is the powerful influence of nonlawyer judges, who do not want their jobs abolished. Another is some people's belief that JPs are easily accessible, whereas more formal courts are miles away. For example, JPs are readily available to sign arrest warrants for the police or to try a motorist accused of driving too fast. Supporters of the current system contend that a knowledge of the local community better prepares JPs to solve minor disputes than does a law degree, mainly because few minor disputes involve any complex legal issues. Thus, JP courts are often viewed as people's courts, forums where people without much money can go to resolve their problems without the necessity of having a lawyer.

 The Massachusetts Justice of the Peace Association offers educational programs to enable justices of the peace to fulfill the duties and responsibilities of their office in a professional and efficient manner: **http://www.mjpa.org/**.

For an up-to-date list of Web links, go to **http://www.wadsworth.com/product/0534563406s**.

Upgrading the Quality of the Personnel

The low pay and equally low status of the JP have not attracted highly qualified personnel. One survey found that only 5 percent of the JPs in Virginia were college graduates. Another showed that between a third and a half of California's lower court judges were not even high school graduates (Ashman and Chapin 1976). Perhaps most shocking of all, the assistant attorney general of Mississippi estimated that "33 percent of the justices of the peace are limited in educational background to the extent that they are not capable of learning the necessary elements of law" (*North v. Russell,* 1976).

High on the judicial reformers' list of priorities is upgrading the quality of lower court judges. Some states have instituted training programs for lay judges, but only a few of the judges have yet received any training in basic legal concepts or the duties and responsibilities of the office. But to many reformers the ultimate goal remains the elimination of nonlawyer judges (see Case Close-Up: *North v. Russell* and Nonlawyer Judges).

MUNICIPAL COURTS

The urban counterparts of the justice of the peace courts are **municipal courts**. Decades ago, the increasing volume of cases in the big cities overwhelmed the ability of the rurally conceived JP system to dispense justice The forerunner of the municipal court was the police magistrate, who had strong ties to local police departments. Municipal courts were also shaped by political machines, which viewed the lower courts as opportunities for patronage. Party bosses controlled the selection of judges. Similarly, the positions of bailiff and clerk were reserved for the party faithful. It is not surprising that municipal courts were often tainted by corruption. Charges would be dropped, or files would mysteriously disappear, in return for political favors or cash. No wonder the judicial reformers of the

 The Delaware (Ohio) Municipal Court offers daily live-streamed court proceedings on the Internet at **http://www.municipalcourt.org/**.

For an up-to-date list of Web links, go to **http://www.wadsworth.com/product/0534563406s**.

Municipal court: A trial court of limited jurisdiction created by a local unit of government.

CASE CLOSE-UP

North v. Russell and Nonlawyer Judges

Judge C. B. Russell made a number of legal errors in the Lynch City Police Court the night he sentenced Lonnie North to jail for drunk driving. Judge Russell refused the defendant's request for a jury trial, did not inform him of his right to a court-appointed lawyer, and failed to advise him of his right to an appeal. Perhaps most glaring of all, Judge Russell listened only to the arresting officer's story and did not allow the defendant to tell his version of events.

The facts of *North v. Russell* (1976) highlight the long-standing issue confronting the American judiciary: Should lower court judges be attorneys? Although judges in the major trial and appellate courts are required to be lawyers, many states impose no such requirement for lower court judges. Nonlawyer judges are more numerous than is usually realized (Bronstein 1981). A disproportionate number of these part-time, nonlawyer judges are located in New York and Texas (Alfini and Passuth 1981).

The U.S. Supreme Court considered the question of nonlawyer judges in *North v. Russell*. Chief Justice Warren Burger's majority opinion argued that nonlawyer judges do not violate the due process clause of the Fourteenth Amendment, nor do they deny equal protection. He described the JP system as courts of convenience for citizens in small towns and spoke favorably of the fact that "the inferior courts are simple and speedy." Burger argued that any defects in the proceedings (which were numerous in this case) could be corrected by the availability of defense attorneys, the right to a jury trial, and a trial de novo. Significantly, though, these were the specific legal matters that Judge Russell failed to inform defendant North about.

In a dissenting opinion, Justice Potter Stewart stated the case for requiring judges to be lawyers. He found it constitutionally intolerable that nonlawyer judges can sentence defendants to jail. He further noted that a defendant's right to a lawyer is eroded if the judge is not capable of understanding a lawyer's argument on the law. Indeed, a later study found that lay judges in New York tended to be slightly more favorable toward police officers and prosecutors than were legally trained officials (Ryan and Guterman 1977).

States are beginning to eliminate nonlawyer judges. The California Supreme Court has ruled that the nonlawyer magistrate violates the state's constitution. Moreover, when states adopt court reorganization, they invariably abolish the nonlawyer JP, although incumbents typically are retained.

Does the elimination of nonlawyer judges alter the decisions reached? After Iowa amended its constitution to require legally trained lower court judges, small claims proceedings became more formal, which frightened away the individual civil plaintiffs. Moreover, decisions in small claims increasingly benefitted the merchants (Green, Russell, and Schmidhauser 1975). A handful of other studies, however, have found few, if any, differences between the behavior of lay and lawyer judges (Provine 1981). A survey in New York concluded that nonlawyer judges are as competent as lawyer judges in carrying out judicial duties in courts of limited jurisdiction (Provine 1986).

 James Dignan, Arnold Wynne, "A Microcosm of the Local Community?"

1920s and 1930s sought to clean up the courts by removing them from politics (Chapter 4).

The Assembly Line

"The Sausage Factories" was the title of a *Time* article on municipal courts (1974). "Hurricanes of Humanity" was the term used by the American Judicature Society in the first national survey of the lower courts. Both phrases draw our attention to the overriding reality of municipal courts in the nation's big cities: the press of cases (Ashman 1975). The

major concern is moving cases; any "obstacles" to speedy disposition—constitutional rights, lawyers, trials—are neutralized. In a process some have labeled an assembly line, shortcuts are routinely taken to keep the docket moving. Thus, the municipal courts more closely resemble a bureaucracy geared to mass processing of cases than an adjudicative body providing consideration for each case.

The emphasis on moving cases begins when the defendant is arraigned. Instead of addressing defendants individually—a time-consuming process—municipal court judges often open court by advising

FIGURE 18-2	Key Developments Concerning the Lower Courts	
Tumey v. Ohio	1927	Paying a justice of the peace a fee only if the defendant is found guilty denies a defendant the right to trial before an impartial judge.
Baldwin v. New York	1970	Defendants have a constitutional right to a trial by jury only if the offense is punishable by imprisonment for more than six months.
Tate v. Short	1971	Defendants may not be jailed because they are unable to pay a fine.
Argersinger v. Hamlin	1972	Misdemeanor defendants sentenced to jail have a right to counsel.
North v. Russell	1976	Nonlawyer judges do not violate the rights to due process or equal protection of the U.S. Constitution.

defendants of their constitutional rights as a group. Few efforts are made to determine whether defendants understand what is said. Notification of rights is treated by the court as a clerical detail to be dispensed with before the taking of guilty pleas can begin (Mileski 1971).

Defense attorneys constitute another potential obstacle to the speedy disposition of cases. Although defendants have a theoretical right to be represented by an attorney, in practice the presence of an attorney in the lower courts is rare. In one Eastern city, 12 percent of the misdemeanor defendants were represented by a lawyer (Mileski 1971). This is partially because of the minor nature of most municipal court cases; some defendants believe the charge is too minor to justify the expense of hiring a lawyer. The more serious the alleged offense, however, the more likely a defendant will have an attorney (Bing and Rosenfeld 1974). The general absence of defense attorneys reinforces the informality of the lower courts and the lack of attention to legal rules and procedures.

What of those too poor to hire a lawyer? In *Argersinger v. Hamlin* (1972), the Supreme Court ruled that "absent a knowing and intelligent waiver, no person may be imprisoned for any offense, whether classified as petty, misdemeanor, or felony unless he was represented by counsel." Thus, an indigent defendant may be fined without having a lawyer, but a judge considering imposing a jail term must give the impoverished defendant the opportunity to have a court-appointed counsel at state expense. Compliance, however, has generally been token in nature, reform has been chaotic and uneven

at best, and the legal right to counsel remains "an empty right for many defendants" (Krantz et al. 1976). (See Figure 18-2 for key developments in the law concerning the lower courts.)

In municipal courts, the defendant's initial appearance is usually the final one. Most people charged with a traffic violation or a minor misdemeanor plead guilty immediately. The quick plea represents the fatalistic view of most defendants: "I did it—let's get it over with." Realistically, a defendant charged with such crimes as public drunkenness and disorderly conduct probably cannot raise a valid legal defense. What has struck all observers of the lower courts is the speed with which the pleas are processed:

> *The Court generally disposes of between 50 and 100 cases per day, but on any Monday there are 200 to 250 and on Monday mornings after holiday weekends the Court may handle as many as 350 cases. I would estimate that, on the average, cases take between 45 seconds and one minute to dispose of. (Wiseman 1976, 235)*

Mileski (1971) calculated the median time to accept a defendant's plea and impose sentence at less than a minute.

Few trials are held in the lower courts. A defendant has a right to a jury trial only if the offense can be punished by imprisonment for more than six months (*Baldwin v. New York* 1970). The absence of attorneys and the minor nature of the offenses combine to make requests for jury trials rare. If there is a trial, it is a bench trial. The informality of the lower court applies to trials, as to almost everything else:

Rules of evidence are not necessarily followed, no trial record is kept, and trials last only a few minutes.

The Courtroom Work Group

It is no accident that most defendants waive their rights to counsel and trial before quickly entering a plea of guilty. The courtroom work group tries to encourage such behavior by controlling the flow of defendants. Some courts manipulate bail to pressure defendants into an immediate disposition. During arraignment, each defendant is informed of the right to a full hearing with a court-appointed attorney. But the hearing cannot be held for two or three weeks, which the defendant will have to spend in jail (Wice 1974). Not surprisingly, the majority of defendants choose to waive their right to counsel in favor of a speedy disposition. Quick pleas reflect defendants' unwillingness to take a chance; they surrender the possibility of an acquittal because they fear a harsher penalty if they try but are unsuccessful (Mileski 1971).

Above all, the routines of the lower courts may be threatened by uncooperative defendants. Those accused who unreasonably take up too much of the court's time can expect sanctions. Judges and prosecutors dislike defendants who "talk too much." Mileski provides an example of a young middle-class white man who made a detailed inquiry into his rights and then gave a relatively lengthy account (roughly two minutes) of his alleged offense of vagrancy. Although the defendant was polite, the judge interrupted him with, "That will be all, Mr. Jones," and ordered him to jail. Other defendants who "talked too much" received sentences that were longer than normal.

Sentencing

In a sense, municipal courts are not trial courts, because few defendants contest their guilt. In actuality, they are a sentencing institution. The courtroom encounter is geared to making rapid decisions about which sentence to impose. The punishments imposed by lower court judges include many of those found in the major trial courts—fines, probation, and jail. In the misdemeanor courts, however, judges can choose alternative sanctions, including community service, victim restitution, placement in substance abuse treatment programs, mandatory counseling, and required attendance in education programs (driver clinics, for example) (Meyer and Jesilow 1997). Despite the diversity of potential sanctions, fines play a predominant role. A study of misdemeanor sentencing in six cities found that few defendants were sentenced to jail. Instead, approximately two-thirds of all defendants paid a fine of some amount (Ragona and Ryan 1983).

The sentencing process in the lower courts involves elements of both routinization and individualization. Lower court judges define their role as "doing justice"; rather than merely being bound by rules of law, judges employ their discretion to achieve what they believe to be a fair and just result (Meyer and Jesilow 1997). In attempting to achieve justice, lower court judges employ readily identifiable characteristics to sort defendants into categories. In the lower courts, sentencing involves a process of quickly determining group averages. The result is a high degree of uniformity; by and large, a defendant gets the same sentence as all others in the same category. To the casual observer, the process appears to be an assembly line, but sentences can also be fitted to the specific defendant. During plea negotiations, there is some individual attention to cases. Despite sentencing consistencies, exceptions are made (Ragona and Ryan 1983). The most important factors in both the routinization and the individualization of sentencing in the lower courts are the nature of the event and the defendant's criminal record.

Offenses are categorized in two ways: the official charge and what actually occurred (the substance). Although the charge is never more serious than the substance, the substance is sometimes more serious than the charge. For example, a defendant may be charged with breach of the peace when he actually

A growing number of municipal courts maintain Web sites, providing information on matters ranging from court calendars to how to pay fines:

Austin (Texas): **http://www.ci.austin.tx.us/court/**

Bernalillo County (New Mexico) Metropolitan Court: **http://www.metrocourt.state.nm.us/**

Hamilton County (Cincinnati): **http://www. hamilton-co.org/MunicipalCourt/**

Milwaukee: **http://www.ci.mil.wi.us/citygov/ court/index.html**

Seattle: **http://www.ci.seattle.wa.us/courts/ house.htm**

Sylvania (Ohio): **http://www.sylvaniacourt.com/**

For an up-to-date list of Web links, go to **http:// www.wadsworth.com/product/0534563406s**.

engaged in a more serious violation—threatening his wife with a knife. When the substance is more serious than the charge, judges usually sentence on the basis of the nature of the event. Even when the charges have been reduced (after plea bargaining, for example), the defendant receives the penalty typical for the more serious charge.

The opposite may also be true. What the police officer perceives as trouble serious enough to warrant an arrest may not be viewed equally seriously by the prosecutor or the judge. On the whole, the court has a higher tolerance for trouble than do the police (Feeley 1979). An arrestee who was loud and threatening at the police station appears quiet and nonthreatening the next day in court. As a result, court officials may treat this case as minor. Indeed, some arrests are regarded as so trivial that prosecutors and judges resent the police for bringing such cases to court.

How defendants are pigeonholed according to their offense emerges in a four-city study (Ragona and Ryan 1983). Drunk driving and traffic cases nearly always resulted in a fine, sometimes combined with a short jail term or probation. By contrast, theft and other miscellaneous criminal offenses resulted much less often in a fine; more commonly, these defendants were sentenced to jail or placed on probation. The basis for a decision not to fine in minor criminal cases may be either that such crimes are too serious to be treated merely with a fine—and that the offenders are in need of ongoing counseling or supervision—or the practical realization that many defendants cannot afford to pay a fine, or some combination of the two.

A key factor in sentencing is the defendant's prior criminal record. First offenders rarely receive a jail term. Indeed, for petty offenses, first offenders may be released without any penalty whatsoever. Repeaters are given more severe sanctions. For example, the jailing of defendants for public intoxication increases strikingly as prior arrests become more numerous and more recent. The importance of a prior criminal record in sentencing partially explains an otherwise unaccountable pattern: Serious misdemeanants are fined, while minor misdemeanants are jailed. The explanation is that few of the serious misdemeanor defendants had prior records, whereas more of the minor misdemeanor defendants did (Mileski 1971).

A study of drunk driving dispositions in Sacramento, California, highlights the importance of prior record and the nature of the event (Kings-north, Barnes, and Coonley 1990). For defendants with no prior convictions, the likelihood of a charge reduction to reckless driving increased three to four times. Similarly, the probability of receiving a jail sentence increased dramatically for those with a prior record. The nature of the event (measured by the level of blood alcohol) also played a role. A low level of blood alcohol was of primary importance in the decision to reduce charges from drunk driving to reckless driving. Similarly, defendants with a high level of alcohol in their systems (.25 and over) were much more likely not only to receive jail but also a lengthy jail term. These two factors, of course, operate together. Defendants with no priors and low levels of blood alcohol fared much better than those with prior convictions and high levels of alcohol in their system. Studies like this one, however, rarely enter the public discourse. (See Controversy: Should Drunk Driving Prosecutions Be Increased?)

Is the Process the Punishment?

Researchers have begun to question the image of the lower courts as assembly-line operations. Susan Silbey (1981) argues that the standard picture of lower courts as wholesale, mechanical processors of a high volume of cases is only partially correct. The operations of the misdemeanor courts are not as chaotic, disordered, or unreasonable as they may first appear. A second consideration is that the lower courts do try to provide justice, but they do so by responding to problems rather than crimes, concentrating their efforts on producing substantive justice rather than focusing on purely formal (due process) justice. Separate studies in New Haven, Connecticut (Feeley 1979), and Columbus, Ohio (Ryan 1980–1981), have assessed the disparate functions served by the lower courts.

To Malcolm Feeley, *the process is the punishment*. This finding is based on several years studying the lower court in New Haven firsthand. The main punishment of defendants occurs during the processing of cases, not after a finding of guilt. Feeley contends that the pretrial process imposes a series of punishments ("price tags") on the accused. These price tags often include staying in jail (briefly), paying a bail agent, hiring a private attorney, and losing time and perhaps wages due to repeated court appearances. These costs far outweigh any punishment imposed after the defendant pleads guilty. These price tags also affect the roughly 40 percent of the defendants eventually found not guilty. In short,

Should Drunk Driving Prosecutions Be Increased?

- "Drunk Driver Kills Mother of Two"
- "Motorist Arrested for Fifth Drunk Driving Offense"

Headlines like these have become all too familiar to readers of the local papers. In a recent year 15,786 persons were killed in alcohol-related automobile accidents (40 percent of all traffic fatalities). Moreover, the police make more arrests—over 1.5 million annually—for drunk driving than any other crime. Public concern over drunk driving has focused attention on the otherwise virtually invisible activities of the nation's lowest (and often forgotten) courts.

Depending on the state, drunk driving is termed driving under the influence (DUI) or driving while intoxicated (DWI). Drinking and driving has been a problem since the invention of the automobile but did not gain recognition as a prominent social concern until the early 1980s (Applegate et al. 1996). The group most responsible for focusing public attention on drunk driving is Mothers Against Drunk Driving (MADD). MADD is not neo-Prohibitionist, recognizing that trying to eliminate alcohol would hamper the organization's ability to recruit members. Rather, MADD is victim-oriented, with many leaders having themselves experienced a family death due to drunk driving. They are closely related to the victims' rights movement (Chapter 9).

Today, MADD has more than 600 chapters and community action teams nationwide. Part of their efforts include victim services—a hotline provides emotional support and guidance to bereaved families and injured victims of drunk driving. But publicly they are recognized as the leading proponents of increasing the criminal penalties for drunk driving (Jacobs 1989; Reinarman 1988).

Getting Tough with Drunk Drivers

In the last two decades, legislatures—under considerable pressure from MADD and other groups like it—have passed a variety of "get tough with drunk drivers" laws including

- Increasing the drinking age to twenty-one
- Lowering from .15 to .10 the blood alcohol content (BAC) level at which a person is presumed legally intoxicated
- Increasing jail penalties for DWI, particularly for repeat offenders

These efforts culminated in 2000 with Congress passing a law mandating states to lower the BAC to .08 by 2007 or face loss of federal highway funds.

But somehow the get-tough laws recently passed never seem to be harsh enough, so in subsequent years legislatures are called upon to crack down even harder on drunk drivers. New legislative agendas are crucial for organizations like MADD because they need to constantly motivate their constituents lest the organization lose momentum and also lose members (Jacobs 1989). Among those new sanctions currently mentioned are

- Lowering the BAC to .08 (MADD's preferred level)
- Confiscation of the automobile for repeat offenders
- Mandatory minimum prison sentence for persons convicted of vehicular homicide while intoxicated

Societal Ambivalence toward Drinking and Driving

Contemporary efforts to get tough with drunk drivers resemble morality plays of old. To sociologist Joseph Gusfield, groups like MADD engage in symbolic politics, portraying drunk drivers as villains. The difficulty with this approach is that DWI arrestees reflect a range of social backgrounds, including ordinary citizens and at times even prominent members of the community. Moreover, the range of behavior varies greatly from a person barely at .08 and having caused no accident to those measuring near .30 (comatose for most people) who have killed several people.

The absence of criminal stereotypes is compounded by the pervasive role of alcoholic beverages in American social and economic life. As a result, there is considerable societal ambivalence toward drinking and driving (Homel 1988): Society is quick to condemn drunk drivers involved in serious accidents, but those who drive after a few drinks often evoke the attitude of "There but for the grace of God go I" (Gusfield 1981).

Adjudicating Drunk Driving Cases

The contradictions in societal attitudes toward drinking and driving (which is different from drunk driving) explain why the enforcement of drunk driving laws is riddled with loopholes. These contradictions help us understand why law in action (actual enforcement) differs greatly from law on the books. Actual enforcement of drunk driving laws blunts the cutting edge of the harsh penalties. Law on the books treats driving and drinking as a serious problem, but law in action (the activities of police, prosecutors, judges, juries, and defense attorneys) sees drunk driving not as a criminal offense but a traffic violation. The end product is not a series of absolutes propounded by MADD but a negotiated reality (Homel 1988). With the imposition of tougher laws:

- Police do not necessarily make more arrests. Faced with serious crime problems, big-city police forces assign higher priority to violent offenders than to drunk drivers (Mastrofski and Ritti 1996).
- Prosecutors are pressured to plea bargain. Given that local jails are already overcrowded and most defendants are not as villainous as public images suggest, pleas to lesser charges such as reckless driving are often arranged.
- Juries are reluctant to convict. As discussed in Chapter 14, if jurors think the penalty is too harsh for the crime, they are less likely to convict.
- As more people go to jail, for longer, following DUI convictions, the prisons become overcrowded, which necessitates shortening actual sentences (Vermont Center for Justice Research 1995).

Overall, DUI filings in state courts have dropped 14 percent since 1985 (Ostrom and Kauder 1996).

Declining Alcohol-Related Traffic Fatalities

There is little doubt that highway deaths linked to drinking have decreased. Data from the National Highway and Traffic Safety Administration show a drop of about a third in recent years. Citizen groups are quick to point to tougher laws on drunk drivers as the reason, but reality is more complex. Other changes were occurring during this period, changes which some say are responsible for the drop in the number of traffic fatalities. Some of these changes are laws mandating use of safety belts, the fifty-five miles per hour speed limit (now largely repealed), and construction of safer automobiles, with the addition of devices such as air bags. There have also been important shifts in public attitudes—Americans increasingly see drinking and driving as unacceptable (indeed, consumption of alcoholic beverages is down). Finally, advances in medicine mean that trauma victims have a better chance of surviving an accident than in earlier decades.

DWI laws are not self-enforcing. Those who lose their license may continue to drive, and those previously convicted may continue to drive drunk. Indeed, one survey found that more than half the persons in local jails charged with DWI had prior sentences for DWI offenses (Cohen 1992).

Overall, studies of drunk driving laws tend to be skeptical of a deterrent effect of get-tough legislation. Typically, new, tougher laws are ushered in with announcements of a major crackdown followed by increased arrests for DWI. But over time, levels of drinking and driving return to previous levels as the perceived certainty of punishment declines with experience (Homel 1988; Ross 1992). Finally, increasing the penalty for DWI makes it more likely that the defendant will fight the charge, resulting in longer delays and fewer convictions; in the long run DWI laws become even harder to enforce.

What do you think? Should there be tougher punishments for drunk driving or are current punishment levels about right? Should more efforts be made to arrest and prosecute drunk drivers or is the current level of effort about right? Overall, how do punishment and enforcement levels of drunk driving compare to other social problems like domestic violence and drug abuse?

 To continue the debate, go to

Mothers Against Drunk Driving: **http://www. madd.org**

The American Beverage Institute: **http://www. abionline.org**

The National Commission Against Drunk Driving: **http://www.ncadd.com**

The National College for DUI Defense, Inc.: **http:// www.ncdd.com**

For an up-to-date list of Web links, go to **http:// www.wadsworth.com/product/0534563406s**.

 Jeanne Mejeur, "Drunk Drivers Beware"

Ralph W. Hingson, Timothy Heeren, Michael R. Winter, "Preventing Impaired Driving"

"All You Ever Wanted to Know About Drunk Drivers"

"Report: More Drunk Drivers Are in Correctional System"

the pretrial process itself is the primary punishment, according to Feeley.

To John Paul Ryan, *the outcome is the punishment.* This contrasting finding is based on statistical analysis of actual court sentences in Columbus, Ohio. Unlike those in New Haven, lower court judges in Columbus routinely impose fines on convicted defendants. Often these fines are substantial. Further, 35 percent of the guilty in Columbus are sentenced to jail—six times as many as in New Haven. Finally, defendants in traffic cases often have their driver's licenses suspended and/or are ordered to attend drunk driver schools. In short, Columbus defendants are more likely to be fined, to pay heavier fines, to go to jail, and to be required to participate in some sort of treatment program than their counterparts in New Haven.

These sharply contrasting conclusions about New Haven and Columbus accentuate the point made earlier in the chapter: Misdemeanor courts are very diverse in their operations and procedures. In short, any assessment of the activities of the lower courts requires an awareness of their diversity.

 The Austin (Texas) Municipal Court provides its fine schedule online: **http://www.ci.austin.tx.us/court/ fine_sch.htm**.

For an up-to-date list of Web links, go to **http:// www.wadsworth.com/product/0534563406s**.

COURT COMMUNITY COLLABORATION

Lower courts have dwindled substantially in number and importance since 1960. Court reform efforts have consolidated the diverse minor courts into more centralized units. In the process most of the justice of the peace and magistrate courts were eliminated. These reforms had unintended consequences. Court activities were consolidated and streamlined for good reasons, but in the process, some of the qualities of locally dispensed justice were lost. Today there is a concerned effort to reestablish court community cooperation (Efkeman and Rottman 1996–97).

The central target of these community justice efforts is minor disputes between parties in ongoing relationships (domestic partners, neighbors, con-

sumers-merchants, landlords-tenants, employees-employers). Examples include unruly children who annoy neighbors, dogs who defecate on the wrong lawns, owners who neglect their property, and acquaintances who dispute small debts. It is not clear what role the criminal justice system can play in resolving such private disputes. Yet private disagreements between friends, neighbors, or significant others are the steady diet of the police and the lower courts. A trial would only obscure the underlying issues because the problem is either irrelevant or immaterial to the legal action. In such interpersonal disputes, the person who files a complaint may be as "guilty" as the defendant. Many of these private disputes are essentially civil matters, yet criminal justice agencies must deal with them to head off the commission of a more serious crime—murder or battery, for example. Thus in addressing problems like those listed above, mediation programs seek solutions not in terms of a formal finding by a judge but through compromise and bargaining. The goal is to seek long-term solutions in hopes the disputants will not return.

Efforts at court community collaboration are but one example of a broader movement termed **alternative dispute resolution (ADR)**, which seeks to settle disputes by less adversarial means than traditional legal processes. Many ADR programs function as alternatives to going to court. Others involve efforts to settle court cases after they have been filed but before they are tried by a judge. ADR efforts most often focus on civil matters but nonserious criminal matters may also be included.

Alternatives to the formal judicial processes, of course, are hardly new. Juvenile courts, small claims courts, and family courts are a few examples of long-standing activities that were established because it was felt they would be more effective than traditional court operations. Today, drug courts and community courts have joined the list (Chapter 4). In recent years, however, there has been a new wave of concern about court congestion and cost, and a new set of alternatives has appeared in response.

Beyond a core concern over essentially minor private disputes, however, community justice programs are diverse in goals and orientations. Some

---

Alternative dispute resolution (ADR): Less adversarial means of settling disputes that may or may not involve a court.

programs, for example, are motivated by concerns that the formal procedures of the lower courts discourage individuals from taking their disputes to these institutions. Thus community dispute settlement centers stress increasing the accessibility of justice to individuals. By contrast, criminal justice officials are often concerned with making the justice system more efficient by reducing caseloads. In essence, the first envisions more cases, while the second wants fewer.

Community justice approaches are diverse and ongoing. We will examine two broad types: community dispute settlement centers (which operate outside of the judicial system) and community courts (which operate within the judicial system).

Hieros Gamos provides a *Guide to Alternate Dispute Resolution:* **http://hg.org/adr.html**.

For an up-to-date list of Web links, go to **http://www.wadsworth.com/product/0534563406s**.

Eileen Barkas Hoffman, "The Impact of the ADR Act of 1998"

Stephanie Schroeder, "Alternative Dispute Resolution Resources"

Julie Brienza, "ADR: Doing Two Things at Once Can Be Problematic"

Community Dispute Settlement Centers

Community dispute settlement centers provide mediation programs for a range of minor civil and criminal matters in nonjudicial settings. These programs go by a variety of names, including citizen dispute resolution programs and community mediation. They were in the vanguard of the ADR movement, serving a catalytic role in rethinking the court-dominated model of dispute resolution.

Community-oriented mediation programs rest on the philosophy that the winner-takes-all approach of adjudication is poorly suited to resolving many minor disputes typically brought to court. Although minor compared to felonies and major civil litigation, these matters are nonetheless major events in the daily lives of the disputants.

Community mediation programs are typically sponsored by private organizations and receive the bulk of their cases from walk-ins or referrals from other community-based organizations. These programs are not particularly concerned with reducing the caseload of courts but instead place a heavy emphasis on providing a more sensible means of settling disputes. They are motivated by the notion that they can offer a dispute resolution process that is superior to the one provided in courts with their stress on legal rights. They place less emphasis on any efficiency advantages to the court (McGillis 1997).

Perhaps the best-known example of the community mediation approach is the San Francisco Community Boards Program, which is extensively probed in a book edited by Sally Engle Merry and Neal Milner (1993). The book's title, *The Possibility of Popular Justice,* highlights the philosophy of the founding director, Raymond Shonholtz, who defined the underlying problem as alienation and based the solution on empowerment. The principal task, therefore, was transforming society by bringing people together. The long-term goal was "not so much the settlement of disagreements, but the long-term rebuilding of community capacities" (Adler, Lovass, and Milner 1988, 321). Popular justice was to be found among the people, not in the corridors of governmental buildings. In essence, the San Francisco program was created in opposition to the formal legal system, and therefore often faced problems of attracting enough cases to keep itself in operation.

A more recent effort is the Dispute Settlement Center of Durham, North Carolina. Originally the program accepted only minor criminal cases referred by the local court but later greatly expanded to include numerous other services such as family and divorce mediation, school conflict resolution programs, and corporate workplace training. It has also recently added court-referred mediation cases involving juveniles (McGillis 1998). Unlike the San Francisco program, the one in Durham tries to work actively with government officials.

You can visit some community dispute settlement centers on the Web:

Cambridge Community Dispute Settlement Center: **http://www.cambridgedispute.org/**

Mountain Dispute Settlement Center (North Carolina): **http://www.dnet.net/mtndsc/**

For an up-to-date list of Web links, go to **http://www.wadsworth.com/product/0534563406s**.

Community Courts

Courts across the nation are searching for ways to reach out in order to be more responsive to the needs of specific communities within their geographical jurisdiction. The phrase "justice community" refers to the range of organizations and people within any specific locale who have a stake in the justice system. It includes judges, court personnel, district attorneys, public defenders, private attorneys, probation departments, law enforcement personnel, community organizers, business groups, and so on (Borys, Banks, and Parker 1999).

Often these outreach efforts lead to an emphasis on mediation of minor disputes. There are important organizational differences, though, between court-based mediation and community mediation programs. For one, they are government-sponsored (either court or prosecutor); as a result these programs receive the bulk of their cases as referrals from criminal justice agencies (something community programs object to). A second difference centers on goals: The dominant goal is to improve the justice system by removing minor cases from the court. In their view, cases such as simple assault, petty theft, and criminal trespass are prime candidates for mediation and not formal processing in the lower courts.

Initially, what today are called community courts were termed criminal justice-based mediation programs, also known as multidoor courthouses or neighborhood justice centers (Adler, Lovass, and Milner 1988). Many of these dispute resolution programs began with a primary emphasis on misdemeanor criminal cases and later added civil matters from the local small claims court and other sources. In a sense, they convert criminal matters to civil ones by treating the cases as matters for discussion between the individual disputants and not for processing between the state and the defendant.

The best-known community court in the nation is the Midtown Community Court in New York City. The Midtown experience was born of a profound frustration with quality-of-life crime in the neighborhood, particularly prostitution, vandalism, and low-level drug offenses. Offenders are sentenced to make restitution to the community through work projects in the neighborhood: removing graffiti, cleaning subway stations, and sorting cans and bottles for recycling. But at the same time the court attempts to link offenders with drug treatment, health care, education, and other social services. Perhaps one of the most unique approaches is that the courthouse includes an entire floor of office space for social workers to assist offenders referred by the judge in the courtroom a few floors below (Feinblatt and Berman 1997). Thus instead of sending an offender to distant bureaucracy the courthouse now incorporates helping institutions within its midst.

 To take an Internet tour of the Midtown Community Court or other community courts around the nation, go to **http://www.communityjustice.org/**, click on "Best Practices," and then "National Scene."

For an up-to-date list of Web links, go to **http://www.wadsworth.com/product/0534563406s**.

 Julie Brienza, "Community Courts Reach Out to Put a Dent in Petty Crime"

CONCLUSION

North v. Russell is a reminder that one out of four Americans get their justice off the main road. Here they often find that justice is dispensed by part-time, nonlawyer justices of the peace who may or may not have much training in the law. Moreover, the justice officials are not only few in number but also bound by long-term social relationships. Thus, compared to their big-city brethren, citizens in rural courthouses experience justice that is convenient and informal, but critics wonder if a little more of the constitution might better serve outsiders. The problems of the lower courts in urban areas are fundamentally different from those of rural courts. Courthouse officials are numerous and often knowledgeable about their tasks. Moreover, although the relationships are cordial, it is obvious that the courtroom is merely a place where representatives of many bureaucracies meet to do their work. Thus, compared to their brethren in more rural settings, citizens in municipal court experience justice that is quick and in many ways certain; sentences are arrived at by applying the group average. Critics argue the process all too often resembles an assembly line geared to rapid dispositions, and the process is the punishment.

Whether lower courts are found in small towns or big cities, they share an important denominator: for most Americans their only first-hand experience with real courtroom justice (as opposed to the courthouse justice they see on TV or read about in newspapers) will be the brief encounter before a lower court judge. The lower courts come into contact with more citizens every year than virtually any other governmental institution. All too often, the average citizen comes away from such encounters with a poor impression, pondering whether the judge was really interested in justice or merely in a hurry to feed the cash register.

The cases processed by the lower courts are indeed minor and have often been referred to as petty. The legal problems of drunks and drunk drivers, vagrants and vagabonds, used to be dismissed as of no interest, something for beat cops and low-level judges to deal with, but certainly not important enough for the real criminal justice system to be concerned about. Until recently, judicial reformers baldly suggested that these cases shouldn't even be in court. No longer. These cases are increasingly important to the public and therefore are now important to criminal justice officials as well. As discussed in Chapter 9, spousal abuse is the subject of serious debate, and no elected official dares dismiss these events as petty. The same holds true for drunk driving, which has catapulted to center stage in national attention. Moreover, some scholars and police officials see minor crimes as an important way to reduce crime, arguing that by cracking down on drunks and punks major crimes will be reduced, thus allowing good citizens to reclaim their community.

CRITICAL THINKING QUESTIONS

1. The justice of the peace system provides quick and convenient access to the courts, but does it cheapen the notion of justice? Or are the critics off-base, seemingly suggesting that every speeding motorist deserves a high-priced lawyer to defend his or her actions?

2. To some, the shorthand used in the lower courts best achieves justice because sentences tend to be uniform. To others, relying on group averages violates a defendant's right to have his or her case considered on its own merits. What do you think?

3. Are the lower courts really courts? With few defense attorneys and even fewer trials, maybe we should label activities in lower courts as hearings, not trials. What are your views on this?

4. Each legislative session, laws are passed getting tougher with drunk drivers. How long do you think this trend will continue?

5. The municipal court studied by Meyer and Jesilow (1997) processed relatively few traditional misdemeanors—assaults and thefts, for example. Instead, much of the court's time was taken up with victimless crimes such as homeless drug addicts, drunks, careless motorists driving on suspended licenses, or streetwalkers plying their trade on busy avenues. Do these cases belong in the courts? Would society be better served by taking many of these types of cases and handling them in social institutions?

 WORLD WIDE WEB RESOURCES AND EXERCISES

Web Guides

http://dir.yahoo.com/Society_and_Culture/ Crime/Types_of_Crime/Drunk_Driving/

http://dir.yahoo.com/Recreation/Automotive/Driving/ Red_Light_Running/

http://dir.yahoo.com/Recreation/Automotive/Driving/ Speeding/

http://dir.yahoo.com/News_and_Media/Television/ Shows/Reality_Television/Courtroom/

http://dir.yahoo.com/Government/Law/Alternative_ Dispute_Resolution/

Web Search Terms

"*Municipal court*"; "*justice of the peace*"; "*drunk driving*"; "*rural crimes*"; "*neighborhood justice centers*"; "*community justice*"

Useful URLs

The National Highway Traffic and Safety Institute makes the case for lowering the BAC to .08: http://www.nhtsa.dot.gov/people/injury/ alcohol/limit.08/.

Visit the Texas Municipal Courts Education Center: http://www.tmcec.com/.

The Community Justice Exchange offers information and assistance to help bring together criminal justice agencies and ordinary citizens to make communities safer: **http://www. communityjustice.org/**.

Uncommon URLs

Don't Go to Municipal Court Alone is presented by the law office of Ronald P. Mondello: **http:// www.municipalcourt.com/**.

Justiceofthepeace.net features the Honorable Rona B. Turano of Arlington, Massachusetts: **http://justicesofthepeace.net/**.

Speedtrap.com bills itself as information for efficiency: **http://www.speedtrap.com**.

Trafficschool.com is a commercial site that allows local courts to sentence traffic offenders to online traffic safety school: **http://www. trafficSchool.com**.

The Definitive Guide to Speeding Tickets offers lots of advice on how to beat speeding tickets: **http://home.att.net/~speeding/**.

See Businesses Against Drunk Driving: **http:// www.baddpage.com**.

Visit the San Francisco Community Courts Initiative: **http://www.ci.sf.ca.us/da/comcourts.htm**.

See the National Center for State Courts, Courts and Communities: **http://www.ncsc.dni.us/ research/cfc.htm**.

The Center for Court Innovation is a public-private partnership located in New York City that works to improve public confidence in justice: **http://www.courtinnovation.org/**.

Web Exercises

1. The homepage for Mothers Against Drunk Driving (MADD) can be found at **http:// www.madd.org**. Critically examine statements made by this organization. Do they document sources? Do they discuss counterarguments? Next, under the heading "Public Policy," examine the policy objectives of MADD. In what ways are their objectives similar to the ones discussed in the text? In what ways are they different?

2. Drunk driving remains a controversial issue. Use this Yahoo guide—**http://dir.yahoo.com/ Society_and_Culture/Crime/Types_of_Crime/ Drunk_Driving/**—to find at least one organization on either side of the issue. How do the groups differ in terms of organization and membership? Do they address the same arguments or different ones?

3. A handful of lower courts have Web sites. Choose the search engine of your choice and use the search term "*municipal courts*." Examine two of these Web sites, first from the perspective of a layperson who is contemplating filing a small claims lawsuit. What types of helpful information does the Web site provide? What additional types of information would you find useful?

   Next, examine the sites from the perspective of a defendant who must go to court in response to a misdemeanor arrest or traffic ticket. Does the site provide useful information to defendants? What additional information might you suggest? Overall, do the municipal court Web pages that you examined seem more oriented toward lawyers or lay citizens?

4. Several groups dedicated to preventing drunk driving can be found on the Web. Yet only a few homepages focus on the law and drunk driving from the arrestee's perspective. The following will yield some of the perspectives of defense lawyers: **http://dir.yahoo.com/ Society_and_Culture/Crime/Type_of_Crime/ Drunk_Driving/**.

5. Find two or more Web sites that provide legal advice to those who might be arrested for drunk driving or those who already have been. In what ways does the tone of these homepages differ from those of organizations against drunk driving? What practical advice do they provide? Overall, do these homepages suggest a high or low probability of being convicted once arrested? In what ways do these homepages try to avoid offending the dominant social culture, which views drunk driving in very negative terms?

 INFOTRAC COLLEGE EDITION RESOURCES AND EXERCISES

Basic Searches

Municipal courts; neighborhood justice centers; small claims courts; rural crimes; drunk driving; mothers against drunk driving; dispute resolution (laws); traffic regulations

Recommended Articles

Cheryl J. Cherpitel, Tammy W. Tam, "Variables Associated with DUI Offender Status among Whites and Mexican Americans"

"Liability Laws Effective in Reducing Harmful Alcohol-Related Behaviors"

Christina Couret, "Courthouse Cameras Save Police Time"

James J. Baxter, "The Mythology of Setting Low Speed Limits"

InfoTrac College Edition Exercises

1. Using the search term *drunk driving, laws, regulations,* find two or more articles that discuss drunk driving enforcement. To what extent do the articles emphasize a law on the books approach as opposed to a law in action perspective? To what extent do the policy recommendations fall along the lines of the crime control or due process model of justice?

2. Using the search term *rural crimes,* find two or more articles that discuss rural justice. To what extent are the problems in small towns similar to big cities? To what extent are they different and why?

REFERENCES

Adler, Peter, Karen Lovass, and Neal Milner. 1988. "The Ideologies of Mediation: The Movement's Own Story." *Law and Policy* 10: 317–339.

Alfini, James, and Patricia Passuth. 1981. "Case Processing in State Misdemeanor Courts: The Effect of Defense Attorney Presence." *Justice System Journal* 6: 100–116.

Applegate, Brandon, Francis Cullen, Bruce Link, Pamela Richards, and Lonn Lanza-Kaduce. 1996. "Determinants of Public Punitiveness Toward Drunk Driving: A Factorial Survey Approach." *Justice Quarterly* 13: 57–79.

Ashman, Allan. 1975. *Courts of Limited Jurisdiction: A National Survey.* Chicago: American Judicature Society.

Ashman, Allan, and Pat Chapin. 1976. "Is the Bell Tolling for Nonlawyer Judges?" *Judicature* 59: 417–421.

Bartol, Anne. 1996. "Structures and Roles of Rural Courts." Pp. 79–92 in *Rural Criminal Justice: Conditions, Constraints, and Challenges,* edited by Thomas McDonald, Robert Wood, and Melissa Pflug. Salem, WI: Sheffield.

Bing, Stephen, and Stephen Rosenfeld. 1974. "The Quality of Justice in the Lower Criminal Courts of Metropolitan Boston." Pp. 259–285 in *Rough Justice: Perspectives on Lower Criminal Courts,* edited by John Robertson. Boston: Little, Brown.

Borys, Bryan, Cynthia Banks, and Darrel Parker. 1999. "Enlisting the Justice Community in Court Improvement." *Judicature* 82: 176–185.

Bronstein, Julie. 1981. *Survey of State Mandatory Judicial Education Requirements.* Washington, D.C.: American University.

Burrell, Diane. 1997. "Financial Analysis of Traffic Court Collections in Ada County, Idaho." *Justice System Journal* 19: 101–116.

Cohen, Robyn. 1992. *Drunk Driving: 1989 Survey of Inmates of Local Jails.* Washington, D.C.: Bureau of Justice Statistics.

Efkeman, Hillery, and David Rottman. 1996–97. "Community-Focused Courts: Progress on a Developmental Initiative." *State Court Journal* 20: 10–16.

Fahnestock, Kathryn. 1991. "The Loneliness of Command: One Perspective on Judicial Isolation." *The Judges' Journal* 30: 13–19.

Feeley, Malcolm. 1979. *The Process Is the Punishment: Handling Cases in a Lower Criminal Court.* New York: Russell Sage Foundation.

Feinblatt, John, and Greg Berman. 1997. *Responding to the Community: Principles for Planning and Creating a Community Court.* Washington, D.C.: Bureau of Justice Assistance, U.S. Department of Justice.

Goerdt, John. 1992. *Small Claims and Traffic Courts: Case Management Procedures, Case Characteristics, and Outcomes in 12 Urban Jurisdictions.* Williamsburg, VA: National Center for State Courts.

Green, Justin, Ross Russell, and John Schmidhauser. 1975. "Iowa's Magistrate System: The Aftermath of Reform." *Judicature* 58: 380–389.

Gusfield, Joseph. 1981. *The Culture of Public Problems: Drinking-Driving and the Symbolic Order.* Chicago: University of Chicago Press.

Homel, Ross. 1988. *Policing and Punishing the Drinking Driver: A Study of General and Specific Deterrence.* New York: Springer-Verlag.

Jacobs, James. 1989. *Drunk Driving: An American Dilemma.* Chicago: University of Chicago Press.

Kingsnorth, Rodney, Carole Barnes, and Paul Coonley. 1990. "Driving Under the Influence: The Role of Legal and Extralegal Factors in Court Processing and Sentencing Practices." Unpublished manuscript, Department of Sociology, California State University, Sacramento.

Krantz, Sheldon, Charles Smith, David Rossman, Paul Froyd, and Janis Hoffman. 1976. *Right to Counsel in Criminal Cases: The Mandate of Argersinger v. Hamlin.* Cambridge, MA: Ballinger.

Mastrofski, Stephen, and R. Richard Ritti. 1996. "Police Training and the Effects of Organization on Drunk Driving Enforcement." *Justice Quarterly* 13: 291–320.

McDonald, Thomas, Robert Wood, and Melissa Pflug, eds. 1996. *Rural Criminal Justice: Conditions, Constraints, and Challenges.* Salem, WI: Sheffield.

McGillis, Daniel. 1997. *Community Mediation Programs: Developments and Challenges.* Washington,

D.C.: National Institute of Justice, U.S. Department of Justice.

———. 1998. *Resolving Community Conflict: the Dispute Settlement Center of Durham, North Carolina.* Washington, D.C.: National Institute of Justice.

Merry, Sally Engle, and Neal Milner, eds. 1993. *The Possibility of Popular Justice: A Case Study of Community Mediation in the United States.* Ann Arbor: University of Michigan Press.

Meyer, Jon'a, and Paul Jesilow. 1997. *Doing Justice in the People's Court: Sentencing by Municipal Court Judges.* Albany: State University of New York Press.

Mileski, Maureen. 1971. "Courtroom Encounters: An Observation Study of a Lower Criminal Court." *Law and Society Review* 5: 473–538.

Ostrom, Brian, and Neal Kauder. 1996. *Examining the Work of State Courts, 1995.* Williamsburg, VA: National Center for State Courts.

President's Commission on Law Enforcement and Administration of Justice. 1967. *Task Force Report: The Courts.* Washington, D.C.: Government Printing Office.

Provine, Doris Marie. 1981. "Persistent Anomaly: The Lay Judge in the American Legal System." *Justice System Journal* 6: 28–43.

———. 1986. *Judging Credentials: Nonlawyer Judges and the Politics of Professionalism.* Chicago: University of Chicago Press.

Ragona, Anthony, and John Paul Ryan. 1983. "Misdemeanor Courts and the Choice of Sanctions: A Comparative View." *Justice System Journal* 8: 199–221.

Reinarman, C. 1988. "The Social Construction of an Alcohol Problem." *Theory and Society* 17: 91–120.

Ross, H. Laurence. 1992. "The Law and Drunk Driving." *Law and Society Review* 26: 219–230.

Ryan, John Paul. 1980–1981. "Adjudication and Sentencing in a Misdemeanor Court: The Outcome Is the Punishment." *Law and Society Review* 15: 79–108.

Ryan, John Paul, and James Guterman. 1977. "Lawyers versus Non-Lawyer Town Justices." *Judicature* 60: 272–280.

"The Sausage Factories." 1974. *Time* (25 November): 91.

Silbey, Susan. 1981. "Making Sense of the Lower Courts." *Justice System Journal* 6: 13–27.

Sitomer, Curtis. 1985. "Rural Justice Affects Many, But May Serve Few." *Christian Science Monitor* (28 May): 23.

Thompson, Kevin. 1996. "The Nature and Scope of Rural Crime." Pp. 3–18 in *Rural Criminal Justice: Conditions, Constraints, and Challenges,* edited by Thomas McDonald, Robert Wood, and Melissa Pflug. Salem, WI: Sheffield.

Vermont Center for Justice Research. 1995. "DUI Adjudication and BAC Level: An Assessment." *DataLine: The Justice Research Bulletin* 4 (May).

Weisheit, Ralph, Edward Wells, and David Falcone. 1995. *Crime and Policing in Rural and Small-Town America: An Overview of the Issues.* Washington, D.C.: National Institute of Justice.

Wice, Paul. 1974. *Freedom for Sale.* Lexington, MA: D. C. Heath.

Wiseman, Jacqueline. 1976. "Drunk Court: The Adult Parallel to Juvenile Court." Pp. 233–252 in *The Criminal Justice Process: A Reader,* edited by William Sanders and Howard Daudistel. New York: Praeger.

FOR FURTHER READING

Church, Thomas. "The Mansion vs. the Gatehouse: Viewing the Courts from a Consumer's Perspective." *Judicature* 75 (1992): 255–268.

Jamieson, Katherine, and Anita Neuberger Blowers. "A Structural Examination of Misdemeanor Court Disposition Patterns." *Criminology* 31 (1993): 243–262.

Kelling, George, and Catherine Coles. *Fixing Broken Windows: Restoring Order and Reducing Crime in Our Communities.* New York: Martin Kessler, 1997.

Laurence, Michael, John Snortum, and Franklin Zimring, eds. *Social Control of the Drinking Driver.* Chicago: University of Chicago Press, 1988.

Legge, Jerome. *Traffic Safety Reform in the United States and Great Britain.* Pittsburgh: University of Pittsburgh Press, 1991.

Lindquist, John. *Misdemeanor Crime: Trivial Criminal Pursuit.* Newbury Park, CA: Sage, 1988.

Matthias, J., G. Lyford, and P. Gomez. *Current Practices in Collecting Fines and Fees in State Courts: A Handbook of Collection Issues and Solutions.* Denver: National Center for State Courts, Court Services Division, 1995.

Meyer, Jon'a, and Tara Gray. "Drunk Drivers in the Courts: Legal and Extra-Legal Factors Affecting Pleas and Sentences." *Journal of Criminal Justice* 25 (1997): 155–163.

Perkins, David. "Indigent or Immune? Constitutional Standards for Incarceration of the Poor in Fine-Only Cases." *Criminal Law Bulletin* 32 (1996): 3–24.

Thurman, Quint, and Edmund McGarrell. *Community Policing in a Rural Setting.* Cincinnati: Anderson, 1996.

Juvenile Courts

GERALD GAULT WAS CHARGED WITH MAKING A LEWD PHONE CALL. If he had been an adult, the maximum sentence was on the lenient side—a fine of fifty dollars and two months in jail. But because he was fifteen years old, the sentence was potentially much stiffer—up to six years in the state industrial school. These substantive differences mirrored important procedural contrasts as well. If he had been an adult, Gerald Gault would have had the right to confront the witness making the accusation and also the right to have a lawyer present. But because he was a juvenile, none of these basic legal protections applied.

In re Gault highlights the duality of juvenile court, which is part court of law and part social welfare agency. It sometimes operates formally, but more often its procedures are informal. These contrasts produce a series of contradictions, which are highlighted in the words of a former judge of the Denver Juvenile Court:

> *It is law, and it is social work; it is control, and it is help; it is the good parent and, also, the stern parent; it is both formal and informal. It is concerned not only with the delinquent, but also with the battered child, the runaway, and many others. . . . The juvenile court has been all things to all people. (Rubin 1984, 79–80)* ∎

The historic mandate of juvenile court was to rescue children from a criminal life by providing the care and protection normally afforded by the natural parents. Thus, helping a child was far more important than protecting constitutional rights. But in certain instances helpful benevolence has been replaced by harsh punishments. In deciding *In re Gault,* the Supreme Court confronted the difficult task of determining the relationship between the social welfare functions of juvenile court and basic due process so important to the American court system.

The best starting point in unraveling these dualities is an examination of the last 100 years of juvenile court.

JUVENILE COURTS 100 YEARS AGO

Juvenile courts are a distinctly twentieth-century development. The major economic and social changes of the late nineteenth century prompted a rethinking of the role of youth. The result was the creation of specialized courts to deal with what were thought to be distinctly youth-oriented problems. Many of the issues that arose 100 years ago remain with us today, shaping the thinking that will affect juvenile courts for the next 100 years.

Industrialization, Cities, and Crime

By the last third of the nineteenth century, the United States was well on its way to becoming the world's greatest industrial nation. What had once been a nation of small farmers was rapidly becoming a nation of city dwellers. The factories were located in the cities, and the workers for these factories were partially drawn from those who wished to escape the hard work of farming. But most of the new jobs were filled by immigrants from foreign lands who sought freedom from the political oppression or economic want in their home countries. The result was a tremendous growth in cities. Indeed, the population of the nation almost doubled, growing from 40 million in 1870 to 76 million in 1900.

America's emerging big cities were truly diverse. The residents spoke different languages, ate strange foods, dressed differently, and worshiped in a variety of churches. The white Anglo-Saxon Protestants who controlled the institutions of the United States at the time did not extend a cordial welcome to these new immigrants. On the contrary, the immigrant urban masses were associated with the poverty, social disorder, and crime of the emerging big cities. Protecting society from the "dangerous poor" became a pressing social concern. Then, as now, there was confusion over what was poverty and what was crime.

The Child Savers and the Progressive Movement

Beginning around 1890, members of the Progressive movement advocated a variety of political, economic, and social reforms. They were genuinely concerned about the economic disparities, social disorders, and excesses of industrialization, particularly as they affected children.

Progressives denounced the evils of child labor and pushed for legislation banning the practice. They were likewise appalled by the violent and exploitive conditions of reform schools. The fact that orphans were thrown into reform schools for the uncontrollable circumstance of having no parents shocked the Progressives' moral values. Taking up the plight of the children of the urban, immigrant poor, they argued that these children were not bad, but were corrupted by the environment in which they grew up.

The Progressives' concern for the plight of the urban masses was also motivated by self-interest. They were largely middle class, and their position in society was threatened by the growth of a competing urban class composed of the poor and the working poor. These white Anglo-Saxon Protestants found the culture of the Southern European Catholics shocking. Anthony Platt's (1969) classic study, *The Child Savers,* notes the types of behavior the Progressives sought to punish—drinking, fighting, begging, frequenting dance halls, staying out late at night, and sexual license. Within a generation many of the social forces unleashed by the Progressive movement would lead to Prohibition, which was directed squarely at the growing political power of big-city Catholic immigrants, whose power base was the neighborhood tavern.

Thus from its origins, the juvenile court movement reflected class distinctions: The children of the poor were processed through the system, but those of the more well-to-do were handled informally. These class differences would mark juvenile court activities throughout the century. Then, as now, there was confusion over what was genuine social concern and what was self-serving class interest.

 Bobbie Wilbur, Colleen Murphy, Kaye Caulkins, "Making a Difference in Juvenile Justice"

Parens Patriae

The Progressives' efforts to save the children of the urban masses reflected a major shift in thinking about children. Historically, children had been viewed as miniature adults. Children under the age of seven were presumed to be incapable of criminal intent and were therefore exempt from prosecution. Those eight and older were considered adults in the eyes of the law, prosecuted as adults, convicted as adults, and served their sentences in the same prison cells as adults.

By the end of the nineteenth century, the notion of children as miniature adults was giving way to a very different conceptualization—children as persons with less than fully developed moral and cognitive capacities. This shift in thinking was reflected in the emerging legal doctrine of **parens patriae** (state as parent). No longer were parents considered to have sole and exclusive legal responsibility over their children. If the parents failed in their responsibility to properly raise a child, the state could intervene to protect children's welfare. This doctrine also meant that in extreme circumstances parental rights over their children could be terminated altogether.

Then, as now, there was confusion over the right of parents to raise their children in their own image and the need of the state to limit social disorder.

HOW JUVENILE COURTS DIFFER FROM ADULT COURTS

The juvenile court is a continuing legacy of the Progressive movement. Not content to tinker with existing procedures, the Progressives insisted upon a radical departure from past practices. Adopting the

Parens patriae: The state as parent; the state as guardian and protector of all citizens (such as juveniles) who are unable to protect themselves.

legal doctrine of parens patriae resulted in juvenile judicial proceedings that differed greatly from those used in adult courts.

The unique legal dimensions of **juvenile court** are reflected in the legal terms employed. Whereas adults are arrested, tried, and sentenced to prison, juveniles are summoned, have a hearing, and are committed to residential placement. Juvenile courts differ from adult courts in five important ways: They emphasize helping the child, they are informal, they are based on civil law, they are secret, and they rarely involve a jury.

Emphasis on Helping the Child

Prosecution of adults at the turn of the century sought to achieve punishment. By contrast, the newly created juvenile courts emphasized helping the child. Benevolence, not punishment, was of paramount importance.

The doctrine of parens patriae became the underlying philosophy of juvenile court; the state should deal with a child who broke the law much as a wise parent would deal with a wayward child (Platt 1969). The Progressives sought to use the power of the state to save children from a life of crime. Juvenile courts would provide flexible procedures for the treatment of the underlying social problems that were seen as the basis of juvenile crime. Guidance would be the norm.

Informal Proceedings

Criminal prosecutions involving adults are formal and adversarial in nature. By contrast, juvenile court proceedings emphasize informality. Although key elements of due process have been integrated into juvenile court in recent years, juvenile proceedings nonetheless retain their informal nature. As a result, rules of evidence and rules of procedure, so important in adult criminal courts, have little relevance in juvenile proceedings.

Flowing from the premise that juvenile courts are meant to help the child, the creators of juvenile court viewed procedural safeguards not only as unnecessary but also as harmful. The concern was that a legal technicality might allow a child to avoid

Juvenile court: Any court that has jurisdiction over matters involving juveniles.

help (Sanborn 1993). In essence, the substance of the decision (helping the child) was more important than the procedures used to reach that decision.

 Denise Casamento Musser, "Kansas' Grassroots Juvenile Justice Reform"

Proceedings Based on Civil Law

Prosecutions of adults are based on the criminal law (Chapter 2). By contrast, juvenile court proceedings are based on the civil law (Chapter 2). This is why the legal terminology used in adult and juvenile courts differs so greatly. The terms *summons* and *commitment,* for example, are borrowed directly from civil practice.

Using civil rather than criminal law reinforced the key notion that juvenile courts were intended to rehabilitate, not punish. It is for this reason, for example, that a child's juvenile court record is not admissible in adult court. Regardless of the frequency or severity of the offenses committed by a juvenile, once he or she becomes an adult in the eyes of the criminal law, the person starts over with no prior record.

Over the years, the Supreme Court, state courts, and legislatures have added some procedural due process features of adult courts to juvenile proceedings. Thus, today it is probably best to view juvenile proceedings as a blend of civil and criminal law.

Secret Proceedings

Criminal proceedings involving adults are open to the public (except grand jury proceedings, and, on the rarest of rare occasions, jury selection in ultrasensitive cases). By contrast, juvenile court proceedings are secret. This means that crime victims who are interested in what happens in their case, or ordinary citizens who are simply curious about what goes on in the courthouse, may freely attend sessions involving adults but not involving juveniles.

In most jurisdictions it is illegal for law enforcement personnel or juvenile court officials to release the names of juveniles to the media. Moreover, even if the media indirectly is able to find out the names, journalistic ethics prohibit that information from being printed or broadcast.

To its supporters, the secrecy of juvenile court proceedings is essential in meeting the key goal of working with children in trouble to prevent future criminal behavior. To critics, this secrecy merely reinforces the informality of the process and prevents much-needed public scrutiny.

Absence of Jury Trials

Adults accused of violating the criminal law have the right to a trial by a jury of their peers. By contrast, juveniles have no such constitutional right. To be sure, a few states have created, often by statute, an extremely limited right to a trial by jury in some matters concerning juveniles. Nonetheless, the central point is clear: Whereas the possibility of a jury trial structures the disposition of adult offenders, the likelihood of a jury trial almost never enters into the discussion in juvenile court.

The absence of jury trials reinforces the informal nature of the proceedings. It also strengthens the control of juvenile court personnel—both judges and probation officers. In adult courts the views of ordinary citizens may prove to differ from those of judge or prosecutor, but there is no such possibility in juvenile court.

A few juvenile courts offer Web sites, including these:

Boston (Massachusetts): **http://www.state.ma.us/ courtsandjudges/courts/juvenilecourt**

Hamilton (Ohio): **http://www.hamilton-co.org/ juvenilecourt/**

Iowa: **http://www.judicial.state.ia.us/families/ juvcourt/**

Ninth Judicial Circuit (Florida): **http://www. ninja9.net/courts/juvenile/juvcrt.htm**

Northampton (Pennsylvania): **http://www. nccpa.org/divs/juvcourtprob.html**

Pierce County (Washington): **http://www.co.pierce. wa.us/abtus/ourorg/supct/abtusjuv.htm**

Pima County (Arizona): **http://www.sc.co.pima. az.us/Juvenile/**

Virginia Beach (Virginia): **http://www.virginia-beach.va.us/courts/jdrcourt/jdrintak.htm**

For an up-to-date list of Web links, go to **http:// www.wadsworth.com/product/0534563406s**.

LAW ON THE BOOKS: THE ORGANIZATION OF JUVENILE COURTS

Today, all states have juvenile courts, but their organizational relationship to other judicial bodies varies greatly. In some ways the term *juvenile court* is a misnomer. Only a few states have created juvenile courts that are completely separate from other judicial bodies.

As Chapter 4 emphasized, important variations exist in state court organization. Nowhere is this diversity more apparent than in the organization of juvenile courts. Along a continuum from the most to the least distinctive, juvenile courts are organized in one of three ways: a separate court, part of family court, or a unit of the trial court.

Juvenile Court as a Separate Court

In a few jurisdictions, juvenile court is completely separate from other judicial bodies. This is the case in the states of Connecticut, Rhode Island, and Utah. A juvenile court as a separate statewide entity means that it has its own administration, judges, probation officers, clerks of court, and other employees. Stated another way, matters concerning juveniles are its exclusive jurisdiction.

A few large cities, such as Boston, also separate juvenile courts from other judicial bodies. Similarly, Denver has a separate juvenile court serving the city and county of Denver. Elsewhere in Colorado, juvenile court is a division of the major trial court.

Juvenile Court as Part of Family Court

A second organizational arrangement is for juvenile court to be a part of family court, which has broad responsibility over family matters. One major type of case is divorce and related issues, including child custody, child support, alimony, and property settlement. In addition, jurisdiction of family courts encompasses paternity matters and adoption of children. Most importantly for our purposes, family court jurisdiction also typically includes matters concerning juveniles (delinquency, status offenses, and child-victim cases).

Six states and the District of Columbia have authorized family courts on a statewide basis. In Delaware, New York, Rhode Island, and South Carolina, family courts are separately organized. In the

District of Columbia, Hawaii, and New Jersey, family courts are a separate division of the trial court of general jurisdiction.

Juvenile Court as a Unit of Trial Court

The third place that juvenile courts are housed organizationally is as part of a trial court. Typically, juvenile court is part of the jurisdiction of the major trial court, but on occasion it is in the minor trial court.

Beyond the legal considerations of jurisdiction, the question of where matters concerning juveniles are heard is largely a function of case volume. In rural areas with few cases, they most often are a type of case on the judge's calendar much like tort and contract. But in most areas there are sufficient cases to justify one or more judges who devote themselves full time to matters concerning juveniles. This specialization is dictated partly by case volume, but also by the requirement that juvenile proceedings be conducted in secret. Administratively, therefore, a separate section of court (sometimes in a different courthouse) makes it easier to keep juvenile proceedings closed to the public.

Law in Action: The Impact of Structure

Since juvenile courts were first established, there has been a debate over the appropriate place in the judicial hierarchy for this new judicial body. Where a state ended up placing its juvenile court was largely determined by broader debates over court organization.

Court reformers recommend that juvenile court be part of family court. But whether this structural arrangement results in "better" justice is at best hard to document. There is some evidence, for example, that the more the judge is a juvenile court specialist, the more likely the judge will handle cases informally rather than conduct a full hearing (Sosin 1978). Similarly, specialists are less likely to find a youth to be a delinquent (Johnson and Secret 1995). The structural differences, however, appear to be far less important than the social environment in which the juvenile court operates; juvenile courts in big cities march to a different drummer than those in rural or suburban areas (Sanborn 1994).

JUVENILE COURT JURISDICTION: AGE

For adults, court jurisdiction is largely determined by the nature of the criminal offense. For **juveniles,** on the other hand, jurisdiction is normally determined by their age. Different states provide complex sets of criteria relating to the **upper age of jurisdiction,** when a child becomes an adult (at least in the eyes of the criminal law), as well as the **lower age of jurisdiction,** when a juvenile may be prosecuted as an adult in court.

No Consensus on Age of Juveniles

Most states consider children to be juveniles until they reach their eighteenth birthday. However, eighteen hardly constitutes a consensus among the states. Three states establish the upper age of juvenile court jurisdiction at fifteen, eight others at age sixteen, and the remaining states at seventeen (see Figure 19-1).

The adjoining states of New York and Pennsylvania illustrate this complex national pattern. In New York a sixteen-year-old is considered an adult and is prosecuted in the adult criminal justice system. But move across the border, and Pennsylvania treats that same sixteen-year-old as a juvenile to be processed in the juvenile court system (DeFrances and Strom 1997). This difference in laws of jurisdictions sometimes no more than a few feet apart illustrates the tremendous diversity of American law, which is highlighted in Chapter 4.

 Richard E. Redding, "Examining Legal Issues: Juvenile Offenders in Criminal Court and Adult Prison"

Transfer to Adult Court

Although a fairly uniform upper age limit for juveniles has been established in the United States, there is far less uniformity involving lower age limits (see

Juvenile: Youth at or below the upper age of juvenile court jurisdiction.

Upper age of jurisdiction: The oldest age at which a juvenile court has original jurisdiction over an individual for behavior that violates the law.

Lower age of jurisdiction: Minimum age at which a youth may be transferred to adult court.

FIGURE 19-1 Upper Age of Juvenile Court Jurisdiction in States

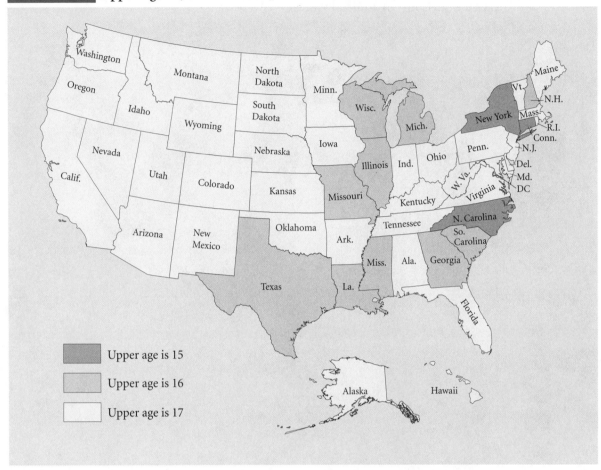

SOURCE: Torbet, P., and Szymanski, L. *State Legislative Responses to Violent Juvenile Crime: 1996–97 Update.* Washington, D.C.: Office of Juvenile Justice and Delinquency Prevention, 1998.

Figure 19-2). Juveniles charged with serious offenses, or who have a history of repeated offenses, may be tried as an adult (Singer 1993). **Transfer to criminal court** (alternatively referred to as certification or waiver) refers to the process whereby the jurisdiction over a juvenile delinquent is moved to adult court. Many states have no lower age for transfer. Vermont sets the age as low as ten, Montana at twelve, Georgia, Illinois, and Mississippi at thirteen. For those stating a lower age limit, fourteen to sixteen is the most common.

The procedures surrounding the decision to transfer juveniles to adult court also vary. In some

---

Transfer to criminal court: A case is moved to a criminal court because of a waiver or transfer hearing in the juvenile court.

---

jurisdictions the juvenile court judge makes the decision, but in the majority the prosecutor has the discretionary authority to decide which juveniles above the lower age will be tried as adults.

In the most recent year for which statistics are available, only a very small proportion of juveniles (1 percent, or approximately 12,000 cases) were transferred to adult court (Puzzanchera et al. 2000). Juveniles transferred to criminal court were generally violent felony offenders. Two-thirds were charged with a violent offense including about 11 percent with murder, 34 percent with robbery, and 15 percent with felony assault (Strom, Smith, and Snyder 1998). A disproportionate number of juveniles transferred to adult criminal court were black males (63 percent). Figures like these lead youth advocacy groups like Building Blocks for Youth (2000) to conclude that the juvenile justice

FIGURE 19-2 Youngest Age at Which Juvenile May Be Transferred to Criminal Court by Judicial Waiver

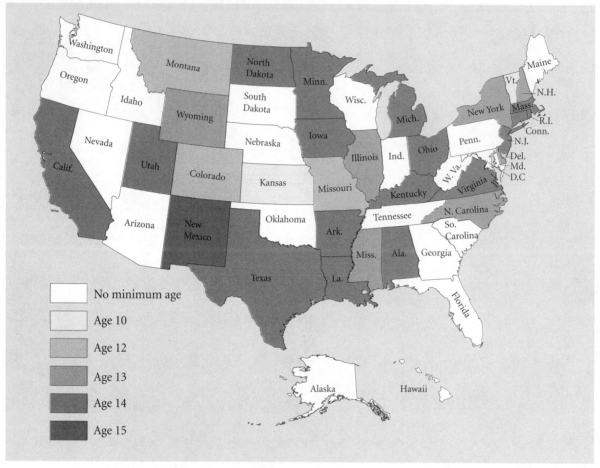

SOURCE: Sickmund, Melissa. "Minimum Transfer Age Specified in Statute, 1997." Adapted from Griffin, P., Torbet, P., and Szymanski, L., *Trying Juveniles as Adults in Criminal Court: An Analysis of State Transfer Provisions.* Washington, D.C.: Office of Juvenile Justice and Delinquency Prevention, 1998.

system is not "racially neural" and that states have not done enough to address racial disparities.

Public pressure to try juveniles as adults is spawned by concerns over violent juvenile crimes. Reality, though, does not match the expectations of elected officials or the public. (See Controversy: Should Juveniles Be Tried as Adults? on page 510) Moreover, once transferred, juveniles do not always receive longer sentences than they would have in juvenile court, because they are appearing in court for the first time and at a relatively young age (Snyder and Sickmund 2000).

The Office of Juvenile Justice and Delinquency Prevention recently evaluated changes in Wisconsin, New Mexico, and Minnesota (Torbet et al. 2000). The final report highlights the following lessons learned:

- A disconnect exists between legislative intent and the actual implementation of new laws.

- The new sentencing laws encourage plea bargaining.

- Blended sentencing provisions expand judicial and prosecutorial discretion.

- Local application of new laws varies widely.

- New sentencing laws have a disproportionate impact on minorities.

Stated another way, alterations of laws on the books do not necessarily produce the intended changes in law in action.

 The National Center for Juvenile Justice provides a dynamic interactive resource called Juvenile Justice State Profiles at **http://www.ncjj.org/**.

For an up-to-date list of Web links, go to **http://www.wadsworth.com/product/0534563406s**.

JUVENILE COURT JURISDICTION: SUBJECT MATTER

Of those children brought before juvenile court because of their age, there is enormous variation in the types of cases. Felons and misdemeanants, petty offenders and truants are all under the jurisdiction of the juvenile court because of their age. And to complicate matters even further, some juveniles are before the court because of neglect or abuse by their parents.

Juvenile court matters fall into three major categories: delinquency, status offenses, and child-victim.

Juvenile Delinquency

Delinquency is a violation of a criminal law that would be a crime if the act were committed by an adult. Common examples include theft, burglary, sale or possession of drugs, and criminal damage to property. Thus, in a juvenile delinquency matter there is no age difference in the substance of the criminal law, although the procedures are considerably different.

A juvenile delinquent may be placed on probation or committed to a juvenile institution. The period of confinement may exceed that of an adult. These criminal-type juvenile cases constitute 64 percent of all matters concerning juveniles.

Delinquency: An act committed by a juvenile that would require an adult to be prosecuted in a criminal court. Because the act is committed by a juvenile, it falls within the jurisdiction of the juvenile court. Delinquent acts include crimes against persons or property, drug offenses, and crimes against public order.

Status Offenses

Status offenses involve acts illegal only for juveniles. Common examples include running away from home, truancy, possession of alcohol, ungovernability, and curfew violations. Each year juvenile courts handle almost 100,000 such cases. Traditionally, juveniles found to be status offenders could be sent to the same juvenile correctional institutions as those found to be delinquent, but this is changing. In recent years some states have decriminalized some of these behaviors; offenders are now treated as dependent children, and child protective-service agencies are given the primary responsibility for addressing the problem.

Child-Victim

Juvenile courts also deal with **child-victim** petitions involving neglect or dependency. Thus, the child is before the court for no fault of his or her own. Common examples include battered children, children abandoned by their parents, and children who are not receiving proper education or medical care. Neglected or dependent children cannot be sentenced to juvenile institutions. Rather, the court has a broad mandate to order social services, foster home or group home care, or medical or mental health services.

Clearly, neglected or dependent children present strikingly different issues from those who are before the court because of their own actions. Child-victim cases are also the ones that evoke considerable public emotion over the child's condition. Because of the complexities inherent in the distinctive nature of these cases, space does not permit further discussion.

Law in Action: One-Pot Jurisdiction

The broad subject matter jurisdiction of juvenile courts complicates the task of addressing the problems facing juvenile justice. At any given time in juvenile court, the judge, prosecutor, probation

Status offense: Behavior that is considered an offense only when committed by a juvenile, for example, running away from home.

Child-victim: Juvenile court case involving a child who has been neglected and/or abused by the parents.

CONTROVERSY

Should Juveniles Be Tried as Adults?

During the mid-1990s the nation's focus on crime began to shift from drugs to juvenile crime, particularly violent juvenile crime. Public concern with crimes committed by juveniles often takes the form of efforts to lower the age at which a juvenile may be prosecuted as an adult.

Beginning in the mid-1980s the juvenile crime rate increased, with juvenile arrests nearly doubling from 197 teen arrests per 100,000 teenagers to 465 per 100,000 (Cannon 1997). What has attracted the most public attention is the increase in violent juvenile crime, which shot up 93 percent (compared with 22 percent in property cases).

To some observers, a juvenile crime wave was on the horizon. Newspaper headlines proclaimed, "Youth Violence Explosion Likely to Worsen" (Bass 1995) and "Violent Children Straining Limit of Justice System" (Hallinan 1993). These concerns were bolstered by the realization that the juvenile population would increase from 27 million to 39 million in 2010. Recent events, however, suggest a different pattern. Arrest data in 1995 and 1996 for violent juvenile crimes were down significantly, and what some had predicted to be a juvenile crime wave now appears to have been only a ripple (Johnson and Fields 1996).

The commonly held belief that juvenile delinquents are becoming younger as a group and committing more serious crimes at earlier ages than in the past does not hold up to scrutiny. The Office of Juvenile Justice and Delinquency Prevention (1996) compared the characteristics of young offenders arrested in recent years with those arrested in 1980 and concluded that today's serious and violent juvenile offenders are not significantly younger than those of ten or fifteen years ago. But downward trends in juvenile crime have apparently had little impact on the public dialogue. The U.S. Congress has been considering a juvenile crime bill that would encourage states to become harsher in prosecuting young offenders.

Numerous states are likewise responding to public perceptions that violent juvenile crime is a growing menace and making it easier to transfer juveniles. Since the late 1970s, for example, forty-four states have changed their laws affecting the transfer of juveniles to adult courts. Some of these efforts involve lowering the age of transfer. Others involve increasing the list of crimes for which juveniles may be transferred. Others seek to mandate transfers in certain situations. In 1994, for example, the state of Georgia enacted a mandatory transfer for juveniles thirteen years and older who have been charged with specified serious offenses. (If convicted, thirteen-year-olds may face a minimum ten-year prison sentence.) Today, at least twenty-four states have laws that automatically send violent kids to adult courts, and several others are considering enacting such laws.

Efforts to greatly increase the number of juveniles tried as adults has prompted tremendous concern in the juvenile justice community. One possibility is that juveniles will be incarcerated with adult offenders. "It is likely that the number of young inmates sentenced to confinement will increase and . . . placing juveniles in adult facilities raises issues such as their risk of being raped or assaulted by the older inmates. If kept in isolation for protection they are then at increased risk for suicide" (Snyder 2000). Advocates of restorative justice (Chapter 15) in particular emphasize that juvenile matters are the prime example of where efforts at reconciliation are likely to yield more positive results than punitive measures.

What do you think? Should juveniles be prosecuted as adults? If you answer yes, under what conditions should juveniles be prosecuted as adults and for what crimes? In what ways are your standards similar to or different from existing practices?

If you answer no, what would you suggest to strengthen rehabilitative efforts in juvenile court? In what ways are your recommendations similar to or different from existing practices?

In forming your answer, also consider the following question: Do you think that the recent decrease in juvenile crime, particularly violent crime, is temporary or long term?

 John Thomas, Dorothy E. Stubbe, Geraldine Pearson, "Race, Juvenile Justice, and Mental Health: New Dimensions in Measuring Pervasive Bias"

officer, and police officer are simultaneously dealing with a wide variety of problems. This has been called the one-pot jurisdictional approach, in which youths who commit serious crimes, status offenders, and deprived children are put into the same "pot" (Springer 1986).

Consider the following three hypothetical cases, all of which would meet a given state's age criteria:

- A juvenile who has burglarized a liquor store;
- A juvenile who has been stopped by the police for possessing liquor;
- A juvenile whose parents drink so heavily that they have given up any efforts to raise their child.

The first is a delinquent, the second a status offender, and the third a child-victim. Yet,

> all three kinds of kids were thought to be the products or victims of bad family and social environments; consequently it was thought, they should be subject, as the wards of the court, to the same kind of solicitous, helpful care. (Springer 1986, 62–63)

It is this broad diversity of juvenile problems that members of the courtroom work group must confront in trying to dispense juvenile court's version of justice.

DUE PROCESS IN JUVENILE COURTS

Juvenile court statutes set forth two standards for deciding the appropriate disposition for a child: the best interests of the child and the best interests of the community. Because the concept of the juvenile court was to aid—not punish—children, the due process guarantees of the adult criminal court were absent. Procedures were more administrative than adversarial, stressing the informal, private, and noncombative handling of cases. It is for this reason that juvenile cases are often captioned *In re,* a Latin phrase meaning "in the matter of." But at what point do juveniles obtain benefits from the special procedures applicable to them that offset the disadvantage of denial of due process?

 Steven H. Rosenbaum, "Civil Rights Issues in Juvenile Detention and Correctional Systems"

Key Court Decisions

The nature of the juvenile court process remained unchanged until the 1960s. When the Warren Court began to scrutinize procedures in adult criminal courts, its attention also turned to juvenile courts. In

a groundbreaking decision the Supreme Court held in *In re Gault* (1967) that the due process clause of the Fourteenth Amendment applied to juvenile court proceedings. The court emphasized that "under our Constitution the condition of being a boy does not justify a kangaroo court." The opinion specified that juveniles have (1) the right to notice, (2) the right to counsel, (3) the right to confront witnesses, and (4) privilege against self-incrimination. (See Case Close-Up: *In re Gault* and Due Process in Juvenile Courts.)

The *Gault* decision points to the constant tension within the juvenile court system between those who think that children should be given all the due process guarantees accorded adults and those who reason that children must be handled in a less adversarial, more treatment-oriented manner so that legal procedures will not interfere with efforts to secure the justice that is in the children's best interests. *Gault* signaled that the juvenile court must become a real court and its procedures must be regularized in accordance with constitutional requirements (Rubin 1984). Juvenile courts, however, afford far fewer due process rights than their adult counterparts. Following *Gault,* the more conservative Burger and Rehnquist Courts have been less enthusiastic about extending due process (see Figure 19-3). Juvenile delinquents, for example, have no constitutional right to a trial by jury (*McKeiver v. Pennsylvania,* 1971) and preventive detention is allowed (*Schall v. Martin,* 1984).

Important Congressional Acts

Congress has also imposed key mandates on the juvenile justice process. The Juvenile Justice and Delinquency Prevention Act of 1974 mandated deinstitutionalization of status offenders by stating that juveniles not charged with acts that would be crimes for adults shall not be jailed. Similarly, the law specifies that juveniles charged with criminal acts shall not be detained in any institution in which they have contact with adult inmates (Snyder and Sickmund 2000). There is little doubt that this law has fundamentally changed the way our nation deals with troubled youth (Holden and Kapler 1995).

Congressional mandates, coupled with *Gault* and other Supreme Court rulings, have had a marked effect on juvenile court procedures. "Today's juvenile court is constantly discarding many of its traditional and fundamental characteristics, and it is

FIGURE 19-3		Key Developments Concerning Juvenile Courts

Ex Parte Crouse	1839	Philadelphia Supreme Court uses term *parens patriae*.
Illinois Juvenile Court Act	1899	First juvenile court created in Cook County, Illinois.
Juvenile Court Act	1938	Federal government adopts principles of juvenile court movement.
Wyoming	1945	Last state to create a juvenile court.
Kent v. U.S.	1966	Court establishes conditions of waiver to criminal court.
In re Gault	1967	Juveniles are entitled to due process guarantees.
In re Winship	1970	Proof must be established "beyond a reasonable doubt" in classifying juveniles as delinquent.
McKeiver v. Pennsylvania	1971	Juvenile delinquents are not entitled to a jury trial.
Juvenile Delinquency and Prevention Act	1974	Mandates deinstitutionalization of status offenders.
Schall v. Martin	1984	Court departs from trend of increasing juvenile rights, upholding the general notion of parens patriae.
Thompson v. Oklahoma	1988	Execution of a person under the age of sixteen at the time of his or her crime is unconstitutional.

adopting many of the features customarily associated with criminal court" (Sanborn 1993).

Some observers see the future of juvenile courts as more formal institutions of law, and they advocate replacing discretion with due process. These critics would open hearings to the public and make juvenile court records accessible. Along the same lines, they would make trials more important. Thus Joseph Sanborn (1993) concludes that it is time for juvenile courts to provide defendants whom the court seeks to punish the right to a public jury trial.

Another proposal would go even further, stripping juvenile courts of their secrecy. The "seemingly hidden juvenile court operations have contributed to the public perception that the court is overly lenient. When open hearings have been tried there have been few negative consequences" (Krisberg and Austin 1993, 184). There seems little doubt that the juvenile courts over the next 100 years will increase the amount of due process provided juveniles, but how much (and how fast) is an open question.

COURTROOM WORK GROUP

At first glance, members of juvenile courtroom work groups are similar to those found in adult courts—prosecutors bring charges, defense attorneys attempt to get the best deal possible for their clients, and judges decide matters that others have not successfully negotiated. These parallels, though, can be deceiving because the tasks of juvenile and adult courts are not the same. More so than courts dealing with adults accused of violating the law, juvenile courts grant judges and other officials unusually wide latitude in making discretionary decisions intended to "individualize justice" (Bazemore 1994). Moreover, although the Supreme Court has imposed minimal due process requirements, juvenile courts remain judicial bodies where informal processing still dominates.

Shared norms are the hallmark of courtroom work groups, Chapter 5 argued. In assessing the worth of a case, members of the juvenile court work group incorporate many of the same factors as those in adult courts—the severity of the offense and the prior record of the offender. The juvenile court tradition of individualized treatment, though, encourages the consideration of another important factor—the characteristics of the family (Matza 1964). The control the parent or parents have over the youth is a major consideration in deciding the disposition of the case. Similarly, members of the juvenile court work group also consider family structure, including the number of parents in the household and patterns of criminality among other family members (Corley, Bynum, and Wordes 1995).

CASE CLOSE-UP

In re Gault and Due Process in Juvenile Courts

 The Sheriff of Gila County, Arizona, took fifteen-year-old Gerald Francis Gault into custody for making a lewd phone call to a neighbor. As to what was actually said, the Supreme Court would only say, "It will suffice for purposes of this opinion to say that the remarks or questions put to her were of the irritatingly offensive, adolescent, sex variety."

Gault was transported to the Children's Detention Home, but no effort was made to contact his parents. Over the next couple of weeks, several brief hearings were held, but no record exists of what happened. What is known, though, is that there is some dispute whether Gerald Gault actually made the phone call. According to one version, he dialed the number, but his friend did the talking. Whatever may have transpired, the hearing would not be able to determine, because the witness was never present.

After another brief hearing, Gerald was found to be a juvenile delinquent and committed to the State Industrial School "for the period of his minority [that is, until 21] unless sooner discharged by due process of law." This harsh sentence was probably influenced by the fact that at the time he was on six months' probation as a result of having been in the company of another boy who had stolen a woman's purse.

It was the lack of procedural regularity in cases like this one that concerned the American Civil Liberties Union (ACLU) (Manfredi 1998). Through a series of complex maneuvers, the ACLU was able to get the case before the Arizona Supreme Court and then the U.S. Supreme Court.

In deciding *Gault*, the Court was essentially writing on a blank slate concerning juveniles. A year earlier the Court had ever so tentatively imposed some due process requirements for juveniles accused of serious felonies (*Kent v. U.S.*, 1966). But now the Court was ready to confront head-on the basic question about juvenile courts: Does the Bill of Rights apply to juveniles, or are children's best interests protected by informal and paternalistic hearings? Justice Abe Fortas's opinion underscored the lack of procedural regularity, stressing that "Due process of law is the primary and indispensable foundation of individual freedom."

At the same time, the opinion in *Gault* supports the purposes of the juvenile court: A juvenile court proceeding is one "in which a fatherly judge touched the heart and conscience of the erring youth by talking over his problems, by paternal advice and admonition" to save him from a downward career. The goodwill and compassion of the juvenile court will not, however, be diminished by due process of law. In one bold stroke, *In re Gault* carved out the following four new constitutional rights in juvenile proceedings:

- Juveniles have the right to timely notice of charges. In the future, parents must be informed that their child has been taken into custody, and written charges must be filed.
- Juveniles have the right to counsel. Following *Gideon*, the Court held that juveniles, like adults, have the right to an attorney present during the proceedings, and if they are indigent, a lawyer will be appointed.
- Juveniles have the right against self-incrimination. *Miranda*, decided by the Court just a year before, greatly extended the right for adults, and many of the same strictures were now extended to juveniles.
- Juveniles have the right to confront and cross-examine complainants and other witnesses.

The Court's opinion in *Gault* was supported by seven justices and partially by an eighth. Only Justice Potter Stewart dissented outright. He viewed the decision as "a long step backwards into the nineteenth century." The danger he saw was that abolishing the flexibility and informality of the juvenile courts would cause children to be treated as adults in courts.

The legally trained members of the courtroom work group rely heavily on professional judgments of nonlawyers in assessing both the background of the youth and the characteristics of the family. This affects the juvenile court work group in a critical way. Whereas in adult court the skills of lawyers are of fundamental importance, in juvenile court they are secondary. Judges, lawyers, and defense attorneys have been trained to interpret and apply the law, but these skills provide little help in making the key decisions in juvenile court cases. Instead, social workers, psychologists, and counselors have been trained to assess the child's problem and devise a treatment plan.

Thomas F. Geraghty, Steven A. Drizin, "Charting a New Course for Juvenile Justice: Listening to Outsiders"

Judges

Judges are the central authority in the juvenile court system. More so than their counterparts in criminal court, they have wide discretion over detention, the adjudicatory hearing, disposition, and other matters. Depending on the size of the court and the rotation system, an individual judge may spend only a little amount of time or a great deal of time in juvenile court (Bazemore and Feder 1997).

In many jurisdictions, assignment to the juvenile court is not a highly sought-after appointment. Although some judges like the challenges of juvenile court, to others it is a dead-end assignment. Judges who specialize in juvenile court matters are often those who enjoy the challenges of working with people rather than those who are intrigued by nuances of legal interpretations (see A Day in Court: "Juvenile Court Judge Finds Peace of Mind"). But even judges deeply committed to the juvenile system may seek rotation to other sections to advance their judicial careers (Krisberg and Austin 1993).

Hearing Officers

In many jurisdictions, judges are assisted by hearing officers (sometimes known as referees, masters, or commissioners). Typically, hearing officers are attorneys appointed by the court to serve on a full- or part-time basis to hear a range of juvenile court matters. These hearing officers enter findings and recommendations that require confirmation by the judge to become an order (Rubin 1989).

Prosecutors

Over the last several decades the power and influence of the prosecutor has grown in U.S. courthouses (Chapter 6). Rising crime rates, coupled with Supreme Court decisions requiring more due process, have contributed to the growing role of the prosecutor in juvenile courts (Shine and Price 1992).

Prosecutors now dominate the intake processing stage in most jurisdictions. At times, intake officers make the initial decision and the prosecutor later reviews that determination. At other times the prosecutor is the chief decision maker (with input

from others, of course). This prosecutorial dominance does not necessarily mean that DAs prefer formal processing. For status offenses and misdemeanor allegations, prosecutors are more likely to opt for informal, rather than formal, processing (Rubin 1989). Similarly, prosecutors, more so than judges, are typically the ones who negotiate the disposition of all but the most serious juvenile delinquency cases.

Although the role of the prosecutor's office has increased in juvenile court, an assignment to a section of juvenile court is not a sought-after promotion. On the contrary, it is the newly hired assistant DAs fresh out of law school who tend to be assigned to juvenile court. Thus, much like judges, assistant DAs typically hope for a promotion to a felony unit, where they can practice "real law," trying and convicting "real criminals."

Defense Attorneys

Defense attorneys play very much a secondary role in the juvenile court. One study found that only half of juveniles had a lawyer (Feld 1988), and another reported a lawyer present during only one-third of formal hearings (Walker and Ostrander 1982). The American Bar Association and other juvenile advocacy groups are concerned that the legal interests of many young people in juvenile court are compromised because of a lack of legal representation (Puritz et al. 1995; Puritz and Shang 1998).

Lack of representation by a lawyer partially reflects the nature of the caseload—many of the cases are minor. As we saw with adults in misdemeanor court, few have lawyers because the penalties are so light. The same holds true for juveniles—most cases will receive some form of probation, supervision, and/or restitution irrespective of whether a lawyer is, or is not, present.

The limited role of the defense attorney is further limited by the informality of juvenile courts. Much more so than in adult court, juvenile court proceedings place little emphasis on the privilege against self-incrimination. From the initial police contact (and often arrest) through the intake proceedings, juveniles are urged to tell the truth. It should be no surprise, therefore, to learn that fewer than 10 percent of juveniles asserted their right to remain silent (Grisso 1981).

Defense attorneys, when they are present at all, become involved after their client has cooperated with police and prosecutor, and perhaps the proba-

A DAY IN COURT

"Juvenile Court Judge Finds Peace of Mind"

 Just across the Trinity River, miles away from downtown Dallas' legal epicenter, is a government building where most of the city's heartbreaking cases are heard. On a daily basis, lawyers, judges, and caseworkers inside the Henry Wade Juvenile Justice Center examine the details of unfathomable crimes, from 15-year-old murderers who kill for a few dollars to parents who sexually abuse their children.

Since 1987, 304th District Judge Hal Gaither has sat in judgment of both parents and children accused of mind-numbing depravity as one of Dallas County's two juvenile court judges. Somehow, he's managed to be at peace with himself. "You learn to leave it all at the office," Gaither says. "If you don't it will kill you." It's easy to see why.

Juvenile judges have incredible power over other people's lives. But with that power comes a mandate to make some rather unpleasant decisions. Juvenile judges decide whether a child accused of a crime will be adjudicated in the juvenile system where rehabilitation is the focus, or sent through the adult system where hope is usually abandoned at the penitentiary gates.

And they decide whether children taken from their parents by Child Protective Services will remain with the family or be placed elsewhere, sometimes in state care—an option few concede is the best place to raise a child.

The easiest way to sleep at night, Gaither says, is to keep one thing in mind while making decisions on matters such as CPS removals. "You've got to focus on who is the most important person in the courtroom," he says. "And that's the kid." . . .

Gaither was Gov. George W. Bush's chief adviser during the 1996 rewrite of the juvenile code, an effort that dropped the age a juvenile can be certified as an adult to 14. But it also expanded the determinate sentencing statutes (offenses that usually involve violent crime) to keep minors in juvenile detention for longer periods of time instead of sending them to adult prison.

Gaither sticks by the tenets of the law he helped create. Very few juveniles are certified as adults in Gaither's court—about 30 per year by his estimation. Although the prosecution decides whether to seek adult certification, Gaither says prosecutors know what he'll certify, so they don't ask unless it's a worthy case.

But as a former juvenile prosecutor with nearly 10 years' experience, Gaither is quick to certify a juvenile as an adult in cases involving violent offenses—especially if the juvenile poses a danger to society, lawyers say. However, Gaither listens to lawyers' suggestions on sentencing matters in unusual cases. . . .

In CPS removal cases, it doesn't matter if the parents are from high-toned North Dallas or impoverished South Dallas, they will be treated the same by Gaither, lawyers say. . . . "He gives folks the benefit of the doubt," says Allison Sartin, a former Dallas juvenile prosecutor who is now in private practice. . . . But there are some types of parents that Gaither has no patience for, Sartin says. "I think he has a firm conviction that you can't be a drug user and an effective parent at the same time. He doesn't have much tolerance for parents who are drug abusers," Sartin says. . . .

On Dec. 31, 2002, Gaither will hang up his robe for the last time and walk out of the juvenile courthouse for good. Gaither says he figures 15 years is a long enough time to be a judge. And he says he told his political supporters that his fourth campaign would be his last. "I just let everybody know this is it," Gaither says. "It's time to smell the roses, I've had a good life." . . .

SOURCE: John Council, "Juvenile Court Judge Finds Peace of Mind," *Texas Lawyer*, September 25, 2000. Copyright 2000 American Lawyer Newspapers Group, Inc.

tion officer and judge as well. For the cases where there is only weak evidence, the defense strategy is to seek a dismissal. For the vast majority of cases where there is strong evidence, defense attorneys negotiate, based on the norms of the work group, the best possible deal for their client. Since most of the cases are, by adult standards, relatively minor, the dispositions reached tend to be on the lenient side—probation, restitution, and community service primarily.

Probation Officers

From the beginning, probation and **probation officers** were a key part of juvenile court. In fact,

> **Probation officer:** Employee of probation agency, responsible for supervision of convicted offenders who have been released to the community under certain conditions of good behavior.

probation in adult court traces its heritage to these developments. Juvenile probation takes several forms. In some states probation officers are part of the judicial branch (either locally or statewide); in other jurisdictions they are part of the executive branch (either locally or statewide) (Rubin 1989).

Similar to adult court, probation officers in juvenile court conduct background reports and supervise those placed on probation. What is strikingly different, though, is the stage at which they become involved. In adult courts, probation officers are brought into the process after the defendant has entered a plea of guilty or been found guilty. In juvenile courts, they become involved from the early stages of the process on. Thus, the probation officer, not a judge or prosecutor, is often the first court official to have contact with the child. Indeed, it is often the probation officer who recommends an informal disposition to the case. Moreover, in more serious cases, the probation officer's recommendation, along with the social worker's, most often becomes the order of the court.

 The Florida Department of Juvenile Justice includes information on prevention and delinquency trends, community-based efforts, innovative sanctions, treatment, and getting involved on its Web site: **http://www.djj.state.fl.us/**.

The Virginia Department of Juvenile Justice develops policies, programs, and institutions to assist the courts in holding juveniles accountable for their actions and affording them opportunities for reform: **http://www.dcjs.state.va.us/juvenile/index.htm**.

For an up-to-date list of Web links, go to **http://www.wadsworth.com/product/0534563406s**.

STEPS OF THE JUVENILE COURT PROCESS

From the perspective of law on the books, the steps of the juvenile court process resemble those for adult courts. Although the terminology is slightly different, juveniles accused of violating the law appear to be treated the same as adults in the same situation (see Figure 19-4).

From the perspective of law in action, however, the steps of the juvenile court process are strikingly different from their adult counterparts. More than

merely differences in terminology, what makes the processing of juveniles so distinctive is the heavy emphasis on informal decision making. The vast majority of decisions are reached not by lawyers and defendants standing before a judge in open court but rather by a juvenile, a parent, and a probation officer sitting around a desk discussing what will happen next.

Delinquency (Crime)

How many crimes are committed by juveniles (as opposed to adults) is impossible to determine with any great precision. As discussed in Chapter 10, the FBI's *Uniform Crime Reports* are based on crimes reported to the police, and most crime victims have no way of knowing the age of the person responsible. Nonetheless, there was a steady increase of juvenile crime beginning in 1985, but this increase declined dramatically after 1995. Two important features related to juvenile crime are worth noting:

- Crimes against juveniles are less likely to be reported to the police.
- Juveniles are twice as likely as adults to be victims of serious violent crime and three times as likely to be victims of assault (Snyder and Sickmund 2000).

Summons (Arrest)

A **summons** is a legal document requiring an individual (in this case a juvenile) to appear in court at a certain time and on a certain date. Although the summons is the official term used in juvenile court, it is informally referred to as an arrest. Last year, law enforcement agencies in the United States made an estimated 2.5 million arrests of persons under eighteen. Overall juveniles were involved in 16 percent of all violent crime index arrests and 32 percent of all property crime index arrests. There are two noteworthy features of juvenile arrest statistics:

- One in four juvenile arrests were of females, and the female proportion of arrests has grown in recent years.
- Juvenile arrests disproportionately involve minorities.

Summons: A legal document ordering an individual to appear in court at a certain time on a certain date.

"Few Options or Safeguards in a City's Juvenile Courts"

 Clarence Richardson, the public defender appointed to represent a 12-year-old boy charged with driving a stolen car, met his client for the first time only a few minutes before the trial began. They talked in the packed waiting area outside the courtroom because Mr. Richardson, like other public defenders here, has no office. Nor does he have a file cabinet, a telephone to contact defendants, or a clerk or secretary to help him draw up motions or conduct investigations.

As Judge Lawrence Lagarde Jr. recited the evidence against his client and swiftly pronounced a two-year sentence in juvenile prison, Mr. Richardson sat largely silent. His defense table was conspicuously bare: no case files, law books, or even the police report on the defendant, to use to challenge the prosecutor.

Welcome to the Orleans Parish Juvenile Court, considered by many lawyers and children's rights advocates to be the most troubled juvenile court system in the country. Juvenile courts nationwide are in crisis, with the public and elected officials denouncing them as overwhelmed and ineffective, a revolving door for young predators. Congress, in fact, may soon pass legislation that would weaken the role of the juvenile courts by pushing large numbers of young people into the adult criminal system. But even as critics clamor for tougher laws dealing with crime by juveniles, an examination of the New Orleans juvenile court reveals another problem with the current system: a lack of constitutional protections like the right to adequate legal representation and due process for young people, an overwhelming majority of whom are poor and black.

In the tradition-bound world of New Orleans, public defenders are expected to play a subservient role, and prosecutors routinely rack up by far the highest conviction rate of any big-city juvenile court in the country. Some young defendants remain in detention centers for up to eight months, without coming to trial,

much longer than the 10- to 30-day limits imposed by most state laws. . . .

But even the judges here are concerned about the system. "The juvenile court is the stepchild of the criminal justice system," said Ernestine Gray, the administrative judge of the New Orleans juvenile court, "and everything about how this court works suggests this is not a place that believes in innocent till proven guilty."

There are about a half-dozen public defenders, one for each courtroom, to handle the 2,200 delinquency cases brought here each year. Others who have worked in the New Orleans court were even blunter than Judge Gray. "It's medieval," said Anne Turissini, who spent five years as a public defender in juvenile court here until she gave up in disgust and moved to a similar job in suburban Jefferson Parish. Her salary, Ms. Turissini said, was $18,000 a year, and with more than 100 cases at a time each, she and her colleagues were "overworked, underpaid, burned out, and demoralized." "You are supposed to go along and get along with your judge," Ms. Turissini said, "and if you object too often in court, they will have you fired."

"All this has an effect on the kids, because they can sense the court is not serious, so they don't take it seriously," she added. "It is absolutely the worst situation, because these are kids with no self-esteem anyway, with parents and teachers telling them they have no value, which is why they shoot people for sneakers."

The ineffectiveness of the public defender system for juveniles here is forcing more and more poor young people to spend unnecessarily long periods in the city's youth detention centers before they are brought to trial or even charged, said James Bell, a lawyer with the Youth Law Center, an advocacy group for children, in San Francisco.

SOURCE: Fox Butterfield, "Few Options or Safeguards in a City's Juvenile Courts," *New York Times,* July 22, 1997.

Intake (Initial Hearing)

Delinquency cases begin with a **referral.** Arrests by law enforcement personnel are by far the biggest

> **Referral:** A request by a law enforcement agency, governmental agency, parent, or individual that a juvenile court take jurisdiction of a youth. A referral initiates court processing.

source of these referrals—85 percent in a typical year. Referrals, though, may originate from several other sources; for example, some juvenile court cases stem from petitions filed by teachers, neighbors, merchants, or even parents unable to control their children. But mainly they follow after a juvenile has been arrested by the police.

These arrests and other referrals produce 1.75 million juvenile court delinquency cases every year. Best estimates indicate that 61 percent of juvenile

| FIGURE 19-4 | Steps of the Juvenile Court Process |

Law on the Books		*Law in Action*
Adult	**Juvenile**	
Crime	*Delinquency* Acts or conduct in violation of criminal laws.	• Juveniles are more likely than adults to be victims of violent crime.
	Status offense Behavior that is considered an offense only when committed by a juvenile.	• Poor young minority males are disproportionately at risk of being victims of violent crime.
Arrest	*Summons* A legal document ordering an individual to appear in court at a certain time on a certain date.	• There are 2.9 million juveniles arrested yearly. • Juveniles are arrested primarily for property offenses.
Initial appearance	*Initial hearing* An often informal hearing during which an intake decision is made.	• There are 1.9 million juvenile cases a year. • Sixty-five percent of juvenile filings involve delinquency.
Bail	*Detention* Holding a youth in custody before case disposition.	There are 100,000 offenders in public and private juvenile detention facilities.
Charging	*Intake decision* The decision made by juvenile court that results in either the case being handled informally at the intake level or more formally and scheduled for an adjudicatory hearing.	• Intake decisions are often informal. • Courtroom work group norms govern decision making.
	Nonpetitioned Cases handled informally by duly authorized court personnel.	• Forty-five percent of juvenile delinquency cases are handled informally (nonpetitioned).
	Petition A document filed in juvenile court alleging that a juvenile is a delinquent or a status offender and asking that the court assume jurisdiction over the juvenile.	• Fifty-five percent of juvenile delinquency cases are handled formally. • Older juveniles with more serious charges are more likely to be handled formally.
Preliminary hearing	*Conference* Proceeding during which the suspect is informed of rights and a disposition decision may be reached.	In the vast majority of petitioned cases, the juvenile admits guilt during the conference.

filings involve delinquency, with the remainder evenly split between status offenses and child-victim.

Juvenile court cases continue to grow. From 1988 to 1997 the total number of filings increased 48 percent. Similar to domestic relations caseloads, juvenile court filings have increased much more rapidly than criminal and civil caseloads (Ostrom and Kauder 1996).

Soon after referral to juvenile court, an **initial hearing** (sometimes called a preliminary inquiry)

is held. As with much of the terminology of juvenile court, *hearing* is often a misnomer. A hearing implies a formal setting in front of a judge, but more typically it is an informal exchange between the police officer, probation officer, child, and parent.

>
>
> For the latest facts and figures about juveniles and crime, go to the Statistical Briefing Book of the Office of Juvenile Justice and Delinquency at **http://ojjdp.ncjrs.org/ojstatbb/index.html**.
>
> For an up-to-date list of Web links, go to **http://www.wadsworth.com/product/0534563406s**.

Initial hearing: In juvenile court, an often informal hearing during which an intake decision is made.

	Law on the Books		Law in Action
	Adult	Juvenile	
Grand jury		Not applicable.	One percent (12,300) of juvenile cases are transferred to adult court.
Arraignment		Occurs during the conference.	Fifty-five percent of juvenile delinquency cases are handled formally (petitioned).
Evidence		Juveniles have the same constitutional protections as adults involving unreasonable search and seizure, and interrogation.	Police gathering of evidence is very rarely contested.
Plea bargaining		*Plea bargaining* Formal and informal discussions resulting in juvenile admitting guilt.	Even more so than adult court, dispositions in juvenile court are the product of negotiations.
Trial		*Adjudicatory hearing* Hearing to determine whether a youth is guilty or not guilty.	Adjudicatory hearings are more informal than adult trials.
Sentencing		*Disposition* A court decision on what will happen to a youth who has not been found innocent.	Dispositions are often referred to as a treatment plan.
		Placement Cases in which youth are placed in a residential facility or otherwise removed from their homes.	Over 150,000 juveniles are placed in residential facilities each year.
		Probation Cases in which youths are placed on informal/voluntary or formal/court-ordered supervision.	Over 500,000 youths each year receive court supervision.
		Dismissal Cases dismissed (including those warned, counseled, and released) with no further disposition anticipated.	Even case dismissals may include a treatment plan or restitution.
		Other Miscellaneous dispositions including fines, restitution, community service.	Teen courts are a modern version of other dispositions.
Appeal		*Appeal* Request that a higher court review the decision of the lower court.	Appeals are very rare in juvenile proceedings.

Detention Hearing

Police make the first **detention** decision shortly after taking the juvenile into custody. Typically the police release the youth to the custody of his or her parents (or guardians). If the crime is serious, however, the police may detain the youth in a police lockup or local jail. In an earlier era, juveniles were held in the same facilities as adult offenders, but no longer. Federal law mandates that juveniles be held in facilities separated by sight and sound from detention facilities for adults. In many communities the number of cells is limited, so even serious violators may be returned to the streets.

A second detention decision may occur after the juvenile has been referred to the juvenile court. Intake personnel review the case and determine whether the youth should be released to parents or detained. Juveniles may be detained if they are thought dangerous to themselves or others if released. Statutes in most states now mandate that, if the juvenile is to be detained, a detention hearing must be held before a judge or other hearing officer within twenty-four to seventy-two hours of arrest.

In a typical year, one out of five juveniles (333,000) are detained prior to the adjudicatory

Detention: Holding a youth in custody before case disposition.

hearing. On any given day 100,000 youths are held in public and private juvenile detention facilities (Perkins, Stephan, and Beck 1995).

Petition

During the initial hearing a decision is made not only about detention but also whether the case will be handled formally (petition) or informally (non-petitioned). This decision is most often referred to as the **intake decision** (the juvenile equivalent of the charging decision for adults accused of violating the criminal law).

As Figure 19-5 shows, 43 percent of delinquency cases are handled informally (termed **non-petitioned**). An informal process is used when the decision makers (police, probation officers, intake workers, and prosecutors) believe that accountability and rehabilitation can be achieved without the use of formal court intervention. Informal sanctions are voluntary. At times they involve no more than a warning and counseling, but more often they consist of voluntary probation, restitution, and community service.

Juvenile cases that are handled formally are referred to as **petition** cases (or petitioned). Figure 19-5 indicates that 57 percent of cases each year receive such treatment. Intake officers are more likely to petition if

- Juveniles are older and have longer court histories.
- The delinquency is serious (involves violence, for example).

Fifty-eight percent of all formally processed delinquency cases result in a finding of delinquency. The sanction may be probation, with the juvenile

released into the custody of a parent or guardian and ordered to undergo some form of training, education, or counseling. But in 28 percent of adjudicated cases the juvenile is ordered by the court to residential placement, such as training school, camp, ranch, or group home. Every year about 100,000 juveniles are committed to long-term facilities (training schools primarily).

Conference

The **conference** is roughly equivalent to a preliminary hearing in an adult proceeding. The more minor the transgression, the more likely the conference will be held at the same time as the initial hearing and the detention hearing. In more serious matters, particularly if the decision has been made to file a petition, the more likely the conference will be held in closed court.

During the conference the judge informs the respondent of the charges in the petition. The person is also informed of constitutional protections, including the right to counsel, right to free counsel, right to subpoena witnesses for the defense, and the opportunity to cross-examine prosecution witnesses.

Vast numbers of juveniles admit to their offense during the conference, waiving the right to counsel and the right to trial. Others request counsel, adjourn to the hallway of the courthouse, and after five or ten minutes with an attorney, come back before the judge and admit their offense (Rubin 1989).

Evidence: Gathering and Suppressing

Challenges to how the police gathered evidence play a very minor role in juvenile cases. The presumption is that the child is in trouble (with the juvenile delinquency charge an indicator of that trouble). This presumption makes it difficult to challenge evidence gathering—the judge might conclude that there is insufficient evidence to find the child a delinquent, but still enough to conclude that the child is in need

Intake decision: The decision made by juvenile court that results in the case either being handled informally at the intake level or more formally by petition and scheduled for an adjudicatory or transfer hearing.

Nonpetitioned case: A case handled informally by duly authorized court personnel.

Petition: A document filed in juvenile court alleging that a juvenile is a delinquent or a status offender and asking that the court assume jurisdiction over the juvenile or that an alleged delinquent be transferred to criminal court for prosecution as an adult.

Conference: Juvenile court proceeding roughly equivalent to a preliminary hearing, in which the suspect is informed of his or her rights and a disposition decision may be reached.

FIGURE 19-5   Juvenile Court Processing of Delinquency Cases (1997 National Estimates)

Note: Detail may not add to totals because of rounding.

SOURCE: Charles Puzzanchera, Anne Stahl, Terrence Finnegan, Howard Snyder, Rowen Poole, and Nancy Tierney. *Juvenile Courts Statistics 1997* (Washington, D.C.: U.S. Department of Justice, Office of Juvenile Justice and Delinquency Prevention, 2000).

of supervision. Moreover, the informal nature of the entire proceedings discourages legal challenges. The general absence of defense attorneys likewise discourages raising issues associated with *Mapp* and *Miranda*.

Plea Bargaining

The informality of juvenile court makes it somewhat difficult to focus on plea bargaining as a distinct phase, because often it is not. Rather, the discretion that runs throughout the juvenile court process is really plea bargaining by a different name (Dougherty 1988).

Efforts to negotiate the matter typically begin during the intake process. Parent, child, and probation officer discuss the matter and often arrive at a solution satisfactory to all parties. Thus, the 43 percent of juvenile delinquency cases that are nonpetitioned clearly represent what in adult court would be labeled plea bargaining.

Efforts to negotiate a settlement continue after a petition is filed. As Figure 19-5 underscores, 41 percent of petitioned cases are in the "nonadjudicated" category. As we shall discuss shortly, even the adjudicatory hearing resembles an informal exchange of settlement possibilities more than a formal, combative trial.

Adjudicatory Hearing

The **adjudicatory hearing** is equivalent to the trial in adult court. The purpose is to determine whether the allegations contained in the petition are supported by a "preponderance of the evidence" (for status offenses) or "beyond a legal doubt" (for juvenile delinquency).

One of the key changes growing out of the due process revolution associated with *In re Gault* is that juveniles have the right to present evidence in favor, which includes cross-examining the government's witnesses and subpoenaing defense witnesses. The juvenile also maintains the privilege against self-incrimination.

Statistics provided by the Office of Juvenile Justice and Delinquency Prevention indicate that 58 percent of petitioned cases are **adjudicated.** This seems like a high "trial" rate, but a closer look indicates that this is not the case. Adjudicatory hearings are much less formal than adult trials. This is due in part to the lack of juries (except in a few exceptional cases in a handful of states). The rules of evidence (Chapter 14) are designed to keep certain information from lay jurors lest they place undue emphasis on some information. But since there are no juries, these rules have considerably less applicability.

Disposition

The more serious the crime and/or the longer the juvenile has been in trouble with the law, the more likely a formal probation report will be prepared. Like its adult counterpart, the probation report (sometimes called the predisposition report) is prepared by the probation officer and based on interviews with the juvenile, the parents, school officials, and others. The report chronicles the juvenile's prior history with the court and also may estimate the economic harm suffered by the victim. Finally, the report makes a **disposition** recommendation.

Adjudicatory hearing: Court hearing to determine whether a youth is guilty or not guilty.

Adjudicated: Judicial determination (judgment) that a youth is a delinquent or status offender.

Disposition: A court decision on what will happen to a youth who has not been found innocent.

The most common disposition is a **dismissal.** Cases dismissed (including those warned, counseled, and released), with no further disposition anticipated, are most likely to occur among cases that are handled informally.

The second most common disposition is **probation.** Probation cases are those in which youths were placed on informal/voluntary or formal/court-ordered supervision.

Another common disposition is **placement.** Placement cases are those in which youth are placed in a residential facility for delinquents or status offenders or cases in which youths are otherwise removed from their homes and placed elsewhere. Consistent with the nonpunishment orientation of the juvenile process, juveniles are not sentenced to prison but rather are placed in residential treatment facilities called training institutes and the like.

Finally, a significant number of dispositions that do not fall under the previous three categories are referred to simply as **other dispositions.** These include fines, restitution, community service, and referrals outside the court for services with minimal or no further court involvement anticipated.

In making disposition decisions juvenile court judges focus primarily on offense characteristics and are influenced only marginally by the offender's social characteristics. These findings are more consistent with the view that juvenile courts are becoming more like adult criminal courts than with the view that individualized justice is the goal (Appelgate et al. 2000).

Juvenile courts in urban areas tend to send proportionally fewer delinquents to state detention facilities than do courts serving less populous areas (Rubin 1989). Officials in rural areas are sometimes

Dismissal: Cases are terminated (including those warned, counseled, and released) with no further disposition anticipated.

Probation: Punishment for a crime that allows the offender to remain in the community without incarceration but subject to certain conditions.

Placement: Cases in which youths are placed in a residential facility or otherwise removed from their homes and placed elsewhere.

Other dispositions: Miscellaneous dispositions, including fines, restitution, community service, referrals outside the court for services with minimal or no further court involvement anticipated.

quicker to "pull the string" and send less serious delinquency cases to state placement, partially because they have fewer institutional resources to deal with these youths but also because the equivalent event is viewed as more harmful in small towns than in big cities.

 For a look at juvenile detention centers, click on any of the following:

> Southwest Idaho: **http://www.canyoncounty.org/ juvdet/swijdc.htm**
>
> Oklahoma City: **http://www.oklahomacounty.org/ jjc/OCJDC.html**
>
> Rankin County (Mississippi): **http://rankincounty. org/SO/RCSOJDC.htm**
>
> Fairfax County (Virginia): **http://www.co.fairfax.va. us/courts/jdr/jdc/Geninfo.htm**
>
> Northwestern Louisiana: **http://www.ghpc.org/ cases/cs0062.htm**
>
> For an up-to-date list of Web links, go to **http:// www.wadsworth.com/product/0534563406s.**

Appeal

Juveniles have a constitutional right to appeal. The opinion in *Gault* discussed the importance of appeals for due process rights but declined to make it a constitutional requirement. Prompted, however, by the possibility that the Supreme Court might indeed make it a constitutional right, state legislatures have passed laws granting juveniles the right to appeal. Thus, today the common practice is to give juveniles the same rights to appeal that apply to adults (Davis 1984). By statute, juveniles also have the right to a transcript and a right to counsel for the first appeal.

The right to appeal is primarily limited to juveniles (and their parents). The state may appeal only in limited circumstances, and this right is seldom activated.

JUVENILE COURTS: THE NEXT 100 YEARS

Juvenile courts, which were once virtually invisible judicial bodies, have in recent years become the central focus in the debate over crime. The war on crime, Chapter 1 argued, is constantly evolving, and as the twenty-first century begins, there are pressures to change the nature of juvenile court justice. A century after the founding of juvenile courts by the Progressive movement, it is appropriate to ask, what will juvenile courts be like 100 years from now? Indeed, some critics argue that this grand experiment has been a failure and should be scrapped.

The debate over the future reflects basic disagreements along the lines of the crime control versus due process models.

Crime Control Model: More Adult Penalties

The crime control model begins with the premise that crime is the product of moral breakdown. This is clearly the theme sounded by Darlene Kennedy (1997) of the National Center for Public Policy Research. "Let's hold juveniles responsible for their crimes," she argues, blaming undue leniency of juvenile court for violent juvenile crimes.

One version of more adult penalties for juvenile offenders involves increasing the number of transfers to adult court. Other proposals include merging adult and juvenile records into one. Argues Marvin Wolfgang: "The dual system of juvenile and criminal

 For contrasting views on juvenile court reform, go to:

> Illinois Juvenile Court Improvement Project Assessment: **http://www.chapin.uchicago.edu/ ProjectsGuide/JuvenileCourt.html**
>
> Amnesty International: **http://www.amnesty-usa. org/** (search for "Juvenile")
>
> Familycourt.com: **http://www.familycourts.com/**
>
> The Coalition for Family Court Reform: **http:// courtreform.hypermart.net/**
>
> ACLU Fact Sheet on the Juvenile Justice System: **http://aclu.org/library/fctsht.html**
>
> For an up-to-date list of Web links, go to **http:// www.wadsworth.com/product/0534563406s.**

 "Comprehensive Juvenile Justice: A Legislator's Guide"

Dan Johnson, "Rehabilitating Criminals Before They Grow Up"

"Juveniles Facing Criminal Sanctions: Three States That Changed the Rules"

A DAY IN COURT

Teen Court

Serving as a juror for the Holland Teen Court has its perks—sometimes after the teen jurors have finished a case the police department kicks in and buys a pizza. Founded in 1991, the Holland Teen Court assigns a punishment appropriate to the defendant's attitude and crime. For level one violations (curfew infractions and cigarette possession, for example) the usual penalty is eight to twelve hours of community service. For level two violations (shoplifting and disorderly conduct, for example) the typical penalty is thirteen to twenty-four hours of community service (Sager 2000).

The Holland Teen Court is but one example of how local government officials are experimenting with a variety of new approaches to juvenile offenders. Teen courts, or youth courts, as they are sometimes called, have been established in over 650 local jurisdictions nationwide as an alternative to traditional juvenile courts. The programs target juvenile first offenders accused of committing minor crimes. Teen court is designed not only to give these first offenders a second chance but also to provide an educational experience to the offender and to its other volunteer participants. The ultimate goal is to increase participants' self-esteem and instill respect for the legal system (Official Teen Court Homepage 1998).

Teen court has also been referred to as peer court. This is most appropriate, considering that teenagers assume the roles of prosecuting and defense attorneys, jury members, and even judge in some jurisdictions. The young officers of the court are volunteers who are trained and supervised by professional volunteers. The structure of teen court varies by jurisdictions. The jury panel usually includes a combination of volunteers from the community, along with former teen court defendants for whom jury duty is part of the punishment for their offense (Zehner 1997).

Most teen court juries do not deliberate the guilt or innocence of a defendant. A prerequisite of being accepted into the program is an admission of guilt by the defendant. Instead, the jury decides the nature of the offender's noninstitutionalized punishment based on preestablished guidelines. The focus of the sentence is on rehabilitation. In addition to jury duty, offenders may be ordered to pay restitution and formally apologize to victims, perform community service, obtain counseling, attend educational seminars, or participate in any other activities the jury finds warranted by the facts of the individual case (Shiff and Wexler 1996).

What is responsible for the growing popularity of teen court programs nationwide is their apparent success in controlling teenage criminal recidivism. In 1995 the Bend, Oregon, teen court reported statistics indicating that 95 percent of its teen participants avoided being rearrested in the first ten years of the court's existence (Oregon Peer 1998). Other jurisdictions report similar success rates. But experts are concerned over the lack of rigorous and comprehensive research evaluations of the effectiveness of teen courts in the prevention of teenage criminal recidivism. It is entirely possible that the statistics look so good because only juveniles viewed as "good risks" are initially selected for the programs.

To view firsthand what teen courts do, click on any of these sites:

Holland Teen Court (Michigan): **http://www.teen-court.org/**

Charlotte County (Florida): **http://www.charlotte-florida.com/community/teen.htm**

Knox County (Illinois): **http://library.thinkquest.org/2640/**

Irving (Texas): **http://www.ci.irving.tx.us/Courts/welcomet.htm**

For an up-to-date list of Web links, go to **http://www.wadsworth.com/product/0534563406s**.

justice that prevents the sharing of information and permits a serious, chronic violent juvenile to become a virgin offender after his 19th birthday is a strange cultural invention" (quoted in Bureau of Justice Statistics 1990, 18).

Some go so far as to argue that it is time to abolish juvenile court altogether. Peter Reinharz, chief of New York City's juvenile prosecution unit argues, "It's time to sell everything off and start over" (quoted in Butterfield 1997). Chronic overcrowding is one problem often mentioned, but it is unclear how merely shuffling the overcrowding problems of juvenile facilities to already overcrowded adult courts and adult prisons will alleviate the problem.

In short, a sharp increase in the public's fear of juvenile crime, particularly gangs, drugs, and violence, has added impetus to a get-tough attitude toward juvenile criminals.

Due Process Model: More Youth Crime Prevention

The due process model starts with the premise that crime is a reflection of social problems. Punishment alone therefore is not necessarily the answer and might even be counterproductive. Placing juveniles in the same prisons as adults, for example, might simply make the youths more hardened and more accomplished crooks.

Amidst numerous voices arguing that the juvenile court created 100 years ago is now outmoded, some respond that the nation should return to those roots. The Progressive movement was concerned about mistreatment of juveniles at the turn of the last century, and we should have the same concern today, argues the American Civil Liberties Union (1996) in a policy statement about "Whatever happened to prevention?"

The core of the argument is that crime prevention works. Instead of pouring increasing amounts of public dollars into prisons (both adult and juvenile), we need to put more into education and prevention. Perhaps what is most needed are programs that work with youth in new and creative ways. Teen Court is but one example (see A Day in Court: Teen Court).

CONCLUSION

The charge against Gerald Gault—making a lewd telephone call—seems tame compared with today's concerns about preteens committing violent crimes. Nonetheless, this irritating but hardly life-threatening behavior was to usher in a new era. Whereas the Progressives saw procedural rights as an impediment to helping children in need, a later generation viewed due process as providing an important safety net against high-handed behavior by government officials.

Court decisions like *In re Gault* and changing patterns of youthful behavior—to say nothing of the types of crimes committed by youths today—could not have been foreseen by the Progressive movement. Whether the founders of juvenile court would recognize their innovation 100 years later is debatable. Initially juvenile court was supposed to make decisions based on the "best interests" of the child. Today, a get-tough attitude has come to dominate discussions of juvenile court. Holding the youth accountable to community standards now plays a major role in dispositions reached (Sanborn 1994).

The future of juvenile courts is rapidly unfolding. To some observers, juvenile courts need to provide more adultlike due process. To others, juvenile courts need to provide more adultlike sentences. Still others would stress the need for new and creative ways of dealing with contemporary problems of America's youth. The Progressive movement, after all, responded to changing conditions in society produced by the Industrial Revolution. To many, the current challenge is to respond to the changing conditions of society produced by the information age.

CRITICAL THINKING QUESTIONS

1. In what ways do juvenile courts differ from courts that process adults accused of violating the criminal law? In what ways are juvenile courts similar?

2. What are the key features of the juvenile courts in your state? How are they organized, what is the upper age limit, and what is the lower age limit?

3. What advantages do you see in adding due process rights to juvenile court? What disadvantages do you see? To what extent are discussions over this matter influenced by atypical cases?

4. Compare the courtroom work group of adult court and juvenile court. What actors are the same? What actors are different? Do the members of the courtroom work group function the same in juvenile court as in adult court?

5. Compare the steps of the adult court process with the steps of juvenile court. In what ways are they similar? In what ways are they different?

6. What do you think juvenile courts will look like 100 years from now? Will they incorporate more adult due process? Will they stress more adult penalties? Or will they develop more innovative helping programs?

 WORLD WIDE WEB RESOURCES AND EXERCISES

Web Guides

http://dir.yahoo.com/Society_and_Culture/Crime/Juvenile/

http://dir.yahoo.com/Society_and_Culture/Crime/Correction_and_Rehabilitation/Juvenile_Detention_Centers/

http://dir.yahoo.com/Society_and_Culture/Crime/Juvenile/Teen_Court/

Web Search Terms

"Juvenile courts"; "teen courts"; "juvenile justice"

Useful URLs

The American Bar Association Juvenile Justice Center works in partnership with other ABA entities, bar associations, and local and state advocacy groups to monitor and influence juvenile justice policy and practice: **http://www.abanet.org/crimjust/juvjus/home.html.**

The Center for Community Alternatives provides services, training, and technical assistance to professionals in the criminal and juvenile justice systems: **http://www.communityalternatives.org/.**

The National Center for Juvenile Justice is the leading source of statistics on juvenile delinquency and the operation of juvenile and family courts: **http://www.ncjj.org/.**

The U.S. Department of Justice, Office of Juvenile Justice and Delinquency Prevention, is charged with leading the fight against juvenile violence and victimization, and promoting practical solutions to the problems challenging the nation's juveniles: **http://ojjdp.ncjrs.org/.**

Visit the National Council of Juvenile and Family Court Judges: **http://www.ncjfcj.unr.edu/.**

Visit the National Juvenile Detention Association: **http://www.njda.com/.**

Uncommon URLs

Building Blocks for Youth is an advocacy group particularly concerned about racial disparities: **http://www.buildingblocksforyouth.org/.**

Juvenile Justice is an online magazine serving juvenile justice professionals in all fifty states involved in youth and human services, law enforcement, probation, and parole: **http://www.juvenilejustice.com/.**

For a close-up view of juvenile court visit Criminon Program in Los Angeles Central Juvenile Hall: **http://www.criminon.org/html/juvenile.htm.**

New Jersey Juvenile Detention Association offers a model Web page: **http://www.njjda.org/.**

Cook County Juvenile Detention Center 4-H and Urban Gardening stresses innovative programs: **http://www.urbanext.uiuc.edu/ptw/03cookjdc.html.**

Web Exercises

1. Update statistics on the number of juvenile arrests and the number of juveniles in placement facilities, using the National Criminal Justice Reference Center homepage, **http://www. ncjrs.org.** Look under "Juvenile Justice" to find the latest government reports.

2. Do a search for homepages dealing with teen courts. Here is an example of how to do the search: Yahoo.com, Society_and_Culture/Crime/Juvenile/Teen Court. Select one homepage that is geographically close to you and another one more distant. In what ways are the programs similar? In what ways are they different? What goals do these programs articulate? What claims do they make for success? Which program would you recommend to your local court? Why?

   If you wish, also use a search engine like Alta Vista.

3. Policies affecting juvenile courts are under intense scrutiny. The American Bar Association's Juvenile Justice Center provides a quick overview of changing legislation. The URL is **http://www.abanet.org/crimjust/juvjus.**

   Click on "Hill Watch" to monitor the progress of pending national legislation. Also click on "State Watch." What current proposals are under consideration in your state?

4. Choose the search engine of your choice and using the search term "*juvenile court*" + "*reform*," choose two or more sites. Are the proposed reforms more representative of the crime control model or the due process model?

INFOTRAC COLLEGE EDITION RESOURCES AND EXERCISES

Basic Searches

Juvenile courts; juvenile justice, administration of; teen courts; juvenile probation; In re Gault

Recommended Articles

Jennifer L. Reichert, "Judges' Group Releases Guidelines for Protecting Victims of Family Violence"

Jerry E. Tyler, Thomas W. Segady, "Parental Liability Laws: Rationale, Theory, and Effectiveness"

Judge David B. Mitchell, "Congress Needs to Consult Profession before Enacting Juvenile Justice Reform"

Sharon Mihalic, "Blueprints for Violence Prevention"

InfoTrac College Edition Exercises

1. Using the search term *juvenile courts, waiver of jurisdiction of,* find two or more articles that discuss the topic. What factors influence decisions to transfer some juvenile offenders to adult court? Are juveniles transferred to adult court sanctioned more severely compared to the punishment they would have received in juvenile court?

2. Using the search term *juvenile courts* or *juvenile justice, administration of,* find two or more articles that discuss juvenile court reform. Analyze the articles. Are the recommendations more consistent with the crime control or the due process model of criminal justice?

REFERENCES

American Civil Liberties Union. 1996. "ACLU Fact Sheet on Juvenile Crime." http://www.aclu.org/congress/juvenile.htm.

Appelgate, Brandon, Michael Turner, Joseph Sanborn, Edward Latessa, and Melissa Moon. 2000. "Individualization, Criminalization, or Problem Resolution: A Factorial Survey of Juvenile Court Judges' Decisions to Incarcerate Youthful Felony Offenders." *Justice Quarterly* 17: 309–332.

Bass, Alison. 1995. "Youth Violence Explosion Likely to Worsen." *Times-Picayune*, 2 July, A-14.

Bazemore, Gordon. 1994. "Understanding the Response to Reforms Limiting Discretion: Judges' Views of Restrictions on Detention Intake." *Justice Quarterly* 11: 429–452.

Bazemore, Gordon, and Lynette Feder. 1997. "Judges in the Punitive Juvenile Court: Organizational, Career and Ideological Influences on Sanctioning Orientation." *Justice Quarterly* 14: 87–114.

Building Blocks for Youth. 2000. *Youth Crime/Adult Time: Is Justice Served?* http://www.buildingblocksforyouth. org/.

Bureau of Justice Statistics. 1990. *Juvenile and Adult Records: One System, One Record?* Washington: D.C.: Author.

Butterfield, Fox. 1997. "Justice Besieged: With Juvenile Courts in Chaos, Critics Propose Their Demise." *The New York Times,* 21 July.

Cannon, Angie. 1997. "Violent Teen Crime Rate Drops Two Years in a Row." *Times-Picayune,* 3 October.

Corley, Charles, Timothy Bynum, and Madeline Wordes. 1995. "Conceptions of Family and Juvenile Court Process: A Qualitative Assessment." *Justice System Journal* 18: 157–172.

Davis, Samuel. 1984. *Rights of Juveniles.* 2d ed. New York: Clark Boardman.

DeFrances, Carol, and Kevin Strom. 1997. "Juveniles Prosecuted in State Criminal Courts." Washington, D.C.: Bureau of Justice Statistics.

Dougherty, Joyce. 1988. "Negotiating Justice in the Juvenile Justice System: A Comparison of Adult Plea Bargaining and Juvenile Intake." *Federal Probation* 52: 72–80.

Feld, Barry. 1988. "*In re Gault* Revisited: A Cross-State Comparison of the Right to Counsel in Juvenile Court." *Crime and Delinquency* 34: 379–392.

Grisso, Thomas. 1981. *Juveniles' Waiver of Rights.* New York: Plenum.

Hallinan, Joe. 1993. "Violent Children Straining Limit of Justice System." *Times-Picayune,* 31 October, A-24.

Holden, Gwen, and Robert Kapler. 1995. "Deinstitutionalizing Status Offenders: A Record of Progress." *Juvenile Justice* 2 (Fall/Winter): 3–10.

Johnson, James, and Philip Secret. 1995. "The Effects of Court Structure on Juvenile Court Decisonmaking." *Journal of Criminal Justice* 23: 63–82.

Johnson, Kevin, and Gary Fields. 1996. "Juvenile Crime 'Wave' May Be Just a Ripple." *USA Today,* 13 December, 3.

Kennedy, Darlene. 1997. "Let's Hold Juveniles Responsible for Their Crimes." The National Center for Public Policy Research. http://www.nationalcenter.inter.net/NPA166.html.

Krisberg, Barry, and James Austin. 1993. *Reinventing Juvenile Justice.* Newbury Park, CA: Sage.

Manfredi, Christopher. 1998. *The Supreme Court and Juvenile Justice.* Lawrence: University Press of Kansas.

Matza, David. 1964. *Delinquency and Drift.* New York: John Wiley & Sons.

Office of Juvenile Justice and Delinquency Prevention. 1996. "Female Offenders in the Juvenile Justice System." Washington, D.C.: U.S. Department of Justice.

Official Teen Court Homepage. 1998. http://library. advanced.org/264.

Oregon Peer. 1998. (Teen) Court Pages. http://www. ncn.com/~snews/peerct/open.htm.

Ostrom, Brian, and Neal Kauder. 1996. *Examining the Work of State Courts, 1995.* Williamsburg, VA: National Center for State Courts.

Perkins, Craig, James Stephan, and Allen Beck. 1995. *Jail and Jail Inmates 1993–1994.* Washington D.C.: Bureau of Justice Statistics.

Platt, Anthony. 1969. *The Child Savers: The Invention of Delinquency.* Chicago: University of Chicago Press.

Puritz, Patricia, S. Burrell, R. Schwartz, M. Soler, and L. Warboys. 1995. *A Call for Justice: An Assessment of Access to Counsel and Quality of Representation in Delinquency Proceedings.* Washington, D.C.: American Bar Association.

Puritz, Patricia, and Wendy Wan Long Shang. 1998. *Innovative Approaches to Juvenile Indigent Defense.* Washington, D.C.: Office of Juvenile Justice and Delinquency Prevention.

Puzzanchera, Charles, Anne Stahl, Terrence Finnegan, Howard Snyder, Rowen Poole, and Nancy Tierney. 2000. *Juvenile Courts Statistics 1997.* Washington, D.C.: U.S. Department of Justice, Office of Juvenile Justice and Delinquency Prevention.

Rubin, H. Ted. 1984. *The Courts: Fulcrum of the Justice System.* New York: Random House.

———. 1989. "The Juvenile Court Landscape." In *Juvenile Justice: Policies, Programs and Services,* edited by Albert Roberts. Chicago: Richard Irwin.

Sager, Jackie. 2000. "Teen Court Offers Disciplinary Alternatives for Youth." *Holland Sentinel,* 11 August.

Sanborn, Joseph. 1993. "The Right to a Public Jury Trial: A Need for Today's Juvenile Court." *Judicature* 76: 230–238.

———. 1994. "The Juvenile, the Court, or the Community: Whose Best Interests Are Currently Being Promoted in Juvenile Court?" *Justice System Journal* 17: 249–266.

Shiff, Allison, and David Wexler. 1996. "Teen Court: A Therapeutic Jurisprudence Perspective." *Criminal Law Bulletin* 32: 342–365.

Shine, J., and D. Price. 1992. "Prosecutors and Juvenile Justice: New Roles and Perspectives." In *Juvenile Justice and Public Policy: Toward a National Agenda,* edited by Ira Schwartz. New York: Lexington Books.

Singer, Simon. 1993. "The Automatic Waiver of Juveniles and Substantive Justice." *Crime and Delinquency* 39: 253–261.

Snyder, Howard. 2000. *Juvenile Arrests, 1999.* Washington, D.C.: Office of Juvenile Justice and Delinquency Prevention.

Snyder, Howard, and Melissa Sickmund. 2000. *Juvenile Offenders and Victims: 1999 National Report.* Washington, D.C.: Office of Juvenile Justice and Delinquency Prevention.

Sosin, M. 1978. "*Parens Patriae* and Dispositions in Juvenile Courts." Madison, WI: Institute for Research on Poverty.

Springer, Charles. 1986. *Justice for Juveniles.* Washington, D.C.: Office of Juvenile Justice and Delinquency Prevention.

Strom, Kevin, Steven Smith, and Howard Snyder. 1998. *Juvenile Felony Defendants in Criminal Courts.* Washington, D.C.: U.S. Department of Justice, Bureau of Justice Statistics.

Torbet, Patricia, Patrick Griffin, Hunter Hurst, and Lynn MacKenzie. 2000. *Juveniles Facing Criminal Sanctions: Three States That Changed the Rules.* Washington, D.C.: U.S. Department of Justice, Office of Juvenile Justice and Delinquency Prevention.

Walker, James, and Susan Ostrander. 1982. "An Observational Study of a Juvenile Court." *Juvenile and Family Court Journal* 33: 53–69.

Zehner, Sharon. 1997. "Teen Court." http://www.fbi. gov/leb/mar971.htm.

FOR FURTHER READING

Bazemore, Gordon. "Judges in the Punitive Juvenile Court: Organizational, Career and Ideological Influences on Sanctioning Orientation." *Justice Quarterly* 14 (1997): 87–114.

Dean, Charles, J. David Hirschel, and Robert Brame. "Minorities and Juvenile Case Dispositions." *Justice System Journal* 18 (1996): 267–285.

Feld, Barry. *Justice for Children: The Right to Counsel and the Juvenile Courts.* Boston: Northeastern University Press, 1993.

———. *Bad Kids: Race and the Transformation of the Juvenile Court.* New York: Oxford University Press, 1999.

Gramckow, Heike, and Elena Tompkins. *Enhancing Prosecutors' Ability to Combat and Prevent Juvenile Crime in Their Jurisdictions.* Washington, D.C.: Office of Juvenile Justice and Delinquency Prevention, 1999.

Guarino-Ghezzi, Susan, and Edward Loughran. *Balancing Juvenile Justice.* New Brunswick, NJ: Transaction, 1996.

Jacobs, Mark. *Screwing the System and Making It Work: Juvenile Justice in the No-Fault Society.* Chicago: University of Chicago Press, 1990.

Kurlychek, Megan, Patricia Torbet, and Melanie Bozynski. *Focus on Accountability: Best Practices for Juvenile Court and Probation.* Washington, D.C.:

Office of Juvenile Justice and Delinquency Prevention, 1999.

Manfredi, Christopher. *The Supreme Court and Juvenile Justice.* Lawrence: University Press of Kansas, 1998.

Moon, Melissa, John Wright, Francis Cullen, and Jennifer Pealer. "Putting Kids to Death: Specifying Public Support for Juvenile Capital Punishment." *Justice Quarterly* 17 (2000): 663–684.

National Center for Juvenile Justice. *Waiting for Justice: Moving Young Offenders Through the Juvenile Court Process.* Pittsburgh, PA: Author, 1996.

Parent, Dale, Terence Dunworth, Douglas McDonald, and William Rhodes. *Key Legislative Issues in Criminal Justice: Transferring Serious Juvenile Offenders to Adult Courts.* Washington, D.C.: National Institute of Justice, U.S. Department of Justice, 1997.

Scalia, John. *Juvenile Delinquents in the Federal Justice System.* Washington, D.C.: Bureau of Justice Statistics, 1997.

Schwartz, Ira. *(In)Justice for Juveniles: Rethinking the Best Interests of the Child.* New York: Lexington Books, 1989.

Torbet, Patricia, Richard Gable, Hunter Hurst, Imogene Montgomery, Linda Szymanski, and Douglas Thomas. *State Responses to Serious and Violent Juvenile Crime.* Pittsburgh, PA: National Center for Juvenile Justice, 1996.

Wright, Linda. "Juvenile Crime in Rural Areas." *Justice System Journal* 19 (1997): 355–364.

Epilogue

Chapter 1 began by noting that crime has been a pressing national concern for more than three decades. This epilogue will return to this initial theme and discuss why crime is a political issue and how the persistence of crime as a political issue influences the judicial process.

CRIME AS AN EMPTY VESSEL

Crime has persisted as a political issue for more than thirty years because it is a vague term, and purposefully so. Indeed, the political dimension of crime has been likened to an empty vessel (Heinz, Jacob, and Lineberry 1983); mention the word and the listener is free to pour in whatever content he or she prefers.

Viewing crime as an empty vessel helps explain why the content changes so much over time. Crime as a political issue has tremendous advantages (political, social, and moral) for entrepreneurs because it is so readily transformed into new and yet more alarming images. To a public that perceives that society is going to hell in a handbasket, the ever-changing nature of the crime problem provides reinforcement. As soon as the public becomes bored or jaded about one issue, a new one can quickly take its place. There is a continuous need to find new types of deviance because the public loses interest in denunciations of sin and degradation that have been around for a while. Consequently, analyzing crime is equivalent to diagnosing illness in a hypochondriac; as soon as the doctor rules out a specific malady, the patient discovers he or she suffers from another illness (which by some mysterious process is closely tied to media attention to that illness).

In a basic sense, crime persists as a political issue that comes close to being all things for all people at all times. As an empty vessel, it is a convenient surrogate for the two persistent underlying political issues of contemporary America—poverty and race.

Poverty and Crime

Crime remains a persistent political issue because it is intimately intertwined with poverty. To quote the old adage: "The law in all its infinite majesty prohibits the rich as well as the poor from sleeping under bridges." In the words of Lawrence Friedman (1993), criminal justice "has always fallen more heavily on the underclass, on the deviants, on the 'outs.' Criminal justice was the strong arm of the stratification system." Not that all the poor are swept up in the net of the criminal justice system, nor are the nonpoor immune to its sting, but as Jonathan Simon (1994) argues, prisons and parole are replacing welfare as forms of controlling the poor.

Race and Crime

Crime also remains a persistent political issue because it is intimately related in the public's mind to race. Race is the major fault line of American politics. Today, overt racism is rare in American politics, but race is nevertheless part of a hidden agenda underlying many domestic issues. Depending on where you live, the specific "out" group varies but includes blacks, Hispanics, Asians, and Native Americans. There is little doubt that when some politicians denounce the ravages of crime voters fill in the gaps and single out racial groups as the primary cause.

The tragic reality is that for most Americans crime has a black face (Marby and Thomas 1992). What gets lost in the discussion is the overriding fact that most crime is intraracial. But some elected officials couch the issue in terms that listeners understand as interracial. Thus, white and black Americans view crime in very different terms (Browning and Cao 1992).

CONSEQUENCES OF POLITICAL RHETORIC FOR THE CRIMINAL COURTS

The continuing political rhetoric of crime has important consequences for the courts. In trying to construct a realistic assessment of the troubled courthouse, one must attempt to walk the fine line between two extremes: the rhetoric of crisis and the endorsement of the status quo.

Increased Expectations

One way in which political rhetoric about crime affects the courts is to increase expectations. The problems of the courthouse are real and should be acknowledged. But this does not mean that the courts are on the brink of collapse. Public perceptions of these problems are often exaggerated, as this book frequently points out. Exaggerated assertions distract attention from realistic assessments of what the problems are and what can be done to solve them. The primary problems of the courts are not the result of external calamities, such as high crime rates and expanded caseloads. Rather, these problems are due to increased attention and raised standards (Feeley 1983).

This tide of rising expectations is clearly legitimate. What is of concern is that some of these increased expectations are unrealistic, and frustration results when lofty goals are not met. We need to ask the right questions. How much delay is too much? How much due process can the lower courts reasonably expect to provide?

The troubled history of the Law Enforcement Assistance Administration (LEAA) is a case in point (Feeley and Sarat 1980). Congress had no clear idea about what needed to be done—only a general sense that change was necessary. Instead of providing policy direction, the act created a planning process. But this left unclear what was to be planned. Overall, the stated goals were overly ambitious. The LEAA did foster important changes and some much-needed improvements. But unrealistic expectations distracted attention from these achievements and contributed to a sense of frustration about reform. Eventually LEAA was disbanded, but some components, like the Bureau of Justice Assistance and the National Institute of Justice, remain in the Justice Department.

Disagreement over Goals

The political rhetoric of crime also has the unfortunate consequence of papering over a lack of agreement on the fundamental goals of the courts. The value of court reform often lies in the eyes of the beholder. What one person applauds as progress, another denounces as a step backward. The essential difficulty is that reform efforts mask these areas of disagreement.

All too often, the emphasis on procedural improvements comes at the expense of substantive policy issues. Government reform movements that purport to be neutral ways of doing things better may actually disguise policy alternatives. Thus, it is necessary to separate the reformers' rhetoric from their underlying and sometimes unarticulated concerns. The emphasis on procedure not only masks substantive policy issues but also diverts attention from questions about the fairness of the system and protection of defendants' rights (Cole and Neubauer 1979). Efforts to improve court efficiency must be considered in substantive terms.

The Dynamics of Courthouse Justice

A flawed understanding of the court process contributes to unrealistic expectations (Feeley 1983). Reformers focus on individual problems in isolation from the broader process. They stress the formal dimensions of the process (law on the books), neglecting the informal ways that discretionary power is controlled and channeled (law in action).

The courts are a community of actors. Throughout this book, the central role of the courtroom work group has been stressed. Judges, prosecutors, defense attorneys, juries, and the police are tied together by more than a shared workplace.

THE MURDER TRIAL OF SHAREEF COUSIN

Uncertainties and Contradictions

 Trials, Americans have come to expect, finally decide matters. After the evidence has been presented and the lawyers have argued about the meaning of that evidence, the public expects an answer to the most basic question: Did he (or she) commit the crime or not? But after trial some cases still seem to be unresolved. To some, unanswered questions remain after the trials of Sacco and Vanzetti and of Julius and Ethel Rosenberg (listed in the inside front and back covers of this book). These cases linger in the national consciousness because of doubts about whether the verdict was correct. In New Orleans, the murder trial of Shareef Cousin likewise remains unsettled, offering uncertainties and contradictions.

One of the most fundamental unanswered questions centers on the defendant himself. The official court records and the unofficial media reports paint two contradictory images of Shareef Cousin. From one vantage point he appears to be a teenager who was in a little more trouble than most, but not much. In school he seemed to excel in math (when he wanted to), and he seemed to experience no major problems while living in the Boston area. From another vantage point, however, Shareef Cousin appears to have been a young man whose life was rapidly spinning out of control. He ran with the wrong crowd, most likely was abusing drugs, and committed four armed robberies in a few short months. Perhaps the answers to some of these questions could be found in Shareef Cousin's medical records, which remain under court seal.

The puzzle of who Shareef Cousin was interacts with one of the dominant issues of American society: race. Newspaper coverage of the trial clearly highlighted the importance of race, for example, by reporting on protests outside the courthouse. By contrast, the official court record shows little if any evidence of race, for example, in the absence of an appeal based on race by the defense during closing arguments. But the reality that a white person was murdered by an African American is bound to fuel the racial divide so prominent in big U.S. cities like New Orleans.

Also striking is the contradictory publicity the case received nationally as opposed to locally. On the na-

tional scene the case was, for a while, prominently featured. For example, Bianca Jagger (ex-wife of rock star Mick Jagger) was to visit New Orleans to lend moral support (but cancelled after the district attorney chose not to retry the boy). Locally, however, the case generated only passing attention, perhaps because Shareef Cousin failed to strike a sympathetic chord (probably because he is serving a twenty-year prison sentence for four armed robberies).

Another set of contradictions relates to how national groups have stated (or misstated) the facts in the case. Anti–death penalty groups, for example, unequivocally proclaim Shareef Cousin innocent. For example, the National Coalition to Abolish the Death Penalty (2001) boldly declares that "Shareef couldn't have killed Michael Gerardi." They support this position by restating the alibi defense, which Chapter 14 stressed was effectively shredded by the prosecutor during cross-examination. Conversely, pro–death penalty groups seem equally convinced that Cousin was a guilty murderer released on a technicality. For example, Pro-Death Penalty.com (2001) states without reservation that the conviction was reversed because the prosecutor improperly impeached a witness with prior inconsistent statements: "Other jurisdictions would not necessarily find this evidence inadmissible." This seems a dubious legal interpretation of the case if for no other reason than that the national group completely ignores the key issue of the prosecutor hiding exculpatory evidence from the defense. If their interpretation was correct, the DA would have retried the case. In short, both sides appear guilty of making absolute statements about matters that are in reality ambiguous.

The contradictions and uncertainties underlay the basic question in the trial of Shareef Cousin: Did he murder Michael Gerardi? I will let readers form their own conclusion. Was Shareef Cousin a brutal murderer whose conviction was overturned on legal technicalities or an innocent on death row falsely convicted because of prosecutorial misconduct and police incompetence?

Because these actors appear daily on the same judicial stage, their interactions combine to create what is best described as a social organization. Limited knowledge about the dynamics of courthouse justice explains why numerous reform efforts have not

been successful. Efforts to limit or control discretion at one point in the process typically result in increased discretion elsewhere. To be successful, reforms must recognize the fundamental role of the courtroom work group.

CONCLUSION

In the final analysis crime is a persistent political issue because the crime problem is insoluble. The public is concerned about crime. Needless to say, politicians respond; it would be strange indeed for politicians not to promise to do something. Alas, once in office public officials discover there is little agreement on the specifics about solving the crime problem and even less money to fund any promising ideas. Thus, elected officials discover that the voters are fearful of crime but often even more fearful of rising taxes (Heinz, Jacob, and Lineberry 1983).

Crime as a political issue often forces government officials to take action for action's sake, and in the end, the politics of promise deteriorate into the politics of scapegoating. Throughout this book we have examined why the most often mentioned areas for change have little if anything to do with the crime rate.

The political rhetoric of crime ignores the basic reality: The courts cannot be expected to solve the problem of crime. This perspective stands in sharp contrast to political rhetoric that lashes out at the criminal courts for their failure to protect the community. For those who want to take advantage of it, crime as a political issue is ideal because it can be associated with action for action's sake. Everyone demands that something be done. What can be done, of course, is unclear to politicians and court officials alike. It is unrealistic to expect that the courts can have much impact on the crime rate.

The elastic nature of crime as a persistent political issue explains why this book repeatedly suggests that a number of major reform efforts should be regarded with a healthy dose of skepticism. However, it should also be noted that in a number of important ways the court process is fairer and more focused than in earlier times. Future efforts require the establishment of realistic expectations about the nature of the court process, how change occurs, and what can be done to make courts better.

Some reform efforts resemble thunderbolts from far-off Mount Olympus. Outsiders proclaim that a problem exists and reform is needed to correct the problem. But those on the working level either fail to see the problem or find that the proposed solution bears little resemblance to how the court system actually operates. When the reform fails because it was poorly tailored to local conditions, the sense that nothing works gains greater momentum. Reform efforts need to refocus by taking into account legitimate practices reflected in the courtroom work group.

REFERENCES

Browning, Sandra Lee, and Liqun Cao. 1992. "The Impact of Race on Criminal Justice Ideology." *Justice Quarterly* 9: 685–701.

Cole, George, and David Neubauer. 1979. "The Living Courtroom: A Critique of the National Advisory Commission Recommendations." *Judicature* 59: 293–299.

Feeley, Malcolm. 1983. *Court Reform on Trial: Why Simple Solutions Fail.* New York: Basic Books.

Feeley, Malcolm, and Austin Sarat. 1980. *The Policy Dilemma: Federal Crime Policy and the Law Enforcement Assistance Administration, 1968–1978.* Minneapolis: University of Minnesota Press.

Friedman, Lawrence. 1993. *Crime and Punishment in American History.* New York: Basic Books.

Heinz, Anne, Herbert Jacob, and Robert Lineberry, eds. 1983. *Crime in City Politics.* New York: Longman.

Marby, Marcus, and Evan Thomas. 1992. "Crime: A Conspiracy of Silences." *Time* (May 18): 37.

Simon, Jonathan. 1994. *Poor Discipline: Parole and the Social Control of the Underclass, 1890–1990.* Chicago: University of Chicago Press.

National Coalition to Abolish the Death Penalty. 2001. "Here's How You Can Get Involved." http://www.ncadp. org/motivate.html, 25 February.

Pro-Death Penalty.com. 2001. "'Innocence' Critique." http://www.prodeathpenalty.com/DPIC.htm, 11 January.

Glossary

A

Acquittal: The decision of the judge or jury that the defendant is not guilty.

Adjudicated: Judicial determination (judgment) that a youth is a delinquent or status offender.

Adjudicatory hearing: Court hearing to determine whether a youth is guilty or not guilty.

Administrative law: Law that governs the duties and proper running of an administrative agency.

Administrative regulations: Rules and regulations adopted by administrative agencies that have the force of law.

Adversary system: A proceeding in which the opposing sides have the opportunity to present their evidence and arguments.

Affirm: In an appellate court, to reach a decision that agrees with the result reached in the case by the lower court.

Affirmative defense: Without denying the charge, defendant raises extenuating or mitigating circumstances, such as insanity, self-defense, or entrapment.

Alibi defense: A defense alleging that the defendant was elsewhere at the time of the crime he or she is charged with.

Alternate juror: Juror(s) chosen in excess of minimum number needed, in case one or more jurors is unable to serve for the entire trial.

Alternative dispute resolution (ADR): Less adversarial means of settling disputes that may or may not involve a court.

American Bar Association (ABA): The largest voluntary organization of lawyers in the United States.

Anglo-American law: The American legal system (see common law).

Appellant: The party, usually the losing one, that seeks to overturn the decision of a lower court by appealing to a higher court.

Appellate court: A court that hears appeals from trial courts on points of law.

Appellate court record: Papers, documents, exhibits, as well as the transcript of the trial, which are submitted to the appellate court for review.

Appellate jurisdiction: The authority of a court to hear, determine, and render judgment in an action on appeal from an inferior court.

Appellee (respondent): A party, usually the winning party, against whom a case is appealed.

Arraignment: The stage of the criminal process in which the defendant is formally told the charges and allowed to enter a plea.

Arrest: The physical taking into custody of a suspected law violator or juvenile.

Arrest warrant: A document issued by a judicial officer authorizing the arrest of a specific person.

Article I: Section of the U.S. Constitution concerning the legislative branch of the national government.

Article III: Section of the U.S. Constitution concerning the judicial branch of the national government.

Assembly-line justice: The operation of any segment of the criminal justice system in which excessive workload results in decisions being made with such speed and impersonality that defendants are treated as objects to be processed rather than as individuals.

Assigned counsel system: Arrangement that provides attorneys for persons who are accused of crimes and are unable to hire their own lawyers. The judge assigns a member of the bar to provide counsel to a particular defendant.

Attempt: An act done with the intent to commit a crime, an overt act toward its commission, the failure to complete the crime, and the apparent possibility of committing it.

Attendant (accompanying) circumstances: Conditions surrounding a criminal act, for example, the amount of money stolen in a theft.

B

Bail: The security (money or bail bond) given as a guarantee that a released prisoner will appear at trial.

Bail agent (bondsman): A person whose business it is to effect release on bail for persons held in custody, by pledging to pay a sum of money if a defendant fails to appear in court as required.

Bankruptcy judge: Judge who presides over the legal procedure under federal law by which a person is relieved of all debts after placing all property under the court's authority. An organization may be reorganized or terminated by the court in order to pay off creditors.

Bench trial: A trial conducted without a jury in which the judge tries the facts.

Bench warrant (*capias*): An order issued by the court itself, or from the bench, for the arrest of a person; it is not based, as is an arrest warrant, on a probable cause showing that a person has committed a crime, but only on the person's failure to appear in court as directed.

Best-evidence rule: Rule requiring that someone coming into court must bring the best available original evidence to prove the questions involved in the case.

Beyond a reasonable doubt: Burden of proof required by law to convict a defendant in a criminal case.

Bill of Rights: The first ten amendments to the U.S. Constitution, guaranteeing certain rights and liberties to the people.

Bind over: If at the preliminary hearing, the judge believes that sufficient probable cause exists to hold a criminal defendant, the accused is said to be bound over for trial.

Boykin **form:** Document intended to show that the defendant entered a guilty plea voluntarily and intelligently, understanding the charges and consequences of conviction (*Boykin v. Alabama* 1969).

Brief: A written statement submitted by the attorney arguing a case in court. It states the facts of the case, presents legal arguments in support of the moving party, and cites applicable law.

Burger Court: The Supreme Court under the leadership of Chief Justice Warren Burger (1969–1986).

C

Capital offense: Any crime punishable by death.

Capital punishment: Use of the death penalty as the punishment for the commission of a particular crime.

Cash bond: Requirement that money be posted to secure pretrial release.

Challenge for cause: Method for excusing a potential juror because of specific reasons such as bias or prejudgment; can be granted only by the judge.

Chambers: The private office of a judge.

Change of venue: The removal of a case from one jurisdiction to another. It is usually granted if the court believes that, due to prejudice, a defendant cannot receive a fair trial in the area where the crime occurred.

Charge bargaining: The defendant pleads guilty to a less serious charge than the one originally filed, which reduces the potential sentence.

Charging conference: Meeting attended by judge, prosecutor, and defense attorney during which the judge's instructions to the jury are discussed.

Charging document: An information, indictment, or complaint that states the formal criminal charge against a named defendant(s).

Child-victim: Juvenile court case involving a child who has been neglected and/or abused by the parents.

Circumstantial evidence: An indirect method of proving the material facts of a case; testimony that is not based on the witness's personal observation of the material events.

Civil law: Law governing private parties; other than criminal law.

Civil protection order: Court order requiring a person to stay away from another person.

Clerk of court: An elected or appointed court officer responsible for maintaining the written records of the court and for supervising or performing the clerical tasks necessary to conduct judicial business.

Closing argument: Statement made by an attorney at the end of the presentation of evidence in which the attorney summarizes the case for the jury.

Common law: Law developed in England by judges who made legal decisions in absence of written law. Such decisions served as precedents and became "common" to all of England. Common law is judge-made, it uses precedent, and it is uncodified.

Complaint: In civil law, the first paper filed in a lawsuit. In criminal law, a charge signed by the victim that a person named has committed a specified offense.

Conditions of confinement lawsuit: Lawsuit brought by a prisoner contesting prison conditions.

Conference: Juvenile court proceeding roughly equivalent to a preliminary hearing, in which the suspect is informed of his or her rights and a disposition decision may be reached.

Consent search: A person, place, or moveable may be lawfully searched by an officer of the law if the owner gives free and voluntary consent.

Constitution: The fundamental rules that determine how those who govern are selected, the procedures by which they operate, and the limits to their powers.

Constitutional courts: Federal courts created by Congress by virtue of its power under Article III of the Constitution to create courts inferior to the Supreme Court.

Contempt (of court): The failure or refusal to obey a court order; may be punished by a fine or imprisonment.

Contract: A legally enforceable agreement between two or more parties.

Contract system: System of providing counsel for indigents under which the government contracts with a law firm to represent all indigents for the year in return for a set fee.

Corpus delicti: The body or substance of a crime, composed of two elements—the act and the criminal agency producing it.

Counseling: Legal advice provided by lawyers to their clients.

Count bargaining: The defendant pleads guilty to some, but not all, of the counts contained in the charging document, which reduces the potential sentence.

Courtroom work group: The regular participants in the day-to-day activities of a particular courtroom: judge, prosecutor, and defense attorney interact on the basis of shared norms.

Crime control model: A perspective on the criminal justice process based on the proposition that the most important function of criminal justice is the repression of crime, focusing on efficiency as a principal measure.

Criminal justice system: Agencies and institutions directly involved in the implementation of public policy concerning crime, mainly the law enforcement agencies, courts, and corrections.

Criminal law: Laws passed by government that define and prohibit antisocial behavior.

Cross-examination: At trial, the questions of one attorney put to a witness called by the opposing attorney.

Cruel and unusual punishment: Punishment, by the government, that is prohibited by the Eighth Amendment.

D

Death penalty: Capital punishment, or executions by the state for purposes of social defense. *Gregg v. Georgia*, 1976, upheld constitutionality of rewritten state capital punishment laws struck down by *Furman v. Georgia*, 1972.

Declaratory judgment: Judicial pronouncement declaring the legal rights of parties involved in an actual case or controversy.

Defendant: The person or party against whom a lawsuit or prosecution is brought.

Delay: Postponement or adjournment of proceedings in a case; lag in case-processing time.

Delinquency: An act committed by a juvenile that would require an adult to be prosecuted in a criminal court. Because the act is committed by a juvenile, it falls within the jurisdiction of the juvenile court. Delinquent acts include crimes against persons or property, drug offenses, and crimes against public order.

Detention: Holding a youth in custody before case disposition.

Determinate sentencing: A term of imprisonment, imposed by a judge, that has a specific number of years.

Deterrence theory: The view that sure and swift punishment will discourage others from similar illegal acts.

Direct evidence: Evidence derived from one or more of the five senses.

Direct restitution: The defendant pays money directly to the victim of the crime.

Discovery: Pretrial procedure in which parties to a lawsuit ask for and receive information such as testimony, records, or other evidence from each other.

Discretion: The lawful ability of an agent of government to exercise choice in making a decision.

Discretionary appellate jurisdiction: Jurisdiction that a court may accept or reject in particular cases. The Supreme Court has discretionary jurisdiction over most cases that come to it.

Discrimination: Illegitimate influences in the sentencing process based on the characteristics of the defendants.

Dismissal: Cases are terminated (including those warned, counseled, and released) with no further disposition anticipated.

Disparity: Unequal sentences resulting from the sentencing process itself.

Disposition: A court decision on what will happen to a youth who has not been found innocent.

Dissenting opinion: An opinion written by a judge of an appellate court in which the judge states the reasons for disagreeing with the majority decision.

District courts: U.S. trial courts established in the respective judicial districts into which the whole United States is divided. These courts are established for the purpose of hearing and deciding cases in limited districts to which their jurisdiction is confined.

Diversity of citizenship: When parties on the opposite sides of a federal lawsuit come from different states, the jurisdiction of the U.S. district courts can be invoked if the case involves a controversy concerning $75,000 or more in value.

Domestic relations: Relating to the home; the law of divorce, custody, support, adoption, and so on.

Double jeopardy: Fifth Amendment prohibition against a second prosecution after a first trial for the same offense.

Dual court system: A court system consisting of a separate judicial structure for each state in addition to a national structure. Each case is tried in a court of the same jurisdiction as that of the law or laws involved.

Due process model: A philosophy of criminal justice based on the assumption that an individual is innocent until proven guilty and has a right to protection from arbitrary power of the state.

Due process of law: A right guaranteed in the Fifth, Sixth, and Fourteenth Amendments of the U.S. Constitution and generally understood to mean the due course of legal proceedings according to the rules and forms established for the protection of private rights.

Duress: Unlawful pressure on a person to do what he or she would not otherwise have done.

E

Elements of a crime: Five principles of a crime that are critical to the statutory definition of crimes: guilty act, guilty intent, relationship between guilty act and guilty intent, attendant circumstances, and results.

En banc: French term referring to the session of an appellate court in which all the judges of the court participate, as opposed to a session presided over by three judges.

Entrapment: The act of a government official or agent inducing a person to commit a crime that the person would not have committed without the inducement.

Error: A mistake made by a judge in the procedures used at trial, or in making legal rulings during the trial, that allows one side in a lawsuit to ask a higher court to review the case.

Error correction: Appellate courts seek to correct legal errors made in lower courts.

Estate: The interest a person has in property; a person's right or title to property.

Evidence: Any kind of proof offered to establish the existence or nonexistence of a fact in dispute, for example, testimony, writings, other material objects, demonstrations.

Exclusionary rule: A rule created by judicial decisions holding that evidence obtained through violations of the constitutional rights of the criminal defendant must be excluded from the trial.

Extradition: Legal process whereby officials of one state surrender an alleged criminal offender to officials of the state in which the crime is alleged to have been committed.

F

Federal question: Case that contains a major issue involving the U.S. Constitution or U.S. laws or treaties.

Fee system: A system that pays the judicial officer directly from fees assessed against the guilty.

Felony: The more serious of the two basic types of criminal behavior, usually bearing a possible penalty of one year or more in prison.

Fine: A sum of money to be paid to the state by a convicted person as punishment for an offense.

Furman v. Georgia: Supreme Court ruling that statutes leaving arbitrary and discriminatory discretion to juries in imposing death sentences are in violation of the Eighth Amendment.

Fusion of the guilty act and guilty intent: One of the components of a crime (see elements of a crime). Criminal law requires that the guilty intent and the guilty act occur together.

G

Gag order: A judge's order that lawyers and witnesses not discuss the trial with outsiders.

General deterrence: Concept stressing that punishment will deter the general populace.

Geographical jurisdiction: Geographical area over which courts can hear and decide disputes.

Good time: A reduction of the time served in prison as a reward for not violating prison rules.

Grand jury: A group of citizens who decide whether persons accused of crimes should be indicted (true bill) or not (no true bill).

Gregg v. Georgia: Supreme Court ruling that (1) the death penalty is not, in itself, cruel and unusual punishment, and (2) a two-part proceeding—one for the determination of innocence or guilt and the other for determination of the sentence—is constitutional and meets the objections noted in *Furman v. Georgia.*

Gubernatorial appointment: Method of judicial selection in which the governor appoints a person to a judicial vacancy without an election.

Guilty act (actus reus): Requirement that, for an act to be considered criminal, the individual must have committed an overt act that resulted in criminal harm (see elements of a crime).

Guilty intent (mens rea): Mental state required for a crime.

H

Habeas corpus: Latin phrase meaning "you have the body"; a writ inquiring of an official who has custody of a person whether that person is being lawfully imprisoned or detained.

Harmless error: An error made at trial that is insufficient grounds for reversing a judgment.

Hearsay: An out-of-court assertion or statement, made by someone other than the testifying witness, which is offered to prove the truth of testimony. Hearsay evidence is excluded from trials unless it falls within one of the recognized exceptions.

Hierarchical jurisdiction: Refers to differences in the functions of courts and involves original as opposed to appellate jurisdiction.

Hung jury: A jury that is unable to reach a verdict.

I

Illegal search and seizure: An act in violation of the Fourth Amendment of the U.S. Constitution.

Immaterial: Evidence that neither proves nor disproves the issue of a trial.

Immunity: A grant of exemption from prosecution in return for evidence or testimony.

Impeach: To question the truthfulness of a witness's testimony.

Impeachment: Official accusation against a public official brought by a legislative body seeking his or her removal.

Imprisonment: Placing a person in a prison, jail, or similar correctional facility as punishment for committing a crime.

Incapacitation: Sentencing philosophy that stresses crime prevention through isolating wrongdoers from society.

Incorporation: The theory that the Bill of Rights has been incorporated or absorbed into the due process clause of the Fourteenth Amendment, thereby making it applicable to the states.

Indeterminate sentence: A sentence that has both a minimum and maximum term of imprisonment, the actual length to be determined by a parole board.

Index crimes: The specific crimes used by the FBI when reporting the incidence of crime in the United States in the *Uniform Crime Reports.*

Indictment: A formal accusation of a criminal offense made against a person by a grand jury.

Indigent: A person too poor to hire a lawyer.

Inferior court: Term for a trial court of limited jurisdiction; also may refer to any court lower in the judicial hierarchy.

Information: A formal accusation charging someone with the commission of a crime, signed by a prosecuting attorney, which has the effect of bringing the person to trial.

Inheritance: Property received from a dead person, either by effect of intestacy or a will.

Initial appearance: Shortly after arrest the suspect is brought before a judicial official who informs the person of the reason for the arrest, and if the case is a felony, bond is set.

Initial hearing: In juvenile court, an often informal hearing during which an intake decision is made.

Injunction: A court order directing someone to do something or refrain from doing something.

In rem: Against a thing; a legal proceeding instituted to obtain decrees or judgments against property.

Intake decision: The decision made by juvenile court that results in the case either being handled informally at the intake level or more formally by petition and scheduled for an adjudicatory or transfer hearing.

Interlocutory: Provisional; temporary; while a lawsuit is still going on.

Intermediate courts of appeals: Judicial bodies falling between the highest, or supreme, tribunal and the trial court; created to relieve the jurisdiction's highest court of hearing a large number of cases.

Intermediate sanctions: Variety of sanctions that lie somewhere between prison and probation.

Irrelevant: Testimony that has no bearing on the issue of a trial.

Irresistible impulse: A test of insanity under which a person is driven to commit an act by an urge that cannot be resisted or overcome because mental disease or derangement has destroyed the freedom of will, the power of self-control, and the ability to choose.

J

Judge-made law: The common law as developed in form and content by judges or judicial decisions.

Judgment: The official decision of a court concerning a legal matter.

Judicial conduct commission: An official body whose function is to investigate allegations of misconduct by judges.

Judicial election: Method of judicial selection in which the voters choose judicial candidates in a partisan or non-partisan election.

Judicial independence: Normative value that stresses a judge should be free from outside pressure in making a decision.

Jurisdiction: The power of a court to hear a case in question.

Jury deliberations: The action of a jury in determining the guilt or innocence, or the sentence, of a defendant.

Jury instructions: Directions given by a judge to the members of the jury informing them of the law applicable to the case.

Jury nullification: Idea that juries have the right to refuse to apply the law in criminal cases despite facts that leave no reasonable doubt that the law was violated.

Just deserts: Punishment for criminal wrongdoing should be proportionate to the severity of the offense.

Justice of the peace (JP): A low-level judge, sometimes without legal training, typically found in rural areas of some states, empowered to try petty civil and criminal cases and to conduct the preliminary stages of felony cases.

Juvenile: Youth at or below the upper age of juvenile court jurisdiction.

Juvenile court: Any court that has jurisdiction over matters involving juveniles.

Juvenile delinquency: An act committed by a juvenile for which an adult could be prosecuted in a criminal court.

L

Law: Body of rules, enacted by public officials in a legitimate manner and backed by the force of the state.

Law clerk: A law student or lawyer employed by a judge, typically for a short time, who assists in legal research and writing.

Legal defense: Legally recognized justification for illegal actions, or acceptance that individuals were not legally responsible for their actions.

Legislative courts: Judicial bodies created by Congress under Article I (legislative article) and not Article III (judicial article).

Local prosecutors: General term for lawyers who represent local governments (cities and counties, for example) in the lower courts; often called city attorneys or solicitors.

Lower age of jurisdiction: Minimum age at which a youth may be transferred to adult court.

M

Mandatory appellate jurisdiction: Jurisdiction that a court must accept. Cases falling under a court's mandatory jurisdiction must be decided officially on their merits, though a court may avoid giving them full consideration.

Mandatory minimum sentencing: Minimum required penalty specified for a certain crime.

Master jury list: A list of potential jurors in a court's district from which a representative cross section of the community in which a crime allegedly was committed can be selected for a trial. It is usually compiled from multiple sources, such as voter registration lists, driver's license lists, utility customer lists, and telephone directories. Also called jury wheel or master wheel.

McNaughton rule: Oldest and most restrictive standard of insanity as legal defense, essentially requiring that the accused not be able to distinguish between right and wrong; currently applied in a modified version in sixteen jurisdictions.

Misdemeanor: Lesser of the two basic types of crime; usually punishable by no more than one year in prison.

Missouri Bar Plan: The name given to a method of judicial selection combining merit selection and popular control in retention elections.

Mistrial: Invalid trial.

Monetary damage: Compensatory damages—payment for actual losses suffered by a plaintiff. Punitive damages—money awarded by a court to a person who has been harmed in a malicious or willful way.

Municipal court: A trial court of limited jurisdiction created by a local unit of government.

Municipal ordinance: Laws passed by local units of government.

N

Negotiate: Discuss, arrange, or bargain about a settlement or compromise between the parties of a lawsuit.

New judicial federalism: Movement in state supreme courts to reinvigorate states' constitutions as sources of individual rights over and above the rights granted by the U.S. Constitution.

Nolle prosequi: The ending of a criminal case because the prosecutor decides or agrees to stop prosecuting. When this happens the case is "nollied," "nolled," or "nol. prossed."

Nolo contendere: Latin phrase meaning "I will not contest it." A plea of "no contest" in a criminal case means that the defendant does not directly admit guilt but submits to sentencing or other punishment.

Nonpetitioned case: A juvenile case handled informally by duly authorized court personnel.

Normal crime: Categorization of crime based on the typical manner in which it is committed, the typical type of defendant who commits it, and the typical penalty to be applied.

Normal penalties: Norms for proper sentencing based on the crime committed and the defendant's prior record.

Notice of appeal: Written document filed with the clerk of court stating that the defendant in the criminal case plans to appeal.

No true bill: The decision of a grand jury not to indict a person for a crime.

O

Objection: The act of taking exception to a statement or procedure during a trial.

Officer of the court: Lawyers are officers of the court and as such must obey court rules, be truthful in court, and generally serve the needs of justice.

Opening statement: Address made by attorneys for both parties at the beginning of a trial in which they outline for the jury what they intend to prove in their case.

Opinion: The reasons given for the decision reached by an appellate court.

Oral argument: The part of the appellate court decision-making process in which lawyers for both parties plead their case in person before the court.

Ordinance: A law enacted by a local governmental body for the regulation of some activity within the community.

Original jurisdiction: Jurisdiction in the first instance; commonly used to refer to trial jurisdiction as compared to appellate jurisdiction. Appellate courts, however, have limited original jurisdiction.

Other dispositions: Miscellaneous dispositions, including fines, restitution, community service, referrals outside the court for services with minimal or no further court involvement anticipated.

P

Pardon: An act of executive clemency that has the effect of releasing an inmate from prison and/or removing certain legal disabilities from persons convicted of crimes.

Parens patriae: The state as parent; the state as guardian and protector of all citizens (such as juveniles) who are unable to protect themselves.

Parole: Early release from prison on the condition of good behavior.

Parole board: An administrative body whose members are chosen by the governor to review the cases of prisoners eligible for release on parole. The board has the authority to release such persons and to return them to prison for violating the conditions of parole.

Peremptory challenge: Method for excusing a potential juror without specifying the reason.

Personal injury: Negligence lawsuits, often involving automobile accidents.

Petition: A document filed in juvenile court alleging that a juvenile is a delinquent or a status offender and asking that the court assume jurisdiction over the juvenile or that an alleged delinquent be transferred to criminal court for prosecution as an adult.

Petit jury: A trial jury as distinguished from a grand jury.

Petty offense: A minor criminal offense that does not entitle the defendant to a trial by jury.

Placement: Cases in which youths are placed in a residential facility or otherwise removed from their homes and placed elsewhere.

Plaintiff: The person or party who initiates a lawsuit.

Plain view: If police happen to come across something while acting within their lawful duty, that item may be used as evidence in a criminal trial even if the police did not have a search warrant.

Plea bargaining: The process by which a defendant pleads guilty to a criminal charge with the expectation of receiving some benefit from the state.

Plea on the nose: The defendant pleads guilty to the charges contained in the indictment or bill of information.

Policy formulation: Function of appellate courts to make new law and adjust existing law to changing circumstances.

Post-verdict motions: Various motions made by the defense after a jury conviction in hopes of gaining a new trial.

Precedent: A case previously decided that serves as a legal guide for the resolution of subsequent cases.

Prejudicial pretrial publicity: Prejudicial information, often inadmissible at trial, which is circulated by the news media before a trial and which reduces the defendant's chances of a trial before an impartial jury.

Preliminary hearing: A pretrial hearing to determine whether there is probable cause to hold the accused for the grand jury.

Preponderance of the evidence: In civil law, the standard of proof required to prevail at trial. To win, the plaintiff must show that the greater weight, or preponderance of the evidence, supports his or her version of the facts.

Pre-sentence investigation: Investigation by a probation department into circumstances surrounding a crime in order to help judges make appropriate sentencing decisions.

Presumption of innocence: The defendant is presumed to be innocent, and the burden is on the state to prove guilt beyond a reasonable doubt.

Preventive detention: Holding a defendant in custody pending trial in the belief that he or she is likely to commit further criminal acts or flee the jurisdiction.

Prisoner petition: Civil lawsuit filed by a prisoner alleging violations of his or her rights during trial or while in prison.

Privileged communications: A recognized right to keep certain communications confidential or private.

Probable cause: Standard used to determine whether a crime has been committed and whether there is sufficient evidence to believe a specific individual committed it.

Probation: Punishment for a crime that allows the offender to remain in the community without incarceration but subject to certain conditions.

Probation officer: Employee of probation agency, responsible for supervision of convicted offenders who have been released to the community under certain conditions of good behavior.

Procedural law: Law that outlines the legal procedures of process to be followed in starting, conducting, and finishing a lawsuit.

Property: Legal right to use or dispose of particular things or subjects.

Property bond: Use of property as collateral for pretrial release.

Prosecutor: A public official who represents the state in a criminal action.

Public defender: An attorney employed by the government to represent indigent defendants.

R

Real evidence: Objects, such as fingerprints, seen by the jury.

Reasonable doubt: The state of mind of jurors when they do not feel a moral certainty about the truth of the charges and when the evidence does not exclude every other reasonable hypothesis except that the defendant is guilty as charged.

Rebuttal: The introduction of contradictory evidence.

Referral: A request by a law enforcement agency, governmental agency, parent, or individual that a juvenile court take jurisdiction of a youth. A referral initiates court processing.

Rehabilitation: The notion that punishment is intended to restore offenders to a constructive role in society; based on the assumption that criminal behavior is a treatable disorder caused by social or psychological ailments.

Rehnquist Court: The Supreme Court under the leadership of Chief Justice William Rehnquist (1986–).

Release on recognizance (ROR): The release of an accused person from jail on his or her own obligation rather than on a monetary bond.

Remand: In an appellate court, to send a case back to the court from which it came for further action.

Remedy: Vindication of a claim of right. A legal procedure by which a right is enforced or the violation of a right is prevented or compensated.

Removal: To dismiss a person from holding office.

Restitution: To restore or to make good on something; for example, to return or pay for a stolen item.

Result: A consequence; an outcome.

Retribution: A concept that implies the payment of a debt to society and thus the expiration of one's offense.

Reverse: In an appellate court, to reach a decision that disagrees with the result reached in the case by the lower court.

Reversed and remanded: Decision of an appellate court that the guilty verdict of the lower court be set aside and the case be retried.

Reversible error: An error made at trial serious enough to warrant a new trial.

Right to counsel: Right of the accused to the services of a lawyer paid for by the government, established by the Sixth Amendment and extended by the Warren Court (*Gideon v. Wainwright*) to indigent defendants in felony cases.

Right to one appeal: U.S. law generally grants the loser in trial court the right to a single appeal, which the upper court must hear.

Routine administration: A matter that presents the court with no disputes over law or fact.

S

Search warrant: A written order, issued by judicial authority, directing a law enforcement officer to search for personal property, and, if found, to bring it before the court.

Selective incapacitation: Sentencing philosophy that stresses targeting dangerous offenders for lengthy prison sentences.

Self-defense: The right to use physical force against another person who is committing a felony, threatening the use of physical force, or using physical force.

Self-incrimination: Forcing a suspect to provide evidence against him- or herself; prohibited by the Fifth Amendment.

Sentence bargaining: The defendant pleads guilty knowing the sentence that will be imposed; the sentence in the sentence bargain is less than the maximum.

Sequester: To isolate members of a jury from the community until they have reached a final verdict.

Small claims court: A lower level court whose jurisdiction is limited to a specific dollar amount, for example, damages may not exceed $1,500.

Solicitor general: Third-ranking official in the U.S. Department of Justice who conducts and supervises government litigation in the Supreme Court.

Special deterrence: Concept stressing that punishment will deter the person being sentenced.

Staff attorneys: Lawyers who work for all the judges of the appellate court.

Stare decisis: Latin phrase meaning "let the decision stand." The doctrine that principles of law established in earlier judicial decisions should be accepted as authoritative in similar subsequent cases.

State attorney general: The chief legal officer of a state, representing that state in civil, and under certain circumstances, criminal cases.

State supreme court: General term for the highest court in a state.

Status offense: Behavior that is considered an offense only when committed by a juvenile, for example, running away from home.

Statute: A written law enacted by a legislature.

Statutory exemptions: Rules adopted by legislatures exempting certain types of persons or occupations from jury duty.

Subject matter jurisdiction: Types of cases courts have been authorized to hear and decide.

Subpoena: An order from a court directing a person to appear before the court and give testimony about a cause of action pending before it.

Substantial capacity: A person is not responsible for criminal conduct if at the time of such conduct and as a result of mental disease or defect he or she lacks substantial capacity either to appreciate the criminality of the conduct or to conform his or her conduct to the regiments of the law.

Substantive law: Law that deals with the content or substance of the law, for example, the legal grounds for divorce.

Summary affirmation: Appellate court affirms the decision of the trial court without providing a written opinion.

Summons: A legal document ordering an individual to appear in court at a certain time on a certain date.

Suppression motion: Request that a court of law prohibit specific statements, documents, or objects from being introduced into evidence in a trial.

Symbolic restitution: The defendant performs community service.

T

Testimony: The giving of evidence by a witness under oath.

Three-judge district court: A special federal trial court for certain limited types of cases specified by federal statute.

Tort: A private or civil wrong, not arising as the result of a breach of contract, in which the defendant's actions cause injury to the plaintiff or to property.

Traffic offenses: A group of offenses, including infractions and minor misdemeanors, relating to the operation of self-propelled motor vehicles.

Transactional immunity: Absolute protection against prosecution for any event or transaction about which a witness is compelled to give testimony or furnish evidence.

Transfer to criminal court: A case is moved to a criminal court because of a waiver or transfer hearing in the juvenile court.

Trial court: Judicial body with primarily original jurisdiction in civil or criminal cases. Juries are used and evidence is presented.

Trial courts of general jurisdiction: The trial courts responsible for major criminal and civil cases.

Trial courts of limited jurisdiction: A lower level state court, such as a justice of the peace court, whose jurisdiction is limited to minor civil disputes or misdemeanors.

True bill: A bill of indictment by a grand jury.

Trustworthiness: Basic criterion for the admissibility of evidence, which seeks to ensure that only the most reliable and credible facts, statements, and testimony are presented to the fact finder.

Type I offenses: Serious crimes of homicide, rape, arson, aggravated assault, robbery, burglary, auto theft, and larceny, according to the FBI's *Uniform Crime Reports*; also called index crimes.

U

Unified court system: Entails a simplified state trial court structure, rule making centered in the supreme court, system governance authority vested in the chief justice of the supreme court, and state funding of the judicial system with a statewide judicial budget.

Unreasonable search and seizure: The Fourth Amendment provides for protection against unreasonable search and seizure, or the illegal gathering of evidence, but was not very effective until the adoption of the exclusionary rule, barring the use of evidence obtained through an unreasonable search and seizure (*Mapp v. Ohio*, 1961, state or federal courts).

Upper age of jurisdiction: The oldest age at which a juvenile court has original jurisdiction over an individual for behavior that violates the law.

U.S. attorney general: Head of the Department of Justice; nominated by the president and confirmed by the Senate.

U.S. attorneys: Officials responsible for the prosecution of crimes that violate the laws of the United States; appointed by the president and assigned to a U.S. district court.

U.S. magistrate judges: Judicial officers appointed by the U.S. district courts to perform the duties formerly performed by U.S. commissioners and to assist the court by serving as special masters in civil actions, conducting pre-trial or discovery proceedings, and conducting preliminary review of applications for post-trial relief made by individuals convicted of criminal offenses.

Use immunity: A witness may not be prosecuted based on grand jury testimony he or she provides but may be prosecuted based on evidence against the witness acquired independently from that testimony.

V

Venire: A group of citizens from which members of the jury are chosen.

Venue: The geographic location of a trial, which is determined by constitutional or statutory provisions.

Verdict: The decision of a trial court.

Voir dire: French legal phrase meaning "to speak the truth." The process by which prospective jurors are questioned to determine whether there is cause to excuse them from the jury.

W

Warrantless search: Search without a search warrant.

Warren Court: The Supreme Court under the leadership of Chief Justice Earl Warren (1953–1969).

Writ of certiorari: Issued from an appellate court for the purpose of obtaining from a lower court the record of its proceedings in a particular case.

Case Index

Index

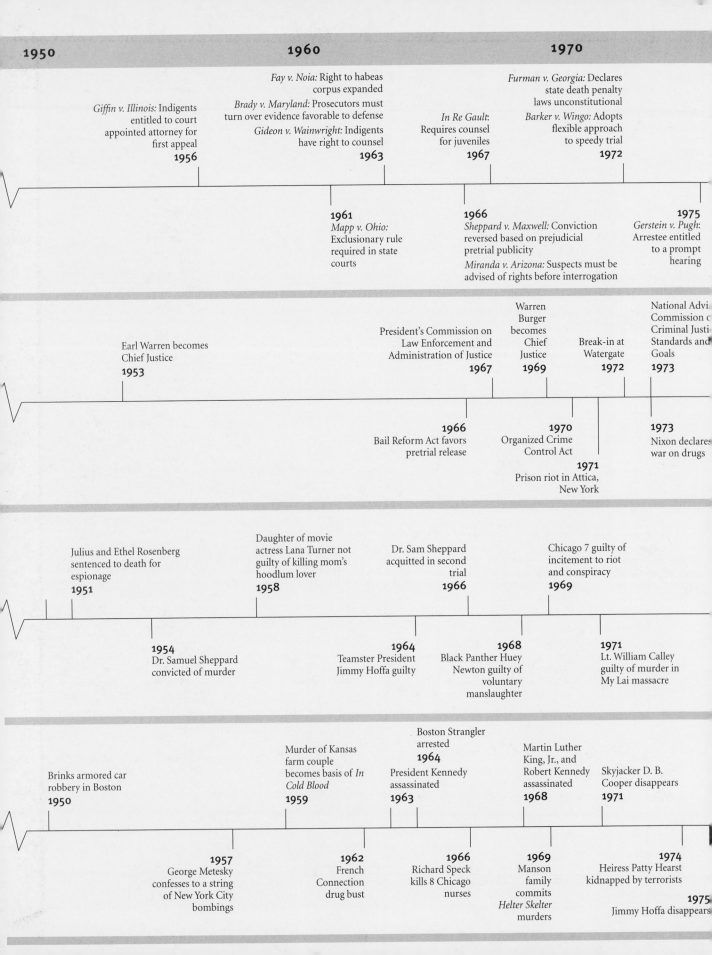

1950   **1960**   **1970**

Giffin v. Illinois: Indigents entitled to court appointed attorney for first appeal
1956

Fay v. Noia: Right to habeas corpus expanded
Brady v. Maryland: Prosecutors must turn over evidence favorable to defense
Gideon v. Wainwright: Indigents have right to counsel
1963

In Re Gault: Requires counsel for juveniles
1967

Furman v. Georgia: Declares state death penalty laws unconstitutional
Barker v. Wingo: Adopts flexible approach to speedy trial
1972

1961
Mapp v. Ohio: Exclusionary rule required in state courts

1966
Sheppard v. Maxwell: Conviction reversed based on prejudicial pretrial publicity
Miranda v. Arizona: Suspects must be advised of rights before interrogation

1975
Gerstein v. Pugh: Arrestee entitled to a prompt hearing

Earl Warren becomes Chief Justice
1953

President's Commission on Law Enforcement and Administration of Justice
1967

Warren Burger becomes Chief Justice
1969

Break-in at Watergate
1972

National Advi Commission c Criminal Justi Standards and Goals
1973

1966
Bail Reform Act favors pretrial release

1970
Organized Crime Control Act

1971
Prison riot in Attica, New York

1973
Nixon declares war on drugs

Julius and Ethel Rosenberg sentenced to death for espionage
1951

Daughter of movie actress Lana Turner not guilty of killing mom's hoodlum lover
1958

Dr. Sam Sheppard acquitted in second trial
1966

Chicago 7 guilty of incitement to riot and conspiracy
1969

1954
Dr. Samuel Sheppard convicted of murder

1964
Teamster President Jimmy Hoffa guilty

1968
Black Panther Huey Newton guilty of voluntary manslaughter

1971
Lt. William Calley guilty of murder in My Lai massacre

Brinks armored car robbery in Boston
1950

Murder of Kansas farm couple becomes basis of *In Cold Blood*
1959

Boston Strangler arrested
1964
President Kennedy assassinated
1963

Martin Luther King, Jr., and Robert Kennedy assassinated
1968

Skyjacker D. B. Cooper disappears
1971

1957
George Metesky confesses to a string of New York City bombings

1962
French Connection drug bust

1966
Richard Speck kills 8 Chicago nurses

1969
Manson family commits *Helter Skelter* murders

1974
Heiress Patty Hearst kidnapped by terrorists

1975
Jimmy Hoffa disappears